ISBN 978-0-260-04346-7
PIBN 10924131

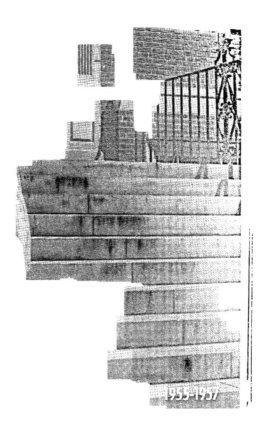
1955-1957

Bulletin

THE UNIVERSITY
OF MASSACHUSETTS

Graduate School Number

1955 - 1956

1956 - 1957

The Graduate School Catalogue for the sessions of 1955-1956, 1956-1957 is part of the Eighty-Ninth Annual Report of the University of Massachusetts and in conjunction with the general catalogue of The University it constitutes Part II of Public Document 31 (Sec. 8, Chapter 75, of the General Laws of Massachusetts).

———

AMHERST, MASSACHUSETTS

Volume XLVII	January, 1955	Number 1

Published six times a year by the University of Massachusetts: January, February, April (two), May, September. Entered at Post Office, Amherst, Mass. as second-class matter.

PUBLICATION OF THIS DOCUMENT APPROVED BY GEORGE J. CRONIN, STATE PURCHASING AGENT

5m-9-54-918184

ACADEMIC CALENDAR

1954-1955

September 20, Monday	Registration of graduate students.
September 22, Wednesday	Classes begin.
September 28, Tuesday	Last day on which registration cards may be handed in.
October 1, Friday	Last day on which thesis outlines may be handed in by Ph.D. candidates who plan to finish their work by the June, 1955 Commencement.
October 7, Thursday	Last day on which Ph.D. candidates who plan to complete their work by the June, 1955 Commencement may take the preliminary comprehensive examination.
October 12, Tuesday	Columbus Day: a holiday.
November 1, Monday	Last day on which graduate students may drop courses without failure.
November 11, Thursday	Armistice Day: a holiday.
November 24, Wednesday, 12:00 M. to November 29, Monday, 8:00 A.M. . .	Thanksgiving recess.
December 18, Saturday 12:00 M. to January 3, Monday, 8:00 A.M. . .	Christmas recess.
January 3, Monday	Last day on which thesis outlines may be handed in by Master's degree candidates who plan to finish their work by the 1955 Commencement.
January 20, Thursday, 5:00 P.M. . . .	Classes stop.
January 21, Friday	Registration of graduate students.
January 24, Monday, to February 2, Wednesday	Final Examinations.
February 7, Monday, 8:00 A.M.	Classes resume.
February 22, Tuesday	Washington's Birthday: a holiday.
March 21, Monday	Last day on which graduate students may drop courses without failure.
April 2, Saturday 12:00 to April 11, Monday, 8:00 A.M.	Spring recess.
April 19, Tuesday	Patriot's Day: a holiday.
May 21, Saturday 12:00 M.	Classes stop
May 23, Monday, to June 2, Thursday, 5:00 P.M.	Final Examinations.
May 30, Monday	Memorial Day: a holiday.
June 1, Wednesday	Last day for bound theses to be handed in.
June 3, Friday, to June 5, Sunday . . .	Commencement.

ACADEMIC CALENDAR
1955-1956

September 19, Monday . . . . . Registration of graduate students.

September 21, Wednesday . . . . Classes begin

September 27, Tuesday . . . . . Last day on which registration cards may be handed in.

September 30, Friday . . . . . Last day on which thesis outlines may be handed in by Ph.D. candidates who plan to finish their work by the June, 1956 Commencement.

October 6, Thursday . . . . . . Last day on which Ph.D. candidates who plan to complete their work by the June, 1956 Commencement may take the preliminary comprehensive examination.

October 12, Wednesday . . . . . Columbus Day: a holiday.

October 31, Monday . . . . . . Last day on which graduate students may drop courses without failure.

November 11, Friday . . . . . . Armistice Day: a holiday.

November 23, Wednesday, 12:00 M., to November 28, Monday . . . . Thanksgiving recess.

December 17, Saturday 12:00 M., to January 3, Tuesday . . . . . Christmas recess.

January 3, Tuesday . . . . . . Last day on which thesis outlines may be handed in by Master's degree candidates who plan to finish their work by the 1956 Commencement.

January 19, Thursday, 5:00 P.M. . . . Classes stop.

January 20, Friday . . . . . . Registration of graduate students.

January 23, Monday to February 1, Wednesday Final Examinations.

February 6, Monday . . . . . . Classes resume.

February 22, Wednesday . . . . Washington's Birthday: a holiday.

March 19, Monday . . . . . . Last day on which graduate students may drop courses without failure.

March 24, Saturday, 12:00 M., to April 2, Monday . . . . Spring recess.

April 19, Thursday . . . . . . Patriot's Day: a holiday.

May 19, Saturday, 12:00 M. . . . . Classes stop.

May 21, Monday, to May 31, Thursday, 5:00 P.M. . . . . Final Examinations.

May 29, Tuesday . . . . Last day for bound theses to be handed in.

May 30, Wednesday . . . . . . Memorial Day: a holiday.

June 1, Friday, to June 3, Sunday . . . Commencement.

September 17, Monday	Registration of graduate students.
September 19, Wednesday	Classes begin.
September 25, Tuesday	Last day on which registration cards may be handed in.
September 28, Friday	Last day on which thesis outlines may be handed in by Ph.D. candidates who plan to finish their work by the June, 1957 Commencement.
October 4, Thursday	Last day on which Ph.D. candidates who plan to complete their work by the June, 1957 Commencement may take the preliminary comprehensive examination.
October 12, Friday	Columbus Day: a holiday.
October 29, Monday	Last day on which graduate students may drop courses without failure.
November 12, Monday	Armistice Day: a holiday.
November 21, Wednesday, 12:00 M., to November 26, Monday	Thanksgiving recess.
December 15, Saturday, 12:00 M., to January 2, Wednesday	Christmas recess.
January 2, Wednesday	Last day on which thesis outlines may be handed in by Master's degree candidates who plan to finish their work by the 1957 Commencement.
January 17, Thursday, 5:00 P.M. . . .	Classes stop.
January 18, Friday	Registration of graduate students.
January 21, Monday, to January 30, Wednesday	Final Examinations.
February 4, Monday	Classes resume.
February 22, Friday	Washington's Birthday: a holiday.
March 18, Monday	Last day on which graduate students may drop courses without failure.
March 23, Saturday, 12:00 M., to April 1, Monday	Spring recess.
April 19, Friday	Patriot's Day: a holiday.
May 18, Saturday, 12:00 M.	Classes stop.
May 20, Monday, to May 29, Wednesday, 5:00 P.M.	Final Examinations.
May 29, Wednesday	Last day for bound theses to be handed in.
May 30, Thursday	Memorial Day: a holiday.
May 31, Friday, to June 2, Sunday . . .	Commencement.

THE TRUSTEES OF THE UNIVERSITY

Organization of 1955

The Graduate School Staff

J. PAUL MATHER, *President of the University.*
GILBERT L. WOODSIDE, *Dean of the Graduate School.*
Deans of the Schools.
Heads of Divisions.
Heads of Departments in which Graduate Courses are offered.
Professors, Associate Professors, Assistant Professors and Instructors in charge of courses offered for graduate credit. The entire staff is listed in the General Catalog of the University.

The Graduate School Council

GILBERT L. WOODSIDE, *Dean of the Graduate School,* Chairman.
EMMETT BENNETT, *Professor of Chemistry,* Secretary.
WILLIAM B. ESSELEN, *Professor of Food Technology.*
CHARLES F. FRAKER, *Head of the Department of Romance Languages.*
JOHN HANSON, *Associate Professor of Insect Morphology.*
FRED P. JEFFREY, *Associate Dean of the School of Agriculture and Horticulture, and Director of the Stockbridge School.*
MILO KIMBALL, *Dean of the School of Business Administration.*
WARREN LITSKY, *Associate Professor of Bacteriology.*
GEORGE A. MARSTON, *Dean of the School of Engineering.*
WARREN P. MCGUIRK, *Head of the Division of Physical Education.*
HELEN S. MITCHELL, *Dean of the School of Home Economics.*
ALBERT W. PURVIS, *Head of the Department of Education.*
FRANK P. RAND, *Dean of the School of Liberal Arts.*
CARL S. ROYS, *Head of the Department of Electrical Engineering.*
DALE H. SIELING, *Dean of the School of Agriculture and Horticulture.*

GENERAL INFORMATION

HISTORY

Graduate courses leading to the degree of doctor of science were offered in botany under President Clark and in chemistry under Professor Goessmann as early as 1876. No candidate, however, completed the requirements for that degree. It was not until 1892, under President Henry H. Goodell, that courses leading to the degree of master of science were offered. This degree was first conferred in June, 1896, on two candidates. Graduate courses leading to the degree of doctor of philosophy were first offered in 1897, with chemistry, botany and entomology as major and minor subjects. The first degree was conferred on one candidate in June, 1902.

In the early years the graduate work was conducted under the direct administration of the President in conjunction with the undergraduate program. The demand for advanced work increased, however, and in June, 1908, the trustees made the Graduate School a separate unit in the College.

LOCATION AND LANDS

The University of Massachusetts is located in Amherst, a town of about nine thousand people, overlooking one of the most picturesque sections of the Connecticut Valley. Amherst is eighty-eight miles from Boston, fifty miles from Worcester, twenty-five miles from Springfield, eighteen miles from Greenfield, and eight miles from Northampton. The campus consists of a tract of approximately seven hundred acres, lying about a mile north of the village center. The University is well provided with modern buildings and equipment, description of which may be found in the general catalog.

PURPOSE AND SCOPE OF THE GRADUATE SCHOOL

The purpose of the Graduate School is to provide qualified students with proper guidance in the methods of advanced study and research. Courses are available leading to the degree of doctor of philosophy, master of science, master of arts, master of landscape architecture, master of science in civil engineering, master of science in electrical engineering, master of science in mechanical engineering, master of science in agricultural engineering, master of business administration, and master of arts in teaching.

DOCTOR OF PHILOSOPHY

The degree is conferred upon graduate students who have met the following requirements:—

1. The preparation of a dissertation satisfactory to the thesis committee and the major department.

2. The earning of at least ninety credits, at least sixty of which must be in the major field, at least fifteen in another field or fields related to, but not part of, the major field and not more than thirty in recognition of the dissertation.

3. The passing of a preliminary written comprehensive examination in the major and minor fields supplemented by an oral examination at the option of the major department, both examinations to be conducted by the department concerned, to be passed not later than eight months before the completion of the candidate's work. In case of failure a candidate may be permitted a second and final opportunity, but not within twelve months.

4. Satisfying the following language requirement:—two languages, foreign to the candidate and not in the same linguistic group, as recommended by the major department. Proficiency tests should be passed as early as possible and must be passed prior to the preliminary examination.

5. The passing of a final examination, at least partly oral, conducted by the Thesis Committee primarily upon, but not limited to, the contents of the candi-

date's dissertation. The Examining Committee shall consist of the Thesis Committee, the Dean of the Graduate School, and such members of the major department as the Head shall appoint.

- 6. Satisfying the residence requirement. At least 30 course credits must have been earned at this University. No credit is valid after 9 years.

7. The payment of all fees and expenses.

MASTER OF SCIENCE, MASTER OF ARTS, MASTER OF SCIENCE IN CIVIL ENGINEER-ING, MASTER OF SCIENCE IN ELECTRICAL ENGINEERING, MASTER OF SCIENCE IN MECHANICAL ENGINEERING, MASTER OF SCIENCE IN AGRICULTURAL ENGINEERING, MASTER OF BUSINESS ADMINISTRATION.

The basic requirements for the above degrees are:—

1. Thirty credits, of which not more than six may be transferred from other institutions. Twenty-one of the thirty credits must be in the major field. If a thesis is offered, six credits must be earned in courses open to graduate students only; if a thesis is not offered, twelve credits must be earned in courses open to graduate students only. Not more than ten credits may be earned by means of a thesis. No credit is valid after 6 years.

2. The thesis is optional with the school or department, but if there is one it shall be under the supervision of a committee appointed by the Scholarship Committee of the Graduate School Council. The thesis must be approved by this committee and by the major department. The candidate must pass an oral examination to be conducted by the thesis committee. If there is no thesis, the candidate shall take a general examination, written or oral, or both under the supervision of the head of his major department. If a student offers a thesis, problem courses shall be limited to three credits; if a thesis is not offered, the limit shall be six credits.

3. All foreign language requirements are optional with the school or departments.

4. All fees and expenses must be paid before the degree will be conferred.

MASTER OF LANDSCAPE ARCHITECTURE

The degree is conferred upon graduate students who have met the following requirements:—

1. Work covering at least two years, of which a minimum of one and one-half years must be devoted to study in residence, and a minimum of one-half year spent in practice, specific requirements concerning the nature of such practice to be laid down by the department.

2. Submission of a written report on the work done in practice, or an oral examination conducted by the department staff.

3. The earning of not less than forty-five credits of which thirty shall conform essentially to the "fifth year program" (see page 74) the remainder to be selected from the "200 series" on page 72, with minor deviations at the discretion of the department.

4. Preparation of a satisfactory thesis.

5. The passing of final examinations, written and oral.

6. Payment of all fees and expenses.

MASTER OF BUSINESS ADMINISTRATION

1. The Master of Business Administration degree will be granted to those who satisfactorily complete sixty semester hours of approved course work as follows:

26-6.	INTRODUCTION TO ACCOUNTING.	6 semester hours.
25-6.	ELEMENTS OF ECONOMICS.	6 semester hours.

179.	ELEMENTS OF STATISTICS.	3 semester hours.
153.	MARKETING PRINCIPLES.	3 semester hours.
155.	FINANCIAL INSTITUTIONS.	3 semester hours.
163.	MANAGEMENT IN INDUSTRY.	3 semester hours.
165.	CORPORATION FINANCE.	3 semester hours.
170.	BUSINESS LAW.	3 semester hours.

The above basic courses may be taken as part of a graduate program, or may have been anticipated in undergraduate course work.

201.	THE BUSINESS ENTERPRISE.	3 semester hours.
211.	ACCOUNTING IN MANAGEMENT.	3 semester hours.
222.	MARKETING MANAGEMENT.	3 semester hours.
231.	FINANCIAL MANAGEMENT.	3 semester hours.
242.	PRODUCTION MANAGEMENT.	3 semester hours.
252.	ADMINISTRATIVE PRACTICES.	3 semester hours.
271.	SEMINAR IN BUSINESS ADMINISTRATION.	3 semester hours.
272.	SEMINAR IN BUSINESS ADMINISTRATION.	3 semester hours.
	ELECTIVES: two from those available for graduate credit and approved by the adviser.	6 semester hours.

2. A candidate for the Master of Business Administration *with Honors* mus submit an acceptable thesis prepared under the direction of a Supervisor ap pointed by the Scholarship Committee of the Graduate School Council. Th thesis may be substituted for one or both of the elective courses as evaluate by the Committee and the Supervisor. If a thesis be adjudged not distinctive it will be accepted only in lieu of required course work as evaluated by th Committee and the Supervisor.

3. Each candidate for the M.B.A. degree is required to pass an oral examina tion.

4. All fees and expenses must be paid before the degree will be conferred.

MASTER OF ARTS IN TEACHING

This is a cooperative program between the College of Arts and Sciences an the Department of Education intended primarily for graduates of approve Liberal Arts Institutions who have had little or no course work in professiona education. The student will register in the Department of Education for eithe the secondary or elementary teaching program.

The special provisions are:—

1. Secondary school program. Eighteen hours in the fundamental educatio courses usually required for certification; at least twelve hours in general edu cation courses of which six hours will be in the two hundred category (course open to graduate students only).

2. Elementary school program. Twenty-four hours in the fundamental ed cation courses usually required for certification; at least twelve hours in gener education courses of which six hours will be in the two hundred category.

Provisions applying to both groups:—

1. Ordinarily the program will be undertaken in one year of residence or one year plus a summer session, and for this degree no credit will be valid after two years.

2. All fees and expenses must be paid before the degree will be conferred.

ADMISSION

Students may be admitted to the Graduate School either on limited status or on full status.

A. Requirements for admission on limited status:—

1. A Bachelor's Degree or its equivalent from any college or university of recognized standing.

2. An official transcript of all previous college work.

3. A letter of recommendation from the head of the department of the applicant's undergraduate major or a letter from his present employer. Under certain circumstances a student may enroll tentatively in courses in the University without having fulfilled requirements 2. (official transcript) and 3. (a letter from the head of the department of the applicant's undergraduate major or a letter from his present employer) but no credit will be given until the requirements are fulfilled.

4. Acceptance by the department and by the Admissions Committee of the Graduate School Council.

Graduate students on limited status will be held to the same standard of performance as Graduate Students on full status. If they wish to become Graduate Students on full status they may petition the Admissions Committee of the Graduate School Council.

They may attain full status on the completion of a satisfactory record at this University, the recommendation of the department concerned, and the approval of the Committee on Admissions.

B. Requirements for admission on full status:—

1. A Bachelor's Degree or the equivalent from any college or university of recognized standing.

2. An official transcript of all previous college work.

3. A letter of recommendation from the head of the department of the applicant's undergraduate major.

4. A letter of recommendation from someone (not connected with the applicant's undergraduate major) who is qualified to judge the student's ability in academic work.

5. The applicant must have been in the upper half of his graduating class. (Those who do not meet this requirement may apply for admission on limited status.) If the transcript does not indicate the rank of the applicant, it is the duty of the Committee on Admissions to evaluate the transcript.

6. Acceptance by the department and by the Admissions Committee of the Graduate School Council.

Admission to the Graduate School on either limited or full status does not imply admission to candidacy for an advanced degree. Such candidacy is subject to specific requirements as laid down by the several departments, and the student must secure the approval of the head of the department in which he desires to major before he can become a candidate for a degree in that subject.

Graduates of Normal Schools are permitted to take courses in the 200 series in the Department of Education, but not as candidates for a University of Massachusetts degree.

With the approval of the Head of the Department concerned, special students are permitted to take graduate courses, but not to exceed a total of six credits.

GENERAL STATEMENT

Graduate credit will be allowed for grades of A, B, and C. Not more than six credits of C will be allowed for a Master's degree. Not more than twelve credits of C will be allowed for the Doctor of Philosophy degree. Thesis work must receive a grade of A or B to be accepted by the Graduate School. No graduate credit will be given for courses numbered below 100.

After registration is completed, courses may be added or dropped or changed from credit to audit only upon the approval of the student's adviser and the Dean of the Graduate School. The consent of the instructor also is necessary for the addition of courses. If the student is not passing a course at the time it is dropped, a failure will be recorded. No student, under any conditions, may drop a course after these dates: First semester, November 1; second semester, March 20; Summer School, two weeks from the beginning of the summer session, without a failure unless granted permission by the Scholarship Committee of the Graduate School Council.

Students in the Graduate School may be dismissed for failure to abide by the rules of the University.

The University reserves the right to make changes in the requirements for degrees without notice.

COURSES OFFERED

Courses available as major subjects for the degree of doctor of philosophy:—

Agronomy	Entomology
Bacteriology	Food Sciences
Botany	Food Technology
Chemistry	Psychology
Economics	

Courses available as major subjects for the master's degree:—

Agricultural Economics	Geology and Mineralogy
Agricultural Engineering	History
Agronomy	Home Economics
Animal Husbandry	Landscape Architecture
Bacteriology	Mathematics
Botany	Mechanical Engineering
Business Administration	Olericulture
Chemistry	Philosophy
Civil Engineering	Pomology
Dairy Industry	Poultry Science
Economics	Public Health
Education	Psychology
Electrical Engineering	Romance Languages
English	Sociology
Entomology	Wildlife Management
Floriculture	Zoology
Food Technology	

Courses available as minor subjects:—

Agricultural Economics and Farm Management	Geology and Mineralogy
Agricultural Engineering	German
Agronomy	Government
Animal Husbandry	History
Bacteriology	Home Economics
Botany	Landscape Architecture
Business Administration	Mathematics
Chemistry	Olericulture
Chemical Engineering	Philosophy
Civil Engineering	Physical Education for Men
Dairy Industry	Physics
Economics	Pomology
Education	Poultry Science
Electrical Engineering	Psychology
English	Public Health
Entomology	Romance Languages
Floriculture	Sociology
Food Technology	Veterinary Science
Forestry	Wildlife Management
	Zoology

THESES

A thesis must be on a topic in the field of the candidate's major subject, and must indicate that its writer possesses the ability and imagination necessary to do independent constructive thinking. The following rules should be adhered to in the preparation and presentation of a thesis:—

The objective of a thesis should be an attempt to make a real contribution to knowledge and practice. When completed it should be of a quality worthy of publication as a contribution from the department concerned.

The thesis, in its completed form, will be judged largely upon the ability of the author to review literature and reach definite deductions; to formulate a problem, plan a method of attack, and work out a solution; and to summarize his material and draw conclusions. Scholastic attainment in writing and presenting the results of the study will also be an important factor in the evaluation. No thesis markedly poor in its English will be accepted.

Four copies of each Master's thesis outline and six copies of each Doctor's thesis outline are to be transmitted to the Dean of the Graduate School by the head of the department in which the student is majoring. The letter of transmittal should contain the name of the professor within the department who is responsible for the direction of the student's research. This professor will be appointed the Chairman of the student's Thesis Committee. Other possible members of the Thesis Committee might be suggested in the letter of transmittal, but the Scholarship Committee of the Graduate School Council has the responsibility of assigning all faculty members to Thesis Committees.

It is the responsibility of the chairman of the Thesis Committee to arrange a conference with other members of the Thesis Committee and the student for the purpose of discussing the research problem before approving the thesis outline. This should be done as soon as possible after the appointment of the Thesis Committee.

The fourth (or sixth, if Ph.D.) copy of the student's thesis outline is then to be signed by each member of the Thesis Committee to indicate approval of the outline and to indicate the fact that a conference with the student has been held. The fourth (or sixth) copy of the thesis outline is then to be returned to the Dean of the Graduate School.

The outline for the thesis for the Master's Degree must be presented not later than January first of the year in which the student expects to get the degree, or five months before he expects to complete the work for the degree.

The outline for the thesis for the Doctor of Philosophy degree must be presented by October first, prior to the June Commencement at which the student expects to get the degree.

The Thesis Committee will have direct charge of all matters pertaining to the thesis, and it is recommended that the student use the advice available from this source in the progress of his research. The thesis must have the unanimous approval of this committee and of the major department before arrangements are made for the final examination for the degree.

Three complete, bound copies of the thesis, including drawings and any other accessories, are required by the Graduate School in order that the files in the Graduate office, the library, and the department in which the thesis was prepared may be supplied. The original copy will be deposited in the Library by the Graduate School. The student is responsible for the binding of the thesis.

If the thesis is printed, whether in periodical or book form, the fact that it is a thesis submitted for an advanced degree at the University of Massachusetts shall be explicitly stated in the title itself or as a footnote on the front page.

Because of the time required to give adequate consideration to the research conducted by the student, it is highly desirable that theses be submitted to the committee, in the case of doctor's theses, not later than March 15, and in the case of master's theses, not later than May 15 of the academic year in which the degrees are to be conferred. The theses in their final bound form shall be deposited with the Dean of the Graduate School by June 1.

If typewritten, whether designed for publication or to remain in the typewritten form, the size of the sheet, the arrangement of the title page, the general structure of the thesis, the character of the paper, and the binding must conform to definite standards.

A. *Size of sheet.* Size of sheet must measure 8½ x 11 inches.

B. *Form of title page.* The title page should be distributed as artistically as possible and must be arranged in this order:

    a. Subject.

    b. Name of author.

    c. "Thesis submitted in partial fulfillment of the requirements for the degree of—."

    d. "University of Massachusetts, Amherst."

    e. Date.

C. Following the title page, the arrangement may take such form, variable of course with the subject matter, as is illustrated below:—

    a. An analytical outline of the thesis.

    b. An introductory statement in which the purposes of the author are set forth.

    c. The body of the thesis composed of literature critically reviewed and deductions made, formulation of method of attack or procedure, and results secured. (All literature reviews and any work done by others should be so separated that no question can be raised as to which portion of the thesis represents the original investigation. It should be clearly kept in mind that *compilation* is not considered original investigation.)

    d. Summary and conclusions.

    e. Bibliography. (This should have the approval of the chairman of the thesis committee before final arrangement.)

    f. Acknowledgments.

    g. Statements of approval signed by members of the thesis committee.

D. *Paper.* See sample in the University store.

E. *Binding.* See sample of binding in the Graduate School Office.

All theses are the property of the University.

ESTIMATE OF EXPENSES

A charge of $50 per semester, payable in advance, which covers tuition, laboratory and student health fees, is imposed on students who are residents of Massachusetts. For residents of other states or foreign countries, this charge is $110 per semester. In cases where students carry less than a full schedule of courses, a special tuition rate is provided. Residents of the State pay $5 per credit; nonresidents pay $10. For purposes of definition, all students claiming residence in the State shall at time of admission provide the treasurer's office with an official statement from their town or city clerk as evidence.

Candidates for a Master's degree who have paid a full year's tuition in the Graduate School are not required to pay an additional amount if they later register for a Master's thesis.

Candidates for the Doctor of Philosophy degree who have paid two full years' tuition in the Graduate School are not required to pay an additional amount if they later register for the Doctor's thesis.

Board should not be in excess of $12 per week. Rooms for graduate students are not available in the dormitories, but can be rented in private homes at from $20 to $25 per month. The cost of books and incidentals should not exceed $150 per year.

LOTTA CRABTREE FELLOWSHIPS

A limited number of fellowships paying $2000 each are available to students in the broad field of agriculture. Students applying for these fellowships must be interested in earning the Doctor of Philosophy degree for the purpose of serving agricultural pursuits. Application should be made to the Dean of the Graduate School.

TEACHING FELLOWSHIPS

The University offers a number of teaching fellowships for the purpose of assisting with the instructional program of various departments. The stipend is $1000 per year, and appointments absolve students from 'tuition and are especially suited to those who desire to gain teaching experience and to make themselves at least partly self-supporting while continuing their education. It should be recognized, however, that, in cases where students render this part-time service in return for the financial assistance extended, the residence time requirement for the degree in question is necessarily longer. Teaching fellows may carry up to 13 credits per semester, but the total in any one academic year may not exceed 24 credits. Application for appointment to these fellowships should be made to the Dean of the Graduate School or to the head of the department in which the candidate's major interest lies.

RESEARCH FELLOWSHIPS

A number of research fellowships are available to qualified graduate students. These are made possible because funds are provided by a). various industries, b). the Experiment Station, or c). research grants awarded to members of the Graduate School Faculty either from sources outside the University or from a fund provided by the University and administered by the Teaching Staff Research Council. Stipends vary with the type of work and the amount of time involved. Interested students should make application to the head of the department in which they plan to work.

THE CRAMPTON RESEARCH FUND

Interest from the Guy Chester Crampton Research Fund is used to help defray the costs of publication of worthy research papers completed by students or occasionally by staff members. Information concerning the fields of work for which grants may be made, and instructions for application, may be obtained from department heads, the chairman of the Crampton Fund Committee or the graduate school office.

GRADUATE COURSES DURING THE SUMMER

The University offers opportunities to pursue graduate courses during the summer in connection with the Summer School. Details regarding courses offered, facilities for study, etc., may be found in the Summer School Catalog, a copy of which is available upon request to the Provost of the University.

DESCRIPTION OF COURSES

Agricultural Economics
ADRIAN H. LINDSEY, major adviser.

COURSES OPEN TO GRADUATE STUDENTS ONLY
(For either major or minor credit)

200. RESEARCH.—Investigations of problems in Agricultural Economics and Farm Management. Credit, 3

Mr. LINDSEY.

202. AGRICULTURAL PRICE THEORY.—The application of economic principles and measurements to the analysis of agricultural prices. Credit, 3.

Mr. LINDSEY.

300. THESIS, Master's Degree. Credit, 4-10.

COURSES OPEN TO BOTH GRADUATE AND UNDERGRADUATE STUDENTS
(For either major or minor credit)

155. MARKETING.—An analysis of the problems, types of marketing agencies, principal marketing functions, marketing costs and margins, price quotations and exchange operations, governmental regulations and the consideration of improvement proposals. Credit, 3.

Mr. LINDSEY.

156. FUNDAMENTALS OF COOPERATION.—A study of the development of co-operative organizations and the economic analysis of cooperative principles and operation. Credit, 3.

Mr. LINDSEY.

157. AGRICULTURAL CREDIT AND LAND APPRAISAL.—The principles and methods of land valuation and credit extension. There is also a study of the operations of institutions granting credit to agriculture. Credit, 3.

Mr. LINDSEY.

171. AGRICULTURAL ECONOMIC THEORY.—A comparative and critical study of the significant contributions of the leading economists from Adam Smith to the present. Credit, 3.

Mr. LINDSEY.

175. FARM ORGANIZATION AND MANAGEMENT.—External and internal economic forces affecting the farm business such as selection and combination of factors of farm production, choice and combination of farm enterprises, and adjusting farm production to markets and prices. Credit, 3.

Mr. BARRETT.

176. ADVANCED FARM MANAGEMENT.—The use of farm records as a basis for planning and budgeting is emphasized. The last part of the course will be given over to the specific study of selected farms. Field trips are required at an estimated cost of not over five dollars. Credit, 2.

Mr. BARRETT.

Prerequisite, Agricultural Economics 175.

Statistics 177. ELEMENTARY EXPERIMENTAL STATISTICS.—"Chi" squire, "t" and analysis of variance tests of significance; frequency distribution, average, dispersion, regression and simple correlation description; and chart and table presentation are the specific fields covered.

Students electing Statistics 177 may not take Statistics 179.   Credit, 3.

Mr. RUSSELL.

178. PRINCIPLES OF LAND ECONOMICS.—A study of the utilization of agricultural land and the economic problems of development, settlement, conservation and policy.   Credit, 3.

Mr. LINDSEY.

Statistics 179. ELEMENTARY ECONOMICS STATISTICS.—"Surveys, tables, charts, frequency distributions, averages, dispersion, standard error and its use, quality control, index numbers, time series, and simple correlation are the specific fields covered."   Credit, 3.

Students electing Statistics 179 may not take Statistics 177.   Mr. RUSSELL.

Statistics 180. ADVANCED STATISTICAL METHOD.—Multiple correlation and analysis of variance.   Credit, 3.

Mr. LINDSEY and Mr. RUSSELL.

182. ADVANCED FARM OPERATION.—A study of farm operations with special emphasis on time and motion experiments.   Credit, 3.

Mr. BARRETT.

189. SEMINAR.—Public and price policy for agriculture.   Credit, 2-3.

Mr. LINDSEY.

190. SEMINAR.—Agricultural Institutions.   Credit, 2-3.

Mr. RUSSELL

COURSES IN OTHER DEPARTMENTS FOR WHICH MAJOR CREDIT WILL BE GIVEN

Economics 153. MONEY, BANKING, AND CREDIT.   Credit, 3.

Mr. GAMBLE.

Economics 155. ECONOMICS OF CONSUMPTION.   Credit, 3.

Mr. HALLER.

Economics 156. BUSINESS CYCLES.   Credit, 3.

Mr. SCHOEFFLER.

Economics 165. CORPORATION FINANCE.   Credit, 3.

Mr. GAMBLE.

Economics 170. MONOPOLIES.   Credit, 3.

Mr. HALLER.

Economics 173. MODERN ECONOMIC THEORY.   Credit, 3.

Mr. SCHOEFFLER.

Economics 178. PUBLIC FINANCE.   Credit, 3.

Mr. GAMBLE.

Agricultural Engineering
H. N. STAPLETON, major adviser.

COURSES OPEN TO GRADUATE STUDENTS ONLY
(For either major or minor credit.)

240. ADVANCED FARM STRUCTURES.—The application of structural theory in the development of high strength structures. The use of building materials and fastening for attaining diaphragms and prestressed components in the development of the structure.

The use of structural factors in the control of environment. Credit, 3.
Prerequisite, Agricultural Engineering 173. Mr. BARTON.

241. CONTROL OF HEAT AND VAPOR FLOW IN AGRICULTURAL BUILDINGS AND PROCESSES.—Application of mass flow theory to heat and vapor transfer. Thermal and vapor interchange between environment and livestock controlling production rates of metabolic and respiratory heat. The application of instruments and controls. Credit, 3.
Prerequisite, Agricultural Engineering 173. Mr. BARTON.

250. UNIT OPERATIONS IN AGRICULTURE.—Machine rates and production standards in the production and handling of crops. The uses of climatic data, water control, and production schedules in crop operations. Plant layout and equipment for processing and storage. Energy requirements of alternate methods of processing. Credit, 3.
Prerequisite, Permission of Instructor. Mr. STAPLETON.

260. AGRICULTURAL PROCESSING.—Heat, refrigeration, and vacuum in dehydrating, storing, and concentrating agricultural products. Critical temperatures, latent heats, fermentation, respiration, and equilibrium moisture content, as they affect the processes and the end products. The effects of modified atmosphere, adsorbents, and dessicants. The application of instruments and controls.
Prerequisite, Agricultural Engineering 173. Credit, 3.
Mr. PATTERSON.

276. ADVANCED AGRICULTURAL MACHINERY DESIGN.—Stress analysis, periodic vibration, and shock leadings, as related to design of agricultural machinery. The mathematical definition of tillage tool surfaces. Dynamics of suspension devices, automatic release equipment, and hydraulic systems. Credit, 3.
Prerequisite, Agricultural Engineering 176. Mr. PATTERSON.

292. SEMINAR.—Review of current literature on research. Credit, 1.
THE STAFF.

300. THESIS, MASTER'S DEGREE. Credit, 4-8.

COURSES OPEN TO BOTH GRADUATE AND UNDERGRADUATE STUDENTS
(For either major or minor credit.)

171. FARM POWER.—The study of internal combustion engines used in farm tractors and power units. Credit, 3.
Prerequisites, Civil Engineering 52 and Mechanical Engineering 65, 68.
Mr. PATTERSON.

173. FARM STRUCTURES.—A study of the strength and durability of building materials, construction systems and the mechanical principles underlying their use in farm-construction. In the drafting room studies will be made of some major farm building and complete working drawings finished in all essential details. Credit, 4.
Prerequisites, Civil Engineering 34, 51, and 61. Mr. STAPLETON.

176. AGRICULTURAL MACHINERY.—The study of design and operational problems of agricultural field machinery. Credit, 3.

Prerequisites, Civil Engineering 52, Mechanical Engineering 68, 83.

Mr. PATTERSON.

178. DRAINAGE, RECLAMATION AND CONSERVATION.—The course covers the engineering phase of drainage and reclamation. The various systems are studied, complete layouts established in the field, and problems of flow and run-off given.

Prerequisites, Civil Engineering 27, 75, or 76; Agronomy 2. Credit, 3.

Mr. STAPLETON.

185. RURAL ELECTRIFICATION.—A course devoted to the utilization of electricity in agriculture. Credit, 3.

Prerequisite, Electrical Engineering 61, 62. Mr. STAPLETON.

COURSES FOR MINOR CREDIT ONLY

151. HOUSE PLANNING.—Plan designs of the small house, will be made. The arrangement of interior equipment, especially in the kitchen, and lighting, heating, water supply, and sewage disposal will be studied, together with a brief history of the house materials, construction methods, equipment, and architectural styles. Consideration will be given to the economics of house building, including financing and to maintenance and overhead expense. Credit, 3.

Mr. MARKUSON.

155. FARM SHOP.—For students in agriculture and horticulture. Laboratory exercises cover instruction and practice in the use of carpenter's tools in construction and in bench work, arc and gas welding, pipe fitting, soldering, use of machinist's tools in machinery repair, and the mixing and placing of concrete. Classroom instruction covers materials of construction and the utilization of local and special materials for these purposes. Credit, 3.

Mr. PIRA and Mr. POWERS.

174. FARM BUILDINGS.—For students without the prerequisites for Agricultural Engineering 173. Credit, 3.

Mr. STAPLETON.

180. FOOD PROCESS ENGINEERING.—A study of food processing machinery and instrumentation. Credit, 3.

MR. PATTERSON.

182. REFRIGERATION.—Fundamentals in planning and operating a refrigerated storage with particular reference to size, details of construction, cooling load, and refrigerating machinery and accessories. For non-engineering majors.

Prerequisite, Agricultural Engineering 180. Credit, 2.

MR. PATTERSON.

Agronomy

WILLIAM G. COLBY, major adviser.

COURSES OPEN TO GRADUATE STUDENTS ONLY
(For either major or minor credit)

200. SPECIAL PROBLEMS.   Credit, 3 or 6.
                                                                  THE STAFF.

211. FIELD CROP PRODUCTION.—A survey course which includes the regional distribution, the cultural requirements, production, and the utilization of the principal field crops grown in the U. S. Given in alternate years, beginning 1953-54.   Credit, 3.
                                                                  Mr. COLBY.

216. FORAGE CROPS.—A survey course which includes the regional distribution, the cultural requirements and the utilization of the principal forage crops grown in the U. S. Given in alternate years, beginning 1952-53.   Credit, 3.
                                                                  Mr. COLBY.

226. CROP IMPROVEMENT.—This is a course in applied genetics involving a study of various plant breeding procedures used in the improvement of important agricultural crops.   Credit, 3.
Prerequisite, Zoology 153, Plant Breeding 152.   Mr. YEGIAN.

263. CHEMISTRY OF THE SOIL.—The chemistry of soil formation, soil acidity, nutrient element availability, ionic exchange and fixation, biological soils reactions, soil-plant-microorganism relationships, and of organic matter of the soil will be discussed. The laboratory work will consist of physical, analytical and biochemical investigations of soils and important soil constituents.   Credit, 5.
                                                                  Mr. STECKEL.

264. EXPERIMENTAL METHODS IN AGRONOMY.—The purpose of this course is to set forth some of the concepts regarding the application of statistics to the analysis and interpretation of data obtained in agricultural research. Such points as choice of field, design of experiments, effect of competition, interpretation of results, and other special factors that need to be considered in well-planned experiments are discussed.   Credit, 3.
                                                                  Mr. YEGIAN.

290. SEMINAR.   Credit, 1 each semester.
                                                                  THE STAFF.

300. THESIS, Master's degree.   Credit, 10.

400. THESIS, Ph. D. degree.   Credit, 30.

COURSES OPEN TO BOTH GRADUATE AND
UNDERGRADUATE STUDENTS

(For either major or minor credit)

151. FIELD CROPS.—A study of the field crops of the U. S. which will include their uses and improvement, with their soil and climatic requirements. Emphasis will be given to the best farm practices of the northeastern states as to rotation, liming, seeding methods, tillage, disease and insect control, and methods of harvesting and storage. As an individual problem, each student must make a detailed plan of crop production for the actual conditions of some New England farm. Credit, 3.

Mr. PARSONS.

152. SOIL UTILIZATION.—The relationship of climate and native vegetation to the broader aspects of soil formation; man's use of land resources; soil use and abuse; soil erosion control and its significance to permanent agriculture. Credit, 3.

Mr. EVERSON.

153. AGROSTOLOGY.—All factors that influence the successful growing of fine turf grasses are studied and correlated to enable the student to have a practical working knowledge of the construction and maintenance of lawns, sports, highways, airport and cemetery turf. Credit, 3.

Mr. DICKINSON.

156. AGROSTOLOGY.—This course considers fine turf management as a business and profession. Emphasis is placed on diagnosis and treatment of turf failures; the selection of equipment and supplies and client approach. Field trips and practical exercises arranged. Credit, 3.

Mr. DICKINSON.

157. SOIL FORMATION.—Physical, chemical, biological, climatic and geological factors involved in soil formation. The relationship of these factors to the kinds of soils formed in the United States. Credit, 3.

Mr. EVERSON.

179. SOIL PHYSICS.—For seniors in Agronomy. The factors in soil which control tilth and energy relationships and the laws of physics which govern these factors are discussed. This includes heat, light, color, particle size and charge, water and gas movement, energy relationships and other physical factors effecting changes in the soil. The laboratory is used to familiarize the students with various methods used in measuring these important physical factors. Credit, 3.

Mr. EVERSON.

184 A. SOIL CHEMISTRY.—For plant science and soil science students. Fundamental inorganic, organic, and biochemical reactions of soils. Plant nutrition and microbiological plant interrelationships. Credit, 3.
Prerequisites, Chemistry 29, Botany 168, Agronomy 157. Mr. STECKEL.

184 B. SOIL CHEMISTRY LABORATORY.—Primarily for seniors in Agronomy. Methods and techniques used in soil chemistry research and in plant science investigations will be studied. The student will be made familiar with methods of determining exchangeable bases, base exchange capacity, soil phosphate fractionation, and many other determinations peculiar to soil investigations. To be taken concurrently with Agronomy 184 A. Credit, 2.
Prerequisites, Chemistry 29, 30, Botany 168, Agronomy 157. Mr. STECKEL.

COURSES IN OTHER DEPARTMENTS FOR WHICH
MAJOR CREDIT WILL BE GIVEN

Bacteriology 211. ADVANCED BACTERIOLOGY.   Credit, 3.
                                                          Miss GARVEY.

Botany 202, 203. ADVANCED PLANT PHYSIOLOGY. Credit, 2-4 each semester.
                                                        Mr. KOZLOWSKI.

Botany 205, 206. ADVANCED PLANT PATHOLOGY. Credit, 2-4 each semester.
                                                        Mr. BANFIELD.

Botany 159, 160. THE ANGIOSPERMS.   Credit, 3-5 each semester.
                                                          Mr. TORREY

Botany 166. GENERAL MYCOLOGY.   Credit, 3.
            •   Mr. BANFIELD

Botany 167, 168. INTRODUCTORY PLANT PHYSIOLOGY. Credit, 3 each semester
                                                        Mr. KOZLOWSKI

Botany 175. METHODS IN PLANT PATHOLOGY.   Credit, 3.
                                                          Mr. BANFIELD.

Botany 181. PLANT ECOLOGY.   Credit, 3.
                                                        Mr. LIVINGSTON.

Botany 182. PLANT GEOGRAPHY.   Credit, 2.
                                                        Mr. LIVINGSTON.

Botany 189. PLANT CYTOGENETICS.   Credit, 3.
                                                        Mr. NICKERSON.

Chemistry 208. CHEMICAL SPECTROSCOPY.   Credit, 3.
                                                          Mr. SMITH.

Chemistry 237. BIOCOLLOIDS.   Credit, 3.
                                                          Mr. BENNETT.

Chemistry 151, 152. ORGANIC CHEMISTRY.   Credit, 4 each semester.
                                        Mr. RITCHIE and Mr. CANNON.

Chemistry 165, 166. PHYSICAL CHEMISTRY.   Credit, 4 each semester.
                                      Mr. FESSENDEN and Mr. SMITH.

Chemistry 179. BIOCHEMISTRY.   Credit, 4.
                                                          Mr. LITTLE.

Civil Engineering 280. APPLIED SOIL MECHANICS.   Credit, 3.
                                                       Mr. HENDRICKSON.

Geology 201. OPTICAL MINERALOGY.   Credilt, 3.
                                                          Mr. NELSON.

Geology 151. MINERALOGY.   Credit, 3.
                                                          Mr. NELSON.

Geology 152. LITHOLOGY.   Credit, 3.
                                                          Mr. NELSON.

Geology 161. GEOMORPHOLOGY.   Credit, 3.
                                                          Mr. WILSON.

Home Economics 203. ADVANCED NUTRITION—METABOLISM OF THE MAJOR
FOODSTUFFS.   Credit, 3.
Miss MITCHELL.

Home Economics 204. ADVANCED NUTRITION—MINERALS AND VITAMINS.
Credit, 3.
Miss MITCHELL.

Plant Breeding 152. ADVANCED PLANT BREEDING.   Credit, 3.
Mr. FRENCH.

Plant Breeding 181. PLANT CYTOLOGICAL TECHNIQUES.   Credit, 2.
Mr. FRENCH.

Plant Breeding 182. SPECIAL PROBLEM IN PLANT BREEDING.   Credit, 2.
Mr. FRENCH.

Poultry Science 203. ADVANCED GENETICS.   Credit, 3.
Mr. HAYS.

Poultry Science 204. ADVANCED GENETICS.   Credit, 3.
Mr. HAYS.

Animal Husbandry

VICTOR A. RICE, Major adviser.

COURSES OPEN TO GRADUATE STUDENTS ONLY
(For either major or minor credit)

Major credit for Animal Husbandry Department students assumes prerequisites in the Animal Husbandry field as covered in undergraduate courses in this University. All hours by arrangement.

200. PROBLEMS IN LIVESTOCK PRODUCTION.—This course will deal with some specific problem in feeding, breeding, production or management as relates to the production of some specific livestock product such as milk, wool, meat and so on. Assistance will be given in outlining the problem and setting up the experimental procedure with the student responsible for collecting and analyzing the data.   Credit, 5.
THE STAFF.

205. ADVANCED ANIMAL NUTRITION.—The chemistry of feed stuffs and the chemistry and physiology of digestion, absorption and utilization of energy, proteins, minerals and vitamins in milk, meat, wool or work production. Recent and current research will be evaluated. Given in alternate years only.   Credit, 5.
Prerequisite, 151 or its equivalent.   Mr. ARCHIBALD and Mr. ELLIOT.

210. ADVANCED ANIMAL BREEDING.—This course will stress selectively the physiology of reproduction, genetics, systems of breeding and selection according to the student's needs and objectives. The student will, in addition, make a thorough review and analysis of available data in the field of his choice. Not a problem course.   Credit, 5.
Prerequisites, 175, 176 or equivalent.   Mr. RICE.

220. MILK SECRETION.—The fundamentals of milk secretion including the gross and microscopic anatomy of the mammary gland. The development of the mammary gland from birth through parturition and lactation will be studied. The physiology of milk secretion will be reviewed both in relation to the endocrine grands which control it and to more practical aspects of successful dairy cattle management.   Credit, 3.
Mr. FOLEY.

230. ANIMAL HUSBANDRY RESEARCH EVALUATION.—Some specific phase or phases of research in Animal Husbandry will be selected and a running critical evaluation will be presented weekly in oral form and at semester's end in writ-ten form. Credit, 5.

THE STAFF.

300. THESIS, MASTER'S DEGREE. Credit, 5-10.

COURSES OPEN TO BOTH GRADUATE AND UNDERGRADUATE STUDENTS

(Minor credit only for Animal Husbandry Department Students.)

151. THE NUTRITION OF FARM ANIMALS.—The mechanics of digestion, absorption, metabolism, and excretion; the functions of proteins, carbohydrates, fats, vitamins, and minerals in body metabolism; the functions of those endocrine glands primarily concerned with nutrition; the nature and value of the various feed stuffs; and methods of calculating rations in order to meet the requirements of various classes of livestock.
3 class hours; one 2-hour laboratory period. Credit, 4.

Mr. ELLIOT.

153. ELEMENTS OF MEAT PACKING. For department majors only. The development of the modern packing industry, the history of meat inspection, the principles of meat preservation, the classification of cattle, calves, sheep and swine into proper market classes and grades and slaughtering and dressing operations. A one-day trip through the packing plants of Boston is a requirement of this course and will cost about ten dollars. Credit, 3.
1 class hour; one 4-hour laboratory period. Mr. BARTLETT.

154. MEAT PROCESSING.—For students not majoring in Animal Husbandry. The physical properties, preservation, processing and identification of meats. The laboratory periods will be devoted to slaughtering, cutting, curing, smoking and freezing of meat. One packing plant field trip will be made—approximate cost $5.00. Credit, 2.
Permission of instructor is required. Mr. BARTLETT.
One 4-hour laboratory period.

156. BEEF AND SHEEP PRODUCTION.—The historical and economic development, present status and probable future trends of beef and sheep production in the United States, especially in New England. Consideration will be given to types of production, systems and methods of feeding, management and marketing. In the laboratory, practice will be obtained in fitting and showing as well as certain practical techniques such as dehorning, ear-tagging, castrating, foot-trimming, shearing, etc., and treatment and prevention of external and internal parasites as well as common ailments.
2 class hours; one 2-hour laboratory period. Credit, 3.

Mr. BAKER.

156A. GENERAL LIVESTOCK JUDGING AND FIELD TRIPS.—This course is given in conjunction with Animal Husbandry 156 and consists of practice in judging and selecting beef cattle, sheep, horses and swine. Throughout the spring, field trips are made to nearby livestock farms and breeding establishments. Credit, 1.
One 4-hour laboratory period. Mr. BAKER.

172. MEAT JUDGING.—The classification, grading, and judging of carcasses and cuts of beef, veal, lamb and pork. Credit, 1.
One 4-hour laboratory period. Mr. BARTLETT.

Prerequisites, Animal Husbandry 151 and 153 or permission of instructor.

174. ADVANCED MEAT STUDIES.—For Animal Husbandry and Food Technology majors.   Credit, 2.
One 4-hour laboratory period.   Mr. BARTLETT.

175. ANIMAL BREEDING.—Reproductive physiology; genetics.   Credit, 4.
Three 2-hour laboratory periods.   Mr. RICE.

176. ANIMAL BREEDING TECHNIQUES.—The practical application of the principles of physiology of reproduction and selection to the improvement of farm animals.   Credit, 1.
One 2-hour laboratory period.   Mr. BAKER.

177. DAIRY CATTLE PRODUCTION.   Credit, 3.
Two class hours, one 2-hour laboratory.   Mr. FOLEY.

178. DAIRY CATTLE PRODUCTION.   Credit, 3.
Two class hours, one 2-hour laboratory.   Mr. FOLEY.

179. HORSE AND SWINE PRODUCTION.   Credit, 3.
Two class hours, one 2-hour laboratory period.   Mr. BAKER.

179A. ADVANCED LIVESTOCK JUDGING.—Beef, sheep, horse, and swine judging and selection. Field trips will be made to breeding establishments. Credit, 1.
One 4-hour laboratory period.   Mr. BAKER.
Prerequisite, Animal Husbandry 156A or permission of instructor.

181. SEMINAR.—For Animal Husbandry majors.   Credit, 1.
One 2-hour laboratory period.   Mr. FOLEY.

182. SEMINAR.—For Animal Husbandry majors.   Credit, 1.
One 2-hour laboratory period.   Mr. Rice.

183. ADVANCED MEAT JUDGING.—A continuation of Course 172.   Credit, 1.
One 4-hour laboratory period, first half of semester.   Mr. BARTLETT.
Prerequisite, Animal Husbandry 172 and permission of instructor.

COURSES IN OTHER DEPARTMENTS FOR WHICH MAJOR CREDIT WILL BE GIVEN.

Bacteriology 185. IMMUNOLOGY.   Credit, 3.
                                                                Miss GARVEY

Chemistry 234. ADVANCED BIOCHEMICAL LECTURES.   Credit, 3
                                                                Mr. LITTLE.

Zoology 220. EXPERIMENTAL EMBRYOLOGY.   Credit, 3
                                                                Mr. WOODSIDE.

Zoology 173. GENERAL CYTOLOGY.   Credit, 3.
                                                                Mr. ROLLASON.

Zoology 184. COMPARATIVE PHYSIOLOGY.   Credit, 4.
                                                                Mr. BISHOP.

Zoology 187. ENDOCRINOLOGY.   Credit, 3.
                                                                Mr. SNEDECOR.

Bacteriology

RALPH L. FRANCE, major adviser.

Registration by permission of the Department. Prerequisite courses required of graduate students in bacteriology are general chemistry, quantitative and qualitative analysis, organic chemistry, and twelve semester hours of undergraduate bacteriology. Students who have not taken these courses as undergraduates will be required to fulfill these requirements here without graduate credit.

COURSES OPEN TO GRADUATE STUDENTS ONLY
(For either major or minor credit)

200. SPECIAL PROBLEMS.—This course is designed especially to provide research experience for students who do not write a thesis. The problem will be carried out in the same manner as a thesis, except that it will be less extensive. A written report of the completed study will be required. Credit, 3-6.
THE STAFF.

201. HISTORY OF BACTERIOLOGY.—Studies in the development of bacteriology from the late seventeenth century to the present time, especially planned to show the developments of bacteriology in relation to agriculture, public health, the arts, industry and medicine. Credit, 2.
Mr. LITSKY and Mr. FULLER.

202. BACTERIAL PHYSIOLOGY.—Lectures, literature reviews, and laboratory exercises in bacterial nutrition, metabolism and growth. The course includes a comprehensive survey of the nutritional requirements of bacteria, their enzyme systems and the chemical changes in substrates that result from enzyme action, and the resulting effect on bacterial growth. Credit, 3-5.
Prerequisites, Bacteriology 51 and Chemistry 179 or 193. Mr. MANDEL.

203. BACTERIAL CYTOLOGY.—Lectures, literature reviews, and laboratory demonstrations, designed to give the student a comprehensive survey of the structure of bacterial cells and the functions of their components. Attention will be given to bacterial mutations. Credit, 3-5.
Prerequisite, College Biology and Bacteriology 31 or equivalent. Mr. FULLER.

204. RESEARCH PROJECT.—This course is designed to permit students to do investigational work on bacteriological problems not related to thesis. Limited to 3 credits per semester. For Ph.D. candidates only. Credit, 1-6.
THE STAFF.

205. ADVANCED IMMUNOLOGY.—Consideration will be given to advanced theories and laboratory procedures basic to bacteriology, immunology, and serology. Credit, 3-6.
Prerequisite, Bacteriology 185. Miss GARVEY.

206. INDUSTRIAL BACTERIOLOGY.—Deals with various industrial processes involving bacterial changes. Specific organisms involved, procedures, and chemistry of changes are discussed. Credit, 3.
Mr. CZARNECKI.

207. VIROLOGY.—A comprehensive study of viruses, including laboratory work covering methods for cultivation and identification. Limited to department majors, except by permission of the instructor. Credit, 3.
Mr. LITSKY.

208. SEMINAR.—Lectures and reports on current literature and special topics. (One credit each semester.) Credit, 1-4.
Mr. LITSKY and Mr. FULLER.

213. ANTIBIOTICS.—The historical background and theory of action of antibiotics are correlated with practical laboratory procedures used in the study of their isolation, methods of assay and effects on morphology and survival of bacteria. Credit, 3.
Prerequisite, Bacteriology 51, 52, or equivalent. Mr. CZARNECKI.

214. MICROBIAL GENETICS.—This course will provide a basic understanding of the genetics of bacteria and viruses. Credit, 3.
Prerequisites, Bacteriology 203 and Zoology 153. THE STAFF.

215. ANTISEPTICS AND DISINFECTANTS.—This course is designed to give the student a critical evaluation of antiseptics and disinfectants, and the procedures used in testing them. Practical aspects of these compounds are considered as to their general use. Studies of the various classes of antiseptics and disinfectants correlate chemical structure to antibacterial activity, mode of action, speed of action, and specificity. Credit, 3.
Prerequisites, Bacteriology 51, 52 and Chemistry 151, or equivalents.

Mr. LITSKY.

300. THESIS, MASTER'S DEGREE. Credit, 10.

400. THESIS, PH.D. DEGREE. Credit, 30.

COURSES OPEN TO BOTH GRADUATE AND UNDERGRADUATE STUDENTS
(For either major or minor credit)

156. (I) and (II). METHODS FOR BACTERIOLOGICAL PREPARATIONS.—This course is intended for students majoring in bacteriology and public health. The material given in the course includes methods of preparation and sterilization of culture media and equipment; the preparation of stains and reagents; and the use, care, and repair of laboratory instruments. Credit, 2.
Two 2-hour laboratory periods. THE STAFF.

181. GENERAL APPLIED BACTERIOLOGY.—This course is designed to give the student a working knowledge of routine and special tests used in present day applied bacteriology. Subjects receiving consideration are: methods for determining the sanitary quality of milk and milk products, water and shellfish; eating and drinking utensils; and air. Credit, 4.
Prerequisite, Bacteriology 31, 31A, or permission of instructor. Mr. FRANCE.

182. FOOD BACTERIOLOGY.—Consideration will be given to (1) bacteriological principles which apply to the preservation, fermentation, and spoilage of foods, (2) the sanitary examination of foods, (3) the causes of food poisoning and (4) microbiological assays. Credit, 3.
Prerequisite, Bacteriology 51, or permission of instructor. Miss GARVEY.

185. IMMUNOLOGY.—Admission by permission of the instructor. This course includes consideration of host reactions which favor the prevention and cure of disease; qualitative and quantitative estimations of toxins and antitoxins; the use of biological products such as antigens and immune sera in differential bacteriology and in disease diagnosis; and a consideration of isohemagglutinins as determinants of blood groups. Credit, 3
Prerequisite, Bacteriology 51 or equivalent. Miss GARVEY.

190. SANITARY BACTERIOLOGY.—A detailed study of public health laboratory methods. Practical application of methods will be made through field studies. By permission of instructor. Credit, 3.
Mr. FRANCE.

192. CLINICAL LABORATORY METHODS.—This course is designated for students majoring in medical technology. The purpose of the course is to familiarize the student with routine clinical laboratory procedures. Credit, 3.
By permission of instructor. Mr. FRANCE.

196. STUDIES OF SPECIAL MICROBIAL GROUPS.—A study of the biology of certain groups of microorganisms not given consideration, or at the most only briefly mentioned, in other courses offered in the department. The course will cover the autotrophic bacteria, photosynthetic bacteria, actinomycetes, myxobacteria, chlamydobacteria, and spirochaetes. Credit, 3.
One class hour, two 2-hour laboratory periods. Mr. MANDEL.
Prerequisite, Bacteriology 51.

COURSES IN OTHER DEPARTMENTS FOR WHICH MAJOR CREDIT MAY BE GIVEN

Agricultural Economics 179. ELEMENTARY STATISTICS. Credit, 3.
Mr. RUSSELL.

Botany 166. GENERAL MYCOLOGY. Credit, 3.
Mr. BANFIELD.

Chemistry 234. ADVANCED BIOCHEMICAL LECTURES. Credit, 3.
Mr. LITTLE.

Chemistry 235. BIOCHEMISTRY LABORATORY METHODS.
Credit, 3-5 each semester.
Mr. LITTLE.

Chemistry 236. ADVANCED BIOCHEMICAL ANALYSIS. Credit, 3-5.
Mr. LITTLE.

Chemistry 237. BIOCOLLOIDS. Credit, 3.
Mr. BENNETT.

Chemistry 251. SEMINAR. Credit, 1 each semester.
Mr. RITCHIE.

Entomology 174. MEDICAL ENTOMOLOGY. Credit, 3.
Mr. SHAW.

Food Technology 210, 211. THERMAL PROCESSING OF FOODS.
Credit, 2, 1st semester.
Credit, 3, 2nd semester.
Mr. ESSELEN.

Food Technology 271, 272. SEMINAR. Credit, 1-2 each semester.
THE STAFF.

Home Economics 203. ADVANCED NUTRITION—METABOLISM OF MAJOR FOODSTUFFS. Credit, 3.
Miss MITCHELL.

Home Economics 204. ADVANCED NUTRITION—MINERALS AND VITAMINS.
Credit, 3.
Miss MITCHELL.

Home Economics 205. LABORATORY METHODS AND TECHNIQUES IN NUTRITION.
Credit, 3.
Mrs. WERTZ.

Home Economics 211, 212. NUTRITION SEMINAR.   Credit, 1, each semester
                                                           Miss MITCHELL.

Public Health 164. MICROSCOPY OF WATER.   Credit, 3.
                                                                Mr. SNOW.

Zoology 169. ANIMAL PARASITOLOGY.   Credit, 3.
                                                              Miss TRAVER.

Zoology 184. CELLULAR PHYSIOLOGY.   Credit, 4.
                                                             Mr. SWENSON.

Zoology 248. PHYSIOLOGICAL GENETICS.   Credit, 3.
                                                               Mr. RAUCH.

COURSES FOR MINOR CREDIT ONLY

151, 152. ADVANCED BACTERIOLOGY.—Studies on bacterial metabolism and the
influence of environmental factors on growth and viability. The differentiation
and identification of bacterial species by morphological, cultural, physiological,
and serological studies. The combined courses not only give the students a comprehensive picture of the various forms of existing bacteria, but develop a special
technique for the isolation, cultivation, and identification of both pathogenic
and non-pathogenic species.   Credit, 3 each semester.
By permission of instructor.   Miss GARVEY.

209. ADVANCED AND APPLIED TECHNIQUES IN BACTERIOLOGY.—For students
majoring in other departments, not for bacteriology majors. Lectures and laboratory. The material offered in this course is designed to help fill in the student's
general knowledge of the biological sciences. Emphasis will be placed on the
position of bacteria in relation to other fields of science and on techniques that
make it possible for the student to use bacteriology as a tool in his particular
major field.   Credit, 3.
                                                         Mr. CZARNECKI.

210. ADVANCED BACTERIOLOGY.—For students majoring in other departments,
not for bacteriology majors. Lectures and laboratory. A systematic study of
pathogenic and nonpathogenic bacteria, disinfectants, and antibiotics. Credit, 3.
Prerequisite, Bacteriology 209.   Mr. CZARNECKI.

Botany

THEODORE T. KOZLOWSKI, major adviser

A thesis will be required of certain candidates for the M.S. in Botany.

COURSES OPEN TO GRADUATE STUDENTS ONLY
(For either major or minor credit)

200. SPECIAL PROBLEMS.—Selected research problems in botany not related
to the candidate's thesis.   Credits, 1-5 per semester.

A. Plant Cytology and Genetics.   Mr. NICKERSON.

B. Plant Ecology.   Mr. LIVINGSTON and Mr. GASIORKIEWICZ.

C. Plant Mycology.   Mr. BANFIELD, Mr. GUBA and Mr. GASIORKIEWICZ.

D. Plant Morphology.   Mr. NICKERSON and Mr. TORREY.

E. Plant Pathology.
            Mr. BANFIELD, Mr. DORAN, Mr. GUBA, Mr. GASIORKIEWICZ.

F. Plant Physiology.   Mr. KOZLOWSKI, Mr. JONES.

G. Plant Taxonomy.   Mr. TORREY, Mr. LIVINGSTON.

202, 203. ADVANCED PLANT PHYSIOLOGY.—Advanced study on metabolism, water relations and mineral nutrition of plants. The course includes lectures, critical anlayses of literature, reports and individual conferences. Given in alternate years.   Credit, 2-4 each semester.
         Mr. KOZLOWSKI.
Prerequisites, Botany 167, 168 or equivalent;
      Chemistry 151, 152 or equivalent.

204. FOREST PATHOLOGY.—A course dealing with the more common and important fungus diseases and with wood decay caused by saprophytic fungi which affect forest trees. Given in alternate years.   Credit, 4.
Prerequisite, Botany 51 or equivalent.   Mr. BANFIELD.

205, 206.—ADVANCED PLANT PATHOLOGY.—A study of biological problems that underlie the diseased state. Consideration is given to the general parasitological and epidermiological aspects of plant disease from the standpoint of critical examination of the variation in and interaction between host plants, parasites and environment. Given in alternate years.   Credit, 2-4 each semester.
Prerequisites, Botany 51 and 166 or equivalent.   Mr. BANFIELD.

207. ADVANCED PLANT ECOLOGY.—Lectures, conferences, critical reading and reports on advanced considerations of synecology and autecology. Given in alternate years.   Credit, 3.
         Mr. LIVINGSTON.

300. THESIS, MASTER'S DEGREE.—Research on an approved problem.
         Credit, 10.

400. THESIS, PH.D. DEGREE.—Research on an approved problem.
         Credit, 30.

COURSES OPEN TO BOTH GRADUATE AND UNDERGRADUATE STUDENTS
(For either major or minor credit)

151, 152. PLANT PATHOLOGY.—A basic course in plant pathology dealing with the nature, causes and control of plant diseases. Attention is given to disease symptoms, infection, parasitism, disease transmission, environmental effects and general principles of plant disease control.   Credit, 3.
         Mr. BANFIELD.

158. MICROTECHNIQUE.—The preparation of microscopic mounts including the use of biological stains with the infiltration, celloidin and paraffin methods, and the use of slide and rotary microtomes. The rewards of careful work are improvement in manipulative technique, better orientation in the field of plant structures, an enhanced aesthetic appreciation and a valuable collection of microscopic mounts.   Credit, 2.
         Mr. TORREY.

159, 160. THE ANGIOSPERMS. A study of the angiosperm orders from the standpoint of reproductive morphology, ecology, evolution, economics and history. Illustrative types are drawn from the State herbarium, while forms for laboratory dissection are supplied from greenhouses or from preserved materials. A course for horticulturalists as well as botanists. Given in alternate years, beginning, 1954-55.   Credit, 3-5 each semester.
         Mr. TORREY.

161, 162. COMPARATIVE ANATOMY OF GREEN PLANTS.—The anatomy, evolution, and taxonomy of chlorophyllus plants, including extinct as well as living forms. Lectures interpret anatomical data in accord with such principles as algal tendencies and parallelisms, isomorphic and heteromorphic alternation, the landward migration, telome concept, rise and development of atracheates and tracheates, stelar evolution and wood anatomy, angiosperms as the ultimate evolutionary types. Given in alternate years, beginning 1955-56.
Prerequisite, one semester of cryptogamic botany.   Credit, 3 each semester.
                                                                  Mr. TORREY.

163, 164. COMPARATIVE MORPHOLOGY OF FUNGI.—Comparative morphology, life history and habitat of representative species of important orders and families. Laboratory work includes collection, identification, and study of common local forms.   Credit, 3 each semester.
                                                                  Mr. BANFIELD.

166. GENERAL MYCOLOGY.—A general course designed to acquaint the student with various classes of fungi, life history and morphology of representative species, their distribution in nature, their significance in plant and animal disease, and their utilization in industrial fermentations.   Credit, 3.
                                                                  Mr. BANFIELD.

167, 168. INTRODUCTORY PLANT PHYSIOLOGY.—A study of the processes occurring in plants and their relation to the complex of activities constituting plant growth.   Credit, 3 each semester.
                                                                  Mr. KOZLOWSKI.

175. METHODS IN PLANT PATHOLOGY.—A study of general techniques and specialized methods used in the investigation of plant diseases. Given in alternate years.   Credit, 3.
Prerequisite, one semester of plant pathology.   Mr. BANFIELD.

181. PLANT ECOLOGY.—The relationships of plants to environment including a study of environmental factors (autecology) and of plant communities (synecology).   Credit, 3.
                                                                  Mr. LIVINGSTON.

182. PLANT GEOGRAPHY.—Lectures and assigned readings of descriptive and historical plant geography as well as basic principles governing the natural distribution of plants.   Credit, 2.
                                                                  Mr. LIVINGSTON.

189. PLANT CYTOGENETICS.—The interpretation of hereditary phenomena, in individuals and in populations, in terms of cell structures. A correlation of plant cytology and genetics which includes embryology, hybridization, polyploidy, apomixis, evolutionary trends and distribution patterns.   Credit, 3.
                                                                  Mr. NICKERSON.

190. INSECT TRANSMISSION OF PLANT DISEASES.—A lecture course on intricate interrelationships of insects and microorganisms, with particular emphasis on the basic role played by insects in inception, distribution and perpetuation of plant diseases.   Credit, 3.
                                                                  Mr. BANFIELD.

Business Administration

MILO KIMBALL, adviser.

The program of graduate courses in Business Administration is designed to prepare for positions of responsibility in business, in organizations that serve business, in government, or in business education.

COURSES OPEN TO GRADUATE STUDENTS ONLY

201. THE BUSINESS ENTERPRISE.—The legal-economic-political environment in which business enterprise operates; the risks of enterprise and profits; market demand analysis; cost-price combinations and production policies; the effects of business fluctuations on the individual enterprise; the enterprise system and public policy as expressed in legislation. Credit, 3.
Mr. SMART.

211. ACCOUNTING IN MANAGEMENT.—The theory of accounts applied to management problems; the established methods of accounting in operating situations; the use of quantitative data as bases for policy decisions. Credit, 3.
Mr. COLWELL.

222. MARKETING MANAGEMENT.—A study of the function of marketing from the point of view of the business executive. The broad aspects of product planning and choice of channels of distribution as well as distribution problems are analyzed. The interrelations between research planning, execution and control of marketing activity is carefully considered. Credit, 3.
Mr. HARDY.

231. FINANCIAL MANAGEMENT.—Attention is first centered on financing current operations: financial analysis and planning; credit management; and the sources and management of working capital. Then, long-term financial policies are stressed: the uses of corporate securities; the capital structure; surplus and dividend policies; financing new enterprises; the recapitalization and reorganization of going concerns. Credit, 3.
Mr. LUDTKE.

242. PRODUCTION MANAGEMENT.—This course deals with the situations which confront executives in charge of manufacturing operations and the direction of people at work. It is designed to develop skill in analyzing production processes in order to determine specific adaptations of production and personnel techniques to the requirements of differing processes. Credit, 3.
Mr. VANCE.

252. ADMINISTRATIVE PRACTICES.—Assuming a knowledge of business processes, this course considers the problems of human relations in business and industry. Consideration is also given to that phase of administration concerned with policy formation. Credit, 3.
Mr. KIMBALL.

271. SEMINAR IN BUSINESS ADMINISTRATION I.—A critical and intensive study of selected problems in Accounting, Finance, Industrial Administration, or Marketing and the application of research methods to these problems. Credit, 3.
THE STAFF.

272. SEMINAR IN BUSINESS ADMINISTRATION II.—A continuation of the Seminar in Business Administration in the field of the student's special interest. Credit, 3.
THE STAFF.

300. THESIS, MASTER'S DEGREE. Credit, 3 or 6.

BASIC COURSES REQUIRED OF GRADUATE STUDENTS IN BUSINESS

Accounting

25-6. INTRODUCTION TO ACCOUNTING.—This course aims to give the students a working knowledge of the principles underlying the gathering, recording, and interpretation of accounting data and is an introduction to valuation and statement interpretation. Credit, 6.

Business Law

170. BUSINESS LAW.—This course consists of a study of the drawing, reading, and interpretation of contracts, and includes agency, sales, and commercial paper. Credit, 3.

Finance

155. FINANCIAL INSTITUTIONS.—A general course which surveys the development and operations of our financial institutions and provides an integrated study of the entire American financial structure. Credit, 3.

165. CORPORATION FINANCE.—This course in business finance is concerned with forms of ownership organization, the nature and uses of corporate securities, provision and maintenance of capital, financial expansion and corporate reorganization. Credit, 3.

Industrial Administration

163. MANAGEMENT IN INDUSTRY.—A study of the principles connected with the organization and management of industrial enterprises. Credit, 3.

Marketing

153. MARKETING PRINCIPLES.—A study of the forces and conditions which determine prices and the organization and methods concerned with transporting, storing and distributing industrial and consumer goods. Credit, 3.

ELECTIVE COURSES OPEN TO GRADUATE STUDENTS

Accounting

161. INTERMEDIATE ACCOUNTING.—An application of accounting principles to problems of income determination and the classification and valuation of assets. Credit, 3.

162. ADVANCED ACCOUNTING.—A continuation of Accounting 161, concerned with the valuation of assets and liabilities, accounting for net worth, statements of application of funds and the analysis of financial statements. Credit, 3.

164. COST ACCOUNTING.—The use of accounting techniques to determine business costs, including process costs, standard costs, distributive costs and cost problems imposed by government regulation. Credit, 3.

176. AUDITING.—A course in the interpretation of accounting records dealing with audit theory and procedure. C.P.A. and American Institute of Accountants examination problems are studied. Credit, 3.

Finance

176. INSURANCE.—A general course concerning risks encountered by individuals and business enterprises and the methods and institutions evolved to insure against loss. Property, casualty, life and other forms of insurance are studied from the point of view of both the insurance carrier and the insured. Credit, 3.

182. INVESTMENTS.—The principles and techniques that are useful for the analysis and selection of investment media; investment policies of individuals and institutions. Credit, 3.

Industrial Administration

164. PERSONNEL MANAGEMENT.—A study of the principles of the management of labor relations. Attention is focused on procuring, developing, maintaining and using personnel. Credit, 3.

166. TRANSPORTATION AND TRAFFIC.—The development of highway, waterway, railway, and air transportation; the operation and control of transportation agencies; the use of freight tariffs, classifications and routing guides; the function of industrial traffic departments. Credit, 3.

Marketing

154. SALESMANSHIP AND SALES MANAGEMENT.—The principles and practices of personal selling; the management of sales personnel; and the control of sales operations. Credit, 3.

171. RETAIL MERCHANDISING.—A study of the operation and productive functions of the business of retailing. Credit, 3.

173. ADVERTISING.—A study of the techniques and media of advertising, its services to business and the organization and economic functions of the advertising industry. Credit, 3.

176. PURCHASING.—A study of the purchasing problems of industrial enterprises and of their market contacts with their sources of supply. Credit, 3.

Chemistry

WALTER S. RITCHIE, major adviser.

The Department of Chemistry provides facilities for students intending to complete the requirements for the Master's degree and the Doctor's degree. Students accepted for graduate study are expected to have met the usual requirements for the Bachelor's degree. Those who have not fulfilled these requirements may be admitted on limited status until the deficiencies have been removed.

First year graduate students will take "placement" examinations during the first week of residence. These examinations are for the purpose of evaluating the background of the student, and to assist in the selection of a course of study. Students are admitted to candidacy for a degree only after the satisfactory passing of written comprehensive examinations, at which time thesis problems are assigned in the following fields of chemistry: physical, organic, inorganic, analytical and biochemical.

COURSES OPEN TO GRADUATE STUDENTS ONLY

(For either major or minor credit)

201. INORGANIC PREPARATIONS.—LABORATORY.—The preparation of chemical products from raw materials. The manufacture and testing of pure chemicals. The laboratory work is essentially synthetic in nature and is designed to aid in acquiring a more adequate knowledge of inorganic chemistry than is to be obtained by chemical analysis alone. Credit, 3-5.

Mr. SMITH.

202. INORGANIC CHEMISTRY OF THE LESS FAMILIAR ELEMENTS.—Lectures and collateral reading on the descriptive chemistry of some of the less familiar elements such as boron, gallium, indium, thallium, the lanthanides, fluorine, titanium, vanadium, tantalum, tungsten, and uranium. Correlations between structure or spatial configurations and chemical properties will be stressed to the extent permitted by modern data. Given in alternate years. Credit, 6.

Mr. ROBERTS.

203. PHYSICAL CHEMICAL MEASUREMENTS.—LABORATORY.—A selection of experiments in Physical Chemistry to meet the needs and background of the individual student. Experiments will be selected from standard texts and from the literature. Credit, 3-5.
Prerequisites, Chemistry 165 and 166 or equivalent.
Mr. FESSENDEN and Mr. SMITH.

205. CHEMICAL THERMODYNAMICS.—The first and second laws of thermodynamics will be reviewed. The concept of the Boltzmann distribution and the partition function will be introduced, and the calculation of thermodynamic function from these quantities will be discussed. The calculation of equilibrium constants from both thermochemical and spectroscopic data will be considered, as will the application to electrochemistry and ionic equilibria. Credit, 3.
Prerequisites, Chemistry 165 and 166. Mr. STEIN.
Given alternate years in Fall Semester (1954).

206. GASES, KINETICS, AND CATALYSIS.—Some of the basic concepts of the kinetic theory of gases and the absorption of gases by solids will be discussed. The kinetics of homogeneous gas reactions and chain reactions will be considered as well as the theory of absolute reaction rates. Homogeneous and heterogeneous catalysis, photochemical, radiation induced reactions, and reactions in solution will be discussed. Credit, 3.
Prerequisite, Chemistry 205 or its equivalent. Mr. STEIN.
Given alternate years in Spring Semester (1955).

208. CHEMICAL SPECTROSCOPY.—This course is designed to give students practice in the use of spectroscopic equipment in solving chemical problems. The lecture work of the course will include discussions of (1) the design and use of instruments, (2) the elementary theory of spectra, and (3) the application of spectroscopy of chemical problems. The laboratory work will include practice in the use of the spectrometer and the spectrograph for the analysis of flame, arc, and spark spectra, and the use of the spectrophotometer for absorption measurements. Photographic procedures will be discussed and used in connection with the operation of the spectrograph. Given in alternate years. Credit, 3.
Prerequisites, Chemistry 165 and 166, or equivalent. Mr. SMITH.

211, 212. QUANTUM CHEMISTRY.—The application of the quantum theory to chemical problems will be discussed. This will include a discussion of the exact theory for describing the structure of simple atoms, the application of approximate methods for complex atoms and molecules, the chemical bond, resonance, and the interaction of radiation and matter. Credit, 3-6.
Prerequisites, Chemistry 186, or equivalent. Mr. STEIN.
Differential Equations is desirable.
Given alternate years in Fall and Spring (1955-56).

214. PHYSICAL CHEMISTRY OF HIGH POLYMERS.—Various aspects of the physical chemistry of natural and synthetic polymers will be discussed. Topics to be considered will include: structure of solid polymers, determination of molecular weights, sizes and shapes, mechanical properties of solid polymers, colligative properties of polymer solutions, polyelectrolytes, and physical chemistry of proteins. Credit, 3.
Prerequisite, Chemistry 205 or equivalent. Mr. STEIN.
Given alternate years in Spring Semester (1956).

221. ADVANCED ANALYTICAL CHEMISTRY.—Laboratory consisting of special work to meet the needs of the individual student. It may consist of ultimate analysis, electro-analysis, the analysis of definite classes of materials such as fertilizers, ores, insecticides, alloy or materials containing the rarer elements, and the use of organic reagents. Credit, 3-5 each semester.
Prerequisite, 183 or equivalent. Mr. ROBERTS.

223. INTRODUCTION TO MICRO-CHEMISTRY.—Laboratory. Designed to illustrate the applications of micro technique to synthesis, analysis, and characterization. The microscopic work may include the optics of the microscope, micrometry, the microscopic study of fibers, crystals, and physiochemical phenomena and an introduction to microscopical qualitative analysis. The quantitative work may include the determination of carbon, hydrogen, nitrogen, and halogen in organic materials and selected inorganic determinations.
Credit, 3-5 each semester.
Prerequisite, Chemistry 183, or equivalent.   Mr. ROBERTS.

227. HETEROCYCLIC CHEMISTRY.—The chemistry of the common organic heterocyclic compounds containing nitrogen, oxygen, and sulfur. Includes considerations of mechanisms of the reactions discussed.
Three class hours   Credit, 3.
Prerequisite, Chemistry 181 or equivalent.   Mr. CANNON.

229, 230. THEORETICAL ORGANIC CHEMISTRY.—Lectures on special topics such as stereochemistry, bond formation, resonance, ionic reactions, free radical reactions, transition state theory, reaction mechanisms, molecular rearrangements, etc. Given in alternate years.   Credit, 3 each semester.
Prerequisite, Chemistry 181 or its equivalent.   Mr. CANNON.
Chemistry 181 may be taken simultaneously with Chemistry 229.

231. ADVANCED ORGANIC CHEMISTRY.—Laboratory. More difficult synthesis of organic compounds will be assigned to the individual student. These compounds will frequently be those desired as starting materials for research. Their preparation will require the use of the original literature.   Credits, 3-5.
Prerequisite, a year course in Organic Chemistry. Mr. CANNON and Mr. RITCHIE.

232. ORGANIC CHEMISTRY.—An intensive survey of certain reactions of organic chemistry with emphasis on their scope and limitations, recent developments, and theoretical aspects. Given every other year, alternating with Chemistry 230.   Credit, 3.
Prerequisite, Chemistry 181.   Mr. CANNON.

234. ADVANCED BIOCHEMICAL LECTURES.—Lectures on recent developments in the chemistry of proteins, lipids, carbohydrates, enzymes, and other materials of biological significance.   Credits, 3.
Mr. LITTLE.

235. BIOCHEMISTRY LABORATORY METHODS.—Advanced laboratory work on preparation, examination, and analytical techniques for protein, carbohydrate, lipids, enzymes, etc. Methods of colloid chemistry will be included. Individual problems and work will be assigned as far as possible to meet individual requirements.   Credit, 3-5 each semester.
Mr. LITTLE.

236. ADVANCED BIOCHEMICAL ANALYSIS.—Advanced laboratory course in analytical methods applicable to naturally occurring materials including foods, feeds, etc. Research methods and techniques will be introduced as well as routine methods.   Credit, 3-5.
Mr. LITTLE.

237. BIOCOLLOIDS.—A consideration of the fundamental principles of colloidal behavior and some applications to industry, agriculture, and biology.   Credit, 3.
Prerequisite, Chemistry 152, or equivalent.   Mr. BENNETT.

239. CHEMISTRY OF NATURAL PRODUCTS.—The lectures and collateral readings will deal with the chemistry of some classes of natural compounds which are of biochemical and economic interest. Proteins, the sugars, starch, cellulose, polyuronides, lignin, glucosides, alkaloids, enzymes, purines, pyrimidines, and pigments will be considered. Credit, 2.
Mr. LITTLE and Mr. CONRAD.

251. SEMINAR.—Conferences, reports, or lectures. Credit, 1 each semester. Maximum credit, 2.
Mr. RITCHIE.

278. ELECTROCHEMISTRY.—A course for students who have had a first course in physical chemistry, or its equivalent. The course will include a study of the fundamentals of oxidation-reduction, galvanic cells, electrolytic cells, conductance transference, and polarography. The concept of activity, and the use of activity co-efficients will be included. To be given in alternate years. Credit, 2.
Mr. FESSENDEN.

300. THESIS, MASTER'S DEGREE.—The preparation of an acceptable thesis in agricultural, analytical, inorganic, organic, biochemical, or physical chemistry, under the direction of the professor in charge of the work. Credit, 10.

400. THESIS, PH.D. DEGREE.—The preparation of an acceptable thesis in agricultural, analytical, inorganic, organic, biochemical or physical chemistry, under the direction of the professor in charge of the work. Credit, 30.

COURSES OPEN TO BOTH GRADUATE AND UNDERGRADUATE STUDENTS
(For either major or minor credit)

177. ADVANCED PHYSICAL CHEMISTRY.—A detailed study of a number of topics such as kinetics, catalysis, chemical thermodynamics and electrochemistry. Three class hours. Credit, 3.
Prerequisites, Chemistry 165 and 166. Mr. STEIN.

181. ORGANIC CHEMISTRY.—A rapid and intensive survey of the important reactions of organic chemistry with emphasis on their scope and limitations, recent developments and theoretical aspects. Credit, 3.
Three class hours. Mr. CANNON.

182. QUALITATIVE ORGANIC CHEMISTRY.—The characterization of organic compounds by means of physical properties, class reactions, and the preparation of suitable derivatives. Credit, 4.
Two class hours; two 3-hour laboratory periods. Mr. CANNON.

183. ADVANCED QUANTITATIVE ANALYSIS.—The laboratory work will include representative determinations in electrolytic and electrometric methods, and an introduction to colorimetry and other optical methods of analysis. Credit, 3.
Two class hours; one 3-hour laboratory period. Mr. ROBERTS.
Prerequisite, Chemistry 130.

186. THEORETICAL INORGANIC CHEMISTRY.—A survey of inorganic chemistry which is largely theoretical and includes such topics as atomic structure, radiochemistry, periodic classification and relationships, valence concepts, acid-base theory, and the chemistry of coordination compounds. To the extent that time permits these topics will be discussed and illustrated with descriptive chemistry of the familiar elements. Credit, 3.
Three class hours. Mr. SMITH.
Prerequisites, Chemistry 165 and 166.

188. HISTORY OF CHEMISTRY.—An historical and biographical study of chemistry and chemists. Credit, 3.
Three class hours; Mr. RITCHIE.

192. INTRODUCTION RESEARCH.—Admission only by permission of the department.
Ten laboratory periods. Credit, 5.
Hours by arrangement. THE STAFF.

193, 194. GENERAL BIOCHEMISTRY.—These courses offer a broad introduction to the general field of biochemistry for students majoring in chemistry or in the biological sciences and provide a background for more advanced or specialized study in this field. A competent preparation in organic chemistry is required. (Chemistry 51 and 52 or their equivalent.) Credit, 5 each semester.
Three class hours; one 3-hour laboratory period. Mr. LITTLE.

COURSES FOR MINOR CREDIT ONLY

151, 152. ORGANIC CHEMISTRY.—A course in the theory of organic chemistry intended to serve the needs of students who will specialize in chemistry, as well as those who may specialize in other fields. Credit, 4.
Three class hours; one 3-hour laboratory period.
Mr. RITCHIE and Mr. CANNON.

163. CHEMISTRY OF WATER, SEWAGE, AND SEWAGE SLUDGE.—The preparation of reagents and standard methods for the analysis of water, sewage, and sewage sludge. Credit, 3.
Two 3-hour laboratory periods. Mr. ———.
Prerequisite, Chemistry 30.

165, 166. PHYSICAL CHEMISTRY.—A study of the fundamental theories and laws of physical chemistry. Credit, 4.
Three class hours; one 3-hour laboratory period.
Mr. FESSENDEN and Mr. SMITH.

179. BIOCHEMISTRY.—An introduction to general biochemistry and physiological chemistry, with particular emphasis on the extension of fundamental organic chemistry to materials and processes of biological significance; proteins, lipids, carbohydrates, enzymes. Credit, 4.
Three class hours; one 3-hour laboratory period. Mr. LITTLE.
Prerequisite, Organic Chemistry.

Chemical Engineering

COURSES FOR MINOR CREDIT ONLY

155. UNIT OPERATIONS I.—A study of the fundamental principles underlying the unit operations of fluid flow, heat transfer, and evaporation. A portion of the course is devoted to a study of the thermodynamic properties of matter.
Three class hours; two 3-hour computation periods. Credit, 5.
Prerequisites, Mathematics 30 or 31, Chemistry 30. Mr. BATKE.

156. UNIT OPERATIONS II.—A continuation of course 155 concerning distillation gas absorption, liquid extraction, crystallization, filtration, mixing, crushing, and grinding.
Three class hours; two 3-hour computation periods. Credit, 5.
Prerequisite, Chemical Engineering 155. Mr. BATKE.

157. INORGANIC CHEMICAL TECHNOLOGY.—A study of the manufacture of some of the important inorganic chemicals. Credit, 3.
Mr. CASHIN.

158. ORGANIC CHEMICAL TECHNOLOGY.—A study of some unit processes involved in the manufacture of organic chemicals; e.g. nitration, amination, halogenation, oxidation. Credit, 3.
Mr. CASHIN.

177. ELEMENTS OF UNIT OPERATIONS.—For other than chemical engineering majors. An introduction to some of the unit operations of process industries. The emphasis is on principles and types of equipment, rather than on the quantitative aspects and design. Credit, 3.
Prerequisites, Chemistry 30, Physics 25 and 26. Mr. LINDSEY.

181. HEAT-ENERGY RELATIONS.—A study of the energy relations in chemical processes. Includes: types of energy, energy balances, second law, thermodynamic functions, P-V-T-relations of fluids, compression and expansion processes. Credit, 3.
Three class hours. Mr. BATKE.
Prerequisites, Chemistry 66, Chemical Engineering 156.

182. INDUSTRIAL EQUILIBRIA AND KINETICS.—A study of phase and chemical equilibria and rates of reaction in chemical processes from the industrial point of view. Credit, 3.
Prerequisites, Chemistry 66, Chemical Engineering 181. Mr. BATKE.

198. ADVANCED UNIT OPERATIONS.—Radiation heat transfer, and multi-component distillation. Credit, 2.
Two class hours. Mr. CASHIN.
Prerequisite, Chemical Engineering 156.

Civil Engineering

MERIT P. WHITE, major adviser.

COURSES OPEN TO GRADUATE STUDENTS ONLY

(For either major or minor credit)

200. SPECIAL PROBLEMS. Credit, 3-6.
THE STAFF.

252. STRUCTURAL DYNAMICS.—This course covers the behavior of simple and complex oscillating systems. It deals particularly with the behavior of structures subjected to periodic forces, to non-periodic forces and to shock loads. Behavior beyond the elastic range is included. Credit, 3.
Prerequisites, C.E. 51 and 52. Mr. WHITE.

261. MATERIALS TESTING TECHNIQUES.—This course is concerned with the machines and auxiliary equipment used in experimental stress analysis for purposes of research. Credit, 3.
Prerequisite, C.E. 51. MR. SHARP.

270. ADVANCED STRUCTURAL THEORY II.—Advanced problems in structural analysis are presented in this course. Topics considered are the analysis of complex rigid frames; influence lines for indeterminate structures; the placing of loads and the determination of stresses in continuous building frames; prestressed concrete. Credit, 3.
Prerequisite, C.E. 172. Mr. OSGOOD.

271. ARCH ANALYSIS.—Methods of analyzing two-hinged and hingeless arches. A design project is included. Credit, 3.
Prerequisites, C.E. 70 and 71. Mr. Osgood.

275. ADVANCED FLUID MECHANICS.—Theory of hydraulic similitude, dimensional analysis, methods of obtaining dynamic similarity in hydraulic models in actual practice, analysis of typical hydraulic models. Credit, 3.
Prerequisite, C.E. 75 or 76. Mr. Marcus.

277. ADVANCED SANITARY ENGINEERING.—This course treats hydraulic and chemical problems encountered in the design and operation of water and sewage works. It also deals with stream sanitation and the latest trends of practice and research in the sanitary engineering field. Credit, 3.
Prerequisites, C.E. 77, 78. Mr. Feng.

279. THEORETICAL SOIL MECHANICS.—A thorough investigation of the phenomena in soil masses subjected to such forces as seepage, frost, and imposed loads. Credit, 3.
Mr. Hendrickson.

280. APPLIED SOIL MECHANICS.—The solution of case problems applying the principles of soil mechanics to the design of embankments, retaining walls, footings, raft foundations, and pile structures. Credit, 3.
Prerequisites C.E. 279. Mr. Hendrickson.

300. RESEARCH AND THESIS, MASTER'S DEGREE. Credit, 6.

COURSES OPEN TO BOTH GRADUATE AND UNDERGRADUATE
STUDENTS
(For either major or minor credit)

172. ADVANCED STRUCTURAL THEORY I.—Methods of analyzing statically indeterminate structures. Credit, 3.
Prerequisite, C.E. 70. Mr. Osgood.

188. ADVANCED STRESS ANALYSIS.—Determination of stresses and strains in elements of machines and structures. Credit, 3.
Prerequisite, C.E. 51 with grade of 75. Mr. White.

196. HYDRAULIC ENGINEERING.—The analysis and design of hydraulic structures such as storage reservoirs, spillways, dams, levees, shore protection and channel works are considered. Credit, 3.
Two class hours; one 3-hour laboratory period. Mr. Marston.
Prerequisites, Civil Engineering 73, 76.

Dairy Industry

D. J. Hankinson, major adviser.

COURSES OPEN TO GRADUATE STUDENTS ONLY
(For either major or minor credit)

200. PROBLEMS IN DAIRY TECHNOLOGY.—A course for individual study in which the student gives attention to specific current problems involved in the processing of dairy products. Credit, 3.
Mr. Hankinson.

202. ADVANCED DAIRY CHEMISTRY.—A study of the physical, colloidal, and chemical properties of dairy products; the role of milk fat, salts, proteins, carbohydrates, and enzyme systems, and their relation to dairy research.
Two 1-hour lectures, one 3-hour laboratory period. .   Credit, 3.
Prerequisite, 175 or equivalent.   Mr. NELSON.

209, 210. SEMINAR.—Reports on current literature.   Credit, 1 each semester.
                                                    Mr. HANKINSON.

300. THESIS, MASTER'S DEGREE.   Credit, 10.

COURSES OPEN TO BOTH GRADUATE AND UNDERGRADUATE STUDENTS
(For either major or minor credit)

175. DAIRY CHEMISTRY.—Physical and chemical principles which explain the behavior of milk and milk products in the various technological operations. Constituents of milk in relation to other organic compounds; physiochemical aspects of certain dairy phenomena such as foaming, coagulation, etc. The laboratory work will include many of the tests used commercially as well as in dairy research, emphasizing the principles and application of both qualitative and quantitative analysis as well as the technique of operating scientific apparatus.   Credit, 3.
Enrollment by permission of instructor.   Mr. NELSON.

COURSES IN OTHER DEPARTMENTS FOR WHICH MAJOR CREDIT WILL BE GIVEN.

No more than two courses may be selected from the following list of courses:
Home Economics 203. ADVANCED NUTRITION.—Metabolism of major foodstuffs.   Credit, 3.
                                                    Miss MITCHELL.

Home Economics 204. ADVANCED NUTRITION.—Minerals and vitamins.
                                                    Credit, 3.
                                                    Miss MITCHELL.

Bacteriology 202. BACTERIAL PHYSIOLOGY.   Credit, 3-5.
                                                    THE STAFF.

Chemistry 165, 166. PHYSICAL CHEMISTRY.   Credit, 4 each semester.
                            Mr. FESSENDEN and Mr. SMITH.

Chemistry 193, 194. GENERAL BIOCHEMISTRY.   Credit, 4 each semester.
                                                    Mr. LITTLE.

Chemistry 237. BIOCOLLOIDS.   Credit, 3.
                                                    Mr. BENNETT.

Food Technology 210. THERMAL PROCESSING OF FOODS.   Credit, 2.
                                                    Mr. ESSELEN.

Food Technology 221. EDIBLE FATS AND OILS.   Credit, 3.
                                                    Mr. ANDERSON.

Food Technology 241. FOOD ACCEPTANCE.—Theory and Methodology.
                                                    Credit, 3.
                                                    Mr. FAGERSON.

COURSES FOR MINOR CREDIT ONLY

152. MARKET MILK.—A study of the various phases of the market milk industry; sanitary production, transportation, pasteurization, and handling in the city plant; marketing, delivery systems, milk and its relation to public health, inspection, milk laws, food value and advertising. Cultured milk and other milk drinks are also included. Some milk plants are visited.   Credit, 4.

Mr. LINDQUIST.

177. BUTTER AND CHEESE MAKING.—Half of the semester is devoted to butter making; the remainder to cheese making, condensed and powdered milk. The various phases of the butter industry studied are: separators and cream separation; pasteurization, neutralization, and ripening of cream; preparation of starter cultures; churning; marketing and scoring of butter; creamery management. The work in cheese making includes cheddar, cream, Neufchatel, cottage, processed cheeses, etc. The manufacture of condensed milk, powdered milk, and commercial casein are also covered.   Credit, 4.
Prerequisite, Dairy 25 or permission of instructor.

MR. LINDQUIST AND MR. NELSON.

178. ICE CREAM MAKING.—The principles and practices of ice cream making. The effects of such factors as composition, quality, pasteurization, homogenization, aging, and freezing on the finished product are considered. Sherbets, ices, fancy and individual forms, and all flavors of ice cream are studied. Some time is devoted to refrigeration, machinery, delivery equipment, and merchandising methods as they are related to the industry.   Credit, 4.
Prerequisite, Dairy 25 or permission of instructor.   Mr. NELSON.

Economics

PHILIP L. GAMBLE, major adviser.

COURSES OPEN TO GRADUATE STUDENTS ONLY

(For either major or minor credit)

200. SPECIAL STUDIES IN ECONOMICS.—The student undertakes a special project under the guidance of a member of the department.
Credit, 2-5 each semester.
THE STAFF.

210. HISTORY OF ECONOMIC THOUGHT.—A general study of economic thought from its ancient beginnings; the contributions of the various schools; recent changes in economic thought. Given as required.   Credit, 3.
Mr. HALLER.

213. CENTRAL BANKING.—A study of the organization and policies of the major central banks with special reference to the Federal Reserve System. Given as required.   Credit, 3.
Mr. GAMBLE.

227. MATHEMATICAL ECONOMICS AND ECONOMIC MODEL-BUILDING.—A study of the various modern applications of mathematics to economic analysis. Special attention is paid to the analysis of interactions among several variables. Both static and dynamic processes will be examined. Given as required.
Admission by consent of instructor.   Credit, 3.
Mr. SCHOEFFLER.
Prerequisites, Economics 173 and Mathematics 29 or the equivalent.

260. MONOPOLY AND PUBLIC UTILITY PROBLEMS.—A study of the problem
of social control of monopolies and industries affected with a public interest.
Given as required.   Credit, 3.
Prerequisite, Economics 170.   Mr. HALLER.

272. ADVANCED ECONOMIC THEORY.—A study of the various theories of value
and distribution.   Credit, 3.
Prerequisite, Economics 173.   THE STAFF.

276. TAXATION.—A study of the assessment and administration of taxes with
particular attention to its economic and social effects of individual taxes and
tax systems.   Credit, 3.
Prerequisite, Economics 25, 78 or 178.   Mr. GAMBLE.

293, 295, 297. COURSES IN AGGREGATIVE ECONOMICS.—(These courses rotate
but not in a consistent cycle.)

293. ECONOMIC PLANNING.—Various economic plans in effect or proposed
throughout the world. Appraisal of the technique of economic planning.
                                                                      Credit, 3.
                                                                    Mr. MORRIS.

294. INSTITUTIONAL ECONOMICS.—Study of the major institutions affecting
economic problems. Given as required.   Credit, 3.
                                                                    Mr. HOWARD.

295. FULL EMPLOYMENT.—Methods of attaining and maintaining full employment in economy.   Credit, 3.
                                                                    Mr. GAMBLE.

297. ECONOMIC FLUCTUATIONS.—Causes, and methods of control of economic
fluctuations.   Credit, 3.
                                                                  Mr. SCHOEFFLER.

300. THESIS, MASTER'S DEGREE.   Credit, 10.

400. THESIS, PH. D. DEGREE.   Credit, 30.

COURSES OPEN TO BOTH GRADUATE AND UNDERGRADUATE STUDENTS
(For either major or minor credit)

Added work required of graduates: (a) extra readings on same or additional
assignments, (b) term paper, (c) special problem or project.

154. MONEY AND MONETARY POLICY.—A study of the relationship between
money, national and personal income and monetary policy. It includes examination of the relationships between individuals, banks, money markets and
central banks.   Credit, 3.
Prerequisite, Economics 53 or Finance 53.   Mr. GAMBLE.

155. ECONOMICS OF CONSUMPTION.—A study of patterns of consumption,
standards of living and the sources and expenditure of individual and family
incomes.   Credit, 3.
(a and b or c)   Mr. HALLER.

156. BUSINESS CYCLES.—A study of business fluctuations and an analysis
of current business cycle theories.   Credit, 3.
                                                                  Mr. SCHOEFFLER.

170. MONOPOLIES.—A study of the growth, development and social control of monopolies. Credit, 3
-(a, b) Mr. HALLER.

174. CURRENT ECONOMIC PROBLEMS.—An intensive study of current economic problems. Students will be encouraged to pursue lines of individual interest
(a, b) Credit, 3
Mr. HOWARD.

177. INTERNATIONAL TRADE.—A study of the policies, principles, and practices of international trade. Credit, 3
(a, b) Mr. G. R. MATTERSDORFF.

178. PUBLIC FINANCE.—A study of the principles underlying public expenditures, public borrowing and taxation. Credit, 3.
(a, b) Mr. GAMBLE

180. LABOR LEGISLATION.—A study of federal and state legislation affecting labor. Credit, 3.
(a, b) Mr. MORRIS.

183. SOCIAL CONTROL OF BUSINESS.—Methods of social control of economic activity including both formal and informal controls. Credit, 3.
(a, b) Mr. HOWARD.

184. COMPARATIVE ECONOMIC SYSTEMS.—An examination of the various forms of economic organization that have been tried and proposed with an analysis of the economic institutions of representative current economics.
(a, b) Credit, 3.
Mr. SCHOEFFLER.

191, 192. SEMINAR. Credit, 1-3.
THE STAFF.

COURSES IN OTHER DEPARTMENTS FOR WHICH MAJOR CREDIT WILL BE GIVEN

Agricultural Economics 200. RESEARCH METHODS AND PROCEDURES.
Credit, 3.
Mr. LINDSEY.

Agricultural Economics 156. FUNDAMENTALS OF COOPERATION. Credit, 3.
Mr. LINDSEY.

Agricultural Economics 171. AGRICULTURAL ECONOMIC THEORY. Credit, 3.
Mr. LINDSEY.

Agricultural Economics 178. PRINCIPLES AND PROBLEMS OF LAND ECONOMICS.
Credit, 3.
Mr. LINDSEY.

Agricultural Economics 180. ADVANCED STATISTICS. Credit, 3.
Mr. LINDSEY and Mr. RUSSELL.

Agricultural Economics 189, 190. PROBLEMS IN AGRICULTURAL ECONOMICS.
Credit, 2-3.
Mr. LINDSEY and Mr. RUSSELL.

Finance 165. CORPORATION FINANCE Credit, 3.
MR. KIMBALL.

COURSES FOR MINOR CREDIT ONLY

153. MONEY, BANKING AND CREDIT.—A critical survey of the development and operation of the monetary and banking systems of the United States.
Credit, 3.
Mr. GAMBLE.

173. MODERN ECONOMIC THEORY.—A study of current theories about value, distribution and prices. Credit, 3.
Mr. SCHOEFFLER.

179. LABOR PROBLEMS.—An analysis of the background and character of the modern labor problems with special references to the United States. Credit, 3. (a and b or c) Mr. MORRIS.

Education

ALBERT W. PURVIS, major adviser.

Before being admitted to full status for the Master's degree with a major in Education, the student must have, in addition to minimum Graduate School requirements:

1. Fifteen hours of such fundamental courses as Education 51, 52, 53, 61, 62, 66, 72, 83, 85, etc., listed in the undergraduate catalog.
2. Experience in teaching. Students entering without teaching experience must arrange for practice teaching as soon as possible.
3. If the major is in secondary education, a major (24 hours) and a minor (12 hours) in the subject-matter fields to be taught.
4. If the major is in elementary school teaching, a minor (18 hours) in some field of general education.

COURSES OPEN TO GRADUATE STUDENTS ONLY

(For either major or minor credit)

200. PROBLEM.—Work necessary to achieve an answer to a particular question in the educational field. Question to be of student's choosing, if possible. It may or may not involve original research and usually has only local significance. This may be chosen instead of a thesis. A bound copy of the written report must be provided for the Department by the student. Credit, 3-6.
Prerequisite, Education 291. THE STAFF.

208. THE TEACHER AND SCHOOL ADMINISTRATION.—Problems in admission, promotion, personnel, discipline, extra-curricular activities, supervision, tenure, salary schedules, etc. Credit, 2-3.
Mr. PURVIS.

209. ADMINISTERING SECONDARY SCHOOLS.—Housing, finance, schedule, the library, guidance, cafeteria, public relations. etc. Credit, 2-3.
Mr. OLIVER.

210. ADMINISTERING EXTRA-CURRICULAR ACTIVITIES.—Scheduling, financing, sponsorship, regulation of pupil participation. (1954-55 and each alternate year.)
Credit, 2-3.
Mr. OLIVER.

211. COMMUNITY RELATIONS FOR SCHOOL PERSONNEL.—Emphasis is placed on the development of good public relations policies and the techniques of assisting lay people in interpreting school activities, policies, and objectives. (1955-56 and each alternate year.) Credit, 2-3.
Mr. OLIVER.

213. ADMINISTERING ELEMENTARY SCHOOLS.—The principal's responsibilities, organization of the school office, scheduling, use of school facilities, curriculum organization, staff relationships, and the place of the school in the community.
Credit, 2-3.
Mr. McCARTHY.

214. SUPERVISING ELEMENTARY SCHOOLS.—Principles and problems of supervision in the elementary school; methods and types of supervision as they are related to the modern elementary curriculum, the content fields, the activity program and the area of unitary teaching. Credit, 2-3.
Mr. McCARTHY.

215. SEMINAR OR WORKSHOP IN EDUCATION.—Group study of current problems in curriculum, instruction, and administration for school personnel in service.
Credit, 2-6.
THE STAFF.

220. SCHOOL LAWS OF MASSACHUSETTS.—A review of the legal relations of the school personnel covering the usual experiences in school and community, presented in a series of selected cases having the support of court decisions.
Credit, 3.
Mr. PURVIS.

254. EVALUATION IN ELEMENTARY SCHOOLS.—Standardized and teacher made tests, rating scales, report cards, growth charts, readiness measures, and diagnosis of educational deficiency in elementary pupils. (To be taken instead of Education 153 by those training for elementary teaching.) 1955-56 and each alternate year.
Credit, 2-3.
Mr. ROURKE.

259. ELEMENTARY SCHOOL SCIENCE.—Methods and materials of instruction.
Credit, 2-3.
Miss O'DONNELL.

265. TECHNIQUES IN REMEDIAL READING.—Methods and materials in diagnosis and remedial instruction. Credit, 2-3.
Prerequisite, Education 61. Miss O'LEARY.

267. AUDIO-VISUAL LABORATORY.—Individual and practical experience in setting up and using common audio-visual equipment and materials. Minor repairs and maintenance will be included. This course should be preceded by Education 166 or a similar course. Credit, 2-3.
Mr. WYMAN.

289. COOPERATIVE CURRICULUM PLANNING.—Approved methods of curriculum planning, group work, consensus studies, used by cities and towns in curriculum development. Credit, 2-3.
Prerequisite, Education 188 or 160. (1954-55 and each alternate year.)
Mr. ROURKE.

291. EDUCATIONAL RESEARCH.—The principles and methods of research with special emphasis upon the technique used in Education. Statistics are studied chiefly from the standpoint of reporting and understanding the results of research. Required in first semester of students who anticipate completion of a thesis or problem in the current year. Credit, 2.
Mr. PURVIS.

300. THESIS, MASTER'S DEGREE.—A completed piece of work on some specific aspect of the educational field with necessary review of the literature pertaining to it. Original research is expected and the study should have more than local significance. Credit, 8.
Prerequisite, Education 291.

COURSES OPEN TO BOTH GRADUATE AND UNDERGRADUATE STUDENTS
(For major or minor credit)

151. HISTORY OF EDUCATION. Credit, 2-3.
Mr. PURVIS and Mr. McCARTHY.

153. EDUCATIONAL TESTS AND MEASUREMENTS. Credit, 2-3.
Mr. ROURKE.

160. ELEMENTARY SCHOOL CURRICULUM. Credit, 2-3.
Miss O'DONNELL.

164. PRINCIPLES OF ELEMENTARY EDUCATION. Credit, 2-3.
Miss O'LEARY.

166. PREPARATION AND USE OF AUDIO-VISUAL AIDS. Credit, 2-3.
Mr. WYMAN.

172. VOCATIONAL EDUCATION IN AGRICULTURE.—By arrangement. Credit, 3.
Mr. OLIVER and Mr. TAFT.

173. APPRENTICE TEACHING IN AGRICULTURE.—By arrangement. Credit, 6.
Mr. OLIVER and Mr. TAFT.

175. TECHNIQUE OF TEACHING VOCATIONAL AGRICULTURE.—By arrangement.
Credit, 3.
Mr. OLIVER and Mr. TAFT.

183. PRINCIPLES OF SECONDARY EDUCATION. Credit, 2-3.
Mr. McCARTHY.

188. SECONDARY SCHOOL CURRICULUM. Credit, 2-3.
Mr. ROURKE.

COURSES FOR MINOR CREDIT ONLY

152. PRINCIPLES AND METHODS OF TEACHING. Credit, 3.
Mr. PURVIS and Mr. McCARTHY.

161. ELEMENTARY READING AND LANGUAGE ARTS. Credit, 3.
Miss O'LEARY.

162. ELEMENTARY ARITHMETIC. Credit, 3.
Miss O'DONNELL.

185. OBSERVATION AND PRACTICE TEACHING.—By arrangement. Credit, 3.
THE STAFF.

Electrical Engineering
CARL S. ROYS, major adviser.

At least 12 credits, including Electrical Engineering 201 and Electrical Engineering 202 and exclusive of thesis, must be obtained in couses open to graduate students only.

COURSES OPEN TO GRADUATE STUDENTS ONLY
(For either major or minor credit)

201. ENGINEERING ANALYSIS I.—Analytical procedures beyond undergraduate levels as applied to the solutions of problems in the various fields of engineering.
Credit, 3.
Prerequisite, B.S. in engineering.   Mr. ROYS and STAFF.

202. ENGINEERING ANALYSIS II.—A continuation of 201.   Credit, 3.
Prerequisite, Electrical Engineering 201.   Mr. ROYS and STAFF.

204. SERVOMECHANISMS II.—A continuation of Electrical Engineering 190 that covers the principles of quantitative dynamic analyses of closed-cycle control systems in terms of differential equations and complex functions. System synthesis on the basis of specified performance characteristics also is a major objective.   Credit, 3.
Prerequisite, Electrical Engineering 190.   THE STAFF.

221. POWER AND MACHINERY LABORATORY.—This is designed to develop testing techniques through class and laboratory studies of the more advanced topics related to electrical machinery and power systems. When taken concurrently with other courses in power and machinery, the laboratory work may be varied to suit individual needs.   Credit, 3.
One class hour; six hours of laboratory.   Mr. KARLSON.
Prerequisite, Electrical Engineering 81.

222. POWER SYSTEMS METERING AND RELAYING.—This course covers metering and protective relaying for electric power systems, and includes modern relay methods used on radial lines, loops and networks, with emphasis upon coordinated protection; circuit interruption problems also are studied. Credit, 3.
Prerequisite, Electrical Engineering 86.   Mr. KARLSON.

223. TRAVELING WAVES IN POWER SYSTEMS.—The fundamental theory of traveling waves and its application to lightning and switching surges in power systems, including reflection and refraction at transition points; insulation levels and coordination; high voltage and current and voltage surge testing standards.
Prerequisite, Electrical Engineering 183.   Credit, 3.
                                                              Mr. ROYS.

224. POWER SYSTEMS OPERATION AND STABILITY.—A continuation of Electrical Engineering 86 with further applications to power systems under unbalanced steady state and transient conditions. This includes the effects of ground wires, ground impedance and mutual coupling impedances; inductive coordination with communication systems; the effects of saturation and pole saliency in synchronous machines upon steady state and transient stability; variability of load impedance; and multimachine problems.   Credit, 3.
Prerequisite, Electrical Engineering 86.   MR. KARLSON.

241. COMMUNICATIONS NETWORKS.—A continuation of Electrical Engineering 79 covering the principles and applications of network analysis and synthesis, noise and information theory.   Credit, 3.
Prerequisite, Electrical Engineering 79 or its equivalent.   Mr. ROYS.

243. ELECTROMAGNETIC ENGINEERING I.—The fundamentals of Electromagnetism, including Ampere's and Faraday's Laws, Gauss' Theorem, retarded potential and Hertz' vector, Maxwell's equations and Poynting's vector. These are applied to the propagation, reflection and refraction of electromagnetic waves, radio-frequency lines, wave guides, cavity resonators, antennas and ionospheric reflections.   Credit, 3.
Prerequisites, Electrical Engineering 201, 202.   MR. ROYS.

246. ELECTROMECHANICAL SYSTEMS AND TRANSDUCERS.—A review of network theory as associated with lumped mechanical systems, vibrating membranes and plates, electromechanical converters and acoustics. Applications are made to microphones, loudspeakers, horns, crystals and electromechanical filters.
Prerequisite, Electrical Engineering 183.   Credit, 3.
                                                              Mr. ROYS.

300. THESIS, MASTER'S DEGREE. GRADUATE RESEARCH.—Independent research under the supervision of a staff member which will serve as the basis for the thesis required for the master's degree in Electrical Engineering. It is expected that a paper covering the project will be presented before the combined A.I.E.E. and I.R.E. student branch at the University.   Credit, 3-6.
Consultation and laboratory hours to be arranged.

COURSES OPEN TO BOTH GRADUATE AND UNDERGRADUATE STUDENTS

(For either major or minor credit)

183. TRANSIENT ANALYSIS.—A study of the transient behavior of electrical, mechanical, and thermal systems. The ordinary and partial differential equations associated with the systems are set up and their solutions obtained by the classical, Heaviside Operational and Fourier and Laplace Transform methods. An introductory survey of Functions of a Complex Variable leads to the evaluation of the Inversion Integral by means of the Method of Residues.   Credit, 3.
Three class hours.   Mr. ROYS.
Prerequisite, Electrical Engineering 58:

184. INDUSTRIAL ELECTRONICS.—Special characteristics of the electron tubes of industry; the theory, design and operation of commercial types of equipment utilizing these tubes, including stroboscopes, grid-controlled and polyphase rectifiers, inverters, welding controllers, speed and voltage regulators, high frequency heating circuits, etc.   Credit, 4.
Three class hours; one 3-hour laboratory period.   Mr. ROYS.
Prerequisite, Electrical Engineering 55.

185. ELECTRICAL MEASUREMENTS.—Theory and practice of electric and magnetic measurements; accuracy, precision, and limitations of measurements and devices.   Credit, 3:
Two class hours; one 3-hour laboratory period.   Mr. LINGO.
Prerequisite, Electrical Engineering 42.

186. POWER SYSTEM NETWORKS.—A study of power system networks including power transfer diagrams, voltage studies, system stability criteria, short-circuit calculations, and protective methods.   Credit, 4.
Three class hours; one 3-hour laboratory period.   Mr. KARLSON.
Prerequisite, Electrical Engineering 58.

187. POWER APPLICATIONS AND CONTROL.—A study of applications of electric machines and their control, power requirements, types of drive, torque relations, speed of response, control and selsyn systems.   Credit, 4.
Three class hours; one 3-hour laboratory period.   Mr. KARLSON.
Prerequisite, Electrical Engineering 54.

188. ELECTRIC POWER DISTRIBUTION.—The general problem of power distribution from bulk substations to the consumer by means of loop and radial systems including such considerations as automatic load transfer, voltage regulation and system protection.   Credit, 3.
Three class hours.   Mr. KARLSON.
Prerequisite, Electrical Engineering 58.

190. SERVOMECHANISMS I.—This is a study of basic types of error-sensitive control systems; proportional, differential and integral controllers; transient behavior; criteria for error-free operation; and practical electrical and mechanical systems. Classical methods of analysis will be employed.   Credit, 4.
Three class hours; one 3-hour laboratory period.   THE STAFF.

194. ULTRA-HIGH-FREQUENCY TECHNIQUES.—This course is a study of U.H.F. oscillators, amplifiers, transmitters, receivers, transmission systems and antennas; multi-vibrators, trigger and gate circuits, electronic switches and controls.
Three class hours; one 3-hour laboratory period.   Credit, 4.
Prerequisites, Electrical Engineering 57 and 58.   THE STAFF.

196. PRINCIPLES OF ELECTRICAL DESIGN.—The fundamentals of electric, dielectric, magnetic and heat-flow systems as applied to the design, rating and life of coils, transformers, machinery and other electrical equipment.   Credit, 3.
Two class hours; one 3-hour laboratory period.   Mr. ROYS.
Prerequisite, Electrical Engineering 54.

198. TELEVISION ENGINEERING.—Application of electronics and radio engineering to the special problems of television. Among the topics considered are system theory and analysis, signal sources, video response, noise limitations, synchronization and scanning, color vision and colorimetry, principles of the NTSC system, picture pickup and display tubes, transmission and reception, and monitoring and testing procedures.   Credit, 4.
Three class hours; one 3-hour laboratory period.   Mr. LANGFORD.
Prerequisites, Electrical Engineering 83 and must be preceded or accompanied by Electrical Engineering 80.

English

FRANK P. RAND, major adviser.

Language requirement: the ability to translate, with the aid of a dictionary, two languages other than English.

COURSES OPEN TO GRADUATE STUDENTS ONLY

(For either major or minor credit)

201. OLD ENGLISH.—A study of Old English grammar with prose translation. This (or 203.) required of all English majors. Given in alternate years. 1955-56.   Credit, 3.
                Mr. LANE.

203. MIDDLE ENGLISH.—A study of the language of Chaucer and the mediaeval romances. This (or 201.) required of all English majors. Given in alternate years. 1954-55.   Credit, 3.
                Mr. HELMING.

251. SHAKESPEARE.—A close study of *Henry 4—Part 1, Twelfth Night, King Lear, and Cymbeline.* 1954-55.   Credit, 3.
Prerequisite, English 155.   Mr. TROY.

254. CARLYLE.—A comprehensive and intensive study of the life and writings of Thomas Carlyle. Relevant biographic, textual, ideational, and esthetic problems will be explored so as to acquaint the student with pertinent scholarly methods and materials, and to develop his competence in research and criticism. Given in various years.   Credit, 3.
Prerequisite, English 165.   Mr. GOLDBERG.

261. MELVILLE.—An exploration of the life, thought and art of the most complex and representative figure of the American Renaissance. Although emphasis will be placed upon the pre-Civil War novels, the later poetry will also be examined. Given in various years. Credit, 3.
Prerequisite, English 167. Mr. KAPLAN.

264. JOYCE, YEATS, AND ELIOT.—An intensive study of the experiments, in expressing personal experience, that established the Twentieth Century literary myths. Given in various years. Credit, 3.
Prerequisite, English 176. Mr. VARLEY.

300. THESIS, MASTER'S DEGREE. Credit, 9.

COURSES OPEN TO BOTH GRADUATE AND UNDERGRADUATE STUDENTS
(For either major or minor credit)

In these courses English majors are required to supplement the undergraduate assignments with a substantial special study.

150. CHAUCER. Credit, 3.
Mr. HELMING.

151. THE RENAISSANCE IN ENGLAND. Credit, 3.
Mr. TROY.

153. LYRICAL POETRY OF THE RENAISSANCE IN ENGLAND.—Given in alternate years, 1954-55. Credit, 3.
MR. BARRON.

154. MILTON. Credit, 3.
Mr. GOLDBERG and Mr. HELMING.

155. SHAKESPEARE. Credit, 3.
Mr. RAND.

157. THE RESTORATION PERIOD. Credit, 3.
Mr. KOEHLER.

158. OTHER ELIZABETHAN DRAMATISTS. Credit, 3.
Mr. O'DONNELL.

159. THE AGE OF POPE. Credit, 3.
Mr. TROY.

160. THE AGE OF JOHNSON. Credit, 3.
Mr. TROY.

161. THE LAKE POETS.—Given in alternate years, beginning 1954-55.
Credit, 3.
Mr. RAND.

162. BYRON, SHELLEY, AND KEATS.—Given in alternate years, beginning 1954-55. Credit, 3.
Miss HORRIGAN.

163. AMERICAN POETRY (1700-1900). Credit, 3.
Mr. WILLIAMS and Mr. O'DONNELL.

165. PROSE OF THE ROMANTIC MOVEMENT. Credit, 3.
Mr. GOLDBERG.

166. VICTORIAN PROSE.   Credit, 3.
                                                       Mr. GOLDBERG.

167. AMERICAN PROSE.   Credit, 3.
                                                       Mr. O'DONNELL.

169. VICTORIAN POETRY.—Given in alternate years, beginning 1955-56.
                                                          Credit 3.
                                                       Mr. RAND.

173. ENGLISH PROSE FICTION.   Credit, 3.
                                              MR. ALLEN AND MR. HELMING.

174. GREEK CLASSICS IN TRANSLATION.   Credit, 3.
                                            Mr. HELMING and Mr. TROY.

179. LITERARY CRITICISM FROM ARISTOTLE TO 1800.—Given in alternate
years, beginning 1955-56.   Credit, 3.
                                                       Mr. GOLDBERG.

180. LITERARY CRITICISM SINCE 1800.—Given in alternate years, beginning
1955-56.   Credit, 3.
                                                       Mr. GOLDBERG.

COURSES FOR MINOR CREDIT ONLY

168. MODERN DRAMA.   Credit, 3.
                                             Mr. RAND and Mr. WILLIAMS.

171. BIOGRAPHY.   Credit, 3.
                                                       Mr. HELMING.

172. THE BIBLE AS LITERATURE.   Credit, 3.
                                                       Mr. RAND.

176. MODERN POETRY.   Credit, 3.
                                            Miss HORRIGAN and Mr. RAND.

177. THE MODERN NOVEL.   Credit, 3.
                                                       Mr. VARLEY.

Entomology

CHARLES P. ALEXANDER, major adviser

COURSES OPEN TO GRADUATE STUDENTS ONLY
(For either major or minor credit)

(Most courses in the department are given on a 3-year cycle, subject to
change on student demand.)

201, 202. ADVANCED INSECT MORPHOLOGY AND PHYLOGENY.—Laboratory,
lecture, and reading assignments in morphology and phylogeny of all orders
of insects, living and fossil.   Credit, 3 each semester
Prerequisites, Entomology 26, 155, 156, 157 or equivalent.   Mr. HANSON.

203. INSECT EMBRYOLOGY.—The embryological development of a generalized
type of insect, after which specific insects are considered. Lectures, assigned
readings, laboratory work.   Credit, 2.
Prerequisite, ENTOMOLOGY 157.   Mr. SHAW.

204. INSECT HISTOLOGY.—Types of tissues and organs of insects. Laboratory
work, discussion and assigned readings.   Credit, 2.
Prerequisites, Entomology 157; Zoology 50.   Mr. SHAW.

207. ADVANCED INSECT PHYSIOLOGY.—Discussion and laboratory work dealing with the functions of the organ systems of insects. Emphasis is placed on methods of analysis and study of physiological processes in insects.   Credit, 3.
Prerequisite, Entomology 181 or equivalent.   Mr. SWEETMAN.

210. INSECT INTERRELATIONSHIPS.—A systematic survey of the various ways in which insects live with, make use of, or are utilized by living organisms, including intra-specific relations; the aim is to present an integrated picture of relationships among insects, and between insects and the living world.
Lectures, readings, papers.   Credit, 2.
Prerequisites, Entomology 26 and 179.   Miss SMITH.

211. INSECT BEHAVIOR.—The honey bee is selected as a type for the study of behavior. Lectures; laboratory work to attempt to interpret the reasons for the actions of this insect. Other species may be included for completeness.
Prerequisites, Entomology 26, 166 or equivalent.   Credit, 3.
                                                                 Mr. SHAW.

212. GEOGRAPHICAL DISTRIBUTION OF ANIMALS AND PLANTS.—The entire field of distribution of life is considered, including a discussion of physical geography, climate, and other materials basic to the subject.   Credit, 3.
                         2 credits 1st semester, 1 credit 2nd semester.
Prerequisites, Botany 1; Zoology 1.   Mr. ALEXANDER.

214. ADVANCED ANIMAL ECOLOGY.—Basic principles of terrestrial, limnological, and marine ecology. Special emphasis is placed on the influence of causal factors, both physical and biotic, that regulate the activities of all organisms.
Prerequisite, Entomology 179, or equivalent.   Credit, 3.
                                                                 Mr. SWEETMAN.

221. ADVANCED CHEMICAL CONTROL OF INSECTS.—The chemistry of insecticides and their physiological effects on insects, man and other animals. Credit, 3.
                                                                 Mr. SWEETMAN.
Prerequisites, Entomology 180 and Pomology 156, or equivalent.

223. ADVANCED BIOLOGICAL CONTROL.—The basic fundamental principles, as well as practical application of biological control of insects. A section is devoted to control of pest weeds with insects.   Credit, 3.
Prerequisite, Entomology 180, or equivalent.   Mr. SWEETMAN.

224. LEGISLATIVE CONTROL OF INSECTS AND INSECTICIDES.—The legal aspects of prevention, control, and eradication of pests; insecticide laws, and health laws regarding use of insecticides. Emphasis is placed on the importance of basic knowledge of the biology and habits of insects and other pest organisms as related to legal and other methods of control and eradication.   Credit, 3.
                                                                 Mr. SWEETMAN.

230. ADVANCED APICULTURE.—This course is designed to provide necessary background for whatever phase of beekeeping the student desires, equipment permitting. Among such topics available are management, biometry, bee poisoning, pollination.   Credit, 2-5.
Prerequisites, Entomology 166, 185, or equivalent.   Mr. SHAW.

240. COCCIDOLOGY.—Lecture and laboratory work on scale insects; their relationships, structure, habits, technique of mounting, identification, damage, and control.   Credit, 2.
Prerequisite, Entomology 26, or equivalent.   Mr. HANSON.

241. CLASSIFICATION OF MINOR ORDERS OF INSECTS.—Laboratory work in taxonomy of the many groups with relatively few species.   Credit, 2.
Prerequisites, Entomology 26, 155, 156, 157, or equivalent.   Mr. HANSON.

242. ADVANCED ARTHROPOD TAXONOMY.—Classification of various groups of insects and insect allies, indicating the latest methods in taxonomy and the principles of classification. In addition to groups listed below, work may be - offered in such groups as Ephemerida, Plecoptera, Diptera (esp. Tipulidae and Mycetophilidae), Lepidoptera, and others upon special arrangement in advance.

Credit, 1-9.

THE STAFF.

A. Culicidae	Miss SMITH
B. Immature stages of insects	Miss SMITH
C. Ticks	Mr. SHAW
D.. Siphonaptera	Mr. SHAW
E. Simuliidae	Mr. SHAW
F. Tabanidae	Mr. SHAW
G. Tipulidae	Mr. ALEXANDER

245. HISTORICAL ENTOMOLOGY.—Lives and works of outstanding entomologists of the world; history of entomology; and classification of insects.

Credit, 3.

(2 credits 1st semester;
1 credit 2nd semester)

Prerequisites, Entomology 26, 153. Mr. ALEXANDER.

248. PRINCIPLES OF SYSTEMATIC ENTOMOLOGY.—Particular stress is placed on a consideration of the International Code of Zoological Nomenclature, and the Opinions thereon; type categories; the species concept; major insect collections; leading entomological specialists. Credit, 3.

(2 credits 1st semester;
1 credit 2nd semester)

Prerequisites, Entomology 26, 155, 156. Mr. ALEXANDER.

250. ADVANCED MEDICAL ENTOMOLOGY.—This course is designed to provide training in whatever phase of medical entomology a student selects (materials and references permitting). Such work might include systematic studies of a family or order of insects involved in medical entomology,. the biology of any particular group of insects, control measures. Credit, 2-5.

Prerequisites, Entomology 174 or its equivalent. Mr. SHAW.

270. ADVANCED RESEARCH METHODS.—The principles, methods of analysis, and presentation of results of research. A section is devoted to statistical treatment and analysis of research. Credit, 3.

Mr. SWEETMAN.

Prerequisites, Research portion of Entomology 181, or equivalent.

280. SEMINAR.—Reports on the current literature of entomology; special reports by resident and visiting speakers. Credit, 1 each semester.

One class hour. (Maximum for M.S. Candidates, 2)
(Maximum for Ph.D. Candidates, 4)

MR. WEIDHAAS.

300. THESIS, MASTER'S DEGREE.—Original work on one or more topics in insect morphology, systematic entomology, medical entomology, insect physiology, insectides,. biological control or apiculture. The thesis requires from one-half to two-thirds of the total working time of the student in his major field. Credit, 10.

400. THESIS, PH.D. DEGREE.—Original work on one or more topics in insect morphology, systematic entomology, medical entomology, insect physiology, insecticides, biological control or apiculture. The thesis requires from one-half to two-thirds of the total working time of the student in his major field.

Credit, 30.

COURSES OPEN TO BOTH GRADUATE AND UNDERGRADUATE STUDENTS

(For either major or minor credit)

185. ADVANCED BEEKEEPING.—A course designed to present more complete knowledge of the more important problems of beekeeping, including management, processing honey and wax, bee diseases, and improvement of honeybees.
Credit, 3.
Prerequisite, Entomology 166. Mr. SHAW.

187, 188. SPECIAL PROBLEMS IN ENTOMOLOGY.—Problem work in many fields, as apiculture, biological control and insectary practice, insecticides, morphology, and classification. Credit, 1, 2, or 3.
Prerequisites, Entomology 26, 53, 155, 157, and should be preceded or accompanied by other courses in the restricted field of the problem.
THE STAFF.

189. ENTOMOLOGICAL TECHNIQUES.—Techniques in the mounting and preservation of insects for study and display by means of fluids, slides, plastics, pinning, and other methods. Credit, 2.
Prerequisite, Entomology 26. Miss SMITH.

190. EVOLUTION.—A course in orientation. Lectures consider evolution of both organic and inorganic matter with attention to the evolution of human behavior and to the effect of evolutionary concepts on human philosophy. Extra supplementary reading required of graduate students. Credit, 2-3.
Mr. HANSON.

COURSES IN OTHER DEPARTMENTS FOR WHICH MAJOR CREDIT WILL BE GIVEN

Zoology 174. LIMNOLOGY. Credit, 4.
Miss TRAVER and STAFF.

Zoology 185. CLASSES OF ARTHROPODS OTHER THAN INSECTS. Credit, 3.
Mr. HANSON.

Botany 190. INSECT TRANSMISSION OF PLANT DISEASES. Credit, 3.
Mr. BANFIELD.

COURSES FOR MINOR CREDIT ONLY

151. PESTS OF SPECIAL CROPS. Credit, 3.
Mr. SHAW.

153. APPLIED ENTOMOLOGY. Credit, 3.
Mr. SHAW.

155, 156. CLASSIFICATION OF INSECTS. Credit, 3.
Mr. ALEXANDER, Miss SMITH.

157. INSECT MORPHOLOGY. Credit, 4.
Mr. HANSON.

166. INTRODUCTORY BEEKEEPING. Credit, 3.
Mr. SHAW.

172. FOREST AND SHADE-TREE INSECTS. Credit, 3.
Mr. HANSON.

174. MEDICAL ENTOMOLOGY.   Credit, 3.
Mr. SHAW.

179. ANIMAL ECOLOGY.   Credit, 3.
Mr. SWEETMAN.

180. INSECT CONTROL.   Credit, 3.
Mr. SWEETMAN.

181. PHYSIOLOGICAL ENTOMOLOGY.   Credit, 3.
Mr. SWEETMAN.

Floriculture

CLARK L. THAYER, major adviser.

All students who major in this department are required to present a thesis as a part of the major requirements.

COURSES OPEN TO GRADUATE STUDENTS ONLY
(For either major or minor credit)

Horticulture 211, 212. SEMINAR.—Each student will present reviews of assigned papers on topics in Horticulture. Departments of Floriculture, Olericulture and Pomology cooperating. Required of all graduate students majoring in Floriculture, Olericulture and Pomology.   Credit, 1 each semester.
THE DEPARTMENTS

226. GARDEN MATERIALS.—Technical studies of a specific genus of plants or a group of plants used in gardening.   Credit, 3.
Prerequisite, Floriculture 26.   Mr. THAYER.

275. ADVANCED COMMERCIAL FLORICULTURE.—Problems dealing with the methods of production of cutflowers and plants under glass. Opportunity is given for a study of factors concerned with methods of marketing such products. Prerequisites, Floriculture 175 and 176.   Credit, 3.
Mr. HUBBARD.

279. CONSERVATORY PLANTS.—Investigations dealing with plant materials which are used primarily in conservatories or in gardens in warm climates. Prerequisite, Floriculture 179.   Credit, 3.
Mr. THAYER.

290. HISTORY OF FLORICULTURE AND FLORICULTURAL LITERATURE.—Consideration of men who have influenced the development of floriculture. Events that have given impetus to the industry. Survey of floricultural literature. Required of all graduate students in the department.   Credit, 3.
Mr. THAYER.

297, 298. SEMINAR.—A review of scientific literature in the field of floriculture or in related fields.   Credit, 1 each semester.
Mr. WHITE and THE STAFF

300. THESIS, MASTER'S DEGREE.—For students having a major in Floriculture. Based on an original investigation of a problem selected by agreement between the student and the staff.   Credit, 10.

COURSES IN OTHER DEPARTMENTS FOR WHICH MAJOR CREDIT WILL BE GIVEN

Agronomy 263. CHEMISTRY OF THE SOIL.   Credit, 5.
                                                        Mr. STECKEL.

Agronomy 264. EXPERIMENTAL METHODS IN AGRONOMY.   Credit, 3.
                                                        Mr. YEGIAN.

Botany 161, 162. THE COMPARATIVE ANATOMY OF GREEN PLANTS.
                                           Credit, 3 each semester.
                                                        Mr. TORREY.

Botany 158. MICROTECHNIQUE.   Credit, 2.
                                                        Mr. TORREY.

Botany 159, 160. THE ANGIOSPERMS.   Credit, 3-5 each semester.
                                                        Mr. TORREY.

Olericulture 201. LITERATURE.   Credit, 3.
                                                        Mr. LACHMAN.

Plant Breeding 152. ADVANCED PLANT BREEDING.   Credit, 3.
                                                        Mr. FRENCH.

Plant Breeding 181. PLANT CYTOLOGICAL TECHNIQUE.   Credit, 2.
                                                        Mr. FRENCH.

Plant Breeding 182. SPECIAL PROBLEMS.   Credit, 2.
                                                        Mr. FRENCH.

COURSES FOR MINOR CREDIT ONLY

151. GREENHOUSE MANAGEMENT.   Credit, 3.
                                           Mr. THAYER and Mr. JESTER.

152. FLORAL ARRANGEMENT.   Credit, 3
                                            Mr. THAYER and Mr. ROSS.

175, 176. COMMERCIAL FLORICULTURE.   Credit, 3 each semester.
                                                        Mr. HUBBARD

179. CONSERVATORY PLANTS (1954-55).   Credit, 2.
                                            Mr. THAYER and Mr. ROSS.

181. HERBACEOUS GARDENS AND BORDERS.   Credit, 3
                                                        Mr. HUBBARD.

182. SEMINAR (Problem course).   Credit, 3
                                                        Mr. THAYER.

Food Sciences

This is a cooperative major designed for Ph.D. candidates who wish to prepare for research in various phases of the food sciences. It is designed to give a broader and somewhat less intensive scientific base for research or its application in industry than is possible when a student takes most of his major work in one department only. This plan provides for a candidate to place the major emphasis in one of the five departments cooperating which may or may not offer a Ph.D. degree in the department.

The departments cooperating are Bacteriology, Chemistry, Dairy Industry, Food Technology, and the School of Home Economics (Foods and Nutrition). Courses, if properly selected, will satisfy both major and minor requirements.

The proportionate contribution of each department will depend upon the student's special interests within the field but a minimum of six credits must be earned in each of the departments contributing to this major.

Candidates for the Ph.D. degree in the Food Sciences are assigned to an advisory committee composed of the heads of the five departments concerned, with the head of the department in which the thesis research is planned serving as chairman. This advisory committee will direct the student's progress, conduct the preliminary examination, and approve the thesis subject. The thesis committee, appointed by the Scholarship Committee of the Graduate School Council with the staff member who is directing the thesis serving as chairman, will have direct charge of all matters pertaining to the thesis investigation.

The 30 major course credits required for the Ph.D. must be distributed among at least 3 of the 5 departments concerned. The minimum requirement of six credits in other departments may be satisfied by either major or minor credits. Courses offered by the 5 departments which are acceptable for major credit toward the degree in Food Sciences have been designated by the advisory committee as follows:

400. THESIS, PH.D. Credit, 30.

Bacteriology

202. BACTERIAL PHYSIOLOGY.

203. BACTERIAL CYTOLOGY.

205. ADVANCED IMMUNOLOGY.

206. INDUSTRIAL BACTERIOLOGY.

207. VIROLOGY.

208. SEMINAR.

213. ANTIBIOTICS.

215. ANTISEPTICS AND DISINFECTANTS.

156. METHODS FOR BACTERIOLOGICAL PREPARATION.

196. STUDIES OF SPECIAL MICROBIAL GROUPS.

182. FOOD BACTERIOLOGY.

185. IMMUNOLOGY.

190. SANITARY BACTERIOLOGY.

Chemistry

237. BIOCOLLOIDS.

239. CHEMISTRY OF NATURAL PRODUCTS.

165, 166. PHYSICAL CHEMISTRY. (For minor credit only)

179. BIOCHEMISTRY. (For minor credit only)

183. ADVANCED QUANTITATIVE ANALYSIS.

193, 194. GENERAL BIOCHEMISTRY

Dairy Industry

175. DAIRY CHEMISTRY.

201. PROBLEMS IN DAIRY TECHNOLOGY.

202. ADVANCED DAIRY CHEMISTRY.

209, 210. SEMINAR.

Food Technology

201, 202. SPECIAL INVESTIGATIONS.
209, 210. THERMAL PROCESSING OF FOODS.
216. FOOD PACKAGING.
221. EDIBLE FATS AND OILS.
241. FOOD ACCEPTANCE—THEORY AND METHODOLOGY.
271, 272. SEMINAR REVIEW OF CURRENT LITERATURE AND RESEARCH.
285, 286. FISHERIES TECHNOLOGY.
161, 162. INDUSTRIAL PRACTICES.
191, 192. FOOD ANALYSIS.
291. ADVANCED FOOD ANALYSIS.

Foods & Nutrition

203. ADVANCED NUTRITION—METABOLISM OF THE MAJOR FOODSTUFFS.
204. ADVANCED NUTRITION—MINERALS AND VITAMINS.
205. LABORATORY METHODS AND TECHNIQUES IN NUTRITION.
207. PROBLEMS IN NUTRITION.
211, 212. NUTRITION SEMINAR.
189. DIET THERAPY.

Food Technology

CARL R. FELLERS, major adviser.

Graduate students who wish to major in Food Technology may not be admitted to candidacy for an advanced degree until such time as the undergraduate requirements in basic sciences and Food Technology have been met substantially.

COURSES OPEN TO GRADUATE STUDENTS ONLY

(For either major or minor credit)

200. RESEARCH PROBLEM.—This course is mainly for candidates for the Master of Science degree. Original research is expected. Two bound copies (flexible binding permissible) are required by the Department. Credit, 3-6.
THE STAFF.

201, 202. SPECIAL INVESTIGATIONS.—A series of individual problems and assignments covering plant layouts, process development, quality control and economics of production. Laboratory, pilot plant and library exercises.
Credit, 1-3 each semester.
THE STAFF.

209, 210. THERMAL PROCESSING OF FOODS.—Biological and Physical Aspects. A study of the factors affecting heat transfer in canned goods. Heating characteristics of canned foods packed in tin, glass, and other containers. Determination of thermal death points of spoilage micro-organisms. Derivation of processing times and temperatures. Causes of spoilage and container failure. Principles of retort operation and control; instrumentation.
First semester—2 lectures or conferences. Credit, 2.
Second semester—1 lecture, one 4-hour laboratory. Credit, 3.
Prerequisites, Food Tech. 162 and Bact. 182. Mr. ESSELEN.

212. FREEZING AND REFRIGERATION.—Lay-out of cold storage plants. Practical refrigeration systems. Equipment and methods used in quick-freezing fruits, vegetables, meats, and marine products. Packaging and quality control. Home freezers and commercial frozen-food lockers. Laboratory and class work.
Prerequisites, Food Tech. 152, Ag. Engin. 180 or 182.   Credit, 2-4.
                                                                          Mr. FELLERS.

216. FOOD PACKAGING.—A study of the characteristics of all packaging materials including flexible films and how they meet the package requirements of various food products. Methods of testing for structural quality and performance, moisture and gas transmission, and other properties. Consideration of adhesives, lacquers and closures included. Occasional lectures by qualified representatives of industry. Plant visits in non-scheduled hours.
One 4-hour laboratory period; one or more class or discussion hours.   Credit, 3.
Prerequisite, Food Tech. 162.   Mr. LEVINE.

221. EDIBLE FATS AND OILS.—The production and uses of edible fats and oils and their chemical nature in relationship to stability. The problem of oxidation and rancidity is considered with emphasis on cause of deterioration and methods of stabilization.   Credit, 2.
One class hour, one 2-hour laboratory period.   Mr. ANDERSON.

232. UNIT PROCESSES.—Unit processes pertaining to the food industries are covered. The work includes instrumentation, temperature measurement, blanching, filtration, comminution, deaeration and extraction, processing, cooling, heat transfer, fluid flow, distillation, dehydration, and evaporation.   Credit, 2.
                                                                          Mr. FAGERSON.
Prerequisites, Food Tech. 162 and Ag. Engin. 180.

241. FOOD ACCEPTANCE—THEORY AND METHODOLOGY.—A critical analysis of objective and subjective methods of evaluation of the quality of processed foods. Physical and chemical means of expressing quality of a product. Sensory methods including difference-preference tests, panel tests, threshold tests, etc. Application of statistical methods including control chart techniques. Psychological and physiological factors affecting flavor appraisal.
1 lecture; 1 conference.
Prerequisites, Food Technology 192, 162.   Credit, 3.
                                                                          Mr. FAGERSON.

271, 272. SEMINAR.—Review of current literature and research.
                                                      Credit, 1-2 each semester.
                                                                          THE STAFF.

285, 286. FISHERIES TECHNOLOGY.—Marine products of commerce. Processed seafoods. Canning, curing, freezing and refrigeration. Spoilage problems. By-products. Chemical and microbiological aspects. Scientific literature. Industrial problems.   Credit, 2-3 each semester.
One class hour plus laboratory work to be arranged.   Mr. FELLERS.

291. ADVANCED FOOD ANALYSIS.—The application of instrumental analysis to the separation, identification, and measurement of food constituents such as vitamins, pigments and trace elements. Includes theory and laboratory experiments in column and paper chromatography, electrodialysis, polarography, colorimetry, absorption and emission spectrophotometry, reflectometry, fluorophotometry, nephelometry and radiosotope dilution methods.   Credit, 3.
Prerequisites, Food Technology 191, Chemistry 165.   Mr. LIVINGSTON.

295. BIOLOGICAL ASSAY OF FOODS.—Provides laboratory training and practice in making animal and microbiological assays of food constituents important in human and animal nutrition.   Credit, 2-5.
Prerequisites, Chem. 179 and Food Tech. 192.   Mr. PARKINSON.

300. THESIS, MASTER'S DEGREE.—Research on some suitable problem in Food Technology. Facilities for nutrition research are provided by well-equipped chemical, physical, and small-animal laboratories and poultry plant.   Credit, 10.

400. THESIS, PH.D. DEGREE.—Research on some suitable problem in Food Technology. Facilities for nutrition research are provided by well-equipped chemical, physical, and small-animal laboratories and poultry plant.   Credit, 30.

COURSES OPEN TO BOTH GRADUATE AND UNDERGRADUATE STUDENTS
(For either major or minor credit)

161, 162. INDUSTRIAL PRACTICES.—Advanced laboratory and pilot plant work in the production of canned, frozen and dehydrated fruits, vegetables, meat, and fish products. The theory and practice in manufacturing jams, jellies and condiments as well as fermented, salted and smoked foods; cereal products and soups. Credit, 3 each semester.
One class hour, one 4-hour laboratory period. Mr. LEVINE.

182. CONFECTIONS AND CEREAL PRODUCTS.—Candy making, maple products, sugar and fountain syrups, corn products such as starch, syrups, dextrose and their uses. Candied fruits and preserves. Flavoring essences, spices, carbonated beverages. This course also considers the principles of baking, doughs, and various prepared cereals and dry mixes. Credit, 3.
One class hour, one 4-hour laboratory period. Mr. LEVINE.

191, 192. ANALYSIS OF FOOD PRODUCTS.—Factory and laboratory methods. Grades and quality factors; physical, chemical, microbiological and microscopical methods, and interpretation of results. Government and trade standards; Federal and State food regulations; mold and insect counts; plant control procedures will be stressed. Food preservatives and flavorings.
Credit, 3 each semester.
Mr. FELLERS and Mr. NEBESKY.
One 4-hour laboratory period, one lecture.
Prerequisites, Chem. 30, Food Tech. 152 or 175.

COURSES IN OTHER DEPARTMENTS FOR WHICH MAJOR CREDIT WILL BE GIVEN

Dairy Industry 152. MARKET MILK. Credit, 4.
Mr. LINDQUIST.

Dairy Industry 177. BUTTER AND CHEESE MAKING. Credit, 4.
Mr. LINDQUIST, Mr. NELSON and Mr. FINNEGAN

Dairy Industry 178. ICE CREAM MAKING. Credit, 4
Mr. NELSON.

Animal Husbandry 154. MEAT PROCESSING. Credit, 2
Mr. BARTLETT.

BACTERIOLOGY 206. INDUSTRIAL BACTERIOLOGY. Credit, 3.
Mr. CZARNECKI.

Chemistry 193-194. GENERAL BIOCHEMISTRY. Credit, 4 or 8.
Mr. LITTLE.

Chemistry 237. BIOCOLLOIDS. Credit, 3.

Mr. BENNETT.

Home Economics 205. LABORATORY METHODS AND TECHNIQUES IN NUTRITION.
Credit, 3.

Mrs. WERTZ.

Olericulture 173. MARKETING AND STORAGE OF VEGETABLE CROPS. Credit, 3.

Mr. SNYDER

Olericulture 174. MARKETING PRACTICES. Credit, 3.

Mr. SNYDER.

Poultry Science 201. ADVANCED POULTRY HUSBANDRY. Credit, 3.

THE STAFF.

COURSES FOR MINOR CREDIT ONLY

151. FRUIT AND VEGETABLE PRODUCTS.—This is a general elementary course covering food economics, production, distribution and processing. The applications of fundamental science to the food industries are pointed out. The laboratory exercises cover both the theory and practice of canning, freezing, and dehydration. The principles of packaging are considered. Fruit and vegetable products are prepared and graded. Credit, 3.
One class hour, one 4-hour laboratory period. Mr. FELLERS.

152. FOOD PRODUCTS AND ADJUNCTS.—This is a continuation of 151. The laboratory work includes pickles and pickle products, maple products, citrus products, fruit syrups, soups, condiments and the preservation of meats, poultry and vegetables. The properties and uses of sugars, syrups, salt, enzymes, pectin, chemical preservatives and anti-oxidants, are considered. Practice is given in the use and handling of instruments and equipment. Credit, 3.
Two class hours, one 2-hour laboratory period. Mr. FELLERS.

175, 176. FOOD PRESERVATION.—This is a general course in food preservation and is intended only for those who desire a survey of the field in a condensed form. Not open to Food Technology majors. Credit 3, either semester.
One class hour, two 2-hour laboratory periods. Mr. NEBESKY.

195, 196. INTRODUCTORY RESEARCH METHODS.—The application of the fundamental sciences to food technology research. Library and laboratory research on assigned individual problems. Credit, 2 each semester.
By arrangement. Mr. FELLERS, Mr. LEVINE

Forestry

COURSES FOR MINOR CREDIT ONLY.

151. FOREST MANAGEMENT OF WATERSHEDS.—A study of forest site and water factor relationships; the measurability of the forest resources and their management toward realizing the multiple values of watersheds. The protection of forested watersheds. Credit, 3.
Three class hours. Mr. RHODES and Mr. HOLDSWORTH.

153. SILVICS.—Forest ecology as the basis for silvacultural practice.
Two class hours; one 4-hour laboratory period. Credit, 3.

Mr. RHODES.

154. FOREST SOILS.—A study of the soils of forests as they influence forest growth and management and as they are influenced by forest trees and forest management. Credit, 3.
Three class hours. Mr. RHODES.

155. ELEMENTS OF FOREST MENSURATION.—Methods of inventorying the volumes of the timber capital or growing stock and other resources of the forest, including growth rates and increase in wood volume. Credit, 3.
Two class hours; one 4 hour laboratory period.
Mr. MacCONNELL and Mr. GANLEY.

156. PRINCIPLES OF APPLIED SILVICULTURE.—Forest establishment and cultural development through silvicultural practice. Credit, 3.
Two class hours; one 4-hour laboratory period. Mr. RHODES and Mr. ABBOTT.

157. ECONOMICS OF FORESTRY.—The resource values of the forest with the history of their economic development. Credit, 3.
Three class hours. Mr. HOLDSWORTH.

159. FOREST PROTECTION.—The principle of protecting forests from all harmful agencies. Credit, 3.
Three class hours. Mr. ABBOTT.

171. AERIAL PHOTOGRAMMETRY.—Interpretation and use of aerial photographs in map making and forest land inventory and management. Credit, 3.
Two class hours, one 4-hour laboratory period.
Mr. MacCONNELL and Mr. GANLEY.

176. WOOD TECHNOLOGY.—A comprehensive survey of the structure, composition and properties of wood in relation to wood utilization. Credit, 3.
Three class hours. Mr. RICH.

180. PRINCIPLES OF FOREST MANAGEMENT.—The organization of the forest for sustained yields management; preparation of forest management plans.
Three class hours. Credit, 3.
Prerequisites, Forestry 155 and 156. Mr. MacCONNELL.

185. SEASONING OF WOOD.—Methods of air seasoning and kiln drying lumber.
Three class hours. Credit, 3.
Mr. RICH.

Geology and Mineralogy

LEONARD R. WILSON, major adviser.

COURSES OPEN TO GRADUATE STUDENTS ONLY.
(For either major or minor credit)

200. SPECIAL PROBLEMS.—For students desiring to pursue special work not covered by courses listed in the curriculum. Permission to take one or both courses must be secured from the head of the department and the instructor under whom the study will be done. The latter will outline and supervise the work. Credit, 6.
THE STAFF.

201. OPTICAL MINERALOGY.—An introduction to the theory, procedure and technique involved in the study of minerals by means of the petrographic microscope. The laboratory work will include the preparation of thin sections of minerals and rocks, together with a study of their optical properties by means of polarized light. Credit, 3.
Given in alternate years, beginning 1954-55. Mr. NELSON.
Prerequisite, Geology 151.

202. ADVANCED PETROLOGY.—A study of physico-chemical principles related to petrogenesis of igneous, metamorphic and sedimentary rocks. The consideration of general principles and specific problems such as differentiation, ore solutions, granitiation, granite tectonics and diagenesis. Credit, 3.
Given in alternate years, beginning 1955-56. Mr. LIGHT.
Prerequisite, Geology 201 or equivalent.

212. SEDIMENTATION.—A course dealing with the sources, depositions, modifying conditions, structures and environmental relationships of sediments and their consolidated equivalents. Credit, 3.
Given in alternate years, beginning 1954-55. Mr. LIGHT.

213. GEOPHYSICS.—A study of the physics of the earth and of the gravitational, magnetic, electrical, and seismic methods of geophysical exploration. The laboratory work consists of problems and computations. Credit, 3.
Prerequisite, Geology 173. Mr. FARRINGTON.

214. MINERAL FUELS.—A course dealing with the geological occurrences of coal, gas and oil. The laboratory work consists of problems related to petroleum geology and the recovery of fluid hydrocarbons. Credit, 3.
Prerequisite, Geology 154. Mr. FARRINGTON.

221. ANIMAL MICROPALEONTOLOGY.—Principles of animal micropaleontology with emphasis on the use of animal microfossils in stratigraphic investigations. Credit, 3.
Mr. WILSON and Mr. JOHANSSON.

222. PLANT MICROPALEONTOLOGY.—Principles of plant micropaleontology with emphasis on the use of plant microfossils in stratigraphic investigations. Credit, 3.
Mr. WILSON.

241. SEMINAR.—Review of current literature or discussion of selected topics. Credit, 1 each semester. Maximum credit, 2.
THE STAFF.

300. THESIS, MASTER'S DEGREE.—Research on an approved problem. Credit, 10.

COURSES OPEN TO BOTH GRADUATE AND UNDERGRADUATE STUDENTS
(For either major or minor credit)

173. STRUCTURAL GEOLOGY.—A study of the origin of rock structures, their occurrence and recognition. Undergraduates must have the permission of the instructor before enrolling. Credit, 3.
Mr. LIGHT.

174. PRINCIPLES OF STRATIGRAPHY.—A study of the principles of stratigraphic correlation as related to the major rock units of the United States. Undergraduates must have the permission of the instructor before enrolling. Credit, 3.
Mr. WILSON.

COURSES FOR MINOR CREDIT ONLY

150. ENGINEERING GEOLOGY.—A general course in engineering geology stressing earth structure, the dynamic processes, and agents of weathering. The laboratory work consists of mineral and rock-determination and map-reading as related to the phenomena of physical geology. Credit, 3.
Two class hours; one 3-hour laboratory period. Mr. LIGHT.

151. MINERALOGY.—A descriptive study. Stress is placed upon the identification and occurrence of minerals. Credit, 3.
One class hour; two 2-hour laboratory periods. Mr. NELSON.

152. LITHOLOGY.—A descriptive study of the classes of rocks with reference to manner of origin, modes of occurrence, structural features and the chemical and petrographic distinction within each group. Credit, 3.
One class hour; two 2-hour laboratory periods. Mr. NELSON.

154. ECONOMIC GEOLOGY.—A course dealing with the origin, classification, and uses of metallic and non-metallic mineral deposits. Credit, 3.
Two class hours; one 2-hour laboratory period. Mr. LIGHT.

161. GEOMORPHOLOGY.—A review of recent studies concerning rock structures, weathering, underground water, streams, alpine and continental glaciers, shorelines, and wind work. Given in alternate years beginning 1954-55.
Credit, 3.
Two class hours; one 2-hour laboratory period. Mr. WILSON.

162. PLEISTOCENE GEOLOGY.—A study of Pleistocene world geology consisting of geological processes, land forms, existing and extinct glaciers, biota and stratigraphy. Field trips by arrangement. Given in alternate years. Credit, 3.
Two class hours; one 2-hour laboratory period. Mr. WILSON.

163. INVERTEBRATE PALEONTOLOGY.—A study of the history, development and identification of invertebrate animal fossils. Field trips by arrangement.
Credit, 3.
Mr. JOHANSSON.

164. PLANT PALEONTOLOGY.—A study of the history, development and identification of plant fossils. Field trips by arrangement. Credit, 3.
One class hour; two 2-hour laboratory periods. Mr. WILSON.

German

COURSES FOR MINOR CREDIT ONLY

151. NINETEENTH CENTURY PROSE I.—A study of the "Novelle" from the death of Goethe to 1890 (early realism to naturalism) with emphasis on literary and social forces in the work of Tieck, Stifter, Keller, and others. Credit, 3.
Three class hours. Given in 1956-57. Mr. SCHROEDER.

152. POETRY AND DRAMA OF THE NINETEENTH CENTURY II.—A study of the development of the drama and of lyric poetry from 1830 to 1890 with special emphasis on dramatic works of Grillparzer, Hebbel, and Hauptmann and the poetry of Mörike, Storm, and C. F. Meyer. Credit, 3.
Three class hours. Given in 1956-57. Mr. SCHROEDER.

153. TWENTIETH CENTURY PROSE I.—Main literary currents in contemporary German prose from Nietzsche to Hesse with particular attention to the work of Thomas Mann, Kafka, and Werfel. Credit, 3.
Three class hours. Given in 1955-56. Mr. SCHROEDER.

154. POETRY AND DRAMA OF THE TWENTIETH CENTURY II.—Reading and discussion of significant lyrical works of Hofmannsthal, George, and Rilke and representative dramas by Hauptmann and Georg Kaiser. Credit, 3.
Three class hours. Given in 1955-56. Mr. GOLDSMITH.

155. STORM AND STRESS I.—A study of storm and stress in German literature centering in the young Goethe. Credit, 3.
Three class hours. Given in 1955-56. Mr. ELLERT.

156. ROMANTICISM II.—A study of the poetry and prose writings of the romantic period from Novalis to Heine. Credit, 3.
Three class hours. Given in 1956-57. Mr. ELLERT.

157. GOETHE'S FAUST I. Credit, 3.
Three class hours. Mr. GOLDSMITH.

158. MIDDLE HIGH GERMAN II.—Reading of Middle High German texts with an introduction to grammar. Credit, 3.
Three class hours. Mr. KRATZ.

159. THE GERMANIC LANGUAGES I.—An introduction to General and Germanic philology for German and English majors; a survey of the relationship between German, English, and the other Indo-European tongues and of the historical development of German and English as the two major Germanic literary languages. Credit, 3.
Three class hours. Mr. KRATZ.

160. THE CLASSICAL PERIOD II.—A study of representative works by Lessing, Goethe, and Schiller. Credit, 3.
Three class hours. Given in 1955-56. Mr. GOLDSMITH.

168. GERMAN LITERATURE OF THE MIDDLE AGES II.—A survey of the literature of the German language from the earliest literary documents to the 15th century, with readings in modern German translation of the Nibelungenlied, Gudrun, Parzival, Tristan, Der arme Heinrich, and the lyrics of Walter von der Vogelweide. Credit, 3.
Three class hours. Given in 1955-56. Mr. ELLERT.

222. ADVANCED SPOKEN GERMAN. Credit, 3.
Prerequisites, German 79 and 80 or their equivalent as determined by a qualifying examination. Mr. SCHROEDER.

Government

COURSES FOR MINOR CREDIT ONLY

154. STATE GOVERNMENT.—A study of state politics, organization and functions, with emphasis on the role of the state in our federal system. Credit, 3.
Mr. GOODWIN.

161. PUBLIC ADMINISTRATION. Credit, 3.
Mr. MAINZER.

162. ADMINISTRATIVE LAW. Credit, 3.
Mr. MAINZER.

163. POLITICAL PARTIES AND ELECTIONS. Credit, 3.
Mr. GOODWIN.

164. MUNICIPAL GOVERNMENT. Credit, 3.
Mr. GOODWIN.

165. CONSTITUTIONAL LAW.   Credit, 3.
                                                           Mr. CAHILL.

166. AMERICAN POLITICAL THOUGHT.   Credit, 3.
                                                           Mr. CAHILL.

167. INTERNATIONAL ORGANIZATION.—A study of international organization in the twentieth century, with emphasis upon the United Nations and regional organizations.   Credit, 3.
                                                           MR. BRAUNTHAL.

168. INTERNATIONAL LAW.—A study of the scope and significance of international law in contemporary international relations.   Credit, 3
                                                           Mr. ALLEN.

171. ANCIENT AND MEDIEVAL POLITICAL THOUGHT.   Credit, 3.
                                                           Mr. TINDER.

172. MODERN POLITICAL THOUGHT.   Credit, 3.
                                                           Mr. TINDER.

173. COMPARATIVE GOVERNMENT.—A functional analysis of contemporary governments with special attention to the ideology, structure, and dynamics of political parties.   Credit, 3.
                                                           Mr. ALLEN.

176. PUBLIC OPINION IN POLITICS.—A study of opinion and communication as aspects of the political process with emphasis upon communication through mass media. Examination of the relations between mass attitudes and communication and political institutions and the formation of public policy.   Credit, 3.
                                                           Mr. MAINZER.

193, 194. SEMINAR.—A study of special problems in the field of government.
                                                           Credit, 3.
                                                           THE STAFF.

History

HAROLD W. CARY, major adviser.

In addition to the general requirements for the Master of Arts degree, candidates in History must fulfill the following departmental requirements:

All candidates are required to take the *Graduate Record Examination*. If possible, this should be taken before admission to the Graduate School; otherwise, it must be taken as soon as possible after admission.

A reading knowledge of one foreign language is required.

The requirement concerning a thesis may be fulfilled by one of the following options: (a) completion of a thesis, for ten credits, (b) completion of two seminar courses, with grades of at least 80, (c) completion of a five credit thesis and one seminar.

A comprehensive written examination, in fields specified by the Department, is required of all candidates.

COURSES OPEN TO GRADUATE STUDENTS ONLY
(For either major or minor credit)

201. SOCIAL AND INTELLECTUAL HISTORY OF THE UNITED STATES.—1815-1896.—An analysis of developments in the principal sections of the U. S.   Credit, 3.
Prerequisites, 159 and 160.   Mr. DAVIS.

210. THE PROGRESSIVE MOVEMENT AND THE NEW DEAL IN THE UNITED STATES, 1896-1940.—Conditions and ideas in the revolt against conservatism.
Credit, 3.
Prerequisites, History 159 and 160. Mr. CARY.

251. SEMINAR IN AMERICAN DIPLOMATIC HISTORY.—Training in historical research.
Credit, 3.
Admission by consent of instructor. Mr. CARY.

256. SEMINAR IN THE WESTWARD MOVEMENT OF THE UNITED STATES.—Training in historical research.
Credit, 3.
Admission by consent of instructor. Mr. DAVIS.

300. THESIS, MASTER'S DEGREE. Credits, 5 or 10.

COURSES OPEN TO BOTH GRADUATE AND UNDERGRADUATE STUDENTS
(For either major or minor credit)

The following courses are open to both graduate and undergraduate students who have fulfilled the prerequisites including History 5 or 6 or their equivalent. Graduate students will be expected to do such additional work as shall be prescribed by the instructor.

151. ANCIENT HISTORY. Credit, 3.
Mr. DAVIS.

153. INTERNATIONAL RELATIONS. Credit, 3.
Mr. PFLANZE.

154. THE FAR EAST IN MODERN TIMES.—Given in alternate years, beginning 1954-55.
Credit, 3.
Mr. GAGNON.

156. THE HISTORY OF MODERN RUSSIA.—Given in alternate years, beginning 1955-56.
Credit, 3.
Mr. GAGNON.

157 and 158. HISPANIC-AMERICAN HISTORY. Credit, 3 each semester.
Mr. POTASH.

165. NINETEENTH AND TWENTIETH CENTURY ENGLAND. Given in alternate years, beginning 1955-56.
Credit, 3.
Prerequisite, History 32 or permission of instructor. Mr. CALDWELL.

167. TUDOR AND STUART ENGLAND. Given in alternate years, beginning 1954-55.
Credit, 3.
Prerequisite, History 31 or permission of instructor. Mr. CALDWELL.

169. EUROPE, 1870-1918. Credit, 3.
Mr. ZEENDER.

170. EUROPE, SINCE 1918. Credit, 3.
Mr. CALDWELL.

172. HISTORY OF AMERICAN WESTWARD EXPANSION, 1763-1893. Credit, 3.
Prerequisite, History 159 or permission of instructor. Mr. DAVIS

175. MEDIEVAL EUROPE. Credit, 3.
Mr. ZEENDER.

176. HISTORY OF THE RENAISSANCE. Credit, 3.
Mr. ZEENDER.

181. DIPLOMATIC HISTORY OF THE UNITED STATES, 1776-1900. Credit, 3.
Prerequisites, History 159 and 160 or permission of instructor. Mr. CARY.

182. DIPLOMATIC HISTORY OF THE UNITED STATES SINCE 1900. Credit, 3.
Prerequisites, History 159 and 160 or permission of instructor. Mr. CARY.

191. HISTORICAL BIBLIOGRAPHY.—Training in assembling a bibliography and
an introduction to the works of some leading historians. Credit, 1.
THE STAFF.

192. SEMINAR.—Instruction in the evaluation of source materials and the
preparation of reports. Credit, 1.
THE STAFF.

COURSES FOR MINOR CREDIT ONLY

159, 160. HISTORY OF THE UNITED STATES. Credit, 3.
Mr. CARY.

Home Economics

HELEN S. MITCHELL, major adviser

Graduate work is primarily in the field of Nutrition Research or Home Economics Education with an emphasis on foods and nutrition. Those applying
for graduate work in Nutrition should have an undergraduate major in Foods
and Nutrition or its equivalent with strong offerings in Organic, Biochemistry,
Physiology, and Bacteriology. Students applying for graduate work in Home
Economics Education should have an undergraduate major in Home Economics
with some courses in Education and Practice Teaching. The major work in
this field is offered jointly by the School of Home Economics and the Department of Education with certain courses in Education accepted for major credit
as listed herewith.

COURSES OPEN TO GRADUATE STUDENTS ONLY

(For either major or minor credit)

200. SPECIAL PROBLEM.—An intensive study of a special problem in the field
of Home Economics. This type of problem is recommended instead of a thesis
for certain students. Credit, 3-6.
THE STAFF.

203. ADVANCED NUTRITION—METABOLISM OF THE MAJOR FOODSTUFFS.—A
study is made of energy metabolism and the metabolism of carbohydrates, fats,
proteins, and related substances, their role in human nutrition, and physiological effects of dietary inadequacies. A critical evaluation of food value tables
and other reference material is made. Students are expected to give special
reports from current literature supplementing class discussion. Credit, 3.
Prerequisites, Physiological Chemistry and/or Physiology. Miss MITCHELL.

204. ADVANCED NUTRITION—MINERALS AND VITAMINS.—A detailed study is
made of mineral metabolism, function in the body and the result of deficiencies.
The vitamins will be discussed from the standpoint of food distribution, function,
chemical nature and stability, assay methods, and result of deficiencies. Credit, 3.
Miss MITCHELL.
Prerequisite, Home Economics 203, or equivalent.

205. LABORATORY METHODS AND TECHNIQUES IN NUTRITION.—Laboratory course designed to acquaint qualified students with the different types of laboratory techniques that are currently used in nutrition research. These methods include fluorometric, colorimetric, spectrophotometric, and microbiological determinations of various nutrients in foods and biological fluids. Credit, 3.
1 class hour, one 4-hour lab. Mrs. WERTZ.
Prerequisites, Quantitative Chemistry, Home Ec. 203, 204, or equivalent.

207. PROBLEMS IN NUTRITION.—Qualified students may be permitted to work on a problem of special interest to them in the fields of vitamin and mineral metabolism, basal metabolism, dietary survey techniques, etc. Credit, 3.
Prerequisite, Home Ec. 203 or 204 or equivalent. Mrs. WERTZ

209. PROBLEMS IN FOODS.—An advanced study of foods. Designed mainly to equip a student of the science in experimental foods procedures. Special emphasis on individual research problems. Credit, 3.
Miss DAVIS.

Prerequisites, Home Economics 193, Quantitative Chemistry, or equivalent, and permission of instructor.

210. HOME ECONOMICS SEMINAR.—Readings, reports and discussions on the current literature of the following areas—family relations, family economics, and home management. Credit, 3.
Miss MERRIAM AND Miss STRATTNER.

211, 212. NUTRITION SEMINAR.—Readings, discussions and preparation of bibliographies on nutrition problems of current interest Credit, 1 each semester.
Miss MITCHELL.

300. THESIS, MASTER'S DEGREE.—Individual research in the field of nutrition and the preparation of an acceptable thesis reporting results and analysis of such studies. Credit, 10.

COURSES OPEN TO BOTH GRADUATE AND UNDERGRADUATE STUDENTS

(For either major or minor credit)

178. ADVANCED TEXTILE DESIGN.—Weaving and handling of complicated looms. Other types of textile design such as stencilling, silk screen printing, batik, block print, with individual problems dependent on special student interests. Credit, 3.
One class hour; two 3-hour laboratory periods. Miss BRIGGS.
Prerequisite, Home Economics 26 or equivalent.

181. METHODS OF TEACHING HOME ECONOMICS.—A study is made of general education philosophy; the application of home economics to the entire school program; development of curricula based upon student needs; exploration of instructional methods and techniques. This course gives credit toward meeting state standards for teachers. During the last month a two-hour laboratory period replaces one lecture. Credit, 3.
Miss STRATTNER.

185. THEORY AND PRACTICE OF NURSERY SCHOOL MANAGEMENT.—This course is planned to give students a background in the history and philosophy of the pre-school program; theory and techniques of nursery school practice; children's activities in music, art, literature and sciences; fundamentals of play and use of play material and methods of observation and recording. Supervised participation in child development laboratory as well as field trips to observe special groups. Credit, 3.
Prerequisite, Home Economics 70. Mrs. THIES.

187. PRINCIPLES AND PRACTICES OF TAILORING.—Emphasis is placed on handling of wool in the making of suits and coats. Credit, 3.
One class hour; one 4-hour laboratory period. Mrs. WILHELM.
Prerequisite, Home Economics 35 or its equivalent.

188. APPLIED DRESS DESIGN.—Costume design through draping and pattern making. An intensive study is made of texture, line, color, and fit as applied to dress design and the figure. Credit, 3.
One class hour; two 2-hour laboratory periods. Mrs. WILHELM.
Prerequisite, Home Economics 35 or its equivalent.

189. DIET THERAPY.—The application of nutrition principles to diet in disease. Recent theories of dietary treatment of gastro-intestinal disorders, obesity, anemia, fevers, diabetes, food allergy, cardiovascular and biliary tract diseases are reviewed critically. Students are required to use and be familiar with current medical literature as it applies to nutrional problems in disease.
Credit, 3.
Prerequisites, Home Economics 52 or 203 and 204; Physiological Chemistry; Physiology. Mrs. COOK.

190. PROFESSIONAL SEMINARS.—Offered in five fields of subject matter—Nutrition, Textiles, Foods, Home Management and Equipment, Family Life and Child Development. Credit, one credit each.
THE STAFF.

191, 192. QUANTITY FOOD PREPARATION AND INSTITUTIONAL MANAGEMENT.—A study of the principles of organization, personnel management, the administration, food costs, operating expenses, and special functions of the dietitian. Laboratory work is at one of the university dining halls and field trips are planned. It is expected that students will enroll for the work of both semesters. Students wishing to qualify for administrative institutional work are advised to take Accounting 25 and Home Economics 71. Credit, 3.
Prerequisite, Home Economics 51 and 52 or equivalent. Miss STECH.
One class hour; one 5-hour laboratory period, first semester.
Two class hours; one 3-hour laboratory period, second semester.

193. EXPERIMENTAL FOODS.—The testing and comparing of different food materials and methods of preparation, including advanced work in the science and techniques of cookery. Special individual problems will be studied.
Two class hours; One 3-hour laboratory period. Credit, 3.
Prerequisites, Home Economics 30 and 51; Chemistry 33 or equivalent, and permission of the instructor. MISS DAVIS.

195. CHILD NUTRITION.—A study is made of nutritional needs from prenatal life through infancy and childhood. Methods of judging nutrition, also causes and effects of malnutrition are discussed. Menus for children and measures to insure the consumption of optimal diets are put in practice with laboratory work in the nursery school. Credit, 3.
Prerequisite, Home Economics 52 or equivalent. Mrs. COOK.
Three class hours. Laboratory by arrangement.

198. PROBLEMS IN HOME ECONOMICS.—An intensive study of some phase of home economics. Credit, 3.
By permission of the Dean of the School. THE STAFF.

COURSES IN OTHER DEPARTMENTS FOR WHICH MAJOR CREDIT WILL BE GIVEN

Chemistry 234. ADVANCED BIOCHEMICAL LECTURES.　　　　Credit, 3.
Mr. LITTLE.

Chemistry 235. BIOCHEMISTRY LABORATORY METHODS.　　　Credit, 3.
Mr. LITTLE.

Chemistry 237. BIOCOLLOIDS.　　　　　　　　　　　　　　Credit 3.
Mr. BENNETT.

Chemistry 239. CHEMISTRY OF NATURAL PRODUCTS.　　　　Credit, 2.
Mr. LITTLE.

Education 153. EDUCATIONAL TESTS AND MEASUREMENTS.　　Credit, 2-3.
Mr. ROURKE.

Education 166. PREPARATION AND USE OF AUDIO-VISUAL AIDS.　Credit, 2-3.
Mr. WYMAN.

Education 291. EDUCATIONAL RESEARCH AND STATISTICS.　　Credit, 2.
Mr. PURVIS.

Food Technology 191, 192. EXAMINATION OF FOOD PRODUCTS.
Credit, 3 each semester.
MR. FELLERS AND MR. NEBESKY.

Food Technology 241. FOOD ACCEPTANCE, THEORY, AND METHODOLOGY.
Credit, 2.
Mr. FAGERSON.

COURSES FOR MINOR CREDIT ONLY

152. NUTRITION AND DIETETICS.—A study is made of the fundamentals of normal nutrition including energy needs, the metabolism of proteins, carbohydrates, fats, vitamins, and minerals; and the quantitative requirements for these various essential nutrients. Laboratory work provides the further study of the composition of foods and their contribution to the diet and the relationship of the nutritive value to cost. Nutritive loss due to cooking, storage, etc., is given consideration.
Three class hours, one 2-hour laboratory period.　　　　　　Credit, 3.
Prerequisites, Home Ec. 30, Chemistry 33 and Physiology.　　Mrs. COOK.

163. ARTS AND CRAFTS.—Introduction to design and execution in crafts particularly adapted to work with children in schools, playgrounds, summer camps; and for any age in recreational leadership and occupational therapy. Opportunity will be offered for work in several of the following: wood and leather work, block printing, fingerpainting, etching, knotting, etc.　Credit, 3.
Prerequisite, Home Economics 31 or equivalent.　　　　　　Miss BRIGGS.

170. CHILD DEVELOPMENT.—The growth and development of the child, his basic needs, the aspects of behavior—routine, creative and social—as they are related to personality development. Planned observation and participation in the Nursery School.
Three class hours; laboratory by arrangement.　　　　　　Credit, 3.
Mrs. THIES.

175. ECONOMICS OF THE HOUSEHOLD.—A study is made of personal and family standards of living in the modern home, the economic relations of the household, and the use of time, energy, and money as a means to influence the home situation.   Credit, 3.
Prerequisite, Economics 25, or equivalent.   Miss MERRIAM.

180. FAMILY LIFE.—A study is made of the modern family; ideals and responsibilities of the home and the individual's share in developing positive family relationships.   Credit, 3.
                                                                Mrs. PIATT.

Landscape Architecture
RAYMOND H. OTTO, major adviser.

COURSES OPEN TO GRADUATE STUDENTS ONLY.
(For either major or minor credit)

200. SPECIAL PROBLEMS.—Individual study by the B. L. A. candidate in lieu of a thesis; or exploratory work preliminary to the thesis by the M.L.A. candidate.   Credit, 3.
                                                                THE STAFF.

290. THEORY.—Special studies in the history and theory of landscape architecture, and planning.   Credit, 3.
                                                                Mr. McLINDON.

291. DESIGN.—Individual problems in any or all branches of public and private work.   Credit, 3.
                                                                Mr. OTTO.

292. CONSTRUCTION.—Including road alignment, computations, and advanced landscape construction.   Credit, 3.
                                                                Mr. PROCOPIO.

293. PRESENTATION.—Studies in drafting, pen and crayon, rendering, water coloring, etc.   Credit, 3.
                                                                Mr. MacIVER.

294. PRACTICE.—Professional field work under supervision, conducted upon going projects as opportunity offers.   Credit, 3
                                                                Mr. BLUNDELL.

297. ARCHITECTURE.—Selected problems as related to landscape architecture.
                                                                Credit, 3.
                                                                Mr. McLINDON.

300. THESIS, MASTER'S DEGREE.   Credit, 10.

COURSES OPEN TO BOTH GRADUATE AND UNDERGRADUATE STUDENTS
(For either major or minor credit)

175. ART APPRECIATION.—An analysis of the principles of critical judgment underlying the fine arts.   Credit, 3.
                                                                Mr. OTTO.

178. HISTORY OF ART.—A chronological survey of the arts from early times to the present.   Credit, 3.
                                                                Mr. HAMILTON.

179. CONSTRUCTION AND MAINTENANCE.—A study of methods and materials of construction, and maintenance procedures. Credit, 3.

Mr. PROCOPIO.

180. LITERATURE OF LANDSCAPE ARCHITECTURE.—A review of the significant literature of all phases of the field, and compiling of bibliographies.

Credit, 2.

Mr. OTTO.

181. ADVANCED DESIGN.—Class "B" Exchange Problems plus specialized study through local projects. Credit, 3.

Mr. HAMILTON.

182. ADVANCED DESIGN. Continuation of 181. Credit, 3.

Mr. HAMILTON.

183. ARCHITECTURE.—Theory and principles of architecture including the development of construction methods and materials. Credit, 3.

Mr. McLINDON.

184. SKETCHING.—Presentation of varied subjects in water color and other mediums. Credit, 2.

Mr. MacIVER.

186. REGIONAL AND CITY PLANNING.—A critical examination of those factors which influence and guide the physical growth and arrangement of communities in harmony with their social and economic needs. Open to non-majors.

Credit, 3.

Mr. McLINDON.

187. REGIONAL AND CITY PLANNING.—An application of the principles of planning through problems on the design of various types of urban land areas.

Credit, 3.

Mr. McLINDON.

COURSES IN OTHER DEPARTMENTS FOR WHICH MAJOR CREDIT WILL BE GIVEN

Agronomy 153. AGROSTOLOGY. Credit, 3.

Mr. DICKINSON.

Agronomy 156. AGROSTOLOGY. Credit, 3.

Mr. DICKINSON.

Botany 181. PLANT ECOLOGY. Credit, 3.

Mr. LIVINGSTON.

Floriculture 181. HERBACEOUS GARDENS AND BORDERS. Credit, 3.

Mr. HUBBARD.

COURSES FOR MINOR CREDIT ONLY

151. ELEMENTS OF TOPOGRAPHY AND CONSTRUCTION.—Contour interpolation, grading and drainage plans, drive design, sections and profiles, computation of earthwork. Credit, 3.

Mr. PROCOPIO.

152. CONSTRUCTION DETAILS.—Problems in structural garden features as walks, steps, walls, gates, pools, and architectural elements. Credit, 3.

Mr. PROCOPIO.

153. GARDEN DESIGN.—Fundamental principles of composition as applied to the design of gardens and small properties.　　　　　Credit, 3.

Mr. OTTO.

154. GENERAL DESIGN.—A series of problems in the design of private and public areas.　　　　　Credit, 3.

Mr. OTTO.

FOR THE DEGREE OF BACHELOR OF LANDSCAPE ARCHITECTURE

To receive this professional bachelor's degree each candidate will be required:

1. To have received the degree of Bachelor of Science or Bachelor of Arts from a recognized institution.

2. To have completed as a prerequisite 24 semester credits in landscape architecture, substantially equivalent to the technical courses now required in the undergraduate major in landscape architecture at this college.

3. In addition, to have completed in residence at this institution, 30 credits in landscape architecture and closely related subjects prescribed by the department. (See Fifth Year Program below.)

4. To have received the unanimous approval of the faculty of the department and the vote of approval of the faculty of the Graduate School.

FIFTH YEAR PROGRAM

The regular program of studies for the Fifth Year, subject to minor changes dependent upon courses taken previously, is as follows:

First Semester

201. GENERAL DESIGN.—Class A Exchange problems and advanced local projects.　　　　　Credit, 3.

Mr. OTTO.

203. ECOLOGY AND PHYSIOGRAPHY.—Plant Associations and ground forms and conditions as related to each other.　　　　　Credit, 3.

Mr. BLUNDELL.

205. ARCHITECTURE.—Studies in principles and problems of architectural design.　　　　　Credit, 3.

Mr. McLINDON.

207. CONTRACTS, SPECIFICATIONS, ESTIMATING COSTS.—Preparation of supporting data for proposed plans.　　　　　Credit, 3.

Mr. HAMILTON.

209. LANDSCAPE SKETCHING.—Graphic expression of suitable subjects in various media.　　　　　Credit, 3

Mr. MacIVER.

Second Semester

202. GENERAL DESIGN.—Continuation of 201.　　　　　Credit, 3.

Mr. OTTO.

204. LANDSCAPE FORESTRY.—Woodland management and silvicultural practices.　　　　　Credit, 3.

Mr. RHODES.

206. ARCHITECTURE.—Studies in principles and problems of architectural design.   Credit, 3.
                                                                        Mr. McLindon.

210. ARCHITECTURAL SKETCHING.—Graphic expression of suitable subjects in various media.   Credit, 3.
                                                                        Mr. MacIver.

212. PROFESSIONAL PRACTICE.—Methods and procedures of the professional office.   Credit, 1.
                                                                        Mr. Otto.

Elective: Suitable subject assigned.

Mathematics

ALLEN E. ANDERSEN, major adviser.

Special Departmental Entrance Requirements:

Candidates for admission who plan to major in this department must have completed at least eighteen semester credit hours in undergraduate mathematics beyond the content of Mathematics 29 and 30 (Differential and Integral Calculus), and also an undergraduate course equivalent to Physics 25 and 26 (Introductory).

Special Degree Requirements:

Six semester credit hours (undergraduate or graduate) in each of the fields of geometry, algebra and appplied mathematics and 12 semester credit hours in the field of analysis. A minimum of 12 semester credit hours chosen from courses in this department which are numbered from 200 to 299.

COURSES OPEN TO GRADUATE STUDENTS ONLY

(For either major or minor credit)

200. TOPICS COURSE.—This course is designed to give the student training in independent study. Readings and reports will be assigned. Weekly conferences will be held between student and instructor. Topics may be chosen from the fields of algebra, geometry, theory of functions, and applied mathematics.
Prerequisite, Consent of instructor.   Credit, 1, 2, or 3.
            Mr. ANDERSEN, Miss CULLEN, Mr. ROSE, and Mr. WAGNER.

201, 202. INTRODUCTION TO MODERN ALGEBRA.—Axiomatic foundation of algebra; groups, rings, fields and vector spaces; linear transformations and matrices.   Credit, 3 each semester.
3 class hours.   Mr. ROSE.
Prerequisite, consent of instructor.

221, 222. THEORY OF FUNCTIONS OF A REAL VARIABLE.—The real number system, limits, continuity and differentiability of functions of one and two real variables, theories of integration, sequences of functions.
3 class hours.   Credit, 3 each semester.
Prerequisite, Mathematics 191.   Mr. WAGNER.

226. THEORY OF FUNCTIONS OF A COMPLEX VARIABLE.—The complex number system, elementary functions and their mappings, line and contour integrals, expansion and representations of analytic functions, introduction to analytic continuation and Riemannian surfaces.   Credit, 3.
3 class hours.   Miss CULLEN.
Prerequisite, Mathematics 221.

241. TOPOLOGY I.—Point Set Topology: Calculus of sets; Topological, Hausdorff and metric spaces; continuous mappings; homeomorphisms; connectivity and compactness. Credit, 3.
Prerequisite, Mathematics 194. Miss CULLEN.

242. TOPOLOGY II.—Combinatorial Topology: Continuous complexes; Jordan's Theorem, Homology and Homotopy. Credit, 3.
Prerequisite, Mathematics 241. Miss CULLEN.

COURSES OPEN TO BOTH GRADUATE AND UNDERGRADUATE STUDENTS
(For either major or minor credit)

151. MODERN SYNTHETIC GEOMETRY.—An extension of the geometry of the triangle and the circle. The course is intended especially for those planning to be high school teachers. Credit, 3.
Three class hours. Mr. ROSE.
Prerequisite, Mathematics 30.

153. 154. HIGHER ALGEBRA.—Permutations, Combinations, probability; mathematical induction, matrices, determinants, linear equations and dependence; quadratic forms and elimination theory; the complex number system; polynominal equations; elementary theory of groups, rings and fields. Credit, 3.
Prerequisite, Mathematics 10. THE STAFF.

156. FINITE DIFFERENCES AND PROBABILITY.
Three class hours. Credit, 3.
Prerequisite, Mathematics 30. Given in alternate years, beginning 1954-55.
THE STAFF.

162. STATISTICS.—The fundamental mathematical principles of statistical analysis. The derivation of the basic formulas used, and the study and discussion of such topics as averages, dispersion, skewness, curve fitting, least squares, linear and curvilinear correlation, probability curve, probable error, sampling, reliability.
Three class hours. Credit, 3.
Prerequisite, Mathematics 10. Mr. WAGNER.

166. INTRODUCTION TO HIGHER GEOMETRY.—A study of various methods employed in the modern treatment of geometry of points, lines, and conics. Such topics as homogeneous point and line coordinates; infinite elements; harmonic division; groups of transformations and their invariants; and the elements of projective and other geometries will be considered. Given in alternate years, beginning 1953-54. Credit, 3.
Prerequisite, Mathematics 30. Mr. ANDERSEN.

171. VECTOR ANALYSIS.—The algebra and calculus of vectors. Applications to physics and other fields will be considered. Given in alternate years.
Prerequisites, Mathematics 30, Physics 26. Credit, 3.
Mr. ANDERSEN.

172. HISTORY OF MATHEMATICS.—Topics considered include classical problems and concepts of mathematics and the lives and times of the great mathematicians. This course is recommended especially for prospective high school teachers. Given in alternate years. Credit, 3.
Three class hours. Mr. ROSE.
Prerequisite, Mathematics 30.

174. THEORY OF NUMBERS.—Euclid's Algorism, Theory of Prime Numbers, Aliquot parts, congruences, further topics in Number Theory.
Three class hours. Given in alternate years. Credit, 3.
Prerequisite, Mathematics 30. THE STAFF.

181. DIFFERENTIAL GEOMETRY.—Theory of the geometry of curves and surfaces in three dimensions.
Three class hours. Given in alternate years. Credit, 3.
Prerequisite, Mathematics 30. THE STAFF.

183. COMPUTATIONAL METHODS.—Errors and approximations in computation, methods of approximating roots of equations, approximation of functions, empirical curve fitting, approximate integration, and numerical integration of ordinary differential equations.
Three class hours. Given in alternate years, beginning 1952-1953. Credit, 3.
Prerequisite, Mathematics 30. Mr. BOUTELLE.

192. DIFFERENTIAL EQUATIONS. Credit, 3.
Three class hours. THE STAFF.
Prerequisite, Mathematics 30.

193. ADVANCED CALCULUS.—The real number system, sequences, elementary theory of functions of one variable and of several variables, Riemannian integration, line integrals, Green's theorem.
Three class hours. Credit, 3.
Prerequisite, Mathematics 91. THE STAFF.

194. ADVANCED CALCULUS.—Double and triple integrals, improper integrals, gamma functions, Beta functions, elliptic functions, calculus of variations, Fourier Series, Laplace Transforms.
Three class hours. Credit, 3.
Prerequisite, Mathematics 193. THE STAFF.

COURSES FOR MINOR CREDIT ONLY

155. MATHEMATICS OF FINANCE.—The mathematical principles of simple and compound interest, annuities, depreciation, valuation of bonds, insurance, building and loan associations. The development and application of aids to computation in problems arising from financial transactions. Credit, 3.
Prerequisite, Mathematics 8 or 10. Mr. BOUTELLE.

160. SPHERICAL TRIGONOMETRY AND SOLID ANALYTICAL GEOMETRY.—The trigonometry of the sphere with application to terrestrial and celestial problems. This is followed by a study of higher plane curves and the analytic representation of points, lines and surfaces in space. Given in alternate years.
Credit, 3.
Prerequisite, Mathematics 30. Mr. BOUTELLE.

191. INTERMEDIATE CALCULUS.—Series, expansion of functions, partial differentiation, envelopes and multiple integrals. Credit, 3.
3 class hours. THE STAFF.
Prerequisite, Mathematics 30.

Mechanical Engineering

WILLIAM H. WEAVER, major adviser.

POWER OPTION

REQUIRED COURSES

First Semester	Second Semester
M.E. 201 ADVANCED THERMODYNAMICS I.	M.E. 202 ADVANCED THERMODYNAMICS II.
M.E. 231 ADVANCED INTERNAL COMBUSTION ENGINES.	M.E. 234 GAS TURBINES.
M.E. 300 RESEARCH & THESIS.	M.E. 300 RESEARCH & THESIS.

RECOMMENDED ELECTIVES

First Semester	Second Semester
M.E. 221 HEAT TRANSFER.	M.E. 254 LUBRICATION & BEARINGS.
M.E. 241 ADVANCED DYNAMICS.	E.E. 202 ENGINEERING ANALYSIS II.
E.E. 201 ENGINEERING ANALYSIS I.	M.E. 182 FLUID DYNAMICS AND MACHINERY.
	M.E. 190 ADVANCED METALLURGY.
	M.E. 194 EXPERIMENTAL MECHANICAL ENGINEERING.

DESIGN OPTION

REQUIRED COURSES

First Semester	Second Semester
M.E. 241 ADVANCED DYNAMICS.	M.E. 254 LUBRICATION & BEARINGS.
M.E. 251 ADVANCED TOPICS IN MACHINE DESIGN.	C.E. 188 ADVANCED STRESS ANALYSIS.
M.E. 300 RESEARCH & THESIS.	M.E. 300 RESEARCH & THESIS.

RECOMMENDED ELECTIVES

First Semester	Second Semester
M.E. 201 ADVANCED THERMODYNAMICS I.	M.E. 202 ADVANCED THERMODYNAMICS II.
M.E. 221 HEAT TRANSFER.	M.E. 234 GAS TURBINES.
M.E. 231 ADVANCED INTERNAL COMBUSTION ENGINES.	E.E. 202 ENGINEERING ANALYSIS II.
E.E. 201 ENGINEERING ANALYSIS I.	M.E. 182 FLUID DYNAMICS AND MACHINERY.
	M.E. 188 STEADY FLOW MACHINERY.
	M.E. 190 ADVANCED METALLURGY.
	M.E. 194 EXPERIMENTAL MECHANICAL ENGINEERING.

COURSES OPEN TO GRADUATE STUDENTS ONLY

(For either major or minor credit)

201. ADVANCED THERMODYNAMICS I.—Advanced course in engineering applications of thermodynamics, including a survey of the physical treatment of thermodynamics. Credit, 3.
Prerequisite, M. E. 164. Mr. LINDSEY and Mr. SWENSON.

202. ADVANCED THERMODYNAMICS II.—A continuation of the work in 201. Mechanical engineering problems in thermodynamics. Credit 3.
Prerequisite, M. E. 201. Mr. LINDSEY and Mr. SWENSON.

221. HEAT TRANSFER.—Fundamentals of heat transfer by convection, conduction and radiation, with engineering applications. Credit, 3.
Prerequisite, M. E. 164. Mr. SWENSON and Mr. LINDSEY.

231. ADVANCED INTERNAL COMBUSTION ENGINES.—Theoretical consideration of fuels, combustion, detonation, lubrication, supercharging, carburetion, and fuel injection as related to gasoline and Diesel engines. Credit, 3.
Prerequisite, M. E. 177. Mr. DITTFACH.

234. GAS TURBINES.—Thermodynamic principles, performance and application of gas turbines as primary and auxiliary power units. Credit, 3.
Prerequisite, M. E. 164. Mr. SWENSON and Mr. DITTFACH.

241. ADVANCED DYNAMICS.—Vibration and stability of systems with many degrees of freedom, normal modes and frequencies; approximate methods. Non-linear systems, self excited vibrations. Gyroscopic effects in mechanical systems. Selected topics of applications to problems in engineering.
Credit, 3.
Prerequisite, M. E. 185. Mr. WHITE and Mr. SOBALA.

251. ADVANCED TOPICS IN MACHINE DESIGN.—Application of advanced theories in elasticity and strength of materials to machine design. Many other theories and their application are included. Credit, 3.
Prerequisite, Mechanical Engineering 186. Mr. BATES.

254. LUBRICATION AND BEARINGS.—Derivation of a generalized Reynold's equation and its application to analysis of sliders, tilted pad bearings, journal bearings, dynamically loaded bearings, partial bearings, and thrust bearings, thermal equilibrium in bearings, bearing loads and design practices. Credit, 3.
Prerequisites, M. E. 186 and C. E. 76. Mr. SOBALA.

300. RESEARCH AND THESIS. Credit, 3-10.

COURSES OPEN TO BOTH GRADUATE AND UNDERGRADUATE STUDENTS

(For either major or minor credit)

146. FUNDAMENTALS OF METALLURGY.—Physical metallurgy involving crystal structure, solid solutions, diffusion in the solid state, freezing of metals, hardening of metals, annealing, and equilibrium diagrams. These fundamentals are then applied to the study of the iron-iron carbide diagram, the S-curve, heat treatment of steel and the properties and uses of the other principal engineering metals. Laboratory work stresses metallographic and radiographic technique.
Two class hours; one 3-hour laboratory period. Credit, 3.
Prerequisites, M. E. 39 or Chemistry 66. Mr. KEYSER.

175. STEAM POWER PLANTS.—This course is a study of the steam power plants, including boilers, stokers, fuels, combustion, steam generation, prime movers, and auxiliary equipment, problems involved in design and operation.
Three class hours, one 2-hour laboratory period. Credit, 3.
Prerequisite, M. E. 164. Mr. SWENSON.

176. REFRIGERATION AND AIR CONDITIONING.—The course content includes a study of the fundamental principles of thermodynamics as applied to refrigeration and air control. Application of refrigeration to industrial processes and the control of temperature, humidity and motion of air in buildings will be studied.
Two class hours, one 3-hour laboratory period. Credit, 3.
Prerequisite, M. E. 164. Mr. SWENSON.

177. INTERNAL COMBUSTION ENGINES.—A study is made of spark-ignition and compression-ignition engines including design, fuels, carburetion, ignition, combustion, lubrication, cooling, and engine performance. The gas turbine and jet propulsion will be included. Credit, 3.
Three class hours. Mr. DITTFACH.
Prerequisite, M. E. 164.

182. FLUID DYNAMICS AND MACHINERY.—Steady one-dimensional compressible flow; compressible flow in channels with friction and heat transfer; boundary layer flow, turbulence, and energy losses; general features of dynamic fluid machines; axial flow fans, pumps, and compressors; centrifugal fans, pumps, and compressors; fluid couplings and torque converters; jet compressors and jet pumps; turbines. Credit, 3.
Prerequisite, Civil Engineering 76. Mr. SWENSON.

183. MACHINE DESIGN.—Principles involved in the design of various machine parts including fastenings, shafts, belts, bearings, gears, and pressure vessels.
Two class hours; one 3-hour laboratory period. Credit, 3.
Prerequisites, C. E. 51 or 53; M. E. 68. Mr. BATES.

185. DYNAMICS OF MACHINERY.—Gyroscopic effects, governors, dynamic balancing of rotating machinery. Analysis of unbalanced forces in a machine containing parts moving with rotation, reciprocation, and their combination. Elements of vibration theory, vibration isolation, vibration analysis of equivalent masses and shaft systems. Vibration absorbers. Credit, 3.
Three class hours. Mr. SOBALA.
Prerequisites, C. E. 52, M. E. 168.

186. ADVANCED MACHINE DESIGN.—A continuation of Course 183. Additional elementary parts are studied which combine into the design of complete machines in the latter part of the course. Credit, 3.
Two class hours, one 3-hour laboratory period. Mr. BATES.
Prerequisite, M. E. 183.

188. STEADY FLOW MACHINERY.—The principles of thermodynamics are applied to steam and internal combustion turbines, condensors, and other heat transfer apparatus. Credit, 3.
Three class hours. Mr. SWENSON.
Prerequisites, M. E. 164 or 166, and C. E. 76.

190. ADVANCED METALLURGY.—Mechanical metallurgy covering the behavior of metals in the plastic state; the shaping of metals by mechanical means such as drawing, rolling, spinning, etc.; the primary methods of metal fabrication such as casting, welding, powder metallurgy, electroforming; the metallurgical applications of radiography. Credit, 3.
Two class hours, one 3-hour laboratory period. Mr. KEYSER.
Prerequisite, M. E. 146.

194. EXPERIMENTAL MECHANICAL ENGINEERING.—Special work in Mechanical Engineering for a senior thesis. Credit, 3.
Prerequisite, Permission of Instructor. THE STAFF.

Industrial Engineering

175. JOB EVALUTION.—A study of the principles used to determine an evaluation of all occupations in order to establish an equitable rating between them, to establish sound wage and salary policies. Credit, 2.
Three class hours. Mr. WEAVER.
Prerequisite, I. E. 51.

176. TIME STUDY.—A study of the principles involved in the establishment of production standards and their application in the management functions of cost accounting, estimating, production control, incentives, budgetary control. Two class hours, one 3-hour laboratory period.   Credit, 3.

Mr. WEAVER.

Prerequisites, I. E. 175, 182 concurrently except for Business Administration majors.

177. PRODUCTION CONTROL.—A study of the principles used to regulate production activities in keeping with the manufacturing plan.   Credit, 3.
Three class hours.   Mr. WEAVER.
Prerequisite, I. E. 51.

178. FACTORY PLANNING AND LAY-OUT.—A study of the principles applying to the determination and development of the physical relationship between plant, equipment and operators working toward the highest degree of economy and effectiveness in operation.   Credit, 2.
One class hour, one 3-hour laboratory period.   Mr. SOBALA.
Prerequisites, M. E. 2 and I. E. 51.

180. PLANT BUDGETARY CONTROL.—A study of the principles used to predetermine expenses for the factors of production and the comparison of results with the estimates to determine and deal with the causes of expense variations as applied by the operating organization in the industrial plant.   Credit, 3.
Three class hours.
Prerequisite, I. E. 51.   Mr. WEAVER.

182. WORK SIMPLIFICATION.—A study of the principles involved in the simplification of means of doing work and in the application and use of these principles.
One class hour, one 3-hour laboratory period.   Credit, 2.
Prerequisites, M. E. 68 and I. E. 176 concurrently.   Mr. WEAVER.

COURSES IN OTHER DEPARTMENTS FOR WHICH MAJOR CREDIT WILL BE GIVEN

Electrical Engineering 201, 202. ADVANCED ENGINEERING ANALYSIS I, II.

Credit, 3 each semester.

Mr. ROYS and STAFF.

Civil Engineering 188. ADVANCED STRESS ANALYSIS.   Credit, 3.

Mr. WHITE.

Olericulture

GRANT B. SNYDER, major adviser

COURSES OPEN TO GRADUATE STUDENTS ONLY

(For either major or minor credit)

201. LITERATURE.—A critical study and analysis of selected scientific papers and reports of past and current research involving vegetable crops.   Credit, 3.
Lectures and assigned readings.   Mr. LACHMAN.

Horticulture 211, 212. SEMINAR.—Each student will be required to present papers on assigned readings related to research work in Horticulture. Departments of Floriculture, Olericulture, and Pomology cooperating.

Credit, 1 each semester.

THE STAFF.

276. ADVANCED VEGETABLE PLANT IMPROVEMENT.—An intensive study of hybridization and selection as related to specific vegetable crops. Special attention will be given to heterosis and its implications in vegetable breeding as well as sterility and its place in seed production of F1 hybrids.   Credit, 3.
Prerequisites, Plant Breeding 152, Zoology 153 or equivalent.

Mr. LACHMAN and Mr. YOUNG.

300. THESIS, MASTER'S DEGREE.—Research on some approved topic relating to a specific phase of Olericulture.   Credit, 10.

COURSES OPEN TO BOTH GRADUATE AND UNDERGRADUATE STUDENTS
(For either major or minor credit)

152. ADVANCED COMMERCIAL CULTURE.—A critical analysis of the factors involved in the commercial culture of vegetable crops including soils, nutrition and the relationship of temperature, light and humidity to production techniques and practices both out of doors and in the greenhouse.   Credit, 3.
Lectures and laboratory.   Mr. SNYDER.

173. MARKETING AND STORAGE OF VEGETABLE CROPS.—A detailed evaluation of factors which may be involved in the market and storage handling of vegetables with particular emphasis on their relationship to quality and deterioration.   Credit, 3.
Mr. SNYDER.

175. ADVANCED SYSTEMATIC OLERICULTURE.—A critical study of vegetable plants as to plant characteristics, nomenclature, identification and classification.   Credit, 3.
Mr. SNYDER.

COURSES IN OTHER DEPARTMENTS FOR WHICH MAJOR CREDIT WILL BE GIVEN

Agronomy 263. CHEMISTRY OF THE SOIL.   Credit, 5.
Mr. STECKEL.

Agronomy 264. EXPERIMENTAL METHODS IN AGRONOMY.   Credit, 3.
Mr. YEGIAN.

Botany 158. MICROTECHNIQUE.   Credit, 2.
Mr. TORREY.

Plant Breeding 152. ADVANCED PLANT BREEDING.   Credit, 3.
Mr. FRENCH.

Plant Breeding 181. PLANT CYTOLOGICAL TECHNIQUE.   Credit, 2.
Mr. FRENCH.

Plant Breeding 182. SPECIAL PROBLEM IN PLANT BREEDING.   Credit, 2.
Mr. FRENCH.

COURSES FOR MINOR CREDIT ONLY

151. PRINCIPLES OF OLERICULTURE.   Credit, 3.
Mr. TUTTLE.

174. MARKETING PRACTICES.   Credit, 3
Mr. SNYDER

178. COMMERCIAL OLERICULTURE.   Credit, 3
Mr. SNYDER

Philosophy

CLARENCE SHUTE, major adviser.

COURSES OPEN TO GRADUATE STUDENTS ONLY
(For either major or minor credit)

266. PHILOSOPHY OF EDUCATION.—An evaluation of various educational theories and practices viewed in the light of historical perspective and contemporary thought.
Credit, 3.
Mr. ROGERS.

267. ORIENTAL PHILOSOPHY.—A study of oriental thought, and its influence upon the modern cultures and ideologies of the Orient—primarily India, China, and Japan.
Credit, 3.
Mr. SHUTE.

271. SOCIAL PHILOSOPHY.—Starting with an analysis of the present world situation, attention will be given to conflicting claims regarding the basis on which social orders are to be criticized. An attempt will be made to formulate a philosophical foundation for democratic society.
Credit, 3.
Mr. ROGERS.

286. CONTEMPORARY PHILOSOPHY.—Representative thinkers of the twentieth century will be read, including Bergson, Dewey, Whitehead, and others selected in conference with the class.
Credit, 3.
Mr. SHUTE.

289, 290. SEMINAR.—Conferences and reports on special studies in philosophy.
Credit, 1-3.
THE STAFF.

300. THESIS, MASTER'S DEGREE.
Credit, 10

COURSES OPEN TO BOTH GRADUATE AND UNDERGRADUATE STUDENTS
(For either major or minor credit)

(These courses require extra work for 3 credits)

163. LOGIC.—A study of the principles, problems, and methods of critical thinking with applications to current problems.
Credit, 2-3.
Mr. ROGERS.

164. ETHICS.—An examination of the many causes and contexts of personal decision and policy formation; an analysis of classical and contemporary theories which attempt to provide an intellectual framework for the guidance and justification of ways of life; and class exploration of concrete cases which focus attention on the realms of value and the place of theory in reflective choice.
Credit, 2-3.
Mr. ROGERS.

181. PHILIOSOPHY OF RELIGION.—A survey of the contrasting types of religious philosophy in the contemporary western world and Asia, with a critical and constructive study of basic issues, such as the meaning of knowledge in the field of religion, the nature of faith, and the religious interpretation of reality.
Credit, 2-3.
Mr. SHUTE.

182. AESTHETICS.—A study of the leading modern theories of the nature of art, the analysis of aesthetic experiences, the distinctive function of art in culture and personality, and the principles of criticism.   Credit, 2-3.

Mr. SHUTE.

183. READINGS IN ANCIENT PHILOSOPHY.—Selections are read from Plato's dialogues and from the works of Aristotle. A study is made of the leading philosophical issues discussed by these writers, with emphasis on ideas which became basic in the development of western thought.   Credit, 2-3.

Mr. SHUTE.

184. READINGS IN MODERN PHILOSOPHY.—Selections are read from Locke, Hume, Kant, and Whitehead, to display the leading ways in which modern thinkers have looked upon the nature of the universe and the possibilities and limitations of knowledge.   Credit, 2-3.

Mr. SHUTE.

185. METAPHYSICS.—The field of metaphysics defined in distinction from the field of science; contrasting theories of reality offered by contemporary naturalism and idealism, especially in the light of recent developments in biological and physical science; anaylsis of basic ideas which will enable the student to continue a fruitful development of his own philosophy.   Credit, 2-3.

Mr. SHUTE.

186. THEORY OF KNOWLEDGE.—Types of knowledge and correlated methods of knowing; questions of certainty, probability, and limits of knowledge; ways of expression, such as mathematical formulae, language, and art, and their involvement in the knowing process; the nature of the relation between the knowing subject and the known object.   Credit, 2-3.

MR. CARMICHAEL.

COURSES IN OTHER DEPARTMENTS FOR WHICH MAJOR CREDIT WILL BE GIVEN

Government 171. ANCIENT AND MEDIEVAL POLITICAL THOUGHT.   Credit, 3

Mr. TINDER.

Government 172. MODERN POLITICAL THOUGHT.   Credit, 3.

Mr. TINDER.

COURSE FOR MINOR CREDIT ONLY

162. HISTORY OF PHILOSOPHY.—A survey of western thought from the early Greeks to the present.   Credit, 3.

Mr. SHUTE.

Physical Education for Men

COURSES FOR MINOR CREDIT ONLY

In addition to the standard requirements of the courses, graduate students must work on a special project requiring research with a resultant term paper.

153. (I) PHYSICAL EDUCATION IN ELEMENTARY SCHOOLS.—Aims and objectives of modern materials and methods of teaching group games, rhythmic activities, dance relays, stunts and lead-up games for the elementary school. Credit, 3.

MR. FOOTRICK.

154. (II) PHYSICAL EDUCATION IN SECONDARY SCHOOLS.—A course in modern methods of teaching physical education in secondary schools. Includes objectives, content material, and organization procedures at the secondary level.

Credit, 3.

MR. RICCI.

155. (I) ORGANIZATION AND ADMINISTRATION OF PHYSICAL EDUCATION.—Problems and procedures in physical education, organization of programs, class schedules, classification of students, equipment, records, finance, intramurals, construction and maintenance of gymnasia, swimming pools, locker rooms, and outdoor play areas. Credit, 3.

MR. McGUIRK.

156. (II) ADAPTIVE PHYSICAL EDUCATION.—A program of developmental activities, games, sports, and rhythms suited to the interests, capacities and limitations of students with disabilities who may not safely engage in unrestricted participation in the vigorous activities of the general physical education program. Prerequisite, Physical Education 42. Credit, 3.

MR. GORBER.

173. (I) PHILOSOPHY AND PRINCIPLES OF PHYSICAL EDUCATION.—Contemporary interpretations and critical analysis. The compilation and organization of material in a functional relationship for the foundation of policies and program construction. Credit, 3.

MR. KAUFFMAN.

176. (II) PHYSIOLOGY OF EXERCISE.—Application of basic physiological concepts to the program of physical education, emphasis upon the physiological effects and adjustments accruing from participation in physical activity. Major factors in diet, conditioning, fatigue, and physical fitness are considered. Prerequisite, Physical Education 42. Credit, 3.

MR. DAVIS.

180. (II) DRIVER EDUCATION INSTRUCTOR COURSE.—This course includes driver education and driver training at the instructor's level, and is designed to orient the student to live safely through skillful and efficient behavior on streets and highways. Leads to certification as instructor in driver education and driver training Credit, 2.

MR. BRIGGS.

Physics

COURSES FOR MINOR CREDIT ONLY

151, 152. MAGNETISM, ELECTRICITY, PHOTO-ELECTRICITY, THERMIONICS AND APPLICATIONS.—Course 151 deals largely with direct currents; Course 152 with alternating currents, applications of thermionics, and photo-electricity.
Two class hours, one 2-hour laboratory period. Credit, 3 each semester.
Prerequisites, Physics 26 and Math. 29. Mr. POWERS.

155, 156.—MECHANICS.—Development of the fundamental concepts of classical dynamics with applications to particles and rigid bodies in translation and rotation. Credit, 3 each semester.
Two class hours; one 2-hour laboratory period. Mr. Ross.
Prerequisites, Physics 26 and Math. 30.

160. SOUND AND ACOUSTICS.—A study of the vibrations, vibrating bodies, coupled systems, sound structure, and acoustic properties. Credit, 3.
Two class hours; one 2-hour laboratory period. Mr. ALDERMAN.
Prerequisite, Physics 155 or equivalent.

161, 162. HEAT AND THERMODYNAMICS.—A study of heat exchanges and energy changes due to heat in systems of matter. Credit, 3 each semester.
Two class hours, one 2-hour laboratory period. Mr. ALDERMAN.

163, 164. OPTICS.—An intermediate course in the theory of light. Geometrical and physical optics. Credit, 3 each semester.
Two class hours, one 2-hour laboratory period. Mr. ALDERMAN.

175, 176. ADVANCED EXPERIMENTAL WORK IN SELECTED TOPICS.—These courses are largely experimental and the subject matter is adapted to the needs of the individual student. Credit, 3 each semester.
One class hour, two 2-hour laboratory periods. Mr. WANG.
Prerequisites, Physics 151, 152 or 155, 156 or 163, 164; and Math. 29 and 30.

185, 186. MODERN PHYSICS.—Typical subjects studied are theories of the atom, radiation, quantum theory; spectra, X-ray analysis, nuclear reactions. Given in alternate years, beginning 1951-52. Credit, 3 each semester.
Prerequisites, 18 junior-senior physics credits, including Physics 52 and 64; Math. 30. Mr. WANG.

195. 196. ELECTRONICS.—Two class hours; one 2-hour laboratory period.
Prerequisites, Physics 151, 152; Math. 29 and 30. Credit, 3 each semester.
.MR. POWERS AND MR. WANG.

Pomology

ARTHUR P. FRENCH, major adviser

All students majoring in this department are required to offer a thesis as part of their major requirements.

COURSES OPEN TO GRADUATE STUDENTS ONLY
(For either major or minor credit)

201, 202. POMOLOGICAL RESEARCH.—A critical review of past and current research work in the field of pomology. Topics selected according to the interests and needs of the individual student. Credit, 2 each semester.
Prerequisite, Pomology 181 and 182. Mr. SOUTHWICK and the STAFF.

205. ADVANCED SYSTEMATIC POMOLOGY.—An intensive study of leaf and tree characters of nursery and orchard trees with reference to identification and the relationship of varieties. This work to be undertaken in the summer. Credit, 3.
Prerequisite, Pomology 175. Mr. FRENCH.

Horticulture 211, 212. SEMINAR.—Each student will present papers on assigned topics in Horticulture. Departments of Pomology, Floriculture and Olericulture cooperating. Required of all graduate students majoring in Floriculture, Olericulture, and Pomology. Credit, 1 each semester.
THE DEPARTMENTS.

300. THESIS, MASTER'S DEGREE. Each student majoring in Pomology will be required to carry out an original investigation on an approved problem and present the results thereof in satisfactory form as a thesis. Credit, 10.

COURSES OPEN TO BOTH GRADUATE AND UNDERGRADUATE STUDENTS
(For either major or minor credit)

181, 182. ADVANCED POMOLOGY.—A consideration of the scientific principles governing the growth and behavior of fruit-bearing plants.
Prerequisite, Pomology 53. Credit, 3 each semester.
Mr. FRENCH, Mr. SOUTHWICK and Mr. WEEKS.

Plant Breeding

Plant Breeding 152. PLANT BREEDING METHODS.—An advanced study of genetic topics peculiar to plants together with consideration of the methods and problems of the plant breeder. Credit, 3.
Prerequisite, Zoology 153 or equivalent. Mr. FRENCH.

Plant Breeding 181. PLANT CYTOLOGICAL TECHNIQUES.—The methods of cytology useful to the plant geneticist. Credit, 2.
Mr. FRENCH.

88

Plant Breeding 182. SPECIAL PROBLEMS IN PLANT BREEDING.—Advanced study of special topics in the field of plant genetics and breeding. Credit, 2. Prerequisite, Plant Breeding 152. Mr. FRENCH.

COURSES IN OTHER DEPARTMENTS FOR WHICH MAJOR CREDIT WILL BE GIVEN

Agronomy 263. CHEMISTRY OF THE SOIL. Credit, 5.
Mr. STECKEL.

Agronomy 264. EXPERIMENTAL METHODS. Credit, 3.
Mr. YEGIAN.

Botany 202, 203. ADVANCED PLANT PHYSIOLOGY. Credit, 4 each semester.
Mr. KOZLOWSKI.

Chemistry 165, 166. PHYSICAL CHEMISTRY. Credit, 4.
Mr. FESSENDEN and Mr. SMITH.

Chemistry 179. BIOCHEMISTRY. Credit, 4.
Mr. LITTLE.

COURSES FOR MINOR CREDIT ONLY

156. ORCHARD PEST CONTROL. Credit, 3.
Mr. ROBERTS.

175. SYSTEMATIC POMOLOGY. Credit, 4.
MR. ANDERSON.

177. COMMERCIAL POMOLOGY. Credit, 3.
Mr. ROBERTS.

183, 184.—SEMINAR. Credit, 1 each semester.
THE STAFF.

Poultry Science

THOMAS W. FOX, major adviser.

The Master of Science degree is offered in the field of genetics and physiology.

COURSES OPEN TO GRADUATE STUDENTS ONLY
(For either major or minor credit)

200. SPECIAL PROBLEMS.—Research problems in avian genetics and physiology. Problems such as heat tolerance, metabolism of chicks, factors affecting feathering have been carried out in the past and are mentioned here to illustrate the type of problem that might be undertaken. Credit, 3.
Mr. HAYS and Mr. SMYTH.

202. POULTRY RESEARCH PROBLEMS.—A critical review of research in genetics or physiology. Required is a comprehensive written report covering some particular phase of the science from its beginning to the present. The final report requires that the student evaluate work in the field and suggest new and unexplored areas. Credit, 3.
Mr. HAYS and Mr. SMYTH.

Prerequisites are standard undergraduate courses in poultry husbandry.

203. ADVANCED GENETICS.—A lecture course dealing with the experimental study of genetics in plants and animals. The major aspects of the science are discussed and illustrated to give the student a good working knowledge and to stimulate his interest in this field of biology. Credit, 3.
3 class hours. Mr. HAYS.
Prerequisites, at least one year's training in biology and Zoology 153 or its equivalent.

204. ADVANCED GENETICS.—A continuation of Poultry 203. The first third of the semester will be devoted to human genetics and the last two-thirds to the application of the latest statistical methods in the interpretation of biological data. Credit, 3.
3 class hours. Mr. HAYS.

205. AVIAN GENETICS.—A lecture course covering the genetics of the principal domesticated birds. Special attention is given to methods of experimentation and interpretation of genetic data. Credit, 3.
Mr. SMYTH.
Prerequisites, at least one year's training in biology and Zoology 153 or its equivalent.

206. AVIAN GENETICS AND PHYSIOLOGY.—This course is a continuation of Poultry 205. Special emphasis will be put on the fields of physiological and population genetics as they apply to poultry genetics and breeding. The physiology of reproduction of avian species will also be considered in detail.
3 class hours. Credit, 3.
Prerequisite, Poultry 205. Mr. Fox.

300. THESIS, MASTER'S DEGREE. Credit, 10.

COURSE FOR MINOR CREDIT ONLY

201. ADVANCED POULTRY HUSBANDRY.—A critical review of research in any one of these fields: (a) genetics and physiology, (b) nutrition, (c) marketing, or (d) incubation and brooding. Three written reports and a comprehensive final examination are required. This course is designed for teachers of vocational agriculture. Credit, 3.
THE STAFF.
Prerequisites are standard undergraduate courses in poultry husbandry.

Psychology

CLAUDE C. NEET, major adviser.

The graduate student majoring in Psychology may orient his program toward either the Doctor of Philosophy degree or the Master's degree. Emphasis may be in the area of child-clinical, general experimental, counseling, industrial, or social psychology.

Students taking the doctorate must satisfy the general requirements of the Graduate School for the degree. They must also include in their programs of study the following psychology courses: 175, 207, 213, 295, 296, and 400. In addition they must elect four of the following courses: 163, 172, 201, 203, 204, 206, and 210. The doctorate program provides practicum courses in each of the applied specialization areas. Institutions and agencies available for such field work include Belchertown State Hospital, Clarke School for the Deaf, Monson State Hospital, Northampton State Hospital, University Guidance and Counseling Services, University Nursery School, and various industrial concerns in nearby towns.

All students qualifying for the Master of Science degree in Psychology must, in addition to meeting the degree requirements of the Graduate School, take course 175 and either 200 or 300. They must also pass a written examination which will cover certain general fields of psychology selected by the Department and certain special fields which may be chosen by the candidate. A final oral examination, given by the problem or thesis committee and the Department, is required. Credits taken to satisfy the requirements for the Master's degree can be applied to the total number of credits required for the doctorate.

Students applying for admission for either the Doctor's or Master's degree program, in addition to meeting the requirements of the Graduate School, should have taken an Introductory course and 21 additional undergraduate credits in Psychology, including a course in laboratory experimental Psychology, and a course in Statistics. In case the student has not taken this number of credits or lacks these courses, he may be allowed to make up the deficiencies in the Undergraduate School of the University. In exceptional cases, students with entrance deficiencies may, at the end of one semester's study, petition the Department to waive remaining undergraduate deficiencies. In completing his application, the student should arrange to take the Miller Analogies Test and have his score submitted to the Head of the Department.

COURSES OPEN TO GRADUATE STUDENTS ONLY
(For either major or minor credit)

200. PROBLEM IN PSYCHOLOGY.—A research project which may be taken in lieu of the master's thesis, or by doctoral students as minor research. Credit, 4-6

THE STAFF.

202. NEURAL CORRELATES OF BEHAVIOR.—A detailed study of the neuroanatomical relationships of sensory-motor systems. Emphasis is placed upon the major fiber systems and their role in behavior. Given in alternate years, beginning 1954-55. Credit, 3.
Prerequisites, 6 credits of Psychology and 6 credits Zoology or the equivalent.

Mr. FELDMAN.

203. LEARNING I.—A consideration of the basic laws of learning, and of relevant research techniques. Given in 1955-56 and in alternate years. Credit, 3.

Mr. GOSS.

204. LEARNING II.—A consideration of the implications of the basic laws of learning for explaining complex behavior. Given in 1955-56 and in alternate years. Credit, 3.
Prerequisite, Psychology 203.

Mr. GOSS.

206. DISCRIMINAL PROCESSES.—An analysis of sensory and perceptual processes. The relationships among physical, physiological and psychological variables are stressed. Given in 1955-56 and in alternate years. Credit, 3.
Prerequisites, 6 hours Psychology and 3 hours Zoology or the equivalent.

Mr. FELDMAN

207. SYSTEMATIC PSYCHOLOGY.—An analysis of the general structure of psychological theory, and an historical and comparative consideration of the backgrounds, viewpoints on scientific methodology, research interests and techniques, and the component variables, hypotheses, and laws of structural, Gestalt functional, and behavioristic movements. Given in alternate years beginning 1954-55. Credit, 3

Mr. GOSS

210. EMOTION AND MOTIVATION.—A study of the nature, determinants, and interrelationships of emotion and motivation, and of the techniques involved in investigating these phenomena. Given in alternate years, beginning 1954-55.
Credit, 3.
Mr. NEET.

213. TEST CONSTRUCTION I.—Logic and methods of psychological scaling; media of testing; item, test, and battery construction; relevance and reliability requirements of items, test, and criteria. Credit, 3
Prerequisite, Psychology 175, or taken concurrently. Mr. ERLICK.

214. TEST CONSTRUCTION II.—The use of correlational and analysis of variance techniques in test construction. The class will statistically analyze a test which they have constructed. Credit, 3.
Prerequisite, Psychology 213. Mr. ERLICK.

221. ADVANCED SOCIAL PSYCHOLOGY.—An investigation of the important areas of social psychology through lectures, discussion, and laboratory exercises. The group will complete two projects or investigations. Topics considered are: experimental study of determinants of social interaction, effect of needs and motives on perception, opinion and attitude measurement, determinants of attitudes, and propaganda. Credit, 3.
Two class hours; one 2-hour laboratory. Mr. MAUSNER.
Prerequisite, Psychology 161 or 162.

226. THEORIES OF PERSONALITY.—Problems and sources of data relating to the study of personality. An evaluation of the contributions of psychological theories, and an approach to an integrated theory. Given in alternate years, beginning 1954-55. Credit, 3.
Prerequisite, Psychology 207. Mr. MAUSNER.

235. ADVANCED ABNORMAL PSYCHOLOGY.—An intensive study of the behavior disorders and their relationships to normal behavior. Major emphasis is on theories of etiology and symptom formation, and on general problems of therapy. Prerequisite, Psychology 183, or the consent of the instructor. Credit, 3.
Mr. NEET.

242. PSYCHOLOGY OF THE PRE-SCHOOL CHILD.—A detailed study of the behavior of the child from the early prenatal period to the school age. Credit, 3.
Prerequisite, Psychology 194, or the consent of the instructor. Mr. CLIFFORD.

251. PROJECTIVE METHODS I.—An intensive study of the methods of administration and of the scoring procedures of a variety of projective media with emphasis upon the Rorschach and Thematic Apperception Test. Credit, 3.
Prerequisite, Psychology 182. Mr. EPSTEIN.

252. PROJECTIVE METHODS II.—Basic interpretive procedures of projective devices with emphasis upon the Rorschach and Thematic Apperception Test.
Prerequisite, Psychology 251. Credit, 3.
Mr. EPSTEIN.

253. ADVANCED CLINICAL PSYCHOLOGY I.—Diagnosis. Application of the principles and techniques of psychological diagnosis to the individual case. Given in alternate years, beginning 1954-55. Credit, 3.
Prerequisites, Psychology 235, 252. Mr. EPSTEIN.

265. COUNSELING AND INTERVIEWING TECHNIQUES.—A study of current counseling and guidance techniques employed with groups and individuals including the organization of counseling services, and the use of occupational information and referral sources. Credit, 3.
Prerequisites, Psychology 181 and 182. Mr. FIELD.

271. ADVANCED INDUSTRIAL PSYCHOLOGY I.—Human relations in industry. Applications of general and social psychological findings to industry and business, with a concentration on the interdependence of morale, leadership and motivation. Given in 1955-56 and in alternate years.   Credit, 3.
Prerequisite, Psychology 186, or the consent of the instructor.   Mr. ERLICK.

283, 284. PRACTICUM—Practice in the application of psychological techniques to the following areas of psychology: child, clinical, guidance and counseling, industrial, and social. Either semester may be elected independently.
Total credit, 3-12.
THE STAFF, with the Staffs of
cooperating institutions and agencies.

295, 296. RESEARCH METHODOLOGY.—A study and evaluation of research methods and of problems in the major fields of psychology. Two semesters are required of students studying toward the doctorate.   Credit, 2 each semester.
THE STAFF.

300. THESIS, MASTER'S DEGREE.—Research, and the preparation of an acceptable thesis.   Credit, 8-10.

400. THESIS, PH.D. DEGREE.—Research, and the preparation of an acceptable thesis.   Credit, 30.

COURSES OPEN TO BOTH GRADUATE AND UNDERGRADUATE STUDENTS

(For either major or minor credit)

156. EDUCATIONAL PSYCHOLOGY.—A study of psychological facts and principles fundamental to education, teaching, and personal relationships between teacher and pupil. Topics considered in relation to school situations are: Physical and mental growth, intelligence, motivation, emotions, learning, transfer of training, and mental hygiene of teacher and pupil.   Credit, 3.
Prerequisite, Psychology 26.   Mr. MAUSNER.

161. SOCIAL PSYCHOLOGY.—The social behavior of the individual. Topics considered will include methods of studying social behavior, "schools" of social psychology, social behavior of animals, foundations of personality development, social (cultural) determinants of personality, social attitudes and their measurement, effects of collective situations on individual behavior, customs and conformity.   Credit, 3.
Prerequisite, Psychology 26.   Mr. MAUSNER.

162. SOCIAL PSYCHOLOGY.—A survey of multiindividual phenomena. Topics to be considered are methods of studying collective action, leadership, morale, propaganda, nature and measurement of public opinion, behavior in crowd situation, social conflict and prejudice. Given in 1955-56 and in alternate years.
Prerequisite, Psychology 161 or the consent of the instructor.   Credit, 3.
Mr. MAUSNER.

163. PHYSIOLOGICAL PSYCHOLOGY.—A study of the relationships between the individual's behavior and his physiological processes. Emphasis will be placed on sensory and motor phenomena, drives, emotional behavior, and learning.
Prerequisite, 6 units of Psychology; Zoology 35.   Credit, 3.
Mr. FELDMAN.

172. ADVANCED EXPERIMENTAL PSYCHOLOGY.—Experimental design, techniques, and apparatus in psychology are considered, and selected projects are carried out individually by the members of the class. Given in 1955-56 and in alternate years.   Credit, 3.
Prerequisite, Psychology 51.   Mr. NEET.

175. PSYCHOLOGICAL STATISTICS.—The application of statistical procedures to the analysis of psychological data and to problems of measurement in psychology and related fields.   Credit, 3.
Prerequisite, one semester of statistics, or the equivalent.   Mr. Goss.

181. PSYCHOLOGICAL TESTS.—A survey of the construction, development, and use of a variety of psychological tests. Emphasis will be placed upon the administration, scoring, interpretation and evaluation of tests of personality, interests, aptitudes, and group tests of intelligence.   Credit, 3.
Prerequisite, Psychology 26.   MISS GRUBLER.

182. PSYCHOLOGICAL TESTS, INDIVIDUAL INTELLIGENCE TESTS.—Theories as to the nature and measurement of intelligence. Emphasis is on the administration, scoring and interpretation of individual intelligence tests such as the Stanford-Binet, Wechsler-Bellevue, Merrill-Palmer, and others.   Credit, 3.
                                                                   MISS GRUBLER.

183. ABNORMAL PSYCHOLOGY.—A study of abnormal behavior. Attention is given to the following: dynamics of behavior abnormalities, the neuroses, psychoses, mental deficiency, speech problems, and sensory and motor disorders.
                                                                      Credit, 3.
Prerequisite, Psychology 26.   Mr. NEET.

186. INDUSTRIAL PSYCHOLOGY.—The course aims to give understanding of psychological principles and methods in business and industrial situations. Topics considered include: employee selection and training, motivation and morale, working conditions, fatigue and accident prevention.   Credit, 3.
Prerequisite, Psychology 26.   Mr. ERLICK.

188. PSYCHOLOGY OF GUIDANCE.—A study of the psychological principles, techniques and tests necessary in guidance. Practice is given in organizing and evaluating relevant data in the analysis of illustrative cases.   Credit, 3.
Prerequisite, Psychology 181.   Mr. FIELD.

. 190. CONTEMPORARY PSYCHOLOGIES.—An introductory historical, logical and systematic analysis of contemporary psychological theories.   Credit, 3.
Prerequisite, Psychology 26.   Mr. Goss.

192. CLINICAL PSYCHOLOGY.—A study of the development, and present status of the techniques and methods used by the psychologist in the diagnosis and treatment of behavior disorders. Consideration is given to the use of diagnostic tests, psycho-therapy, and the general role of the clinical psychologist.
Prerequisite, Psychology 183.   Credit, 3.
                                                                   Mr. EPSTEIN.

193. ADOLESCENT PSYCHOLOGY.—The application of the basic principles of learning, primary and secondary motivation, frustration and conflict to the facts and problems of adolescent behavior. Given in 1954-55 and in alternate years.   Credit, 3.
Prerequisite, Psychology 26.   Mr. CLIFFORD.

194. CHILD PSYCHOLOGY.—The course aims to develop an understanding of the behavior of the child. Psychological aspects of the following are considered: Original nature, maturation, play, social behavior, personality and mental hygiene. Nursery school observation and practice.   Credit, 3.
Prerequisite, Psychology 26.   Mr. CLIFFORD.

Public Health

RALPH L. FRANCE, major adviser.

The following courses are offered to students interested in environmental sanitation and who intend to prepare for positions as industrial and public health sanitarians. With the cooperation of the Massachusetts Department of Public Health, field training is integrated into the curriculum. Applicants must have satisfied the entrance requirements of the Graduate School and should have completed an undergraduate major in the physical or biological sciences. Experience as a full time employee in environmental sanitation may be accepted in lieu of specific undergraduate requirements.

COURSES OPEN TO GRADUATE STUDENTS ONLY
(For either major or minor credit)

200. SPECIAL PROBLEMS IN PUBLIC HEALTH.—Special investigational or research problems in public health for advanced students. The scope of this work can be varied to meet specific conditions. Credit, 3-6.

THE STAFF.

201. PUBLIC HEALTH LAW.—A discussion of the laws governing health activities of federal, state and local health agencies including methods of preparation and mediation of health legislation and regulations. Rules of evidence and conduct of witnesses will be included. Credit, 3.

Mr. WISNIESKI.

202. METHODS OF PUBLIC HEALTH EDUCATION.—The object of this course is to give the health educator an opportunity to study, use, and evaluate some of the special methods, tools, and skills in health education. Opportunity for practice in the preparation of health education materials is provided. Credit, 3.

Mr. WISNIESKI.

203. THE PLANNING OF ENVIRONMENTAL SANITATION PROGRAMS.—The practical techniques of putting the principles of environmental sanitation into practice in a health department program are studied. The level of application and the field of application will be determined by the students' own needs. Topics considered are the development of standards, rating systems and field forms, the uses and execution of sanitary surveys, the training of sub-professional sanitarians in areas outside the United States, the planning of schools in food handling, the use of milk-shed rating systems, the job analysis of a balanced sanitation program. Credit, 3.

Mr. WISNIESKI.

206. ADVANCED EPIDEMIOLOGY.—Lectures, discussions, and laboratory work on the principles, and methods of epidemiological investigation with laboratory work in assembling and analyzing crude data resulting from field investigations of epidemics. Credit, 3.
Prerequisite, P. H. 188 or equivalent. Mr. LEE.

207. SEMINAR.—Lectures and reports on current literature and special topics. (One each semester.) Credit, 1-2.

THE STAFF.

300. THESIS, MASTER'S DEGREE.—Independent research leading to the preparation of a thesis that will make an original contribution to the literature in public health. Results should be suitable for publication. The thesis is optional for M.S. candidates who have had sufficient training in public health before entering the graduate school to profit more from thesis research than from additional courses. Credit, 10.

COURSES OPEN TO BOTH GRADUATE AND UNDERGRADUATE STUDENTS
(For either major or minor credit)

161, 162. GENERAL AND COMMUNITY SANITATION.—A study of the problems of general and community sanitation. Subjects discussed will include insect and rodent control, housing and slum clearance, ventilation, lighting, bathing places, sanitation of eating utensils, nuisances, camp sanitation, industrial hygiene, water supplies, sewerage and sewage, refuse and garbage, food and milk sanitation.

Credit, 3.

Mr. PERRIELLO or Mr. WISNIESKI.

163. INDUSTRIAL HYGIENE AND SANITATION. Credit, 3.
Permission of instructor. Mr. PERRIELLO.

164. MICROSCOPY OF WATER.—Counting and control of plankton in potable waters.
Credit, 3.
Prerequisite, Bacteriology 31A. Mr. SNOW.

184. PUBLIC HEALTH ADMINISTRATION. Credit. 3.
Mr. PERRIELLO.

186. FIELD STUDIES IN SANITATION.—Trips will be taken into the field for the observation of public health practices. Credit, 2.
Prerequisites, Public Health 161, 162. Mr. WISNIESKI.

188. EPIDEMIOLOGY AND COMMUNICABLE DISEASE CONTROL.—Admission by approval of the instructor. Credit, 3.
Mr. LEE.

192. SUPERVISED FIELD TRAINING.—To be taken during the summer session. All graduates majoring in sanitary technology must complete a prescribed thirteen-week field training program conducted by the New England Field Training Center under the direction of the Training Division of the Communicable Disease Center, U. S. Public Health Service, with the assistance of the staff and State Department of Health personnel. This course is a prerequisite for placement in federal, state, and municipal agencies. Credit, 6.
THE STAFF.

COURSES IN OTHER DEPARTMENTS FOR WHICH MAJOR CREDIT WILL BE GIVEN.

Bacteriology 181. GENERAL APPLIED BACTERIOLOGY. Credit, 4.
Mr. FRANCE.

Bacteriology 182. FOOD BACTERIOLOGY. Credit, 3.
Miss GARVEY.

Bacteriology 190. SANITARY BACTERIOLOGY. Credit, 3.
Mr. FRANCE.

Agricultural Economics 179. ELEMENTARY STATISTICS. Credit, 3.
Mr. RUSSELL.

Botany 166. GENERAL MYCOLOGY. Credit, 3.
Mr. BANFIELD.

Home Economics 203. ADVANCED NUTRITION—METABOLISM OF THE MAJOR FOODSTUFFS. Credit, 3.
Miss MITCHELL.

Home Economics 204. ADVANCED NUTRITION—MINERALS AND VITAMINS.
Credit, 3.
Miss MITCHELL.

Food Technology 175. FOOD PRESERVATION.
Credit, 3.
Mr. NEBESKY.

Food Technology 192. ANALYSIS OF FOOD PRODUCTS.
Credit, 3.
Mr. FELLERS and Mr. NEBESKY.

Dairy 152. MARKET MILK.
Credit, 4.
Mr. LINDQUIST.

Dairy 209, 210. SEMINAR.
Credit, 1 each semester.
Mr. HANKINSON.

Education 267. AUDIO-VISUAL LABORATORY.
Credit, 2-3.
Mr. WYMAN.

Zoology 169. ANIMAL PARASITOLOGY.
Credit, 3.
Miss TRAVER.

COURSES FOR MINOR CREDIT ONLY

Government 162. ADMINISTRATIVE LAW.

Entomology 174. MEDICAL ENTOMOLOGY.

Forestry 151. FOREST MANAGEMENT OF WATERSHEDS.

Animal Husbandry 153. ELEMENTS OF MEAT PACKING.

Civil Engineering 179. PRINCIPLES OF SANITARY ENGINEERING.

Agricultural Engineering 180. FOOD PROCESS ENGINEERING.

Education 166. PREPARATION AND USE OF AUDIO-VISUAL AIDS.

Geology 150. ENGINEERING GEOLOGY.

Veterinary Science 178. GENERAL VETERINARY PATHOLOGY.

Romance Languages

CHARLES F. FRAKER, major adviser.

Requirements for admission to candidacy for the M.A. in Romance Languages:

1. A working knowledge of Latin.

2. Oral proficiency in at least one of the Romance Languages.

3. A reading knowledge of a second language (Latin, German or another Romance Language).

All candidates for the M.A. degree are required to take either Romance Languages 201-202, or 203-204.

COURSES OPEN TO GRADUATE STUDENTS ONLY
(For either major or minor credit)

200. PROBLEM COURSE.—Independent study of some phase of linguistics or literature.　　　　　　　　　　　Credit, 3 each semester; maximum credit, 6.
THE STAFF.

201, 202. AN INTRODUCTION TO ROMANCE PHILOLOGY.—Studies in the laws of vowel and consonantal change; the provenience of words.
Credit, 3 each semester.
Mr. FRAKER.

203, 204. OLD FRENCH READINGS.—Early monuments of French Literature; The Arthurian and Carolingian Cycles. Given as needed.
Credit, 3 each semester.
Mr. GODING and Mr. FRAKER.

205, 206. OLD SPANISH READINGS.—Early monuments of Spanish Literature; The Cronicas and the Poema del mio Cid. · Given as needed.
Credit, 3 each semester.
Mr. FRAKER.

300. THESIS, MASTER'S DEGREE.　　　　　　　　　　Credit, 10.

COURSES OPEN TO BOTH GRADUATE AND UNDERGRADUATE STUDENTS
(For either major or minor credit)

151, 152. FRENCH LITERATURE OF THE EIGHTEENTH CENTURY.—Given in alternate years, beginning 1954-55.　　　　　　　Credit, 3 each semester.
Mr. FRAKER.

153, 154. CONTEMPORARY FRENCH LITERATURE.—Given as needed. ·
Credit, 3 each semester.
Miss CLARKE.

155, 156. FRENCH CLASSICISM.—A ·survey of the Classic period, with readings from representative works. Given in alternate years, beginning 1955-56. Prerequisites, French 15 and 16 or their equivalent.　　　　Credit, 3.
Mr. FRAKER.

157. FRENCH ROMANTICISM.—A detailed study of the Romantic Period. Readings from Hugo, de Vigny, Lamartine, de Musset, and others. Conducted in French. Given in alternate years, beginning 1954-55.　　　Credit, 3.
Prerequisites, French 15 and 16 or their equivalent. ·　　　Mr. GODING.

158. FRENCH REALISM.—A detailed study of the Realistic period and the modern writers. Readings from Balzac, Flaubert, Stendhal, Loti, Daudet, Anatole France, and others. Conducted in French. Given in alternate years, beginning 1955-56.　　　　　　　　　　　　　　Credit, 3.
Prerequisite, French 31.　　　　　　　　　　　　Mr. GODING.

180. ADVANCED GRAMMAR AND COMPOSITION.—A thorough review of grammar, pronunciation, and the phonetic method. A course for prospective teachers.
Credit, 3.
Mr. GODING.

181. SPANISH ROMANTICISM.—Readings from representative authors; written and oral composition. Given in alternate years, beginning 1954-55.
Credit, 3.
Prerequisite, a reading knowledge of Spanish.　　　　　　Mr. FRAKER.

182. THE MODERNISTS.—Dario, Nervo, and their contemporaries; composition and conversation. Given in alternate years, beginning 1955-56.   Credit, 3.
Prerequisite, a reading knowledge of Spanish.   Mr. FRAKER.

183, 184. THE GOLDEN AGE.—Readings from Cervantes, Lope de Vega, Calderon, Garcilaso, and others. Composition and conversation. Given in alternate years, beginning 1955-56.   Credit, 3 each semester.
Prerequisites, Spanish 7 and 8.   Mr. FRAKER.

Sociology

J. H. KORSON, major adviser.

Special Departmental Entrance Requirements:

Candidates for admission who plan to major in Sociology must have completed an undergraduate major, or have taken a minimum of 15 credits in Sociology. A minimum of three credits in Statistics must be offered. A deficiency in Statistics can be made up by taking Agricultural Economics 179. In certain cases students will be advised to take Agricultural Economics 180. A student lacking this minimum undergraduate training will be expected to make up deficiencies in the undergraduate college of the University. Exceptions to this rule will be made only on petition of the student to the department. Students who desire to direct their training toward Correctional Administration will be expected to take certain courses in Government and Psychology.

In addition to the general requirements for the Master of Arts degree, found elsewhere in this Bulletin, candidates in Sociology are required to take the Graduate Record Examination before admission, or as soon after as possible.

Degree requirements: 30 credits, of which a minimum of 12 are to be earned in courses at the 200 level, 6 of which must be in Sociology 281 and 282. Students who elect the program in Correctional Administration are expected to earn a minimum of 15 credits at the 200 level. A student may be granted the option of writing a Master's thesis (10 credits) or working on a special problem (3-6 credits). All candidates for the Master of Arts degree must take a final oral examination given by the Department covering their problem or thesis.

COURSES OPEN TO GRADUATE STUDENTS ONLY
(Courses for major or minor credit)

200. SPECIAL PROBLEM.—A special project in Sociology which may serve in lieu of thesis.   Credit, 3-6.
Prerequisite, Sociology 179, or equivalent.   THE DEPARTMENT.

214. (II) CRIMINOLOGY.—A consideration of criminological theories, past and present. Special emphasis on present research trends as they relate to theoretical formulations. Given as required.   Credit, 3.
Prerequisite, Sociology 78, or equivalent.   Mr. DRIVER.

217. (I) JUVENILE DELINQUENCY.—A consideration of various theories of causation and treatment of delinquency. Given as required.   Credit, 3.
Prerequisite, Sociology 78, or equivalent.   Mr. DRIVER.

268. (II) INDUSTRIAL SOCIOLOGY.—A study of the role, status, and function of the worker in the industrial community. A consideration of the impact of technological change on the community. An analysis of selected occupational functions.   Credit, 3.
Prerequisite, Economics 79, or equivalent.   Mr. KORSON.

281. (I) HISTORY OF SOCIOLOGICAL THEORY.—A survey of the literature from classical times to the Utilitarians. Credit, 3.
Prerequisite, Sociology 82, or equivalent. Mr. MANFREDI.

282. (II) CONTEMPORARY SOCIOLOGICAL THEORY.—A survey of the literature from Auguste Comte to the present. Credit, 3.
Prerequisite, Sociology 82, or equivalent. Mr. MANFREDI.

291. (I) SOCIAL CHANGE.—Emphasis is placed upon planned innovations and reforms in political, religious and economic areas and upon the possibilities and problems of social planning. Consideration is also given to social changes resulting indirectly from invention and group contact. Credit, 3.
Admission by consent of the instructor. Mr. KING.

298. INTERNSHIP.—Supervised training and practice in the administration of a state correctional institution or organization. Students chosen for this training will serve with one of the following: Women's Reformatory (Framingham), Men's Reformatory (Concord), The Bureau of Classification (Department of Correction), Youth Service Board (Department of Education), The United Prison Association (Boston). A minimum of three months (40-hour weeks) is required and will normally take place the summer following completion of the major part of the student's course work. Credit, 3.
Prerequisites, Sociology 176, 214, 217. THE DEPARTMENT.

300. THESIS, MASTER'S DEGREE. Credit, 10.

(Courses for major or minor credit)

151. URBAN SOCIOLOGY. Credit, 3.
Mr. MANFREDI.

152. RURAL SOCIOLOGY. Credit, 3.
Mr. MANFREDI.

153. SOCIAL ANTHROPOLOGY. Credit, 3.
Mr. WILKINSON.

154. RACE RELATIONS. Credit, 3.
Mr. KING, Mr. KORSON.

157. THE FAMILY. Credit, 3.
Mr. KING, Mr. KORSON.

162. POPULATION PROBLEMS. Credit, 3.
Mr. WILKINSON.

175. SOCIAL PROBLEMS. Credit, 3.
Mr. DRIVER.

176. SOCIAL WELFARE. Credit, 3.
Mr. DRIVER.

179. SEMINAR. RESEARCH METHODS. Credit, 3.
Mr. DRIVER.

180. SEMINAR. RESEARCH METHODS. Credit, 3.
Mr. DRIVER.

Veterinary Science

COURSES FOR MINOR CREDIT ONLY

175. COMPARATIVE VETERINARY ANATOMY.
Credit, 3.
Mr. SMITH.

176. GENERAL VETERINARY PATHOLOGY.
Credit, 3.
Mr. SMITH.

178. GENERAL VETERINARY PATHOLOGY.
Credit, 3.
Mr. SMITH.

188. AVIAN PATHOLOGY.
Credit, 3.
Mr. BULLIS.

Wildlife Management

REUBEN E. TRIPPENSEE, major adviser.

Graduate work in Wildlife Management is closely tied in with the Cooperative Wildlife Research Station which is now a part of the Department of Forestry and Wildlife Management. Financial support for the Unit is received from the U. S. Fish and Wildlife Service, the Wildlife Management Institute and the State Fish and Game Department. Dr. William G. Sheldon, director of the Research Unit spends approximately half of his time assisting the research activities of the students who work under fellowships received through the Unit. The director of research is automatically on the graduate committee of each student who receives funds through the Unit.

Students graduating in Wildlife Management at the University of Massachusetts are strongly urged to pursue graduate work at another University. Opportunities for fellowships in this field are usually available at other Cooperative Units.

COURSES OPEN TO GRADUATE STUDENTS ONLY
(For either major or minor credit)

200. SPECIAL PROBLEMS IN WILDLIFE MANAGEMENT.
Credit, 3 per semester maximum credit, 6.
THE STAFF.

201. NORTH AMERICAN ANIMALS.—A review of the taxonomy, life histories and ecological inter-relationships of certain North American vertebrates.
Credit, 3.
Mr. TRIPPENSEE.

202. WILDLIFE ADMINISTRATION.—A study of the organization and operation of state and federal agencies and certain associations concerned with wildlife management.
Credit, 3.
Prerequisite, Wildlife Management 27 or equivalent.
Mr. TRIPPENSEE.

203. WILD ANIMAL ABUNDANCE.—A study of the factors which influence wild animal abundance.
Credit, 3.
Mr. TRIPPENSEE.

204. LAND USE AND WILDLIFE.—A study of wildlife populations on different ecological sites with special emphasis on the indirect influence of land use practices and natural vegetative succession.
Credit, 3.
Prerequisites, Agronomy 2, Botany 181, Forestry 55 and 56 or equivalents.
Mr. SHELDON and Mr. TRIPPENSEE.

205. MANAGEMENT OF WET LANDS AND WATER IN RELATION TO WILDLIFE.
Credit, 3.
Mr. SHELDON and Mr. TRIPPENSEE.

300. THESIS, MASTER'S DEGREE. Credit, 10.

COURSES OPEN TO BOTH GRADUATE AND UNDERGRADUATE STUDENTS

(For either major or minor credit)

170. GAME BIRDS AND MAMMALS.—Life histories, ecology methods of management. Credit. 3.
Mr. TRIPPENSEE.

171. WATERFOWL MANAGEMENT.—Life histories and factors which affect abundance of waterfowl. Credit, 3.
Mr. TRIPPENSEE.

173. PREDACEOUS BIRDS AND INJURIOUS RODENTS.—Life histories, ecology and control. Credit, 3.
Mr. TRIPPENSEE.

174. TECHNIQUES IN WILDLIFE MANAGEMENT.—Includes analysis of cover, census methods, food habit studies, and determination of flock and herd age and sex composition of game animals. Credit, 3.
Mr. TRIPPENSEE.

175. MANAGEMENT OF FURBEARERS.—Life histories and management of furbearers and nomenclature of the fur trade. Credit, 3.
Mr. TRIPPENSEE.

COURSES IN OTHER DEPARTMENTS FOR WHICH MAJOR CREDIT WILL BE GIVEN

Agricultural Economics 179. ELEMENTARY STATISTICS THROUGH SIMPLE CORRELATION. Credit, 3.
Mr. RUSSELL.

Botany 167, 168. INTRODUCTORY PLANT PHYSIOLOGY. Credit, 3 each semester.
Mr. KOZLOWSKI.

Botany 181. PLANT ECOLOGY. Credit, 3.
Mr. LIVINGSTON.

Entomology 179. ADVANCED ANIMAL ECOLOGY. Credit, 3.
Mr. SWEETMAN.

Entomology 190. EVOLUTION. Credit, 2.
Mr. HANSON.

Entomology 212. GEOGRAPHICAL DISTRIBUTION. Credit, 3.
Mr. ALEXANDER.

Education 166. PREPARATION AND USE OF AUDIO-VISUAL AIDS. Credit, 2-3.
Mr. WYMAN.

Forestry 171. AERIAL PHOTOGRAMMETRY. Credit, 3.
Mr. MACCONNELL.

Forestry 180. PRINCIPLES OF FOREST MANAGEMENT.   .Credit, 3.
                                                   Mr. MacCONNELL.

Poultry Science. 203, 204. ADVANCED GENETICS.   · Credit, 3 each semester.
                                                         Mr. HAYS.

Zoology 171. COMPARATIVE VERTEBRATE ANATOMY. ˙   Credit, 3.
                                  Mr. BARTLETT and Mr. DEARDEN.

Zoology 174. LIMNOLOGY.—A study of· inland waters.   Credit, 4.
                                                    Miss TRAVER.

Zoology 182. MAMMOLOGY.   Credit, 3.
                                                   Mr. DEARDEN.

Zoology 183. GENERAL CELLULAR PHYSIOLOGY.   Credit, 4.
                                                   Mr. SWENSON.

Zoology 184. COMPARATIVE PHYSIOLOGY.   Credit, 4.
                                                   Mr. ROBERTS.

Zoology 186. FISHERY BIOLOGY.   ·   Credit, 3.
                                                   Mr. ANDREWS

Zoology 187. ENDOCRINOLOGY.   Credit, 3.
                                                   Mr. SNEDECOR.

Zoology 200. SPECIAL PROBLEMS.   Credit, 3 or 6.
                                                   THE STAFF.

Zoology

GILBERT L. WOODSIDE, major adviser.

A thesis is required of all graduate students in the Department of Zoology
who become candidates for the Master's degree.

Candidates who have fulfilled the requirements of the Graduate School and
the Department of Zoology will be awarded the Master of Arts degree.

COURSES OPEN TO GRADUATE STUDENTS ONLY
(For either major or minor credit)

200. SPECIAL PROBLEMS.   Credit, 3 or 6.
                                                   THE STAFF.

202. ADVANCED INVERTEBRATE ZOOLOGY.—Invertebrate fauna of local ponds,
streams and bogs. Morphology, classification, habits and life cycles of such
groups as freshwater sponges, flatworms, bryozoans, annelids and crustaceans,
with a survey of the important literature on each group. Several field trips.
Term paper required. This course permits the student to become familiar with
animals of each of the above groups, the study of which can barely be touched
in courses 170 and 174.   Credit, 3.
Discussion period and two 3-hour laboratory periods.   Miss TRAVER.
Prerequisite, Zoology 25, 170 or 174.

204. HELMINTHOLOGY.—The course has two aims: first to acquaint the student with the morphology, classification and life histories of the principal groups of parasitic helminths, only a few of which can be studied in Zoology 169; and second to provide opportunity for the practical application of such knowledge. Included, in addition to the study of the helminth groups, are: methods of preparation of helminths for study; instruction and practice in the use of such reference sources as Biological Abstracts; an individual problem involving the collection, preparation and identification of helminth parasites from some species of animal; and the preparation of a term report embodying these findings. Credit, 3.

One class hour; two 3-hour laboratory periods. Miss TRAVER.

Prerequisites, Zoology 169 or equivalent.

220. EXPERIMENTAL EMBRYOLOGY.—Lectures, seminar reports and laboratory work dealing with the chief factors in the mechanics and physiology of development; the germ cells; fertilization, establishment of the primary axis; embryonic induction, and differentiation. Given in alternate years, beginning 1955-56.

Prerequisite, Zoology 172 or equivalent. Credit, 3.

Mr. WOODSIDE.

245. ADVANCED VERTEBRATE PHYSIOLOGY.—An opportunity for the student to gain experience in small animal surgery and in making standard experimental preparations. Suitable techniques for recording results will be employed, and the proper interpretation of the acquired data will be stressed. Credit, 3.

One class hour; one 4-hour laboratory period. Mr. SNEDECOR.

Prerequisites, Zoology 35 and 171, or equivalent.

248. PHYSIOLOGICAL GENETICS.—The nature of the gene and its action in the developmental and physiological processes of the organism. Credit, 3.

Prerequisite, Zoology 153, or equivalent, and permission of instructor.

Mr. RAUCH.

255. DEPARTMENTAL SEMINAR. Credit, 1 each semester.
Maximum credit, 4.

THE STAFF.

260. PHYSIOLOGY SEMINAR. Credit, 1 each semester.
Maximum credit, 3.

Mr. SWENSON.

300. THESIS, MASTER'S DEGREE. Credit, 10.

COURSES OPEN TO BOTH GRADUATE AND UNDERGRADUATE STUDENTS
(For either major or minor credit)

164. BIOLOGY OF PROTOZOA.—An introduction to the morphology, systematics, physiology, and ecology of Protozoa with a consideration of the contributions to the problems of biology made through the study of these organisms. Given in alternate years, beginning 1954-55. Credit, 3.

One lecture hour; one 2-hour and one 3-hour laboratory period. Mr. HONIGBERG.

Prerequisite, Zoology 1 and permission of the instructor.

169. ANIMAL PARASITOLOGY.—Representative protozan and helminthic parasites of man and domestic animals are studied, with special reference to their morphology and life cycles. Emphasis is placed upon parasitism as a mode of life, on host-parasite relationship, on vectors, and other modes of transmission, and on methods of control of certain of the more important human parasites. Graduate students taking this course prepare a term paper on some phase of parasitism. Credit, 3.

One class hour; two 2-hour laboratory periods. Miss TRAVER.
Prerequisite, Zoology 1.

170. INVERTEBRATE ZOOLOGY.—A survey of the phyla of invertebrate animals from evolutionary and phylogenetic aspects. Morphology, modes of nutrition and reproduction, interrelationships with other animals, and distribution in time and space are considered as well as classification. For each phylum, representatives of the principal classes are studied. Marine, terrestrial and freshwater forms are included. Given in alternate years, beginning 1954-55.

One class hour; two 3-hour laboratory periods. Credit, 3.
Prerequisite, Zoology 1. Miss TRAVER.

173. GENERAL CYTOLOGY.—A consideration of the morphological features of cells in relation to their function. Lectures, seminar reports and individual laboratory work. Given in alternate years, beginning 1954-55. Credit, 3.
Prerequisite, Zoology 150. Mr. ROLLASON.

174. LIMNOLOGY.—The study of inland waters, emphasizing the geological, physical, chemical and biological aspects of this problem. Standard methods for making physical and chemical tests and measurements, and for the collection of biological materials, are used by students in the numerous field trips. Biological material collected in the field is studied in the laboratory. Given in alternate years, beginning 1955-56. Credit, 4.

Two class hours; two 3-hour laboratory periods. Miss TRAVER in cooperation
Prerequisites, Botany 1, Zoology 1, Chemistry 1 with the departments of
and 2 and permission to register. Strongly Botany, Entomology, Ge-
recommended: Botany 25, 26, Entomology 26, ology, Public Health and
Zoology 25, Geology 27, 28, Chemistry 29, 30. Zoology.

178. GENETICS OF ANIMAL POPULATIONS.—The principles of the genetics of animal populations with emphasis upon its basic techniques and methods, its goals and contributions. The population approach to the study of the origin of species and human genetics will also be considered. Given in alternate years, beginning 1955-56. Credit, 2.
Enrollment limited to 10. Mr. RAUCH.
One 2-hour lecture-discussion period per week.
Prerequisite, Zoology 53 or equivalent and permission of the instructor.

182. MAMMALOGY.—The paleontology, taxonomy, speciation, natural history, range and distribution of the class Mammalia. Primary emphasis will be placed upon the study of local fauna, including at least one week-end collecting trip as part of the laboratory exercises. Course limited to fifteen students. Given in alternate years, beginning 1954-55. Credit, 3.
Two class hours; one 2-hour laboratory period. Mr. DEARDEN.

183. GENERAL AND CELLULAR PHYSIOLOGY.—A course designed to introduce the student to modern trends in physiology. Emphasis is on the chemical and physical activities of the single cell. Topics include: protoplasmic organization, cellular metabolism, permeability, bioelectric phenomena, muscle contraction and radiation biology. Credit, 4.
Three class hours; one 3-hour laboratory period. Mr. SWENSON.
Prerequisites, one year biology; organic chemistry.

184. COMPARATIVE PHYSIOLOGY.—A course designed to acquaint students with physiological principles involved in adaptations of animals to their environments. In the laboratory, experimental methods used to study adaptive mechanisms will be emphasized.   Credit, 4.
Three class hours; one 3-hour laboratory period.   Mr. ROBERTS.
Prerequisites, Zoology 1, 35 (or 183).

186. FISHERY BIOLOGY.—Theory in the practice of regulating fresh-water fisheries; the physical and biological conditions of the environment and their influence on fish populations.   Credit, 3.
Prerequisite, Zoology 181 and permission of the instructor.   Mr. ANDREWS.

187. ENDOCRINOLOGY.—The importance of the endocrines in their control over normal functions (growth, metabolism, reproduction, etc.) in a variety of animals.   Credit, 3.
Two class hours; one 3-hour laboratory period.   Mr. SNEDECOR.

COURSES IN OTHER DEPARTMENTS FOR WHICH MAJOR CREDIT WILL BE GIVEN

Chemistry 193-194. BIOCHEMISTRY.   Credit, 4 each semester.
                                                                    Mr. LITTLE.

Entomology 212. GEOGRAPHICAL DISTRIBUTION.—Geographic distribution of animals and plants, with partciular reference to insects, insect migrations.
                                                                    Credit, 2.
                                                                    Mr. ALEXANDER.

COURSES FOR MINOR CREDIT ONLY

150. HISTOLOGY OF VERTEBRATES.   Credit, 3.
                                                                    Mr. ROLLASON.

153. GENETICS.   Credit, 3.
                                                                    Mr. RAUCH.

171. COMPARATIVE VERTEBRATE ANATOMY.   Credit, 4.
                                            Mr. BARTLETT and Mr. DEARDEN.

172. VERTEBRATE EMBRYOLOGY.   Credit, 4.
                                    Mr. WOODSIDE, Mr. RAUCH and Mr. BARTLETT.

180. ORNITHOLOGY.   Credit, 3.
                                            Mr. BARTLETT and Mr. NUTTING.

181. VERTEBRATE ZOOLOGY.   Credit, 3.
                                            Mr. ANDREWS and Mr. BARTLETT.

185. THE CLASSES OF ARTHROPODS OTHER THAN INSECTS.   Credit, 3.
                                                                    Mr. HANSON

INDEX

INDEX *(Continued)*

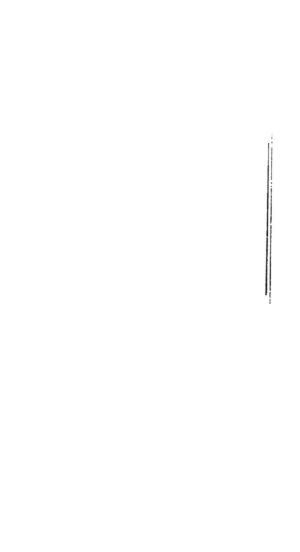

Other University of Massachusetts
Catalogs:

- Annual Undergraduate Cata
- Stockbridge School Catalog
- Summer School Catalog

NDERGRADUATE SCHOO

University
of
Massachusetts
at Amherst

Catalogue of the University
1955-1956

CONTENTS

FOREWORD

This Catalogue of the University presents announcements concerning courses, admission, etc., for the sessions of 1955-56.

The University reserves, for itself and its departments, the right to withdraw or change the announcements made in its catalogue.

VOLUME XLVII   FEBRUARY, 1955   NUMBER 2

Published six times a year by the University of Massachusetts, January, February, April (two), May, September.

Entered at Post Office, Amherst, Mass., as second class matter.

The University Catalogue for the sessions 1955-56 is part of the Ninety-first Annual Report of the University of Massachusetts and as such is part II of Public Document 31. Sec. 8, Chapter 75, of the General Laws of Massachusetts.

PUBLICATION OF THIS DOCUMENT APPROVED BY
GEORGE J. CRONIN, STATE PURCHASING AGENT

12m-1-55-913951

CALENDAR

1955

September

16-20 — Friday through Tuesday. Freshman Orientation.
19 — Monday. Registration of sophomore, junior, senior and graduate students.
20 — Tuesday. Registration of freshman students.
21 — Wednesday, 8 a.m. Classes begin.
22 — Thursday, 10:45 a.m. All University Convocation.

October

12 — Wednesday. Columbus Day. No University exercises.

November

11 — Friday. Veteran's Day. No University exercises.
23-28 — Wednesday, 12 noon to Monday, 8 a.m. Holiday recess.

December

17 — Saturday, 12 noon to January 3, Tuesday, 8 a.m. Holiday recess.

1956

January

19 — Thursday, 5 p.m. Classes stop.
20 — Friday. Registration of sophomore, junior, senior and graduate students.
21 — Saturday. Registration of freshmen students.
23 — Monday to February 1, Wednesday. Examinations.

February

6 — Monday, 8 a.m. Second semester begins.
22 — Wednesday. Washington's Birthday. No University exercises.

March

24 — Saturday, 12 noon to April 2, Monday, 8 a.m. Spring recess.

April

19 — Thursday, Patriot's Day. No University exercises.

May

19 — Saturday, 12 noon. Classes stop.
21 — Monday to May 31, Thursday. Final examinations.
30 — Wednesday. Memorial Day. No University exercises.

June

1-3 — Friday to Sunday. Commencement.

BOARD OF TRUSTEES

6

STANDING TRUSTEE COMMITTEES[1]

Committee on Faculty and Program of Study

FRANK L. BOYDEN, *Chairman*
GRACE A. BUXTON
DENNIS M. CROWLEY
JOHN J. DESMOND
MRS. ELIZABETH L. MCNAMARA
LEWIS PERRY

Committee on Agriculture and Horticulture

ALDEN C. BRETT, *Chairman*
HARRY D. BROWN
DENNIS M. CROWLEY
L. ROY HAWES
ERNEST HOFTYZER
PHILIP F. WHITMORE

Committee on Buildings and Grounds

PHILIP F. WHITMORE, *Chairman*
ALDEN C. BRETT
JOHN W. HAIGIS
F. ROLAND MCDERMOTT
RALPH F. TABER

Committee on Finance

JOHN W. HAIGIS, *Chairman*
ALDEN C. BRETT
WILLIAM M. CASHIN
F. ROLAND MCDERMOTT
PHILIP F. WHITMORE

Committee on Recognized Student Activities

FRANK L. BOYDEN, *Chairman*
HARRY D. BROWN
GRACE A. BUXTON
ERNEST HOFTYZER
RALPH F. TABER

Committee on Legislation

WILLIAM M. CASHIN, *Chairman*
HARRY D. BROWN
JOHN W. HAIGIS
MRS. ELIZABETH L. MCNAMARA
RALPH F. TABER

Executive Committee

JOSEPH W. BARTLETT, *Chairman*
FRANK L. BOYDEN
ALDEN C. BRETT
WILLIAM M. CASHIN
PHILIP F. WHITMORE

---

[1] The President of the University and the Chairman of the Board are ex officio members of each committee.

OFFICERS OF ADMINISTRATION

President
JEAN PAUL MATHER   South College

Secretary
JAMES WILLIAM BURKE   South College

Treasurer
KENNETH WILLIAM JOHNSON   South College

Dean of Men
ROBERT STODDART HOPKINS, JR.   South College

Dean of Women
HELEN CURTIS   South College

Registrar
MARSHALL OLIN LANPHEAR   South College

Dean of Graduate School
GILBERT LLEWELLYN WOODSIDE   Fernald Hall

Director of Experiment Station
DALE HAROLD SIELING   East Experiment Station

Director of Extension Service
JAMES WILLIAM DAYTON   Munson Hall

Director of Stockbridge School
FRED PAINTER JEFFREY   South College

Librarian
HUGH MONTGOMERY   Goodell Library

Business Manager
HOBART HAYES LUDDEN   South College

Director of Publications
ROBERT JOSEPH MCCARTNEY   South College

Senior Physician
ERNEST JAMES RADCLIFFE   Out Patient Department

Director of Placement
EMORY ELLSWORTH GRAYSON   South College

Alumni Secretary
ROBERT LEAVITT   Memorial Hall

GENERAL INFORMATION

The University of Massachusetts is the state university of the Commonwealth, founded under provisions of the Morrill Land Grant Act of Congress of 1862.

Location

The University of Massachusetts is located near the geographical center of the state at Amherst. This town of about 7,000 overlooks one of the most picturesque sections of the Connecticut River Valley. The valley is noted both for its scenic beauty and its educational institutions. The setting for the University, therefore, is ideal. The surrounding country is a rich agricultural region providing an excellent outdoor laboratory for the work in Agriculture and Horticulture as well as for the Biological Sciences and Geology. Those interested in other Sciences and Liberal Arts study under equally favorable conditions both because of the facilities at the University and its location in this educational area of the valley.

Amherst is eighty-seven miles from Boston and may be reached by bus connections from Northampton, Greenfield, Springfield, and Worcester. The campus consists of a tract of approximately seven hundred acres, lying about a mile north of the village center. In addition, the University owns one area of 755 acres six miles north of the campus on Mt. Toby and has recently been given another tract of 1200 acres of readily accessible forest land on Mt. Lincoln several miles to the east of the campus. These holdings are administered by the Department of Forestry and are used in instruction as demonstration forests.

The University also operates a horticultural field station at Waltham and a cranberry field station at East Wareham.

Functions

The University of Massachusetts now serves the Commonwealth in the three important fields of resident instruction, research, and extension. Since all three services are organized on the campus, students have the advantages that come from contact with persons carrying education to the state at large, with others conducting original investigation as well as those engaged in formal instruction.

9

BRANCHES OF INSTRUCTION.

The Undergraduate College

The University offers four-year undergraduate instruction leading to the following degrees: Bachelor of Science, Bachelor of Arts, Bachelor of Science in Agricultural, Chemical, Civil, Electrical and Mechanical Engineering, Bachelor of Business Administration and Bachelor of Vocational Agriculture.

This instruction is assigned to the College of Arts and Sciences, the Schools of Agriculture and Horticulture, Business Administration, Engineering, Home Economics, Nursing and to the Division of Physical Education. The aim of the four-year course is to give as high a degree of proficiency in some particular branch of learning as is possible without sacrificing the breadth, knowledge, and training which should characterize a well-rounded college education.

The degree of Bachelor of Science is conferred upon those candidates who complete the curriculum requirements of the freshman and sophomore years, and 60 junior-senior credits including the specialization requirements in a particular biological or physical science department of the College of Arts and Sciences. The Bachelor of Sciences degree is awarded also to students who complete the curriculum requirements of the Schools of Agriculture and Horticulture, Home Economics, Nursing, and the Division of Physical Education for men. This degree may be granted to students majoring in Education or Psychology who complete a minimum of 15 junior-senior credits in science departments of the College.

The degree of Bachelor of Arts is awarded to all candidates who complete the curriculum requirements of the freshman and sophomore years in the College of Arts and Sciences and 60 junior-senior credits including the specialization requirements of a liberal arts department in the College. This degree may be awarded also to majors in a biological or physical science department who select a minimum of 18 junior-senior credits in liberal arts departments of the College.

All graduates from the School of Engineering will receive the appropriate degrees of Bachelor of Science in Chemical Engineering, Civil Engineering, Electrical Engineering, Mechanical Engineering or Agricultural Engineering.

All graduates from the School of Business Administration will receive the degree of Bachelor of Business Administration.

Special arrangements are made for some graduates, of county agricultural schools and of agricultural departments of certain high schools to complete the college course with majors in agriculture or horticulture. Upon the completion of their course they will be granted a Bachelor of Vocational Agriculture degree.

The Graduate School

Graduate courses leading to the Doctor of Philosophy degree may be taken in the following fields: Agronomy, Bacteriology, Botany, Chemistry, Economics, Entomology, Food Science, Food Technology and Psychology.

The following departments offer major work leading to a Master's degree: Agricultural Economics, Agronomy, Animal Husbandry, Bacteriology, Botany, Chemistry, Civil Engineering, Dairy Industry, Economics, Education, Electrical Engineering, English, Entomology, Floriculture, Food Technology, Geology and Mineralogy, History, Home Economics, Landscape Architecture, Mathematics, Mechanical Engineering, Olericulture, Philosophy, Physical Education for Men, Pomology, Poultry Science, Psychology, Public Health, Romance Languages, Wildlife Management, Zoology.

The degree of Master of Landscape Architecture is granted to students completing the two years' graduate work offered by the Department of Landscape Architecture; while students taking the equivalent of one year's graduate work in that major may be granted the degree of Bachelor of Landscape Architecture.

Several other departments in the University, while not regularly organized for major work in the Graduate School, do, nevertheless, offer courses which may be selected for minor credit. These are: Forestry, Physics, and Veterinary Science.

The general requirements of the Graduate School regarding admission, residence, credits, tuition, etc., together with specific information concerning details of interest to prospective students, are outlined in a separate bulletin, which may be obtained upon request from the Dean of the Graduate School.

The School of Business Administration offers, through the Graduate School of the University, a program of advanced study in Business leading to the degree of Master of Business Administration.

The Summer School

A Summer Session is available for those desiring to accelerate their program. This Summer Session is planned to serve the needs of (1) all students enrolled as candidates for a degree at any college, (2) persons desiring refresher or professional improvement courses, (3) graduate students desirous of meeting specific requirements in certain fields, and (4) any adult person who finds courses suited to his preparation and needs. Applications for the Summer

School may be obtained by writing to the Director of the Summer Session.

Non-Degree Short Courses

The University, through its Short Course division, as a special service under the Land-Grant Act by which it was established, provides a complete program of two-year technical and vocational courses in the fields of agriculture and horticulture. These train for all types of commercial farming operations as practiced in New England.

Other short courses, varying in length from one to ten weeks, furnish supplementary training for city and town sanitary inspectors, tree wardens and city foresters, golf course greenkeepers, and skilled workers in dairy and ice cream plants.

The Stockbridge School of Agriculture

This School was organized at the University in 1918 under the name of "The Two Year Course in Practical Agriculture." Its purpose was to meet the demand for shorter courses in agriculture which might be taken by high school graduates who could not satisfy college entrance requirements or who, for one reason or another, were unable to take the four year college course. In 1928 the School was given its present name in honor of Levi Stockbridge, first professor of agriculture at the University and its fifth president.

This program trains men and women primarily for the practice of farming or associated agricultural industries. Graduation from the School does not fulfill the requirements for entrance into the degree course, nor are credits earned during the course regularly transferable toward credit for a degree. A diploma is awarded for satisfactory completion of any two-year course; for other short courses certificates are presented.

As the two-year program is now organized a student may choose any one of eleven vocational courses including dairy farming, dairy manufactures or milk plant operation; poultry farming, arboriculture or the care of trees; fine turf maintenance for golf courses, cemeteries, park, and play-grounds; commercial flower growing, both retail and wholesale; food management for clubs, hotels, and restaurants; commercial fruit farming, ornamental horticulture or landscape gardening; commercial vegetable farming, and applied forestry for timber growing and forest products industries.

On-the-job placement training is required of all first year students in the second semester for a period of four to seven months, depending on type of employment. No student can earn a diploma of graduation without this applied training experience. Wages earned can pay a large part of second year expenses if the student is forced to economize.

Limited enrollment quotas in each major course make necessary early filing of application. No formal entrance examinations are required for non-degree short courses.

A catalogue, giving complete description of all two-year courses offered in The Stockbridge School of Agriculture, as well as full details on estimated costs, employment opportunities in each field, and entrance arrangements is available. Application form is printed in the catalogue. Write to Director of Short Courses, University of Massachusetts, Amherst.

NOTE: (For interview or personal conference the Short Course Office is open Monday through Friday from 8:30 to 12:00 and 1:00 to 5:00, state and national holidays excepted.)

Research and Regulatory Services

The University of Massachusetts serves the fields of agriculture and horticulture through its Experiment Station, which provides research and regulatory services. Experiment stations were established in all states as the need of development of practical information on subjects relating to agriculture became apparent. Through the efforts of experiment stations a fund of scientific knowledge applicable to agriculture and horticulture has been accumulated, and research workers in the experiment stations continue to contribute to this knowledge by constant research and experimentation.

At the University of Massachusetts, the Experiment Station service has expanded until it now deals with problems in the following fields of specialization: Agricultural Economics and Farm Management, Agronomy, Animal Husbandry, Bacteriology, Botany, Chemistry, Dairy Industry, Economics, Engineering, Entomology, Horticulture, Floriculture, Food Technology, Nutrition, Olericulture, Pomology, Poultry Science, and Veterinary Science. Most of the research activities of the University of Massachusetts are undertaken at the main Experiment Station at Amherst. There are, however, two substations, one at Waltham, devoted largely to the problems of horticulture as applied to olericulture, floriculture, and nursery culture, and one at East Wareham, where attempts are in progress to solve the problems of the cranberry and blueberry growers.

In addition to the work described above, the administration of certain regulatory services, as pertaining to the sale of feeds, fertilizers, and seeds and to the use of dairy glassware, is also assigned to the Experiment Station which is equipped with the necessary laboratory facilities and personnel for that purpose.

13

Extension Service

The Massachusetts Extension Service is a cooperative teaching effort between the United States Department of Agriculture, the University of Massachusetts and the several counties of the State. The work of the Extension Service is carried on through unified teaching programs in all parts of Massachusetts. The Extension Service assists the people of the farm, the home, and the rural communities to improve agriculture, home making, and rural life. The University of Massachusetts is the State Extension Service headquarters. Extension educational teaching plans are made in council with the people who determine their problems and help to suggest methods and practices for their solution.

The Extension effort was brought about by the Smith-Lever Law, passed by Congress on May 8, 1914. Since that time, the service has grown to a staff of over 100 State and County workers who conduct an educational program in all phases of agriculture and home-making among the adults and young people (4-H Club work) of the State. All types of methods, including subject matter, meetings, demonstrations, farm and home visits, publications, visual aid, and radio are used in carrying out this educational program directly in the farm and rural areas of the State. During the war emergency, the Extension Service extended its home food production and preservation program to the urban areas.

ADMISSION

Persons interested in applying for admission to the University of Massachusetts should write to the Registrar to obtain an application form. The first two pages of the application form are completed by the candidate himself. The last two are completed by high school or preparatory school authorities who mail the application form directly to the Registrar of the University.

Because of the increasing interest in college level study and the consequent increase in the number of applications, candidates are advised to file their applications early in the senior year of high school and certainly not later than March 1 of the year in which they plan to enter.

Candidates for the freshman class are accepted only for the opening of the college year in September. Students enrolled in other colleges may apply for admission to the Summer Session, but admission to the Summer Session does not necessarily constitute regular admission and enrollment in the undergraduate program of the University.

The University admits young men and women to the freshman class chiefly on the basis of character and scholarship. The general record must indicate promise of success and ability to profit by the opportunities which the University has to offer. Due regard is given to special achievement in specified subject matter fields.

Methods

Plan A. Students applying from accredited schools and making the college recommendation grade of their school in accordance with the subject requirements listed above are considered certified for admission.

Superior graduates of Vocational Schools of Agriculture in Massachusetts and Vocational Agricultural Departments in Massachusetts High Schools may be accepted for the Degree of Bachelor of Vocational Agriculture provided:

a. They are unqualifiedly recommended by the Vocational Division of the Department of Education as bona fide Vocational Graduates with superior ranks; and

b. That they can present at least 16 units of certified entrance credits, approved as to quality and quantity by the State Department of Vocational Education.

Plan B. Students who are not fully certified will be required to take the Scholastic Aptitude Test of the College Entrance Examination Board. In some cases three Achievement Tests will be required also. The applicant will be informed what tests are to be taken as soon as his application is received or at the time of his personal interview. Candidates will ordinarily take these examinations in the spring of their senior year. Application blanks and a bulletin of general information concerning the tests may be obtained from the College Entrance Examination Board, P. O. Box 592, Princeton, New Jersey.

The University realizes that though almost all students will qualify under either Plan A or B, there will be a few promising candidates who, for one reason or another, are unable to meet fully the subject requirements for enrollment. Such applicants are requested to present their individual problems to the Registrar in order that the Admissions Committee may outline for them what must be done to qualify for enrollment.

Advanced Standing

A limited number of students from approved colleges may be admitted on transfer to advanced standing. Since applicants for such admission usually exceed the number that can be accepted, they are placed on a competitive basis. Acceptance will thus depend upon recommendations and quality of record.

Candidates desiring to transfer to the University of Massachusetts from other institutions should write to the Registrar for a regular application form, inasmuch as a student applying for transfer must first of all be able to meet the entrance requirements of the University. Such candidates should also submit the following:

a. A letter outlining reasons for wishing to transfer and describing briefly the type of major work to be followed if accepted for admission.

b. An official transcript of entrance credits and college record to be sent by the Registrar of the College from which he wishes to transfer. This should be forwarded as soon as possible after the close of the semester preceding the one for which transfer is sought.

At least forty-five semester hours of work in residence are required of any transfer student desiring to be recommended for the Bachelor's degree.

Subject Requirements

The subjects of preparatory study required for admission call for the satisfactory completion of a four-year high school course or its equivalent and are stated in terms of units. A unit is the equivalent of at least four recitations a week for a school year. High school graduation alone is not sufficient. The applicant's record must indicate capacity for handling the quality of scholastic work which the University has established as its standard of achievement.

Sixteen units of secondary school work must be offered, selected according to the following requirements:

Algebra	1½
Plane Geometry	1
English	4
Foreign Language (2 years of 1 language) . . .	2
U.S. History	1

The remaining units are elective and may be selected from the following subject matter:

a. Mathematics.
b. Science
c. Foreign Language
d. History and Social Studies
e. Free electives (not more than four units)

Free elective subjects are those not included in groups a-d, as for example: Music, Art, Drawing, Typewriting, Aeronautics, Agriculture, Home Economics, etc. Such free electives are allowed in order that the student who wishes may have some opportunity to elect other high school offerings, while at the same time covering the fundamental requirements for college work.

Students planning to pursue an engineering curriculum should offer two years of Algebra, one of Plane Geometry, and one-half year each of Trigonometry and Solid Geometry, Chemistry and Physics are also advised. Those deficient in the Mathematics should plan to cover it during the summer prior to entrance or expect to take five years to complete the college course.

In high schools organizing agricultural club work under the supervision and rules of the Junior Extension Service of the University, one credit is granted for each full year of work approved by the State Leaders.

Candidates of exceptional ability and promise may be considered for admission even though some of the prescribed courses were not included in their high school program.

Physical Examination

Physical examination by their local doctor is required of all entering freshmen, re-entering students and all students participating in athletics. Physical report forms for this examination will be mailed to each student with the bill for the first semester and must be completed and returned to the University Health Service 10 days before the opening of the semester. Evidence of a *successful* smallpox vaccination is required.

Veterans' Affairs

The Veterans' Coordinator is a member of the Placement Service.

Veterans enrolling for the first time under Public Law 346 must file a Certificate of Eligibility with the Placement Office prior to or at registration. All veterans should clear their affairs through the Placement Service.

EXPENSES

The sections of the catalogue that follow are primarily for undergraduate students in the four year degree course. Those interested in graduate study are referred to the Graduate School catalogue and in short courses to the catalogue of the Stockbridge School of Agriculture and other short course publications.

University Fees

Expenses vary from approximately $750 to $850 per year for the normally economical student. First year costs are usually greater than those of the other three years and there is less opportunity to earn. A student is advised to have a definite plan for meeting the expenses of the first year before entering.

Freshmen entering the School of Engineering should be prepared to meet an expense of approximately $35 for drawing equipment and a slide rule.

The following estimate of a year's expenses, based upon last year's costs, includes only those items which are strictly college and does not include amounts for clothing, laundry, travel, etc. These costs vary slightly from year to year. Tuition for residents of Massachusetts is $100 per year and for others $400.

	Normal
Tuition (citizens of Massachusetts)	$100.00
Room in college dormitory or private home (ave.) .	165.00
Board at University Dining Hall	430.00
Books, stationery, and other supplies . . .	90.00
Athletic Fee	20.00
Student Tax (approx.)	18.50
	$823.50

Initial Payment for Freshmen

The initial payment required of freshmen at the time of fall registration is indicated below and is made up of the following items:

Tuition (citizens of Massachusetts)	$50.00
Room rent (dormitory) approximately . . .	82.50
Board (University Dining Hall)	165.00
Military Uniform (men students)	30.00

Athletic Fee	.	.	.	.	.	.	.	.	20.00
Student Tax (approx.)	.	.	.	.	..	.	.		10.00
Books, Stationery, etc.	.	.	.	.	.	.	.		45.00

$402.50

The above are only approximate figures. A bill will be rendered to the parent of each student prior to the opening of the University.

Tuition

As a state institution the University of Massachusetts offers a low rate of tuition to all students entering from the Commonwealth. Eligibility for admission under the low residential rate is determined in accordance with the following policy established by the Board of Trustees.

A student must present evidence satisfactory to the Treasurer of the University that his domicile is in the Commonwealth of Massachusetts in order to be considered eligible to register in the University as a resident student. This means that he must have established a *bona fide* residence in the Commonwealth with the intention of continuing to maintain it as such.

The domicile of a minor shall follow that of the parents unless such minor has been emancipated. In case of emancipation the student, in addition to the requirements of these regulations, respecting residence, shall present satisfactory proof respecting emancipation. Minors under guardianship shall be required to present, in addition to the certification of the domicile of the guardian, satisfactory documentary evidence of the appointment of the guardian.

No student shall be considered to have gained residence by reason of his attendance in the University nor shall a student lose residential preference during his continuous attendance at the University.

The residence of a wife shall follow that of the husband.

The prescribed form of application for classification as to residence status must be executed by each student. Misrepresentation of facts in order to evade the payment of out-of-state tuition shall be considered sufficient cause for suspension or permanent exclusion from the University.

Discretion to adjust individual cases within the spirit of these rules is lodged with the President of the University.

Board

The University provides three dining halls for students at Butterfield House, Greenough House and University Dining Commons. The dining halls at Butterfield and Greenough dormitories are intended primarily to provide for students housed in that area, including residents of Chadbourne, Mills and Brooks Houses.

All freshmen except commuters will be required to board at University dining halls on a five-day week basis.

Sophomores and juniors residing in University dormitories and other campus buildings will also be required to board at University Dining Halls except that such students who are members of fraternities or sororities may be permitted upon request to board at their respective fraternities or sororities.

Any student who wishes may board at University dining halls on the ticket plan or cash basis.

Military Uniform

All students taking military drill are required to make a deposit of $30 for the uniform. A rebate of this amount is made when the uniform is returned.

Student Activity Tax

This tax, authorized by vote of the undergraduate students with the approval of the Board of Trustees, provides each student with the Collegian, the student newspaper; Index, University annual; Social Union privileges, student government, class and other activities.

PAYMENTS

Advanced Payment

New students will be expected to make an advance payment of $15 to the Treasurer of the University as soon as they are notified by the Registrar that they are accepted for admission. This will be considered as first payment on registration fee, which will be due at time of matriculation in September. It is not refundable and will be considered as payment for admissions and registration expense if the student does not matriculate.

A Certificate of Residence form furnished by the University must be properly filled out by the parent and the town or city clerk and returned with the $15.00 advance payment.

When Payments Are Due

In accordance with policy established by the Board of Trustees, all charges for tuition, fees, board, and room rent in University Dormitories are due and payable seven days prior to the date of registration of each semester. Bills will be rendered in advance

21

and payment may best be made by mail. Students may not register until registration charges are paid.

Late Payment and Registration

Any student who does not make payment of his semester charges within the time specified may be required to pay a fine of $5.00. Similarly, any student who does not report for registration on the dates specified or fails to complete his registration within the prescribed time may be required to pay a late registration fee of $5.00.

Tuition and Fee Refunds

A student who leaves the University for any reason except as specified below before a semester is completed will be granted a refund of tuition and fees in accordance with the following schedule:

Regular Term
   a. Within the first two weeks from the beginning of semester or term — 80%
   b. During the third week — 60%
   c. During the fourth week — 40%
   d. During the fifth week — 20%
   e. After the fifth week — no refund

Six-Week Summer Session
   a. During the first week — 60%
   b. During the second week — 20%
   c. After the second week — no refund

A student who makes an advance payment and then for any reason does not attend any part of the next semester or term at the University will be given a full refund of tuition and fees. The $15.00 advance payment fee required of new students is not refundable.

A student who is involuntarily called into military service before the completion of a semester will be given a pro rata refund of tuition and fees provided that he receives no academic credit for the work of that semester. If academic credit is given, there will be no refund.

Room Rent Refunds

It is the policy of the University that there will be no refund of prepaid room rent after the semester has commenced except in the case of a student who is involuntarily called to military service who will be granted a refund on a pro rata basis.

A student who has made an advance payment of room rent who fails to attend any part of the next semester or term or does not reside in a dormitory or other housing will be granted a full refund of prepaid room rent.

Board Refunds

Prepaid board will be refunded on a pro rata basis.

A student who is expelled or suspended from the University for disciplinary reasons forfeits all rights to a refund.

Veterans' Information

Veterans who are entering the University for the first time under the old G.I. Bill (P.L. 346) must present a Certificate of Eligibility at registration. This may be obtained from your nearest Veterans Administration office. Veterans failing to obtain the Certificate of Eligibility must make payment of tuition and fees in order to register. Board and room fees must be paid in advance whether enrolled under the G.I. Bill or not.

Veterans (under P.L. 346) who are transferring to the University of Massachusetts from another institution or who have done summer work at another institution will be required to submit a supplemental Certificate of Eligibility at registration. This may be obtained by applying through the veterans' office at the institution last attended.

Veterans entering under the new G.I. Bill (P.L. 550) must meet all expenses personally. Presentation of a Certificate of Eligibility should insure the receipt of subsistence checks from the Veterans Administration.

Financial Requirements for Graduation

Diplomas, transcripts of record, and letters of honorable dismissal will be withheld from all students who have not paid all bills and all loans due the University or all legitimate bills for room rent and board due fraternities or private individuals. All such bills due the University must be paid ten days preceding Commencement. If paid after that date and the student is otherwise eligible, he may graduate the following year.

FINANCIAL AID

Scholarships, loans, and part-time employment are available for a limited number of needy and deserving students. See page 33.

Aid for Freshman Year

Freshmen are eligible for scholarships and part-time employment. A freshman also becomes eligible for assistance from loan funds after satisfactorily completing one semester of academic work. Scholarship application blanks may be secured from the Registrar and should be filed by May 1. Part-time employment application forms may be obtained from the Director of Placement Service and filed after a candidate has been accepted for admission.

Because of the time required for preparation of studies, few students should plan to spend more than ten hours per week in part-time employment.

Aid for Upperclassmen

To become eligible for financial assistance, whether scholarship, loan, or part-time employment students must file completed financial aid application forms with the Student Aid Committee in the Placement Service office by March 1 previous to the college year for which assistance is asked.

Aid for Graduates of the University

The Lotta M. Crabtree Agricultural Funds make available to graduates of the University of Massachusetts funds to be used for farm financing.

The purpose of loans from these funds is to assist meritorious graduates who are without means in establishing themselves in agricultural pursuits. These loans are made without interest or service charges other than the cost of title search and legal papers. They must, however, be paid back in full amount within a reasonable length of time and there are certain restrictions on their use.

Applications for the "Lotta Agricultural Fund" should be addressed to the Trustees of the Lotta M. Crabtree Estate, 619 Washington Street, Boston, Massachusetts, or may be secured at the Placement Office at the University. Decisions regarding the granting of a loan rest entirely with the Trustees under the terms of Miss Crabtree's will.

UNIVERSITY REGULATIONS

Standards of Deportment
The customary high standard of college men and women in honor, self-respect, and consideration for the rights of others constitutes the ideal of student deportment.

The privileges of the University may be withdrawn from any student at any time if such action is deemed advisable.

It should be understood that the University, acting through its President or any administrative officer designated by him, distinctly reserves the right, not only to suspend or dismiss students, but also to name conditions under which they may remain in the institution. For example, if a student is not doing creditable work, he may not only be disciplined, but he may also be required to meet certain prescribed conditions in respect to his studies even though under the foregoing rules his status as student be not affected. The same provision applies equally to the matter of absences. According to the rules, juniors and seniors are allowed a certain percentage of absences from class and other exercises. This permission, which implies a privilege and not a right, may be withdrawn at any time for any cause.

Similarly, it applies to participation in student activities. Though this will ordinarily be governed by the rules as already laid down, yet if in the judgment of the University authorities, a student is neglecting his work on account of these activities, the privilege of participating in them may be withdrawn for such time as is considered necessary; moreover, it may be withdrawn as a punishment for misconduct.

Hazing in the sense of the punishment or humiliation of students is not permitted.

Registration
Every student must report for registration on the appointed day. All late registrants must pay a $5.00 fine. No student will be admitted to any class until he has completed the prescribed registration procedure. Changes of courses on the registration card shall be made only by the Registrar's Office.

Any student who does not complete his registration, including payment of semester charges, on the regular registration days will be required to pay a fine of $5.00.

No course will be recorded on the permanent records of the University nor will a student receive credit for it, unless such course appears on the registration card for the semester and has been properly countersigned by the instructor.

Freshman Week

All members of the incoming freshman class are required to be in residence on the campus for the period known as Freshman Week. During this period an attempt will be made to orient the student. He will be given psychological and mental tests, and a physical examination. Schedules and section assignments will also be arranged. In addition there will be lectures on student activities, customs, and curricula, and a scheduled meeting with the student's adviser.

GRADING SYSTEM

The scholastic record of each student is reported to his parents at the end of each semester. Mid-semester marks are sent to parents for the first semester only. A complete report of the scholarship record of each student during his first semester is sent to the principal of the school from which the student entered.

Marking

All undergraduate marking shall be done according to a letter system under which the classwork of students will be rated as follows:

A — exceptional
B — excellent
C — average
D — passing
F — failure

Inc — the mark, Incomplete, will be reported only when a portion of assigned or required classwork has *not* been completed because of necessary absence of the student or other reason equally satisfactory to the instructor, and then only when the instructor judges the work already done to be of passing quality. Students may obtain credit for course marks of Incomplete only by completing the work of the course before the end of the fourth week of the next semester in which they are enrolled.

Quality Points

Four points are allowed for each credit of work of A grade;.
Three points for each credit of B grade;
Two points for each credit of C grade;
One point for each credit of D grade;

No points are given for grades of F or Inc.

A 2.00 grade point average is required for graduation.

Grade Point Averages

A. *Semester Point Averages:* To compute the semester grade point average, the total points earned will be divided by the total credits carried. Credits carried are defined as total credits earned and failed.

B. *Cumulative Average:* To compute the cumulative grade point average, the total points earned will be divided by total credits carried. Total credits carried will be the sum of the total credits earned and failed. In case courses are repeated only the last grade, credits, and points are considered in computing the cumulative average.

C. In computing grade point averages, the following will *not* be included:

   1. Required military and physical education courses of the Freshman and Sophomore years.

   2. Courses for which students do not receive credit toward a college degree (e.g., Math 01)

Dismissal

Dismissal from the University for scholastic reasons shall be based on the following regulations, to be administered by the Committee on Admissions and Records. A student is dismissed from the University as deficient in scholarship:

A. If at the end of his first semester, he has failed three academic courses and has not earned a grade of C in each of the remaining two academic courses.

B. If at the end of his second semester he has earned fewer than one and one-half (1.5) times as many quality points as the total number of credits for which he has been registered.

C. If at the end of his fourth or of any subsequent semester he has earned fewer than one and seven tenths (1.7) times as many quality points as the total number of credits for which he has been registered.

D. Any student, subject to dismissal under the quality point rule alone will not be dismissed if his work in the current semester is sufficient in quality and quantity that, if he continues such work until he has been in residence ten semesters, he will meet graduation requirements. Any freshman whose cumulative quality point ratio would make him subject to dismissal but whose work in the second semester alone would meet the quality point ratio rule in paragraph C above, will not be dismissed.

27

E. Any student who is dismissed, or any member of the faculty in his behalf, may request reconsideration of the case by the Committee on Admissions and Records.

F. When a student is dismissed from the University for scholastic reasons only, any certificate or transcript issued must contain the statement, "Dismissed for scholastic deficiency but otherwise entitled to honorable dismissal".

G. Dismissal involves non-residence on the University campus or in fraternity or sorority residences coming under University supervision.

Changes in registration—Adding and dropping courses

A. No course will be recorded on the permanent records of the University nor will a student receive credit for it unless the student has registered for such a course in accordance with the established procedure on a regularly scheduled registration day or unless his registration shall have been made official by the signature of the Registrar. A student may not add or drop a course except in accordance with these regulations. A course will not be considered dropped without the signature of the Registrar. A course dropped without approval will be recorded as a failure.

B. A student may add or drop a subject only upon the written recommendation of his advisor (or Dean of the School, College, or Division in which he is enrolled) and the Registrar.

C. The normal time for adding or dropping courses will be established and recorded in the official University Calendar by the selection of the nearest practicable date which will allow approximately three weeks from the last scheduled official registration day of each semester. The selection of this date shall be the responsibility of the Provost of the University. A student adding a course without written approval of his advisor and confirmation by the Registrar, will not receive credit for the course. A student may not enroll in a course after the established registration date without the approval of the instructor. A student dropping a course without approval will receive a failure in the course. A course dropped with approval within the three week period will not be counted in calculating quality points.

D. A course dropped after the date regularly established in the University Calendar will receive a mark of WF (withdrawn failing). This mark will be computed in the quality point average. If a student presents a valid reason for dropping a course after the established date, with a statement from his instructor that he is passing at the time and after approval (as indicated in B above), the course will be recorded as WP (withdrawn passing). No substitute course may be added for a course so dropped, and the WP grade is not computed in the quality point average.

E. In case of voluntary withdrawal from the University, the rules for WF and WP grades will apply to the entire course program of the student withdrawing.

Change of Major

A student wishing to change his major must get a Program Change Card at the Registrar's Office. This change is to be approved by the head of the Department or School in which he is now majoring and also by his new major adviser. This card, properly indorsed, must be returned to the Registrar's Office before the change receives final approval.

Graduation Requirements

At the beginning of his freshman year each student selects a school or division in which he will carry his major work. One of the fundamental objectives of all programs, however, regardless of School, is a general cultural education which should be the mark of every college graduate.

With this end in view all candidates for the B.S. or A.B. degree must take certain required courses: English 1, 2, 25, 26; Speech 3 and 4; two social sciences to be selected from Economics 25, Psychology 26, and Sociology 28; and twelve semester hours of science. In addition, at least three hours must be elected from one of the following: History 5, 6, 59, 60, or Government 25.

The requirements in Physical Education must also be satisfied. All physically fit men students must take Military 1, 2, 25, and 26.

Since the work of the first two years is directed toward a broad, general education as a foundation for the more specialized training of juniors and seniors, it follows that the program of studies for all schools is fairly uniform up to the junior year. Because of this, students can readily change from one curriculum to another or even from one school to another as both freshmen and sophomores.

Regardless of major, students who plan to teach should register early, in their freshman year if possible, with the Department of Education, although their work there does not begin until the junior year.

The minimum requirement for graduation is 60 junior-senior credits in addition to the satisfactory completion of the required and elective work of the first two years. Except upon special permission from the Provost or Registrar, no junior or senior shall enroll for more than 17 or less than 14 credits each semester.

29

During the junior and senior years, each student shall complete not less than 15, and not more than 30 credits in junior-senior courses in the department in which he is specializing.

It is the policy of the University that the final forty-five semester hours of scholastic work be taken in residence. Residence, for this purpose, is defined as a period of continuous enrollment and regular attendance in classes conducted on the campus of the University.

Transcripts

Two transcripts of a student's record will be furnished without cost. For each additional copy there will be a charge of one dollar.

Student Housing

It is the policy of the Board of Trustees that freshman men and women students shall be housed in campus dormitories and be required to eat at University dining halls unless given permission to commute. Sophomore and upper-class students will also be required to live in University dormitories in so far as accommodations are available. Those who cannot be so housed will be given permission to live in fraternity or sorority houses or in private homes.

Students who are assigned to housing operated by the University, or homes approved by the University, are expected to occupy them for the entire school year and may not be released sooner except as their places are taken by suitable substitutes.

Dormitories will be open for occupancy at 1 p.m. on the day immediately preceding the opening of the University.

Students assigned to dormitory rooms will be responsible for the room rent of the entire semester. Room rent is not refundable.

Rooms are furnished except for necessary bedding and linen are cared for by the students occupying them. Each occupant is held responsible for any damage.

All student property must be removed from the rooms and the key turned in to the Treasurer's Office immediately after final examinations in June. Such property not removed by the owner will be removed by the University and stored at the owner's expense.

Rooms for Women Students.

Dormitory rooms are available for women students at Abigail Adams, Crabtree, Leach, Hamlin, Knowlton, Lewis and Thatcher Houses and at a new dormitory completed in September, 1954, and still to be named.

Under the supervision of the Dean of Women, life in each dormitory is directed by a council of student leaders, advised by a full-time Housemother, so that conditions in the residence halls are conducive to study and good living habits. Through the women's branch of the Student Government, the responsibility is put upon each student to live according to her own best standards as well as according to the standards of the group.

Freshman girls will be assigned rooms in the dormitory and will be notified of the assignment prior to the beginning of college.

Near the close of each year, upperclass women will draw numbers to determine the order in which rooms may be chosen for the coming year.

Only students living in their own homes may commute. Upperclass women may apply to the Dean of Women for permission to live in a sorority house, or to earn room and board in a private home.

Rooms for Men Students.

Dormitory rooms are available for male students at Baker, Butterfield, Brooks, Chadbourne, Greenough, Berkshire, Middlesex and Plymouth Houses, and at a new dormitory to be completed by September, 1955.

Upperclassmen should make dormitory room reservations at the Housing Office before May 1. Those who cannot be accommodated in dormitories will be given permission to live in fraternities or private homes. Assignment of dormitory rooms will be under the supervision of the Housing Office.

Rooms for Married Students.

The University cannot guarantee facilities for married students; however, those married students who can be accommodated will be housed in the University Apartment Units. Assignments are under the direction of the Housing Office and all inquiries should be addressed to that office. Some students may be able to locate rooms or apartments off campus.

The University of Massachusetts reserves the right to change room assignments whenever necessary.

Advisory System

In order that from the day he enrolls the freshman may have some one to whom he may go for consultation and assistance, each student is assigned to a faculty adviser at the time of registration. It is the function of this adviser to help the student in adjusting himself to the work and life of the University. Academic progress reports issued by the Provost's Office are sent to the advisers periodically, and the students are expected to report to their advisers from time to time to discuss their academic standing. The adviser also forwards reports of academic standing to the parents. Both students and parents are encouraged to consult with the adviser whenever there are problems regarding studies or personal adjustments to college life.

At the beginning of the second semester of the freshman year each student will discuss his vocational and specialization plans with his adviser. If he can decide definitely upon the department in which he wishes to specialize, and the adviser approves, the student takes his election card to the head of that department for approval. In cases where students are not ready to designate a department of specialization they continue as general majors during the sophomore year under the direction of an adviser assigned by the head of the School in which the student is enrolled. Such general majors must select their field of specialization by the end of the sophomore year.

During the junior and senior years the student is under the guidance of the head of the department in which he is majoring or an adviser assigned by him.

Automobiles

Members of the freshmen and sophomore classes, also students who are on probation of any kind are not permitted to have automobiles on the campus or in the town of Amherst. All students who are privileged to have automobiles on campus are required to register their vehicles with the Campus police at the time of registration, or immediately after bringing their automotive equipment to the campus for the first time.

SCHOLARSHIPS AND LOANS

Scholarships are awarded only to needy and deserving students of high character whose habits of life are economical and whose scholastic records are satisfactory. A limited number of these scholarships are available for entering freshmen.

Scholarships are paid in installments at the beginning of each semester in the form of a credit on the student's bill. A scholarship may be discontinued at the close of any semester.

If the scholarship student withdraws from the University, any refund of of University fees or charges must first be applied to reimburse the scholarship fund for the full amount of the scholarship received by the student for the semester.

GENERAL SCHOLARSHIPS

COMMONWEALTH SCHOLARSHIPS. The Commonwealth of Massachusetts annually provides 25 scholarships of not more than $250 for members of each of the four undergraduate classes of the University. Upperclass students may obtain application forms at the Dean of Men's office. Entering freshmen may obtain application forms at the Registrar's Office.

LUCIUS CLAPP FUND to provide scholarships and loans to deserving students.

HENRY GASSETT SCHOLARSHIP for a worthy undergraduate student.

CHARLES A. GLEASON SCHOLARSHIPS. General scholarship for worthy students.

WHITING STREET SCHOLARSHIP. Scholarships of $50 each for deserving students.

UNIVERSITY SCHOLARSHIP. A limited number of scholarships of $100 or more, awarded on the basis of leadership, need, scholarship and participation in extra-curricular activities.

DANFORTH KEYES BANGS SCHOLARSHIP for the aid of industrious and deserving students.

RESTRICTED SCHOLARSHIPS

Area Scholarships

FREDERICK G. CRANE SCHOLARSHIPS for the aid of worthy undergraduate students, preference being given to residents of Berkshire County.

BETSEY C. PINKERTON SCHOLARSHIPS. Two general scholarships for graduates of the schools of the city of Worcester.

WILBUR H. H. WARD SCHOLARSHIPS. Twenty-five scholarships of approximately $100, known as the Wilbur H. H. Ward Scholarships. The Wilbur H. H. Ward Fund is administered by a Board of Trustees independent of the University. Applicants for these scholarships write to Sumner R. Parker, 1 Sunset Court, Amherst. They are available only to Hampshire County Boys.

Class Eligibility Scholarships

CLASS OF 1882 SCHOLARSHIPS for the aid of a worthy student of the junior or senior class.

School of Agriculture and Horticulture

ALVORD. For students specializing in the study of dairy husbandry or dairy manufacturing with the intention of becoming an investigator, teacher, or special practitioner in the dairy industry. Restricted to students who do not use tobacco or fermented beverages.

O. G. ANDERSON MEMORIAL FUND. For needy and worthy students in Pomology. To be used for the purchase of books and supplies. Granted only on the recommendation of the Department of Pomology.

ASCENSION FARM. For men students in the School of Agriculture and Horticulture. Residents of Berkshire County have preference, but awards may be made to students from Hampshire, Hampden, and Franklin Counties.

BORDEN. One scholarship of $300 to be awarded to a Senior in the School of Agriculture and Horticulture who has the highest scholarship average in all work through the Junior year and who has completed two or more courses in dairying.

BOSTON MARKET GARDENERS' ASSOCIATION. A $100 scholarship for a Sophomore in agriculture. Applications should be made to the Secretary of the Boston Market Gardeners' Association, 240 Beaver Street, Waltham 54, Massachusetts.

BOSTON STEWARDS' CLUB. For students in Food Management. Three $100 scholarships awarded as recommended by that department.

BUTTRICK. For junior, senior or graduate students majoring in Dairy Industry or Food Technology. Scholarships will range from $100 to $500 per year depending upon scholarship achievement and need.

THE CHARLES M. COX TRUST FUND SCHOLARSHIP of $300 is awarded to a student or students in the School of Agriculture and Horticulture on the basis of need, character and scholarship ability. Preferably the scholarships will be awarded to undergraduate majors in dairy husbandry or poultry husbandry.

LOTTA CRABTREE. For students in Agriculture and Horticulture. Based on scholarship and need.

DANFORTH FOUNDATION. Summer scholarships for outstanding freshman and senior students in Agriculture. For attending a summer camp sponsored by the Danforth Foundation.

ESSO. Scholarships are based on membership in 4-H Club, and applications should be sent to county 4-H Club agents. Scholarship is for $400–$100 per year for students enrolled in some course of agriculture.

J. W. D. FRENCH FUND. For students in Dairy and Forestry, and allied subjects.

CHARLES H. HOOD FOUNDATION awarded to two Juniors and two Seniors in the School of Agriculture and Horticulture, with preference given to those studying the production of milk. Based on scholastic standing, character, industry, and personality.

MARGARET MOTLEY. For a woman student majoring in Floriculture or Landscape Gardening. Need, scholarship, and promise of success form the basis of award.

NEW ENGLAND CLUB MANAGERS' ASSOCIATION. For students in Food Management who are recommended by that department.

PORTER L. NEWTON. For students majoring in Agriculture who are residents of Middlesex County.

FRANK H. PLUMB. For students majoring in Agriculture and Horticulture.

SEARS-ROEBUCK FOUNDATION. Four scholarships for outstanding freshmen in Agriculture and Horticulture, based on scholarship, leadership, personality, business ability, or special achievement. The outstanding freshman recipient is eligible for a special Sophomore scholarship.

SPRINGFIELD GARDEN CLUB. For students living in the vicinity of Springfield, Massachusetts and majoring in some phase of Horticulture.

STATLER HOTEL. For a student in Food Management, and recommended by that department.

TREADWAY HOTELS. For students in Food Management who have worked for the Treadway organization and who are recommended by the Department of Food Management.

UNION AGRICULTURAL MEETING. A $250 scholarship for the Senior in the School of Agriculture and Horticulture having the highest scholastic standing and who has not been given another award based primarily on scholarship.

Engineering Alumni Scholarships

Provided by annual contributions from graduates and friends of the School of Engineering to provide tuition scholarships to deserving and well-qualified students pursuing work in a major field of Engineering. They are available to freshmen and upperclassmen.

Military Scholarships

UNITED STATES ARMY ROTC SCHOLARSHIP. The U. S. Army Reserve Officers Training Corps provides a scholarship, renewable for three years, to a young man with a good scholastic record in secondary school who possesses leadership qualities and can meet the physical requirements for commission as a second lieutenant in the Army Reserve. The applicant must agree to enroll in the basic course, Army ROTC, and to apply for the advanced course, ROTC.

UNITED STATES AIR FORCE ROTC SCHOLARSHIP. The U. S. Air Force Reserve Officers Training Corps in conjunction with the Department of Physical Education offers a scholarship of $100 to an entering male student. This scholarship is solely for tuition and fees and may be renewed for three additional years. It is awarded to a student who possesses leadership qualities, meets the physical standards required for commission in Air Force Reserve, has a good scholastic record in secondary school and agrees to enroll in the basic course, Air Force ROTC and to apply for the advanced course, Air Force ROTC.

4-H Scholarships

COTTING MEMORIAL SCHOLARSHIP. All college expenses of freshman year—for a woman student. Recipient of this scholarship is selected by a committee of the New England Branch of the Farm and Garden Association from among candidates proposed by State Leaders of 4-H Club work in the New England states.

GEORGE L. FARLEY SCHOLARSHIPS. The Massachusetts Society for Promoting Agriculture has established a scholarship in memory of George L. Farley. The income of approximately $60 per semester is awarded to deserving 4-H Club members, men or women, recommended by the State Leader of 4-H Clubs from applications submitted by County 4-H Club Agents.

Scholarships for Women Students Only

CHI OMEGA AWARD. The local chapter of the Chi Omega Sorority offers an annual scholarship of $25 to that woman student majoring in the department of economics or psychology who has the highest scholastic average at the end of the first semester of the senior year.

HELEN A. WHITTIER SCHOLARSHIP for a deserving woman student in art as applied to living.

THE ISOGON AWARD. An award by Isogon, the senior women's honorary society, to a young woman student at the end of her junior year. This award is made on the basis of character and personality, scholastic achievement, campus influence and service.

POLISH JUNIOR LEAGUE SCHOLARSHIP. An award by the Polish Junior League to a woman student of Polish descent, at the end of her junior year, paying full tuition for the senior year. The basis of this award is character and scholastic achievement.

LOANS

Through the generosity of friends of the University, funds have been donated to provide loans for a limited number of students of the three upper classes to assist in paying tuition or other college expenses. These loans are granted, after proper consideration, to needy students of good scholarship whose habits are economical. All loans are secured by a note endorsed by a responsible party as collateral. All such loans must be paid before graduation. Upon withdrawal from the University, loans automatically become due. Interest is charged at the rate of 3% to maturity, 5% thereafter on loans from all funds except the Lotta Agricultural Fund, from which loans are made without interest. Application for loans should be made to the Student Aid Committee, Placement Service Office, South College. No loan will be granted in excess of $200 in any one year.

If funds are available at the beginning of the second semester, loans may be made in exceptional cases to members of the Freshman class whose scholastic record is satisfactory and whose budget calculations have been upset through circumstances beyond their control.

DANFORTH KEYES BANGS FUND. This is a gift of $6,000 from Louisa A. Baker of Amherst, the income of which is used in aiding poor, industrious and deserving students to obtain an education in the University of Massachusetts.

LOTTA AGRICULTURAL FUND. A limited number of loans are made to students from the income of this fund. Such loans are made without interest but only to deserving students of high scholastic rank. This fund is administered by a Board of Trustees independent of the University although loans are made only upon the recommendation of the President of the University.

VINCENT GOLDTHWAIT MEMORIAL LOAN FUND. A gift of $5,000 from Dr. Joel E. Goldthwait in memory of his son. This fund is used almost entirely for students in the Stockbridge School of Agriculture.

FRANK A. WAUGH FOUNDATION. Graduates of the Department of Landscape Architecture and friends of Professor Frank Waugh have established this fund, to be used in part for loans to deserving seniors and fifth year students of that department. Requests for loans shall be reviewed and approved by the head of the department of Landscape Architecture and submitted to the Board of Trustees of the Foundation, who shall make final decision as to granting of the loans and amounts thereof.

4-H SCHOLARSHIP AND LOAN FUND. This fund is under the supervision of the State Leader of the 4-H Clubs and is used to aid students preparing for agricultural and home economics service.

NATIONAL PEST CONTROL ASSOCIATION LOAN FUND. A fund established by the National Pest Control Association for needy students in the field of Entomology.

HONORS, PRIZES, AWARDS

Scholarship Honors

DEPARTMENTAL HONORS. A student who has shown outstanding promise within some department and has maintained a general scholastic average of B or better is permitted to apply for the privilege of registering for departmental honors. If his application is accepted by his department and the Honors Committee, he is allowed to pursue a course of independent study within the department of his choice throughout his senior year. This may include intensive reading, investigation or laboratory work in connection with some problem that he chooses for his consideration. The objective is to create initiative power of independent investigation and to develop the spirit of research. Although the student is responsible for his undertaking he is encouraged to consult with his department in regard to his work should the need arise. At the close of his study the student presents a thesis covering his investigation. In addition he may be required to appear for an oral or written examination. If by the excellence of his work he satisfies all the requirements of his department and the Honors Committee, his name will appear on the commencement program as receiving honors in the field of his specialization.

Scholastic Prizes

PHI KAPPA PHI AWARD FOR SCHOLARSHIP. Massachusetts Chapter of the Phi Kappa Phi, scholarship honor society, offers an award of $50 for outstanding work in scholarship. This is given to some member of the senior class at the opening of school in the fall. The award is based on the record of the first three years.

THE BURNHAM PRIZES. These were made possible through the generosity of Mr. T. O. H. P. Burnham of Boston. Prizes of $15 and $10 are awarded to those students delivering the best and second best declamations in the Burnham contest. The preliminary contests are open under certain restrictions to freshmen and sophomores.

THE FLINT PRIZES. The Flint Oratorical Contest was established in 1881 by a gift of the late Charles L. Flint, a former president of the College. After his death the prizes were continued by college appropriation. Prizes of $30 and $15 are awarded as first and second prizes respectively to those two students delivering the best orations in this contest.

THE HILLS BOTANICAL PRIZE. This is given through the generosity of Henry F. and Leonard M. Hills of Amherst, for the first and second best herbaria. Competition is open to members of the senior, junior and sophomore classes. First prize is $20, second prize $15.

THE BETTY STEINBUGLER PRIZE IN ENGLISH. This prize was endowed by John L. Steinbugler, New York City, in honor of his daughter Elizabeth Steinbugler Robertson, a graduate of this College in 1929. It is awarded to a woman in the junior or senior class who has written the best long paper on a subject of literary investigation in a course in English during the year.

MASSACHUSETTS SOCIETY FOR PROMOTING AGRICULTURE PRIZES. Three prizes of $25, $15, and $10 are awarded to those senior students who are judged to have made the best records in the theoretical and practical work in agriculture required in their course of study, and in the special written and oral examination prepared for this award.

Athletic Prizes

THE ALLAN LEON POND MEMORIAL MEDAL. This medal is awarded for general excellence in football in memory of Allan Leon Pond of the class of 1920, who died February 26, 1920. He was a congenial companion, a devoted lover of Alma Mater, a veteran of World War I, a fine all-round athlete and a true amateur. He would rather win than lose, but he would rather play fair than win. He has been characterized as a typical student of the University.

THE WILLIAM T. EVANS MEMORIAL TROPHY. This trophy is given each year to that member of the varsity football team who through his sportsmanship, football ability, character and personality, has thus exemplified the character and spirit of the person in whose memory this memorial trophy is dedicated. The trophy is dedicated to the memory of William T. Evans, a former member of the class of 1942, who died December 9, 1941. This trophy is presented annually by the class of 1942.

THE THOMAS E. MINKSTEIN MEMORIAL AWARD. This award is made by the class of 1931 in memory of their classmate who died July 16, 1930 while he was captain-elect of football. The award is given to one of the outstanding men in the Junior class who has as nearly as possible attained those standards of athletics, scholarship and leadership set by him whose memory this award honors.

THE GEORGE HENRY RICHARDS MEMORIAL CUP. This cup is awarded annually to the member of the basketball team who shows the greatest improvement in leadership, sportsmanship, and individual and team play during the year. It is in memory of George Henry Richards of the Class of 1921 who died suddenly while a student at the College.

THE JOSEPH LOJKO MEMORIAL PLAQUE. This plaque is presented to a senior who must be a letter man, have a satisfactory scholastic record and show those qualities of enthusiasm and cooperation which make for leadership. It is awarded in honor of Joseph Lojko of the Class of 1934, outstanding athlete who died while a senior in the College.

THE SAMUEL B. SAMUELS BASKETBALL CUP. This cup is presented annually in the name of Samuel B. Samuels of the Class of 1925 who was an outstanding basketball player during the early years of basketball as a varsity sport at the University. The trophy is awarded to that letter man who is a regular member of the varsity team and who has performed with excellence during scheduled varsity games.

THE E. JOSEPH THOMPSON MEMORIAL TROPHY. This baseball trophy is given by Thomas Thompson in memory of his brother, E. Joseph Thompson who graduated from Massachusetts State College in 1932. He was president of the Student Senate, a varsity letter man in football and baseball, and an outstanding campus citizen. The award goes to that member of the varsity baseball team who best exemplifies the best characteristics of the sport each year.

MILITARY HONORS AND AWARDS

Leadership, scholarship, and proficiency in the work of the military department are recognized by honors and awards announced at the Annual Federal Inspection in May.

United States Army Reserve Officers Training Corps, Armor Branch

DISTINGUISHED MILITARY STUDENTS. Each year the Professor of Military Science and Tactics designates as distinguished military students those members of the first year advanced course who possess outstanding qualities of leadership, high moral character, and a definite aptitude for the military service. Students who are so designated must possess an academic standing in the upper half of their class or in the upper ten per cent of their class in military subjects. All distinguished military students are authorized to wear the distinguished military student badge.

DISTINGUISHED MILITARY GRADUATES. Each year the Professor of Military Science and Tactics designates as distinguished military graduates those members of the graduating class who were previously designated as distinguished military students and have maintained the same high standards required for such designation and have successfully completed training at the Reserve Officers' Training Camp.

THE MILITARY ORDER OF THE LOYAL LEGION TROPHY. Awarded annually by the Military Order of the Loyal Legion to the senior armor cadet ranking No. 1 in military scholarship and proficiency. Winner's name is engraved on a plaque and a sterling silver goblet, appropriately engraved, is given to the individual to keep in his permanent possession.

THE U. S. ARMOR ASSOCIATION SCROLL. Awarded annually by the U. S. Armor Association to the outstanding Armor cadet graduating from the Senior ROTC class. An engraved scroll bearing the name of the winner is presented to the winning cadet to keep in his personal possession.

ARMED FORCES COMMUNICATIONS ASSOCIATION HONOR AWARD. Awarded annually by the Armed Forces Communications Association to the outstanding Senior ROTC cadet majoring in electrical engineering. The winner is presented with an appropriately engraved gold medal and scroll.

41

THE MILITARY SCIENCE TROPHY. Awarded annually by the Department of Military Science, University of Massachusetts, to the Junior Armor cadet ranking No. 1 in military scholarship. The name of the winner is engraved on a sterling silver goblet given to the individual to keep in his permanent possession.

THE RESERVE OFFICERS ASSOCIATION MEDAL. Awarded annually by the Reserve Officers Association of the United States, Massachusetts Department, to the Junior Armor cadet who is outstanding in military proficiency. The winner's name is engraved on a plaque and a medal, appropriately engraved, is given to the individual to keep in his personal possession.

THE ELIZABETH L. MCNAMARA TROPHY. Awarded annually by Mrs. Elizabeth L. McNamara, a trustee of the University of Massachusetts for many years, to the Armor cadet ranking No. 1 in scholarship in the second year basic course. The winner's name is engraved on a plaque and a sterling silver goblet, appropriately engraved, is given to the individual to keep in his permanent possession.

THE JOHN C. HALL TROPHY. Awarded annually by the Military Science Department, University of Massachusetts, to the Armor cadet ranking No. 1 in military proficiency in the second year basic course. The winner's name is engraved on a loving cup donated by the class of '02 in the name of John C. Hall.

THE AMHERST ROTARY CLUB TROPHY. Awarded annually by the Amherst Rotary Club to the Armor cadet ranking No. 1 in scholarship in the first year basic course. The winner's name is engraved on a plaque and a sterling silver goblet, appropriately engraved, is presented to the winner to keep in his personal possession.

THE MILITARY SCIENCE AWARD. Awarded annually by the Department of Military Science, University of Massachusetts, to the Armor cadet ranking No. 1 in military proficiency in the first year basic course. The winner's name is engraved on a gold medal which is presented to him to keep in his personal possession.

RIFLE TEAM AWARD. Awarded annually by the Varsity Rifle Team, University of Massachusetts, to the team member who fires the highest cumulative match score for the season. The winner's name is engraved on a gold cup which is presented to him to keep in his personal possession.

United States Air Force Reserve Officers Training Corps

DISTINGUISHED MILITARY STUDENT. Each year the Professor of Air Science and Tactics will select from the students who are completing the second year advanced course, AFROTC, those who possess outstanding qualities of character, leadership, and a definite aptitude for the military service for designation as Distinguished Military Students.

DISTINGUISHED MILITARY GRADUATE. Each year the Professor of Air Science and Tactics will designate the distinguished Military Graduates from those Distinguished Military Students who have completed the advanced course, AFROTC, and who will receive their baccalaureate degree. The Distinguished Military Graduates, with their consent, may compete for a regular Air Force Commission after serving on active duty for eighteen months.

AIR SCIENCE TROPHY. Awarded annually by the Department of Air Science to the Air Science freshman cadet most outstanding in Military and Academic Scholarship. The trophy is a silver cup appropriately engraved which is given to the winner.

SONS OF AMERICAN REVOLUTION MEDAL. Awarded annually by the Sons of the American Revolution to an Air Science Sophomore cadet selected for Leadership, Soldierly Bearing and General Excellence. The winner's name is appropriately engraved on a medal which is presented to the individual.

AMHERST POST AMERICAN LEGION TROPHY. Awarded annually by the Amherst Post American Legion to the Air Science sophomore cadet who has demonstrated the most outstanding abilities in Military Drill and Scholarship. The trophy is a suitably engraved silver cup which is presented.

AIR CADET SQUADRON TROPHY. Awarded annually by the Air Cadet Squadron to an Air Science sophomore cadet who has been an outstanding member of the Air Cadet Squadron and Drill Team. A silver cup appropriately engraved with the individual's name is presented to the winner.

AIR SCIENCE TROPHY. Awarded annually by the Department of Air Science to the Air Science junior cadet who has displayed outstanding military proficiency and maintained a high scholastic standing. A silver cup appropriately engraved with the individual's name is presented to the winner.

AIR FORCE ASSOCIATION MEDAL. Awarded by the Air Force Association to the most outstanding Air Science junior cadet. The award is a suitably engraved medal which is presented to the winner.

RESERVE OFFICERS ASSOCIATION MEDAL. Awarded by the Massachusetts Reserve Officers Association to the graduating Air Force cadet who has been outstanding in Scholarship and Military Proficiency. The award is a medal appropriately engraved, which is presented to the winner.

HONORS, PRIZES, AWARDS

NORTHAMPTON BENEVOLENT PROTECTIVE ORDER OF ELKS TROPHY. Awarded annually by the Northampton Lodge, BPOE, to the Air Science senior who by his zeal, effort and initiative has contributed most to the Corps of Air Cadets. The trophy is a suitably engraved silver cup which is presented to the winner.

DANIEL FUNGAROLI TROPHY. Awarded annually by Mr. Daniel Fungaroli to the Air Science senior cadet who has been most outstanding at Summer Camp. The trophy is a silver cup appropriately engraved, which is presented to the winner.

AIR SCIENCE TROPHY. Awarded by the Department of Air Science annually to the graduating Air Science senior cadet who has demonstrated superior qualities of Leadership, Military Bearing and Scholarship. The trophy is a silver cup appropriately engraved, which is presented to the winner.

STUDENT ORGANIZATIONS

One of the values received from the University course is the training one acquires through participation in student activities. Student organizations offer excellent opportunities for development of leadership and broadening of outlook.

Student Government

The student Senate operating under the student constitution and composed of elected representatives from the student body is the governing council of undergraduates. Its aim is to promote the general welfare of the University and, in doing so, groups of both students and faculty meet to further their mutual interests. The student Senate directs student conduct and represents the interests of the student body before the faculty.

Academic Honor Societies

Phi Kappa Phi. The Massachusetts Chapter of the Honor Society of Phi Kappa Phi was installed on the campus in 1904. Its prime object is to emphasize scholarship and character. Senior students from all departments of the University are eligible for election to membership provided the scholastic and character requirements of the Society are met.

Sigma Xi. The Society of Sigma Xi is a scientific fraternity to which members are elected on the basis of outstanding scientific research. The local chapter was established in 1938.

Upsilon Mu Epsilon. The Society of Upsilon Mu Epsilon was established at the University of Massachusetts in 1952. Its prime objectives are to emphasize engineering scholarship and character. Senior and junior students in the School of Engineering are eligible for election to membership if they meet scholastic and character requirements of the Society.

Student Honor Societies

Adelphia. The men's senior honor society, recognizing students who have been leaders in the extra-curricular activities of the campus.

Isogon. The women's senior honor society. Its purpose is to recognize women students who have demonstrated outstanding qualities of character and leadership.

Fraternities and Sororities

Social fraternities on the campus include Alpha Epsilon Pi, Alpha Gamma Rho, Delta Phi Gamma, Delta Sigma Chi, Kappa Sigma, Lamdba Chi Alpha, Phi Mu Delta, Phi Sigma Kappa, Q.T.V., Sigma Alpha Epsilon, Sigma Phi Epsilon, Tau Epsilon Phi, Theta Chi. An Inter-Fraternity council, consisting of representatives of these fraternities, has charge of rushing and all general matters dealing with fraternity life.

Sororities include Chi Omega, Kappa Alpha Theta, Kappa Kappa Gamma, Phi Delta Nu, Pi Beta Phi, Sigma Delta Tau, and Sigma Kappa. The Pan-Hellenic Council, made up of representatives from the sororities, supervises rushing and other sorority matters.

Extra Curricular Activities

All extra-curricular activities are supervised by the Committee on Recognized Student Organizations composed of alumni, faculty, and students. Recognition is given in the annual award of gold and silver medals.

The Collegian. This is a weekly newspaper published by undergraduates.

The Quarterly. A magazine in which the literary and artistic efforts of the students are published.

Index. The year book.

University Handbook. Published annually as a campus book of reference.

University Musical Organizations. Open to all students of the University. For instrumentalists: Band, Dance Band, Orchestra and Ensembles; for vocalists: Chorus, Chorale, Operetta Guild and small combinations. A Women's Drill Team performs at home games and ceremonies. The University Concert Association provides an annual series of major concerts by famous artists.

Drama is represented on the campus by the Roister Doisters, open to all four-year students interested in the art of the theater; and the University Players, open to those students who have shown outstanding ability, effort, and interest in some phase of dramatics through the Roister Doisters.

Inter-Collegiate Athletics

The University is represented in inter-collegiate athletics by teams in all the leading sports including football, soccer, cross country, basketball, swimming, indoor track, hockey, rifle and pistol, baseball, track, tennis, and golf. General policies governing athletics are directed by the Joint Committee on the Inter-Collegiate Athletics composed of alumni, faculty, and students.

Professional Clubs

There are numerous professional clubs, established in connection with the various major courses of study. These clubs stimulate the students' professional interest in their chosen subject-matter fields and afford opportunity for discussion of technical subjects of mutual interest.

SPECIAL SERVICES

Religious Life

The University makes an effort to provide a wholesome and stimulating spiritual atmosphere for the students by cooperating with official agencies of the three faiths most largely represented at the University.

On the campus the religious life of Catholic students is enriched by the Newman Club, of which Father David j. Power of Saint Brigid's Parish is chaplain. Jewish students may participate in services and activities at the local Hillel House, under the chaplaincy of Rabbi Louis Ruchames of Northampton; and Protestant students may join in worship and other religious activities conducted by the Student Christian Association, under the guidance of the Reverend Albert Seely, chaplain to Protestant students.

The churches of Amherst provide not only the usual opportunities for worship and participation in church work, but special events for students. Students are particularly encouraged to attend Sunday service in the local church of their respective faiths.

Health Service

The Health Service is a separate administrative unit dealing with all matters directly or indirectly influencing or affecting the health of staff members, employees, students, or campus visitors.

The University endeavors to safeguard the health of all students while on the campus. Basic medical attention is provided, including preliminary diagnosis, primary treatment of injuries, and temporary care of the sick. A group of three infirmary buildings and a staff of resident physicians and resident nurses are available to perform these functions.

(1) The Student Health physicians have offices in the out-patient Infirmary Building, where they may be consulted during college hours.

(2) The Infirmary consists of three buildings, one for bed patients, one for contagious cases, and one for out-patient cases, where the out-patient clinic is conducted daily by the Student Health physicians.

(3) The students are urged to consult the resident physicians at the first sign of physical disorder, or even for minor accidents. Many severe illnesses and much lost time may be avoided by early or preventive treatment.

(4) House calls cannot be made to dormitories, sororities, or fraternities except in the case of emergency. The University cannot assure each student that a resident physician will always be available. In such instances students are encouraged to consult a town physician, although any expense connected with such service shall be borne entirely by the student. One resident physician is on call at all times to care for emergencies beyond the scope of the nurse on duty.

(5) No charge is made to Infirmary bed patients up to seven days in each school year; time in excess of seven days will be charged at the rate of $4 per day. A nominal charge may be made to out-patients for miscellaneous treatments.

(6) In addition to the fee charged as specified in paragraph 6, the following additional expenses will be charged to the patient:

Nurses. If a special nurse is required for the proper care of an individual, the services and board of this nurse will be paid by the patient. Such a nurse will be under the general supervision of the resident nurse.

Professional Service. If a student requires continuous medical attention by a physician, he may be required to select a town physician and become responsible for fees charged by that physician.

Supplies. Special medical supplies prescribed by a physician will be charged to the patient.

Laundry. Expenses for personal laundry incurred by students while in the infirmary will be charged to the individual student.

(7) The Health Service recommends strongly that students participate in the blanket insurance program described in literature accompanying the initial bill rendered students each year. This program is a reimbursement insurance plan providing medical, surgical, and hospital care for both accident and illnesses at a very low cost. During the past years this plan has saved numerous patients from serious unexpected expense and the insurance payments have enabled the student to stay in school. The University has no financial interest in this and acts only as a clearing

49

house to receive premiums, in order to give the low group rate.

The Placement Service

The University maintains a centralized Placement Service, the function of which is to assist students to secure part-time, summer, or permanent employment and to administer the required Placement Training Program.

The University is keenly interested that each graduate has an opportunity to serve his fellow men in a socially desirable occupation consistent with his interests, abilities, aptitudes, and education. To assist students to accomplish their objectives, the following aids are available: cumulative student personnel records, occupational information, library, counselling and guidance in job hunting techniques, preparation of credentials and personal data sheets and personal interviews.

The Placement Service is the clearing center for all part-time jobs at the University. Students are assisted in obtaining part-time work during the college year and full-time work during the summer vacation. Employment is not guaranteed, but every effort is made to help those students who must work to meet their college expenses. In order to give assistance to as many needy students as possible, the Student Aid Committee has adopted the policy of limiting the maximum financial aid per student to the equivalent of board. The average earnings of students engaged in part-time work is approximately $100.00 per year.

Publications and News Office

The University recognizes its obligation to provide the public with accurate information about its educational program.

Providing such information is the function of the Publications and News Office which edits the University catalogues and the school bulletin series and services communications media such as newspapers and radio stations. This is a public service program and not a publicity operation.

The Publications and News Office also supervises a Student News Bureau which affords internship training in news writing to a limited number of students.

Alumni Association

The Associate Alumni is the general organization of the Alumni, men and women, of the University of Massachusetts. The association maintains headquarters at Memorial Hall, erected by Alumni and friends in honor of those men of the University who died in World War I.

It publishes a magazine, *The Massachusetts Alumnus,* as the alumni publication of the University.

According to its By-Laws the Corporation is constituted for the purpose of promoting the general usefulness of the University of Massachusetts; of cultivating among its graduates and former students a sentiment of mutual regard; and of strengthening their attachment to their Alma Mater.

Under alumni sponsorship, 13 self-liquidating dormitories have been built on campus, and one is under construction.

The governing body of the Associate Alumni consists of its officers and a Board of Directors. Four directors are elected each year and serve a term of four years. All graduating seniors become members of, and contributors to, the Association at graduation, according to a tradition set by the Class of 1940.

UNIVERSITY BUILDINGS

The campus is laid out in the form of an oval attractively set off by the College Pond in the center. Around this oval are grouped the main buildings of the University.

South College. Here are located the administrative offices including those of the President, Treasurer, Secretary, Provost, Registrar, Director of Placement Service, the Dean of Women, the Dean of Men and Director of Publications. Erected 1885.

North College. The University Store and faculty offices. Erected 1868.

Farley 4-H Club Building and Bowditch Lodge. Headquarters for 4-H Club Activities. Erected 1933 and 1936 respectively by funds contributed by 4-H Club members and interested friends and organizations. The former was named to honor George L. Farley for twenty-five years State Leader of County Club Agents; the latter for Nathaniel Bowditch, Trustee of the University from 1896-1945.

Power Plant. General Maintenance.

University Farm. In the University barns are maintained Percheron and Morgan horses; Aberdeen-Angus, Ayrshire, Guernsey, Hereford, Jersey and Holstein cattle; Shropshire and Southdown sheep; and Chester White swine. The university farm is operated as a livestock farm, producing all its necessary roughage in the form of pastures, hay and silage and a portion of its required grain.

Liberal Arts Building. Classrooms, laboratories and offices for Foreign Lnaguages, Psychology and Education. A temporary structure erected in 1947.

Grinnell Arena and Abattoir. Erected in 1910 primarily for livestock judging. An abattoir was constructed in 1930 as an addition to the original building. Named in honor of James S. Grinnell, for twenty-two years a trustee of the University.

Flint Laboratory. Laboratories and classrooms for Dairy Industry. Erected in 1911 and named for Charles L. Flint, fourth president of the University.

Stockbridge Hall. Departments of Agronomy, Animal Husbandry and Poultry Husbandry. Erected in 1914 and named for Levi Stockbridge, first Professor of Agriculture and a former President of the University. Bowker Auditorium, the main auditorium of the University, is located here. It is named for William H. Bow-

GOODELL LIBRARY

A Fast Growing

Campus ◆ ◆ ◆

LEWIS HALL—WOMEN'S RESIDENCE AREA

More Than 700 Acres

in the

HEART OF CAMPUS
LIBRARY AND OLD CHAPEL

Beautiful

Connecticut River Valley

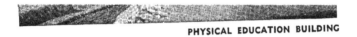

PHYSICAL EDUCATION BUILDING

A Multi-Million Dollar ··

THE UNIVERSITY DINING COMMONS

HASBROUCK (TOP) AND PAIGE LABORATORIES

Expansion Program . . .

TO MEET THE NEEDS OF MASSACHUSETTS YOUTH

SKINNER HALL—HOME ECONOMICS

High Quality Education ◊ ◊ ◊

AERIAL VIEW—WOMEN'S AREA AND COMMONS

OLD
CHAPEL

t Low Cost

ker, a member of the first graduating class, trustee of the University, and one of the pioneers in the fertilizer industry.

Chenoweth Laboratory. Classrooms and laboratories including Commercial Practices Laboratory for the Department of Food Technology. Erected 1929 and named in honor of Walter W. Chenoweth, pioneer in the field of Food Technology and first Head of the Department.

Dramatic Workshop. A headquarters for instruction in stagecraft.

Draper Hall. Classrooms and offices of the School of Business Administration. Headquarters also of the Department of Agricultural Economics and Farm Management. School of Nursing offices are located in the basement. Erected in 1903 and renovated in 1954.

Hatch Laboratory. A laboratory where small animals and chickens are used in connection with investigations into human, animal, and poultry nutrition.

Engineering Annex. Laboratories, classrooms, and offices for the School of Engineering. Erected 1948.

Engineering Shop. Laboratories and shop for machine tools, woodworking, motors, and welding instruction. Erected 1916.

Poultry Plant. Consisting of a number of modern buildings, in which instruction and research in ventilation, breeding, feeding, incubation, brooding, marketing and management of poultry and poultry enterprises take place. Rhode Island Reds, Barred Plymouth Rocks, White Plymouth Rocks, New Hampshires, and S.C. White Leghorns and several other breeds are maintained here on a commercial basis.

Paige Laboratory. Erected in 1950 and named in honor of James B. Paige, a graduate of the College in 1882 and Professor of Veterinary Science from 1891-1922. The building contains classrooms and laboratories. Laboratories for State Control and research work in animal diseases are located here.

Gunness Laboratory. Laboratories for industrial combustion engines, materials testing, fluid mechanics, heating, air conditioning and refrigeration, electrical machinery, electrical circuits, as well as classrooms and offices for the School of Engineering. Built in 1948 and named in honor of Christian I. Gunness, Professor of Agricultural Engineering from 1914 to 1946.

Electrical Engineering Wing. Completed in 1950, this portion of the main Engineering building provides laboratories for Industrial Electronics, Communications, Ultra High Frequency, Electrical Measurements, Illumination and Metallurgy, as well as classrooms and offices for the School of Engineering. This structure is a wing of the main Engineering building of the University, now under construction.

Goessmann Laboratory. Contains eight large laboratories, an auditorium, chemical library, and lecture rooms. The east wing of the third floor is used by the Experiment Station chemists. The remainder of the building is for resident instruction in Chemistry. Erected in 1924 and named in honor of Charles A. Goessmann, first Professor of Chemistry at the University. A large addition to this building will be under construction during 1955-56.

West Experiment Station. The State Control Service is centralized here. Fertilizers, seeds, and feeds are analyzed or inspected in accordance with the state law. Erected 1886.

Crabtree House. A self-liquidating dormitory housing 154 students. This building was erected under the sponsorship of the Associate Alumni and completed in 1953. Named for Lotta Crabtree, benefactress of the University.

Abigail Adams House. Women's dormitory accommodating 100 students. Erected in 1919 and named for Abigail Adams, wife of John Adams, second President of the United States.

The Homestead. Girls majoring in Home Economics receive their Home Management practice here. This is a fine old colonial homestead newly equipped with all the modern conveniences of the home.

Hamlin House. A self-liquidating dormitory housing 175 students. Erected under the sponsorship of the Associate Alumni and completed in 1949. Named for Margaret P. Hamlin, first Placement Officer for Women from 1919 to 1948.

Knowlton House. A self-liquidating dormitory with accommodations for 175 students. Erected under the sponsorship of the Associate Alumni and completed in 1950. Named in honor of Helen Knowlton, Associate Professor of Home Economics, 1924-1941.

Leach House. A self-liquidating dormitory housing 154 students. This building was erected under the sponsorship of the Associate Alumni and completed in 1953. Named in honor of Mrs. Joseph A. Leach, chairman of the Women's Advisory Council and former trustee.

Lewis House. Women's dormitory accommodating 150 students. A self-liquidating dormitory erected under the sponsorship of the Associate Alumni in 1940 and named in honor of Edward M. Lewis, Dean of the College 1914-25 and President 1925-27.

Thatcher House. Women's dormitory with facilities for 150 students. Erected in 1935 and named in honor of Roscoe W. Thatcher, President of the College 1927-32.

University Dining Commons. The central University dining commons for men and women students.

University Infirmary. A group of three buildings, one for bed patients, one for out patients and a third for contagious cases.

Marshall Hall. Erected in 1915 and named for Dr. Charles

Marshall, a former Professor of Bacteriology and Director of the Graduate School. The building provides laboratories and classroom space, for the Department of Bacteriology and the Department of Zoology.

Skinner Hall. Laboratories, classrooms and offices for the School of Home Economics. Erected in 1947 and named in honor of Edna L. Skinner, first Dean of the School of Home Economics.

Hasbrouck Physics Laboratory. Completed in 1949. Contains laboratories and lecture rooms designed for the various main divisions of Physics. Named in honor of Philip B. Hasbrouck, Professor of Physics and Registrar of the College during the period 1905 to 1924.

Conservation Building. Formerly the Old Botany Museum, erected 1867. Houses laboratories, classrooms and offices for the Department of Forestry and Wildlife Management.

Fisher Laboratory. Erected in 1910 and named for Jabez Fisher, one of the foremost early horticulturists of the state. Laboratories for Pomology. Included are a quick freezing room, six refrigerator rooms, two rooms for the storage of frozen products, two classrooms, and three packing rooms.

Wild Life Laboratory. Laboratories for graduate students in Wild Life Management.

Wilder Hall. Contains classrooms, drafting rooms, and offices of the Department of Landscape Architecture. Erected in 1905 and named for Marshall P. Wilder, a pioneer in the movement for agricultural education in Massachusetts, and one of the first trustees of the College.

French Hall. Erected in 1908 and named in honor of Henry F. French, the first President of the College, this building houses the Departments of Floriculture, Pomology, and Olericulture. In the rear of the building is the Edward A. White range of greenhouses, built in 1908 and devoted to the growing of carnations, roses, chrysanthemums, etc. One house is maintained as a conservatory and contains a collection of plants used primarily for decorative purposes. The old Durfee range just north of French includes a collection of tropical and semi-tropical plants of botanical and horticultural importance. It was erected in 1867 from money given by Dr. Nathan Durfee of Fall River, treasurer of the board of trustees.

Stockbridge House. Faculty Club House.

Shade Tree Laboratories. Constructed in 1948 for research on shade tree problems including Dutch Elm Disease.

Clark Hall. Offices, lecture rooms, laboratories, and greenhouses of the Department of Botany are located here. The herbarium contains about 122,000 sheets of seed plants and ferns, 5000 sheets of liverworts, mosses, algae, lichens, and a collection of 20,000 specimens of fungi. The building was erected in 1906 and named in honor of William S. Clark, President of the College and Professor of Botany from 1867 to 1879.

Fernald Hall. Erected in 1909 and named in honor of Professor Charles H. Fernald who served the College from 1886 to 1909, built a strong Department of Zoology, created the Department of Entomology, and acted as Director of the Graduate School. Fernald Hall houses the Departments of Entomology and Geology and offices and classrooms of the Department of Zoology. Offices and laboratories of the Western Sanitary District, Massachusetts Department of Public Health, are also located here. The Entomology collection includes over 160,000 insects. There are also Geological and Zoological museums.

Mathematics Building. Classrooms and offices of the Mathematics Department.

Mills House. A self-liquidating dormitory for 150 students. Erected in 1948 under the sponsorship of the Associate Alumni. Named in honor of George F. Mills, teacher of English from 1890 to 1914 and Head of the Division of Humanities.

Brooks House. Men's self-liquidating dormitory. Named in honor of William Penn Brooks, Professor of Agriculture and Director of the Experiment Station, 1888-1921.

Butterfield House. A self-liquidating dormitory with dining hall. Accommodates 147 students. Erected in 1941 under the sponsorship of the Associate Alumni. Named in honor of Kenyon L. Butterfield, President of the College 1906-1924.

Chadbourne House. Men's self-liquidating dormitory for one hundred and fifty students. Erected in 1946 under the sponsorship of the Associate Alumni. Named in honor of Paul Ansel Chadbourne, President 1866-67 and 1882-83.

Baker House. A self-liquidating dormitory for men accommodating 360 students. Erected in 1951 by the Alumni Building Corporation. Named in honor of Hugh P. Baker, President of the University from 1933 to 1947.

Greenough House. Men's dormitory and Dining Hall. Houses one hundred and forty-eight students. A self-liquidating dormitory erected in 1946 under the sponsorship of the Associate Alumni. Named in honor of James Carruthers Greenough, President from 1883-86.

Munson Hall. Headquarters for the Massachusetts Extension Service. Named in honor of Willard A. Munson, a graduate of the College in 1905 and Director of the Extension Service from 1926 to 1951.

Curry S. Hicks Physical Education Building. Erected in 1931 from funds contributed by Alumni and friends of the College plus an appropriation by the state legislature. Contains a large swimming pool, an exercise hall, basketball floor, and locker room.

Named for Curry S. Hicks, Professor and Head of the Division of Physical Education from 1911 to 1949.

Alumni Field. So called because both funds and labor for its construction were contributed by alumni and students. Included are a baseball diamond, football and soccer fields, and a cinder track. Tennis courts are adjacent to the Physical Education Building.

Athletic Field for Women. A large field west of the Physical Education Building provides space for Archery, Softball, Field Hockey, and other women's activities.

County Circle. Five residence halls erected in 1948 by the Commonwealth. Hampshire and Suffolk Houses contain 30 two-room and three-room apartments for married persons and their families. Plymouth, Berkshire, and Middlesex Houses contain dormitory rooms for approximately 144 students each.

Drill Hall. Contains, in addition to the offices of the Departments of Military Science and Air Science, the offices, locker and dressing rooms, and exercise hall for the Department of Physical Education for Women.

Memorial Hall. Erected in 1921 by Alumni and friends in memory of those men of the College who died in World War I. Included is a Memorial Room in which the names of those members of the College family who died in the service of their country are appropriately enshrined. This building is a social center of student life. Alumni headquarters are here as well as the offices of student organizations including the Senate, Collegian, and Index.

Old Chapel. Erected in 1885. Auditorium, seminar room, classrooms, and offices for English and History.

Goodell Library. Goodell Library is named in honor of Henry Hill Goodell who served the College from 1867-1905. He was President from 1886 to 1905 and because of his deep enthusiasm for books also acted as Librarian of the College.

This library houses the main collection of the University library system and has the central card catalog and the catalog and processing units for both the main and departmental libraries.

Goodell Library is a fireproof building erected in 1935. Its plan is virtually unique among University libraries in that the greater part of its book-stacks are open for inspection and borrowing. The present collection in the building amounts to approximately 152,000 volumes including books and extensive files of periodicals.

The collections in the Goodell Library include the books and periodicals in the Humanities and Social Sciences together with some of the material in the Natural and Applied Sciences.

The main floor includes a large reading room, a reference room, circulation desk, reference and current periodical desk, both in the main lobby, and cataloging and administrative offices. On the second floor is another large reading room, commonly used for reserve book reading. There is a study for faculty and a University History Room in memory of Dean William L. Machmer in which the historical records of the University are kept and exhibited.

Besides the Goodell Library there are thirty-seven department libraries totaling about 38,000 books and bound periodicals located in the several University buildings with the teaching departments and laboratories. These libraries vary from small working libraries to extensive collections in special fields. Particularly worthy of note are the Botany, Chemistry, and Entomology libraries.

The complete library system contains 190,055 volumes (Sept. 1, 1954) and is growing at the rate of over 7,000 volumes a year. The library regularly receives over 1,000 periodicals, and also the serial publications of learned societies. It is also a depository for government documents of the United States Department of Agriculture and the various State Experiment Stations.

Under Construction

Classroom Building. A $1,000,000 structure, adjacent to North College, providing instruction facilities for several departments in Arts and Sciences.

Dormitories no. 13 (housing 225 men) and no. 14 (housing 400 men). Completion dates of September 1955 and September 1956 respectively.

Engineering Wing to house offices and laboratories of the Electrical Engineering department, to be completed by September 1955.

Goessmann Laboratory Addition. A $1,747,000 addition to the chemistry laboratory facilities. Expected date of completion

Student Union Building. A $2,000,000 structure for recreational facilities for all students, located in the center of the campus adjacent to the pond. Expected date of completion, September 1956.

Women's Physical Education Building. A $1,621,000 structure located adjacent to the women's residence area, providing complete facilities for the Department of Physical Education for Women, including gymnasium and swimming pool.

UNDERGRADUATE CURRICULA

Undergraduate instruction is organized into a College of Arts and Sciences, the Schools of Agriculture and Horticulture, Business Administration, Engineering, Home Economics, Nursing, and the Division of Physical Education for Men.

This section of the catalogue deals with the opportunities for study and the curricula available in each of these departments of the University.

COLLEGE OF ARTS AND SCIENCES

_____, *Dean*

The College of Arts and Sciences includes the usual subject matter departments in which are offered the courses in general education essential for enlightened citizenship and for specialized and professional training. Most of the courses in the common prescribed curriculum for all freshman and sophomore students, regardless of their field of specialization, are taught in the College.

Each department offers the usual requirements of undergraduate specialization in its particular field. In addition, special curricula are provided to meet the needs of special groups of students. These include curricula for pre-medical, pre-dental, and pre-veterinary students; for those who plan to train as laboratory technicians and to enter the public health service; and for those interested in social work.

The work of the first two years is largely prescribed, specialization occurring in the junior and senior years. The concentration of the junior and senior years gives the students as high a proficiency in their fields of specialization as is possible without sacrificing the objectives and requirements of a well-rounded education. The curriculum for the first two years follows:

FRESHMAN YEAR

1st Semester	Credits	2nd Semester	Credits
English 1	2	English 2	2
Speech 3	1	Speech 4	1
Math. 7 or 5	3-4	Math. 8 or 10 or 6	3-4
2Zoology 1 or Botany 1	3	2Botany 1 or Zoology 1	3
Foreign Language	3	Foreign Language	3
1Elective	3	1Elective	3
Military 1 (men)	3	Military 2 (men)	2
Physical Education 3 (men)	1	Physical Education 4 (men)	1
Physical Education 7 (women)	2	Physical Education 8 (women)	2
		Hygiene (women)	1

1 Those majoring in biological and physical science departments take Chemistry 1 and 2 (or 4); others take History 5 and 6 .

2 Those not majoring in biological and physical science departments may take Chemistry 1 and 2 in place of Zoology 1 and Botany 1, or substitute Geology 27 for either Botany 1 or Zoology 1.

SOPHOMORE YEAR

1st Semester	Credits	2nd Semester	Credits
English 25	3	English 26	3
Sociology 28, Psychology 26, or Economics 25	3	Economics 25, Sociology 28, or Psychology 26	3
1Science	3-4	1Science	3-4
12 electives	6-7	12 electives	6-7
Military 25 (men)	2	Military 26 (men)	2
Physical Education 27 (women)	2	Physical Education 28 (women)	2
Physical Education 33 (men)	1	Physical Education 34 (men)	1

1 In selecting the required science course and the two electives, students should be guided by the recommendations for sophomore work given under the descriptions of junior-senior curricula that follow.

JUNIOR-SENIOR CURRICULA

Major work is available in the following departments during the last two years. The department offers three curricula: one in Bacteriology, one in Public Health, and the other in Medical Technology.

Bacteriology   R. L. FRANCE, *Adviser*

The courses in bacteriology have been planned to furnish (1) a general and applied training for students majoring in other departments who must have some knowledge of bacteria and (2) specialization for those contemplating a professional career in bacteriology.

Students majoring in bacteriology should complete the following courses in their sophomore year: Chemistry 29 and 30, Zoology 35 and Bacteriology 31. Physics 25 and 25 should be elected the junior year.

During junior and senior years the following courses should be taken: Chemistry 51, 52, and 79; Zoology 69 and 84; Public Health 61, 62, and 88; Bacteriology 51, 52, 56, 81, 82, 85, and 96.

Public Health   R. L. FRANCE, *Adviser*

Through the cooperation of several departments of the university and the Massachusetts Department of Public Health, curricula are provided for (1) a limited number of students interested in the many phases of public health service for which graduate work in medical or engineering schools is not essential; and (2) students planning graduate work in sanitary engineering.

Particular attention will be given to the training of sanitarians, district sanitary officers, food and milk inspectors, water and sewage treatment plant operators, technicians for public health laboratories, and agents for local boards of health. Students planning graduate work in sanitary engineering must also take Mathematics 29 and 30 (calculus) before the end of their junior year.

Students electing this major should complete the following courses during their sophomore year: Chemistry 29, Physics 25 and 26, Zoology 35 and Bacteriology.

During junior and senior years the following courses should be completed: Chemistry 51 and 52; Bacteriology 81 and 90; Public Health 61, 62, 63, 84, and 88. Supporting courses in other departments will be selected with the guidance of an adviser.

Medical Technology   R. L. FRANCE, *Adviser*

This curriculum provides a broad basic training in the physical and biological sciences for young women who plan to qualify as medical technologists. The program more than meets the basic collegiate requirements of the Registry of Medical Technologists of the American Society of Clinical Pathologists. Students taking this curriculum should be prepared to spend a year's internship in a certified hospital laboratory after graduation.

The following courses should be completed in the sophomore year: Chemistry 29 and 30, Zoology 35 and Bacteriology 31. Physics 25 and 26 may be taken in the junior year.

During junior and senior years the following courses should be elected: Chemistry 51, 52, 79, and 80; Zoology 51 and 69; Public Health 61, 62, and 88; Bacteriology 51, 52, 56, 81, 82, 85, and 92.

Botany   T. T. KOZLOWSKI, *Adviser*

The purpose of the courses in botany is to provide a thorough background for specialization in the science, and to support and supplement the work of other fields in which knowledge of plant life is held to be important. Certain courses should likewise prove of interest and value to the general student.

Those who wish to specialize in botany will find here an ample field and an adequate opportunity for advanced undergraduate study. Post-graduate training, often with provision for financial aid, is available in most graduate institutions, and many teaching, research and industrial positions in schools and colleges, experiment stations, federal and state services and private enterprise are open to the trained botanist.

The curriculum offers to the student an opportunity to acquire either a broad general knowledge of botany, or to devote himself to more extensive study in one of the major divisions of the science, such as Plant Morphology and Taxonomy, Plant Physiology, Mycology and Plant Pathology. Under the direction of his adviser each student selects a program of courses in botany and other sciences, humanities and arts which seems best adapted to his particular botanical objectives.

Specialization in botany assumes the satisfactory completion of certain basic and supporting courses prior to the junior year. These include Botany 1, 25 and 26; Chemistry 1, 2 and 29; and a modern language. Two years of German are advised.

The junior-senior program requires that courses in botany to the amount of 15-30 credits be chosen under the guidance of the adviser. He will also make recommendations in regard to electives.

Chemistry   W. S. RITCHIE, Adviser

The objectives in chemistry are to give the student an understanding of the subject which will enable him to appreciate the relation of chemistry to other sciences, and to industry, and to provide training for those who intend to become teachers and workers in the allied sciences, and for those who wish to go on to graduate study and into a professional career in chemistry. Completion of the course in chemistry fits the student for positions in the chemical industries and related fields as well as in the agricultural industry, for employment in state and Federal agricultural experiment stations and commercial laboratories, for teaching and for graduate study.

Students planning to major in chemistry should elect German in the freshman year. The sophomore program should include Chemistry 29, 30; Mathematics 29, 30; and Physics 25, 26.

In the junior year the chemistry major takes Chemistry 51, 52, 65, and 66. In the senior he takes German 81 and 82, Chemistry 83, and elects at least three of the following courses: Chemistry 77, 81, 82, 86, 93, 94.

Economics   P. L. GAMBLE, *Adviser*

In economics the aims are twofold: (1) to give the student an understanding of economic theory and of the application of economic principles to the organization of society; (2) to provide students with the elementary training necessary for further study of economic and business problems.

The department requires that all majors irrespective of the career desired take the following courses: Economics 53, 73, 79, Accounting 25, and Agricultural Economics 79 or Mathematics 62. In addition, each student must select an additional 12 credit hours of work from the Economics curriulum. No major student is permitted to take more than 36 junior-senior credit hours of economics, agricultural economics and business administration courses. In choosing elective courses students are urged to select courses in the humanities and preferably some from the allied fields of history, philosophy, government, psychology, and sociology. Those intending to major in economics should elect Economics 26 in the sophomore year.

For the majors in the Economics department, there are offered courses which may be combined to serve as preparation toward a number of different careers. Among others, possible careers in the following fields are open:

Banking and Finance	Public Utilities
Government Service	Social Security
International Trade	Statistics
Labor and Personnel Relations	Transportation and Communication

Education   A. W. PURVIS, *Adviser*

The department through its undergraduate program seeks to utilize the forces of the University to prepare teachers for elementary and secondary schools and through its graduate offering to prepare administrators and specialists in public education. Its program is based upon the assumption that teachers and other school personnel should have a broad liberal education, considerable mastery of at least one field, and professional courses which should lead to a knowledge of the persons to be taught, familiarity with the problems to be met, and practice in the best techniques of teaching and supervision.

In order to realize these aims, all students who contemplate teaching as a career should register early, in their freshman year if possible, with the department of education although their work there does not begin until the junior year. Admission to the teacher-training program will be determined largely by a composite rating based on scholarship as shown by University grades (a three-year average at least as high as the University median is

71

desired), success in the beginning course in History of Education, and on personality ratings by members of the staff.

The various programs in Education are as follows:

FOR ELEMENTARY SCHOOL TEACHING (D. J. McCarthy, adviser) Either a major or minor in Education. Majors in Education will be expected to elect a junior-senior minor of eighteen hours in a general education field. For both majors and minors:

Junior Year: Education 51, 64, Psychology 94 or Home Economics 70.

Senior Year: One full semester Education 60, 61, 62, 85.

For candidates with artistic or musical ability Art 33, 34, and Music 62 are strongly recommended.

FOR SECONDARY SCHOOL TEACHING. Students who wish to teach in secondary schools should major in the field to be taught and minor in Education.

Junior Year: Education 51, 52, 88, Psychology 56.

Senior Year: Education 85 in either semester together with another Education course selected from Education 53, 66, or 83. (The most usual certification requirement is eighteen hours.)

In years when there is sufficient demand the Block system for Secondary School Teacher Training will be opened to selected students from Arts and Sciences. These students will take Education 51 in the first semester and Education 52, 85, 88, Psychology 56 in the second semester. In this plan the courses are so scheduled as to permit eight full weeks of practice teaching for six credits.

Several cooperative special-field programs for teachers have been developed as follows:

TEACHER-TRAINING IN AGRICULTURE. (C. F. Oliver, adviser.) By a cooperative agreement with the State Division of Vocational Education, persons otherwise qualified may prepare to teach vocational agriculture by the satisfactory completion of Education 72, 73, and 75. Education 52 is also recommended. To insure a desirable range of preparation, students who contemplate vocational teaching should consult (early in the freshmen year if possible) Professor Oliver and the State Supervisor of Agricultural Teacher-Training. A vocational teacher-training certificate is awarded by the Vocational Division to those who fully qualify.

TEACHER-TRAINING IN HOME ECONOMICS. (Miss Strattner, adviser.) These students will major in home economics and elect Education 51, 53, 83, and 85, Psychology 56, and Home Economics 81.

TRAINING OF TEACHER-COACHES. (S. W. Kauffman, adviser.) These students should major in the subject-field to be taught and minor in Education. They should elect Education 51, 52, 85, and 88, Psychology 56, and Physical Education 54.

TEACHER-TRAINING IN MUSIC. (D. Alviani, adviser.) These students should major in Music and elect Education 51, 52, 85, 88, and Psychology 56.

English   F. P. RAND, *Adviser*

The department of English offers courses in English composition and literature and in speech. Students majoring in this department must conform to the institutional and school requirements for freshmen and sophomore years, and in choosing sophomore electives should include two semesters of modern language and one semester of English history.

The courses in English are intended to enable students to express themselves effectively and to appreciate humanistic values and the ideals of English-speaking people throughout their history. They also offer an appropriate, and in some instances an adequate, classroom training for work in such fields as teaching, authorship and editing.

The student majoring in English must earn 30 credits in elective courses in English. However, for six of these he may substitute elective courses in technical writing, other languages or speech.

Journalism

The journalism courses are designed to provide professional guidance for students interested in newspaper work or related fields. Such students are advised to compete for membership on the college newspaper while freshmen or sophomores, take the introductory course (Journalism 85) as juniors, and elect other courses in social science and literature. Selected seniors will be provided a limited amount of actual professional experience.

Entomology   C. P. ALEXANDER, *Adviser*

Courses in entomology serve a variety of functions, such as to give students a broad knowledge of insects, particularly in their relations to man, his crops, his animals, and his health. Students are trained to become entomologists in the service of the United States, or in various state, territorial, or foreign services, especially in the field of agriculture. Other fields of training include forest entomology; medical entomology; control of pests in buildings; research, technical service or sales work with manufacturers of insecticides; teachers of zoology, particularly entomology, at the university level; and various other branches.

The courses in beekeeping are offered with the following aims: (1) to meet the increase in vocational opportunities for the production of bees or honey as a business; (2) to study the beekeeping needs of fruit and truck-crop industries and the part that bees play

73

in the pollination of flowers; (3) to acquaint the student with a recreational field that can be made profitable.

Majors are required to take Entomology 26 in the sophomore year. Strongly recommended sophomore subjects include Botany 25, 26; Zoology 25, 35; Chemistry 29, 30; and either French or German, or both.

Juniors and seniors should support their work in entomology with the following courses: Botany 51, 52; Bacteriology 61, 62; Chemistry 51, 52; Zoology 51, 69, 70; Pomology 56; English 84, and selected courses in education, floriculture, forestry, horticulture, and other subjects.

Geology and Mineralogy L. R. WILSON, Adviser

The offerings in geology and mineralogy are intended chiefly for those who wish to gain some acquaintance with one or more branches of earth science. For the general student prerequisite requirements are reduced to a minimum. A program of moderate specialization may be provided for science majors who are interested in geology.

To major in geology a student must complete thirty credit hours of work in the department. Those who have completed nine or more credits in geology in addition to the sophomore courses by the end of the junior year, and who wish to satisfy major requirements for graduation in the field of geology, will be given individual or group problems in the senior year. The nature of the work will depend upon student interest and preparation. In any junior or senior course in geology an additional period per week without credit may be required of students who specialize in this field. Chemistry through qualitative analysis and a year's work in college physics represent minimum requirements in these respective fields for undergraduate specialization in physical geology. For those interested in pursuing studies in stratigraphy or paleontology, work beyond the freshman year in the systematic aspects of both botany and zoology is essential for satisfactory progress.

German F. C. ELLERT, Adviser

The courses in German are intended to give a practical knowledge of the language for the purpose of wider reading, research, and oral communication.

During the junior and senior years each student will complete not less than 24 and not more than 30 credits in the junior-senior German courses. German 59, 79, and 80 are required of all major students. Students planning to use the language professionally are also urged to supplement their courses here with a summer session at an approved school of German.

History and Government
H. W. CARY, *History Adviser*
FRED V. CAHILL, *Government Adviser*

The courses in history are intended to impart an understanding of the people of the world and their problems through an analysis of man's development in the past. A major in this field should provide the student with a broad cultural background and a basis for good citizenship. History may have special value for the following groups:

(1) Those who plan to teach history or the social studies.

(2) Those who plan careers in which considerable knowledge of history is desirable. These might be in fields such as law, government service, journalism, and library work.

Prospective majors should ordinarily elect History 31 and 32 in the sophomore year. Government 25 is recommended. Major students must earn a minimum of 26 credit hours in history from the junior and senior courses. The following courses are required: History 59, 60, 91, 92. The student must elect one of the following courses which deal with a period prior to 1500: History 51, 75, 76. In addition, he should select, in consultation with his adviser, a program of elective courses from fields related to the major.

The study of government is intended to give the student an understanding of the principles of government and politics and their application to the organization of society, and to provide him with training necessary for positions in government service or further study on the graduate level. It thus may be considered either as pre-law or pre-professional work, in addition to its general cultural value.

Majors in the field should elect Government 25 and 26 in their sophomore year. In the junior and senior years a minimum of eight additional courses in government is recommended; these may be elected from the following: Government 54, 61, 62, 63, 64, 65, 66, 68, 70, 73, 76, 93, 94, or History 53. In addition supporting courses in other fields are recommended; these may be chosen from the fields of history, economics, sociology, psychology, or philosophy.

Mathematics
A. E. ANDERSEN, *Adviser*

The department offers courses designed to furnish a cultural background as well as a foundation for both undergraduate and graduate work in such fields of science as physics and chemistry, in engineering and in other technical subjects.

The courses recommended for majors in the department are designed to prepare students for high school teaching, graduate study in mathematics, actuarial work, statistical work, or work as engineering aides:

All majors are required to take Mathematics 29 and 30 and Physics 25 and 26 in the sophomore year. In the junior and senior years each major must take Mathematics 53, 54, 91, and 92 and must, in addition, complete at least 12 credits in other junior-senior courses. Prospective majors should consult the department, for a list of recommended courses.

Music   D. J. ALVIANI, *Adviser*

The courses in music are open to all university students depending on their training, experience, ability and talent. The department of music supervises and directs the activities of a number of musical organizations which offer opportunities to students for the development of skill in playing, singing, acting, and attitudes for artistic growth of intellectual, practical, and social intelligence. Music courses furnish an understanding of the history and interpretation of music, a knowledge of basic theory, and training in applied music.

The music major student is expected to adjust his elective courses to fit his individual needs in preparation for work in the fields of: music education, music merchandising, private teaching, the ministry, the armed forces, church music, private school music, kindergarten music, bi-subject teaching, music library administration, music in radio, television, recreation and industry, institutional music therapy, and advanced study in music.

During the sophomore year all music majors must elect Music 25 and 26. They must pass a piano examination and they may be expected to study voice or an instrument privately before graduation.

Philosophy   C. SHUTE, *Adviser*

Philosophy in general attempts to offer a comprehensive understanding of the universe and makes an effort to decide what one should do while living in it. The distinctive purpose of the courses in philosophy is to concentrate on methods of inquiry, standards of thought, search for values in personal and community life, and the analysis of artistic expression and standards of criticism.

The student majoring in this subject will complete a minimum of 21 credits in junior-senior courses in philosophy. A wide range of supplementary courses is advised, among which the following are acceptable: Chemistry 88, Government 66, 71, 82, Education 51, English 51, 74, 79, 80, Art 75, 77, 78, Music 51, 52, History 77, 78, Mathematics 72, Psychology 61, 90, French 51, 52, Sociology 53, 82.

Majors must take Physics 25, 26 and Mathematics 29, 30 in the Sophomore year. Juniors and seniors are advised to support their physics major courses by electives in mathematics, such as differential equations and vector analysis. Since the interests of major students vary, the department adviser will be glad to make suggestions regarding programs of study.

Psychology   C. C. NEET, *Adviser*

The courses in the psychology department are designed (1) to impart an understanding of behavior and the application of this knowledge to problems of human adjustment; and (2) to give preparation for professional work in psychology and related fields.

Careers open to psychology majors include: teaching and research, guidance, psychometrics, personnel and industrial work, child welfare, abnormal and clinical psychology, opinion polling, social work and government service. Additional training is required for certain of these careers.

Students planning to major in psychology should elect Psychology 26 and Psychology 28 in the sophomore year. In the junior and senior years majors are advised to take a minimum of 24 credits in psychology. Courses 51 and 90 are required. As broad a cultural background as major programs will permit is advised.

Majors planning careers primarily in experimental and physiological psychology should plan to take one or more courses during their four years in mathematics, physics, and zoology. Those planning careers in abnormal and clinical psychology and in child welfare should elect specified courses in education, English, sociology, and zoology; while those planning careers in psychometrics, guidance, personnel and industrial work, and government service should take certain courses in business administration, economics, education, industrial engineering, and sociology.

Recreation Leadership   W. E. RANDALL, *Adviser*

The students who desire to train for various positions in the field of recreation will major in the department of recreation leadership. Positions open to majors in this field include leadership in such activities as park, community, nature, camping, and institutional recreation. During junior and senior years the students will undertake a core program consisting of Recreation 51, 52, 54, 75, 76, and 77. After consultation with his adviser the student will elect Recreation 53 or 78 or any other course which seems to meet his individual needs.

Romance Languages   C. F. FRAKER, S. C. GODING, *Advisers*

Two majors are offered: French and Spanish. The courses in these curricula are intended to give rounded and practical knowledge of the languages for the purpose of wider reading, research, and oral communication, leading to a better understanding of all aspects of the intellectual, spiritual, and material attainments of the nations concerned.

Students majoring in French or Spanish are required to complete at least 30 approved junior-senior credits, six of which may be in English or another foreign language. Those preparing to use the language professionally are urged to supplement their courses with a summer session at an approved school of languages.

Sociology   J. H. KORSON, *Adviser*

The courses in sociology are planned with two aims in view:

(1) To give the student an understanding of the factors which influence men in their activities and interests as members of society, and

(2) To prepare those students who are interested in teaching at the elementary or high school level; or those students interested in careers with government agencies; or in careers as social workers with state or private agencies to gain the pre-professional courses necessary before embarking on such careers. Some agencies require work on the graduate level before full-time employment is obtained, while others offer in-training opportunities to graduate majors in sociology. Programs for students interested in teaching are prepared in cooperation with the Education department.

All major students are required to take Economics 25 and Psychology 26. At least 24 junior-senior credits in sociology are required. Students are required to take Sociology 53 and 82 and are urged also to select courses in economics, history, government, psychology, and as many in the humanities as possible.

Social Work

The American Association of Schools of Social Work indicates that the pre-professional subjects most closely related to professional work in this field are economics, political science, psychology, and sociology. The Association recommends that prospective students of social work or social administration take not fewer than 12 semester hours in one of these subjects while taking less in others. It also recognizes the value of courses in biology, history, English, as well as other subjects contributing to a broad cultural background for the student.

6

Speech   A. E. NIEDECK, *Adviser*

The program in speech is planned to assist students in the entire university who wish training in oral communication, and to provide an opportunity for students in the College of Arts and Sciences to major in speech and drama. All students planning to major in speech should elect Psychology 26 in their sophomore year. In addition to the courses in the department, speech majors must take English 55 and 68, and Philosophy 82 to fulfill the requirements for graduation.

Zoology   G. L. WOODSIDE, *Adviser*

The courses in zoology have two major aims: (1) to offer students an opportunity to develop an understanding and appreciation of the scientific method as a part of a liberal education; and (2) to provide training for prospective graduate students in biology, medicine, dentistry, and related fields, as well as future teachers and laboratory technicians in the biological sciences.

The minimum requirements for majors are: Zoology 1, 35, 50, 53, 71, 72, and either 83 or 84; Chemistry 1, 2, 29, 30, 51, 52; Physics 25, 26.

The minimum requirements for graduation are Zoology 1, 71, 72; 69 or 70 or 74; 50 or 53; and two of the following three: 35, 83, 84; Chemistry 1, 2, 29, 30, 51, and 52 (33 may be substituted for 51 and 52); Physics 25 and 26.

SPECIAL CURRICULUM IN ARTS AND SCIENCES

In addition to the major work provided in the departments previously listed, the following special curriculum is available.

Pre-Medical Curriculum

Advisory Committee: G. L. WOODSIDE, *Chairman*, G. W. ALDERMAN, L. M. BARTLETT, W. S. RITCHIE, J. H. SMITH.

Pre-medical and pre-dental students should register with a member of the pre-medical advisory committee as soon as possible after entering the university. Pre-veterinary students may register with the pre-medical advisory committee or with the school of their choice. Pre-medical or pre-dental students will be assigned a member of the committee as adviser, and as long as they remain premedical or pre-dental students they will continue under this adviser. The assignment is made alphabetically as follows: A-C, Dr. Woodside; D-G, Dr. Smith; H-L, Dr. Ritchie; M-R, Dr. Bartlett; S-Z, Mr. Alderman. During the second semester of the student's sophomore year the committee will review his academic record and will schedule an interview for the purpose of considering his general qualifications. After careful study, specific recommendations will be made as to whether the student should continue with the curriculum or change his objective and choose another major. Each student remaining in the program will again be interviewed during his junior year.

Medical schools do not look with favor on over-specialization in any field. They stress the importance of a broad general education. Therefore, in addition to a major of the student's own choosing, he should include courses beyond the introductory level in other fields, especially the humanities and social sciences. The student is to decide upon his electives only after consultation with his adviser.

FRESHMAN YEAR

1st Semester	Credits	2nd Semester	Credits
Mathematics 7	3	Methematics 8 or 10	3
English 1, Composition	2	English 2, Composition	2
Speech 3	1	Speech 4	1
Chemistry 1, General	3	Chemistry 2 or 4, Gen.	3 or 4
Botany 1 or Zoology 1	3	Zoology 1 or Botany 1	3
German 1 or 5, or French 1, 5, 15	3	German 2 or 6, or French 2, 6, 16	3
Military 1 (men)	3	Military 2 (men)	2
Physical Education 3 (men)	1	Physical Education 4 (men)	1
Physical Education 7 (women)	2	Physical Education 8 (women)	2

SOPHOMORE YEAR

1st Semester	Credits	2nd Semester	Credits
English 25, Humane Letters	3	English 26, Humane Letters	3
Econ. 25 or Psych. 26 or Soc. 28	3	Econ. 25 or Psych. 26 or Soc. 28	3
Physics 25	4	Physics 26	4
Foreign Language	3	Foreign Language	3
Elective*	3	Chem. 29	4
Military 25 (men)	2	Military 26 (men)	2
Physical Education 33 (men)	1	Physical Education 34 (men)	1
Physical Education 27 (women)	2	Physical Education 28 (women)	2

*Students who plan to major in Chemistry elect Chemistry 29, to be followed by Chemistry 30 during the second semester. The second social science is then deferred until the junior year.

JUNIOR YEAR

1st Semester	Credits	2nd Semester	Credits
Chemistry 51, Organic	4	Chemistry 52, Organic	4
Zoology 71, Comp. Vert. Anatomy	4	Zoology 72, Vert. Embryology	4
History	3	1Electives	9
1Electives	6		

SENIOR YEAR

1st Semester	Credits	2nd Semester	Credits
Chemistry 30	4	1Electives	15
1Electives	11		

1 The electives must bring the total junior-senior credits in some one department to 15 to meet the University requirement for graduation.

SCHOOL OF AGRICULTURE AND HORTICULTURE

D. H. SIELING, Dean

The School of Agriculture and Horticulture with its several departments offers a broad general education with specific training in some phase of agriculture or horticulture. Upon the completion of the requirements for graduation, the student will have devoted about one-quarter of his time to pure science, one-quarter to social and humanistic studies, and about one-half to applied science and technology in agriculture and horticulture.

A broad choice of electives within the required courses of each curriculum gives the student the opportunity to prepare for (1) actual agricultural production; (2) research, teaching, or extension work; or (3) industrial work.

Each department of the school has specific requirements for graduation which are included in the descriptive matter under the name of the department. To prevent overspecialization, each student is required to elect at least 12 junior-senior credits in some other school of the University, one-half of these credits to be in the humanities and social sciences.

During the first semester of the freshman year, students interested in teaching vocational agriculture, extension work, or specializing in research work, should consult with the head of the department in which they plan to major.

The School comprises the following departments: Agricultural Economics and Farm Management, Agronomy, Animal Husbandry, Dairy Industry, Floriculture, Food Technology, Forestry and Wildlife Management, Landscape Architecture, Olericulture, Pomology, Poultry Science, and Veterinary Science. Students may major in any of these departments except Veterinary Science.

Curricula in Agriculture and Horticulture

All students will take the following uniform curriculum during the first two years:

81

AGRICULTURE AND HORTICULTURE

FRESHMAN YEAR

1st Semester	Credits	2nd Semester	Credits
English 1, Composition	2	English 2, Composition	2
Speech 3	1	Speech 4	1
1Mathematics 7, Algebra and		1Mathematics 8 or 10	3
Trigonometry	3	2Chemistry 2, General	3
2Chemistry 1, General	3	Zoology 1, General	3
Botany 1, General	3	Agronomy 2, Soils	3
Military 1 (men)	3	Military 2 (men)	2
3Elective	3	Physical Education 4 (men)	1
Physical Education 3 (men)	1	Physical Education 8 (women)	2
Physical Education 7 (women)	2	Hygiene (women)	1

1 Candidates for the Bachelor of Vocational Agriculture degree will take Government 25 and 26 in place of Mathematics.

Students who expect to take Calculus in the sophomore year should elect. Mathematics 10.

2 Those intending to major in Landscape Architecture and Ornamental Horticulture will take Chemistry 1 the first semester and Botany 1 the second semester. They may substitute a foreign language or History 5 and 6 for Zoology 1 and Chemistry 2.

3 Students intending to major in Agricultural Economics, Agronomy, Animal Husbandry, Dairy Industry or Poultry Husbandry will take Animal Husbandry 1, Agriculture. Students intending to major in Floriculture, Forestry, Landscape Architecture, Olericulture or Pomology will take Horticulture 1, Plant Propagation. Forestry majors will take Forestry 26, Dendrology, in place of Agronomy 2. Wildlife Management majors are required to take a year of modern language and Agronomy 2 during freshman and sophomore years. Food Technology majors will take Mechanical Engineering 1, Drawing. One year of foreign language may be substituted for Drawing 1 and Agronomy 2 by special permission.

SOPHOMORE YEAR

1st Semester	Credits	2nd Semester	Credits
English 25, Humane Letters	3	English 26, Humane Letters	3
Econ. 25, Psych. 26 or Soc. 28	3	Econ. 25, Psych. 26 or Soc. 28	3
1A Science	3-4	1A Science	3-4
2Electives	6	2Electives	6
Military 25 (men)	2	Military 26 (men)	2
Physical Education 27 (women)	2	Physical Education 28 (women)	2
Physical Education 33 (men)	1	Physical Education 34 (men)	1

1 To be selected from the following:

Bacteriology 31, 31A
Botany 25, 26, 28
Chemistry 29, 30, 33
Geology 27, 28
Mathematics 29, 30

Physics 25, 26
Zoology 25, 35
Entomology 26
Civil Engineering 27

2 The student will be guided in his selections by his major adviser.

JUNIOR-SENIOR CURRICULA

At the end of the sophomore year each student selects one of the following curricula as his major to complete his collegiate training.

Agricultural Economics and
Farm Management
A. H. LINDSEY, *Adviser*

The purpose of the Agricultural Economics and Farm Management major is to train students for positions in those private and government institutions servicing the agricultural industry and to assist in the training of farm managers.

The department maintains an inventory of current price information and agricultural production reports from which price study and analysis may be made. Statistical machines are also available for computation and analysis. The laboratories of the department must be found in business institutions and on farms in Massachusetts with which contact is maintained.

Two curricula are available.

AGRICULTURAL ECONOMICS

JUNIOR YEAR

1st Semester	Credits	2nd Semester	Credits
Ag. Ec. 55, Mark'g Farm Prod.	3	Ag. Ec. 56, Coop. in Agri	3
Ag. Ec. 57, Agri. Credit	3	Agricultural Electives	6
Agricultural Electives	6	General Electives	6
General Electives	3		

SENIOR YEAR

1st Semester	Credits	2nd Semester	Credits
Accounting 25	3	Agri. Ec. 76, Farm Mgt.	2
Agri. Ec. 79, El. Statis.	3	Agricultural Electives	3
Ag. Ec. 75, Farm Mgt.	3	General Electives	11
Agricultural Electives	3		
General Electives	3		

All Agricultural Economics majors must take the courses listed above. Specialization may be one of the three following fields: (1) Animal products, (2) Fruits and Vegetables, (3) Feeds and Fertilizers.

The following courses should be completed for each of these specialized fields:

Animal Products	Fruits and Vegetables	Feed and Fertilizer
An. Husb. 53	Pomology 53	Agronomy 51
An. Husb. 54	Pomology 77	Agronomy 52
Dairy 52	Olericulture 74	Agronomy 78
Dairy 77	Olericulture 78	An. Husb. 51
Dairy 78	Food Technology 75	An. Husb. 78
Poultry 75		An. Husb. 78
		Poultry 56

FARM MANAGEMENT

JUNIOR YEAR

1st Semester	Credits	2nd Semester	Credits
Agri. Ec. 55, Mktg. Farm Prod.	3	Agri. Ec. 56, Coop. Agri.	3
Agri. Ec. 57, Agri. Cr.	3	Agronomy 52, Soil Util.	3
An. Husb. 51, Nutrition	3	Agri. Ec. 78, Land Econ.	3
Electives	6	Bus. Law 70	3
		Electives	3

SENIOR YEAR

1st Semester	Credits	2nd Semester	Credits
Agri. Ec. 71, Theory	3	Agri. Ec. 76, Farm Mgt.	2
Ag. Ec. Farm Mgt.	3	An. Husb. 78, Dairy Cattle Prod.	4
Agronomy 51, Field Crops	3	Poultry 78, Management	2
Forestry 55, Mgt. Woodlands	3	Electives	8
Electives	3		

Agronomy   W. G. COLBY, *Adviser*

The department of agronomy is equipped with modern soils, crops and chemical laboratories, greenhouses, and utilizes parts of the university farm for fertilizer and plant growth experimentation, and for demonstration of soil utilitization and conservation.

The courses are designed to give instruction concerning the basic knowledge of the soil and its management, fertilizers, and their uses as related to the principal products of the field. Crop improvement practices and the science of crop improvement are stressed for those who are interested in agronomy as a specialty.

There is sufficient flexibility within the curriculum to allow the student to specialize in soil science, plant science, soil conservation or general agronomy. Those students who have a desire to receive training which will qualify them for investigational work in these fields may obtain it by selecting appropriate supporting science or vocational subjects as electives. This training equips them to serve as specialists in one of these selected fields for industrial corporations and may serve also as training for extension or teaching work.

JUNIOR YEAR

1st Semester	Credits	2nd Semester	Credits
Agron. 57, Soil Formation	3	Agron. 52, Soil Utilization	3
Zoology 53, Genetics	3	Electives	9
Electives	6		

SENIOR YEAR

1st Semester	Credits	2nd Semester	Credits
Agron. 51, Field Crops	3	Agron. 78, Fertilizer and Soil	
Chem. 51, Organic	4	Fertility	3
Electives	9	Chem. 52, Organic	4
		Electives	9

Animal Husbandry   V. A. RICE, *Adviser*

The broad purpose of the animal husbandry major is that of providing the basic training for specialists in animal husbandry. Upon graduation, opportunities are available in the practical, scientific or commercial fields of animal husbandry; i.e., livestock farming, research, teaching, administration, or in the business phases of the livestock industry.

Students who major in the department of animal husbandry must successfully complete one summer of placement training as a requirement for graduation.

JUNIOR YEAR

1st Semester	Credits	2nd Semester	Credits
An. Husb. 51, Nutrition of Farm An.	3	An. Husb. 56, 56A, Beef and Sheep Production	4
An. Husb. 53, El. Meat Packing	3	Electives	
Electives			

SENIOR YEAR

1st Semester	Credits	2nd Semester	Credits
An. Husb. 75, An. Breeding	4	An. Husb. 76, Animal Breeding Practice	
An. Husb. 81, Seminar	1	An. Husb. 78, Dairy Cattle Production	3
Electives		An. Husb. 82, Seminar	1
		Electives	

Dairy Industry   D. J. HANKINSON, *Adviser*

Major students in dairy industry receive training in the testing, handling, and processing of milk, ice cream, butter, cheese, and other milk products. Practical application is made of chemistry, bacteriology, economics, and engineering in the many phases of dairy work.

The dairy industry department, with student laboratories for the testing and manufacture of dairy products, research laboratories, and commercial scale milk and ice cream plant facilities, is housed in Flint Laboratory, a building devoted solely to dairy work.

Dairy industry graduates may secure responsible positions with commercial dairy manufacturing firms, or with equipment and supply firms. Opportunities are offered also for positions as teachers in high schools and colleges, for service in the fields of extension and research, and for sanitation and public health work with city, state or federal agencies.

Major students in dairy industry must successfully complete one summer of placement training in a dairy plant. It is recommended that this requirement be met during the summer immediately following the sophomore year of University residence.

JUNIOR YEAR

1st Semester	Credits	2nd Semester	Credits
Dairy Ind. 77, Butter and Cheese	4	Dairy Ind. 50, Judging	1
Chem. 51, Organic	4	Dairy Ind. 52, Mkt. Milk	4
Bact. 61, Public Health	3	Chem. 52, Organic	4
Electives	6	Electives	6

SENIOR YEAR

1st Semester	Credits	2nd Semester	Credits
Dairy Ind. 75, Chemistry	3	Dairy Ind. 78, Ice Cream	4
Dairy Ind. 79, Seminar	1	Dairy Ind. 80, Seminar	1
Bact. 81, Applied	4	Bact. 90, sanitary	3
Agr. Engin. 80 Food Process Eng.	3	Electives	9
Electives	6		

Floriculture   C. L. THAYER, *Adviser*

The courses in floriculture provide for a comprehensive and detailed study of the practices and principles involved in the production, marketing and uses of cut flowers, flowering and foliage plants grown outdoors and under glass. Opportunities available to graduates may include: positions in various fields of commercial floriculture, such as production, wholesale marketing and retailing; employment in nurseries, on private estates and in conservatories; positions in the professional field, including graduate study, teaching in colleges and secondary schools, research and extension work under state, Federal, or other supervision.

It is advantageous for the student to determine, as soon as possible, the type of position for which he wishes to fit himself since the choice of elective courses will depend largely on his decision.

All major students in floriculture must successfully complete one summer of placement training in work related to their major objective and approved by the head of the department. It is recommended that this requirement for graduation be met during the summer following the freshman or sophomore year.

As sophomores majors are advised to take Chemistry 29 and Botany 26 for their sciences. First semester electives should be Botany 25 and Olericulture 25; second semester Entomology 26 and Floriculture 26.

JUNIOR YEAR

1st Semester	Credits	2nd Semester	Credits
Flori. 51, Greenhouse Mgt.	3	Flori. 52, Flower Arrangement	3
Flori. 79, Conservatory Plants or	2	Flori. 54, Greenhouse Const.	3
Flori. 81, Gardens and		Plant Breeding 52, Methods	3
borders	3	Botany 52, Advanced Plant	
Zoology 53, Prin. of Genetics	3	Pathology	3
Entomology 51, Pests of Special		Electives	3
Crops	3		
Botany 51, Plant Pathology	3		
Electives	2-3		

SENIOR YEAR

1st Semester	Credits	2nd Semester	Credits
Flori. 75, Commercial	3	Flori. 76, Commercial	3
Flori. 79 or	2	Flori. 82, Seminar	3
Flori. 81	3	Botany 68, Physiology	3
Botany 67, Physiology	3	Electives	8
Electives	5-9		

Food Technology   C. R. FELLERS, Adviser

The department offers a curriculum in food technology, and is preparing curricula for two new options recently approved—one in fisheries technology and one in food management.

The curriculum in food technology provides scientific and applied training in the principles concerned with the processing, preservation, and packaging of foods and food products. Both home and commercial methods of food preservation are considered. Practical work includes canning, freezing, dehydration, fermentation and salting. Methods of manufacture of jams, jellies, fruit juicies, and beverages are a part of the course work. An effort is made to apply the student's background in chemistry, physics, and bacteriology to food technology problems and food analysis.

The curriculum gives the student a broad science background with specialized knowledge in food processing and preservation. Special courses are offered for home economics majors who plan to teach or do extension work in foods. Major fields open to graduates include: (1) commercial work in cannery, freezer and other plant operations; (2) control and analytical work related to food products; (3) government food inspection and grading; (4) technological work in government and industry.

Ambitious students are encouraged to acquire the background which will enable them to pursue graduate work and research in the application of scientific knowledge to the technology of foods.

The selection of supporting courses depends upon the objective of the student, which should be determined as early as possible.

Food technology majors should take Physics 25 and 26 and Chemistry 29 and 30 in the sophomore year; also, if possible, Bacteriology 31. Students planning to take Physical Chemistry should complete Mathematics 29 and 30.

JUNIOR YEAR

1st Semester	Credits	2nd Semester	Credits
Food Tech. 51, Introductory	3	Food Tech. 52, Food Prod.	3
Chemistry 51, Organic	4	Chemistry 52, Organic	4
Bacteriology 51	3	Bacteriology 82, Applied	3
Agr. Engin. 80, Food Eng.	3	Agr. Engin. 82, Refrigeration	2
Elective		Electives	

SENIOR YEAR

1st Semester	Credits	2nd Semester	Credits
Food Tech. 61, Industrial Technology	3	Food Tech. 62, Industrial Technology	3
Food Tech. 71, Food Science Literature	2	Food Tech. 72, Food Science Literature	2
Food Tech. 91, Analysis of Food Prod.	3	Food Tech. 92, Exam. of Food Prod.	3
Chemistry 79, Elem. Biol. or	4	Food Tech. 82, Confections and Cereal Products or	2
Chemistry 65, Physical	3	Chemistry 65, Physical	3
Electives		Electives	

SUGGESTED JUNIOR-SENIOR ELECTIVES

Public Health 61, 62, 63
A Foreign Language
Mechanical Engin. 1, 63
Pomology 77
Dairy Ind. 75, 77, 52 or 78
Animal Husbandry 53

Poult. Husbandry 75
Olericulture 73, 74
Botany 66
Home Ec. 30, 52, 54
Food Tech. 85, 95
Chem. Engin. 77, 75
Indus. Engin. 25, 51

FORESTRY AND WILDLIFE MANAGEMENT

This department offers two curricula, one in Forest Production and Management and one in Wildlife Management.

Forestry R. P. HOLDSWORTH, *Adviser*

The technical curriculum in forestry in concentrated in the field of forest production and management, and leads to the degree of Bachelor of Science. It has professional status, being accredited by Society of American Foresters.

The freshman and sophomore years are devoted to studies of basic sciences, English, and other subjects of cultural-foundational value. A required group of three courses—forest mensuration, forest harvesting, and plane surveying—is presented in a nine-weeks summer term immediately following the freshman year. During the summer following the sophomore year qualified students are recommended for work giving practical field experience in forestry. Such employment may be with the United States Forest Service or other public and private agencies.

Ten technical courses in forestry are grouped in the junior and senior years in addition to three supporting courses presented by other departments, a required course in history, and six student electives. It is intended that the forestry curriculum be as sound professionally and as broad from the viewpoint of general education as is possible within the limits of four undergraduate years.

Students who complete the forestry curriculum with high academic standing may be admitted to graduate professional schools for work toward a Master of Forestry degree. This is usually obtainable with one year. Seniors are eligible to compete in Federal and State Civil Service examinations.

The forestry courses are open with few exceptions to students other than those concentrating in forestry but should be elected only after consultation with the student's major adviser and with the instructor teaching the course.

Sophomore majors in forestry take Physics 26 and Geology 27 the first semester; Entomology 26, Physics 26, Botany 28 and Agronomy 2 the second semester.

SUMMER (Following Freshman Year)

Forestry 55, Forest Mensuration	Credit, 3
Forestry 78, Forest Harvesting	Credit, 3
Civil Engineering 27, Plane Surveying	Credit, 3

JUNIOR YEAR

1st Semester	Credits	2nd Semester	Credits
Forestry 53, Silvics	3	Forestry 56, Prin. of Silviculture	3
Forestry 59, Protection	3	Forestry 54, Forest Soils	3
Forestry 75, Products	3	Wildlife Mgt. 72, Forest-Animal	
History	3	Relationships	3
Elective (not Forestry)	3	Entomology 72, Forest Ent.	3
		Elective (not Forestry)	3

SENIOR YEAR

1st Semester	Credits	2nd Semester	Credits
Forestry 81, Regional Silvicul.	3	Forestry 82, Seeding and Planting	3
Forestry 57, Forest Policy & Econ.	3	Forestry 80, 52, Photogrammetry,	
Botany 51, Plant Pathology	3	Forest Mgt.	3
Electives (not Forestry)	6	Forestry 52, Photogrammetry	3
		Electives (not Forestry)	6

Wildlife Management   R. E. Trippensee, *Adviser*

The courses in conservation and wildlife management are designed for those who desire a general understanding of the renewable natural resources as well as those who expect to make a living in the professional field of wildlife management. Courses are available also to students who expect to major in other fields including agriculture, agronomy, economics, forestry, entomology, and education.

Wildlife management is both an applied science and an art and is concerned with the production and control of animal populations on many types of land including farms, forests, and on waste lands and water areas. Thus an understanding of both the origin and management of land and water is necessary. These background phases included geology, agronomy, forestry, and agriculture. Fields of specialization include fisheries management, game, and furbearer management and control of injurious animals, and related fields such as soil conservation, conservation education, and industrial biology.

Studies in wildlife management are closely correlated with the work of the State Conservation Department and the U. S. Fish and Wildlife Service. During the junior and senior years trips are planned to the bait-mixing station of the U. S. Fish and Wildlife Service, the John C. Phillips, Wildlife Laboratory at Upton, Mass. and to numerous wildlife projects in the state. Students are urged to attend the northeastern and the American wildlife conferences.

Graduates in this field are eligible to both state and federal civil service examinations, and most of the permanent job opportunities are in public service either with the state or federal government. A limited number of positions are open in private enterprises. Training in the wildlife field is an excellent background for teaching of science in the public schools and for employment as conservation officers. Much research data and many research operations are available to undergraduates through the Massachusetts Cooperative Wildlife Research Station, and students with sufficiently high grades are eligible for graduate work at other universities.

The courses during the first two years are basic educational subjects required to build a background of sound professional training. Sophomores are expected to take Geology 27, Zoology 35, Wildlife Management 27, Agronomy 2, Entomology 26, and Forestry 26:

JUNIOR YEAR

1st Semester	Credits	2nd Semester	Credits
Wildlife Management 71 or 75	3	Botany 26	3
Fores. 55	3	Wildlife Management 70	3
Gov't. 25	3	Wildlife Management 74 or 84	3
Electives*		Gov't. 28	3
		Forestry 56	3
		Electives*	

SENIOR YEAR

1st Semester	Credits	2nd Semester	Credits
Wildlife Management 75 or 71	3	Wildlife Management 74 or 84	3
Botany 53	3	Forestry 52	3
Electives*		Electives*	

* Electives should be chosen in consultation with the student's adviser.

Landscape Architecture   R. H. OTTO, *Adviser*

Instruction in this department has two objectives: first a contribution to general education; second, a preparation of students for the practice of landscape architecture. The department offers optional curricula, (1) Professional Landscape Architecture, and (2) Ornamental Horticulture.

The department also offers several elective courses in art (listed and described under Directory of Courses, page 121, which do not constitute a major. These courses are primarily cultural rather than technical and are intended to provide a better appreciation of the arts.

Students following this curriculum are prepared to take up work in landscape architecture, which leads through field experience or post-graduate study to permanent establishment in the profession.

Sophomores in the first semester elect either Botany 25 or Geology 27 for their science and take Landscape Architecture 25 (Drawing) and Civil Engineering 27 as electives. In the second semester the science is either Entomology 26 or Geology 28 and the electives Landscape Architecture 26 (Drafting) and Horticulture 26 (Plant Materials).

JUNIOR YEAR

1st Semester	Credits	2nd Semester	Credits
Landscape Arch. 51, Topography	3	Landscape Arch. 52, Elements of Landscape Arch.	3
Landscape Arch. 53, Intro. Design	3	Landscape Arch. 54, General Design	3
Hort. 51, Plant Materials	3	Landscape Arch. 86, City Planning	3
Landscape Arch. 79, Construction & Maintenance alternates with Landscape Arch. 83	3	Hort. 52, Planting Design	3
Elective	3	Electives	3

SENIOR YEAR

1st Semester	Credits	2nd Semester	Credits
Landscape Arch. 81, Advanced Design	3	Landscape Arch. 84, Sketching	2
Landscape Arch. 87, City Planning	3	Landscape Arch. 82, Advanced Design	3
Landscape Arch. 83, alternates with Landscape Arch. 79	3	Art 78, History of Art	3
Electives	6	Landscape Arch. 80, History & Lit. of Landscape Arch.	2
		Electives	5

SUGGESTED ELECTIVES FOR JUNIOR AND SENIOR YEARS

Agronomy 53, 56, Agrostology
Civil Engin. 90, Contracts, Specifications, and Estimating
Agri. Engin. 51, House Planning

Floriculture 81, Herbaceous Borders
Philosophy 82, Aesthetics
Art 33, 34, 75

Ornamental Horticulture

The curriculum in ornamental horticulture is suggested for those preferring to follow the horticultural phase of landscape including (1) nursery practice; (2) landscape planting and construction; and (3) maintenance of landscaped areas, such as parks and semi-public institution grounds.

Sophomores in this major will take Botany 25, Civil Engineering 27, Landscape Architecture 25 in the first semester; Entomology 26, Floriculture 26, and Horticulture 26 in the second.

JUNIOR YEAR

1st Semester	Credits	2nd Semester	Credits
Hort. 51, Plant Materials	3	Hort. 52, Planting Design	3
Landscape Arch. 51, Topography	3	Landscape Arch. 52, Construction	
Landscape Arch. 53, Garden		details	3
Design	3	Pomology 26, Small Fruits	3
Landscape Arch. 79, Construction		Landscape Arch. 54, General	
& Maintenance	3	Design	3
Elective	3	Elective	3

SENIOR YEAR

1st Semester	Credits	2nd Semester	Credits
Flori. 81, Herbaceous Borders		Agrostology 56, Turf Mgt.	3
Agrostology 53, Turf Grasses		Pomology 56, Spraying	3
Zoology 53, Genetics		Plant Breeding 52, Methods	3
Ent. 51, Pests of Sp. Crops		Electives	6
Botany 51, Plant Physiology	3		

SUGGESTED ELECTIVES FOR JUNIOR AND SENIOR YEARS

Botany 67, 68, 81	Agronomy 78
Entomology 72	Forestry 56

Olericulture   G. B. SNYDER, *Adviser*

The courses in olericulture offer a comprehensive training in the scientific principles and commercial practices related to the culture and marketing of vegetable crops. The studies and training involved are set up to prepare graduates to undertake work in the following fields: (1) practical work in operating commercial market garden or truck farms or greenhouse establishments, (2) teaching olericulture and related subjects in college, secondary or high schools, (3) extension work in horticulture and agriculture, (4) research studies with state, Federal, or private agencies, (5) state, Federal, or private inspection service agencies, and (6) the wholesale and retail marketing of vegetables and other perishable commodities.

The department of olericulture has facilities in greenhouses, plant houses, hot beds, machinery and equipment used in production and marketing procedures as well as land to provide the student ample opportunity to become acquainted with modern techniques and practices used in handling vegetable crops. Nearby truck farms, wholesale and retail market outlets, variety trial plots of seed companies and inspection agencies are used to demonstrate laboratory and classroom points of discussion.

The rather broad objectives of the training mean that the selection of supporting courses depends upon the specific field in which the student wishes to engage on graduation. This objective should, therefore, be determined as early as possible during the sophomore year.

Majors in olericulture should take the following courses during the first semester of the sophomore year: Botany 25, and Olericulture 25. In the second semester they should include Chemistry 29, Entomology 26, and Pomology 26.

JUNIOR YEAR

1st Semester	Credits	2nd Semester	Credits
Oleri. 51, Nutrient Requirements	3	Oleri. 52, Environment and Plant Culture	3
Zoology 53, Genetics	3		
Botany 51, Plant Pathology	3	Oleri. 76, Greenhouse Crops	3
Botany 67, Plant Physiology	3	Botany 68, Plant Physiology	3
Electives	5	Electives	6-8

SENIOR YEAR

1st Semester	Credits	2nd Semester	Credits
Oleri. 73, Marketing Practices	3	Oleri. 74, Merchandising of Perishables	3
Oleri. 75, Systematic	3		
Oleri. 81, Seminar	1	Oleri. 78, Commercial	3
Entomology 51, Pests of Special Crops	3	Oleri. 82, Seminar	1
Electives	7	Electives	10

Pomology   A. P. FRENCH, *Adviser*

The pomology courses provide a comprehensive training in the scientific and commercial principles concerned in the growing and marketing of apples, pears, peaches, plums, cherries, and small fruits. Major fields open to graduates include: (1) practical work in connection with the operation of fruit farms; (2) teaching in college, high school, or secondary schools of agriculture; (3) extension work in county, state, or nation; (4) research work with state, federal or private concerns; and (5) commercial work in connection with the manufacture and sale of such supplies as machinery, packages, and spraying and dusting materials. Certain supporting courses are required and their selection depends upon the objective of the student. That objective should, therefore, be determined as early as possible.

First semester sophomores are advised to elect Geology 27, Physics 25, and Olericulture 25. In the second semester they should take Chemistry 29, Entomology 26 and Pomology 26.

The selection of junior-senior electives should be undertaken with the help of the departmental adviser. They will depend for the most part on the interests and objectives of the student and his class record to date. The student who wishes to do college teaching, extension work, or research is advised to secure a broad foundation in science and liberal arts, and to plan to enter a graduate school sooner or later. The student whose objective is growing fruit or teaching in secondary school may need to broaden his training in horticulture and agriculture and, again, will need all the science and liberal arts that can be included in the program.

Students majoring in Pomology must successfully complete one summer of placement training on a fruit farm before the beginning of the senior year.

JUNIOR YEAR

1st Semester	Credits	2nd Semester	Credits
Pomology 53, General		Pomology 56, Orchard Pest	
Pomology 75, Systematic or	3	Control	3
Pomology 77, Commercial		Botany 68, Psychology	3
Botany 51, Plant Pathology		Botany 30, Plant Anatomy	3
Botany 67, Physiology		English 84, Tech. Writing	3
Elective	6	Electives	3

SENIOR YEAR

1st Semester	Credits	2nd Semester	Credits
Pomology 81, Advanced	3	Pomology 82, Advanced	3
Pomology 75, Systematic or	4	Pomology 84, Seminar	1
Pomology 77, Commercial	3	Electives	12
Pomology 83, Seminar	1		
Zoology 53, Genetics	3		
Electives	5		

Curriculum in Cranberry Technology

This curriculum is designed to provide a broad training in the fields of knowledge which serve as the foundation of the cranberry industry. Its purpose is to provide future leaders and specialists for the industry.

Students who follow this curriculum must satisfactorily complete a minimum of two summers' practical experience in the cranberry industry before the beginning of the senior year.

Courses taken during the freshman and sophomore year will be the same as those outlined for others majoring in Pomology. The choice of junior-senior electives will depend upon the objective of the student and will be made with the assistance of the adviser.

JUNIOR YEAR

1st Semester	Credits	2nd Semester	Credits
Chem. 33	3	Pomology 56, Spraying	3
Botany 51, Plant Pathology	3	Ag. Econ. 26, Ag'l Prod.	3
Ent. 51, Pests of Special Crops	3	Electives	
Electives			

SENIOR YEAR

1st Semester	Credits	2nd Semester	Credits
Bot. 67, Plant Psychology	3	Bot. 68, Plant Physiol.	3
Ag. Econ. 55, Marketing	3	Ag. Econ. 56, Cooperatn.	3
Pom. 85, Cranberry Prob.	2	Pom. 86, Cranberry Prob.	2
Electives		Electives	

Poultry Husbandry ——————, *Adviser*

The department gives instruction in the science, art and practices of poultry keeping, not only to students specializing in this department, but also to those in other departments who desire supporting work in poultry husbandry. The major courses prepare men for the successful operation of commercial poultry and breeding farms and hatcheries either as owners or managers; for high school, college and federal work in teaching, extension and research; and as service men, specialists and managers in industrial fields allied to the poultry industry.

Students must successfully complete one summer of placement training on a poultry farm or in some business allied to poultry.

Sophomores may choose electives from the list of sophomore sciences or Dairy 25, Animal Husbandry 26, Agricultural Economics 26, Olericulture 25, Pomology 26, Floriculture 26, or Wildlife Management 27.

JUNIOR YEAR

1st Semester	Credits	2nd Semester	Credits
Poultry Husb. 55, Housing and Sanitation	2	Poultry Husb. 52, Incubation and Brooding	3
Poultry Husb. 53, Judging	3	Poultry Husb. 56, Nutrition	3
Zoology 53	3	Electives	
Electives			

SENIOR YEAR

1st Semester	Credits	2nd Semester	Credits
Poultry Husb. 75, Marketing	2	Poultry Husb. 78, Seminar and Farm Management	3-4
Poultry Husb. 77, Breeding	3	Poultry Husb. 76, Turkey Prod.	2
Vet. Sci. 75, Comp. Vet. Anat	3	Vet. Sci. 88, Avian Path.	3
Electives		Electives	

Veterinary Science

Though major work in Veterinary Science is not available, the department does offer supporting courses to assist students who expect to enter the various fields of agriculture, wildlife management, public health, teaching and laboratory work in the biological sciences or veterinary medicine.

SCHOOL OF BUSINESS ADMINISTRATION

Milo Kimball, *Dean*

The School of Business Administration prepares students eventually to assume positions of responsibility in business. An objective of the School is the education of young men and women who will regard management in business as a profession with high ethical standards and broad social responsibilities. The curricula provide preparation for specialized tasks in accounting, finance, industrial administration, marketing, and merchandising. When less specialization is desired, the student selects the General Business program. Each course of study leads to the professional degree of Bachelor of Business Administration.

Curricula in Business Administration

In keeping with the objectives of the School, the curricula encourage breadth of training for business. General education is emphasized by providing fundamental courses in the humanities, mathematics, science, and social studies. The courses for the first two years are therefore largely prescribed.

FRESHMAN YEAR

1st Semester	Credits	2nd Semester	Credits
English 1, Composition	2	English 2, Composition	2
Speech 3	1	Speech 4	1
Industrial Adm. 11, Indust. Geography or Foreign Language	3	Economics 12, Ec. Hist of U. S. or Foreign Language	3
Government 25, American	3	History 6, Mod. European Civ.	3
Mathematics 7 or 5	3	Mathematics 8 or 10 or 6	3
Elective, Science	3	Elective, Science	3
Military 1	3	Military 2	2
Physical Ed. 7 (women)	2	Physical Ed. 8 (women)	2
Physical Ed. 3 (men)	1	Physical Ed. 4 (men)	1

SOPHOMORE YEAR

1st Semester	Credits	2nd Semester	Credits
English 25, Humane Letters	3	English 26, Humane Letters	3
Accounting 25, Introduction o	3	[1]Accounting 26, Introduction to	3
Economics 25, Elements	3	Economics 26, Prob. of Nat'l Economy	3
Psychology 26, General	3	Sociology 28, Elements	3
Elective	3	Elective	3
Military 25	2	Military 26	2
Physical Ed. 33 (men)	1	Physical Ed. 34 (men)	1
Physical Ed. 27 (women)	2	Physical Ed. 28 (women)	2

[1] Students majoring in Merchandising take Home Ec. 2 in place of Acct. 26.

JUNIOR-SENIOR CURRICULA IN BUSINESS ADMINISTRATION

The channels to specialization in a particular area of business lead through basic courses in production, marketing, finance, accounting, statistics and business law. The junior-senior programs are based on this core. Students acquire an awareness of each of the fundamental functions of business and develop facility in the use of the basic tools of management. They develop understanding of the relationship of their particular interest to all business activities as well as competence in a special field.

General Business Management

This program is for students whose interest is in general business management. It is designed to provide understanding of the broad administrative aspects of business, and specialized courses are subordinated to a comprehensive program of training. It prepares also for study of a more specialized nature in graduate school.

JUNIOR YEAR

1st Semester	Credits	2nd Semester	Credits
Ind. Adm. 63, Mgt. in Ind.	3	Ind. Adm. 66, Transportation & Traffic	3
Fin. 55, Financial Inst.	3	Fin. 65, Corp. Fin.	3
Mkt. 53, Marketing Prin.	3	Fin. 76, Insurance	3
Statistics 79, Elem. Ec. Stat.	3	Ec. 56, Business Fluctuations	3
Elective	3	Elective	3

SENIOR YEAR

1st Semester	Credits	2nd Semester	Credits
Bus. Law 70, Bus. Law I		Bus. Law 72, Bus. Law II	3
Ec. 73, Modern Econ. Theory		Ind. Adm. 80, Adm. Proced.	3
Ec. 79, Labor Problems		Ec. 78, Public Finance	3
Professional Elective		Professional Elective	3
Elective	3	Elective	3

Accounting

Accounting deals with the problems of measuring, recording, reporting and interpreting business transactions. The courses in this program are designed for the student who wishes to undertake preparation for employment as auditor, controller, cost analyst, industrial accountant, public accountant, or teacher of accounting.

JUNIOR YEAR

1st Semester	Credits	2nd Semester	Credits
Acct. 61, Intermediate Acct.	3	Acct. 62, Advanced Acct.	3
Fin. 55, Finan. Inst.	3	Acct. 64, Cost Acct.	3
Statistics 79, Elem. Ec. Stat.	3	Bus. Law 70, Bus. Law I	3
Mkt. 53, Marketing Prin.	3	Fin. 65, Corp. Fin.	3
Elective	3	Elective	3

SENIOR YEAR

1st Semester	Credits	2nd Semester	Credits
Acct. 73, Tax Acct.	3	Acct. 74, Acctg. Systems	3
Acct. 75, Adm. Acct. & Control	3	Acct. 76, Auditing.	3
Ec. 73, Modern Ec. Theory	3	Ec. 78, Public Finance	3
Ind. Adm. 63, Mgt. in Ind.	3	Fin. 82, Investments	3
Elective	3	Elective	3

Finance

Courses in banking, finance and insurance are provided for students who expect to assume responsibility for financing a business or to work for banks, investment institutions, brokerage houses, insurance companies, or governmental agencies concerned with finance. The curriculum provides for study of our financial institutions, the procedures of financial organization and administration, the principles of insurance, and training for investment analysis and management.

JUNIOR YEAR

1st Semester	Credits	2nd Semester	Credits
Fin. 55, Fin. Institutions	3	Bus. Law 70, Business Law I	3
Fin. 65, Corp. Finance	3	Ec. 56, Business Fluctuations	3
Ind. Adm. 63, Mgt. in Ind.	3	Statistics 79, Elem. Ec. Stat.	3
Mkt. 53, Mkt. Principles	3	Professional Elective	3
Elective	3	Elective	3

SENIOR YEAR

1st Semester	Credits	2nd Semester	Credits
Fin. 81, Problems of Bus. Fin.	3	Fin. 82, Investments	3
Ec. 73, Modern Ec. Theory	3	Fin. 76, Insurance	3
Ec. 79, Labor Problems	3	Ec. 78, Public Finance	3
Professional Elective	3	Professional Elective	3
Elective	3	Elective	3

Industrial Administration

American industry offers to qualified students the opportunity to find satisfying careers in the various fields of industrial management, labor relations, or personnel management. The program offered is designed to give the student specialized training in these fields and a comprehensive understanding of the problems of industrial enterprises.

JUNIOR YEAR

1st Semester	Credits	2nd Semester	Credits
Ind. Adm. 63, Mgt. in Ind.		Ind. Adm. 64, Personnel Mgt.	3
Fin. 55, Finan. Inst.		Bus. Law 70, Bus. Law I	3
Mkt. 53, Mkt. Principles		Ind. Adm. 66, Transp. & Traffic	3
Statistics 79, Elem. Ec. Stat.		Acct. 64, Cost Acct.	3
Elective	3	Elective	3

SENIOR YEAR

1st Semester	Credits	2nd Semester	Credits
Ind. Adm. 73, Probs. in Ind. Mgt.	3	Ind. Adm. 80, Admin. Procedure	3
Acct. 75, Adm. Acct. & Control	3	Mkt. 56, Purchasing	3
Fin. 65, Corp. Finance	3	Psych. 86, Industrial	3
Ec. 79, Labor Problems	3	Ind. Engin. 88, Time & Motion	
Elective	3	Study	3
		Elective	3

Marketing

Students in marketing prepare for occupations in wholesale and retail enterprises, the selling activities of industry and advertising and auxiliary services to business. The program offers some general training in business and specialized study of basic types of market operations.

JUNIOR YEAR

1st Semester	Credits	2nd Semester	Credits
Mktg. 53, Mktg. Prin.	3	Mktg. 54, Sales Mgt. &	
Fin. 55, Finan. Inst.	3	Salesmanship	3
Ind. Adm. 63, Mgt. in Industry	3	Bus. Law 70, Bus. Law	
Statistics 79, Ec. Stat.	3	Mkgt. 62, Mkt. Research	3
Elective	3	Ind. Adm. 66, Transportation	
		& Traffic	3
		Bus. Law 70, Bus. Law I	3
		Elective	3

SENIOR YEAR

1st Semester	Credits	2nd Semester	Credits
Mktg. 71, Retail Merchandising	3	Mkt. 80, Probs. in Mkt.	3
Mktg. 73, Advertising	3	Mkt. 76, Purchasing	3
Ec. 73, Modern Ec. Theory	3	Psych. 86, Industrial Psych.	3
Ec. 79, Labor Problems	3	Professional Elective	3
Elective	3	Elective	3

Merchandising

This program has been planned in cooperation with the School of Home Economics to meet the demand for women with technical training to fill positions of responsibility in merchandising.

JUNIOR YEAR

1st Semester	Credits	2nd Semester	Credits
Mkt. 53, Mkt. Prin.	3	Mkt. 62, Market Research	3
Ec. 55, Ec. of Consumption	3	Bus. Law 70, Bus. Law I	3
Home Ec. 51, Food Selection or		Home Ec. 52, Nutrition or	
Home Ec. 57, Clothing Select.	3	Home Ec. 62, Home Furnishing	3
Professional Elective	3	Professional Elective	3
Elective	3	Elective	3

99

BUSINESS ADMINISTRATION

SENIOR YEAR

1st Semester	Credits	2nd Semester	Credits
Mkt. 71, Retail Merchandising	3	Mkt. 80, Mkt. Problems	3
Mkt. 73, Advertising	3	Ind. Adm. 64, Personnel Mgt.	3
Home Ec. 87, Tailoring or		Home Ec. 88, Appld. Dres Dsn. or	
Home Ec. 91, Inst. Mgt.	3	Home Ec. 92, Inst. Mgt.	3
Professional Elective	3	Professional Elective	3
Elective	3	Electives	3

SCHOOL OF ENGINEERING

G. A. MARSTON, *Dean*

The departments of agricultural engineering, chemical engineering, civil engineering, mechanical engineering and electrical engineering comprise the School of Engineering. Each department offers a curriculum leading to a Bachelor of Science Degree in that particular branch. An optional curriculum in industrial engineering is offered in the mechanical engineering department.

The Civil, Electrical, Mechanical, and the Industrial optional curricula have been accredited by the Engineers Council for Professional Development.

Engineering can be defined as the combination of science and art by which materials and power are made useful to mankind. An engineer requires intensive technical training but at the same time he should acquire the broad education that distinguishes the professional man from the technician. His education does not end with formal schooling but continues throughout his life as he accumulates experience.

The curricula in engineering have been carefully prepared to offer each student the opportunity to acquire a sound training in the fundamental work of the various branches of his chosen field. At the same time he receives a thorough training in the sciences and mathematics, which are the important tools of the engineer. About twenty per cent of his time is devoted to the social and humanistic studies. Some opportunity to pursue his particular interest is offered in the senior year.

The curriculum of the freshman year is the same for all. Specialization to a limited extent begins in the sophomore year.

FRESHMAN YEAR

1st Semester	Credits	2nd Semester	Credits
English I, Composition	2	English 2, Composition	2
Speech 3	1	Speech 4	1
Mathematics 5, Analytical Geom.	4	Mathematics 6, Diff. Calculus	4
Chem. 1, General	3	Chem. 2 or 4, General	3 or 4
Mechanical Engineering 1, Drawing	2	Mechanical Engr. 2, Drawing	3
*Hist. 5, Fren., Ger., or Span.	3	*Hist. 6, Fren., Ger., or Span.	3
Military 1	3	Military 2	2
Physical Ed. 3	1	Physical Ed. 4	1

* French or German recommended for Chem. Engin. majors.

SOPHOMORE-JUNIOR-SENIOR CURRICULA

Majors in Engineering will select one of the following curricula.

Agricultural Engineering   H. N. STAPLETON, *Adviser*

Agricultural engineering is concerned with the application of scientific engineering principles to the agricultural industry in which mechanical and electrical power, processing equipment, design and development of a farm structure, soil and water conservation, research, extension, teaching, and promotional activities form parts.

The curriculum is designed to prepare students soundly in basic sciences, engineering, and humanistic subjects for service in this expanding field. There is opportunity for limited specialization and generous provision for electives in the third and fourth years.

SOPHOMORE YEAR

1st Semester	Credits	2nd Semester	Credits
Eng. 25, Humane Letters	3	English 26, Humane Letters	3
Math. 31, Integ. Calculus	4	Math. 32, Diff. Equations	4
Physics 25, Mech., Sound, Heat	4	Physics 26, Light, Elect.	4
Civil Engin. 27, Surveying	3	Civil Engin. 34, Statics	3
Mech. Engin. 39, Materials		Psych. 26, or Soc. 28	3
of Construction	2	Miltary 26	2
Military 25	2	Phys. Ed. 34	1
Phys. Ed. 33	1		

SUMMER (6 WEEKS)

Civ. Engin. 28, Prop. &		Civ. Engin. 30, Route Surveying	
Topog. Surveying	3	Practice	3

(or approved industrial or farm employment)

JUNIOR YEAR

1st Semester	Credits	2nd Semester	Credits
Engl. 83, Tech. Writing	2	Econ. 25, General	3
Civ. Eng. 52, Dynamics	3	Agron. 2, Soils	3
Civ. Eng. 51, Strength of Mat'l	4	Civ. Eng. 61, Testing Mat'ls	2
Elec. Eng. 61, Principles of	4	Elec. Eng. 62' Principles of	4
Mech. Eng. 65, Heat Eng.	3	Mech. Eng. 68, Kinematics	3
Ag. Eng. 71, Mech. Power	3	Ag. Eng. 73, Farm Structures	4

SENIOR YEAR

1st Semester	Credits	2nd Semester	Credits
Ag. Eng. 85, Farm Electrifi.	3	Ag. Eng. 92, Seminar	1
Ag. Econ. 75, Mgt.	3	Ag. Eng. 76, Agr. Machinery	3
Mech. Eng. 83, Machine Design	3	Ag. Eng. 78, Drain, Recl., Consv.	3
Civ. Eng. 75, Fluid Mech.	3	Civ. Eng. 90, Constr., Spec., Est.	3
Ag.* & Tech.* Electives	6	Ag.* & Tech.* Electives	8-9

* Electives to be selected in consultation with the student's adviser.

Chemical Engineering
E. E. LINDSEY, *Adviser*

Chemical Engineering is that branch of engineering concerned with the development of manufacturing processes in which chemical or certain physical changes of materials are involved. These processes may usually be resolved into a coordinated series of unit operations (physical changes) and unit processes (chemical changes). The work of the chemical engineer is primarily concerned with the design, construction, and operation of equipment and plants in which series of these unit operations and processes are applied. Chemistry, physics, and mathematics are the underlying sciences of chemical engineering, and economics is its guide in practice.

Chemical engineers are employed not only in these industries manufacturing chemicals but in many others where there occur chemical changes and physical changes other than forming and shaping which is the province of mechanical engineering. Examples are: petroleum refining, coal processing, refractories and clay products, cement, waste treatment, pulp and paper, rayon and textiles, paint and varnish, natural and synthetic rubber, foods, leather, plastics, soap, penicillin and other antibiotics. Much of the work of the atomic energy program is chemical engineering. The types of work done by chemical engineers include: design, construction, research, development, production, financial and patent appraisal, management, and sales.

SOPHOMORE YEAR

1st Semester	Credits	2nd Semester	Credits
Chem. 29, Qualitative Analy.	4	Chem. 30, Quantitative Analy.	4
Physics 27, General	4	Physics 28, General	4
Math. 31, Applied Calculus	4	Math. 32, Diff. Equations	4
English 25, Humane Letters	3	English 26, Humane Letters	3
Military 25	2	Chem. Engin. 26, Calculations	2
Physical Education 33	1	Military 26	2
		Physical Education 34	1

JUNIOR YEAR

1st Semester	Credits	2nd Semester	Credits
Chemistry 51, Organic	4	Chemistry 52, Organic	4
Chemistry 65, Physical	4	Chemistry 66, Physical	4
Civil Engin. 34, Statics	3	Civil Engin. 51, Strength of Mat.	4
Chem. Engin. 55, Unit Opera. I	5	Chem. Engin. 56, Unit Opera. II	5
[1]Economics 25, Elements	3	[1]Psych. 26 or Sociology 28	3

SUMMER (6 WEEKS)

Chem. Engin. 75, Instrumentation	2	Chem. Engin. 88, Chem. Engin. Lab.	3

[1] Advanced military students will take Economics 25 and either Psychology 26 or Sociology 28 as two of their senior electives.

SENIOR YEAR

1st Semester	Credits	2nd Semester	Credits
Chem. Engin. 81, Heat-Energy Rel.	3	Chem. Engin. 82, Ind. Equil.	
Chem. Engin. 93, Comprehen.		& Kinetics	3
Prob.	3	Chem. Engin. 94, Comprehen.	
Chem. Engin. 91, Seminar	1	Prob.	3
Elec. Engin. 63, Elements	3	Chem. Engin. 92, Seminar	1
Chem. Eng. 89, Lab. Projects	3	Elec. Engin. 64, Indus. Applic.	3
1Electives	6	1Electives	8

1 Advanced military students will take Economics 25 and either Psychology 26 or Sociology 28 as two of their senior electives.

Recommended electives include history, government, French, German, Math. 83, English 83, Chem. 57, 58, 95, 98, Chemistry 77, 79, 86, 93, 94, Mech. Engin. 39, 46, Business Law 70. Other courses may be chosen with the approval of the Head of the Department.

Civil Engineering   M. P. WHITE, Adviser

Civil engineering is concerned with structures, transportation, movement of fluids, use and storage of water, sanitation, and surveying and mapping. A civil engineer may be engaged in research, in planning and designing, in construction, or in maintenance and operation. Consequently, civil engineering contains room for a wide range of interests—from highly theoretical to very practical.

The curriculum gives a thorough training in the fundamental sciences and at the same time prepares a student for work in any branch of civil engineering. During his senior year a student takes two or three elective technical courses, allowing him to specialize to some extent in whatever branch of civil engineering is most interesting to him — sanitation, mechanics and structures, hydraulics, foundation engineering, highway engineering.

SOPHOMORE YEAR

1st Semester	Credits	2nd Semester	Credits
English 25, Humane Letters	3	English 26, Humane Letters	3
Math. 31, Integ. Calculus	4	Math. 32, Diff. Equations	4
Physics 27, General	4	Physics 28, General	4
Civ. Engin. 25, Surveying	5	Elec. Engin. 63, Elements of	3
Military 25	2	Civ. E. 34, Statics	3
Phys. Ed. 33	1	Military 26	2
		Phys. Ed. 34	1

SUMMER (6 WEEKS)

Civ. E. 28, Prop. & Topog.		Civ. Eng. 30, Route Surveying	
Surveying	3	Practice	3

JUNIOR YEAR

1st Semester	Credits	2nd Semester	Credits
Psych. 26, Econ. 25 or Soc. 28	3	Econ. 25, Psych. 26 or Soc. 28	3
Civ. Eng. 51, Strength of Mat'ls	4	Civ. Eng. 70, Theory of Structures	4
Civ. Eng. 55, Highway Engin.	3	Civ. Eng. 61, Testing Mat'ls	2
Civ. Eng. 52, Dynamics	3	Civ. Engin. 80, Soil Mechanics	3
Mech. Eng. 65, Thermodynamics*	3	Mech. Engin. 39, Mat'ls. of	
Geol. 50, Engin. Geol.	3	Constr.*	2
		Civ. Eng. 76, Fluid Mechanics	4

SENIOR YEAR

1st Semester	Credits	2nd Semester	Credits
Civ. Eng. 71, Structural Design	3	Civ. Eng. 78, Sanitary Engin. II	4
Civ. Eng. 73, Concrete & Masonry	4	Civ. Eng. 90, Contracts,	
Civ. Eng. 77, Sanitary Engin. I	3	Specif. & Est.	3
Civ. Eng. 81, Foundations .	3	Civ. Eng. 92, Professional Sem.	1
English 83, Technical Writing	2	Technical Electives (Civ.	
Non-Tech. Elective*	3	Eng. 72, 86, 88, 94, 96,	
		Bact. 54, recommended)	6
		Non-Tech. Elective*	3

* Replaced by military for military majors.

Electrical Engineering   C. S. Roys, *Acting Adviser*

Electrical engineering is that branch of the profession covering the engineering applications of electricity. It reaches into practically every profession, every branch of activity, either through performance of the tasks involved, or through their measurement and control. Because it is so diversified in its applications, it is considered to be divided into various fields such as power, communications, electronics, illumination, measurements and control and others, each of these having specialized subdivisions.

The undergraduate curriculum is designed to prepare the student for work in any of these fields, and to serve as a basis for specialization in any of them, either in advanced courses or in the field. At the same time, about one-fifth of the student's work is devoted to the humanistic-social courses so that he may have an understanding of the broader aspects of engineering and its relation to other fields of human endeavor.

SUMMER (Following Freshman Year)

Mechanical Engineering 23, Shop and Civil Engineering 27, Surveying, 6 credit hours.

SOPHOMORE YEAR

1st Semester	Credits	2nd Semester	Credits
English 25, Humane Letters	3	English 26, Humane Letters	3
Math. 31, Integ. Calculus	4	Math. 32, Diff. Equations	4
Physics 27, General	4	Physics 28, General	4
Elec. Engin. 41, Fundemantals	4	Civ. E. 34, Statics	3
Military 25	2	Elec. Engin. 42, A-C. Circuits	3
Physical Ed. 33	1	Military 26	2
		Physical Ed. 34	1

JUNIOR YEAR

1st Semester	Credits	2nd Semester	Credits
Elec. Engin. 53, D-C. Machinery	4	Elec. Engin. 54, A-C. Machinery	4
Elec. Engin. 55, Electronics	3	Elec. Engin. 56, Appld. Electrn.	4
Elec. Engin. 57, Engin. Analysis	3	Elec. Engin. 58, Elec. Trans.	3
Mech. Engin. 65, Heat Engin. I	3	Mech. Engin. 66, Heat Engin. II	3
Civ. Engin. 53, Strength of Mat.	3	‡Civ. Engin. 52, Dynamics	3
**Econ. 25, Psych. 26, or Soc. 28	3	English 83, Tech. Writing	2

SENIOR YEAR

1st Semester	Credits	2nd Semester	Credits
Elec. Engin. 83, Transient		Elec. Engin. 92, Prof. Seminar	1
Analysis	3	Elec. Engin. 78, Special Projects	1
Elec. Engin. 85, Elec.		‡Ind. Engin. 86, Ind. Mgt.	3
Measurements	3	Econ. 25, Psych. 26 or Soc. 28	3
‡Mech. Engin. 79, M. E. Lab. I	2	Technical Elective (Elec.	
Civ. Engin. 75, Fluid Mechanics	3	Engin. 80, 84, 86, 88, 90, 94,	
Technical Elective (Elec.		96, 98)	6 to 8
Engin. 79, 81, 87)	4	Non-Tech. Elective*	3
Non-Tech. Elective*	3		

* Recommended as non-technical electives: Govt. 26, Bus. Law 70, Psych. 86.

‡ Not required of advanced military students.

** Postponed to senior year replacing M. E. 79 for advanced military students.

Mechanical Engineering   W. H. WEAVER, *Adviser*

Mechanical engineering is that branch of the profession which, broadly speaking, covers the fields of heat, power, design of machinery, industrial management and manufacturing problems.

Building upon the foundation laid by the departments of mathematics, physics, and chemistry, the department of mechanical engineering undertakes to show the student how fundamental physical laws apply to this field of the profession. The courses selected give the student thorough training in the basic principles so that particular applications can be mastered in professional practice. Therefore, no attempt is made to give highly specialized instruction.

It must be realized that the modern engineer lives in a time of rapid social and technological change. Only the man who has had a well-balanced cultural and technical program of study can adjust quickly enough to the needs of a continually changing social order. The following curricula emphasize the fundamentals of the four M's of engineering: materials, methods, men, and money, a knowledge of which is vital to the modern engineer.

SUMMER (Following Freshman Year)

Mechanical Engineering 27 and 28, Shop 6 credit hours.

SOPHOMORE YEAR

1st Semester	Credits	2nd Semester	Credits
English 25, Humane Letters	3	English 26, Humane Letters	3
Math. 31, Integ. Calculus	4	Math. 32, Diff. Equations	4
Physics 27, General	4	Physics 28, General	4
Mech. Eng. 39, Mat'l of Constr.	2	Civ. Eng. 34, Statics	3
Ind. Engin. 25, Prod. Processes	2	Mech. Eng. 46, Fund. of Metallurgy	3
Military 25	2	Military 26	2
Physical Ed. 33	1	Physical Ed. 34	1

JUNIOR YEAR

1st Semester	Credits	2nd Semester	Credits
‡English 83, Tech. Writing	2	Psych. 26, Econ. 25 or Soc. 28	3
Civ. Engin. 52, Dynamics	3	Civ. Engin. 76, Fluid Mech.	4
Mech. Eng. 63, Eng. Thermo-		Mech. Eng. 68, Kinematics	3
dynamics	4	Mech. Eng. 64, Eng. Thermo-	
Elec. E. 61, Principles	4	dynamics	3
Civ. Eng. 51, Strength of Mat'ls.	4	Mech. E. 67, Mech. Instr. Lab.	1
Civ. Eng. 61, Testing of Mat'ls.	2	Elec. Eng. 62, Principles	4

SENIOR YEAR

1st Semester	Credits	2nd Semester	Credits
Mech. Eng. 75, Power Plants	3	Psych. 26, Econ. 25 or Soc. 28	3
Mech. E. 77, Internal		Mech. E. 76, Ref. & Air Cond.	3
Combust. Engines	3	Mech. E. 80, Mech. Eng. Lab.	2
Mech. Eng. 79, Mech. Eng. Lab.	2	Mech. E. 86, Adv. Mach. Des.	3
Mech. Eng. 83, Machine Design	3	‡Technical Elect.†	6
Mech. Engin. 85, Dynamics		‡Non-Tech. Elect. (Bus. Law	
of Mach.	3	70 or Psych. 86, Ind.	
Mech. Eng. 91, Sem.	1	recommended	3
‡Non-Technical Elect. (Am.			
Govt. 25 recommended)	3		

‡ Not required of advanced military students.
†Mech. Engin. 88, Steady Flow Mach.
†Mech. Eng. 90, Adv. Metallurgy
†Elec. Eng. 64, Ind. Electricity
†Ind. Engin. 86, Ind. Mgt.
†Ind. Engin. 54, Engin. Econ.
†Mech. Eng. 94, Exp. Mech.
†Civil Engin. 88, Adv. Stress Analy.

Industrial Engineering Option   W. H. WEAVER, *Adviser*

Industrial engineering is concerned with the engineering aspects of the organization, operation and management of manufacturing plants. It is based on the premise that the operation of a manufacturing plant is fundamentally an engineering activity. Consequently, the industrial engineering curriculum is built on a foundation of mechanical engineering. To the technical knowledge and scientific attitude developed through the study of engineering is added the study of certain courses in the humanities, in economics, and in management.

JUNIOR YEAR

1st Semester	Credits	2nd Semester	Credits
Econ. 25	3	Ind. Engin. 82, Work	
Mech. Eng. 65, Heat Engin.	3	Simplification	2
Civ. Eng. 53, Strength of Mat'ls.	3	Mech. Eng. 66, Heat Eng.	3
Elec. Eng. 61, Prin. of Elec. Eng.	4	Civ. E. 52, Dynamics	3
Acct. 25, Prin. of Bus.	3	Elec. Eng. 62, Prin. of E. E.	4
Ind. Engin. 51, Ind. Mgt.	3	Acct. 26, Prin. of Bus.	3
		Mech. Eng. 68, Kinematics	3

ENGINEERING

SENIOR YEAR

1st Semester	Credits	2nd Semester	Credits
Civ. Eng. 75, Fluid Mech.	3	Psych. 26, or Soc. 28	3
Mech. Engin. 79, Lab. I	2	Statistics 79, Elem.	3
Mech. Engin. 83, Mach. Design	3	Ind. Engin. 78, Factory Pl.	2
Ind. Engin. 75, Job Evaluation	2	Ind. Engin. 80, Budget Con.	3
Ind. Engin. 76, Time Study	3	Ind. Engin. 54, Eng. Econ.	3
Ind. Engin. 77, Prod. Control	3	Ind. Engin. 92, Sem.	1
Non-Technical Elective	3	Non-Technical Elective	3

SCHOOL OF HOME ECONOMICS

HELEN S. MITCHELL, *Dean*

General education for living is the main objective of the several four-year curricula in home economics. Non-majors as well as majors, men and women, may elect courses for which they have the necessary prerequisites. Electives during the junior and senior years allow for specialization in preparation for several professional fields: preschool work with children, dietetics, nutrition, teaching of home economics, Extension, and merchandising. The American Dietetic Association sets educational standards for which students in this school may qualify.

When registering for the sophomore year, each student should make a decision as to which home economics curriculum she intends to follow. Some change in emphasis may be made later, but the student is often at a disadvantage if a change in the field of specialization is made later in the college career.

The program of studies for the first two years is largely prescribed.

FRESHMAN YEAR

1st Semester	Credits	2nd Semester	Credits
English 1, Composition	2	English 2, Composition	2
Speech 3	1	Speech 4	1
Chemistry 1, General	3	Chemistry 2, General	3
Foreign Language	3	Foreign Language	3
Home Ec. 1, Introduction	3	Home Ec. 2, Cloth. Select.	
Physical Education 7	2	& Constr.	3
Hygiene	1	Math. 12	3
1Elective	3	Physical Education 8	2

1 Elective to be chosen from the following:

Zoology 1, recommended for majors in Foods and Nutrition, Pre-research, or Child Development.

History 5, recommended for majors in Applied Art, Textiles and Clothing, and Merchandising.

Math 7.

Botany 1.

SOPHOMORE YEAR

1st Semester	Credits	2nd Semester	Credits
English 25, Humane Letters	3	English 26, Humane Letters	3
Economics 25, Elements	3	Psychology 26, General	3
Chem. 33, Organic	4	Zool. 1 or 35 or	3
Physical Education 27	2	Bact. 31	4
1Home Ec. Elective	3	3Home Ec. 30, Foods	3
2Elective	3	Physical Education 28	2
		2Elective	3

1 One of the following electives may be taken during the sophomore year: Home Ec. 31, Applied Art; Home Ec. 26, Textiles, Home Ec. 35, Clothing Con-

struction. If none of these is elected Home Ec. 62 should be elected junior year:

2 Other electives: Accounting 25, 26; Art 31, 34; Bacteriology 31; Chem. 29 and 30; Physics 25, 26; Econ. 26; Government 25; Sociology 28; Zoology 35; Language.

3 Merchandising majors may elect Home Ec. 26 in place of Home Ec. 30.

JUNIOR-SENIOR CURRICULA IN HOME ECONOMICS

A student may specialize in one of several fields of Home Economics during the junior and senior years. In consultation with her faculty adviser, each student will choose courses directly related to her objective. To qualify for a B.S. degree in Home Economics a student during the junior and senior years must have at least 15 but not more than 30 credits in the major field and not more than 42 credits in the School of Home Economics. The following courses or their equivalent are required for all majors: Home Economics 51, 52, 75, 77. The following curricula are suggestive. Those interested in other types of professional work should consult with advisers about desirable electives. For students not interested in professional work, a more liberal choice of electives is possible.

Child Development and Family Life Education

Students interested in child development, nursery school work and social service work should choose this curriculum. The University has arranged for two affiliations for qualified students interested in taking one semester of specialized work elsewhere: with Merrill-Palmer School in Detroit, which specializes in education for home and family life, and with the Nursery Training School in Boston which gives professional training for teaching in nursery schools and kindergartens.

JUNIOR YEAR

1st Semester	Credits	2nd Semester	Credits
Home Ec. 51, Foods	3	Home Ec. 52, Nutrition	3
Home Ec. 75, Ec. of Household	3	Home Ec. 70, Child Developm't	3
Psych. 55, Educational	3	Home Ec. 80, Family	3
Electives	6	Electives	6

SENIOR YEAR

1st Semester	Credits	2nd Semester	Credits
Home Ec. 85, Nursery Sch. Mgt.	3	Ed. 85, Practice Teaching	3
Home Ec. 81, Methods	3	Home Ec. 77, Household Mgt.	3
Home Ec. 95, Child Nutr.	3	Home Ec. 90, Seminar	1
Electives	6	Electives	9

Foods and Nutrition and Institution Management

This curriculum prepares for such professions as therapeutic or administrative dietitian or nutritionist and meets the require-

110

ments of internships approved by the American Dietetic Association. This curriculum is also advised for those interested in home service, food testing and commercial demonstrating related to foods.

Bacteriology 31 and Zoology 35 should be elected sophomore year to satisfy requirements of the American Dietetics Association.

JUNIOR YEAR

1st Semester	Credits	2nd Semester	Credits
Home Ec. 51, Food Selection	3	Home Ec. 52, Nutrition	3
Home Ec. 75, Ec. of Household	3	Home Ec. 60, Household Equip.	3
Home Ec. 81, Methods	3	Home Ec. 70, Child Develop.	3
Chem. 79, Biochemistry	4	Electives	6
Acct. 25, Bus. Acct.	3		

SENIOR YEAR

1st Semester	Credits	2nd Semester	Credits
Home Ec. 71, Retail Fd. Buy.		Home Ec. 77, Home Mgt.	3
Home Ec. 89, Diet Therapy		Home Ec. 90, Nutr. Sem.	1
Home Ec. 91, Institution. Mgt.		Home Ec. 92, Inst. Mgt.	3
Home Ec. 93, Experimental Fds.		Electives	9
Elective	3		

Pre-Research in Nutrition

This curriculum is planned for the students who wish to prepare for graduate work in nutrition or biochemical research. The course should be planned with the advice of the Dean of the School.

Pre-research majors are advised to elect Physics 25 and 26, and take Chemistry 29 in place of Chemistry 33 in the sophomore year.

JUNIOR YEAR

1st Semester	Credits	2nd Semester	Credits
Chemistry 51, Organic	4	Chemistry 52, Organic	4
Home Ec. 51, Foods	3	Home Ec. 52, Nutrition	3
Home Ec. 75, Ee. of Household	3	Home Ec. 60, Equipment	3
Chemistry 30, Quantitative	4	Electives	6
Elective	3		

SENIOR YEAR

1st Semester	Credits	2nd Semester	Credits
Chemistry 79, Biochemistry	4	Home Ec. 77, Home	
Home Ec. 89, Diet Therapy	3	Management	3
Home Ec. 93, Experimental		Home Ec. 90, Nutrition Sem.	1
Foods	3	Home Ec. 98, Special Problems	3
Home Ec. 95, Child Nutrition	3	Electives	9
Elective	3		

Home Economics Education and Extension

Preparation for teaching demands the same basic courses whether a student plans to teach adults or 4-H club groups in Extension, or young people at the high school or junior high school level. In addition to courses required of all home economics students, certain electives are recommended for those planning for any form of teaching. Courses in speech and writing are important. Electives should be chosen in line with special interests or needs. Teachers should be ready to teach some subject other than home economics if demanded; extension workers need special work in rural sociology and adult education. Camp teaching or apprentice training is recommended between junior and senior year.

JUNIOR YEAR

1st Semester	Credits	2nd Semester	Credits
Home Ec. 51, Foods	3	Home Ec. 52, Foods	3
Home Ec. 31, Applied Art or		Home Ec. 60, Equipment	3
Home Ec. 35, Clothing Constr.	3	Home Ec. 62, Home Furnish. or	
Home Ec. 75, Ec. of Household	3	Home Ec. 26, Textiles	2
Home Ec. 81, Methods	3	Home Ec. 70, Child Develop.	3
Education 53, Tests & Measrmts.	3	Elective	3

SENIOR YEAR

1st Semester	Credits	2nd Semester	Credits
Home Ec. 77, Home Mgt.	3	Home Ec. 80, Family Life	3
Home Ec. 91, Institution Mgt.	3	Ed. 85, Practice Teaching	3
Home Ec. 93, Experimental		Home Ec. 90, Seminar	1
Foods	3	Electives	9
Psychology 55, Educational	3		
Elective	3		

Any of these junior-senior courses may be taken either year.
Home Ec. 26, 31, 35 may be taken sophomore year.

Merchandising and Retailing

This curriculum is planned in cooperation with the School of Business Administration and provides an opportunity for girls interested in preparing for the merchandising field. The junior and senior curriculum includes courses in home economics and in business administration and should be planned with the faculty adviser by the end of the freshman year if possible. Students choosing this program are expected to take Home Economics 31, Accounting 25, and Economics 26 in the sophomore year, and should plan on at least a year of in-service training after college. If the interest is primarily in business, see the Merchandising major under the School of Business Administration.

JUNIOR YEAR

1st Semester	Credits	2nd Semester	Credits
Home Ec. 35, Clothing Constr.	3	Home Ec. 56, Foods	3
Home Ec. 75, Ec. of Household	3	Home Ec. 52, Nutrition	3
Mktg. 53, Mktg. & Mktg.		Home Ec. 62, Home	
Problems	3	Furnishings	3
Elective	6	Mktg. 54, Salesmanship & Mgt.	3
		Electives	3

SENIOR YEAR

1st Semester	Credits	2nd Semester	Credits
Home Ec. 87, Tailoring	3	Home Ec. 77, Home Management	3
Home Ec. 79, Textile Testing	3	Home Ec. 78, Adv. Textile Design	3
Mktg. 71, Retail Merchandising	3	Home Ec. 88, Dress Design	3
Mktg. 73, Advertising	3	Mktg. 72, Mktg. Research	3
Electives	3	Home Ec. 90, Seminar	1
		Electives	3

Textiles, Clothing, and Applied Art

This curriculum is of interest to students who may wish to use clothing and related art in a general and aesthetic sense for their personal and family development. Students with ability and professional interest in the artistic and technical aspects of textiles, clothing, and related art are encouraged to go further in this field. They are expected to take Home Economics 31 and Home Economics 26 in the sophomore year. Art 31 is recommended.

JUNIOR YEAR

1st Semester	Credits	2nd Semester	Credits
Home Ec. 51, Foods	3	Home Ec. 52, Nutrition	3
Home Ec. 35, Clothing Constr.	3	Home Ec. 62, Home Furnishing	3
Home Ec. 75, Ec. of Household	3	Electives	9
Home Ec. 81, Methods	3		
Elective	3		

SENIOR YEAR

1st Semester	Credits	2nd Semester	Credits
Home Ec. 77, Home Mgt.	3	Home Ec. 88, Dress Design	3
Home Ec. 79, Textile Testing	3	Home Ec. 78, Adv. Textile Design	3
Ed. 85, Practice Teaching	3	Home Ec. 90, Seminar	1
Home Ec. 87, Tailoring	3	Electives	9
Electives	3		

SCHOOL OF NURSING

MARY A. MAHER, *Head and Director*

The basic professional nursing program is designed for qualified high school graduates who are interested in preparing themselves for a way of life as professional nurses which may be expressed through service to the individual, the family, and the community.

The four calendar year program plus 8 weeks (total 216 weeks) aims to provide its graduates with the basic understandings, appreciations, skills and attitudes which are essential for a beginning professional nurse practitioner in the hospital and in the community; leadership in the hospital nursing team; an increased competency as an active participant in the therapeutic and health teams; and citizen participation. It further aims to provide the foundation for advancement to head nurse positions, graduate study in nursing, and candidacy for positions in teaching, supervision, administration, clinical specialities, consultation and research.

The desired outcomes of the educational program are directed toward helping the student to increase her self-understanding so that she may function constructively and creatively in her personal and professional relationships; enhance and improve her emotional, physical, social and spiritual well-being; extend her understanding of the health needs of the individual and the family and community organizations primarily concerned with the promotion of health and prevention of illness; improve her professional competency as she ministers to the individual and the family in a selected clinical situation; more fully understand and appreciate her role in the nursing care, the therapeutic and the health team; become sensitive to the need of and responsibility for periodic appraisal and improvement of professional nursing practice; enable her to become a more self-directive and responsible member of the profession and of the community; and improve her professional competency through continued study.

The first four academic semesters at the University enable the student to gain an educational foundation upon which to develop the more specialized portion of the program in nursing. The summer following the second academic semester is free. During the 141 weeks (including 16 weeks vacation) which follow the fourth academic semester, the professional courses (including instruction and correlated clinical experience) are given in selected cooperating hospitals and community agencies by the nursing faculty of the University School of Nursing and the allied professional staffs of the cooperating agencies. Following the clinical portion of the program, the student returns to the University for a fifth academic

114

semester and is granted a Bachelor of Science degree in June. Upon the satisfactory completion of the State Board Examinations, the candidate receives legal status as a Registered Nurse (R.N.).

PROGRAM SEQUENCE

First and Second Academic Semesters (Sept. to June)   *Credits*

English 1 & 2	English Composition	4
Speech 3 & 4	Speech	2
Chemistry 1 & 2	General Chemistry	6
Zoology 1	Introductory Zoology	3
Zoology 35	Vertebrate Physiology	3
Mathematics 12	Functional Mathematics	3
History 5	Modern European Civilization	3
Sociology 28	Introduction to Sociology	3
Psychology 26	General Psychology	3

Third and Fourth Academic Semesters (Sept. to June)

English 25	Humane Letters	3
Chemistry 33	Organic Chemistry	4
Sociology 53	Intro. to Cultural Anthropology	3
Psychology 56	Educational Psychology	3
Home Economics 41	Foods and Nutrition	4
Home Economics 42	Medical Dietetics	2
Bacteriology 31	Introductory Bacteriology	4
Philosophy 65	Ethics	3
Home Economics 70	Child Development	3
Nursing 26	Orientation to Nursing	4

First Clinical Period: June to June (34 days vacation)

Nursing S27	Fundamentals of Nursing	9
Nursing S28	Social and Historical Foundations of Nursing	2
Nursing 51	Medical and Surgical Nursing I	16
Nursing 52A	Nursing of Children I	2
Nursing 54	Psychiatric Nursing	4

Second Clinical Period: June to June (30 days vacation)

Nursing 54 (cont.)	Psychiatric Nursing	2
Nursing S56	Tuberculosis Nursing	3
Nursing 57	Maternity Nursing	5
Nursing 52B	Nursing of Children II	5
Nursing 58	Public Health Nursing	3
Nursing 60	Medical and Surgical Nursing II	3

Third Clinical Period: June to February (39 days vacation)

Nursing 60 (cont.)	Medical and Surgical Nursing II	2
Nursing S61	Hospital Team Nursing	2
Nursing 63	Advanced Medical and Surgical Nursing	3
Nursing 65	Senior Elective (Internship)	4

Fifth Academic Semester (February to June)

English 26	Humane Letters	3
History 6	Modern European Civilization	3
Nursing 66	Senior Nursing Seminar	4
Electives (academic)		5

DEPARTMENTS OF MILITARY SCIENCE AND AIR SCIENCE RESERVE OFFICERS TRAINING CORPS

COLONEL RAYMOND P. TARR, JR., *U. S. Army, Head*
COLONEL RICHARD H. SMITH, *U. S. Air Force, Head*

An Act of Congress, July 2, 1862, required the Commonwealth of Massachusetts to provide a two-year course in military instruction at the Massachusetts Agricultural College when it was established. All able-bodied male students who were enrolled for four years were required to take this training. This requirement has continued until today, although The National Defense Act of 1916, as amended in later years, created a Reserve Officers' Training Corps at those colleges which were giving military instruction.

The National Security Act of 1947, which created the United States Air Force as a separate armed service, also resulted in separate Army and Air Force Reserve Officers' Training Corps units being organized at the University of Massachusetts and other colleges and universities.

The general objective of the courses of instruction (Army and Air Force) is to produce junior officers who by their education, training and inherent qualities are suitable for continued development in the United States Army or the United States Air Force Reserve. Training in military leadership is emphasized. It is intended to obtain this objective during the time the students are pursuing their general or professional studies, with the least practicable interference with their civil careers.

All physically qualified male candidates for a degree in any four-year course at the University, except veterans, are required to take the basic course (Army or Air) for at least three hours a week for two years.

The choice of service, Army or Air Force, must be made by each student when he initially enrolls. The student in the basic course is provided with a uniform of the service in which he is enrolled. A deposit of $30.00 is required to cover the cost of loss or damage to any of the articles issued.

The courses of instruction include theoretical and practical work in all phases of military and air science, such as military organization, hygiene and first aid, weapons, maps, military administration, world political geography, military law and boards, and leadership, drill, and the exercise of command.

DIVISION OF PHYSICAL EDUCATION

W. P. McGuirk, *Head*

The Division of Physical Education includes the Departments of Athletics, Physical Education for Men, and Physical Education for Women. It offers one major, that in Physical Education for Men.

INTERCOLLEGIATE ATHLETICS

W. P. McGuirk, *Director*

The following men are in charge of the coaching of the intercollegiate teams:

Charles C. O'Rourke, head coach of football and coach of golf; Chester S. Gladchuk, assistant coach of football and coach of freshman basketball; Robert T. Curran, coach of basketball and coach of freshman baseball; Earl E. Lorden, assistant director of athletics, coach of baseball, assistant coach of football, coach of track and cross country; Lawrence E. Briggs, coach of soccer and skiing; Henry B. Woronicz, assistant coach of hockey, coach of freshman football and director of intramural sports; Stephen R. Kosakowski, coach of tennis and supervisor of Stockbridge School athletics; Benjamin Ricci, Jr., coach of lacrosse; Joseph R. Rogers, Jr., coach of swimming; Gerald Healy, Director of Sports Information.

Physical Education for Men   S. W. Kauffman, *Adviser*

The department of physical education for men offers physical activity courses for four years and the opportunity to major in physical education or teacher coaching.

The activity courses which are required the first two years are designed to assist the student to meet minimum standards of physical health and through regularity and continuity of progressively planned exercises, maintain sound physical condition throughout his college career.

Students are expected to attain minimum physical standards established by the department which includes the ability to swim.

The major in physical education leading to a degree of Bachelor of Science in physical education is designed primarily to train the student for a career as a teacher of physical education. It also includes adequate training in other fields of teaching and coaching of interschool athletics. It is contemplated that physical education majors will be well trained in general scientific and cultural subjects. They are urged to elect advanced military and those planning on teacher-coaching should take additional work in their particular subject matter fields.

117

PHYSICAL EDUCATION

The outline of the physical education major follows:

FRESHMAN YEAR

1st Semester	Credits	2nd Semester	Credits
English I	2	English II	2
Speech 3	1	Speech 4	1
P. E. 23, Princples of Health Ed.	3	Government 25, American	
P. E. 21, Intro. to Phys. Ed.	3	Government	3
Psych. 26, General Psychology	3	Mathematics 12 or 14	3
Military I	3	P. E. 22, First Aid and Safety	3
P. E. 5, Skills and Techniques	1	Military 2	2
Elect one:		P. E. 6, Skills and Techniques	1
Chemistry I	3	Elect one:	
Botany I	3	Chemistry II	3
Zoology I	3	Botany I	3
		Zoology 1	3

SOPHOMORE YEAR

1st Semester	Credits	2nd Semester	Credits
English 25	3	English 26	3
Bacteriology 31	4	Zoology 35, Physiology	3
P. E. 41, Anatomy	3	P. E. 42, Kinesiology	3
Economics 25 or Sociology 28	3	Psychology 56, Educ. Psychology	3
P. E. 35, Skills and Techniques	1	P. E. 36, Skills and Techniques	1
Military 25	2	Military 26	2
Electives	3	Electives	3

JUNIOR YEAR

1st Semester	Credits	2nd Semester	Credits
Ed. 83, Principles of Second Ed.	3	Ed. 52, Prin. and Methods of	
P. E. 53, Phys. Ed. Elem. Schools	3	Teach.	3
P. E. 55, Org. and Adm. of		P. E. 54, Phys. Ed. Second. Schools	3
Phys. Ed.	3	P. E. 56, Adaptive Phys. Ed.	3
P. E. 57, Meth. and Mat. Coaching	3	Psych. 94, Child Psychology	3
(Football-Basketball)		P. E. 58, Meth. and Mat. Coaching	3
P. E. 63, Skills and Techniques	1	(Swimming-Baseball)	
Electives	6	P. E. 64, Skills and Techniques	1
		Electives	3

SENIOR YEAR

1st Semester	Credits	2nd Semester	Credits
Ed. 85, Practice Teaching	3	Education 85, Practice Teaching	3
P. E. 73, Phil. & Princ. of		Ed. 64, Princ. of Elem. Education	3
Phys. Ed.	3	P. E. 74, Tests and Meas. in	
Speech 91, Extempore Speech	3	Phys. Ed.	3
Rec. Ed. 77, Org. & Adm. of		P. E. 76, Physiology of Exercise	3
Comm. Rec.	3	P. E. 84, Skills and Techniques	1
P. E. 81, Meth. & Mat. Coaching	3	Electives	6
(Soccer-Track)			
P. E. 83, Skills and Techniques	1		
Electives	3		

Physical Education for Women RUTH J. TOTMAN, *Adviser*

The courses in physical education for women are planned to provide recreative activity, to develop body grace and efficiency, and to increase health and vigor. No major is available.

The first and second year women students are required to take physical education three times a week and are given two credits for each semester of satisfactory work. Third and fourth year students may elect Physical Education 63, 64, 65, 66. They may elect also Physical Education 42 in the department of physical education for men.

Girls who are restricted from unlimited activity are placed in classes suitable to their ability. Girls who are restricted from all class activity are assigned to rest periods three times a week and receive their regular physical education credit for satisfactory attendance. A similar rest program is substituted for the regular activity program when girls are temporarily incapacitated.

Credits

Credits

Credits

RELIGION

CHAPLAINS POWER, RUCHAMES, AND SEELY, *Advisers*

The courses in the history of religion, the articles of belief and the application of religious principles are given by the Counselors in Religion of the three major western faiths and by others designated by the churches represented. They are financially independent of the University although the facilities of the University are available as for other courses.

Courses are offered in this field for the sake of the student who is interested in rounding out his educational program with the acquiring of a mature perspective in religion. The opportunity is offered for the student to gain a wide knowledge of the forces which have been basic to his culture, an understanding of the religious influences in his own life, and an evaluation of the part that religion plays in current social movements.

Students register for these courses at the regular registration period and may do so in addition to a normal semester load. No academic credit accrues from participation in the courses in religion, but the grade is recorded on the student's permanent card in the Registrar's office.

DIRECTORY OF COURSES

This section contains a list of courses offered in the regular sessions of the University. Course descriptions are arranged alphabetically according to subject matter fields. If any course cannot be found readily, refer to the General Index in the back of the catalogue. A separate bulletin will outline those available during the summer. The University reserves the right to withdraw any course for which an insufficient number of students enroll.

Courses are designated by numbers as follows: freshman 1-24 inclusive; sophomore 25-49 inclusive; junior 50-74 inclusive; senior 75-99 inclusive. Odd numbers designate courses given in the first semester, even numbers those offered during the second. Credit is indicated in terms of semester hours. Where possible, the class schedule follows the course description. A complete schedule of class hours is published at the beginning of each semester.

Students are referred to the section on Divisions of Study and Curricula for a statement of graduation requirements and majors available.

AGRICULTURAL ECONOMICS AND FARM MANAGEMENT

PROFESSOR LINDSEY, PROFESSOR BARRETT,
ASSISTANT PROFESSOR RUSSELL†, MR. CALLAHAN.

26. (II) Economics of Agricultural Production

This course considers the principles of production economics. An analysis of specialization, comparative advantage, diminishing, constant, and increasing costs and returns applied to the individual establishment as well as to the nation. A careful study of the combination of the factors of production is made considering the individual's adjustment when operating under monopolistic competition, laissez-faire, and monopoly. Finally, dynamic and static factors are considered in relation to their effects on the individual's production, on the economy of cities and nations, and on the international economy.

3 class hours.   Credit, 3.
8:00-8:50 M. W. F.   MR. BARRETT.
Prerequisite, Economics 25.
    † On leave of absence.

55. (I) Marketing Farm Products

Not open to students who have taken or are taking Marketing 53. An analysis of present and past systems of assembling, transporting, distributing, and grading agricultural products. Such aspects as the adjustment of production and consumption, price formation, channels of distribution, price differentials and margins, public policy, market reporting and forecasting, and a study of the marketing of major agriculture products are considered. Geographic, future, and quality differentials are studied from the agricultural and commercial standpoint. A field trip may be arranged.

3 class hours.   Credit, 3.
8:00-8:50 M. W. F,   THE DEPARTMENT.

56. (II) The Fundamentals of Cooperation

A study of the philosophy and principles of cooperation in Europe and in the United States. The history of cooperation, legal consideration, management, financing, membership relations, methods of formation, sales methods and policies are given full attention. Progress in the cooperative marketing of different agricultural products is studied.

3 class hours.   Credit, 3.
8:00-8:50 M. W. F.   MR. CALLAHAN.

57. (I) Agricultural Credit and Land Appraisal (1956-57)

A study of the development, use, functions, and operations of public and private credit institutions which are available to agriculture. Special emphasis is given to the practical aspects of credit policy and land appraisal. Given in alternate years.

3 class hours.   Credit, 3.
11:00-11:50 M. W. F.   MR. LINDSEY.

71. (I) Agricultural Economic Theory (1955-56)

The course is a comparative and critical study of the significant contributions of the leading economists to the theory of agricultural economics from the time of Adam Smith to the present. Given in alternate years.

3 class hours.   Credit, 3.
11:00-11:50 M. W. F.   MR. LINDSEY.

75. (I) Farm Organization and Management

This course analyzes the functions of the farmer as a business proprietor. Both the external and internal economic forces affecting the farm business are considered, such as selection and combination of factors of farm production, choice and combination of farm enterprises, the economical use of funds, the nature of farming costs, adjusting farm production to markets and prices, and the management of equipment and labor.

3 class hours.   Credit, 3.
9:00-9:50 M. W. F.   MR. BARRETT.
Prerequisite, Agricultural Economics 26.

76. (II) Advanced Farm Organization and Management

The use of farm records and accounts as a basis for planning and budgeting is emphasized. Measures of success and factors in success in farming, and work simplification as applied to efficient farm techniques are considered. The last part of the course will be given over to the specific study of selected farms and the practical application of the principles and practices already discussed. Field trips are required at an estimated cost of not over five dollars.

1 class hour; 1 4-hour laboratory period.   Credit, 2.
10:00-10:50 Th.; 1:00-4:50 M.   MR. BARRETT.
Prerequisite, Agricultural Economics 75.

78. (II) Principles and Problems of Land Economics

A study of the major contributions by outstanding economic writers to theoretical land economics; a review of American land policies; a presentation of the principles, techniques, and objectives involved in modern land use planning; and a discussion of contemporary land problems in the United States.

3 class hours.   Credit, 3.
11:00-11:50 M. W. F.   MR. LINDSEY.

83. (I) Advanced Farm Operation

For seniors specializing in agriculture; others by permission of instructor. A study of the efficiency of operations on a specific farm.

3 hours or equivalent.   Credit, 3.
Hours by arrangement.   MR. BARRETT.

89. (I) 90. (II) Seminar in Agricultural Economics

A study of special problems in agricultural policy, agricultural institutions, market and price analysis.

Hours by arrangement.   THE DEPARTMENT.

STATISTICS

77. (I) Elementary Experimental Statistics

Primarily for students in psychology, biology, chemistry, agronomy, poultry, animal husbandry, food technology, education, and public health, who are interested in obtaining and handling data of small samples. Chi square, "t" and analysis of variance tests of significance; frequency distribution, averages, dispersion, regression and simple correlation description; and chart and table presentation are the specific fields covered. Students taking this course may not take Statistics 79.

1 class hour; 2 2-hour laboratory periods. Credit, 3.
MR. LINDSEY, MR. RUSSELL.

79. (I) Elementary Economics Statistics

Primarily for students in economics, business administration, mathematics, and industrial engineering, who are interested in obtaining and presenting the data of large samples. Surveys, tables, charts, frequency distributions, averages, dispersion, standard error and its use, quality control, index numbers, time series, and simple correlation are the specific fields covered. Students taking this course may not take Statistics 77.

1 class hour; 2 2-hour laboratory periods. Credit, 3.
MR. LINDSEY, MR. RUSSELL.

80. (II) Advanced Statistics

This course is primarily devoted to linear and curvilinear multiple correlation analysis. Machine and shortcut graphic methods are used. Some time will also be devoted to probability and analysis of variance.

1 class hour; 2 2-hour laboratory periods. Credit, 3.
1:00-1:50 W.; 1:00-2:50 M. F.   MR. LINDSEY, MR. RUSSELL.

AGRONOMY

PROFESSOR COLBY, PROFESSOR DICKINSON, PROFESSOR STECKEL, AS-
SISTANT PROFESSOR THAYER, ASSISTANT PROFESSOR EVERSON,
ASSISTANT PROFESSOR ZAK.

2. (II) Soils

This is an elementary course relating soils and their management to crop growth. This course is designed to give the student a broad background in soil science and its direct application to practical field problems. The course itself is presented with the object of introducing to the student the properties of soils and their influence upon the production of crops. The laboratory work consists of investigation of the fundamental characteristics of soil and basic principles of fertilizer and liming practices.

2 class hours; 1 2-hour laboratory period. Credit 3.
8:00-8:50 Tu. Th.; 3:00-4:50 W. or Th.
MR. EVERSON, MR. ZAK, MR. PARSONS.

51. (I) Field Crops

A study of the field crops of the United States which include their uses and improvement, with their soil and climatic requirements. Emphasis will be given to the best farm practices of the northeastern states as to rotation, liming, fertilizing, seeding methods, tillage, disease and insect control, and to methods of harvesting and storage. As an individual problem, each student must take a detailed plan of crop production for the actual conditions of some New England farm.

2 class hours; 1 2-hour laboratory period.   Credit, 3.
9:00-9:50 Tu. Th.; 1:00-2:50 Th.   Mr. THAYER.

52. (II) Soil Utilization

The relationship of climate and native vegetation to the broader aspects of soil formation is described. Man's use of land resources is connected to show how the agricultural background of settlers has been active in soil use and abuse. Soil erosion control and its significance to permanent agriculture is considered.

3 class hours.   Credit, 3.
8:00-8:50 M. W. F.   Mr. EVERSON.

57. (I) Soil Formation

The first part of this course considers those physical, chemical, biological, climate and geological factors involved in soil formation. The relationship of these factors to the kinds of soil formed in the United States is discussed.

3 class hours.   Credit, 3.
    Mr. EVERSON.

77. (I) Crop Improvement

Theory and practice of the improvement of field crops by breeding and selection.

2 class hours; 1 2-hour laboratory period.   Credit, 3.
Hours by arrangement.   THE DEPARTMENT.
Prequisites, Argronomy 51, Pomology 52, Zoology 53.

78. (II) Fertilizers and Soil Fertility

The primary purpose of this course is to relate soils and fertilizers to plant growth. Studies are made of fertilizer practices in the United States and Europe. In the early part of the course consideration is given to the history of fertilizer development, with special emphasis upon early discoveries and causes of failure in early research. Later in the course, studies are made of factors which relate fertilizers and soils to plant growth. Fertilizer formulation

125

technology and practice are considered in detail in the laboratory phase of this course.

2 class hours 1 2-hour laboratory period.   Credit, 3.

9:00-9:50 Tu. Th.; 1.00-2:50 Th.   MR. EVERSON.

79. (I) Soil Physics

For seniors specializing in agronomy. The factors in soil which control tilth and energy relationships and the laws of physics which govern these factors are discussed. This includes heat, light, color, particle size and charge, water and gas movement, energy relationships and other physical factors effecting changes in the soil. The laboratory is used to familiarize the students with various methods used in measuring these important physical factors.

1 class hour; 2 2-hour laboratory periods.   Credit, 3.

                         MR. EVERSON.

81. (I) 82. (II) Special Problems in Agronomy

For seniors specializing in agronomy. This course is designed to acquaint students with agronomic research methods and practical agronomic procedures.

3 2-hour laboratory periods.   Credit, 3.

                      MR. COLBY.

84. (II) Soil Chemistry

For plant science and soil science students. Fundamental inorganic, organic, and bio-chemical reactions of soils are discussed and related to plant nutrition and microbiological activities. Colloidal aspects of soil chemical reactions and soil-plant interrelationships will be studied.

3 class hours.   Credit, 3.

            THE DEPARTMENT.

Prerequisites: Chemistry 29; Botany 68; Agronomy 57.

84B. (II) Soil Chemistry Laboratory

Primarily for seniors majoring in agronomy. Methods and techniques used in soil chemistry research and in plant science investigations will be studied. The student will be made familiar with methods of determining exchangeable bases, base exchange capacity, soil phosphate fractionation, and many other determinations peculiar to soil investigations. To be taken concurrently with Agronomy 84.

2 3-hour laboratory periods.   Credit, 2.

           THE DEPARTMENT.

Prerequisites, Chemistry 29, 30; Botany 68; Agronomy 57.

AGROSTOLOGY

53. (I) Agrostology

All factors that influence the successful growing of fine turf grasses are studied and correlated to enable the student to have a practical working knowledge of the construction and maintenance of lawns, sports, highway, airport and cemetery turf.

2 class hours; 1 2-hour laboratory period. Credit, 3.

MR. DICKINSON.

56. (II) Agrostology

This course considers fine turf management as a business and profession. Emphasis is placed on diagnosis and treatment of turf failures; the selection of equipment and supplies and client approach. Field trips and practical exercises are arranged.

1 class hour; 2 2-hour laboratory periods. Credit, 3.

MR. DICKINSON.

ANIMAL HUSBANDRY

PROFESSOR RICE, PROFESSOR FOLEY, ASSISTANT PROFESSOR ELLIOT, ASSISTANT PROFESSOR BAKER, MR. CHADWICK, MR. BARTLETT.

1. (I) Agriculture

This course is designed to provide the student with a perspective of the whole field of agriculture. It will orient the student relative to the position of agriculture in relation to other primary and secondary industries. The course will introduce the student briefly to some of the physical characteristics, economic elements, social and political factors concerned with agricultural pursuits and rural living. It will attempt to assist the student in finding his or her proper niche in the broad field of agriculture.

2 class hours; 1 2-hour laboratory period. Credit, 3.

9:00-9:50 Tu. Th.; 1:00-2:50 M., W., or F. MR. FOLEY.

26. (II) Breeds of Livestock and Dairy Cattle Judging

This course considers the economic desirability of thirty breeds of domestic livestock. The origin, history, characteristics and distribution of the breeds of cattle, sheep, swine, and horses commercially important in the United States will be discussed.

2 class hours; 1 2-hour laboratory period. Credit, 3.

11:00-11:50 Tu. Th.; 3:00-4:50 F. MR. ELLIOT.

26A. (II) Judging Dairy Cattle

This is an intensive course in judging dairy cattle and is required of animal husbandry majors. Others may take only by in-

127

structor's permission. During April and May, trips to leading
dairy cattle breeding farms will be made on Saturdays. The highest ranking students will represent the University in the Intercollegiate Dairy Cattle Judging contest at the Eastern States Exposition and the Dairy Cattle Congress at Waterloo, Iowa the
following fall.
1 2-hour laboratory period, February and March, 3-5 Th.
1 4-8 laboratory period, April and May, Saturday.

Credit, 1.
MR. ELLIOT.

51. (I) Nutrition of Farm Animals

This course will present the fundamental principles of animal
nutrition together with the identification, composition, properties
and uses of the common feed stuffs. The application of these
basic principles in calculating balanced rations for all classes of
livestock will be stressed, followed by practical feeding problems
assigned outside the classroom. Feeding practices in use with
the university livestock will be analyzed and demonstrated.
3 class hours; 1 2-hour laboratory period.   Credit, 4.
8:00-8:50 M. W. F.; 3:00-4:50 Tu. or Th.   MR. ELLIOT.

53. (I) Elements of Meat Packing

For department majors only. The lectures will discuss the development of the modern packing industry, the history of meat
inspection, the principles of meat preservation and the opportunities in this field. Laboratories include the classification of
cattle, calves, and swine into proper market classes and grades and
slaughtering and dressing operations with animals provided by
the university farm. Wholesale and retail cuts are prepared. A
one-day trip through the packing plants of Boston is a requirement
of this course and will cost about ten dollars.
1 class hour; 1 4-hour laboratory period.   Credit, 3.
1:00-1:50 W.; 1:00-5:00 M. or F.   MR. BARTLETT.

54. (II) Meat Processing

For students not majoring in animal husbandry, by permission
of the instructor. A few periods will be devoted to a discussion
of the meat packing industry and to the preserving and care of
meat products. The remainder will be spent on the classification
of meat animals with practice slaughtering and the making of
wholesale and retail cuts with stress on identification of retail cuts.
A one-day trip through the packing plants of Boston is a requirement of this course and will cost about ten dollars.
1 4-hour laboratory period.   Credit, 2.
1:00-5:00 W. or F.   MR. CHADWICK.

56. (II) Beef and Sheep Production

This course considers the historical and economic development, present status and probable future trends of beef and sheep production in the United States, especially New England. Consideration will be given to types of production; systems and methods of feeding, management and marketing. In the laboratory, practice will be obtained in fitting and showing as well as certain practical techniques such as dehorning, ear-tagging, castrating, foot-trimming, shearing, etc., and the treatment and prevention of external and internal parasites as well as common ailments.

2 class hours; 1 2-hour laboratory period. Credit, 3.
10:00-10:50 Tu. Th.; 8:00-9:50 Tu. or 3:00-4:50 Th.

MR. BAKER.

56A. (II) General Livestock Judging and Field Trips

This course is given in conjunction with Animal Husbandry 56 and consists of practice in judging and selecting beef, cattle, sheep, horses, and swine. Throughout the spring, field trips are made to nearby livestock farms and breeding establishments. The five highest ranking students in judging will represent the university in the Intercollegiate Livestock Judging Contest at Eastern States Exposition the succeeding fall.

1 4-hour laboratory period. Credit, 1.
8:00-12:00 S.

MR. BAKER.

72. (II) Meat Judging

This course deals with the classification, grading and judging of carcasses and cuts of beef, veal, lamb and pork. Class work will be carried on at Amherst and nearby packing and distributing plants. The team to represent the university in the Intercollegiate Meat Judging Contest held in connection with the Eastern States Exposition will be chosen from students in this course.

1 4-hour laboratory period. Credit, 1.
1:00-4:50 Tu.

MR. BARTLETT.

Prerequisites, Animal Husbandry 53 or permission of instructor.

74. (II) Advanced Meats

This course deals with the advanced techniques in preparing, preserving, and utilizing the various meat products from cattle, sheep and swine.

2 2-hour laboratory periods. Credit, 2.

MR. CHADWICK.

Prerequisites, Animal Husbandry 53 or 54 and permission of instructor.

75. (I) Animal Breeding

This course is planned to acquaint the student with the facts of reproductive physiology, with the facts and theories of modern genetics, and to show how such knowledge may be utilized through genetic analysis, selection, and systems of breeding for the creation of more beautiful and more efficient animal types.

3 2-hour periods.   Credit, 4.
1:00-2:50 M. W. F.   Mr. Rice.
Prerequisite, Zoology 53.

76. (II) Animal Breeding Techniques

This course deals with the practical application of the principles of physiology of reproduction and selection to the improvement of farm animals. It includes practice in semen collection and evaluation, artificial insemination procedures and techniques, and in the study of genitalia at different stages of estrus and gestation periods in live and deal animals. Methods of easing and aiding parturition will be discussed and observed.

1 2-hour laboratory period.   Credit, 1.
1:00-2:50 Tu. or Th.   Mr. Elliot.

77. (I) 78. (II) Dairy Cattle Production

This is an intensive course covering all phases of dairy cattle and milk production. It affords an opportunity to seek the solution to the economic, nutritional, genetic, and managerial problems concerned in successful dairying.

1 2-hour laboratory period.   Credit, 3.
                                                           Mr. Foley.

79. (I) Horse and Swine Production

This course is the same as Animal Husbandry 56 except that it deals with horses and swine instead of beef and sheep.

2 class hours; 1 2-hour laboratory period.   Credit, 3.
10:00-10:50 Tu. Th.; 1:00-2:50 Th.   Mr. Baker.

79A. (I) Advanced Livestock Judging

This course is devoted entirely to beef, sheep, horse, and swine judging and selection. Field trips will be made to breeding establishments and a team will be selected to represent the University at the Intercollegiate Livestock Judging Contest at the International Livestock Exposition in Chicago and at any other contests in which the University may occasionally or regularly participate.

1 4-hour laboratory period, first half of semester.   Credit, 1.
8:00-12:00 S.   Mr. Baker.
Prerequisite, Animal Husbandry 56A or permission of instructor.

81. (I) Seminar
For Animal Husbandry majors.
1 2-hour laboratory period. Credit, 1.
3:00-4:50 Tu. or Th. Mr. Foley.

82. (II) Seminar
For Animal Husbandry majors.
1 2-hour laboratory period. Credit, 1.
3:00-4:50 Tu., W., or Th. Mr. Rice.

83. (I) Advanced Meat Judging
This course is a continuation of Course 72. The team to represent the University in the Intercollegiate Meats Judging Contest held in connection with the International Livestock Exposition will be chosen from students in this course.
1 4-hour laboratory period, first half of semester. Credit, 1.
1:00-4:50 Tu. Mr. Bartlett.
Prerequisite, Animal Husbandry 72 or permission of instructor.

91. (I) Genetics and Eugenics
This course, open to students other than those specializing in animal husbandry, deals with the general problems concerned in human reproduction and inheritance. The main topics studied will consist of the physiology of reproduction, the physical basis of inheritance, and the mode of transmission of human characteristics. Consideration will also be given to such questions as the causes of variation, the relative importance of genetic and environmental influences, the mechanism of sex determination as well as population trends, differential birth rates, sterilization, and kindred eugenic problems.
3 class hours. Credit, 3.
9:00-9:50 M. W. F. Mr. Rice.

ART
Instructors in Landscape Architecture.

27. Modeling
A course in elementary modeling, of seeing, analyzing, and reproducing form in clay and modeling wax to develop sculptural technique.
6 laboratory hours. Credit, 3.
Mr. McLindon.

28. Modeling

A continuation of Course 27 in advanced design and the making of plaster casts from original problems in small sculpture, such as plaques, masks, and medals or other such pieces.

6 laboratory hours.   Credit, 3.
                                                   MR. McLINDON.

Prerequisite, Art 27.

31. (I) Elementary Design

For women. Elementary principles of design as applied to textiles, fabrics, interior decorations, etc.

3 2-hour laboratory periods.   Credit, 3.
                                                   MR. MacIVER.

33. (I) Freehand Drawing

A non-professional course in elementary drawing and painting in various media in black and white. The work is more or less personal and is adapted to the individual capacities and backgrounds of each student as far as possible. Limited to two sections of 20 students each.

6 laboratory hours.   Credit, 3.
                                                   MR. MacIVER.

34. (II) Freehand Drawing

This non-professional course is essentially one in which the use of color is stressed in various media, freehand drawing is emphasized and paintings in still-life and landscape subjects are produced. Limited to two sections of 20 students each.

6 laboratory hours.   Credit, 3.
                                                   MR. MacIVER.

75. (I) Art Appreciation

An analysis of the principles of critical judgment underlying the fine arts, leading toward the enjoyment of art and its application to every day life.

3 class hours.   Credit, 3.
9:00-9:50 M. W. F.   MR. OTTO.

78. (II) Early and Medieval Art

An appreciative survey of art and history from early times to the present. Works in painting, sculpture, architecture, and the minor arts are examined in the light of their contributions to the history of civilization, and to the development of art forms.

3 class hours.   Credit, 3.
11:00-11:50 M. W. F.   MR. HAMILTON.

BACTERIOLOGY AND PUBLIC HEALTH

PROFESSOR FRANCE, ASSOCIATE PROFESSOR GARVEY, ASSOCIATE PROFESSOR PERRIELLO, ASSISTANT PROFESSOR CZARNECKI, ASSISTANT PROFESSOR MANDEL, MR. WISNIESKI, MR. LARKIN, in cooperation with DR. WALTER W. LEE, State District Health Officer; MR. ERNEST A. SNOW of the Division of Sanitary Engineering of the Massachusetts Department of Public Health; MR. JOEL COHEN of the Springfield Hospital.

31. (I) and (II) Introductory Bacteriology

Students majoring in Liberal Arts, Business Administration, and Agriculture taking this course to satisfy a science requirement should take it first semester. Designed to present to students interested in general science, agriculture, horticulture, and home economics the fundamental concepts of bacteriological science; make microorganisms real and significant; and demonstrate their importance in the problems of agriculture, general science, industry, public health, and medicine. The laboratory work covers the use and care of the compound microscope, the preparation of culture media, methods of sterilizing equipment, the isolation and aseptic handling of pure cultures, simple and differential staining, bacterial classification and differential studies on type species of pathogenic and non-pathogenic bacteria.

2 class hours; 2 2-hour laboratory periods. Credit, 4.
12:00-12:50 M. F. or Tu. Th.; 1:00-2:50 or 3:00-4:50 M. F. or Tu. Th. MR. CZARNECKI AND STAFF.

51. (I) 52. (II) Advanced Bacteriology

A continuation of introductory bacteriology. Studies on bacterial metabolism and the influence of environmental factors on growth and viability. The identification and differentiation of bacterial species by morphological, cultural, physiological, and serological studies; disinfectants and antibiotics. The combined courses give to the student not only a comprehensive picture of various forms of existing bacteria but develop a specialized technique for their cultivation, isolation, and identification.

2 3-hour laboratory periods. Credit, 3.
1:00-3:50 Tu. Th. MISS GARVEY.
Prerequisite, for 51, Bacteriology 31; for 52, Bacteriology 51.

54. (I) and (II) Water and Sewage Bacteriology

For students majoring in Engineering. Elementary bacteriology with emphasis placed upon the importance of bacteria found in water and sewage. Work will include routine analysis used in the

examination of water and sewage and in the laboratory control of
water and sewage treatment plants.

2 3-hour laboratory periods. Credit, 3.

2:00-4:50 Tu. Th. MR. PERRIELLO.

Prerequisite, Civil Engineering 77 or permission of the instructor.

55. (I) Fundamentals of Soil Microbiology

This course is designed for students majoring in agricultural
and related fields. Subjects included will be: fundamental laboratory procedures and techniques; quantitative and qualitative microbiological analysis of various types of soils; studies on the carbon
and nitrogen cycles as affected by soil microorganisms.

2 3-hour laboratory periods. Credit, 3.

MR. MANDEL.

56. (I) and (II) Methods for Bacteriological Preparations

This course is intended for students majoring in bacteriology
and public health. The material given in the course includes
methods of preparation and sterilization of culture media and
equipment, the preparation of stains and reagents, and the use,
care and repair of laboratory instruments.

2 2-hour laboratory periods. Credit, 2.

THE STAFF.

81. (I) General Applied Bacteriology

This course is designed to give the student a working knowledge
of routine and special tests used in present day applied bacteriology.
Subjects receiving consideration are: methods for determining
the sanitary quality of milk and milk products, water and shellfish; eating and drinking utensils; and air.

1 class hour; 2 3-hour laboratory periods. Credit, 4.

1:00-3:50 M. F. or 1:00-3:50 W.; 9:00-11:50 S.

MR. FRANCE, MR. PERRIELLO.

Prerequisite, Bacteriology 51 or permission of the instructor.

82. (II) Food Bacteriology

Consideration will be given to (1) bacteriological principles
which apply to the preservation, fermentation and spoilage of
foods, (2) the sanitary examination of foods, (3) the causes of food
poisoning, and (4) microbiological assays.

2 3-hour laboratory periods. Credit, 3.

1:00-3:50 M. F. or Tu. Th. MISS GARVEY.

Prerequisite, Bacteriology 51 or permission of the instructor.

85. (I) Bacteriology (Immunology)

Admission by permission of the instructor. This course includes consideration of host reactions which favor the prevention and cure of disease; qualitative and quantitative estimations of toxins and antitoxins; the use of biological products such as antigens and immune sera in differential bacteriology and in disease diagnosis; and a consideration of isohemagglutinins as determinants of blood groups.

2 3-hour laboratory periods.   Credit, 3.
1:00-3:50 M. F.   MISS GARVEY.

90. (II) Sanitary Bacteriology

A detailed study of public health laboratory methods. Practical application of methods will be made through field studies.

1 4-hour and 1 2-hour laboratory period.   Credit, 3.
1:00-4:50 M., 1:00-2:50 F.   MR. FRANCE, MR. PERRIELLO.
Prerequisite, Bacteriology 81.

92. (II) Clinical Laboratory Methods

This course is designed for students majoring in medical technology. The purpose of the course is to familiarize the student with routine clinical laboratory procedures.

1 4-hour laboratory period.   Credit, 3.
1:00-4:50 W., 3:00-4:50 F.   MR. FRANCE, MR. COHEN.
Prerequisites, Bacteriology 85; Zoology 35, 69.

93. (I) 94. (II) Problems

Qualified seniors who have obtained permission from the department may arrange for independent work on special problems in bacteriology.

Credit, 3.
THE DEPARTMENT.

96. (II) Studies of Special Microbial Groups

A study of the biology of certain groups of microorganisms considered only briefly or not at all in other courses offered in the department. The course will cover the autotrophic bacterial, photosynthetic bacterial, actinomycetes, myxobacteria, chlamydobacteria and spirochaetes.

1 class hour; 2 2-hour laboratory periods.   Credit, 3.
MR. MANDEL.

Prerequisite, Bacteriology 51.

135

61. (I) 62. (II) General and Community Sanitation

A study of the problems of general and community sanitation. Subjects discussed will include insect and rodent control, housing and slum clearance, ventilation, lighting, bathing places, sanitation of eating utensils, nuisances, camp sanitation, industrial hygiene, water supplies, sewerage and sewage, refuse and garbage, food and milk sanitation.

3 class hours. Credit, 3.
9:00-9:50 Tu. Th., 12:00-12:50 F. or 10:00-10:50 M. W. F.

MR. PERRIELLO, MR. WISNIESKI.

63. (I) Industrial Hygiene and Sanitation

A comprehensive study of the practices and principles of industrial processes which may constitute problems in sanitation; industrial wastes, smoke abatement, and the health of the worker. Subject matter includes organization of programs and the formation of policies for the inspection of sanitary and mechanical facilities of factories, food processing plants and other industries.

3 class hours. Credit, 3.

MR. PERRIELLO.

64. (II) Microscopy of Water

A study of microscopic forms of life exclusive of the bacteria. Counting and control of plankton in potable waters. Elements of limnology.

2 class hours; 1 2-hour laboratory period. Credit, 3.
9:00-9:50 M. F.; 8:00-9:50 or 10:00-11:50 W. MR. SNOW.
Prerequisite, Bacteriology 31.

66. (I) and (II) Principles of Sanitation

The application of sanitary engineering and related sanitary sciences to health problems in the environment of urban and rural communities.

2 class hours. Credit, 2.
11:00-11:50 Tu. Th. MR. PERRIELLO.
Prerequisite, Civil Engineering 77 or permission of the instructor.

84. (II) Public Health Administration

Admission by approval of the instructor. The organization, function, and administration of governmental health agencies; the

136

relationship of official and volunteer health agencies; preparation and presentation of lectures, demonstrations, and exhibits. Public health laws, regulations, and sanitary codes, their origin and enforcement.

3 class hours.   Credit, 3.
10:00-10:50 M. W. F.   MR. PERRIELLO.

86. (II) Field Studies in Sanitation

Trips will be taken into the field for the observation of public health practices in sewerage; sewage treatment and disposal; the production and purification of public water supplies; housing and slum clearance; insect and rodent nuisances; milk production, handling, and distribution; garbage and refuse collection and disposal; slaughter houses and rendering plants; cold storage warehouses; and bakery and restaurant sanitation. A comparative study of urban and rural services will be made. Although transportation will be furnished, students are expected to finance their own meals.

1 class hour; 1 4-hour laboratory period.   Credit. 2.
Hours by arrangement.   MR. WISNIESKI.
Prerequisites, Public Health 61 and 62.

92. (Summer) Supervised Field Training

All students majoring in sanitary technology must complete a prescribed thirteen-week field training program conducted by the New England Field Training Center under the direction of the Training Division of the Communicable Disease Center, U. S. Public Health Service, with the assistance of the staff and State Department of Health personnel. This course is a prerequisite for placement in federal, state and municipal agencies.

13 weeks.   Credit, 6.
                                                                      THE STAFF.

88. (II) Epidemiology and Communicable Disease Control

Admission by approval of the instructor. Consideration of the factors involved in the spread of infections; a detailed discussion of the communicable diseases, their distribution, cause, epidemiology, and means of prevention and control. The use of vaccines, serums and drugs for prevention and treatment. Mass immunization programs.

3 class hours.   Credit, 3.
8:00-8:50 M. W. F.   MR. LEE.

BOTANY

PROFESSOR KOZLOWSKI, PROFESSOR TORREY, PROFESSOR LIVINGSTON,
ASSISTANT PROFESSOR BANFIELD, ASSISTANT PROFESSOR PUTALA, MR.
SCARBOROUGH, MR. NICKERSON, MR. DAVIS†, MR. KETCHLEDGE.

1. (I) and (II) Introductory Botany

The course sets forth a body of facts dealing with the morphology
and physiology of plants which is not only a foundation for future
professional work in biological science, but of intrinsic value to the
educated layman. The topics of seed germination, ecological
adaptations, floral structures, taxonomy, botanical history, cytology,
wood-anatomy, plant physiology, and plant reproduction receive
appropriate elementary treatment. The lectures attempt to interpret the facts of plant structure and function in the light of the
major biological principles.

2 class hours; 1 3-hour laboratory period. Credit 3.
MR. NICKERSON.

25. (I) The Plant Kingdom

Selected forms typifying the slimemolds, bacteria, algae, fungi,
lichens, liverworts, mosses, fernworts, and seed plants. The course
has a two-fold purpose: (1) it is intended for students who desire
to extend their knowledge to the principal branches of the plant
kingdom, thus rounding out a general course of which Botany 1
constitutes the first part; (2) it is also planned as an introduction
to certain advanced courses for which it is prerequisite.

2 class hours; 1 2-hour laboratory period. Credit, 3.
Prerequisite, Botany 1. MR. TORREY.

26. (II) Spring Flora

Designed primarily to acquaint the student with the local spring
flora through the identification of the commoner tracheate plants
(lycopods, horsetails, ferns, gymnosperms, angiosperms) and the
families they represent. In addition, laboratory and field work
will include the study of native woody plants in the winter condition; the techniques of collection; the use of a standard manual
in the identification of plants; and the preparation of a representative herbarium. The course is designed for students majoring in
botany, forestry, floriculture, recreational leadership, and wildlife
management. Enrolment limited to 40. Expense of required
materials approximately $20.

1 class hour; 2 2-hour laboratory periods. Credit, 3.
8:00-8:50 W.; 1:00-2:50 Tu. Th. or 1:00-2:50 M. F.
MR. LIVINGSTON.

Prerequisite, Botany 1, Botany 25 recommended.
† On leave of absence.

138

28. (II) Plant Physiology

Only for students intending to major in forestry. The processes occurring in plants with special emphasis on tree physiology and its relation to forestry problems.

2 class hours; 1 2-hour laboratory period. Credit 3.

MR. KOZLOWSKI.

30. (II) Plant Anatomy

A study of the origin and structure of vegetative and reproductive organs of seed plants.

2 class hours; 1 2-hour laboratory period. Credit 3.

MR. PUTALA.

51. (I) Plant Pathology

A basic course in plant pathology dealing with the nature, cause and control of plant disease. Particular attention is given to disease symptoms, the phenomena of infection and of parasitism, the sources of inoculum, the agents of disease transmission, the relation of environment to disease incidence and development and to general principles of plant disease control. The laboratory phase is devoted to intensive study of a relatively few representative diseases induced by bacteria and fungi of the various classes.

1 class hour; 2 2-hour laboratory periods. Credit, 3.

9:00-9:50 W.; 3:00-4:50 Tu. Th. MR. BANFIELD.

52. (II) Advanced Plant Pathology (1954-55)

An extension of Course 51. The objective is that of providing the student with a general knowledge of the more common and representative plant disease problems. Students are granted the option in the laboratory of specializing in disease problems in their major field of interest. Given in alternate years.

1 class hour; 2 2-hour laboratory periods. Credit, 3.

9:00-9:50 W.; 3:00-4:50 Tu. Th. MR. BANFIELD.

Prerequisite, Botany 51.

58. (II) Microtechnique

A course in the preparation of microscopic mounts including the celloidin and paraffin methods of involving the use of microtomes and of differential stains. Enrolment limited to ten students.

2 2-hour laboratory periods. Credit, 2.

1:00-2:50 Tu. Th. MR. TORREY.

Prerequisite, Botany 25.

59. (I) 60. (II) The Angiosperms (1954-55)

Alternate with Courses 61 and 62. The angiosperms are here treated from the standpoints of their structure and evolution, their

taxonomy, their habits and distribution, and their economic or other special appeal to man's interests. Representatives of the dominant families, both temperate and tropical, are studied in the laboratory. The course is designed for students who want a broad knowledge of the flowering plants of the world.
2 class hours; 1 2-hour laboratory period. Credit, 3.
MR. TORREY.
Prerequisite, Botany 1.

61. (I) 62. (II) The Comparative Anatomy of Green Plants (1955-56)

Alternate with Courses 59 and 60. The first semester is devoted to algae and mosses; the second to tracheates, including the extinct forms.
2 class hours; 1 2-hour laboratory period. Credit, 3.
10:00-10:50 M. F.; 1:00-2:50 W. MR. TORREY.
Prerequisite, Botany 25.

63. (I) Comparative Morphology of Fungi— Basidiomycetes and Fungi Imperfecti (1956-57)

The lectures deal with the comparative morphology, life history, and habitat of representative species of the important orders and families. The laboratory periods are devoted to the collection, identification, and study of common local forms. Given in alternate years.
1 class hour; 2 2-hour laboratory periods. Credit, 3.
9:00-9:50 F.; 3:00-4:50 M. F. MR. BANFIELD.

64. (II) Comparative Morphology of Fungi— Phycomycetes and Ascomycetes (1955-56)

The lectures deal with the comparative morpology, life history, and habitat of representative species of the important orders and families. The laboratory periods are devoted to the collection, identification, and study of common local forms. Given in alternate years.
2 class hours; 1 2-hour laboratory period. Credit, 3.
9:00-9:50 Tu.; 10:00-10:50 Th.; 3:00-4:50 M.
MR. BANFIELD.

66. (II) General Mycology

A survey course in mycology designed to acquaint the student with the various classes of fungi, their distribution in nature, their significance in plant and animal disease, their utilization in industrial fermentations. The laboratory phase is devoted to a study of common representative forms and practice in the use of keys for their identification.

1 class hour; 2 2-hour laboratory periods. Credit, 3.
11:00-11:50 Tu.; 3:00-4:50 Tu. Th. MR. BANFIELD.

67. (I) 68. (II) Introductory Plant Physiology

A study of the processes occurring in plants and their relation to the complex of activities constituting plant growth. Topics include colloidal systems, osmotic phenomena, absorption, transpiration, and internal water relations of plants, photosynthesis, fat and protein synthesis, digestion, translocation, respiration, and growth. This is a basic course for students planning for advanced work in any branch of plant science.

1 class hour; 2 2-hour laboratory periods. Credit, 3.
10:00-10:50 W.; 3:00-4:50 M. W. or Tu. Th.
MR. KOZLOWSKI.

75. (I) Methods in Plant Pathology (1956-57)

A course in the general techniques and specialized methods used in the investigation of plant diseases, including isolation, culture and pathogenicity studies of representative plant pathogens, the preparation and sterilization of various culture media, elementary staining and histological techniques, the use of the microscope, study of fungicides, and training in elementary photographic procedures. Given in alternate years.

1 class hour; 2 2-hour laboratory periods. Credit, 3.
2:00-2:50 Tu.; 10:00-11:50 Tu.; 3:00-4:50 F. MR. BANFIELD.
Prerequisite, Botany 51.

77. (I) 78. (II) Advanced Plant Physiology (1955-56)

Advanced study in physiology. Given in alternate years.

1 class hour; 2 2-hour laboratory periods. Credit, 3.
Hours by arrangement. MR. KOZLOWSKI.
Prerequisites, Botany 67, 68; Chemistry 51, 52.

81. (I) Plant Ecology

A general survey of the relationship of plants to their environment including a study of environmental factors (autecology)—soil, water, temperature, light, atmosphere, and the biotic factors—and of plant communities (synecology) with special emphasis on the structure and succession of plant communities in North America.

1 class hour; 2 2-hour laboratory periods. Credit, 3.
MR. LIVINGSTON.
Prerequisite, Botany 1; Botany 26 recommended.

82. (II) Plant Geography

A survey of descriptive and historical plant geography as well as the basic principles governing the natural distributions of plants. Included as topics are problems of dispersal and migration, endemism, species senescence, discontinuous distributions, polyphlesis, continental drift, and geographical aspects of polyploidy. The course is designed for advanced undergraduates or qualified graduate students.

2 class hours.   Credit, 2.

MR. LIVINGSTON.

Prerequisite, Botany 81 or equivalent recommended.

85. (I) 86. (II) Problems in Botany

Supervised problem work for qualified students.

Hours by arrangement.   Credit, 1-3.

THE STAFF.

89. (I) Plant Cytogenetics

The interpretation of hereditary phenomena in plants in terms of cell structures. A correlation of plant cytology and genetics which is of applied as well as theoretical importance.

1 class hour; 2 2-hour laboratory periods.   Credit, 3.

MR. NICKERSON.

90. (II) Insect Transmission of Plant Diseases

The intricate interrelationships of insects and microorganisms with particular emphasis on the basic role played by insects in inception, distribution and perpetuation of plant diseases.

3 class hours.   Credit, 3.

MR. BANFIELD.

BUSINESS ADMINISTRATION

PROFESSOR KIMBALL, PROFESSOR HARDY, PROFESSOR VANCE, ASSOCIATE PROFESSOR COLWELL, ASSOCIATE PROFESSOR SMART, ASSOCIATE PROFESSOR LUDTKE, ASSISTANT PROFESSOR SINGER, ASSISTANT PROFESSOR RIVERS, ASSISTANT PROESSOR LENTILHON, ASSISTANT PROFESSOR GILLIS, ASSISTANT PROFESSOR ANDERSON, ASSISTANT PROFESSOR HACKAMACK, ASSISTANT PROFESSOR SHERMAN, MR. ROBINSON, MR. ZANE.

ACCOUNTING

25. (I) Introduction to Accounting I

This course aims to give the student a working knowledge of the principles underlying the gathering, recording, and use of accounting data.

1 class hour; 2 2-hour laboratory periods.   Credit, 3.

MR. COLWELL, MR. ANDERSON, MR. SINGER, MR. LENTILHON.

26. (II) Introduction to Accounting II

This course covers the principles and procedures of corporation accounting and is an introduction to valuation and statement interpretation.

1 class hour; 2 2-hour laboratory periods.   Credit, 3.

MR. COLWELL, MR. ANDERSON, MR. SINGER, MR. LENTILHON.

61. (I) Intermediate Accounting

An application of accounting principles to problems of income determination and the classification and valuation of assets.

1 class hour; 2 2-hour laboratory periods.   Credit, 3.

MR. LENTILHON, MR. SINGER.

Prerequisite, Accounting 26.

62. (II) Advanced Accounting

A continuation of Accounting 61, concerned with the valuation of assets and liabilities, accounting for net worth, statements of application of funds and the analysis of financial statements.

1 class hour; 2 2-hour laboratory periods.   Credit, 3.

MR. SINGER.

Prerequisite, Accounting 61.

64. (II) Cost Accounting

The use of accounting techniques to determine business costs, including process costs, standard costs, distributive costs and cost problems imposed by government regulation.

2 class hours; 1 2-hour laboratory period.   Credit, 3.

MR. LENTILHON.

Prerequisite, Accounting 26.

73. (I) Tax Accounting

This course examines the principles of income taxation as applied to individuals and emphasizes the application of income tax laws in corporate accounting.

3 class hours.   Credit, 3.

MR. ANDERSON.

Prerequisite, Accounting 61.

74. (II) Accounting Systems

The application of accounting procedures to representative types of business including mechanized accounting systems.

3 class hours.   Credit, 3.

MR. COLWELL.

Prerequisite, Accounting 64.

75. (I) Administrative Accounting and Control

The preparation and analysis of budgets, reports, and internal checks, using accounting techniques and data as control devices in business and industry.

3 class hours.   Credit, 3.

MR. COLWELL.

Prerequisite, Accounting 26.

76. (II) Auditing

A course in the verification of accounting records dealing with audit theory and procedure. C.P.A. and American Institute of Accountants examination problems are studied.

3 class hours.   Credit, 3.

MR. ANDERSON.

Prerequisites, Accounting 62 and 64.

BUSINESS LAW

70. (I) and (II) Business Law I

This course consists of a study of the drawing, reading, and interpretation of contracts, and includes agency, sales, and commercial paper.

3 class hours.   Credit, 3.

MR. SMART.

72. (II) Business Law II

A continuation of Business Law 70 including the study of the legal aspects of business organization and some laws of public regulation.

3 class hours.   Credit, 3.

MR. SMART.

Prerequisite, Business Law 70.

FINANCE

55. (I) Financial Institutions

A general course which surveys the development and operations of our financial institutions and provides an integrated study of the entire American financial structure.

3 class hours.   Credit, 3.

MR. LUDTKE, MR. GILLIS.

65. (I) and (II) Corporation Finance

This course in business finance is concerned with forms of ownership organization, the nature and uses of corporate securities, provision and maintenance of capital, financial expansion, and corporate reorganization.

3 class hours. Credit, 3.

MR. KIMBALL, MR. LUDTKE, MR. GILLIS.

76. (II) Insurance

A general course concerning risks encountered by individuals and business enterprises and the methods and institutions evolved to insure against loss. Property, casualty, life and other forms of insurance are studied from the point of view of both the insurance carrier and the insured.

3 class hours. Credit, 3.

MR. LUDTKE.

81. (I) Problems in Business Finance

A study of problems of financial management of various types of business corporations and the formation of their financial policies.

3 class hours. Credit, 3.

MR. LUDTKE.

Prerequisite, Finance 65 or consent of instructor.

82. (II) Investments

The principles and techniques that are useful for the analysis and selection of investment media; investment policies of individuals and institutions.

3 class hours. Credit, 3.

MR. LUDTKE.

Prerequisite, Finance 65 or consent of instructor.

INDUSTRIAL ADMINISTRATION

11. (I) Industrial Geography

A study of the distribution of natural and human resources and the industrial and physiographic bases of the extractive and manufacturing industries.

3 class hours. Credit, 3.

MR. VANCE, MR. RIVERS, MR. HACKAMACK, MR. ROBINSON.

63. (I) Management in Industry

A study of the principles connected with the organization and management of manufacturing enterprises.

3 class hours. Credit, 3.

MR. VANCE, MR. HACKAMACK, MR. RIVERS.

MARKETING

64. (II) Personnel Management
A study of the principles of the management of labor relations. Attention is focused on procuring, developing, maintaining and using personnel.
3 class hours. Credit, 3.

MR. VANCE, MR. HACKAMACK, MR. RIVERS.

66. (II) Transportation and Traffic
The development of highway, waterway, railway, and air transportation; the operation and control of transportation agencies; the use of freight tariffs, classifications and routing guides; the functions of industrial traffic departments.
3 class hours. Credit, 3.

MR. RIVERS, MR. ROBINSON.

73. (I) Problems of Industrial Management
An intensive analysis, through study of actual cases, of the problems that confront managers in the manufacturing division of a business.
3 class hours. Credit, 3.

MR. VANCE.

Prerequisite, Industrial Administration 63.

80. (II) Administrative Procedure
Theory and practice of administrative organization; planning and direction in business situations; formation and execution of business policies; coordinated and effective operations through group action.
3 class hours. Credit, 3.

MR. VANCE.

MARKETING

53. (I) Marketing Principles
A study of the forces and conditions which determine prices and the organization and methods concerned with transporting, storing, and distributing industrial and consumer goods.
3 class hours. Credit, 3.

MR. HARDY, MR. SHERMAN, MR. ROBINSON, MR. ZANE.

54. (II) Salesmanship and Sales Management
The principles and practices of selling; the management of sales personnel; and the control of sales operations.
3 class hours. Credit, 3.

MR. HARDY.

62. (II) Market Research
The aims, sources and fact-gathering methods of market research activities. General study and individual research projects.
3 class hours.   Credit, 3.
                                                    MR. SHERMAN.

71. (I) Retail Merchandising
A study of the operation and productive functions of the business of retailing.
3 class hours.   Credit, 3.
                                                    MR. SHERMAN.

73. (I) Advertising
A study of the techniques and media of advertising, its services to business and the organization and economic functions of the advertising industry.
3 class hours.   Credit, 3.
                                            MR. HARDY, MR. ZANE.

74. (II) New England Markets
Individual and group study of the marketing problems of New England industrial and marketing enterprises.
3 class hours.   Credit, 3.
                                    BUSINESS ADMINISTRATION STAFF.

76. (II) Purchasing
An intensive study of the purchasing problems of industrial enterprises and their market contacts with their sources of supply.
3 class hours.   Credit, 3.
                                                    MR. ROBINSON.

80. (II) Problems in Marketing
A study of problems of market management, especially the interrelations between research planning, execution of sales programs, and market control. Effects of various marketing policies upon individual firms and the industry are examined.
3 class hours.   Credit, 3.
                                            MR. HARDY, MR. SHERMAN.
Prerequisite, Marketing 53.

Field Work in Merchandising
Open only to students in the Merchandising curriculum who have been assigned to supervised field work positions.
                                    BUSINESS ADMINISTRATION STAFF.

CHEMISTRY

PROFESSOR RITCHIE, PROFESSOR FESSENDEN, PROFESSOR SMITH, ASSO-
CIATE PROFESSOR CANNON, ASSOCIATE PROFESSOR LITTLE, AS-
SISTANT PROFESSOR RICHASON, ASSISTANT PROFESSOR ROBERTS,
ASSISTANT PROFESSOR STEIN, MR. PARROTT*, MR. OBERLANDER,
MR. TYLER, MR. SCHEUFELE, MR. CHRISTOFFERS, MISS KENDROW,
MR. CONRAD, MISS JUDGE, MR. LEVITT, MR. McWHORTER, MR.
GARPINI.

1. (I) 2. (II) General Chemistry

A study of the fundamental chemical laws and theories. A considerable amount of descriptive material will be included in connection with discussions of the periodic system, atomic structure,
and in various applications of the principles. The object of the
course is to give the student a sound scientific training through a
course in chemistry. Students who have had no previous work in
chemistry will be grouped together in recitation sections so that
they may have special attention.

2 class hours; 1 quiz hour; 1 2-hour laboratory period.   Credit, 3.
MR. FESSENDEN, MR. RICHASON, MR. STEIN, MR. OBERLANDER.

4. (II) General Inorganic Chemistry

For students planning to major in chemistry or chemical engineering, and others who plan to continue the study of this science
in preparation for their field of specialization. The course will
include ionic equilibria; oxidation and reduction; electro-chemistry; the descriptive chemistry of some nonmetallic and metallic
elements; the metallurgy of some common metals, and a discussion
of the production of some of the more important inorganic chemicals. Applications of atomic structure and the electronic theory
of valence to these subjects will be stressed.

2 class hours; 1 quiz hour; 2 2-hour laboratory periods.   Credit, 4.
MR. FESSENDEN, MR. RICHASON.
Prerequisite, Chemistry 1.

29. (I) and (II) Qualitative Analysis

A study of the fundamental principles and laws concerning the
behavior of solutions of electrolytes. The laboratory work deals
with the characteristic properties, reactions, and the systemic separation and identification of the common cations and anions. The
semi-micro technique is used throughout for the analysis of salts,
salt mixtures, and alloys. A considerable portion of the laboratory
work is devoted to the identification of substances unknown to

* On leave of absence for military service.

the student. This course is designed to meet the needs not only of those students specializing in chemistry, but also of those students specializing in other subjects where inorganic chemistry is of importance.

2 class hours; 6 laboratory hours.   Credit, 4.
8:00-8:50 or 10:00-10:50 Tu. Th.; 8:00-9:50 or 10:00-11:50 M. W. F. or 1:00-3:50 M. F. or 1:00-3:50 Tu. Th.

MR. SMITH.

30. (I) and (II) Quantitative Analysis

The theory and practice of representative determinations in gravimetric and volumetric analysis are considered in detail together with analytical calculations. The laboratory work emphasizes the techniques required for accurate chemical measurements.

2 class hours; 2 3-hour laboratory periods.   Credit, 4.
11:00-11:50 Tu. Th.; 1:00-3:50 M. F. or Tu. Th. or 1:00-3:50 W., 9:00-11:50 S.

MR. ROBERTS.

Prerequisite, Chemistry 29.

33. (I) and (II) Organic Chemistry

A short course intended to satisfy the requirements in this field for all students who do not specialize in chemistry.

3 class hours; 1 3-hour laboratory period.   Credit, 4.
9:00-9:50 Tu. Th. S.; 1:00-3:50 M. T. W. or Th.   MR. CONRAD.
Prerequisites, Chemistry 1 and 2.

51. (I) 52. (II) Organic Chemistry

A course in the theory of organic chemistry intended to serve the needs of students who will specialize in chemistry, as well as those who may specialize in other fields where a more comprehensive course is desired than Chemistry 33. The first semester deals largely with compounds of the aliphatic series, while the benzene series is taken up in the second semester. Students electing this course should take both 51 and 52.

3 class hours; 1 3-hour laboratory period.   Credit, 4.
9:00-9:50 M. W. F.; 1:00-3:50 M. W. or F.

MR. RITCHIE, MR. CANNON.

Prerequisite, Chemistry 29.

63. (I) Chemistry of Water, Sewage and Sewage Sludge

Admission by permission of the instructor. The preparation of reagents and standard methods for the analysis of water, sewage and sewage sludge. Lectures and discussions on the sanitary significance of analytical data.

2 3-hour laboratory periods. Credit, 3.
1:00-3:50 W.; 9:00-11:50 S.

MR. SNOW.

Prerequisite, Chemistry 30.

65. (I) 66. (II) Physical Chemistry

A study of the fundamental theories and laws of physical chemistry, together with the solution of problems involved in their application. The laboratory work will include practice in making physico-chemical measurements and the preparation of reports.

3 class hours; 1 3-hour laboratory period. Credit, 4.
8:00-8:50 or 11:00-11:50 M. W. F.; 1:00-3:50 M. W. or F.

MR. FESSENDEN, MR. SMITH.

Prerequisites, Chemistry 30; Mathematics 30; Physics 26.

77. (I) Advanced Physical Chemistry

A detailed study of a number of topics such as kinetics, catalysis, chemical thermodynamics and electrochemistry.

3 class hours. Credit, 3.

MR. STEIN.

Prerequisites, Chemistry 65 and 66.

79. (I) Elementary Biochemistry

A consideration of the more important facts relating to biological materials and processes. This course is designed primarily for students not eligible for courses 93 or 94. It is not open to chemistry majors and is not offered for graduate credit.

3 class hours; 1 3-hour laboratory period. Credit, 4.

MR. LITTLE.

80. (II) Clinical Chemistry (Blood and Urine Analysis)

Work to be covered will include the collection and preparation of samples for analysis; standardization of glassware and the preparation of reagents; description of colorimeters and the determination of certain significant compounds in the samples. The latter group will include at least sugars, proteins, non-protein, nitrogen, fatty substances and inorganic elements.

1 class hour; 1 2-hour laboratory period. Credit, 2.

MR. LITTLE.

81. (I) Organic Chemistry

A rapid and intensive survey of the important reactions of organic chemistry with emphasis on their scope and limitations, recent developments and theoretical aspects. Admission by permission of instructor.

3 class hours. Credit, 3.
9:00-9:50 Tu. Th. S.

MR. CANNON.

Prerequisite, one year of organic chemistry.

82. (II) Qualitative Organic Chemistry

The characterization of organic compounds by means of physical properties, class reactions and the preparation of suitable derivatives. The laboratory work will involve the identification of a number of simple unknown compounds followed by the separation, purification, and identification of the individual components in several unknown mixtures of organic compounds.

Admission by permission of instructor.

2 class hours; 2 3-hour laboratory periods. Credit, 4.
1:00-1:50 Tu. Th.; 2:00-4:50 Tu. Th.

MR. CANNON.

Prerequisite, one year of organic chemistry.

83. (I) Advanced Analytical Chemistry

The theory and techniques of special methods of analysis such as colorimetry, potentiometry, microscopy, ion exchange, electrodeposition and other recently developed methods of analysis. Primarily for chemistry majors but open to others with the permission of the instructor.

2 class hours; 1 3-hour laboratory period. Credit, 3.

MR. ROBERTS.

Prerequisite, Chemistry 30.

86. (II) Theoretical Inorganic Chemistry

A survey of inorganic chemistry which is largely theoretical and includes such topics as atomic structure, periodic classification and relationships, valence concepts, acid-base theory, and the chemistry of the commercially important elements and their compounds based upon the periodic table.

3 class hours. Credit, 3.
8:00-8:50 M. W. F.

MR. SMITH.

Prerequisite, Chemistry 65.

88. (II) History of Chemistry

An historical and biographical study of chemistry and chemists. The aim of the course is: (1) to give the student a comprehensive view of the science as a whole, through a study of the development of new ideas and the establishment of new theories and laws; and

151

(2) to arouse an enthusiastic interest in the subject and an appreciation of the true spirit of scientific research, through a sympathetic presentation of the work and lives of the great chemists who have been the creators of the chemistry of today.

3 class hours.   Credit, 3.
10:00-10:50 M. W. F.   MR. RITCHIE.

92. (II) Introduction Research

Admission only by permission of the department. The aim of the course is to give the student an opportunity to learn the purpose and methods of research. To each student is assigned some special subject or problem in one of the following fields of chemistry, viz., analytical, biochemical, inorganic, organic, physical.

10 laboratory hours.   Credit, 5.
Hours by arrangement.   THE DEPARTMENT.

93. (I) 94. (II) General Biochemistry

These courses offer a broad introduction to the general field of biochemistry for students majoring in chemistry or in the biological sciences, and provide a background for more advanced or specialized study in this field.

3 class hours; 1 3-hour laboratory period.   Credit, 4.
                                   MR. LITTLE.

Prerequisites, Chemistry 51 and 52 or their equivalent.

DAIRY INDUSTRY

PROFESSOR HANKINSON, ASSISTANT PROFESSOR LINDQUIST,
MR. ————.

25. (I) General Dairying

This course is introductory to all other courses in dairy industry and gives a general knowledge of the subject to those who wish to take only one course in dairying. The lecture portion includes the importance of the dairy industry, the composition and properties of milk, the secretion of milk, production of quality milk on the farm, methods of processing milk and cream, and the elements of ice cream, butter and cheese making. The laboratory work includes the testing of milk and milk products for fat and acidity, lactometry, and a general study of dairy plant equipment and processes.

2 class hours; 1 2-hour laboratory period.   Credit, 3.
1:00-1:50 Tu. Th.; 2:00-3:50 Tu. or Th.   MR. HANKINSON.

50. (II) Judging Dairy Products

A study of market standards and grades of dairy products, with practice in judging milk, ice cream, butter, and cheese. The emphasis is on recognizing quality in dairy products, detecting specific defects, and learning the causes and means of preventing common defects. A team is chosen from this class to represent the University in two contests: Eastern States Intercollegiate Dairy Products Judging Contest, and Collegiate Students' International Contest in Judging Dairy Products.

1 2-hour laboratory period.   Credit, 1.
3:00-4:50 F.   MR. ————.

52. (II) Market Milk

A study of the various phases of the market milk industry; sanitary production, transportation, pasteurization and handling in the city plant; marketing, delivery systems, milk and its relation to public health, inspection, milk laws, food value, and advertising. Cultured milk and other milk drinks also are included. Some milk plants are visited, the cost of the trip not exceeding five dollars.

2 class hours; 2 2-hour laboratory periods.   Credit, 4.
8:00-8:50 Tu. Th.; 9:00-10:50 Tu. Th. or 3:00-4:50 Tu. Th.
                                   MR. LINDQUIST.

75. (I) Dairy Chemistry

This course is a particular study of those physical and chemical principles which not only explain the behavior of milk and milk products in the various technological operations, but also provide a basic viewpoint for dairy research. The lectures will include discussions (1) of the constituents of milk in relation to other organic compounds, and (2) the physiochemical aspects of certain dairy phenomena such as foaming, coagulation, etc. The laboratory work will include many of the tests used commercially and in dairy research, emphasizing the principles and application of both qualitative and quantitative analysis as well as the technique of operating scientific apparatus.

1 class hour; 2 2-hour laboratory periods.   Credit, 3.
8:00-10:50 Tu., 8:00-9:50 Th.   MR. ————.
Prerequisites, Dairy 25, Dairy 52, and Chemistry 52 or permission of the instructor.

77. (I) Butter and Cheese Making

Half of the semester is devoted to butter making; the remainder to cheese making, condensed and powdered milk. The various phases of the butter industry studied are: separators and cream separation; pasteurization, neutralization, and ripening of cream; preparation of starter cultures; churning; marketing and scoring of butter; creamery management. The work in cheese making includes cheddar, cream, Neufchatel, cottage, processed cheeses, etc. The manufacture of condensed milk, powdered milk, and commercial casein is also covered.

2 class hours; 2 3-hour laboratory periods.   Credit, 4.
11:00-11:50 W. F., 1:00-3:50 M. F.
                            MR. LINDQUIST, MR. ————.
Prerequisite, Dairy 25.

78. (II) Ice Cream Making
The course includes a study of the principles and practices of ice-cream making. The effects of such factors as composition, quality, pasteurization, homogenization, aging, and freezing on the finished products are considered. Sherbets, ices, fancy and individual forms, and all flavors of ice cream are studied. Some time is devoted to refrigeration, machinery, delivery equipment, and merchandising methods as they are related to the industry.

2 class hours; 2 3-hour laboratory periods.   Credit, 4.
11:00-11:50 W. F.; 1:00-3:50 Tu. Th.   MR. ————.

79. (I) 80. (II) Seminar
For students specializing in dairy industry.
1 class hour.   Credit, I.
11:00-11:50 M.   THE DEPARTMENT.

ECONOMICS

PROFESSOR GAMBLE, PROFESSOR MORRIS, ASSISTANT PROFESSOR HALLER, ASSISTANT PROFESSOR HOWARD, ASSISTANT PROFESSOR SCHOEFFLER, MR. ROTHENBERG, MR. MATTERSDORFF, MR. WILL.

12. (II) Economic History of the United States
A study of the significant factors in the economic development of the nation.
3 class hours.   Credit, 3.
                            MR. HALLER, MR. HOWARD.

25. (I) and (II) Elements of Economics
Definitions and introductory principles of production, exchange, and the financial organization of society, with a short survey of the economics of distribution and the use of wealth and income.
3 class hours.   Credit, 3.
                                THE DEPARTMENT.

26. (II) Problems of the National Economy

A continuation of course 25 with emphasis on the study of wealth and income distribution.

3 class hours. Credit, 3.

Prerequisite, Economics 25. THE DEPARTMENT.

53. (I) Money, Banking and Credit

A critical survey of the development and operation of the monetary and banking systems of the United States.

3 class hours. Credit, 3.

MR. GAMBLE.

54. (II) Money, Income and Monetary Policy

A study of the relationship between money, income and monetary policy. It includes examination of the relationships between individuals, banks, money markets and central banks.

3 class hours. Credit, 3.

MR. GAMBLE.

Prerequisite, Economics 53 or Finance 53.

55. (I) Economics of Consumption

A study of patterns of consumption, standards of living and the sources and expenditure of individual and family incomes.

3 class hours. Credit, 3.

MR. HALLER.

56. (II) Business Fluctuations and Forecasting

A study of business fluctuations and an analysis of current business cycle theories.

3 class hours. Credit, 3.

MR. SCHOEFFLER.

70. (II) Monopolies

A study of the growth, development, and social control of monopolies.

3 class hours. Credit, 3.

MR. HALLER.

73. (I) Modern Economic Theory

A study of current theories about value, distribution and prices.

3 class hours. Credit, 3.

MR. SCHOEFFLER.

74. (II) Current Economic Problems

An advanced course for those desirous of studying more intensively some current economic problems. Students will be encouraged to pursue lines of individual interest.

3 class hours. Credit, 3.

MR. HOWARD.

77. (I) Economics of International Trade (1954-55)

A study of the policies, principles, and practices of international trade. Given in alternate years.

3 class hours. Credit, 3.
MR. WEINER.

78. (II) Public Finance

Principles of public revenues and expenditures with special emphasis on the systems and problems of taxation.

3 class hours. Credit, 3.
MR. GAMBLE.

79. (I) Labor Problems

An analysis of the background and character of the modern labor problem with special references to the United States. Topics to be considered include: the problems of wages, hours, working conditions and unemployment; the trade union movement; and some agencies for the promotion of industrial peace.

3 class hours. Credit, 3.
MR. MORRIS.

80. (II) Labor Legislation

A study of federal and state legislation affecting labor.

3 class hours. Credit, 3.
MR. MORRIS.

83. (I) Social Control of Business

Methods of social control of economic activity including both formal and informal controls.

3 class hours. Credit, 3.
MR. HOWARD.

84. (II) Comparative Economic Systems

An examination of the various forms of economic organization that have been tried and proposed with an analysis of the economic institutions of representative current economies.

3 class hours. Credit, 3.
MR. SCHOEFFLER.

91. (I) 92. (II) Seminar

Research in economic theory; problems of labor, commerce, and industry. If desirable, some other economic study may be substituted.

1 or 2 2-hour conferences. Credit, 1 to 3.
THE DEPARTMENT.

EDUCATION

PROFESSOR PURVIS, ASSISTANT PROFESSOR OLIVER, ASSISTANT PROFESSOR ROURKE, ASSISTANT PROFESSOR McCARTHY, ASSISTANT PROFESSOR WYMAN, ASSISTANT PROFESSOR O'LEARY, MISS O'DONNELL, MR. TAFT.[1]

51. (I) History of Education

Educational movements are traced from early Greece to the present with the aim of better understanding of modern problems. Special emphasis is placed upon the function of the school in the various societies.

3 class hours. Credit, 3.

MR. PURVIS, MR. McCARTHY.

52. (II) Principles and Methods of Teaching

By means of discussion, case studies, and current educational literature, teaching ideals and procedures are set up. Application of the general principles are made in the major fields represented by the class. Given also in the one-semester program.

3 class hours. Credit, 3.

MR. PURVIS, MR. McCARTHY.

53. (I) Educational Tests and Measurements

The most serviceable tests and scales for measuring achievement are considered; test construction, administration, scoring, and interpretation of results are studied and practiced. Considerable attention is given to preparation of informal tests for diagnostic and grading purposes. Given also in the one-semester program.

2 class hours; 1 2-hour laboratory period. Credit, 3.

MR. ROURKE.

60. (I) and (II) Elementary School Curriculum

This course is designed to present a picture of the elementary school curriculum from the standpoint of content and methodology. Emphasis will be placed on the unit method and the activity program.

3 class hours. Credit, 3.

MISS O'DONNELL

61. (I) and (II) Teaching of Elementary Reading and Language Arts

The main emphasis will be placed upon a development program in reading instruction. Discussions, demonstrations, and principles

[1] State Supervisor for Agricultural Teacher-Training representing the State Department of Education in the administration of vocational agricultural acts.

of effective reading practices will form a major part of the course. Methods of teaching oral and written language will be included.
3 class hours. Credit, 3.
MISS O'LEARY.

63. (I) and (II) Teaching of Elementary Arithmetic

This course will discuss and demonstrate accepted methods and materials in the teaching of arithmetic in the elementary grades. Attention will be given to methods of correlating arithmetic with the total program of the school.
3 class hours. Credit, 3.
MISS O'DONNELL

64. (II) Principles of Elementary Education

This course is designed to acquaint the student with the aim, organization, program, pupil population, etc., of the elementary school and the relationship between this level of education and the secondary school level which follows.
3 class hours. Credit, 3.
MISS O'LEARY.

66. (I) and (II) Preparation and Use of Audio-Visual Aids

Study is made of available media of audio-visual aids to instruction, construction of visual material, and accepted methods of use.
2 class hours; 1 2-hour laboratory period. Credit, 3.
MR. WYMAN.

72. (II) Vocational Education in Agriculture

This course demands certain requisites of experience and a definite objective on the part of the student to enter the field of vocational agricultural teaching which makes it necessary for the student to seek permission to enter the course. It is the first of the series of special courses (72, 73, 75) required of candidates for the vocational teacher-training certificate. A survey of vocational agricultural education and an introduction to teaching of vocational agriculture at the secondary school level is the basis of the course. Certain information and observations in preparation for the apprenticeship course are offered.
2 class hours; 1 2-hour laboratory period. Credit, 3.
MR. OLIVER and VOCATIONAL DIVISION
of STATE DEPARTMENT of EDUCATION.

73. (I) and (II) Apprentice Teaching in Agriculture

For a limited number of qualified candidates in vocational agriculture education. A full year in absentia normally following the junior year in college, teaching agriculture, horiculture, and related subjects. Candidates should have completed the course in

Education 72, and in Education 52, if possible and must apply early to the instructor of the course.

Maximum Credit, 6.

MR. OLIVER and VOCATIONAL DIVISION
of STATE DEPARTMENT of EDUCATION.

75. (I) Technique of Teaching Vocational Agriculture

By arrangement with the instructor. Preferably this course should follow courses 72 and 73. It covers the materials, methods, policies, and special requirements of Massachusetts for teaching vocational agriculture and related subjects in high schools and special county schools. This is one of three courses required of candidates for. agricultural teacher training certificates.

2 class hours; 1 2-hour laboratory period.   Credit, 3.

MR. OLIVER and VOCATIONAL DIVISION
of STATE DEPARTMENT of EDUCATION.

79. (I) Methods in Adult Education

Admission only by permission of instructor. The beginning Education course for juniors and seniors who are training for extension work and for others interested in teaching adults. Generally accepted methods of group and individual instruction with adults, and methods of developing leaders to carry on the work in the field.

2 class hours; 1 2-hour laboratory period.   Credit, 3.

MR. —————.

83. (I) Principles of Secondary Education

This course presents a picture of the secondary school as a social agency, its relation to elementary and collegiate education, its aims, organizations, administration, curriculum procedures, and such other phases as are necessary to acquaint the student with the predominant level of our educational ladder. Given also in the one-semester program.

3 class hours.   Credit, 3.

MR. McCARTHY.

85. (I) and (II) Observation and Practice Teaching

Admission by permission of the Department. An opportunity to do regular teaching in cooperating schools within commuting distance of the University. The student works under the supervision of a teacher with frequent visits from some member of. the university staff.   Credit, 3-6.

THE DEPARTMENT.

Prerequisites, Education 51, 52, 88 or their equivalent for secondary teaching, and Education 51, 64, Psychology 94 or Home Economics 70 for elementary teaching.

159

88. (II) Secondary School Curriculum

For senior majors in Education. A consideration of learning material and activities and their organization in the subjects which these students are teaching, and the preparation of courses of study in those fields in the light of accepted educational practices. Given also in the one-semester program.

2 class hours; 1 2-hour laboratory period. Credit, 3.

MR. ROURKE.

AGRICULTURAL ENGINEERING

PROFESSOR STAPLETON, ASSOCIATE PROFESSOR MARKUSON†, ASSISTANT PROFESSOR TAGUE, ASSISTANT PROFESSOR PATTERSON, MR. POWERS, MR. PIRA.

51. (I) House Planning

Plan designs of the small house will be made. The arrangement of interior equipment, especially in the kitchen, and lighting, heating, water supply, and sewage disposal will be studied, together with a brief history of the house materials, construction methods, equipment, and architectural styles. Consideration will be given to the economics of house building, including financing, and to maintenance and overhead expense.

1 class hour; 2 2-hour laboratory periods. Credit, 3.

MR. MARKUSON.

55. (I) Farm Shop

For students in agriculture and horticulture. Laboratory exercises cover instruction and practice in the use of carpenter's tools in construction and in bench work, arc and gas welding, pipe fitting, soldering, use of machinist's tools in machinery repair, and the mixing and placing of concrete. Classroom instruction covers materials of construction and the utilization of local and special materials for these purposes.

1 class hour; 2 2-hour laboratory periods. Credit, 3.

MR. POWERS.

71. (I) Farm Power

The study of internal combustion engines used in farm tractors and power of units.

1 class hours; 2 2-hour laboratory periods. Credit, 3.

MR. PATTERSON.

Prerequisites, Civil Engineering 52, Mechanical Eng. 65, 68.

† On leave of absence.

72. (II) Drainage and Irrigation Engineering

This course is an abridgement of Agricultural Engineering 78 for students not majoring in Engineering who do not have the prerequisites for Course 78.

1 class hour; 1 2-hour laboratory period. Credit, 3

MR. STAPLETON.

73. (I) Farm Structures

A study of the strength and durability of building materials, construction systems and the mechanical principles underlying their use in farm construction. In the drafting room studies will be made of some major farm building and complete working drawings finished in all essential details.

1 class hour; 3 2-hour laboratory periods. Credit, 4.

MR. STAPLETON.

Prerequisites, Civil Engineering 34, 51; Mechanical Eng. 61.

74. (II) Farm Structures

This course is an abridgment of Agricultural Engineering 73 for students not majoring in engineering who do not have the prerequisites for Course 73.

1 class hour; 2 2-hour laboratory periods. Credit, 3.

MR. MARKUSON.

76. (II) Agricultural Machinery

The study of design and operational problems of agricultural field machinery.

2 class hours; 1 2-hour laboratory period. Credit, 3.

MR. PATTERSON.

Prerequisites, Civil Engineering 52, Mechanical Eng. 68, 83.

78. (II) Drainage, Reclamation and Conservation

This course covers the engineering phase of drainage and reclamation. The various systems are studied, complete layouts established in the field, and problems of flow and run-off given.

1 class hour; 2 2-hour laboratory periods. Credit, 3.

MR. STAPLETON.

Prerequisites, Civil Engineering 25, 75 or 76 Agronomy 2.

80. (I) and (II) Food Process Engineering

A study of food processing machinery and instrumentation.

2 class hours; 1 2-hour laboratory period. Credit, 3.

MR. ————.

82. (II) Refrigeration

Fundamentals in planning and operating a refrigerated storage with particular reference to size, details of construction, cooling load, and refrigerating machinery and accessories. For non-engineering majors.

1 class hour; 1 3-hour laboratory period.　　　　　Credit, 2.

MR. ————.

83. (I) 84. (II) Agricultural Engineering Problems

Open only to seniors specializing in agricultural engineering. This course consists of individual problems chosen by the students under guidance of the department.

Hours by arrangement.　　　　　Credit, 3.

THE DEPARTMENT.

85. (I) Rural Electrification

A course devoted to the utilization of electricity in agriculture.

2 class hours; 1 2-hour laboratory period.　　　　　Credit, 3.

Prerequisites, Electrical Engineering 61, 62.　　MR. ————.

92. (II) Professional Seminar

For seniors majoring in agricultural engineering.

1 class hour.　　　　　Credit, 1.

THE DEPARTMENT.

CHEMICAL ENGINEERING

PROFESSOR LINDSEY, ASSISTANT PROFESSOR CASHIN†, ASSISTANT PROFESSOR BATKE.

26. (II) Fundamentals

An introduction to the nature and scope of chemical engineering and certain fundamental concepts, to be amplified in later courses, particularly problems dealing with material and energy balances. There is a review of the chemical, mathematical, and physical principles which are particularly applicable.

2 class hours.　　　　　Credit, 2.

MR. CASHIN.

Prerequisites, Chemistry 2 or 4, Physics 25.

55. (I) Unit Operations I

A study of the fundamental principles underlying the unit operations of fluid flow, heat transfer and evaporation. A portion of the

† On leave of absence.

course is devoted to a study of the thermodynamic properties of matter.

3 class hours; 2 3-hour computation periods. Credit, 5.

MR. BATKE.

Prerequisites, Chemical Engineering 26; Mathematics 30 or 31; Physics 25.

56. (II) Unit Operations II

A continuation of Course 55, including the additional unit operations of distillation, gas absorption, liquid extraction, crystallization, filtration, mixing, crushing and grinding.

3 class hours; 2 2-hour computation periods. Credit, 5.

MR. BATKE.

Prerequisite, Chemical Engineering 55.

57. (I) Inorganic Chemical Technology

A study of manufacture of some of the important inorganic chemicals. Topics studied include sulfuric acid, nitric acid, hydrochloric acid, ammonia, sodium carbonate, and sodium hydroxide with particular stress on unit operations. Field trips will be included where possible.

3 class hours. Credit, 3.

MR. CASHIN.

Prerequisites, Chemistry 30; Physics 26.

58. (II) Organic Chemical Technology

A study of some of the unit processes involved in the manufacture of organic chemicals. Unit processes studied include nitration, amination, halogenation, oxidation and esterification. Field trips will be included where possible.

3 class hours. Credit, 3.

MR. CASHIN.

Prequisite, Chemistry 51.

75. (S) Instrumentation

A detailed study of the underlying principles and practices in indicating, recording and controlling instruments used on industrial process equipment.

4 class hours; 2 3 hour laboratory periods per week for six weeks.

Credit, 3

MR. CASHIN.

Prerequisites, Physics 26 or 28; Chemical Engineering 55.

77. (I) Elements of Unit Operations

For other than chemical engineering majors. An introduction to some of the unit operations of process industries. The emphasis is on the principles and types of equipment, rather than on the quantitive aspects and design.

2 class hours; 1 2-hour laboratory period. Credit, 3.

MR. LINDSEY.

Prerequisites, Chemistry 30; Physics 25, 26.

81. (I) Heat-energy Relations

A study of the energy relations in chemical processes. Includes: types of energy, energy balances, second law, thermodynamic functions, P-V-T relations of fluids, compression and expansion on processes.

3 class hours. Credit, 3.

MR. BATKE.

Prerequisites, Chemistry 66; Chemical Engineering 56.

82. (II) Industrial Equilibria and Kinetics

A study of phase and chemical equilibria and rates of reaction in chemical processes from the industrial point of view.

3 class hours. Credit, 3.

MR. BATKE.

Prerequisites, Chemistry 66; Chemical Engineering 81.

88. (S) Chemical Engineering Laboratory

A quantitative study of pilot plant size equipment illustrating some unit operations. Special emphasis is placed on the securing of accurate data, correct operating techniques, and on report writing. Field trips will be made when possible.

4 8-hour laboratory days per week for six weeks. Credit, 3.

THE STAFF.

Prerequisite, Chemical Engineering 56.

89. (I) 90. (II) Laboratory Projects

Investigation and report on an elementary chemical engineering problem.

2 4-hour laboratory periods. Credit, 3.

THE STAFF.

Prerequisites, Chemical Engineering 56, 88.

91. (I) 92. (II) Seminar

Preparation and discussion of professional topics of interest to chemical engineers.

1 class hour. Credit, 1.

THE STAFF.

93. (I) 94. (II) Comprehensive Problems

The solution of comprehensive problems which requires the application and integration of a number of the principles studied in previous courses in chemistry and chemical engineering. Course 93 is a prerequisite for Course 94.

2 class hours; 1 3-hour computation period.   Credit, 3.

MR. LINDSEY.

Prerequisites, Chemical Engineering 56; Chemistry 52, 66.

95. (I) Process Equipment Design

The design of process equipment for the chemical industries: riveted pressure vessels, welded pressure vessels, piping, attachments and closures, etc.

1 class hour; 1 3-hour laboratory period.   Credit, 2.

MR. LINDSEY.

Prerequisites, Chemical Engineering 55; Civil Engineering 53.

98. (II) Advanced Unit Operations

A more detailed study of certain unit operations such as unsteady-state heat transfer, and multicomponent-distillation.

2 class hours.   Credit, 2.

MR. CASHIN.

Prerequisites, Chemical Engineering 56.

CIVIL ENGINEERING

PROFESSOR MARSTON, PROFESSOR WHITE, PROFESSOR OSGOOD, ASSOCIATE PROFESSOR HENDRICKSON, ASSISTANT PROFESSOR FENG, ASSISTANT PROFESSOR MARCUS, ASSISTANT PROFESSOR GROW, ASSISTANT PROFESSOR SHARP, ASSISTANT PROFESSOR BOYER, MR. NEVEL.

25. (I) Surveying

The theory of surveying for both measurement and layout work, description of field and office computation, notes, and drafting procedure are given in the classroom. Topics covered are use of tape, transit, level, and plane table; methods of carrying out property surveys, layout surveys, computation and field work for simple and compound horizontal and vertical curves, determination of geographic position, determination of azimuth from the sun and Polaris, and a finished map of a small area.

3 class hours; 2 3-hour laboratory periods.   Credit, 5.

MR. BOYER.

Prequisite, Trigonometry.

27. (I) and (II) Plane Surveying

The basic principles of mensuration are discussed in class. Instruction and problems involving the use of tape, transit and level are given in the field, and the preparation of a map of a small area is carried out in the drafting room. Route surveying is considered briefly. This course is not open to civil engineering students.

2 class hours; 1 3-hour laboratory period. Credit, 3.

Prequisite, Mathematics 5 or 7. MR. BOYER.

28. (Summer) Property and Topographic Surveying

This course consists of a transit and tape property survey in which reference to Registry of Deeds records is required, and a topographic survey of a selected area using the plane table. Certain advanced topics such as triangulation and conformal coordinate systems are discussed as they relate to the topographic survey.

3 40-hour weeks. Credit, 3.

MR. BOYER.

Prerequisite, Civil Engineering 25 or 27.

30. (Summer) Route Surveying Practice

This practice course consists of a preliminary survey for a short highway location and of the preparation of maps and profile from the data recorded on the survey. The maps are to be used in C.E. 55 in choosing the final location of the route and in estimating earthwork quantities and cost.

3 40-hour weeks. Credit, 3.

MR. BOYER.

Prerequisite, Civil Engineering 25 or 27.

34. (I) and (II) Statics

The following topics are considered: equilibrium of forces, friction, first and second moments, center of gravity. Algebraic and graphical methods are covered.

3 class hours. Credit, 3.

MR. WHITE, MR. MARCUS, MR. GROW.

Prerequisites, Physics 25; Mathematics 31.

51. (I) Strength of Materials

The following topics are considered: simple stresses and strains; combined stresses; torsion; shear and bending moments in beams; stresses and deflection of beams; columns.

3 class hours; 1 3-hour laboratory period. Credit, 4.

MR. WHITE, MR. MARCUS, MR. GROW.

Prerequisites, Civil Engineering 34; Mathematics 32.

52. (I) and (II) Dynamics

The following topics are considered: kinematics, motion of particles, motion of rigid bodies, work and energy, power, impulse and momentum.
3 class hours.   Credit, 3.

MR. WHITE, MR. MARCUS, MR. GROW.

Prerequisites, Civil Engineering 34; Mathematics 32.

53. (I) and (II) Strength of Materials

A shortened version of C.E. 51 for electrical and mechanical engineers in the industrial option.
3 class hours.   Credit, 3.

MR. WHITE, MR. SHARP, MR. MARCUS.

Prerequisites, Civil Engineering 34; Mathematics 32.

55. (I) Highway Engineering

The design features of highway construction and relative merits of various types of highway surfaces are discussed in class. Plans, profiles, cross sections, and specifications for a short section of highway are prepared.
2 class hours; 1 3-hour laboratory period.   Credit, 3.

MR. BOYER.

Prerequisite, Civil Engineering 30.

61. (I) and (II) Testing of Materials

A study of laboratory methods for the determination of the physical properties of engineering materials and their behavior under stress.
1 class hour; 1 3-hour laboratory period.   Credit, 2.

MR. SHARP.

Prerequisite, Civil Engineering 51 or 53.

70. (II) Theory of Structures

The course treats the analysis of statically determinate structures of wood and steel, with reference to particular types of structures, such as industrial and office buildings, highway and railway bridges.
3 class hours; 1 3-hour laboratory period.   Credit, 4.

MR. OSGOOD.

Prequisite, Civil Engineering 51.

71. (I) Structural Design

This course is an application of the theory of structures to engineering practice through the preparation of designs and drawings for structural frames, girders and trusses in steel and wood that

CIVIL ENGINEERING

together make up a complete building frame or bridge. Emphasis
is placed upon the design of structural members and joints.
2 class hours; 1 3-hour laboratory period. Credit, 3.
MR. OSGOOD.
Prerequisite, Civil Engineering 70.

72. (II) Advanced Structural Theory
The analysis of space frames and methods of finding deflections
of trusses and beams are studied. Several methods of analysis of
statically indeterminate structures are introduced. Application of
the theories considered is made in the solution of practical problems during the laboratory periods.
2 class hours; 1 3-hour laboratory period. Credit, 3.
MR. OSGOOD.
Prerequisite, Civil Engineering 70.

73. (I) Concrete Design
This course deals with the general methods of analyzing and designing plain and reinforced concrete structures. Application is
made to slabs, beams, girders, columns, walls and foundations for
buildings, retaining walls and bridges. Drawings are prepared for
a reinforced concrete building.
2 class hours; 2 3-hour laboratory periods. Credit, 4.
MR. OSGOOD.
Prerequisite, Civil Engineering 51.

75. (I) Fluid Mechanics
This course is an abridgment of Civil Engineering 76 for electri-
cal and industrial engineering majors.
3 class hours. Credit, 3.
MR. MARSTON, MR. MARCUS.
Prerequisite, Civil Engineering 52.

76. (I) and (II) Fluid Mechanics
The following topics are considered: properties of fluids, gas
laws, viscosity, static pressure, gages, buoyant forces, dynamics of
fluids, Bernoulli's theorem, flow in pipes, orifices, nozzles, weirs and
open channels, hydraulic similitude and dimensional analysis.
3 class hours, 1 3-hour laboratory period. Credit, 4.
MR. MARCUS, MR. FENG.
Prerequisite, Civil Engineering 52.

77. (I) Sanitary Engineering I
This course treats the following topics: demand of water and
quantity of sewage, hydrology relating to water resources and

drainage, hydraulics of water supply systems and sewers, pumps and pumping stations, water collecting and distributing works and sewerage systems.

3 class hours. Credit, 3.

MR. FENG.

Prerequisite, Civil Engineering 75 or 76 concurrently.

78. (II) Sanitary Engineering II

Consideration is given to hydraulic aspects of sedimentation, flotation, aeration and recirculation, quality of water supplies, characteristics of sewage, water purification works, sewage treatment works and industrial waste problems. The laboratory periods are devoted to the practice of designing water distribution systems and sewer systems.

3 class hours; 1 3-hour laboratory period. Credit, 4.

MR. FENG.

Prerequisite, Civil Engineering 75 or 76.

79. (I) Principles of Sanitary Engineering

This course is designed for students in the Department of Public Health. It covers phases of Civil Engineering 77 and 78 with consideration of the non-engineering background of the student. Admission by permission of the instructor.

2 class hours; 1 3-hour laboratory period. Credit, 3.

MR. FENG.

80. (II) Soil Mechanics

This course is a study of the mechanical classification of soil based upon field and laboratory work and the validity of these classifications as a means of predicting soil behavior. The student is guided through case studies in embankment stability, seepage and consolidation.

2 class hours; 1 3-hour laboratory period. Credit, 3.

MR. HENDRICKSON.

Prerequisite, Geology 50.

81. (I) Foundations

A survey of modern theories and practice in transferring structural loads to earth masses. Pile foundations, spread footings, cassions, and buoyant systems are discussed.

2 class hours; 1 3-hour laboratory period. Credit, 3.

MR. HENDRICKSON.

Prerequisite, Civil Engineering 80.

86. (II) Sanitary Engineering Design

This is a laboratory course devoted to the design of sanitary engineering facilities, water supply and conditioning and sewerage and sewage treatment plants. Stream sanitation is considered and the latest practice and research in the sanitary engineering field are discussed.

1 class hour; 2 3-hour laboratory periods.   Credit, 3.

MR. FENG.

Prerequisites, Civil Engineering 77 and 78, or concurrently.

88. (II) Advanced Stress Analysis

This course is concerned with the determination of stresses and strains in structural and machine elements.

3 class hours.   Credit, 3.

MR. WHITE.

Prerequisite, Civil Engineering 51 (with a grade of 75).

90. (II) Contracts, Specifications and Estimating

A study of the essentials of contracts as applied to business procedures in the construction field, the purposes and makeup of specifications, and the processes of estimating through quantity surveys and unit cost applications.

3 class hours.   Credit, 3.

MR. MARKUSON.

92. (II) Professional Seminar

For seniors majoring in civil engineering. Current engineering projects are described by student reports. The professional aspect of the civil engineer's work is stressed.

3 class hours.   Credit, 3.

THE DEPARTMENT.

94. (II) Advanced Surveying

The following topics are included: elements of astronomy, precise methods of surveying, adjustment of observations and the elements of photogrammetry.

2 class hours. 1 3-hour laboratory period.   Credit, 3.

MR. HENDRICKSON.

Prerequisites, Civil Engineering 25, 28.

96. (II) Hydraulic Engineering

The analysis and design of hydraulic structures such as storage reservoirs, spillways, dams, levees, and shore protection and channel works are considered.

2 class hours, 1 3-hour laboratory period.   Credit, 3.

MR. MARSTON.

Prerequisite, Civil Engineering 76.

ELECTRICAL ENGINEERING

PROFESSOR ROYS, ASSOCIATE PROFESSOR LANGFORD, ASSOCIATE PRO-
FESSOR MOHN, ASSISTANT PROFESSOR SMITH, ASSISTANT PROFESSOR
KARLSON, ASSISTANT PROESSOR LINGO, MR. KNUDSEN.

41. (I) Fundamentals of Electrical Engineering

Direct current, circuit analysis by means of Ohm's and Kirchoff's
laws, nodal equations, determinants, superposition principle, reciprocity and Thevenin's theorem. The fundamental laws of electricity and magnetism and their application to problems in electrostatics, magnetostatics and electromagnetism.
3 class hours; 1 3-hour laboratory period. Credit, 4.
MR. LINGO, MR. SMITH.
Prerequisites, Math. 6, and 31 previously or concurrently.

42. (II) Alternating Current Circuits

The fundamentals of alternating—current circuit theory. This
includes instantaneous voltage and current relations, effective
values, average power, representation of sinusoids by means of complex quantities, resonance phenomena, coupled and polyphase circuits, Fourier Series and metering in A-C circuits.
2 class hours; 1 quiz hour; 1 2-hour laboratory period. Credit, 3.
MR. LINGO, MR. MOHN.
Prerequisite, Electrical Engineering 41.

53. (I) Direct Current Machinery

The theory, construction, and operation of D-C motors and generators with emphasis upon analysis of performance, design features, applications and methods of control.
3 class hours; 1 3-hour laboratory period. Credit, 4.
Prerequisite, Electrical Engineering 41. MR. KARLSON.

54. (II) Alternating Current Machinery

A basic study of single and polyphase A-C machinery, covering
synchronous and induction motors and generators, converters,
transformers and magnetic amplifiers. This includes analysis, design considerations, applications and an introductory study of
transient behavior and unbalanced operations.
3 class hours; 1 3-hour laboratory period. Credit, 4.
Prerequisites, Electrical Engineering 42, 53. MR. KARLSON.

55. (I) Electronics

The theory and application of electron tubes and solid state
devices. Basic theory consists of electron ballistics, electron emis-

sion, photoelectric effects and conduction in a vacuum, gases and semi-conductors. Applications are made to the characteristics of electron tubes, varistors and transitors, together with their use for rectification, amplification and control. Amplifiers are analyzed by means of equivalent circuits, load-line methods and harmonic analysis.

2 class hours; 1 quiz hour; 1 2-hour laboratory period.   Credit, 3.

MR. LANGFORD, MR. MOHN, MR. SMITH.

Prerequisite, Electrical Engineering 42.

56. (II) Applied Electronics

Analysis and design of vacuum tube circuits from the standpoints of response, distortion and stability. Applications include Class A, B and C, grounded cathode, grounded grid, cathode-follower and inverse feedback circuits, cascaded amplifiers, and the fundamental theory and characteristics of vacuum tube oscillators and multi-vibrators.

3 class hours; 1 3-hour laboratory period.   Credit, 4.

MR. LANGFORD, MR. MOHN, MR. SMITH.

Prerequisite, Electrical Engineering 55.

57. (I) Engineering Analysis

Ordinary differential equations as applied to electrical and mechanical systems; vector algebra and calculus; electro-magnetic field theory through the derivation of Maxwell's field equations and the Poynting and Schelkunoff radiation vectors; reflection and refraction of plane waves; skin effect in round conductors and Bessel's functions.

3 class hours.   Credit, 3.

MR. MOHN, MR. ROYS.

Prerequisites, Mathematics 32; Electrical Engineering 42.

58. (II) Electrical Transmission

A continuation of Course 57 consisting of the fundamental theory and characteristics of waveguides and long lines, analysis of filters by means of difference calculus and traveling waves in transmission systems.

3 class hours.   Credit, 3.

Prerequisite, Electrical Engineering 57.   MR. MOHN, MR. ROYS.

61. (I) 62. (II) Principles of Electrical Engineering

For mechanical, industrial and agricultural engineering students. A study of D-C and A-C circuits and machinery and basic electronics.

3 class hours; 1 3-hour laboratory period.   Credit, 4.

Prerequisites, Physics 26, Mathematics 32.   MR. KNUDSEN.

172

63. (I) and (II) Elements of Electrical Engineering

For civil and chemical engineering students. A study of D-C and A-C circuits and machines with application to industrial problems.

2 class hours; 1 3-hour laboratory period.   Credit, 3.

MR. SMITH.

Prerequisites, Physics 26; Mathematics 32.

64. (II) Industrial Electricity

An elective for mechanical, industrial and chemical engineering students which deals principally with the applications of electronics to measurement and control in industry.

2 class hours; 1 3-hour laboratory period.   Credit, 3.

MR. SMITH.

Prerequisite, Electrical Engineering 62 or 63.

78. (II) Special Projects

A laboratory course, associated with a selected technical elective (as approved by the student's major adviser), in which the student carries out a study or project of particular interest to himself, with a minimum of supervision, and wherein he is expected to learn to do independent work. A written report is required at the conclusion of the project.

1 3-hour laboratory period.   Credit, 1.

THE DEPARTMENT.

Prerequisite, a suitable technical elective concurrently.

79. (I) Electrical Communications I

The general theory of four-terminal, and selective circuits and of the use of distributed parameter systems as circuit elements. Among the special expedients employed are matrices, duality, Foster's reactance theorem, and transmission charts. Applications are made to attenuators, filters, equalizer and delay networks, and to long lines and waveguides.

3 class hours; 1 3-hour labortory period.   Credit, 4.

MR. LANGFORD.

Prerequisite, Electrical Engineering 58.

80. (II) Electrical Communications II

Theory and applications of circuits for radio communication, in which wideband and R-F amplifiers, oscillators, modulation, demodulation and frequency conversion are studied. Consideration is given also to pulse techniques, noise and interference, antennas, radiation and propagation phenomena.

3 class hours; 1 3-hour laboratory period.   Credit, 4.

Prerequisite, Electrical Engineering 56.   MR. LANGFORD.

173

81. (I) Advanced Electrical Machinery

A continuation of Course 54 dealing with modern methods of machine analysis. These are developed and applied to the pre-determination of the transient and short circuit behavior and stability of synchronous machines and to variable speed and single phase motors.

3 class hours; 1 3-hour laboratory period. Credit, 4.

MR. KARLSON.

Prerequisite, Electrical Engineering 54.

83. (I) Transient Analysis

A study of the transient behavior of electrical, mechanical and thermal systems. The ordinary and partial differential equations associated with the systems are set up and their solutions obtained by the classical, Heaviside operational and Fourier and Laplace transform methods. An introductory survey of functions of a complex variable leads to the evaluation of the inversion integral by means of the method of residues.

3 class hours. · Credit, 3.

MR. ROYS.

Prerequisite, Electrical Engineering 58.

84. (II) Industrial Electronics

A study of special characteristics of the electron tubes of industry, the theory, design and operation of commercial types of circuits utilizing these tubes, including stroboscope, grid-controlled and polyphase rectifiers, inverters, welding controllers, speed and voltage regulators, high frequency heating circuits, and others.

3 class hours; 1 3-hour laboratory period. Credit, 4.

MR. ROYS.

Prerequisite, Electrical Engineering 55.

85. (I) Electrical Measurements

Theory and practice of electric and magnetic measurements; accuracy, precision, and limitations of measurements devices.

2 class hours; 1 3-hour laboratory period. Credit, 3.

THE DEPARTMENT.

Prerequisite, Electrical Engineering 42.

86. (II) Power System Networks

This course is a study of power system networks including power transfer diagrams, voltage studies, system stability criteria, short-circuit calculations, and protective methods.

3 class hours; 1 3-hour laboratory period. Credit, 4.

MR. KARLSON.

Prerequisites, Electrical Engineering 54, 58.

87. (I) Power Applications and Control

A study of applications of electric machines and their controls, power requirements, types of drive, torque relations, speed of response, control systems, selsyn systems.

3 class hours; 1 3-hour laboratory period. Credit, 4.

MR. KARLSON.

Prerequisite, Electrical Engineering 54.

88. (II) Electric Power Distribution

The general problem of power distribution from bulk substations to the consumer by means of loop and radial systems including such considerations as automatic load transfer, voltage regulation and system protection.

3 class hours. Credit, 3.

MR. KARLSON.

Prerequisite, Electrical Engineering 58.

90. (II) Servomechanisms I

A study of basic types of error-sensitive control systems; proportional differential and integral controllers; transient behavior; criteria for error-free operation; and practical electrical and mechanical systems. Classical methods of analysis will be employed.

3 class hours; 1 3-hour laboratory period. Credit, 4.

MR. LINGO, MR. MOHN.

Prerequisite, Electrical Engineering 57 or Mechanical Engineering 85.

92. (II) Professional Seminar

Current engineering developments are discussed through student reports. The professional aspects of the electrical engineer's work is stressed. Instruction is given in the preparation of engineering papers for publication and in their presentation before technical audiences.

1 class hour. Credit, 1.

THE DEPARTMENT.

94. (II) Ultra-high-frequency Techniques

A study of u.h.f. oscillators, amplifiers, transmitters, receivers, transmission systems, antennas, multi-vibrators, trigger and gate circuits, electronics switches, and controls.

3 class hours; 1 3-hour laboratory period. Credit, 4.

MR. MOHN.

Prerequisite, Electrical Engineering 56.

96. (II) Principles of Electrical Design.

The fundamentals of electric, dielectric, magnetic and heat-flow systems as applied to the design, rating and life of coils, transformers, machinery and other electrical equipment.

2 class hours; 1 3-hour calculation period. Credit, 3.

MR. ROYS.

Prerequisite, Electrical Engineering 54.

98. (II) Television Engineering

Application of electronics and radio engineering to the special problems of television. Among the topics considered are system theory and analysis, signal sources, video response, noise limitations, synchronization and scanning, color vision and colorimetry, principles of the NTSC system, picture pickup and display tubes, transmission and reception, and monitoring and testing procedures.

3 class hours; 1 3-hour laboratory period. Credit, 4.

MR. LANGFORD.

Prerequisites, Electrical Engineering 83, and 80 previously or concurrently.

MECHANICAL ENGINEERING

PROFESSOR WEAVER, PROEESSOR BATES, PROFESSOR SWENSON, ASSOCIATE PROFESSOR KEYSER, ASSOCIATE PROFESSOR DITTFACH, ASSOCIATE PROFESSOR LONGSTAFF, ASSISTANT PROFESSOR EMERSON, ASSISTANT PROFESSOR LAKE†, ASSISTANT PROFESSOR SOBALA, ASSISTANT PROFESSOR WEIDMANN, ASSISTANT PROFESSOR DAY, MR. COSTA, MR. ALLIO, MR. BUTLER.

1. (I) Engineering Drawing

The purpose of the course is to develop skill in the use of drafting equipment with a working knowledge of orthographic projections, lettering, auxiliary views, sectional views, tracings and pictorial representation of machine parts.

2 3-hour laboratory periods. Credit, 2.

MR. WEIDMANN, MR. GROW.

2. (II) Drawing and Descriptive Geometry

During the first part of the course a study of dimensioning, fastenings, and conventional representations is made. The remainder of the course is devoted to descriptive geometry and encompasses a study of graphical methods applicable to engineering problems.

1 class hour; 2 3-hour laboratory periods. Credit, 3.

MR. WEIDMANN, MR. GROW.

Prerequisite, Mechanical Engineering 1.

† On leave of absence.

23. (Summer) Shop

The course is designed primarily for engineers other than mechanical. Approximately half the semester is spent in welding; in the other half the student gains experience in the machine shop, where he becomes familiar with the various machine and hand tools used in metal working.

3 40-hour weeks.   Credit, 3.

MR. COSTA.

27. (Summer) Shop

The course covers weldability of metals, manual and automatic welding processes. Experience is gained in the manual welding of various metals.

3 40-hour weeks.   Credit, 3.

MR. PATTERSON.

28. (Summer) Machine Shop

A knowledge of metal-working equipment is obtained by using the fundamental machine tools such as the lathe, planer, shaper, milling machine and drill press. A reasonable amount of bench work is included. Classroom work is devoted to the theory of machine tool operation, fits, tolerances and measurement.

3 40-hour weeks.   Credit, 3.

MR. COSTA.

39. (I) and (II) Materials of Construction

Properties of engineering materials; failure by (a) exceeding the elastic limit, (b) creep, (c) fatigue, and (d) corrosion. The crystalline nature of metals. Properties and uses of the structural metals, wood, stone, clay products, cementing materials, concrete, plastics, protective coatings, and water.

2 class hours.   Credit, 2.

MR. KEYSER.

Prerequisites, Chemistry 2 or 4; Physics 27, taken previously or concurrently.

46. (II) Fundamentals of Metallurgy

Physical metallurgy involving crystal structure, solid solutions, diffusion in the solid state, freezing of metals, hardening of metals, annealing, and equilibrium diagrams. These fundamentals are applied to a study of the iron-iron carbide diagrams, time-temperature-transformation relationships for steel, the heat treatment of steel, and heat-treating equipment. Laboratory work is intended to substantiate some of the principles developed in lecture work and to acquire basic skill in metallographic technique.

2 class hours; 1 3-hour laboratory period.   Credit, 3.

MR. KEYSER.

Prerequisites, Mechanical Engineering 39 or Chemistry 66.

63. (I) Engineering Thermodynamics I

This course is a treatment of the application of the laws of heat to various energy-transforming devices. Topics include ideal and actual cycles of steam, internal combustion engines, and air compressors together with problems pertaining to these machines, energy transformations in fluid flow, variable specific heats and mixtures of gases.

4 class hours.   Credit, 4.

MR. SWENSON, MR. LONGSTAFF.

Prerequisites, Physics 28; Mathematics 30 or 32.

64. (II) Engineering Thermodynamics II

A continuation of the work of Course 63. Study will be made of liquids and vapors, thermodynamic cycles, energy transformations and the transfer of heat, together with engineering problems pertaining to these devices.

4 class hours.   Credit, 3.

MR. SWENSON, MR. LONGSTAFF.

Prerequisite, Mechanical Engineering 63.

65. (I) Heat Engineering I

This course is a survey of the field of applied energy and is designed for engineering students outside of the mechanical engineering field. The application of the laws of heat to energy transforming devices is studied, but not as extensively as in Courses 63 and 64. A study will be made of gases, vapors, fuels, combustion, heat transfer, measurement of power, and internal combustion engines.

3 class hours.   Credit, 3.

THE DEPARTMENT.

Prerequisites, Physics 28; Mathematics 6.

66. (II) Heat Engineering II

A continuation of the work of Course 65. Air compressors, fans, refrigeration, and air conditioning turbines, jet propulsion and power plants will be studied.

3 class hours.   Credit, 3.

THE DEPARTMENT.

Prerequisite, Mechanical Engineering 65.

67. (I) Mechanical Instrumentation Laboratory

The calibration and application of instruments used in the testing of mechanical engineering apparatus.

1 3-hour laboratory period.   Credit, 1.

THE DEPARTMENT.

Prerequisite, Mechanical Engineering 63 concurrently.

68. (II) Kinematics

Principles of mechanism, including velocity and acceleration diagrams, instant centers, gear teeth and gear trains, eams, and various speed transmissions.

2 class hours; 1 3-hour laboratory period. Credit, 3.

Mr. Bates, Mr. Sobala.

Prerequisites, Mechanical Engineering 1; Civil Eng. 52.

75. (I) Steam Power Plants

This course is a study of the steam power plant, including boilers, stokers, fuels, combustion, steam generation, prime movers, and auxiliary equipment, and engineering problems involved in design and operation.

3 class hours; 1 2-hour laboratory period. Credit, 3.

Mr. Swenson.

Prerequisite, Mechanical Engineering 64.

76. (II) Refrigeration and Air Conditioning

The course content includes a study of the fundamental principles of thermodynamics as applied to refrigeration and air control. Application of refrigeration to industrial processes and the control of temperature, humidity and motion of air in buildings will be studied.

2 class hours; 1 3-hour laboratory period. Credit, 3.

Mr. Swenson.

Prerequisite, Mechanical Engineering 64.

77. (I) Internal Combustion Engines

A study is made of spark-ignition and compression-ignition engines including design, fuels, carburetion, ignition, combustion, lubrication, cooling, and engine performance. The gas turbine and jet propulsion will be included.

3 class hours. Credit, 3.

Mr. Dittfach.

Prerequisite, Mechanical Engineering 64.

79. (I) Mechanical Engineering Laboratory I

Tests of fuels and lubricants. Performance tests of steam engines and turbines, gasoline and Diesel engines, fans, hydraulic apparatus, refrigeration systems and other typical engineering equipment. Emphasis on laboratory procedure and orderly presentation of results.

2 3-hour laboratory periods. Credit, 2.

The Department.

Prerequisites, Civil Engineering 76 or 75 concurrently; Mechanical Engineering 64 or 66; Mechanical Engineering 67 for Mechanical Engineering majors.

80. (II) Mechanical Engineering Laboratory II

This course continues the work of the first semester in more advanced phases.

2 3-hour laboratory periods.   Credit, 2.

                                                   THE DEPARTMENT.

Prerequisite, Mechanical Engineering 79.

83. (I) Machine Design

Principles involved in the design of various machine parts including fastenings, shafts, belts, bearings, gears, and pressure vessels.

2 class hours; 1 3-hour laboratory period.   Credit, 3.

                                                        MR. BATES.

Prerequisites, Civil Engineering 51 or 53; Mechanical Engineering 2, 68.

85. Dynamics of Machinery

Gyroscopic effects, governors, dynamic balancing of rotating machinery. Analysis of unbalanced forces in a machine containing parts moving with rotation, reciprocation, and their combination. Elements of vibration theory, vibration isolation, vibration analysis of equivalent masses and shaft systems. Vibration absorbers.

3 class hours.   Credit, 3.

                                                       MR. SOBALA.

Prerequisites, Civil Engineering 52; Mechanical Eng. 68.

86. (II) Advanced Machine Design

A continuation of Course 83. Additional elementary parts are studied which combine into the design of complete machines in the latter part of the course.

2 class hours; 1 3-hour laboratory period.   Credit, 3.

                                                        MR. BATES.

Prerequisite, Mechanical Engineering 83.

88. (II) Steady Flow Machinery

The principles of thermodynamics are applied to steam and internal combustion turbines, condensers, and other heat transfer apparatus.

3 class hours.   Credit, 3.

                                                       MR. SWENSON.

Prerequisites, Mechanical Engineering 64 or 66; Civil Engineering 76.

90. (II) Advanced Metallurgy

Advanced topics in engineering metallurgy, such as the effects of alloying elements in steel, aluminum, magnesium, and copper alloys. The significant properties of, the fabricating methods for, and the applications of ferrous and nonferrous metals. Admission by permission of instructor.

2 class hours; 1 3-hour laboratory period.   Credit, 3.

                                                            MR. KEYSER.

Prerequisite, Mechanical Engineering 46.

91. (I) Professional Seminar

For senior and graduate students only. Presentation of papers on various important subjects in the field of mechanical engineering with principle emphasis on recent developments.

                                                            Credit, 1.

                                                    THE DEPARTMENT.

94. (I) or (II) Experimental Mechanical Engineering

Special work in mechanical engineering for a senior thesis. Admission by permission of instructor.

                                                            Credit, 3.

                                                    THE DEPARTMENT.

INDUSTRIAL ENGINEERING

25. (I) Manufacturing Processes

The methods of producing and fabricating the basic engineering materials: metals, cementing materials, ceramics, plastics, rubber, and lumber. Production methods (excluding machining) of metal parts and their assembly in a typical mass production industry is discussed. Laboratory periods involve inspection trips and movies.

1 class hour; 1 3-hour laboratory period.   Credit, 2.

                                                            MR. KEYSER.

26. (Summer) Tool Engineering

This course includes the determination of the manufacturing operations necessary to produce a finished product. This is followed by consideration of the principles embodied in the design of jigs, fixtures, dies, and gauges necessary to perform each operation. The economics of tooling as influenced by intermittent or continuous type manufacturing and the effect of volume are also included.

3 44-hour weeks.   Credit, 3.

                                                            MR. COSTA.

51. (I) Industrial Management

A course designed to acquaint the student with the principles of industrial engineering and their application to the solution of the problems of industrial plant operation.

3 class hours.   Credit, 3.

                                                            MR. WEAVER.

54. (II) Engineering Economy

This course includes a study of the bases for comparison of alternatives in engineering projects, break-even and minimum cost points, evaluation of proposals for new activities, economy of operations, the evaluation of public activities, the output and life of typical items of engineering and industrial equipment, manufacturing lot sizes, economic purchase quantities, the selection and replacement of structures and machines.

3 class hours.   Credit, 3.

MR. WEAVER.

Prerequisites, Economics 25; Mathematics 6 or 29.

75. (I) Job Evaluation

A study of the principles used to determine an evaluation of all occupations in order to establish an equitable rating between them, to establish sound wage and salary policies.

3 class hours.   Credit, 2.

MR. WEAVER.

Prerequisite, Industrial Engineering 51.

76. (I) Time Study

A study of the principles involved in the establishment of production standards and their application in the management functions of cost accounting, estimating, production control, incentives, budgetary control.

2 class hours; 1 3-hour laboratory period.   Credit, 3.

MR. EMERSON.

Prerequisites, Industrial Engineering 75.

77. (I) Production Control

A study of the principles used to regulate production activities in keeping with the manufacturing plan.

3 class hours.   Credit, 3.

MR. EMERSON.

Prerequisite, Industrial Engineering 51.

78. (II) Factory Planning and Layout

A study of the principles applying to the determination and development of the physical relationship between plant, equipment and operators working toward the highest degree of economy and effectiveness in operation.

1 class hour; 1 3-hour laboratory period.   Credit, 2.

MR. WEAVER.

Prerequisites, Mechanical Engineering 2; Industrial Engineering 51.

80. (II) Plant Budgetary Control

A study of the principles used to pre-determine expenses for the factors of production and the comparison of results with the estimates to determine and deal with the causes of expense variations as applied by the operating organization in the industrial plant.

3 class hours.   Credit, 3.

MR. WEAVER.

Prerequisite, Industrial Engineering 51.

82. (II) Work Simplification

A study of the principles involved in the simplification of means of doing work and in the application and use of these principles.

1 class hour; 1 3-hour laboratory period.   Credit, 2.

MR. WEAVER.

Prerequisite, Mechanical Engineering 68.

86. (II) Industrial Management

Designed for students other than industrial engineers. A broad course dealing with the many problems encountered in a modern industry. Topics include types of organization, management, plant location, arrangement of equipment, product design, methods of production control, costs, wage payment systems and personnel relations.

3 class hours.   Credit, 3.

MR. EMERSON.

88. (II) Motion and Time Study

This course covers the combined fields of motion study and time study for junior and senior students outside the industrial engineering field.

2 class hours; 1 3-hour laboratory period.   Credit, 3.

MR. EMERSON.

92. (I) Professional Seminar

For seniors and graduate students.

Credit, 1.

THE DEPARTMENT.

183

ENGLISH

PROFESSOR RAND, PROFESSOR GOLDBERG, PROFESSOR HELMING, PRO-
FESSOR TROY, PROFESSOR O'DONNELL, ASSOCIATE PROFESSOR
VARLEY, ASSISTANT PROFESSOR HORRIGAN, ASSISTANT PROFESSOR
LANE, ASSISTANT PROFESSOR ALLEN, ASSISTANT PROFESSOR WIL-
LIAMS, ASSISTANT PROFESSOR KOEHLER, ASSISTANT PROFESSOR
KAPLAN, MRS. WRIGHT, MRS. HOGAN,† ASSISTANT PROFESSOR
BARRON, MRS. DUBOIS, MR. CLARK, MR. MADEIRA, MR. TUCKER,
MR. HAVEN, MR. SAVAGE, MR. COLLINS, MR. RUDIN.

COMPOSITION

1. (I) 2. (II) English Composition

Intended to teach straight thinking, sound structure, clear and correct expression. Scheduled hours include Speech 3. (I) 4. (II).
2 class hours.   Credit, 2.

THE DEPARTMENT.

81. (I) (II) Creative Writing

A course in critical and imaginative composition based upon the examples of standard authors and the experience of the student. It provides an opportunity for work in description, narrative, verse and drama as well as in exposition.
3 class hours.   Credit, 3.

THE DEPARTMENT.

Prerequisite, a mark of A or B in English 2 (U. of M.) or permission of instructor.

83. (I) (II) Technical Writing

For majors in engineering. A course in factual and inductive exposition with special emphasis upon process reports and theses.
2 class hours.   Credit, 2.

MR. MADEIRA.

Prerequisites, English 1, 2.

84. (II) Technical Writing

For students not majoring in engineering. A course in factual and inductive exposition with special emphasis upon library research and the preparation of reports, and theses.

Credit, 3.

MR. KAPLAN.

Prerequisites, English 1, 2.

† On leave of absence.

184

LITERATURE

25. (I) 26. (II) Humane Letters

A general reading course based upon a chronological selection of masterpieces: classical, continental, and English.

3 class hours.   Credit, 3.

THE DEPARTMENT.

50. (II) Chaucer

A study of Chaucer's development and preeminence as a creative artist and an attempt to appreciate his humanism.

3 class hours.   Credit, 3.

MR. HELMING.

51. (I) The Renaissance in England

A study of various aspects of the Renaissance as revealed in such writers as Spenser, Bacon, Sir Thomas Browne, Burton, and Hobbes. Special emphasis is given to Spenser's *Faerie Queene*.

3 class hours.   Credit, 3.

MR. TROY.

53. (I) Lyrical Poetry of the Renaissance in England (1956-57)

A study of lyrical poets such as Sidney, Campion, Jonson, Herrick, Lovelace, Suckling, Carew, Donne, Herbert, Vaughn, Crashaw, Traherne and Marvell. Special emphasis is given to "Metaphysical" tradition. Given in alternate years.

3 class hours.   Credit, 3.

MR. GOLDBERG.

54. (II) Milton

The development of the mind and art of Milton as a Renaissance writer. Emphasis is placed upon *Paradise Lost, Paradise Regained,* and *Samson Agonistes.*

3 class hours.   -   Credit, 3.

MR. GOLDBERG, MR. HELMING.

55. (I) Shakespeare

This course is based upon the reading of about twenty-five of Shakespeare's plays, and attempts both to indicate the evolution of the dramatist and to emphasize the various phases of his art.

3 class hours.   Credit, 3.

MR. RAND.

57. (I) English Literature of the Restoration

A study of the social problems and literary values of the Restoration period as they reflect in prose, verse, and drama. Emphasis

will be placed on the Theater, both tragic and comic, with particular attention to the role of wit, "humours", and satire in the Restoration Comedy of Manners.
3 class hours.   Credit, 3.
MR. KOEHLER.

58. (II) Elizabethan Dramatists
A study of English drama from the death of Elizabeth to the closing of the theaters. Special consideration will be given to the plays of Jonson, Beaumont, Fletcher, Webster, Middleton, Massinger, and Shirley.
3 class hours.   Credit, 3.
MR. O'DONNELL.

59. (I) English Literature of the Eighteenth Century
A study of the literature of the Augustan Age, with special emphasis on the writing of Swift and Pope.
3 class hours.   Credit, 3.
MR. TROY.

60. (II) English Literature of the Eighteenth Century
A continuation of English 59, but may be elected independently. A study of the literature of the later Eighteenth Century with special emphasis on the Johnson Circle.
3 class hours.   Credit, 3.
MR. TROY.

61. (I) Romantic Poetry (1956-57)
A study of the Lake Poets (primarily Wordsworth and Coleridge) and their precursors. Given in alternate years.
3 class hours.   Credit, 3.
MR. RAND.

62. (II) Romantic Poetry (1954-55)
A continuation of English 61 but may be elected independently. A study of Byron, Shelley and Keats. Given in alternate years.
3 class hours.   Credit, 3.
MISS HORRIGAN.

63. (I) American Poetry
A study of American poetry from Colonial times to 1900, with special emphasis upon the work of Freneau, Bryant, Emerson, Longfellow, Whittier, Poe, Whitman, and Emily Dickinson.
3 class hours.   Credit, 3.
MR. O'DONNELL, MR. WILLIAMS.

65. (I) English Prose of the Nineteenth Century

A study of the chief Romantic prose writers in relation to literary techniques and main currents of epochal thought and feeling. Among the authors treated are Coleridge, Lamb, Hazlitt, De-Quincey, Carlyle, and Ruskin.

3 class hours. Credit, 3.

MR. GOLDBERG.

66. (II) English Prose of the Nineteenth Century

A continuation of English 65, but may be elected independently. A study of the chief Victorian prose writers in relation to literary techniques and main currents of epochal thought and feeling. Among the authors treated are Macaulay, Newman, Arnold, Huxley, Pater, and Stevenson.

3 class hours. Credit, 3.

MR. GOLDBERG.

67. (I) American Prose

A course in the chief American prose writers of the nineteenth and twentieth centuries. Among the authors studied are Emerson, Thoreau, Hawthorne, Melville, Mark Twain, Henry Adams, and Henry James.

3 class hours. Credit, 3.

MR. O'DONNELL.

68. (II) Modern Drama

This course traces the development of English and American drama from the time of Ibsen to the present day. Its purpose is to impart an intelligent and enthusiastic interest in the theatre of the twentieth century.

3 class hours. Credit, 3.

MR. RAND, MR. WILLIAMS.

69. (I) Victorian Poetry (1955-56)

A study of Tennyson and Browning. Given in alternate years.

3 class hours. Credit, 3.

MR. RAND.

71. (I) Biography

The history of the biography as a literary type; discussion of leading biographers from Boswell to Maurois, with special emphasis upon the development of the modern biographical method.

3 class hours. Credit, 3.

MR. HELMING.

72. (II) The Bible as Literature

A study of the King James version of the Bible, with emphasis upon the Hebrew as discernible in translation, the poetic qualities characteristic of Tudor England, and the varied influence of the Bible upon subsequent English poetry.

3 class hours.   Credit, 3.
                                                    MR. RAND.

73. (I) The Novel from Defoe through the Victorians

The development of the novel; the reading and discussion of eight or nine great English novels of the eighteenth and nineteenth centuries.

3 class hours.   Credit, 3.
                                    MR. ALLEN, MR. HELMING.

74. (II) Greek Classics in Translation

Readings and discussion of the epics of Homer, representative dramas of Aeschylus, Sophocles, Euripides, and Aristophanes, the "Socratic" dialogues of Plato, and Thucydides' history of the Peloponnesian War. Intended to acquaint students with the famous myths and stories of classical antiquity, and the literary forms and ideas which have contributed most to subsequent literatures.

3 class hours.   Credit, 3.
                                    MR. HELMING, MR. TROY.

76. (II) Modern Poetry

This course attempts to trace the spirit of twentieth century poetry from such authors as Hardy, Whitman, and Emily Dickinson to those of the present day.

3 class hours.   Credit, 3.
                                    MR. RAND, MISS HORRIGAN.

77. (I) The Modern Novel

An analytical presentation of eleven novels written between 1890 and 1930, in which the expanding form and the extension of critical themes will be stressed.

3 class hours.   Credit, 3.
                                                    MR. VARLEY.

79. (I) Literary Criticism (1955-56)

A study of major critical attitudes and principles, in relation to philosophic background and to practice. Emphasis is placed upon important critics and theorists from Plato and Aristotle through those of the eighteenth century. Given in alternate years.

3 class hours.   Credit, 3.
                                                    MR. GOLDBERG.

80. (II) Literary Criticism (1955-56)

A continuation of English 79, but may be elected independently. Emphasis is placed upon important critics and theorists of the nineteenth and twentieth centuries. Given in alternate years.

3 class hours.   Credit, 3.
                                                    MR. GOLDBERG.

ENTOMOLOGY

PROFESSOR ALEXANDER, PROFESSOR SWEETMAN, ASSOCIATE PROFESSOR
SHAW, ASSISTANT PROFESSOR HANSON, MISS SMITH, MR. FIELD,*
. MR. WEIDHASS.

26. (II) General and Field Entomology

The lectures are devoted to a brief survey of the entire field of
entomology; structure and metamorphosis; the more important
methods and materials for control.of injurious species; a survey of
the more conspicuous and important insects with particular attention to the fauna of New England. A laboratory period will be
devoted to the preparation and formation of a collection of insects.
Until about April 10th, this work will be done indoors and will
consist of lectures and practical work preparatory to the field work
after that date. Collections made by the students are studied in
later courses.

2 class hours; 1 2-hour laboratory period. Credit, 3.
8:00-8:50 or 10:00-10:50 M. F.; 1:00-2:50 M. Tu. W. Th. F.

MR. ALEXANDER, MISS SMITH.

51. (I) Pests of Special Crops

For students not specializing in entomology who desire a more
complete knowledge of the insects connected with their major
lines of work. Work in the laboratory consists of identification,
life-history studies and control measures of important insect pests.
Work of this nature is available on pests of field crops, market-
garden crops, fruits, flowers, shade trees and shrubs, forest trees,
household articles, domestic animals, and man.

1 class hour; 2 2-hour laboratory periods. Credit, 3.
10:00-10:50 M.; 1:00-2:50 Tu.; 2:30-3:50 Th.

MR. WEIDHAAS.

Prerequisite, Entomology 26.

53. (I) Applied Entomology

Studies on the more important insect pests, their life-histories,
damage, identification, and methods of control. Special attention
is devoted to the use of entomological literature, methods of preparing scientific papers, and the general principles of insect control.

1 class hour; 2 2-hour laboratory periods. Credit, 3.
10:00-10:50 W.; 3:00-4:50 M. F. MR. SHAW.

Prerequisite, Entomology 26.

* On leave of absence for military service.

55. (II) 56. (II) Classification of Insects

Laboratory work on the identification of the major orders of insects. In Course 56, the immature stages of insects, with particular stress on their structures and recognition.

3 2-hour laboratory periods. Credit, 3.

8:00-9:50 Tu. Th. S. MR. ALEXANDER, MISS SMITH.

Prerequisites, Entomology 26; Entomology 57, previously or concurrently.

57. (I) Insect Morphology

The lectures treat of the external and internal anatomy, particularly of the major orders, stress being placed upon the phylogenetic relationships, as backgrounds for parallel and subsequent work in taxonomy and physiology of insects.

1 class hour; 3 2-hour laboratory periods. Credit, 4.

10:00-10:50 F.; 1:00-2:50 M. Tu. Th. MR. HANSON.

Prerequisite, Entomology 26.

60. (II) Structural Pest Control

For students specializing in entomology, especially those desiring to enter the structural pest field, and others interested in gaining knowledge of methods of combating insect and rodent pests. The emphasis will be placed on the control of those pests attacking buildings and other structures, foods, fabrics, and other stored products in private homes or other establishments. The life history, feeding habits, methods of reproduction, and dispersal of the various species will be stressed in so far as these influence control measures.

2 class hours. Credit, 2.

11:00-11:50 M. F. MR. SWEETMAN.

Prerequisite, Zoology 1; Entomology 26 desirable.

72. (II) Forest and Shade Tree Insects

The lecture work deals with the principles and methods of controlling insects which attack shade trees, forests and forest products. The laboratory periods are devoted to a study of the more important species, their identification, biology, and specific

74. (II) Medical and Veterinary Entomology

The relationships of insects and their allies to the health of man and animals. The classification, biology and control of these pests is studied in detail.

1 class hour; 2 2-hour laboratory periods.   Credit, 3.
10:00-10:50 W.; 3:00-4:50 Tu. Th.   MR. SHAW.
Prerequisite, Entomology 26.

79. (I) Animal Ecology

Designed for students specializing in entomology, zoology, and related fields. The course deals with the relation of animals to their environment, covering the physical factors as temperature, moisture, light, etc., and biotic factors as neighbors, competitors, predators, etc. Both terrestrial and aquatic communities are studied. The student is shown not only that animals do things, but why they make definite responses to the environmental factors. Actual measurements of the environmental factors and responses of the animals in the field and laboratory are included.

2 class hours; 1 2-hour laboratory period.   Credit, 3.
9:00-9:50 M. F.; 3:00-4:50 M.   MR. SWEETMAN.
Prerequisite, Entomology 26 or Zoology 1 or equivalent.

80. (II) Insect Control

The scientific basis of insect control is considered from the chemical, biological, ecological, mechanical, and legislative approaches. Special emphasis is placed on the composition, manufacture, preparation, and reaction of insecticides, and the use of resistant hosts, micro-organisms and the larger parasites and predators that might be used in the control of insects.

1 class hour; 2 2-hour laboratory periods.   Credit, 3.
9:00-9:50 M.; 3:00-4:50 M. F.   MR. SWEETMAN.
Prerequisites, Entomology 53, 55, and 57; 79 and 81 desirable.

81. (I) Physiological Entomology

A detailed consideration is given to the organ systems, showing the functions such as nutrition, respiration, and growth, and the relationship of physiology to behavior. A portion of the laboratory time will be devoted to assigned individual problems dealing with any phase of insect biology or control and conducted on a research basis.

1 class hour; 2 2-hour laboratory periods.   Credit, 3.
9:00-9:50 Th.; 3:00-4:50 W. F.   MR. SWEETMAN.
Prerequisite, Entomology 26; 55, 56, and 57 desirable.

ENTOMOLOGY

87. (I) 88. (II) Special Problems in Entomology
Problem work in many fields, as apiculture, biological control and insectary practice, insecticides, morphology, and classification. Intended primarily to introduce qualified students to research methods in some branch of entomology. Excess departmental credits are necessary for election.

Hours by arrangement. Credit, 1, 2, or 3.

THE DEPARTMENT.

Prerequisites, Entomology 26, 53, 55, 57, and should be preceded or accompanied by any other courses in the restricted field of the problem.

89. (I) Entomological Techniques
Theory and practice in the preservation, preparation, and mounting of insects for study and display. Excess departmental credits are necessary for election.

2 2-hour laboratory periods. Credit, 2.

Hours by arrangement. MISS SMITH.

Prerequisites, Entomology 26 and permission of instructor.

90. (II) Evolution
The phylogeny of plants and animals is outlined at some length in conjunction with consideration of factors and forces influencing and guiding evolution. Especial consideration is given throughout the course to the implications and applications of evolutionary concept to human behavior, welfare and philosophy.

2 class hours. Credit, 2.

10:00-10:50 M. F. MR. HANSON.

APICULTURE

66. (II) Introductory Beekeeping
This course is designed to give the student a broad grasp of the general field of apiculture. The lectures cover honeybees and their relatives, biology of the bee, methods of management, diseases, pollination, queen rearing, honey production, and history of bee-keeping. The laboratory will acquaint the student with the structure of the bee, equipment for keeping bees and its construction, costs of beekeeping, plants of value for bees, and as much as possible the actual management of bees in the apiary.

2 class hours; 1 2-hour laboratory period. Credit, 3.

11:00-11:50 M. F.; 1:00-2:50 M. MR. SHAW.

85. (I) Advanced Beekeeping
This course is designed for the student who wants more detailed knowledge of the management of bees. It will cover such topics

as fall management, wintering, the care of the honey crop, grading and packaging of honey, judging honey, bee diseases, beeswax, and some simple biometrical problems relating to bees. If possible, one or more visits to commercial apiaries will be made.

1 class hour; 1 2-hour laboratory period. Credit, 2.
Mr. Shaw.

Prerequisite, Entomology 66.

FLORICULTURE

Professor Thayer, Assistant Professor Hubbard,
Assistant Professor Ross, Mr. Jester.

26. (II) Garden Materials

A study of the annuals, biennials, herbaceous perennials, bulbs, bedding plants, and roses that are valuable for use in floricultural or landscape gardening work. Methods of propagation, culture, and uses of the various plants are considered as well as identification of materials.

2 class hours; 1 2-hour laboratory period. Credit, 3.
11:00-11:50 M. F.; 3:00-4:50 Th. Mr. Jester.

51. (I) Greenhouse Management

This course is intended to familiarize students with the methods and principles involved in the management of greenhouses and greenhouse crops; history and development of the floricultural industry, preparation of soils, fertilizers, potting, watering, ventilation, control of insects and diseases, methods of plant propagation, forcing plants, soilless methods of plant culture. At some time during the semester the members of the class will be required to take a one-day trip to visit large commercial establishments at an approximate cost of five dollars.

2 class hours; 1 2-hour laboratory period. Credit, 3.
9:00-9:50 M. F.; 1:00-2:50 F. Mr. Thayer, Mr. Jester.

52. (II) Floral Arrangement

A study of the principles involving the arrangement and use of cut flowers and plants; funeral designs, basket and vase arrangements, corsages, wedding bouquets, table decorations, home, church, and other interior decorations. A study of color and color harmony as applied to such work. This course is limited to ten students, preference being given to students specializing in floriculture and landscape architecture.

1 class hour; 2 2-hour laboratory periods. Credit, 3.
8:00-8:50 Th.; 1:00-2:50 M. F. Mr. Thayer, Mr. Ross.

54. (II) Greenhouse Construction and Heating

The location, types, arrangement, construction, cost, equipment, heating, and ventilation of greenhouse structures; the drawings of plans and study of specifications. Special emphasis laid on heating problems.

2 class hours; 1 2-hour laboratory period.   Credit, 3.
9:00-9:50 M. F.; 3:00-4:50 M.   MR. THAYER, MR. JESTER.

58. (II) Amateur Floriculture

This course is intended primarily for major students in the School of Home Economics and for other women students. Three phases of floriculture will be considered: (1) the arrangement and use of cut flowers for decorative purposes in the home and elsewhere, (2) house plants, methods of propagation, (3) garden flowers and their uses on the home grounds.

2 class hours; 1 2-hour laboratory period.   Credit, 3.
10:00-10:50 Tu. Th.; 3:00-4:50 Tu. or 1:00-2:50 Th.
       MR. THAYER, MR. ROSS.

75. (I) 76. (II) Commercial Floriculture

A detailed study of the cultural methods for the important commercial cut-flower crops and potted plants. The marketing of flowers and plants, including the management of wholesale markets and retail stores, a study of systems of record keeping, cost analysis, inventory methods, and other phases of this important part of the floricultural industry. Trips may be taken to nearby commercial establishments.

2 class hours; 1 2-hour laboratory period.   Credit, 3.
9:00-9:50 Tu., Th.; 1:00-2:50 Tu.   MR. HUBBARD.
Prerequisite, Floriculture 51.

79. (I) Conservatory Plants (1954-55)

Alternates with Course 81 for students specializing in floriculture. A study of the foliage and flowering plants used in conservatory work; methods of propagation; identification of materials.

1 class hour; 1 2-hour laboratory period.   Credit, 2.
12:00-12:50 Th.; 1:00-2:50 M.   MR. THAYER, MR. ROSS.

81. (I) Herbaceous Gardens and Borders

Alternates with Course 79 for students specializing in floriculture; given annually for students specializing in landscape architecture. This course is a continuation of Course 26 with emphasis on the use of herbaceous materials in various types of planting of borders and gardens.

1 class hour; 1 4-hour laboratory period.   Credit, 3.
10:00-10:50 Tu.; 1:00-4:50 Th.   Mr. Hubbard.
Prerequisite, Floriculture 26.

82. (II) Seminar

For seniors specializing in floriculture. Presentation and discussion of research work in floriculture and other related fields and individual problems.

1 class hour; 4 laboratory hours.   Credit, 3.
11:00-11:50 W.; laboratory hours by arrangement.
        The Department.

FOOD TECHNOLOGY

Professor Fellers, Associate Professor Levine, Assistant Professor Culbertson,† Assistant Professor Baker, Assistant Professor Francis, Mr. Feliciotti.

51. (I) Introductory Course

This is a general elementary course covering food economics, production, distribution and processing. The applications of fundamental science to the food industries are pointed out. The laboratory exercises cover both the theory and practice of canning, freezing and dehydration. The principles of packaging are considered. Fruit and vegetable products are prepared and graded.

2 class hours; 1 2-hour laboratory period.   Credit, 3.
8:00-8:50 Tu., Th.; 1:00-2:50 W. or Th.   Mr. Fellers.

52. (II) Food Products and Adjuncts

This is a continuation of Course 51. The laboratory work includes pickles and pickle products, maple products, citrus products, fruit syrups, soups, condiments, and the preservation of meat, fish, poultry, and vegetables. The properties and uses of sugars, syrups, brines, enzymes, acids, salt, pectin, preservatives and antioxidants are considered. Experience is given in the use and handling of instruments and equipment. Enrollment is limited to 25.

2 class hours; 1 2-hour laboratory period.   Credit, 3.
8:00-8:50 Tu., Th.; 1:00-2:50 W. or Th.   Mr. Fellers.
Prerequisite, Food Technology 51.

† On leave of absence.

61. (I) Industrial Technology

A survey of commercial practices in the manufacture and preservation of food products. This will involve a study of equipment, factory arrangement, sanitation, government regulations, and the operation of types of commercial equipment in quantity production.

1 class hour; 1 4-hour laboratory period. Credit, 3.
10:00-10:50 Th.; 1:00-4:50 M. or Tu. MR. LEVINE.
Prerequisites, Food Technology 52; Bacteriology 31.

62. (I) Industrial Technology

This is a continuation of Course 61. The class exercises will deal largely with a survey study of the sources of raw material, commercial methods of manufacture, packing and distribution of the more common foods. The important contributions of research to food technology will be studied. Laboratory work will include the formation of research projects, interpretation of research data, the use of preservatives, the simple analysis of foods and the commercial practices as applied to preservation of such materials as are available: fish, meats, poultry, and spring vegetables. The inspection and grading of canned food will be studied. Sometime during the semester a two-day field trip to food plants in the Boston area will be taken. The trip will cost the student about fifteen dollars.

1 class hour; 1 4-hour laboratory period. Credit, 3.
10:00-10:50 Th.; 1:00-4:50 M. or Tu. MR. LEVINE.
Prerequisite, Food Technology 61.

71. (I) 72. (II) Food Science Literature

For seniors who specialize in food technology.
2 class hours. Credit, 2.
11:00-11:50 M. W. THE DEPARTMENT.

75. (I) and (II) Food Preservation

For students not majoring in food technology. A survey is made of the causes of food spoilage and of the methods commonly used in preserving foods. The important food products are discussed with emphasis on raw materials used, processing methods and examination of packaged foods. Methods of detecting and preventing spoilage are studied. The laboratory exercises cover the preservation of the major food groups. The theory and use of the pressure cooker are included.

2 class hours; 1 2-hour laboratory period. Credit, 3.
12:00-12:50 Tu. Th.; 3:00-4:50 M. or Th. MR. ————.

82. (II) · Confections and Cereal Products

The materials offered in this course are as follows: the home manufacture of fruit preserves, candied and glacéed fruits, pastes, confections, candies, and other specialties. Approximately one-half the semester is devoted to elementary work in candy making. This course will also consider the principles of baking, doughs, various cereal products and dry mixes.

2 2-hour laboratory periods. Credit, 2.
1:00-2:50 M. F. or 3:00-4:50 M. F. MR. LEVINE.

85. (I) 86. (II) Marine Products Technology

A survey of marine products of commerce and industry. Canning, curing, and freezing of seafoods. Chemical and micro-biological aspects of the industry. By-products, industrial problems and scientific literature. Emphasis is placed on the New England fisheries.

1 class hour; 1 2-hour laboratory period. Credit, 2.
MR. FELLERS.

91. (I) Analysis of Food Products

Laboratory studies on the grading of foods, examination of foods for adulteration, testing accessory products for quality, and determining the causes of spoilage or deterioration in processed food products. Physical, chemical, microbiological, and microscopical methods will be employed. Enrollment limited to 18.

1 class hour; 1 4-hour laboratory period. Credit, 3.
9:00-9:50 Th.; 1:00-4:50 Th. or F.
MR. FELLERS, MR. LIVINGSTON.

Prerequisites, Food Technology 52; Bacteriology 31; Chemistry 30.

92. (II) Examination of Food Products

For students specializing in food technology. This is a continuation of Course 91. It includes interpretation of analysis, sanitation and food laws, government grading of processed foods, use of manuals and the technical work of trade associations. Laboratory work includes use of all kinds of laboratory and field equipment and apparatus used in food plants. A separate laboratory section is given for Bacteriology and Public Health majors.

1 class hour; 1 4-hour laboratory period. Credit, 3.
9:00-9:50 Th.; 1:00-4:50 Th. or F.
MR. FELLERS, MR. LIVINGSTON.

Prerequisite, Food Technology 91.

95. (I) and (II) Introductory Research Methods

For food technology majors. The application of the fundamental sciences to food technology research.

Hours by arrangement. Credit, 2.

MR. THE DEPARTMENT.

98. (II) Sensory Evaluation Methods

An introduction to sensory measurements in the evaluation and acceptance of foods. Panel tests and their statistical interpretation; taste, odor, color, and texture measurements; application to food quality control and grading. For seniors only.

1 class hour; 1 2-hour laboratory period. Credit, 2.

MR. FAGERSON.

FORESTRY AND WILDLIFE MANAGEMENT

PROFESSOR HOLDSWORTH, PROFESSOR TRIPPENSEE, PROFESSOR RHODES, ASSOCIATE PROFESSOR RICH, ASSISTANT PROFESSOR MACCONNELL, MR. COLE*, MR. GANLEY, MR. ABBOTT.

25. (I) Wood Anatomy and Identification

A basic anatomical study of wood elements, their various structural characteristics and functions. Relation of structure and properties to use. Microscopic study of wood elements. Practice in identification.

1 class hour; 2 2-hour laboratory periods. Credit, 3.

MR. RICH.

26. (II) Dendrology

The taxonomic features, silvical characteristics and geographical distribution of the principal forest trees of temperate North America, and the description of the forests in which they occur; identification of the native and naturalized woody plants occurring in the forests of the Northeastern United States, in summer and winter condition, by means of keys and first-hand examination.

2 class hours; 2 2-hour laboratory and field periods. Credit, 3.

MR. RHODES, MR. GANLEY.

51. (I) Forest Management of Watersheds

For students majoring in bacteriology and public health. Admission on recommendation of student's major adviser. A study of forest site—water factor relationships; the improvement of watershed forests through applied silviculture; relative suitability of tree species for watershed uses; forest protection measures.

3 class hours; special field trips. Credit, 3.

MR. RHODES, MR. HOLDSWORTH.

* On leave of absence for military service.

53. (I) Silvics

Forest ecology as a foundation for silvicultural practice: the physiological basis of forest ecology; environmental factors, their effect upon vegetation, and how they are influenced by it; the development and silvical habits of the individual tree; the development, characteristics and classification of forest communities; plant indicators; methods for the study and analysis of vegetation and its environment.

2 class hours; 1 4-hour laboratory and field period. Credit, 3.

MR. RHODES.

54. (II) Forest Soils

The structure, development and maintenance of forest soils; their relationship to applied silviculture and forest productivity; the literature of forest soils with special reference to American experience.

3 class hours. Credit, 3.

MR. RHODES.

55. (I) and (Summer) The Elements of Forest Mensuration

Methods of determining the volume and value of the forest growing stock; type mapping as it pertains to timber cruising; the field work includes mapping and timber estimating on forests realistic in size and condition and the submission of inventory reports.

2 class hours; 1 4-hour laboratory and field period. Credit, 3.
Summer course: 3 44-hour weeks.

MR. MacCONNELL, MR. GANLEY.

56. (II) The Principles of Silviculture

The methods of establishing and developing forest stands through the application of correct silvicultural practice. Intermediate cuttings and reproduction systems. Field work in applied silviculture, including the marking of forest stands for silvicultural treatment, is given on University forest property.

2 class hours; 1 4-hour laboratory period. Credit, 3.

MR. RHODES, MR. ABBOTT.

57. (I) Forest Economics and Policy

This course considers the forest as a resource yielding direct forest values and social benefits. The history of American forestry and the development of a forest policy together with the role of the forest in American economy are considered.

3 class hours. Credit, 3.

MR. HOLDSWORTH.

59. (I) Forest Protection

The principle of protecting forests from all harmful agencies but with special reference to the prevention and control of forest fires, insects, and disease. Other agencies are treated in accordance with their importance.

3 class hours.   Credit, 3.

MR. ABBOTT.

62. (II) The Management and Uses of Farm Forests

A study of the production of wood as a crop from forest land associated with farm enterprise. Silvicultural methods to improve wood quality and increase quantity; the measurement of timber volumes and growth rates; the grading, measurement, and use of forest products. Open to non-majors only.

2 class hours; 1 4-hour laboratory period.   Credit, 3.

MR. GANLEY.

71. (I) Aerial Photogrammetry

A course designed to familiarize the student with the use of aerial photographs in present-day forest management practice. Map making, forest inventory and other phases of forest management involving the application of photogrammetry are considered in detail. Field trips for checking photographic detail on the ground will be made. Texts and equipment costing about $10.00 are required.

2 class hours; 1 4-hour laboratory period.   Credit, 3.

MR. MacCONNELL, MR. GANLEY.

75. (I) Manufacture and Distribution of Forest Products

A study of the techniques of manufacturing forest products, including production and cost studies; also the seasoning, grading and special processing prerequisite to marketing.

3 class hours.   Credit, 3.

MR. RICH.

76. (II) Wood Technology

The structure, composition and properties of wood in relation to its economic utilization; wood-liquid relationships as they affect seasoning, preservation, and technological process for industrial purposes. A survey of the technological advances in the use of wood.

3 class hours.   Credit, 3.

MR. RICH.

78. (Summer) Harvesting of Forest Products

Primarily a field course designed to give students practice in the actual harvesting and preparation of direct forest products from the felling of standing timber through the log-making, skidding, transportation and sawing processes to the stacking of lumber. This part of the course is given on University owned forest land and at the mill of a private cooperator. Short field trips are made to active forest properties where harvesting is proceeding and a longer trip is made to New Hampshire and Maine to visit pulpwood and timber operations and manufacturing plants. Lectures and classwork survey the theory and practice of forest harvesting in the several U. S. forest regions.

3 44-hour weeks. Credit, 3.

MR. GANLEY, MR. MacCONNELL.

80. (II) Principles of Forest Management

The organization of the forest for sustained yield management with a study of the underlying principles. Forest regulation. The preparation of forest management plans.

3 class hours. Credit, 3.

MR. MacCONNELL.

81. (I) Regional Silviculture

The practice of silviculture as applied in the several forest regions of the United States with special reference to the treatment of the tree species of commercial importance. Emphasis is given to the factors, both natural and economic, which govern silviculture in these regions.

3 class hours. Credit, 3.

MR. RHODES.

82. (II) Seeding and Planting in the Practice of Forestry

A study of forest tree seeds and their characteristics, production, harvest, storage, and qualities of germination. The production, distribution, and forest use of planting stock.

1 class hour; 2 2-hour laboratory periods. Credit, 3.

MR. ABBOTT.

85. (I) Air Seasoning and Kiln Drying

A study of the proper conditioning of wood products by air seasoning and kiln drying, of moisture relations in the wood, and of kiln operation.

3 class hours. Credit, 3.

MR. RICH.

WILDLIFE MANAGEMENT

27. (I) Conservation of Natural Resources

Natural resources of the United States including soil, water, forests, wildlife, and the important minerals, the historic back-ground of their use and their present status in relation to the social and economic welfare. Includes the discussion of various conservation problems in relation to national prosperity.

3 class hours.   Credit, 3.
10:00-10:50 M. W. F.   MR. TRIPPENSEE.

70. (II) Wildlife Management

Life histories, ecology, and management of common game birds and mammals. Includes a study of natural habitats and methods of management.

1 class hour; 2 2-hour laboratory periods.   Credit, 3.
                                              MR. TRIPPENSEE.

71. (I) Wildlife Management (1954-55)

Life histories, ecology, and management of waterfowl. Includes a study of natural habitats and method of management. Given in alternate years.

1 class hour; 2 2-hour laboratory periods.   Credit, 3.
11:00-11:50 Tu.; 3:00-4:50 Tu. Th.   MR. TRIPPENSEE.

72. (II) Forest-Animal Relationships

For students majoring in Forestry. Effects of animals on the forest; the effects of forest practices on wild animal production; economic aspects of forest-animal relationships.

3 class hours.   Credit, 3.
10:00-10:50 M. W. F.   MR. TRIPPENSEE.

73. (I) Wildlife Management

Life histories, ecology, and management of predaceous birds and injurious mammals. Particularly designed for those who seek employment with rodent control division of U. S. Fish and Wildlife Service.

1 class hour; 2 2-hour laboratory periods.   Credit, 3.
                                              MR. TRIPPENSEE.

74. (II) Techniques in Wildlife Management (1954-55)

Admission by permission of instructor. Quantitative field studies of wild animals of forest and farm. Includes cover mapping, habitat studies, census, food habits, and damage of game animals. For

students interested in state and federal employment through civil service, Given in alternate years.
1 class hour; 1 4-hour laboratory period.   Credit, 3.
1:00-1:50 W.; 1:00-4:50 M.   MR. TRIPPENSEE.

75. (I) Wildlife Management (1955-56)
Life histories, ecology, and management of the furbearers. Includes a study of natural habitats, management and fur farm problems. Given in alternate years.
1 class hour; 2 2-hour laboratory periods.   Credit, 3.
11:00-11:50 Tu.; 3:00-4:50 Tu. Th.   MR. TRIPPENSEE.

84. (II) Seminar (1955-56)
Study and discussion of problems in relation to agriculture, forestry, and the use and control of wildlife resources. For juniors and seniors majoring in wildlife management. Given in alternate years.
3 class hours.   Credit, 3.
MR. TRIPPENSEE.

GEOLOGY AND MINERALOGY

PROFESSOR WILSON, ASSISTANT PROFESSOR NELSON, ASSISTANT PROFESSOR JOHANSSON, ASSISTANT PROFESSOR ————————, MR. FARRINGTON, MR. RICE, MR. WOODLAND.

27. (I) Physical Geology
An introduction to the agents and processes that modify the earth's crust. Field trips by arrangement.
2 class hours; 1 quiz hour; 1 2-hour laboratory period.   Credit, 3.
THE DEPARTMENT.

28. (II) Historical Geology
A survey of geological time, stressing the development of continents and the history of plants and animals. Field trips by arrangement.
2 class hours; 1 quiz hour; 1 2-hour laboratory period.   Credit, 3.
THE DEPARTMENT.

50. (I) Engineering Geology
A general course in engineering geology stressing earth structure, the dynamic processes, and agents of weathering. The laboratory work consists of mineral and rock-determination and map-reading as related to the phenomena of physical geology.
2 class hours; 1 3-hour laboratory period.   Credit, 3.
MR. ————————.

51. (I) Mineralogy

A descriptive study. Stress is placed upon the identification and occurrence of minerals.

1 class hour; 2 2-hour laboratory periods.   Credit, 3.

MR. NELSON.

52. (II) Lithology

A descriptive study of the classes of rocks with reference to manner of origin, modes of occurrence, structural features and the chemical and petrographic distinction within each group.

1 class hour; 2 2-hour laboratory periods.   Credit, 3.

MR. NELSON.

54. (II) Economic Geology

A course dealing with the origin, classification, and uses of metallic and non-metallic mineral deposits.

2 class hours; 1 2-hour laboratory period.   Credit, 3.

MR. ————.

60. (II) Principles of Physical Geography

A systematic study of the world's physiographic provinces, climate, vegetation, soils, mineral resources, and their effects upon mankind. The geographic relationships to land forms will be stressed.

3 class hours.   Credit, 3.

MR. JOHANSSON.

61. (I) Geomorphology (1956-57)

A review of recent studies concerning rock structures, weathering, streams, underground water, shorelines, wind work, volcanoes, and mountains. Field trips by arrangement. Given in alternate years.

2 class hours; 1 2-hour laboratory period.   Credit, 3.

MR. WILSON.

62. (II) Pleistocene Geology (1954-55)

A study of Pleistocene world geology consisting of geological processes, land forms, existing and extinct glaciers, biota and stratigraphy. Field trips by arrangement. Given in alternate years.

2 class hours; 1 2-hour laboratory period.   Credit, 3.

MR. WILSON.

63. (I) Invertebrate Paleontology

A study of the history, development and identification of invertebrate animal fossils. Field trips by arrangement.

1 class hour; 2 2-hour laboratory periods.   Credit, 3.

MR. JOHANSSON.

64. (II) Plant Paleontology
A study of the history, development, and identification of plant fossils. Field trips by arrangement.
1 class hour; 2 2-hour laboratory periods. Credit, 3.
MR. WILSON.

71. (I) 72. (II) Special Problems
For seniors specializing in geology.
6 laboratory hours. Credit, 3.
Hours by arrangement. THE DEPARTMENT.

73. (I) Structural Geology (1956-57)
A study of the origin of rock structures, their occurrence, and recognition. Field and laboratory problems emphasize the structure present in the Connecticut valley. Given in alternate years.
1 class hour; 2 2-hour laboratory periods. Credit, 3.
MR. ————.

74. (II) Principles of Stratigraphy (1955-56)
An examination of the principles of stratigraphic correlation and their application to the problems of the major rock units of the United States. Field and laboratory work consists primarily of problems related to the eastern United States. Given in alternate years.
1 class hour; 2 2-hour laboratory periods. Credit, 3.
MR. WILSON.

GERMAN

PROFESSOR ELLERT, ASSOCIATE PROFESSOR GOLDSMITH, ASSOCIATE PROFESSOR SCHROEDER, MR. STAWIECKI, MR. LEA, MR. KRATZ, MR. TAUBE.

1. (I) 2. (II) Elementary German
Grammar, prose composition, and reading. No credits in this course may be applied toward a degree until the close of the second semester, except upon special recommendation from the Provost.
3 class hours. Credit, 3.
THE DEPARTMENT.

5. (I) 6. (II) Advanced German Prose
Reading of representative German authors. Grammar review.
3 class hours. Credit, 3.
8:00-8:50 Tu. Th. S. MR. LEA, MR. GOLDSMITH.
Prerequisite, Entrance German.

25. (I) 26. (II) Intermediate German

German prose and poetry; the simple German drama; grammar review. Passages of prose and poetry to commit to memory.

3 class hours.   Credit, 3.

Prerequisites, German 1 and 2.   THE DEPARTMENT.

28. (II) Scientific German

Admission by arrangement with the instructor. Intensive and extensive readings of scientific texts in various fields taken from standard German works.

3 class hours.   Credit, 3.

Prerequisites, German 25.   MR. TAUBE.

51. (I) Nineteenth Century (1956-57)

A study of the "Novelle" from the death of Goethe to 1890 (early realism to naturalism) with emphasis on literary and social forces in the work of Tieck, Stifter, Keller, and Hauptmann. Given in alternate years.

3 class hours.   Credit, 3.

Prerequisites, German 25 and 26.   MR. SCHROEDER.

52. (II) Poetry and Drama of the Nineteenth Century (1954-55)

A study of the development of the drama and of lyric poetry from 1830 to 1890 with special emphasis on dramatic works of Grillparzer, Hebbel, and Hauptmann and the poetry of Mörike, Storm, and C. F. Meyer. Given in alternate years.

3 class hours.   Credit, 3.

Prerequisites, German 25 and 26.   MR. GOLDSMITH.

53. (I) Twentieth Century Prose

Main literary currents in contemporary German prose from Nietzsche to Hesse with particular attention to the work of Thomas Mann, Kafka, and Warfel.

3 class hours.   Credit, 3.

MR. SCHROEDER.

54. (II) Poetry and Drama of the Twentieth Century

Reading and discussion of significant lyrical works of Hofmannsthal, George, and Rilke, and representative dramas by Hauptmann and Georg Kaiser.

3 class hours.   Credit, 3.

Prerequisites, German 25 and 26.   MR. GOLDSMITH.

55. (I) Storm and Stress (1955-56)

A study of storm and stress in German literature centering in the young Goethe. Given in alternate years.

3 class hours. Credit, 3.
MR. ELLERT.

Prerequisites, German 25 and 26.

56. (II) Romanticism (1954-55)

A study of the poetry and prose writings of the romantic period from Novalis to Heine. Given in alternate years.

3 class hours. Credit, 3.
MR. ELLERT.

Prerequisites, German 25 and 26.

57. (I) Goethe's Faust

3 class hours. Credit, 3.
MR. GOLDSMITH.

Prerequisites, German 25 and 26.

58. (II) Middle High German

Readings of Middle High German texts in the original with an introduction to the grammar.

3 class hours. Credit, 3.
MR. KRATZ.

Prerequisites, German 25 and 26.

59. (I) The Germanic Languages

An introduction to general and Germanic linguistics for German and English majors; a survey of the relationship between German, English, and the other Indo-European tongues and of the historical development of German and English as the two principal Germanic literary languages.

3 class hours. Credit, 3.
MR. KRATZ.

60. (II) The Classical Period (1955-56)

A study of representative works by Lessing, Goethe, and Schiller. Given in alternate years.

MR. SCHROEDER.

Prerequisites, German 25 and 26.

68. (II) German Literature of the Middle Ages (1955-56)

A survey of the literature of the German language from the earliest literary documents to the 15th century, with readings in modern German translation of the Nibelungenlied, Gudrun, Par-

zival, Tristan, Der arme Heinrich, and the lyrics of Walter von der Vogelweide. Given in alternate years.
3 class hours.   Credit,. 3.
                                                        MR. ELLERT.

79. (I) 80. (II) Conversational German and Advanced German Composition

Admission by arrangement with the instructor. Practice in the oral and written language.
4 class hours.   Credit, 3.
3:00-4:50 Tu. Th.   MR. SCHROEDER.
Prerequisites, German 25 and 26.

GOVERNMENT

PROFESSOR CAHILL, ASSISTANT PROFESSOR GOODWIN, MR. TINDER,
MR. ALLEN, MR. MAINZER, MR. BRAUNTHAL.

25. (I) and (II) American Government

A study of the principles, machinery, dynamics and problems of government in the United States.
3 class hours.   Credit, 3.
                                                     THE DEPARTMENT.

26. (II) European Government

A survey of the politics and governmental institutions of Great Britain, France, U. S. S. R., and other European countries.
3 class hours.   Credit, 3.
                                               MR. ALLEN, MR. TINDER.

54. (II) State Government (1955-56)

A study of state politics, organization and functions, with emphasis on the role of the state in our Federal system. Given in alternate years.
3 class hours.   Credit, 3.
                                                       MR. GOODWIN.

61. (I) Public Administration

A study of organization and management in modern government, with emphasis on the bureaucracy's role in public policy formation.
3 class hours.   Credit, 3.
                                                       MR. MAINZER.

62. (II) Administrative Law

A study of governmental activities in the regulation of industry, agriculture, and labor, with emphasis on the legal framework within which these activities operate. Not offered 1955-56.
3 class hours. Credit, 3.
MR. MAINZER.

63. (I) Political Parties and Elections

A study of the American political process, with emphasis on parties, pressure groups, and public opinion.
3 class hours. Credit, 3.
MR. GOODWIN.

64. (II) Municipal Government (1956-57)

A survey of the governmental structure and function of American municipalities. Given in alternate years.
3 class hours. Credit, 3.
MR. GOODWIN.

65. (I) Constitutional Law

An historical study of the United States Constitution as interpreted by decisions of the Supreme Court.
3 class hours. Credit, 3.
MR. CAHILL.

66. (II) American Political Thought

A study of the development of American political thought from colonial times to the present.
3 class hours. Credit, 3.
MR. CAHILL.

68. (II) International Law

A study of the origin, character, and function of international law.
3 class hours. Credit, 3.
MR, ALLEN.

70. (II) International Organization

A study of international organization in the twentieth century, with emphasis upon the United Nations and regional organizations. Not offered 1955-56.
3 class hours. Credit, 3.
MR, ALLEN.

71. (I) Ancient and Medieval Political Thought
A study of the development of political thought and its relation to cultural and institutional growth from the time of the Greeks to the end of the Middle Ages.
3 class hours.   Credit, 3.
                                                          MR. TINDER.

72. (II) Modern Political Thought
A study of the development of political thought and its relation to cultural and institutional growth from the rise of the modern state to the present.
3 class hours.   Credit, 3.
                                                          MR. TINDER.

73. (I) Comparative Government
A functional analysis of contemporary governments with special attention to the ideology, structure, and dynamics of political parties.
3 class hours.   Credit, 3.
                                                           MR,. ALLEN.
Prerequisite, Government 26.

76. (II) Public Opinion in Politics
A study of opinion and communication as aspects of the political process with emphasis upon communication through mass media. Examination of the relations between mass attitudes and communication and political institutions and the formation of public policy.
3 class hours.   Credit, 3.
                                                         MR. MAINZER.

93. (I) 94. (II) Seminar
A study of special problems in the field of government.
3 class hours.   Credit, 3.
                                                      THE DEPARTMENT.

HISTORY
PROFESSOR CALDWELL, PROFESSOR CARY, ASSOCIATE PROFESSOR DAVIS, ASSISTANT PROFESSOR ZEENDER†, ASSISTANT PROFESSOR PFLANZE, MR. POTASH, MR. GAGNON†, MR. KINGDON, MR. SOLT, MR. DIETEL, MR. HIGHAM, MR. HILL.

5. (I) 6. (II) Modern European Civilization
The first semester covers the period from the later Middle Ages to 1815; the second semester, the period from 1815 to the present. These courses are required of candidates for the B.A. degree but may be elected independently by other students.
3 class hours.   Credit, 3.
  † On leave of absence.   THE DEPARTMENT.

31. (I) 32. (II) English History

Emphasis on economic, social, and cultural influences, as well as on constitutional development. Either semester may be elected independently.

3 class hours. Credit, 3.

MR. CALDWELL, MR. SOLT.

51. (I) Ancient History

A general survey of Mesopotamian, Egyptian, Greek, and Roman history, with primary emphasis on cultural and intellectual achievements.

3 class hours. Credit, 3.

MR. DAVIS.

53. (I) International Relations

The nation-state system and conceptions of national interest in modern world politics. The forms and distribution of power by which states seek to implement national interests. The making of foreign policy and methods of adjusting international conflict. Attention will be given to current international problems.

3 class hours. Credit, 3.

MR. PFLANZE.

54. (II) The Far East (1954-55)

A general historical introduction to the civilization and contemporary problems of China and Japan. The first half covers the traditional civilization of China and Japan and the early impact of the west to 1890. The second half deals with revolutionary developments of the twentieth century and the place of the Far East in the world balance of power. Given in alternate years.

3 class hours. Credit, 3.

MR. —————.

56. (II) History of Russia (1955-56)

A general historical introduction to the civilization and contemporary problems of Russia. Growth of the Russian state, society, culture and ideology, and their relations to the non-Russian world. Emphasis on the Soviet period. Given in alternate years.

3 class hours. Credit, 3.

MR. GAGNON.

57. (I) 58. (II) Hispanic-American History

The first semester deals with the colonial period: the age of the "conquistadores", political, economic, and cultural developments, and growth of the independence movement; the second semester with the period of national development from 1810 to the present. Emphasis will be given to the history of Mexico and the more im-

portant South American countries. Either semester may be elected
independently.
3 class hours. Credit, 3.

MR. POTASH.

59. (I) 60. (II) History of the United States

A survey of the national development including political, social,
economic, and cultural factors in the growth of American democracy. The first semester covers the period to 1865; the second, from
1865 to the present. Either semester may be elected independently.
3 class hours. Credit, 3.

MR. CARY.

65. (I) Nineteenth and Twentieth Century England (1955-56)

A topical study of England since 1815. Emphasis is given to
social change and to movements of thought. Subjects treated include: Victorian society and ideals; growth of democracy; imperial
development; socialist Britain. Considerable biographical reading.
Given in alternate years.
3 class hours. Credit, 3.

MR. CALDWELL.

Prerequisite, History 32.

67. (I) Tudor and Stuart England (1956-57)

A brief survey of the Tudor Period followed by a detailed study
of Early Stuart England. Emphasis is placed on social, religious,
and intellectual aspects of English life in the period. Given in
alternate years.
3 class hours. Credit, 3.

MR. CALDWELL.

Prerequisite, History 31 or 32.

69. (I) Europe, 1870-1918

Internal developments of the principal countries, including political and economic changes, social unrest, and intellectual currents; the development of imperialism; a detailed study of conditions and diplomacy which led to the World War; military history
of the War.
3 class hours. Credit, 3.

MR. ZEENDER.

Prerequisite, History 6.

70. (II) Europe Since 1918

Approximately half of the course is devoted to international
affairs, including the Peace Settlement, the development of German, Italian, and Japanese aggression, and World War II. The

other half of the course is a study of internal developments in the principal European nations.

3 class hours. Credit, 3.

MR. CALDWELL.

72. (II) History of American Westward Expansion, 1763-1893

Advance of settlement from the Appalachians to the Pacific and influence of the frontier upon social, economic, and political conditions in the country as a whole.

3 class hours. Credit, 3.

MR. DAVIS.

Prerequisite, History 59.

75. (I) Medieval History

Europe from the collapse of Roman civilization to the Renaissance. Fusion of the Graeco-Roman inheritance, Christianity, and Germanic traditions in the building of Western European civilization. The medieval outlooks as expressed in the thought and culture of the High Middle Ages.

3 class hours. Credit, 3.

MR. ZEENDER.

76. (II) History of the Renaissance

The later Middle Ages; the Church at the height of power; the rise of nationalities; the Italian towns; the New Learning and its relation to art, science, invention, geographical discoveries; spread and effects of the Renaissance.

3 class hours. Credit, 3.

MR. ZEENDER.

77. (I) 78. (II) The History of Science in Western Civilization

This course will trace the growth of the community of science as it exists in the world today. Emphasis will be placed upon the mutual relations between science and the economic, social, and intellectual forces in society at large. Not offered in 1954-55.

2 class hours. Credit, 2.

MR. ————.

81. (I) 82. (II) Diplomatic History of the United States

The development of American foreign relations, 1776 to the present. Either semester may be elected independently.

3 class hours. Credit, 3.

MR. CARY.

Prerequisites, History 59, 60, or permission of the instructor.

91. (I) Historical Bibliography
Training in assembling a bibliography and an introduction to the works of some leading historians.

1 class hour. Credit, 1.

THE DEPARTMENT.

92. (II) Seminar
Instruction in the evaluation of source materials and the preparation of reports.

1 class hour. Credit, 1.

THE DEPARTMENT.

HOME ECONOMICS

PROFESSOR MITCHELL, ASSOCIATE PROFESSOR BRIGGS, ASSISTANT PROFESSOR MERRIAM, ASSISTANT PROFESSOR COOK†, ASSISTANT PROFESSOR DAVIS, ASSISTANT PROFESSOR McCULLOUGH, ASSISTANT PROFESSOR STRATTNER, MRS. THIES, MRS. WILHELM, MISS HAWES, MISS FORBES, MRS. IRVIN, MRS. SULLIVAN.

1. (I) Introduction to Home Economics
The course introduces the student to the objectives in Home Economics and the fields of specialization for which it prepares. Consideration is given to a philosophy of living which emphasizes the responsibility of a woman to her family, to her community wherever she is, and to the world. Introductory work is offered in food and nutrition, child development and family life. Laboratory work includes food selection and simple preparation, and observation in the Nursery School.

3 class hours. Credit, 3.

THE DEPARTMENT.

2. (II) Clothing Selection
A study of the principles of clothing selection in order to assist each student to choose satisfactorily line, color, and texture; a study of the principles of buymanship in relation to ladies' ready-to-wear; fundamentals of construction for cotton and linen.

2 class hours; 1 2-hour laboratory period. Credit, 3.

MRS. WILHELM, MISS HAWES.

26. (II) Textiles
This course is designed to give the student an introduction to the characteristic properties and uses of natural and synthetic fibers; the conversion of fiber to finished fabrics; fabric identifications; buying and use of fabrics for clothing and home use.

2 class hours; 1 2-hour laboratory period. Credit, 3.

Miss Hawes.

† On leave of absence.

30. (II) Food Science and Preparation

A study of the fundamental scientific principles and comparative methods of food preparation. The nutritional and economic aspects of foods are also stressed.

2 class hours; 1 3-hour laboratory period. Credit, 3.

MISS DAVIS, MISS FORBES.

31. (I) Applied Art

Art principles are studied with many practical applications for selecting and arranging. Specific problems in decorating cloth, wood, and leather afford opportunity for individual expression.

1 class hour; 2 2-hour laboratory periods. Credit, 3.

MISS BRIGGS, MRS. SULLIVAN.

35. (I) Clothing Construction

Advanced construction and fitting problems with emphasis on new fabrics. In the latter part of the semester provision is made for individual development in the field of clothing in which the student is most interested. Sections offered are: more advanced construction and fitting problems; visual aids for teaching clothing; creative pattern drafting and merchandising women's ready-to-wear.

1 class hour; 2 2-hour laboratory periods. Credit, 3.

MRS. WILHELM, MISS HAWES.

Prerequisite, Home Economics 2 or equivalent.

41. (I) Nutrition and Food Preparation

This course combines the fundamentals of nutrition with food preparation and meal planning to meet nutritional requirements. The content and emphasis is appropriate for nurses whose responsibilities will be mostly with their patients. Admission by permission of instructor.

3 class hours; 1 2-hour laboratory period. Credit, 4.

MRS. COOK, MISS FORBES.

Prerequisites, Chemistry 1 and 2; Zoology 35.

42. (II) Medical Dietetics

The principles and practice of dietary restrictions and modifications recommended for certain diseases, always keeping in mind the nutritional needs of the individual. Students learn to use current medical literature for supplementary reference in connection with new developments.

2 class hours. Credit, 2.

MRS. COOK.

Prerequisite, Home Economics 41 or equivalent.

215

51. (I) Food Selection and Meal Planning

Meal planning, serving and etiquette and emphasis on well-balanced meals as to nutritive value and economy of money, time, and labor in preparation. Further study of food principles and techniques of cookery and a unit in food preservation, freezing and canning is included.

2 class hours; 1 4-hour laboratory period.   Credit, 3.

MISS DAVIS, MISS FORBES.

Prerequisite, Home Economics 30; Chemistry 33.

52. (II) Nutrition and Dietetics

A study of the fundamentals of normal nutrition including energy needs, the metabolism of proteins, carbohydrates, fats, vitamins, and minerals; and the quantitative requirements for these various essential nutrients. Laboratory work provides for further study of the composition of foods and their contribution to the diet and the relationship of the nutritive value to cost. Nutritive loss due to cooking, storage, etc. is given consideration.

3 class hours; 1 2-hour laboratory period.   Credit, 3.

MRS. COOK.

Prerequisites, Home Economics 30; Chemistry 33 and Zoology 1 to 35.

54. (II) Nutrition

For students who are not majoring in Home Economics and who do not have prerequisites for Home Economics 52. This course is designed to interpret the technical knowledge of foods and nutrition in terms of its practical application for optimum health.

3 class hours.   Credit, 3.

MRS. COOK.

56. (II) Food Preparation and Meal Planning

This course is designed to meet the needs of those who wish a general knowledge of the basic food principles. It includes latest methods and techniques of cookery, conservation of nutrients, menu planning and food preparation, buying of food, consumer education and table service, decoration and etiquette. It is recommended for students who want a scientific as well as practical knowledge of food and its preparation for everyday use.

2 class hours; 1 3-hour laboratory period.   Credit, 3.

MISS FORBES.

57. (I) Clothing Selection and Simple Construction

For students not majoring in home economics. This course is designed to stimulate an interest in good workmanship. Emphasis is given to construction technique such as fitting, pattern use and altering.

1 class hour; 1 3-hour laboratory period.   Credit, 2.

MISS HAWES.

60. (II) Household Equipment

A study of selection, care, and operation of household equipment and the mechanical principles involved. Actual work with equipment and field trips are included.

1 class hour; 1 3-hour laboratory period.   Credit, 2.

MISS MERRIAM.

61. (I) Demonstration Techniques

Emphasis is given to the purposes and techniques of demonstration both in preparation of food and the use of equipment, with application to teaching, extension, and business.

2 2-hour laboratory periods.   Credit, 2.

MISS MERRIAM.

Prerequisites, Home Economics 30, 51.

62. (II) Home Furnishing

A study of the fundamental principles which underlie the successful planning and furnishing of a satisfying home. A study of period homes and furnishings is included. Many applications of these principles are worked out in practical problems.

1 class hour; 2 2-hour laboratory periods.   Credit, 3.

MISS BRIGGS.

63. (I) Arts and Crafts

Introduction to design and execution in crafts particularly adapted to work with children in schools, playgrounds, summer camps; and for any age in recreational leadership and occupational therapy. Opportunity will be offered for work in several of the following: wood and leather work, block printing, fingerpainting, etching, knotting, etc.

1 class hour; 2 2-hour laboratory periods.   Credit, 3.

MISS BRIGGS.

70. (II) Child Development

The growth and development of the child, his basic needs, aspects of behavior—routine, creative and social—as they are related to personality development. Planned observation and participation in nursery school.

3 class hours; 1 1-hour laboratory period.   Credit, 3.

MRS. THIES.

71. (I) Retail Food Buying

This course is offered jointly by the departments of olericulture, animal husbandry, and poultry husbandry for all students interested in retail marketing. First 5 weeks: vegetables and fruits, retail buying, varieties and adaptability to various uses, season of availability, grades, packs and packages. Second 5 weeks; poultry and eggs—dressed poultry is graded and prepared in various ways for the table and home freezing. Demonstrations are given of handling and market classification of eggs. Third 5 weeks: meats— demonstration and laboratory practices in identification and classi- fication of meat cuts, in preservation (freezing and curing) and in judging quality.

2 class hours; 1 2-hour laboratory period.   Credit, 3.

MR. SNYDER, MR. VONDELL, MR. BARTLETT.

MISS ———— coordinator.

75. (I) Economics of the Household

A study of personal and family standards of living in the modern home, the economic relations of the household, and the use of time, energy, and money as a means to influence the home situa- tion.

3 class hours.   Credit, 3.

MISS MERRIAM.

77. (I) and (II) Home Management Practice

Successive groups of seniors live in the home management house or apartment and assume responsibilities involved in managing a home. Meals are planned on low, medium, and high income levels.

Credit, 3.

MISS MERRIAM, MRS. IRVIN.

Prerequisites, Home Economics 51, 52, and 75, or by special permis- sion.

78. (II) Advanced Textile Design

Weaving and handling of complicated looms. Other types of textile design such as stencilling, silk screen printing, batik, block print, with individual problems dependent on the student's special interests.

1 class hour; 2 3-hour laboratory periods.   Credit, 3.

MISS BRIGGS.

Prerequisite, Home Economics 26.

79. (I) Textile Testing (1955-56)

Testing and analysis of textile fibers and fabrics, emphasis placed on testing techniques for composition, thread count, tensile strength, color fastness and finishes. The subject matter is of value to students interested in scientific or commercial textile testing. Given in alternate years.

2 class hours; 1 3-hour laboratory period.   Credit, 3.

MISS HAWES.

Prerequisite, Home Economics 26.

80. (II) Family Life

A study of the modern family; ideals and responsibilities of the home and the individual's share in developing postive family relationships.

3 class hours. Credit, 3.

MISS STRATTNER.

81. (I) Methods of Teaching Home Economics

A study of the philosophy of general education; the application of home economics to the entire school program; development of curricula based upon student needs; exploration of instructional methods and techniques. This course gives credit toward meeting state standards for teachers.

3 class hours. Credit, 3.

MISS STRATTNER.

85. (I) Theory and Practice of Nursery School Management

This course is planned to give students a background in the history and philosophy of the pre-school program; theory and techniques of nursery school practice; children's activities in music, art, literature, and science; fundamentals of play and use of play materials, and methods of observation and recording. Supervised participation in child development laboratory as well as field trips to observe special groups.

2 class hours; 1 3-hour laboratory period. Credit, 3.

MRS. THIES.

Prerequisite, Home Economics 70.

87. (I) Principles and Practices of Tailoring

Emphasis on handling of wool in the making of suits and coats.

1 class hour; 2 2-hour laboratory periods. Credit, 3.

MRS. WILHELM.

Prerequisite, Home Economics 35 or equivalent.

88. (II) Applied Dress Design

Costume design through draping and pattern making. An intensive study is made of texture, line, color and fit as applied to dress design and the figure.

3 2-hour laboratory periods. Credit, 3.

MRS. WILHELM.

Prerequisite, Home Economics 35 or equivalent.

89. (I) Diet Therapy

The application of nutrition principles to diet in disease. Recent theories of dietary treatment of gastro-intestinal disorders, obesity, anemia, fevers, diabetes, food allergy, cardiovascular and biliary tract diseases are reviewed critically. Students are required to use and be familiar with current medical literature as it applies to nutritional problems in disease and at the same time be open-minded regarding new developments in this field. Scientific and medical terminology is emphasized.

3 class hours. Credit, 3.

MRS. COOK.

Prerequisites, Home Economics 52; Chemistry 79; Zoology 35.

90. (II) Professional Seminars

A one-credit seminar is offered in each of the five fields of subject matter: Nutrition, Textiles, Foods, Home Management and Equipment, Family Life and Child Development. One seminar is required of each senior and permission may be granted to take as many as three of the five.

Credit, 1-3.

HOME ECONOMICS STAFF.

91. (I) 92. (II) Quantity Food Preparation and Institutional Management

For qualified juniors or seniors interested in institutional food service. A study of the principles of organization, personnel management, the administration, food costs, operating expenses, and the special functions of the dietitian. Laboratory work is at one of the university dining halls and field trips are planned. It is expected that students will enroll for the work of both semesters. Students wishing to qualify for administrative institutional work are advised to take Accounting 25 and Home Economics 71.

2 class hours, 1 4-hour laboratory period or field work. Credit, 3.

MRS. McCULLOUGH.

Prerequisites, Home Economics 51 and 52.

93. (I) Experimental Foods

The testing and comparing of different food materials and methods of preparation, including advanced work in the science and techniques of cookery. Special individual problems will be studied. The course is helpful to those interested in commercial food testing and valuable to those wishing to develop a scientific approach to the study of foods.

2 class hours; 1 3-hour laboratory period. Credit, 3.

MISS DAVIS.

Prerequisite, Home Economics 30.

95. (I) Child Nutrition

A study is made of nutritional needs from prenatal life through infancy and childhood. Methods of judging nutrition, also causes and effects of malnutrition are discussed. Menus for children and measures to insure the consumption of optimal diets are put in practice with laboratory work in the Nursery School.

3 class hours. Laboratory by arrangement. Credit, 3.

MRS. COOK.

Prerequisite, Home Economics 52 or 54.

98. (I) and (II) Problems in Home Economics

An intensive study of some phase of home economics. By permission of the Staff adviser.

Credit, 3.

HOME ECONOMICS STAFF.

HYGIENE

Hygiene

All freshmen are required to attend a series of lectures on personal hygiene. For men students these lectures are included in the Military program; for women students they are scheduled as a separate course.

Credit, 1.

THE HEALTH SERVICE STAFF.

JOURNALISM

PROFESSOR MUSGRAVE.

84. (II) Community Journalism

A study of the weekly newspaper, the small-city daily, and the scholastic press, combined with training in copyediting. The University and town weeklies are used as laboratories. Given in alternate years.

3 class hours. Credit, 3.

MR. MUSGRAVE.

85. (I) Introduction to Journalism

A basic course in reporting designed to acquaint the student with the scope, principles, and practice of contemporary journalism. Stress is placed upon the role of the press as a social institution and upon the relationships between a general education and effective journalism.

3 class hours. Credit, 3.

MR MUSGRAVE.

86. (II) Feature Article Writing

Instruction in writing feature or magazine articles, combined with a study of the field of magazine journalism. The practice work is related to problems of interpretive writing, communication, and public opinion. Each student is expected to publish a feature article in a newspaper, a trade journal or other magazines.
3 class hours.   Credit, 3.

MR. MUSGRAVE.

88. (II) Newspaper Internship

Advanced reporting and copyediting, with laboratory work on daily newspapers in the area. Limited to seniors who intend to go into newspaper or public relations or radio news or editing work. Admission only by permission of instructor.
2 class hours; 1 laboratory period.   Credit, 3.

MR. MUSGRAVE.

Prerequisites, Journalism 85, and 84 or 86.

LANDSCAPE ARCHITECTURE

PROFESSOR OTTO, PROFESSOR BLUNDELL, ASSISTANT PROFESSOR MC-
LINDON, ASSISTANT PROFESSOR PROCOPIO, MR. MACIVER, MR.
HAMILTON.

LANDSCAPE ARCHITECTURE

25. (I) Freehand Drawing and Elementary Design

The work in this course is to supply the student with technical aspects of freehand drawing and design necessary to proficiency in that field.
3 2-hour laboratory periods.   Credit, 3.
1:00-2:50 M. W. F.   MR. MACIVER.

26. (II) Landscape Drafting

This course continues the work in Landscape Architecture 25, but draws on the mechanical aspects of the designers problems and includes simple projections—orthographic, perspective, and isometric—and architectural shades and shadows.
3 2-hour laboratory periods.   Credit, 3.
1:00-2:50 M. W. F.   MR. MACIVER.

51. (I) Elements of Topography and Construction

Contour interpolation, grading and drainage, plans, drive design, profiles and sections, computation of earth work. Application of surveying to landscape construction.

3 2-hour laboratory periods.   Credit, 3.
3:00-4:50 M. W. F.   Mr. PROCOPIO.
Prerequisites, Civil Engineering 27; Landscape Architecture 26.

52. (II) Construction Details

A series of problems in architectural garden features as walks, steps, walls, gates, pools, and small structures.

3 2-hour laboratory periods.   Credit, 3.
3:00-4:50 M. W. F.   Mr. PROCOPIO.
Prerequisites, Landscape Architecture 51.

53. (I) Introductory Design

Fundamental principles of composition with application to problems in the design of gardens and small home grounds.

3 2-hour laboratory periods.   Credit, 3.
1:00-2:50 M. W. F.   Mr. OTTO.
Prerequisites, Landscape Architecture 25 and 26 or permission of the instructor.

54. (II) General Design

A series of problems in the design of private properties and public works. Members of this class will be required to take a two-day field trip to visit typical examples of design; approximate cost, $15.00.

3 2-hour laboratory periods.   Credit, 3.
1:00-2:50 M. W. F.   Mr. OTTO.
Prerequisites, Landscape Architecture 51, 53, and concurrently 52.

79. (I) Construction and Maintenance (1955-56)

A study of construction methods and materials as applied to the landscape field. Given in alternate years.

3 class hours.   Credit, 3.
10:00-10:50 M. W. F.   Mr. PROCOPIO.

80. (II) History and Literature of Landscape Architecture

A review of the history and literature of landscape architecture and allied fields. Compilation of bibliographies of significant works.

2 class hours.   Credit, 2.
8:00-8:50 Tu. Th.   Mr. OTTO.

81. (I) 82. (II) Advanced Design
Class B Exchange Problems plus specialized study of landscape details and a summary of general design. Members of the class may be required to take a two-day field trip to visit typical examples of design; approximate cost, $15.00.

3 2-hour laboratory periods. Credit, 3.

3:00-4:50 M. W. F. MR. HAMILTON.

Prerequisites, Landscape Architecture 53 and 54.

83. (I) Architecture (1956-57)
The history of architectural development, including styles of architecture and construction principles of value to landscape architects when working with architectural problems. Given in alternate years.

3 class hours. Credit, 3.

8:00-8:50 M. W. F. MR. McLINDON.

84. (II) Sketching
Drawing and sketching in various mediums from outdoor and indoor subjects.

2 2-hour laboratory periods. Credit, 2.

MR. MACIVER.

86. (II) City Planning
A critical examination of those factors which influence and guide the physical growth and arrangement of communities in harmony with their social and economic needs.

3 class hours. Credit, 3.

8:00-8:50 M. W. F. MR. McLINDON.

87. (I) City Planning
An application of the principles of modern civic art through a series of problems on the design of various types of urban land areas.

3 2-hour laboratory periods. Credit, 3.

MR. McLINDON.

Prerequisite, Landscape Architecture 86.

HORTICULTURE

1. (I) Plant Propagation
This course serves as an introduction to the field of horticulture, emphasizing the methods and principles involved in the propagation of horticultural plants.

2 class hours; 1 2-hour laboratory period. Credit, 3.

MR. THAYER, MR. PROCOPIO.

26. (II) Plant Materials

Detailed study of deciduous and evergreen trees, with special reference to their mature form and character, means of identification, natural associations, and uses of the various types of trees in landscape work.

1 class hour; 2 2-hour laboratory periods.   Credit, 3.

Mr. Blundell.

51. (I) Plant Materials

Detailed study of shrubs and woody vines, and their identification, with especial emphasis being given to their adaptability to the various landscape uses, methods of handling, and care.

1 class hour; 2 2-hour laboratory periods.   Credit, 3.

Mr. Blundell.

52. (II) Planting Design

A study of the utilization of plant materials in combination as applied to the many conditions and demands of landscape work.

1 class hour; 2 2-hour laboratory periods.   Credit, 3.

Mr. Blundell.

Prerequisites, Horticulture 26 and 51.

LATIN

Instructors in Romance Languages.

51. (I) 52. (II) Elementary Latin

An intensive course in Latin grammar and reading. Recommended for prospective language teachers and those planning graduate work in foreign languages or English who have had no previous Latin. No credits in this course may be applied toward a degree until the close of the second semester, except upon special recommendation from the Provost.

3 class hours.   Credit, 3.

Mr. Greenfield.

55. (I) 56. (II) Advanced Latin

A survey of classical Latin literature: dialogues and oratory (Cicero), the epic (Virgil), lyric poetry (Catullus and Horace), historical prose (Livy), satire, comedy, and other genres. Recommended for prospective language teachers and those planning graduate work in foreign languages or English who have had two or more years of high school Latin.

3 class hours.   Credit, 3.

Mr. Greenfield.

Prerequisites, Latin 51 and 52 or 2 years of high school Latin.

MATHEMATICS

PROFESSOR ANDERSEN, PROFESSOR WAGNER, ASSOCIATE PROFESSOR
BOUTELLE, ASSOCIATE PROFESSOR ROSE, ASSISTANT PROFESSOR
SCHOONMAKER, ASSISTANT PROFESSOR CULLEN,. MR. BUZZELL,
MR. SKILLINGS, MR. ALLEN, MR. MIENTKA,† MR. MOSER, MR.
BUSSEL, MR. WATSON, MR. NAYLOR, MISS LAVALLE, MISS
ROSTON, MR. SCHWARTZ, MR. WALLACE.

01. (I) Elementary College Algebra

A course intended for those students who offer only one unit of
algebra for entrance. It contains a review of elementary algebra
and a more thorough study of such topics as quadratic equations,
exponents and radicals, and progressions. No college credit is
given for this course, but the successful completion of this course
and Mathematics 14 which follows in the second semester, may
satisfy the freshman mathematics requirement unless the student's
major requires further mathematics.

3 class hours. Credit, 0.

THE DEPARTMENT.

1. (I) Introductory Mathematics I

Basic set-theoretic and axiomatic concepts, number systems and
equations. A study of elementary functions, algebraically and by
the methods of analytic geometry.

3 class hours. Credit, 3.

MR. ————.

2. (II) Introductory Mathematics II

A terminal course intended for students whose curriculum calls
for just one year of mathematics. A continuation of Mathematics
1, including topics from the calculus, statistics, and mathematics
of finance.

3 class hours. Credit, 3.

MR. ————.

Prerequisite, Mathematics 1.

4. (II) Introductory Mathematics IV

A continuation of Mathematics 1 for those students intending
to take further courses in mathematics. Analytic geometry and
trigonometry.

3 class hours. Credit, 3.

MR. ————.

Prerequisite, Mathematics 1.

† On leave of absence.

5. (I) Introductory Engineering Mathematics

Trigonometry and algebra: a rapid basic review, theory of equations, simple determinants and the slide rule. Plane analytic geometry: the straight line, conic sections, selected higher plane curves, polar coordinates and parametric equations.

4 class hours. Credit, 4.

THE DEPARTMENT.

6. (II) Introductory Calculus for Engineering

Differentiation, with applications, technique of integration.

4 class hours. Credit, 4.

THE DEPARTMENT.

Prerequisite, Mathematics 5.

7. (I) Algebra and Trigonometry

For all freshmen, except majors in Engineering, who are required to take a full year of college mathematics. Fractions, quadratic equations, exponents, logarithms, variation, determinants of the second and third orders, and plane trigonometry.

3 class hours. Credit, 3.

THE DEPARTMENT.

8. (II) Algebra

This course is designed for the freshmen who do not plan to proceed to Calculus. Theory of equations, progressions, mensuration, number systems, and the elements of statistics and mathematics of investments.

3 class hours. Credit, 3.

THE DEPARTMENT.

10. (II) Algebra and Analytic Geometry

This course is designed for the freshmen who plan to take Calculus. Theory of equations, binominal theorem, determinants of higher order, and plane analytic geometry.

3 class hours. Credit, 3.

THE DEPARTMENT.

Prerequisite, Mathematics 7.

12. (II) Functional Mathematics

For freshmen who are not required to take a full year of college mathematics. Fractions, percentage, linear and quadratic equations with applications, exponents, logarithms, slide rule, proportion, graphs, statistics, progressions, and the elements of mathematics of investments.

3 class hours. Credit, 3.

THE DEPARTMENT.

227

14. (II) Trigonometry and Analytic Geometry

A study of the essential elements of elementary trigonometry and selected topics in algebra.

3 class hours.   Credit, 3.

THE DEPARTMENT.

Prerequisite, Mathematics 01.

29. (I) Differential Calculus

The basic ideas and methods of the differential calculus.

3 class hours.   Credit, 3.

THE DEPARTMENT.

Prerequisite, Mathematics 10.

30. (II) Integral Calculus

A continuation of Mathematics 29 into the field of the integral calculus, with special emphasis on application to problems.

3 class hours.   Credit, 3.

THE DEPARTMENT.

Prerequisite, Mathematics 29.

31. (I) Applied Calculus for Engineers

Area, volume, length of curve, centroid, moment of inertia, liquid pressure, work, partial differentiation.

4 class hours.   Credit, 4.

THE DEPARTMENT.

Prerequisite, Mathematics 6.

32. (II) Applied Calculus for Engineers

Multiple integrals, infinite series, expansion of functions, hyperbolic functions, differential equations.

4 class hours.   Credit, 4.

THE DEPARTMENT.

Prerequisite, Mathematics 31.

51. (I) Modern Synthetic Geometry

An extension of the geometry of the triangle and the circle. The course is intended especially for those planning to be high school teachers.

3 class hours.   Credit, 3.

MR. ROSE.

Prerequisite, Mathematics 30.

53. (I) 54. (II) Higher Algebra

Permutations, combinations, probability; mathematical induction, matrices, determinants, linear equations and dependence;

quadratic forms and elimination theory; the complex number system; polynomial equations; elementary theory of groups, rings and fields.

3 class hours. Credit, 3.

THE DEPARTMENT.

Prerequisite, Mathematics 10.

55. (I) Mathematics of Finance

The mathematical principles of simple and compound interest, annuities, depreciation, valuation of bonds, insurance. The development and applications of aids to computation in problems arising from ·financial transactions.

3 class hours. Credit, 3.

MR. BOUTELLE.

Prerequisite, Mathematics 7.

56. (II) Finite Differences and Probability (1954-55)

Given in alternate years.

3 class hours. Credit, 3.

MR. WAGNER.

Prerequisite, Mathematics 30.

60. (II) Spherical Trigonometry and Solid Analytic Geometry (1955-56)

The trigonometry of the sphere with application to terrestrial and celestial problems. This is followed by a study of higher plane curves and the analytic representation of points, lines, and surfaces in space. Given in alternate years.

3 class hours. Credit, 3.

MR. BOUTELLE.

Prerequisite, Mathematics 30.

62. (II) Statistics

The fundamental mathematical principles of statistical analysis. The derivation of the basic formulas used, and the study and discussion of such topics as averages, dispersion, skewness, curve fitting, least squares, linear and curvilinear correlation, probability and its application to statistics.

3 class hours. Credit, 3.

MR. WAGNER.

Prerequisite, Mathematics 30, previously or concurrently.

66. (II) Introduction to Higher Geometry (1955-56)

A study of various methods employed in the modern treatment of the geometry of points, lines, and conics. Such topics as homogenous point and line coordinates; infinite elements; harmonic division; groups of transformations and their invariants; and the elements of projective and other geometrics, will be considered. Given in alternate years.

3 class hours.   Credit, 3.
                                                          MR. ANDERSEN.
Prerequisite, Mathematics 10.

71. (I) Vector Analysis (1956-57)

The algebra and calculus of vectors. Applications to physics and other fields will be considered. Given in alternate years.

3 class hours.   Credit, 3.
                                                          MR. ANDERSEN.
Prerequisites, Mathematics 30; Physics 26.

72. (II) History of Mathematics (1954-55)

A study of mathematics as it has developed historically. Topics considered include classical problems and concepts of mathematics and the lives and times of the great mathematicians. This course is recommended especially for prospective high school teachers. Given in alternate years.

3 class hours.   Credit, 3.
                                                             MR. ROSE.
Prerequisite, Mathematics 30.

74. (II) Theory of Numbers (1955-56)

Euclid's Algorism, Theory of Prime Numbers, Aliquot parts, congruences, further topics in number theory. Given in alternate years.

3 class hours.   Credit, 3.
                                                        THE DEPARTMENT.
Prerequisite, Mathematics 30.

81. (I) Differential Geometry (1955-56)

Theory of the geometry of curves and surfaces in three dimensions. Given in alternate years.

3 class hours.   Credit, 3.
                                                        THE DEPARTMENT.
Prerequisite, Mathematics 30.

83. (I) Computational Methods (1956-57)

Errors and approximations in computation, methods of approximating roots of equations, approximation of functions, empirical curve, fitting, approximate integration, and numerical integration of ordinary differential equations. Given in alternate years.

3 class hours.   Credit, 3.
                                                        THE DEPARTMENT.
Prerequisite, Mathematics 30.

91. (I) (Intermediate) Calculus

Series, expansion of functions, partial differentation, envelopes, and multiple integrals.

3 class hours.   Credit, 3.

Prerequisite, Mathematics 30.   THE DEPARTMENT.

92. (II) Differential Equations

3 class hours.   Credit, 3.

Prerequisite, Mathematics 30.   THE DEPARTMENT.

93. (I) Advanced Calculus

The real number system, sequences, elementary theory of functions of one variable and of several variables, Riemannian integration, line integrals, Green's theorem.

3 class hours.   Credit, 3.

Prerequisite, Mathematics 91.   THE DEPARTMENT.

94. (II) Advanced Calculus

Double and triple integrals, improper integrals, gamma functions, Beta functions, elliptic functions, calculus of variations, Fourier Lines, Laplace Transforms.

3 class hours.   Credit, 3.

Prerequisite, Mathematics 93.   THE DEPARTMENT.

MILITARY SCIENCE AND TACTICS

COLONEL TARR, PMST, LIEUTENANT COLONEL GAUTHIER, ASSISTANT PMST, MAJOR EASTLAKE, ASSISTANT PMST, MAJOR TRAGLE, ASSISTANT PMST, MAJOR PETERS, ASSISTANT PMST, MAJOR WILSON, ASSISTANT PMST.

1. (I) 2. (II)

Theoretical and practical instruction in leadership, drill and exercise of command; first aid and hygiene; small arms weapons, maps and aerial photographs; military organization; tactics of the rifle squad; combat formations; and military problems and policy of the United States, National Defense Act and ROTC.

3 scheduled hours.   First semester, Credit, 3.
                                        Second semester, Credit, 2.
                                        ARMY INSTRUCTORS.

25. (I) 26. (II)

Theoretical and practical instruction in leadership, drill and exercise of command; the tactics and techniques of armor to include basic communications, basic automotive maintenance, history and missions of armor, familiarization with tank fighting compartment; scouting and patrolling; and crew-served weapons. Emphasis is placed on the functions, duties, and responsibilities of junior noncommissioned officers in the capacity of squad leaders, assistant squad leaders, and guidon bearers.

3 scheduled hours.   Credit, 2.
                                              ARMY INSTRUCTORS.

51. (I) 52. (II)

Theoretical and practical instruction in leadership, drill and exercise of command; the tactics and techniques of armor to include communications; tank gunnery; automotive maintenance; organization of armored units; platoon tactics; tank driving; troop leading; and map and aerial photographs. Emphasis is placed on the functions, duties, and responsibilities of senior non-commissioned officers.

5 scheduled hours.   Credit, 3.
                                              ARMY INSTRUCTORS.

75. (I) 76. (II)

Theoretical and practical instruction in leadership, drill and exercise of command; military administration; military law and boards; military teaching methods; psychological warfare; geographical foundations of national power; the tactics and techniques of armor to include combat intelligence, communications, tank gunnery; automotive maintenance; supply and evacuation; tactics; and tank driving. Emphasis is placed on the functions, duties, and responsibilities of junior commissioned officers.

5 scheduled hours.   Credit, 3.
                                              ARMY INSTRUCTORS.

AIR SCIENCE

COLONEL SMITH, PAS, LIEUTENANT COLONEL EWBANK, ASSISTANT PAS, MAJOR GRAPENTINE, ASSISTANT PÁS, MAJOR WELLS, ASSISTANT PAS, CAPTAIN COLE, ASSISTANT PAS, CAPTAIN HAMLIN, ASSISTANT PAS, CAPTAIN MCCOLLOR, ASSISTANT PAS, CAPTAIN SAGE, ASSISTANT PAS.

1. (I) 2. (II)

Theoretical and practical instruction in leadership, drill and exercise of command, history and development of aviation, fundamentals of global geography, international tensions and security organizations, and instruments of national military security.

3 scheduled hours.   First semester, Credit, 3.
                                   Second semester, Credit, 2.
                                      AIR FORCE INSTRUCTORS.

25. (I) 26. (II)

Theoretical and practical instruction in leadership, drill and exercise of command, careers in the United States Air Force, and elements of aerial warfare, consisting of a study of targets, weapons, aircraft, the air, ocean, bases, and forces.

3 scheduled hours.   Credit, 2.

AIR FORCE INSTRUCTORS.

51. (I) 52. (II)

Theoretical and practical instruction in leadership, drill and exercise of command, the air force commander and his staff, problem solving techniques, the communication process and air force correspondence, military law, courts and boards, air force base functions, and applied air science, consisting of a study of aircraft engineering, navigation, and weather.

5 scheduled hours.   Credit, 3.

AIR FORCE INSTRUCTORS.

75. (I) 76. (II)

Theoretical and practical instruction in leadership, drill and exercise of command, military aspects of world political geography, military aviation, and the evolution of warfare. Emphasis will be placed on preparation for commissioned service, and career guidance.

5 scheduled hours.   Credit, 3.

AIR FORCE INSTRUCTORS.

MUSIC

PROFESSOR ALVIANI†, MR. CONTINO.

Applied Music

Practical work in vocal or instrumental music at an approximate cost of $60.00 per semester.

15 1-hour lessons.   No credit.

25. (I) 26. (II) Fundamentals of Music

A study of the structure of music to meet the practical needs of the listener, performer, or creator. Sight singing, ear training, and keyboard practice are used to give context to the acquired music theory. All music majors are required to study piano while following this course.

1 class hour; 2 2-hour laboratory periods.   Credit, 3.
1:00-3:50 Tu., 1:00-2:50 Th.   THE DEPARTMENT.

† On leave of absence.

27. (I)   28. (II)   Vocal or Instrumental Music

This course is designed to improve the playing of instruments and/or the use of the singing voice, and to create further appreciation of music by actual performance. Students electing this course should take both Courses 27 and 28. Admission by permission of the instructor.

1 class hour.	Credit, 1.
Hour by arrangement.	THE DEPARTMENT.

29. (I)   30. (II)   Advanced Instrumental or Vocal Ensemble

A continuation of Music 27 and 28 for the training of performers in combination for voices or instruments. Solo performance and program planning are discussed and practiced. Students taking Course 29 should also take Course 30.

1 class hour.	Credit, 1.
Hour by arrangement.	THE DEPARTMENT.

51. (I) and (II)   Discovering Music

This elementary course is non-technical and is designed primarily for those students who would like to acquire a general background and knowledge of this art. With learning to listen its motive, the course deals with the elements of music, forms in music, musical composition, and selected composers. Excerpts from works most frequently heard and performed will be used as illustrations.

3 class hours.	Credit, 3.
10:00-10:50 or 11:00-11:50 M. W. F.	MR. ALVIANI.

52. (II)   Discovering Music

A continuation of Music 51. Students may register for this course without Music 51 if permission is granted by the instructor.

3 class hours.	Credit, 3.
	MR. ALVIANI.

55. (I)   Organization and Direction of Choral Groups

The aim of this course is to demonstrate the methods of developing school and community choral groups. Techniques and factors of good vocal performance are studied and practiced. The student may conduct choral groups during the semester. Previous musical experience is desirable. Admission by permission of the instructor.

2 class hours.	Credit, 2.
Hours by arrangement.	MR. ALVIANI.

56. (II)   Organization and Direction of Instrumental Groups

Different types of instrumental music, the problems of balancing instrumentation, the functioning of instruments are introduced

by the members of the class. Previous musical experience is desirable. Admission by permission of the instructor.
2 class hours. Credit, 2.
Hours by arrangement. MR. CONTINO.

61. (I) Masterpieces of Music

Selected masterpieces from musical literature are intensively analyzed, and a relationship is drawn between the compositions and the social-cultural periods in the history of music.
3 class hours. Credit, 3.
9:00-9:50 Tu. Th. S. MR. CONTINO.
Prerequisite, Music 51 or 52 recommended but not required.

62. (I) and (II) Music in the Elementary Grades

Designed for the classroom teacher having little or no formal training in music, this course deals with the principles of musical development with particular emphasis on classroom presentation. Using the class as a laboratory, rote and reading songs are examined and processes of presentation are evaluated.
3 class hours. Credit, 3.
9:00-9:50 M. W. F. MR. CONTINO.

75. (I) 76. (II) Music Theory

The development of skill in the use of music fundamentals. Elementary and advanced harmony are studied and practiced. Techniques of elementary counterpoint are presented to show their relationship to vocal and instrumental music.
2 class hours; 1 2-hour laboratory period. Credit, 3.
10:00-10:50 Tu. Th.; 1:00-2:50 W. THE DEPARTMENT.

77. (I) 78. (II) Form and Analysis.

An approach to the study of music through observation of its forms, analysis of its rhythms, melodies, and harmonies as used in the vocal and instrumental compositions of various periods in the historical development of music. The theory of conducting is discussed, studied, evaluated, and its techniques practiced.
1 class hour; 2 2-hour laboratory periods. Credit, 3.
10:00-10:50 F.; 10:00-11:50 M. W. THE DEPARTMENT.

79. (I) Score Reading and Analysis

Through listening and reading assignments the characteristics of voices and instruments are studied and the results are applied to practical arranging for vocal and instrumental groups of various types, sizes, and combinations.
3 class hours. Credit, 3.
THE DEPARTMENT.

80. (II) Score Reading and Composition

A continuation of Music 79. In this course the student is expected to study the methods and materials of original composition. Procedures for processing, printing, publishing, and marketing are examined. Laws and regulations governing performance, publication, personnel, and other related activities are discussed.
3 class hours.   Credit, 3.

THE DEPARTMENT.

81. (I) Music and History

A comprehensive study of the periods in music history—Renaissance, Baroque, Classic, Romantic, and Modern—so that the student may feel their quality, understand their enthusiasms, recognize their resources and limitations, and identify their habits of thought and style.
3 class hours.   Credit, 3.

THE DEPARTMENT.

82. (II) Music and Research Methods

Recommended to students interested in bibliography, references, source materials, rental libraries, etc., who expect to work in the field of music or related fields. In addition to compilation, the student will investigate a special area of study and report the findings in written form.
3 class hours.   Credit, 3.

THE DEPARTMENT.

Each student will be required to study two semesters of Piano and will be expected to pass an examination, required for graduation, not later than the end of the junior year. In addition, each student will be required to study two semesters of a major instrument or voice. If the major instrument is Piano, the student will be advised to study four semesters.

NURSING

PROFESSOR MAHER, ASSOCIATE PROFESSOR GILMORE,
ASSOCIATE PROFESSOR MACDONALD, MISS DIMAGGIO.

26. (II) Orientation to Nursing

An introductory course in nursing. Unit I is designed to familiarize the beginning student with the scope of professional nursing in the community and in the hospital, and the privileges and responsibilities of one who has chosen nursing as a profession. Unit II provides an opportunity for the student to gain a foundation upon which to build the subsequent nursing courses. Emphasis is placed upon the development of interpersonal skills and the principles and methods óf teaching in nursing.

90 hours in the 4th academic semester.   Credit, 4.

THE NURSING DIVISION.

27. (S) Fundamentals of Nursing

The basic course in nursing practice. It is designed as a foundation course for subsequent clinical nursing courses. Beginning with a consideration of the basic needs of patients in general, the student is guided, through a case study approach, to become increasingly able to identify the particular needs of selected patients, and to design an individualized nursing care plan. Emphasis is placed on the understanding of the scientific principles of the nursing procedure, the acquisition of manipulative skills, the significance of nurse-patient relationships, individualized patient teaching, and the unique role of the nurse in the therapeutic plan. Direct nursing care of selected patients on the medical and surgical units will be an integral part of this course.

10 hours per week of clinical practice for 9 weeks
    in the summer following the 4th academic
    semester.   Credit, 9.

MISS GILMORE AND ASSISTANTS.

28. (S) Social and Historical Foundations of Nursing

A survey course of nursing from the pre-Christian era to the present. The influence of society upon nursing in the various historical periods will serve to familiarize the student with the development of nursing as a profession.

30 hours in the summer following the 4th aca-
    demic semester.   Credit, 2.

MISS MAHER.

51. (I) Medical and Surgical Nursing I

A combined course which enables the nurse to become familiar with the major health problems of the community as reflected by the adults receiving care on the medical and surgical units, and to acquire the specialized nursing abilities essential to provide comprehensive nursing care. The significance of the individual's total response to threats of living as reflected in illness; the relationships of prevention and early detection and medical resources to treatment, rehabilitation and prognosis will be emphasized. Pertinent course content regarding the pathological findings, nutrition in illness, the pharmacological and special therapies are presented in

relation to the health problems under consideration and the particular needs of patients in various age groups and different sexes. 28 weeks of correlated clinical nursing practice in
the care of selected patients on the Medical
and Surgical Units and in the Out-Patient Service; 8 weeks Operating Room Services and 4
weeks Therapeutic Diet Practice.   Credit, 16.

MISS GILMORE AND ASSISTANTS; MEDICAL AND
ALLIED PROFESSIONAL STAFFS OF THE HOSPITAL.

52A. (II) Nursing of Children I

The course is designed to help the student to identify the persistent behavior patterns of children which enhance or impede emotional maturity. Through case studies, conferences and discussions the student will be helped to understand more fully the child's behavior and to consider family and community responsibility for preventing emotional disturbances.

2 weeks clinical experience with young children.   Credit, 2.

INSTRUCTORS IN PEDIATRIC AND PSYCHIATRIC NURSING.

52B. (II) Nursing of Children II

The physical, educational, social, and spiritual needs of the child in health are reviewed as a basis for understanding the child who is acutely ill; the child whose hospital experience is extended over a period of time, and the child displaying evidences of emotional stress. Basic principles of the care of children with special needs are taught concurrently with the clinical experience.

12 weeks clinical experience in the care of selected children.   Credit, 5.

MEDICAL AND PROFESSIONAL STAFFS OF
COOPERATING HOSPITALS AND AGENCIES.

54. (II) Psychiatric Nursing

Through the presentation and discussion of the dynamics of human behavior, the content of the course is extended to include the fundamentals of psychopathology related to the basic origin of conflict in patients. The specialized abilities and skills of the nurses in providing care to the mentally ill patients are presented in order that the understanding of the patient's behavior will lead to a constructive nurse-patient relationship thereby enabling the students to participate more fully in the therapeutic plan. The relationship of selected patient's behavior pathology to early manifestations of behavior deviation, early diagnosis, treatment, rehabilitation and prevention will be discussed in case conferences.

Community planning resources and responsibility in regard to this major health problem will be explored.

12 weeks clinical experience with care of selected
  patients in a Psychiatric Hospital. Credit, 6.
    INSTRUCTOR IN PSYCHIATRIC NURSING; MEDICAL AND
    ALLIED PROFESSIONAL STAFFS OF THE HOSPITALS.

56. (S) Tuberculosis Nursing

The principles and practice of nursing the patient with tuberculosis will be utilized as a basis for extending the student's knowledge of tuberculosis; its significance as a major health problem, the special needs of patients with long-term illnesses and the epidemiological aspects of communicable diseases. Clinical experience in the care of selected patients will be combined with clinics, conferences, and group discussion.

6 weeks clinical experience in the care of selected
  patients with tuberculosis. Credit, 3.
    MEDICAL AND ALLIED PROFESSIONAL
    STAFFS OF THE HOSPITAL.

57. (I) Maternity Nursing

The course content is developed around the meaning of pregnancy to the patient and the family with special emphasis on the understanding of the mother's physiological and psychological needs before, during, and after the birth of the infant. The specialized abilities of the nurse are taught in relation to an understanding of the phenomena of pregnancy, the birth process, immediate care of the mother and infant, newborn care, the importance for early constructive mother-child relationship and patient teaching.

12 weeks clinical practice including prenatal
  clinic, labor and birth room, newborn and premature nurseries, post-partal units and clinics. Credit, 5.
    MEDICAL AND ALLIED PROFESSIONAL
    STAFFS OF THE MATERNITY HOSPITAL.

58. (II) Public Health Nursing

An introduction to the role of the public health nurse in a family health service. Through a study of an experience with selected families the student will be helped to acquire an understanding of abilities essential for public health nursing practice.

8 weeks field experience with selected families. Credit, 3.
    MISS MAHER AND EDUCATIONAL DI-
    RECTORS OF COOPERATING AGENCIES.

60. Medical and Surgical Nursing II

Instruction and clinical practice in the nursing care of patients admitted to the gynecological, urological, neurological, ear, eye, nose and throat, dermatological outpatient and emergency services. 12 weeks clinical practice in the care of selected

patients in the above services.   Credit, 5.

MISS GILMORE AND ASSISTANTS; MEDICAL AND ALLIED PROFESSIONAL STAFFS OF THE HOSPITAL.

61. (Summer) Team Nursing

The purpose, organization and functioning of the nursing team in the ward units will be presented. Emphasis will be placed on the privileges and responsibilities of the team leader and team members in providing nursing care to patients.

4 weeks clinical experience.   Credit, 2.

THE NURSING DIVISION.

63. (I) Advanced Medical and Surgical Nursing

Nursing care of selected patients with major health problems who require extensive medical and/or surgical therapy and nursing care.

8 weeks clinical experience.   Credit, 3.

MISS GILMORE AND ASSISTANTS; MEDICAL AND PROFESSIONAL STAFF MEMBERS OF THE HOSPITAL.

65. (I) Senior Elective (Internship)

Public Health Nursing Service or Psychiatric Nursing or Hospital Team Leader or Tuberculosis Nursing or Maternity Nursing or Pediatric Nursing or Health Services for the Ambulant Patient or Operating Room Nursing or Advanced Medical and Surgical Nursing or Rehabilitation in Nursing or Community Nursing.

12 weeks.   Credit, 4.

66. (II) Senior Nursing Seminar

Through a group approach to the study of persistent problems in nursing, this course will provide an opportunity for the student to gain an understanding of the methodology and techniques involved in a study of a problem, the role of professional nursing organizations and the opportunities and responsibilities of graduate nurses in modern society.

Credit, 4.

THE NURSING DIVISION AND CONSULTANTS.

OLERICULTURE

PROFESSOR SNYDER, ASSISTANT PROFESSOR TUTTLE, MR. JOHNSON.

25. (I) General Olericulture

A study of the factors affecting the growth of plants which are essential to a basic understanding of the cultural requirements of vegetable and other horticultural crops.

2 class hours; 1 2-hour laboratory period. Credit, 3.
MR. JOHNSON.

51. (I) Plant Nutrition

A critical study of the water and nutrient requirement of vegetable plants as applied to irrigation, soils and their preparation, manures, fertilizers, lime, green manures and crop residues.

3 class hours. Credit, 3.
8:50-8:50 M. W. F. MR. TUTTLE.

52. (II) Plant Culture

A study of certain environmental factors which influence the culture of vegetables as applied to actual commercial practices.

3 class hours. Credit, 3.
8:00-8:50 M. W. F. MR. JOHNSON.

73. (I) Vegetable Marketing Practices

A consideration of the various factors, techniques, and methods in harvesting and preparing vegetables for market, including marketing centers, production areas, market and consumer preference, packing house facilities and equipment, and pre-market storage. Trips to nearby growers and markets will be required at a cost of not over ten dollars.

3 class hours. Credit, 3.
10:00-10:50 M. W. F. MR. SNYDER.
Prerequisite, Agricultural Economics 55.

74. (II) Merchandising of Perishables

Discussion and demonstrations in this course will include the various techniques, practices, and methods that are used in selling and distributing horticultural commodities through both wholesale and retail outlets from the farm to the ultimate consumer. Trips to the Boston and New York markets may be elected by the student at a reasonable cost.

3 class hours. Credit, 3.
10:00-10:50 M. W. F. MR. SNYDER.

241

75. (I) Systematic Olericulture

A detailed study of variety identification; nomenclature and classification; history, variety improvement and seed sources; judging and exhibiting.

1 class hour; 2 2-hour laboratory periods.   Credit, 3.
Hours by arrangement.   MR. SNYDER.

76. (II) Greenhouse Crops and Plant Growing (1954-55)

A study of the culture of greenhouse crops including cucumbers, tomatoes, lettuce, rhubarb, and mushrooms; the growing of seeding plants both under glass and in the open for local retail or wholesale business. Given in alternate years.

2 class hours; 1 2-hour laboratory period.   Credit, 3.
Hours by arrangement.   MR. JOHNSON.

78. (II) Commercial Olericulture

A study of the problems in the commercial production of vegetables; general culture, fertilizers and manures, machinery, labor, harvesting, and marketing. One or two trips to important markets and truck growing sections are required. Twenty-five dollars will cover the cost of these trips.

2 class hours; 1 2-hour laboratory period.   Credit, 3.
Hours by arrangement.   MR. TUTTLE.

81. (I)   82. (II) Seminar

Advanced study of problems relating to vegetable production.

1 class hour.   Credit, 1.
Hours by arrangement.   THE DEPARTMENT.

PHILOSOPHY

ASSOCIATE PROFESSOR SHUTE, ASSISTANT PROFESSOR ROGERS,
MR. CARMICHAEL.

61. (I) Introduction to Philosophy

A general approach to philosophy both from the standpoint of method and content; an attempt to understand and evaluate contemporary ideas.

3 class hours.   Credit, 3.
MR. ROGERS, MR. CARMICHAEL.

62. (II) History of Philosophy

A survey of the development of western thought from the early Greeks to the present.

3 class hours.   Credit, 3.
MR. SHUTE.

63. (I) Logic

A study of the principles, problems and methods of critical thinking; emphasis upon principles and methods of formal logic; critical study of inductive reasoning and scientific method with applications to current problems.

3 class hours.   Credit, 3.

MR. ROGERS.

64. (II) Ethics

The meaning of good and evil, right and wrong; survey of ethical theories and practices both historical and contemporary; an attempt to evaluate these theories with reference to modern ethical problems.

3 class hours.   Credit, 3.

MR. ROGERS, MR. CARMICHAEL.

65. (I) History of Philosophy — Ancient and Medieval

A survey of development of western thought with emphasis on the cultural factors which generated and interacted with the successive philosophical interpretations of man's experience.

3 class hours.   Credit, 3.

MR. SHUTE.

66. (II) History of Philosophy—Modern

Attention is centered on the impact of modern science on the development of man's comprehensive understanding of the world, of the powers and limitations of knowledge, and of the basis of his valuations.

3 class hours.   Credit, 3.

MR. SHUTE.

72. (II) Philosophy of Science

A study of the backgrounds, presuppositions, methods and general theories of modern physical, biological and social sciences. Readings selected from the works of leading scientists and philosophers will be used as the basis of class discussions which will attempt to explore the great scientific achievements of our time and to assess their importance in the student's construction of a mature philosophic orientation.

3 class hours.   Credit, 3.

MR. ROGERS.

81. (I) Philosophy of Religion

A survey of the contrasting types of religious philosophy in the contemporary western world and Asia, with a critical and construc-

PHILOSOPHY

tive study of basic issues, such as the meaning of knowledge in the
field of religion, the nature of faith, and the religious interpretation of reality.
3 class hours.   Credit, 3.
                                                       MR. SHUTE.

82. (II) Aesthetics

A study of the leading modern theories of the nature of art, the
analysis of aesthetic experience, the distinctive function of art in
culture and personality, and the principles of criticism.
3 class hours.   Credit, 3.
                                                       MR. SHUTE.

83. (I) Readings in Ancient Philosophy

Selections are read from Plato's dialogues and from the works of
Aristotle. A study is made of the leading philosophical issues discussed by these writers, with emphasis on ideas which became basic
in the development of western thought.
3 class hours.   Credit, 3.
                                                       MR. SHUTE.

84. (II) Readings in Modern Philosophy

Selections are read from Locke, Hume, Kant, and Whitehead, to
display the leading ways in which modern thinkers have looked
upon the nature of the universe and the possibilities and limitations of knowledge.
3 class hours.   Credit, 3.
                                                       MR. SHUTE.

85. (I) Metaphysics

The field of metaphysics defined in distinction from the field of
science, contrasting theories of reality offered by contemporary naturalism and idealism, especially in the light of recent developments in biological and physical science; analysis of basic ideas
which will enable the student to continue a fruitful development
of his own philosophy.
3 class hours.   Credit, 3.
                                                       MR. SHUTE.

86. (II) Theory of Knowledge

Types of knowledge and correlated methods of knowing; questions of certainty, probability, and limits of knowledge; ways of
expression, such as mathematical formulae, language, and art, and

their involvement in the knowing process; the nature of the relation between the knowing subject and the known object.
3 class hours.   Credit, 3.
MR. CARMICHAEL.

PHYSICAL EDUCATION FOR MEN

PROFESSOR McGUIRK, PROFESSOR KAUFFMAN, ASSOCIATE PROFESSOR
BRIGGS, ASSISTANT PROFESSOR RICCI, ASSISTANT PROFESSOR SAL-
WAK, ASSISTANT PROFESSOR DAVIS, MR. BOSCO, MR. GARBER.

ACTIVITY COURSES

3. (I) 4. (II) Physical Activity Course

The object of the course is to help every student, through regularity and continuity of physical activity, to realize not only his physical and mental capacities, but learn to use them as an intelligent, cooperative, and efficient citizen. The students are given motor ability tests, expected to learn to swim and to meet minimum standards in the basic skills through participation in team sports and exercise.
3 class hours.   Credit, 1.
THE DEPARTMENT.

33. (I) 34. (II) Physical Education

A continuation of Physical Education 3 and 4.
3 class hours.   Credit, 1.
THE DEPARTMENT.

SKILLS AND TECHNIQUES IN PHYSICAL EDUCATION

The following courses are concerned with the methods and techniques of applied physical education. Classroom presentation, field, court, and floor demonstrations are emphasized. These courses are primarily for students enrolled for a Bachelor of Science degree with a major in physical education. Non-major admission only by permission of the instructor.

5. (I) Skills and Techniques

Development of fundamental skills and methods of teaching and organizing groups for participation in track and field, basketball.
60 clock hours per semester.   Credit, 1.
MR. CURRAN.

6. (II) Skills and Techniques

Fundamental skills in life-saving and water-safety methods. Successful completion resulting in qualification as American Red Cross Water Safety Instructor.

60 clock hours per semester.   Credit, 1.
                                                MR. ROGERS.

35. (I) Skills and Techniques

Development of fundamental skills, methods of teaching and organizing groups for participation in soccer, speedball, volleyball.

60 clock hours per semester.   Credit, 1.
                                       MR. BRIGGS, MR. RICCI.

36. (II) Skills and Techniques

Fundamental skills and instruction in techniques of teaching elementary apparatus, tumbling exercises, pyramids, construction of elementary gymnastic routines.

60 clock hours per semester.   Credit, 1.
                                                MR. BOSCO.

63. (I) Skills and Techniques

Fundamental skills and techniques of teaching golf and badminton.

60 clock hours per semester.   Credit, 1.
                                   MR. O'ROURKE, MR. RICCI.

64. (II) Skills and Techniques

Fundamentals of movement and rhythmic response basic to elementary dance techniques. Instruction in skills in archery and participation in various types of competitive events.

60 clock hours per semester.   Credit, 1.
                                       MR. BRIGGS, MR. BOSCO.

83. (I) Skills and Techniques

Fundamental skills, instruction in techniques of teaching tennis and wrestling.

60 clock hours per semester.   Credit, 1.
                                 MR. KOSAKOWSKI, MR. ————.

84. (II) Skills and Techniques

Instruction and participation in indoor and outdoor games of high and low organization. Emphasis on student teaching within class.

60 clock hours per semester.   Credit, 1.
                                       MR. DAVIS, MR. GARBER.

MAJOR COURSES

21. (I) Introduction to Physical Education

Origins of physical education, fundamental concepts, current status in education, qualifications and professional opportunities in the field.

3 class hours. Credit, 3.

MR. KAUFFMAN.

22. (II) First Aid and Safety

Materials applicable to the immediate care of the injured, causes of accidents and procedures designed to develop habits and attitudes leading to safe behavior through desirable safety practices. Certified by American Red Cross for First Aid Instructor training.

3 class hours. Credit, 3.

MR. BRIGGS.

23. (I) Principles and Practices in Health Education

Principles of maintaining and improving individual health, pupil needs, fundamentals related to planning instruction on the elementary and secondary school level, resources in health education, evaluation of materials.

3 class hours. Credit, 3.

MR. SALWAK.

41. (I) Human Anatomy

A study of the gross structure and function of the human body.

3 class hours. Credit, 3.

MR. RICCI.

42. (II) Kinesiology

A course aimed to give the anatomical application basic to a thorough understanding of the mechanical problems in motor skills.

3 class hours. Credit, 3.

MR. KAUFFMAN.

Prerequisite, Physical Education 41.

43. (I) Officiating

Technique and practice in officiating football and soccer.

1 class hour; 1 2-hour laboratory period. Credit, 1.

MR. —————.

44. (II) Officiating

Technique and practice in officiating basketball and baseball.

1 class hour; 1 2-hour laboratory period. Credit, 1.

MR. —————.

53. (II) Physical Education in Elementary Schools

Aims and objectives of modern materials and methods of teaching group games, rhythmic activities, dance relays, stunts and lead-up games for the elementary school.

2 class hours; 1 2-hour laboratory period.   Credit, 3.

MR. —————.

54. (II) Physical Education in Secondary Schools

A course in modern methods of teaching physical education in secondary schools. Includes objectives, content material, and organization procedures at the secondary level.

3 class hours.   Credit, 3.

MR. RICCI.

55. (I) Organization and Administration of Physical Education

Problems and procedures in physical education, organization of programs, class schedules, classification of students, equipment, records, finance, intramurals, construction and maintenance of gymnasia, swimming pools, locker rooms, and outdoor play areas.

3 class hours.   Credit, 3.

MR. McGUIRK.

56. (II) Adaptive Physical Education

A program of developmental activities, games, sports, and rhythms suited to the interests, capacities and limitations of students with disabilities who may not safely engage in unrestricted participation in the vigorous activities of the general physical education program.

2 class hours; 1 2-hour laboratory period.   Credit, 3.

MR. GARBER.

Prerequisite, Physical Education 42.

57. (I) Methods and Materials; Coaching Football, Basketball

The analysis of and instruction in individual skills and team play, types of offense and defense, teaching techniques.

2 class hours; 1 2-hour laboratory period.   Credit, 3.

MR. O'ROURKE, MR. CURRAN.

58. (II) Methods and Materials; Coaching Swimming, Baseball

Designed to develop individual skills and techniques of teaching and coaching swimming and diving, stroke analysis, conduct of

meets, water sports. Fundamentals of individual skills, position and team play, offensive and defensive strategy in baseball.
2 class hours; 1 2-hour laboratory period. Credit, 3.

MR. ROGERS, MR. LORDEN.

60. (II) Organized Camping Administration

This course includes the history and philosophy of organized camping, minimum standards of health and safety, modern trends, and the camping industry.
3 class hours. Credit, 3.

MR. BRIGGS.

70. (II) Resources in Recreation

Including types of recreational areas, recreational resources, recreational needs of the people, geography of recreation, competitors of recreational land use, economic aspects of federal, state, and local recreational systems.
3 class hours. Credit, 3.

MR. BRIGGS.

71. (I) 72. (II) Special Problems Course

Presentation and discussion of research work in physical education, health, or athletics.
3 class hours. Credit, 3.

THE DEPARTMENT.

73. (I) Philosophy and Principles of Physical Education

Contemporary interpretations and critical analysis. The compilation and organization of material in a functional relationship for the foundation of policies and program construction.
3 class hours. Credit, 3.

MR. KAUFFMAN.

74. (II) Tests and Measurements

This course considers the status of measurements in physical education, an historical sketch, typical of contributions in anthropometrics, strength tests, ability and achievement tests, cardiac functional tests, neuro-muscular control tests, and sports technique tests; and it includes the tools of measurement, indices, and the theory and practice of test administration.
2 class hours; 1 2-hour laboratory period. Credit, 3.

MR. SALWAK.

75. (I) Physiology of Exercise

Application of basic physiological concepts to the program of physical education, emphasis upon the physiological effects and adjustments accruing from participation in physical activity. Major factors in diet, conditioning, fatigue, and physical fitness are considered.

3 class hours.   Credit, 3.
                                                        Mr. Davis.

Prerequisite, Physical Education 42.

80. (II) Driver Education Instructor Course

This course includes driver education and driver training at the instructor's level, and is designed to orient the student to live safely through skillful and efficient behavior on streets and highways. Leads to certification as instructor in driver education and driver training.

2 class hours.   Credit, 2.
                                                        Mr. Briggs.

81. (I) Methods and Materials; Coaching Soccer, Track

Analyses of and instruction in individual skills and team play, types of offense and defense, teaching techniques in soccer. Analyses of form and coaching technique in fundamental skills in track and field events.

2 class hour; 1 2-hour laboratory period.   Credit, 3.
                                   Mr. Briggs, Mr. ————.

83. (I) Athletic Injuries—Prevention and Care

The use of proper personal and field equipment, support methods, conditioning exercises, the medical examination, therapeutic aids, and the clinical use of physiotherapy equipment.

2 class hours.   Credit, 2.

Prerequisite, Physical Education 42.   Mr. Ricci.

PHYSICAL EDUCATION FOR WOMEN

Professor Totman, Miss Hubbard, Miss Riggs†, Miss
Ogilvie, Miss Reid, Miss Robertson, Miss Wallace.

7. (I) 8. (II) Physical Education

Students are required to participate in one term of dancing, in one team sport, and to pass a safety test in swimming. Except for these requirements, all unrestricted students may select any ac-

† On leave of absence.

tivity which is offered. Fall season: field hockey, volleyball, soccer, archery, tennis, swimming. Winter season: basketball, volleyball, badminton, swimming, life saving (by permission), modern dance, square dance, calisthenics, posture training. Spring season: softball, soccer, archery, swimming, modern dance.

3 class hours.   Credit, 2.

THE DEPARTMENT.

27. (I) 28. (II) Physical Education

The activities offered in Courses 7 and 8 are continued. In addition, advanced modern dance is offered in the fall season and water safety instruction in the winter season. Unrestricted students may select any activity which is offered.

3 class hours.   Credit, 2.

THE DEPARTMENT.

63. (I) 64. (II) Teaching Sports for Secondary Schools

Designed to give the fundamentals of teaching and officiating of team sports for women appropriate for the secondary school level. Course content includes development and knowledge of techniques, knowledge of rules, teaching progressions, class procedures, and instruction in officiating related to the following activities: hockey, soccer, speedball, volleyball, basketball, and softball.

1 class hour; 3 laboratory hours.   Credit, 2.

MISS RIGGS.

65. (I) Play Activities and Games for Elementary Schools

A study of the place of physical education in the schools with emphasis on procedures, organization and teaching techniques. There will be more opportunity to learn games and other play activities for children from 5 to 14 years.

1 class hour; 3 laboratory hours.   Credit, 2.

MISS TOTMAN.

66. (II) Rhythms and Dancing for the Elementary School

The course will include the development of rhythmic sense through basic motor skills; dramatizations; the construction of simple dance forms; folk dances and singing games. There will be practice in planning the rhythm and dance program in the elementary school from nursery school through sixth grade.

1 class hour; 3 laboratory hours.   Credit, 2.

MISS HUBBARD.

251

PHYSICS

PROFESSOR POWERS, PROFESSOR ALDERMAN, ASSOCIATE PROFESSOR ROSS, ASSISTANT PROFESSOR MATHIESON, ASSISTANT PROFESSOR FISHER, ASSISTANT PROFESSOR WANG, MR. CROOKER, MR. NICHOLSON.

25. (I) Mechanics, Sound, and Heat

This course is largely a study of the following and related topics; equilibrium of bodies; forms of energy; motion, fluids; surface tension; molecular phenomena; elasticity; wave-motion; sound; thermometry; expansion; hygrometry; transmission of heat; changes of state; radiation.

3 class hours; 1 2-hour laboratory period.   · Credit, 4.

THE DEPARTMENT.

Prerequisite, Mathematics 5, 7, or 14.

26. (II) Light and Electricity

Includes wave-theory of light; optical instruments; analysis of light; interference; polarization; magnetism; electrostatics; production and properties of electric currents; electrical appliances and machines; oscillatory circuits; vacuum tubes, and related topics.

3 class hours; 1 2-hour laboratory period.   Credit, 4.

THE DEPARTMENT.

27. (I) General Physics

The topics covered are mechanics, sound, and heat with special emphasis on the mathematical development of· statics, centroids, and Gauss' theorem.

3 class hours; 1 2-hour laboratory period.   Credit, 4.

THE DEPARTMENT.

Prerequisites, Mathematics 5, 6, or equivalent; Mathematics 31 previously or concurrently.

28. (II) General Physics

The topics covered are light and electricity with special emphasis on the mathematical development of Gauss' theorem, dielectrics and A.C. electricity.

3 class hours; 1 2-hour laboratory period.   Credit; 4.

THE DEPARTMENT.

Prerequisites, Physics 27.

51. (I) 52. (II) Magnetism, Electricity, Photo-electricity, Thermionics and Applications

Course 51 deals with direct currents (mesh currents often used); Course 52 with alternating currents (low and high frequency), applications of thermionics, and photo-electricity. These courses are planned to give the student a good training in the theory and methods of measurement in the indicated and allied subjects. Modern methods are stressed and instruments of precision are used.
2 class hours; 1 2-hour laboratory period. Credit, 3.
8:00-8:50 Tu., Th.; 10:00-11:50 Tu. or 1:00-2:50 W. or Th.

MR. POWERS.

Prerequisites, Physics 26 and Mathematics 29 for Course 51; Physics 51 for Course 52.

54. (II) Meteorology

The course deals with the application of certain concepts of mechanics and thermodynamics to the consideration of various atmospheric phenomena such as condensation, pressure, radiation, motion, fronts, etc. The treatment is theoretical in nature but the observed phenomena are correlated to the theory with a descriptive approach. The laboratory deals with weather observations, preparation of weather charts, and the techniques of weather forecasting.
2 class hours; 1 2-hour laboratory period. Credit, 3.
2:00-2:50 Tu. Th.; laboratory hours by arrangement.

MR. CROOKER.

Prerequisites, Physics 26; Mathematics 30.

55. (I) 56. (II) Mechanics

Development of the fundamental concepts of dynamics with applications to particles and rigid bodies in translation and rotation. One laboratory period may be substituted for one class hour.
3 class hours. Credit, 3.
9:00-9:50 Tu., Th.; laboratory by arrangement. MR. Ross.
Prerequisites, Physics 26; Mathematics 30.

57. (I) Introduction to Astronomy

The general facts and principles of astronomy, mainly qualitative, starting with basic physical principles. Periods of evening observation will be substituted for lecture hours when feasible. This course may not be taken for major credit in Physics.
3 class hours. Credit, 3.
8:00-8:50 M. W. F. MR. Ross.
Prerequisite, Mathematics 7 or equivalent.

PHYSICS

58. (II) Photography
Class work and laboratory practice in the fundamentals of photography. Types of cameras, characteristics of photographic emulsions, exposure and exposure meters, processing of negatives and prints, enlarging, composition, photomicrography. Limited to ten students. This course may not be taken for major credit in Physics.
2 class hours; 1 4-hour laboratory period. Credit, 3.
3:00-3:50 M. W.; 1:00-5:00 F.   Mr. Powers.
Prerequisites, Physics 25, 26; Chemistry 1, 2; Mathematics 10.

60. (II) Sound and Acoustics
A study of vibrations, vibrating bodies, coupled systems, sound structure, and acoustic properties. The work will include many applications of sound to technical and commercial fields.
2 class hours; 1 2-hour laboratory period. Credit, 3.
                                                        Mr. Alderman.
Prerequisites, Physics 55 or its equivalent.

61. (I) 62. Heat and Thermodynamics
A study of heat exchanges and energy changes due to heat in systems of matter. The subject material and experimental methods are useful in other branches of science.
2 class hours; 1 2-hour laboratory period. Credit, 3.
10:00-10:50 Tu., Th.; laboratory by arrangement.
                                                        Mr. Alderman.
Prerequisites, Physics 26; Mathematics 29.

63. (I) 64. (II) Optics
An intermediate course in the theory of light. Work in geometrical and physical optics is done. Precision instruments are used in the laboratory.
2 class hours; 1 2-hour laboratory period. Credit, 3.
1:00-1:50 Tu., Th.; laboratory hours by arrangement.
                                                        Mr. Alderman.
Prerequisites, Physics 26; Mathematics 29.

75. (I) 76. (II) Advanced Experimental Work in Selected Topics
These courses are largely experimental and the subject matter is adapted to the needs of the individual student. The research viewpoint is emphasized. The class hour is used for a course in precision of measurements.
1 class hour; 2 2-hour laboratory periods. Credit, 3.
                                                        Mr. Wang.
Prerequisites, Mathematics 29, 30; two of the following year courses: Physics 51-52, 55-56, 61-62, 53-64.

254

85. (I) 86. (II) · Modern Physics

Typical subjects studied are theories of the atom, radiation, quantum theory; spectra, X-ray analysis, nuclear reactions.
3 class hours.   Credit, 3.
9:00-9:50 M. W. F.   Mr. Wang.
Prerequisites, Physics 52, 64, and 12 other junior-senior physics credits; Mathematics 30.

95. (I) 96. (II) Electronics

2 class hours; 1 2-hour laboratory period.   Credit, 3.
10:00-10:50 M. F.; 10:00-11:50 W.   Mr. Wang.
Prerequisites, Physics 51, 52; Mathematics 29, 30.

POMOLOGY

Professor French, Associate Professor Roberts,
Mr. J. F. Anderson, Mr. Fish

26. (II) Small Fruits

A study of the·growing of raspberries, blackberries, strawberries, currants, blueberries, cranberries, and grapes, dealing with such questions as varieties, selecting a site for the plantation, soils, fertilizers, pruning, harvesting, and marketing.
2 class hours; 1 2-hour laboratory period.   Credit, 3.
10:00-10:50 M. F.; 1:00-2:50 W. or F.   Mr. Anderson.

53. (I) General Pomology

A study of the most improved practices in tree fruit production, including orchard sites and soils, laying out and setting the orchard, the structure and growth of fruit plants; the bearing habits, pruning, fertilizers, pollination; pest control; harvesting and marketing the crop.
2 class hours; 1 2-hour laboratory period.   Credit, 3.
10:00-10:50 Tu., Th.; 3:00-4:50 Th. or F.
Mr. Roberts, Mr. Anderson.

56. (II) Orchard Pest Control

This course is especially designed to familiarize the student with: (a) spraying and dusting machinery; (b) methods in the application of materials used in orchards, with the important considerations for spraying each fruit and for combating each orchard pest; (c) preparation for use of the common fungicides and insecticides.
2 class hours; 1 2-hour laboratory period.   Credit, 3.
8:00-8:50 Tu., Th.; 1:00-2:50 Tu.   Mr. Roberts.

255

57. (I) Fruit Judging

Practice in the identification, selection, and judging of fruit for exhibition purposes. From this class a team is selected to represent the University in Intercollegiate Fruit Judging Contests.

1 class hour.   Credit, 1.
Hours by arrangement.   MR. ANDERSON.

75. (I) Systematic Pomology (1956-57)

A study of the more important kinds and varieties of fruits grown in the United States, their relationships and nomenclature. Particular emphasis is placed upon the identification, classification and value of varieties including a study of the characters of the plant as well as the fruit. Given in alternate years.

1 class hour; 3 2-hour laboratory periods.   Credit, 4.
8:00-8:50 Tu.; 1:00-2:50 M. W. F.   MR. ANDERSON.

77. (I) Commercial Pomology (1955-56)

A critical consideration of the picking, grading, packing, storing, and marketing of fruits. This course also considers the leading American and foreign centers of fruit production as they affect our own fruit industry through competition here or abroad. A two-day market trip will be required at an approximate cost of ten dollars. Given in alternate years.

2 class hours; 1 2-hour laboratory period.   Credit, 3.
8:00-8:50 Tu., Th.; 1:00-2:50 Tu.   MR. ROBERTS.

81. (I) 82. (II) Advanced Pomology

A consideration of the scientific principles governing the growth and behavior of fruit-bearing plants. Special attention is given to the more important research work in the field of pomology.

2 class hours; 1 2-hour laboratory period.   Credit, 3.
Hours by arrangement.   MR. FRENCH.
Prerequisite, Pomology 53.

83. (I) 84. (II) Seminar

Advanced study of problems relating to fruit production.

1 class hour.   Credit, 1.
Hours by arrangement.   THE DEPARTMENT.

85. (I) 86. (II) Cranberry Problems

For seniors specializing in cranberry technology. Selected readings and individual work to familiarize students with the literature, research, and problems of the cranberry industry.

Credit, 2.

Hours by arrangement.   MR. FRENCH.

52. (II) Plant Breeding Methods

An advanced study of genetic topics peculiar to plants, also the methods and problems of the plant breeder. Laboratory work in genetic analysis and the breeding of plants.

2 class hours; 1 2-hour laboratory period.　　　Credit, 3.
11:00-11:50 M. F.; 3:00-4:50 W.　　　Mr. French.
Prerequisite, Zoology 53.

81. (I) 82. (II) Special Problems in Plant Breeding

Qualified seniors may carry on advanced study on special topics or undertake such original investigations as time and available material will permit.

Hours by arrangement.　　　Credit, 2.
　　　Mr. French.
Prerequisite, Plant Breeding 52.

POULTRY HUSBANDRY

Professor Jeffrey, Professor Sanctuary, Associate Professor Vondell, Assistant Professor Banta.

25. (I) General Poultry

For students not majoring in poultry husbandry. A general course giving an introduction to the breeds of poultry, the principles and practice of breeding, incubation, and poultry nutrition, brooding and rearing, houses and equipment, management practices, disease control, marketing poultry products, and the business of poultry keeping.

2 class hours; 1 2-hour laboratory period.　　　Credit, 3.
9:00-9:50 M. F.; 10:00-11:50 or 3:00-4:50 Tu.　　　Mr. Jeffrey.

52. (II) Incubation and Brooding

This course is based upon the actual operation of incubators and brooders. Each year a research project is planned and data obtained concerning the effects of various incubator adjustments upon malpositions and maldevelopment of embryos and the percentage of hatch. Studies of temperature gradients, chick behavior and development are made in brooding with various types of equipment. Analysis is made of common and unusual field problems.

1 class hour; 2 2-hour laboratory periods.　　　Credit, 3.
11:00-11:50 W.; 3:00-4:50 M.; other hours by arrangement.
　　　Mr. Sanctuary.

257

POULTRY HUSBANDRY

53. (I) Poultry Judging
Physiological and anatomical characters are used in production judging. The American Standard of Perfection is employed in a study of the more popular breeds and varieties, and for exhibition judging. Judging teams competing in the Eastern Intercollegiate Contest are trained in this course.

1 class hour; 2 2-hour laboratory periods.　　　　Credit, 3.
8:00-8:50 Tu.; 1:00-2:50 Th. F.　　　　Mr. Banta.

55. (I) Poultry Housing and Sanitation
In this course are considered the biological factors related to the proper physical environment necessary for growth, health, and reproduction. Various systems of ventilation and methods of insulation are studied and demonstrated by models. Humidity, temperature, and condensation studies are made at the poultry plant with varying adjustments of ventilation devices. A study is made of modern equipment. Sanitation from the standpoint of disease prevention practices is also considered.

1 class hour; 1 2-hour laboratory period.　　　　Credit, 2.
9:00-9:50 Th.; 1:00-2:50 Tu.　　　　Mr. Sanctuary.

56. (II) Poultry Nutrition
A study of the scientific principles of nutrition, classification and identification of feedstuffs, formulation and calculation of rations for specific purposes. A class trip may be arranged.

2 class hours; 1 2-hour laboratory period.　　　　Credit, 3.
9:00-9:50 Tu. Th.; 1:00-2:50 W.　　　　Mr. Banta.

75. (I) Marketing Poultry Products
A study of the preparation and grading methods of eggs and poultry products to meet the requirements of the northeastern markets. The laboratories are designed to cover the fields of modern dressing, processing and packaging poultry; as well as grading, candling and quality studies of eggs. A one-half day class trip to Springfield markets in December is required. Estimated cost, two dollars.

1 class hour; 1 2-hour laboratory period.　　　　Credit, 2.
10:00-10:50 Tu.; 3:00-4:50 W.　　　　Mr. Vondell.

76. (II) Turkey Production
This course includes the production of ducks and geese but most of the time is given to the turkey industry; its importance, breeds, breeding, incubation, brooding, feeding, finishing, marketing, etc.

1 class hour 1 2-hour laboratory period.　　　　Credit, 2.
1:00-1:50 M.; 3:00-4:50 W.　　　　Mr. Vondell.

77. (I) Poultry Breeding

The improvement of poultry by selection is developed through a study of the principles of heredity. The inheritance of morphological and physiological characters including plumage color, egg production, meat production, hatchability, egg traits, and disease resistance.

2 class hours; 1 2-hour laboratory period. Credit, 3.
11:00-11:50 M. W.; 1:00-2:50 W. MR. ————

78. (II) Seminar and Farm Management

A combination seminar and lecture course designed to give the student a comprehensive view of all phases of the poultry industry. A field trip covering approximately three days will be arranged. Poultry majors with an average of 80 or more in poultry courses may elect an additional problem credit.

3 class hours; 1 2-hour laboratory period may be elected.
Credits, 3, 4.
9:00-9:50 M. W. F. THE STAFF.

PSYCHOLOGY

PROFESSOR NEET†, ASSOCIATE PROFESSOR FELDMAN, ASSOCIATE PROFESSOR GOSS, ASSISTANT PROFESSOR MAUSNER, ASSISTANT PROFESSOR EPSTEIN, ASSISTANT PROFESSOR FIELD, MR. ERLICK, MR. CLIFFORD, MRS. FIELD.

26. (I) and (II) General Psychology

This is an introductory course dealing with the basic principles and applications of psychology with regard to the understanding and control of behavior. Topics considered include the nature and development of behavior, motivation, learning, problems of adjustment, intelligence, aptitudes, and personality.

3 class hours. Credit, 3.
THE DEPARTMENT.

28. (II) General Psychology

A continuation of Psychology 26. Topics considered include neural relationships, sensory processes, perception, thinking, emotions, social behavior, and individual differences.

3 class hours. Credit, 3.
9:00-9:50 or 11:00 to11:50. THE DEPARTMENT.
Prerequisite, Psychology 26.

51. (I) Experimental Psychology

This course is designed to give an understanding of the problems, methods, and data of experimental psychology. One of the basic

† On leave of absence.

functions of the course is to acquaint the student with the scientific method as applied to psychological studies of behavior.

2 class hours; 1 2-hour laboratory period.   Credit, 3.

10:00-10:50 Tu. Th.; 1:00-2:50 Tu. W. or Th.   Mr. NEET.

Prerequisite, Psychology 26.

56. (II) Educational Psychology

A study of psychological facts and principles fundamental to education, teaching, and personal relationships between teacher and pupil. Topics considered in relation to school situations are: physical and mental growth, intelligence, motivation, emotions, learning, transfer of training, and mental hygiene of teacher and pupil.

3 class hours.   Credit, 3.

9:00-9:50 Tu. Th. S.   Mr. MAUSNER.

Prerequisite, Psychology 26.

61. (I) Social Psychology

The social behavior of the individual. Topics considered will include methods of studying social behavior, schools of social psychology, social behavior of animals, foundations of personality development, social (cultural) determinants of personality, social attitudes and their measurements, effects of collective situations on individual behavior, custom and conformity.

3 class hours.   Credit, 3.

9:00-9:50 M. W. F.   Mr. MAUSNER.

Prerequisite, Psychology 26.

62. (II) Social Psychology (1955-56)

A survey of multi-individual phenomena. Topics to be considered are methods of studying collective action, leadership, morale, propaganda, nature and measurement of public opinion, behavior in crowd situations, social conflict and prejudice. Given in alternate years.

3 class hours.   Credit, 3.

11:00-11:50 M. W. F.   Mr. MAUSNER.

Prerequisite, Psychology 26.

63. (I) Physiological Psychology

A study of the relationships between physiological processes and behavior. Major emphasis will be placed upon the structure and mechanisms of the central nervous system and sense organs, endocrine functions, and drives.

3 class hours.   Credit, 3.

11:00-11:50 M. W. F.   Mr. FELDMAN.

Prerequisites, Psychology 26; Zoology 35.

72. (II) Advanced Experimental Psychology

The literature, techniques, and apparatus of experimental psychology are considered, and selected projects are carried out individually by the members of the class.

1 class hour; 2 2-hour laboratory periods.   Credit, 3.
10:00-10:50 Th.; 1:00-2:50 Tu. Th.   MR. NEET.
Prerequisite, Psychology 51.

75. (I) Statistics in Psychology

The application of statistical procedures to the analysis of psychological data and to problems of measurement in psychology and related fields.

2 class hours; 1 2-hour laboratory period.   Credit, 3.
200-2:50 M. F.; 2:00-3:50 W.   MR. GOSS.
Prerequisites, Psychology 26; Statistics 77 or Mathematics 62.

81. (I) 82. (I) and (II) Psychological Tests

Different varieties of psychological tests are studied. The first semester surveys the field of testing and introduces the student to tests of intelligence, aptitude, interest, personality, and adjustment. The second semester is devoted to a more intensive study of individual intelligence tests with the aim of teaching the student to administer, score and interpret those in most common use. Either semester may be elected independently.

2 class hours; 1 2-hour laboratory period.   Credit, 3.
Course 81 (I) and 82 (II) 9:00-9:50 Tu. Th.; 3:00-4:50 W.
Course 82 (I) 3:00-3:50 Tu. Th.; laboratory by arrangement.
                                                            MR. EPSTEIN.
Prerequisite, Psychology 26.

83. (I) Abnormal Psychology

A study of the principles relative to the causes, symptoms, and treatment of behavior abnormalties. Special attention is given to the following: dynamics of behavior abnormalties, speech problems, emotional extremes, memory losses and other disorders of association, the neuroses and psychoses, and mental deficiency. Hospital trips and clinics.

3 class hours.   Credit, 3.
10:00-10:50 M. W. F.   MR. NEET.
Prerequisite, Psychology 26.

86. (I) and (II) Industrial Psychology

A study of psychological principles and methods in business and industrial situations. Topics considered include: job analysis, job evaluation, employee selection and training, fatigue, techniques of motivation, measurement of morale and problems of leadership.

3 class hours. Credit, 3.

1:00-1:50 M. W. F. or 9:00-9:50 Tu. Th. S. MR. ERLICK.

Prerequisite, Psychology 26.

88. (II) Psychology of Guidance

A study of the psychological principles, techniques and tests necessary in guidance. Practice is given in organizing and evaluating relevant data in the analysis of illustrative cases

2 class hours; 1 2-hour laboratory period. Credit, 3.

10:00-10:50 Tu. Th.; 2:00-3:50 M. MR. FIELD.

Prerequisites, Psychology 26 and 81 or consent of the instructor.

90. (II) Contemporary Psychologies

A logical, historical, and systematic analysis of contemporary psychological theories, including structuralism, functionalism, Gestalt and organismic psychologies, psychoanalysis, and behaviorisms from Thorndike and Watson to the contemporary scene.

3 class hours. Credit, 3.

2:00-2:50 M. W. F. MR. GOSS.

Prerequisite, Psychology 26.

92. (II) Clinical Psychology

A study of the techniques and methods involved in the diagnosis and treatment of behavior disorders. Diagnostic clinical testing, counselling, and other psychotherapeutic procedures are given consideration. Hospital trips and clinics.

2 class hours; 1 2-hour laboratory period. Credit, 3.

11:00-11:50 M. W. F. MR. EPSTEIN.

Prerequisite, Psychology 83 or consent of the instructor.

93. (II) Psychology of Adolescence (1954-55)

A consideration of the development, and emotional, social, and intellectual adjustment of the individual during the adolescent years. Given in alternate years.

3 class hours. Credit, 3.

9:00-9:50 Tu. Th. S. MR. ————.

94. (II) Child Psychology

This course aims to develop an understanding of the behavior of the child. Psychological aspects of the following topics are considered: original nature, maturation and development of behavior, language, habit formation, emotional behavior, development of intelligence and understanding, social behavior, motivation,

personality, and mental hygiene. Nursery school observation and practice.
3 class hours.   Credit, 3.
10:00-10:50 M. W. F.   Mr. ————
Prerequisite, Psychology 26.

95. (I) 96. (II) Problems in Psychology

For qualified seniors. The student will be allowed to do independent work and study on special problems or in certain fields of psychological interest. By arrangement with the members of the department.
Credit, 1.
THE DEPARTMENT.

RECREATION LEADERSHIP
ASSOCIATE PROFESSOR RANDALL.

51. (I) Principles of Recreation

This course considers recreation as an important social force in education and community living. Emphasis is given to the study and discussion of established principles and their applicability to functional recreation programs.
3 class hours.   Credit, 3.
MR. RANDALL.

52. (II) Group Leadership and Camp Counseling

A study of principles and practices dealing with leadership problems, group work methods, camp counselling, and organization. Application is made to youth-serving agencies and organized camps through practical observations and demonstrations. Special attention is given to social and educational outcomes for adolescents.
3 class hours.   Credit, 3.
MR. RANDALL.
Prerequisite, Recreation 51.

53. (I) Social Recreation (1955-56)

Provides leadership preparation in a wide range of social recreation for various age levels. Selecting and developing materials for use in actual situations is required. Opportunity is provided for practical experience in planning and conducting party games and mixers, group singing, social and square dancing, outings and

263

picnics, and other mass activities for home, church, club, camp, playground, hospital and institutional use. Given in alternate years.

3 class hours.   Credit, 3.

MR. ————.

Prerequisite, Recreation 51.

54. (Summer) Field Work Experience

Supervised off-campus field work experience is required of students preparing for leadership and teaching responsibilities in recreation and outdoor education. Assignments of one month are arranged for field experience during the summer following the junior year. Cooperating recreation centers, camps, schools, hospitals, industries, and other youth-serving organizations provide students with actual leadership preparation. Students are guided in their study through the use of a workbook adapted for the purpose and personal supervision. Placement arrangements should be made with the guidance of the major advisor as early as possible in the junior year. Required as excess graduation credits.

MR. RANDALL.

75. (I) Field Work Analysis

A seminar for recreation majors. The course is planned primarily to discuss and evaluate supervised student leadership experience in community recreation, camping, and outdoor education. Student reports, staff appraisals, and workbook problems contribute to the analysis of field experience and student accomplishments.

3 class hours.   Credit, 3.

MR. RANDALL.

Prerequisite, Recreation 54.

76. (II) Public Relations in Recreation

This course is intended to provide opportunity for a study of the purposes and methods in developing and maintaining interest and understanding in public recreation. The course explores recommended programs and procedures for establishing good public relations and securing recreation as an important community affair. Provision is made for practical application and evaluation of selected techniques and their effectiveness in creating favorable public opinion.

3 class hours.   Credit, 3.

MR. RANDALL.

Prerequisite, Recreation 51.

77. (I) Organizing and Conducting Community Recreation

This course gives special attention to program planning for rural and urban recreation areas, neighborhood centers, adult education projects, and community activities. Organization and management including scheduling, staff assignments, record keeping, reports, special events, promotion and other departmental problems are considered.

3 class hours.   Credit, 3.

MR. RANDALL.

78. (I) or (II) Special Problems in Recreation

Admission with the approval of the major adviser. A qualified senior may elect to undertake independent study of a selected problem in the area of his primary interest or specialization.

3 class hours.   Credit, 3.

MR. RANDALL.

Prerequisite, Recreation 54.

RELIGION
(Non-credit courses)

REV. FR. DAVID J. POWER, A.B.; RABBI LOUIS RUCHAMES, PH.D.;
REV. ALBERT L. SEELY, B.A., B.D.; REV. SYDNEY TEMPLE, PH.D.

15. (I)   16. (II)   A History of Jewish Thought and Culture

A survey of Jewish thought and culture from the Bible to contemporary times. Particular emphasis will be placed upon the relevance of such thought to contemporary religious and philosophical problems. Among the thinkers to be discussed will be Jeremiah, Ecclesiastes, Philo, Maimonides, Spinoza, Achad-Ha'am, and Will Herberg.

1 hour.   No credit.

MR. RUCHAMES.

17. (I)   18. (II)   Basic Beliefs of Judaism

Discussions of the basic principles and pratices of the Jewish faith.

1 hour.   No credit.

MR. RUCHAMES.

20. (II)   21' (I)   Religious Foundations of the West

The development of religious consciousness is considered against the background of the Old Testament record. The Bible text is critically surveyed in the light of national, cultural, and rational influences and as applicable to the contemporary religious situation. Course 20: The Law and Former Prophets; Course 21: Prophets and Writings.

1 hour. No credit.
MR TEMPLE.

30. (II) 31. (I) Elements of Christianity

The fundamentals of the Christian faith as found in the New Testament writings are studied critically and empirically, with special reference to their relevance for individual and social life in the contemporary world. Course 30: The Four Gospels; Course 31: Acts and Epistles.

1 hour. No credit.
MR. TEMPLE, MR. SEELY.

41. (I) 42. (II) Catholic Faith and Practice

Discussions of the Catholic Church dogmas and practices.

1 hour. No credit.
FR. POWER.

61. (I) The Understanding of Personality

The findings of modern psychology and psychiatry are interpreted in the light of the Christian faith so as to lead to a better understanding of the human personality. Courtship and marriage, vocation, personal and social attitudes are considered.

1 hour. No credit.
MR. ————.

63. (I) Biblical Thought and Contemporary Ideologies

A review of the great themes of the Bible and a comparison with contemporary, challenging ideologies, with special reference to the conflict between Communism and Christianity

MR. SEELY.

71. (I) Religion in Life

A practical approach to theology. The primary doctrines of the Christian Church are considered in the light of God's action and man's response, the place of the Church, and the task of the Christian today.

1 hour. No credit.
MR TEMPLE.

72. (II) Christian Belief

An exposition and discussion of the articles of the Christian faith, with special attention to the scriptural basis of belief and its confirmation in the experience of the Church.

1 hour. No credit.

Mr. ————.

Courses in Elementary and Intermediate Hebrew, and Elementary Yiddish are offered by Rabbi Ruchames. These are open to all students.

ROMANCE LANGUAGES

PROFESSOR FRAKER†, PROFESSOR GODING, ASSOCIATE PROFESSOR FERRIGNO, ASSISTANT PROFESSOR CLARKE, ASSISTANT PROFESSOR JOHNSON, ASSISTANT PROFESSOR WEXLER, MISS TILLONA, MR. GREENFIELD, MISS GEORGANTAS, MISS VEUM, MR. GORE, MR. FRAKER, MR. MERMIER, MR. ROUGÉ.

FRENCH

1. (I) 2. (II) Elementary French

For those who have had no previous courses in French. Intensive drill for rapid reading, writing, speaking and understanding. No credits in this course may be applied toward a degree until the close of the second semester, except upon special recommendation from the Provost.

3 class hours; 1 laboratory hour. Credit, 3.

THE DEPARTMENT.

5. (I) 6. (II) Advanced Intermediate French

Readings from representative masterpieces of French literature. Composition, grammar review, intensive oral practice.

3 class hours; 1 laboratory hour. Credit, 3.

THE DEPARTMENT.

Prerequisites, French 1 and 2, or 2 years of high school French.

9. (I) 10. (II) Oral Practice

Not open to freshmen except in conjunction with another course in French. Intensive oral practice, vocabulary study, grammar essentials for fluent speech. Recommended for those who desire a reasonably good command of the spoken language.

3 class hours; 1 laboratory hour. Credit, 3.

THE DEPARTMENT.

Prerequisites, French 5 and 6 or equivalent or permission of the instructor.

† On leave of absence.

15. (I) 16. (II) Survey of French Literature

Readings from representative masterpieces of French literature. Review of grammar. Composition, outside reading.

3 class hours; 1 laboratory hour.   Credit, 3.

THE DEPARTMENT.

Prerequisites, French 5 and 6 or 3 years of high school French.

ADVANCED COURSES

Prerequisites, French 15 and 16, or French 5 and 6 and permission of the instructor. Since most of the advanced courses are conducted in French, the student should have a reasonable oral command of the language before electing these courses. For this purpose the student is advised to take French 9 and 10, or spend one year in the French House.

29. (I) 30. (II) French Literature of the Seventeenth Century (1955-56)

A survey of the Classic period, with readings from representative works. Given in alternate years.

3 class hours; 1 laboratory hour.   Credit, 3.

MR. FRAKER.

31. (I) 32. (II) French Literature of the Nineteenth Century (1954-55)

A detailed study of the more important authors and movements. Given in alternate years.

3 class hours; 1 laboratory hour.   Credit, 3.

MR. GODING.

51. (I) French Literature of the Eighteenth Century (1954-55)

Rousseau: The Encyclopedists. Given in alternate years.

3 class hours; 1 laboratory hour.   Credit, 3.

MR. FRAKER.

52. (II) Voltaire (1954-55)

A study of the Eighteenth Century through the life and works of Voltaire. Given in alternate years.

3 class hours; 1 laboratory hour.   Credit, 3.

MR. FRAKER.

53. (I) 54. (II) French Literature of the Twentieth Century

3 class hours; 1 laboratory hour.   Credit, 3.
                                                                    MISS CLARKE.

75. (I) 76. (II) Cours de Style

A study of syntax and idioms at an advanced level. The student is taught how to express himself clearly and logically in living French.

3 class hours; 1 laboratory hour.   Credit, 3.
                                                                    MR. ————.

79. (I) French Civilization (1955-56)

A study of those elements which lie back of the cultural contribution of France to the world civilization. Subjects studied will include arts, sciences, school systems, the press, the family, social classes, influences of history and geography. The assigned readings will be drawn from contemporary French literature. Given in alternate years.

3 class hours; 1 laboratory hour.   Credit, 3.
                                                                    MR. GODING.

80. (II) Advanced Language Study (1955-56)

Methods of teaching; review of grammar and pronunciation; outside reading and reports.

3 class hours; 1 laboratory hour.   Credit, 3.
                                                                    MR. GODING.

ITALIAN

1. (I) 2. (II) Elementary Italian

For those who have had no previous courses in Italian. The essentials of Italian grammar, intensive drill in pronunciation, conversation and composition. Extensive reading of modern Italian writings. No credits in this course may be applied toward a degree until the close of the second semester except upon special recommendation from the Provost.

3 class hours; 1 laboratory hour.   Credit, 3.
                                                                    MISS TILLONA.

25. (I) 26. (II) Intermediate Italian

Readings from modern authors and from Dante, Petrarch and Boccaccio. Intensive oral drill, continued composition and conversation. Systematic review of grammar.

3 class hours; 1 laboratory hour.   Credit, 3.
                                                                    MR. FERRIGNO.

Prerequisites, Italian 1 and 2 or two years of high school Italian.

SPANISH

1. (I) 2. (II) Elementary Spanish

For students who have had no training in Spanish. The essentials of Spanish grammar, intensive oral drill in pronunciation, fundamentals of conversation and composition, and extensive reading of short stories. No credits in this course may be applied toward a degree until the close of the second semester, except upon special recommendation from the Provost.

3 class hours; 1 laboratory hour. Credit, 3.

THE DEPARTMENT.

7. (I) 8. (II) Intermediate Spanish

Systematic grammar review, intensive oral drill, continued composition and conversation; intensive and extensive readings from selected modern texts.

3 class hours; 1 laboratory hour. Credit, 3.

THE DEPARTMENT.

Prerequisites, Spanish 1 and 2 or two years of high school Spanish.

19. (I) 20. (II) Oral Spanish

Primary emphasis is placed on the oral aspects of the language; pronunciation, vocabulary building, reading, comprehension, preparation of speeches, group discussions, and conversations. Considerable attention is also paid to those elements of grammar required for correct and fluent use of the language. Recommended for major students and for those who desire a good command of the spoken language.

3 class hours; 1 laboratory hour. Credit, 3.

MR. WEXLER.

Prerequisites, Spanish 7 and 8 or permission of the department.

25. (I) 26. (II) Survey of Spanish Literature

This course traces the development of Spanish literature from the 12th through the 20th centuries. Lectures, readings from some of the most important works, reports and discussions. The course is conducted largely in Spanish.

3 class hours; 1 laboratory hour. Credit, 3.

MR. FERRIGNO.

Prerequisites, Spanish 7 and 8 or equivalent.

29. (I) The Romantic Period (1956-57)

Readings from representative authors; written and oral composition. Given in alternate years.
2 class hours; 1 2-hour laboratory period.   Credit, 3.

MR. FRAKER.
Prerequisites, Spanish 25 and 26.

30. (II) The Modernists (1954-55)

Dario, Nervo and their contemporaries; composition and conversation. Given in alternate years.
2 class hours; 1 2-hour laboratory period. ʹ   Credit, 3.

MR. FRAKER.
Prerequisite, Spanish 29.

73. (I) 74. (II) The Golden Age (1955-56)

Readings from Cervantes, Lope de Vega, Calderon, Garcilaso and others. Composition and conversation. Given in alternate years.
2 class hours; 1 2-hour laboratory period.   Credit, 3.

MR. FRAKER.
Prerequisites, Spanish 25 and 26.

RUSSIAN

· Instructor in Romance Languages.

51. (I) 52. (II) Elementary Russian

Grammar, exercises in composition and conversation, selected readings. No credits in this course may be applied toward a degree until the close of the second semester, except upon special recommendations from the Provost.
3 class hours; 1 laboratory hour.   Credit, 3.

MRS. JOA.
Prerequisite, previous language training.

SOCIOLOGY

PROFESSOR KORSON, ASSOCIATE PROFESSOR KING, ASSISTANT PROFESSOR DRIVER, MR. MANFREDI, MR. WILKINSON, MR. ————.

28. (I) and (II) Introduction to Sociology

An outline study of the social order, and of the individual considered as a member of his various groups.
3 class hours.   Credit, 3.

THE DEPARTMENT.

51. (I) Urban Sociology

A comparative study of modern social conditions, and methods of adjustment, with special reference to city environment. Characteristics of the population, urban ecology, and problems of adjustment in the fields of housing, health, education, and recreation are considered.

3 class hours.   Credit, 3.

2:00-2:50 Tu. Th., third hour by arrangement.   MR. MANFREDI.

Prerequisite, Sociology 28.

52. (II) Rural Sociology

A study of rural society from the standpoint of its population, institutions, standards of living, and their relation to urban society.

3 class hours.   Credit, 3.

MR. MANFREDI.

Prerequisite, Sociology 28.

53. (I) An Introductory Study of Cultural Anthropology

A non-technical sociological study of man in preliterate societies.

3 class hours.   Credit, 3.

MR. WILKINSON.

Prerequisite, Sociology 28.

54. (II) Race Relations

The social, economic, and political aspects of racial problems in the United States, with particular reference to the Negro and major ethnic groups. A rabbi, minister, and priest are invited to address the class, and visits are made to the respective churches.

3 class hours.   Credit, 3.

MR. KORSON, MR. KING.

Prerequisite, Sociology 28.

57. (I) The Family

The study of the development of the customs of courtship and marriage of the contemporary American family. The basic causes of changes and trends of the family are considered. Such topics as mate selection, marriage laws, marital prediction, husband-wife relations, and the role of the child are considered.

3 class hours.   Credit, 3.

MR. KING, MR. KORSON.

Prerequisite, Sociology 28.

61. (I) Population Problems

An analytical study of population trends and problems of the world; the origin, composition, growth, migration, and urbanization of the American population. A consideration of population pressure as a cause of migratory movements.

3 class hours.   Credit, 3.

MR. WILKINSON.

Prerequisite, Sociology 28.

68. (II) Industrial Sociology

A study of the role, status, and function of the worker in the industrial community. A consideration of changing technology, resulting social change and the adjustments made in the industrial community.

3 class hours.   Credit, 3.

MR. KORSON.

Prerequisite, Sociology 28.

75. (I) Social Problems

A consideration of the incidence, distribution and interrelations among the major types of social tensions in human societies. Various theories of causation are evaluated. In addition to regular classroom work, research projects and field trips are required.

3 class hours.   Credit, 3.

MR. DRIVER.

Prerequisite, Sociology 28.

76. (II) Introduction to Social Welfare

For senior majors and others who qualify. Contemporary problems of social concern: causes of poverty; methods of caring for adult and child dependents and defectives. A consideration of public and private agency administration and techniques, and an examination of federal, state, and local community programs.

3 class hours.   Credit, 3.

MR. DRIVER.

Prerequisites, Sociology 28, 75.

78. (II) Criminology

A study of the nature of crimes and the factors underlying criminal behavior. Attention is also given to the machinery of justice in criminal behavior; the law, the courts, police enforcement, penal and correctional institutions.

3 class hours.   Credit, 3.

MR. DRIVER.

Prerequisites, Sociology 28, 75.

79. (I) 80. (II) Seminar

Admission by permission of instructor. A study of the methods of research employed by social scientists. Students, under direction of the instructor, analyze and organize such sociological material as they gather through their own research. Projects must be approved in advance by the instructor.

Credit, 3.

Hours by arrangement.   MR. DRIVER.

82. (II) Sociological Theory

An examination of the contributions of European and American writers who have concerned themselves with theories of the origin, growth, and development of human social organization.

3 class hours.   Credit, 3.

MR. MANFREDI.

Prerequisites, Sociology 28, 53.

SPEECH

PROFESSOR NIEDECK, ASSISTANT PROFESSOR ZAITZ, MR. PEIRCE, MISS ABRAMSON, AND THE INSTRUCTORS IN ENGLISH.

3. (I) 4. (II) Public Speaking

This course is designed to give the student introductory instruction and opportunity in oral self-expression and includes both public speaking and literary interpretation. Scheduled under English 1, 2.

1 class hour.   Credit, 1.

THE DEPARTMENT.

51. (I) Voice and Diction and Oral Interpretation

The course is divided into five weeks of training and drill in the correct production of speech, followed by ten weeks of practice in the fundamentals of vocal interpretation of literature. It is possible for a student to take the five weeks of voice and diction and receive one credit.

3 class hours.   Credit, 1 or 3.

MISS ABRAMSON.

61. (I) Fundamentals of Broadcasting

A general introduction to broadcasting: practice in preparing, rehearsing, and producing programs of various types.

2 class hours; 1 2-hour laboratory period.   Credit, 3.

MR. ZAITZ.

62. (II) Advanced Radio Production

An advanced course in broadcasting to provide practice in preparing and producing radio talks, radio plays and documentary programs.

2 class hours; 1 2-hour laboratory period.   Credit, 3.

MR. ZAITZ.

63. (I) Television Programming and Production

An exploration of the television medium for orientation in producing, directing and writing: network, local and educational operations both studio and remote.

2 class hours; 1 2-hour laboratory period.   Credit, 3.

MR. ZAITZ.

64. (II) Television Programming and Production

Practical television techniques from effective planning through effective execution by people off camera and on camera.

2 class hours; 1 2-hour laboratory period.   Credit, 3.

MR. ZAITZ.

Prerequisite, Speech 63.

65. (I) Writing for Television

A consideration of television writing methods for the successful production of all types of formats.

3 class hours.   Credit, 3.

MISS ABRAMSON.

66. (II) Film Production and Staging for Television

Preparation and execution of 16mm films for television: the course will prepare a 10-minute film project from the idea to editing, processing, screening and narration.

2 class hours; 1 2-hour laboratory period.   Credit, 3.

MR. NIEDECK.

Prerequisite, Speech 63.

71. (I) Scene Design and Construction

Theories and design in the modern theatre with assignments in developing stage settings from sketches to working drawing; from scenery construction to painting.

2 class hours; 1 2-hour laboratory period.   Credit, 3.

MR. PEIRCE.

75. (I) Acting and Make-up

The course is roughly divided into ten weeks of study of emotion and imagination in acting, reading lines, rehearsing, diction, and bodily action; and five weeks of study and application of the principles of stage make-up.

2 class hours; 1 2-hour laboratory period.   Credit, 3.

MR. NIEDECK.

76. (II) Stage Direction
Study and practice in the fundamentals of directing a play. Recommended for those taking only one course in Drama.
2 class hours; 1 2-hour laboratory period. Credit, 3.
MR. NIEDECK.

78. (II) Stage Lighting
Introduction to lighting a stage. Analysis of basic types of equipment and their application in artistic productions. Simple wiring and installations.
2 class hours; 1 2-hour laboratory period. Credit, 3.
MR. PEIRCE.

91. (I) (II) Extempore Speech
The theory and practice of public speaking for business and professional purposes.
3 class hours. Credit, 3.
MR. NIEDECK.

92. (II) Formal Discussion
Most of the semester is devoted to formal discussion: its organization and presentation. Students are given the opportunity to lead and to participate in discussions of current problems.
3 class hours. Credit, 3.
MISS ABRAMSON.
Prerequisite, Speech 91.

94. (II) Persuasion
Advanced study and practice in appeals to beliefs and actions through extemporaneous speech.
3 class hours. Credit, 3.
MR. ZAITZ.
Prerequisite, Speech 91.

VETERINARY SCIENCE
PROFESSOR BULLIS, PROFESSOR SMITH.

75. (I) Comparative Veterinary Anatomy
A study of the structure of vertebrates with emphasis upon the comparative structure of domesticated animals, both mammals and birds.
3 class hours. Credit, 3.
11:00-11:50 M. W. F. MR. SMITH.

76. (II) General Veterinary Pathology

An introduction to the study of disease — causes, transmission, structural changes, and defense mechanisms; and the application of these principles to the prevention, control, and eradication of the common communicable and non-communicable diseases of farm animals.

3 class hours.   Credit, 3.

11:00-11:50 M. W. F.   Mr. Smith.

Prerequisite, Veterinary Science 75.

78. (II) General Veterinary Pathology

This course is similar to Veterinary Science 76 except that diseases of importance to wildlife, and diseases of animals transmissible to man will be considered.

3 class hours.   Credit, 3.

                                           Mr. Smith.

Prerequisites, Bacteriology 31, Zoology 35 or 71.

88. (II) Avian Pathology

This course is similar to Veterinary Science 76 but with application to specific communicable and non-communicable diseases of poultry.

3 class hours.   Credit, 3.

8:00-8:50 M. W. F.   Mr. Bullis.

Prerequisite, Veterinary Science 75.

ZOOLOGY

Professor Woodside, Associate Professor Snedecor†, Associate Professor Bartlett, Assistant Professor Traver, Assistant Professor Rollason, Assistant Professor Andrews, Assistant Professor Nutting, Assistant Professor Rauch, Assistant Professor Honiberg, Assistant Professor Swenson, Assistant Professor Roberts, Mr. Dearden.

1. (I) and (II) Introductory Zoology

This course provides an introduction to the principles of biology, with special reference to the zoological aspects. The structure and activities of a representative vertebrate animal, the frog, are considered in detail and the knowledge thus gained is utilized in a comprehensive survey of the major groups of the animal kingdom. Brief introductions are given to the principles of classification,.

† On leave of absence.

nutrition, structure, and functions of protoplasm, genetics, heredity, development, and evolution.

2 class hours; 1 3-hour laboratory period. Credit, 3.
11:00-11:50 M. W. or 2:00-2:50 M. W. or 3:00-3:50 Tu. Th.; laboratory hours as sectioned.

THE DEPARTMENT.

25. (I) Survey of the Animal Kingdom

Lectures emphasize those aspects of the zoological sciences which are least stressed in the introductory course; the principles of classification; ecology; economic importance; and the history of zoology in relation to man's progress. The laboratory work will include several exercises in field work; studies on representatives of phyla not covered previously; the morphological adaptations of animals to special modes of existence; and some simple zoological techniques.

2 class hours; 1 2-hour laboratory period. Credit, 3.
10:00-10:50 M. F.; 1:00-2:50 Tu. or W. or Th. MR. NUTTING.
Prerequisite, Zoology 1.

35. (I) and (II) Vertebrate Physiology

An introductory course which will include consideration of circulation, respiration, digestion, metabolism, excretion, chemical and nervous coordination, muscular activity, and reproduction. The laboratory work will acquaint the student with some of the equipment and methods used in physiological studies, with emphasis on the experimental approach to the laboratory exercises.

2 class hours; 1 3-hour laboratory period. Credit, 3.
MR. SNEDECOR, MR. SWENSON, MR. ROBERTS.

50. (II) Histology of the Vertebrates

A study of the types of tissues found in the body of vertebrate animals, and of the organs in which these tissues occur. Tissues and organs of mammals are emphasized. A knowledge of comparative anatomy is advised.

2 class hours; 1 3-hour laboratory period. Credit, 3.
8:00-8:50 Tu. Th.; 2:00-4:50 Tu. or 1:00-3:50 W.

MR. ROLLASON.

Prerequisite, Zoology 1.

51. (I) and (II) Microtechnique of Animal Tissues

The course comprises (1) a consideration of the principles and methods of microtechnique as applied to animal tissues, and (2) a series of practical exercises in the preparation of animal tissues

for microscopic examination. Registration is limited to 12 students per semester. Consult instructor for section assignments.
2 2-hour laboratory periods.   Credit, 2.
MR. HONIGBERG.

Prerequisite, Zoology 1.

53. (I) Principles of Genetics
Lectures and laboratory experiments concerning the laws governing the transmission of hereditary factors in plants and animals, expression and action of genes, population genetics, and the relationship of genetics to other biological sciences.
2 class hours; 1 3-hour laboratory period.   Credit, 3.
MR. RAUCH.

Prerequisite, Zoology 1.

54. (II) Natural History—Physical
Designed to orient students to the features of sky, climate and terrain which are of prime importance to the teaching naturalist. Collection, recording, preservation, and the use of natural objects will be stressed. Biological data will also be obtained as the season dictates.
1 class hour; 1 4-hour laboratory period.   Credit, 3.
11:00-11:50 Tu.; 1:00-5:00 F.   MR. NUTTING.
Prerequisites, Botany 1; Zoology 1.

55. (I) Natural History—Biotic
An extension of Zoology 54 with emphasis upon the fauna and flora. This course is primarily concerned with the development, local distribution, responses, and interrelationships of these organisms. Their position with respect to the physical environment will be discussed in some detail.
1 class hour; 1 4-hour laboratory period.   Credit, 3.
11:00-11:50 Tu.; 1:00-5:00 F.   MR. NUTTING.
Prerequisites, Botany 26; Geology 27; Zoology 54.

56. (II) Natural History—Field Studies
A program of extensive field work growing out of preparation in Zoology 54 and 55. Emphasis upon seasonal differences in abundance and stage of development of our fauna and flora.
1 class hour; 1 2-hour laboratory period.   Credit, 2.
1:00-1:50 W.; 2:00-3:50 W.   MR. NUTTING.
Prerequisites, Zoology 55 and permission of instructor.

64. (II) Biology of Protozoa (1954-55)
An introduction to the morphology, systematics, physiology, and ecology of protozoa with a consideration of the contributions to

the problems of biology made through the study of these organisms. Given in alternate years.

1 class hour; 1 2-hour and 1 3-hour laboratory period.   Credit, 3.

MR. HONIGBERG.

Prerequisites, Zoology 1 and permission of the instructor.

69. (I) Animal Parasitology

Representative protozoan and helminthic parasites of man and domestic animals are studied, with special reference to their morphology and life cycles. Emphasis is placed upon parasitism as a mode of life; on hostparasite relationships; on vectors, and other modes of transmission; and on methods of control of certain of the more important human parasites.

1 class hour; 2 2-hour laboratory periods.   Credit, 3.

MISS TRAVER.

Prerequisite, Zoology 1.

70. (II) Invertebrate Zoology (1954-55)

A survey of the phyla of invertebrate animals from evolutionary and phylogenetic aspects. Morphology, modes of nutrition and reproduction, interrelationships with other animals, and distributions in time and space, are considered, as well as classification. For each phylum, representatives of the principal classes are studied. Marine, terrestrial and freshwater forms are included. Given in alternate years.

1 class hour; 2 3-hour laboratory periods.   Credit, 3.

MISS TRAVER.

Prerequisite, Zoology 1.

71. (I) Comparative Vertebrate Anatomy

A thorough study of the anatomy of the vertebrates, with emphasis on the evolution, special modifications, and functional interrelationships of each of the organ systems. A systemic approach in both lecture and laboratory work. Animals studied in the laboratory are: protochordates, lamprey, dogfish, mudpuppy, and cat.

2 class hours; 2 3-hour laboratory periods.   Credit, 4.

1:00-1:50 Tu. Th.; 1:00-3:50 W. F. or 2:00-4:50 Tu. Th.

MR. BARTLETT, MR. DEARDEN.

Prerequisite, Zoology 1.

72. (II) Vertebrate Embryology

Lectures and laboratory work dealing with the development of representative animals, special emphasis being placed on the amphibian, bird and mammal.

2 class hours; 2 3-hour laboratory periods.   Credit, 4.

MR. WOODSIDE, MR. RAUCH.

Prerequisite, Zoology 71.

73. (I) General Cytology (1954-55)

A consideration of the morphological features of cells in relation to their function. Lectures, seminar reports and laboratory work will deal with cytoplasmic structure and inclusions and nuclear phenomena. Given in alternate years.

2 class hours; 1 3-hour laboratory period. Credit, 3.

MR. ROLLASON.

Prerequisites, Zoology 50.

74. (II) Limnology (1955-56)

The study of inland waters, emphasizing the geological, physical, chemical and biological aspects of this problem. Standard methods for making physical and chemical tests and measurements, and for the collection of biological materials, are used by students in the numerous field trips. Biological material collected in the field is studied in the laboratory. Given in alternate years.

2 class hours; 2 3-hour laboratory periods. Credit, 4.

MISS TRAVER.

in cooperation with the departments of Botany, Entomology, Geology, Public Health, and Zoology.

Prerequisites, Botany 1; Zoology 1; Chemistry 1, 2; and permission to register. Strongly recommended: Botany 25, 26; Entomology 26; Zoology 25; Geology 27, 28; Chemistry 29, 30.

78. (II) Genetics of Animal Populations (1955-56)

The principles of the genetics of animal populations with emphasis upon its basic techniques and methods, its goals and contributions. The population approach to the study of the origin of species and human genetics will be considered also. Given in alternate years. Enrolment is limited to ten.

1 2-hour lecture-discussion period per week. Credit, 2.

MR. RAUCH.

Prerequisites, Zoology 53 or its equivalent and permission of the instructor.

80. (II) Ornithology

An introduction to the study of avian biology with emphasis on structural and functional adaptations, and particularly the behavioral patterns of birds. Laboratory periods include discussions of assigned readings in current literature in addition to field trips for identification and methods of field study.

1 class hour; 2 2-hour laboratory periods. Credit, 3.
8:00-8:50 Th; 3:00-4:50 M. F. or 9:00-11:00 Tu.; 3:00-4:50 F.

MR. BARTLETT, MR. NUTTING.

Prerequisite, Zoology 1.

81. (I) Vertebrate Zoology

An introduction to the vertebrates, their classification and ecology, with particular emphasis on the fishes. Field trips for the study of local fauna will be included as a part of the laboratory exercises. Course limited to eighteen students.

1 class hour; 2 2-hour laboratory periods.   Credit, 3.
9:00-9:50 W.; 1:00-2:50 Tu. Th.   MR. ANDREWS, MR. BARTLETT.
Prerequisite, Zoology 1.

82. (II) Mammalogy (1954-55)

The paleontology, taxonomy, speciation, natural history, range and distribution of the class Mammalia. Primary emphasis will be placed upon the study of local fauna, including at least one weekend collecting trip as part of the laboratory exercises. Course limited to fifteen students. Given in alternate years.

2 class hours; 1 2-hour laboratory period.   Credit, 3.
                                                          MR. DEARDEN.
Prerequisites, Zoology 1 and permission of instructor.

83. (I) General and Cellular Physiology

A course designed to introduce the student to modern trends in physiology. Emphasis is on the chemical and physical activities of the single cell. Topics include: protoplasmic organization, cellular metabolism, permeability, bioelectric phenomena, muscle contraction and radiation biology.

3 class hours; 1 3-hour laboratory period.   Credit, 4.
                                                          MR. SWENSON.
Prerequisites, 1 year of biology; organic chemistry.

84. (II) Comparative Physiology

A course designed to acquaint students with physiological principles involved in adaptations of animals to their environments. In the laboratory, experimental methods used to study adaptive mechanisms will be emphasized.

3 class hours; 1 3-hour laboratory period.   Credit, 4.
                                                          MR. ROBERTS.
Prerequisites, Zoology 1, 35 or 83.

85. (I) Classes of Arthropods Other Than Insects

Arthropods are studied from the phylogenetic standpoint, with special reference to their relationship to the origin and evolution of insects.

1 class hour; 2 2-hour laboratory periods.   Credit, 3.
12:00-12:50 W.; 1:00-2:50 W. F.   MR. HANSON.

86. (II) Fishery Biology

Theory in the practice of regulating freshwater fisheries; the physical and biological conditions of the environment and their influence on fish populations.

2 class hours; 1 2-hour laboratory period.

9:00-9:50 Tu. Th.; laboratory hours by arrangement.

MR. ANDREWS.

Prerequisite, Zoology 81 and permission of instructor.

87. (I) Endocrinology

Emphasis will be directed toward the importance of the endocrines in their control over normal functions (growth, metabolism, reproduction, etc.), in a variety of animals.

2 class hours; 1 3-hour laboratory period. Credit, 3.

MR. SNEDECOR.

Prerequisite, Zoology 1.

91. (I) 92. (II) Special Problems in Zoology

Qualified seniors who have met departmental requirements for specialization in the field of zoology may arrange for work on a special problem in zoology.

Credit, 1-3.

THE DEPARTMENT.

Invertebrate Zoology, Marine Biological Laboratory, Woods Hole, Massachusetts.

Credit, 3.

Invertebrate Embryology, Marine Biological Laboratory, Woods Hole, Massachusetts.

Credit, 3.

OFFICERS OF ADMINISTRATION

Office of the President

JEAN PAUL MATHER, B.S.C., M.B.A. (University of Denver),
M.A. (Princeton University), *President of the University*. South College
AFFIE MAY COOK, *Secretary to the President*.   South College

Office of the Secretary

JAMES WILLIAM BURKE, B.S. (University of Massachusetts),
Secretary of the University.   South College

Office of the Provost

MARSHALL OLIN LANPHEAR, B.S., M.S. (University of Massachusetts),
Registrar.   South College
ROBERT STODDART HOPKINS, JR., B.A., M.ED. (Rutgers University),
Dean of Men.   South College
HELEN CURTIS, A.B. (Iowa State Teachers College),
A.M. (Columbia University), *Dean of Women*.   South College
DONALD WINSLOW CADIGAN, B.S., M.S. (University of Massachusetts),
Associate Registrar.   South College
WILLIAM CHANDLER STARKWEATHER, B.S. (University of Massachusetts),
Assistant Registrar.   South College
WILLIAM FRANKLIN FIELD, B.S. (West Chester State Teachers College),
ED. M. (Temple University), PH.D. (University of Maryland), *Director
of Guidance*.   South College
MILDRED PIERPONT, A.B. (Mount Holyoke College),
Schedule Supervisor.   South College
EMILY MAY LARKIN,
Administrative Assistant to the Dean of Men.   South College

Office of the Dean of the Graduate School

GILBERT LLEWELLYN WOODSIDE, B.A. (DePauw University), A.M., PH.D.
(Harvard University), *Dean of the Graduate School*. ·   Fernald Hall
MRS. ELIZABETH W. CADIGAN,
Secretary to the Dean of the Graduate School. East Experiment Station

Office of the Treasurer

KENNETH WILLIAM JOHNSON, B.S. (University of Vermont),
Treasurer of the University.   South College
L. LAWRENCE TAYLOR, B.B.A. (Northeastern University),
Assistant Treasurer.   South College

FRANCIS JOSEPH TEAHAN,
  Administrative Assistant to the Treasurer.   South College
MRS. GAMER H. PAUL, *Secretary to the Treasurer.*   South College

Business Office

HOBART HAYES LUDDEN, B.B.A. (Boston University),
  Business Manager.   South College
EDWARD MARCUS MANOOKIAN,
  Administrative Assistant to the Business Manager.   South College
GEORGE CHARLES BREHM,
  Superintendent of Buildings and Grounds.   Service Building
LIONEL GEORGE DAVID, *Engineer.*   Service Building
WALTER OSCAR JOHNSON, B.S. (University of Massachusetts),
  Manager of Boarding Halls.   University Commons
AUGUSTINE JOSEPH RYAN, A.B. (Dartmouth College), M.B.A. (Harvard
  University), *Manager of the University Store.*   North College

Office of Director of Experiment Station

DALE HAROLD SIELING, B.S., M.S. (Kansas State College), PH.D. (Iowa State
  College), *Director of the Experiment Station.*
                                            East Experiment Station
MARGARET HELEN O'DONNELL,
  Administrative Director.   East Experiment Station
MATTHEW LOUIS BLAISDELL, B.S. (University of Massachusetts), *Associate
  Professor, Superintendent of Farms and Head of Station Service.*
                                            East Experiment Station
DONALD MARKHAM KINSMAN, B.S. (University of Massachusetts), M.S. (University of New Hampshire), *Assistant Professor, Assistant to Superintendent of Farms.*   Stockbridge Hall
MRS. DOROTHY MALLORY ROSE,
  Secretary to the Director.   East Experiment Station

Office of Director of Extension Service

JAMES WILSON DAYTON, B.S. (University of Massachusetts), *Associate Dean
  and Director of Extension Service.*   Munson Hall
IRENE ELISABETH CHANDLER, *Secretary to the Director.*   Munson Hall

Office of Director of Stockbridge School

FRED PAINTER JEFFREY, B.S. (Pennsylvania State University), M.S. (University of Massachusetts), *Associate Dean of the School of Agriculture
  and Director of the Stockbridge School.*   South College
KATHARINE MARY MARTIN, *Secretary to the Director.*   South College

Office of Publications

ROBERT JOSEPH McCARTNEY, B.A. (University of Massachusetts),
  University Editor.   South College

ADMINISTRATION

MRS. PEARL THOMAS KLIMCYK,
Secretary to the University Editor. South College

Health Service

ERNEST JAMES RADCLIFFE, M.B., M.D. (University of Toronto),
Senior Physician. Out Patient Department

MRS. SANDRA GULBEN GODING, B.S. (University of Massachusetts), M.D.
(Woman's Medical College of Pennsylvania), *Assistant Physician.*
Out Patient Department

HARRY HIRSH MICHELSON, M.D. (University of Kiel),
Consulting Psychiatrist. Northampton

Placement Office

EMORY ELLSWORTH GRAYSON, B.S. (University of Massachusetts),
Director of Placement. South College

ROBERT JOHN MORRISSEY, B.S. (State Teachers College, Buffalo, New York),
M.S. (St. Bonaventure College), *Placement Officer for Men.*
South College

MRS. CAROL BURR CORNISH, A.B. (Grinnell College), M.A. (Syracuse University), *Placement Officer for Women.* South College

GEORGE EDWARD EMERY, B.S. (University of Massachusetts),
Assistant Placement Officer. South College

Library

HUGH MONTGOMERY, B.S. (Harvard University), B.S. in L.S.
(Columbia University), *Librarian.* Goodell Library

BENTON LeROY HATCH, B.A. (Yale University),
Assistant Librarian for Acquisitions. Goodell Library

MRS. MARIE VAN WIEREN MAYER, B.S. (Simmons College),
Cataloguer. Goodell Library

KENNETH LEAMAN HULBERT, A.B. (Clark University, B.S. (Simmons College),
ED.M. (Boston University), *Reference Librarian.* Goodell Library

MRS. EILEEN ANN ANDERSON, *Librarian's Secretary.* Goodell Library

MRS. BEATRICE LOUISE CAMPBELL, *Circulation Assistant.* Goodell Library

MRS. BARBARA-ALLEN DOYLE ERICKSON,
Circulation Assistant. Goodell Library

MRS. ELIZABETH ANN GEHLING, *Acquisitions Assistant.* Goodell Library

MRS. DELORES BERNARDO HEBERT, *Circulation Assistant.* Goodell Library

MRS. SOSIE KATCHIKIAN, *Catalogue Assistant.* Goodell Library

MRS. NANCY WARDICK MURDY, *Administrative Secretary.* Goodell Library

MRS. JANICE FAY TYLER, *Serials Assistant.* Goodell Library

Audio Visual Center

RAYMOND WYMAN, B.S. (University of Massachusetts), ED.M. (Boston
University), *Director, Audio Visual Center.* South College

DONALD CURTIS, B.S. (Pennsylvania State University), M.S. (University of
Massachusetts), *Assistant Director, Audio Visual Center.*
South College

Alumni Office

ROBERT LEAVITT, B.S. (University of Massachusetts),
  Executive Secretary, Associate Alumni.   Memorial Hall
CHRISTINE PATRICIA MURPHY, *Office Secretary.*   Memorial Hall

Heads of Residence

MRS. MADELINE LEWIS CARTWRIGHT, A.B. (Boston University,
  M.A. (Columbia University).   Crabtree House
MRS. JEAN THOMPSON CHURCHILL, A.B. (Mount Holyoke College).
                                                    Lewis House
MRS. LUCIE KNOWLES DAVEY.   Thatcher House
MME. MARINA SKARZYNSKA GUTOWSKA, PH.D. (University of Warsaw).
                                                    Leach House
MRS. AMY STONE JUDGE, A.B. (Mount Holyoke College). Knowlton House
MRS. ELSIE McCAUSLAND RICH.   Hamlin House
MRS. NADINE BOLLES WHIPPLE.   Abigail Adams House

Chaplains

REV. DAVID JOHN POWER, A.B. (Georgetown University), (Seminary of
  Philosophy of Montreal, Grand Seminary of Theology of Montreal),
  Chaplain to Catholic Students.   North College
RABBI LOUIS RUCHAMES (Jewish Institute of Religion), PH.D. (Columbia
  University), *Chaplain to Jewish Students.*   Hillel House
REV. ALBERT LYNUS SEELY, B.A. (Oberlin College), B.D. (Yale University),
  Chaplain to Protestant Students.   North College

EMERITI

WILLIAM HENRY ARMSTRONG, B.S. (University of Massachusetts), B.S., M.L.A.C.P. (Harvard University), *Assistant Professor of Mechanical Drawing*, Emeritus.

LORIN EARL BALL, B.S. (University of Massachusetts), *Assistant Professor of Physical Education*, Emeritus.

ARTHUR BISHOP BEAUMONT, B.S. (Kentucky State University), PH.D. (Cornell University), *Professor of Agronomy*, Emeritus.

ALEXANDER EDMOND CANCE, A.B. (Macalester College), M.A., PH.D. (University of Wisconsin), *Professor of Economics*, Emeritus.

ORTON LORING CLARK, B.S. (University of Massachusetts), *Associate Professor of Botany*, Emeritus.

PAUL WHEELER DEMPSEY, B.S. (University of Massachusetts), *Assistant Professor of Horticulture*, Emeritus.

LLEWELLYN LIGHT DERBY, B.S. (Springfield College), M.S. (University of Massachusetts), *Associate Professor of Physical Education*, Emeritus.

WALTER SAMUEL EISENMENGER, B.S., M.S. (Bucknell University), A.M., PH.D. (Columbia University), *Professor of Agronomy*, Emeritus.

CLIFFORD J. FAWCETT, B.S. (Ohio State University), *Extension Professor of Animal Husbandry*, Emeritus.

F. ETHEL FELTON, A.B. (Smith College), *Experiment Station Editor*, Emeritus.

JULIUS HERMAN FRANDSEN, B.S., M.S. (Iowa State College), *Professor of Dairy Industry*, Emeritus.

HENRY JAMES FRANKLIN, B.S., PH.D. (University of Massachusetts), *Professor of Horticulture*, Emeritus.

EDWIN FRANCIS GASKELL, B.S. (University of Massachusetts), *Assistant Professor of Agronomy*, Emeritus.

GUY VICTOR GLATFELTER, B.S. (Pennsylvania State University), M.S. (Iowa State College), *Placement Officer*, Emeritus.

HAROLD MARTIN GORE, B.S. (University of Massachusetts), *Professor of Physical Education for Men*, Emeritus.

JOHN CAMERON GRAHAM, B.S., AGR. (University of Wisconsin), *Professor of Poultry Husbandry*, Emeritus.

MARGARET POMEROY HAMLIN, A.B. (Smith College), *Placement Officer*, Emeritus.

HENRI DARWIN HASKINS, B.S. (University of Massachusetts), *Professor of Agricultural Chemistry*, Emeritus.

ROBERT DORMAN HAWLEY, B.S. (University of Massachusetts), M.B.A. (Boston University), *Treasurer*, Emeritus.

Mrs. HARRIET JULIA HAYNES, B.S. (Columbia University), *Extension Professor of Home Economics*, Emeritus.

CURRY STARR HICKS, B.PD., M.ED. (Michigan State Normal College), *Professor of Physical Education*, Emeritus.

ARTHUR DUNHAM HOLMES, B.S. (Dartmouth College), PH.D. (Johns Hopkins University), *Research Professor of Chemistry*, Emeritus.

GAY TETLEY KLEIN, B.S. (University of Missouri), M.S. (Kansas State College), *Extension Professor of Poultry Husbandry*, Emeritus.

JOHN BECKLEY LENTZ, A.B. (Franklin and Marshall College), V.M.D. (University of Pennsylvania), *Professor of Veterinary Science*, Emeritus.

FREDERICK ADAMS McLAUGHLIN, B.S. (University of Massachusetts), *Associate Professor of Botany*, Emeritus.

FRANK COCHRANE MOORE, A.B. (Dartmouth College), *Professor of Mathematics*, Emeritus.

WILLARD ANSON MUNSON, B.S. (University of Massachusetts), *Director of Extension Service*, Emeritus.

JOHN BAXTER NEWLON, *Assistant Professor of Engineering*, Emeritus.

SUMNER RUFUS PARKER, B.S. (University of Massachusetts), *Extension Professor of Agriculture*, Emeritus.

CHARLES ADAMS PETERS, B.S. (University of Massachusetts), PH.D. (Yale University), *Professor of Chemistry*, Emeritus.

JACOB KINGSLEY SHAW, B.S. (University of Vermont), M.S., PH.D. (University of Massachusetts), *Research Professor of Pomology*, Emeritus.

EDNA LUCY SKINNER, B.S., M.A. (Columbia University), M.ED. (Michigan State Normal College), *Dean of the School of Home Economics*, Emeritus.

CHARLES HIRAM THAYER, B.AGR. (University of Massachusetts), *Assistant Professor of Agronomy*, Emeritus.

RALPH ALBERT-VAN METER, B.S. (Ohio State University), M.S. (University of Massachusetts), PH.D. (Cornell University), LL.D. (Amherst College, University of Massachusetts), *President*, Emeritus.

ROLAND HALE VERBECK, B.S. (University of Massachusetts), *Director of Short Courses*, Emeritus.

WILLIAM GOULD VINAL, B.S., M.A. (Harvard University), PH.D. (Brown University), *Professor of Nature Education*, Emeritus.

WINTHROP SELDEN WELLES, B.S. (University of Illinois), M.ED. (Harvard University), *Professor of Education*, Emeritus.

BASIL BOISE WOOD, A.B. (Brown University), *Librarian*, Emeritus.

FACULTY OF RESIDENT INSTRUCTION

JEAN PAUL MATHER, B.S.C., M.B.A. (University of Denver),
M.A. Princeton University), *President.*   South College

HERSCHEL GEORGE ABBOTT, B.S. (University of Maine), M.F. (Harvard
University), *Instructor in Forestry.*   Conservation Building

DORIS ELIZABETH ABRAMSON, B.A. (University of Massachusetts),
M.A. (Smith College), *Instructor in Speech.*   Dramatic Workshop

GEORGE WILLIAM ALDERMAN, B.A. (Williams College),
Professor of Physics.   Hasbrouck Laboratory

CHARLES PAUL ALEXANDER, B.S., PH.D. (Cornell University),
Professor of Entomology and Head of Department.   Fernald Hall

ELIOT DINSMORE ALLEN, B.A. (Wesleyan University), A.M. (Harvard University), M.A., PH.D. (Princeton University), *Assistant Professor of English.*   Chapel

LUTHER ALFRED ALLEN, A.B. (Williams College), M.A. (State
University of Iowa), *Instructor in Government.*   North College

STEPHEN IVES ALLEN, A.B. (Amherst College), A.M. (Harvard University),
Instructor in Mathematics.   Mathematics Building

ROBERT JOHN ALLIO, B.MET.E. (Rensselaer Polytechnic Institute), M.S.
(Ohio State University), *Instructor in Mechanical Engineering.*
Engineering Wing

[1]DORIC ALVIANI, MUS.B., ED.M. (Boston University),
Professor of Music.

ALLEN EMIL ANDERSEN, A.B., M.A. (University of Nebraska), PH.D. (Harvard
University), *Professor of Mathematics and Head of Department.*
Mathematics Building

[1]JAMES FRANKLIN ANDERSON, B.S., M.S. (West Virginia University),.
Instructor in Pomology.

JOHN WILLIAM ANDERSON, B.S., M.B.A. (Indiana University),
Assistant Professor of Business Administration.   Draper Hall

THOMAS JOSEPH ANDREWS, B.S. (University of Massachusetts), A.M.
(Williams College), *Assistant Professor of Zoology.*   Fernald Hall

JOHN HARRIS BAKER, B.S. (Cornell University),
Assistant Professor of Food Technology.   University Commons

LOUIS NELSON BAKER, B.S. (University of New Hampshire), M.S. (University
of Kentucky), *Assistant Professor of Animal Husbandry.*
Stockbridge Hall

WALTER MILLER BANFIELD, B.S. (Rutgers University), PH.D. (University of
Wisconsin), *Assistant Professor of Botany.*   Clark Hall

---

[1] On leave of absence.

LUTHER BANTA, B.S. (Cornell University),
Assistant Professor of Poultry Husbandry.   Stockbridge Hall

ROLLIN HAYES BARRETT, B.S. (University of Connecticut), M.S. (Cornell
University), Professor of Farm Management.   Stockbridge Hall

LEON OSER BARRON, B.A. (University of Massachusetts), M.A. (University of
Minnesota), Assistant Professor of English.   Chapel

FRANK DANA BARTLETT, JR., B.S. (University of Massachusetts),
Instructor in Animal Husbandry.   Stockbridge Hall

LAWRENCE MATTHEWS BARTLETT, B.S., M.S. (University of Massachusetts),
PH.D. (Cornell University), Associate Professor of Zoology.
                                                        Fernald Hall

MAURICE EDWARD BATES, B.S.E. (M.E.) (University of Michigan), S.M.
(Massachusetts Institute of Technology), PH.D. (University of Michigan), Professor of Mechanical Engineering.   Gunness Laboratory

THEODORE LOUIS BATKE, B.A.SC., M.A.SC., PH.D. (University of Toronto),
Assistant Professor of Chemical Engineering.   Engineering Annex

MATTHEW LOUIS BLAISDELL, B.S. (University of Massachusetts), Associate
Professor, Superintendent of Farms and Head of Station Service.
                                                East Experiment Station

LYLE LINCOLN BLUNDELL, B.S. (Iowa State College),
Professor of Horticulture.   Wilder Hall

JAMES SALVATORE BOSCO, B.S. (Springfield College), M.S. (University of
Illinois), Instructor in Physical Education.
                                        Physical Education Building

REGINA BOUIN, B.S. (Tufts College),
Instructor in Physical Education for Women.   Drill Hall

HAROLD DANFORTH BOUTELLE, B.S., C.E. (Worcester Polytechnic Institute),
Associate Professor of Mathematics.   Mathematics Building

WILLIAM WELCH BOYER, B.S., C.E., M.S., C.E. (North Carolina State College),
Assistant Professor of Civil Engineering.   Stockbridge Hall

GERARD BRAUNTHAL, B.A. (Queen's College), M.A. (University of Michigan),
PH.D. (Columbia University), Instructor in Government.
                                                        North College

LAWRENCE ELLIOTT BRIGGS, B.S., M.S. (University of Massachusetts),
Associate Professor of Physical Education.
                                        Physical Education Building

MILDRED BRIGGS, A.B. (DePauw University), M.S. (Iowa State College),
Associate Professor of Home Economics.   Edna Skinner Hall

KENNETH LLOYD BULLIS, D.V.M. (Iowa State College), M.S. (University of
Massachusetts), Professor of Veterinary Science and Head of Department.   Paige Laboratory

JAMES WILLIAM BURKE, B.S. (University of Massachusetts),
Secretary of the University.   South College

BERNARD PHILIP BUSSEL, B.S. (University of Massachusetts), M.A. (Columbia
University), Instructor in Mathematics.   Mathematics Building

RICHARD WENDELL BUTLER, B.S. in M.E. (University of Massachusetts),
Instructor in Mechanical Engineering.   Engineering Wing

HALL GERALD BUZZELL, A.B. (Dartmouth College), M.S. (University of Massachusetts), *Instructor in Mathematics.*   Mathematics Building

FRED VIRGIL CAHILL, JR., B.A., M.A. (University of Nebraska), PH.D. (Yale University), *Professor of Government.*   North College

THEODORE CUYLER CALDWELL, B.A. (College of Wooster), A.M. (Harvard University), PH.D. (Yale University), *Professor of History.*   Chapel

GEORGE WESLEY CANNON, B.A. (Dakota Wesleyan University), M.S., PH.D. (University of Illinois), *Associate Professor of Chemistry.*
Goessmann Laboratory

DOUGLAS CARMICHAEL, A.B. (Bowdoin College), A.M. (Harvard University), PH.D. (Indiana University), *Instructor in Philosophy.*   North College

HAROLD WHITING CARY, A.B. (Williams College), A.M. (Harvard University), PH.D. (Yale University), *Professor of History and Head of Department.*
Chapel

[1]KENNETH DELBERT CASHIN, B.S. in CH.E., M.S. in CH.E. (Worcester Polytechnic Institute), *Assistant Professor of Chemical Engineering.*

JAMES WARREN CHADWICK, JR., B.S. (University of Massachusetts), *Instructor in Animal Husbandry.*   Stockbridge Hall

HARRY JOHN CHRISTOFFERS, B.S., M.S. (University of Washington), *Instructor in Chemistry.*   Goessmann Laboratory

DAVID RIDGLEY CLARK, B.A. (Wesleyan University), M.A. (Yale University), *Instructor in English.*   Chapel

KATHERINE ALLEN CLARKE, A.B. (Goucher College), M.A. (Middlebury College), *Docteur de l'Universite de Grenoble, Assistant Professor of French.*   Liberal Arts Annex

EDWARD CLIFFORD, A.B. (Roosevelt College), M.A. (University of Chicago), *Instructor in Psychology.*   Liberal Arts Annex

WILLIAM GEORGE COLBY, B.S.A. (University of Illinois), M.S., PH.D. (Rutgers University), *Professor of Agronomy and Head of Department.*
Stockbridge Hall

ALTON BRIGHAM COLE, B.S. (University of Massachusetts), M.F. (Yale University), *Captain, USAF, Assistant Professor of Air Science.*
Drill Hall

DAN STEAD COLLINS, B.S. (University of Pennsylvania), M.A. (University of North Carolina), *Instructor in English.*   Chapel

RICHARD MOWRY COLWELL, B.S., M.S. (University of Rhode Island), PH.D. (University of Massachusetts), *Associate Professor of Accounting.*
North College

WALTER E. CONRAD, B.S., M.S. (Wayne University), PH.D. (University of Kansas), *Instructor in Chemistry.*   Goessmann Laboratory

JOSEPH CONTINO, B. MUS. (Oberlin College), M.A. (Columbia University), *Instructor in Music.*   Memorial Hall

MRS. GLADYS MAE COOK, B.S. (Battle Creek College), M.S. (University of Massachusetts), *Assistant Professor of Home Economics.*
Edna Skinner Hall

---

[1] On leave of absence.

THOMAS ALBERT COOKINGHAM, B.S. (Cornell University), *Captain, Armor, U.S.A., Assistant Professor of Military Science and Tactics.*
Drill Hall

ARMAND J. COSTA, B.A. (American International College), *Instructor in Mechanical Engineering.*
Engineering Shop

BENJAMIN CHARLES CROOKER, JR., B.S. (University of Massachusetts), *Instructor in Physics.*
Hasbrouck Laboratory

[1]THOMAS ALOYSIUS CULBERTSON, B.S. (University of Massachusetts), *Assistant Professor of Food Technology.*

HELEN FRANCES CULLEN, A.B. (Radcliffe College), M.A., PH.D. (University of Michigan), *Assistant Professor of Mathematics.*
Mathematics Building

ROBERT THOMAS CURRAN, B.S. in BUS.AD. (College of the Holy Cross), *Associate Professor of Physical Education.*
Physical Education Building

REYNOLD BERNARD CZARNECKI, B.S. (Pennsylvania State University), M.S., PH.D. (University of Illinois), *Assistant Professor of Bacteriology.*
Marshall Hall Annex

DOROTHY DAVIS, B.S. (Syracuse University), M.A. (Columbia University), *Assistant Professor of Home Economics.*
Edna Skinner Hall

[1]EDWARD LYON DAVIS, A.B. (Harvard University), M.S. (University of Massachusetts), *Instructor in Botany.*

JACK FARR DAVIS, B.A. (Livingston State Teachers College, Alabama), M.A. (State University of Iowa), D.ED. (University or Oregon), *Assistant Professor of Physical Education.*
Physical Education Building

WILLIAM ALLEN DAVIS, B.A. (Colgate University), A.M. (Harvard University), *Associate Professor of History.*
Chapel

ROBERT WILLIAM DAY, B.S. in M.E. (University of Massachusetts), M.M.E. (Rensselaer Polytechnic Institute), *Assistant Professor of Mechanical Engineering.*
Gunness Laboratory

LYLE CONWAY DEARDEN, B.A., M.A. (University of Utah), *Instructor in Zoology.*
Fernald Hall

LAWRENCE SUMNER DICKINSON, B.S., M.S. (University of Massachusetts), *Professor of Agrostology.*
Stockbridge Hall

WILLIAM MOORE DIETEL, A.B. (Princeton University), M.A. (Yale University), *Instructor in History.*
Chapel

GELLESTRINA TERESA DiMAGGIO, A.B. (Connecticut College for Women), M.N. (Yale University), *Instructor in Nursing.*
Draper Hall

JOHN HARLAND DITTFACH, B.M.E., M.S. (University of Minnesota), *Associate Professor of Mechanical Engineering.* Gunness Laboratory

EDWIN DOUGLAS DRIVER, A.B. (Temple University), M.A. (University of Pennsylvania), *Assistant Professor of Sociology.*
North College

MRS. MARRON SHAW DuBOIS, B.A. (St. Lawrence University), *Instructor in English.*
Chapel

[1] On leave of absence.

DONALD EGGLESTON EASTLAKE, JR., B.S. in BUS.AD. (Lehigh University), *Major, Armor, U.S.A., Assistant Professor of Military Science and Tactics.* Drill Hall

FRED CHARLES ELLERT, B.S. (University of Massachusetts), M.A. (Amherst College), *Professor of German and Acting Head of Department.* Liberal Arts Annex

J. MURRAY ELLIOT, B.S. (McGill University), *Assistant Professor of Animal Husbandry.* Stockbridge Hall

EDWARD DONALD EMERSON, B.S. in M.E. (Harvard University), M.M.E. (University of Delaware), *Assistant Professor of Mechanical Engineering.* Engineering Wing

MRS. ALICE HOPPER EPSTEIN, B.S. (New Jersey College for Women), M.S. (University of Wisconsin), *Instructor in Mathematics.* Mathematics Building

SEYMOUR EPSTEIN, B.A. (Brooklyn College), M.A., PH.D. (University of Wisconsin), *Assistant Professor of Psychology.* Liberal Arts Annex

DWIGHT EDMUND ERLICK, A.B. (Colby College), M.A., PH.D. (Columbia University), *Instructor in Psychology.* Liberal Arts Annex

JOHN NELSON EVERSON, B.S., M.S. (University of Massachusetts), *Assistant Professor of Agronomy.* Stockbridge Hall

WILLIAM LANCELOT EWBANK, B.S. in ED. (Kansas State Teachers College), *Lieutenant Colonel, USAF, Assistant Professor of Air Science.* Drill Hall

ROBERT SIMION FELDMAN, B.S., M.S., PH.D. (University of Michigan), *Associate Professor of Psychology.* Liberal Arts Annex

CARL RAYMOND FELLERS, A.B. (Cornell University), M.S., PH.D. (Rutgers University), *Professor of Food Technology and Head of Department.* Chenoweth Laboratory

TSUAN HUA FENG, B.S. in C.E. (National Pei-Yang University), M.S., PH.D. (University of Wisconsin), *Assistant Professor of Civil Engineering.* Gunness Laboratory

JAMES M. FERRIGNO, A.B., A.M., PH.D. (Boston University), *Associate Professor of Romance Languages.* Liberal Arts Annex

RICHARD WILLIAM FESSENDEN, B.S., M.S. (University of Massachusetts), PH.D. (Columbia University), *Professor of Inorganic Chemistry.* Goessmann Laboratory

ARTHUR JORDAN FIELD, B.S.E. (University of Pennsylvania), M.A. (Columbia University), *Instructor in Sociology.* North College

[2]GORDON FIELD, B.S., M.S. (University of Massachusetts), *Instructor in Entomology.*

ALMON SUTPHEN FISH, JR., A.B. (Bates College), M.S. (Kansas State College), *Instructor in Pomology.* French Hall

JOHN C. FISHER, B.S. (University of Massachusetts), *Instructor in Geology and Mineralogy.* Fernald Hall

ROY MARSHALL FISHER, A.B. (Clark University), *Assistant Professor of Physics.* Hasbrouck Laboratory

[1] On leave of absence.   [2] On leave of absence for military service.

RICHARD CAROL FOLEY, B.S., M.S. (University of Massachusetts), PH.D. (Rutgers University), *Professor of Animal Husbandry.*
Stockbridge Hall

WILLIAM FOOTRICK, B.S., M.P.E. (Springfield College), *Associate Professor of Physical Education.* Physical Education Building

EDITH COLBURN FORBES, B.S. in ED. (Framingham State Teachers College). M.ED. (Boston University), *Instructor in Home Economics.*
Edna Skinner Hall

[1]CHARLES FREDERIC FRAKER, A.B. (Colorado College), A.M., PH.D. (Harvard University), *Professor of Romance Languages and Head of Department.*

CHARLES FREDERIC FRAKER, JR., A.B. (University of Massachusetts), B.MUS. (Yale University), M.A. (Middlebury College), *Instructor in Romance Languages.* Liberal Arts Annex

RALPH LYLE FRANCE, B.S. (University of Delaware), M.S. (University of Massachusetts), *Professor of Bacteriology and Head of Department.*
Marshall Hall Annex

ARTHUR PERKINS FRENCH, B.S. (Ohio State University), M.S. (University of Massachusetts), PH.D. (University of Minnesota), *Professor of Pomology and Plant Breeding and Head of Department of Pomology.*
French Hall

[1]PAUL ADELARD GAGNON, B.A. (University of Massachusetts), M.A. (Harvard University), *Instructor in History*

PHILIP LYLE GAMBLE, B.S., M.A. (Wesleyan University), PH.D. (Cornell University), *Professor of Economics and Head of Department.*
North College

ROBERT VERRILL GANLEY, B.S. (University of Massachusetts), M.F. (Duke University), *Instructor in Forestry.* Conservation Building

RICHARD FRANKLIN GARBER, B.S. (Springfield College), M.ED. (Pennsylvania State University), *Instructor in Physical Education.*
Physical Education Building

MARY ELLEN MONICA GARVEY, B.S. (University of Massachusetts), *Associate Professor of Bacteriology.* Marshall Hall Annex

ARCHIE PETER GAUTHIER, B.S. (Louisiana State University), *Lieutenant Colonel Armor, USA., Assistant Professor of Military Science and Tactics.* Drill Hall

RICHARD McIVER GILLIS, B.B.A. (Tulane University), M.B.A. (University of Pennsylvania), *Assistant Professor of Business Administration.*
Draper Hall

MARY ELIZABETH GILMORE, B.S. (Simmons College), M.S. (The Catholic University of America), *Associate Professor of Nursing.* Draper Hall

CHESTER STEPHEN GLADCHUK, B.S.ED. (Boston College), *Assistant Football Coach.* Physical Education Building

STOWELL COOLIDGE GODING, A.B. (Dartmouth College), A.M. (Harvard University), PH.D. (University of Wisconsin), *Professor of French*
Liberal Arts Annex

---

[1] On leave of absence.

MAXWELL HENRY GOLDBERG, B.S. (University of Massachusetts), M.A., PH.D. (Yale University), *Professor of English.* Chapel

ULRICH KARL GOLDSMITH, B.A., M.A. (University of Toronto), PH.D. (University of California), *Associate Professor of German.*
Liberal Arts Annex

GEORGE GOODWIN, JR., B.A. (Williams College), M.A. (Harvard University), *Assistant Professor of Government.* North College

ALBERT EDWARD GOSS, B.A., M.A., PH.D. (State University of Iowa), *Associate Professor of Psychology.* Liberal Arts Annex

JACK ERWIN GRAPENTINE, B.A. (Mount Union College), *Major, USAF, Assistant Professor of Air Science.* Drill Hall

SUMNER MELVIN GREENFIELD, A.B. (Boston College), A.M. (Boston University and Harvard University), *Instructor in Romance Languages.*
Liberal Arts Annex

THOMAS AUGUSTUS GROW, B.S. (University of Connecticut), M.S. (Virginia Polytechnic Institute), *Assistant Professor of Civil Engineering.*
Engineering Wing

EVA RUTH GRUBLER, B.A. (Hunter College), M.A. (Columbia University), *Instructor in Psychology.* Liberal Arts Annex

HERBERT WILLIAM HAAS, B.S. in C.E. (University of Wisconsin), *Lecturer in Public Health.* Marshall Hall Annex

LAWRENCE CARROLL HACKAMACK, B.A. (Culver-Stockton College), M.S. (Western Illinois State College), *Assistant Professor of Industrial Administration.* Draper Hall

WILLIAM HALLER, JR., A.B. (Amherst College), M.A., PH.D. (Columbia University), *Assistant Professor of Economics.* North College

TOM SHERMAN HAMILTON, JR., B.F.A. in LAND ARCH. (University of Illinois), *Instructor in Landscape Architecture.* Wilder Hall

ROSS ELDON HAMLIN, B.S. (Purdue University), *Captain, USAF, Assistant Professor of Air Science.* Drill Hall

DENZEL J. HANKINSON, B.S. (Michigan State College), M.S. (University of Connecticut), PH.D. (Pennsylvania State University), *Professor of Dairy Industry and Head of Department.* Flint Laboratory

JOHN FRANCIS HANSON, B.S., M.S., PH.D. (University of Massachusetts), *Associate Professor of Insect Morphology.* Fernald Hall

HAROLD ERNEST HARDY, A.B. (Pomona College), PH.D. (University of Minnesota), *Professor of Marketing.* Draper Hall

RICHARD HAVEN, A.B. (Harvard University), M.A. (Princeton University), B.LITT. (Oxford University), *Instructor in English.* Chapel

SARAH LOUISE HAWES, B.S. (Northern Michigan College of Education), M.S. (Cornell University), *Instructor in Home Economics.*
Edna Skinner Hall

GERALD M. HEALY, A.B. (St. Michael's College), *Instructor,* (Director of Sports Information). Physical Education Building

VERNON PARKER HELMING, B.A. (Carleton College), PH.D. (Yale University), *Professor of English.* Chapel

KARL NEWCOMB HENDRICKSON, B.S., M.S. (University of Maine),
Associate Professor of Civil Engineering. Gunness Laboratory

ROBIN DAVID STEWART HIGHAM, A.B. (Harvard University), M.A. (Claremont Graduate School), *Instructor in History.* Chapel

ALBERT SEYMOUR HILL, A.B. (Boston University), A.M. (Harvard University), *Instructor in History.* North College

[1]MRS. FLORIANA TARANTINO HOGAN, B.S., A.M. (Boston University),
Instructor in English

ROBERT POWELL HOLDSWORTH, B.S. (Michigan State College), M.F. (Yale University), *Professor of Forestry and Head of Department.*
Conservation Building

BRONISLAW MARK HONIGBERG, A.B., M.A., PH.D. (University of California),
Assistant Professor of Zoology. Fernald Hall

LEONTA GERTRUDE HORRIGAN, B.S. (University of Massachusetts), M.A.
(Smith College), *Assistant Professor of English.* Chapel

MARSHALL CHAPMAN HOWARD, A.B. (Princeton University), PH.D. (Cornell University), *Assistant Professor of Economics.* North College

ELISABETH VICKERY HUBBARD, B.S. (University of Wisconsin), M.A. (University of Chicago), *Instructor in Physical Education for Women.*
Drill Hall

SAMUEL CHURCH HUBBARD, *Assistant Professor of Floriculture.* French Hall

ALEXANDER HULL, JR., B.A., M.A. (University of Washington),
Instructor in French. Liberal Arts Annex

ANGELO IANTOSCA, S.B. (Massachusetts Institute of Technology),
Visiting Lecturer in Public Health. Marshall Hall Annex

FRED PAINTER JEFFREY, B.S. (Pennsylvania State University), M.S. (University of Massachusetts), *Associate Dean of the School of Agriculture and Director of the Stockbridge School.* Stockbridge Hall

RANDOLPH ANTHONY JESTER, B.S. (Virginia Polytechnic Institute), M.S.
(Rutgers University), *Instructor in Floriculture.* French Hall

WARREN IRVING JOHANSSON, B.S., M.S. (University of Massachusetts)),
Assistant Professor of Geology and Mineralogy. Fernald Hall

ROBERT BROWN JOHNSON, A.B. (Ohio University), M.A., PH.D. (University of Wisconsin), *Assistant Professor of Romance Languages.*
Liberal Arts Annex

WILLIAM BRADFORD JOHNSON, B.S. (Pennsylvania State University), M.S.
(University of Massachusetts), *Instructor in Olericulture.* French Hall

SIDNEY KAPLAN, B.A. (College of the City of New York), M.A. (Boston University), *Assistant Professor of English.* Chapel

JOHN HOPKINS KARLSON, B.S. in E.E. (University of Wisconsin), M.S. in E.E.
(Northwestern University), *Assistant Professor of Electrical Engineering.* Gunness Laboratory

SIDNEY WILLIAM KAUFFMAN, B.S., M.ED. (Springfield College), *Professor of Physical Education and Head of Department of Physical Education for Men.* Physical Education Building

[1] On leave of absence.

RESIDENT FACULTY

CAROLYN HELEN KENDROW, B.S. (University of Massachusetts),
Instructor in Chemistry. Goessmann Laboratory

EDWIN HERBERT KETCHLEDGE, B.S., M.S. (New York State College of
Forestry), *Instructor in Botany.* Clark Hall

CARL ANTON KEYSER, B.S. (Carnegie Institute of Technology), B.S., M.S.
(Worcester Polytechnic Institute), *Associate Professor of Metallurgy.*
Engineering Wing

MILO KIMBALL, B.S. (Ohio Northern University), B.B.A., M.B.A. (Boston
University), *Dean of the School of Business Administration.*
Draper Hall

CLARENCE WENDELL KING, B.A., M.A., PH.D. (Yale University),
Associate Professor of Sociology. North College

GORDON STEPHENSON KING, B.S. (Michigan State College),
Assistant Professor of Arboriculture. Wilder Hall

ROBERT McCUNE KINGDON, B.A. (Oberlin College), M.A. (Columbia
University), *Instructor in History.* North College

DAVID WARREN KNUDSEN, B.S. in E.E. (University of Maine),
Instructor in Electrical Engineering. Engineering Wing

STANLEY KOEHLER, A.B., A.M. (Princeton University), A.M. (Harvard University), PH.D. (Princeton University), *Assistant Professor of English.*
Chapel

JAY HENRY KORSON, B.S. (Villanova College), M.A., PH.D. (Yale University),
Professor of Sociology and Head of Department. North College

STEPHEN RAYMOND KOSAKOWSKI,
Instructor in Physical Education. Physical Education Building

STEPHEN EARNEST KOELZ, B.S., M.S. (University of Illinois), M.P.H. (University of Michigan), *Lecturer in Public Health.*
Marshall Hall Annex

THEODORE THOMAS KOZLOWSKI, B.S. (Syracuse University), M.A., PH.D.
(Duke University), *Professor of Botany and Head of Department.*
Clark Hall

HENRY KRATZ, JR., B.A. (New York State College for Teachers), M.A., PH.D.
(Ohio State University), *Instructor in German.* Liberal Arts Annex

[1]WALTER SIDELINGER LAKE, B.S., M.ED. (Fitchburg State Teachers College),
Assistant Professor of Mechanical Engineering.

ROBERT PHILIPS LANE, A.B. (Columbia University), A.M. (Harvard
University), *Assistant Professor of English.* Chapel

JOSEPH WALTON LANGFORD, JR., B.S. (University of New Hampshire), S.M.
(Massachusetts Institute of Technology), *Associate Professor of Electrical Engineering.* Engineering Wing

MARSHALL OLIN LANPHEAR, B.S., M.S. (University of Massachusetts),
Registrar. South College

EDWARD PETER LARKIN, B.S., M.S., PH.D. (University of Massachusetts),
Instructor in Public Health. Marshall Hall Annex

HENRY ARTHUR LEA, B.S. in ED., M.A. (University of Pennsylvania),
Instructor in German. Liberal Arts Annex

[1] On leave of absence.

298

WALTER WILFRED LEE, M.B., M.D. (Toronto University), M.P.H. (Harvard University), *Lecturer in Public Health.* Marshall Hall Annex

ROBERT WARD LENTILHON, B.S. (University of Rhode Island), M.B.A. (Boston University), *Assistant Professor of Business Administration.*
Draper Hall

ARTHUR SIDNEY LEVINE, B.S., M.S., PH.D. (University of Massachusetts), *Associate Professor of Food Technology.* Chenoweth Laboratory

ARNOLD EDWIN LEVITT, B.A. (Reed College), M.A., PH.D. (Oregon State College), *Instructor in Chemistry.* Goessmann Laboratory

HARRY GOTTFRED LINDQUIST, B.S. (University of Massachusetts), M.S. (University of Maryland), *Assistant Professor of Dairy Industry.*
Flint Laboratory

ADRIAN HERVE LINDSEY, B.S. (University of Illinois), M.S., PH.D. (Iowa State College), *Professor of Agricultural Economics and Head of Department of Agricultural Economics and Farm Management.* Draper Hall

EDGAR ERNEST LINDSEY, B.S. in CH.E. (Georgia School of Technology), D.ENG. (Yale University), *Professor of Chemical Engineering and Head of Department.* Engineering Annex

LOWELL EDWIN LINGO, B.E., M.E. (Yale University), *Assistant Professor of Electrical Engineering.* Engineering Wing

HENRY NELSON LITTLE, B.S. (Cornell University), M.S., PH.D. (University of Wisconsin), *Associate Professor of Chemistry.* Goessmann Laboratory

GIDEON ELEAZAR LIVINGSTON, B.A. (New York University), M.S., PH.D. (University of Massachusetts), *Assistant Professor of Food Technology.*
Chenoweth Laboratory

ROBERT BLAIR LIVINGSTON, A.B. (Colorado College), M.A., PH.D. (Duke University), *Professor of Botany.* Clark Hall

JOHN BAILEY LONGSTAFF, B.S. (United States Naval Academy), M.S. (Pennsylvania State University), *Associate Professor of Mechanical Engineering.* Gunness Laboratory

EARL EASTMAN LORDEN, B.S., M.ED. (University of New Hampshire), *Professor of Physical Education.* Physical Education Building

JAMES BUREN LUDTKE, B.A., M.A., PH.D. (State University of Iowa), *Associate Professor of Business Finance.* Draper Hall

DANIEL JUSTIN McCARTHY, B.S.E., ED.M. (Bridgewater State Teachers College), *Assistant Professor of Education.* Liberal Arts Annex

WILLIAM PRESTON MacCONNELL, B.S. (University of Massachusetts), M.F. (Yale University), *Assistant Professor of Forestry.*
Conservation Building

ROSSLYN CLAYTON McCOLLOR, B.A. (University of Minnesota), *Captain, USAFR, Assistant Professor of Air Science.* Drill Hall

MRS. JANE FRANCES McCULLOUGH, B.S., M.S. (Ohio University), *Assistant Professor of Home Economics.* Edna Skinner Hall

MARY ELIZABETH MACDONALD, A.B. (Emmanuel College), M.A. (Columbia University), *Associate Professor of Nursing.* Draper Hall

WARREN PIERCE McGUIRK, PH.B. (Boston College), ED.M. (Boston University), *Professor of Physical Education and Head of Division.*
Physical Education Building

IAN TENNANT MORRISON MacIVER,
Instructor in Landscape Architecture. Wilder Hall

GERALD JOSEPH McLINDON, B.ARCH., DIPL.C.D. (University of Liverpool), *Assistant Professor of Landscape Architecture.* Wilder Hall

EARL JAMES McWHORTER, B.S. (Rensselaer Polytechnic Institute), *Instructor in Chemistry.* Goessmann Laboratory

ALBERT PIERPONT MADEIRA, A.B. (Bowdoin College), M.A. (University of New Hampshire), *Instructor in English.* Stockbridge Hall

MARY ANN MAHER, B.S., A.M. (Columbia University), *Professor of Nursing and Head of the Division of Nursing.* Draper Hall

LEWIS CASPER MAINZER, B.A. (New York University), M.A. (University of Chicago), *Instructor in Government.* North College

MANLEY MANDEL, B.A. (Brooklyn College), M.S., PH.D. (Michigan State College), *Assistant Professor of Bacteriology.* Marshall Hall

JOHN FRANCIS MANFREDI, B.S. (University of Pennsylvania), M.A., PH.D. (Harvard University), *Instructor in Sociology.* North College

JOSEPH SOL MARCUS, B.S. (Worcester Polytechnic Institute), M.S. (University of Massachusetts), *Assistant Professor of Civil Engineering.*
Engineering Wing

[1]MINER JOHN MARKUSON, B.S. in ARCH. (University of Minnesota), *Associate Professor of Agricultural Engineering.*

GEORGE ANDREWS MARSTON, B.S., C.E. (Worcester Polytechnic Institute), M.S. (University of Iowa), *Dean of the School of Engineering.*
Engineering Wing

ALFRED HERMAN MATHIESON, JR., S.B. (State Teachers College, East Stroudsburg, Pennsylvania), M.A. (Columbia University), *Assistant Professor of Physics.* Hasbrouck Laboratory

GUENTER H. MATTERSDORFF, A.B., A.M. (Harvard University), *Instructor in Economics.* North College

BERNARD MAUSNER, B.A., M.A., PH.D. (Columbia University), *Assistant Professor of Psychology.* Liberal Arts Annex

GUY RENE MERMIER, A.B. (Lycee Champollion), CERTIFICAT DE LITTERATURE ET CIVILISATION AMERICIANE, DIPLOME D'ETUDES SUPERIEUR (University de Grenoble), *Instructor in Romance Languages.* Liberal Arts Annex

OREANA ALMA MERRIAM, B.S. (University of Vermont), M.S. (University of Massachusetts), *Associate Professor of Home Economics.*
Edna Skinner Hall

[1]WALTER EUGENE MIENTKA, B.S. (University of Massachusetts), M.A. (Columbia University), *Instructor in Mathematics.*

HELEN SWIFT MITCHELL, A.B. (Mt. Holyoke College), PH.D. (Yale University), *Dean of the School of Home Economics.* Edna Skinner Hall

JOHN HOWARD MITCHELL, B.S. (Bowdoin College), A.M. (Harvard University), *Assistant Professor of English.* Chapel

---

[1] On leave of absence.

JOHN WILLIAM MOHN, M.E. (Stevens Institute of Technology), B.S. (Worcester Polytechnic Institute), M.S. (Stanford University), *Associate Professor of Electrical Engineering.* Engineering Wing

BRUCE ROBERT MORRIS, A.B. (Western Reserve University), M.A. (Ohio State University), PH.D. (University of Illinois), *Professor of Economics.* North College

DONALD EUGENE MOSER, A.B. (Amherst College), A.M. (Brown University), *Instructor in Mathematics.* Mathematics Building

ARTHUR BENSON MUSGRAVE, B.S., M.S. (Boston University), NIEMAN FELLOW IN JOURNALISM (Harvard University), *Professor of Journalism.* North College

CLAIR WAYLAND NAYLOR, PH.B., M.A. (Yale University), *Instructor in Mathematics.* Mathematics Building

[1]CLAUDE CASSELL NEET, A.B. (University of California, Los Angeles), M.A., PH.D. (Clark University), *Professor of Psychology and Head of Department.*

ALBERT BIGELOW NELSON, B.S. (Colby College), M.S. (Middlebury College), *Assistant Professor of Geology and Mineralogy.* Fernald Hall

D. HORACE NELSON, B.S. (University of New Hampshire), M.S. (University of Missouri), PH.D. (Pennsylvania State University), *Assistant Professor of Dairy Industry.* Flint Laboratory

AUGUST NEWLANDER, JR., B.S. (University of Denver), M.S. (University of Chicago), *Instructor in Mathematics.* Mathematics Building

JOHN CARTLIDGE NICHOLSON, B.S. (Sir John Cass College, London), *Instructor in Physics.* Hasbrouck Laboratory

NORTON HART NICKERSON, B.S. (University of Massachusetts), M.A. (University of Texas), PH.D. (Washington University), *Instructor in Botany.* Clark Hall

ARTHUR ELLSWORTH NIEDECK, B.S. (Ithaca College), M.A. (Cornell University), *Professor of Speech.* Dramatic Workshop

WILLIAM BROWN NUTTING, B.S., M.S. (University of Massachusetts), PH.D. (Cornell University), *Assistant Professor of Zoology.* Fernald Hall

GEORGE JAMES OBERLANDER, B.S. (Tufts College), *Instructor in Chemistry.* Goessmann Laboratory

ANN HELEN O'DONNELL, B.S. (University of Vermont), M.S. (University of Massachusetts), *Instructor in Education.* Liberal Arts Annex

WILLIAM GREGORY O'DONNELL, B.S. (University of Massachusetts), M.A., PH.D. (Yale University), *Professor of English.* Chapel

SALLY ANN OGILVIE, B.S., M.ED. (University of North Carolina), *Instructor in Physical Education for Women.* Drill Hall

HELEN FRANCES O'LEARY, B.S. in ED., ED.M. (Boston University), *Assistant Professor of Education.* Liberal Arts Annex

CHARLES FRANK OLIVER, B.S., M.S. (University of Massachusetts), *Assistant Professor of Education.* Liberal Arts Annex

DONALD JAMES OLSEN, B.A., M.A.. PH.D. (Yale University), *Instructor in History.* Chapel

---

[1] On leave of absence.

CHARLES CHRISTOPHER O'ROURKE, B.S. (Boston College),
Head Coach. Physical Education Building

ELMER CLAYTON OSGOOD, C.E., D.ENG. (Rensselaer Polytechnic Institute),
Professor of Civil Engineering. Stockbridge Hall

RAYMOND HERMAN OTTO, B.S. (University of Massachusetts), M.L.A. (Harvard University), *Professor of Landscape Architecture and Head of Department.* Wilder Hall

[2]ERNEST MILFORD PARROTT, B.S. (Union University), M.S. (University of Massachusetts), PH.D. (University of Missouri), *Instructor in Chemistry.*

ROBERT KINCAID PATTERSON, B.S. (University of Maine),
Assistant Professor of Agricultural Engineering. Engineering Shop

HENRY BROWN PEIRCE, JR., B.A. (University of Massachusetts), M.F.A. (Carnegie Institute of Technology), *Instructor in Speech.*
Dramatic Workshop

ROBERT CHARLES PERRIELLO, B.S. (University of Massachusetts),
Associate Professor of Bacteriology. Marshall Hall Annex

KENNETH ARTHUR PETERS, A.B. (Ripon College), *Major, Armor, U.S.A.,*
Assistant Professor of Military Science and Tactics. Drill Hall

OTTO PAUL PFLANZE, B.A. (Maryville College), M.A., PH.D. (Yale University),
Assistant Professor of History. Chapel

EDWARD STANLEY PIRA, B.S. (University of Connecticut),
Instructor in Agricultural Engineering. Engineering Shop

ROBERT AARON POTASH, A.B., A.M., PH.D. (Harvard University),
Instructor in History. Chapel

ALFRED XAVIER POWERS, B.S. in ED. (Fitchburg State Teachers College),
Instructor in Agricultural Engineering. Engineering Shop

WALLACE FRANK POWERS, A.B., A.M., PH.D. (Clark University),
Professor of Physics and Head of Department. Hasbrouck Laboratory

PAUL NICHOLAS PROCOPIO, B.S., M.S. (University of Massachusetts),
Assistant Professor of Horticulture. Wilder Hall

ALBERT WILLIAM PURVIS, A.B. (University of New Brunswick), M.ED., D.ED. (Harvard University), *Professor of Education and Head of Department.* Liberal Arts Annex

EUGENE CHARLES PUTALA, B.S., M.S. (University of Massachusetts),
Assistant Professor of Botany. Clark Hall

FRANK PRENTICE RAND, A.B. (Williams College), A.M. (Amherst College),
Professor of English and Head of Department; Acting Dean of School of Liberal Arts. Chapel

WILLIAM EDWIN RANDALL, JR., B.S. (University of Massachusetts), M.S., PH.D. (University of Wisconsin), *Associate Professor of Recreation Leadership.* North College

HAROLD RAUCH, B.S. (Queens College), M.S. (University of Illinois), PH.D. (Brown University), *Assistant Professor of Zoology.* Fernald Hall

GEORGIA REID, B.S. (State University of New York at Cortland),
Instructor in Physical Education for Women. Drill Hall

RESIDENT FACULTY

ARNOLD DENSMORE RHODES, B.S. (University of New Hampshire), M.F. (Yale University), *Professor of Forestry.*   Conservation Building

BENJAMIN RICCI, JR., B.S., M.ED. (Springfield College), *Assistant Professor of Physical Education.* Physical Education Building

THOMAS EDWIN RICE, B.S. (University of Massachusetts), *Instructor in Geology.*   Fernald Hall

VICTOR ARTHUR RICE, B.S., D.AGR. (North Carolina State College), M.AGR. (University of Massachusetts), *Professor of Animal Husbandry and Head of Department.*   Stockbridge Hall

JOSEPH HARRY RICH, B.S., M.F. (New York State College of Forestry), *Associate Professor of Forestry.*   Conservation Building

GEORGE ROBERT RICHASON, JR., B.S., M.S. (University of Massachusetts), *Assistant Professor of Chemistry.*   Goessmann Laboratory

[1]MAIDA LEONARD RIGGS, B.S. (University of Massachusetts), *Instructor in Physical Education for Women.*

WALTER STUNTZ RITCHIE, B.S. (Ohio State College), A.M., PH.D. (University of Missouri), *Goessmann Professor of Chemistry and Head of Department; Acting Dean of School of Science.*   Goessmann Laboratory

ROBERT LOUIS RIVERS, A.B. (Clark University), M.S. (University of Illinois), *Assistant Professor of Industrial Administration.*   Draper Hall

JOHN EDWIN ROBERTS, B.S., M.S. (University of New Hampshire), PH.D. (Cornell University), *Assistant Professor of Chemistry.*
Goessmann Laboratory

JOHN LEWIS ROBERTS, B.S., M.S. (University of Wisconsin), PH.D. (University of California), *Assistant Professor of Physiology.*   Marshall Hall

OLIVER COUSENS ROBERTS, B.S. (University of Massachusetts), M.S. (University of Illinois), *Associate Professor of Pomology.*   French Hall

GRACE ROBERTSON, A.B. (Barnard College), M.S. (Smith College), *Instructor in Physical Education for Women.*   Drill Hall

NEWTON YOUNG ROBINSON, B.S., M.S. (Columbia University), *Instructor in Business Administration.*   Draper Hall

DONALD WILLIAM ROGERS, B.S. (Northwestern University), M.A., PH.D. (Yale University), *Assistant Professor of Philosophy.*   North College

JOSEPH RICHARD ROGERS, JR., *Associate Professor of Physical Education.*
Physical Education Building

HERBERT DUNCAN ROLLASON, JR., A.B. (Middlebury College), M.A. (Williams College), A.M., PH.D. (Harvard University), *Assistant Professor of Zoology.*   Fernald Hall

ISRAEL HAROLD ROSE, B.A., M.A. (Brooklyn College), PH.D. (Harvard University), *Associate Professor of Mathematics.*   Mathematics Building

DONALD ERNEST ROSS, B.S. (University of Massachusetts), *Assistant Professor of Floriculture.*   French Hall

WILLIAM HAROLD ROSS, B.A., M.A. (Amherst College), PH.D. (Yale University), *Associate Professor of Physics.*   Hasbrouck Laboratory

[1] On leave of absence.

303

WILLIAM MARTIN ROURKE, B.A. (Beloit College), M.S. (Northwestern University), *Assistant Professor of Education.* Liberal Arts Annex

CARL SHERWOOD ROYS, B.S. (Worcester Polytechnic Institute), M.S. in E.E., PH.D. (Purdue University), *Professor of Electrical Engineering and Acting Head of Department.* Engineering Wing

SEYMOUR RUDIN, B.A., M.S. (College of the City of New York), PH.D. (Cornell University), *Instructor in English.* Chapel

SARGENT RUSSELL, B.S. (University of Maine), M.S. (Cornell University), *Assistant Professor of Agricultural Economics.* Stockbridge Hall

WILLIAM MORRIS SAGE, A.B. (Colorado State College of Education), ED.M. (Boston University), *Captain, USAF, Assistant Professor of Air Science.* Drill Hall

STANLEY FRANCIS SALWAK, B.S., M.S. (University of Massachusetts), D.ED. (Pennsylvania State University), *Assistant Professor of Physical Education.* Physical Education Building

WILLIAM CROCKER SANCTUARY, B.S., M.S. (University of Massachusetts), *Professor of Poultry Husbandry.* Stockbridge Hall

RICHARD CHASE SAVAGE, B.A. (University of North Carolina), M.A. (Columbia University), *Instructor in English.* Chapel

HENRY HERBERT SCARBOROUGH, JR., B.S. (University of Texas), *Instructor in Botany.* Clark Hall

SIDNEY SCHOEFFLER, B.S. (New York University), A.M. (University of Pennsylvania), PH.D. (The New School for Social Research), C.P.A. (New Jersey), *Assistant Professor of Economics.* North College

NORMAN JAMES SCHOONMAKER, B.S. (University of Massachusetts), S.M. (University of Chicago), PH.D. (University of Pittsburgh), *Assistant Professor of Mathematics.* Mathematics Building

ADOLF ERNST SCHROEDER, B.A. (University of Illinois), M.A. (Louisiana State University), PH.D. (Ohio State University), *Associate Professor of German.* Liberal Arts Annex

RALPH EDGAR SCHWARTZ, PH.B., S.M. (University of Chicago), *Instructor in Mathematics.* Mathematics Building

ARNOLD GIDEON SHARP, B.S. in M.E. (Tufts College), M.S. in M.E. (Worcester Polytechnic Institute), *Assistant Professor of Civil Engineering.* Gunness Laboratory

FRANK ROBERT SHAW, B.S. (University of Massachusetts), PH.D. (Cornell University), *Associate Professor of.Entomology and Beekeeping.* Fernald Hall

LAWRENCE WILLIAM SHERMAN, JR., B.S. in B.A. (Miami University), M.B.A. (Indiana University), *Assistant Professor of Business Administration.* Draper Hall

CLARENCE SHUTE, A.B. (Asbury College), A.M., PH.D. (Columbia University), *Associate Professor of Philosophy.* North College

DALE HAROLD SIELING, B.S., M.S. (Kansas State College), PH.D. (Iowa State College), *Dean of Agriculture and Director of the Experiment Station.* East Experiment Station

FRANK ALBERT SINGER, B.S., M.B.A. (Indiana University),
Assistant Professor of Accounting. Draper Hall

HENRY HILLS SKILLINGS, A.B. (Amherst College),
Instructor in Mathematics. Mathematics Building

HAROLD WILLIAM SMART, LL.B. (Boston University), A.B. (Amherst College),
Associate Professor of Business Law. Draper Hall

J. HAROLD SMITH, B.S., M.A. (University of Utah), PH.D. (University
of Wisconsin), *Professor of Chemistry.* Goessmann Laboratory

MARION ESTELLE SMITH, B.S., M.S. (University of Massachusetts), PH.D.
(University of Illinois), *Assistant Professor of Entomology.*
Fernald Hall

RICHARD HENRY SMITH, B.S. (United States Military Academy), *Colonel,
USAF, Professor of Air Science and Head of Division.* Drill Hall

RUSSELL EATON SMITH, B.S. (University of Massachusetts), V.M.D. (University of Pennsylvania), *Professor of Veterinary Science.*
Paige Laboratory

WALTER WORCESTER SMITH, B.E.E. (Northeastern University),
Assistant Professor of Electrical Engineering. Engineering Wing

[1]JAMES GEORGE SNEDECOR, B.S. (Iowa State College), PH.D. (Indiana
University), *Associate Professor of Physiology.*

ERNEST AUGUSTUS SNOW, B.S., M.S. (Harvard University),
Lecturer in Public Health. Fernald Hall

GRANT BINGEMAN SNYDER, B.S.A. (University of Toronto), M.S. (Michigan
State College), *Professor of Olericulture and Head of Department.*
French Hall

DANIEL SOBALA, S.B. (Massachusetts Institute of Technology),
Assistant Professor of Mechanical Engineering. Gunness Laboratory

ODDVAR SOLSTAD, B.S. (Tufts College), M.S. (University of Massachusetts),
Instructor in Chemical Engineering. Engineering Annex

LEO FRANK SOLT, B.A. (Iowa State Teachers College), M.A. (University of
Iowa), *Instructor in History.* Chapel

RICHARD ARTHUR SOUTHWICK, B.S., M.S. (University of Vermont),
Instructor in Agronomy. Stockbridge Hall

HERBERT NORMAN STAPLETON, B.S., M.S. (Kansas State College), *Professor
of Agricultural Engineering and Head of Department.*
Stockbridge Hall

EDMUND JOSEPH STAWIECKI, B.S. (University of Massachusetts), M.A. (University of Iowa), *Instructor in German.* Liberal Arts Annex

RICHARD STEPHEN STEIN, B.S. (Brooklyn Polytechnic Institute), M.A., PH.D.
(Princeton University), *Assistant Professor of Chemistry.*
Goessmann Laboratory

MARY JANE STRATTNER, B.S. (College of St. Elizabeth), M.A. (University of
Minnesota), *Assistant Professor of Home Economics.* Edna Skinner Hall

HARVEY LEROY SWEETMAN, B.S. (Colorado State College), M.S. (Iowa State
College), PH.D. (University of Massachusetts), *Professor of Entomology.*
Fernald Hall

---

[1] On leave of absence.

305

JOHN DAVID SWENSON, B.S. (New York University), M.A. (Columbia University), *Professor of Mechanical Engineering.*   Gunness Laboratory

PAUL ARTHUR SWENSON, B.S. (Hamline University), PH.D. (Stanford University), *Assistant Professor of Physiology.*   Marshall Hall

WILLIAM HENRY TAGUE, B.S. (Iowa State College),
Assistant Professor of Agricultural Engineering.   Engineering Shop

RAYMOND PORTER TARR, JR., *Colonel, Infantry, U.S.A., Professor of Military Science and Tactics and Head of Division.*   Drill Hall

RENE SIMON TAUBE, DR.CHEM. (Central University, Quito, Ecuador), M.A. (Johns Hopkins University), *Instructor in Spanish and German.*
Liberal Arts Annex

CLARK LEONARD THAYER, B.S. (University of Massachusetts),
Professor of Floriculture and Head of Department.   French Hall

MRS. EMILY PERRY THIES, B.S. (Michigan State College), M.S. (Cornell University), *Instructor in Home Economics.*   Edna Skinner Hall

ZINA JOAN TILLONA, B.A. (Hunter College), M.A. (Wellesley College),
Instructor in Romance Languages.   Liberal Arts Annex

GLENN ERIN TINDER, B.A., M.A. (Pomona College), PH.D. (University of California), *Instructor in Government.*   North College

RAY ETHAN TORREY, B.S. (University of Massachusetts), A.M., PH.D. (Harvard University), *Professor of Botany.*   Clark Hall

RUTH JANE TOTMAN, B.S. (New Jersey College for Women), M.ED. (University of Pittsburgh), *Professor and Director of Physical Education for Women.*   Drill Hall

HENRY IRVING TRAGLE, *Major, Armor, U.S.A.,*
Assistant Professor of Military Science and Tactics.   Drill Hall

JAY R. TRAVER, B.A., M.A., PH.D. (Cornell University),
Assistant Professor of Zoology.   Fernald Hall

REUBEN EDWIN TRIPPENSEE, B.S. (Michigan State College), M.S., PH.D. (University of Michigan), *Professor of Wildlife Management.*
Conservation Building

FREDERICK SHERMAN TROY, B.S. (University of Massachusetts), M.A. (Amherst College), *Professor of English.*   Chapel

ROBERT GARLAND TUCKER, A.B. (Amherst College), A.M. (Harvard University), *Instructor in English.*   ·   Chapel

ALDEN PARKER TUTTLE, B.S. (University of Massachusetts), M.S. (Pennsylvania State University), *Assistant Professor of Vegetable Gardening.*
French Hall

STANLEY VANCE, B.A. (St. Charles College), M.A., PH.D. (University of Pennsylvania), *Professor of Industrial Administration.*   Draper Hall

HENRY LELAND VARLEY, A.B., A.M. (Wesleyan University), PH.D. (University of Wisconsin), *Associate Professor of English.*   Chapel

JOHN HENRY VONDELL,
Associate Professor of Poultry Husbandry.   Stockbridge Hall

ROBERT WANNER WAGNER, A.B. (Ohio University), M.A., PH.D. (University of Michigan), *Professor of Mathematics.*   Mathematics Building

ESTHER MARIE WALLACE, B.S. (Boston University), M.S. (Wellesley College), *Instructor in Physical Education for Women.* Drill Hall

THEODORE JOSEPH WANG, B.S., PH.D. (University of Illinois), *Assistant Professor of Physics.* Hasbrouck Laboratory

NEAL THOMAS WATSON, B.A. (Duke University), A.M. (Harvard University), *Instructor in Mathematics.* Mathematics Building

WILLIAM HENRY WEAVER, B.S. in I.E., M.S. in I.E., I.E. (Pennsylvania State University), *Professor of Mechanical Engineering and Head of Department.* Gunness Laboratory

JOHN AUGUST WEIDHAAS, JR., B.S., M.S. (University of Massachusetts), *Instructor in Entomology.* Fernald Hall

GEORGE PHILIP WEIDMANN, B.S. (College of the City of New York), M.A. (Columbia University), *Assistant Professor of Mechanical Engineering.* Engineering Wing

HAROLD GEORGE WELLS, JR., B.S. (University of Connecticut), *Major, USAFR, Assistant Professor of Air Science.* Drill Hall

SIDNEY FREDERICK WEXLER, B.S. (New York University), M.A. (University of Colorado), PH.D. (New York University), *Assistant Professor of Romance Languages.* Liberal Arts Annex

MERIT PENNIMAN WHITE, A.B., C.E. (Dartmouth College), M.S., PH.D. (California Institute of Technology), *Professor of Civil Engineering and Head of Department.* Stockbridge Hall

MRS. MARGARET KOERBER WILHELM, B.S., M.S. (University of Massachusetts), *Assistant Professor of Home Economics.* Edna Skinner Hall

THOMAS OBERSON WILKINSON, A.B. (University of North Carolina), M.A. (Duke University), *Instructor in Sociology.* North College

ROBERT ERWIN WILL, B.A. (Carleton College), M.A. (Yale University), *Instructor in Economics.* North College

ARTHUR ROBERT WILLIAMS, A.B. (Clark University), A.M., PH.D. (Cornell University), *Assistant Professor of English.* Chapel

HENRY RITCHIE WILSON, *Major Armor, U.S.A., Assistant Professor of Military Science and Tactics.* Drill Hall

LEONARD RICHARD WILSON, PH.B., PH.M., PH.D. (University of Wisconsin), *Professor of Geology and Mineralogy and Head of Department.* Fernald Hall

KAROL STANLEY WISNIESKI, B.S. (University of Massachusetts), M.P.H. (University of Michigan), *Instructor in Bacteriology.* Marshall Hall Annex

BERTRAM GEORGE WOODLAND, B.S. (University College of South Wales and Monmouthshire, Cardiff, Wales), *Instructor in Geology and Mineralogy.* Fernald Hall

GILBERT LLEWELLYN WOODSIDE, B.A. (DePauw University), A.M., PH.D. (Harvard University), *Professor of Biology and Head of Department of Zoology; Dean of Graduate School.* Fernald Hall

HENRY BRONISLAW WORONICZ, B.S. (Boston College), *Instructor in Physical Education.* Physical Education Building

MRS. MARTHA ROCKHOLD WRIGHT, B.S. (Miami University), *Instructor in English.* Chapel

PART TIME FACULTY

RAYMOND WYMAN, B.S. (University of Massachusetts), ED.M. (Boston University), *Assistant Professor of Education and Director, Audio Visual Center.* South College

ANTHONY WILLIAM ZAITZ, B.S.O. (Curry College), M.A. (Boston University), *Assistant Professor of Speech.* Dramatic Workshop

JOHN MICHAEL ZAK, B.S., M.S. (University of Massachusetts), *Assistant Professor of Agronomy.* Stockbridge Hall

EDWARD ALLAN ZANE, B.B.A. (University of Alaska), M.B.A. (Boston University), *Instructor in Business Administration.* Draper Hall

[1]JOHN KARL ZEENDER, B.A., M.A. (The Catholic University of America), PH.D. (Yale University), *Assistant Professor of History.*

PART TIME FACULTY.

LOUIS ALBERT CARPINO, B.S. (Iowa State College), M.S., PH.D. (University of Illinois), *Instructor in Chemistry.* Goessmann Laboratory

MRS. ESTHER STRONG CLAPP, A.B. (Smith College), *Instructor in Music.* Memorial Hall

ENIO FELICIOTTI, B.A., M.A. (Boston University), *Instructor in Food Technology.* Chenoweth Laboratory

ALICE GEORGANTAS, B.A. (University of Massachusetts), *Instructor in Romance Languages.* Liberal Arts Annex

ALLEN WENTWORTH HIXON, JR., B.S. (University of Massachusetts), *Instructor in Landscape Architecture.* Wilder Hall

MRS. KATHERINE WILLIS IRVIN, B.S. (University of North Carolina), *Instructor in Home Economics.* Edna Skinner Hall

MRS. VILMA VERONICA JOA, B.S. (University of Tartu), *Instructor in Russian.* Liberal Arts Annex

JANE T. JUDGE, B.A. (Mt. Holyoke College), M.A. (Smith College), *Instructor in Chemistry.* Goessmann Laboratory

LORRAINE DORIS LAVALLEE, A.B. (Mt. Holyoke College), *Instructor in Mathematics.* Mathematics Building

DONALD EUGENE NEVEL, B.S. in C.E. (Pennsylvania State University), *Instructor in Civil Engineering.* Stockbridge Hall

JEAN ROBERT ROUGE, LICENCE D'ANGLAIS; DIPLOME D'ETUDES SUPERIEURES D'ANGLAIS (Universite de Paris), *Instructor in Romance Languages.* Liberal Arts Annex

DONALD SEWALL SCHEUFELE, B.S., M.S. (Tufts College), *Instructor in Chemistry.* Goessmann Laboratory

BENJAMIN MARTIN SHAUB, M.E., M.S., PH.D. (Cornell University), *Assistant Professor of Geology and Mineralogy.* Fernald Hall

VERA A. SICKELS, *Instructor in Speech.* Dramatic Workshop

HELEN BINKERD STOTT, A.B. (Smith College), *Instructor in Music.* Memorial Hall

---
[1] On leave of absence.

MRS. MARJORIE FIELD SULLIVAN, B.S. (Framingham State Teachers College),
Instructor in Home Economics. Edna Skinner Hall

JOHN EDWARD TYLER, JR., A.B., A.M. (College of the Holy Cross),
Instructor in Chemistry. Goessmann Laboratory

ANA MARGARITA VEUM, PROFESSORA NORMAL CON ESPECIALIDAD EN INGLES,
Instructor in Romance Languages. Liberal Arts Annex

ALBERT WILLIS WALLACE, B.S. (Northeastern University),
Instructor in Mathematics. Mathematics Building

DONALD ELVIN WESTCOTT, B.S., M.S., PH.D. (University of Massachusetts),
Instructor in Food Technology. Chenoweth Laboratory

TEACHING FELLOWS

EDWARD STEPHEN BERESTKA, B.S. (Northeastern University),
Teaching Fellow in Chemistry. Goessmann Laboratory

PAUL RAYMOND BOURDEAU, B.S. (University of Massachusetts),
Teaching Fellow in Education. Liberal Arts Annex

FRANK ROWLAND BRIDGES, JR., B.A. (Norwich University), M.S. (University
of Massachusetts), *Teaching Fellow in Bacteriology and Public Health.*
Marshall Hall

AURORA GARCIA CORPUZ, B.S. (University of the Philippines),
Teaching Fellow in Home Economics. Edna Skinner Hall

STANLEY MICHAEL DEC, B.S. (University of Massachusetts),
Teaching Fellow in Chemistry. Goessmann Laboratory

ROBERT WARREN DELAND, B.S. (University of Massachusetts),
Teaching Fellow in Mathematics. Mathematics Building

JOHN PAUL DUSZA, B.S. (University of Massachusetts),
Teaching Fellow in Chemistry. Goessmann Laboratory

OLIVER SIMEON FLINT, JR., B.S. (University of Massachusetts),
Teaching Fellow in Entomology. Fernald Hall

RAYMOND ROY GAGNON, B.S. (University of Massachusetts),
Teaching Fellow in Education. Liberal Arts Annex

CHARLES LEWIS GOLDMAN, B.S. (Providence College), M.S. (Tufts College),
Teaching Fellow in Bacteriology and Public Health. Marshall Hall

EDITH WINIFRED HADDOCK, B.A. (University of Redlands),
Teaching Fellow in Landscape Architecture. Wilder Hall

JOHN SYLVESTER HALL, B.S. (University of Massachusetts),
Teaching Fellow in Zoology. Fernald Hall

WILLIAM DANIEL HASKINS, B.S. (Boston College),
Teaching Fellow in Bacteriology and Public Health. Marshall Hall

HERBERT DUNKERLY HILL, JR., B.A. (University of Maryland),
Teaching Fellow in Education. Liberal Arts Annex

JOSEPH RAYMOND HILYARD, B.A. (University of Massachusetts),
Teaching Fellow in English. Chapel

TEACHING FELLOWS

KENNETH JOSEPH JACKSON, B.A., (University of Massachusetts),
Teaching Fellow in Economics. North College

HERBERT MARCUS KAGAN, B.S. (University of Massachusetts),
Teaching Fellow in Bacteriology and Public Health. Marshall Hall

HELEN CATHERINE KEEFE, B.A. (University of Massachusetts),
Teaching Fellow in Education. Liberal Arts Annex

MAUREEN CATHERINE KERRIGAN, B.A. (Brandeis University),
Teaching Fellow in Botany. Clark Hall

DONALD GEORGE LEGRAND, B.A. (Boston University),
Teaching Fellow in Chemistry. Goessmann Laboratory

HARVEY ROBERT LEVINE, B.S. (College of the City of New York),
Teaching Fellow in Entomology. Fernald Hall

NORMAN HENRY MACLEOD, B.A. (University of Chicago),
Teaching Fellow in Agronomy. Stockbridge Hall

DALI NARIMAN MALOO, B.S. (Burjorji Pastonji Baria Science Institute),
Teaching Fellow in Food Technology. Chenoweth Laboratory

HERBERT KENNEY MAXFIELD, B.S. (University of Massachusetts),
Teaching Fellow in Wildlife Management. Conservation Building

ROBERT EDWARD MILKEY, B.A. (Hamilton College),
Teaching Fellow in Business Administration. Draper Hall

IRA MINTZ, B.S. (Long Island University), M.A. (New York University),
Teaching Fellow in Psychology. Liberal Arts Annex

MRS. CYNTHIA WILKINS PERCY, B.A. (Mt. Holyoke College),
Teaching Fellow in Geology and Mineralogy. Fernald Hall

DAN EDWIN PRATT, B.S., M.S. (University of Georgia),
Teaching Fellow in Food Technology. Chenoweth Laboratory

RALPH ROTHSTEIN, B.A. (University of Michigan),
Teaching Fellow in Psychology. Liberal Arts Annex

BERNARD L. RYACK, B.S. (University of Connecticut), M.A. (University of
Pennsylvania), *Teaching Fellow in Psychology.* Liberal Arts Annex

NELSON JAMES SARRIS, B.S. (Amherst College),
Teaching Fellow in Geology and Mineralogy. Fernald Hall

SIDNEY GEORGE SPECTOR, B.A. (Harvard University), M.S. (University of
Massachusetts), *Teaching Fellow in Bacteriology and Public Health.*
Marshall Hall

VICTOR ANTHONY TRIOLO, B.S. (Brooklyn College),
Teaching Fellow in Zoology. Fernald Hall

MADELEINE MARIE ODETTE VUATEAU, B.A. (Jeanne de France, Nice),
Teaching Fellow in Romance Languages. Liberal Arts Annex

LYNN WETHERILL, B.S. (University of the South),
Teaching Fellow in Chemistry. Goessmann Laboratory

EXPERIMENT STATION STAFF

DALE HAROLD SIELING, B.S., M.S. (Kansas State College), PH.D. (Iowa State College), *Dean of Agriculture and Director of the Experiment Station.*
East Experiment Station

EDWARD EVERETT ANDERSON, B.S., M.S., PH.D. (University of Massachusetts), *Associate Professor, Research, Food Technology.*
Chenoweth Laboratory

JOHN GEDDIE ARCHIBALD, B.S. (Toronto University), M.S. (University of Massachusetts), *Professor, Research, Animal Husbandry.*
Goessmann Laboratory

JOHN SEARLS BAILEY, B.S. (Michigan State College), M.S. (Iowa State College), *Associate Professor, Research, Cranberry Station.*
East Wareham

ALLEN BROWN BARTON, B.S. (University of Minnesota), M.S. (University of Connecticut), *Associate Professor, Research, Agricultural Engineering.*
Stockbridge Hall

WILLIAM BERNARD BECKER, B.S. (New York State College of Forestry), M.S., PH.D. (University of Massachusetts), *Assistant Professor, Research, Entomology.*
Fernald Hall

EMMETT BENNETT, B.S. (Ohio State University), M.S. (University of Massachusetts), PH.D. (Pennsylvania State University), *Professor, Research, Chemistry.*
Goessmann Laboratory

WALLACE GORDON BLACK, B.S., M.S., PH.D. (University of Wisconsin), *Associate Professor, Research, Animal Husbandry.*
Stockbridge Hall

MATTHEW LOUIS BLAISDELL, B.S. (University of Massachusetts), *Associate Professor; Superintendent of Farms and Head of Station Service.*
East Experiment Station

PAUL FREDERICK BOBULA, B.S. (University of Massachusetts), M.S. (Ohio State University), *Instructor, Research, Nursery Culture.*
Waltham Field Station

ARTHUR ISRAEL BOURNE, A.B. (Dartmouth College), *Professor, Research, Entomology.*
Fernald Hall

ALFRED ALEXANDER BROWN, B.S., M.S. (University of Massachusetts), *Professor, Research, Agricultural Economics.*
Draper Hall

ROBERT WELLS BRUNDAGE, B.S., M.S. (University of Maine), *Instructor, Research, Agricultural Economics.*
Draper Hall

JAMES WILLIAM CALLAHAN, B.S., M.S. (University of Massachusetts), *Instructor, Research, Agronomy.*
Stockbridge Hall

FRANKLIN JAMES CAMPBELL, B.S. (Pennsylvania State University), *Instructor, Research, Floriculture.*
Waltham Field Station

EXPERIMENT STATION STAFF

FREDERICK BARKER CHANDLER, B.S. (University of Maine), PH.D. (University of Maryland), *Professor, Research, Cranberry Station.* East Wareham

CHESTER ELLSWORTH CROSS, B.S., M.S. (University of Massachusetts), PH.D. (Harvard University), *Professor, Research, Head of Cranberry Station.* East Wareham

BRADFORD DEAN CROSSMON, B.S., M.S. (University of Connecticut), M.P.A. (Harvard University), *Associate Professor, Research, Agricultural Economics.* Draper Hall

WILLIAM LEONARD DORAN, B.S., M.S. (University of Massachusetts), *Professor, Research, Botany.* Clark Hall

MACK DRAKE, B.S., M.S., PH.D. (Purdue University), *Professor, Research, Chemistry.* Goessmann Laboratory

WILLIAM BRIGHAM ESSELEN, B.S., M.S., PH.D. (University of Massachusetts), *Professor, Research, Food Technology.* Chenoweth Laboratory

GEORGE PETER FADDOUL, D.V.M. (Middlesex University), M.S. (University of New Hampshire), *Professor, Research, Poultry Disease.* Waltham Field Station

IRVING SEYMOUR FAGERSON, S.B. (Massachusetts Institute of Technology), M.S., PH.D. (University of Massachusetts), *Assistant Professor, Research, Food Technology.* Chenoweth Laboratory

GORDON WALLACE FELLOWS, A.B. (University of Connecticut), *Instructor, Research, Poultry Disease.* Waltham Field Station

ROBERT ALAN FITZPATRICK, B.S., M.S. (University of Massachusetts), *Assistant Professor, Research, Agricultural Economics.* Draper Hall

LESLIE WAYNE FLEMING, A.B., M.A. (University of Kansas), *Instructor, Research, Veterinary Science.* Paige Laboratory

THOMAS WALTON FOX, B.S., M.S. (University of Massachusetts), PH.D. (Purdue University), *Assistant Professor, Research, Poultry Husbandry.* Stockbridge Hall

FREDERICK JOHN FRANCIS, B.A., M.A., PH.D. (University of Toronto), *Assistant Professor, Research, Food Technology.* Chenoweth Laboratory

JAMES EVERARD FULLER, A.B., A.M. (Colorado College), PH.D. (Yale University), *Professor, Research, Bacteriology.* Marshall Hall

WILLIAM GARLAND, *Instructor, Research, Entomology.* Waltham Field Station

EUGENE C. GASIORKEWICZ, B.A., M.S. (Marquette University), PH.D. (University of Wisconsin), *Assistant Professor, Research, Botany.* Waltham Field Station

JULIUS SYDNEY GREENSTEIN, A.B. (Clark University), M.S., PH.D. (University of Illinois), *Assistant Professor, Research, Animal Husbandry.* Stockbridge Hall

EMIL FREDERICK GUBA, B.S. (University of Massachusetts), PH.D. (University of Illinois), *Professor, Research, Botany.* Waltham Field Station

JOHN RALPH HAVIS, B.S. (Texas Technical College), M.S., PH.D. (Cornell University), *Professor, Research, Horticulture; Head of Waltham Field Station.* Waltham Field Station

312

FRANK ALFRED HAYS, B.S. (Oklahoma Agricultural College), M.A. (University of Nebraska), PH.D. (Iowa State College), *Professor, Research, Poultry Husbandry.* Stockbridge Hall

PORTIA ADELE IERARDI, B.S., M.A. (Boston University), *Experiment Station Editor.* East Experiment Station

ELMAR JARVESOO, AGR.DIP., MAG.AGR. (Tartu University), DR.AGRI. (Berlin University), *Instructor, Research, Agricultural Economics.* Draper Hall

LINUS HALE JONES, B.S., M.S. (University of Massachusetts), PH.D. (Rutgers University), *Assistant Professor, Research, Botany.* Clark Hall

PEARL KANE, B.S., M.S. (Pennsylvania State University), *Instructor, Research, Home Economics.* Edna Skinner Hall

CLIFFORD VAUGHN KIGHTLINGER, B.S., M.S. (Grove City College), *Professor, Research, Agronomy.* Stockbridge Hall

DONALD MARKHAM KINSMAN, B.S. (University of Massachusetts), M.S. (University of New Hampshire), *Assistant Professor, Assistant to Superintendent of Farms.* Stockbridge Hall

KAROL JOSEPH KUCINSKI, B.S., M.S., PH.D. (University of Massachusetts), *Assistant Professor, Research, Agronomy.* Stockbridge Hall

WILLIAM HENRY LACHMAN, JR., B.S., M.S. (Pennsylvania State University), *Associate Professor, Research, Vegetable Gardening.* French Hall

WARREN LITSKY, A.B. (Clark University), M.S. (University of Massachusetts), PH.D. (Michigan State College), *Associate Professor, Research, Bacteriology.* Marshall Hall

MRS. MARY EUGENE LOJKIN, B.S., M.S. (Polytechnic Institute, Petrograd), PH.D. (Columbia University), *Assistant Professor, Research, Home Economics Nutrition.* Edna Skinner Hall

MALCOLM ARTHUR MCKENZIE, PH.B., A.M., PH.D. (Brown University), *Director, Shade Tree Laboratories.* Shade Tree Laboratory

JOHN WALTER MASTALERZ, B.S. (University of Massachusetts), M.S. (Purdue University), PH.D. (Cornell University), *Assistant Professor, Research, Floriculture.* Waltham Field Station

WILLIAM SAMUEL MUELLER, B.S. (University of Illinois), M.S. (Rutgers University), PH.D. (University of Massachusetts), *Associate Professor, Research, Dairy Industry.* Flint Laboratory

MARGARET HELEN O'DONNELL, *Administrative Director of Experiment Station.* East Experiment Station

LEONARD RAYMOND PARKINSON, B.S. (University of New Hampshire), M.S., PH.D. (University of Massachusetts), *Assistant Professor, Research, Food Technology.* Hatch Laboratory

RICHARD E. PRIDE, B.S., M.S. (Pennsylvania State University), *Assistant Professor, Research, Horticulture.* Waltham Field Station

ELIOT COLLINS ROBERTS, B.S. (University of Rhode Island), M.S., PH.D. (Rutgers University), *Assistant Professor, Research, Agronomy.* Stockbridge Hall

DAVID ROZMAN, B.A., M.A. (University of Wisconsin), PH.D. (Northwestern University), *Professor, Research, Agricultural Economics.*
Draper Hall

EDWARD HARTLEY SEADALE, B.S. (University of Massachusetts), *Instructor, Research, Veterinary Science.* Paige Laboratory

RUTH EVELYN SHERBURNE, B.S. (Simmons College), *Instructor, Research, Agricultural Economics.* Draper Hall

NATHAN L. SHIPKOWITZ, B.S., M.S. (University of Illinois), PH.D. (Michigan State College), *Assistant Professor, Research, Bureau of Animal Industry.* Paige Laboratory

J. ROBERT SMYTH, JR., B.S. (University of Maine), M.S., PH.D. (Purdue University), *Associate Professor, Research, Poultry Husbandry.*
Stockbridge Hall

FRANKLIN WALLBURG SOUTHWICK, B.S. (University of Massachusetts), M.S. (Ohio State University), PH.D. (Cornell University), *Professor, Research, Pomology.* French Hall

HERBERT GEORGE SPINDLER, B.A. (University of Wisconsin), M.B.A. (Boston University), *Assistant Professor, Research, Agricultural Economics.*
Draper Hall

JOSEPH ERIS STECKEL, B.S.A., PH.D. (Purdue University), *Professor, Research, Agronomy.* Stockbridge Hall

BERYL STONE, B.S. (University of Massachusetts), *Instructor, Research, Home Economics.* Edna Skinner Hall

ROBERT LEWIS TICKNOR, B.S. (Oregon State College), M.S., PH.D. (Michigan State College), *Assistant Professor, Research, Nurseryculture.*
Waltham Field Station

WILLIAM EDWARD TOMLINSON, JR., B.S. (Tufts College), M.S. (University of Massachusetts), *Associate Professor, Research, Cranberry Station.*
East Wareham

JONAS VENGRIS, M.AGR. (Agricultural College, Dotnuva, Lithuania), D.AGR.SC. (University of Bonn), *Assistant Professor, Research, Agronomy.*
Stockbridge Hall

WALTER DRURY WEEKS, B.S., M.S. (University of New Hampshire), PH.D. (University of Massachusetts), *Assistant Professor, Research, Pomology.*
French Hall

MRS. ANNE WILLIAMS WERTZ, A.B. (Connecticut College), PH.D. (University of Massachusetts), *Professor, Research, Home Economics Nutrition.*
Edna Skinner Hall

WARREN DRAPER WHITCOMB, B.S. (University of Massachusetts), *Professor, Research, Entomology.* Waltham Field Station

HAROLD EVERETT WHITE, B.S., M.S. (Purdue University), *Professor, Research, Floriculture.* French Hall

ROLAND WHALEY WINTERFIELD, B.S. in AGR., D.V.M. (Iowa State College), *Professor, Research, Veterinary Science.* Paige Laboratory

HRANT MISSAK YEGIAN, B.S. (Iowa State College), M.S. (University of Massachusetts), *Assistant Professor, Research, Agronomy.* Stockbridge Hall

Robert Ellsworth Young, b.s.a. (Oklahoma Agricultural College), m.s. (Ohio State University), *Professor, Research, Olericulture.*
Waltham Field Station

John Walter Zahradnik, b.s. (Pennsylvania State University), m.s. (Iowa State College), *Assistant Professor, Research, Agricultural Engineering.*
Engineering Annex

Heads of those departments functioning in the Experiment Station although not listed here, are also recognized as members of the staff.

PART TIME EXPERIMENT STATION STAFF

William Makepeace Atwood, b.s. (University of Massachusetts),
Instructor, Research, Agronomy. Stockbridge Hall

Martin Sherman Cryan, b.s., m.s. (University of Massachusetts),
Instructor, Research, Food Technology. Chenoweth Laboratory

Johannes Delphendahl, dip.ldw. (Hohenheim Agricultural College),
Instructor, Research, Agricultural Economics. Draper Hall

Mrs. Georgia Perkins French, b.s. (University of Massachusetts),
Instructor, Research, Home Economics. Edna Skinner Hall

Rauno Andrew Lampi, b.s. (University of Massachusetts),
Instructor, Research, Food Technology. Chenoweth Laboratory

REGULATORY SERVICE STAFF

JESSIE LOUISE ANDERSON,
  Assistant Professor, Research, Seeds. West Experiment Station

LEO PAUL BENINATO, B.S. (Boston College), M.S. (University of Massachusetts), *Instructor, Research, Veterinary Science.* Paige Laboratory

ROBERT ALVIN BENNETT, B.S., M.S. (University of Massachusetts),
  Instructor, Research, Poultry Disease. Paige Laboratory

KENNETH LLOYD BULLIS, D.V.M. (Iowa State College), M.S. (University of Massachusetts), *Professor of Veterinary Science and Head of Department.* Paige Laboratory

CLIFFORD SPENCER CHATER, B.S.A. (University of Rhode Island), M.S. (Kansas State College), *Assistant Professor, Shade Tree Laboratories.*
  Waltham Field Station

MIRIAM KEITH CLARKE, A.B. (Mt. Holyoke College), M.S. (University of Massachusetts), *Assistant Professor, Research, Poultry Disease.*
  Paige Laboratory

[2]LEO VINCENT CROWLEY, B.S. (University of Massachusetts),
  Assistant Professor, Research, Feeds and Fertilizers.

[2]ELMO JAMES FRESIA, B.S. (University of Massachusetts),
  Instructor, Research, Feeds and Fertilizers.

BERTRAM GERSTEN, B.S. (University of Rhode Island), *Assistant Professor, Research, Feeds and Fertilizers.* West Experiment Station

HENRY WALTER GILBERTSON, B.S. (University of Idaho), M.S. (University of Maryland), *Instructor, Shade Tree Laboratories.*
  Waltham Field Station

JACK ELLSWORTH GRAY, D.V.M., M.S. (Michigan State College),
  Professor, Research, Veterinary Science. Paige Laboratory

WILLIAM KENNETH HARRIS, D.V.M. (Ohio State University),
  Professor, Research, Mastitis. Stockbridge Hall

FRANCIS WILLIAM HOLMES, B.A. (Oberlin College), *Assistant Professor, Research, Shade Tree Laboratories.* Shade Tree Laboratory

JOHN WILLIAM KUZMESKI, B.S. (University of Massachusetts), *Professor, Research, Feeds and Fertilizers.* West Experiment Station

WALDO CHANDLER LINCOLN, JR., B.S. (University of Massachusetts),
  Instructor, Research, Seeds. West Experiment Station

OLGA MARION OLESIUK, B.A. (Mt. Holyoke College), M.S. (University of Massachusetts), *Assistant Professor, Research, Poultry Disease.*
  Paige Laboratory

---

[2] On leave of absence for military service.

IONA MAE REYNOLDS, B.S. (University of Massachusetts),
Instructor, Research, Mastitis. Paige Laboratory

MRS. MARION BROWN RHODES, B.S. (University of Connecticut),
Instructor, Research, Feeds and Fertilizers. West Experiment Station

C. TYSON SMITH, B.S., M.S. (Princeton University), *Associate Professor,
Research, Feeds and Fertilizers.* West Experiment Station

CHARLES FREDERICK SMYSER, B.S. (University of Maryland), M.S. (University
of Connecticut), *Assistant Professor, Research, Veterinary Science.*
Paige Laboratory

GLENN HOWARD SNOEYENBOS, D.V.M. (Michigan State College),
Professor, Research, Avian Pathology. Paige Laboratory

ALBERT FRANCIS SPELMAN, B.S. (University of Massachusetts), *Associate
Professor, Research, Feeds and Fertilizers.* West Experiment Station

HENRY VAN ROEKEL, D.V.M. (Iowa State College), M.S. (Virginia Polytechnic
Institute), PH.D. (Yale University), *Professor, Research, Veterinary
Science.* Paige Laboratory

RESEARCH FELLOWS

HERBERT DAVID BRODY, B.S. (Massachusetts Institute of Technology), M.S. (University of Massachusetts), *Research Fellow in Food Technology.*
Chenoweth Laboratory

PAUL VINCENT DECAREAU, B.S., M.S. (University of Massachusetts),
Research Fellow in Food Technology.   Chenoweth Laboratory

PAUL ECK, B.S. (Rutgers University),
Research Fellow in Agronomy.   Stockbridge Hall

ELIZABETH MARY ELBERT, A.B. (University of California), M.S. (Cornell University), *Research Fellow in Food Technology.*
Chenoweth Laboratory

HANS JOA, B.S. (University of Tartu),
Research Fellow in Agronomy.   Stockbridge Hall

TILFORD DAY MILLER, B.S., M.A. (Amherst College),
Research Fellow in Food Technology.   Chenoweth Laboratory

CHARLES EDWIN REDMAN, JR., B.S. (University of Massachusetts),
Research Fellow in Poultry Husbandry.   Stockbridge Hall

ARNOLD SAUL ROSEMAN, B.S. (Northeastern University),
Research Fellow in Food Technology.   Chenoweth Laboratory

MAYNARD ALBERT STEINBERG, B.S. (University of Massachusetts), M.S. (Oregon State College), *Research Fellow in Food Technology.*
Chenoweth Laboratory

THEODORE WISHNETSKY, B.S., M.S. (Cornell University),
Research Fellow in Food Technology.   Chenoweth Laboratory

EMPLOYEES OF FEDERAL GOVERNMENT

with Headquarters
at the University of Massachusetts

ARTHUR BISHOP BEAUMONT, B.S. (Kentucky State University), PH.D. (Cornell University), *State Conservationist, Soil Conservation Service.*
South College

WILLIAM H. COATES, B.S. TECHNOLOGY, B.S.A., M.S. (University of New Hampshire), *State Soil Scientist, Soil Conservation Service.*
South College

WESLEY ROBERT JONES, B.S. (University of Connecticut), M.S. (University of Massachusetts), *Mammal Control Supervisor, U. S. Fish and Wildlife Service.*
South College

PAUL CHARLES LYNCH, *State Administrative Assistant, Soil Conservation Service.*
South College

ANNE URSULA ROGERS, *Secretary, U. S. Fish and Wildlife Service.*
South College

WILLIAM GULLIVER SHELDON, B.A. (Yale University), M.S., PH.D. (Cornell University), *Leader of the Massachusetts Cooperative Wildlife Research Unit.*
Conservation Building

MRS. ELEANOR ISABELLE STARZYK, *Administrative Assistant, Agricultural Stabilization and Conservation Office.*
South College

HAROLD FOSS TOMPSON, B.S. (University of Massachusetts), *Chairman, Agricultural Stabilization and Conservation Office.*
South College

JESSE ALDERMAN TAFT, B.S., M.S. (University of Massachusetts), *Supervisor of Agricultural Teacher-Training.*
Liberal Arts Annex
(Member of Staff of State Department of Education.)

EXTENSION SERVICE STAFF

JAMES WILSON DAYTON, B.S. (University of Massachusetts),
Associate Dean and Director of Extension Service.   Munson Hall

DONALD PEARSON ALLAN, B.A. (University of Massachusetts), *Associate Extension Professor, Secretary of Extension Service.*   Munson Hall

JAMES RICHARD BEATTIE, B.S., M.S. (University of New Hampshire),
Extension Professor of Horticulture.   East Wareham

ELLSWORTH WILLIAM BELL, B.S. (Pennsylvania State University), M.S. (University of Vermont), *Extension Professor of Agricultural Economics.*   Draper Hall

ALFRED WORDEN BOICOURT, B.S., M.S. (Cornell University),
Extension Professor of Horticulture.   French Hall

FAYETTE HINDS BRANCH, B.S. (Cornell University),
Extension Professor of Agricultural Economics.   Draper Hall

RADIE HAROLD BUNN, B.S. (South Dakota State College),
Assistant Extension Professor, Extension Editor.   Munson Hall

NORMAN WESLEY BUTTERFIELD, B.S. (University of Massachusetts), M.S. (Purdue University), *Extension Professor of Floriculture.*
Waltham Field Station

EARLE STANTON CARPENTER, B.S. (University of Massachusetts), M.S. (Iowa State College), *Extension Professor of Visual Education.* Munson Hall

BYRON EARLE COLBY, B.S. (University of New Hampshire),
Extension Professor of Animal Husbandry.   Stockbridge Hall

FREDERICK EUGENE COLE, B.S. (University of Massachusetts),
Extension Professor of Fruit and Vegetable Marketing. Draper Hall

VERDA MAE DALE, B.S. (Kansas State College), M.S. (Cornell University),
Associate Extension Professor of Home Economics. Edna Skinner Hall

VIRGINIA DAVIS, B.S. (Skidmore College), *Assistant Extension Professor of Home Economics.*   Edna Skinner Hall

RALPH WILFRED DONALDSON, B.A. (Acadia University), B.S.A. (Toronto University), *Extension Professor of Agronomy.*   Stockbridge Hall

WINIFRED ISABEL EASTWOOD, A.B. (Sterling College), M.A. (Columbia University), *Extension Professor; Head, Extension Division of Home Economics.*   Edna Skinner Hall

MAY ESTELLA FOLEY, B.S. (Michigan State College), M.A. (Columbia University), *Extension Professor of Home Economics.*
Edna Skinner Hall

STANLEY NEWKIRK GAUNT, B.S. (Rutgers University),
Extension Professor of Dairy Husbandry.   Stockbridge Hall

CONSTANTINE JOSEPH GILGUT, B.S., M.S. (University of Massachusetts), A.M., PH.D. (Harvard University), *Extension Professor of Plant Pathology.*
Clark Hall

WELLESLEY CARL HARRINGTON, M.E. (Cornell University),
· *Extension Professor of Engineering.* Stockbridge Hall

KIRBY MAXWELL HAYES, B.S., M.S. (University of Massachusetts),
Associate Extension Professor of Food Technology.
Chenoweth Laboratory

BARBARA HIGGINS, B.S. (University of Maine), M.S. (Cornell University),
Associate Extension Professor of Home Economics. Edna Skinner Hall

MILDRED LOUISE HOWELL, B.S. (Buffalo State Teachers College),
Associate Extension Professor of Home Economics. Munson Hall

HORACE MANFRED JONES, B.S. (South Dakota State College), *Extension Professor; Head, Extension Division of Youth Work.* Munson Hall

MRS. N. MAY LARSON, B.S. (University of Wisconsin), M.S. (Iowa State College), *Extension Professor of Home Economics.* Edna Skinner Hall

HARLEY ALANSON LELAND, B.S. (University of Vermont),
Extension Professor of Agriculture. Munson Hall

LAWRENCE VERNELLE LOY, B.S., M.S. (Iowa State College),
Extension Professor in Charge of Youth Programs. Munson Hall

H. RUTH MCINTIRE, B.S. (Cornell University),
Extension Professor of Recreation. Edna Skinner Hall

ROY EDGAR MOSER, B.S. (Ohio State University), M.S. (Cornell University),
Extension Professor of Agricultural Economics. Draper Hall

EARLE HARRISON NODINE, B.S. (University of Connecticut), M.ED. (Springfield College), *Associate Extension Professor of Agriculture.*
Munson Hall

GRUNOW OTTO OLESON, B.S., M.S. (University of Wisconsin),
Extension Professor of Information. Munson Hall

ROBERT BROWN PARMENTER, B.S.F. (University of Maine),
Extension Professor of Forestry. Conservation Building

CLARENCE HOWARD PARSONS, B.S., M.S. (University of Massachusetts),
Extension Professor of Dairy Husbandry. Stockbridge Hall

ROBERT CLEMENS SIMMONS, B.S. in AGR. JOURNALISM (Iowa State College),
Instructor, Extension Editor. Munson Hall

ROSA MARY STARKEY, B.S. (Nasson College), *Assistant Extension Professor of Home Economics.* Edna Skinner Hall

DOUGLAS NEFF STERN, B.A. (Lehigh University), V.M.D. (University of Pennsylvania), *Extension Professor of Animal Pathology.*
Paige Laboratory

WILBUR HERMAN THIES, B.S., M.S. (Michigan State College),
Extension Professor of Horticulture. French Hall

CECIL LYMAN THOMSON, B.S.A. (University of Toronto), M.S. (University of Minnesota), *Extension Professor of Vegetable Crops.* French Hall

HERBERT SIDNEY VAUGHAN, B.S. (University of Massachusetts), M.P.A. (Harvard University), *Extension Professor; Head, Extension Division of Agriculture.* Munson Hall

321

EXTENSION SERVICE STAFF

GEORGE WILLIAM WESTCOTT, B.S., M.S. (Iowa State College), M.P.A. (Harvard University), *Extension Professor of Agricultural Economics.*
Draper Hall

ELLSWORTH HAINES WHEELER, B.S. (University of Massachusetts), M.S., PH.D. (Cornell University), *Extension Professor of Entomology.*
Fernald Hall

ROGER AUGUSTUS WOLCOTT (Massachusetts College of Art), *Assistant Extension Professor of Visual Aids.*
Munson Hall

AGENTS WITH HEADQUARTERS
IN COUNTIES

Barnstable County, Barnstable

MYRTIS EDITH BEECHER, B.S.E. (Framingham State Teachers College),
  Home Demonstration Agent.

GEORGE E. BRODIE, JR., B.S. (University of Rhode Island),
  Assistant Club Agent.

[1]CARL ARTHUR FRASER, B.S., M.S. (University of Massachusetts), *Club Agent.*

CORINNE WANDA FULLER, B.S. (Simmons College), *Assistant Club Agent.*

OSCAR SHIRLEY JOHNSON, B.S. (University of Rhode Island),
  Associate Agricultural Agent.

BERT TOMLINSON, *County Agent-Manager.*

Berkshire County, Pittsfield

ROBERT MERRILL HALL, B.S. (University of Rhode Island), *Club Agent.*

MILES REES MCCARRY, B.S. (Iowa State College), *Agricultural Agent.*

JEANNE ELIZABETH MANGUM, B.S. (University of Massachusetts),
  Associate Home Demonstration Agent.

FRANK ALBERT SKOGSBERG, B.V.A. (University of Massachusetts),
  County Agent-Manager.

Bristol County, Segreganset

PHYLLIS JANE BOWDEN, B.S. (Nasson College), *Assistant Club Agent.*

CAROL C. FABER, A.B. (Regis College),
  Assistant Home Demonstration Agent.

ROGER MCKEE HARRINGTON, B.S. (Pennsylvania State University),
  Club Agent.

BARBARA RUTH O'BRIEN, B.S. (University of Massachusetts),
  Home Demonstration Agent.

HAROLD OLIVER WOODWARD, B.S. (University of Connecticut),
  Associate Agricultural Agent.

Dukes County, Vineyard Haven

JANET DANITIS, B.S. (University of Massachusetts),
  Associate Home Demonstration Agent.

MRS. EDITH F. MORRIS, B.S. (Framingham State Teachers College),
  Club Agent.

---

[1] On leave of absence for military service.

COUNTY AGENTS

Essex County, Hathorne

CHARLES EDWARD BLANCHARD, B.S. (University of Massachusetts),
Club Agent.

CALTON OLIVER CARTWRIGHT, B.V.A., M.S. (University of Massachusetts),
Agricultural Agent.

MARGARET MARY FITZPATRICK, B.S. (Framingham State Teachers College),
Associate Club Agent.

DANIEL PATRICK HURLD, JR., B.S. (University of Massachusetts),
Agricultural Agent.

KATHERINE MAY LAWLER, B.S. (Simmons College), M.S. (University of
Massachusetts), *Home Demonstration Agent.*

JOHN EVERETT MILTIMORE, B.S. (University of New Hampshire),
Associate Agricultural Agent.

VERA ARLAYNE SULLIVAN, A.B. (Regis College),
Assistant Home Demonstration Agent.

Franklin County, Greenfield

MILFORD WALTER ATWOOD, B.S. (University of Massachusetts), *Club Agent.*

MARGUERITA COSTANZA, B.S. (Nasson College),
Associate Home Demonstration Agent.

MRS. ELIZABETH ANNE MANNHEIM, B.S. (University of Massachusetts),
Assistant Club Agent.

MRS. MARJORIE HALL McGILLICUDDY, B.S. (Framingham State Teachers
College), *Home Demonstration Agent.*

DONALD TURNER THAYER, B.V.A. (University of Massachusetts),
Associate Agricultural Agent.

OSCAR LEWIS WYMAN, B.S. (University of Maine), *County Agent-Manager.*

Hampden County, West Springfield

MRS. HELEN HINMAN BARWELL, B.S. (University of Connecticut),
Associate Home Demonstration Agent.

*ROBERT ANTHONY BIEBER, B.S. (University of Massachusetts),
Agricultural Agent.

MRS. ETHEL MERLE CROSS, B.S. (Springfield College), *Associate Club Agent.*

ALBERT HENRY FULLER, *Director of County Extension Service.*

CARL ANTON HEDIN, B.S. (Cornell University), *Associate Agricultural Agent.*

MOLLY MARGARET HIGGINS, B.S. (Framingham State Teachers College),
Home Demonstration Agent.

ROBERT KENDALL MARSH, B.S. (University of Massachusetts), *Club Agent.*

MRS. MEREDYTHE BARKER OLSON, B.S. (Simmons College),
Associate Home Demonstration Agent.

JAMES NATHANIEL PUTNAM, B.S. (University of Massachusetts),
Agricultural Agent.

* Time divided between Hampden and Hampshire Counties.

Hampshire County, Northampton

REBECCA JANE DEA, B.S. (Nasson College), *Associate Club Agent.*

FLORENCE IRENE GATES, B.S. (Framingham State Teachers College),
Home Demonstration Agent.

ALLEN SANFORD LELAND, B.S. (University of Massachusetts),
County Agent-Manager.

WALTER MELNICK, B.S. (University of Massachusetts), *Agricultural Agent.*

WILLIAM WARNER METCALFE, B.S. (University of New Hampshire),
Club Agent.

ELIZABETH A. THAYER, B.S. (Framingham State Teachers College),
Associate Home Demonstration Agent.

Middlesex County, Concord

MRS. IRENE HOLMES BROWN, B.S. (Framingham State Teachers College),
Assistant Club Agent.

ALFRED WHITNEY CARLSON, B.S. (Rutgers University), *Agricultural Agent.*

BLANCHE WOODBURY EAMES, B.S. (Framingham State Teachers College),
Home Demonstration Agent.

MAX GEORGE FULTZ, B.S. (Purdue University), *Agricultural Agent.*

JESSE JAMES, B.S., M.S. (University of Georgia), *Club Agent.*

ALLISTER FRANCIS MACDOUGALL, B.S. (University of Massachusetts),
Director and Agricultural Agent.

FRANCIS GOULD MENTZER, JR., B.S. (University of Massachusetts),
Associate Agricultural Agent.

SIDNEY ARTHUR MONTAGUE, B.S. (University of Massachusetts),
Associate Club Agent.

MRS. JANICE BOWEN MORRIS, B.S. (Russell Sage College),
Assistant Club Agent.

MRS. ETHEL WADSWORTH VEENENDAAL, B.S. (Cornell University),
Associate Home Demonstration Agent.

Norfolk County, Walpole

CATHERINE COOK, B.S. (Framingham State Teachers College), M.ED. (Boston
University), *Associate Club Agent.*

MRS. SANTINA RILEY CURRAN, B.S. (Framingham State Teachers College),
Home Demonstration Agent.

FRANK LESLIE DAVIS, B.S. (University of Massachusetts),
Agricultural Agent.

ALBERT JOHN HEALEY, B.S. (University of Massachusetts), *Club Agent.*

HURON MAYBEE SMITH, B.S. (Michigan State College),
Associate Agricultural Agent.

MRS. JEAN ECKERSON WOODWARD, B.S. (Russell Sage College),
Associate Home Demonstration Agent.

COUNTY AGENTS

Plymouth County, Brockton

JOSEPH TRUE BROWN, B.S. (University of New Hampshire),
County Agent-Manager.

ROBERT BRUCE EWING, *Club Agent.*

DOMINIC ALEXANDER MARINI, B.S. (University of Massachusetts),
Associate Agricultural Agent.

MRS. NANCY TUCKER MCLAUGHLIN, B.S. (Simmons College),
Assistant Club Agent.

BETSEY DEAN POOL, B.S. (Simmons College),
Assistant Home Demonstration Agent.

LAWRENCE DUNCAN RHOADES, B.S. (University of Massachusetts),
Agricultural Agent.

EDGAR WINFRED SPEAR, B.S. (University of Massachusetts),
Associate Agricultural Agent.

BEATRICE ISABELLE WHITE, B.S. (Framingham State Teachers College),
Home Demonstration Agent.

Worcester County, Worcester

IRENE MARGARET DAVIS, B.S. (Framingham State Teachers College),
Associate Home Demonstration Agent.

ERNEST ARTHUR GEORGE, B.S. (University of New Hampshire),
Associate Agricultural Agent.

EVELYN MAY LYMAN, B.S. (Cornell University),
Associate Home Demonstration Agent.

LEON OTIS MARSHALL, B.S. (University of Maine), *Club Agent.*

ELDINE JUNE NYLANDER, B.S. (University of Massachusetts),
Assistant Club Agent.

WALTER BRUCE SHAW, *Associate Agricultural Agent.*

MRS. EVANGELINE D. STANDISH, B.S. (University of Rhode Island),
Associate Club Agent.

MILDRED CAROLINE THOMAS, *Home Demonstration Agent.*

CHARLES WINFIELD TURNER, B.S. (University of Rhode Island), M.S. (Nort
Carolina State College), *Director of County Extension Service.*

INDEX

UNIVERSITY OF MASSACHUSETTS ENROLLMENT — September, 1954

UNDERGRADUATE COLLEGE

CLASS	1955		1956		1957		1958		TOTAL		TOTAL
	MEN	WOMEN	MEN	WOMEN	MEN	WOMEN	MEN	WOMEN	MEN	WOMEN	
Liberal Arts	107	135	118	136	121	191	106	216	452	678	1,130
Engineering	86	0	115	0	208	5	310	4	719	9	728
Science	71	42	87	60	106	70	139	82	403	254	657
Bus. Administration	117	7	113	9	151	6	141	7	522	29	551
Agric. & Hort.	80	3	87	10	67	5	90	8	324	26	350
Home Economics	0	65	0	45	0	63	0	55	0	228	228
Physical Education	6	0	12	0	17	0	24	0	59	0	59
	467	252	532	260	670	340	810	372	2,479	1,224	3,703
Specials									45	40	85
									2,524	1,264	3,788

GRADUATE SCHOOL

MEN	WOMEN	TOTAL
243	56	299

STOCKBRIDGE SCHOOL

	1955	1956	TOTAL
Men	124	188	312
Women	2	6	8
			320

SUMMER SCHOOL

653

SUMMARY

Undergraduate College	3,788
Graduate School	299
Stockbridge School	320
TOTAL ENROLLMENT	4,407

Office of Publications
November, 1954

GIFTS AND BEQUESTS

For the information of those who may wish to make a gift or a bequest to this University, the following suggestion is made as to a suitable form which may be used.

There are a number of worth-while activities of the University which are handicapped by lack of funds and for which small endowments would make possible a greater measure of service to our students and to the Commonwealth. The religious work on the Campus is an example. This is now carried on in a very limited way by current private contributions. Further information concerning this and other activities in similar need will be gladly furnished by the President.

SUGGESTED FORM

"I give and bequeath to the Trustees of the University of Massachusetts, at Amherst, Massachusetts, the sum of ....
.... dollars."

(1) (Unrestricted)

"To be used for the benefit of the University of Massachusetts in such manner as the Trustees thereof may direct."

or (2) (Permanent Fund: income unrestricted)

"to constitute an endowment fund to be known as the ....
.... Fund, such fund to be kept invested by the Trustees of the University of Massachusetts and the income used for the benefit of the College in such manner as the Trustees thereof may direct."

or (3) (Specific Purposes)

"to be used for the following purposes,"

(Here specify in detail the purposes.)

BIRTH

_n_

A

ic Higher Education

ersity of Massachusetts"

February 14, 1955

The Honorable Joseph W. Bartlett
Chairman, Board of Trustees
The University of Massachusetts

Dear Mr. Bartlett:

I have the honor to present through you to the Board of Trustees, and to the Governor and Citizens of the Commonwealth a Report of Progress for the University of Massachusetts covering the year January 1, 1954 to January 1, 1955.

Respectfully yours,

JEAN PAUL MATHER

President

VOLUME XLVII   APRIL 1955   NUMBER 3

Published six times a year by the University of Massachusetts: January, February, April (two), May, September. Entered at Post Office, Amherst, Mass., as second class matter.

The report of the President for the year ending January 1, 1955, is part of the 92nd annual report of the University of Massachusetts, and as such is Part I of Public Document 31. (Section 8, Chapter 75, of the General Laws of Massachusetts.)

PUBLICATION OF THIS DOCUMENT APPROVED BY
GEORGE J. CRONIN, STATE PURCHASING AGENT.
1500-3-55-914420

UNIVERSITY OF MASSACHUSETTS ENROLLMENT

SEPTEMBER, 1954

UNDERGRADUATE COLLEGE

Class	1955		1956		1957		1958		Total		
	Men	Women	Men	Women	Men	Women	Men	Women	Men	Women	Tot.
Liberal Arts	107	135	118	136	121	191	106	216	452	678	113
Engineering	86	0	115	0	208	5	310	4	719	9	72
Science	71	42	87	60	106	70	139	82	403	254	65
Business Administration	117	7	113	9	151	6	141	7	522	29	55
Agric. & Hort.	80	3	87	10	67	5	90	8	324	26	35
Home Economics	0	65	0	45	0	63	0	55	0	228	22
Physical Education	6	0	12	0	17	0	24	0	59	0	5
	467	252	532	260	670	340	810	372	2479	1224	370
Specials									45	40	8
									2524	1264	378

GRADUATE SCHOOL

Men	Women	Total
243	56	299

STOCKBRIDGE SCHOOL

	1955	1956	Total
Men	124	188	312
Women	2	6	8
			320

SUMMER SCHOOL

653

SUMMARY

Undergraduate College	3788
Graduate School	299
Stockbridge School	320
TOTAL ENROLLMENT	4407

(Office of Publications, November, 1954)

Report of the President
To the Board of Trustees, the Governor, and the Citizens of the Commonwealth

---

The Rebirth of an Idea

THE fundamental concepts of educational opportunity, as well as religious freedom, came with the early settlers in New England. You might say they came over on the Mayflower. For shortly afterward, in 1636, the General Court of the Massachusetts Bay Colony made the first appropriation of 400 pounds to establish a University, later to be known as Harvard College. This was a remarkable performance of faith in education, for the amount appropriated was almost exactly equal to the whole colony tax for that entire year.

Three hundred eighteen years, then, before the writing of this report, the General Court of the Commonwealth gave financial support to the birth of an idea—the idea of public, tax-supported, higher education. And in 1954 the same idea experienced a *rebirth* in the largest appropriation ever recorded for the University of Massachusetts—$10,836,645 or $2,783,720 more than the previous record budget of 1952. By this action the people of Massachusetts reestablished their faith in a great historical heritage—the belief that the productivity and progress of a state or nation are founded upon the nature and extent of education of the people. By recognizing the need for greater public higher education facilities a step forward in democracy has been taken and opportunities for the youth of the Commonwealth have been related to the "ability for learning" rather than the limited concept of "ability to pay."

3

The Pressures on Admissions and Enrollment

The annual enrollment statistics of the University are again placed at the beginning of this report. It is essential that admissions and enrollments give a true picture to every taxpayer of the pressures currently placed upon the University by an increasing collegeage population in a State where 93 % of the enrollment is in private colleges and universities and only 7 % in public institutions of higher learning.

There were in the Commonwealth at the date of these admissions figures an estimated 237,738 young men and women of college age, who received most of their elementary and secondary education in the *public* tax-supported schools of Massachusetts. Of this number 58,310 were eighteen years of age, and hence were born in 1936, a depression, low-birth-rate, year.[1] From this group of 58,310 a Freshman class of 1,182 entered the University.

Under policy adopted by the Board of Trustees in the Fall of 1953 it was planned to restrict enrollment in September 1954 and again in September 1955 until additional instructional facilities could be provided. Accordingly the Freshman class is but twelve students in excess of the Freshman enrollment in 1953. The 1,182 new enrollees were admitted from a total of over 7,500 applications. Applications requested by mail from Massachusetts resident students numbered 4,756. Over 1,000 additional applications were distributed at interviews and in the office of the Registrar. Requests for admission application blanks were received from over 2,000 out of state students, but since the "hold the line" policy of the administration and Board restricted admission to Massachusetts residents, there were no application forms issued to non-residents. 3,281 applications were finally returned and from these the 1,182 admitted were finally selected.

When teaching staff members were requested in the budget planning for this year a total student body of 4,145 was estimated. The final total of 4,407, after admitting a static freshman class, resulted from increased numbers of students in the upper classes. Economic attrition as well as academic failure apparently de-

---

[1] "College Age Population Trends" (American Association of Collegiate Registrars and Admissions Officers, August 1953) p. 38.

creased, and noticeably at the sophomore level. What this means internally is an overload against staff and physical facilities that is presently straining maximum limits, particularly in the College of Arts and Sciences.

The planning policy of the past year is looking toward a total enrollment of 10,000 students by 1965. Private universities and colleges have again and again affirmed their intention of remaining relatively fixed in enrollment for the next ten years. But the youngsters already born guarantee a college age population in Massachusetts that by 1970 will reach 152 per cent of the college age group of 1953. In 1965, for example, the college age population of the Commonwealth is estimated at 337,214 as compared with 237,738 in 1954.[2] These figures direct the program and planning of the University by the language of the land grant act that established this institution. This is truly a state "where a much larger number of people need wider educational advantages and impatiently await their possession."

The slight decrease in the numbers of women enrolled is due chiefly to admitting more veterans. Students receiving Veterans Administration educational benefits increased 44% over similar enrollment for the academic year 1953-54. At the same time Korean veterans on campus increased by 72%. Total veterans in the fall of 1954 numbered 556 or in excess of 10% of the student body. Two dormitories formerly assigned to women are currently assigned to men to accommodate this increased veteran enrollment.

THE COLLEGES, SCHOOLS, AND DIVISIONS
The College of Arts and Sciences

With a total enrollment of 1787 the College of Arts and Sciences represents 44 per cent of the undergraduate student body. Housing the basic or core curriculum of the University as heart and home, the College provides a common lower division experience in the humanities, the social and physical sciences, and the arts for all those who specialize in the last two years as students in one of the professional schools. And many prefer to stay in this major college as evidenced by the preponderant

[2] Ibid, op. cit. p. 38.

numbers of seniors moving toward Bachelor of Arts or Bachelor of Science degrees.

Research, original creative effort, and teaching all go hand in hand. Each is complementary to the other and inspiration is a function of interest and participation by the staff in all three. In both arts and sciences progress has marked this year. A foundation grant enabled the English Department to prepare a notable recording series by living poets entitled *New England Anthology*. Off-campus grants have extended the research program in Psychology. Grants-in-aid and allocations of funds amounted to over $80,000 in total from the American Cancer Society, the Office of Naval Research, Army Ordnance, Research Corporation of New York, Petroleum Research Fund (American Chemical Society), the Atomic Energy Commission, Standard Oil of New Jersey, the American Petroleum Institute and Sigma XI. Requests for research funds came from all grades of teaching personnel, from instructors to full professors.

Nearly a hundred papers have originated from research and creative activity, and many were presented before appropriate scientific and professional societies.

Actually the total amount of research carried on at the University for both public and private agencies and institutions is extremely limited in comparison to the magnitude and diversity of the Commonwealth economy, and the total contributions of the Massachusetts populace in taxes and prices at both a state and national level. Practically this problem is related to the extreme pressure of current enrollments on staff and facilities. Current teaching loads simply do not permit faculty to develop the research and creative potential inherent in the background and training of the staff. Limited equipment further hampers research effort. The net result is that teaching is not stimulated to the degree it might be through new investigation and exploration of the everlasting frontiers of art and science.

Expansion of staff and facilities with an expanding student body for the future *must* include additional allocations of funds, time, and effort for research and originality. Dependence of a dynamic and growing Engineering School upon the Chemistry, Physics, Mathematics, and English departments of the College of Arts and Sciences will require that these departments have the

6

best in up-to-date facilities as well as highly competent professional personnel and service staff.

The School of Engineering

This was the seventh year since the establishment of the School of Engineering in the University, and marked a further increase in enrollment (728), the start of construction of the next unit of the engineering development, the graduation of the smallest senior class (45) since 1949, and the completion of the first major research project in the Engineering Research Institute. Each year brings its problems, its accomplishments and its disappointments, but there is no doubt that the School is dynamic and showing continued growth and improvement.

The teaching faculty of 35 included two half-time instructors who were continuing with graduate work. Of these, 7 were new staff members. The market for engineers continues high. Applications for faculty positions in engineering are almost non-existent, and the fact that the School attracts new men is a credit to the efforts of the department heads and other members of the staff. A growing organization, good facilities, the town of Amherst, New England, and a friendly faculty group are some of the most attractive factors.

The faculty continued active in research, consulting work, writing and general professional activities. Consulting activity of an engineering faculty during the summer contributes to their professional development and is definitely encouraged. This past summer of 1954 many of the staff were employed as consultants and engineers on work in Massachusetts and elsewhere. The organizations employing included the Bell Laboratories, Western Massachusetts Electric Company, Westinghouse, Rodney-Hunt, Dupont, Hessey Eastern, Colonial Engineering, U. S. Air Force, Daniel O'Connell & Sons, and Tighe & Bond. Several of the faculty continued their writing, others taught required "summer shop" courses and still others carried on research work on the campus.

The student body is above average academically when compared with many other state universities and colleges. Furthermore, engineering attracts a higher percentage of good students than some other disciplines. About 35 per cent of the boys admitted to the freshman class in 1953 selected engineering as a major. Of these, about 19 per cent were on the University Honors List (80% or above) the second semester, as compared with 26.5 per cent for the total University. About 36 per cent of the engineers had second semester averages below 70, and 23 students failed out of the University. These figures seem reasonable and consistent with high quality academic work when it is recognized that most of the engineering students are taking one more course than their colleagues in the other schools. Forty-five received B.S. degrees in a professional engineering field in June 1953. These included the School's first girl engineer, Miss Bettie Ann Francis who was awarded a B.S. in E.E.

An engineering school with student chapters of the national engineering societies provides a unique opportunity in the educational field for the development of leadership and a sense of responsibility. Chapters of A.S.C.E., A.S.M.E., A.I.E.E. and I.R.E., A.I.Ch.E. and A.S.A.E., were active. The Engineers' Council made up of two elected representatives from each of these student chapters organized and put on the annual Engineering Open House viewed by well over 2000 visitors. The amateur Radio Club as well as the W.M.U.A. broadcast group attract many engineers, although their membership is campus-wide. Other campus extra-curricula activities, including athletics, attract many but participation has to be tempered with moderation, or the major objective of a college experience suffers. Engineering students soon learn this.

Seniors who graduated in June of 1954 took positions with 19 different companies, government agencies or universities. Practically all of these contacts were made through the University Placement Service. Big industry continues to attract most of the engineering graduates and the majority go out of the state.

Construction was started in May on the $850,000 addition to the Electrical Engineering Wing, with M. Spinelli & Sons Company, Inc. of Cambridge, the General Contractor. Completion is planned for September 1955. This will provide seven additional laboratories, seven much needed classrooms, three conference rooms, three drafting rooms, and a library or reading room. Also included are studios for the University radio station. A new C.F.R. engine has been added to the internal combustion laboratory. A new large steam line will provide an adequate supply for a rapidly improving steam laboratory in the Engineering Annex. Additional test tables and equipment have been added in the electrical machinery laboratory. Thirty different companies have donated equipment.

Engineering Education appears to be headed in the direction of more science and less of the applied courses. Changes will come in the physics offered engineering students by physics departments. The department should be alert to these trends. The humanistic-social courses required of engineers will hold at about one-fifth of their total program but a trend toward vertical sequences so common in science and engineering is developing. This will, however, narrow the breadth and should be approached cautiously but not ignored. Graduate work in engineering, especially part-time evening programs, will become more common and probably show less specialization and even include some humanities. There is nothing dormant about engineering education today but it is conservative and permanent changes will come slowly. Experimentation within reason is encouraged by those responsible for accreditation but the professional societies themselves appear reluctant to recommend radical changes.

For the future, Engineering extension for small industry in the state, somewhat similar to the agricultural extension service to agriculture, may be an important factor in maintaining Massachusetts in an industrially competitive position. This should center at the University and would seem to offer an opportunity to be of real service to the state at a very modest outlay of funds.

A re-examination of curricula by the Engineers' Council for Professional Development for continued accreditation will take place in 1954-1955. The Chemical Engineering curriculum will be inspected for the first time. This is an important event for the School, for it offers an opportunity for a complete review of the educational program offered engineering students.

An evening graduate program probably in Electrical and Mechanical Engineering appears to be the best approach to graduate education. Western Massachusetts industry employs many engineers, many of whom are interested in continuing their education towards a master's degree. This should be organized and financed by the University with the help of industry.

9

Staff members cannot be asked to teach days and evenings also. Their schedules must be adjusted when they teach evenings to keep their work program within reason. This program will undoubtedly be offered on staff rotating basis.

The School of Business Administration

The faculty of the School of Business Administration accepts the responsibility for providing professional education for a business career. Prerequisite to such training is a competent staff, an interested student body, varied curricula and adequate equipment.

Measured both by education and business experience, there is a solid corps of competent instructors in the School. Every man on the staff has had some practical business experience: the average for the staff is between three and four years. Each of the men has a broad general education and also specialized training in his chosen field. Six of the staff have secondary graduate degrees. Nine have a first graduate degree and of these, four have completed all the work for a doctorate except the dissertation.

Three of the staff, during the summer, were in residence at middle-western universities working on the doctor's dissertation. Two spent the summer on a research job. And two taught in the University Summer School. The Professor of Industrial Administration meantime completed his book on "American Industries," which is now in press and will be published this winter.

The table below shows that there is a continually increasing demand for training young men and women for responsible positions in business organizations of every kind. The School is providing instruction for 70 per cent more students than it was five years ago. Meantime, the total enrollment of the University has increased 25 per cent.

	Total	Men	Women	Per cent Increase or Decrease
1954-1955	551	522	29	+14.2
1953-1954	482	444	38	+16.9
1952-1953	413	380	33	+ 8.4
1951-1952	381	351	30	+16.9
1950-1951	326	312	14	−12.0

The table above covers business administration majors, but 945 were registered in undergraduate courses in the School a year ago compared with 1213 this fall semester; an increase of nearly 28 per cent. This increase in number of registrants in courses shows the number of students in other Schools on campus who elect one or more Business courses.

To the faculty of the School, growth in enrollment is gratifying, but growth should not be more rapid than is possible to acclimate the student population to the standards, purposes and ideals of professional education for business.

During the past year a few significant changes were made in the established curricula. To the curriculum in Accounting an important course in Tax Accounting was added. A much needed course in Problems of Industrial Management has been inserted in the first semester of the senior year in the curriculum in Industrial Administration. Although there have always been several specialized courses in Marketing, there has been no specific course to integrate the specialties. This situation has been remedied by the introduction in the second semester of the senior year of a course in Problems of Marketing.

An important addition to the curriculum has been approved. This is a junior-senior program, based on two years of liberal studies, in Management training particularly for Young Women. This curriculum was introduced not to attract students, but to provide for an insistent demand that young women be given appropriate training for middle management positions in business offices.

The program of Graduate Study in Business, which started off last year with a small group, continues to attract an increasing number of competent graduate students who have their bachelor's degree from other institutions.

For the first time in the history of the School of Business adequate facilities have been provided by occupancy of renovated Draper Hall. The School now has two well-equipped laboratories for classes in Accounting. A beginning has been made in equipping a laboratory for classes in Industrial Management. Once the new course in Office Procedures is under way, machinery is available to conduct this course in a competent manner. The

School has essential duplicating equipment, files and other office machinery, and two large, well-furnished general classrooms. Each man on the instructional staff has a modestly equipped office in which he can work and where he can have conferences with students. The "Mark Hopkins on one end of a log and a student on the other" concept will not apply for modern business training, which demands facilities that will acquaint students with the environment in which they will work in the future.

Inquiries are constantly received from individuals and from business firms concerning work in research. These inquiries, for the most part, relate to research problems of business management especially of the "small business" type. It is perhaps not the province of the School to duplicate the research *about* business conducted by other types of organizations on university campuses. Research in the schools of business is a continuing process of investigation and study of managerial problems encountered in the conduct of business. It is designed to aid individual firms of the community in meeting organizational and operational problems. It is as necessary and distinct an activity as are the activities of an agriculture or engineering research organization. It will be a high priority requirement for the future. Not only is this research of value to the management of business, it also assists the teaching faculty by supplying case-problems derived from actual business situations.

Another area in which the School has requests for service is that for extension courses in centers other than Amherst. At present, there is pressure upon the School to offer, in extension, our graduate courses in Business Administration. To discharge adequately the School's responsibility to the business community plans are essential for work beyond the University campus.

It is the policy of the School of Business to avoid a trade school type of training. In line with the trend in business management toward the development of would-be executives of the future, the School of Business hopes to participate in the professionalization of business by supplying lieutenants, if not "captains of industry."

The School of Agriculture and Horticulture

Having a wheel and four legs of its own
Has never availed the cumbersome grindstone
To get anywhere that I can see.
These hands have helped it go, and even race;
Not all the motion, though, they ever lent,
Not all the miles it may have though it went
Have got it one step from the starting place.

—from "The Grindstone"
by ROBERT FROST

The advantage of an annual report is to determine how far from the "starting place" the organization one belongs to has moved during this period.

The progress made during the past year has been outstanding. In addition to the usual activities and routine accomplishments, the School of Agriculture and Horticulture has made two significant gains: (1) the adoption of the Reorganization Plan, and (2) the initiation of an expanded program of Research and Extension.

The greatest accomplishment of the year (possibly for the half century), was the adoption of the Reorganization Plan with these results:

A. The elimination of arbitrary administrative segregation of the professional staff by agricultural service groups so that the personnel can now be used interchangeably between the various services according to duty assignments.

B. All programs may now be developed, organized, initiated, and carried out at the departmental level and may be based on the use of all personnel within the department on the calendar year basis.

C. Resident instruction programs may be geared to actual demands by students for classes. Classes normally required for certain majors in which small numbers of students usually register can be scheduled in alternate years for the simple reason that teachers are no longer employed only to teach, but are expected to have other duties when they are

13

not teaching. There should no longer be a tendency to schedule classes for the primary purpose of keeping the teacher occupied. This should result in a net reduction in the cost of instruction and a more effective total program in research and extension.

D. The quality of professional employees should increase because of the establishment of a realistic salary scale for calendar year employees and the development of a wholesome attitude because the administration recognizes the need for equalization of pay.

Also of great importance has been the expansion of the Research and Extension programs during this past year. America needs an efficient agricultural industry. Reduction of costs of production, improvement of quality of produce, and efficient marketing of produce are vital steps in the maintenance of this industry on a profitable basis, but these factors also have a real effect on the welfare of the consuming public. The traditional methods of agriculture, based on beliefs and folklore, are not adequate for today's society, nor will they be adequate in the future. Agriculture must be based on the foundation of knowledge gained from fundamental and applied research. The application of this knowledge to improving the effectiveness of this basic industry comes through the educational program of the extension service. Research and education are an effective team that guarantees adequate food and fibre of high quality and low cost for the expanding population of America.

This new expanded program for strengthening agriculture in Massachusetts received its primary support from funds made available through Federal grants-in-aid and through the transfer of teaching staff from a school year basis.

The expanded Extension program, which has been emphasizing marketing, consumer education, farm and home planning, and urban horticulture has been made possible through the employment of four new specialists at the state level and eight in the counties. Research projects which emphasize mechanization of crop production, marketing of farm produce, improvement of quality of produce, improvement of varieties and breeds, control of diseases, and studies in basic animal physiology have

14

been initiated or expanded with the employment of 22 professional persons in 10 departments. For the Extension program, $56,400 came from Federal sources, and of this 85 % was assigned to counties for support of programs at the grass roots, while 15 % was maintained at the State level for supervising and organizing State-wide programs.

New research has been supported by $86,400 from Federal grants-in-aid and allotments made to this University from regional research funds. Between $90,000 and $100,000 of new money is being applied to the research and extension programs by the reassignment of instructional personnel, including the department heads, with the result that more research will be done, more extension programs supported, and the agricultural instruction program will have a parallel reduction in cost equalling the amount transferred to these other activities.

Personnel changes are always important and significant. Fred P. Jeffrey has been appointed Associate Dean of the School of Agriculture and Horticulture and Director of the Stockbridge School of Agriculture to succeed Roland H. Verbeck who retired. Dr. John R. Havis took over the important position of Head of the Waltham Field Station to succeed the late Ray M. Koon. Dr. Thomas W. Fox has been promoted to Head of the Poultry Department, and some of the other important appointments include Dr. Roland Winterfield and Dr. William E. Meehl as Professors in Veterinary Science. During the year, over 30 new professional people joined the staff of this School. Several staff members have been on sabbatical leave during the year. Professor Wilbur H. Thies represented the University in a FAO assignment for three months in Yugoslavia.

Outstanding results and performances were obtained during the year. The job done by all personnel in the School in developing emergency educational material for use in the areas affected by the hurricane Carol and Edna, and the actual professional help given to the people in these areas by staff members, deserves special recognition. Staff and students cooperated to put on a great Horticultural Show under difficult conditions, but were adequately rewarded when 26,000 persons attended.

New space in Draper Hall for the Agricultural Economics Department will free space in Stockbridge Hall so that, for the first time, Agricultural Administration can be bought together there. The new Durfee conservatory added materially to the appearance of the campus and is significant in the teaching program of the plant science subjects. Thirteen new motor vehicles in the School, and the repairs to the farm buildings are welcome improvements.

The School of Home Economics

Last spring and summer, as in previous years, the demand for Home Economics graduates so far exceeded the supply that administrators in colleges, high schools and hospitals were literally begging for candidates. This situation contrasts markedly with an abundant number of graduates in some other fields and should serve to focus the attention of high school girls on a field in which women are in great demand.

Of the 57 Home Economics graduates in the class of 1954 at the University of Massachusetts, 13 are teaching home economics, 9 are teaching elementary grades, 6 are in the Extension service, 8 are dietetic interns or assistant dietitians, 1 is in home service, 1 in market research, and 11 are married home makers. Thus 49 are using their professional training in a variety of ways, and it is hoped that the others in insurance or other offices, in libraries and art school, may find their home economics training useful.

For those who go on to graduate school there are college teaching and research positions waiting. Graduate programs at the University are in the fields of Foods and Nutrition and Home Economics Education.

The service to non-majors has increased with 65 non-majors during the first semester this year contrasted to 22 the first semester 1953-54. The second semester offerings drew 96 non-majors second semester last year.

The School of Home Economics is responsible for a 15-minute weekly television program "Homecoming" over Channel 4, Boston (WBZ-TV). The Extension staff carried the major responsibility during the summer and fall but the teaching staff with student participants are assuming their share during the school year.

16

A new course in the Teaching of Arts and Crafts was introduced in Summer School, 1954 at the suggestion of the Education and Recreational Leadership Departments and has had capacity registration. Courses in foods and nutrition for nurses and for majors in Food Management are taught by the Home Economics staff. A new course in Demonstration Techniques has filled a long felt need and students are gaining much needed poise in public speaking.

The Division of Nursing

A basic collegiate program of nursing aims to prepare qualified high school graduates for a career in professional nursing, for marriage, and family living. The graduate of such a program is ready for a beginning position in a variety of nursing situations, including public health; for leadership in the hospital nursing team; and for participation with allied personnel in providing comprehensive patient care. A foundation is laid for advanced study, through which the nurse may prepare for positions in teaching, supervision, administration, consultation and research.

The basic collegiate program of nursing was inaugurated at the University of Massachusetts with the opening of the fall semester in September 1954. At this time, five sophomore students, previously enrolled in the general program of arts and sciences, transferred to become the first class in the Division of Nursing. In addition, thirteen entering freshmen were enrolled in this program. A study of the home addresses and high schools of these students gives evidence of a representative group of young women from a variety of communities and secondary schools within the state. Of this group of 18 students, 15 are students in residence at the University and three from local communities are enrolled as day students.

Since the programs for both groups, as planned by the Director and accepted by the various University and State approving boards, called for the utilization of selected on-going courses offered by other University schools and departments, the efforts of the faculty of this division have been directed toward the further development and implementation of a nursing program which is authentically collegiate, with the faculty of the division assuming responsibility for the major in nursing, both in its theoretical and clinical aspects. The nature of these faculty efforts has been varied, as have the role and responsibilities of the individual faculty member.

The nine-week summer session in the sophomore year (scheduled for the first time for June 13 to August 12, 1955) marks the beginning of the study of the nursing care of the ambulatory and hospitalized patients with medical and surgical conditions. This study will extend through and somewhat beyond the next clinical semester. Initial agreements had been reached previously with the Springfield Hospital and other health agencies in that area for the utilization of selected clinical resources for field instruction and practice. Specific contractural arrangements are in process with the Springfield Hospital regarding the use of its classroom and clinical facilities during the summer session.

A Division of Nursing brochure has been developed by the faculty, in cooperation with the Department of Publications, for publicity and recruitment purposes. This material should be ready for circulation in the near future.

Aptitude, health and other requirements for admission to the University program of nursing have been defined in cooperation with the University Registrar. A pre-admission nursing test battery has been developed in cooperation with the Department of Guidance.

The details of an organized and continuous health program for students of nursing are being worked out cooperatively with the University Health Office and the Springfield Hospital. This program is planned to provide the needed health counseling as well as preventive and remedial health services throughout the academic and clinical terms.

Division of Physical Education

A broad professional program in physical education, plus efficient and meaningful athletic and service activity programs, continues to be the goal of the Division of Physical Education. An awareness of the need for preparation in general education, as well as specialization in a chosen field, has resulted in a revised professional program. Increased participation of students on varsity teams and intramural teams, due to an expansion of programs in these areas, is a trend which is being encouraged. Activity for as many students as possible should be part of every student's experience, regardless of his major interest in an academic field.

Every attempt was made during the past year to meet the ever-increasing demand of the student body for intramural activity. Volleyball was added to the winter program for the first time, with the possibility of adding indoor track and tennis as other activities on the intramural level.

A redesign of existing indoor play areas has resulted in covering the entire dirt area with flooring. The improvement in design and larger floor area enabled more students to participate during the past year.

The revised major curriculum in Physical Education was instituted in September 1954, with 24 freshmen enrolled bringing the total enrolled to 59 students for the four classes. Five students currently enrolled in other departments in the University have requested permission to transfer their major to Physical Education at the close of the Fall semester.

With current facilities and staff, enrollment in the major program must now be limited to 30 entering students. Essential facilities for the future should include separate indoor and outdoor areas necessary for the diversified program of Physical Education.

It is significant to note that an ever-increasing number of students have been requesting information relative to advanced degrees in Physical Education at the University.

offered next spring. Badminton will be offered under the outdoor category but will be taught inside the gymnasium.

Coeducational courses have increased in popularity. In keeping with the needs of college-age students, we are planning to increase the number of coeducational courses as facilities become available.

In fulfilling the two-year requirement in Physical Education, all students, with the exception of students who are members of athletic teams or students who are excused for medical reasons, must have participated in:

1. Aquatics
2. Three team sports elected from the following: softball, volleyball, track, or membership on freshman or varsity athletic teams
3. Four individual activities elected from the following: archery, badminton, boxing, fly and bait casting, folk dancing, golf, gymnastics, tennis, track and field, trampoline and wrestling.

Our program of adapted Physical Education, to which students with physical or organic abnormalties are assigned, has been greatly expanded. Approximately 40 students are presently classified as adaptive cases. The improvement and expansion of the adapted program brings closer to realization a program of Physical Education for all—regardless of any degree of deviation from normal.

Fall semester figures indicate that 1115 students are enrolled in the Physical Education activity program. The breakdown by class is:

1955 — 33   1956 — 43   1957 — 486   1958 — 553

Beginning with the fall of 1954, written tests were administered to all students in our program. The computation of a grade in Physical Education reflects objective testing: skill testing results plus knowledge testing.

During the year of 1954 there has been little change in the number of students served or in the program offered for women due to the limitations of present facilities. Every possible effort is made to keep both the service activity program for undergraduates and women's athletics on as high a standard as possible. Fall semester enrollment figures show that 729 and 821 students participated in the service activity program during the first and second semesters.

The two professional courses for future secondary and elementary teachers, "The Teaching of Team Sports" and "Physical Education for Elementary Schools", were taught to women during the college year 1953-54 for the first time with 16 and 26 students enrolled in the former and latter courses respectively. Both courses are being offered again during the year 1954-55.

The 1954 appropriation of $1,621,000 for a Women's Physical Education Building and Athletic Field will greatly facilitate the entire women's program. It is hoped that ground will be broken in the spring of 1955 and that the building will be completed by September 1956.

Important research was conducted in the reading laboratory this past year. The laboratory was established last year after two years of planning and research. Based on the fact that good reading ability is important for success in college work, a course was initiated in "Speeded Reading and Increased Comprehension". The instruction, which commenced a year ago, was offered to freshman major students in Physical Education and athletes (majors and non-majors in Physical Education). The results were most gratifying. The group had an initial average reading rate of 225 words a minute with 65 per cent comprehension. At the end of the course, the group, as a whole, improved its rate of reading by 150 words a minute without any loss in comprehension. In fact, comprehension was improved by 11 per cent on the average.

The Graduate School

During the past year approval was granted for offering two new degrees in the Graduate School. These are Master of Science in Agricultural Engineering and Master of Arts in Teaching. The Master of Arts in Teaching is a cooperative program involving the several departments of the College of Arts and Sciences as well as the Department of Education. It is intended primarily for graduates of approved liberal arts colleges who have had little or no course work in professional education. Students registering in this program may prepare themselves for work in either secondary or elementary schools. It is hoped that the new degree will help to stimulate an increase in the number of college graduates entering the field of teaching.

Enrollment in the Graduate School continues to increase. During the first semester of 1954-55, 341 students were registered including 42 listed as special graduate students. At the 1954 Commencement, the following degrees were awarded: 7 Ph.D., 67 M.S., 8 M.A., 1 B.L.A., 2 M.L.A., 1 M.C.E., 1 M.E.E., and 3 M.B.A. degrees.

Two of the most important needs of the Graduate School relate to Teaching Fellowships and Research Fellowships. The University should have at least double the present number of Teaching Fellows (at present there are 35 Fellows for a total of 34 departments offering major graduate work), and the stipend should be increased to attract high quality candidates. State-supported Research Fellowships are also needed in order that members of the graduate faculty may receive technical assistance with their research and other creative work. The eventual establishment of what might be called University Professorships would be of great value to the Graduate School as well as to the entire University. These Professorships could be awarded to men of truly outstanding ability who should be free to work in any field and should not be restricted to the confines of a single department. Their very presence on the campus would prove a stimulus to all students and especially to graduate students.

People—The Vital Ingredient

There were 59 new appointments to the resident instruction staff during 1954 — 43 at the rank of instructor, 14 as assistant professors and 2 as associate professors. This turnover figure is but one position in excess of last year and from an enlarged total staff. New members of the Experiment Station and Extension Service number 20 — 13 instructors, 5 assistant professors, 1 associate and 1 full professor.

In recognition of excellent service, promotions were granted to 31 members of the instructional staff. Four were newly ranked as Heads of Departments; 5 as full Professors; 9 as Associate Professors; and 12 as Assistant Professors.

22

Seven promotions recognized professional staff in the Experiment Station—one to Professor, three to Associate Professor and three to Assistant Professor.

Nine people retired during 1954. President Ralph Van Meter retired May 14, 1954 after seven years as President and 30 additional years as a devoted and tireless staff member and public servant at the University. To retirement, concluding long and devoted professional service records: Roland H. Verbeck, Director of Short Courses; Ray M. Koon, Head of the Waltham Field Station; Harry N. Glick, Head of Department of Philosophy; Arthur D. Holmes, Research Professor of Chemistry; Frederick A. McLaughlin, Associate Professor of Research, Seed Control; Llewellyn L. Derby, Associate Professor of Physical Education; Charles H. Thayer, Assistant Professor of Agronomy; Lorin E. Ball, Assistant Professor of Physical Education; Mrs. Lena C. Mory, Library Reference Assistant.

No written tribute can adequately express the debt of gratitude and appreciation owed by the entire Commonwealth of Massachusetts to the staff of the University, both retired and in service. Again this University is uniquely strong in the people who do its work.

The University Library — Problem Number One — Present and Future

The past year for the University of Massachusetts Library has been one of continuing effort to improve service in the face of increasing demands with a static complement of personnel and only "token" increases in book and periodical funds. In 1935, when the present Goodell Library was dedicated, the building, with a few minor physical changes, was estimated to accommodate a maximum student population of 1,200. The same building is now in use with a student body of over 4,400.

During the past fiscal year, June 30, 1953 to July 1, 1954, the total amount expended for books and periodicals was $24,503, or $1,270 more than in 1952-53. Per student this is an expenditure of $19.66 and considerably less than the median of $44 derived from a recent survey of 70 university libraries including nearly all state universities.

23

The library operation now utilizes four library-trained staff members and nine clerical personnel. Lack of trained personnel has prevented fullest use of clerical staff since the supervisory staff is constantly loaded with reference, acquisition, and cataloging problems which cannot be delegated to clerical personnel because of lack of technical knowledge.

7,094 volumes were catalogued while approximately 8,000 volumes were taken in through purchase and gift. Over 1,000 volumes have been added to an already sizable backlog of uncatalogued arrears.

An increase in the total use of Reserved Books during the year is shown by 8,091 overnight circulations as against 4,916 last year, or an increase of 75 per cent.

The current record of the Library is bluntly that of a heroic and conscientious attempt on the part of a limited staff to hold together a technical service unit of the University, the position of which is becoming more untenable day by day because of demands related to a paucity of collections to work with the the technical staff to make them available. In short it spells out a desperate need for greater *financial support* and more *library trained personnel*.

CIRCULATION STATISTICS—JULY 1953 - JUNE 1954

Total circulation	25,938
Largest circulation by classes:	
Literature	5,052
History	2,642
Social Sciences	2,640
Fine Arts	1,496
Useful Arts	1,360
Science	997
Months having largest circulation:	
March	4,363
April	4,855
May	3,448
Number of days library was open July 1 - June 30	311
Acquisition and Cataloging Statistics	
Total Books Catalogued July 1, 1953 - June 30, 1954	7,094
Total Books Discarded July 1, 1953 - June 30, 1954	61
Net Total	7,033

24

Fort Devens Books recatalogued	1,061
Replacements	40
Total purchases	4,792
Total gifts	2,302
Total added	7,094
Total books in Library System	189,670

The Extra-Curricular Services

The morale and personal welfare of the student body are the daily concern of a vitally necessary contingent, a regular staff of "regular" people in the Guidance Office, the Placement Service, the offices of the Dean of Men and Dean of Women, and the Health Service.

Vocational and personal guidance services, sought voluntarily by individual students, remained the primary focus of the Guidance Office. Expansion of guidance services within the high schools seems to be producing a greater interest on the part of incoming students in vocational guidance at the college level.

Efforts have been made to develop group services in 1954 beyond the individual requests. Meetings were held in four freshman dormitories to instruct incoming students in effective study methods and to assist in acquiring sound attitudes toward academic achievement. In "study skill" groups of 15, a total of over 230 members of the freshman class participated.

In addition to regular administration of scholastic aptitude and reading tests for all freshmen, a more extensive preadmission test battery was administered to 260 veteran applicants.

The Placement Service is one of the most necessary general services of a state university. This is true because the student body is recruited largely from lower and middle income class groups, with limited business and professional contacts that will aid in employment after college. The same lack of financial and personal backing makes it necessary for a larger portion of our students to find summer and part-time employment to continue university careers to completion of degree requirements.

25

Last year 135 company recruiting representatives visited the campus and conducted 1,493 interviews with male seniors. 85 employers interviewed 694 women students during the year.

And to keep students in school the same Placement Service allocated $115,037 to 964 student employees at the University for average annual earnings per student of $119.00.

As a University contribution to the teacher shortage problem in elementary and secondary schools, 40 men and 67 women graduates of the class of 1954 went out as teachers and teacher-coaches. The impending shortage of secondary teachers, as crowded elementary classes move up, was obvious in the excess of requests for these teachers over available candidates, either from past graduates or the current class.

The Placement Service continued to handle the assignment of Stockbridge School students to training jobs and also to positions upon graduation. Again the demand for these Agriculture and Horticulture graduates exceeded the supply.

The Placement Office for women published a new brochure, "Launching Your Career" containing essential information on interviews, letters of application, job opportunities, etc. and a copy was given each senior this past fall.

Offices of the Dean of Men and Dean of Women continued to serve as nerve centers for the extra curriculum. A marked improvement in student social activities was evidenced during the year by dormitory dances, parties, suppers, faculty-student coffee hours, and regular Saturday night open dorm parties for freshmen. The two major and newly formed faculty-student committees, one for Recognized Student Organization and one for Social Activities have gone far in establishing extra-curricular life on a sound and constructive basis. The joint student-faculty committee on planning of the new Student Union, to be built in 1955-56 by the Alumni Building Corporation envisions a new era of adequacy and advancement of student organizations and activities dedicated to a wholesome and stimulating campus recreational opportunity for the entire student body.

Fraternity and sorority chapter houses had installed, by the opening of the 1954 fall semester, minimum acceptable fire escape, fire alarm, and fire detection facilities.

For the third consecutive year the number of bed patients treated in the Infirmary has dropped, due to no epidemic disease during the period. This is indeed fortunate, because the present Infirmary is not large enough to handle even a small epidemic. Figures for the 12 month period are: Bed Patients 467; Patient Days 932; Out Patients 9,052. The number of out-patients is steadily increasing and perhaps early out-patient treatment is a factor in the decreasing number of bed patients. On November 1, 1954 a full-time Assistant Physician, Dr. Malcolm J. Chisholm joined the staff. For the first time in many years all positions in the Health Service are permanent and full-time.

The Dollars that Translate Possibilities

During the past fiscal year the University received an operating and maintenance appropriation of $5,466,627 of which $18,631 reverted to the State Treasurer as unused funds. Money received by the University and returned to the Treasurer and Receiver General of the Commonwealth amounted to $1,861,872. The total *net cost* of operation and maintenance was $3,602,256. Of this the net cost of providing instruction for 4,091 students was $1,952,160 or 54 per cent of the total. The remaining 46 per cent was expended in providing the other services required of the University by law, including agricultural research, adult education through the Extension Service, and maintaining the control and regulatory services. It should be noted again that the housing of students, extra curricular activities and dining hall operations are, in net, self-supporting out of fees, prices, and assessments paid in full by the student body.

The net tax cost for operation and maintenance of the University amounted to about 75 cents for each person in Massachusetts. The State of Illinois for exactly the same net item spent $3.63 of tax money per person in Illinois for the University of Illinois.

Endowment funds of the University were increased by the gift of the David Buttrick Company of 750 shares of Preferred Stock, the income to be used for scholarships in Dairy Industry and Food Technology. At the close of the year, the principal of Endowment Funds at book value totaled $305,188.94.

A sum of $41,450 of which $25,000 comes from Commonwealth tax appropriated scholarships, was available for scholarship awards by the University Scholarship Committee. Of the
total amount $13,139 was loaned to 111 students from funds
available for this purpose. Limited funds make it necessary to
limit loans to a maximum of $200 per student.

During the year the Dining Commons went into service
adding $800,400 to value of buildings. Completion of Arnold
House by the Alumni Building Corporation added housing for
214 women and construction was started on Dormitory Number 13
for men to accommodate 173 additional students in September
1955. Construction of the $850,000 addition to Engineering is
underway to be completed by September 1955. Durfee Conservatory and Draper Hall construction and renovation were
completed at a net cost of $345,000 and remodeling of Bowker
auditorium is underway at the time of writing this report. Plans
are coming off the drawing boards now for the New Classroom
Building ($1,000,000), the Women's Physical Education Build-
ing ($1,621,000), and the Addition to Chemistry ($1,747,000).
These buildings should all be under construction in 1955.

The Elements of Rebirth

In conclusion I would say that all the elements necessary
for the rebirth of the whole philosophy of public higher education
in this Commonwealth are evident in the current position of the
University of Massachusetts. Appropriations to the writing of
this report promise adequate and improved facilities *for the
current enrollment.* Expansion of the staff and facilities to provide
adequate educational facilities for the coming generation will be
public recognition by this State that the progress and productivity
of the American people have always far exceeded, even in material
rewards, the cost of the education that is the foundation for
every advance. That the spiritual rewards are immeasurable is
obvious. The tone for the challenge and opportunity, and
necessity of this people's University for the future may be expressed to the entire people of the Commonwealth in the moral
imperative of the statesman Henry L. Stimson. He was summing
up his thoughts after a long and distinguished career but as is
so often true his words were for the future of those to follow:

"Let them learn from our adventures what they can. Let them charge us with our failures and do better in their turn. But let them not turn aside from what they have to do, nor think that criticism excuses inaction. Let them have hope, and virtue, and let them believe in mankind, and its future, for there is good as well as evil, and the man who tries to work for the good, believing in its eventual victory, while he may suffer occasional setback, will never know defeat."

JEAN PAUL MATHER
President

THE UNIVERSITY
OF MASSACHUSETTS

Bulletin

1955 Summer Session Catalogue

Amherst, Massachusetts

SIX WEEK SUMMER SESSION
JULY 5 - AUGUST 15

OFFICERS OF ADMINISTRATION

J. PAUL MATHER, B.S.C., M.B.A., M. A.............................President
BRUCE R. MORRIS, B.A., M.A., Ph.D. ....Director, 1955 Summer Session
GILBERT L. WOODSIDE, B.A., M.A., Ph.D. ....Dean of the Graduate School
MARSHALL O. LANPHEAR, B.S., M.S. ....Registrar
DONALD W. CADIGAN, B.S., M.S. ....Assistant Registrar
ROBERT S. HOPKINS, Jr., B.A., M.Ed. ....Dean of Men
HELEN CURTIS, A.B., A. M.................................Dean of Women
JAMES W. BURKE, B.S. ....Secretary
HUGH MONTGOMERY, B.S., B.S. in L.S. ....Librarian
GEORGE E. EMERY, B.S.....Assistant Placement Officer and Veteran's Coordinator
KENNETH W. JOHNSON, B.S. ....Treasurer

FACULTY OF THE SUMMER SESSION, 1955

LUTHER ALLEN, Instructor in Government
ALLEN E. ANDERSEN, Professor of Mathematics
WILLIAM W. BOYER, Assistant Professor of Civil Engineering
GERARD BRAUNTHAL, Instructor in Government
MILDRED BRIGGS, Associate Professor of Home Economics
THEODORE C. CALDWELL, Professor of History
HAROLD W. CARY, Professor of History
DAVID R. CLARK, Instructor in English
WALTER E. CONRAD, Instructor in Chemistry
GAIL E. COSGROVE, Supervisor of Elementary Education, Natick
ARMAND J. COSTA, Instructor in Mechanical Engineering
DOROTHY DAVIS, Assistant Professor of Home Economics
EDWIN D. DRIVER, Assistant Professor of Sociology
SEYMOUR EPSTEIN, Assistant Professor of Psychology
EDWARD G. FENNELL, Assistant Professor of Education
WILLIAM F. FIELD, Director of Guidance
ROBERT V. GANLEY, Instructor in Forestry
SUMNER M. GREENFIELD, Instructor in Romance Languages
THOMAS A. GROW, Assistant Professor of Civil Engineering
LAWRENCE C. HACKAMACK, Assistant Professor of Industrial Administration
SARAH L. HAWES, Instructor in Home Economics
VERNON P. HELMING, Professor of English
KARL N. HENDRICKSON, Associate Professor of Civil Engineering
LEONTA G. HORRIGAN, Assistant Professor of English
WARREN I. JOHANSSON, Assistant Professor of Geology and Mineralogy
STANLEY KOEHLER, Assistant Professor of English
ARTHUR S. LEVINE, Associate Professor of Food Technology
E. ERNEST LINDSEY, Professor of Chemical Engineering
WILLIAM P. MACCONNELL, Assistant Professor of Forestry
WILLIAM G. O'DONNELL, Professor of English
HELEN F. O'LEARY, Assistant Professor of Education
CHARLES F. OLIVER, Assistant Professor of Education
ELMER C. OSGOOD, Professor of Civil Engineering
ROBERT K. PATTERSON, Assistant Professor of Agricultural Engineering
ALFRED X. POWERS, Instructor in Agricultural Engineering

2

ALBERT W. PURVIS, Professor of Education
JOHN E. ROBERTS, Assistant Professor of Chemistry
DONALD W. ROGERS, Assistant Professor of Philosophy
NORMAN J. SCHOONMAKER, Assistant Professor of Mathematics
ADOLF E. SCHROEDER, Associate Professor of German
ARNOLD G. SHARP, Assistant Professor of Civil Engineering
J. HAROLD SMITH, Professor of Chemistry
LEO F. SOLT, Instructor in History
HERBERT J. STACK, Director of the Center for Safety Education, New York Un
WARREN J. TARRANT, Associate Professor of French, State University of N(
THOMAS O. WILKINSON, Instructor in Sociology
ARTHUR R. WILLIAMS, Assistant Professor of English
KENNETH E. WRIGHT, Associate Professor of Botany, Smith College
RAYMOND WYMAN, Assistant Professor of Education

COMMITTEE ON SUMMER SESSION

BRUCE R. MORRIS, Professor of Economics, Chairman
EDWIN D. DRIVER, Assistant Professor of Sociology, Secretary
JAMES M. FERRIGNO, Associate Professor of Romance Languages
ROBERT S. HOPKINS, Dean of Men
WILLIAM P. MACCONNELL, Assistant Professor of Forestry
GEORGE A. MARSTON, DEAN, School of Engineering
HELEN S. MITCHELL, DEAN, School of Home Economics
CLAUDE C. NEET, HEAD, Department of Psychology
ALBERT W. PURVIS, HEAD, Department of Education
WALTER S. RITCHIE, ACTING DEAN, School of Science
HENRY H. SCARBOROUGH, JR., Instructor in Botany

CALENDAR

July 5, Tuesday, 1:00 - 5:00 p.m. Registration, Drill Hall
July 6, Wednesday, 8:00 a.m. Classes Begin
August 12, Friday - August 13, Saturday. Final Examinations
August 15, Monday, 5:00 p.m. End of Summer Session

Volume XLVII   APRIL, 1955   ]

Published six times a year by the University of Massachusetts, Janu
ruary, April (two), May, September. Entered at Post Office, Amherst,
second-class matter.

UNIVERSITY OF MASSACHUSETTS
SUMMER SESSION
1955

JULY 5 -- AUGUST 15

SHORT TERMS:
Driver Education
June 27 - July 9

Home Economics Workshop
July 5 - July 25

Programs Offered

The University of Massachusetts will conduct a regular six-week summer session with opportunity for study in many basic courses and special fields. The program will give special attention to teachers and school administrators, as well as undergraduate students, and will afford an opportunity for veterans to accelerate their education.

In cooperation with the Center for Safety Education of New York University, a special two-week *Driver Education Instructor* course will be offered. This course is intended to prepare teachers seeking certification to teach Driver Education in secondary schools. Qualified persons may pursue this offering for graduate or undergraduate credit.

Special courses in Engineering and Forestry and two three-week workshops in Home Economics will also be offered.

Degree Credit

All courses offered carry degree credit and are equivalent in method, content and credit to courses offered in the University during the regular academic year. Credits obtained in these courses are ordinarily accepted as transfer credits by other colleges and universities. Students attending the Summer Session usually carry two courses, enabling them to earn six or seven semester hours credit. In exceptional cases students may be granted special permission to schedule additional credit hours. This permission will not be granted to students whose past record does not indicate a capacity to carry such a program. Students desiring to pursue courses for advanced degrees must seek the approval of the Dean of the Graduate School.

Expenses

Tuition for residents of Massachusetts (entire session)	$20.00
Tuition for residents of Massachusetts (Special Course)	$10.00
Tuition for non-resident undergraduate students (entire session)	$80.00
Tuition for non-resident undergraduate students (Special Course)	$40.00
Tuition for non-resident graduate students per semester credit hour	$10.00
Student Health and Activities Fee..	$ 2.00
Room rent for six weeks at $4.00 per week	$24.00
Board for six weeks (Monday through Friday) at $9.50 per week..........	$57.00

Payment for Summer Session fees is due June 28 and must be paid at or before registration. No student will be eligible to attend classes until fees are paid.

Living Accomodations and Health Services

Students, not commuting from home, are expected to live in the University Dormitories and board at the University Dining Halls.

The University Infirmary will be kept open during the session with a staff doctor on call.

Advance Enrollment: Veterans and Civilians

In order to facilitate arrangements, students contemplating attendance should notify the Director of the Summer Session at once, using the application form on page 12.

Veterans who plan to enroll under the G. I. Bill (P.L. 346, 16 & 894) must present at the time of registration evidence of eligibility (V.A. certificate of eligibility or, if previously enrolled, a clearance through the University Coordinator). Veterans failing to obtain certification must make payment of tuition and fees.

New students who are not under G. I. Bills must file certificate of residence with the Treasurer's Office.

Recreation

Under the direction of a faculty-student committee, programs for recreation offering many informal sports such as swimming, soft ball, baseball, tennis and hiking will be arranged.

A limited number of special lectures and entertainments will also be provided. Efforts are being made, for example, to provide a trip to a concert at Tanglewood and a play at Mountain Park. Dances and one major picnic will be scheduled by the Social Committee.

The surrounding area offers many opportunities for informal picnics and hiking. Square dance festivals are ordinarily held in surrounding towns.

COURSE DIRECTORY

The University reserves, for itself and its departments, the right to withdraw or change the announcements made in this catalogue.

Courses numbered 1-99 carry undergraduate credit only. Those numbered 200 or over admit graduate students only. Courses numbered 100-199 are undergraduate courses for which graduate students may receive graduate credit with the completion of additional requirements as determined by the instructor.

BOTANY 1. Introductory Botany. The morphology and physiology of plants.
1-1:50 MTWTF, Clark Hall 105   Credit 3
2-3:50 MTWT, Clark Hall 202   Mr. Wright

CHEMISTRY 29. Qualitative Analysis. Systematic semi micro analysis in a study of the principles and laws of the behavior of solutions of electrolytes.
1-2:00 MTWTF, Goessmann 26   Credit 4
2-4:50 MTWTF, Goessmann 7   Mr. Smith
Prerequisites, Chemistry 1 and 2 (or equivalent)

CHEMISTRY 30. Quantitative Analysis. The theory and practice of representative determinations, both gravimetric and volumetric.
8-9:10 MTWTF, Goessmann 28   Credit 4
9:20 - 11:50 MTWTF, Goessmann 228   Mr. Roberts
Prerequisite, Chemistry 29

CHEMISTRY 33. Organic Chemistry. A short course intended to satisfy the requirements in this field for all students who do not specialize in chemistry.
9:20 - 10:30 MTWTF, Goessmann 28   Credit 4
1 - 4:50 TT Goessmann 112   Mr. Conrad
Prerequisites, Chemistry 1 and 2

EDUCATION 53, 153. Educational Tests and Measurements. Construction, administration, scoring and interpretation of results of educational tests.
8 - 9:10 MTWTF, Liberal Arts Annex 32   Credit 3
                                          Mr. Fennell

EDUCATION 61, 161. Elementary School Reading. Purposes, methods, and materials of oral and written language and reading, with special attention to emerging methods of preventing reading difficulties.
10:40 - 11:50 MTWTF, Liberal Arts Annex 12A   Credit 3
                                         Miss O'Leary

EDUCATION 62, 162. Elementary School Arithmetic. Method and materials in arithmetic and correlating of arithmetic with the total program of the elementary school.
8 - 9:10 MTWTF, Liberal Arts Annex 12   Credit 3
                                        Mr. Cosgrove

EDUCATION 66, 166. Preparation and Use of Audio-Visual Aids. A wide variety of aids studied from the point of view of how they may be used effectively in teaching.
9:20 - 10:30 MTWTF, Liberal Arts Annex 32   Credit 3
                                         Mr. Wyman

EDUCATION 72, 172. Vocational Education in Agriculture. A survey of vocational education and an introduction to teaching of vocational agriculture at the secondary school level.
8 - 9:10 MTWTF, Liberal Arts Annex 30   Credit 3
                                         Mr. Oliver

EDUCATION 75, 175. Technique of Teaching Vocational Agriculture.
Materials, methods, policies, and special requirements of Massachusetts for teaching vocational agriculture. Credit 3
9:20 - 10:30 MTWTF, Liberal Arts Annex 30 Mr. Oliver

**EDUCATION 181. Workshop in The Teaching of Modern Foreign Lang-
uages in Elementary Schools.** The latest techniques, methods and materials
will be presented and demonstrated. Some roundtable discussions with Education,
Romance Language and Psychology departments. The course is especially designed
for present and prospective elementary school teachers and for teachers in a Modern
Foreign Language. Minor credit for students who have a major in a Modern
Foreign Language. Credit 3
9:20 - 10:30 MTWTF, Liberal Arts Annex 8 Mr. Tarrant

EDUCATION 83, 183. Principles of Secondary Education. Aims, pupil
population, program, guidance, problems and trends of junior and senior high
school. Credit 3
10:45 - 11:50 MTWTF, Liberal Arts Annex 32 Mr. Fennell

EDUCATION 208. The Teacher and School Administration. Problems in
admission, promotion, discipline, personnel, supervision, tenure, salary, schedules,
etc. Credit 3
9:20 - 10:30 MTWTF, Liberal Arts Annex 11A Mr. Purvis

EDUCATION 259. Teaching Elementary School Science. Methods and
materials and their place in the activity program. Credit 3
10:40 - 11:50 MTWTF, Liberal Arts Annex 12 Mr. Cosgrove

EDUCATION 265. Techniques in Remedial Reading. Methods and materials
in diagnosis and remedial instruction. Credit 3
9:20 - 10:30 MTWTF, Liberal Arts Annex 12A Miss O'Leary

EDUCATION 267. Audio-Visual Laboratory. Practical experience in setting
up and using common audio-visual equipment and materials. Credit 3
10:45 - 11:50 MTWTF, South College Mr. Wyman

EDUCATION 291. Educational Research. Common types of research in
Education, writing of the Problem report, evaluation of research studies, and the
elementary statistics needed in this evaluation of research. Credit 3
8 - 9:10 MTWTF, Liberal Arts Annex 11A Mr. Purvis

ENGLISH 2 & SPEECH 4. English Composition. Intended to teach straight
thinking, sound structure, clear and correct expression. Credit 3
8 - 9:10 MTWTF, Old Chapel A Mr. Clark

ENGLISH 25. Humane Letters. A general reading course based upon a chronological selection of masterpieces: classical, continental and English Credit 3
10:40 - 11:50 MTWTF, Old Chapel B Mr. Clark

ENGLISH 26. Humane Letters. A continuation of English 25, but may be
elected independently. Credit 3
9:20 - 10:30 MTWTF, Old Chapel B Mr. Koehler

ENGLISH 67, 167. American Prose. A course in the chief American prose
writers of the nineteenth and twentieth centuries. Credit 3
8 - 9:10 MTWTF, Old Chapel D Mr. O'Donnel

ENGLISH 68, 168. **Modern Drama.** The development of English and American drama from the time of Isben to the present day. Credit 3
8 - 9:10 MTWTF, Old Chapel B   Mr. Williams

ENGLISH 71, 171. **Biography.** The history of biography as a literary type; discussion of leading biographers from Boswell to Maurois, with special emphasis upon the development of the modern biographical method. Credit 3
9:20 - 10:30 MTWTF, Old Chapel A.   Mr. Helming

ENGLISH 76, 176. **Modern Poetry.** This course attempts to trace the spirit of twentieth century poetry from such authors as Hardy, Whitman, and Emily Dickinson to those of the present day. Credit 3
10:40 - 11:50 MTWTF, Old Chapel A.   Miss Horrigan

FOOD TECHNOLOGY 61, 161. **Industrial Technology.** A survey of theory and practices of commercial operations in the manufacture and preservation of food products. Includes equipment, sanitation, government regulations, and operation of types of commercial equipment in quantity production. The chemical, microbiological and physical factors directly related to canning and other food processing are discussed in detail. Credit 3
1 - 5:00 TWT, Chenoweth Lab, 110   Mr. Levine
Prerequisites, Food Technology 52; Bacteriology 31; or equivalents

FRENCH. **Graduate Reading Course.** For graduate students wishing to prepare for the graduate reading examination.
8 - 9:10 MTWTF, Liberal Arts Annex 8   Mr. Tarrant

GEOLOGY 27. **Physical Geology.** An introduction to the agents and processes that modify the earth's crust. Credit 3
8 - 10:30 MTWTF, Fernald K and B   Mr. Johannsson

GERMAN. **Graduate Reading Course.** For graduate students wishing to prepare for the graduate reading examination.
8 - 9:10 MTWTF, Liberal Arts Annex 1   Mr. Schroeder

GOVERNMENT 25. **American Government.** A study of the principles, machinery, dynamics and problems of American national government. Credit 3
9:20 - 10:30 MTWTF, Goessmann 26   Mr. Braunthal

GOVERNMENT 26. **European Government.** A study of the politics and institutions of Great Britain, France, U.S.S.R. and other European countries.
8 - 9:10 MTWTF, Goessmann 26   Credit 3
          Mr. Allen

GOVERNMENT 55, 155. **The Presidency in American Government.** The growth of the executive in the United States Government; varying conceptions of the Presidential office. Constitutional and political aspects of the office in legislation, administration, the conduct of foreign affairs. The president as party leader. Credit 3
10:40 - 11:50 MTWTF, Goessmann 26   Mr. Braunthal
Prerequisite, Government 25

HISTORY 6. **Modern European Civilization.** A basic survey course covering the period from 1815 to the present. Credit 3
10:40 - 11:50 MTWTF, Old Chapel C   Mr. Solt

HISTORY 60, 160. History of the United States. A survey of the natio development including political, social, economic, and cultural factors in growth of American democracy from 1865 to the present. Credi
9:20 - 10:30 MTWTF, Old Chapel C   Mr. C

HISTORY 70, 170. Europe Since 1918. Approximately half of the course devoted to international affairs, the other half to a study of recent internal devel ments in the principal European countries. Credi
8 - 9:10 MTWTF, Old Chapel C   Mr. Caldw

HOME ECONOMICS 63, 163. Arts and Crafts. Introduction to design a execution in crafts particularly adapted to work with children in schools, pl grounds, summer camps; and for any age in recreational leadership and occu tional therapy.
8 - 10:30 MTWTF, 1 - 3 T T, Skinner 20 & 17   Credi
Prerequisite Home Economics 31 or equivalent   Miss Bri

HOME ECONOMICS WORKSHOPS. See listing under special courses.

INDUSTRIAL ADMINISTRATION 11. Industrial Geography. A study the distribution of natural and human resources and the industrial and phys graphic bases of the extractive and manufacturing industries. Credi
9:20 - 10:30 MTWTF, Draper 124   Mr. Hackam

MATHEMATICS 6. Introductory Calculus for Engineers. May be used a substitute for Mathematics 29, Differential Calculus. Differentiation, with ap cations; technique of integration. Credi
Section 1, 10:40 - 12:20 MTWTF, Math Bldg. B   Mr. Andersen, Mr. Schoomal
Section II, 10:40 - 12:20 MTWTF, Math Bldg. A
Prerequisites, Algebra, Trigonometry, and Plane Analytic Geometry.

MATHEMATICS 7. Algebra and Trigonometry. Fractions, quadratic eq tions, exponents, logarithms, variation, determinants of the second and th orders, and plane trigonometry. Credi
9:20 - 10:30 MTWTF, Math Bldg. A   Mr. Schoonma

MATHEMATICS 92, 192. Differential Equations. May be used in some ca as a substitute for Mathematics 32. Cred
9:20 - 10:30 MTWTF, Math Bldg. B   Mr. Ander
Prerequisite, Mathematics 30

PHILOSOPHY 64, 164. Ethics. The meaning of good and evil, right and wro a survey of ethical theories and practices and an attempt to evaluate these theo with reference to modern ethical problems. Cred
9:20 - 10:30 MTWTF, Draper 117   Mr. Ro

PHILOSOPHY 266. Philosophy of Education. An evaluation of various cational theories and practices viewed in the light of historical perspective contemporary thought. Crec
10:40 - 11:50 MTWTF, Draper 117   Mr. Ro

PSYCHOLOGY 26. General Psychology. An introductory course des with the basic principles and applications of psychology with regard to the un standing and control of behavior. Crec
8 - 9:10 MTWTF, Liberal Arts Annex 27

PSYCHOLOGY 82, 182. Psychological Tests. Different varieties of psychological tests are studied. Practice will be given in administering, scoring, interpreting and evaluating tests.   Credit 3
9:20 - 10:30 MTWTF, Liberal Arts Annex 22   Mr. Epstein
One 3-hour laboratory by arrangement
Prerequisite, Psychology 26

PSYCHOLOGY 88, 188. Psychology of Guidance. A study of the psychological principles relevant to counseling and guidance with special emphasis on the methods and techniques of the counseling interview; the selection and interpretation of tests and group approaches to guidance. Laboratory practice is devoted to the development of interviewing skills and to the organization and evaluation of illustrative case materials.   Credit 3
8 - 9:10 MTWTF, Liberal Arts Annex 22   Mr. Field
One 3-hour laboratory by arrangement
Prerequisite, Psychology 26 and 81, Psychological Tests, or consent of instructor.

PSYCHOLOGY 94, 194. Child Psychology. The course aims to develop an understanding of the behavior of the child. Psychological aspects of the following are considered: original nature, maturation, play, social behavior, personality and mental hygiene.   Credit 3
10:40 - 11:50 MTWTF, Liberal Arts Annex 27
Prerequisite Psychology 26

SOCIOLOGY 28. Introduction to Sociology. An outline study of the social order, and of the individual considered as a member of his various groups.
9:20 - 10:30 MTWTF, Old Chapel D   Credit 3
                                                                                          Mr. Wilkinson
SOCIOLOGY 53, 153. Cultural Anthropology. A non-technical sociological study of man in pre-literate societies.   Credit 3
8 - 9:10 MTWTF, Liberal Arts Annex 3   Mr. Wilkinson
Prerequisite, Sociology 28

SOCIOLOGY 75, 175. Social Problems. A consideration of the incidence, distribution and interrelations among the major types of social tensions in human societies. Various theories of causation are evaluated. Research projects are required.   Credit 3
9:20 - 10:30 MTWTF, Liberal Arts Annex 3   Mr. Driver
Prerequisite, Sociology 28

SOCIOLOGY 78. Criminology. A study of the nature of crimes and the factor underlying criminal behavior. Attention is also given to the machinery of justice in criminal behavior; the law, the courts, police enforcement, penal and correctional institutions.   Credit 3
10:40 - 11:50 MTWTF, Old Chapel D   Mr. Driver
Prerequisite, Sociology 28

SPANISH 2. Elementary Spanish. The essentials of Spanish grammar, intensive oral drill and intensive reading of short stories.   Credit 3
8 - 9:10 MTWTF, Liberal Arts Annex 2   Mr. Greenfield
Prerequisite, Spanish 1

SPECIAL COURSES

CHEMICAL ENGINEERING 75. Instrumentation. A detailed study of tl
underlying principles and practices of indicating, recording and controlling instr
ments used on industrial process equipment.   Credit
Three 40-hour weeks: (Aug. 8-26)   Mr. Linds
Engineering Annex
Prerequisites, Physics 27, 28; Chemical Engineering 55, Calculations

CHEMICAL ENGINEERING 88. Chemical Engineering Laboratory.
quantitative study of pilot plant size equipment illustrating some unit operation
Three 40-hour weeks. (Aug. 29 - Sept. 16)   Credit
Engineering Annex   Mr. Linds
Prequisite: Chemical Engineering 56, Unit Operations II

CIVIL ENGINEERING 27. Plane Surveying. The basic principles of me
suration; use of tape, transit, and level; a brief consideration of route surveyi.ı
Three 40-hour weeks: (Aug. 8-26; Aug. 29 - Sept. 16)   Credit
                                 Mr. Hendrickson, Mr. Boyer, Mr. Gro
Engineering Building
Prerequisite, Mathematics 5, Introductory Engineering Mathematics, or Mat
ematics 7, Algebra and Trigonometry.

CIVIL ENGINEERING 28. Property and Topographic Surveying. A trans
and tape property survey requiring reference to Registry of Deeds records; al:
a topographical survey.   Credit
Three 40-hour weeks: (June 6-24; June 27-July 15) Mr. Hendrickson, Mr. Gro
Engineering Building
Prerequisite, Civil Engineering 25, Surveying or Civil Engineering 27, Pla
Surveying

CIVIL ENGINEERING 30. Route Surveying Practice. A preliminary surv
for a short highway location and the preparation of maps and profile.
Three 40-hour weeks: (June 6 - 24; June 27 - July 15)   Credi
Engineering Building   Mr. Osgood, Mr. Boy
Prerequisite, Civil Engineering 25 or 27

MECHANICAL ENGINEERING 23. Shop. Welding and machine shop, ı
of various machine and hand tools used in metal working.   Credi
Three 40-hour weeks: (Aug. 8 - 26; Aug. 29 - Sept. 16)
Engineering Shop   Mr. Patterson, Mr. Costa, Mr. Pow

MECHANICAL ENGINEERING 27. Shop. Welding, manual and automa
For mechanical engineering majors..   Credi
Three 40-hour weeks: (June 6 - 24; June 27 - July 15   Mr. Patterson, Mr. Pow
Engineering Shop

MECHANICAL ENGINEERING 28. Machine Shop. The fundamental mach
tools; lathe, planer, shaper, milling machine and drill press.   Cred
Three 40-hour weeks: (June 6-24; June 27-July 15)   Mr. Sharp, Mr. Co
Engineering Shop

FORESTRY 55, 155. The Elements of Forest Mensuration. Methods
determining the volume and value of the forest growing stock; type mappi
methods of predicting growth of trees and stands.   Cred
Three 44-hour weeks: (June 6-24)   Mr. MacConnell, Mr. Gar
Conservation Building

FORESTRY 78. Harvesting of Forest Products. Practice in the harvesting and preparation of direct forest products. Field trips to active forest properties and to visit pulpwood operations and manufacturing plants.   Credit 3
Three 44-hour weeks: (June 27 - July 15)   Mr. MacConnell, Mr. Ganley
Conservation Building

HOME ECONOMICS 86, 186. Workshop in Recent Developments in Textiles. A concentrated study of recent developments in the field of textiles. Characteristics and properties of the thermoplastic, protein, cellulose, and mineral fibres (natural and synthetic); blends, fabric finishes and fabric care. Field trips.
8-12 noon MTWTF (July 5-25) 2 hour lecture, 2 hour laboratory daily. Credit 3
Skinner Hall 118   Miss Hawes
Prerequisites, Home Economics 26 or equivalent

HOME ECONOMICS 94, 194. Workshop in Foods. An intensive three weeks course dealing with the planning and preparation of family meals. Consideration to new products, cost levels, new trends toward international foods, and outdoor cookery. Designed for home economics teachers and others with a background knowledge of scientific food preparation. (Maximum of 16 and minimum of 4 students).   Credit 3
8 - 1 MTWTF (July 5 - 25)   Miss Davis
Skinner Hall 220
Prerequisite, Home Economics 30 or equivalent.

PHYSICAL EDUCATION 80, 180. Driver Education and Driver Training. Objectives, scope, content, and problems of driver training; teaching materials; psycho-physical tests; motor vehicle construction, operation, and maintenance; advanced driving practices; administrative standards; practice teaching and behind-the-wheel instruction. Offered in cooperation with the Center for Safety Education, New York University, and the Massachusetts Registry of Motor Vehicles.
8 - 12 MTWTF (June 27 - July 9)   Credit 2
Curry Hicks Gymnasium   Mr. Stack and Staff

APPLICATION FOR ADMISSION

Prospective students may use the form below in applying for admission to
1955 Summer Session. This should be sent to the Director of the Summer Sessi
University of Massachusetts at Amherst.

- -

UNIVERSITY OF MASSACHUSETTS—1955 SUMMER SESSION

Name. . . . .

Address . . . .

Courses :   *Name and No.*   *Descriptive Title*

. . . .

. . . .

Previous school or college training beyond high school (degrees, when, whei
ceived) : . . . .

. . . .

. . . .

Are you now enrolled as a student (where, degree to be received, when) . . . . .

. . . .

. . . .

. . . .

Will you be studying under the G.I. Bill? . . . .

Will you require a dormitory room? . . . .

Will you commute from home? . . . .

High School Guest Day

~~~~~~ BULLETIN ~~~~~~

CURRY HICKS PHYSICAL EDUCATION BUILDING

UNIVERSITY OF MASSACHUSETTS
AT AMHERST

Se tember 24

❧ THE PROGRAM ❧

THIS YEAR ALL REGISTRATION WILL BE DONE
MAIL. THIS MEANS STUDENTS AND OTHER VISITORS MU
PICK UP PREREGISTRATION CARDS, PROGRAMS, AI
CAMPUS MAPS FROM THEIR PRINCIPAL OR HEAD MASTI
READ CAREFULLY ALL INFORMATION AND PLEASE FC
LOW DIRECTIONS. WHEN YOU ARRIVE ON CAMPUS, Y(
WILL FIND SIGNS DESIGNATING PARKING AREAS. PLEA
PREDETERMINE AREA NEAREST BUILDING YOU WISH '
VISIT AND GO THERE DIRECTLY. PLEASE OBSERVE VIS
ING HOURS. PLAN NOW FOR YOUR TRIP TO THE UNIVE
SITY TO AVOID LAST-MINUTE CONFUSION.

9:00 A.M. - 1:30 P.M.   Visiting Hours — Schools and Divisions.

11:45 A.M. - 12:45 P.M.   Visitors may have luncheon at moder
cost in the dining commons.

2:00 P.M.   Football game — Massachusetts vs. American Internatic
College. Alumni Field.

(The Red Registration Card is your pass to the ga
These are *not* available on campus. You *must* pick th
up from your principal or head master.)

❧ ❧

COED DRILL TEAM IN ACTION

**STUDENT
RADIO
STATION**

A Note From President Mather:

The University of Massachusetts extends a cordial invitation to high school juniors and seniors and their parents and teachers to visit he campus on Saturday, September 24, High School Guest Day. If you re a good student but have felt that a college education was beyond our reach, we would make the invitation a particularly urgent one. Possibly we can help you.

We are proud of our beautiful campus. We take particular pride n the strength and soundness of our educational program and what it ffers the serious student. We should like to give you a glimpse of tudent life and activities.

We hope that you can spend a day with us and that your determina-ion will be strengthened to get a college education.

Sincerely,

J. PAUL MATHER, *President*

From 8:30 A.M. Until 3:30 P.M.

The Offices of the Registrar Will Be Open

for

Personal Interviews Regarding Admission

COLLEGE OF ARTS AND SCIENCES

COLLEGE OF AGRICULTURE

SCHOOL OF BUSINESS
ADMINISTRATION

SCHOOL OF ENGINEERING

SCHOOL OF HOME ECONOMICS

SCHOOL OF NURSING

DIVISION OF PHYSICAL
EDUCATION

DIVISION OF MILITARY SCIENCE
(Armor and Air Force R.O.T.C.)

From 9 A.M. to 1:30 P.M. Mr. Fred Jeffrey, Director of Short Courses, will be in his office in South College to interview applicants for admission to the two-year vocational Stockbridge School of Agriculture.

~~~~~~~~~✤~~~~~~~~~

SEE YOUR HEADMASTER
OR PRINCIPAL
AT ONCE
FOR REGISTRATION CARDS

~~~~~~~~~✤~~~~~~~~~

September 24, 1955

Form 30. 6m-8-55-915500

in

UNIVERSITY OF MASSACHUSETTS

Stockbridge School of Agriculture
1956-1958

The University of Massachusetts is both a State University and a Land rant College and as such has been established by Acts of Congress and of the egislature of Massachusetts.

The two year course in practical agriculture at The University of Massachutts is known as The Stockbridge School of Agriculture, named after an early ·esident of the University. Included herein are descriptions of the various ·urses offered, information concerning expenses, enrollment and regulations. ι the back of catalogue will be found forms for application and certification of tizenship.

The University reserves, for itself and its departments, the right to withdraw change the announcements made in its catalogue.

UNIVERSITY BULLETIN
Amherst, Massachusetts

VOLUME XLVIII	JANUARY, 1956	NUMBER 1

Published five times a year by the University of Massachusetts, January, bruary, April (two), September.

plication for re-entry as second-class matter applied for at Post Office, Amherst, Mass.

BLICATION OF THIS DOCUMENT APPROVED BY GEORGE J. CRONIN, STATE PURCHASING AGENT
-12-55-916316

CALENDAR
THE STOCKBRIDGE SCHOOL OF AGRICULTURE
1956

January 3, Tuesday, 8:00 A. M..Classes Be
January 26, Thursday to February 1, Wednesday......................Final Examinat
February 6, Monday, 8:00 A.M.................................Second Semester Be
February 22, Wednesday...................................Holiday, Washington's Birth
March 24.................................Second Semester ends for Freshman stud
                   except Food Management and Forestry Ma
March 24, Saturday, 12 M. to April 2, Monday. 8 A.M.......................Spring Re
March 26...Placement Begins for Fresh
April 2, Monday, 8:00 A.M..Classes Be
April 19, Thursday ....Holiday, Patriot's
May 16, Wednesday, 5:00 P.M..Classes S
May 17, Thursday to May 23, Wednesday............................Final Examinat
May 24-27, Thursday to Sunday.......................................Commencen

1956-1957

September 17, Monday............................Registration of Senior Forestry Stud
September 24, Monday..................................Registration of Fresh
September 25, Tuesday.....................................Registration of Sen
September 26, Wednesday, 8:00 A.M................................Classes Be
October 12, Friday ....Holiday, Columbus
November 12, Monday..................................Observance of Veteran's
November 21-26, Wednesday, 12 M. to Monday, 8:00 A.M...............Thanksgiving Re
December 15, Saturday, 12 M. to January 2, Wednesday, 8:00 A.M........Christmas Re
January 2, Monday, 8:00 A.M.......................................Classes Be
January 23, Wednesday, 5:00 P.M.....................................Classes S
January 24, Thursday to January 30, Wednesday......................Final Examinati
February 4, Monday, 8:00 A.M.................................Second Semester Beg
February 22, Friday....................................Holiday, Washington's Bir
March 23, Saturday, 12 M. to April 1, Monday, 8:00 A.M..................Spring Re
March 23, Saturday ....Second Semester ends for Freshmen ex
          Food Management and Forestry Ma
April 1, Monday, 8:00 A.M..Classes Be
April 1, Monday.......................................Placement Begins for Fresh
April 19, Friday...Holiday, Patriot's
May 15, Wednesday, 5:00 P.M......................................Classes
May 16, Thursday to May 22, Wednesday............................Final Examinat
May 23-26, Thursday to Sunday.......................................Commencer

1957-1958

September 16, Monday............................Registration of Senior Forestry Stud
September 23, Monday..................................Registration of Fresh
September 24, Tuesday.....................................Registration of Se
September 25, Wednesday, 8:00 A.M................................Classes B
October 12, Saturday...................................Holiday, Columbus
November 11, Monday ....Holiday, Veteran's
November 27, Wednesday, 12:00 M to December 2, Monday, 8:00 A.M.....Thanksgiving R
December 21, Saturday, 12:00 M. to January 6, Monday 8:00 A.M..........Christmas R
January 6, Monday, 8:00 A.M..Classes F
January 22, Wednesday, 5:00 P.M....................................Classes
January 23, Thursday to January 29, Wednesday......................Final Examina
February 3, Monday, 8:00 A.M.................................Second Semester B
February 22, Saturday.................................Holiday, Washington's Bir
March 29, Saturday, 12:00 M. to April 7, Monday, 8:00 A.M................Spring R
March 29, Saturday...............................Second Semester ends for Fres
          except Food Management and Forestry M
March 31, Monday.......................................Placement Begins for Fres
April 19, Saturday...Holiday, Patriot's
May 14, Wednesday, 5:00 P.M......................................Classes
May 15, Thursday to May 21, Wednesday............................Final Examin
May 22-25...Commenc

STAFF

Officers of General College Administration

JEAN PAUL MATHER, LL.D., D.Sc.
President of the University

SHANNON McCUNE, Ph.D.
Provost
KENNETH WILLIAM JOHNSON, B.S.
Treasurer of the University
DALE HAROLD SIELING, Ph.D.
Dean of the College of Agriculture
JAMES WILLIAM BURKE, B.S.
Secretary of the University

HUGH MONTGOMERY, B.S. in L.S.
Librarian of the University
FRED PAINTER JEFFREY, M.S.
Director of the Stockbridge School of Agriculture and Associate Dean the College of Agriculture

STOCKBRIDGE ADVISORY COMMITTEE

ROLLIN H. BARRETT
LYLE L. BLUNDELL
THOMAS A. CULBERTSON
RICHARD C. FOLEY
JULIAN M. FORE
EMORY E. GRAYSON
ROBERT P. HOLDSWORTH
FRED P. JEFFREY, *Chairman*

RANDOLPH A. JESTER
GORDON S. KING
ELLIOT C. ROBERTS
OLIVER C. ROBERTS
RUSSELL E. SMITH
GRANT B. SNYDER
JOHN H. VONDELL
JOHN M. ZAK

The Faculty of Instruction

HERSCHEL G. ABBOTT, M.F.......................................Conservation Buil
    Instructor in Forestry
VERNE A. ADAMS, B.S...Stockbridge
    Instructor in Dairy and Animal Science
DORIC ALVIANI, M.Ed...Memorial
    Professor of Music
JAMES F. ANDERSON, M.S..French
    Instructor in Pomology
JOHN H. BAKER, B.S..University Com
    Assistant Professor of Food Technology
LOUIS N. BAKER, Ph.D..Stockbridge
    Assistant Professor of Dairy and Animal Science
WALTER M. BANFIELD, Ph.D..Clark
    Assistant Professor of Botany
LUTHER BANTA, B.S...Stockbridge
    Assistant Professor of Poultry Husbandry
ROLLIN H. BARRETT, M.S..Draper
    Professor of Farm Management
ALLEN B. BARTON, M.S..Stockbridge
    Associate Professor of Agricultural Engineering
LYLE L. BLUNDELL, B.S...Wilder
    Professor of Horticulture
KENNETH L. BULLIS, D.V.M..Paige Labor
    Professor of Veterinary Science and Head of Department
JAMES W. CALLAHAN, M.S..Draper
    Instructor in Agricultural Economics
WILLIAM G. COLBY, Ph.D..Stockbridge
    Professor of Agronomy and Head of Department
MRS. GLADYS M. COOK, M.S..Edna Skinner
    Assistant Professor of Home Economics
MRS. CAROL B. CORNISH, M.S......................................South C
    Placement Officer for Women
THOMAS A. CULBERTSON, B.S.......................................University Com
    Assistant Professor of Food Technology
HELEN CURTIS, A.M...South C
    Dean of Women
LAWRENCE S. DICKINSON, M.S......................................East Experiment St
    Professor of Agrostology
MRS. MARRON S. DuBOIS, B.A......................................C
    Instructor in English
J. MURRAY ELLIOT, B.S...Stockbridge
    Assistant Professor of Dairy and Animal Science
DAVID A. EVANS, M.S...Flint Labor
    Assistant Professor of Dairy and Animal Science

CARL R. FELLERS, Ph.D...Chenoweth Laboratory
Professor of Food Technology and Head of Department
RICHARD C. FOLEY, Ph.D..Stockbridge Hall
Professor of Dairy and Animal Science
WILLIAM FOOTRICK, M.P.E.......................................Physical Education Building
Associate Professor of Physical Education
JULIAN M. FORE, M.S..Stockbridge Hall
Professor of Agricultural Engineering and Head of Department
THÓMAS W. FOX, Ph.D..Stockbridge Hall
Professor of Poultry Husbandry and Head of Department
ARTHUR P. FRENCH, Ph.D...French Hall
Professor of Pomology and Plant Breeding, Head of Department
ROBERT V. GANLEY, M.F...Conservation Building
Instructor in Forestry
GEORGE B. GODDARD, B.S...French Hall
Instructor in Floriculture
EMORY E. GRAYSON, B.S...South College
Director of Placement
TOM S. HAMILTON, JR., B.F.A...Wilder Hall
Assistant Professor of Landscape Architecture
DENZEL J. HANKINSON, Ph.D...Stockbridge Hall
Professor of Dairy and Animal Science and Head of Department
JOHN F. HANSON, Ph.D...Fernald Hall
Assistant Professor of Entomology
JOHN L. HOBART, B.S..Stockbridge Hall
Instructor in Dairy and Animal Science
ROBERT P. HOLDSWORTH, M.F.....................................Conservation Building
Professor of Forestry and Head of Department
RANDOLPH A. JESTER, M.S...French Hall
Assistant Professor of Floriculture
WALTER O. JOHNSON, B.S...University Commons
Manager of University Commons
GORDON S. KING, B.S...Wilder Hall
Assistant Professor of Arboriculture
STEPHEN R. KOSAKOWSKI ....Physical Education Building
Instructor in Physical Education
THEODORE T. KOZLOWSKI, Ph.D..Clark Hall
Professor of Botany and Head of Department
RAUNO A. LAMPI, M.S..Chenoweth Laboratory
Instructor in Food Technology
EDWARD P. LARKIN, Ph.D.:..Marshall Hall Annex
Instructor in Bacteriology
ARTHUR S. LEVINE, Ph.D..Chenoweth Laboratory
Associate Professor of Food Technology
ADRIAN H. LINDSEY, Ph.D..Draper Hall
Professor of Agricultural Economics and Head of Department of Agricultural Economics and Farm Management
WILLIAM P. MACCONNELL, M.F.....................................Conservation Building
Assistant Professor of Forestry
MINER J. MARKUSON, B.S..Stockbridge Hall
Associate Professor of Agricultural Engineering
HELEN S. MITCHELL Ph.D...Edna Skinner Hall
Dean of the School of Home Economics
RAYMOND H. OTTO, M.L.A...Wilder Hall
Professor of Landscape Architecture and Head of Department
HENRY B. PEIRCE, JR., M.F.A. ....South College
Instructor in Speech
EDWARD S. PIRA, B.S..Stockbridge Hall
Instructor in Agricultural Engineering
FRANK E. POTTER, Ph.D..Flint Laboratory
Assistant Professor of Dairy and Animal Science
ALFRED X. POWERS, B.S..Stockbridge Hall
Instructor in Agricultural Engineering
PAUL N. PROCOPIO, B.S...Wilder Hall
Assistant Professor of Horticulture
ERNEST J. RADCLIFFE, M.D...Infirmary
Senior Physician
ARNOLD D. RHODES, M.F...Conservation Building
Professor of Forestry
J. HARRY RICH, M.F...Conservation Building
Associate Professor of Forestry
ELIOT C. ROBERTS, Ph.D. ....Stockbridge Hall
Assistant Professor of Agrostology
OLIVER C. ROBERTS, M.S...French Hall
Associate Professor of Pomology
DONALD E. ROSS, B.S..French Hall
Assistant Professor of Floriculture

WILLIAM C. SANCTUARY, M.S...Stockbridg
    Professor of Poultry Husbandry

FRANK R. SHAW, Ph.D..,........Fernal
    Associate Professor of Entomology and Beekeeping

RUSSELL E. SMITH, D.V.M...........................,.....................Paige Lab
    Professor of Veterinary Science

J. ROBERT SMYTH, JR., Ph.D..Stockbridg
    Associate Professor of Poultry Husbandry

GRANT B. SNYDER, M.S............................... ......Frenc
    Professor of Olericulture and Head of Department

RICHARD A. SOUTHWICK, M.S..Stockbridg
    Instructor in Agronomy

HERBERT G. SPINDLER, M.B.A...Drape
    Assistant Professor of Agricultural Economics

HARVEY L. SWEETMAN, Ph.D..Fernal
    Professor of Entomology

WILLIAM H. TAGUE, B.S...Stockbridg
    Assistant Professor of Agricultural Engineering

CLARK L. THAYER, B.S..Frenc
    Professor of Floriculture and Head of Department

REUBEN E. TRIPPENSEE, Ph.D................................Conservation B
    Professor Wildlife Management

ALDEN P. TUTTLE, M.S..Frenc
    Assistant Professor of Vegetable Growing

JOHN H. VONDELL...Stockbridg
    Associate Professor of Poultry Husbandry

JOHN A. WEIDHAAS, JR., M.S...Fernal
    Instructor in Entomology

KAROL S. WISNIESKI, M.P.H...Marsha
    Instructor in Bacteriology

HENRY B. WORONICZ, B.S..............................Physical Education B
    Instructor in Physical Education

JOHN W. ZAHRADNIK, M.S..................................Agricultural Engineering
    Assistant Professor of Agricultural Engineering

JOHN M. ZAK, M.S...................................,...................Stockbridg
    Assistant Professor of Agronomy

CHARLES ZAPSALIS, B.S..Stockbridg
    Teaching Fellow in Agronomy

THE STOCKBRIDGE SCHOOL OF AGRICULTURE

he Stockbridge School of Agriculture is the vocational non-degree department
he University providing training of post high school grade in the College of
iculture.

he Stockbridge School program is set up to fully meet requirements of a
)erative course as defined in Veterans Administration regulation 12205.

leven programs of study are. offered, one of which must be selected by each
lent and completed as specified for the school diploma. The present list of
rings includes:

nce its organization in 1918 at the request of the Massachusetts Legislature
school has registered more than 3,500 students and graduated thirty-three
ses. The value of this kind of concentrated technical schooling aiming di-
ly toward preparation for a definite field of work, is amply demonstrated
.he successful careers of our graduates.

General Information

ntrance Conditions:—The school program is open to any student who
:venteen years old or over and who has completed a secondary school
rse or its equivalent, but some major courses do require personal in-
'iews with applicants to insure proper qualifications. All eleven pro-
ns of study have limited enrollment quotas which cannot be exceeded
iuse placement, employment, or teaching facilities will not permit a
'er student registration. There are no formal entrance examinations.

ow to Enroll.—Fill out application blank, Form 1, page 62 giving all in-
\ation requested. Be sure to indicate course you wish to elect. Mail this
t, with citizenship certificate, Form II, on page 63 to Director of Short
rses. If application is accepted you will be notified, and certificate of citizen-
will be kept on file until you register.

egistration. —For registration dates see calendar in front of catalog.

.struction. —Instruction is given by the University teaching staff through
:room teaching, laboratory exercises and practical work. The work of the
:room is supplemented by demonstration work in the barns, dairy plant,
nhouses, orchards, gardens, engineering shops, quick freezing plant, canning
t, forest, and abattoir. The courses are planned to offer fundamental in-
\ation; and to establish the underlying reasons as well as the special methods
loyed in the various operations. The combined advantages of university
uction and a university plant with all its varied resources are thus made
lable to young men and women training for successful business careers in
:ultural vocations.

The usual University holidays are indicated on calendar, Page 2. First year Arboriculture students report two weeks prior to the opening of regular class work for preliminary training in the use of ropes and climbing. Forestry seniors report one week early or at time of four year registration. Freshman classes continue to April first, when most students are assigned to placement jobs, excepting Food Management and Forestry freshmen who complete two full semesters to June first. Class work is required at the University in the months of October to March inclusive; placement training for practical experience on jobs away from the University, on a wage basis, is required of all first year students from April to September inclusive, with exceptions noted.

Diploma Requirements.—In order to obtain a diploma a student must complete satisfactorily the entire program of study in which he has registered. A student who fails to pass the requirements of his summer placement training, after a suitable job has been assigned him, is not eligible for graduation until this deficiency is made up, and may not be allowed to enroll for the second year, if the Director of Placement Service considers his record to be unsatisfactory.

Transfer Credits.—Students who make excellent scholastic and placement records in this two-year course, and whose high school preparation has been satisfactory, may transfer to the same major program in the University with credit allowances of one to two semesters, depending on the individual record. This arrangement is limited strictly to students who meet the stipulated requirements, and each case is considered individually by the Registrar.

Evaluation of Stockbridge School Credits.—A student who has completed the work of the Stockbridge School may be recommended for transfer to the four year course if he has an average of B or above for his Stockbridge School course.

A student who has completed all the Stockbridge School work with an average of B or above shall be granted 30 credits in the four year course.

A student who has completed two semesters of the Stockbridge School course shall be granted 10 credits.

A student who has completed one semester of Stockbridge School work shall be granted 5 credits.

A student who has completed three semesters of work in the Stockbridge School should complete his course before transferring to the four year course.

A Stockbridge School student who has satisfactorily completed his period of placement training will have satisfied this requirement of a department in a four year major if this major is closely related to his Stockbridge School major. Otherwise, the Head of the Department will determine whether placement training for the four year course is to be required.

Graduation Requirements.—No student will be graduated unless all bills due the University are paid on or before the Wednesday preceding graduation exercises.

Diplomas and letters of honorable dismissal will be withheld from all students who have not paid bills due the University, or legitimate bills due private individuals or business concerns.

A diploma will not be awarded to any senior if arrears are reported by his fraternity. All bills for second semester, senior year, must be settled not later than the Wednesday before graduation.

Attendance at graduation exercises is required of all seniors before diploma will be awarded.

Seniors who have borrowed from the Goldthwait Loan Fund will have diplomas held as collateral by the University until they have paid up loans in full. This in no way interferes with the privileges of graduation.

Scholarship Regulations.—At the close of each semester students receive a formal report showing the standings given in the subjects pursued by them.

If a student's average in any subject is below D, he is failed (F) in the course and must repeat it with the following class.

The instructor has the privilege of turning in a condition (#) mark which allows the student to repeat the final examination with the hope of receivin a passing grade. The instructor also has the privilege of turning in a withhel (wh) mark in case a student has not turned in all required work.

Students will be graded by instructors at mid-semester to show general stand ing and at end of semester for permanent record. The Faculty Advisory Com mittee will consider all questionable grades after each marking period, and whe a student's scholastic record indicates failures or uniformly poor work, ma recommend close supervision of his class work by the major department con cerned, or that he be asked to withdraw from School.

A first year student will not be eligible for placement training if in th opinion of his major department his scholastic work has not been satisfactory

At the end of any semester a student who has failed in two courses, or ha conditions in more than two courses, is dismissed. A student failing a cours in his major department may or may not be dismissed depending on the recom mendation of his major department.

Rules and Regulations

Absences from Class

    (1) Attendance at all lectures, laboratories, and class trips is ex pected of all students.

    (2) Each instructor will establish his own attendance rules and th Director will support whatever rules are established.

    (3) All students are required to report promptly to University in firmary, if ill, and condition permits. Bring doctor's statemen for absence excuse if treated elsewhere.

Student Expenses

Tuition.—A tuition fee of $50 per semester is charged students, resi dents of Massachusetts, enrolled in the Stockbridge School of Agricultur Students who are not residents of Massachusetts are charged a tuition c $200 each semester. The tuition per semester, charged persons not citizen of the United States is $200. **Students entering from Massachusetts, unles of voting age themselves, are required to file a statement signed by eithe town or city clerk, stating that the applicant's parent is a legal residen of Massachusetts.** (See Form II in back of catalog.)

Variation in Course Charges:

Food Management and Forestry Courses:—Placement jobs are not availabl until after June 1, and students have to complete two semesters of residen study each year. Students majoring in these two programs of work pay f semester fees both the first and second years as indicated in the following tabl

Summary of Expenses Estimated:

	FIRST YEAR	SECOND YEA
Tuition (Citizens of Mass.)	$75.00-$100.00	$100.00
Room in University Dormitory	130.25- 170.00	170.00
Board at University Commons (5-day week)	225.00- 308.00	308.00
Books, stationery, and other supplies	90.00- 90.00	90.00
Athletic Fee	15.00- 20.00	20.00
Student Union Fee	15.00- 20.00	20.00
*Student Taxes	18.00- 18.75	20.75
	$568.25-$726.75	$728.75

These figures for board and room are estimates based on prevailing prices and may subject to change.

*Student Taxes:

	FIRST YEAR	SECOND YEA
Class Tax	$2.00	$2.00
Collegian	2.25-3.00	3.00
Concert Tax	3.00	3.00
Shorthorn (School Yearbook)	7.00	10.00
Stockbridge School Activities	3.00	2.00
Student Handbook	.75	.75
	$18.00-18.75	$20.75

Advance Payment

New students will be expected to make an advance payment of $15
the Treasurer of the University as soon as they are notified by the Dire
that they are accepted for admission. This will be considered as first p
ment on registration fees which will be due at time of matriculation
the fall. It is not refundable and will be considered as payment for admiss
and registration expense if the student does not matriculate.

Refund of Student Payments

Prepaid tuition and fees will be refunded to students withdrawing as follo

a. Within the first two weeks from the date of registration 80%
b. Within the third week 60%
c. Within the fourth week 40%
d. Within the fifth week 20%
e. After fifth week, no refund.

Prepaid board—pro rata refund.

Prepaid room rent—no refund.

When Payments Are Due

In accordance with policy established by the Board of Trustees, all cha
for tuition, fees, board and room rent in University dormitories are due at
beginning of each semester and must be paid on or before the opening dat
each semester. Bills will be rendered in advance by the University Treasu
and payment may best be made by mail. Students may not attend classes u
registration charges are paid.

Late Registration

Any student who does not complete his registration, including payment
semester charges on the regular registration days will be required to pay a
of five dollars.

Dormitory Facilities

Men Students: All Stockbridge students except commuters, married
dents, or those living in Stockbridge fraternities, are required to live in Uni
sity dormitories. Rooms are furnished except for study lamps, metal wa
baskets, bed linen and blankets. Freshman students will be required to b
at the University Commons. This requirement will not apply to seniors.

Women Students: Women students of the Stockbridge School are ho
in University dormitories and have their meals at the University Comr
unless given permission to commute from home.

Under the supervision of the Dean of Women, life in each dormitor
directed by a council of student leaders, advised by a full-time Housemo
so that conditions in the residence hall are conducive to study and good l
habits. Through Women's branch of the Student Government, the resp
bility is put upon each student to live according to her own best standar
well as according to the standards of the group.

Room furnishings include mattress and pillow; students furnish bedding; l
towels, desk lamp and wastebasket. Rooms are cared for by students occuj
them.

Dormitories are open at 1:00 o'clock on Sunday preceding Stockbridge
tration.

Board

All freshmen, both men and women living in dormitories are required to secure meals at the University Commons. This same rule applies to senior girls living in dormitories. Senior men living in dormitories may have their meals at the University Commons or make other arrangements. Preparation of food in dormitory rooms is *not permitted* under any circumstances. It is recommended that senior men living in dormitories eat at the University Commons.

Student Cars

Freshman students living in dormitories are not permitted to have cars. Senior students are permitted to have cars although this practice is not encouraged.

Books and Supplies

For the convenience of students, the University maintains a store service in North College. Here all textbooks may be purchased at cost plus transportation charges. Students are informed at the first class session in each course what books are required and must secure individual copies according to order list sent in by instructor.

There is little opportunity to secure secondhand books because most students find the texts assigned of value to retain as reference sources after completing a course.

Student Aid

Students desiring financial aid from the University in the form of part-time employment, are required to file applications with the Placement Service not later than May 15 of each year. Incoming freshmen are allowed an extension of time.

These application forms are used to determine the comparative need of the applicants and are passed on by the Student Aid Committee. No student is eligible for any kind of financial assistance from the University unless he or she has filed the required form and has been certified as deserving by the Student Aid Committee. Application forms may be secured at the Placement Service Office, South College.

The placement training period between the first and second year usually enables a student to earn from $500 to $1,000 depending upon his skill and general ability, and the type of work. This will pay a large part of the second year expenses.

Prospective students should understand that the above estimates cover expenses which may be called strictly University expenses, and that there are other financial obligations voluntarily assumed by students which they should expect to meet. Such expenses vary from $40 to $50 a year. Additional financial responsibility is also assumed by students joining fraternities or entering into other social activities of the University. Besides the amount necessary for clothes and traveling, the economical student will probably spend between $600 and $700 for the first year for one and one-half semesters in residence, and $800 to $900 for the second year of two semesters.

Student Employment Projects

Part-time work is available for a limited number of needy students. The type of work to which students may be assigned is as follows: clerical and office, building and grounds maintenance, farm, greenhouse and orchard duties, helpers in livestock and cattle barns, and other miscellaneous jobs.

Self Help.—The University does not encourage students to enter without money in the expectation of earning their way entirely. The student will find it better to work and accumulate sufficient funds before coming to the University, or else to take more than two years in completing his course.

No student should undertake work that interferes with his studies, and students should understand that no one may receive any large amount of work at the University.

First year students particularly should not risk failure in their beginning studies by taking on such extra work until they have, at least, tested themselves in the study program of the first semester. It is advised to proceed cautiously in combining both extra work and athletics at the same time, if the student's scholastic record is at all questionable.

Loans

Bartlett Loan Fund.—This fund was given to the Stockbridge School by the F. A. Bartlett Tree Expert Company of Stamford, Connecticut. This fund is available only to students majoring in Arboriculture and is handled in a manner similar to the one used in administering the Stockbridge Emergency Loan Fund.

The Vincent Goldthwait Loan Fund.—This fund was established by Dr Joel E. Goldthwait, U. of M. 1885, of Boston, as a memorial to his son who died in 1922 during his junior year at Harvard. Its purpose is to aid worthy students in financial difficulties. Amounts in excess of $200.00 are rarely granted and most loans range from $50.00 to $150.00.

A regular promissory note must be executed, endorsed by parent or guardian, and repayment may be made within any reasonable period after graduation up to one year. There is no interest charge.

Stockbridge Emergency Loan Fund.—This fund was started by the Class of 1951 and added to by the Classes of 1952, 1953 and 1955 as their commencement gifts to the School. It provides immediate loans for short periods of time one week to on month usually, to any student who finds his funds running short or has an emergency expense not anticipated. These are temporary loans without interest charge to meet emergency situations only, developing during the school year.

All requests for such aid should be made in person to the Director of Short Courses who issues the necessary order to the Treasurer's Office.

SCHOLARSHIPS

Prospective senior students should file scholarship applications before starting placement training in the spring. First year students will receive a scholarship application blank when notified of their acceptance. This application should be filed within one month after its receipt.

Ascension Farm School Scholarships.—Trust funds from the Ascension Farm School Corporation of Great Barrington were given to the University trustees in 1952 the income from which shall be used to provide for the "education and training in agriculture of boys resident in Western Massachusetts" as stated in its original charter. This makes possible the award of scholarship to men students residing in Hampden, Hampshire, Franklin, and Berkshire counties with special consideration to be given applicants from the last named county.

The Margaret Fitz Barnes Scholarship.—A $100 scholarship awarded annually to a young man or young woman interested in Ornamental Horticulture who is in need of financial aid and has been accepted or is enrolled in the Stockbridge School of Agriculture.

13

The Boston Market Gardeners Association Scholarship.—An annual scholarship of $100 to be awarded to a deserving student majoring in Vegetable Crops. This scholarship may be awarded either to a four year or Stockbridge student.

The Cape Cod Farm Bureau Scholarship.—An annual $50.00 scholarship to a student of agriculture at the University of Massachusetts who may be taking either Stockbridge or four year course.

Lotta Crabtree Scholarships.—By special arrangement with the Lotta Crabtree Foundation trustees of Boston, a number of scholarships are available to Stockbridge students.

The Holbrook Garden Club Scholarship.—An annual scholarship of $100 to be awarded to a Stockbridge student who has graduated from a Norfolk County high school. Preference is given to a Holbrook High School graduate or resident who is recommended by the High School Principal and approved by the Holbrook Garden Club awards committee.

Holyoke and Northampton Florists' and Gardeners' Club Scholarship. An annual scholarship of $100 to be awarded to a senior student (man or woman) in the Stockbridge School who is majoring in Floriculture or Ornamental Horticulture.

The V. A. Rice Scholarship Fund.—A $100 scholarship for a worthy student majoring in Animal Husbandry—either Stockbridge or four year.

Wilbur H. H. Ward Scholarships.—The Wilbur H. H. Ward Fund is administered by a Board of Trustees independent of the University. Applicants for these scholarships should write to Sumner R. Parker, who may be addressed at 1 Sunset Court, Amherst, Mass. They are available only to Hampshire County boys.

Convocation

No classes are scheduled on Wednesdays from 11:00-12:00 m, with the idea that a convocation may be held during this hour. On occasion a convocation for either freshmen or seniors will be compulsory. The number of convocations held per year will be based on recommendations from the Student Council.

STUDENT ACTIVITIES

A large number of student organizations furnish opportunity to students for work and leadership.

Memorial Hall is the center of student activities and contains offices for the various student organizations, including the Stockbridge School Student Council. On the first floor are located a lounging room, the Memorial Room, and the offices; in the basement, bowling alleys, pool and ping pong tables; and on the second floor an auditorium for meetings and dances. This building was erected by the alumni, students, faculty, and friends in honor of the fifty-one "Aggie" men who gave their lives in World War I.

For those students who play musical instruments there are opportunities with the University Orchestra and the University Band.

Student Council.—The Stockbridge School Council is composed of representatives of the first and second year classes. This body serves as a general committee on student government and helps to maintain the best traditions and customs of the school.

Shorthorn.—A student yearbook called "The Shorthorn" is published annually by the members of the graduating class, and is usually issued in June. All students subscribe to it.

Fraternities.—There are two Stockbridge fraternities for men in the student body. Alpha Tau Gamma and Kappa Kappa, both owning houses, serving as social and residential centers for their groups.

Blue and White Octet—The Blue and White Octet has built up a reputation for good quality singing. It is directed by a capable four year student during the year and makes many appearances at social events on the campus.

Scholastic Society.—A Stockbridge Honorary Scholastic Society called "Stosag" was established in 1935 to encourage high scholarship. Students whose record for the first three semesters is 3.0 quality points or better, are elected to membership in the society each June. Engraved certificates are awarded to members of the graduating class who have achieved this distinction.

Athletics and Physical Education.—The school has its own separate athletic program with regular schedules in football, basketball, ice hockey, cross-country and winter track. Sweaters and letters are awarded to team members and managers in these sports. The official insigne is the letter S.

The football team plays a schedule of 6-7 games with preparatory school teams. The basketball team plays a 12 game schedule; the cross-country team usually runs 3 races while 2 or 3 meets are scheduled for the winter track squad. Ice hockey affords 6 to 8 games depending on the weather.

Due to the fact that most freshmen are on placement training by April first, which leaves only seniors available, no regular team is maintained in baseball. Men desiring to play soft ball are organized into teams and an intramural league is arranged.

This athletic program is entirely under the supervision and direction of the Athletic Department of the University and coaches are provided for all sports. Instructor Stephen R. Kosakowski, director of the Stockbridge physical education work, is coach of football and hockey. Associate Professor William Footrick, coach of the varsity track team, has charge of the cross-country. Instructor Henry B. Woronicz coaches the basketball team.

A physical education building containing a swimming pool, an indoor cage 150 by 180 feet for all kinds of sports and games, and locker room and shower bath facilities are provided. Individual equipment is supplied to all members of the football, hockey, basketball, cross-country, and track squads, and for students wanting general recreation. They may avail themselves of facilities in cage and swimming pool during scheduled hours in school year, when not assigned for other activities.

STUDENT RELATIONS

The customary high standard of university men in honor, manliness, self-respect, and consideration for the rights of others constitute the standards of student deportment.

Any student known to be guilty of dishonest conduct or persistent violation of rules must be reported by the instructor to the Director for discipline.

The privileges of the university may be withdrawn from any student at any time if such action is deemed advisable.

It should be understood that the university, acting through its President or any administrative officer designated by him, distinctly reserves the right not only to suspend or dismiss students, but also to name conditions under which students may remain in the institution. For example, if a student is not doing creditable work he may not only be disciplined, but he may be required to meet certain prescribed conditions in respect to his studies, even though under the foregoing rules his status as a student be not affected. The same provision applies equally to the matter of absences.

Similarly, also, it applies to participation in student activities. Though this will ordinarily be governed by the rules as already laid down, yet if in the judgment of the university authorities a student is neglecting his work on account of these activities, the privilege of participating in them may be withdrawn for such time as is considered necessary. Moreover, it may be withdrawn as punishment for misconduct.

HEALTH SERVICE

The Health Service is a separate administrative unit dealing with all matters directly or indirectly influencing or affecting the health of staff members, employees, students, or campus visitors.

The University endeavors to safeguard the health of all students while on the campus. Basic medical attention is provided, including preliminary diagnosis, primary treatment of injuries, and temporary care of the sick. A group of three infirmary buildings and a staff of resident physicians and resident nurses are available to perform these functions.

(1) Physical examination by your local doctor is required of all entering freshmen and re-entering students. Physical report forms for this examination will be mailed to each student prior to October 1, and must be returned to the Short Course Office not later than that date.

(2) The Student Health physicians have offices in the out-patient Infirmary Building, where they may be consulted during college hours.

(3) The Infirmary consists of 3 buildings, one for bed patients, one for contagious cases, and one for out-patient cases, where the out-patient clinic is conducted daily by one of the Student Health physicians.

(4) The students are urged to consult the resident physicians at the first sign of physical disorder, or even for minor accidents. Many severe illnesses and much lost time may be avoided by early or preventive treatment.

(5) House calls cannot be made to dormitories, private homes, or fraternities except in the case of emergency. The University cannot assure each student that a resident physician will always be available. In such instances students are encouraged to consult a town physician, although any expense connected with such service shall be borne entirely by the student. One resident physician is on call at all times to care for emergencies beyond the scope of the nurse on duty.

(6) No charge is made to Infirmary bed patients up to seven days in each school year; time in excess of seven days will be charged at the rate of $4 per day. A nominal charge may be made to out-patients for miscellaneous treatments.

(7) In addition to the fee charged as specified in paragraph 6, the following additional expenses will be charged to the patient.

   (a) *Nurses.*—If a special nurse is required for the proper care of an individual, the services and board of this nurse will be paid by the patient. Such a nurse will be under the general supervision of the resident nurse.

   (b) *Professional Service.*—If a student requires continuous medical attention by a physician, he may be required to select a town physician and become responsible for fees charged by that physician.

   (c) *Supplies.*—Special medical supplies prescribed by a physician will be charged to the patient.

   (d) *Laundry.*—Expenses for personal laundry incurred by students while in the infirmary will be charged to the individual student.

(8) The Health Service recommends strongly that students participate in the blanket insurance program described in literature accompanying the initial bill rendered students each year. This program is a reimbursement insurance plan providing medical, surgical, and hospital care for both accidents and illnesses at a very low cost. During the past years this plan has saved numerous patients from serious unexpected expenses and the insurance payments have enabled the student to stay in school. The University has no financial interest in this and acts only as a clearing house to receive premiums, in order to give the low group rate.

GOODELL LIBRARY

The Goodell Library forms the central unit of the University Library and contains the largest portion of the book collections of the University numbering 194,729 books and periodicals. A central card catalog lists all books to be found in the University. The agricultural and scientific collections are especially strong in the literature of entomology, botany, chemistry, horticulture, land architecture, soil science and animal husbandry. In addition there are extensive collections in literature, history, economics and sociology. There are over 850 current periodical titles (popular, literary, and scientific) subscribed to by the Library. The publications of the several state Agricultural Experiment Stations are well represented in the collections. The Library is also a Federal Government Depository Library for a portion of the publications of the United States Government including Department of Agriculture publications.

The Library hours during regular term time are Mondays through Fridays 8:00 a.m. to 10:00 p.m.; Saturdays, 8:00 a.m. to 12:30 p.m., and Sundays and holidays, 2:00 p.m. to 10:00 p.m.

Goodell Library is named in memory of Henry Hill Goodell, President of the University from 1886 to 1904 and Librarian from 1886 to 1898 and was built in 1935.

AGRICULTURAL OPPORTUNITIES FOR WOMEN

Agriculture is a field in which women have always found some opportunity. There are women farming independently in all branches of agriculture. As a rule poultry raising, small fruits and vegetable growing and floriculture, seem to offer women an easier opportunity than dairy, stock, and general farming. There is little demand for women to fill paid positions on farms or estates. From time to time some positions are available such as the position of agricultural officer in state correctional institutions.

For the woman or girl whose home is already upon the farm the opportunity is better. With the help of an agricultural education there are open to her many means of increasing her own or the farm income. With the knowledge of farm life which she already possesses, and with the possibility of securing occasional help from her family, she may be able to carry on and develop a profitable enterprise of her own. The Stockbridge School of Agriculture offers to the women who wish to engage in farming the practical training which they will need to fit for such work.

POSITIONS

The University does not guarantee positions to students registered in any of its courses, but through the Placement Service it has an opportunity to recommend students for a large number of positions. A record is kept of each student's work and experience, and of his success in positions for which he has been recommended after he has finished his course. Opportunities for trained men and women, especially those who have had experience, are good.

A student desiring a recommendation from the university must meet the following conditions:—

(1) He must be of good character.

(2) His previous record must be good.

(3) His work in all courses must be satisfactory.

Students who have not previously had a considerable amount of practical experience cannot, as a rule, be recommended for positions of responsibility. This is especially true of the better positions for which managers or superintendents are wanted.

VOCATIONAL PLACEMENT

The work of locating first year students for apprentice training from April to October, after the resident term is completed, is in charge of the Director of Placement Service. Placement training for women students is in charge of Mrs. Carol Burr Cornish of the Placement Office. Every effort is made to secure satisfactory positions affording the kind of training desired by the student, but the Placement Office cannot guarantee to place every student for training, when positions are not available. In normal times placement positions are secured for all students who are eligible under these conditions.

1. Positions are secured that will enable a student to gain practical experience in his particular vocation.

2. A student desiring placement at home may arrange for such assignment if the Director of Placement approves. As a rule, it will be found more desirable for a student to spend this six months away from home even though he plans to be employed there after finishing the course. This statement is based on the experience of students who have already taken the course. The parent must request in writing, placement on the home project.

3. If credit is to be secured for the six months' placement training the following rules must be carefully observed.

Rules for Stockbridge Students on Placement

1. The student must interview the Director of Placement early in his first year in order that his qualifications, the type of work he wishes to pursue, and his general fitness may be determined.

2. No final arrangement for placement training may be made by the student himself until the Director of Placement has been consulted.

3. Students are required to complete their period of training without unnecessary absences.

4. No transfers are to be made by a student if he is to receive credit, until permission has been had from the Director of Placement.

5. A position may not be given up by the student until the Director of Placement has been notified.

6. A monthly report must be furnished on the form supplied, and submitted not later than the fifth of each month during his training period.

7. Students must satisfactorily complete all reports as required by the various departments.

8. When a student fails to complete the requirements of his placement training with a satisfactory grade, he is not allowed to take the work of the second year.

9. All students are required to submit a report of physical examination at time of registration. Any disabilities liable to affect the student's placement work are noted, and, if of a serious nature, recommendations for corrective measures are supplied. Parents should understand that most kinds of agricultural work require a well-balanced combination of brawn and brain. No student whose physical condition is questionable will be accepted for placement training without a physician's certificate, and parents' approval.

It should be clearly understood by both employer and employee that the same energy, regularity and general conduct will be expected of the student during his period of placement training as is expected in his work in classes and on the campus.

It should also be noted that this six months' experience is educational in its nature. Students are expected to earn and receive a reasonable wage, but the purpose of the training is the experience gained rather than the wage earned. The scale of wages may vary in different localities, but each man's ability is given very careful thought, that he may obtain a wage that is fair to him. In the event of any misunderstanding the supervisor should be immediately informed.

ANIMAL HUSBANDRY

PROFESSOR HANKINSON, PROFESSOR FOLEY, ASSISTANT PROFESSOR ELLIOT,
ASSISTANT PROFESSOR BAKER, MR. ADAMS, MR. HOBART

A major program of study in the Department of Dairy and Animal Science.

Animal Husbandry, in this School, refers to the breeding, feeding and management of dairy cattle, beef cattle, horses, sheep and swine.

The purposes of the curriculum in Animal Husbandry are (1) to provide the student with a thorough understanding of the basic principles involved in the creation of more efficient and more beautiful animal types, said principles being those involved in the biology of animal reproduction, the chemistry of animal growth and nutrition and the economics of livestock production; (2) to show the practical workings of these principles in the selection, feeding and management of the various classes of livestock and (3) to provide practice in judging, fitting, showing and general management of livestock as well as the production of milk and other products, and the slaughtering, curing and marketing of meat products.

The University dairy herd comprises about 150 animals in the Ayrshire, Guernsey, Holstein and Jersey breeds. In beef cattle, we maintain a herd of Aberdeen-Angus and a herd of Herefords; in sheep, flocks of Southdowns and Shropshires; in swine, a herd of Chester Whites; and in horses, a stallion and several mares and foals in the Morgan breed. Modern barns house the above animals and modern equipment is available for practice work with them.

The University Farm of about 250 acres is handled primarily as a livestock farm, producing pasture, hays, silages and some grain for livestock feeding. The farm is equipped with up-to-date machinery for agricultural production. The farm and barns are our laboratories, the animals and accessories our equipment.

The Charles H. Hood Dairy Foundation Prize for Animal Husbandry Seniors

The Charles H. Hood Dairy Foundation Prize of $200 is awarded annually to seniors who in the judgment of a faculty committee have made an outstanding scholastic record in this major course and who because of their practical qualifications, personality, and character, seem best qualified to receive this honor.

Trains for Jobs Like These:

Owners and operators of dairy farms; farm managers; superintendents or foremen; herdsmen in various kinds of livestock enterprises; dairy herd association testers; inseminators in artificial breeding units; businesses allied to agriculture such as farm cooperative fieldmen, sales and service men for feed, fertilizer and farm machinery companies.

Field trips will be required during the two years at an estimated cost of $40 per student.

Special equipment needed for the course in Meats is: Knives, boots, and wash suits, at an estimated cost of $15.

Animal Husbandry

First Year

First Semester	Second Semester
(Sixteen Weeks Resident Instruction)	(Eight Weeks Resident Instruction Followed
Agricultural Economics S3 (Marketing)	by Six Months Placement Training) .
Agronomy S1 (Soil Management)	Agricultural Engineering S4 (Farm Shop)
Animal Husbandry S1 (Principles of Feeding)	Agronomy S2 (Fertilizers)
Bacteriology S1 (Bacteriology and Rural Hygiene)	Animal Husbandry S2 (Types and Breeds)
Dairy S1 (General Dairying)	Fruit Growing S10 (General Course)
Farm Management S3 (Efficiency in Farming Operations)	Poultry Husbandry S10 (General Course)
Milking (Practice periods only, by arrangement)	

Elective

Physical Education S1 (Football)

Elective

Physical Education S4 (Basketball and Hockey)

First Semester

(Sixteen Weeks Resident Instruction)
Agricultural Engineering S1 (Farm Power)
Animal Husbandry S3 (Animal Breeding)
Animal Husbandry S5 (Farm Meats)
Business English S1
Farm Management S1 (Farm Management and Accounts)
Public Speaking S1
Veterinary Science S1 (Animal Sanitary Science)

Elective

Physical Education S5 (Football)

Second Semester

(Sixteen Weeks Resident Instruction)
Agricultural Engineering S10 (Farm Structures and Drainage)
Agronomy S4 (Field Crops)
Animal Husbandry S4 (Livestock Production)
Animal Husbandry S6 (Dairy Cattle and Milk Production)
Public Speaking S2

Electives

Physical Education S4 (Basketball and Hockey)
Physical Education S6 (Baseball)

ANIMAL HUSBANDRY S-1. (Principles of Feeding) I.

This course includes a study of the organs of digestion, the digestion and absorption of feeds, the classification and characteristics of the common feed-stuffs, the utilization of feeds in maintenance, growth, fattening; meat, work and milk production. Some time will be spent on the importance of minerals and vitamins. Methods of calculating balanced rations; feeding standards, and feeding practices will be studied. A visit to a feed mill is a requirement of this course.

Textbook: Morrison, "Feeds and Feeding."

4 class hours and 1 2-hour laboratory period a week.

Credit, 5.
MR. ELLIOT.

ANIMAL HUSBANDRY S-2. (Types and Breeds) II.

This course considers the origin, history, development, characteristics and distribution of the breeds of cattle, sheep, swine and horses commercially important in the United States. The conditions to which each class of livestock and each breed seem best adapted will be discussed. Laboratory work consists of judging and evaluating as many rings of dairy, beef cattle, sheep, swine and horses as time permits.

3 class hours and 2 2-hour laboratory periods a week.

Credit, 5.
MR. BAKER, MR. ADAMS.

ANIMAL HUSBANDRY S-3. (Animal Breeding) I.

This course is planned to acquaint the student with the facts of reproductive physiology, with the facts and theories of modern genetics, and to show how such knowledge may be utilized through genetic analyses, selection, and systems of breeding for the creation of more beautiful and more efficient animal types. A field trip is made to the Massachusetts Selective Breeding Association. Textbook: Rice and Andrew, "Breeding and Improvement of Farm Animals."

3 class hours and 2 2-hour laboratory periods a week.

Credit, 5.
MR. BAKER.

ANIMAL HUSBANDRY S-4. (Livestock Production) II.

This course deals briefly with the problems of selection, breeding and care of horses, beef cattle, sheep, and swine, with emphasis on their place in New England Agriculture. Attention is given to the general situation, equipment, feeding, and management problems. The laboratory periods consist of practice in fitting and showing, shearing, docking and castrating. As a part of the laboratory work, each student will be assigned an animal for fitting and showing in the "Little International" which will be held on a Saturday in March. Trips to other purebred livestock establishments in New England will be required during the semester. The cost of transportation will not exceed $5.00. Four students in this course will be selected to participate in the New England two-year s‹ judging contest. Textbook: Ensminger, "Animal Science."

Prerequisites: Animal Husbandry S1 and Animal Husbandry S2.

3 class hours, 1 2-hour and one 4-hour laboratory periods a week and trips.
                                                                            Cred
                                                      MR. ADAMS, MR. HOBAI

ANIMAL HUSBANDRY S-5. (Farm Meats) I.

This course includes a survey of the packing industry and follows the pr‹ (i.e., beef, pork, lamb and veal) from the feed-lot to the consumer's t Practice is afforded in classifying animals as to market class and grade ar slaughtering, dressing, and cutting beef, pork, lamb and veal. At the end o course, a trip will be taken to several large packing houses in Boston consu one day and costing about $10.00. Textbook: Ziegler, "The Meat We Eat
Special equipment needed for this course includes knives, boots and suits, estimated cost $15.00.

1 class hour and 2 2-hour laboratory periods a week.   Cred
                                                      MR. ADAMS, MR. HOBAI

ANIMAL HUSBANDRY S-6. (Dairy Cattle and Milk Production) II.

For Seniors.—This course treats all phases of dairy cattle production and ɪ agement. The student is provided with an opportunity to study and seel solution to the various economic, nutritional, genetic and managerial prob concerned in successful dairying. Lectures will be supplemented with talk specialists in the various fields. Laboratory will consist of a detailed stud methods used on the university farm, with practice in the various skills neces for the herdsman or showman. A dairy cattle judging team will represen1 Stockbridge School of Agriculture in the New England two-year school juc contest. Special judging laboratories will be scheduled to train this team.

Trips to purebred livestock farms for the purpose of inspection and adva dairy cattle judging will be required during the spring semester. The cos transportation will not exceed $15.00. Textbook: Petersen, "Dairy Scienc

3 class hours and 2 2-hour laboratory periods a week, plus special judging pr2 and a two-day field trip.   Cred
                                                      MR. FOLEY, MR. ADA1

ANIMAL HUSBANDRY S-8. (Food Management Meats) II.

For majors in the Food Management Course. This course is designed t‹ part a knowledge of the fundamental principles involved in judging, purch and efficiently utilizing meat and meat products. Laboratories will in actual slaughtering, dressing, wholesale and retail cutting and preparati‹ by-products. Judging practice will be secured in a nearby packer cooler at the end of the course a one-day trip costing $10.00 will be schedul several large packing houses in Boston. Textbook: Ziegler, "The Mea Eat." Special equipment needed for this course includes knives, boots, and suits—estimated cost $15.00.

1 class hour and 2 2-hour laboratory periods a week.   Cre
                                                               MR. ADA

ANIMAL HUSBANDRY S-9. (Special Dairy Cattle Course) I.

For Dairy Technology Seniors and Poultry Husbandry Freshmen. This will consider briefly the origin, history, development, characteristics and bution of the five major dairy breeds in the United States. The princip genetics and the art of breeding better dairy cattle will be emphasized balance of the course will include basic principles of dairy cattle feeding ɛ profitable management of the dairy herd. Laboratories will be devoted to lging dairy cattle and to various exercises and problems concerned with the ding, breeding and management of dairy cattle. A half-day field trip to rby beef and sheep operations and a one-day field trip to successful dairy ms are required in the course. Estimated cost $5.00. Textbook: Petersen, airy Science."

lass hours and 1 2-hour laboratory period a week.   Credit, 3.
                                                                MR. FOLEY.

Note—Every student in this major must pass a qualifying test in milking. rangements for practice periods and examinations by special assignment. No dent will be put in placement training who has not satisfied this preliminary quirement.

ARBORICULTURE

Assistant Professor King

Arboriculture, the care of shade and ornamental trees, is becoming more portant here in Massachusetts as the citizens realize the necessity of tree their everyday life. It includes tree planting; large tree moving; diagnosis treatment of tree diseases, defects, and mechanical injuries; identification control of tree insect pests; fertilizing; pruning and repair of storm or other damaged trees; and removal of dead or undesirable trees. A growing app ation of the value of trees and a demand for a tree maintenance service ha to the development of organizations to supply it. These firms desire tre men. All Massachusetts towns are required to elect tree wardens. At pre there are over one thousand men actively engaged in municipal and pr tree care in Massachusetts and the future is unlimited on a state basis. Natior over 300 million dollars is spent annually on shade and ornamental trees. men who accept this responsibility should be trained in the requirement trees and their care. This course is designed to give basic training in the ca shade and ornamental trees to supply these needs.

This University offered the first course in the country on shade tree ea 1895, and now offers the only complete two-year Arboriculture course in United States. Annually in March, a school of one week's duration for wardens is held on the campus. This school brings together tree wardens men interested in tree care to discuss their problems. Parts of the program o school will be of interest to students in this course.

Our large campus has a wide variety of trees of all ages with which the dent becomes acquainted, and which also serves as a laboratory for prob similar to those one will have to meet in practice. The research laborato shade tree diseases for the state is also located on the campus.

The Massachusetts Arborists' Association and the Massachusetts Tree War and Foresters Association have approved this course as a basic training prog

New class group limited to twenty students each year.

Those electing Arboriculture must register two weeks prior to the openii the fall semester for the preliminary training period. Applicants will be no of the date of registration. This two-week period before the start of re class work will be used for intensive training in the use of ropes, climbing the use of knots and safety practices. Eight hours a day will be given completely to this purpose. Only those who qualify in this preliminary pro will be permitted to take the course in Arboriculture. Those who do not qu may take the Ornamental Horticulture course. All students applying fo course must have a doctor's certification that they are physically fit. Any ailment or other serious weakness automatically disqualifies an applicant.

The University campus of about 700 acres affords an excellent ou laboratory for plant identification, tree work and tree diseases.

Field trips will be required during the two years at an estimated cost of dollars, other than those conducted during laboratory periods.

Trains for Jobs Like These:

Operators, foremen and salesmen for arboriculture firms, utility line clea foremen, deputy tree wardens and eventually tree wardens in towns and tree care in estates, parks, state highways, college campuses or grounds of public institutions, developing one's own service organization for the pract arboriculture.

Recommended clothes for tree climbing: breeches, good heavy work sh

All students qualifying will be required to obtain personal tools for work, a hand saw, and a pair of 14" or 16" high top shoes with rubber o position soles and heels at an approximate cost of $50.00.

An accident insurance policy will be required of all prospective students. Such a policy will be available at the University at time of registration.

Arboriculture

First Year

First Semester	Second Semester
(Eighteen Weeks Resident Instruction)	(Eight Weeks Resident Instruction Followed by Six Months Placement Training)
Agronomy S1 (Soil Management)	Agricultural Engineering S2 (Power Units)
Agrostology S5 (Basic Factors and Uses of Turf Areas)	Agronomy S2 (Fertilizers)
Arboriculture S0 (Tree Climbing. Special-Qualifying Course)	Arboriculture S2 (Continuation of S1)
Arboriculture S1 (Practices and Policies)	Botany S2 (Diseases of Trees and Shrubs)
Botany S1 (Tree Physiology)	Entomology S4 (Insect and Related Pests of Shade and Ornamental Trees and Shrubs)
Horticulture S1 (Plant Materials, Trees)	Horticulture S2 (Plant Propagation)
Public Speaking S1	Public Speaking S2

Elective	Elective
Physical Education S1 (Football)	Physical Education S4 (Basketball and Hockey)

Second Year

First Semester	Second Semester
(Sixteen Weeks Resident Instruction)	(Sixteen Weeks Resident Instruction)
Arboriculture S3 (Diagnosis and Control)	Arboriculture S6 (Shade Tree Spraying)
Arboriculture S7 (Shade Tree Surveys and Cost Estimates)	Arboriculture S8 (Shade Tree Surveys and Cost Estimates)
Business English S1	Business Management S4
Entomology S5 (Control of Insect and Related Pests of Shade and Ornamental Trees and Shrubs)	Fruit Growing S4 (Fruit Pests and Spraying)
	Horticulture S4 (Landscape Construction)
Forestry S3 (Farm Forestry)	Horticulture S6 (Plant Materials, Shrubs)
Horticulture S3 (Surveying and Mapping)	

Elective	Electives
Physical Education S5 (Football)	Physical Education S4 (Basketball and Hockey)
	Physical Education S6 (Basketball)

ARBORICULTURE S-0. (Tree Climbing) I.

For two weeks previous to the regular opening of school, all students electing this major will attend a special qualifying course in tree climbing. This course will be conducted on the campus for eight hours each day for two weeks to acquaint the student with ropes, tools and climbing techniques. To be enrolled in the arboriculture major all students must pass this qualifying tree climbing practice.

MR. KING.

ARBORICULTURE S-1. (Practice and Policies) I.

Factual material covering the phases or types of work; pruning, cabling, bracing, fertilization and line clearance. Laboratory work in the application of class discussion. A one-day trip to attend the annual meeting of the Massachusetts Arborists' Association.

2 class hours and 1 4-hour laboratory period a week.   Credit, 4.
MR. KING.

ARBORICULTURE S-2. (Continuation of S-1) II.

Soils, their origin, structure and function as pertaining to tree growth and development. Fertilizers, their use, sources, application and functions of their elements in the growth and development of a tree. Common tree diseases and their treatment and simple cavity treatments. Attendance required at the annual meeting of the Massachusetts Arborists' Association.

2 class hours and 1 4-hour laboratory period a week.   Credit, 4.
MR. KING.

ARBORICULTURE S-3. (Diagnosis and Control) I.

Individual and class assignments in the diagnosis of infectious and infectious diseases and the proper treatments and corrective measures. An: of symptoms and effects common to infectious diseases and environmenta fluences. Methods and techniques used to determine the causes and their t ments.

1 class hour and 2 2-hour laboratory periods a week.   Cred
                                                                         MR. KI

ARBORICULTURE S-6. (Shade Tree Spraying) II.

Spray materials, equipment, and charts for shade tree insects, fungi, weed control. The laboratory periods will be devoted to the actual applic of spray material in the field. Attendance required at the annual meeting o Massachusetts Tree Wardens and Foresters' Association.

1 class hour and 2 2-hour laboratory periods a week.   Cred
                                                                         MR. KI

ARBORICULTURE S-7 and S-8. (Shade Tree Surveys and Cost Estimates) 1

The use and determination of shade tree surveys. Time and cost estin and shade tree maintenance programs as determined by shade tree surveys. planting and planning programs essential for city and street tree care and velopment. Line clearance, and tree laws of various states. Arboriculture A one day trip to attend the Annual Meeting of the Massachusetts Arbo Association. Arboriculture S8—A three day field trip to Connecticut and York Botanical Garden to visit private, municipal and research organization

1 class hour and 1 4-hour laboratory period a week for Arboriculture S7.
                                                                         Cred

2 class hours and 1 4-hour laboratory period a week for Arboriculture S8
                                                                         Cred
                                                                         MR. KI

ONE YEAR ARBORICULTURE COURSE

ASSISTANT PROFESSOR KING

This course is available to a limited number of Stockbridge graduates ((mental Horticulture, Forestry, or Floriculture are prerequisites) who wi take one year of Arboriculture. The courses to be taken will be those i Arboriculture major not covered by the above major in which the st graduated. Prospective students must show ability to climb and must con three months' placement before starting this course.

Private and municipal tree organizations usually prefer a graduate wh had both Horticulture and Arboriculture courses, since most of these org: tions do general landscaping, nursery and tree work.

A one year certificate is granted upon satisfactory completion of the work, subject to the scholastic requirement of the School.

DAIRY TECHNOLOGY

PROFESSOR HANKINSON, ASSISTANT PROFESSOR POTTER,
ASSISTANT PROFESSOR EVANS.

A major program of study in the Department of Dairy and Animal Science.

The Dairy Technology course is designed to fit men for positions with market milk concerns, creameries, ice cream plants, and specialized dairy farms.

All dairy technology courses are given in the dairy building (Flint Laboratory), a building devoted especially to dairy work. The building is well equipped with dairy and creamery machinery.

The market milk department contains two complete pasteurizing units, a clarifier, separator, automatic bottle filler and capper, rotary can washer and automatic soaker type bottle washer with conveyor transfer of bottles to the bottle filler and capper.

The ice cream making room contains a pasteurizing vat, homogenizer, cooler, brine and direct expansion freezers, continuous freezer, and additional equipment such as is found in ice cream plants.

The room designed for cheese making is equipped with cheese vats, draining racks, presses, etc. The butter making room contains power churns, workers, scales and other accessories.

The testing laboratories are well equipped with apparatus for the Babcock, Mojonnier, and other tests for the determination of chemical and bacteriological quality of milk products.

Trains for Jobs Like These:

Skilled workers in wholesale and retail dairy plants including laboratory technicians, pasteurizer operators, ice cream mix makers, freezer operators and fancy form decorators, cheesemakers, salesworkers; also dairy equipment and supply salesmen, fieldmen and Dairy Herd Improvement Association testers. Such training supplemented with sufficient practical experience may lead to positions such as assistant plant superintendents and plant managers.

Field trips will be required during the two years at an estimated cost of $20 per student.

While working in the dairy laboratories, white suits and rubber footwear are required, at an estimated cost of $10.00.

DAIRY TECHNOLOGY

First Year

First Semester	Second Semester
(Sixteen Weeks Resident Instruction)	(Eight Weeks Resident Instruction Followed
Agricultural Economics S1 (Farm Economic	by Six Months Placement Training)
Problems)	Agricultural Economics S6 (Dairy Business
Agricultural Engineering S1 (Farm Power)	Accounting)
Bacteriology S1 (Bacteriology and Rural	Dairy S2 (Testing Milk Products)
Hygiene)	Food Technology S2 (Basic Principles and
Dairy S1 (General Dairying)	Freezing)
Entomology S3 (Structural Pests)	Food Technology S4 (Special Products)
Nutrition S3 (Elementary Nutrition)	Practical Science S8
Practical Science S7	Public Speaking S2
Public Speaking S1	
Elective	**Elective**
Physical Education S1 (Football)	Physical Education S4 (Basketball and Hockey)

Second Year

First Semester	Second Semester
(Sixteen Weeks Resident Instruction)	(Sixteen Weeks Resident Instruction)
Animal Husbandry S9 (Special Dairy Cattle Course)	Agricultural Economics S2 (Marketing)
Business English S1	Agricultural Engineering S6 (Dairy chanics)
Business Management S3	Bacteriology S4 (Dairy Bacteriology)
Dairy S3 (Ice Cream Making, Cheese, and other Milk Products)	Dairy S4 (Market Milk and Butter Makir
Dairy S5 (Judging Dairy Products)	
Veterinary Science S1 (Animal Sanitary Science)	**Electives**
	Physical Education S4 (Basketball a Hockey)
Elective	Physical Education S6 (Baseball)
Physical Education S5 (Football)	

DAIRY TECHNOLOGY S-1. (General Dairying) I.

This course takes up the question of the importance of dairying in the Ur States, and especially in the New England States, giving the developmen dairying from the earliest to the present time. It covers the secretion, com] tion and properties of milk; reasons for variation in the per cent in fat in ferent samples of milk; the Babcock test for fat in milk and other dairy prodt other common milk tests; the advantage of testing herds, Herd Improver Associations, advanced registry work; the handling of market milk; soft ch making, ice cream making, and butter making as applied to general farm cc tions. The laboratory work consists in testing milk and dairy products for bt fat, solids, and acidity, together with some dairy plant experience in handling, butter making, cheese making, and ice cream making.

2 class hours and 1 2-hour laboratory period a week.   Credi
MR. EVAN

DAIRY TECHNOLOGY S2. (Testing Milk Products) II.

In this course a study is made of the common tests used in dairy indu processes.

The lectures in this course include a discussion of the application of t what they indicate and their importance in the dairy plant.

The laboratory work consists of a study of the various dairy labora tests such as sediment, flavor, and total solids of milk; moisture, fat salt determination in butter; moisture test of cheese; the operation of Mojonnier tester and the modified Babcock tests for fat in dairy products

In addition to the testing work students will be required to arrange work about the plant in order to become familiar with dairy plant tices and the operation of dairy machinery.

1 class hour and 2 2-hour laboratory periods a week.   Cred
MR. POTTI

DAIRY TECHNOLOGY S3. (Ice Cream Making, Cheese, and Other Milk F ducts) I.

This course deals with the making of ice cream, cheese, condensed, evapo and powdered milk.

The ice cream making portion of the course includes a careful study of mc methods of manufacturing the common frozen dairy products (ice cream, sher ices, frozen puddings, punches, mousses, etc.).

The lecture work includes a discussion of the history of ice cream ma the ingredients found in ice cream, methods of preparing and standard mixes, the freezing process, methods of hardening, marketing, and distrib of the finished product.

The laboratory work involves the preparation and standardization o cream mixes, the freezing of ice cream and other frozen dairy products, laboratory tests for butterfat and total solids in ice cream.

In that part of the course dealing with cheese making, a study is made o different methods of manufacturing hard and soft cheese (cheddar, brick, cream, neufchatel, olive, nut, cottage, cheese spreads, etc.).

In the lectures the manufacture of the different cheeses is considered, either from the standpoint of marketing the entire milk supply of the dairy or as an economical means of disposing of surplus milk. In the laboratory work the different kinds of cheese are made.

Lectures are also given on the manufacture of the various concentrated products as sweetened condensed, evaporated, and powdered milk, casein, semi-solid buttermilk, dried whey; malted milk, etc.

3 class hours and 3 3-hour laboratory periods a week.   Credit, 8.
MR. POTTER, MR. EVANS.

DAIRY TECHNOLOGY S-4. (Market Milk and Butter Making) II.

In that part of the course on market milk, a study of the development of the market milk industry is made. Attention is given to the necessary essentials in producing a high grade milk; the economics of milk production and distribution; food value and uses; the advantages and disadvantages of cooperative milk producers' organizations; the various methods of marketing milk; the transportation, processing and delivery of milk; manufacture and marketing of surplus milk in the form of by-products as cream, cultured buttermilk, chocolate milk, etc.

The laboratory work consists of receiving and making quality tests on milk and the operation of the machinery used in processing market milk.

The butter making portion of the course includes studies of milk separation with the selection, care, and use of separators; the pasteurization and ripening of cream; the making and use of starters; a study of churns and churning; modern methods of making butter; tests for moisture, salt, fat, and curd content of butter.

3 class hours and 3 3-hour laboratory periods a week.   Credit, 8.
MR. POTTER, MR. EVANS.

DAIRY TECHNOLOGY S-5. (Judging Dairy Products) I.

This course is a study of the grading and evaluating of dairy product quality based upon product flavor, odor, appearance, and body and texture characteristics. Consideration is given to identification and correction of quality defects. Judging of milk, ice cream, butter, cheese, chocolate milk, buttermilk and sour cream will be emphasized.

2-hour laboratory period a week.   Credit, 1.
MR. POTTER.

DAIRY TECHNOLOGY S-6. (General Course for Poultry Majors) II.

This course takes up the importance of dairying in the United States, and especially in the New England States.

Lectures will be given on secretion, composition, and properties of milk, reasons for variation in per cent of butter fat in different samples of milk. The Babcock test for fat in milk, cream, skim milk and buttermilk, the advantages of testing herds, herd improvement associations, advanced registry work; the handling of market milk, soft cheese making, ice cream making, and butter making, as applied to general farm conditions.

The laboratory work consists mainly in testing milk and dairy products for butter fat.

3 class hours and 1 2-hour laboratory period a week.   Credit, 4.
PROFESSOR HANKINSON.

DAIRY TECHNOLOGY S-8. (Grading and Marketing of Dairy Products) II.

This course is arranged for students specializing in Food Management provide a basis for the more intelligent selection of dairy products.

It includes a consideration of the composition, food value, selection, a use of the different dairy products; a careful study of the methods of marketi and grading; a survey of processing methods and types of packages; a laboratory practice in testing milk products and in evaluating and identifyi eating quality of milk, butter, cheese, and ice cream.

During the semester a trip will be made to leading dairy wholesale marke in Boston, at an estimated cost of $15.00.

1 class hour and 2 2-hour laboratory periods a week.   Credit,
                                                                 MR. POTTER.

FLORICULTURE

PROFESSOR THAYER, ASSISTANT PROFESSOR ROSS, ASSISTANT PROFESSOR JESTER, MR. GODDARD.

Students who complete the major in Floriculture are fitted primarily for work in commercial and private estate greenhouses and retail flower stores. After gaining experience such students may be able to start in business for themselves. With courses required of Floriculture majors in Ornamental Horticulture they are also qualified for positions on private estates, in parks and nurseries.

The offices and classrooms of the Department are located in French Hall, named in honor of Henry F. French, the first president of the Massachusetts Agriculture College.

The glass area of the Department consists of approximately 19,000 square feet: (1) the French Hall Range of 11,800 square feet, a commercial type of range with separate houses devoted to various crops; automatic ventilation has been installed in four of the units; (2) the new Durfee Conservatories, erected in 1954, 5,000 square feet; curved eave construction, steel frame and aluminum members, aluminum barcaps, automatic ventilation and automatic steam control; the five units provide a Desert House, Cool House, Show House with pool, Orchid House and Camellia House; (3) approximately 2,200 square feet in hotbeds and coldframes.

Land is available for the outdoor culture of florists' crops. At present an extensive perennial garden is being developed by Floriculture and Ornamental Horticulture.

Trains for Jobs Like These:

Skilled workers in commercial greenhouses and on private estates, growing all types of flower crops; wholesale and retail florists, growers, salesmen, managers; flower arrangement work, designers and decorators in retail flower stores; salesmen for florists' supplies and equipment.

Students who major in Floriculture are required to purchase in the first semester of the first year, Taylor's Garden Dictionary, estimated at $5.00.

Field trips will be required during the two years at an estimated cost of $20.00.

Floriculture

First Year

First Semester	Second Semester
(Sixteen Weeks Resident Instruction)	(Eight Weeks Resident Instruction Followed by Six Months Placement Training)
Agronomy S1 (Soil Management)	Agronomy S2 (Fertilizers)
Floriculture S1 (Garden Materials)	Botany S2 (Diseases of Trees and Shrubs)
Floriculture S3 (Greenhouse Management)	Entomology S2 (Insect and Related Pests of Florists' Crops)
Horticulture S1 (Plant Materials)	Floriculture S2 (Greenhouse Construction and Heating)
Public Speaking S1	Horticulture S2 (Plant Propagation)
Vegetable Growing S1 (Principles of Vegetable Culture)	Public Speaking S2
	Vegetable Growing S2 (Principles of Vegetable Culture)

Elective	Elective
Physical Education S1 (Football)	Physical Education S4 (Basketball and Hockey)

Second Year

First Semester	Second Semester
(Sixteen Weeks Resident Instruction)	(Sixteen Weeks Resident Instruction)
Agricultural Engineering S3 (Farm Shop)	Business Management S2 (Fundamentals
Business English S1	Business Management)
Floriculture S5 (Commercial Production)	Floriculture S6 (Commercial Production)
Floriculture S7 (Flower Arrangement)	Floriculture S8 (The Uses of Herbaceous
Fruit Growing S7 (Small Fruits)	Plants)
Horticulture S7 (Grounds Maintenance)	Floriculture S10 (Conservatory Plants)
	Horticulture S6 (Plant Materials)
	Vegetable Growing S4 (Vegetable Forcing)

Elective

Physical Education S5 (Football)

Electives

Physical Education S4 (Basketball and Hockey)
Physical Education S6 (Baseball)

FLORICULTURE S-1. (Garden Materials) I.

A study of the annuals, biennials, herbaceous perennials bulbs, and bed plants which are commonly used in commercial floriculture and in private e work. Methods of propagation, culture and uses are considered. Laboratory ercises include work in propagation, planting, identification of materials planning of beds and borders.

3 class hours and 1 2-hour laboratory period a week.   Cred
                                        MR. JESTER, MR. GODDAI

FLORICULTURE S-2. (Greenhouse Construction and Heating) II.

The origin, growth, and importance of the floricultural industry; type greenhouses, types of construction, painting, glazing, ventilators, beds benches, and methods of heating. Trips may be taken to visit greenhouse ra in the vicinity of Amherst with university transportation.

2 class hours and 1 2-hour laboratory period a week.   Cred
                                                   MR. THAYE

FLORICULTURE S-3. (Greenhouse Management) I.

A study of the principles of greenhouse management including the consi tion of location, soils, fertilizers, watering, ventilation, temperature regula insect and disease control. Methods of wrapping and packaging of plants instruction in elementary plant breeding.

3 class hours and 1 2-hour laboratory period a week.   Cred
                                                  MR. ROSS, MR. GODDA

FLORICULTURE S-5. (Commercial Production) I.

Courses S-5 and S-6 are devoted to a consideration of the important mercial crops. Special attention is given to the culture (under glass) of c tions, roses, chrysanthemums, sweet peas and snapdragons. Other cutf crops and seasonal pot plants are also considered. Modern methods of pr tion including soilless culture and subirrigation practices are discussed in (

All members of the class may be required to take a one-day trip to visit a commercial greenhouse range at an approximate cost of $10.00 each.

2 class hours and 1 2-hour laboratory period a week.   Cre
                                                   MR. GODD

FLORICULTURE S-6. (Commercial Production) II.

A continuation of Floriculture S-5.

2 class hours and 1 2-hour laboratory period a week.   Cre
                                                  MR. GODD

_ORICULTURE S-7. (Flower Arrangement) 1.

The lectures include a discussion of the principles and techniques underlying
e use of flowers in corsages, wedding bouquets, vase, bowl, and basket arrange-
ents, table decorations, funeral designs and sprays, and decorations for public
nctions. The study of color and color harmonies is also considered in this
urse. The laboratory periods provide opportunity for actual practice in making
e various types of arrangements which are considered in the classroom.

Students enrolled in this course are required to take a one day trip to attend
e Untied Florists' Trade Fair and School in Boston.

class hour and 2 2-hour laboratory periods a week.   Credit, 3.
MR. ROSS.

_ORICULTURE S-8. (The Uses of Herbaceous Plants) II.

This course is a continuation of Floriculture S-1 and is intended for students
ajoring in Floriculture and Ornamental Horticulture. It provides opportunity
r a more detailed study of many of the plants considered in the preceding
urse with special emphasis on their uses in gardens and in other types of land-
ape planting. Lectures, assigned readings, study and identification of plants,
anning of borders and gardens.

Students enrolled in this course take a one-half day trip to attend the Western
assachusetts Flower Show in Springfield.

class hours and 1 4-hour laboratory period a week.   Credit, 4.
MR. THAYER, MR. GODDARD.

_ORICULTURE S-10. (Conservatory Plants) II.

A study of the plants, both foliage and flowering, used in conservatories
d in decorative work or sold in the retail flower shop. Methods of propaga-
n, culture, uses and identification of plants are included in the course. Trips
ay be taken to visit the conservatories at Smith and Mount Holyoke Colleges
th university transportation.

class hour and 1 2-hour laboratory period a week.   Credit, 2.
MR. THAYER, MR. ROSS.

FOOD MANAGEMENT

PROFESSOR FELLERS, ASSISTANT PROFESSOR CULBERTSON,
ASSISTANT PROFESSOR BAKER

Food management work, in all its various trade sub-divisions, is closely allie
food production work. Purchasing agents for wholesale and retail food ch
must know vegetables and fruits of all kinds, meats, and dairy products .sucl
milk, butter, cheese and ice cream; poultry products such as fowl, du
turkeys, and all kinds of eggs, and egg products. This same knowledge
superior grades, varieties, and packs of all agricultural products, as well as
modern methods of cooling, freezing, preserving, processing, and serving
highly essential to the hotel and restaurant industry for its supply of fu
managers, stewards, and operators. Lunchroom, tearoom and all summer re
operators should have thorough training in the procurement of food supf
of superior quality if trade competition and public demands are to be efficie
and economically controlled.

Modern methods of food processing including canning, freezing, dehydra
and packing, place a greater responsibility on institutional buyers. Sound kn
edge in food production methods may be considered essential to the comp
training of stewards, food managers, and restaurant operators. "In-pla
feeding installations for large factories and shops, now offer tremendous fi
for food management efficiency and service.

Planning of menus and preparation of food is studied and practiced in
course, along with a complete survey of the whole food production program
agriculture. The excellent equipment of the farms, orchards, food, technol
laboratories and dining halls, is a major factor for thorough training which
University provides.

This course is sponsored by the Massachusetts Hotel Association, New E
land Club Managers, Boston Stewards' Club, and by the Massachusetts F
taurant Association, whose members are cooperating in the placement and
ployment of students and graduates. The Boston Stewards' Club has generou
donated an annual scholarship prize fund and the state hotel association
established a loan fund for student aid.

Due to the nature of the course and need for careful selection of candid
based on scholastic preparation, business objectives, and experience factors de
mining choice of course, a personal interview here is required of all applic
before final acceptance can be given. Students who select Food Managen
as a major should have completed a full high school course and must pre
school record at interview.

Trains for Jobs Like These:

Stewards, assistant stewards, and supervisory positions in restaurants, c
terias, hotels, country inns and vacation resorts serving both summer and wi
clientele. All New England states have a huge business in their country ar
providing home-grown foods and food products for the year-round vaca
trade. Many farm homes and boarding houses rely on this type of business
a considerable part of their income. New England foods from shore and f
have earned a distinctive quality which this course seeks to maintain.

Field trips will be required during the two years at an estimated cost of $5
per student.

Food Management

First Year

First Semester	Second Semester
(Sixteen Weeks Resident Instruction)	(Sixteen Weeks Resident Instruction Followed by Four Months Placement Training)
...ods and Nutrition S1 (Basic Food Principles, Meal Planning and Service)	Agricultural Engineering S12 (Food Handling Equipment)
...neral Mathematics S1	Dining Room Management S2
...ultry Husbandry S9	Food Technology S2 (Basic Principles, Freezing and Canning)
...actical Science S7	Practical Science S8
...iblic Speaking S1	Public Speaking S2
...iantity Foods S1 (Preparation and Service)	Quantity Foods S2 (Preparation and Service)
...iecial Lectures S1	Vegetable Growing S10 (Marketing Methods)
...ewarding S1	

Elective

...iysical Education S1 (Football)

Elective

Physical Education S4 (Basketball and Hockey)

Second Year

First Semester	Second Semester
(Sixteen Weeks Resident Instruction)	(Sixteen Weeks Resident Instruction)
...cteriology S3 (Food Sanitation)	Agricultural Economics S4 (Marketing)
...itomology S3 (Structural Pests)	Animal Husbandry S8 (Food Management Meats)
...ood Service Practice S3	Business English S2
...od Technology S5 (Food Manufacturing)	Dairy S8 (Grading and Marketing of Dairy Products)
...otel Accounting S3	Food Service Practice S4
...tchen Administration S3	Hotel Accounting S4
...rsonnel Management S1	Hotel Practices S4
...iecial Lectures S3	

Elective

...iysical Education S5 (Football)

Electives

Physical Education S4 (Basketball and Hockey)
Physical Education S6 (Baseball)

...INING ROOM MANAGEMENT S-2. II.

A study of all types of table service for restaurants, hotels, and clubs. Self ...rvice operations, cafeterias, coffee shops, in-plant feeding, etc. Time is spent ...udying various types of banquet, buffet service and dining room organization, ...nd supervision with breakdown of various positions—hostess, headwaiter, cap-...ins, waiters, and omnibus boys, etc.

...class hours a week.   Credit, 3.

MR. CULBERTSON.

...OOD SERVICE PRACTICE S-3 and S-4. I. II.

This course is a practice course in food service. Students will work under ...ipervision of instructor and regular employees of Dining Commons in table ...rvice of special parties and functions. Time will also be spent on cafeteria ...ne.service. Course must be taken in conjunction with Kitchen Administration ...-3, and Hotel Practices S-4. There will be obligatory field trips to study vari-...us commercial operations.

4-hour laboratory period a week.   Credit, 2.

MR. CULBERTSON.

...IOTEL ACCOUNTING S-3 and S-4. I. II.

An introductory course in bookkeeping and accounting. Principles of double ...ntry system, journalizing; posting and closing a practice set of accounts. Study ...lso of balance sheet, and profit and loss statements.
Hotel Accounting S-4 is a continuation of S-3. Use of a practice kit for

restaurant, or small hotel. Subsidiary records, inventory controls, food operating expense percentages.

2 class hours and 1 2-hour laboratory period a week. Credi
Mr. Bake

Hotel Practices S-4. II.

A survey course of hotel procedures and practices pertaining to room serv banquets, front office, telephone, reservations, transportation and housekeep This course is designed to give an overall picture of the interdependence of e operating department.

3 class hours a week. Credit
Mr. Bake

Kitchen Administration S-3. I.

This course will be a study of kitchen floor plans and layouts, with con eration given to equipment, design, maintenance and operation. Purchase depreciation principles of food cost control will be studied at length. Field t are required in this course.

2 class hours a week. Credit
Mr. Bake

Personnel Management S-1. I.

A course designed to stimulate group employee relations. Covered during course: Analyzing, simplifying, and evaluating the job; recruiting, selecting, placing employees; training and rating employees; defining and measu morale; fire and accident prevention; organizing personnel relations; increas cooperation.

3 class hours a week. Credit
Mr. Bake

Quantity Foods S-1 and S-2. (Preparation and Service) I, II.

This course is planned to give the student an insight into the problems the kitchen department of the hotel, restaurant or club. Students will be un the supervision of the manager of the University Commons and will be app ticed to the regular employees there and will assist the cooks, baker, st clerk, etc., during the laboratory periods. The course is planned so that e student will have the opportunity to do actual work in quantity food prepara and service.

1 4-hour laboratory period a week. Credi
Mr. Culbertso

Special Lectures S-1 and S-3. I.

Registration restricted to Food Management students. These lectures be presented weekly by men within the hotel and restaurant industry and a professions and by members of the university faculty. They will cover a var of subjects, all of which will be of interest and value to young people plan to enter the hotel and restaurant business.

1 class hour a week. Credi
The Departmen

Stewarding S-1. I.

A study of principles and practices used in the purchasing, receiving, sto and issuing of all food stuffs. Employee practices, menu planning and pri and a study of proper cooking methods.

4 class hours a week. Credi
Mr. Culbertso

APPLIED FORESTRY

PROFESSOR HOLDSWORTH, PROFESSOR RHODES, PROFESSOR TRIPPENESEE,
ASSOCIATE PROFESSOR RICH, ASSISTANT PROFESSOR MacCONNELL,
MR. GANLEY, MR. ABBOTT

The two year course in applied forestry is intended to equip young men with sound understanding of the principles of growing wood and doing the work necessary to the handling of forests as productive enterprises.

The men who elect to take the course should fully understand that the vocation for which they are preparing will involve hard work, much of it physical character. They should also keep in mind that a man trained in forestry techniques will be in a position to advance through apprenticeship to jobs of genuine responsibility.

There is a definite place in the broad field of forestry for trained workers who are capable of understanding and intelligently carrying out the tasks of a sub-professional character which are so necessary to forest maintenance and development.

Men who successfully complete the curriculum in applied forestry are qualified for places with timber growing and forest products industries, for supervision of forested estates, watershed properties, town forests and for work with certain public agencies which are concerned with forestry.

Entrance Requirements: A personal interview with each applicant is required. Mathematics preparation through elementary algebra and plane geometry is necessary. Copy of high school record must be presented at time of interview. Good command of English is essential for report writing on survey and mapping projects.

Student Limitation: Each entering class is limited to eighteen men and must be selected on basis of scholastic preparation, sound purpose, and adequate physical ability.

Facilities: The University owns 2000 acres of forest easily accessible from the campus. This land is used for laboratory and field studies in forestry.

Placement Training: The program of study and vocational preparation requires the students of Applied Forestry to spend four months in suitable placement training. The placement jobs in forestry often require the student to work considerable distances from home and he should be prepared to do this.

Equipment: The forestry department has good technical equipment for laboratory and field study purposes.

Student Needs: In addition to the regular expense of the Stockbridge School the student must be prepared to buy a hand compass costing about $12.00; aerial photographs costing about $8.00, and other drafting and special equipment costing about $30.00.

Forestry Club: This is a student organization to membership in which all students of Forestry, both Stockbridge and University are eligible. The programs are professional in character and present valuable material not otherwise available to students.

Applied Forestry

First Year

First Semester	Second Semester
(Sixteen Weeks Resident Instruction)	(Sixteen Weeks Resident Instruction Followed by Four Months Placement Training)
Agronomy S1 (Soil Management)	Business English S2
Forestry S1 (Dendrology)	Forestry S2 (Wood Identification)
Forestry S5 (Forest Measurement)	Forestry S4 (Forest Improvements)
Forestry S7 (Forest Physiology)	Forestry S6 (Insects and Diseases)
Review Mathematics S3	Forestry S8 (History of Forestry; Forest Economics)

Elective

Physical Education S1 (Football)

Electives

Physical Education S4 (Basketball and Hockey)
Physical Education S6 (Baseball)

Second Year

First Semester .	Second Semester

<table>
<tr><td>

(Sixteen Weeks Resident Instruction)
Forestry S11 (Silvics)
Forestry S13 (Harvesting)
Forestry S15 (Protection)
Forestry S17 (Professional Literature and Reports)
Forestry S21 (Photogrammetry)
Horticulture S3 (Surveying and Mapping)

</td><td>

(Sixteen Weeks Resident Instruction)
Forestry S10 (Forest Management)
Forestry S12 (Applied Silviculture)
Forestry S14 (Forest Products)
Forestry S16 (Seeding and Planting)
Forestry S18 (Wildlife Management)

</td></tr>
</table>

<table>
<tr><td>

Elective

Physical Education S5 (Football)

</td><td>

Electives

Physical Education S4 (Basketball Hockey)
Physical Education S6 (Baseball)

</td></tr>
</table>

FORESTRY S-1. (Dendrology) I.

The identifying features of the principal North American trees; their bota classification and geographical distribution; their importance in American estry. The vegetation regions of the United States and Canada.

1 class hour and 2 2-hour field or laboratory periods a week. Credi

MR. GANLE

FORESTRY S-2. (Wood Identification) II.

The gross structural and identification features of our most used North A ican woods. Lectures and laboratory. Each student must equip himself a 10 power hand lens and a sturdy pocket knife. Instruction is given in use of identification keys.

3 2-hour periods a week. (For lecture or for exercise in identification).

Credi

MR. RIC

FORESTRY S-4. (Forest Improvements. Draughtsmanship) II.

One entire day each week is given to this course. Weather permitting, day is spent in the field on boundary work, roads, forest structures, internal veys, mapping. The inevitable portion of bad weather is used in the drafting in drafting exercises or compiling and recording data.

8 hours practical field work or laboratory a week. Cred

MR. MACCONNELL, MR. GANLI

FORESTRY S-5. (Forest Measurement) I.

Determination of the volume and value of the growing stock by severa proved methods. This requires the making of a chain and compass land vey; forest type mapping and the use of tools and instruments comme timber estimating and growth studies.

Exercises in the use and care of ordinary woods tools and equipment incl' tractor. Construction of usable "home-made" equipment.

2 class hours and 1 8-hour laboratory period a week. Cre

MR. MACCONNE

FORESTRY S-6. (Forest Insects and Fungi) II.

A study of the principal forest insects and fungi. Their life histories identification and the nature of the damage they inflict or the good that do in the forest.

3 class hours and 1 3-hour laboratory and field period a week. Cre

MR. ABB

:STRY S-7. (Forest Physiology) I.

ie structure and physiological functions of forest trees and other forest
tation. Classroom course with demonstrations.

.ss hours a week.   Credit, 3.
                                                            MR. ABBOTT.

:STRY S-8. (History of Forestry and Forest Economics) II.

ie development of forestry and forest policy in America. Certain economic
cts of the developing field of American forestry.

.ss hours a week.   Credit, 3.
                                                       MR. HOLDSWORTH.

:STRY S-10. (Forest Management) II.

ie management of American forests; a review of existing management plans
esenting several forest regions; the preparation of operational management
s.

.ss hours and 1 4-hour field and laboratory period a week.   Credit, 5.
                                                        MR. MACCONNELL.

:STRY S-11. (Silvics) I.

ie forest qualities and requirements of forest trees including a study of
relationships, growth rates, tolerance, temperature and moisture factors.
ial emphasis is laid on the experience of others in the forest use of tree
ies.

.ss hours and 1 4-hour field period a week.   Credit, 4.
                                                            MR. ABBOTT.

:STRY S-12. (Applied Silviculture) II.

ie intermediate cuttings necessary to the production of wood as a crop;
reproduction methods used in assuring the continuity of the forest in con-
ion with harvesting the mature trees.

ss hours and 1 4-hour field or laboratory period a week.   Credit, 4.
                                                            MR. RHODES.

:STRY S-13. (Harvesting) I.

ie methods of harvesting various classes of direct forest products used in
arts of the United States. The use of woods tools and machines; practical
work.

ss hours and 1 4-hour field period a week.   Credit, 4.
                                                            MR. GANLEY.

STRY S-14. (Forest Products) II.

study of the products of American Forest and wood-using industries.

ss hours a week.   Credit, 3
                                                            MR. GANLEY.

STRY S-15. (Forest Protection) I.

thods of protecting the forest against fire and the other forest destructive
ies; regional problems and protective organizations.

s hours a week.   Credit, 3.
                                                            MR. ABBOTT.

FORESTRY S-16. (Seeding and Planting) II.

Study of forest tree seed; its preparation and use in the forest nurser' production of forest planting stock and its use in reforestation.

2 class hours and 2 2-hour laboratory periods a week.   Cre

MR. ABB

FORESTRY S-17. (Professional Literature and Reports) I.

Library reading and study on assigned forestry subjects. Written repor original papers.

3 class hours and 2 hours of supervised library research a week.   Cre

MR. HOLDSWOF

FORESTRY S-18. (Wildlife Management) II.

Effects of animals on the forest; the effects of forest practices on wild ɛ habitats and production.

3 class hours a week.   Cre

MR. TRIPPEN

FORESTRY S-21. (Forest Photogrammetry) I.

The use of aerial photographs in forest mapping and estimating. Int tation of photographs; the use of stereoscope, sketchmaster, other sta equipment. A map covering several thousands acres is prepared.

2 class hours and 1 4-hour laboratory period a week.   Cre

MR. MACCONN

FRUIT GROWING

Professor French, Associate Professor Roberts, Mr. James Anderson

The course in Fruit Growing prepares the student for successful participation in the activities of our many sided fruit industry. An essentially practical course, it emphasizes also the basic principles of plant growth which underlie sound cultural practices and the economic principles which bear upon marketing procedures and the business side of fruit growing. It provides a foundation on which increasing effectiveness may be developed through continued practical experience.

The University has about fifty acres of fruits easily reached from the classroom, which are used freely for purposes of illustration and study. Most of the trees and small fruits commonly found in New England are grown here on a commercial scale. Many experiments and tests are in progress in the plantations, offering exceptional opportunities to the student for the practical study of plant reactions under many and varied conditions. Excellent commercial orchards near the campus provide a wealth of additional material for observation and study. Large markets are visited to afford valuable contacts with the main channels of crop distribution.

Equipment for instruction includes a modern storage and packing house in which there are several types of refrigerated storage, a quick freezing unit, and zero temperature holding rooms. The principal types of orchard tools and machines, such as tractors, plows, harrows, cultivators, sprayers, dusters, and pruning and grafting tools are available for study and trial by students. Emphasis is placed on life histories and methods of control of all important insect, fungus and other pests. Materials used in pest control are also studied.

Graduates of the course in Fruit Growing are found in positions of responsibility all over the Northeast. Some have established successful fruit farms of their own. Others, after gaining added practical experience, have risen to positions as managers or foremen in large orchards. Still others have entered the industrial field and are employed by supply and equipment firms or are engaged in marketing activities. Fruit Growing is an active and thriving industry which offers a field of continuing interest and many opportunities for profitable development to the earnest student.

Trains for Jobs Like These:

Skilled workers on fruit farms, operators, foremen, owners; packing house operators, managers of sales and distribution. Salesmen for commercial spray materials, orchard equipment, and fertilizers; fruit inspection and grading. Growers of specialty fruit crops.

Field trips will be required during the two years at an estimated cost of $25 per student.

Fruit Growing

First Year

First Semester	Second Semester
(Sixteen Weeks Resident Instruction)	(Eight Weeks Resident Instruction Followed by Six Months Placement Training)
Agricultural Engineering S1 (Farm Power)	Agricultural Engineering S14 (Repair of Farm Equipment)
Agronomy S1 (Soil Management)	Agronomy S2 (Fertilizers)
Forestry S3 (Farm Forestry)	Entomology S4 (Insect and Related Pests of Shade and Ornamental Trees and Shrubs)
Fruit Growing S1 (Growing Tree Fruits)	Fruit Growing S2 (Orchard Pruning)
Public Speaking S1	Poultry Husbandry S10 (General Poultry Husbandry)
Vegetable Growing S1 (Principles of Vegetable Culture)	Public Speaking S2

Elective	Elective
Physical Education S1 (Football)	Physical Education S4 (Basketball and Hockey)

Second Year

<table>
<tr><td>

First Semester

(Sixteen Weeks Resident Instruction)
Agricultural Economics S1 (Farm Economic Problems)
Beekeeping S1 (Fall Management, Wintering, Honey, and Bee Diseases)
Botany S1 (Tree Physiology)
Business English S1
Fruit Growing S5 (Harvesting, Packing, Storage, and Marketing)
Fruit Growing S7 (Small Fruits)
Vegetable Growing S7 (Commercial Vegetable Culture)

Elective

Physical Education S1 (Football)

</td><td>

Second Semester

(Sixteen Weeks Resident Instruction)
Agricultural Engineering S10 (Farm Structures and Drainage)
Beekeeping S2 (Spring Management, Pollination and Honey Production)
Fruit Growing S4 (Fruit Pests and Spraying)
Fruit Growing S6 (Orchard Management)
Vegetable Growing S6 (Marketing Methods)
Vegetable Growing S8 (Commercial Vegetable Culture)

Electives

Physical Education S4 (Basketball and Hockey)

</td></tr>
</table>

FRUIT GROWING S-1. (Growing Tree Fruits) I.

This course covers the planting and development of orchards and the management of bearing trees. The nature of the tree itself is stressed as the basis of sound cultural practices. The selection of sites and soils and varieties is studied for plantations of apples, pears, peaches, plums, and cherries. The handling of young trees to bring them into early profitable bearing is given special attention.

The culture of bearing orchards is studied in detail to give an understanding of the factors that influence yield and quality of fruit. Methods of soil management are considered with reference to their long-time effects on tree and soil. The experimental plots afford exceptional opportunities to study cultural methods and many subjects are discussed in the orchards.

2 class hours and 1 2-hour laboratory period a week.   Credit, 3,

MR. FRENCH, MR. ANDERSON.

FRUIT GROWING S-2. (Orchard Pruning) II.

This course aims to give the student a thorough training in the underlying principles and the practice of pruning apples, pears, peaches, cherries and plums. The bearing habit of each fruit is studied as a basis for effective pruning. Practice pruning in the University orchards is stressed as an important feature of the course. Instruction and practice in budding and grafting are included in this course. Bridge grafting and top working are given special attention.

1 class hour and 2 2-hour laboratory periods a week.   Credit, 3.

MR. ROBERTS, MR. ANDERSON.

FRUIT GROWING S-4. (Fruit Pests and Spraying) II.

This course deals with the characteristics and behavior of insect and disease pests which attack fruit plants. Particular attention is given to the vulnerable points in their life cycles at which control measures are directed. A study of the principal spray materials and their uses is an essential part of the course.

The construction and care of spraying and dusting equipment is emphasized and students are required to use various types of implements in spraying and dusting trees in the orchard.

2 class hours and 1 2-hour laboratory period a week.   Credit, 3.

MR. ROBERTS.

FRUIT GROWING S-5. (Harvesting, Packing, Storage and Marketing) I.

Handling the crop from tree to consumer is the field covered by this course. Methods of harvesting and appliances used are studied in the orchards. Practice in packing the most popular containers forms a prominent part of the laboratory work.

The principles of common and refrigerated storage are considered in detail and storage house construction is discussed with a critical examination of several storages in use on or near the campus. Marketing methods as they relate both to distant and to local markets are given special consideration. A two-day field trip is a part of the course. Estimated cost, $10.00.

2 class hours and 1 2-hour laboratory period a week.   Credit, 3.

MR. ROBERTS.

FRUIT GROWING S-6. (Orchard Management) II.

This course is a critical study of fruit growing as a business. It is the aim of the course to familiarize the student with conditions under which fruit must be grown here, with current thought on the more recent developments, and with adjustments which are being made in the fruit industry of the Northeastern States.

Each student must be prepared to take one or more trips to prominent orchards. Estimated cost, $15.00.

2 class hours and 1 2-hour laboratory period a week.   Credit, 3.

MR. ROBERTS.

FRUIT GROWING S-7. (Small Fruits) I.

There are many unusual opportunities in Massachusetts for success in growing small fruits. This course deals with the establishment and management of plantations of strawberries, raspberries, blackberries, blueberries, currants, cranberries, and grapes. The aim is to make the course of the utmost practical value as well as to give an understanding of the fundamental principles on which practices are based.

The University has plantations of these fruits except cranberries which are used freely for laboratory purposes. Berries which ripen in summer are frozen and held in excellent condition for study in this course.

2 class hours and 1 2-hour laboratory period a week.   Credit, 3

MR. ANDERSON.

FRUIT GROWING S-9. (General Course) I.

This course is intended to meet the needs of students in other majors who can devote one semester only to the subject of Fruit Growing. It deals with the practical side of growing tree and small fruits for home use and market. Special attention is given to such questions as selection of sites, choice of varieties, grafting, pruning, spraying, soil management, harvesting, and storing. (Horticulture and Poultry majors.)

2 class hours and 1 2-hour laboratory period a week.   Credit, 3.

MR. ANDERSON.

FRUIT GROWING S-10. (General Course) II.

This course is a repetition of Fruit Growing S-9 primarily for the benefit of first year students who are specializing in Animal Husbandry.

4 class hours and 1 2-hour laboratory period a week.   Credit, 5.

MR. ANDERSON.

ORNAMENTAL HORTICULTURE

PROFESSOR BLUNDELL, ASSISTANT PROFESSOR PROCOPIO,
ASSISTANT PROFESSOR HAMILTON

The constantly increasing interest in development of grounds, both public
private, for use and enjoyment, has created a demand for men trained to ha
the varied problems in the construction and maintenance of these grounds.
course in Ornamental Horticulture aims to make the student familiar with tl
various problems.

Men who have taken this course are to be found in such different jobs as f
men in nurseries, or proprietors of nurseries which they themselves have de
oped; superintendents on private estates, cemeteries, parks, and various pu
and private institution grounds; foremen for landscape construction firms,
some have organized their own business in landscape construction and grou
maintenance service.

With the whole campus as a laboratory, the student every day finds probl
about him comparable to those he will meet when he goes out to work. '
broad lawns, the walks and drives, the gardens, the greenhouses, the orcha
the vegetable plots, as well as the farms, supply all the various phases of w
which will be encountered on estates, in parks, or in institution grounds. As
as practicable the student is given the opportunity to determine what tl
problems are and to solve them himself under expert supervision.

On the campus is to be found a large and excellent collection of mature tr
shrubs, and vines. From these plants the student is able to build up a ba
ground of plant knowledge; in identification; in propagation which is carried
in a special greenhouse for the purpose; in the handling of plants in vari
stages of their growth, in the nursery and on the campus; and in their ultim
care, pruning and protection against injuries of all kinds. Construction of ro
walks, drainage and other problems involving the moving of earth are especi
valuable to those looking forward to landscape construction.

Trains for Jobs Like These:

Skilled workers in plant nurseries; gardeners, foremen or superintendents
private estates, public parks, cemeteries, and various public and private inst
tion grounds such as state and government cantonments and hospitals, coll
and private schools; workers or foremen with landscape construction compar
real estate developments; owners and operators of small landscape maintena
businesses and nurseries, salesmen for seed and nursery concerns, plant pr
gators, town or city watershed foresters, botanic garden foremen.

A special requirement for students in Ornamental Horticulture is one dra
man's set estimated at $25 and secured at the University store.

Field trips will be required during the two years at an estimated cost of
per student.

Ornamental Horticulture

First Year

First Semester	Second Semester
(Sixteen Weeks Resident Instruction)	(Eight Weeks Resident Instruction Foll
Agronomy S1 (Soil Management)	by Six Months Placement Training)
Agrostology S1 (Basic Factors and Uses of	Agronomy S2 (Fertilizers)
Turf Areas)	Agrostology S2 (Turf Maintenance)
Floriculture S1 (Garden Materials)	Botany S2 (Disease of Trees and Shrubs)
Horticulture S1 (Plant Materials)	Entomology S4 (Insect and Related Pes
Public Speaking S1	Shade and Ornamental Trees and Sh1
Vegetable Growing S1 (Principles of Vegetable	Horticulture S2 (Plant Propagation)
Culture)	Horticulture S10 (Horticultural Practice:
	Public Speaking S2
	Vegetable Growing S2 (Principles of Veg(
	Culture)

Elective	Elective
Physical Education S1 (Football)	Physical Education S4 (Basketball
	Hockey)

Second Year

First Semester	Second Semester
een Weeks Resident Instruction)	(Sixteen Weeks Resident Instruction)
·iculture S1 (Practices and Policies—	Arboriculture S2 (Practices and Policies—
:tures only)	Lectures only)
ıess English S1	Floriculture S8 (Uses of Herbaceous Plants)
nology S5 (Control of Insect and Re-	Fruit Growing S4 (Fruit Pests and Spraying)
ıd Pests of Shade and Ornamental Trees	Horticulture S4 (Landscape Construction
l Shrubs)	Problems)
·ulture S3 (Greenhouse Management)	Horticulture S6 (Plant Materials)
try S3 (Farm Forestry)	Horticulture S8 (Nursery Practices and Man-
Growing S9 (General Course)	agement)
culture S3 (Surveying and Mapping)	
:ulture S7 (Grounds Maintenance)	

Elective

cal Education S5 (Football)

Electives

Physical Education S4 (Basketball and Hockey)
Physical Education S6 (Baseball)

rICULTURE S-1. (Plant Materials) I.

udy of evergreen and deciduous trees used in landscape work, their distinguish-
characters, and culture, with special reference to nursery and planting
tice.

ıss hour and 2 2-hour laboratory periods a week.   Credit, 3.
                                                MR. BLUNDELL.

rICULTURE S-2. (Plant Propagation) II.

ıis course will present the principles of plant propagation with special refer-
to their application to plant materials in nursery and greenhouse practice.
lectures are concerned with careful explanation of seedage, cuttage, graftage,
rage and division. In the laboratory the student propagates plants by each
ıese methods.

ss hours and 2 2-hour laboratory periods a week.   Credit, 4.
                                                MR. PROCOPIO.

rICULTURE S-3. (Surveying and Mapping) I.

·actice in the use of simple surveying instruments as tapes, compasses, and
s used in the measurement of land surfaces, and the application of these
uments in landscape construction.

ss hour and 2 2-hour laboratory periods a week.   Credit, 3.
                                                MR. HAMILTON.

rICULTURE S-4. (Landscape Construction Problems) II.

ntinuation of Horticulture S-3, including the reading of landscape plans,
ıng construction costs on grading work and garden construction problems,
ıetting stakes for landscape development from working drawings.

ıs hour and 2 2-hour laboratory periods a week.   Credit, 3.
                                                MR. HAMILTON.

rICULTURE S-6. (Plant Materials) II.

ıdy of shrubs, both evergreen and deciduous, woody vines, to enable the
ınt to recognize the plants used in ornamental plantings and to familiarize
with the handling of these plants both in nursery practice and landscape
. A two-day field trip will be required. Estimated cost, $20.00.

ıs hour and 2 2-hour laboratory periods a week.   Credit, 3.
                                                MR. BLUNDELL.

HORTICULTURE S-7. (Grounds Maintenance) I.

A course based upon the formulation and study of a work program which considers those essential operations contributing to successful horticultural management of grounds. The care of woody ornamental plants is included under the following heads: planting, pruning, maintenance of soil fertility, winter protection, and pest control. For non-majors only.

2 class hours and 1 2-hour laboratory period a week. Credit, 3.

MR. PROCOPIO.

HORTICULTURE S-8. (Nursery Practices and Management) II.

For Ornamental Horticulture majors only. This course deals with the propagation, maintenance and planting of nursery plants. Laboratory work includes experience in advanced methods of propagation, lining out stock in cold frames and in the field, pruning, root pruning, and planting. Emphasis is placed on development of supervisory capacity. The student is given the opportunity to develop a nursery program. A one day field trip to Education Day of the Annual Convention of the New England Nurserymen's Association will be required. Estimated cost: $5.00.

2 class hours and 1 2-hour laboratory period a week, first half of semester.
1 class hour and 1 4-hour laboratory period a week, last half of semester.

Credit, 3.

MR. PROCOPIO.

HORTICULTURE S-10. (Horticultural Practices) II.

This course is in preparation for placement and takes up such horticultural practices as pruning, planting, winter protection, and pest control, as relating to a gardening or nursery program.

1 4-hour laboratory period a week. Credit, 2.

MR. BLUNDELL.

POULTRY HUSBANDRY

Professor Fox, Professor Sanctuary, Associate Professor Vondell,
Associate Professor Smyth, Assistant Professor Banta

There are excellent opportunities in poultry work for men and women who have had the proper training. Graduates from this department have taken their places as leaders in the industry and have filled them capably. Some of them own their own breeding farms, manage or assist in the management of commercial egg farms, while others are in those industries which are closely allied with the production and marketing of poultry products.

Seven specialized courses and two general courses are offered by this department. Those students who specialize in poultry culture take all seven of the specialized courses. The general course is designed to give the students specializing in other branches of agriculture and horticulture the fundamental principles underlying successful poultry raising when a sideline on the farm.

The facilities for practical instruction in poultry husbandry include quarters and equipment in Stockbridge Hall for efficient classroom teaching and demonstrations.

The University Poultry Farm, our practical laboratory, comprises classrooms and laboratories which provide facilities for practice in incubation, breeding, feeding, killing, picking, candling and grading eggs, caponizing, judging, sexing, construction of poultry houses and appliances, and other phases of poultry work.

The well-bred flock of about 1,500 adult birds consists principally of White Plymouth Rocks, Single Comb Rhode Island Reds, Barred Plymouth Rocks, Single Comb White Leghorns and New Hampshires. The largest flocks of approximately 150 birds are used primarily for practical experiments and demonstrations in housing, feeding, breeding and management. Equipment includes several types of lamp and mammoth type incubators; many styles of coal and electric brooders and chick batteries for brooding and rearing approximately 5,000 chicks. A flock of several hundred Jersey Buff and improved White Holland turkeys is maintained.

The practical phases of commercial poultry production are stressed in the courses offered.

Trains for Jobs Like These:

Skilled workers on poultry farms, owner operators and managers; poultry breeding farms; operation of incubators and brooders; wholesale and retail poultry meats; testing, grading and packing eggs; poultry cooperative sales work with eggs, dressed and live fowl; salesmen for poultry feeds and equipment; broiler production and day-old chicks; turkey and duck farms, breeding (record of performance) and disease control (Pullorum) field men.

Field trips will be required during the two years at an estimated cost of $37 per student. All poultry Stockbridge students will be required to make a trip to the Boston Poultry Show which is held sometime during the month of January. Estimated cost $6.00.

Poultry Husbandry

First Year

First Semester

(Sixteen Weeks Resident Instruction)
Agronomy S1 (Soil Management)
Animal Husbandry S9 (Special Dairy Cattle Course)
Bacteriology S1 (Bacteriology and Rural Hygiene)
Poultry Husbandry S1 (Judging and Housing)
Practical Science S7
Public Speaking S1
Vegetable Growing S9 (General Course)

Elective

Physical Education S1 (Football)

Second Semester

(Eight Weeks Residence Instruction Followed by Six Months Placement Training)
Agronomy S2 (Fertilizers)
Animal Husbandry S2 (Tpyes and Breeds)
Dairy S6 (General Course)
Poultry Husbandry S2 (Incubation and Brooding)
Poultry Husbandry S12 (Specialties)
Public Speaking S2

Elective

Physical Education S4 (Basketball and Hockey)

Second Year

First Semester

(Sixteen Weeks Resident Instruction)
Agricultural Economics S1 (Farm Economic
 Problems)
Agricultural Engineering S7 (Farm Struc-
 tures)
Fruit Growing S9 (General Course)
Poultry Husbandry S5 (Marketing)
Poultry Husbandry S7 (Breeding)
Veterinary Science S1 (Animal Sanitary
 Science)

Elective

Physical Education S5 (Football)

Second Semester

(Sixteen Weeks Resident Instruction)
Agricultural Engineering S2 (Farm Pow
Agricultural Engineering S4 (Farm Sh
Business English S2
Farm Management S2 (Farm Mana
 and Accounts)
Poultry Husbandry S4 (Feeding)
Poultry Husbandry S8 (Supervised R
 and Management)
Veterinary Science S2 (Applied Anima
 tary Science)

Elective

Physical Education S4 (Basketbal
 Hockey)
Physical Education S6 (Baseball)

POULTRY HUSBANDRY S-1. (Judging and Housing) I.

This course embraces a study of the various economically important ty
breeds of domestic fowl, judging for egg production capacity, and for exhi
quality. This course also covers the principles and practices of constructin
equipping houses on a commercial poultry farm. A few trips to nearby p
plants may be taken to study poultry house ventilation. Two credits for juc
three credits for housing.

3 class hours and 2 2-hour laboratory periods a week.   Cre

MR. SANCTUARY, MR. BAN

POULTRY HUSBANDRY S-2. (Incubation and Brooding) II.

A study of incubation and brooding is made by means of the operati
standard incubators and brooders and through a consideration of basic
ciples. Students select and grade hatching eggs, operate small incubator.
observe mammoth incubators for a period of time. Under supervision
student has charge of a brood of chicks.

2 class hours and 2 2-hour laboratory periods a week.   Cre

MR. SANCTU

POULTRY HUSBANDRY S-4. (Feeding) II.

A study of the scientific principles of nutrition essential to commercial s
with particular emphasis on vitamins. Rations properly balanced for v
purposes will be calculated. A comparative analysis of the different meth
feeding is included. Textbook: "Feeding Poultry" by Heuser—Publish
John Wiley & Sons.

2 class hours and 1 2-hour laboratory period a week.   Cr

MR. BA

POULTRY HUSBANDRY S-5. (Marketing) I.

A study of preparing eggs and poultry products to meet the requirem
the northeastern markets. Grades, prices and reports are studied in conj
with different marketing methods. The laboratories are designed to co
field of practical grading, internal study, candling and packing of eggs as
selection, fattening and killing and dressing of poultry by the latest ap
methods.

A one-half day class trip to Springfield markets in December is require
mated cost, $2.00. Textbook: Benjamin, Pierce and Termohlen's "Ma
Poultry Products."

2 class hours and 1 2-hour laboratory period a week.   C

MR. VON

,TRY HUSBANDRY S-7. (Breeding) I.

lis course includes the study of the improvement of poultry by means of
selection, cockerel progeny, flock improvement, and pedigree methods of
ling. Students follow through each step of a pedigree hatch and assist in
election of the breeders used at the university plant. Basic principles of
lity necessary for an understanding of good breeding practices are studied.
xtbook costing $3.00 to $4.00 will be required.

ss hours; 1 2-hour laboratory; 1-hour practice laboratory a week. Credit, 5.

MR. SANCTUARY.

,TRY HUSBANDRY S-8. (Supervised Reading and Management) II.

.ch student will be assigned references in the field in which he is most inter-
. Oral reports will be required. A major part of the work will be the
ng of a term paper and students will be graded on their ability to summarize
ence reading and on the neatness of their work. Required day trips totalling
: or four days to representative commercial poultry areas are made at an
oximate cost of $30.00 per student. The basic factors essential to a finan-
/ successful poultry enterprise are analyzed.

ss hours a week. Credit, 3.

MR. BANTA.

,TRY HUSBANDRY S-9. I.

lis course covers candling and grading of eggs, market classification, a study
:gs in the local markets, dressing poultry and various ways of preparing
:ry for the table. Prices and market operations form an active part of the
;e.

one-half day class trip to the Springfield markets in December is required.
nated cost, $2.00.

ss hour and 1 2-hour laboratory period a week. Credit, 2.

MR. VONDELL.

,TRY HUSBANDRY S-10. (General Poultry Husbandry) II.

'ultry keeping as a national industry; its importance and geographical dis-
tion; opportunities and possibilities in poultry culture in Massachusetts;
:iples of feeding; utility classification of fowl; incubation; the production of
1ing eggs; the baby chick industry and brooding and rearing. Practical
:ises will be closely correlated with the study of breeds and varieties, various
s of incubators, brooders, brooder-houses, etc. Textbook: Jull, "Successful
try Management." Note: Students who take course S-10 must get permis-
from the Poultry Department to take advanced poultry courses.

ss hours and 2 2-hour laboratory periods a week. Credit, 4.

MR. VONDELL.

,TRY HUSBANDRY S-12. (Specialties) II.

irkeys, ducks, geese, and game birds are considered. Breeding, incubation,
ng, rearing, management, marketing, housing, and disease control methods
practices are studied. Most of the course is devoted to the study of turkeys.
book: Jull, "Raising Turkeys."

ss hours and 1 2-hour laboratory period a week. Credit, 3.

MR. SMYTH.

TURF MAINTENANCE

PROFESSOR DICKINSON, ASSISTANT PROFESSOR ROBERTS

There is an immediate need for skilled supervisors and assistants to park cemetery, and recreation area superintendents. Municipal and private golf club are expecting that their superintendents shall be trained in turf maintenanc Every city and large town offers splendid opportunities for the private busine: horticulturist who is especially well trained to "take care of the lawn."

As the many proposed memorial parks, play fields, public buildings and go courses are being constructed and completed, the demand for specialists in tu: maintenance will be increased and the number of replacements needed annuall will be large.

This course is arranged and taught in such a manner that a student who h: completed the work will be well qualified to accept a position as assistant or tl actual superintendency of a small park, cemetery, or golf course, òr to establis a business in his community.

Laboratory and field exercises give practical experience and demonstration Good equipment is supplemented by loans from manufacturers and suppl houses. The supporting courses are strong and have been carefully chosen fc their close alliance to the problems of turf maintenance and general estate worl

Each student's placement training and special interest will be considered i his chosen field, whether it be park, cemetery, golf course, or private busines and professional men will visit the classes to give of their experiences. Ever student will be required to keep a record of work done, results obtained, an observations made during the placement training period, for use during th senior year.

Positions Capable of Holding at Graduation:

Assistant to superintendents or as an actual superintendent on golf cours cemetery, a park, or with a commercial nursery or landscape service compan; also with golf course construction companies and equipment supply dealers.

At least one field trip will be required during the second semester of the seni year. The total cost of such a trip or trips to each student will not exceed $20.0

TURF MAINTENANCE

First Year

First Semester	Second Semester
(Sixteen Weeks Resident Instruction)	(Eight Weeks Resident Instruction Follow
Agronomy S1 (Soil Management)	by Six Months Placement Training)
Agrostology S1 (Basic Factors and Uses of	Agricultural Engineering S14 (Repair of Fa:
Turf Areas)	Equipment)
Floriculture S1 (Garden Materials)	Agronomy S2 (Fertilizers)
Horticulture S1 (Plant Materials)	Agrostology S2 (Turf Maintenance)
Public Speaking S1	Botany S2 (Diseases of Trees and Shrubs)
Vegetable Growing S1 (Principles of Plant	Business English S2
Growth)	Entomology S6 (Turf Insects)
	Public Speaking S2

Elective	Elective
Physical Education S1 (Football)	Physical Education S4 (Basketball s Hockey)

Second Year

First Semester	Second Semester
(Sixteen Weeks Resident Instruction)	(Sixteen Weeks Resident Instruction)
Agricultural Engineering S9 (Structures and	Agricultural Engineering S16 (Irrigation :
Drainage)	Soil Conservation)
Agrostology S3 (Business of Turf Manage-	Agrostology S4 (Practical Problems) .
ment)	Arboriculture S2 (Lectures)
Aboriculture S1 (Lectures)	Floriculture S8 (The Uses of Herbace
Business English S3	Plants)
Horticulture S3 (Surveying and Mapping)	Horticulture S4 (Landscape Construction)
Horticulture S7 (Grounds Maintenance)	
Business English S3	

Elective	Electives
Physical Education S5 (Football)	Physical Education S4 (Basketball Hockey)
	Physical Education S6 (Baseball)

AGROSTOLOGY S-1. (Basic Factors and Uses of Turf Areas) I.

Starting with an appreciation of the grass plant the course carries the fine turf grasses from seed through uses. Identification of seed and vegetative growth. The limits of tolerance and factors affecting them are studied and correlated with the adaptation of the species to the user's specifications for various conditions.

class hours and 2 2-hour laboratory periods a week.   Credit, 5.

MR. ROBERTS.

AGROSTOLOGY S-2. (Construction and Maintenance of Turf Areas) II.

The student will adapt factors determined in the first semester to the practical construction of new turf areas and maintenance of existing turf. Fertilizing, controlling disease, clipping, watering, etc.

class hours and 2 2-hour laboratory periods a week.   Credit, 6.

MR. ROBERTS.

AGROSTOLOGY S-3. (Turf Maintenance as a Business) I.

This course is primarily for those students desiring to become professional turf growers such as superintendents of golf courses, cemeteries, or parks. The cultural costs as well as the monetary costs are studied. Equipment, fungicides, insecticides and herbicides are evaluated. Experiences gained during summer placement are thoroughly discussed.

class hours and 2 2-hour laboratory periods a week.   Credit, 5.

MR. DICKINSON.

AGROSTOLOGY S-4. (Practical Problems) II.

Designing, report making and presenting, field trips, equipment maintenance and practical problems to summarize the work of preceding courses.

class hours and 1 3-hour laboratory period a week.   Credit, 5.

MR. DICKINSON.

AGROSTOLOGY S-5. (Basic Factors, Construction and Maintenance of Fine Turf Areas) I.

At the completion of this course the student should have a knowledge and appreciation of the requirements for the growing of lawns and sports turf.

He will have considered the construction of turf areas; seed identification, selection and sowing; identification of turf grasses and their soil and fertilizer preferences, correct cultural practices and control of turf pests and diseases.

This course is for Arboriculture majors only.

class hour and 2 2-hour laboratory periods a week.   Credit, 3.

MR. ZAK.

VEGETABLE GROWING

PROFESSOR SNYDER, ASSISTANT PROFESSOR TUTTLE.

There are many opportunities for both men and women who complet Stockbridge School vegetable growing courses. These include the operatioi market garden, truck crop, or greenhouse business; skilled employees of mercial operators; operators or trained employees in the many types of v sale and retail marketing; employees in responsible positions on private es private and state institutions as well as with commercial companies hai agricultural products such as fertilizers, seed and various supplies and equip

The production and marketing of vegetable crops is a highly specialized ness involving a background of technical training as well as a knowled practical skills. The staff and facilities of the Department of Vegetable Gr are well qualified and adequate to give a thorough training to students i fundamentals essential to growing, harvesting and marketing the many vege crops commonly grown in New England.

In addition to the facilities of the Department, trips will be mai several production areas and markets to observe actual operations.

Trains for Jobs Like These:

Skilled workers on market garden and truck farms, growers of comm vegetable crops in greenhouses, cold frames, and fields. Operating all tyi farm machinery, tractors, cultivators, seeders, both motor and horse-di preparing crops for market, sorting, grading, bunching, packing. Wholesal retail sales and distribution. Workers for seed-growing firms, plant breedin, field work on testing plots. Operators, owners, managers of vegetable farms. State and federal market inspectors on commercial grades and i Buyers and inspectors for dehydration and quick freezer plants. Institu farm managers.

Field trips will be required during the two years at an estimated cost o per student.

Vegetable Growing

First Year

First Semester	Second Semester
(Sixteen Weeks Resident Instruction)	(Eight Weeks Resident Instruction Fo
Agronomy S1 (Soil Management)	by Six Months Placement Training)
Business English S1	Agronomy S2 (Fertilizers)
Floriculture S3 (Greenhouse Management)	Floriculture S2 (Greenhouse Constructi
Fruit Growing S1 (Growing Tree Fruits)	Heating)
Public Speaking S1	Fruit Growing S2 (Orchard and Vi
Vegetable Growing S1 (Principles of Vegetable Culture)	Pruning)
Vegetable Growing S3 (Systematic Vegetable Growing)	Poultry Husbandry S10 (General Cours
	Public Speaking S2
	Vegetable Growing S2 (Principles of Ve Culture)
	Vegetable Growing S12 (Diseases, Insec their Control)

Elective	Electives
Physical Education S1 (Football)	Physical Education S4 (Basketball and Hockey)

Second Year

First Semester	Second Semester
(Sixteen Weeks Resident Instruction)	(Sixteen Weeks Resident Instruction)
Agricultural Engineering S1 (Farm Power)	Beekeeping S2 (Spring Management, tion and Honey Production)
Agricultural Engineering S9 (Drainage and Farm Structures)	Farm Management S2 (Farm Managem Accounts)
Beekeeping S1 (Fall Management, Wintering, Honey, and Bee Diseases)	Food Technology S2 (Basic Principles, ing, Canning and Pickling)
Fruit Growing S7 (Small Fruits)	Fruit Growing S4 (Fruit Pests and Sp
Vegetable Growing S5 (Market Practices)	Vegetable Growing S4 (Vegetable For
Vegetable Growing S7 (Commercial Vegetable Culture)	Vegetable Growing S6 (Marketing Metl
	Vegetable Growing S8 (Commercial V Culture)

Elective	Electives
Physical Education S5 (Football)	Physical Education S4 (Basketball and Hockey)
	Physical Education S6 (Baseball)

VEGETABLE GROWING S-1. (Principles of Vegetable Culture) I.

Lecture periods are devoted to discussions covering certain fundamental principles of plant structure and growth as they influence and regulate commercial vegetable culture. The work in the laboratory includes detailed studies in seedage, plant growing, manures and fertilizers, garden planting, pests, storage and marketing.

2 class hours and 1 2-hour laboratory period a week. Credit, 3.
MR. TUTTLE.

VEGETABLE GROWING S-2. (Principles of Vegetable Culture) II.

Lectures are devoted to discussions of the more important environmental factors of the soil and climate which regulate plant growth and reproduction, including water, temperature, light, humidity and wind.

3 class hours a week. Credit, 3.
MR.

VEGETABLE GROWING S-3. (Systematic Vegetable Growing) I.

This course is designed to acquaint the student with the identification, nomenclature and classification of the standard types and varieties of vegetables; judging and exhibiting; seed production and variety improvement work.

class hour and 2 2-hour laboratory periods a week. Credit, 3.
MR. TUTTLE.

VEGETABLE GROWING S-4. (Vegetable Forcing) II.

A study of the principles and practices involved in growing, harvesting and marketing of vegetable crops commonly grown in forcing structures, especially tomatoes, cucumbers, lettuce, mushrooms and rhubarb. Discussions will also include the growing and handling of vegetable plants for field setting, in plant houses, hotbeds and cold frames.

class hours and 1 2-hour laboratory period a week. Credit, 3.
MR.

VEGETABLE GROWING S-5. (Marketing Practices) I.

A study of the various factors and practices involved in harvesting, preparing for market (bunching, tying, wrapping, waxing), grading, packaging, packages used, brands and inspection of vegetables for various market outlets as well as packing house facilities and storage. Trips to nearby and Boston markets will cost approximately $10.

class hours and 1 2-hour laboratory period a week. Credit, 3.
MR. SNYDER.

VEGETABLE GROWING S-6. (Marketing Methods) II.

A continuation of the studies in S-5 covering the marketing of vegetables with emphasis on advertising, salesmanship, roadside markets, wholesale and retail outlets, market reports and transportation by truck, rail and plane.

class hours a week. Credit, 3.
MR. SNYDER.

VEGETABLE GROWING S-7. (Commercial Vegetable Culture) I.

Problems and practices of the commercial grower are discussed as they involve seedage, planting, cultivation, irrigation, tools, machinery, farm organization, and management.

class hours and 1 2-hour laboratory period a week. Credit, 3.
MR.

VEGETABLE GROWING S-8. (Commercial Vegetable Culture) II.

This is a continuation of Vegetable Growing S-7 in which the disc involve the cultural practices for the various vegetables that are of comi importance in the New England area. Organized trips to market gai areas are required which cover a period of approximately three days ar about $30.

2 class hours and 1 2-hour laboratory period a week.　　　　Cr
　　　　　　　　　　　　　　　　　　　　　　　　　　MR. Tui

VEGETABLE GROWING S-9. (General Course) I.

This course is designed to meet the needs of students in other majoi cannot devote more than one semester to a study of vegetable growing. Ati is to be given to starting plants early, transplanting, seeding, fertilizing, sp: dusting, harvesting, marketing, and storing the more important vegetable

2 class hours and 1 2-hour laboratory period a week.　　　　Cri
　　　　　　　　　　　　　　　　　　　　　MR.

VEGETABLE GROWING S-10. (Marketing Methods) II.

A course in the purchasing of vegetables designed only for students speci in Food Management. It includes studies of the more important vegε sources of supplies, seasons of availability, grades, containers, and packs markets, and the characteristics associated with quality. Market outlets, of dealers, and business methods of the vegetable trade will be examined.

A field trip to a wholesale market is required. Estimated cost—$10.00.

2 class hours and 1 2-hour laboratory period a week.　　　　Cr
　　　　　　　　　　　　　　　　　　　　　　　　　MR. Tui

VEGETABLE GROWING S-12. (Diseases, Insects and their Control) II.

This course is intended to give those students majoring in vegetable an understanding of the more common insects and diseases which attac table plants and the most satisfactory methods for controlling these pests

2 class hours and 2 2-hour laboratory periods a week.　　　　Cr
　　　　　　　　　　　　　　　　　　　　　　　　MR. Tu

RELATED SUBJECTS IN OTHER DEPARTMENTS

GRICULTURAL ECONOMICS S-1. (Farm Economic Problems) I.

The purpose of this course is to introduce students to the more important eco-
omic problems facing New England farmers. Increasing competition with other
arm sections, long-time movements of farm prices and farm profits, farm credit,
arm taxation; tariffs and other farm relief measures are some of the problems
b be considered.

class hours a week.   Credit, 2.

MR. CALLAHAN.

GRICULTURAL ECONOMICS S-2 and S-3. (Marketing) I. II.

This course deals largely with economic problems arising out of marketing
arm products. Particular attention is given to marketing methods used in
ew England and to the comparison of local methods with methods used by
armers in competing sections. Principles and methods of co-operative market-
g used by successful co-operative associations are studied in detail in order to
ow how New England farmers may meet competition from associations in
ther sections, either as individual producers or as officers or members of local
associations.

class hours a week.   Credit, 3.

MR. CALLAHAN.

GRICULTURAL ECONOMICS S-4. (Marketing) II.

This course is designed to give instruction in purchasing and in management
r Hotel Stewards. A study of the distribution system for food products will
b given as well as merchandising practices, store location, advertising and per-
nnel management.

class hours a week.   Credit, 2.

MR. LINDSEY.

GRICULTURAL ECONOMICS S-6. (Dairy Business Accounting) II.

Business arithmetic and bookkeeping are given consideration. The mathe-
atics of fat determination, ice cream mixes, etc., are studied. An understanding
elementary bookkeeping principles involved in milk distribution also forms
part of the course.

class hours and 2 2-hour laboratory periods a week.   Credit, 5.

MR. SPINDLER.

GRICULTURAL ENGINEERING S-1 and S-2. (Farm Power) I. II.

A study of the principles of the gasoline engine and its accessories, as used
trucks, tractors and power units; and the application of electricity to farm
perations, with particular emphasis on the selection, care and maintenance of
ectric motors. Exercises cover trouble shooting and minor repairs to gasoline
gines; and the selection of proper wire size, overload protection, and the elec-
ical equipment for farm electric appliances.

2-hour laboratory periods a week.   Credit, 3.

MR. TAGUE, MR. PIRA.

GRICULTURAL ENGINEERING S-3 and S-4. (Farm Shop) I. II.

The purpose of this course is to teach the student the manner in which
dequate tools in a farm shop can assist in solving farm construction and main-
nance problems. Instruction is given in the care and use of carpenter's tools

through exercises in bench work, repair of farm equipment, and building
struction, including the mixing and placing of concrete. Exercises coverir
mestic water systems and the repair of farm machinery give the student e
ence in arc and gas welding, pipe fitting, soldering, and the use of mach
tools. While the time is too limited for the student to develop much ski
capabilities of the equipment can be adequately demonstrated.

3 2-hour laboratory periods a week. Cre

MR. PIRA, MR. POW

AGRICULTURAL ENGINEERING S-6. (Dairy Mechanics) II.

Designed for men who are fitting themselves for work in dairy plant
allied work, this course covers the principles and equipment involved in pr
ing and refrigeration of milk products, together with the instrumentation
sary for process control.

2 class hours and 1 2-hour laboratory period a week. Cre

MR. ZAHRADM

AGRICULTURAL ENGINEERING S-7. (Farm Structures) I.

A study of principles of design of farm buildings, utilizing elementary
tural mechanics and the characteristics of building materials. Experier
developing construction details results from the complete planning of a
farm building by the individual student.

1 class hour and 2 2-hour laboratory periods a week. Cre

MR. MARKUS

AGRICULTURAL ENGINEERING S-9 and S-10. (Farm Structures and Drai
I. II.

A study of building materials, details of construction, simple structura
chanics, and the principles of design applied to farm buildings. Each st
will design in detail one of the major farm buildings in which he is partic
interested.

About one-fourth of the time is given to the study of land drainage pi
and the use of the engineer's level in laying out drainage systems.

1 class hour and 3 2-hour laboratory periods a week. Cre

MR. MARKU

AGRICULTURAL ENGINEERING S-12. (Food Handling Equipment) II.

A study of the principles of operation, the care and maintenance of l
and other equipment used in food preparation for large groups. Refrige
heating and cooking, cleaning, and lighting equipment, as well as pum
electrical appliances are covered in exercises which give incidental prac
soldering, pipe fitting, and the selection of proper wire size.

Through the cooperation of commercial agencies, a one-day period of
instruction on industrial kitchen equipment and commercial lighting appli
is provided.

1 class hour and 2 2-hour laboratory periods a week. Cr

MR. T.

AGRICULTURAL ENGINEERING S-14. (Repair of Farm Equipment) II.

Instruction in the capabilities of arc and gas welding, soldering, pipe fitti
machinist's tools in the repair and construction of farm machinery and
laneous farm equipment. Exercises cover the repair of machines and th
of pumps and water systems.

3 2-hour laboratory periods a week. C

MR. Po

AGRICULTURAL ENGINEERING S-16. (Irrigation and Soil Conservation) II.

The principles of design for irrigation systems and soil conservation practices applicable to the management of large turf areas.

1 class hour and 2 2-hour laboratory periods a week. Credit, 3.

MR. BARTON.

AGRONOMY S-1. (Soil Management) I.

Every agricultural interest is vitally concerned with the soil, its adaptations and its management for plant production. This course treats of the selection of suitable soils for the special purpose of agriculture, horticulture and floriculture.

Laboratory includes training in the use and interpretation of the maps of the U. S. Soil Survey and in tests of soil texture, organic matter and soil acidity. Practical field work will be given in judging the crop adaptation and value of soils.

As a field project the student will be required to make a study of some farm, nursery or florist's plant, from the standpoint of soil conditions and methods of soil management in relation to the enterprise as a whole.

2 class hours and 1 3-hour laboratory period a week. Credit, 3.

MR. ZAK, MR. SOUTHWICK,
AND TEACHING FELLOWS.

AGRONOMY S-2. (Fertilizers) II.

This course deals with the origin, manufacture, purchase and use of commercial fertilizer materials. A study will be made of the interpretation of fertilizer formula, analysis and guarantee. Special attention will be given to the newer concentrated fertilizer materials and to those produced from atmospheric nitrogen. The laboratory work will give practice in the identification of fertilizer materials, in the calculation of fertilizer formulas, and in the preparation of fertilizer mixtures.

2 class hours and 1 2-hour laboratory period a week. Credit, 3.

MR. ZAK, MR. SOUTHWICK,
AND TEACHING FELLOWS.

AGRONOMY S-4. (Field Crops) II.

The lecture hours of this course will be devoted to presentation and discussion of the most successful methods of fertilizing, cultivating, harvesting, and storing the field crops grown in New England. Special attention will be given to the choice of the best adapted varieties for the production of hay, pasture, corn, potatoes, and root crops.

The laboratory work will include the study of corn and potato varieties, identification of grass and weed species, and studies of purity and germination. Field observations of growing crops will be included as the season permits.

2 class hours and 1 2-hour laboratory period a week. Credit, 3.

MR. SOUTHWICK.

BACTERIOLOGY S-1. (Bacteriology and Rural Hygiene) I.

The purpose is to present the problems of applied bacteriology in health, agriculture, and industry. Milk, water supply, sewage disposal, and food production are considered.

3 class hours a week. Credit, 3.

MR. LARKIN.

BACTERIOLOGY S-3. (Food Sanitation) I.

This course is designed to give students interested in the practical problems of food sanitation, spoilage, handling, and preservation a better understanding of bacteria and an appreciation of their importance in the sanitary production and handling of foods.

3 class hours a week. Credit, 3.

MR. WISNIESKI.

BACTERIOLOGY S-4. (Dairy Bacteriology) II.

Various bacteriological tests for the estimation of the numbers and types of organisms in milk are studied. Special attention is given to the interpretation of results indicated by the standard plate, Breed, methylene blue, and Burri methods of testing milk quality.

2 class hours and 2 3-hour laboratory periods a week. Credit, 5.

MR. LARKIN.

BEEKEEPING S-1. (Fall Management, Wintering, Honey, and Bee Diseases) I.

The students are given an opportunity for individual handling of bees in the early fall, and field studies are made of the bee colony and its organization. Studies and practice in fall management are followed by a similar treatment of winter protection and the bees are then prepared for winter. During the latter part of the semester the surplus honey is extracted and prepared for market, a laboratory study made of the product and, finally, the commoner bee diseases are discussed and methods of control pointed out.

1 class hour and 1 2-hour laboratory period a week. Credit, 2.

MR. SHAW.

BEEKEEPING S-2. (Spring Management, Pollination, and Honey Production) II.

The first part of the semester is occupied in assembling and studying the equipment used in beekeeping, but as soon as the weather permits, work is resumed on the bees in the apiary. Studies are made in spring management; pollination in the apple orchards is particularly stressed, and attention is then turned to the preparation of the colonies for honey production.

1 class hour and 1 2-hour laboratory period a week. Credit, 2.

MR. SHAW.

BOTANY S-1. (Tree Physiology) I.

A study of the processes occurring in trees and their relation to the complex of activities constituting plant growth. Topics include basic considerations of anatomy and physiology of roots, stems and leaves. Absorption, transpiration, internal water relations, food synthesis, digestion, translocation and growth receive appropriate elementary treatment.

1 class hour and 2 2-hour laboratory periods a week. Credit, 3.

MR. KOZLOWSKI.

BOTANY S-2. (Diseases of Trees and Shrubs) II.

A survey course dealing with the cause, nature, and general procedures of plant disease control. The profound influence environment exerts on plant disease, the role played by insects in their transmission and the major classes of plant pathogens, fungi, viruses and bacteria are briefly considered.

3 class hours a week. Credit, 3.

MR. BANFIELD.

BUSINESS ENGLISH S-1 and S-2. I. II.

This course is designed to cover review work in the fundamentals of grammar and composition, and to give students training and practice in writing various types of business letters and reports.

3 class hours a week. Credit, 3.

MRS. DUBOIS.

BUSINESS ENGLISH S-3. (Report Writing) I.

A discussion and writing course concerned with planning and setting up the different kinds of reports necessary in many occupations.

3 class hours a week.   Credit, 3.
                                                                    MRS. DuBOIS.

BUSINESS MANAGEMENT S-2. II.

This course is designed primarily for students majoring in Floriculture. It involves a study of records and accounts used by florists; costs and prices; uses of capital and credit; house and store management; advertising; buying and selling; economic use of labor and equipment; general business trends as affecting the flower business; how the florist should make adjustments to meet economic changes; analyses of going concerns; and finally a bringing together of all information studied and applying it to the successful organization of a business. The entire course is to be made as applicable and practical as possible.

2 class hours and 1 2-hour laboratory period a week.   Credit, 3.
                                                                    MR. LINDSEY.

BUSINESS MANAGEMENT S-3. I.

This course is designed primarily for students majoring in Dairy Technology. The principles of business organization and management are considered in relation to the successful operation of a dairy plant. The course includes a study of the following: various records and accounts used by dairies; costs and prices; uses of capital and credit; economic trends as affecting the business; how to make adjustments in the business to meet economic changes; analyses of different types of going concerns; and finally a bringing together of all the information studied and applying it to the successful organization of a business.

2 class hours and 1 2-hour laboratory period a week.   Credit, 3.
                                                                    MR. CALLAHAN.

BUSINESS MANAGEMENT S-4. II.

This course will be given to Aboriculture majors. It will cover contracts, labor and property law. The accounting will involve principles and interpretation of accounts and the business management will bring together forming and financing a business, location theory and personnel relations.

3 class hours a week.   Credit, 3.
                                                                    MR. LINDSEY.

ENTOMOLOGY S-2. (Insect and Related Pests of Florists' Crops) II.

Course material is designed to provide a comprehensive study of insect pests of greenhouse and garden plants primarily for Floriculture majors. It is devoted to an understanding of the nature of the pests encountered; types of damage, life histories, associations with environment, and the more important aspects of their control.

2 class hours and 1 2-hour laboratory period a week.   Credit, 3.
                                                                    MR. WEIDHAAS.

ENTOMOLOGY S-3. (Structural Pests) I.

A course for majors in Dairy Technology, Food Management, and others, designed to acquaint students with the common structural pests (household, stored food, etc.) and how to prevent and eradicate them.

1 class hour and 1 2-hour laboratory period a week.   Credit, 2.
                                                                    MR. SWEETMAN.

ENTOMOLOGY S-4. (Insect and Related Pests of Shade and Ornamental Tr and Shrubs) II.

Course material, for Freshmen in Horticulture, Arboriculture, and Pomolo is devoted to an introduction to Entomology and a study of major pest speci their recognition, and development. The course is basic to a further study pests and their control for those in Horticulture and Arboriculture who will t; Entomology S-5. A summer collection of important pests may be required.

2 class hours and 1 2-hour laboratory period a week.   Credit,

MR. WEIDHAAS

ENTOMOLOGY S-5. (Control of Insect and Related Pests of Shade and Or. mental Trees and Shrubs) I.

This course is designed for seniors in Horticulture and Arboriculture who h; completed Entomology S-4. It is devoted to a more detailed study of import; pests; their damage, life histories, environment, and distribution and to an derstanding of the principles and practical methods of controlling those pe; Summer collections will be classified and studied during laboratory periods

1 class hour and 2 2-hour laboratory periods a week   Credit

MR. WEIDHAAS

ENTOMOLOGY S-6. (Turf Insects) II.

A course designed to acquaint the student with the principal pests of tu General introduction to Entomology, followed by study of specific pests of tu

1 class hour and 1 2-hour laboratory period a week.   Credit,

MR. HANSON

FARM MANAGEMENT S-1 and S-2. (Farm Management and Accounts) I. II.

The work in this course involves a study of farm records and accounts; co and prices of farm products; uses of capital and credit; types of farming, sel tion of crop and live stock enterprises; size, diversity and production as rela to the successful farm business; farm layout and arrangement; economic of labor, power and equipment; detailed analysis of both successful and uns nessful farms, how the farmer should make adjustments to meet econo changes; and finally, a bringing together of the information gained and apply it to the successful organization of a farm business.

Actual farm records are used to illustrate the above points. The entire cou is made as applicable and practical as possible.

2 class hours and 1 2-hour laboratory period a week.   Credit

MR. BARRETT

FARM MANAGEMENT S-3. (Efficiency in Farming Operations) I.

For Freshmen. This is an introductory course to the regular Farm Mana ment work which comes in the second year. It is in no sense a theoretical c sideration but rather a study of the practical aspects of the efficiency of many day-to-day jobs found on various types of farms. In brief, a careful an ysis is made of the "one best way" of doing the jobs. The course involve study of farm layout, building layout, economical use of machinery and equ ment, and efficiency in hand operations. The primary objective is to po out ways of reducing farm labor costs. Motion pictures will be used to illustr good methods versus poor or inefficient methods.

2 class hours and 1 2-hour laboratory period a week.   Credit

MR. BARRET.

FOODS AND NUTRITION S-1. (Basic Food Principles, Meal Planning and Service) I.

This course aims to teach the basic scientific principles of food preparation and to give a general survey of the fundamental principles of nutrition. It includes a study of the nutritive value of foods, conservation of the nutritive values; planning, preparation and serving of family meals; and recent developments in foods. Emphasis is placed upon organization, high standards of work techniques, quality of finished products.

3 class hours and 1 3-hour laboratory period a week. Credit, 4.

THE DEPARTMENT.

FOOD TECHNOLOGY S-2. (Basic Principles, Freezing, Canning and Pickling) II.

Principles of food preservation including refrigeration and modern locker storage management are covered. Work is given in the use of packaging materials and the examination and grading of food products. Three field trips will be required. Estimated cost $10.00.

Note: This is a full semester course for Freshman Food Management and Senior Vegetable Growing majors; one-half semester course for Freshman Dairy Technology majors.

2 class hours and 1 2-hour laboratory period a week. Credit, 3.

MR. LAMPI.

FOOD TECHNOLOGY S-4. (Special Products) II.

The class and laboratory exercises in this course are planned to meet the needs of students majoring in Dairy Technology. General principles of food preservation and their application to the subject of dairying are discussed in class exercises. Crushed fruits, fruit juices, syrups, flavored syrups and other products which are utilized in the dairy trade are manufactured and tested.

2 class hours and 1 2-hour laboratory period a week. Credit, 3.

MR. LEVINE.

FOOD TECHNOLOGY S-5. (Food Manufacturing) I.

Class work consists of study and laboratory exercises on phases of the food industry of major interest to the students. The studies include food preservation methods, manufacture of carbonated beverages, pickled products, confectionery production and commercial bakery procedures and operations. Some field trips to local commercial food plants will be made.

1 class hour and 1 4-hour laboratory period a week. Credit, 3.

MR. LEVINE.

FORESTRY S-3. (Farm Forestry) I.

A course designed to give in one semester a working knowledge of the treatment of farm woodlands. Methods of determining the volume and value of standing timber are practiced in the first half of the course; this is followed by practice in the application of silvicultural intermediate cuttings.

2 class hours and 1 4-hour field period a week. Credit, 4.

MR. GANLEY.

GENERAL MATHEMATICS S-1. I.

This course provides a thorough drill in those fundamentals which are used in practical arithmetic. Fractions, ratio and proportion, percentage, formulas of area and volume, graphs, logarithms, and the use of the slide rule will be studied.

2 class hours a week. Credit, 2.

THE DEPARTMENT.

NUTRITION S-3. (Elementary Nutrition) I.

This course is designed to give a general survey of the fundamental prir on which the normal person may plan an adequate dietary. It includes a of the nutritive value of foods so as to make wise selection possible.

3 class hours a week. Cree
MRS. Cc

PRACTICAL SCIENCE S-7 and S-8. I. II.

This is a course in applied sciences, chiefly in the fields of chemistr physics, as they are tools serving the needs of the food and dairy industrie general, the course is designed to give an introduction to scientific though phenomena by means of lectures, textbook study and classroom demonstra The emphasis is entirely built around the practical problems in the stu field of work. Practical Science S-8 is a full semester course for Food Ma ment majors.

2 class hours and 1 2-hour laboratory period a week. Cree
MR. ZAPSA

PUBLIC SPEAKING S-1 and S-2. I. II.

The aim of the course is to give the student confidence in himself while s ing before groups, and to have him acquire some knowledge of, and pr in, the more practical types of public speaking.

1 class hour a week. Cre
MR. PEII

REVIEW MATHEMATICS S-3. I.

A course intending to bring into sharp focus the simple mathematics is used in vocational forestry and without which such forestry cannot be ligently practiced. Arithmetic, plane geometry and certain vocational u trigonometry are taught.

3 class hours a week. Cre
THE DEPARTME

VETERINARY SCIENCE S-1. I.

For Animal Husbandry and Dairy Technology Majors. Conservation health of animals is the keystone of successful animal husbandry.

Animal Husbandry: This course acquaints students with the causes, de ment, control, eradication, and prevention of diseases common to cattle, swine, and horses.

Dairy Technology: Content of this course is restricted to dairy cattl considers normal structure and function of various systems of the body. tation—and diseases that might effect milk supply and the public health.

3 class hours a week. Cre
MR. SM

VETERINARY SCIENCE S-1 and S-2. I. II.

For Poultry Husbandry Majors. Students in the first semester will b cerned with the anatomy and physiology of poultry, and hygienic me applicable to poultry management.

The second semester will cover the causes, development, control, eradi and prevention of diseases of economic importance to the poultry indi

3 class hours a week. Cre
MR. BU

[ORT COURSES AT THE UNIVERSITY OF MASSACHUSETTS

Short courses are based on the idea that the motive which inspires study is
most significant factor in study itself, and that this motive rises when the
dent himself realizes he faces a problem that calls for a solution. Therefore
re is no age limit. Enrolled in short courses are the young and the old, the
erienced and the inexperienced, the theoretical and the practical. In this
uping there is a value, since students learn from each other as well as from
instructors. Practically all Short Course students intend to make a direct
plication of the knowledge given. Hence the aim of Short Course work is to
er the largest amount of information and training in agricultural and horti-
tural lines in the shortest possible time. During the past thirty years Short
urses have served thousands of students in this Commonwealth, and the
nand for these courses since the war has increased greatly due to both veteran
l non-veteran demand.

DIRECTORY OF INFORMATION

The University

Those desiring University catalogs and other pamphlets giving full information
ative to entrance requirements, courses of study, expenses, opportunities for
dent labor, and so forth, and those with questions regarding admission to
university, either to the freshman class or to advanced standing should
ress Marshall O. Lanphear, Registrar of the University, Amherst, Mass.

The Graduate School

Questions relating to courses offered leading to the degrees of Master of Sci-
e and Doctor of Philosophy, admission and work required, should be addressed
Gilbert L. Woodside, Director of the Graduate School, Amherst, Mass.

Short Courses

For information concerning the Short Course Units, the Stockbridge School
Agriculture, write or apply to Fred P. Jeffrey, Director of Short Courses,
herst, Mass.

Please forward with your application the following: (1) a letter of recommendation from your high school principal; (2) a letter written in long hand giving your reasons for wanting to attend Stockbridge; (3) a transcript of your high school or preparatory school grades; and (4) the certificate of citizenship form to be found on the next page, if lower Massachusetts tuition rate is claimed.

FORM 1

APPLICATION FOR ENROLLMENT
IN THE
STOCKBRIDGE SCHOOL OF AGRICULTURE

Name ....Date ....

City or
Town .... Street .... State ....

Present Occupation .... Age ....
School or College Attended:
                                    Years in
Name of School .... High School? .... Graduate? ....

Place ....Are you a Veteran trainee?..........

Indicate by a check mark the course in which you desire to register. Do not check more than one.

1. Animal Husbandry	7. Fruit Growing
2. Arboriculture	8. Ornamental Horticulture
3. Dairy Technology	9. Poultry Husbandry
4. Floriculture	10. Turf Maintenance
5. Food Management	11. Vegetable Growing
6. Forestry	

References. — I am personally acquainted with the above applicant, and know ....
to be of good moral character, industrious, studious, and physically capable.

1. Name .... Position ....

   Address ....

2. Name .... Position ....

   Address ....
             (Two references are required and should not be members of your own family. Your teacher, your neighbor, or a former employer, are desirable. These persons should sign the application themselves.)

Mail this blank to FRED P. JEFFREY, Director of Short Courses.
                 UNIVERSITY OF MASSACHUSETTS, AMHERST, MASS.
Important.—Be sure to file citizenship certificate if State tuition rate is claimed.

CERTIFICATE OF CITIZENSHIP

e University of Massachusetts charges a tuition fee of $200 a semester to students who residents of Massachusetts. In order to satisfy the university authorities that an applientitled to state tuition of $50 a semester, they require a statement signed by the clerk city or town in which .the applicant resides, certifying to the fact that the parent or n of the applicant is. a legal resident of said city or town. Where the guardian is ng to this statement, it will be necessary for him to furnish copies of his appointment court. Such a statement may be made on the form below. If this is not presented he student registers, the Treasurer has no option but to collect tuition on the above basis. requesting the City Clerk to sign this certificate, an applicant for admission to the unishould give the name and. address of the parent or legal guardian unless he himself ral age.

is is to certify that I am the father.........mother.........legal guardian.........

....
Student's Name

Signed ....

is is to certify that on the date specified below (Insert name of parent or guardian)

.... is a legal resident of.......................
Parent's Name

......................; Massachusetts.
Town or City

Signed ....
Town or City Clerk

....
Seal

this blank to FRED P. JEFFREY, Director of Short Courses

UNIVERSITY OF MASSACHUSETTS, AMHERST, MASS.

rtificate must be filed with application blank if lower tuition rate. for citizens of Massa-
i is to be secured.

Other University of Massachusetts Catalogues:

- Summer School Catalogue
- Graduate School Catalogue
- Undergraduate Catalogue

UNIVERSITY
of
MASSACHUSETTS
at Amherst

Catalogue of the University
1956-1957

FOREWORD

This Catalogue of the University presents announcements concerning courses, admission, etc., for the sessions of 1956-57.

The University reserves, for itself and its departments, the right to withdraw or change the announcements made in its catalogue.

VOLUME XLVIII   FEBRUARY, 1956   NUMBER 2

Published five times a year by the University of Massachusetts, January, February, April (two), September.

Entered at Post Office, Amherst, Mass., as second class matter.

The University Catalogue for the sessions 1956-57 is part of the Ninety-second Annual Report of the University of Massachusetts and as such is part II of Public Document 31. Sec. 8, Chapter 75, of the General Laws of Massachusetts.

PUBLICATION OF THIS DOCUMENT APPROVED BY
GEORGE J. CRONIN, STATE PURCHASING AGENT

12m-1-56-916558

2

CONTENTS

3

CALENDAR

1956

February
6 — Monday, 8 a.m. Second semester begins.
22 — Wednesday. Washington's Birthday. No University exercises.

March
24 — Saturday, 12 noon to April 2, Monday, 8 a.m. Spring recess.

April
19 — Thursday, Patriot's Day. No University exercises.

May
19 — Saturday, 12 noon. Classes stop.
21 — Monday to May 31, Thursday. Final examinations.
30 — Wednesday. Memorial Day. No University exercises.

June
1-3 — Friday to Sunday. Commencement.

September
16-20 — Friday through Tuesday. Freshman Orientation.
19 — Monday. Registration of sophomore, junior, senior and graduate students.
20 — Tuesday. Registration of freshman students.
19 — Wednesday, 8 a.m. Classes begin.
20 — Thursday, 10:45 a.m. All University Convocation.

October
15 — Monday. Columbus Day observance. No University exercises.

November
12 — Monday. Veteran's Day. No University exercises.
21-26 — Wednesday, 12 noon to Monday, 8 a.m. Holiday recess.

December
15 — Saturday, 12 noon to January 2, Wednesday, 8 a.m. Holiday recess.

1957

January
17 — Thursday, 5 p.m. Classes stop.
18 — Friday. Registration of sophomore, junior, senior and graduate students.
19 — Saturday. Registration of freshman students.
21 — Monday to January 30, Wednesday. Examinations.

February
4 — Monday, 8 a.m. Second semester begins.
22 — Friday. Washington's Birthday. No University exercises.

March
23 — Saturday, 12 noon to April 1, Monday, 8 a.m. Spring recess.

April
19 — Friday, Patriot's Day. No University exercises.

May
18 — Saturday, 12 noon. Classes stop.
20 — Monday to May 29, Wednesday. Final examinations.
30 — Thursday. Memorial Day. No University exercises.
31 - June 2 — Friday to Sunday. Commencement.

Correspondence regarding various phases of the
University program should be directed as follows:

Admission and registration
    MARSHALL O. LANPHEAR, *Registrar*

Fees, expenses, payments
    AVERY BARRETT, *Cashier*

Loans
    EMORY GRAYSON, *Director of Placement*

Scholarships
    ROBERT S. HOPKINS, *Dean of Men*

Student housing
    HERBERT RANDOLPH, *Housing Supervisor*

Student employment
    ROBERT MORRISSEY, *Placement Officer for Men*

Veterans' Affairs
    GEORGE EMERY, *Veterans Coordinator*

Short Courses
    FRED JEFFREY, *Director of Short Courses*

Stockbridge School of Agriculture
    FRED JEFFREY, *Director*
    Stockbridge School of Agriculture

Graduate School
    GILBERT WOODSIDE, *Dean of the Graduate School*

Summer Session
    SHANNON McCUNE, *Provost*

Transcript of records
    MARSHALL O. LANPHEAR, *Registrar*

Extra-curricular activities
    ROBERT S. HOPKINS, *Dean of Men*

General academic problems
    SHANNON McCUNE, *Provost*

Women's affairs
    MISS HELEN CURTIS, *Dean of Women*

UNDERGRADUATE MAJORS

College of Arts and Science

Bacteriology
Botany
Chemistry
Economics
Education
English
Geology
German
Government
History
Mathematics
Medical Technology
Mineralogy

Music
Philosophy
Physics
Pre-Dental
Pre-Medical
Pre-Veterinary
Public Health
Psychology
Recreation Leadership
Romance Languages
Sociology
Speech
Zoology

College of Agriculture

Agricultural Economics and
   Farm Management
Agronomy
Animal Husbandry
Dairy and Animal Science
Floriculture
Food Technology

Forestry
Landscape Architecture
Ornamental Horticulture
Olericulture
Pomology
Poultry Husbandry
Wildlife Management

School of Business Administration

General Business Manage-
   ment
Accounting
Finance

Industrial Administration
Marketing
Merchandising

School of Engineering

Agricultural Engineering
Chemical Engineering
Civil Engineering

Electrical Engineering
Industrial Engineering
Mechanical Engineering

School of Home Economics

Child Development and Family Life Education
Foods, Nutrition and Institution Management
Pre-research in Nutrition
Home Economics Education and Extension
Merchandising and Retailing
Textiles, Clothing and Applied Art

School of Nursing

General Nursing

Division of Physical Education

Physical Education for Men

BOARD OF TRUSTEES

8

OFFICERS OF ADMINISTRATION

President
JEAN PAUL MATHER   South College

Provost
SHANNON McCUNE   South College

Secretary
JAMES WILLIAM BURKE   South College

Treasurer
KENNETH WILLIAM JOHNSON   South College

Dean of Men
ROBERT STODDART HOPKINS, JR.   South College

Dean of Women
HELEN CURTIS   South College

Registrar
MARSHALL OLIN LANPHEAR   South College

Dean of Graduate School
GILBERT LLEWELLYN WOODSIDE   Fernald Hall

Dean of the College of Agriculture and
Director of Experiment Station
DALE HAROLD SIELING   Stockbridge Hall

Associate Dean of the College of Agriculture and
Director of Extension Service
JAMES WILLIAM DAYTON   Stockbridge Hall

Associate Dean of the College of Agriculture and
Director of Stockbridge School
FRED PAINTER JEFFREY   Stockbridge Hall

Librarian
HUGH MONTGOMERY   Goodell Library

Business Manager
HOBART HAYES LUDDEN   South College

Director of Publications
ROBERT JOSEPH McCARTNEY   South College

Senior Physician
ERNEST JAMES RADCLIFFE   Out Patient Department

Director of Placement
EMORY ELLSWORTH GRAYSON   South College

Alumni Secretary
ROBERT LEAVITT   Memorial Hall

GENERAL INFORMATION

The University of Massachusetts is the state university of the Commonwealth, founded under provisions of the Morrill Land Grant Act of Congress of 1862.

Location

The University of Massachusetts is located near the geographical center of the state at Amherst. This town of about 7,000 overlooks one of the most picturesque sections of the Connecticut River Valley. The valley is noted both for its scenic beauty and its educational institutions. The setting for the University, therefore, is ideal. The surrounding country is a rich agricultural region providing an excellent outdoor laboratory for the work in Agriculture and Horticulture as well as for the Biological Sciences and Geology. Those interested in other Sciences and Liberal Arts study under equally favorable conditions both because of the facilities at the University and its location in this educational area of the valley.

Amherst is eighty-seven miles from Boston and may be reached by bus connections from Northampton, Greenfield, Springfield, and Worcester. The campus consists of a tract of approximately seven hundred acres, lying about a mile north of the village center. In addition, the University owns one area of 755 acres six miles north of the campus on Mt. Toby and has recently been given another tract of 1200 acres of readily accessible forest land on Mt. Lincoln several miles to the east of the campus. These holdings are administered by the Department of Forestry and are used in instruction as demonstration forests.

The University also operates a horticultural field station at Waltham and a cranberry field station at East Wareham.

Functions

The University of Massachusetts now serves the Commonwealth in the three important fields of resident instruction, research, and extension. Since all three services are organized on the campus, students have the advantages that come from contact with persons carrying education to the state at large, with others conducting original investigation as well as those engaged in formal instruction.

11

BRANCHES OF INSTRUCTION.

The Undergraduate College

The University offers four-year undergraduate instruction leading to the following degrees: Bachelor of Science, Bachelor of Arts, Bachelor of Science in Chemical, Civil, Electrical and Mechanical Engineering, Bachelor of Business Administration and Bachelor of Vocational Agriculture.

This instruction is assigned to the College of Arts and Science, the College of Agriculture, the Schools of Business Administration, Engineering, Home Economics, Nursing and to the Division of Physical Education. The aim of the four-year course is to give as high a degree of proficiency in some particular branch of learning as is possible without sacrificing the breadth, knowledge, and training which should characterize a well-rounded college education.

The degree of Bachelor of Science is conferred upon those candidates who complete the curriculum requirements of the freshman and sophomore years, and 60 junior-senior credits including the specialization requirements in a particular biological or physical science department of the College of Arts and Science. The Bachelor of Science degree is awarded also to students who complete the curriculum requirements of the College of Agriculture, the Schools of Home Economics and Nursing, and the Division of Physical Education for men. This degree may be granted to students majoring in Education or Psychology who complete a minimum of 15 junior-senior credits in science departments of the College of Arts and Science.

The degree of Bachelor of Arts is awarded to all candidates who complete the curriculum requirements of the freshman and sophomore years in the College of Arts and Science and 60 junior-senior credits including the specialization requirements of a liberal arts department in the College. This degree may be awarded also to majors in a biological or physical science department who select a minimum of 18 junior-senior credits in liberal arts departments of the College.

All graduates from the School of Engineering will receive the appropriate degrees of Bachelor of Science in Chemical Engineering, Civil Engineering, Electrical Engineering or Mechanical Engineering.

All graduates from the School of Business Administration will receive the degree of Bachelor of Business Administration.

Special arrangements are made for some graduates of county agricultural schools and of agricultural departments of certain high schools to complete the college course with majors in agriculture or horticulture. Upon the completion of their course they will be granted a Bachelor of Vocational Agriculture degree.

The Graduate School

Graduate courses leading to the Doctor of Philosophy degree may be taken in the following fields: Agronomy, Bacteriology, Botany, Chemistry, Economics, Entomology, Food Sciences, Food Technology and Psychology.

The following departments offer major work leading to a Master's degree: Agricultural Economics, Agricultural Engineering, Agronomy, Bacteriology, Botany, Business Administration, Chemistry, Chemical Engineering, Civil Engineering, Dairy and Animal Science, Economics, Education, Electrical Engineering, English, Entomology, Floriculture, Food Technology, Geology and Mineralogy, History, Home Economics, Landscape Architecture, Mathematics, Mechanical Engineering, Olericulture, Philosophy, Pomology, Poultry Science, Psychology, Public Health, Romance Languages, Sociology, Wildlife Management, Zoology.

The degree of Master of Landscape Architecture is granted to students completing the two years' graduate work offered by the Department of Landscape Architecture; while students taking the equivalent of one year's graduate work in that major may be granted the degree of Bachelor of Landscape Architecture.

Several other departments in the University, while not regularly organized for major work in the Graduate School, do, nevertheless, offer courses which may be selected for minor credit. These are: Forestry, German, Government, Physical Education for Men, Physics, and Veterinary Science.

The general requirements of the Graduate School regarding admission, residence, credits, tuition, etc., together with specific information concerning details of interest to prospective students, are outlined in a separate bulletin, which may be obtained upon request from the Dean of the Graduate School.

The School of Business Administration offers, through the Graduate School of the University, a program of advanced study in Business leading to the degree of Master of Business Administration.

The Summer School

A Summer Session is available for those desiring to accelerate their program. This Summer Session is planned to serve the needs of (1) all students enrolled as candidates for a degree at any college, (2) persons desiring refresher or professional improvement courses, (3) graduate students desirous of meeting specific requirements in certain fields, and (4) any adult person who finds courses

13

suited to his preparation and needs. Applications for the Summer School may be obtained by writing to the Director of the Summer Session.

The Stockbridge School of Agriculture

The University, through its Short Course division, as a special service under the Land-Grant Act by which it was established, provides a complete non-degree program of two-year technical and vocational courses in the fields of agriculture and horticulture.

This School was organized at the University in 1918 under the name of "The Two Year Course in Practical Agriculture." Its purpose was to meet the demand for shorter courses in agriculture which might be taken by high school graduates who could not satisfy college entrance requirements or who, for one reason or another, were unable to take the four year college course. In 1928 the School was given its present name in honor of Levi Stockbridge, first professor of agriculture at the University and its fifth president.

This program trains men and women primarily for the practice of farming or associated agricultural industries. A diploma is awarded for satisfactory completion of the course.

As the two-year program is now organized a student may choose any one of eleven vocational courses including dairy farming, dairy manufactures or milk plant operation; poultry farming, arboriculture or the care of trees; fine turf maintenance for golf courses, cemeteries, park, and play-grounds; commercial flower growing, both retail and wholesale; food management for clubs, hotels, and restaurants; commercial fruit farming, ornamental horticulture or landscape gardening; commercial vegetable farming, and applied forestry for timber growing and forest products industries.

On-the-job placement training is required of all first year students in the second semester for a period of four to seven months, depending on type of employment. No student can earn a diploma of graduation without this applied training experience. Wages earned can pay a large part of second year expenses if the student is forced to economize.

Limited enrollment quotas in each major course make necessary early filing of application. No formal entrance examinations are required for non-degree short courses.

A catalogue, giving complete description of all two-year courses offered in The Stockbridge School of Agriculture, as well as full details on estimated costs, employment opportunities in each field, and entrance arrangements is available. Application form is printed in the catalogue. Write to Director of Short Courses, University of Massachusetts, Amherst.

NOTE: (For interview or personal conference the Short Course Office is open Monday through Friday from 8:30 to 12:00 and 1:00 to 5:00, state and national holidays excepted.)

Other Non-Degree Short Courses

Other short courses, varying in length from one to ten weeks, furnish supplementary training for city and town sanitary inspectors, tree wardens and city foresters, golf course greenkeepers, and skilled workers in dairy and ice cream plants. A certificate is presented upon the satisfactory completion of the course.

Research and Regulatory Services

The University of Massachusetts serves the fields of agriculture and horticulture through its Experiment Station, which provides research and regulatory services. Experiment stations were established in all states as the need of development of practical information on subjects relating to agriculture became apparent. Through the efforts of experiment stations a fund of scientific knowledge applicable to agriculture and horticulture has been accumulated, and research workers in the experiment stations continue to contribute to this knowledge by constant research and experimentation.

At the University of Massachusetts, the Experiment Station service has expanded until it now deals with problems in the following fields of specialization: Agricultural Economics and Farm Management, Agronomy, Animal Husbandry, Bacteriology, Botany, Chemistry, Dairy Industry, Economics, Engineering, Entomology, Horticulture, Floriculture, Food Technology, Nutrition, Olericulture, Pomology, Poultry Science, and Veterinary Science. Most of the research activities of the University of Massachusetts are undertaken at the main Experiment Station at Amherst. There are, however, two substations, one at Waltham, devoted largely to the problems of horticulture as applied to olericulture, floriculture, and nursery culture, and one at East Wareham, where attempts are in progress to solve the problems of the cranberry and blueberry growers.

In addition to the work described above, the administration of certain regulatory services, as pertaining to the sale of feeds, fertilizers, and seeds and to the use of dairy glassware, is also assigned to the Experiment Station which is equipped with the necessary laboratory facilities and personnel for that purpose.

15

Extension Service.

The Massachusetts Extension Service is a cooperative teaching effort between the United States Department of Agriculture, the University of Massachusetts and the several counties of the State. The work of the Extension Service is carried on through unified teaching programs in all parts of Massachusetts. The Extension Service assists the people of the farm, the home, and the rural communities to improve agriculture, home making, and rural life. The University of Massachusetts is the State Extension Service headquarters. Extension educational teaching plans are made in council with the people who determine their problems and help to suggest methods and practices for their solution.

The Extension effort was brought about by the Smith-Lever Law, passed by Congress on May 8, 1914. Since that time, the service has grown to a staff of over 100 State and County workers who conduct an educational program in all phases of agriculture and home-making among the adults and young people (4-H Club work) of the State. All types of methods, including subject matter, meetings, demonstrations, farm and home visits, publications, visual aid, and radio are used in carrying out this educational program directly in the farm and rural areas of the State. During the war emergency, the Extension Service extended its home food production and preservation program to the urban areas.

ADMISSION

Persons interested in applying for admission to the University of Massachusetts should write to the Registrar to obtain an application form. The first two pages of the application form are completed by the candidate himself. The last two are completed by high school or preparatory school authorities who mail the application form directly to the Registrar of the University.

Because of the increasing interest in college level study and the consequent increase in the number of applications, candidates are advised to file their applications early in the senior year of high school and certainly not later than March 1 of the year in which they plan to enter.

Candidates for the freshman class are accepted only for the opening of the college year in September. Students enrolled in other colleges may apply for admission to the Summer Session, but admission to the Summer Session does not necessarily constitute regular admission and enrollment in the undergraduate program of the University.

The University admits young men and women to the freshman class chiefly on the basis of character and scholarship. The general record must indicate promise of success and ability to profit by the opportunities which the University has to offer. Due regard is given to special achievement in specified subject matter fields.

Methods

Plan A. Students applying from accredited schools and making the college recommendation grade of their school in accordance with the subject requirements listed above are considered certified for admission.

Superior graduates of Vocational Schools of Agriculture in Massachusetts and Vocational Agricultural Departments in Massachusetts High Schools may be accepted for the Degree of Bachelor of Vocational Agriculture provided:

a. They are unqualifiedly recommended by the Vocational Division of the Department of Education as bona fide Vocational Graduates with superior ranks; and

b. That they can present at least 16 units of certified entrance credits, approved as to quality and quantity by the State Department of Vocational Education.

Plan B. Students who are not fully certified will be required to take the Scholastic Aptitude Test of the College Entrance Examination Board. In some cases three Achievement Tests will be required also. The applicant will be informed what tests are to be taken as soon as his application is received or at the time of his personal interview. Candidates will ordinarily take these examinations in the spring of their senior year. Application blanks and a bulletin of general information concerning the tests may be obtained from the College Entrance Examination Board, P. O. Box 592, Princeton, New Jersey.

The University realizes that though almost all students will qualify under either Plan A or B, there will be a few promising candidates who, for one reason or another, are unable to meet. fully the subject requirements for enrollment. Such applicants are requested to present their individual problems to the Registrar in order that the Admissions Committee may outline for them what must be done to qualify for enrollment.

Advanced Standing

A limited number of students from approved colleges may be admitted on transfer to advanced standing. Since applicants for such admission usually exceed the number that can be accepted, they are placed on a competitive basis. Acceptance will thus depend upon recommendations and quality of record.

Candidates desiring to transfer to the University of Massachusetts from other institutions should write to the Registrar for a regular application form, inasmuch as a student applying for transfer must first of all be able to meet the entrance requirements of the University. Such candidates should also submit the following:

a. A letter outlining reasons for wishing to transfer and describing briefly the type of major work to be followed if accepted for admission.

b. An official transcript of entrance credits and college record to be sent by the Registrar of the College from which he wishes to transfer. This should be forwarded as soon as possible after the close of the semester preceding the one for which transfer is sought.

At least forty-five semester hours of work in residence are required of any transfer student desiring to be recommended for the Bachelor's degree.

Subject Requirements

The subjects of preparatory study required for admission call for the satisfactory completion of a four-year high school course or its equivalent and are stated in terms of units. A unit is the equivalent of at least four recitations a week for a school year. High school graduation alone is not sufficient. The applicant's record must indicate capacity for handling the quality of scholastic work which the University has established as its standard of achievement.

Sixteen units of secondary school work must be offered, selected according to the following requirements:

Algebra	1½
Plane Geometry	1
English	4
Foreign Language (2 years of 1 language)	2
U.S. History	1

The remaining units are elective and may be selected from the following subject matter:

a. Mathematics
b. Science
c. Foreign Language
d. History and Social Studies
e. Free electives (not more than four units)

Free elective subjects are those not included in groups a-d, as for example: Music, Art, Drawing, Typewriting, Aeronautics, Agriculture, Home Economics, etc. Such free electives are allowed in order that the student who wishes may have some opportunity to elect other high school offerings, while at the same time covering the fundamental requirements for college work.

Students planning to pursue an engineering curriculum should offer two years of Algebra, one of Plane Geometry, and one-half year each of Trigonometry and Solid Geometry, Chemistry and Physics are also advised. Those deficient in the Mathematics should plan to cover it during the summer prior to entrance or expect to take five years to complete the college course.

In high schools organizing agricultural club work under the supervision and rules of the Junior Extension Service of the University, one credit is granted for each full year of work approved by the State Leaders.

Candidates of exceptional ability and promise may be considered for admission even though some of the prescribed courses were not included in their high school program.

Physical Examination

Physical examination by their local doctor is required of all entering freshmen, re-entering students and all students participating in athletics. Physical report forms for this examination will be

ADMISSION

mailed to each student with the bill for the first semester and must
be completed and returned to the University Health Service 10
days before the opening of the semester. Evidence of a *successful*
smallpox vaccination is required.

Veterans' Affairs

The Veterans' Coordinator is a member of the Placement Service.
Veterans enrolling for the first time under Public Law 346 must
file a Certificate of Eligibility with the Placement Office prior to or
at registration. All veterans should clear their affairs through the
Placement Service.

EXPENSES

The sections of the catalogue that follow are primarily for undergraduate students in the four year degree course. Those interested in graduate study are referred to the Graduate School catalogue and in short courses to the catalogue of the Stockbridge School of Agriculture and other short course publications.

University Fees

Expenses vary from approximately $860 to $900 per year for the normally economical student. First year costs are usually greater than those of the other three years and there is less opportunity to earn. A student is advised to have a definite plan for meeting the expenses of the first year before entering.

Freshmen entering the School of Engineering should be prepared to meet an expense of approximately $35 for drawing equipment and a slide rule.

The following estimate of a year's expenses, based upon last year's costs, includes only those items which are strictly college and does not include amounts for clothing, laundry, travel, etc. These costs vary slightly from year to year. Tuition for residents of Massachusetts is $100 per year and for others $400.

	Normal
Tuition (citizens of Massachusetts)	$100.00
Room in college dormitory or private home (average)	180.00
Board at University Dining Hall	430.00
Books, stationery, and other supplies	100.00
Athletic Fee	20.00
Student Tax (approximate)	38.50
	$868.50

Initial Payment for Freshmen

The initial payment required of freshmen at the time of fall registration is indicated below and is made up of the following items:

Tuition (citizens of Massachusetts)	$50.00
Room rent (dormitory) approximately	90.00
Board (University Dining Hall)	165.00
Military Uniform (men students)	30.00
Physical Education Equipment Fee (men only) . .	10.00

Athletic Fee	20.00
Student Tax (approximate)	20.00
Books, Stationery, etc.	60.00
	$445.00

The above are only approximate figures. A bill will be rendered to the parent of each student prior to the opening of the University.

Tuition

As a state institution the University of Massachusetts offers a low rate of tuition to all students entering from the Commonwealth. Eligibility for admission under the low residential rate is determined in accordance with the following policy established by the Board of Trustees.

A student must present evidence satisfactory to the Treasurer of the University that his domicile is in the Commonwealth of Massachusetts in order to be considered eligible to register in the University as a resident student. This means that he must have established a *bona fide* residence in the Commonwealth with the intention of continuing to maintain it as such.

The domicile of a minor shall follow that of the parents unless such minor has been emancipated. In case of emancipation the student, in addition to the requirements of these regulations, respecting residence, shall present satisfactory proof respecting emancipation. Minors under guardianship shall be required to present, in addition to the certification of the domicile of the guardian, satisfactory documentary evidence of the appointment of the guardian.

No student shall be considered to have gained residence by reason of his attendance in the University nor shall a student lose residential preference during his continuous attendance at the University.

The residence of a wife shall follow that of the husband.

The prescribed form of application for classification as to residence status must be executed by each student. Misrepresentation of facts in order to evade the payment of out-of-state tuition shall be considered sufficient cause for suspension or permanent exclusion from the University.

Discretion to adjust individual cases within the spirit of these rules is lodged with the President of the University.

Board

The University provides three dining halls for students at Butterfield House, Greenough House and University Dining Commons. The dining halls at Butterfield and Greenough dormitories are intended primarily to provide for students housed in that area, including residents of Chadbourne, Mills and Brooks Houses.

All freshmen except commuters will be required to board at University dining halls on a five-day week basis.

Sophomores and juniors residing in University dormitories and other campus buildings will also be required to board at University Dining Halls except that such students who are members of fraternities or sororities are permitted to board at their respective fraternities or sororities.

Any student who wishes may board at University dining halls on the ticket plan or cash basis.

Military Uniform

All freshmen students taking military drill are required to make a deposit of $30 for the uniform at the time the first semester bill is paid. Charges for loss or damage of the government issued uniforms will be deducted from this deposit. Should the amount on deposit drop below $20, because of charges, the student will be required to make additional deposit to restore the balance to $30. The deposit will be refunded to the student less any charges after clearance from the Air Force or the Army after the student has completed the requirements of the basic course, has been excused from the course or has left the University.

Student Activity Tax

This tax, authorized by vote of the undergraduate students with the approval of the Board of Trustees, provides each student with the Collegian, the student newspaper; Index, University annual; Social Union privileges, student government, class and other activities.

PAYMENTS

Advanced Payment

New students will be expected to make an advance payment of $15 to the Treasurer of the University as soon as they are notified by the Registrar that they are accepted for admission. This will be considered as first payment on registration fee, which will be due at time of matriculation in September. It is not refundable and will be considered as payment for admissions and registration expense if the student does not matriculate.

A Certificate of Residence form furnished by the University must be properly filled out by the parent and the town or city clerk and returned with the $15.00 advance payment.

When Payments Are Due

In accordance with policy established by the Board of Trustees, all charges for tuition, fees, board, and room rent in University Dormitories are due and payable seven days prior to the date of registration of each semester. Bills will be rendered in advance and payment may best be made by mail. Students may not register until registration charges are paid.

Late Payment and Registration

Any student who does not make payment of his semester charges within the time specified may be required to pay a fine of $5.00. Similarly, any student who does not report for registration on the dates specified or fails to complete his registration within the prescribed time may be required to pay a late registration fee of $5.00.

Tuition and Fee Refunds

A student who leaves the University for any reason except as specified below before a semester is completed will be granted a refund of tuition and fees in accordance with the following schedule:

Regular Term
- a. Within the first two weeks from the beginning of semester or term — 80%
- b. During the third week — 60%
- c. During the fourth week — 40%
- d. During the fifth week — 20%
- e. After the fifth week — no refund

Six-Week Summer Session
- a. During the first week — 60%
- b. During the second week — 20%
- c. After the second week — no refund

A student who makes an advance payment and then for any reason does not attend any part of the next semester or term at the University will be given a full refund of tuition and fees. The $15.00 advance payment fee required of new students is not refundable.

A student who is involuntarily called into military service before the completion of a semester will be given a pro rata refund of tuition and fees provided that he receives no academic credit for the work of that semester. If academic credit is given, there will be no refund.

A student who is suspended or expelled from the University for disciplinary reasons forfeits all rights to a refund.

Room Rent Refunds

It is the policy of the University that there will be no refund of prepaid room rent after the semester has commenced except in the case of a student who is involuntarily called to military service who will be granted a refund on a pro rata basis.

A student who has made an advance payment of room rent who fails to attend any part of the next semester or term or does not reside in a dormitory or other housing will be granted a full refund of prepaid room rent.

Board Refunds

Prepaid board will be refunded on a pro rata basis.

Veterans' Information

Veterans who are entering the University for the first time under the old G.I. Bill (P.L. 346) must present a Certificate of Eligibility at registration. This may be obtained from your nearest Veterans Administration office. Veterans failing to obtain the Certificate of Eligibility must make payment of tuition and fees in order to register. Board and room fees must be paid in advance whether enrolled under the G.I. Bill or not.

Veterans (under P.L. 346) who are transferring to the University of Massachusetts from another institution or who have done summer work at another institution will be required to submit a supplemental Certificate of Eligibility at registration. This may be obtained by applying through the veterans' office at the institution last attended.

Veterans entering under the new G.I. Bill (P.L. 550) must meet all expenses personally. Presentation of a Certificate of Eligibility should insure the receipt of subsistence checks from the Veterans Administration.

FINANCIAL AID

Scholarships, loans, and part-time employment are available for a limited number of needy and deserving students. See page 36.

Aid for Freshman Year

Freshmen are eligible for scholarships and part-time employment. A freshman also becomes eligible for assistance from loan funds after satisfactorily completing one semester of academic work. Scholarship application blanks may be secured from the Registrar and should be filed by March 15. Part-time employment application forms may be obtained from the Director of Placement Service and filed after a candidate has been accepted for admission.

Because of the time required for preparation of studies, few students should plan to spend more than ten hours per week in part-time employment.

Aid for Upperclassmen

To become eligible for financial assistance, whether scholarship, loan, or part-time employment students must file completed financial aid application forms with the Student Aid Committee in the Placement Service office by March 15 previous to the college year for which assistance is asked.

Aid for Graduates of the University

The Lotta M. Crabtree Agricultural Funds make available to graduates of the University of Massachusetts funds to be used for farm financing.

The purpose of loans from these funds is to assist meritorious graduates who are without means in establishing themselves in agricultural pursuits. These loans are made without interest or service charges other than the cost of title search and legal papers. They must, however, be paid back in full amount within a reasonable length of time and there are certain restrictions on their use.

. Applications for the "Lotta Agricultural Fund" should be addressed to the Trustees of the Lotta M. Crabtree Estate, 619 Washington Street, Boston, Massachusetts, or may be secured at the Placement Office at the University. Decisions regarding the granting of a loan rest entirely with the Trustees under the terms of Miss Crabtree's will.

Standards of Deportment

The customary high standard of college men and women in honor, self-respect, and consideration for the rights of others constitutes the ideal of student deportment.

The privileges of the University may be withdrawn from any student at any time if such action is deemed advisable.

It should be understood that the University, acting through its President or any administrative officer designated by him, distinctly reserves the right, not only to suspend or dismiss students, but also to name conditions under which they may remain in the institution. For example, if a student is not doing creditable work, he may not only be disciplined, but he may also be required to meet certain prescribed conditions in respect to his studies even though under the foregoing rules his status as student be not affected. The same provision applies equally to the matter of absences.

Hazing in the sense of the punishment or humiliation of students is not permitted.

Registration

Every student must report for registration on the appointed day. All late registrants must pay a $5.00 fine. No student will be admitted to any class until he has completed the prescribed registration procedure. Changes of courses on the registration card shall be made only by the Registrar's Office.

Any student who does not complete his registration, including payment of semester charges, on the regular registration days will be required to pay a fine of $5.00.

No course will be recorded on the permanent records of the University nor will a student receive credit for it, unless such course appears on the registration card for the semester and has been properly countersigned by the instructor.

Freshman Week

All members of the incoming freshman class are required to be in residence on the campus for the period known as Freshman Week. During this period an attempt will be made to orient the student. He will be given psychological and mental tests, and a physical examination. Schedules and section assignments will also be arranged. In addition there will be lectures on student activities, customs, and curricula, and a scheduled meeting with the student's adviser.

GRADING SYSTEM

Graduation from the University involves the elements of both quality and quantity of work. The mere accumulation of credits earned with D grades will not suffice for the degree. In addition to completing the semester hours required for graduation, a student must have made a quality point average of 2.0 or higher.

I. Grades

Grades shall be reported according to the following letter system. No other interpretation of this letter system shall be authorized.

> A — Excellent
> B — Good
> C — Average
> D — Passing (but not satisfactory)
> F — Failure
> Inc — Incomplete

The grade of Incomplete shall be reported.

A. When a portion of the assigned or required class work has not been completed because of necessary absence of the student or other reasons equally satisfactory to the instructor and then only when he considers the work already done to be of passing quality.

B. When because of serious illness or other cause beyond the control of the student, he is unable to take the final examination. In this case an Incomplete is to be given only if the instructor judges that the quality of the student's work is such that by satisfactory performance in the examination he could complete the work of the course with a passing grade. If the student's record is such that he would fail the course regardless of the result of the examination, he is to be given a failure.

A student can obtain credit for an Incomplete only by finishing the work of the course before the end of the fourth week of the next semester in which he is enrolled. A mark of Incomplete will be automatically converted to a failure if the course requirement has not been satisfied by this time. The initiative in arranging for the removal of the Incomplete rests with the student.

II. Quality Points

A. Quality points per semester hour will be assigned as follows: A, 4; B, 3; C, 2; D, 1; F, 0.

B. *Semester Grade Point Average.* To compute the semester grade point average, the total points earned will be divided by the total credits carried. Credits carried are defined as total credits earned and failed. Grade point averages will be recorded to one decimal place. For example, averages from 2.65 to 2.74 will be recorded as 2.7. At the end of the senior year, the cumulative average will be recorded to two decimal places. A student with an Inc. will not have his semester quality point average computed until these marks have been converted to letters except in those cases where obvious dismissal would be involved regardless of the Incomplete.

C. *Cumulative Average.* To compute the cumulative grade point average, the total points earned will be divided by total credits carried. Total credits carried will be the sum of the total credits earned and failed. When a failed course is repeated, only the last grade, credits and points are considered in computing the cumulative average. A course once passed cannot be repeated for a higher grade.

D. In computing grade point averages the following will not be included:

1. Required Military and Physical Education courses of the freshman and sophomore years.
2. Courses for which a student does not receive credit toward a college degree (Mathematics or Foreign Language to satisfy an entrance deficiency).

E. Only grades earned at the University will be included in computing the Cumulative Quality Point Average.

F. *Warning.* Any student whose semester quality point average falls below the cumulative quality point average requirement of his class will be warned of his status by the Registrar and informed of the rules governing dismissal. A copy will be sent to his parent.

III. Dismissal

Dismissal from the University for scholastic reasons shall be based upon the following regulations to be administered by the Committee on Admissions and Records. Changes in these regulations may be made by the Educational Policies Council and the University faculty. A student is dismissed from the University as deficient in scholarship:

A. If at the end of the first semester freshman year, he has failed three academic courses with a combined aggregate of eight or more semester hours and has not made a C grade in each of his other academic subjects.

B. If at the end of the second semester freshman year or first semester sophomore year his cumulative quality point average is less than 1.5. He will not be dismissed, however, if his quality point average for the current semester is such that a continuation of this performance would result in a cumulative quality point average of 1.7 at the end of the second semester sophomore year.

C. If at the end of the second semester sophomore year or any subsequent semester, his cumulative quality point average is less than 1.7. He will not be dismissed, however, if his quality point average for the current semester is such that if continued until he has the equivalent of ten semesters of work, including residence in another college, his cumulative quality point average will be at least 2.0.

D. A transfer student must satisfy the cumulative quality point average of the class to which he is assigned.

E. Any student upon recommendation of the Dean of his School may request reconsideration of his case by the Committee on Admissions and Records.

F. When a student is dismissed for scholastic reasons only, any certificate or transcript issued must contain the statement "Dismissed for scholastic deficiency but otherwise entitled to honorable dismissal."

G. Dismissal involves non-residence on the University campus or in fraternity or sorority residences coming under University supervision.

IV. Honors

A. *University Honors Groups.* At the beginning of each semester a list is posted of those students who, during the previous semester, made a semester grade point average of 3.0 or higher. Three groups are recognized as follows:

First Honors . . . . . 3.8 or higher
Second Honors . . . . . 3.4 to 3.7 inclusive
Third Honors . . . . . 3.0 to 3.3 inclusive

B. *Graduation with Distinction.* High ranking students will be graduated as follows:

Summa Cum Laude—Cumulative average 3.8 or higher.
Magna Cum Laude—Cumulative average 3.4-3.7 inclusive.
Cum Laude—Cumulative average 3.0-3.3 inclusive.

A transfer, to be eligible for consideration for graduation with distinction, must have earned his final 60 semester hours of credit in residence at the University.

V. Changes in Registration—Adding and Dropping Courses

A. No course will be recorded on the permanent records of the University nor will a student receive credit for it unless he has registered for such a course in accordance with established procedure on a regularly scheduled registration day or unless his registration shall have been made official by the signature of the Registrar. In the latter case a Program Change Card must be signed by the student's Adviser and the Registrar approving the course. No instructor should allow a student to enter his class unless the student was officially enrolled on a regularly scheduled registration day or submits such a Program Change Card authorizing his admission to the class.

A student may not drop a course without the approval of his Adviser and the Registrar on a Program Change Card. A course dropped without this approval will be recorded as a Failure.

B. No new course can be added to a student's program after ten calendar days from the first scheduled day of classes of each semester.

The normal time for dropping a course without a failure will be established and recorded on the official University Calendar by the selection of the nearest practicable date which will allow three weeks from the first scheduled day of classes of each semester. The selection of this date will be the responsibility of the Provost.

C. A course dropped after the date regularly established on the University Calendar will receive a mark of WF (withdrew failing). This grade will be computed in the quality point average. If a student presents a valid reason from his Adviser for dropping a course after the established date together with a statement from his instructor certifying that he is passing, and it is so recorded on a program change card, the course may be dropped with the mark WP (withdrew passing). The WP is not computed in the quality point average.

D. In case of voluntary withdrawal from the University after the mid-semester report the rules for WF and WP will apply to the entire course program of the student.

Change of Major

A student wishing to change his major must get a Program Change Card at the Registrar's Office. This change is to be approved by the head of the Department or School in which he is now majoring and also by his new major adviser. This card, properly indorsed, must be returned to the Registrar's Office before the change receives final approval.

Graduation Requirements

At the beginning of his freshman year each student selects a school or division in which he will carry his major work. One of the fundamental objectives of all programs, however, regardless of School, is a general cultural education which should be the mark of every college graduate.

With this end in view all candidates for the B.S. or B.A. degree must take certain required courses: English 1, 2, 25, 26; Speech 3 and 4; two social sciences to be selected from Economics 25, Psychology 26, and Sociology 28; and twelve semester hours of science. In addition, at least three hours must be elected from one of the following: History 5, 6, 59, 60, or Government 25.

The requirements in Physical Education must also be satisfied. All physically fit men students must take Military 1, 2, 25, and 26.

Since the work of the first two years is directed toward a broad, general education as a foundation for the more specialized training of juniors and seniors, it follows that the program of studies for all schools is fairly uniform up to the junior year. Because of this, students can readily change from one curriculum to another or even from one school to another as both freshmen and sophomores.

Regardless of major, students who plan to teach should register early, in their freshman year if possible, with the Department of Education, although their work there does not begin until the junior year.

The minimum requirement for graduation is 60 junior-senior credits in addition to the satisfactory completion of the required and elective work of the first two years. Except upon special permission from the Provost or Registrar, no junior or senior shall enroll for more than 17 or less than 14 credits each semester.

During the junior and senior years, each student shall complete not less than 15, and not more than 30 credits in junior-senior courses in the department in which he is specializing.

It is the policy of the University that the final forty-five semester hours of scholastic work be taken in residence. Residence, for this purpose, is defined as a period of continuous enrollment and regular attendance in classes conducted on the campus of the University.

Financial Requirements for Graduation

Diplomas, transcripts of record, and letters of honorable dismissal will be withheld from all students who have not paid all bills and all loans due the University or all legitimate bills for room rent and board due fraternities. All such bills due the University must be paid ten days preceding Commencement. If paid after that date and the student is otherwise eligible, he may graduate the following year.

Transcripts

Two transcripts of a student's record will be furnished without cost. For each additional copy there will be a charge of one dollar.

Student Housing

It is the policy of the Board of Trustees that freshman men and women students shall be housed in campus dormitories and be required to eat at University dining halls unless given permission to commute. Sophomore and upper-class students will also be required to live in University dormitories in so far as accommodations are available. Those who cannot be so housed will be given permission to live in fraternity or sorority houses or in private homes.

Students who are assigned to housing operated by the University, or homes approved by the University, are expected to occupy them for the entire school year and may not be released sooner except as their places are taken by suitable substitutes.

Dormitories will be open for occupancy at 10 a.m. on the day immediately preceding the opening of the University.

Students assigned to dormitory rooms will be responsible for the room rent of the entire semester. Room rent is not refundable.

Rooms are furnished except for necessary bedding and linen and cared for by the students occupying them. Each occupant is held responsible for any damage.

All student property must be removed from the rooms and the key turned in to the Treasurer's Office immediately after final examinations in June. Such property not removed by the owner will be removed by the University and stored at the owner's expense.

Rooms for Women Students.

Dormitory rooms are available for women students at Abigail Adams, Crabtree, Leach, Hamlin, Knowlton and Arnold Houses.

Under the supervision of the Dean of Women, life in each dormitory is directed by a council of student leaders, advised by a full-time Housemother, so that conditions in the residence halls are conducive to study and good living habits. Through the women's branch of the Student Government, the responsibility is put upon each student to live according to her own best standards as well as according to the standards of the group.

Freshman girls will be assigned rooms in the dormitory and will be notified of the assignment prior to the beginning of college.

Near the close of each year, upperclass women will draw numbers to determine the order in which rooms may be chosen for the coming year.

Only students living in their own homes may commute. Upperclass women may apply to the Dean of Women for permission to live in a sorority house, or to earn room and board in a private home.

Rooms for Men Students.

Dormitory rooms are available for male students at Baker, Butterfield, Lewis, Thatcher, Van Meter, Brooks, Mills, Chadbourne, Greenough, Berkshire, Middlesex and Plymouth Houses.

Upperclassmen should make dormitory room reservations at the Housing Office before May 1. Those who cannot be accommodated in dormitories will be given permission to live in fraternities or private homes. Assignment of dormitory rooms will be under the supervision of the Housing Office. Requests for permission to live off campus must be made in writing to the Dean of Men.

Rooms for Married Students.

The University cannot guarantee facilities for married students; however, those married students who can be accommodated will be housed in the University Apartment Units. Assignments are under the direction of the Housing Office and all inquiries should be addressed to that office. Some students may be able to locate rooms or apartments off campus.

The University of Massachusetts reserves the right to change room assignments whenever necessary.

Advisory System

In order that from the day he enrolls the freshman may have some one to whom he may go for consultation and assistance, each student is assigned to a faculty adviser at the time of registration. It is the function of this adviser to help the student in adjusting himself to the work and life of the University. Academic progress reports issued by the Provost's Office are sent to the advisers periodically, and the students are expected to report to their advisers from time to time to discuss their academic standing. The adviser also forwards reports of academic standing to the parents. Both students and parents are encouraged to consult with the adviser whenever there are problems regarding studies or personal adjustments to college life.

At the beginning of the second semester of the freshman year each student will discuss his vocational and specialization plans with his adviser. If he can decide definitely upon the department in which he wishes to specialize, and the adviser approves, the student takes his election card to the head of that department for approval. In cases where students are not ready to designate a department of specialization they continue as general majors during the sophomore year under the direction of an adviser assigned by the head of the School in which the student is enrolled. Such general majors must select their field of specialization by the end of the sophomore year.

During the junior and senior years the student is under the guidance of the head of the department in which he is majoring or an adviser assigned by him.

Automobiles

Members of the freshmen and sophomore classes, also students who are on probation of any kind are not permitted to have automobiles on the campus or in the town of Amherst. All students who are privileged to have automobiles on campus are required to register their vehicles with the Campus police at the time of registration, or immediately after bringing their automotive equipment to the campus for the first time.

SCHOLARSHIPS AND LOANS

Scholarships are awarded only to needy and deserving students of high character whose habits of life are economical and whose scholastic records are satisfactory. A limited number of these scholarships are available for entering freshmen.

Scholarships are paid in installments at the beginning of each semester in the form of a credit on the student's bill. A scholarship may be discontinued at the close of any semester.

If the scholarship student withdraws from the University, any refund of University fees or charges must first be applied to reimburse the scholarship fund for the full amount of the scholarship received by the student for the semester.

Applications for scholarships may be obtained from the Registrar or the Dean of Men and must be completed and returned by March 15 to be considered.

GENERAL SCHOLARSHIPS

COMMONWEALTH SCHOLARSHIPS. The Commonwealth of Massachusetts annually provides 25 scholarships of not more than $250 for members of each of the four undergraduate classes of the University. Upperclass students may obtain application forms at the Dean of Men's office. Entering freshmen may obtain application forms at the Registrar's Office.

LUCIUS CLAPP FUND to provide scholarships and loans to deserving students.

HENRY GASSETT SCHOLARSHIP for a worthy undergraduate student.

CHARLES A. GLEASON SCHOLARSHIPS. General scholarship for worthy students.

WHITING STREET SCHOLARSHIP. Scholarships of $50 each for deserving students.

UNIVERSITY SCHOLARSHIP. A limited number of scholarships of $100 or more, awarded on the basis of leadership, need, scholarship and participation in extra-curricular activities.

DANFORTH KEYES BANGS SCHOLARSHIP for the aid of industrious and deserving students.

THE ALPHA SIGMA PHI SCHOLARSHIP for needy students.

36

RESTRICTED SCHOLARSHIPS

Area Scholarships

FREDERICK G. CRANE SCHOLARSHIPS for the aid of worthy undergraduate students, preference being given to residents of Berkshire County.

BOSTON ALUMNI CLUB SCHOLARSHIP. A limited number of scholarships awarded on the basis of leadership, need, scholarship and participation in extra-curricular activities. Available only to incoming freshmen from Greater Boston.

BETSEY C. PINKERTON SCHOLARSHIPS. Two general scholarships for graduates of the schools of the city of Worcester.

WILBUR H. H. WARD SCHOLARSHIPS. Twenty-five scholarships of approximately $100, known as the Wilbur H. H. Ward Scholarships. The Wilbur H. H. Ward Fund is administered by a Board of Trustees independent of the University. Applicants for these scholarships write to Sumner R. Parker, 1 Sunset Court, Amherst. They are available only to Hampshire County Boys.

Class Eligibility Scholarships

CLASS OF 1882 SCHOLARSHIPS for the aid of a worthy student of the junior or senior class.

College of Agriculture

ALVORD. For students specializing in the study of dairy husbandry or dairy manufacturing with the intention of becoming an investigator, teacher, or special practitioner in the dairy industry. Restricted to students who do not use tobacco or fermented beverages.

O. G. ANDERSON MEMORIAL FUND. For needy and worthy students in Pomology. To be used for the purchase of books and supplies. Granted only on the recommendation of the Department of Pomology.

ASCENSION FARM. For men students in the College of Agriculture. Residents of Berkshire County have preference, but awards may be made to students from Hampshire, Hampden, and Franklin Counties.

BORDEN. One scholarship of $300 to be awarded to a Senior in the College of Agriculture who has the highest scholarship average in all work through the Junior year and who has completed two or more courses in dairying.

BOSTON MARKET GARDENERS' ASSOCIATION. A $100 scholarship for a Sophomore in agriculture. Applications should be made to

37

the Secretary of the Boston Market Gardeners' Association, 240 Beaver Street, Waltham 54, Massachusetts.

BOSTON STEWARDS' CLUB. For students in Food Management. Three $100 scholarships awarded as recommended by that department.

BUTTRICK. For junior, senior or graduate students majoring in Dairy Industry or Food Technology. Scholarships will range from $100 to $500 per year depending upon scholarship achievement and need.

THE CHARLES M. COX TRUST FUND SCHOLARSHIP of $300 is awarded to a student or students in the College of Agriculture on the basis of need, character and scholarship ability. Preferably the scholarships will be awarded to undergraduate majors in dairy husbandry or poultry husbandry.

LOTTA CRABTREE. For students in the College of Agriculture. Based on scholarship and need.

DANFORTH FOUNDATION. Summer scholarships for outstanding freshman and senior students in Agriculture. For attending a summer camp sponsored by the Danforth Foundation.

ESSO. Scholarships are based on membership in 4-H Club, and applications should be sent to county 4-H Club agents. Scholarship is for $400—($100 per year) for students enrolled in some course of agriculture.

J. W. D. FRENCH FUND. For students in Dairy and Forestry, and allied subjects.

CHARLES H. HOOD FOUNDATION. Awarded to two Juniors and two Seniors in the College of Agriculture, with preference given to those studying the production of milk. Based on scholastic standing, character, industry, and personality.

MARGARET MOTLEY. For a woman student majoring in Floriculture or Landscape Gardening. Need, scholarship, and promise of success form the basis of award.

NEW ENGLAND CLUB MANAGERS' ASSOCIATION. For students in Food Management who are recommended by that department.

PORTER L. NEWTON. For students majoring in Agriculture who are residents of Middlesex County.

FRANK H. PLUMB. For students majoring in the College of Agriculture.

V. A. RICE SCHOLARSHIP FUND. A $100 scholarship for a worthy student majoring in Animal Husbandry.

SEARS-ROEBUCK FOUNDATION. Four scholarships for outstanding freshman in the College of Agriculture, based on scholarship, leadership, personality, business ability, or special achievement. The outstanding freshman recipient is eligible for a special Sophomore scholarship.

SPRINGFIELD GARDEN CLUB. For students living in the vicinity of Springfield, Massachusetts and majoring in some phase of Horticulture.

STATLER HOTEL. For a student in Food Management, and recommended by that department.

TREADWAY HOTELS. For students in Food Management who have worked for the Treadway organization and who are recommended by the Department of Food Management.

UNION AGRICULTURAL MEETING. A $250 scholarship for the Senior in the College of Agriculture having the highest scholastic standing and who has not been given another award based primarily on scholarship.

Engineering Alumni Scholarships

Provided by annual contributions from graduates and friends of the School of Engineering to provide tuition scholarships to deserving and well-qualified students pursuing work in a major field of Engineering. They are available to freshmen and upperclassmen.

Military Scholarships

UNITED STATES ARMY ROTC SCHOLARSHIP. The U. S. Army Reserve Officers Training Corps provides a scholarship, renewable for three years, to a young man with a good scholastic record in secondary school who possesses leadership qualities and can meet the physical requirements for commission as a second lieutenant in the Army Reserve. The applicant must agree to enroll in the basic course, Army ROTC, and to apply for the advanced course, ROTC.

UNITED STATES AIR FORCE ROTC SCHOLARSHIP. The U. S. Air Force Reserve Officers Training Corps in conjunction with the Department of Physical Education offers a scholarship of $100 to an entering male student. This scholarship is solely for tuition and fees and may be renewed for three additional years. It is awarded to a student who possesses leadership qualities, meets the physical standards required for commission in Air Force Reserve, has a good scholastic record in secondary school and agrees to enroll in the basic course, Air Force ROTC and to apply for the advanced course, Air Force ROTC.

4-H Scholarships

COTTING MEMORIAL SCHOLARSHIP. All college expenses of freshman year—for a woman student. Recipient of this scholarship is selected by a committee of the New England Branch of the Farm and Garden Association from among candidates proposed by State Leaders of 4-H Club work in the New England states.

GEORGE L. FARLEY SCHOLARSHIPS. The Massachusetts Society for Promoting Agriculture has established a scholarship in memory of George L. Farley. The income of approximately $60. per semester is awarded to deserving 4-H Club members, men or women, recommended by the State Leader of 4-H Clubs from applications submitted by County 4-H Club Agents.

Scholarships for Women Students Only

CHI OMEGA AWARD. The local chapter of the Chi Omega Sorority offers an annual scholarship of $25 to that woman student majoring in the department of economics or psychology who has the highest scholastic average at the end of the first semester of the senior year.

HELEN A. WHITTIER SCHOLARSHIP for a deserving woman student in art as applied to living.

THE MORTARBOARD AWARD. An award by Mortarboard, the senior women's honorary society, to a young woman student at the end of her junior year. This award is made on the basis of character and personality, scholastic achievement, campus influence and service.

POLISH JUNIOR LEAGUE SCHOLARSHIP. An award by the Polish Junior League to a woman student of Polish descent, at the end of her junior year, paying full tuition for the senior year. The basis of this award is character and scholastic achievement.

LOANS

Through the generosity of friends of the University, funds have been donated to provide loans for a limited number of students of the three upper classes to assist in paying tuition or other college expenses. These loans are granted, after proper consideration, to needy students of good scholarship whose habits are economical. All loans are secured by a note endorsed by a responsible party as collateral. All such loans must be paid before graduation. Upon withdrawal from the University, loans automatically become due. Interest is charged at the rate of 3% to maturity, 5% thereafter on loans from all funds except the Lotta Agricultural Fund, from which loans are made without interest. Application for loans should be made to the Student Aid Committee, Placement Service Office, South College. No loan will be granted in excess of $200 in any one year.

If funds are available at the beginning of the second semester, loans may be made in exceptional cases to members of the Freshman class whose scholastic record is satisfactory and whose budget calculations have been upset through circumstances beyond their control.

DANFORTH KEYES BANGS FUND. This is a gift of $6,000 from Louisa A. Baker of Amherst, the income of which is used in aiding poor, industrious and deserving students to obtain an education at the University of Massachusetts.

LOTTA AGRICULTURAL FUND. A limited number of loans are made to students from the income of this fund. Such loans are made without interest but only to deserving students of high scholastic rank. This fund is administered by a Board of Trustees independent of the University although loans are made only upon the recommendation of the President of the University.

VINCENT GOLDTHWAIT MEMORIAL LOAN FUND. A gift of $5,000 from Dr. Joel E. Goldthwait in memory of his son. This fund is used almost entirely for students in the Stockbridge School of Agriculture.

FRANK A. WAUGH FOUNDATION. Graduates of the Department of Landscape Architecture and friends of Professor Frank Waugh have established this fund, to be used in part for loans to deserving seniors and fifth year students of that department. Requests for loans shall be reviewed and approved by the head of the department of Landscape Architecture and submitted to the Board of Trustees of the Foundation, who shall make final decision as to granting of the loans and amounts thereof.

4-H SCHOLARSHIP AND LOAN FUND. This fund is under the supervision of the State Leader of the 4-H Clubs and is used to aid students preparing for agricultural and home economics service.

NATIONAL PEST CONTROL ASSOCIATION LOAN FUND. A fund established by the National Pest Control Association for needy students in the field of Entomology.

HONORS, PRIZES, AWARDS

Scholarship Honors

DEPARTMENTAL HONORS. A student who has shown outstanding promise within some department and has maintained a general scholastic average of B or better is permitted to apply for the privilege of registering for departmental honors. If his application is accepted by his department and the Honors Committee, he is allowed to pursue a course of independent study within the department of his choice throughout his senior year. This may include intensive reading, investigation or laboratory work in connection with some problem that he chooses for his consideration. The objective is to create initiative power of independent investigation and to develop the spirit of research. Although the student is responsible for his undertaking he is encouraged to consult with his department in regard to his work should the need arise. At the close of his study the student presents a thesis covering his investigation. In addition he may be required to appear for an oral or written examination. If by the excellence of his work he satisfies all the requirements of his department and the Honors Committee, his name will appear on the commencement program as receiving honors in the field of his specialization.

Scholastic Prizes

PHI KAPPA PHI AWARD FOR SCHOLARSHIP. Massachusetts Chapter of the Phi Kappa Phi, scholarship honor society, offers an award of $50 for outstanding work in scholarship. This is given to some member of the senior class at the opening of school in the fall. The award is based on the record of the first three years.

THE BURNHAM PRIZES. These were made possible through the generosity of Mr. T. O. H. P. Burnham of Boston. Prizes of $25 and $15 are awarded through the Department of Speech to those students delivering the best and second best declamations in the Burnham contest. Preliminary contests are open under certain conditions to freshmen and sophomores.

THE FLINT PRIZES. The Flint Speaking Contest was established in 1881 by a gift of the late Charles L. Flint, a former president of the College. After his death the prizes were continued by college appropriation. Awards of $25 and $15 are presented through the Department of Speech as first and second prizes respectively to those two upperclassmen delivering the best extemporaneous speeches in the contest.

THE HILLS BOTANICAL PRIZE. This is given through the generosity of Henry F. and Leonard M. Hills of Amherst, for the first and second best herbaria. Competition is open to members of the senior, junior and sophomore classes. First prize is $20, second prize $15.

THE BETTY STEINBUGLER PRIZE IN ENGLISH. This prize was endowed by John L. Steinbugler, New York City, in honor of his daughter Elizabeth Steinbugler Robertson, a graduate of this

College in 1929. It is awarded to a woman in the junior or senior class who has written the best long paper on a subject of literary investigation in a course in English during the year.

MASSACHUSETTS SOCIETY FOR PROMOTING AGRICULTURE PRIZES. Three prizes of $25, $15, and $10 are awarded to those senior students who are judged to have made the best records in the theoretical and practical work in agriculture required in their course of study, and in the special written and oral examination prepared for this award.

Athletic Prizes

THE ALLAN LEON POND MEMORIAL MEDAL. This medal is awarded for general excellence in football in memory of Allan Leon Pond of the class of 1920, who died February 26, 1920. He was a congenial companion, a devoted lover of Alma Mater, a veteran of World War I, a fine all-round athlete and a true amateur. He would rather win than lose, but he would rather play fair than win. He has been characterized as a typical student of the University.

THE WILLIAM T. EVANS MEMORIAL TROPHY. This trophy is given each year to that member of the varsity football team who through his sportsmanship, football ability, character and personality, has thus exemplified the character and spirit of the person in whose memory this memorial trophy is dedicated. The trophy is dedicated to the memory of William T. Evans, a former member of the class of 1942, who died December 9, 1941. This trophy is presented annually by the class of 1942.

THE THOMAS E. MINKSTEIN MEMORIAL AWARD. This award is made by the class of 1931 in memory of their classmate who died July 16, 1930 while he was captain-elect of football. The award is given to one of the outstanding men in the Junior class who has as nearly as possible attained those standards of athletics, scholarship and leadership set by him whose memory this award honors.

THE GEORGE HENRY RICHARDS MEMORIAL CUP. This cup is awarded annually to the member of the basketball team who shows the greatest improvement in leadership, sportsmanship, and individual and team play during the year. It is in memory of George Henry Richards of the Class of 1921 who died suddenly while a student at the College.

THE JOSEPH LOJKO MEMORIAL PLAQUE. This plaque is presented to a senior who must be a letter man, have a satisfactory scholastic record and show those qualities of enthusiasm and cooperation which make for leadership. It is awarded in honor of Joseph Lojko of the Class of 1934, outstanding athlete who died while a senior in the College.

THE SAMUEL B. SAMUELS BASKETBALL CUP. This cup is presented annually in the name of Samuel B. Samuels of the Class of 1925 who was an outstanding basketball player during the early years of basketball as a varsity sport at the University. The trophy is awarded to that letter man who is a regular member of the varsity team and who has performed with excellence during scheduled varsity games.

THE E. JOSEPH THOMPSON MEMORIAL TROPHY. This baseball trophy is given by Thomas Thompson in memory of his brother, E. Joseph Thompson who graduated from Massachusetts State College in 1932. He was president of the Student Senate, a varsity letter man in football and baseball, and an outstanding campus citizen. The award goes to that member of the varsity baseball team who best exemplifies the best characteristics of the sport each year.

MILITARY HONORS AND AWARDS

Leadership, scholarship, and proficiency in the work of the military department are recognized by honors and awards announced at the Annual Federal Inspection in May.

United States Army Reserve Officers Training Corps, Armor Branch

DISTINGUISHED MILITARY STUDENTS. Each year the Professor of Military Science and Tactics designates as distinguished military students those members of the first year advanced course who possess outstanding qualities of leadership, high moral character, and a definite aptitude for the military service. Students who are so designated must possess an academic standing in the upper half of their class or in the upper ten per cent of their class in military subjects. All distinguished military students are authorized to wear the distinguished military student badge.

DISTINGUISHED MILITARY GRADUATES. Each year the Professor of Military Science and Tactics designates as distinguished military graduates those members of the graduating class who were previously designated as distinguished military students and have maintained the same high standards required for such designation and have successfully completed training at the Reserve Officers' Training Camp.

THE MILITARY ORDER OF THE LOYAL LEGION TROPHY. Awarded annually by the Military Order of the Loyal Legion to the senior armor cadet ranking No. 1 in military scholarship and proficiency. Winner's name is engraved on a plaque and a sterling silver goblet, appropriately engraved, is given to the individual to keep in his permanent possession.

THE U. S. ARMOR ASSOCIATION SCROLL. Awarded annually by the U. S. Armor Association to the outstanding Armor cadet graduating from the Senior ROTC class. An engraved scroll bearing the name of the winner is presented to the winning cadet to keep in his personal possession.

ARMED FORCES COMMUNICATIONS ASSOCIATION HONOR AWARD. Awarded annually by the Armed Forces Communications Association to the outstanding Senior ROTC cadet majoring in electrical engineering. The winner is presented with an appropriately engraved gold medal and scroll.

THE MILITARY SCIENCE TROPHY. Awarded annually by the Department of Military Science, University of Massachusetts, to the Junior Armor cadet ranking No. 1 in military scholarship. The name of the winner is engraved on a sterling silver goblet given to the individual to keep in his permanent possession.

THE RESERVE OFFICERS ASSOCIATION MEDAL. Awarded annually by the Reserve Officers Association of the United States, Massachusetts Department, to the Junior Armor cadet who is outstanding in military proficiency. The winner's name is engraved on a plaque and a medal, appropriately engraved, is given to the individual to keep in his personal possession.

THE ELIZABETH L. MCNAMARA TROPHY. Awarded annually by Mrs. Elizabeth L. McNamara, a trustee of the University of Massachusetts for many years, to the Armor cadet ranking No. 1 in scholarship in the second year basic course. The winner's name is engraved on a plaque and a sterling silver goblet, appropriately engraved, is given to the individual to keep in his permanent possession.

THE JOHN C. HALL TROPHY. Awarded annually by the Military Science Department, University of Massachusetts, to the Armor cadet ranking No. 1 in military proficiency in the second year basic course. The winner's name is engraved on a loving cup donated by the class of '02 in the name of John C. Hall.

THE AMHERST ROTARY CLUB TROPHY. Awarded annually by the Amherst Rotary Club to the Armor cadet ranking No. 1 in scholarship in the first year basic course. The winner's name is engraved on a plaque and a sterling silver goblet, appropriately engraved, is presented to the winner to keep in his personal possession.

THE MILITARY SCIENCE AWARD. Awarded annually by the Department of Military Science, University of Massachusetts, to the Armor cadet ranking No. 1 in military proficiency in the first year basic course. The winner's name is engraved on a gold medal which is presented to him to keep in his personal possession.

RIFLE TEAM AWARD. Awarded annually by the Varsity Rifle Team, University of Massachusetts, to the team member who fires the highest cumulative match score for the season. The winner's name is engraved on a gold cup which is presented to him to keep in his personal possession.

United States Air Force Reserve Officers Training Corps

DISTINGUISHED MILITARY STUDENT. Each year the Professor of Air Science and Tactics will select from the students who are completing the second year advanced course, AFROTC, those who possess outstanding qualities of character, leadership, and a definite aptitude for the military service for designation as Distinguished Military Students.

DISTINGUISHED MILITARY GRADUATE. Each year the Professor of Air Science and Tactics will designate the distinguished Military Graduates from those Distinguished Military Students who have completed the advanced course, AFROTC, and who will receive their baccalaureate degree. The Distinguished Military Graduates, with their consent, may compete for a regular Air Force Commission after serving on active duty for eighteen months.

AIR SCIENCE TROPHY. Awarded annually by the Department of Air Science to the Air Science freshman cadet most outstanding in Military and Academic Scholarship. The trophy is a silver cup appropriately engraved which is given to the winner.

SONS OF AMERICAN REVOLUTION MEDAL. Awarded annually by the Sons of the American Revolution to an Air Science Sophomore cadet selected for Leadership, Soldierly Bearing and General Excellence. The winner's name is appropriately engraved on a medal which is presented to the individual.

AMHERST POST AMERICAN LEGION TROPHY. Awarded annually by the Amherst Post American Legion to the Air Science sophomore cadet who has demonstrated the most outstanding abilities in Military Drill and Scholarship. The trophy is a suitably engraved silver cup.

AIR CADET SQUADRON TROPHY. Awarded annually by the Air Cadet Squadron to an Air Science sophomore cadet who has been an outstanding member of the Air Cadet Squadron and Drill Team. A silver cup appropriately engraved with the individual's name is presented to the winner.

AIR SCIENCE TROPHY. Awarded annually by the Department of Air Science to the Air Science junior cadet who has displayed outstanding military proficiency and maintained a high scholastic standing. A silver cup appropriately engraved with the individual's name is presented to the winner.

AIR FORCE ASSOCIATION MEDAL. Awarded by the Air Force Association to the most outstanding Air Science junior cadet. The award is a suitably engraved medal which is presented to the winner.

RESERVE OFFICERS ASSOCIATION MEDAL. Awarded by the Massachusetts Reserve Officers Association to the graduating Air Force cadet who has been outstanding in Scholarship and Military Proficiency. The award is a medal appropriately engraved, which is presented to the winner.

NORTHAMPTON BENEVOLENT PROTECTIVE ORDER OF ELKS TROPHY. Awarded annually by the Northampton Lodge, BPOE, to the Air Science senior who by his zeal, effort and initiative has contributed most to the Corps of Air Cadets. The trophy is a suitably engraved silver cup which is presented to the winner.

DANIEL FUNGAROLI TROPHY. Awarded annually by Mr. Daniel Fungaroli to the Air Science senior cadet who has been most outstanding at Summer Camp. The trophy is a silver cup appropriately engraved, which is presented to the winner.

AIR SCIENCE TROPHY. Awarded by the Department of Air Science annually to the graduating Air Science senior cadet who has demonstrated superior qualities of Leadership, Military Bearing and Scholarship. The trophy is a silver cup appropriately engraved, which is presented to the winner.

STUDENT ORGANIZATIONS

One of the values received from the University course is the training one acquires through participation in student activities. Student organizations offer excellent opportunities for development of leadership and broadening of outlook.

Student Government

The student Senate operating under the student constitution and composed of elected representatives from the student body is the governing council of undergraduates. Its aim is to promote the general welfare of the University and, in doing so, groups of both students and faculty meet to further their mutual interests. The student Senate directs student conduct and represents the interests of the student body before the faculty.

Academic Honor Societies

Phi Kappa Phi. The Massachusetts Chapter of the Honor Society of Phi Kappa Phi was installed on the campus in 1904. Its prime object is to emphasize scholarship and character. Senior students from all departments of the University are eligible for election to membership provided the scholastic and character requirements of the Society are met.

Sigma Xi. The Society of Sigma Xi is a scientific fraternity to which members are elected on the basis of outstanding scientific research. The local chapter was established in 1938.

Omicron Nu. The Alpha Pi chapter of the Society of Omicron Nu was installed on the campus in 1952. The purpose of the Society is to recognize superior scholarship and to promote leadership and research in home economics. Membership is open to juniors and seniors majoring in home economics who meet the requirements of the Society.

Phi Tau Sigma. Phi Tau Sigma Honorary Society is the international honor society for food science. It was founded at the University of Massachusetts in 1953, and its executive headquarters are permanently located here. Its purpose is to encourage and recognize achievement in food science. Senior students from all departments related to food science are eligible for election to membership if they meet scholastic and character requirements of the University Chapter.

Sigma Gamma Epsilon. The Beta Theta chapter of the Sigma Gamma Epsilon Fraternity was installed at the University of Massachusetts in 1951. The purpose of the Fraternity is to stimulate scholastic, scientific, and social advancement of its members and the extension of the relations of friendship and assistance between the universities and scientific schools with recognized standings in the United States and Canada, which are devoted to the advancement of the earth sciences. Membership is open to men majoring in geology, mining, metallurgy, ceramics, petroleum engineering, or other branches of earth sciences, who meet the requirements of the Fraternity.

Phi Eta Sigma. The Society of Phi Eta Sigma was installed on the campus in 1955 to recognize outstanding scholastic achievement by freshmen men.

Tau Beta Pi. The Massachusetts Zeta chapter of Tau Beta Pi was installed on the campus in the fall of 1955. The Society exists for the purpose of honoring engineering students of high scholarship and character, and who also participate in campus activities. Senior and junior students in the School of Engineering are eligible for election to membership if they meet the requirements of the Society.

Student Honor Societies

Adelphia. The men's senior honor society, recognizing students who have been leaders in the extra-curricular activities of the campus.

Mortarboard. The Isogon Chapter of Mortarboard was installed at the University of Massachusetts in 1955. The purpose of the Society is to promote college loyalty, to advance the spirit of service and fellowship among University women, to maintain a high standard of scholarship, to recognize and encourage leadership, and to stimulate and develop a finer type of college women. Membership is composed of a total of not less than five or more than twenty-five girls from the senior class selected on the basis of service, scholarship, and leadership.

Maroon Key. Men's sophomore honorary society comprised of 25 students elected at the end of the freshman year.

Scrolls. Women's sophomore honorary society comprised of 15 students elected at the end of the freshman year.

Fraternities and Sororities

Social fraternities on the campus include Alpha Epsilon Pi, Alpha Gamma Rho, Alpha Sigma Phi, Alpha Tau Gamma, Delta

49

Sigma Chi, Kappa Kappa, Kappa Sigma, Lamdba Chi Alpha, Phi Mu Delta, Phi Sigma Kappa, Q.T.V., Sigma Alpha Epsilon, Sigma Phi Epsilon, Tau Epsilon Phi, Theta Chi. An Inter-Fraternity council, consisting of representatives of these fraternities, has charge of rushing and all general matters dealing with fraternity life.

Sororities include Chi Omega, Kappa Alpha Theta, Kappa Kappa Gamma, Phi Delta Nu, Pi Beta Phi, Sigma Delta Tau, and Sigma Kappa. The Pan-Hellenic Council, made up of representatives from the sororities, supervises rushing and other sorority matters.

Extra-Curricular Activities

All extra-curricular activities are supervised by the Committee on Recognized Student Organizations composed of alumni, faculty, and students. Recognition is given in the annual award of gold and silver medals.

The Collegian. This is a bi-weekly newspaper published by undergraduates.

The Quarterly. A magazine in which the literary and artistic efforts of the students are published.

Index. The year book.

University Handbook. Published annually as a campus book of reference.

University Musical Organizations. Open to all students of the University. For instrumentalists: Band, Dance Band, Orchestra and Ensembles; for vocalists: Chorus, Chorale, Operetta Guild and small combinations. A Women's Drill Team performs at home games and ceremonies. The University Concert Association provides an annual series of major concerts by famous artists.

Drama. Drama is represented on the campus by the Roister Doisters, open to all four-year students interested in the art of the theater; and the University Players, open to those students who have shown outstanding ability, effort, and interest in some phase of dramatics through the Roister Doisters.

Ya Hoo is the campus humor magazine published twice a year.

In addition, there are approximately 100 student organizations which offer an opportunity to interested students who participate in small group meetings.

Inter-Collegiate Athletics

The University is represented in inter-collegiate athletics by teams in all the leading sports including football, soccer, cross country, basketball, swimming, indoor track, hockey, rifle and pistol, baseball, track, tennis, and golf. General policies governing athletics are directed by the Joint Committee on the Inter-Collegiate Athletics composed of alumni, faculty, and students.

Professional Clubs

There are numerous professional clubs, established in connection with the various major courses of study. These clubs stimulate the students' professional interest in their chosen subject-matter fields and afford opportunity for discussion of technical subjects of mutual interest.

SPECIAL SERVICES

Religious Life

The University makes an effort to provide a wholesome and stimulating spiritual atmosphere for the students by cooperating with official agencies of the three faiths most largely represented at the University.

On the campus the religious life of Catholic students is enriched by the Newman Club, of which Father David J. Power of Saint Brigid's Parish is chaplain. Jewish students may participate in services and activities at the local Hillel House, under the chaplaincy of Rabbi Louis Ruchames of Northampton; and Protestant students may join in worship and other religious activities conducted by the Student Christian Association, under the guidance of the Reverend Albert Seely, chaplain to Protestant students.

The churches of Amherst provide not only the usual opportunities for worship and participation in church work, but special events for students. Students are particularly encouraged to attend Sunday service in the local church of their respective faiths.

Health Service

The Health Service is a separate administrative unit dealing with all matters directly or indirectly influencing or affecting the health of staff members, employees, students, or campus visitors.

The University endeavors to safeguard the health of all students while on the campus. Basic medical attention is provided, including preliminary diagnosis, primary treatment of injuries, and temporary care of the sick. A group of three infirmary buildings and a staff of resident physicians and resident nurses are available to perform these functions.

(1) The Student Health physicians have offices in the out-patient Infirmary Building, where they may be consulted during college hours.

(2) The Infirmary consists of three buildings, one for bed patients, one for contagious cases, and one for out-patient cases, where the out-patient clinic is conducted daily by the Student Health physicians.

(3) The students are urged to consult the resident physicians at the first sign of physical disorder, or even for minor accidents. Many severe illnesses and much lost time may be avoided by early or preventive treatment.

(4) House calls cannot be made to dormitories, sororities, or fraternities except in the case of emergency. The University cannot assure each student that a resident physician will always be available. In such instances students are encouraged to consult a town physician, although any expense connected with such service shall be borne entirely by the student. One resident physician is on call at all times to care for emergencies beyond the scope of the nurse on duty.

(5) No charge is made to Infirmary bed patients up to seven days in each school year; time in excess of seven days will be charged at the rate of $4 per day. A nominal charge may be made to out-patients for miscellaneous treatments.

(6) In addition to the fee charged as specified in paragraph 5, the following additional expenses will be charged to the patient:

Nurses. If a special nurse is required for the proper care of an individual, the services and board of this nurse will be paid by the patient. Such a nurse will be under the general supervision of the resident nurse.

Professional Service. If a student requires continuous medical attention by a physician, he may be required to select a town physician and become responsible for fees charged by that physician.

Supplies. Special medical supplies prescribed by a physician will be charged to the patient.

Laundry. Expenses for personal laundry incurred by students while in the infirmary will be charged to the individual student.

(7) The Health Service recommends strongly that students participate in the blanket insurance program described in literature accompanying the initial bill rendered students each year. This program is a reimbursement insurance plan providing medical, surgical, and hospital care for both accident and illnesses at a very low cost. During the past years this plan has saved numerous patients from serious unexpected expense and the insurance payments have enabled the student to stay in school. The University has no financial interest in this and acts only as a clearing

house to receive premiums, in order to give the low group rate.

The Placement Service

The University maintains a centralized Placement Service, the function of which is to assist students to secure part-time, summer, or permanent employment and to administer the required Placement Training Program.

The University is keenly interested that each graduate has an opportunity to serve his fellow men in a socially desirable occupation consistent with his interests, abilities, aptitudes, and education. To assist students to accomplish their objectives, the following aids are available: cumulative student personnel records, occupational information, library, counselling and guidance in job hunting techniques, preparation of credentials and personal data sheets and personal interviews.

The Placement Service is the clearing center for all part-time jobs at the University. Students are assisted in obtaining part-time work during the college year and full-time work during the summer vacation. Employment is not guaranteed, but every effort is made to help those students who must work to meet their college expenses. In order to give assistance to as many needy students as possible, the Student Aid Committee has adopted the policy of limiting the maximum financial aid per student to the equivalent of board. The average earnings of students engaged in part-time work is approximately $100.00 per year.

Publications and News Office

The University recognizes its obligation to provide the public with accurate information about its educational program.

Providing such information is the function of the Publications and News Office which edits the University catalogues and the school bulletin series and services communications media such as newspapers and radio stations. This is a public service program and not a publicity operation.

The Publications and News Office also supervises a Student News Bureau which affords internship training in news writing to a limited number of students.

Alumni Association

The Associate Alumni is the general organization of the Alumni, men and women, of the University of Massachusetts. The association maintains headquarters at Memorial Hall, erected by Alumni and friends in honor of those men of the University who died in World War I.

It publishes a magazine, *The Massachusetts Alumnus,* as the alumni publication of the University.

According to its By-Laws the Corporation is constituted for the purpose of promoting the general usefulness of the University of Massachusetts; of cultivating among its graduates and former students a sentiment of mutual regard; and of strengthening their attachment to their Alma Mater.

Under alumni sponsorship, 13 self-liquidating dormitories have been built on campus, and one is under construction.

The governing body of the Associate Alumni consists of its officers and a Board of Directors. Four directors are elected each year and serve a term of four years. All graduating seniors become members of, and contributors to, the Association at graduation, according to a tradition set by the Class of 1940.

SPECIAL INSTITUTES AND SERVICES

Bureau of Government Research

A Bureau of Government Research was established at the University of Massachusetts on October 1, 1955. The Bureau is to be staffed by professional personnel experienced in local government research. Its work will consist of research, publication and cooperative activities with local government officials of the Commonwealth.

College English Association

The offices of the Executive Secretary of the College English Association are maintained in South College. This is a national association of teachers of college English. The organization's monthly publication, *The CEA Critic,* is edited and published on the campus.

New England Field Training Center

For health department sanitarians. Has been located on the campus since 1949. Sponsored jointly by the U. S. Department of Public Health and the University's department of bacteriology and public health, the center instructs a limited number of health department sanitarians through in-service training.

UNIVERSITY BUILDINGS

The campus is laid out in the form of an oval attractively set off by the College Pond in the center. Around this oval are grouped the main buildings of the University.

South College. Here are located the administrative offices including those of the President, Treasurer, Secretary, Provost, Registrar, Director of Placement Service, the Dean of Women, the Dean of Men and Director of Publications. Erected 1885.

North College. The University Store and faculty offices. Erected 1868.

Farley 4-H Club Building and Bowditch Lodge. Headquarters for 4-H Club Activities. Erected 1933 and 1936 respectively by funds contributed by 4-H Club members and interested friends and organizations. The former was named to honor George L. Farley for twenty-five years State Leader of County Club Agents; the latter for Nathaniel Bowditch, Trustee of the University from 1896-1945.

Power Plant. General Maintenance.

University Farm. In the University barns are maintained Percheron and Morgan horses; Aberdeen-Angus, Ayrshire, Guernsey, Hereford, Jersey and Holstein cattle; Shropshire and Southdown sheep; and Chester White swine. The university farm is operated as a livestock farm, producing all its necessary roughage in the form of pastures, hay and silage and a portion of its required grain. .

Liberal Arts Annex. Classrooms, laboratories and offices for Foreign Languages, Psychology and Education. A temporary structure erected in 1947.

Grinnell Arena and Abattoir. Erected in 1910 primarily for livestock judging. An abattoir was constructed in 1930 as an addition to the original building. Named in honor of James S. Grinnell, for twenty-two years a trustee of the University.

Flint Laboratory. Laboratories and classrooms for Dairy Industry. Erected in 1911 and named for Charles L. Flint, fourth president of the University.

Stockbridge Hall. Departments of Agronomy, Animal Husbandry and Poultry Husbandry. Erected in 1914 and named for Levi Stockbridge, first Professor of Agriculture and a former President of the University. Bowker Auditorium, the main auditorium of the University, is located here. It is named for William H. Bow-

GOODELL LIBRARY

A Fast Growing

Campus ◊ ◊ ◊

LEWIS HOUSE—WOMEN'S RESIDENCE AREA

More Than 700 Acres

in the

HEART OF CAMPUS
LIBRARY AND OLD CHAPEL

Beautiful

Connecticut River Valley

PHYSICAL EDUCATION BUILDING

A Multi-Million Dollar • • •

THE UNIVERSITY DINING COMMONS

HASBROUCK (TOP) AND PAIGE LABORATORIES

ansion P*rogram* ♦ ♦ ♦

TO MEET THE NEEDS OF MASSACHUSETTS YOUTH

High Quality Education ◇ ◇

AERIAL VIEW—WOMEN'S AREA AND COMMONS

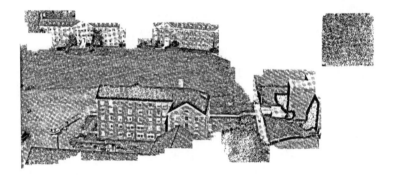

OLD
CHAPEL

Low Cost

DORMITORIES — MEN'S RESIDENCE AREA

CAMPUS KEY

No.	Utilization

- E1 — Butjek House — Dormitory
- E1 — Plymouth House — Dormitory
- E1 — Middlesex House — Dormitory
- E1 — Hampshire House — Dormitory
- E1 — Berkshire House — Dormitory
- E1 — Arm — ROTC Tanks
- E1 — Ato Garage
- E1 — Alumni Field — Athletic Fields
- E1 — Mem Hall — Extension Service
- B1 — Gian's Hall — Division of Physical Education
- E1 — Curry Hicks Physical Education Building
- B1 — Stockbridge Hall — Parking
- B1 — Mem Hall — Alumni Office–Music Department
- B1 — Drill Hall — ROTC Headquarters Physical Education for Women
- — — — Liberal Arts Headquarters
- D1 — Old Chapel — Library
- D1 — Goodell Library — Administration
- D1 — na h College — Faculty Office–Econ. Gov't.
- D1 — na h College — Music
- D1 — na h College — 4-H Club House
- D1 — Machmer Lodge — 4-H Club House
- C1 — Fak 4-H Club House — Undergrad
- C1 — Power Plant — Utilities Service
- C1 — Liberal Arts Ann — Class Rooms
- C1 — Old Dairy Barn — Cat & Building
- A1 — Chenoweth Laboratory — Food Technology Dept.
- A1 — Engineering Annex — Engineering
- A1 — Brooks Workshop — Agricultural Engineering
- A1 — University Farm — Poultry Building
- A1 — Poultry Lab — Poultry Science
- A1 — Draper Hall — Dairy Industry
- B1 — Research Laboratory — Food Industries
- B1 — Stockbridge Hall — Bowker Auditorium, Classroom Agricultural Faculty Office
- — — — School of Business, Nursing
- B4 — Hal Park Area — Parking
- B4 — Germann Laboratory — Chemistry Department
- B4 — Wes Experiment Station — Exper., and Con l Service
- B4 — Hasbrouck House — Dormitory
- B4 — The Homestead — Home Management Pla t House
- A5 — Gunness Lab — Engineering
- A5 — Annt Isolation Bldg — Engineering
- A4 — Paige Laboratory — Veterinary Science
- A4 — Engineering Bldg — Mass Veterinary Science Building
- A4 — New Physical Education Building for Wom — Under Construction
- B4 — Leach House — Dorm
- B4 — Hamlin House — Dormitory
- B4 — Arnold House — Dormitory
- B4 — Knowlton House — Dormitory
- B4 — Crabtree House — Dormitory
- B4 — Lewis House — Dorm
- B4 — Thatcher House — Dorm
- C4 — University Cot —
- C4 — Eas Experiment Stat — Research and Control
- C4 — Public Hlth Building — To Be Cor
- C4 — Fernbrook L Laboratory — Department
- C4 — Skinner Hall — Home Economics
- C4 — Marshall Hall — Zoonomics
- C4 — University Infirmary — Bo ing and Public Health
- C4 — Conservation Building — Landscape Architecture
- B4 — Wilder Hall — Tropical Plant Hou
- B4 — New Drape r ange — Horticulture
- B4 — President's House — Residence
- B4 — Fisher Laboratory — Pomology
- B4 — Wildlife ? Laboratory — Animal Dis rvation Research
- B4 — French Hall — Floriculture
- C4 — Clark Hall — Botany
- C4 — East Parking Lot — Parking
- B4 — Mathematics Building — Math ematics
- B4 — Fernald Hall — Ento mology of Mat Ge ology Zoology and Min eralogy
- — — — Zoology
- B5 — Brooks House — Dormitory
- B5 — Mills House — Dormitory
- B5 — Baker House — Dormitory
- B5 — Greenough House — Dormitory
- B5 — Chadbourne House — Dormitory
- B5 — Van Meter House — Dormitory
- B5 — Butterfield House — Dormitory
- C4 — University Apartments — Faculty Rm

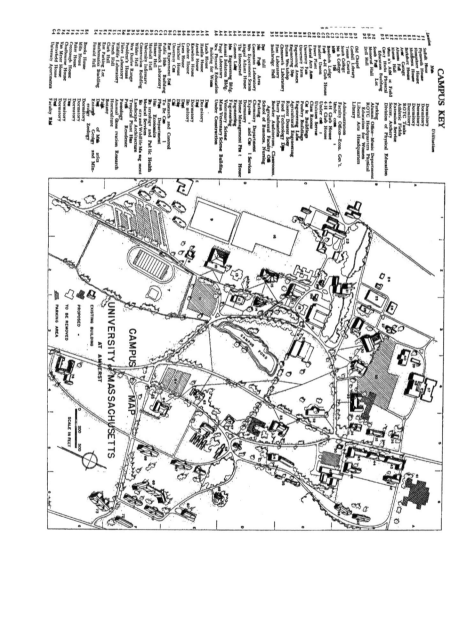

CAMPUS MAP

UNIVERSITY of MASSACHUSETTS
AT AMHERST

CAMPUS POND

EXISTING BUILDING
PROPOSED ·
TO BE REMOVED
PARKING AREA

SCALE IN FEET
0   300   600

ker, a member of the first graduating class, trustee of the University, and one of the pioneers in the fertilizer industry.

Chenoweth Laboratory. Classrooms and laboratories including Commercial Practices Laboratory for the Department of Food Technology. Erected 1929 and named in honor of Walter W. Chenoweth, pioneer in the field of Food Technology and first Head of the Department.

Dramatic Workshop. A headquarters for instruction in stagecraft.

Draper Hall. Classrooms and offices of the School of Business Administration. Headquarters also of the Department of Agricultural Economics and Farm Management. Erected in 1903 and renovated in 1954. Named in honor of James Draper, for twenty years a Trustee of the College.

Hatch Laboratory. A laboratory where small animals and chickens are used in connection with investigations into human, animal, and poultry nutrition.

Engineering Annex. Laboratories, classrooms, and offices for the School of Engineering. Erected 1948.

Engineering Shop. Laboratories and shop for machine tools, woodworking, motors, and welding instruction. Erected 1916.

Poultry Plant. Consisting of a number of modern buildings, in which instruction and research in ventilation, breeding, feeding, incubation, brooding, marketing and management of poultry and poultry enterprises take place. Rhode Island Reds, Barred Plymouth Rocks, White Plymouth Rocks, New Hampshires, and S.C. White Leghorns and several other breeds are maintained here on a commercial basis.

Paige Laboratory. Erected in 1950 and named in honor of James B. Paige, a graduate of the College in 1882 and Professor of Veterinary Science from 1891-1922. The building contains classrooms and laboratories. Laboratories for State Control and research work in animal diseases are located here.

Gunness Laboratory. Laboratories for industrial combustion engines, materials testing, fluid mechanics, heating, air conditioning and refrigeration, electrical machinery, electrical circuits, as well as classrooms and offices for the School of Engineering. Built in 1948 and named in honor of Christian I. Gunness, Professor of Agricultural Engineering from 1914 to 1946.

Main Engineering Building. First wing completed in 1950 provides laboratories for industrial electronics, communications, ultra high frequency, electrical measurements, illumination and metallurgy, as well as classrooms and offices for the School of Engineering. Building completed in 1955. Addition contains laboratories for civil engineering in soil mechanics, sanitary engineering, applied

65

mechanics and structural engineering, industrial engineering laboratories for time and motion studies and work simplification. New metallurgical facilities include new processing laboratory, X-ray and non-destructive testing equipment. Mechanical engineering and the School of Engineering laboratories are also housed here. The University radio studio, together with its transmitter are housed on the first floor and the campus weather station will be located on the third floor. This building serves also as temporary headquarters for the School of Nursing and contains office space for several members of the history department.

Goessmann Laboratory. Contains eight large laboratories, an auditorium, chemical library, and lecture rooms. The east wing of the third floor is used by the Experiment Station chemists. The remainder of the building is for resident instruction in Chemistry. Erected in 1924 and named in honor of Charles A. Goessmann, first Professor of Chemistry at the University. A large addition to this building will be under construction during 1955-56.

West Experiment Station. The State Control Service is centralized here. Fertilizers, seeds, and feeds are analyzed or inspected in accordance with the state law. Erected 1886.

Crabtree House. A self-liquidating dormitory housing 154 students. This building was erected under the sponsorship of the Associate Alumni and completed in 1953. Named for Lotta Crabtree, benefactress of the University.

Abigail Adams House. Women's dormitory accommodating 100 students. Erected in 1919 and named for Abigail Adams, wife of John Adams, second President of the United States.

The Homestead. Girls majoring in Home Economics receive their Home Management practice here. This is a fine old colonial homestead newly equipped with all the modern conveniences of the home.

Hamlin House. A self-liquidating dormitory housing 175 students. Erected under the sponsorship of the Associate Alumni and completed in 1949. Named for Margaret P. Hamlin, first Placement Officer for Women from 1919 to 1948.

Arnold House. Women's dormitory accommodating 205 students. A self-liquidating dormitory erected under the sponsorship of the Associate Alumni in 1954 and named in honor of Sarah Louise Arnold, former trustee of the University.

Knowlton House. A self-liquidating dormitory with accommodations for 175 students. Erected under the sponsorship of the Associate Alumni and completed in 1950. Named in honor of Helen Knowlton, Associate Professor of Home Economics, 1924-1941.

Leach House. A self-liquidating dormitory housing 154 students. This building was erected under the sponsorship of the Associate Alumni and completed in 1953. Named in honor of Mrs.

Joseph A. Leach, chairman of the Women's Advisory Council and former trustee.

Lewis House. Women's dormitory accommodating 150 students. A self-liquidating dormitory erected under the sponsorship of the Associate Alumni in 1940 and named in honor of Edward M. Lewis, Dean of the College 1914-25 and President 1925-27.

Thatcher House. Women's dormitory with facilities for 150 students. Erected in 1935 and named in honor of Roscoe W. Thatcher, President of the College 1927-32.

University Dining Commons. The central University dining commons for men and women students.

University Infirmary. A group of three buildings, one for bed patients, one for out patients and a third for contagious cases.

Marshall Hall. Erected in 1915 and named for Dr. Charles Marshall, a former Professor of Bacteriology and Director of the Graduate School. The building provides laboratories and classroom space for the Department of Bacteriology and the Department of Zoology.

Skinner Hall. Laboratories, classrooms and offices for the School of Home Economics. Erected in 1947 and named in honor of Edna L. Skinner, first Dean of the School of Home Economics.

Hasbrouck Physics Laboratory. Completed in 1949. Contains laboratories and lecture rooms designed for the various main divisions of Physics. Named in honor of Philip B. Hasbrouck, Professor of Physics and Registrar of the College during the period 1905 to 1924.

Conservation Building. Formerly the Old Botany Museum, erected 1867. Houses laboratories, classrooms and offices for the Department of Forestry and Wildlife Management.

Fisher Laboratory. Erected in 1910 and named for Jabez Fisher, one of the foremost early horticulturists of the state. Laboratories for Pomology. Included are a quick freezing room, six refrigerator rooms, two rooms for the storage of frozen products, two classrooms, and three packing rooms.

Wild Life Laboratory. Laboratories for graduate students in Wild Life Management.

Wilder Hall. Contains classrooms, drafting rooms, and offices of the Department of Landscape Architecture. Erected in 1905 and named for Marshall P. Wilder, a pioneer in the movement for agricultural education in Massachusetts, and one of the first trustees of the College.

French Hall. Erected in 1908 and named in honor of Henry F. French, the first President of the College, this building houses the Departments of Floriculture, Pomology, and Olericulture. In the rear of the building is the Edward A. White range of greenhouses, built in 1908, enlarged in 1939, and devoted to the growing of

67

carnations, roses, chrysanthemums, etc. One house is maintained as a conservatory and contains a collection of plants used primarily for decorative purposes.

Durfee Conservatories. The new Durfee Conservatories were erected in 1954. They contain collections of plants of various types, including desert, tropical and sub-tropical, of botanical and horticultural importance. These greenhouses replace the Durfee Planthouses erected in 1867 from money given by Dr. Nathan Durfee of Fall River, treasurer of the board of trustees.

Stockbridge House. Faculty Club House.

Shade Tree Laboratories. Constructed in 1948 for research on shade tree problems including Dutch Elm Disease.

Clark Hall. Offices, lecture rooms, laboratories, and greenhouses of the Department of Botany are located here. The herbarium contains about 122,000 sheets of seed plants and ferns, 5000 sheets of liverworts, mosses, algae, lichens, and a collection of 20,000 specimens of fungi. The building was erected in 1906 and named in honor of William S. Clark, President of the College and Professor of Botany from 1867 to 1879.

Fernald Hall. Erected in 1909 and named in honor of Professor Charles H. Fernald who served the College from 1886 to 1909, built a strong Department of Zoology, created the Department of Entomology, and acted as Director of the Graduate School. Fernald Hall houses the Departments of Entomology and Geology and offices and classrooms of the Department of Zoology. Offices and laboratories of the Western Sanitary District, Massachusetts Department of Public Health, are also located here. The Entomology collection includes over 160,000 insects. There are also Geological and Zoological museums.

Mathematics Building. Classrooms and offices of the Mathematics Department.

Mills House. A self-liquidating dormitory for 150 students. Erected in 1948 under the sponsorship of the Associate Alumni. Named in honor of George F. Mills, teacher of English from 1890 to 1914 and Head of the Division of Humanities.

Brooks House. Men's self-liquidating dormitory. Named in honor of William Penn Brooks, Professor of Agriculture and Director of the Experiment Station, 1888-1921.

Butterfield House. A self-liquidating dormitory with dining hall. Accommodates 147 students. Erected in 1941 under the sponsorship of the Associate Alumni. Named in honor of Kenyon L. Butterfield, President of the College 1906-1924.

Chadbourne House. Men's self-liquidating dormitory for one hundred and fifty students. Erected in 1946 under the sponsorship of the Associate Alumni. Named in honor of Paul Ansel Chadbourne, President 1866-67 and 1882-83.

Baker House. A self-liquidating dormitory for men accommodating 360 students. Erected in 1951 by the Alumni Building Corporation. Named in honor of Hugh P. Baker, President of the University from 1933 to 1947.

Greenough House. Men's dormitory and Dining Hall. Houses one hundred and forty-eight students. A self-liquidating dormitory erected in 1946 under the sponsorship of the Associate Alumni. Named in honor of James Carruthers Greenough, President from 1883-86.

Van Meter House. A self-liquidating dormitory for men. The building was completed in 1955 and houses 165 students. It was named for Dr. Ralph A. Van Meter, 13th president of the University, who retired in 1954. A second wing is now under construction.

Munson Hall. Headquarters for the Massachusetts Extension Service. Named in honor of Willard A. Munson, a graduate of the College in 1905 and Director of the Extension Service from 1926 to 1951.

Curry S. Hicks Physical Education Building. Erected in 1931 from funds contributed by Alumni and friends of the College plus an appropriation by the state legislature. Contains a large swimming pool, an exercise hall, basketball floor, and locker room. Named for Curry S. Hicks, Professor and Head of the Division of Physical Education from 1911 to 1949.

Alumni Field. So called because both funds and labor for its construction were contributed by alumni and students. Included are a baseball diamond, football and soccer fields, and a cinder track. Tennis courts are adjacent to the Physical Education Building.

Athletic Field for Women. A large field west of the Physical Education Building provides space for Archery, Softball, Field Hockey, and other women's activities.

County Circle. Five residence halls erected in 1948 by the Commonwealth. Hampshire and Suffolk Houses contain 30 two-room and three-room apartments for married persons and their families. Plymouth, Berkshire, and Middlesex Houses contain dormitory rooms for approximately 144 students each.

Drill Hall. Contains, in addition to the offices of the Departments of Military Science and Air Science, the offices, locker and dressing rooms, and exercise hall for the Department of Physical Education for Women.

Memorial Hall. Erected in 1921 by Alumni and friends in memory of those men of the College who died in World War I. Included is a Memorial Room in which the names of those members of the College family who died in the service of their country are appropriately enshrined. This building is a social center of

69

student life. Alumni headquarters are here as well as the offices of student organizations including the Senate, Collegian, and Index.

Old Chapel. Erected in 1885. Auditorium, seminar room, classrooms, and offices for English and History.

Goodell Library. Goodell Library is named in honor of Henry Hill Goodell who served the College from 1867-1905. He was President from 1886 to 1905 and because of his deep enthusiasm for books also acted as Librarian of the College.

This library houses the main collection of the University library system and has the central card catalog and the catalog and processing units for both the main and departmental libraries.

Goodell Library is a fireproof building erected in 1935. Its plan is virtually unique among University libraries in that the greater part of its book-stacks are open for inspection and borrowing. The present collection in the building amounts to approximately 152,000 volumes including books and extensive files of periodicals.

The collections in the Goodell Library include the books and periodicals in the Humanities and Social Sciences together with some of the material in the Natural and Applied Sciences.

The main floor includes a large reading room, a reference room, circulation desk, reference and current periodical desk, both in the main lobby, and cataloging and administrative offices. On the second floor is another large reading room, commonly used for reserve book reading. There is a study for faculty and a University History Room in memory of Dean William L. Machmer in which the historical records of the University are kept and exhibited.

Besides the Goodell Library there are thirty-seven department libraries totaling about 38,000 books and bound periodicals located in the several University buildings with the teaching departments and laboratories. These libraries vary from small working libraries to extensive collections in special fields. Particularly worthy of note are the Botany, Chemistry, and Entomology libraries.

The complete library system contains 190,055 volumes (Sept. 1, 1954) and is growing at the rate of over 7,000 volumes a year. The library regularly receives over 1,000 periodicals, and also the serial publications of learned societies. It is also a depository for government documents of the United States Department of Agriculture and the various State Experiment Stations.

Under Construction

Machmer Hall. A $1,000,000 structure, adjacent to North College, providing instruction facilities for several departments in Arts and Science.

Van Meter House. An addition to the wing completed in 1955 is now in progress. Expected completion date, September 1956.

Goessmann Laboratory Addition. A $1,747,000 addition to the chemistry laboratory facilities. Expected date of completion, September 1957.

Student Union Building. A $2,000,000 structure for recreational facilities for all students, located in the center of the campus adjacent to the pond. Expected date of completion, September 1957.

Women's Physical Education Building. A $1,621,000 structure located adjacent to the women's residence area, providing complete facilities for the Department of Physical Education for Women, including gymnasium and swimming pool. Expected date of completion, September 1957.

Public Health Building. A $1,281,000 structure to accommodate public health services in western Massachusetts, the University's department of bacteriology and public health and the School of Nursing. This building will form the core unit of a $3,500,000 science center.

UNDERGRADUATE CURRICULA

Undergraduate instruction is organized into the College of Arts and Science, the College of Agriculture, the Schools of Business Administration, Engineering, Home Economics, Nursing, and the Division of Physical Education for Men.

This section of the catalogue deals with the opportunities for study and the curricula available in each of these departments of the University.

COLLEGE OF ARTS AND SCIENCE

FRED V. CAHILL, JR., *Dean*

The College of Arts and Science includes those departments offering instruction in the humanities, the physical and biological sciences, and the social sciences. Its curricula comprise both general education courses essential for enlightened citizenship and those necessary for specialized and professional training.

The work of the first two years is largely prescribed, specialization occurring in the junior and senior years. The concentration of the junior and senior years gives the student as high a proficiency in his field of specialization as is possible without sacrificing the objectives and requirements of a well-rounded education.

The majority of the curriculum prescribed for all freshmen and sophomores, regardless of their fields of specialization, is taught in the College. In addition, each of the departments of the College offers courses leading to undergraduate specialization in its particular field. There are also curricula designed to meet the special needs of pre-medical, pre-dental, and pre-veterinary students; of those planning to train as laboratory technicians or to enter the public health service; and of those interested in social work.

In sum, the College provides training for: persons primarily seeking a liberal education; those who, wishing to go on to specialization in one of the fields of the College, seek a liberal education and the beginnings of specialization; those, in other parts of the University, whose basic professional interests are outside the range of, but who receive liberal education within, the College.

72

FRESHMAN YEAR

1st Semester	Credits	2nd Semester	Credits
English 1	2	English 2	2
Speech 3	1	Speech 4	1
Math. 7 or 5	3-4	Math. 8 or 10 or 6	3-4
2Zoology 1 or Botany 1	3	2Botany 1 or Zoology 1	3
Foreign Language	3	Foreign Language	3
1Elective	3	1Elective	3
Military 1 (men)	3	Military 2 (men)	2
Physical Education 3 (men)	1	Physical Education 4 (men)	1
Physical Education 7 (women)	2	Physical Education 8 (women)	2

1 Those majoring in biological and physical science departments take Chemistry 1 and 2 (or 4); others take History 5 and 6 .

2 Those not majoring in biological and physical science departments may take Chemistry 1 and 2 in place of Zoology 1 and Botany 1, or substitute Geology 27 for either Botany 1 or Zoology 1.

SOPHOMORE YEAR

1st Semester	Credits	2nd Semester	Credits
English 25	3	English 26	3
Sociology 28, Psychology 26, or Economics 25	3	Economics 25, Sociology 28, or Psychology 26	3
1Science	3-4	1Science	3-4
12 electives	6-7	12 electives	6-7
Military 25 (men)	2	Military 26 (men)	2
Physical Education 27 (women)	2	Physical Education 28 (women)	2
Physical Education 33 (men)	1	Physical Education 34 (men)	1

1 In selecting the required science course and the two electives, students should be guided by the recommendations for sophomore work given under the descriptions of junior-senior curricula that follow.

JUNIOR-SENIOR CURRICULA

Major work is available in the following departments during the last two years.

Bacteriology - R. L. FRANCE, Adviser

The courses in bacteriology have been planned to furnish (1) a general and applied training for students majoring in other departments who must have some knowledge of bacteria and (2) specialization for those contemplating a professional career in bacteriology. An optional curriculum in medical technology is offered for young women who plan to qualify as medical technologists. This program provides a broad basic training in the physical and biological sciences and more than meets the basic collegiate requirements of the Registry of Medical Technologists of the American Society of Clinical Pathologists.

Students majoring in bacteriology or taking the optional curriculum in medical technology should complete the following

73

courses in their sophomore year: Chemistry 29 and 30, Zoology 35, and Bacteriology 31. Physics 25 and 26 should be elected junior year by bacteriology majors and may be elected by majors in medical technology.

During the junior and senior years the following courses should be taken: Chemistry 51, 52, and 79; Zoology 69 and 84; Public Health 61, 62, and 88; Bacteriology 51, 52, 56, 81, 82, 85, and 96. Students in medical technology take Chemistry 80 as an additional course in Chemistry and elect Zoology 51 in place of Zoology 84, and Bacteriology 92 in place of Bacteriology 96; and should be prepared to spend a year's internship in a certified hospital laboratory after graduation.

Botany   T. T. KOZLOWSKI, Adviser

The purpose of the courses in botany is to provide a thorough background for specialization in the science, and to support and supplement the work of other fields in which knowledge of plant life is held to be important. Certain courses should likewise prove of interest and value to the general student.

Those who wish to specialize in botany will find here an ample field and an adequate opportunity for advanced undergraduate study. Post-graduate training, often with provision for financial aid, is available in most graduate institutions, and many teaching, research and industrial positions in schools and colleges, experiment stations, federal and state services and private enterprise are open to the trained botanist.

The curriculum offers to the student an opportunity to acquire either a broad general knowledge of botany, or to devote himself to more extensive study in one of the major divisions of the science, such as Plant Morphology and Taxonomy, Plant Physiology, Mycology and Plant Pathology. Under the direction of his adviser each student selects a program of courses in botany and other sciences, humanities and arts which seems best adapted to his particular botanical objectives.

Specialization in botany assumes the satisfactory completion of certain basic and supporting courses prior to the junior year. These include Botany 1, 25 and 26; Chemistry 1, 2 and 29; and a modern language. Two years of German are advised.

The junior-senior program requires that courses in botany to the amount of 15-30 credits be chosen under the guidance of the adviser. He will also make recommendations in regard to electives.

Chemistry   W. S. RITCHIE, Adviser

The objectives in chemistry are to give the student an understanding of the subject which will enable him to appreciate the relation of chemistry to other sciences, and to industry, and to provide training for those who intend to become teachers and workers in the allied sciences, and for those who wish to go on to graduate study and into a professional career in chemistry. Completion of the course in chemistry fits the student for positions in the chemical industries and related fields as well as in the agricultural industry, for employment in state and Federal agricultural experiment stations and commercial laboratories, for teaching and for graduate study.

Students planning to major in chemistry should elect German in the freshman year. The sophomore program should include Chemistry 29, 30; Mathematics 29, 30; and Physics 25, 26, German 25, 28.

In the junior year the chemistry major takes Chemistry 51, 52, 65, and 66. In the senior he takes Chemistry 83, and elects at least three of the following courses: Chemistry 77, 81, 82, 86, 93, 94.

Economics   P. L. GAMBLE, *Adviser*

In economics the aims are twofold: (1) to give the student an understanding of economic theory and of the application of economic principles to the organization of society; (2) to provide students with the elementary training necessary for further study of economic and business problems.

The department requires that all majors irrespective of the career desired take the following courses: Economics 53, 73, 79, Accounting 25, and Agricultural Economics 79 or Mathematics 62. In addition, each student must select an additional 12 credit hours of work from the Economics curriulum. No major student is permitted to take more than 36 junior-senior credit hours of economics, agricultural economics and business administration courses. In choosing elective courses students are urged to select courses in the humanities and preferably some from the allied fields of history, philosophy, government, psychology, and sociology. Those intending to major in economics should elect Economics 26 in the sophomore year.

For the majors in the Economics department, there are offered courses which may be combined to serve as preparation toward a number of different careers. Among others, possible careers in the following fields are open:

Banking and Finance	Public Utilities
Government Service	Social Security
International Trade	Statistics
Labor and Personnel Relations	Transportation and Communication

75

Education   A. W. Purvis, *Adviser*

The department through its undergraduate program seeks to utilize the forces of the University to prepare teachers for elementary and secondary schools and through its graduate offering to prepare administrators and specialists in public education. Its program is based upon the assumption that teachers and other school personnel should have a broad liberal education, considerable mastery of at least one field, and professional courses which should lead to a knowledge of the persons to be taught, familiarity with the problems to be met, and practice in the best techniques of teaching and supervision.

In order to realize these aims, all students who contemplate teaching as a career should register early, in their freshman year if possible, with the department of education although their work there does not begin until the junior year. Admission to the teacher-training program will be determined largely by a composite rating based on scholarship as shown by University grades (a three-year average at least as high as the University median is desired), success in the beginning course in History of Education, and on personality ratings by members of the staff.

The various programs in Education are as follows:

For ELEMENTARY SCHOOL TEACHING. (Miss O'Leary, adviser.) Either a major or minor in Education. Majors in Education will be expected to elect a junior-senior minor of eighteen hours in a general education field. For both majors and minors:
Junior Year: Education 51, 64, Psychology 94 or Home Economics 70.
Senior Year: One semester block, Education 60, 61, 62, 85 (either semester).
For candidates with artistic or musical ability Art 33, 34, and Music 62 are strongly recommended.

For SECONDARY SCHOOL TEACHING. Students who wish to teach in secondary schools should major in the field to be taught and minor in Education.
Junior Year: Education 51, Psychology 56.
Senior Year: One semester block, Education 52, 85, 88 (either semester).

Note: In both elementary and secondary school teacher training, the schedule is arranged so that the student in his senior year semester block of Education has eight full weeks of Practice Teaching (Ed. 85).

Several cooperative special-field programs for teachers have been developed as follows:

TEACHER-TRAINING IN AGRICULTURE. (C. F. Oliver, adviser.) By a cooperative agreement with the State Division of Vocational

Education, persons otherwise qualified may prepare to teach vocational agriculture by the satisfactory completion of Education 72, 73, and 75. Education 52 is also recommended. To insure a desirable range of preparation, students who contemplate vocational teaching should consult (early in the freshmen year if possible) Professor Oliver and the State Supervisor of Agricultural Teacher-Training. A vocational teacher-training certificate is awarded by the Vocational Division to those who fully qualify.

TEACHER-TRAINING IN HOME ECONOMICS. (Miss Strattner, adviser.) These students will major in Home Economics and elect Education 51, Psychology 56 in the junior year, and Education 52, 85 in the senior year semester block.

TRAINING OF TEACHER-COACHES. (S. W. Kauffman, adviser.) These students will major in Physical Education or the subject field to be taught and elect Psychology 56 in the junior year and Education 52, 85 and 88 in the senior year semester block.

TEACHER-TRAINING IN MUSIC. (D. Alviani, adviser.) These students will major in Music and elect Education 51, Psychology 56 in the junior year and Education 52, 85, and 88 in the senior year semester block.

English   M. H. GOLDBERG, *Adviser*

The department of English offers courses in English composition and literature and in speech. Students majoring in this department must conform to the institutional and school requirements for freshman and sophomore years, and in choosing sophomore electives should include two semesters of modern language and one semester of English history.

The courses in English are intended to enable students to express themselves effectively and to appreciate humanistic values and the ideals of English-speaking people throughout their history. They also offer an appropriate, and in some instances an adequate, classroom training for work in such fields as teaching, authorship and editing.

The student majoring in English must earn 30 credits in elective courses in English. However, for six of these he may substitute elective courses in technical writing, other languages or speech.

Entomology   C. P. ALEXANDER, *Adviser*

Courses in entomology serve a variety of functions, such as to give students a broad knowledge of insects, particularly in their relations to man, his crops, his animals, and his health. Students are trained to become entomologists in the service of the United States, or in various state, territorial, or foreign services, especially in the field of agriculture. Other fields of training include forest entomology; medical entomology; control of pests in buildings;

research, technical service or sales work with manufacturers of insecticides; teachers of zoology, particularly entomology, at the university level; and various other branches.

The courses in beekeeping are offered with the following aims:
(1) to meet the increase in vocational opportunities for the production of bees or honey as a business; (2) to study the beekeeping
needs of fruit and truck-crop industries and the part that bees play
in the pollination of flowers; (3) to acquaint the student with a
recreational field that can be made profitable.

Majors are required to take Entomology 26 in the sophomore
year. Strongly recommended sophomore subjects include Botany
25, 26; Zoology 25, 35; Chemistry 29, 30; and either French or
German, or both.

Juniors and seniors should support their work in entomology
with the following courses: Botany 51, 52; Bacteriology 61, 62;
Chemistry 51, 52; Zoology 51, 69, 70; Pomology 56; English 84, and
selected courses in education, floriculture, forestry, horticulture,
and other subjects.

Geology and Mineralogy   L. R. WILSON, *Adviser*

The offerings in geology and mineralogy are intended chiefly
for those who wish to gain some acquaintance with one or more
branches of earth science. For the general student prerequisite
requirements are reduced to a minimum. A program of moderate
specialization may be provided for science majors who are interested in geology.

To major in geology a student must complete thirty credit hours
of work in the department. Those who have completed nine or
more credits in geology in addition to the sophomore courses by
the end of the junior year, and who wish to satisfy major requirements for graduation in the field of geology, will be given individual or group problems in the senior year. The nature of the
work will depend upon student interest and preparation. In any
junior or senior course in geology an additional period per week
without credit may be required of students who specialize in this
field. Chemistry through qualitative analysis and a year's work
in college physics represent minimum requirements in these respective fields for undergraduate specialization in physical geology.
For those interested in pursuing studies in stratigraphy or paleontology, work beyond the freshman year in the systematic aspects
of both botany and zoology is essential for satisfactory progress.

German   F. C. ELLERT, *Adviser*

The courses in German are intended to give a practical knowledge of the language for the purpose of wider reading, research,
and oral communication.

During the junior and senior years each student will complete not less than 24 and not more than 30 credits in the junior-senior German courses. German 59, 79, and 80 are required of all major students. Students planning to use the language professionally are also urged to supplement their courses here with a summer session at an approved school of German.

Government   G. GOODWIN, JR., *Adviser*

The study of government, as presented by the department of history and government, is intended to give the student an understanding of the principles of government and politics and their application to the organization of society, and to provide him with training necessary for positions in government service or further study on the graduate level. It thus may be considered either as pre-law or pre-professional work, in addition to its general cultural value.

Majors in the field should elect Government 25 and 26 in their sophomore year. In the junior and senior years a minimum of eight additional courses in government is recommended; these may be elected from the following: Government 54, 61, 62, 63, 64, 65, 66, 68, 70, 73, 76, 93, 94, or History 53. In addition supporting courses in other fields are recommended; these may be chosen from the fields of history, economics, sociology, psychology, or philosophy.

History   H. W. CARY, *Adviser*

The courses in history, offered by the department of history and government, are intended to impart an understanding of the people of the world and their problems through an analysis of man's development in the past. A major in this field should provide the student with a broad cultural background and a basis for good citizenship. History may have special value for the following groups:

(1) Those who plan to teach history or the social studies.

(2) Those who plan careers in which considerable knowledge of history is desirable. These might be in fields such as law, government service, journalism, and library work.

Prospective majors should ordinarily elect History 31 and 32 in the sophomore year. Government 25 is recommended. Major students must earn a minimum of 26 credit hours in history from the junior and senior courses. The following courses are required: History 59, 60, 91, 92. The student must elect one of the following courses which deal with a period prior to 1500: History 51, 62, 73.

79

In addition, he should select, in consultation with his adviser, a program of elective courses from fields related to the major.

Journalism   A. B. MUSGRAVE, *Adviser*

The journalism program is concerned with (1) the study of communication problems relevant to the media of mass communication, and (2) the best utilization of the University's liberal education resources by students who plan careers in newspaper work, communications research, public relations, magazine and radio journalism, or some other field of communications.

For such students the journalism courses are intended to provide both increased communication skill and relevant background. The courses may have special value also for students who plan to go into government service, law, education, and similar fields in which knowledge of the process and effects of communication is particularly useful.

The courses emphasize (1) the professional responsibilities of the mass media in a free society, (2) communications research, and (3) study of the reporting of those issues in public affairs which may be evaluated as contemporary history.

English-Journalism majors take five literature courses, English 84, and four journalism courses. Such students should select, in consultation with their adviser, an integrated program of elective courses to obtain the broadest and most liberal training.

Mathematics   A. E. ANDERSEN, *Adviser*

The department offers courses designed to furnish a cultural background as well as a foundation for both undergraduate and graduate work in such fields of science as physics and chemistry, in engineering and in other technical subjects.

The courses recommended for majors in the department are designed to prepare students for high school teaching, graduate study in mathematics, actuarial work, statistical work, or work as engineering aides.

All majors are required to take Mathematics 29 and 30 and Physics 25 and 26 in the sophomore year. In the junior and senior years each major must take Mathematics 53, 54, 91, and 92 and must, in addition, complete at least 12 credits in other junior-senior courses. Prospective majors should consult the department, for a list of recommended courses.

Music   D. J. ALVIANI, *Adviser*

The courses in music are open to all university students depending on their training, experience, ability and talent. The department of music supervises and directs the activities of a number of musical organizations which offer opportunities to students for the development of skill in playing, singing, acting, and attitudes for artistic growth of intellectual, practical, and social intelligence. Music courses furnish an understanding of the history and interpretation of music, a knowledge of basic theory, and training in applied music.

The music major student is expected to adjust his elective courses to fit his individual needs in preparation for work in the fields of: music education, music merchandising, private teaching, the ministry, the armed forces, church music, private school music, kindergarten music, bi-subject teaching, music library administration, music in radio, television, recreation and industry, institutional music therapy, and advanced study in music.

During the sophomore year all music majors must elect Music 25 and 26. They are required to take four semesters of Applied Music before graduation, two of which must be in Piano. Each major student will be required to pass an examination in Piano not later than junior year.

Philosophy   C. SHUTE, *Adviser*

Philosophy seeks a comprehensive understanding of the various areas of man's experience in their interrelatedness. In the context of the historically important theories, the courses concentrate on methods of inquiry into the persisting questions of philosophy, standards of thought, clarification of ethical and aesthetic values, and the bases of criticism.

The student majoring in this subject will complete a minimum of 21 credits in junior-senior courses in philosophy. A wide range of supplementary courses is advised, among which the following are suggested: Art 75, 78; Chemistry 88; Education 51; English 72, 74, 79, 80; French 51, 52; German 56, 57; Government 66, 71, 72; Mathematics 72; Music 51, 52; Psychology 61, 90; Sociology 53, 82.

Physics   W. F. POWERS, *Adviser*

The courses give opportunity for the study of basic physical laws. From these courses students may make a selection to satisfy a major in physics, or to comply with requirements for graduate study.

Majors must take Physics 25, 26 and Mathematics 29, 30 in the sophomore year. Juniors and seniors are advised to support their physics major courses by electives in mathematics, such as differential equations and vector analysis. Since the interests of major students vary, the department adviser will be glad to make suggestions regarding programs of study.

Pre-Medical and Pre-Dental Curriculum

Advisory Committee: G. L. Woodside, *Chairman,* G. W. Alderman, L. M. Bartlett, W. S. Ritchie, J. H. Smith.

Pre-medical and pre-dental students should register with a member of the pre-medical advisory committee as soon as possible after entering the university. Pre-veterinary students may register with the pre-medical advisory committee or with the school of their choice. Pre-medical or pre-dental students will be assigned a member of the committee as adviser, and as long as they remain pre-medical or pre-dental students they will continue under this adviser. The assignment is made alphabetically as follows: A-C, Dr. Woodside; D-G, Dr. Smith; H-L, Dr. Ritchie; M-R, Dr. Bartlett; S-Z, Mr. Alderman. During the second semester of the student's sophomore year the committee will review his academic record and will schedule an interview for the purpose of considering his general qualifications. After careful study, specific recommendations will be made as to whether the student should continue with the curriculum or change his objective and choose another major. Each student remaining in the program will again be interviewed during his junior year.

Medical schools do not look with favor on over-specialization in any field. They stress the importance of a broad general education. Therefore, in addition to a major of the student's own choosing, he should include courses beyond the introductory level in other fields, especially the humanities and social sciences. The student is to decide upon his electives only after consultation with his adviser.

FRESHMAN YEAR

1st Semester	Credits	2nd Semester	Credits
Mathematics 7	3	Mathematics 8 or 10	3
English 1, Composition	2	English 2, Composition	2
Speech 3	1	Speech 4	1
Chemistry 1, General	3	Chemistry 2 or 4, Gen. 3 or 4	
Botany 1 or Zoology 1	3	Zoology 1 or Botany 1	3
German 1 or 5, or French 1, 5, 15	3	German 2 or 6, or French 2, 6, 16	3
Military 1 (men)	3	Military 2 (men)	2
Physical Education 3 (men)	1	Physical Education 4 (men)	1
Physical Education 7 (women)	2	Physical Education 8 (women)	2

SOPHOMORE YEAR

1st Semester	Credits	2nd Semester	Credits
English 25, Humane Letters	3	English 26, Humane Letters	3
Econ. 25 or Psych. 26 or Soc. 28	3	Econ. 25 or Psych. 26 or Soc. 28	3
Physics 25	4	Physics 26	4
Foreign Language	3	Foreign Language	3
Elective*	3	Chem. 29	4
Military 25 (men)	2	Military 26 (men)	2
Physical Education 33 (men)	1	Physical Education 34 (men)	1
Physical Education 27 (women)	2	Physical Education 28 (women)	2

  * Students who plan to major in Chemistry elect Chemistry 29, to be followed by Chemistry 30 during the second semester. The second social science is then deferred until the junior year.

JUNIOR YEAR

1st Semester	Credits	2nd Semester	Credits
Chemistry 51, Organic	4	Chemistry 52, Organic	4
Zoology 71, Comp. Vert. Anatomy	4	Zoology 72, Vert. Embryology	4
History	3	1Electives	9
1Electives	6		

SENIOR YEAR

1st Semester	Credits	2nd Semester	Credits
Chemistry 30	4	1Electives	15
1Electives	11		

1 The electives must bring the total junior-senior credits in some one department to 15 to meet the University requirement for graduation.

Psychology   C. C. NEET, Adviser

The courses in the psychology department are designed (1) to impart an understanding of behavior and the application of this knowledge to problems of human adjustment; and (2) to give preparation for professional work in psychology and related fields.

Careers open to psychology majors include: teaching and research, guidance, psychometrics, personnel and industrial work, child welfare, abnormal and clinical psychology, opinion polling, social work and government service. Additional training is required for certain of these careers.

Students planning to major in psychology should elect Psychology 26 and Psychology 28 in the sophomore year. In the junior and senior years majors are advised to take a minimum of 24 credits in psychology. Courses 51 and 90 are required. As broad a cultural background as major programs will permit is advised.

Majors planning careers primarily in experimental and physiological psychology should plan to take one or more courses during their four years in mathematics, physics, and zoology. Those planning careers in abnormal and clinical psychology and in child welfare should elect specified courses in education, English, sociology, and zoology; while those planning careers in psychometrics, guidance, personnel and industrial work, and government service should take certain courses in business administration, economics, education, industrial engineering, and sociology.

Public Health   R. L. FRANCE, *Adviser*

The Department of Bacteriology, through the cooperation of several departments of the university and the Massachusetts Department of Public Health, offers curricula for (1) a limited number of students interested in the many phases of public health service for which graduate work in medical or engineering schools is not essential; and (2) students planning graduate work in sanitary engineering.

Particular attention will be given to the training of sanitarians, district sanitary officers, food and milk inspectors, water and sewage treatment plant operators, technicians for public health laboratories, and agents for local boards of health. Students planning graduate work in sanitary engineering must also take Mathematics 29 and 30 (calculus) before the end of their junior year.

Students electing this major should complete the following courses during their sophomore year: Chemistry 29, Physics 25 and 26, Zoology 35 and Bacteriology.

During junior and senior years the following courses should be completed: Chemistry 51 and 52; Bacteriology 81 and 90; Public Health 61, 62, 63, 84, and 88. Supporting courses in other departments will be selected with the guidance of an adviser.

Recreation Leadership   W. E. RANDALL, *Adviser*

The department seeks to prepare students for positions involving administrative, supervisory, and program leadership responsibilities in municipal recreation agencies, voluntary and youth-serving agencies, hospitals, and industrial and institutional organizations. Students who plan a career in recreation should register as early as possible with the department.

The program is designed to provide opportunities for a broad liberal education, a knowledge and understanding of people and society, activity skills and resource knowledge, professional competency, and practical experience in various leadership situations. Major students are required to take the following courses: Recreation Leadership 51, 52, 74, 77, 79, 80; Education 66; Psychology 62, and 93 or 94; Sociology 51, and one of the following: Sociology 52, 53, 54, 57, 68, 75. Two summers of leadership experience are required, without course credit: one summer should be in an organized camp and the other on a playground or in an institutional program. Each major student should have a working knowledge and some skill in each of the following: arts and crafts, music, dramatics, nature, sports, social recreation, public speaking, and first aid and safety.

Sophomores should elect Psychology 26, Sociology 28, and Government 25. Economics 25 and Philosophy 25 are recommended.

Romance Languages
S. C. GODING, *French Adviser*
J. M. FERRIGNO, S. F. WEXLER, *Spanish Advisers*

Two majors are offered: French and Spanish. The courses in these curricula are intended to give rounded and practical knowledge of the languages for the purpose of wider reading, research, and oral communication, leading to a better understanding of all aspects of the intellectual, spiritual, and material attainments of the nations concerned.

Students majoring in French or Spanish are required to complete at least 30 approved junior-senior credits, six of which may be in English or another foreign language.

Sociology
J. H. KORSON, *Adviser*

The courses in sociology are planned with two aims in view:

(1) To give the student an understanding of the factors which influence men in their activities and interests as members of society, and

(2) To prepare those students who are interested in teaching at the elementary or high school level; or those students interested in careers with government agencies; or in careers as social workers with state or private agencies to gain the pre-professional courses necessary before embarking on such careers. Some agencies require work on the graduate level before full-time employment is obtained, while others offer in-training opportunities to graduate majors in sociology. Programs for students interested in teaching are prepared in cooperation with the Education department.

All major students are required to take Economics 25 and Psychology 26. At least 24 junior-senior credits in sociology are required. Students are required to take Sociology 53 and 82 and are urged also to select courses in economics, history, government, psychology, and as many in the humanities as possible.

Social Work
J. H. KORSON, *Adviser*

The American Association of Schools of Social Work indicates that the pre-professional subjects most closely related to professional work in this field are economics, political science, psychology, and sociology. The Association recommends that prospective students of social work or social administration take not fewer than 12 semester hours in one of these subjects while taking less in others. It also recognizes the value of courses in biology, history, English, as well as other subjects contributing to a broad cultural background for the student.

Speech   A. E. NIEDECK, *Adviser*

The program in speech is planned to serve the students in the entire university who wish training in oral communication, and to provide an opportunity for students in the College of Arts and Sciences to major in speech. Areas of specialization within the major include Rhetoric and Public Address, Oral Interpretation, Theater, Radio and Television. All students planning to major in speech should elect Psychology 26 in their sophomore year. Required electives in other departments during the junior or senior year include English 55 and 68, and Philosophy 82.

Zoology   G. L. WOODSIDE, *Adviser*

The courses in zoology have two major aims: (1) to offer students an opportunity to develop an understanding and appreciation of the scientific method as a part of a liberal education; and (2) to provide training for prospective graduate students in biology, medicine, dentistry, and related fields, as well as future teachers and laboratory technicians in the biological sciences.

The minimum requirements for graduation are Zoology 1, 71, 72; 69 or 70 or 74; 50 or 53; and two of the following three: 35, 83, 84; Chemistry 1, 2, 29, 30, 51, and 52 (33 may be substituted for 51 and 52); Physics 25 and 26.

COLLEGE OF AGRICULTURE

DALE H. SIELING, *Dean*

The College of Agriculture with its several departments offers a broad general education with specific training in some phase of agriculture or horticulture. Upon the completion of the requirements for graduation, the student will have devoted about one-quarter of his time to pure science, one-quarter to social and humanistic studies, and about one-half to applied science and technology in agriculture and horticulture.

A broad choice of electives within the required courses of each curriculum gives the student the opportunity to prepare for (1) actual agricultural production; (2) research, teaching, or extension work; or (3) industrial work.

Each department of the school has specific requirements for graduation which are included in the descriptive matter under the name of the department. To prevent overspecialization, each student is required to elect at least 12 junior-senior credits in some other school of the University; one-half of these credits to be in the humanities and social sciences.

During the first semester of the freshman year, students interested in teaching vocational agriculture, extension work, or specializing in research work, should consult with the head of the department in which they plan to major.

The School comprises the following departments: Agricultural Economics and Farm Management, Agricultural Engineering, Agronomy, Animal Husbandry, Dairy Industry, Floriculture, Food Technology, Forestry and Wildlife Management, Landscape Architecture, Olericulture, Pomology, Poultry Science, and Veterinary Science. Students may major in any of these departments except Veterinary Science and Agricultural Engineering.

Curricula in Agriculture

All students will take the following uniform curriculum during the first two years:

AGRICULTURE

FRESHMAN YEAR

1st Semester	Credits	2nd Semester	Credits
English 1, Composition	2	English 2, Composition	2
Speech 3	1	Speech 4	1
[1]Mathematics 7, Algebra and Trigonometry		[1]Mathematics 8 or 10	3
[2]Chemistry 1, General		[2]Chemistry 2, General	3
Botany 1, General		Zoology 1, General	3
Military 1 (men)		[3]Elective	3
Agriculture 1		Military 2 (men)	2
Physical Education 3 (men)		Physical Education 4 (men)	1
Physical Education 7 (women)	2	Physical Education 8 (women)	2
		Hygiene (women)	1

[1] Candidates for the Bachelor of Vocational Agriculture degree will take Government 25 and 26 in place of Mathematics.

Students who expect to take Calculus in the sophomore year should elect Mathematics 10.

[2] Those intending to major in Landscape Architecture and Ornamental Horticulture will take Chemistry 1 the first semester and Botany 1 the second semester. They may substitute a foreign language or History 5 and 6 for Zoology 1 and Chemistry 2.

[3] Students intending to major in Agricultural Economics, Floriculture, Food Management, Food Technology, Landscape Architecture and Ornamental Horticulture, Olericulture, and Pomology will take Horticulture 2. Animal Husbandry and Dairy Industry majors will take Animal Husbandry 2. Forestry and Wildlife Management majors will take Forestry 26. Students undecided as to major as well as those majoring in Agronomy and Poultry Husbandry will take History 6.

SOPHOMORE YEAR

1st Semester	Credits	2nd Semester	Credits
English 25, Humane Letters	3	English 26, Humane Letters	3
Econ. 25, Psych. 26 or Soc. 28	3	Econ. 25, Psych. 26 or Soc. 28	3
[1]A Science	3-4	[1]A Science	3-4
[2]Electives	6	[2]Electives	6
Military 25 (men)	2	Military 26 (men)	2
Physical Education 27 (women)	2	Physical Education 28 (women)	2
Physical Education 33 (men)	1	Physical Education 34 (men)	1

[1] To be selected from the following:

Bacteriology, 31	Physics 25, 26
Botany 25, 26, 28, 30	Zoology 25, 35
Chemistry 29, 30, 33	Entomology 26
Geology 27, 28	Civil Engineering 27
Mathematics 29, 30	

[2] The student will be guided in his selections by his major adviser.

JUNIOR-SENIOR CURRICULA

At the end of the sophomore year each student selects one of the following curricula as his major to complete his collegiate training.

Agricultural Economics and
Farm Management   A. H. LINDSEY, *Adviser*

The purpose of the Agricultural Economics and Farm Management major is to train students for positions in those private and government institutions servicing the agricultural industry and to assist in the training of farm managers.

The department maintains an inventory of current price information and agricultural production reports from which price study and analysis may be made. Statistical machines are also available for computation and analysis. The laboratories of the department must be found in business institutions and on farms in Massachusetts with which contact is maintained.

Two curricula are available.

AGRICULTURAL ECONOMICS
JUNIOR YEAR

1st Semester	Credits	2nd Semester	Credits
Ag. Ec. 55, Mark'g Farm Prod.	3	Ag. Ec. 56, Coop. in Agri	3
Ag. Ec. 57, Agri. Credit	3	Agricultural Electives	6
Agricultural Electives	6	General Electives	6
General Electives	3		

SENIOR YEAR

1st Semester	Credits	2nd Semester	Credits
Accounting 25	3	Agri. Ec. 76, Farm Mgt.	2
Stat. 79, El. Statis.	3	Agricultural Electives	3
Ag. Ec. 75, Farm Mgt.	3	General Electives	11
Agricultural Electives	3		
General Electives	3		

All Agricultural Economics majors must take the courses listed above. Specialization may be one of the three following fields: (1) Animal products, (2) Fruits and Vegetables, (3) Feeds and Fertilizers.

The following courses should be completed for each of these specialized fields:

Animal Products	Fruits and Vegetables	Feed and Fertilizer
An. Husb. 53	Pomology 53	Agronomy 51
An. Husb. 54	Pomology 77	Agronomy 52
Dairy 52	Olericulture 74	Agronomy 78
Dairy 77	Olericulture 78	An. Husb. 51
Dairy 78	Food Technology 75	An. Husb. 78
Poultry 75		An. Husb. 78
		Poultry 56

FARM MANAGEMENT
JUNIOR YEAR

1st Semester	Credits	2nd Semester	Credits
Agri. Ec. 55, Mktg. Farm Prod.	3	Agri. Ec. 56, Coop. Agri.	3
Agri. Ec. 57, Agri. Cr.	3	Agronomy 52, Soil Util.	3
An. Husb. 51, Nutrition	3	Agri. Ec. 78, Land Econ.	3
Electives	6	Bus. Law 70	3
		Electives	3

SENIOR YEAR

1st Semester	Credits	2nd Semester	Credits
Agri. Ec. 71, Theory	3	Agri. Ec. 76, Farm Mgt.	2
Ag. Ec. 75, Farm Mgt.	3	An. Husb. 78, Dairy Cattle Prod.	4
Agronomy 51, Field Crops	3	Poultry 78, Management	2
Forestry 55, Mgt. Woodlands	3	Electives	8
Electives	3		

Agricultural Engineering   W. G. COLBY, *Adviser*

The department offers various courses in support of the various fields of agriculture. Those wishing major work in this field may get it under an option in the School of Engineering (page 113).

Agronomy

The courses are designed to give instruction concerning the basic knowledge of the soil and its management, fertilizers, and their uses as related to the principal products of the field. Crop improvement practices and the science of crop improvement are stressed for those who are interested in agronomy as a specialty.

There is sufficient flexibility within the curriculum to allow the student to specialize in soil science, plant science, soil conservation or general agronomy. Those students who have a desire to receive training which will qualify them for investigational work in these fields may obtain it by selecting appropriate supporting science or vocational subjects as electives. This training equips them to serve as specialists in one of these selected fields for industrial corporations and may serve also as training for extension or teaching work.

JUNIOR YEAR

1st Semester	Credits	2nd Semester	Credits
Agron. 57, Soil Formation	3	Agron. 52, Soil Utilization	3
Zoology 53, Genetics	3	Electives	9
Electives	6		

SENIOR YEAR

1st Semester	Credits	2nd Semester	Credits
Agron. 51, Field Crops	3	Agron. 78, Fertilizer and Soil	
Chem. 51, Organic	4	Fertility	3
Electives	9	Chem. 52, Organic	4
		Electives	9

Animal Husbandry
D. J. HANKINSON, *Adviser*

The broad purpose of the animal husbandry major is that of providing the basic training for specialists in animal husbandry. Upon graduation, opportunities are available in the practical, scientific or commercial fields of animal husbandry; i.e., livestock farming, research, teaching, administration, or in the business phases of the livestock industry.

Students who major in the department of animal husbandry must successfully complete one summer of placement training as a requirement for graduation.

JUNIOR YEAR

1st Semester	Credits	2nd Semester	Credits
An. Husb. 51, Nutrition of Farm An.	3	An. Husb. 56, 56A, Beef and Sheep Production	
An. Husb. 53, El. Meat Packing	3	Electives	
Electives			

SENIOR YEAR

1st Semester	Credits	2nd Semester	Credits
An. Husb. 75, An. Breeding	4	An. Husb. 76, Animal Breeding Practice	
An. Husb. 81, Seminar	1	An. Husb. 78, Dairy Cattle Production	3
Electives		An. Husb. 82, Seminar	1
		Electives	

Dairy Industry
D. J. HANKINSON, *Adviser*

Major students in dairy industry receive training in the testing, handling, and processing of milk, ice cream, butter, cheese, and other milk products. Practical application is made of chemistry, bacteriology, economics, and engineering in the many phases of dairy work.

Dairy industry graduates may secure responsible positions with commercial dairy manufacturing firms, or with equipment and supply firms. Opportunities are offered also for positions as teachers in high schools and colleges, for service in the fields of extension and research, and for sanitation and public health work with city, state or federal agencies.

Major students in dairy industry must successfully complete one summer of placement training in a dairy plant. It is recommended that this requirement be met during the summer immediately following the sophomore year of University residence.

JUNIOR YEAR

1st Semester	Credits	2nd Semester	Credits
Dairy Ind. 77, Butter and Cheese	4	Dairy Ind. 50, Judging	1
Chem. 51, Organic	4	Dairy Ind. 52, Mkt. Milk	4
Bact. 61, Public Health	3	Chem. 52, Organic	4
Electives	6	Electives	6

SENIOR YEAR

1st Semester	Credits	2nd Semester	Credits
Dairy Ind. 75, Chemistry	3	Dairy Ind. 78, Ice Cream	4
Dairy Ind. 79, Seminar	1	Dairy Ind. 80, Seminar	1
Bact. 81, Applied	4	Bact. 90, sanitary	3
Agr. Engin. 80 Food Process Eng.	3	Electives	9
Electives	6		

Fisheries Technology
C. R. FELLERS, *Adviser*

An optional curriculum in fisheries technology has been prepared by the Food Technology department. Excellent opportunities exist for employment by Federal, State, and private industry in this rapidly expanding field.

Students taking this curriculum will follow the regular Food Technology curriculum with certain substitutions and additions. The department head should be consulted before the student begins his second year.

Floriculture
C. L. THAYER, *Adviser*

The courses in floriculture provide for a comprehensive and detailed study of the practices and principles involved in the production, marketing and uses of cut flowers, flowering and foliage plants grown outdoors and under glass. Opportunities available to graduates may include: positions in various fields of commercial floriculture, such as production, wholesale marketing and retailing; employment in nurseries, on private estates and in conservatories; positions in the professional field, including graduate study, teaching in colleges and secondary schools, research and extension work under state, Federal, or other supervision.

It is advantageous for the student to determine, as soon as possible, the type of position for which he wishes to fit himself since the choice of elective courses will depend largely on his decision.

All major students in floriculture must successfully complete one summer of placement training in work related to their major objective and approved by the head of the department. It is recommended that this requirement for graduation be met during the summer following the freshman or sophomore year.

As sophomores majors are advised to take Chemistry 29 and Botany 26 for their sciences. First semester electives should be Botany 25 and Olericulture 25; second semester Entomology 26 and Floriculture 26.

JUNIOR YEAR

1st Semester	Credits	2nd Semester	Credits
Flori. 51, Greenhouse Mgt.	3	Flori. 52, Flower Arrangement	3
Flori. 79, Conservatory Plants or	2	Flori. 54, Greenhouse Const.	3
Flori. 81, Gardens and		Plant Breeding 52, Methods	3
Borders	3	Botany 52, Advanced Plant	
Zoology 53, Prin. of Genetics	3	Pathology	3
Entomology 51, Pests of Special		Electives	3
Crops	3		
Botany 51, Plant Pathology	3		
Electives	2-3		

SENIOR YEAR

1st Semester	Credits	2nd Semester	Credits
Flori. 75, Commercial	3	Flori. 76, Commercial	3
Flori. 79 or	2	Flori. 82, Seminar	3
Flori. 81	3	Botany 68, Physiology	3
Botany 67, Physiology	3	Electives	8
Electives	5-9		

Food Management   C. R. FELLERS, *Adviser*

The curriculum in food management is offered as an option in the Food Technology department. The program is designed to give the student a general well-rounded background of arts and sciences, coupled with training in subjects useful to the hotel and restaurant industries. The nature of the food service industry requires persons with broad, general backgrounds of business training coupled with a scientific knowledge of foods.

In the sophomore year food management majors should take Food Management 33, Chemistry 33, and Accounting 25 the first semester and Home Economics 30, Bacteriology 31, and Accounting 26 the second semester.

JUNIOR YEAR

1st Semester	Credits	2nd Semester	Credits
Food Mgt. 67, Food Prep. &		Food Mgt. 68, Kitchen Adm.	3
Serv.	3	Food Tech. 52, Food Prod.	3
Food Tech. 51, Introductory	3	Home Ec. 52, Nutrition & Diet	3
*Dairy 25, General	3	Accounting 64, Cost Acct.	3
†Electives	6	An Hus. 54, Meat Processing	2
		†Elective	2-3

SENIOR YEAR

1st Semester	Credits	2nd Semester	Credits
Food Tech. 71, Food Sci. Lit.	2	Food Tech. 72, Food Sci. Lit.	2
Food Mgt. 77, Food Service Prac.	3	Food Mgt. 78, Stewarding	3
Home Ec. 91, Quant. Food Prep.		Ind. Adm. 64, Personnel Mgt.	3
& Institutional Mgt.	3	Bus. Law 70, Bus. Law I	3
Poult. 75, Marketing Poult.		†Electives	4
Prod.	2		
†Electives	5		

† Suggested electives:

Dairy 52, 78	Speech 91
Economics 79	Journalism 85
Finance 65, 75	Marketing 52, 54
Home Economics 62	Olericulture 74
Industrial Administration 83	Public Health 61, 63

* An additional elective may be substituted for Dairy 25.

Food Technology   C. R. FELLERS, *Adviser*

The curriculum in food technology provides scientific and applied training in the principles concerned with the processing, preservation, and packaging of foods and food products. Both home and commercial methods of food preservation are considered. Practical work includes canning, freezing, dehydration, fermentation and salting. Methods of manufacture of jams, jellies, fruit juicies, and beverages are a part of the course work. An effort is made to apply the student's background in chemistry, physics, and bacteriology to food technology problems and food analysis.

The curriculum gives the student a broad science background with specialized knowledge in food processing and preservation. Special courses are offered for home economics majors who plan to teach or do extension work in foods. Major fields open to graduates include: (1) commercial work in cannery, freezer and other plant operations; (2) control and analytical work related to food products; (3) government food inspection and grading; (4) technological work in government and industry.

Ambitious students are encouraged to acquire the background which will enable them to pursue graduate work and research in the application of scientific knowledge to the technology of foods.

The selection of supporting courses depends upon the objective of the student, which should be determined as early as possible.

Food technology majors should take Physics 25 and 26 and Chemistry 29 and 30 in the sophomore year; also, if possible, Bacteriology 31. Students planning to take Physical Chemistry should complete Mathematics 29 and 30.

JUNIOR YEAR

1st Semester	Credits	2nd Semester	Credits
Food Tech. 51, Introductory	3	Food Tech. 52, Food Prod.	3
Chemistry 51, Organic	4	Chemistry 52, Organic	4
Bacteriology 51	3	Bacteriology 82, Applied	3
Agr. Engin. 80, Food Eng.	3	Agr. Engin. 82, Refrigeration	2
Elective		Electives	

SENIOR YEAR

1st Semester	Credits	2nd Semester	Credits
Food Tech. 61, Industrial Technology	3	Food Tech. 62, Industrial Technology	3
Food Tech. 71, Food Science Literature	2	Food Tech. 72, Food Science Literature	2
Food Tech. 91, Analysis of Food Prod.	3	Food Tech. 92, Anal. Meth. & Instrumentation	3
Chemistry 79, Elem. Biol. or	4	Food Tech. 98, Sensory Evaluation Meth.	2
Chemistry 65, Physical	3	Chemistry 65, Physical	3
Electives		Electives	

SUGGESTED JUNIOR-SENIOR ELECTIVES

Public Health 61, 62, 63
A Foreign Language
Mechanical Engin. 1, 63
Pomology 77
Dairy Ind. 75, 77, 52 or 78
Animal Husbandry 53

Poult. Husbandry 75
Olericulture 73, 74
Botany 66
Home Ec. 30, 52, 54
Food Tech. 85, 95
Chem. Engin. 77, 75
Indus. Engin. 25, 51

Forestry   R. P. HOLDSWORTH, Adviser

The technical curriculum in forestry is concentrated in the field of forest production and management, and leads to the degree of Bachelor of Science. It has professional status, being accredited by the Society of American Foresters.

The freshman and sophomore years are devoted to studies of basic sciences, English, and other subjects of cultural-foundational value. A required group of three courses—forest mensuration, forest harvesting, and plane surveying—is presented in a nine-weeks summer term immediately following the freshman year. During the summer following the sophomore year qualified students are recommended for work giving practical field experience in forestry. Such employment may be with the United States Forest Service or other public and private agencies.

Ten technical courses in forestry are grouped in the junior and senior years in addition to three supporting courses presented by other departments, a required course in history, and six student electives. It is intended that the forestry curriculum be as sound professionally and as broad from the viewpoint of general education as is possible within the limits of four undergraduate years.

Students who complete the forestry curriculum with high academic standing may be admitted to graduate professional schools for work toward a Master of Forestry degree. This is usually obtainable with one year. Seniors are eligible to compete in Federal and State Civil Service examinations.

The forestry courses are open with few exceptions to students other than those concentrating in forestry but should be elected only after consultation with the student's major adviser and with the instructor teaching the course.

Sophomore majors in forestry take Physics 26 and Geology 1 the first semester; Entomology 26, Physics 26, Botany 28 and Agronomy 2 the second semester.

SUMMER (Following Freshman Year)

Forestry 55, Forest Mensuration	Credit, 3
Forestry 78, Forest Harvesting	Credit, 3
Civil Engineering 27, Plane Surveying	Credit, 3

JUNIOR YEAR

1st Semester	Credits	2nd Semester	Credits
Forestry 53, Silvics	3	Forestry 56, Prin. of Silviculture	3
Forestry 59, Protection	3	Forestry 54, Forest Soils	3
Forestry 75, Products	3	Wildlife Mgt. 72, Forest-Animal	
History	3	Relationships	3
Elective (not Forestry)	3	Entomology 72, Forest Ent.	3
		Elective (not Forestry)	3

SENIOR YEAR

1st Semester	Credits	2nd. Semester	Credits
Forestry 81, Regional Silvicul.	3	Forestry 82, Seeding and Planting	3
Forestry 57, Forest Policy & Econ.	3	Forestry 80, 52, Photogrammetry,	
Botany 51, Plant Pathology	3	Forest Mgt.	3
Electives (not Forestry)	6	Forestry 71, Photogrammetry	3
		Electives (not Forestry)	6

Landscape Architecture   R. H. OTTO, *Adviser*

Instruction in this department has two objectives: first a contribution to general education; second, a preparation of students for the practice of landscape architecture. The department offers optional curricula, (1) Professional Landscape Architecture, and (2) Ornamental Horticulture.

The department also offers several elective courses in art (listed and described under Directory of Courses, page 132, which do not constitute a major. These courses are primarily cultural rather than technical and are intended to provide a better appreciation of the arts.

Students following this curriculum are prepared to take up work in landscape architecture, which leads through field experience or post-graduate study to permanent establishment in the profession.

Sophomores in the first semester elect either Botany 25 or Geology 1 for their science and take Landscape Architecture 25 and Civil Engineering 27 as electives. In the second semester the science is either Entomology 26 or Geology 28 and the electives Landscape Architecture 26 and Horticulture 26.

JUNIOR YEAR

1st Semester	Credits	2nd Semester	Credits
Land. Arch. 51, Topography	3	Land. Arch. 52, Elem. of Land.	
Land. Arch. 53, Intro. Design	3	Arch.	3
Hort. 51, Plant Materials	3	Land. Arch. 54, Gen. Design	3
Land. Arch. 79, Const. & Maint.		Land. Arch. 86, City Plan.	3
alternates with Land. Ach.		Hort. 52, Planting Design	3
83, Architecture	3	Electives	3
Elective	3		

SENIOR YEAR

1st Semester	Credits	2nd Semester	Credits
Land. Arch. 81, Adv. Design	3	Land. Arch. 88, Projects in Plan.	3
Land. Arch. 87, Projects in Plan.	3	Land. Arch. 82, Advanced Design	3
Land. Arch. 83, alternates with		Land. Arch. 80, His. & Lit. of	
Land. Arch. 79	3	Land. Arch.	2
Electives	6	Electives	7

SUGGESTED ELECTIVES FOR JUNIOR AND SENIOR YEARS

Agronomy 53, 56	Floriculture 81
Civil Engin. 90	Philosophy 82
Agri. Engin. 51	Art 33, 34, 75, 78
	Land. Arch. 84

Olericulture   G. B. SNYDER, *Adviser*

The courses in olericulture provide a basic training in the scientific principles and applied practices relative to the culture and marketing of vegetable crops. The major courses prepare students for the operation of commercial vegetable farms; for high school, college, and federal work in teaching, research and extension; for state, federal and private produce inspection work; for various opportunities in the retail and wholesale marketing of perishables; and as service men, specialists, and managers in industrial fields allied to the vegetable industry.

The rather broad objectives of the training means that the selection of supporting courses depends upon the specific field in which the student wishes to engage on graduation. This objective should, therefore, be determined as early as possible during the sophomore year.

Majors in olericulture should take the following courses during the first semester of the sophomore year: Botany 25 or Geology 1 and Olericulture 25. In the second semester they should include Chemistry 29, Entomology 26, and Pomology 26.

JUNIOR YEAR

1st Semester	Credits	2nd Semester	Credits
Oleri. 51, Nutr. of Veg. Crops	3	Oleri, 52, Comm. Veg. Prod.	3
Zoology 53, Genetics	3	Botany 68, Plant Physiology	3
Botany 51, Plant Pathology	3	*Electives	9-11
Botany 67, Plant Physiology	3		
*Electives	5		

SENIOR YEAR

1st Semester	Credits	2nd Semester	Credits
Oleri. 73, Prod. Marketing		Oleri. 74, Merchandising of	
Practices	3	Perishables	3
Oleri, 75, Systematic	4	Oleri. 80, Sp. Problems	3
Entomology 51, Pests of Special		*Electives	9-11
Crops	3		
*Electives	5-7		

* Suggested electives:

Agric. Ec. 55, 75, 76	Plant Breed. 52
Agron. 78	Pomology 52
Botany 58	Agric. Engin. 72, 82
Bacteriology 56	Flori. 54
Chem. 33, 79	Food Tech. 51, 75

Ornamental Horticulture

The curriculum in ornamental horticulture offered by the department of landscape architecture is suggested for those preferring to follow the horticultural phase of landscape including (1) nursery practice; (2) landscape planting and construction; and (3) maintenance of landscaped areas, such as parks and semi-public institution grounds.

Sophomores in this major will take Botany 25, Civil Engineering 27, Landscape Architecture 25 in the first semester; Entomology 26, Floriculture 26, and Horticulture 26 in the second.

JUNIOR YEAR

1st Semester	Credits	2nd Semester	Credits
Hort. 51, Plant Materials	3	Hort. 52, Planting Design	3
Land. Arch 51, Topography	3	Land. Arch. 52, Constr. Details	3
Land. Arch. 53, Intro. Design	3	Pomology 26, Small Fruits	3
Landscape Arch. 79, Constr. &		Land. Arch. 54, Gen. Design	3
Maint.	3	Elective	3
Elective	3		

SENIOR YEAR

1st Semester	Credits	2nd Semester	Credits
Flori. 81, Herbaceous Borders	3	Agrostology 56, Turf Mgt.	3
Agrostology 53, Turf Grasses	3	Pomology 56, Spraying	3
Zoology 53, Genetics	3	Plant Breeding 52, Methods	3
Ent. 51, Pests of Sp. Crops	3	Electives	6
Botany 51, Plant Pathology	3		

SUGGESTED ELECTIVES FOR JUNIOR AND SENIOR YEARS

Botany 67, 68, 81	Agronomy 78
Entomology 72	Forestry 56

Pomology

A. P. French, *Adviser*

The pomology courses provide a comprehensive training in the scientific and commercial principles concerned in the growing and marketing of apples, pears, peaches, plums, cherries, and small fruits. Major fields open to graduates include: (1) practical work in connection with the operation of fruit farms; (2) teaching in college, high school, or secondary schools of agriculture; (3) extension work in county, state, or nation; (4) research work with state, federal or private concerns; and (5) commercial work in connection with the manufacture and sale of such supplies as machinery, packages, and spraying and dusting materials. Certain supporting courses are required and their selection depends upon the objective of the student. That objective should, therefore, be determined as early as possible.

An optional curriculum in cranberry technology is offered by the department and is designed to provide a broad training in the fields of knowledge which serve as the foundation of the cranberry industry. Its purpose is to provide future leaders and specialists for the industry.

Sophomores are advised to elect Geology 1, Physics 25, and Olericulture 25 in the first semester; in the second semester they should take Chemistry 29, Entomology 26, and Pomology 26.

Two separate curricula are offered during junior and senior year: one for pomology majors and one for majors in cranberry technology.

Pomology majors follow the curriculum outlined below. The student who wishes to do college teaching, extension work, or research is advised to secure a broad foundation in science and liberal arts, and to plan to enter a graduate school sooner or later. The student whose objective is growing fruit or teaching in a secondary school may need to broaden his training in horticulture and agriculture and will need also all the science and liberal arts courses that can be included in the program. Students majoring in Pomology must successfully complete one summer of placement training on a fruit farm before the beginning of the senior year.

JUNIOR YEAR

1st Semester	Credits	2nd Semester	Credits
Pomology 53, General	3	Pomology 56, Orchard Pest	
Pomology 75, Systematic or	4	Control	3
Pomology 77, Commercial	3	Botany 68, Psychology	3
Botany 51, Plant Pathology	3	Botany 30, Plant Anatomy	3
Botany 67, Physiology	3	English 84, Tech. Writing	3
Elective	3	Electives	3

SENIOR YEAR

1st Semester	Credits	2nd Semester	Credits
Pomology 81, Advanced	3	Pomology 82, Advanced	3
Pomology 75, Systematic or	4	Pomology 84, Seminar	1
Pomology 77, Commercial	3	Electives	12
Pomology 83, Seminar	1		
Zoology 53, Genetics	3		
Electives	5		

Majors in cranberry technology will take the following curriculum. They also must satisfactorily complete a minimum of two summers' practical experience in the cranberry industry before the beginning of the senior year.

JUNIOR YEAR

1st Semester	Credits	2nd Semester	Credits
Chem. 33	3	Pomology 56, Spraying	3
Botany 51, Plant Pathology	3	Ag. Econ. 26, Ag'l Prod.	3
Ent. 51, Pests of Special Crops	3	Electives	
Electives			

SENIOR YEAR

1st Semester	Credits	2nd Semester	Credits
Bot. 67, Plant Psychology	3	Bot. 68, Plant Physiol.	3
Ag. Econ. 55, Marketing	3	Ag. Econ. 56, Cooperatn.	3
Pom. 85, Cranberry Prob.	2	Pom. 86, Cranberry Prob.	2
Electives		Electives	

Poultry Husbandry   T. W. Fox, *Adviser*

The department gives instruction in the science, art and practices of poultry keeping, not only to students specializing in this department, but also to those in other departments who desire supporting work in poultry husbandry. The major courses prepare men for the successful operation of commercial poultry and breeding farms and hatcheries either as owners or managers; for high school, college and federal work in teaching, extension and research; and as service men, specialists and managers in industrial fields allied to the poultry industry.

Students must successfully complete one summer of placement training on a poultry farm or in some business allied to poultry.

Sophomores may choose electives from the list of sophomore sciences or Dairy 25, Animal Husbandry 26, Agricultural Economics 26, Olericulture 25, Pomology 26, Floriculture 26, or Wildlife Management 27.

JUNIOR YEAR

1st Semester	Credits	2nd Semester	Credits
Poultry Husb. 55, Housing and Sanitation	2	Poultry Husb. 52, Incubation and Brooding	3
Poultry Husb. 53, Judging	3	Poultry Husb. 56, Nutrition	3
Zoology 53	3	Electives	
Electives			

SENIOR YEAR

1st Semester	Credits	2nd Semester	Credits
Poultry Husb. 75, Marketing	2	Poultry Husb. 78, Seminar and Farm Management	3-4
Poultry Husb. 77, Breeding	3	Poultry Husb. 76, Turkey Prod.	2
Vet. Sci. 75, Comp. Vet. Anat	3	Vet. Sci. 88, Avian Path.	3
Electives		Electives	

Veterinary Science

Though major work in Veterinary Science is not available, the department does offer supporting courses to assist students who expect to enter the various fields of agriculture, wildlife management, public health, teaching and laboratory work in the biological sciences or veterinary medicine.

Wildlife Management   R. E. Trippensee, *Adviser*

The courses in conservation and wildlife management offered by the department of forestry and wildlife management are designed for those who desire a general understanding of the renewable natural resources as well as those who expect to make a living in the professional field of wildlife management. Courses are available also to students who expect to major in other fields including agriculture, agronomy, economics, forestry, entomology, and education.

Wildlife management is both an applied science and an art and is concerned with the production and control of animal populations on many types of land including farms, forests, and on waste lands and water areas. Thus an understanding of both the origin and management of land and water is necessary. These background phases include geology, agronomy, forestry, and agriculture. Fields of specialization include fisheries management, game, and furbearer management and control of injurious animals, and related fields such as soil conservation, conservation education, and industrial biology.

Studies in wildlife management are closely correlated with the work of the State Conservation Department and the U. S. Fish and Wildlife Service. During the junior and senior years trips are planned to the bait-mixing station of the U. S. Fish and Wildlife Service, the John C. Phillips Wildlife Laboratory at Upton, Mass. and to numerous wildlife projects in the state. Students are urged to attend the northeastern and the American wildlife conferences.

Graduates in this field are eligible to both state and federal civil service examinations, and most of the permanent job opportunities are in public service either with the state or federal government. A limited number of positions are open in private enterprises. Training in the wildlife field is an excellent background for teaching of science in the public schools and for employment as conservation officers. Much research data and many research operations are available to undergraduates through the Massachusetts Cooperative Wildlife Research Station, and students with sufficiently high grades are eligible for graduate work at other universities.

The courses during the first two years are basic educational subjects required to build a background of sound professional training. Sophomores are expected to take Geology 1, Zoology 35, Wildlife Management 27, Agronomy 2, Entomology 26, and Forestry 26.

JUNIOR YEAR

1st Semester	Credits	2nd Semester	Credits
Wildlife Management 71 or 75	3	Botany 26	3
Fores. 55	3	Wildlife Management 70	3
Gov't. 25	3	Wildlife Management 74 or 84	3
Electives*		Gov't. 28	3
		Forestry 56	3
		Electives*	

SENIOR YEAR

1st Semester	Credits	2nd Semester	Credits
Wildlife Management 75 or 71	3	Wildlife Management 74 or 84	3
Botany 53	3	Forestry 52	3
Electives*		Electives*	

* Electives should be chosen in consultation with the student's adviser.

SCHOOL OF BUSINESS ADMINISTRATION

MILO KIMBALL, *Dean*

The School of Business Administration prepares students eventually to assume positions of responsibility in business. An objective of the School is the education of young men and women who will regard management in business as a profession with high ethical standards and broad social responsibilities. The curricula provide preparation for specialized tasks in accounting, finance, industrial management, insurance, marketing, merchandising, office management or personnel management. When specialization is not desired, the student selects the General Business Managment program. Each course of study leads to the professional degree of Bachelor of Business Administration.

Curricula in Business Administration

In keeping with the objectives of the School, the study programs encourage breadth of training for business. General education is emphasized by providing fundamental courses in the humanities, mathematics, science, and social studies. The courses for the first two years are therefore largely prescribed.

FRESHMAN YEAR

1st Semester	Credits	2nd Semester	Credits
English 1, Composition	2	English 2, Composition	2
Speech 3	1	Speech 4	1
Industrial Adm. 11, Indust. Geography or Foreign Language	3	Economics 12, Ec. Hist of U. S. or Foreign Language	3
Mathematics 1, 5, or 7	3	Mathematics 2, 4, 6, 8, or 10	3
Government 25, American	3	History 6, Mod. European Civ.	3
Elective, Science	3	Elective, Science	3
Military 1	3	Military 2	2
Physical Ed. 7 (women)	2	Physical Ed. 8 (women)	2
Physical Ed. 3 (men)	1	Physical Ed. 4 (men)	1

SOPHOMORE YEAR

1st Semester	Credits	2nd Semester	Credits
English 25, Humane Letters	3	English 26, Humane Letters	3
Economics 25, Elements	3	Economics 26, Prob. of Nat'l Economy	3
Accounting 25, Introduction to	3	1Accounting 26, Introduction II	3
Psychology 26, General	3	Sociology 28, Elements	3
Elective	3	Elective	3
Military 25	2	Military 26	2
Physical Ed. 33 (men)	1	Physical Ed. 34 (men)	1
Physical Ed. 27 (women)	2	Physical Ed. 28 (women)	2

1 Students majoring in Merchandising take Home Economics 12.

JUNIOR-SENIOR CURRICULA IN BUSINESS ADMINISTRATION

The channels to specialization in a particular area of business lead through basic courses in production, marketing, finance, accounting, statistics, business law, and administration. The junior-senior programs are based on this core. Students thus acquire an awareness of each of the fundamental functions of business and develop facility in the use of the basic tools of management. They develop understanding of the relationship of their particular interest to all business activities as well as competence in a special field.

General Business Management

This program is given for students whose interest is in general management in business. It is designed to provide understanding of the broad administrative aspects of business, and specialized courses are subordinated to a comprehensive program of training.

JUNIOR YEAR

1st Semester	Credits	2nd Semester	Credits
I. A. 63, Mgt. in Industry	3	Fin. 65, Corporation Finance	3
Mkt. 53, Marketing Principles	3	Fin. 76, Insurance	3
Fin. 55, Financial Institutions	3	I. A. 66, Transporation & Traffic	3
Stat. 79, Elem. Ec. Stat.	3	Ec. 56, Business Fluctuations	3
Elective	3	Elective	3

SENIOR YEAR

1st Semester	Credits	2nd Semester	Credits
Bus. Law 70, Bus. Law I	3	Bus. Law 72, Bus. Law II	3
Ec. 73, Modern Econ. Theory	3	I. A. 80, Adm. Procedure	3
Ec. 79, Labor Problems	3	Ec. 78, Public Finance	3
Elective in Business	3	Elective in Business	3
Elective	3	Elective	3

Accounting

Accounting deals with the problems of measuring, recording, reporting and interpreting business transactions. This program is for the student who wishes to prepare for employment as auditor, controller, cost analyst, industrial accountant, public accountant, or teacher of accounting.

JUNIOR YEAR

1st Semester	Credits	2nd Semester	Credits
Acct. 61, Intermediate Accounting	3	Acct. 62, Advanced Accounting	3
Fin. 55, Financial Institutions	3	Acct. 64, Cost Accounting	3
Statistics 79, Elem. Ec. Stat.	3	Bus. Law 70, Bus. Law I	3
Mkt. 53, Marketing Principles	3	Fin. 65, Corporation Finance	3
Elective	3	Elective	3

SENIOR YEAR

1st Semester	Credits	2nd Semester	Credits
Acct. 73, Tax Accounting	3	Acct. 74, Accounting Systems	3
Acct. 75, Adm. Accounting &		Acct. 76, Auditing	3
Control	3	Fin. 82, Investments	3
I. A. 63, Management in Industry	3	Ec. 78, Public Finance	3
Ec. 73, Modern Ec. Theory	3	Elective	3
Elective	3		

Finance

Courses in banking, finance and insurance are provided for students who expect to assume responsibility for financing a business or to work for banks, investment institutions, brokerage houses, insurance companies, or governmental agencies concerned with finance.

JUNIOR YEAR

1st Semester	Credits	2nd Semester	Credits
Fin. 55, Financial Institutions	3	Bus. Law 70, Business Law I	3
Fin. 65, Corporation Finance	3	Ec. 56, Business Fluctuations	3
I. A. 63, Management in Industry	3	Stat. 79, Elem. Ec. Stat.	3
Mkt. 53, Marketing Principles	3	Elective in Business	3
Elective	3	Elective	3

SENIOR YEAR

1st Semester	Credits	2nd Semester	Credits
Fin. 81, Problems of Bus. Finance	3	Fin. 76, Insurance	3
Ec. 73, Modern Economic Theory	3	Fin. 82, Investments	3
Ec. 79, Labor Problems	3	Ec. 78, Public Finance	3
Electives	6	Electives	6

Industrial Administration

Industry offers to qualified students an opportunity to find satisfying careers in industrial management, or personnel management. The program offered is designed to give the student specialized training in these fields and a comprehensive understanding of the problems of industrial enterprises.

JUNIOR YEAR

1st Semester	Credits	2nd Semester	Credits
I. A. 63, Mgt. in Industry	3	I. A. 64, Personnel Management	3
Fin. 55, Financial Institutions	3	I. A. 66, Transportation & Traffic	3
Mkt. 53, Marketing Principles	3	Bus. Law 70, Bus. Law I	3
Stat. 79, Elem. Ec. Stat.	3	Acct. 64, Cost Accounting	3
Elective	3	Elective	3

SENIOR YEAR

1st Semester	Credits	2nd Semester	Credits
I. A. 73, Problems in Industrial		I. A. 80, Administrative	
Management	3	Procedure	3
Acct. 75, Administrative		Mkt. 76, Purchasing	3
Accounting & Control	3	Psych. 86, Industrial Psychology	3
Fin. 65, Corporation Finance	3	I. E. 88, Motion & Time Study	3
Ec. 79, Labor Problems	3	Elective	3
Elective	3		

Management Training

A curriculum in Management Training for young women has been approved and is being developed.

Marketing

Students in marketing prepare for a variety of occupations in wholesale and retail enterprises and the sales activities of manufacturers. The program offers specialized study of basic types of market operations.

JUNIOR YEAR

1st Semester	Credits	2nd Semester	Credits
Mktg. 53, Marketing Principles	3	Mktg. 54, Salesmanship &	
Fin. 55, Financial Institutions	3	Sales Mgt.	3
I. A. 63, Management in		Mkgt. 62, Market Research	3
Industry	3	I. A. 66, Transportation	
Stat. 79 Elem. Ec. Statistics	3	& Traffic	3
Elective	3	Bus. Law 70, Bus. Law I	3
		Elective	3

SENIOR YEAR

1st Semester	Credits	2nd Semester	Credits
Mkt. 71, Retail Merchandising	3	Mkt. 80, Problems in Mgt.	3
Mkt. 73, Advertising	3	Mkt. 76, Purchasing	3
Ec. 79, Labor Problems	3	Psych. 86, Industrial Psychology	3
Ec. 73, Modern Ec. Theory	3	Elective in Business	3
Elective	3	Elective	3

Merchandising

This program has been planned to meet the growing demand for women with technical training to fill positions of responsibility in retail merchandising.

JUNIOR YEAR

1st Semester	Credits	2nd Semester	Credits
Mkt. 53, Marketing Principles	3	Mkt. 62, Market Research	3
Ec. 55, Ec. of Consumption	3	I. A. 64, Personnel Management	3
Fin. 55, Financial Institutions	3	Home Ec. 26, Textiles	3
Elective in Business	3	Elective in Business	3
Elective	3	Elective	3

SENIOR YEAR

1st Semester	Credits	2nd Semester	Credits
Mkt. 71, Retail Merchandising	3	Mkt. 80, Marketing Problems	3
Mkt. 73, Advertising	3	B. L. 70, Business Law I	3
Home Ec. 35, Tailoring or		H. Ec. 62, Home Furnishing	3
Clothing Construction	3	Elective in Business	3
Elective in Business	3	Electives	3
Elective	3		

SCHOOL OF ENGINEERING

G. A. MARSTON, *Dean*

The departments of chemical engineering, civil engineering, mechanical engineering and electrical engineering comprise the School of Engineering. Each department offers a curriculum leading to a Bachelor of Science Degree in that particular branch. An optional curriculum in industrial engineering is offered in the mechanical engineering department.

The Civil, Electrical, Mechanical, and the Industrial optional curricula have been accredited by the Engineers Council for Professional Development.

Engineering can be defined as the combination of science and art by which materials and power are made useful to mankind. An engineer requires intensive technical training but at the same time he should acquire the broad education that distinguishes the professional man from the technician. His education does not end with formal schooling but continues throughout his life as he accumulates experience.

The curricula in engineering have been carefully prepared to offer each student the opportunity to acquire a sound training in the fundamental work of the various branches of his chosen field. At the same time he receives a thorough training in the sciences and mathematics, which are the important tools of the engineer. About twenty per cent of his time is devoted to the social and humanistic studies. Some opportunity to pursue his particular interest is offered in the senior year.

The curriculum of the freshman year is the same for all. Specialization to a limited extent begins in the sophomore year.

FRESHMAN YEAR

1st Semester	Credits	2nd Semester	Credits
English I, Composition	2	English 2, Composition	2
Speech 3	1	Speech 4	1
Mathematics 5, Analytical Geom.	4	Mathematics 6, Diff. Calculus	4
Chem. 1, General	3	Chem. 2 or 4, General	3 or 4
Mechanical Engineering 1, Drawing	2	Mechanical Engr. 2, Drawing	3
*Hist. 5, Fren., Ger., or Span.	3	*Hist. 6, Fren., Ger., or Span.	3
Military 1	3	Military 2	2
Physical Ed. 3	1	Physical Ed. 4	1

* French or German recommended for Chem. Engin. majors.

SOPHOMORE-JUNIOR-SENIOR CURRICULA

Majors in Engineering will select one of the following curricula.

Chemical Engineering   E. E. LINDSEY, *Adviser*

Chemical Engineering is that branch of engineering concerned with the development of manufacturing processes in which chemical or certain physical changes of materials are involved. These processes may usually be resolved into a coordinated series of unit operations (physical changes) and unit processes (chemical changes). The work of the chemical engineer is primarily concerned with the design, construction, and operation of equipment and plants in which series of these unit operations and processes are applied. Chemistry, physics, and mathematics are the underlying sciences of chemical engineering, and economics is its guide in practice.

Chemical engineers are employed not only in these industries manufacturing chemicals but in many others where there occur chemical changes and physical changes other than forming and shaping which is the province of mechanical engineering. Examples are: petroleum refining, coal processing, refractories and clay products, cement, waste treatment, pulp and paper, rayon and textiles, paint and varnish, natural and synthetic rubber, foods, leather, plastics, soap, penicillin and other antibiotics. Much of the work of the atomic energy program is chemical engineering. The types of work done by chemical engineers include: design, construction, research, development, production, financial and patent appraisal, management, and sales.

SOPHOMORE YEAR

1st Semester	Credits	2nd Semester	Credits
Chem. 29, Qualitative Analy.	4	Chem. 30, Quantitative Analy.	4
Physics 27, General	4	Physics 28, General	4
Math. 31, Applied Calculus	4	Math. 32, Diff. Equations	4
English 25, Humane Letters	3	English 26, Humane Letters	3
Military 25	2	Chem. Engin. 26, Calculations	2
Physical Education 33	1	Military 26	2
		Physical Education 34	1

JUNIOR YEAR

1st Semester	Credits	2nd Semester	Credits
Chemistry 51, Organic	4	Chemistry 52, Organic	4
Chemistry 65, Physical	4	Chemistry 66, Physical	4
Civil Engin. 34, Statics	3	Civil Engin. 51, Strength of Mat.	4
Chem. Engin. 55, Unit Opera. I	5	Chem. Engin. 56, Unit Opera. II	5
[1]Economics 25, Elements	3	[1]Psych. 26 or Sociology 28	3

SUMMER (6 WEEKS)

Chem. Engin. 75, Instrumentation	2	Chem. Engin. 88, Chem.	
		Engin. Lab.	3

[1] Advanced military students will take Economics 25 and either Psychology 26 or Sociology 28 as two of their senior electives.

SENIOR YEAR

1st Semester	Credits	2nd Semester	Credits
Chem. Engin. 81, Heat-Energy Rel.	3	Chem. Engin. 82, Ind. Equil.	
Chem. Engin. 93, Comprehen.		& Kinetics	3
Prob.	3	Chem. Engin. 94, Comprehen.	
Chem. Engin. 91, Seminar	1	Prob.	3
Elec. Engin. 63, Elements	3	Chem. Engin. 92, Seminar	1
Chem. Eng. 89, Lab. Projects	3	Elec. Engin. 64, Indus. Applic.	3
1Electives	6	1Electives	8

1 Advanced ·military students will take Economics 25 and either Psychology 26 or Sociology 28 as two. of their senior electives.

· Recommended electives include history,. government, French, German, Math. 83, English 83, Chem. 57, 58, 95, 98, Chemistry 77, 79, 86, 93, 94, Mech. Engin. 39, 46, Business Law·70. Other courses may be chosen with the approval of the Head of the Department.

Civil Engineering   M. P. WHITE, *Adviser*

Civil engineering is concerned with structures, transportation, movement of fluids, use and storage of water, sanitation, and surveying and mapping. A civil engineer may be engaged in research, in planning and designing, in construction, or in maintenance and operation. Consequently, civil engineering contains room for a wide range of interests—from highly theoretical to very practical.

The curriculum gives a thorough training in the fundamental sciences and at the same time prepares a student for work in any branch of civil engineering. During his senior year a student takes two or three elective technical courses, allowing him to specialize to some extent in · whatever branch of civil engineering is most interesting to him — sanitation, mechanics and structures, hydraulics, foundation engineering, highway engineering.

SOPHOMORE YEAR

1st Semester	Credits	2nd Semester	Credits
English 25, Humane Letters	3	English 26, Humane Letters	3
Math. 31, Integ. Calculus	4	Math. 32, Diff. Equations	4
Physics 27, General	4	Physics 28, General	4
Civ. Engin. 25, Surveying	5	Elec. Engin. 63, Elements of	3
Military 25	2	Civ. E. 34, Statics	3
Phys. Ed. 33	1	Military 26	2
		.Phys. Ed. 34	1

SUMMER (6 WEEKS)

Civ. E. 28, Prop. & Topog.		Civ. Eng. 30, Route Surveying	
Surveying	3	Practice	˄

JUNIOR YEAR

1st Semester	Credits	2nd Semester	Credits
Psych. 26, Econ. 25 or Soc. 28	3	Econ. 25, Psych. 26 or Soc. 28	3
Civ. Eng. 51, Strength of Mat'ls	4	Civ. Eng. 70, Theory of Structures	4
Civ. Eng. 55, Transportation		Civ. Eng. 61, Testing Mat'ls.	2
Engin.	3	Civ. Engin. 80, Soil Mechanics	3
Civ. Eng. 52, Dynamics	3	Mech. Engin. 39, Mat'ls. of	
Mech. Eng. 65, Thermodynamics*	3	Constr.*	2
Geol. 50, Engin. Geol.	3	Civ. Eng. 76, Fluid Mechanics	4

SENIOR YEAR

1st Semester	Credits	2nd Semester	Credits
Civ. Eng. 71, Structural Design	3	Civ. Eng. 78, Sanitary Engin. II	4
Civ. Eng. 73, Reinforced		Civ. Eng. 90, Contracts,	
Concrete Design	4	Specif. & Est.	3
Civ. Eng. 77, Sanitary Engin. I	3	Civ. Eng. 92, Professional Sem.	1
Civ. Eng. 81, Foundations	3	Technical Electives (Civ.	
English 83, Technical Writing	2	Eng. 72, 86, 88, 94, 96, 98,	
Non-Tech. Elective*	3	Bact. 54, recommended)	6
		Non-Tech. Elective*	3

   * Replaced by military for military majors.

Electrical Engineering   C. S. Roys, *Adviser*

Electrical engineering is that branch of the profession covering the engineering applications of electricity. It reaches into practically every profession, every branch of activity, either through performance of the tasks involved, or through their measurement and control. Because it is so diversified in its applications, it is considered to be divided into various fields such as power, communications, electronics, illumination, measurements and control and others, each of these having specialized subdivisions.

The undergraduate curriculum is designed to prepare the student for work in any of these fields, and to serve as a basis for specialization in any of them, either in advanced courses or in the field. At the same time, about one-fifth of the student's work is devoted to the humanistic-social courses so that he may have an understanding of the broader aspects of engineering and its relation to other fields of human endeavor.

SUMMER (Following Freshman Year)

   Mechanical Engineering 23, Shop and Civil Engineering 27, Surveying, 6 credit hours.

SOPHOMORE YEAR

1st Semester	Credits	2nd Semester	Credits
English 25, Humane Letters	3	English 26, Humane Letters	3
Math. 31, Integ. Calculus	4	Math. 32, Diff. Equations	4
Physics 27, General	4	Physics 28, General	4
Elec. Engin. 41, Fundamentals	4	Civ. E. 34, Statics	3
Military 25	2	Elec. Engin. 42, A-C. Circuits	3
Physical Ed. 33	1	Military 26	2
		Physical Ed. 34	1

JUNIOR YEAR

1st Semester	Credits	2nd Semester	Credits
Elec. Engin. 53, D-C. Machinery	4	Elec. Engin. 54, A-C. Machinery	4 .
Elec. Engin. 55, Electronics	3	Elec. Engin. 56, Appld. Electrn.	4
Elec. Engin. 57, Engin. Analysis	3	Elec. Engin. 58, Elec. Trans.	3
Mech. Engin. 65, Heat Engin. I	3	Mech. Engin. 66, Heat Engin. II	3
Civ. Engin. 53, Strength of Mat.	3	Civ. Engin. 52, Dynamics	3
**Econ. 25, Psych. 26, or Soc. 28	3	‡English 83, Tech. Writing	2

SENIOR YEAR

1st Semester	Credits	2nd Semester	Credits
†Elec. Engin. 78, Special Projects	1	Elec. Engin. 92, Prof. Seminar	1
Elec. Engin. 83, Transient Analysis	3	†Elec. Engin. 78, Special Projects	1
Elec. Engin. 85, Elec. Measurements	3	‡Ind. Engin. 86, Ind. Mgt.	3
‡Mech. Engin. 81, M. E. Lab. I	2	Econ. 25, Psych. 26 or Soc. 28	3
Civ. Engin. 75, Fluid Mechanics	3	Technical Elective (Elec. Engin. 80, 84, 86, 88, 90, 94, 96, 98)	6 to 8
Technical Elective (Elec. Engin. 79, 81, 87)	4	Non-Tech. Elective*	3
Non-Tech. Elective*	3		

* Recommended as non-technical electives: Govt. 26, Bus. Law 70, Psych. 86.
‡ Not required of advanced military students.
** Postponed to senior year replacing M. E. 79 for advanced military students.
† May be taken either semester.

Mechanical Engineering   W. H. WEAVER, Adviser

Mechanical engineering is that branch of the profession which, broadly speaking, covers the fields of heat, power, design of machinery, industrial management and manufacturing problems.

Building upon the foundation laid by the departments of mathematics, physics, and chemistry, the department of mechanical engineering undertakes to show the student how fundamental physical laws apply to this field of the profession. The courses selected give the student thorough training in the basic principles so that particular applications can be mastered in professional practice. Therefore, no attempt is made to give highly specialized instruction.

It must be realized that the modern engineer lives in a time of rapid social and technological change. Only the man who has had a well-balanced cultural and technical program of study can adjust quickly enough to the needs of a continually changing social order. The following curricula emphasize the fundamentals of the four M's of engineering: materials, methods, men, and money, a knowledge of which is vital to the modern engineer.

SUMMER (Following Freshman Year)

Mechanical Engineering 27 and 28, Shop 6 credit hours.

SOPHOMORE YEAR

1st Semester	Credits	2nd Semester	Credits
English 25, Humane Letters	3	English 26, Humane Letters	3
Math. 31, Integ. Calculus	4	Math. 32, Diff. Equations	4
Physics 27, General	4	Physics 28, General	4
Mech. Eng. 39, Mat'l of Constr.	2	Civ. Eng. 34, Statics	3
Ind. Engin. 25, Prod. Processes	2	Mech. Eng. 46, Fund. of Metallurgy	3
Military 25	2	Military 26	2
Physical Ed. 33	1	Physical Ed. 34	1

JUNIOR YEAR

1st Semester	Credits	2nd Semester	Credits
‡English 83, Tech. Writing	2	Psych. 26, Econ. 25 or Soc. 28	3
Civ. Engin. 52, Dynamics	3	Civ. Engin. 76, Fluid Mech.	4
Mech. Eng. 63, Eng. Thermo-		Mech. Eng. 68, Kinematics	3
dynamics	4	Mech. Eng. 64, Eng. Thermo-	
Elec. E. 61, Principles	4	dynamics	3
Civ. Eng. 51, Strength of Mat'ls.	4	Mech. E. 67, Mech. Instr. Lab.	1
Civ. Eng. 61, Testing of Mat'ls.	2	Elec. Eng. 62, Principles	4

SENIOR YEAR

1st Semester	Credits	2nd Semester	Credits
Mech. Eng. 75, Power Plants	3	Psych. 26, Econ. 25 or Soc. 28	3
Mech. E. 77, Internal		Mech. E. 76, Ref. & Air Cond.	3
Combust. Engines	3	Mech. E. 80, Mech. Eng. Lab.	2
Mech. Eng. 79, Mech. Eng. Lab.	2	Mech. E. 86, Adv. Mach. Des.	3
Mech. Eng. 83, Machine Design	3	‡Technical Elect.†	6
Mech. Engin. 85, Dynamics		‡Non-Tech. Elect. (Bus. Law	
of Mach.	3	70 or Psych. 86, Ind.	
Mech. Eng. 91, Sem.	1	recommended	3
‡Non-Technical Elect. (Am.			
Govt. 25 recommended)	3		

‡ Not required of advanced military students.
†Mech. Engin. 88, Steady Flow Mach.
†Mech. Eng. 90, Adv. Metallurgy
†Elec. Eng. 64, Ind. Electricity
†Ind. Engin. 86, Ind. Mgt.
†Ind. Engin. 54, Engin. Econ.
‡Mech. Eng. 94, Exp. Mech.
†Civil Engin. 88, Adv. Stress Analy.

Industrial Engineering Option   W. H. WEAVER, *Adviser*

Industrial engineering is concerned with the engineering aspects of the organization, operation and management of manufacturing plants. It is based on the premise that the operation of a manufacturing plant is fundamentally an engineering activity. Consequently, the industrial engineering curriculum is built on a foundation of mechanical engineering. To the technical knowledge and scientific attitude developed through the study of engineering is added the study of certain courses in the humanities, in economics, and in management.

JUNIOR YEAR

1st Semester	Credits	2nd Semester	Credits
Econ. 25	3	Ind. Engin. 82, Work	
Mech. Eng. 65, Heat Engin.	3	Simplification	2
Civ. Eng. 53, Strength of Mat'ls.	3	Mech. Eng. 66, Heat Eng.	3
Elec. Eng. 61, Prin. of Elec. Eng.	4	Civ. E. 52, Dynamics	3
Acct. 25, Prin. of Bus.	3	Elec. Eng. 62, Prin. of E. E.	4
Ind. Engin. 51, Ind. Mgt.	3	Acct. 26, Prin. of Bus.	3
		Mech. Eng. 68, Kinematics	3

SENIOR YEAR

1st Semester	Credits	2nd Semester	Credits
Civ. Eng. 75, Fluid Mech.	3	Psych. 26, or Soc. 28	3
Mech. Engin. 79, Lab. I	2	Statistics 79, Elem.	3
Mech. Engin. 83, Mach. Design	3	Ind. Engin. 78, Factory Pl.	2
Ind. Engin. 75, Job Evaluation	2	Ind. Engin. 80, Budget Con.	3
Ind. Engin. 76, Time Study	3	Ind. Engin. 54, Eng. Econ.	3
Ind. Engin. 77, Prod. Control	3	Ind. Engin. 92, Sem.	1
Non-Technical Elective	3	Non-Technical Elective	3

Agricultural Engineering

The University has discontinued the professional curriculum in Agricultural Engineering as of July 1, 1955. However, agricultural engineering is concerned with the application of engineering principles to the agricultural industry. Mechanical and electrical power, processing equipment, planning and design of farm structures, soil and water conservation, research, and resident and extension instruction all form parts.

A student interested in pursuing a career in this applied field of engineering should major in one of the engineering departments offering work according to his particular interest as follows:

Drainage, irrigation and farm structures	Civil Engineering
Farm machinery, maintenance and design	Mechanical Engineering
Electrical machinery and electrification	Electrical Engineering
Food processing	Chemical Engineering

He will have the opportunity to elect some courses in agriculture and related fields his senior year. No formal curriculum for this year is planned so that individual interests can be met. Programs will be arranged by the head of the agricultural engineering department and the head of the major department concerned. The student will receive the degree of the department in which he majors.

SCHOOL OF HOME ECONOMICS

HELEN S. MITCHELL, *Dean*

General education for living is the main objective of the several four-year curricula in home economics. Electives during the junior and senior years allow for specialization in preparation for several professional fields: preschool work with children, dietetics, nutrition, teaching of home economics, Extension, and merchandising. The American Dietetic Association sets educational standards for which students in this school may qualify.

When registering for the sophomore year, each student should make a decision as to which home economics curriculum she intends to follow. Some change in emphasis may be made later, but the student is often at a disadvantage if a change in the field of specialization is made later in the college career.

The program of studies for the first two years is largely prescribed.

FRESHMAN YEAR

1st Semester	Credits	2nd Semester	Credits
English 1, Composition	2	English 2, Composition	2
Speech 3	1	Speech 4	1
Chemistry 1, General	3	Chemistry 2, General	3
Foreign Language	3	Foreign Language	3
Home Ec. 11, Euthenics	3	Home Ec. 12, Consumer	
Physical Education 7	2	Clothing Problems	3
1Elective	3	Math. 12	3
		Physical Education 8	2

1 Elective to be chosen from the following:

Zoology 1, recommended for majors in Foods and Nutrition, Pre-research, or Child Development.

History 5, recommended for majors in Applied Art, Textiles and Clothing, and Merchandising.

Math 7 recommended for Pre-research majors planning to take Physics 25 and 26.

Botany 1.

SOPHOMORE YEAR

1st Semester	Credits	2nd Semester	Credits
English 25, Humane Letters	3	English 26, Humane Letters	3
Economics 25, Elements	3	Psychology 26, General	3
Chem. 33, Organic	4	Zool. 1 or 35 or	3
Physical Education 27	2	Bact. 31	4
1Electives	6	2Home Ec. 30, Foods	3
		Physical Education 28	2
		1Elective	3

1 One of the following electives must be taken and two may be taken during the sophomore year: Home Ec. 31, Applied Art; Home Ec. 26, Textiles, Home Ec.

35, Clothing Construction. Other electives: Accounting 25; Art 31, 34; Bacteriology 31; Chem. 29 and 30; Physics 25, 26; Econ. 26; Government 25; Sociology 25; Zoology 35; Language.

[2]Merchandising majors take Home Ec. 30 sophomore year and Home Ec. 51 junior year, or Home Ec. 26 sophomore year and Home Ec. 56 junior year.

JUNIOR-SENIOR CURRICULA IN HOME ECONOMICS

A student may specialize in one of several fields of Home Economics during the junior and senior years. In consultation with her faculty adviser, each student will choose courses directly related to her objective. To qualify for a B.S. degree in Home Economics a student during the junior and senior years must have at least 15 but not more than 30 credits in the major field and not more than 42 credits in the School of Home Economics. The following courses or their equivalent are required for all majors: Home Economics 51, 52, 75, 77, 90. The following curricula are suggestive. Those interested in other types of professional work should consult with advisers about desirable electives. For students not interested in professional work, a more liberal choice of electives is possible.

Child Development and Family Life Education

Students interested in child development, nursery school work and social service work should choose this curriculum. The University has arranged for two affiliations for qualified students interested in taking one semester of specialized work elsewhere: with Merrill-Palmer School in Detroit, which specializes in education for home and family life, and with the Nursery Training School in Boston which gives professional training for teaching in nursery schools and kindergartens. Students interested in combining this major with elementary education should elect Education 61 and 64 as juniors.

JUNIOR YEAR

1st Semester	Credits	2nd Semester	Credits
Home Ec. 51, Meal Planning	3	Home Ec. 52, Nutrition	3
Home Ec. 75, Ec. of Household	3	Home Ec. 70, Child Developm't	3
Home Ec. 63, Arts and Crafts	3	Home Ec. 80, Family	3
Electives	6	Psych. 56, Educational	3
		Electives	3

SENIOR YEAR

1st Semester	Credits	2nd Semester	Credits
Home Ec. 85, Nursery Sch. Mgt.	3	Ed. 85, Practice Teaching	3
Home Ec. 81, Methods	3	Home Ec. 77, Household Mgt.	3
Home Ec. 95, Child Nutr.	3	Home Ec. 90, Seminar	1
Electives	6	Electives	9

115

Foods and Nutrition and Institution Administration

This curriculum prepares for such professions as therapeutic dietitian or administrative dietitian or nutritionist and meets the requirements of internships approved by the American Dietetic Association. This curriculum is also advised for those interested in home service, food testing and commercial demonstrating related to foods.

Bacteriology 31, Zoology 35, and Accounting 25 should be elected sophomore year, if possible, to satisfy requirements of the American Dietetics Association.

JUNIOR YEAR

1st Semester	Credits	2nd Semester	Credits
Home Ec. 51, Meal Planning	3	Home Ec. 52, Nutrition	3
Home Ec. 75, Ec. of Household	3	Home Ec. 60, Household Equip.	2
Home Ec. 81, Methods	3	Home Ec. 70, Child Develop.	3
Chem. 79, Biochemistry	4	Electives	6-8
Elective	3		

SENIOR YEAR

1st Semester	Credits	2nd Semester	Credits
Home Ec. 61, Demonst. Tech.	2	Home Ec. 77, Home Mgt.	3
Home Ec. 71, Retail Fd. Buy.	3	Home Ec. 90, Sem.	1
Home Ec. 89, Diet Therapy	3	Home Ec. 92, Inst. Adm.	3
Home Ec. 91, Institution Adm.	3	Home Ec. 93, Experimental Fds.	3
Elective	4	Electives	6

Pre-Research in Nutrition

This curriculum is planned for the students who wish to prepare for graduate work in nutrition or biochemical research. The course should be planned with the advice of the Dean of the School.

Pre-research majors are advised to take Chemistry 29 and 30 in place of Chemistry 33, Zoology 35, and Bacteriology 31 in the sophomore year, and may elect Physics 25 and 26.

JUNIOR YEAR

1st Semester	Credits	2nd Semester	Credits
Chemistry 51, Organic	4	Bacteriology 31, Intro.	4
Home Ec. 51, Meal Planning	3	Chemistry 52, Organic	4
Home Ec. 75, Ec. of Household	3	Home Ec. 52, Nutrition	3
Zool. 35, Physiol.	3	Electives	4-6
Elective	3		

SENIOR YEAR

1st Semester	Credits	2nd Semester	Credits
Chemistry 79, Biochemistry	4	Home Ec. 77, Home Management	3
Home Ec. 89, Diet Therapy	3	Home Ec. 90, Sem.	1
Home Ec. 95, Child Nutrition	3	Home Ec. 93, Experimental Foods	3
Electives	6	Home Ec. 98, Special Problems	3
		Electives	6

Home Economics Education and Extension

Preparation for teaching demands the same basic courses whether a student plans to teach adults or 4-H club groups in Extension, or young people at the high school or junior high school level. Teachers should be ready to teach some subject other than home economics if demanded; extension workers need special work in rural sociology and adult education. Courses in speech and writing are important. Camp teaching or apprentice training is recommended between junior and senior year.

Two of the following electives should be taken in sophomore year and the third in junior year: Home Economics 26, 31, 35. Students who wish to take 6 credits in teaching under the Block System for Secondary School Teacher Training must reserve one semester of their senior year for this program.

JUNIOR YEAR

1st Semester	Credits	2nd Semester	Credits
Home Ec. 51, Meal Planning	3	Home Ec. 52, Nutri. & Diet	3
Home Ec. 75, Ec. of Household	3	Home Ec. 70, Child Develop.	3
Home Ec. 81, Methods	3	Home Ec. 80, Family Life	3
Education 51, History	3	Psych. 56, Educational	3
Elective	3	Elective	3

SENIOR YEAR

1st Semester	Credits	2nd Semester	Credits
Home Ec. 61, Demonst. Tech.	2	Home Ec. 62, Home Furnish.	3
Home Ec. 77, Home Mgt.	3	Home Ec. 90, Seminar	1
Home Ec. 87, Tailoring	3	*Electives	11
*Electives	7		

*Electives recommended for teachers: Education 85 and 88; for extension workers: Education 79, Home Economics 98, Sociology 52.

Merchandising and Retailing

This curriculum provides an opportunity for girls interested in preparing for the merchandising field. The junior and senior curriculum includes courses in home economics and in business administration and should be planned with the faculty adviser by the end of the freshman year if possible. Students choosing this program are expected to take Home Economics 31 or 26, Accounting 25, and Economics 26 in the sophomore year, and should plan on at least a year of in-service training after college. If the interest is primarily in business, see the Merchandising major under the School of Business Administration.

JUNIOR YEAR

1st Semester	Credits	2nd Semester	Credits
Home Ec. 35, Clothing Constr.	3	Home Ec. 56 or 51, Meal Planning	3
Home Ec. 75, Ec. of Household	3	Home Ec. 52, Nutrition	3
Mktg. 53, Mktg. & Mktg. Problems	3	Home Ec. 62, Home Furnishings	3
Elective	6	Mktg. 54, Salesmanship & Mgt.	3
		Electives	3

SENIOR YEAR

1st Semester	Credits	2nd Semester	Credits
Home Ec. 87, Tailoring (optional)	3	Home Ec. 77, Home Management	3
Mktg. 71, Retail Merchandising	3	Home Ec. 88, Dress Design (optional)	3
Mktg. 73, Advertising	3	Mktg. 72, Mktg. Research	3
Electives	6	Home Ec. 90, Seminar	1
		Electives	6

Textiles, Clothing, and Applied Art

This curriculum is of interest to students who may wish to use clothing and related art in a general and aesthetic sense for their personal and family development. Students with ability and professional interest in the artistic and technical aspects of textiles, clothing, and related art are encouraged to go further in this field. They are expected to take Home Economics 31 and Home Economics 26 in the sophomore year. Art 31 is recommended.

JUNIOR YEAR

1st Semester	Credits	2nd Semester	Credits
Home Ec. 51, Meal Planning	3	Home Ec. 52, Nutrition	3
Home Ec. 35, Clothing Constr.	3	Home Ec. 62, Home Furnishing	3
Home Ec. 75, Ec. of Household	3	Home Ec. 78, Adv. Text. Design	3
Home Ec. 81, Methods (optional)	3	Electives	6

SENIOR YEAR

1st Semester	Credits	2nd Semester	Credits
Home Ec. 63, Arts & Crafts (optional)	3	Home Ec. 88, Dress Design	3
Home Ec. 77, Home Mgt.	3	Home Ec. 90, Seminar	1
Home Ec. 61, Demonst. Tech.	2	Electives	11
Home Ec. 87, Tailoring	3		
Electives	4-7		

SCHOOL OF NURSING

MARY A. MAHER, *Head and Director*

The basic professional nursing program is designed to prepare qualified high school graduates for a career in professional nursing, for marriage and family living. It aims to equip the student with those understandings, attitudes, skills and appreciations which are essential for a competent practitioner and health teacher.

The program is planned specifically to help the student increase her self-understanding so that she may function constructively and creatively in her personal and professional relationships; enhance and improve her emotional, physical, social and spiritual well-being; extend her understanding of the health needs of the individual and family and of the community organizations primarily concerned with the promotion of health and prevention of illness; improve her professional competency as she ministers to the individual and the family in selected clinical situations; more fully understand and appreciate her role in the nursing, the therapeutic and the health team; become sensitive to the need and responsibility for periodic appraisal and improvement of professional nursing practice; become a more self-directive and responsible member of the profession and of the community; and improve her professional competency through continued study.

The graduate of such a program is ready for a beginning position in a variety of nursing situations, including public health; for leadership in the hospital nursing team; and for participation with allied personnel in providing comprehensive patient care. A foundation is laid for advanced study, through which the nurse may prepare for positions in teaching, supervision, administration, consultation and research.

During the first two academic years at the University, the student builds an educational foundation upon which to base the more specialized portion of the program. Courses in the humanities and in the sciences—biological, physical and social—are taken with other students on the campus.

The clinical aspects of the program are developed in the next two and one half years, when instruction and correlated clinical practice is given in selected cooperating agencies by the nursing faculty of the University and allied professional staffs. These agencies include: the Springfield Hospital; the Wesson Maternity Hospital, Springfield; the Visiting Nurse Association of Springfield; the Springfield Health Department; and the New England Medical Center, Boston.

NURSING

The student returns to the campus for a fifth academic semester, upon completion of which a Bachelor of Science degree is awarded. This qualifies the graduate for State Board Examinations in Nursing. If achievement in these examinations is satisfactory, the candidate receives legal status as a registered nurse within the state.

PROGRAM SEQUENCE

First Year

1st Semester	Credits	2nd Semester	Credits
English 1, English Comp.	2	English 2, English Comp.	3
Speech 3	1	Speech 4	1
Chemistry 1, General	3	Chemistry 2, General	3
Zoology 1, Introductory	3	Zoology 35, Vert. Physiol.	3
Mathematics 12, Functional	3	Psychology 26, General	3
History 5, Mod. European Civil.	3	Sociology 25, Introduction	3

Second Year

1st Semester	Credits	2nd Semester	Credits
English 25, Humane Letters	3	Bacteriology 31, Introductory	4
Chemistry 33, Organic	4	Philosophy 64, Ethics	3
Sociology 53, Intro. Study, Cultural Anthrop.	3	Home Economics 42, Med. Diet.	2
Home Economics 41, Nutri. & Food Prep.	4	Home Economics 70, Child Devel.	3
Psychology 56, Educational	3	Nursing 26, Orient. to Nursing	4

Summer Session

		Credits
Nursing 27,	Fundamentals of Nursing	9
Nursing 28,	Social and Historical Foundations of Nursing	2

Third Year

Nursing 51,	Medical and Surgical Nursing I	16
Nursing 52A,	Nursing of Children I	2
Nursing 54,	Psychiatric Nursing	6
Nursing 57,	Maternity Nursing	5

Fourth Year

Nursing 52B,	Nursing of Children II	5
Nursing 60,	Medical and Surgical Nursing II	8
Nursing 58,	Public Health Nursing	3
Nursing 56,	Tuberculosis Nursing	3
Nursing 70,	Management of Hospital Nursing Unit	2

Fifth Year

Nursing 65,	Senior Internship	4
Nursing 66,	Senior Nursing Seminar	4
English 26,	Humane Letters	3
History 6,	Modern European Civilization	3
Electives		5

DEPARTMENTS OF MILITARY SCIENCE AND AIR SCIENCE RESERVE OFFICERS TRAINING CORPS

COLONEL RAYMOND P. TARR, JR., *U. S. Army, Head*
COLONEL DONALD B. WHITE, *U. S. Air Force, Head*

An Act of Congress, July 2, 1862, required the Commonwealth of Massachusetts to provide a two-year course in military instruction at the Massachusetts Agricultural College when it was established. All able-bodied male students who were enrolled for four years were required to take this training. This requirement has continued until today, although The National Defense Act of 1916, as amended in later years, created a Reserve Officers' Training Corps at those colleges which were giving military instruction.

The National Security Act of 1947, which created the United States Air Force as a separate armed service, also resulted in separate Army and Air Force Reserve Officers' Training Corps units being organized at the University of Massachusetts and other colleges and universities.

The general objective of the courses of instruction (Army and Air Force) is to produce junior officers who by their education, training and inherent qualities are suitable for continued development in the United States Army or the United States Air Force Reserve. Training in military leadership is emphasized. It is intended to obtain this objective during the time the students are pursuing their general or professional studies, with the least practicable interference with their civil careers.

All physically qualified male candidates for a degree in any four-year course at the University, except veterans, are required to take the basic course (Army or Air) for at least three hours a week for two years.

The choice of service, Army or Air Force, must be made by each student when he initially enrolls. The student in the basic course is provided with a uniform of the service in which he is enrolled. A deposit of $30.00 is required to cover the cost of loss or damage to any of the articles issued.

The courses of instruction include theoretical and practical work in all phases of military and air science, such as military organization, hygiene and first aid, weapons, maps, military administration, world political geography, military law and boards, and leadership, drill, and the exercise of command.

DIVISION OF PHYSICAL EDUCATION
W. P. McGuirk, *Head*

The Division of Physical Education includes the Departments of Athletics, Physical Education for Men, and Physical Education for Women. It offers one major, that in Physical Education for Men.

INTERCOLLEGIATE ATHLETICS
W. P. McGuirk, *Director*

The following men are in charge of the coaching of the intercollegiate teams:

Charles C. O'Rourke, head coach of football and coach of golf; Chester S. Gladchuk, assistant coach of football and coach of freshman basketball; Robert T. Curran, coach of basketball and coach of freshman baseball; Earl E. Lorden, assistant director of athletics, coach of baseball, assistant coach of football; William Footrick, coach of track and cross country; Lawrence E. Briggs, coach of soccer and skiing; Henry B. Woronicz, assistant coach of hockey, coach of freshman football and director of intramural sports; Stephen R. Kosakowski, coach of tennis and supervisor of Stockbridge School athletics; Benjamin Ricci, Jr., coach of lacrosse; Joseph R. Rogers, Jr., coach of swimming; Gerald Healy, Director of Sports Information.

Physical Education for Men   S. W. Kauffman, *Adviser*

The department of physical education for men offers physical activity courses for four years and the opportunity to major in physical education or teacher coaching.

The activity courses which are required the first two years are designed to assist the student to meet minimum standards of physical health and through regularity and continuity of progressively planned exercises, maintain sound physical condition throughout his college career.

Students are expected to attain minimum physical standards established by the department which includes the ability to swim.

The major in physical education leading to a degree of Bachelor of Science in physical education is designed primarily to train the student for a career as a teacher of physical education. It also includes adequate training in other fields of teaching and coaching of interschool athletics. It is contemplated that physical education majors will be well trained in general scientific and cultural subjects. They are urged to elect advanced military and those planning on teacher-coaching should take additional work in their particular subject matter fields.

The outline of the physical education major follows:

FRESHMAN YEAR

1st Semester	Credits	2nd Semester	Credits
English I	2	English II	2
Speech 3	1	Speech 4	1
P. E. 23, Princples of Health Ed.	3	Government 25, American	
P. E. 21, Intro. to Phys. Ed.	3	Government	3
Psych. 26, General Psychology	3	Mathematics 12 or 14	3
Military I	3	P. E. 22, First Aid and Safety	3
P. E. 5, Skills and Techniques	1	Military 2	2
Elect one:		P. E. 6, Skills and Techniques	1
Chemistry I	3	Elect one:	
Botany I	3	Chemistry II	3
Zoology I	3	Botany I	3
		Zoology 1	3

SOPHOMORE YEAR

1st Semester	Credits	2nd Semester	Credits
English 25	3	English 26	3
Bacteriology 31	4	Zoology 35, Physiology	3
P. E. 41, Anatomy	3	P. E. 42, Kinesiology	3
Economics 25 or Sociology 28	3	Psychology 56, Educ. Psychology	3
P. E. 35, Skills and Techniques	1	P. E. 36, Skills and Techniques	1
Military 25	2	Military 26	2
Electives	3	Electives	3

JUNIOR YEAR

1st Semester	Credits	2nd Semester	Credits
Ed. 83, Principles of Second Ed.	3	Ed. 52, Prin. and Methods of	
P. E. 53, Phys. Ed. Elem. Schools	3	Teach.	3
P. E. 55, Org. and Adm. of		P. E. 54, Phys. Ed. Second. Schools	3
Phys. Ed.	3	P. E. 56, Adaptive Phys. Ed.	3
P. E. 57, Meth. and Mat. Coaching	3	Psych. 94, Child Psychology	3
(Football-Basketball)		P. E. 58, Meth. and Mat. Coaching	3
P. E. 63, Skills and Techniques	1	(Swimming-Baseball)	
Electives	6	P. E. 64, Skills and Techniques	1
		Electives	3

SENIOR YEAR

1st Semester	Credits	2nd Semester	Credits
Ed. 85, Practice Teaching	3	Education 85, Practice Teaching	3
P. E. 73, Phil. & Princ. of		Ed. 64, Princ. of Elem. Education	3
Phys. Ed.	3	P. E. 74, Tests and Meas. in	
Speech 91, Extempore Speech	3	Phys. Ed.	3
Rec. Ed. 77, Org. & Adm. of		P. E. 76, Physiology of Exercise	3
Comm. Rec.	3	P. E. 84, Skills and Techniques	1
P. E. 81, Meth. & Mat. Coaching	3	Electives	6
(Soccer-Track)			
P. E. 83, Skills and Techniques	1		
Electives	3		

Physical Education for Women   Ruth j. Totman, *Adviser*

The courses in physical education for women are planned to provide recreative activity, to develop body grace and efficiency, and to increase health and vigor. No major is available.

The first and second year women students are required to take physical education three times a week and are given two credits for each semester of satisfactory work. Third and fourth year students may elect Physical Education 63, 64, 65, 66. They may elect also Physical Education 42 in the department of physical education for men.

Girls who are restricted from unlimited activity are placed in classes suitable to their ability. Girls who are restricted from all class activity are assigned to rest periods three times a week and receive their regular physical education credit for satisfactory attendance. A similar rest program is substituted for the regular activity program when girls are temporarily incapacitated.

RELIGION

Chaplains Power, Ruchames, and Seely, *Advisers*

The courses in the history of religion, the articles of belief and the application of religious principles are given by the Chaplains of the three major western faiths and by others designated by the churches represented. They are financially independent of the University although the facilities of the University are available as for other courses. .

Courses are offered in this field for the sake of the student who is interested in rounding out his educational program with the acquiring of a mature perspective in religion. The opportunity is offered for the student to gain a wide knowledge of the forces which have been basic to his culture, an understanding of the religious influences in his own life, and an evaluation of the part that religion plays in current social movements.

Students register for these courses at the regular registration period and may do so in addition to a normal semester load. No academic credit accrues from participation in the courses in religion.

DIRECTORY OF COURSES

This section contains a list of courses offered in the regular sessions of the University. Course descriptions are arranged alphabetically according to subject matter fields. If any course cannot be found readily, refer to the General Index in the back of the catalogue. A separate bulletin will outline those available during the summer. The University reserves the right to withdraw any course for which an insufficient number of students enroll.

Courses are designated by numbers as follows: freshman 1-24 inclusive; sophomore 25-49 inclusive; junior 50-74 inclusive; senior 75-99 inclusive. Odd numbers designate courses given in the first semester, even numbers those offered during the second. Credit is indicated in terms of semester hours. Where possible, the class schedule follows the course description. A complete schedule of class hours is published at the beginning of each semester.

Students are referred to the section on Divisions of Study and Curricula for a statement of graduation requirements and majors available.

AGRICULTURAL ECONOMICS AND FARM MANAGEMENT

PROFESSOR LINDSEY, PROFESSOR BARRETT,

ASSISTANT PROFESSOT RUSSELL, MR. CALLAHAN.

26. (II) Economics of Agricultural Production

This course considers the principles of production economics. An anlysis of specialization, comparative advantage, diminishing, constant, and increasing costs and returns applied to the individual establishment as well as to the nation. A careful study of the combination of the factors of production is made considering the individual's adjustment when operating under monopolistic competition, laissez-faire, and monopoly. Finally, dynamic and static factors are considered in relation to their effects on the individual's production, on the economy of cities and nations, and on the international economy.

3 class hours.   Credit, 3.
8:00-8:50 M. W. F.   MR. BARRETT.

55. (I) Marketing Farm Products

Not open to students who have taken or are taking Marketing 53. An analysis of present and past systems of assembling, transporting, distributing, and grading agricultural products. Such aspects as the adjustment of production and consumption, price formation, channels of distribution, price differentials and margins, public policy, market reporting and forecasting, and a study of the marketing of major agricultural products are considered. Geographic, future, and quality differentials are studied from the agricultural and commercial standpoint. A field trip may be arranged.

3 class hours.   Credit, 3.
8:00-8:50 M. W. F.   THE DEPARTMENT.

56. (II) The Fundamentals of Cooperation

A study of the philosophy and principles of cooperation in Europe and in the United States. The history of cooperation, legal consideration, management, financing, membership relations, methods of formation, sales methods and policies are given full attention. Progress in the cooperative marketing of different agricultural products is studied.

3 class hours.   Credit, 3.
8:00-8:50 M. W. F.   MR. CALLAHAN.

57. (I) Agricultural Credit and Land Appraisal (1956-57)

A study of the development, use, functions, and operations of public and private credit institutions which are available to agriculture. Special emphasis is given to the practical aspects of credit policy and land appraisal. Given in alternate years.

3 class hours.   Credit, 3.
11:00-11:50 M. W. F.   MR. LINDSEY.

71. (I) Agricultural Economic Theory (1957-58)

The course is a comparative and critical study of the significant contributions of the leading economists to the theory of agricultural economics from the time of Adam Smith to the present. Given in alternate years.

3 class hours.   Credit, 3.
11:00-11:50 M. W. F.   MR. LINDSEY.

75. (I) Farm Organization and Management

This course analyzes the functions of the farmer as a business proprietor. Both the external and internal economic forces affecting the farm business are considered, such as selection and combination of factors of farm production, choice and combination of farm enterprises, the economical use of funds, the nature of farming costs, adjusting farm production to markets and prices, and the management of equipment and labor.

3 class hours.   Credit, 3.
9:00-9:50 M. W. F.   MR. BARRETT.
Prerequisite, Agricultural Economics 26.

76. (II) Advanced Farm Organization and Management

The use of farm records and accounts as a basis for planning and budgeting is emphasized. Measures of success and factors in success in farming, and work simplification as applied to efficient farm techniques are considered. The last part of the course will be given over to the specific study of selected farms

STATISTICS

and the practical application of the principles and practices already discussed.
Field trips are required at an estimated cost of not over five dollars.

1 class hour; 1 4-hour laboratory period. Credit, 2
10:00-10:50 Th.; 1:00-4:50 M. MR. BARRETT.
Prerequisite, Agricultural Economics 75.

78. (II) Principles and Problems of Land Economics

A study of the major contributions by outstanding economic writers to
theoretical land economics; a review of American land policies; a presentation
of the principles, techniques, and objectives involved in modern land use planning; and a discussion of contemporary land problems in the United States.

3 class hours. Credit, 3.
11:00-11:50 M. W. F. MR. LINDSEY.

83. (I) Advanced Farm Operation

For seniors specializing in agriculture; others by permission of instructor.
A study of the efficiency of operations on a specific farm.

3 hours or equivalent. Credit, 3.
Hours by arrangement. MR. BARRETT.

89. (I) 90. (II) Seminar in Agricultural Economics

A study of special problems in agricultural policy, agricultural institutions,
market and price analysis.

Hours by arrangement. THE DEPARTMENT.

STATISTICS

77. (I) Elementary Experimental Statistics

Primarily for students in psychology, biology, chemistry, agronomy, poultry,
animal husbandry, food technology, education, and public health, who are
interested in obtaining and handling data of small samples. Chi square, "t" and
analysis of variance tests of significance; frequency distribution, averages, dispersion, regression and simple correlation description; and chart and table
presentation are the specific fields covered. Students taking this course may
not take Statistics 79.

1 class hour; 2 2-hour laboratory periods. Credit, 3
MR. LINDSEY, MR. RUSSELL.

79. (I) Elementary Economics Statistics

Primarily for students in economics, business administration, mathematics,
and industrial engineering, who are interested in obtaining and presenting
the data of large samples. Surveys, tables, charts, frequency distributions, averages, dispersion, standard error and its use, quality control, index numbers, time
series, and simple correlation are the specific fields covered. Students taking
this course may not take Statistics 77.

3 1-hour periods; 1 2-hour laboratory period. Credit, 3.
MR. LINDSEY, MR. RUSSELL.

80. (II) Advanced Statistics

This course is primarily devoted to linear and curvilinear multiple correlation analysis. Machine and shortcut graphic methods are used. Some time will
also be devoted to probability and analysis of variance.

1 class hour; 2 2-hour laboratory periods. Credit, 3.
1:00-1:50 W.; 1:00-2:50 M. F. MR. LINDSEY, MR. RUSSELL.

AGRICULTURE

1. (I) Economic Geography of the World's Agriculture

The agriculture of North America is given first consideration but special emphasis is placed on the study of southeastern Asia and the Soviet Union.

3 class hours. Credit, 3.

MR. JEFFREY.

AGRICULTURAL ENGINEERING

PROFESSOR FORE, ASSOCIATE PROFESSOR MARKUSON, ASSISTANT PROFESSOR TAGUE, MR. POWERS, MR. PIRA.

51. (I) House Planning

Plan designs of the small house will be made. The arrangement of interior equipment, especially in the kitchen, and lighting, heating, water supply, and sewage disposal will be studied, together with a brief history of the house materials, construction methods, equipment, and architectural styles. Consideration will be given to the economics of house building, including financing, and to maintenance and overhead expense.

1 class hour; 2 2-hour laboratory periods. Credit, 3.

MR. MARKUSON.

55. (1) Farm Shop

For students in agriculture and horticulture. Laboratory exercises cover instruction and practice in the use of carpenter's tools in construction and in bench work, arc and gas welding, pipe fitting, soldering, use of machinist's tools in machinery repair, and the mixing and placing of concrete. Classroom instruction covers materials of construction and the utilization of local and special materials for these purposes.

1 class hour; 2 2-hour laboratory periods. Credit, 3.

MR. POWERS.

72. (II) Drainage and Irrigation Engineering

This course is an abridgement of Agricultural Engineering 78 for students not majoring in Engineering who do not have the prerequisites for Course 78.

1 class hour; I 2-hour laboratory period. Credit, 3.

MR. FORE.

74. (II) Farm Structures

This course is an abridgement of Agricultural Engineering 73 for students not majoring in engineering who do not have the prerequisites for Course 73.

1 class hour; 2 2-hour laboratory periods. Credit, 3.

MR. MARKUSON.

80. (I) and (II) Food Process Engineering

A study of food processing machinery and instrumentation.

2 class hours; 1 2-hour laboratory period. Credit, 3.

MR. —————.

82. (II) Refrigeration

Fundamentals in planning and operating a refrigerated storage with particular reference to size, details of construction, cooling load, and refrigerating machinery and accessories. For non-engineering majors.

1 class hour; 2 3-hour laboratory period. Credit, 2.

MR. —————.

AGRONOMY

PROFESSOR COLBY, PROFESSOR DICKINSON, PROFESSOR STECKEL, ASSISTANT PRO-
FESSOR ROBERTS, ASSISTANT PROFESSOR EVERSON, ASSISTANT PROFESSOR ZAK,
MR. SOUTHWICK.

2. (II) Soils

This is an elementary course relating soils and their management to crop growth. This course is designed to give the student a broad background in soil science and its direct application to practical field problems. The course itself is presented with the object of introducing to the student the properties of soils and their influence upon the production of crops. The laboratory work consists of investigation of the fundamental characteristics of soil and basic principles of fertilizer and liming practices.

2 class hours; 1 2-hour laboratory period.   Credit, 3.
8:00-8:50 Tu. Th.; 3:00-4:50 W. or Th.
           MR. EVERSON, MR. ZAK, MR. COLBY.

51. (I) Field Crops

A study of the field crops of the United States which include their uses and improvement, with their soil and climatic requirements. Emphasis will be given to the best farm practices of the northeastern states as to rotation, liming, fertilizing, seeding methods, tillage, disease and insect control, and to methods of harvesting and storage. As an individual problem, each student must take a detailed plan of crop production for the actual conditions of some New England farm.

2 class hours; 1 2-hour laboratory period.   Credit, 3.
9:00-9:50 Tu. Th.; 1:00-2:50 Th.   MR. SOUTHWICK.

52. (II) Soil Utilization

The relationship of climate and native vegetation to the broader aspects of soil formation is described. Man's use of land resources is connected to show how the agricultural background of settlers has been active in soil use and abuse. Soil erosion control and its significance to permanent agriculture is considered.

3 class hours.   Credit, 3.
8:00-8:50 M. W. F.   MR. EVERSON.

57. (I) Soil Formation

The first part of this course considers those physical, chemical, biological, climate and geological factors involved in soil formation. The relationship of these factors to the kinds of soil formed in the United States is discussed.

3 class hours.   Credit, 3.
         MR. EVERSON.

77. (I) Crop Improvement

Theory and practice of the improvement of field crops by breeding and selection.

2 class hours; 1 2-hour laboratory period.   Credit, 3.
Hours by arrangement.   THE DEPARTMENT.
Prerequisites, Agronomy 51, Pomology 52, Zoology 53.

78. (II) Fertilizers and Soil Fertility

The primary purpose of this course is to relate soils and fertilizers to plant growth. Studies are made of fertilizer practices in the United States and

Europe. In the early part of the course consideration is given to the history of fertilizer development, with special emphasis upon early discoveries and causes of failure in early research. Later in the course, studies are made of factors which relate fertilizers and soils to plant growth. Fertilizer formulation technology and practice are considered in detail in the laboratory phase of this course.

2 class hours; 1 2-hour laboratory period. Credit, 3.
9:00-9:50 Tu. Th.; 1:00-2:50 Th. MR. EVERSON.

79. (I) Soil Physics

For seniors specializing in agronomy. The factors in soil which control tilth and energy relationships and the laws of physics which govern these factors are discussed. This includes heat, light, color, particle size and charge, water and gas movement, energy relationships and other physical factors effecting changes in the soil. The laboratory is used to familiarize the students with various methods used in measuring these important physical factors.

1 class hour; 2 2-hour laboratory periods. Credit, 3.
MR. EVERSON.

81. (I) 82. (II) Special Problems in Agronomy

For seniors specializing in agronomy. This course is designed to acquaint students with agronomic research methods and practical agronomic procedures.

3 2-hour laboratory periods. Credit, 3.
MR. COLBY.

84. (II) Soil Chemistry

For plant science and soil science students. Fundamental inorganic, organic, and bio-chemical reactions of soils are discussed and related to plant nutrition and microbiological activities. Colloidal aspects of soil chemical reactions and soil-plant interrelationships will be studied.

3 class hours. Credit, 3.
MR. STECKEL.

Prerequisites: Chemistry 29; Botany 68; Agronomy 57.

84B. (II) Soil Chemistry Laboratory

Primarily for seniors majoring in agronomy. Methods and techniques used in soil chemistry research and in plant science investigations will be studied. The student will be made familiar with methods of determining exchangeable bases, base exchange capacity, soil phosphate fractionation, and many other determinations peculiar to soil investigations. To be taken concurrently with Agronomy 84.

2 3-hour laboratory periods. Credit, 2.
MR. STECKEL.

Prerequisites: Chemistry 29, 30; Botany 68; Agronomy 57.

AGROSTOLOGY

53. (I) Agrostology

All factors that influence the successful growing of fine turf grasses are studied and correlated to enable the student to have a practical working knowledge of the construction and maintenance of lawns, sports, highway, airport and cemetery turf.

2 class hours; 1 2-hour laboratory period. Credit, 3.
MR. DICKINSON.

ART

56. (II) Agrostology

This course considers fine turf management as a business and profession. Emphasis is placed on diagnosis and treatment of turf failures; the selection of equipment and supplies and client approach. Field trips and practical exercises are arranged.

1 class hour; 2 2-hour laboratory periods.   Credit, 3.

MR. DICKINSON.

ART

Instructors in Landscape Architecture.

27. Modeling

A course in elementary modeling, of seeing, analyzing, and reproducing form in clay and modeling wax to develop sculptural technique.

6 laboratory hours.   Credit, 3.

28. Modeling

A continuation of Course 27 in advanced design and the making of plaster casts from original problems in small sculpture, such as plaques, masks, and medals or other such pieces.

6 laboratory hours.   Credit, 3.

MR. ——————.

Prerequisite, Art. 27.

31. (I) Elementary Design

For women. Elementary principles of design as applied to textiles, fabrics, interior decorations, etc.

3 2-hour laboratory periods.   Credit, 3.

MR. MacIVER.

33. (I) Freehand Drawing

A non-professional course in elementary drawing and painting in various media in black and white. The work is more or less personal and is adapted to the individual capacities and backgrounds of each student as far as possible. Limited to three sections of 20 students each.

6 laboratory hours.   Credit, 3.

MR. MacIVER.

34. (II) Freehand Drawing

This non-professional course is essentially one in which the use of color is stressed in various media, freehand drawing is emphasized and paintings in still-life and landscape subjects are produced. Limited to three sections of 20 students each.

6 laboratory hours.   Credit, 3.

MR. MacIVER.

75. (I) Art Appreciation

An analysis of the principles of critical judgment underlying the fine arts, leading toward the enjoyment of art and its application to every day life.

3 class hours.   Credit, 3.

9:00-9:50 M. W. F.   MR. OTTO.

78. (II) Early and Medieval Art

An appreciative survey of art and history from early times to the present. Works in painting, sculpture, architecture, and the minor arts are examined in the light of their contributions to the history of civilization, and to the development of art forms.

3 class hours.   Credit, 3.
11:00-11:50 M. W. F.   MR. HAMILTON.

BACTERIOLOGY AND PUBLIC HEALTH

PROFESSOR FRANCE, ASSOCIATE PROFESSOR GARVEY, ASSOCIATE PROFESSOR PERRIELLO, ASSISTANT PROFESSOR CZARNECKI, ASSISTANT PROFESSOR MANDEL, MR. WISNIESKI, MR. LARKIN, in cooperation with DR. WALTER W. LEE, State District Health Officer; MR. ERNEST A. SNOW of the Division of Sanitary Engineering of the Massachusetts Department of Public Health; MR. JOEL COHEN of the Springfield Hospital.

31. (I) and (II) Introductory Bacteriology

Students majoring in Liberal Arts, Business Administration, and Agriculture taking this course to satisfy a science requirement should take it first semester. Designed to present to students interested in general science, agriculture, horticulture, and home economics the fundamental concepts of bacteriological science; make microorganisms real and significant; and demonstrate their importance in the problems of agriculture, general science, industry, public health, and medicine. The laboratory work covers the use and care of the compound microscope, the preparation of culture media, methods of sterilizing equipment, the isolation and aseptic handling of pure cultures, simple and differential staining, bacterial classification and differential studies on type species of pathogenic and non-pathogenic bacteria.

2 class hours; 2 2-hour laboratory periods.   Credit, 4.
12:00-12:50 M. F. or Tu. Th.; 1:00-2:50 or 3:00-4:50 M. F. or Tu. Th.
                                                        MR. CZARNECKI.

51. (I) 52. (II) Advanced Bacteriology

A continuation of introductory bacteriology. Studies on bacterial metabolism and the influence of environmental factors on growth and viability. The identification and differentiation of bacterial species by morphological, cultural, physiological, and serological studies; disinfectants and antibiotics. The combined courses give to the student not only a comprehensive picture of various forms of existing bacteria but develop a specialized technique for their cultivation, isolation, and identification.

2 3-hour laboratory periods.   Credit, 3.
1:00-3:50 Tu. Th.   MISS GARVEY.
Prerequisite, for 51, Bacteriology 31; for 52, Bacteriology 51.

54. (I) and (II) Water and Sewage Bacteriology

For students majoring in Engineering. Elementary bacteriology with emphasis placed upon the importance of bacteria found in water and sewage. Work will include routine analysis used in the examination of water and sewage and in the laboratory control of water and sewage treatment plants.

2 3-hour laboratory periods.   Credit, 3.
2:00-4:50 Tu. Th.   MR. PERRIELLO.
Prerequisite, Civil Engineering 77 or permission of the instructor.

55. (I) Fundamentals of Soil Microbiology

This course is designed for students majoring in agricultural and related fields. Subjects included will be: fundamental laboratory procedures and techniques; quantative and qualitative microbiological analysis of various types of soils; studies on the carbon and nitrogen cycles as affected by soil microorganisms.

2 3-hour laboratory periods.   Credit, 3.
                                                                      MR. MANDEL.

56. (I) and (II) Methods for Bacteriological Preparations

This course is intended for students majoring in bacteriology and public health. The material given in the course includes methods of preparation and sterilization of culture media and equipment, the preparation of stains and reagents, and the use, care and repair of laboratory instruments.

2 2-hour laboratory periods.   Credit, 2.
                                                                      THE STAFF.

81. (I) General Applied Bacteriology

This course is designed to give the student a working knowledge of routine and special tests used in present day applied bacteriology. Subjects receiving consideration are: methods for determining the sanitary quality of milk and milk products, water and shellfish; eating and drinking utensils; and air.

1 class hour; 2 3-hour laboratory periods.   Credit, 4.
1:00-3:50 M. F. or 1:00-3:50 W.; 9:00-11:50 S.
                                              MR. FRANCE, MR. PERRIELLO.
Prerequisite, Bacteriology 51 or permission of the instructor.

82. (II) Food Bacteriology

Consideration will be given to (1) bacteriological principles which apply to the preservation, fermentation and spoilage of foods, (2) the sanitary examination of foods, (3) the causes of food poisoning, and (4) microbiological assays.

2 3-hour laboratory periods.   Credit, 3.
1:00-3:50 M. F. or Tu. Th.   MISS GARVEY.
Prerequisite, Bacteriology 51 or permission of the instructor.

85. (I) Bacteriology (Immunology)

Admission by permission of the instructor. This course includes consideration of host reactions which favor the prevention and cure of disease; qualitative and quantitative estimations of toxins and antitoxins; the use of biological products such as antigens and immune sera in differential bacteriology and in disease diagnosis; and a consideration of isohemagglutinins as determinants of blood groups.

2 3-hour laboratory periods.   Credit, 3.
1:00-3:50 M. F.   MISS GARVEY.

90. (II) Sanitary Bacteriology

A detailed study of public health laboratory methods. Practical application of methods will be made through field studies.

1 4-hour and 1 2-hour laboratory period.   Credit, 3.
1:00-4:50 M., 1:00-2:50 F.   MR. FRANCE, MR. PERRIELLO.
Prerequisite, Bacteriology 81.

92. (II) Clinical Laboratory Methods

This course is designed for students majoring in medical technology. The purpose of the course is to familiarize the student with routine clinical laboratory procedures.

1 4-hour laboratory period.   Credit, 3.
1:00-4:50 W., 3:00-4:50 F.   MR. FRANCE, MR. COHEN.
Prerequisites, Bacteriology 85; Zoology 35, 69.

93. (I) 94. (II) Problems

Qualified seniors who have obtained permission from the department may arrange for independent work on special problems in bacteriology.

Credit, 3.
THE DEPARTMENT.

96. (II) Studies of Special Microbial Groups

A study of the biology of certain groups of microorganisms considered only briefly or not at all in other courses offered in the department. The course will cover the autotrophic bacterial, photo-synthetic bacterial, actinomycetes, myxobacteria, chlamydobacteria and spirochaetes.

1 class hour; 2 2-hour laboratory periods.   Credit, 3.
MR. MANDEL.

Prerequisite, Bacteriology 51.

PUBLIC HEALTH

61. (I) 62. (II) General and Community Sanitation

A study of the problems of general and community sanitation. Subjects discussed will include insect and rodent control, housing and slum clearance, ventilation, lighting, bathing places, sanitation of eating utensils, nuisances, camp sanitation, industrial hygiene, water supplies, sewerage and sewage, refuse and garbage, food and milk sanitation.

3 class hours.   Credit, 3.
9:00-9:50 Tu. Th., 12:00-12:50 F. or 10:00-10:50 M. W. F.
MR. PERRIELLO, MR. WISNIESKI.

63. (I) Industrial Hygiene and Sanitation

A comprehensive study of the practices and principles of industrial processes which may constitute problems in sanitation; industrial wastes, smoke abatement, and the health of the worker. Subject matter includes organization of programs and the formation of policies for the inspection of sanitary and mechanical facilities of factories, food processing plants and other industries.

3 class hours.   Credit, 3.
MR. PERRIELLO.

64. (II) Microscopy of Water

A study of microscopic forms of life exclusive of the bacteria. Counting and control of plankton in potable waters. Elements of limnology.

2 class hours; 1 2-hour laboratory period.   Credit, 3.
9:00-9:50 M. F.; 8:00-9:50 or 10:00-11:50 W.   MR. SNOW.
Prerequisite, Bacteriology 31.

135

BACTERIOLOGY AND PUBLIC HEALTH

66. (I) and (II) Principles of Sanitation

The application of sanitary engineering and related sanitary sciences to health problems in the environment of urban and rural communities.

2 class hours. Credit, 2.

11:00-11:50 Tu. Th. Mr. Perriello.

Prerequisite, Civil Engineering 77 or permission of the instructor.

84. (II) Public Health Administration

Admission by approval of the instructor. The organization, function, and administration of governmental health agencies; the relationship of official and volunteer health agencies; preparation and presentation of lectures, demonstrations, and exhibits. Public health laws, regulations, and sanitary codes, their origin and enforcement.

3 class hours. Credit, 3.

10:00-10:50 M. W. F. Mr. Perriello.

86. (II) Field Studies in Sanitation

Trips will be taken into the field for the observation of public health practices in sewerage; sewage treatment and disposal; the production and purification of public water supplies; housing and slum clearance; insect and rodent nuisances; milk production, handling, and distribution; garbage and refuse collection and disposal; slaughter houses and rendering plants; cold storage warehouses; and bakery and restaurant sanitation. A comparative study of urban and rural services will be made. Although transportation will be furnished, students are expected to finance their own meals.

1 class hour; 1 4-hour laboratory period. Credit, 2.

Hours by arrangement. Mr. Wisnieski.

Prerequisites, Public Health 61 and 62.

92. (Summer) Supervised Field Training

All students majoring in sanitary technology must complete a prescribed thirteen-week field training program conducted by the New England Field Training Center under the direction of the Training Division of the Communicable Disease Center, U. S. Public Health Service, with the assistance of the staff and State Department of Health personnel. This course is a prerequisite for placement in federal, state and municipal agencies.

13 weeks. Credit, 6.

The Staff.

88. (II) Epidemiology and Communicable Disease Control

Admission by approval of the instructor. Consideration of the factors involved in the spread of infections; a detailed discussion of the communicable diseases, their distribution, cause, epidemiology, and means of prevention and control. The use of vaccines, serums and drugs for prevention and treatment, Mass immunization programs.

3 class hours. Credit, 3.

8:00-8:50 M. W. F. Mr. Lee.

BOTANY

PROFESSOR KOZLOWSKI, PROFESSOR TORREY, PROFESSOR LIVINGSTON, ASSISTANT PROFESSOR BANFIELD, ASSISTANT PROFESSOR PUTALA, MR. SCARBOROUGH, MR. NICKERSON, MR. DAVIS†, MR. MILLER.

1. (I) and (II) Introductory Botany

The course sets forth a body of facts dealing with the morphology and physiology of plants which is not only a foundation for future professional work in biological science, but of intrinsic value to the educated layman. The topics of seed germination, ecological adaptations, floral structures, taxonomy, botanical history, cytology, wood-anatomy, plant physiology, and plant reproduction receive appropriate elementary treatment. The lectures attempt to interpret the facts of plant structure and function in the light of the major biological principles.

2 class hours; 1-3hour laboratory period. Credit 3.

THE STAFF.

25. (I) The Plant Kingdom

Selected forms typifying the slimemolds, bacteria, algae, fungi, lichens, liverworts, mosses, fernworts, and seed plants. The course has a two-fold purpose: (1) it is intended for students who desire to extend their knowledge to the principal branches of the plant kingdom, thus rounding out a general course of which Botany 1 constitutes the first part; (2) it is also planned as an introduction to certain advanced courses for which it is prerequisite.

2 class hours; 1-2hour laboratory period. Credit, 3.

Prerequisite, Botany 1. MR. ——————.

26. (II) Spring Flora

Designed primarily to acquaint the student with the local spring flora through the identification of the commoner tracheate plants (lycopods, horsetails, ferns, gymnosperms, angiosperms) and the families they represent. In addition, laboratory and field work will include the study of native woody plants in the winter condition; the techniques of collection; and the use of a standard manual in the identification of plants.

1 class hour; 2 2-hour laboratory periods. Credit, 3.
8:00-8:50 W.; 1:00-2:50 Tu. Th. or 1:00-2:50 M. F.

MR. LIVINGSTON.

Prerequisite, Botany 1, Botany 25 recommended.

28. (II) Plant Physiology

Only for students intending to major in forestry. The processes occurring in plants with special emphasis on tree physiology and its relation to forestry problems.

2 class hours; 1 2-hour laboratory period. Credit 3.

MR. KOZLOWSKI.

30. (II) Plant Anatomy

A study of the origin and structure of vegetative and reproductive organs of seed plants.

2 class hours; 1 2-hour laboratory period. Credit 3.

MR. PUTALA.

† On leave of absence.

137

BOTANY

51. (I) Plant Pathology

A basic course in plant pathology dealing with the nature, cause and control of plant disease. Particular attention is given to disease symptoms, the phenomena of infection and of parasitism, the sources of inoculum, the agents of disease transmission, the relation of environment to disease incidence and development and to general principles of plant disease control. The laboratory phase is devoted to intensive study of a relatively few representative diseases induced by bacteria and fungi of the various classes.

1 class hour; 2 2-hour laboratory periods.　　　　　　　　　Credit, 3.
9:00-9:50 W.; 3:00-4:50 Tu. Th.　　　　　　　　　　　Mr. Banfield.

52. (II) Plant Pathology (1956-57)

An extension of Course 51. The objective is that of providing the student with a general knowledge of the more common and representative plant disease problems. Students are granted the option in the laboratory of specializing in disease problems in their major field of interest. Given in alternate years.

1 class hour; 2 2-hour laboratory periods.　　　　　　　　　Credit, 3.
9:00-9:50 W.; 3:00-4:50 Tu. Th.　　　　　　　　　　　Mr. Banfield.
Prerequisite, Botany 51.

58. (II) Microtechnique

A course in the preparation of microscopic mounts including the celloidin and paraffin methods of involving the use of microtomes and of differential stains. Enrolment limited to ten students.

2 2-hour laboratory periods.　　　　　　　　　　　　Credit, 2.
1:00-2:50 Tu. Th.　　　　　　　　　　　Mr. ——————.
Prerequisite, Botany 25.

59. (I) 60. (II) The Angiosperms (1956-57)

Alternate with Courses 61 and 62. The angiosperms are here treated from the standpoints of their structure and evolution, their taxonomy, their habits and distribution, and their economic or other special appeal to man's interests. Representatives of the dominant families, both temperate and tropical, are studied in the laboratory. The course is designed for students who want a broad knowledge of the flowering plants of the world.

2 class hours; 1 2-hour laboratory period.　　　　　　　　　Credit, 3.
　　　　　　　　　　　Mr. ——————.
Prerequisite, Botany 1.

61. (I) 62. (II) The Comparative Antomy of
　　　　　　　　　　　Green Plants (1955-56)

Alternate with Courses 59 and 60. The first semester is devoted to algae and mosses; the second to tracheates, including the extinct forms.

2 class hours; 1 2-hour laboratory period.　　　　　　　　　Credit, 3.
10:00-10:50 M. F.; 1:00-2:50 W.　　　　　　　　　Mr. ——————.
Prerequisite, Botany 25.

63. (I) Comparative Morphology of Fungi—
　　　　　　　Basidiomycetes and Fungi Imperfecti (1956-57)

The lectures deal with the comparative morphology, life history, and habitat of representative species of the important orders and families. The laboratory

138

periods are devoted to the collection, identification, and study of common local forms. Given in alternate years.

1 class hour; 2 2-hour laboratory periods.   Credit, 3.
9:00-9:50 F.; 3:00-4:50 M. F.   MR. BANFIELD.

64. (II) Comparative Morphology of Fungi
Phycomycetes and Ascomycetes (1955-56)

The lectures deal with the comparative morpology, life history, and habitat of representative species of the important orders and families. The laboratory periods are devoted to the collection, identification, and study of common local forms. Given in alternate years.

2 class hours; 1 2-hour laboratory period.   · Credit, 3.
9:00-9:50 Tu.; 10:00-10:50 Th.; 3:00-4:50 M.

MR. BANFIELD.

66. (II) General Mycology

A survey course in mycology designed to acquaint the student with the various classes of fungi, their distribution in nature, their significance in plant and animal disease, their utilization in industral fermentations. The laboratory phase is devoted to a study of common representative forms and practice in the use of keys for their identification.

1 class hour; 2 2-hour laboratory periods.   Credit, 3.
11:00-11:50 Tu.; 3:00-4:50 Tu. Th.   MR. BANFIELD.

67. (I) 68. (II) Introductory Plant Physiology

A study of the processes occurring in plants and their relation to the complex of activities constituting plant growth. Topics include colloidal systems, osmotic phenomena, absorption, transpiration, and internal water relations of plants, photosynthesis, fat and protein synthesis, digestion, translocation; respiration, and growth. This is a basic course for students planning for advanced work in any branch of plant science.

1 class hour; 2 2-hour laboratory periods.   Credit, 3.
10:00-10:50 W.; 3:00-4:50 M. W. or Tu. Th.   MR. KOZLOWSKI.

69. (I) Forest and Shade Tree Pathology

The nature, cause and control of the principal types of disease in trees, including decay of forest products, standing and structural timber; insects and environment in relation to fungi and disease development; morphology and identification of fungi that induce disease or decay in trees.

2 class hours; 1 3-hour laboratory period.   Credit, 3.

MR. BANFIELD.

75. (I) Methods in Plant Pathology (1956-57)

A course in the general techniques and specialized methods used in the investigation of plant diseases, including isolation, culture and pathogenicity studies of representative plant pathogenes, the preparation and sterilization of various culture media, elementary staining and histological techniques, the use of the microscope, study of fungicides, and training in elementary photographic procedures. Given in alternate years.

1 class hour; 2 2-hour laboratory periods.   Credit, 3.
2:00-2:50 Tu.; 10:00-11:50 Tu.; 3:00-4:50 F.   MR. BANFIELD.
Prerequisite, Botany 51.

77. (I) 78. (II) Advanced Plant Physiology (1955-56)

Advanced study in physiology. Given in alternate years.

1 class hour; 2 2-hour laboratory periods.
Hours by arrangement.
Prerequisites, Botany 67, 68; Chemistry 51, 52.

Credit, 3.
MR. KOZLOWSKI.

81. (I) Plant Ecology

A general survey of the relationship of plants to their environment including a study of environmental factors (autecology)—soil, water, temperature, light, atmosphere, and the biotic factors—and of plant communities (synecology) with special emphasis on the structure and succession of plant communities in North America.

1 class hour; 2 2-hour laboratory periods.

Credit, 3.
MR. LIVINGSTON.

Prerequisite, Botany 1; Botany 26 recommended.

82. (II) Plant Geography

A survey of descriptive and historical plant geography as well as the basic principles governing the natural distributions of plants. Included as topics are problems of dispersal and migration, endemism, species senescence, discontinuous distributions, polyphlesis, continental drift, and geographical aspects of polyploidy. The course is designed for advanced undergraduates or qualified graduate students.

2 class hours.

Credit, 2.
MR. LIVINGSTON.

Prerequisite, Botany 81 or equivalent recommended.

85. (I) 86. (II) Problems in Botany

Supervised problem work for qualified students.

Hours by arrangement.

Credit, 1-3.
THE STAFF.

89. (I) Plant Cytogenetics

The interpretation of hereditary phenomena in plants in terms of cell structures. A correlation of plant cytology and genetics which is of applied as well as theoretical importance.

1 class hour; 2 2-hour laboratory periods.

Credit, 3.
MR. NICKERSON.

90. (II) Insect Transmission of Plant Diseases

The intricate interrelationships of insects and microorganisms with particular emphasis on the basic role played by insects in inception, distribution and perpetuation of plant diseases.

3 class hours.

Credit, 3.
MR. BANFIELD.

BUSINESS ADMINISTRATION

PROFESSOR KIMBALL, PROFESSOR HARDY, PROFESSOR VANCE, ASSOCIATE PROFESSOR COLWELL, ASSOCIATE PROFESSOR SMART, ASSOCIATE PROFESSOR LUDTKE, ASSISTANT PROFESSOR SINGER, ASSISTANT PROFESSOR RIVERS,† ASSISTANT PROFESSOR LENTILHON, ASSISTANT PROFESSOR GILLIS, ASSISTANT PROFESSOR HACKAMACK, ASSISTANT PROFESSOR ANDERSON, ASSISTANT PROFESSOR SHERMAN, MR. ROBINSON, MR. ZANE..

ACCOUNTING

25. (I) Introduction to Accounting I

This course aims to give the student a working knowledge of the principles underlying the gathering, recording, and interpretation of accounting data.

1 class hour; 2 2-hour laboratory periods.   Credit, 3.

MR. COLWELL, MR. ANDERSON, MR. LENTILHON, MR. SINGER.

26. (II) Introduction to Accounting II

This course covers the principles and procedures of corporation accounting and the construction of corporate financial statements.

1 class hour; 2 2-hour laboratory periods.   Credit, 3.

MR. COLWELL, MR. ANDERSON, MR. LENTILHON, MR. SINGER.

61. (I) Intermediate Accounting

An application of accounting principles to problems of income determination and the classification and valuation of assets.

1 class hour; 2 2-hour laboratory periods.   Credit, 3.

Prerequisite, Accounting 26.   MR. LENTILHON, MR. SINGER.

62. (II) Advanced Accounting

A continuation of Accounting 61, concerned with the valuation of assets and liabilities, accounting for net worth, statements of application of funds and the analysis of financial statements.

1 class hour; 2 2-hour laboratory periods.   Credit, 3.

Prerequisite, Accounting 61.   MR. SINGER.

64. (II) Cost Accounting

The use of accounting techniques to determine business costs, including process costs, standard costs, distributive costs and cost problems imposed by government regulation.

2 class hours; 1 2-hour laboratory period.   Credit, 3.

Prerequisite, Accounting 26.   MR. LENTILHON.

73. (I) Tax Accounting

This course examines the principles of income taxation as applied to individuals and emphasizes the application of income tax laws in corporate accounting.

3 class hours.   Credit, 3.

Prerequisite, Accounting 26.   MR. ANDERSON.

† On leave of absence.

74. (II) Accounting Systems

The application of accounting procedures to representative types of business including mechanized accounting.

3 class hours.   Credit, 3.
                                                          MR. COLWELL.

Prerequisite, Accounting 64.

75. (I) Administrative Accounting and Control

The preparation and analysis of budgets, reports, and internal checks, using accounting techniques as control devices in business and industry.

3 class hours.   Credit, 3.
                                                          MR. COLWELL.

Prerequisite, Accounting 26.

76. (II) Auditing

A course in the verification of accounting records dealing with audit theory and procedure.

3 class hours.   Credit, 3.
                                                          MR. ANDERSON.

Prerequisites, Accounting 62 and 64.

BUSINESS LAW

70. (I) and (II) Business Law I

This course consists of a study of the drawing, and interpretation of contracts, and includes agency, sales, and commercial paper.

3 class hours.   Credit, 3.
                                                          MR. SMART.

72. (II) Business Law II

A continuation of Business Law 70 including the study of the legal aspects of business organization and some laws of public regulation.

3 class hours.   Credit. 3.
                                                          MR. SMART.

Prerequisite, Business Law 70.

FINANCE

55. (I) Financial Institutions

A general course which surveys the development and operations of our financial institutions and provides an integrated study of the entire American financial structure.

3 class hours.   Credit, 3.
                                          MR. KIMBALL, MR. LUDTKE, MR. GILLIS.

65. (I) and (II) Corporation Finance

This course in business finance is concerned with the nature and uses of corporate securities, provision and maintenance of capital, financial expansion, and corporate reorganization.

3 class hours.   Credit, 3.
                                          MR. KIMBALL, MR. LUDTKE, MR. GILLIS.

76. (II) Insurance

A general course concerning risks encountered by individuals and business enterprises and the methods and institutions evolved to insure against loss. Property, casualty, life and other forms of insurance are studied from the point of view of both the insurance carrier and the insured.

3 class hours. Credit, 3.

MR. LUDTKE.

81. (I) Problems in Business Finance

A study of problems of financial management of various types of business enterprises and the formation of their financial policies.

3 class hours. Credit, 3.

Prerequisite, Finance 65 or consent of instructor. MR. LUDTKE.

82. (II) Investments

The principles and techniques that are useful for the analysis and selection of investment media; investment policies of individuals and institutions.

3 class hours. Credit, 3.

Prerequisite, Finance 65 or consent of instructor. MR. LUDTKE.

INDUSTRIAL ADMINISTRATION

11. (I) Industrial Geography

A study of the distribution of natural and human resources and the industrial and physiographic bases of the extractive and manufacturing industries.

3 class hours. Credit, 3.

MR. VANCE, MR. HACKAMACK, MR. RIVERS, MR. ROBINSON.

53. (I) Office Procedures

This course provides instruction and laboratory practice in office organization and procedures and the operation of office machines. Not offered 1956-57.

1 class hour; 4 1-hour laboratory periods. Credit, 3.

MR. ————.

54. (II) Office Procedures

A continuation of Course 53, including the use of systems and records as managerial aids in the business office. Not offered 1956-57.

1 class hour; 4 1-hour laboratory periods. Credit, 3.

MR. ————.

62. (II) Market Research

The aims, sources and fact-gathering methods of market research activities. General study and individual research projects.

3 class hours. Credit, 3.

MR. SHERMAN.

71. (I) Retail Merchandising

A study of the operation and productive functions of the business of retailing.

3 class hours. Credit, 3.

MR. SHERMAN.

INDUSTRIAL ADMINISTRATION

73. (I) Advertising

A study of the techniques and media of advertising, its services to business and the organization and economic functions of the advertising industry.

3 class hours.   Credit, 3.
                                                            MR. HARDY.

74. (II) New England Markets

Individual and group study of the marketing problems of New England industrial enterprises.

3 class hours.   Credit, 3.
                                                            MR. HARDY.

76. (II) Purchasing

A study of the purchasing organization and practices of industrial enterprises.

3 class hours.   Credit, 3.
                                                          MR. ROBINSON.

80. (II) Problems in Marketing

A study of problems of market management, especially the interrelation between research planning and the execution of sales programs. Effects of various marketing policies upon individual firms and the industry are examined.

3 class hours.   Credit, 3.
                                                          MR. SHERMAN.

Prerequisite, Marketing 53.

63. (I) Management in Industry

A study of the principles connected with the organization and management of industrial enterprises.

3 class hours.   Credit, 3.
                        MR. VANCE, MR. HACKAMACK, MR. RIVERS.

64. (II) Personnel Management

A study of the principles of the management of labor relations. Attention is focused on procuring, developing, maintaining and using personnel.

3 class hours.   Credit, 3.
                        MR. VANCE, MR. HACKAMACK, MR. RIVERS.

66. (II) Transportation and Traffic

The development of highway, waterway, railway, and air transportation; the operation and control of transportation agencies; the use of freight tariffs, classifications and routing guides; the functions of industrial traffic departments.

3 class hours.   Credit, 3.
                                      MR. RIVERS, MR. ROBINSON.

73. (I) Problems of Industrial Management

An intensive analysis, through study of actual cases, of the problems that confront managers in the manufacturing division of a business.

3 class hours.   Credit, 3.
                                                            MR. VANCE.

Prerequisite, Industrial Administration 63.

144

80. (II) Administrative Procedure

Theory and practice of administrative organization; planning and direction in business situations; formation and execution of business policies; coordinated and effective operations through group action.

3 class hours.   Credit, 3.
                                                                                                  MR. VANCE.

MARKETING

53. (I) Marketing Principles

Not open to students who have taken or are taking Agricultural Economics 55. A study of the institutions, methods, and problems concerned with the distribution of industrial and consumer goods.

3 class hours.   Credit, 3.
                                                     MR. HARDY, MR. SHERMAN, MR. ROBINSON.

54. (II) Salesmanship and Sales Management

The principles and practices of selling; the management of sales personnel; and the control of sales operations.

3 class hours.   Credit, 3.
                                                                                                  MR. HARDY.

CHEMISTRY

PROFESSOR RITCHIE, PROFESSOR FESSENDEN, PROFESSOR SMITH, ASSOCIATE PROFESSOR CANNON, ASSOCIATE PROFESSOR LITTLE, ASSISTANT PROFESSOR RICHASON, ASSISTANT PROFESSOR ROBERTS, ASSISTANT PROFESSOR STEIN, MR. PARROTT*, MR. OBERLANDER, MR. TYLER, MR. CHRISTOFFERS†, MISS KENDROW, MISS JUDGE, MR. LEVITT, MR. McWHORTER, MR. CARPINO.

1. (I) 2. (II) General Chemistry

A study of the fundamental chemical laws and theories. A considerable amount of descriptive material will be included in connection with discussions of the periodic system, atomic structure, and in various applications of the principles. The object of the course is to give the student a sound scientific training through a course in chemistry. Students who have had no previous work in chemistry will be grouped together in recitation sections so that they may have special attention.

2 class hours; 1 quiz hour; 1 2-hour laboratory period.   Credit, 3.
                    MR. FESSENDEN, MR. RICHASON, MR. STEIN, MR. OBERLANDER.

4. (II) General Inorganic Chemistry

For students planning to major in chemistry or chemical engineering, and others who plan to continue the study of this science in preparation for their field of specialization. The course will include ionic equilibria; oxidation and reduction; electro-chemistry; the descriptive chemistry of some nonmetallic and metallic elements; the metallurgy of some common metals, and a discussion of the production of some of the more important inorganic chemicals. Applications of atomic structure and the electronic theory of valence to these subjects will be stressed.

2 class hours; 1 quiz hour; 2 2-hour laboratory periods.   Credit, 4.

Prerequisite, Chemistry 1.   MR. FESSENDEN, MR. RICHASON.

  * On leave of absence for military service.
  † On leave of absence.

29. (I) and (II)   Qualitative Analysis

A study of the fundamental principles and laws concerning the behavior of solutions of electrolytes. The laboratory work deals with the characteristic properties, reactions, and the systematic separation and identification of the common cations and anions. The semi-micro technique is used throughout for the analysis of salts, salt mixtures, and alloys. A considerable portion of the laboratory work is devoted to the identification of substances unknown to the student. This course is designed to meet the needs not only of those students specializing in chemistry, but also of those students specializing in other subjects where inorganic chemistry is of importance.

2 class hours; 6 laboratory hours.   Credit, 4.
8:00-8:50 or 10:00-10:50 Tu. Th.; 8:00-9:50 or 10:00-11:50 M. W. F. or 1:00-3:50
M. F. or 1:00-3:50 Tu. Th.   MR. SMITH.
Prerequisites, Chemistry 2 or 4.

30. (I) and (II)   Quantitative Analysis

The theory and practice of representative determinations in gravimetric and volumetric analysis are considered in detail together with analytical calculations. The laboratory work emphasizes the techniques required for accurate chemical measurements.

2 class hours; 2 3-hour laboratory periods.   Credit, 4.
10:00-10:50 Tu. Th.; 1:00-3:50 M. F. or Tu. Th. or 1:00-3:50 W., 9:00-11.50 S.
MR. ROBERTS.
Prerequisite, Chemistry 29.

33. (I) and (II)   Organic Chemistry

A short course intended to satisfy the requirements in this field for all students who do not specialize in chemistry.

3 class hours; 1 3-hour laboratory period.   Credit, 4.
9:00-9:50 Tu. Th. S.; 1:00-3:50 M. T. W. or Th.   MR. CARPINO.
Prerequisites, Chemistry 1 and 2.

51. (I)   52. (II)   Organic Chemistry

A course in the theory of organic chemistry intended to serve the needs of students who will specialize in chemistry, as well as those who may specialize in other fields where a more comprehensive course is desired than Chemistry 33. The first semester deals largely with compounds of the aliphatic series, while the benzene series is taken up in the second semester. Students electing this course should take both 51 and 52.

3 class hours; 1 3-hour laboratory period.   Credit, 4.
9:00-9:50 M. W. F.; 1:00-3:50 M. W. or F.   MR. RITCHIE, MR. McWHORTER.
Prerequisite, Chemistry 29.

63. (I)   Chemistry of Water, Sewage and Sewage Sludge

Admission by permission of the instructor. The preparation of reagents and standard methods for the analysis of water, sewage and sewage sludge. Lectures and discussions on the sanitary significance of analytical data.

2 3-hour laboratory periods.   Credit, 3.
1:00-3:50 W.; 9:00-11:50 S.   MR. SNOW.
Prerequisite, Chemistry 30.

146

65. (I) 66. (II) Physical Chemistry

A study of the fundamental theories and laws of physical chemistry, together with the solution of problems involved in their application. The laboratory work will include practice in making physico-chemical measurements and the preparation of reports.

3 class hours; 1 3-hour laboratory period. Credit, 4.
8:00-8:50 or 11:00-11:50 M. W. F.; 1:00-3:50 M. W. or F.

MR. FESSENDEN, MR. SMITH.

Prerequisites, Chemistry 30; Mathematics 30; Physics 26.

77. (I) Advanced Physical Chemistry

A detailed study of a number of topics such as kinetics, catalysis, chemical thermodynamics and electrochemistry.

3 class hours. Credit, 3.

MR. STEIN.

Prerequisites, Chemistry 65 and 66.

79. (I) Elementary Biochemistry

A consideration of the more important facts relating to biological materials and processes. This course is designed primarily for students not eligible for courses 93 or 94. It is not open to chemistry majors and is not offered for graduate credit.

3 class hours; 1 3-hour laboratory period. Credit, 4.
Prerequisite, Chemistry 33 or 51.

MR. LITTLE.

80 (II) Clinical Chemistry (Blood and Urine Analysis)

Work to be covered will include the collection and preparation of samples for analysis; standardization of glassware and the preparation of reagents; description of colorimeters and the determination of certain significant compounds in the samples. The latter group will include at least sugars, proteins, non-protein, nitrogen, fatty substances and inorganic elements.

1 class hour; 1 3-hour laboratory period. Credit, 2.

MR. LITTLE.

81. (I) Organic Chemistry

A rapid and intensive survey of the important reactions of organic chemistry with emphasis on their scope and limitations, recent developments and theoretical aspects. Admission by permission of instructor.

3 class hours. Credit, 3.
9:00-9:50 Tu. Th. S. MR. CANNON.
Prerequisite, one year of organic chemistry.

82. (II) Qualitative Organic Chemistry

The characterization of organic compounds by means of physical properties, class reactions and the preparation of suitable derivatives. The laboratory work will involve the identification of a number of simple unknown compounds followed by the separation, purification, and identification of the individual components in several unknown mixtures of organic compounds.

Admission by permission of instructor.

2 class hours; 2 3-hour laboratory periods. Credit, 4.
1:00-1:50 Tu. Th.; 2:00-4:50 Tu. Th. MR. CANNON.
Prerequisite, one year of organic chemistry.

CHEMISTRY

83. (I) Advanced Analytical Chemistry

The theory and techniques of special methods of analysis such as color-imetry, potentiometry, microscopy, ion exchange, electro-deposition and other recently developed methods of analysis. Primarily for chemistry majors but open to others with the permission of the instructor.

2 class hours; 1 3-hour laboratory period.   Credit, 3.
                                                         Mr. Roberts.

Prerequisite, Chemistry 30.

86. (II) Theoretical Inorganic Chemistry

A survey of inorganic chemistry which is largely theoretical and includes such topics as atomic structure, periodic classification and relationships, valence concepts, acid-base theory, and the chemistry of the commercially important elements and their compounds based upon the periodic table.

3 class hours.   Credit, 3.
8:00-8:50 M. W. F.   Mr. Smith.
Prerequisite, Chemistry 65.

88. (II) History of Chemistry

An historical and biographical study of chemistry and chemists. The aim of the course is: (1) to give the student a comprehensive view of the science as a whole, through a study of the development of new ideas and the establishment of new theories and laws; and (2) to arouse an enthusiastic interest in the subject and an appreciation of the true spirit of scientific research, through a sympathetic presentation of the work and lives of the great chemists who have been the creators of the chemistry of today.

3 class hours.   Credit, 3.
11:00-11:50 M. W. F.   Mr. Ritchie.

92. (II) Introduction Research

Admission only by permission of the department. The aim of the course is to give the student an opportunity to learn the purpose and methods of research. To each student is assigned some special subject or problem in one of the following fields of chemistry, viz., analytical, biochemical, inorganic, organic, physical.

10 laboratory hours.   Credit, 5.
Hours by arrangement.   The Department.

93. (I) 94. (II) General Biochemistry

These courses offer a broad introduction to the general field of biochemistry for students majoring in chemistry or in the biological sciences, and provide a background for more advanced or specialized study in this field.

3 class hours; 1 3-hour laboratory period.   Credit, 4.
                                                         Mr. Little.

Prerequisites, Chemistry 51 and 52 or their equivalent.

DAIRY AND ANIMAL SCIENCE

PROFESSOR HANKINSON, PROPESSOR FOLEY, PROFESSOR GAUNT, ASSOCIATE PROFESSOR BLACK, ASSISTANT PROFESSOR LINDQUIST, ASSISTANT PROFESSOR ELLIOT, ASSISTANT PROFESSOR BAKER, ASSISTANT PROFESSOR POTTER, ASSISTANT PROFESSOR GREENSTEIN, MR. ADAMS, MR. HOBART.

ANIMAL HUSBANDRY

26. (II) Breeds of Livestock and Dairy Cattle Judging

This course considers the economic desirability of thirty breeds of domestic livestock. The origin, history, characteristics and distribution of the breeds of cattle, sheep, swine, and horses commercially important in the United States will be discussed.

2 class hours; 1 2-hour laboratory period.   Credit, 3.
11:00-11:50 Tu. Th,: 3:00-4:50 F.   MR. ELLIOT.

26A. (II) Judging Dairy Cattle

This is an intensive course in judging dairy cattle and is required of animal husbandry majors. Others may take only by instructor's permission. During April and May, trips to leading dairy cattle breeding farms will be made on Saturdays. The highest ranking students will represent the University in the Intercollegiate Dairy Cattle Judging contest at the Eastern States Exposition and the Dairy Cattle Congress at Waterloo, Iowa the following fall.

1 2-hour laboratory period, February and March, 3-5 Th.
1 4-8 laboratory period, April and May, Saturday.   Credit, 1.
     MR. ELLIOT.

51. (I) Nutrition of Farm Animals

This course will present the fundamental principles of animal nutrition together with the indentification, composition, properties and uses of the common feed stuffs. The application of these basic principles in calculating balanced rations for all classes of livestock will be stressed, followed by practical feeding problems assigned outside the classroom. Feeding practices in use with the university livestock will be analyzed and demonstrated.

3 class hours; 1 2-hour laboratory period.   Credit, 4.
8:00-8:50 M. W. F.; 3:00-4:50 Tu. or Th.   MR. ELLIOT.

53. (I) Elements of Meat Packing

For department majors only. The lectures will discuss the development of the modern packing industry, the history of meat inspection, the principles of meat preservation and the opportunities in this field. Laboratories include the classification of cattle, calves, and swine into proper market classes and grades and slaughtering and dressing operations with animals provided by the university farm. Wholesale and retail cuts are prepared. A one-day trip through the packing plants of Boston is a requirement of this course and will cost about ten dollars.

1 class hour; 1 4-hour laboratory period.   Credit, 3.
1:00-1:50 W.; 1:00-5:00 M. or F.   MR. HOBART.

54. (II) Meat Processing

For students not majoring in animal husbandry, by permission of the instructor. A few periods will be devoted to a discussion of the meat packing

149

industry and to the preserving and care of meat products. The remainder will be spent on the classification of meat animals with practice slaughtering and the making of wholesale and retail cuts with stress on identification of retail cuts. A one-day trip through the packing plants of Boston is a requirement of this course and will cost about ten dollars.

1 4-hour laboratory period. Credit, 2.
1:00-5:00 W. or F. MR. ADAMS.

56. (II) Beef and Sheep Production

This course considers the historical and economic development, present status and probable future trends of beef and sheep production in the United States, especially New England. Consideration will be given to types of production; systems and methods of feeding, management and marketing. In the laboratory, practice will be obtained in fitting and showing as well as certain practical techniques such as dehorning, ear-tagging, castrating, foot-trimming, shearing, etc., and the treatment and prevention of external and internal parasites as well as common ailments.

2 class hours; 1 2-hour laboratory period. Credit, 3.
10:00-10:50 Tu. Th.; 8:00-9:50 Tu. or 3:00-4:50 Th. MR. BAKER.

56A. (II) General Livestock Judging and Field Trips

This course is given in conjunction with Animal Husbandry 56 and consists of practice in judging and selecting beef, cattle, sheep, horses, and swine. Throughout the spring, field trips are made to nearby livestock farms and breeding establishments. The five highest ranking students in judging will represent the university in the Intercollegiate Livestock Judging Contest at Eastern States Exposition the succeeding fall.

1 4-hour laboratory period. Credit, 1.
8:00-12:00 S. MR. BAKER.

72. (II) Meat Judging

This course deals with the classification, grading and judging of carcasses and cuts of beef, veal, lamb and pork. Class work will be carried on at Amherst and nearby packing and distributing plants. The team to represent the university in the Intercollegiate Meat Judging Contest held in connection with the Eastern States Exposition will be chosen from students in this course.

1 4-hour laboratory period. Credit, 1.
1:00-4:50 Tu. MR. ADAMS.
Prerequisites, Animal Husbandry 53 or permission of instructor.

74. (II) Advanced Meats

This course deals with the advanced techniques in preparing, preserving, and utilizing the various meat products from cattle, sheep and swine.

2 2-hour laboratory periods. Credit, 2.
MR. HOBART.
Prerequisites, Animal Husbandry 53 or 54 and permission of instructor.

75. (I) Reproduction in Farm Animals

This course deals with the comparative aspects of anatomy, embryology, endocrinology and physiology of the reproductive system of farm mammals, concepts of fertility and sterility, and practice in semen collection, artificial insemination and pregnancy diagnosis.

2 class hours; 1 2-hour laboratory period.

Credit, 3.

Prerequisites, Zoology 53.

MR. BLACK.

76. (II) Animal Breeding

This course is designed to acquaint the student with the workings of heredity and variation in farm mammals and the role of breeding systems and selection procedures in animal improvement.

2 class hours; 1 2-hour laboratory period.

Credit, 3.

Prerequisite, Animal Husbandry 75.

MR. GAUNT.

77 (I) 78. (II) Dairy Cattle Production

This is an intensive course covering all phases of dairy cattle and milk production. It affords an opportunity to seek the solution to the economic, nutritional, genetic, and managerial problems concerned in successful dairying.

1 2-hour laboratory period.

Credit, 3.

MR. FOLEY.

79. (I) Horse and Swine Production

This course is the same as Animal Husbandry 56 except that it deals with horses and swine instead of beef and sheep.

2 class hours; 1 2-hour laboratory period.
10:00-10:50 Tu. Th.; 1:00-2:50 Th.

Credit, 3.

MR. BAKER.

79A. (I) Advanced Livestock Judging

This course is devoted entirely to beef, sheep, horse, and swine judging and selection. Field trips will be made to breeding establishments and a team will be selected to represent the University at the Intercollegiate Livestock Judging Contest at the International Livestock Exposition in Chicago and at any other contests in which the University may occasionally or regularly participate.

1 4-hour laboratory period, first half of semester.
8:00-12:00 S.

Credit, 1.

MR. BAKER.

Prerequisite, Animal Husbandry 56A or permission of instructor.

81. (I) Seminar

For Animal Husbandry majors.

1 2-hour laboratory period.
3:00-4:50 Tu. or Th.

Credit, 1.

MR. GREENSTEIN.

82. (II) Seminar

For Animal Husbandry majors.

1 2-hour laboratory period.
3:00-4:50 Tu., W., or Th.

Credit, 1.

THE DEPARTMENT.

83. (I) Advanced Meat Judging

This course is a continuation of Course 72. The team to represent the University in the Intercollegiate Meats Judging Contest held in connection with the International Livestock Exposition will be chosen from students in this course.

1 4-hour laboratory period, first half of semester.
1:00-4:50 Tu.

Credit, 1.

MR. ADAMS.

Prerequisite, Animal Husbandry 72 or permission of instructor.

DAIRY INDUSTRY

25. (I) General Dairying

This course is introductory to all other courses in dairy industry and gives a general knowledge of the subject to those who wish to take only one course in dairying. The lecture portion includes the importance of the dairy industry, the composition and properties of milk, the secretion of milk, production of quality milk on the farm, methods of processing milk and cream, and the elements of ice cream, butter and cheese making. The laboratory work includes the testing of milk and milk products for fat and acidity, lactometry, and a general study of dairy plant equipment and processes.

2 class hours; 1 2-hour laboratory period. Credit, 3.
1:00-1:50 Tu. Th.; 2:00-3:50 Tu. or Th. MR. HANKINSON.

50. (II) Judging Dairy Products

A study of market standards and grades of dairy products, with practice in judging milk, ice cream, butter, and cheese. The emphasis is on recognizing quality in dairy products, detecting specific defects, and learning the causes and means of preventing common defects. A team is chosen from this class to represent the University in two contests: Eastern States Intercollegiate Dairy Products Judging Contest, and Collegiate Students' International Contest in Judging Dairy Products.

1 2-hour laboratory period. Credit, 1.
3:00-4:50 F. MR. POTTER.

52. (II) Market Milk

A study of the various phases of the market milk industry; sanitary production, transportation, pasteurization and handling in the city plant; marketing, delivery systems, milk and its relation to public health, inspection, milk laws, food value, and advertising. Cultured milk and other milk drinks also are included. Some milk plants are visited, the cost of the trip not exceeding five dollars.

2 class hours; 2 2-hour laboratory periods. Credit, 4.
8:00-8:50 Tu. Th.; 9:00-10:50 Tu. Th. or 3:00-4:50 Tu. Th. MR. LINDQUIST.

75. (I) Dairy Chemistry

This course is a particular study of those physical and chemical principles which not only explain the behavior of milk and milk products in the various technological operations, but also provide a basic viewpoint for dairy research. The lectures will include discussions (1) of the constituents of milk in relation to other organic compounds, and (2) the physiochemical aspects of certain dairy phenomena such as foaming, coagulation, etc. The laboratory work will include many of the tests used commercially and in dairy research, emphasizing the principles and application of both qualitative and quantitative analysis as well as the technique of operating scientific apparatus.

1 class hour; 2 2-hour laboratory periods. Credit, 3.
8:00-10:50 Tu., 8:00-9:50 Th. MR. POTTER.
Prerequisites, Dairy 25, Dairy 52, and Chemistry 52 or permission of the instructor.

77. (I) Butter and Cheese Making

Half of the semester is devoted to butter making; the remainder to cheese making, condensed and powdered milk. The various phases of the butter industry studied are: separators and cream separation; pasteurization, neutralization, and ripening of cream; preparation of starter cultures; churning; marketing and scoring of butter; creamery management. The work in cheese making includes cheddar, cream, Neufchatel, cottage, processed cheeses, etc. The manufacture of condensed milk, powdered milk, and commercial casein is also covered.

2 class hours; 2 3-hour laboratory periods.   Credit, 4.
11:00-11:50 W. F., 1:00-3:50 M. F.   MR. LINDQUIST, MR. POTTER.
Prerequisite, Dairy 25.

78. (II) Ice Cream Making

The course includes a study of the principles and practices of ice-cream making. The effects of such factors as composition, quality, pasteurization, homogenization, aging, and freezing on the finished products are considered. Sherbets, ices, fancy and individual forms, and all flavors of ice cream are studied. Some time is devoted to refrigeration, machinery, delivery equipment, and merchandising methods as they are related to the industry.

2 class hours; 2 3-hour laboratory periods.   Credit, 4.
11:00-11:50 W. F.; 1:00-3:50 Tu. Th.   MR. POTTER.

79. (I) 80. (II) Seminar

For students specializing in dairy industry.

1 class hour.   Credit, 1.
11:00-11:50 M.   THE DEPARTMENT.

ECONOMICS

PROFESSOR GAMBLE, PROFESSOR MORRIS, ASSOCIATE PROFESSOR SCHOEFFLER, ASSISTANT PROFESSOR HALLER, ASSISTANT PROFESSOR HOWARD, MR. MATTERSDORF, MR. WILL, VISITING PROFESSOR HAYN.

12. (II) Economic History of the United States

A study of the significant factors in the economic development of the nation.

3 class hours.   Credit, 3.
     MR. HALLER, MR. HOWARD.

25. (I) and (II) Elements of Economics

Definitions and introductory principles of production, exchange, and the financial organization of society, with a short survey of the economics of distribution and the use of wealth and income.

3 class hours.   Credit, 3.
     THE DEPARTMENT.

26. (II) Problems of the National Economy

A continuation of course 25. Current problems, including international economic relations, the determination and distribution of the national income, and the place of economic planning in peace and war are discussed.

3 class hours.   Credit, 3.
Prerequisite, Economics 25.   THE DEPARTMENT.

53. (I) Money, Banking and Credit

A critical survey of the development and operation of the monetary and banking systems of the United States.

3 class hours.   Credit, 3.
     MR. GAMBLE.

54. (II) Money, Income and Monetary Policy

A study of the relationship between money, income and monetary policy. It includes examination of the relationships between individuals, banks, money markets and central banks.

3 class hours. Credit, 3.
MR. GAMBLE.

Prerequisite, Economics 53 or Finance 53.

55. (I) Economics of Consumption

A study of patterns of consumption, standards of living and the sources and expenditure of individual and family incomes.

3 class hours. Credit, 3.
MR. HALLER.

56. (II) Business Fluctuations and Forecasting

A study of business fluctuations and an analysis of current business cycle theories.

3 class hours. Credit, 3.
MR. SCHOEFFLER, MR. HOWARD.

70. (II) The Structure of American Industry

A study of enterprise, market competition and economic development in American industries.

3 class hours. Credit, 3.
MR. HALLER.

73. (I) Modern Economic Theory and Analysis

An analysis of the mode of operation of a non-controlled free-enterprise economy. The principles of rational economic planning by business firms; the operation of various types of markets; and the balancing of conflicting forces in the entire economy.

3 class hours. Credit, 3.
MR. SCHOEFFLER.

74. (II) Current Economic Problems

An advanced course for those desirous of studying more intensively some current economic problems. Students will be encouraged to pursue lines of individual interest.

3 class hours. Credit, 3.
MR. HOWARD, MR. MORRIS.

77. (I) Economics of International Trade (1956-57)

A study of the policies, principles, and practices of international trade. Given in alternate years.

3 class hours. Credit, 3.
MR. MATTERSDORF.

78. (II) Public Finance

Principles of public revenues and expenditures with special emphasis on the systems and problems of taxation.

3 class hours. Credit, 3.
MR. GAMBLE.

154

79. (I) Labor Problems

An analysis of the background and character of the modern labor problem with special reference to the United States. Topics to be considered include: the problems of wages, hours, working conditions and unemployment; the trade union movement; and some agencies for the promotion of industrial peace.

3 class hours. Credit, 3.

MR. MORRIS, MR. WILL.

80. (II) Labor Legislation

A study of federal and state legislation affecting labor.

3 class hours. Credit, 3.

MR. MORRIS.

83. (I) Social Control of Business

Methods of social control of economic activity including both formal and informal controls.

3 class hours. Credit, 3.

MR. HOWARD.

84. (II) Comparative Economic Systems

An examination of the various forms of economic organization that have been tried and proposed with an analysis of the economic institutions of representative current economies.

3 class hours. Credit, 3.

MR. SCHOEFFLER.

91. (I) 92. (II) Seminar

Research in economic theory; problems of labor, commerce, and industry. If desirable, some other economic study may be substituted.

1 or 2 2-hour conferences. Credit, 1 to 3.

THE DEPARTMENT.

EDUCATION

PROFESSOR PURVIS, ASSISTANT PROFESSOR OLIVER, ASSISTANT PROFESSOR ROURKE, ASSISTANT PROFESSOR WYMAN, ASSISTANT PROFESSOR O'LEARY, ASSISTANT PROFESSOR FENNELL, MISS O'DONNELL, MISS DOWER, MR. TAFT.[1]

51. (I) and (II) History of Education

Educational movements are traced from early Greece to the present with the aim of better understanding of modern problems. Special emphasis is placed upon the function of the school in the various societies.

3 class hours. Credit, 3.

MR. PURVIS, MR. FENNELL.

52. (II) Principles and Methods of Teaching

By means of discussion, case studies, and current educational literature, teaching ideals and procedures are set up. Application of the general principles are made in the major fields represented by the class. Given also in the one-semester program.

3 class hours. Credit, 3.

MR. PURVIS, MR. FENNELL.

[1] State Supervisor for Agricultural Teacher-Training representing the State Department of Education in the administration of vocational agricultural acts.

53. (I) Educational Tests and Measurements

The most serviceable tests and scales for measuring achievement are considered; test construction, administration, scoring, and interpretation of results are studied and practiced. Considerable attention is given to preparation of informal tests for diagnostic and grading purposes.

2 class hours; 1 2-hour laboratory period. Credit, 3.
MR. ROURKE.

60. (I) and (II) Elementary School Curriculum

This course is designed to present a picture of the elementary school curriculum from the standpoint of content and methodology. Emphasis will be placed on the unit method and the activity program. Given only in the one-semester program.

3 class hours. Credit, 3.
MISS O'DONNELL.

61. (I) and (II) Teaching of Elementary Reading and Language Arts

The main emphasis will be placed upon a development program in reading instruction. Discussions, demonstrations, and principles of effective reading practices will form a major part of the course. Methods of teaching oral and written language will be included. Given only in the one-semester program.

3 class hours. Credit, 3.
MISS O'LEARY.

62. (I) and (II) Teaching of Elementary Arithmetic

This course will discuss and demonstrate accepted methods and materials in the teaching of arithmetic in the elementary grades. Attention will be given to methods of correlating arithmetic with the total program of the school. Given only in the one-semester program.

3 class hours. Credit, 3.
MISS O'DONNELL.

64. (I) and (II) Principles of Elementary Education

This course is designed to acquaint the student with the aim, organization, program, pupil population, etc., of the elementary school and the relationship between this level of education and the secondary school level which follows.

3 class hours. Credit, 3.
MISS O'LEARY.

66. (I) and (II) Preparation and Use of Audio-Visual Aids

Study is made of available media of audio-visual aids to instruction, construction of visual material, and accepted methods of use.

2 class hours; 1 2-hour laboratory period. Credit, 3.
MR. WYMAN.

72. (II) Vocational Education in Agriculture

This course demands certain requisites of experience and a definite objective on the part of the student to enter the field of vocational agricultural teaching which makes it necessary for the student to seek permission to enter the course. It is the first of the series of special courses (72, 73, 75) required of candidates for the vocational teacher-training certificate. A survey of vocational agricultural education and an introduction to teaching of vocational agriculture at the secondary school level is the basis of the course. Certain information and observations in preparation for the apprenticeship course are offered.

2 class hours; 1 2-hour laboratory period.   Credit, 3.
MR. OLIVER AND VOCATIONAL DIVISION
OF STATE DEPARTMENT OF EDUCATION.

73. (I) and (II) Apprentice Teaching in Agriculture

For a limited number of qualified candidates in vocational agriculture education. A full year in absentia normally following the junior year in college, teaching agriculture, horticulture, and related subjects. Candidates should have completed the course in Education 72, and in Education 52, if possible and must apply early to the instructor of the course.

Maximum Credit, 6.
MR. OLIVER AND VOCATIONAL DIVISION
OF STATE DEPARTMENT OF EDUCATION.

75. (I) Technique of Teaching Vocational Agriculture

By arrangement with the instructor. Preferably this course should follow courses 72 and 73. It covers the materials, methods, policies, and special requirements of Massachusetts for teaching vocational agriculture and related subjects in high schools and special country schools. This is one of three courses required of candidates for agricultural teacher training certificates.

2 class hours; 1 2-hour laboratory period.   Credit, 3.
MR. OLIVER AND VOCATIONAL DIVISION
OF STATE DEPARTMENT OF EDUCATION.

79. (I) Methods in Adult Education

Admission only by permission of instructor. The beginning Education course for juniors and seniors who are training for extension work and for others interested in teaching adults. Generally accepted methods of group and individual instruction with adults, and methods of developing leaders to carry on the work in the field.

2 class hours; 1 2-hour laboratory period.   Credit, 3.
MR. ——————.

81. (S) Teaching Foreign Language in Elementary School

The latest techniques, methods, and materials will be presented by instructors from the Departments of Education and Foreign Language. For trainees in elementary education or elementary teachers who have a major in foreign language.

5 periods a week for 6 weeks.   Credit, 3.
THE COOPERATING DEPARTMENTS.

83. (I) Principles of Secondary Education

This course presents a picture of the secondary school as a social agency, its relation to elementary and collegiate education, its aims, organizations, administration, curriculum procedures, and such other phases as are necessary to acquaint the student with the predominant level of our education ladder. Given also in the one-semester program.

3 class hours.   Credit, 3.
MR. MCCARTHY.

157

85. (I) and (II) Observation and Practice Teaching

Admission by permission of the Department. An opportunity to do regular teaching in cooperating schools within commuting distance of the University. The student works under the supervision of a teacher with frequent visits from some member of the university staff.   Credit, 3-6.

THE DEPARTMENT.

Prerequisites, the courses in the one-semester plan or their equivalent.

88. (I) and (II) Secondary School Curriculum

For senior majors in Education. A consideration of learning material and activities and their organization in the subjects which these students are teaching, and the preparation of courses of study in those fields in the light of accepted educational practices. Given also in the one-semester program.

2 class hours; 1 2-hour laboratory period.   Credit, 3.

MR. ROURKE.

CHEMICAL ENGINEERING

PROFESSOR LINDSEY, ASSISTANT PROFESSOR CASHIN, MR. SOLSTAD.

26. (II) Fundamentals

An introduction to the nature and scope of chemical engineering and certain fundamental concepts, to be amplified in later courses, particularly problems dealing with material and energy balances. There is a review of the chemical, mathematical, and physical principles which are particularly applicable.

2 class hours.   Credit, 2.

MR. CASHIN.

Prerequisites: Chemistry 2 or 4; Physics 25.

55. (I) Unit Operations I

A study of the fundamental principles underlying the unit operations of fluid flow, heat transfer and evaporation. A portion of the course is devoted to a study of the thermodynamic properties of matter.

3 class hours; 2 3-hour computation periods.   Credit, 5.

MR. CASHIN.

Prerequisites: Chemical Engineering, 26; Mathematics 30 or 31; Physics 25.

56. (II) Unit Operations II

A continuation of Course 55, including the additional unit operations of distillation, gas absorption, liquid extraction, crystallization, filtration, mixing, crushing and grinding.

3 class hours; 2 2-hour computation periods.   Credit, 5.

MR. CASHIN.

Prerequisite, Chemical Engineering 55.

57. (I) Inorganic Chemical Technology

A study of manufacture of some of the important inorganic chemicals. Topics studied include sulfuric acid, nitric acid, hydrochloric acid, ammonia, sodium carbonate, and sodium hydroxide with particular stress on unit operations. Field trips will be included where possible.

3 class hours.   Credit, 3.

Prerequisites: Chemistry 30; Physics 26.   MR. CASHIN.

58. (II) Organic Chemical Technology

A study of some of the unit processes involved in the manufacture of organic chemicals. Unit processes studied include nitration, amination, halogenation, oxidation and esterification. Field trips will be included where possible.

3 class hours.   Credit, 3.

Prerequisite, Chemistry 51.   MR. CASHIN.

75. (S) Instrumentation

A detailed study of the underlying principles and practices in indicating, recording and controlling instruments used on industrial process equipment.

4 class hours; 2 3-hour laboratory periods per week for six weeks.   Credit, 3.

Prerequisites: Physics 26 or 28; Chemical Engineering 55.   MR. CASHIN.

77. (I) Elements of Unit Operations

For other than chemical engineering majors. An introduction to some of the unit operations of process industries. The emphasis is on the principles and types of equipment, rather than on the quantitive aspects and design.

2 class hours; 1 2-hour laboratory period.   Credit, 3.

Prerequisites: Chemistry 30; Physics 25, 26.   MR. LINDSEY.

81. (I) Heat-energy Relations

A study of the energy relations in chemical processes. Includes: types of energy, energy balances, second law, thermodynamic functions, P-V-T relations of fluids, compression and expansion on processes.

3 class hours.   Credit, 3.

Prerequisites: Chemistry 66; Chemical Engineering 56.   MR. LINDSEY.

82. (II) Industrial Equilibria and Kinetics

A study of phase and chemical equilibria and rates of reaction in chemical processes from the industrial point of view.

3 class hours.   Credit, 3.

Prerequisites: Chemistry 66; Chemical Engineering 81.   MR. LINDSEY.

88. (S) Chemical Engineering Laboratory

A quantitative study of pilot plant size equipment illustrating some unit operations. Special emphasis is placed on the securing of accurate data, correct operating techniques, and on report writing. Field trips will be made when possible.

4 8-hour laboratory days per week for six weeks.   Credits, 3.

Prerequisite, Chemical Engineering 56.   THE STAFF.

89. (I) 90. (II) Laboratory Projects

Investigation and report on an elementary chemical engineering problem.

2 4-hour laboratory periods.   Credit, 3.

Prerequisites, Chemical Engineering 56, 88.   THE STAFF.

CIVIL ENGINEERING

91. (I) 92. (II) Seminar

Preparation and discussion of professional topics of interest to chemical engineers.

1 class hour.   Credit, 1.
                                                                     THE STAFF.

93. (I) 94. (II) Comprehensive Problems

The solution of comprehensive problems which requires the application and integration of a number of the principles studied in previous courses in chemistry and chemical engineering. Course 93 is a prerequisite for Course 94.

2 class hours; 1 3-hour computation period.   Credit, 3.

Prerequisites: Chemical Engineering 56; Chemistry 52, 66.   MR. LINDSEY.

95. (I) Process Equipment Design

The design of process equipment for the chemical industries: riveted pressure vessels, welded pressure vessels, piping, attachments and closures, etc.

1 class hour; 1 3-hour laboratory period.   Credit, 2.

Prerequisites: Chemical Engineering 55; Civil Engineering 53.   MR. LINDSEY.

98. (II) Advanced Unit Operations

A more detailed study of certain unit operations such as unsteady-state heat transfer, and multicomponent-distillation.

2 class hours.   Credit, 2.

Prerequisite, Chemical Engineering 56.   MR. CASHIN.

CIVIL ENGINEERING

PROFESSOR MARSTON, PROFESSOR WHITE, PROFESSOR OSGOOD, ASSOCIATE PROFESSOR HENDRICKSON, ASSISTANT PROFESSOR FENG, ASSISTANT PROFESSOR MARCUS, ASSISTANT PROFESSOR GROW, ASSISTANT PROFESSOR SHARP, ASSISTANT PROFESSOR BOYER, MR. BARTLETT.

25. (I) Surveying

The theory of surveying for both measurement and layout work, description of field and office computation, notes, and drafting procedure are given in the classroom. Topics covered are use of tape, transit, level, and plane table; methods of carrying out property surveys, layout surveys, computation and field work for simple and compound horizontal and vertical curves, determination of geographic position, determination of azimuth from the sun and Polaris, and a finished map of a small area.

3 class hours; 2 3-hour laboratory periods.   Credit, 5.

Prerequisite, Trigonometry.   MR. BOYER.

27. (I) and (II) Plane Surveying

The basic principles of mensuration are discussed in class. Instruction and problems involving the use of tape, transit and level are given in the field, and the preparation of a map of a small area is carried out in the drafting room. Route surveying is considered briefly. This course is not open to civil engineering students.

2 class hours; 1 3-hour laboratory period.   Credit, 3.

Prerequisite, Mathematics 5 or 7.   MR. BOYER.

28. (Summer) Property and Topographic Surveying

This course consists of a transit and tape property survey in which reference to Registry of Deeds records is required, and a topographic survey of a selected area using the plane table. Certain advanced topics such as triangulation and conformal coordinate systems are discussed as they relate to the topographic survey.

3 40-hour weeks. Credit, 3.

Prerequisite, Civil Engineering 25 or 27. MR. BOYER.

30. (Summer) Route Surveying Practice

This practice course consists of a preliminary survey of a short highway location, and of the preparation of a set of plans including plan, profile and cross sections and earthwork quantities from the data recorded on the survey.

3 40-hour weeks. Credit, 3.

Prerequisite, Civil Engineering 25. MR. BOYER.

34. (I) and (II) Statics

The following topics are considered: equilibrium of forces, friction, first and second movements, center of gravity. Algebraic and graphical methods are covered.

3 class hours. Credit, 3.

MR. WHITE, MR. MARCUS, MR. GROW.

Prerequisites: Physics 25; Mathematics 31.

51. (I) Strength of Materials

The following topics are considered: simple stresses and strains; combined stresses; torsion; shear and bending moments in beams; stresses and deflection of beams; columns.

3 class hours; 1 3-hour laboratory period. Credit, 4.

MR. WHITE, MR. MARCUS, MR. GROW.

Prerequisites: Civil Engineering 34; Mathematics 32.

52. (I) and (II) Dynamics

The following topics are considered: Kinematics, motion of particles, motion of rigid bodies, work and energy, power, impulse and momentum.

3 class hours. Credit, 3.

MR. WHITE, MR. MARCUS, MR. GROW.

Prerequisites: Civil Engineering 34; Mathematics 32.

53. (I) and (II) Strength of Materials

A shortened version of C.E. 51 for electrical and mechanical engineers in the industrial option.

3 class hours. Credit, 3.

MR. WHITE, MR. MARCUS, MR. GROW.

Prerequisites: Civil Engineering 34; Mathematics 32.

55. (I) Transportation Engineering

A study of transportation systems with major emphasis on geometric design of highways, transportation and traffic studies, and design and operation of

161

railroads. The laboratory periods are devoted to location and design of highways and intersections, and the design of railroad facilities.

2 class hours; 1 3-hour laboratory period.
Prerequisite, Civil Engineering 30.

Credit, 3.
MR. BOYER.

61. (I) and (II) Testing of Materials

A study of laboratory methods for the determination of the physical properties of engineering materials and their behavior under stress.

1 class hour; 1 3-hour laboratory period.
Prerequisite, Civil Engineering 51 or 53.

Credit, 2.
MR. SHARP.

70. (II) Theory of Structures

The course treats the analysis of statically determinate structures of wood and steel, with reference to particular types of structures, such as industrial and office buildings, highway and railway bridges.

3 class hours; 1 3-hour laboratory period.
Prerequisite, Civil Engineering 51.

Credit, 4.
MR. OSGOOD.

71. (I) Structural Design

This course is an application of the theory of structures to engineering practice through the preparation of designs and drawings for structural frames, girders and trusses in steel and wood that together make up a complete building frame or bridge. Emphasis is placed upon the design of structural members and joints.

2 class hours; 1 3-hour laboratory period.
Prerequisite, Civil Engineering 70.

Credit, 3.
MR. OSGOOD.

72. (II) Advanced Structural Theory

The analysis of space frames and methods of finding deflections of trusses and beams are studied. Several methods of analysis of statically indeterminate structures are introduced. Application of the theories considered is made in the solution of practical problems during the laboratory periods.

2 class hours; 1 3-hour laboratory period.
Prerequisite, Civil Engineering 70.

Credit, 3.
MR. OSGOOD.

73. (I) Reinforced Concrete Design

This course deals with the general methods of analyzing and designing reinforced concrete structures. Application is made to slabs, beams, girders, columns, walls and foundations for buildings, retaining walls and bridges. Drawings are prepared for a reinforced concrete building.

2 class hours; 2 3-hour laboratory periods.
Prerequisite, Civil Engineering 51.

Credit, 4.
MR. OSGOOD.

75. (I) and (II) Fluid Mechanics

The following topics are considered: properties of fluids, gas laws, viscosity, static pressure, gages, buoyant forces, dynamics of fluids, Bernoulli's theorem, flow in pipes, orifices, nozzles, weirs and open channels, hydraulic similitude and dimensional analysis.

3 class hours.
Prerequisite, Civil Engineering 52.

Credit, 3.
MR. ——————.

162

76. (I) and (II) Fluid Mechanics Laboratory

1 3-hour laboratory period. .   Credit, 1.

MR. ——————.

Prerequisite, Civil Engineering 75 previously or concurrently.

77. (I) Sanitary Engineering I

This course treats the following topics: demand of water and quantity of sewage, hydrology relating to water resources and drainage, hydraulics of water supply systems and sewers, pumps and pumping stations, water collecting and distributing works and sewerage systems.

3 class hours.   Credit, 3.

Prerequisite, Civil Engineering 75 or 76 concurrently.   MR. FENG.

78. (II) Sanitary Engineering II

. Consideration is given to hydraulic aspects of sedimentation, flotation, aeration and recirculation, quality of water supplies, characteristics of sewage, water purification works, sewage treatment works and industrial waste problems. The laboratory periods are devoted to the practice of designing water distribution systems and sewer systems.

3 class hours; 1 3-hour laboratory period.   Credit, 4.

Prerequisite, Civil Engineering 75 or 76.   MR. FENG

79. (I) Principles of Sanitary Engineering

This course is designed for students in the Department of Public Health. It covers phases of Civil Engineering 77 and 78 with consideration of the non-engineering background of the student. Admission by permission of the instructor.

2 class hours; 1 3-hour laboratory period.   Credit, 3.

MR. FENG.

80. (II) Soil Mechanics

This course is a study of the mechanical classification of soil based upon field and laboratory work and the validity of these classifications as a means of predicting soil behavior. The student is guided through case studies in embankment stability, seepage and consolidation.

2 class hours; 1 3-hour laboratory period.   Credit, 3.

Prerequisite, Geology 50.   MR. HENDRICKSON.

81. (I) Caissons

A survey of modern theories and practice in transferring structural loads to earth masses. Pile foundations, spread footings, cassions, and buoyant systems are discussed.

2 class hours; 1 3-hour laboratory period.   Credit, 3.

Prerequisite, Civil Engineering 80.   MR. HENDRICKSON.

86. (II) Sanitary Engineering Design

This is a laboratory course devoted to the design of sanitary engineering facilities, water supply and conditioning and sewerage and sewage treatment plants. Stream sanitation is considered and the latest practice and research in the sanitary engineering field are discussed.

1 class hour; 2 3-hour laboratory periods.   Credit, 3.

Prerequisites: Civil Engineering 77 and 78, or concurrently.   MR. FENG.

163

88. (II) Advanced Stress Analysis

This course is concerned with the determination of stresses and strains in structural and machine elements.

3 class hours.
Prerequisite, Civil Engineering 51 (with a grade of 75).
Credit, 3.
MR. WHITE.

90. (II) Contracts, Specifications and Estimating

A study of the essentials of contracts as applied to business procedures in the construction field, the purposes and makeup of specifications, and the processes of estimating through quantity surveys and unit cost applications.

3 class hours.
Credit, 3.
MR. MARKUSON.

92. (II) Professional Seminar

For seniors majoring in civil engineering. Current engineering projects are described by student reports. The professional aspect of the civil engineer's work is stressed.

3 class hours.
Credit, 3.
THE DEPARTMENT.

94. (II) Advanced Surveying

The following topics are included: Elements of astronomy, precise methods of surveying, adjustment of observations and the elements of photogrammetry.

2 class hours; 1-3-hour laboratory period.
Prerequisites, Civil Engineering 25, 28.
Credit, 3.
MR. HENDRICKSON.

96. (II) Hydraulic Engineering

The analysis and design of hydraulic structures such as storage reservoirs, spillways, dams, levees, and shore protection and channel works are considered.

2 class hours; 1 3-hour laboratory period.
Prerequisite, Civil Engineering 76.
Credit, 3.
MR. MARSTON.

98. (II) Advanced Transportation Engineering

The engineering aspects of traffic problems, urban and rural highways and airports are discussed in the lecture periods. The laboratory periods are devoted to the design of various facilities including urban streets, traffic signals, intersections and an airport.

2 class hours; 1 3-hour laboratory period.
Prerequisite, Civil Engineering 55.
Credit, 3.
MR. BOYER.

ELECTRICAL ENGINEERING

PROFESSOR ROYS, ASSOCIATE PROFESSOR LANGFORD, ASSOCIATE PROFESSOR MOHN, ASSISTANT PROFESSOR SMITH†, ASSISTANT PROFESSOR KARLSON, ASSISTANT PROFESSOR LINGO, ASSISTANT PROFESSOR EDWARDS, ASSISTANT PROFESSOR LAESTADIUS, MR. TROCCHI.

41. (I) Fundamentals of Electrical Engineering

Direct current circuit analysis by means of Ohm's and Kirchoff's laws, nodal equations, determinants, superposition principle, reciprocity and Theven-

† On leave of absence.

in's theorem. The fundamental laws of electricity and magnetism and their application to problems in electrostatics, magnetostatics and electromagnetism.
3 class hours; 1 3-hour laboratory period. Credit, 4.

Mr. Lingo, Mr. Mohn.

Prerequisites, Math 6, and 31 previously or concurrently.

42. (II) Alternating Current Circuits

The fundamentals of alternating—current circuit theory. This includes instantaneous voltage and current relations, effective values, average power, representations of sinusoids by means of complex quantities, resonance phenomena, coupled and polyphase circuits, Fourier Series and metering in a-c circuits.
2 class hours; 1 quiz hour; 1 2-hour laboratory period. Credit, 3.

Prerequisite, Electrical Engineering 41. Mr. Lingo, Mr. Mohn.

53. (I) Direct Current Machinery

The theory, construction, and operation of d-c motors and generators with emphasis upon analysis of performance, design features, applications and methods of control.
3 class hours; 1 3-hour laboratory period. Credit, 4.
Prerequisite, Electrical Engineering 41.

Mr. Edwards, Mr. Karlson.

54. (II) Alternating Current Machinery

A basic study of single and polyphase a-c machinery, covering synchronous and induction motors and generators, converters, transformers and magnetic amplifiers. This includes analysis, design considerations, applications and an introductory study of transient behavior and unbalanced operations.
3 class hours; 1 3-hour laboratory period. Credit, 4.

Prerequisites, Electrical Engineering 42, 53. Mr. Edwards, Mr. Karlson.

55. (I) Electronics

The theory and application of electron tubes and solid state devices. Basic theory consists of electron ballistics, electron emission, photoelectric effects and conduction in vacuum, gases and semi-conductors. Applications are made to the characteristics of electron tubes, varistors and transistors, together with their use for rectification, amplication and control. Amplifiers are analyzed by means of equivalent circuits and graphical methods.
2 class hours; 1 quiz hour; 2 laboratory hours. Credit, 3.

Prerequisite, Electrical Engineering 42. Mr. Langford, Mr. Mohn.

56. (II) Applied Electronics

Analysis and design of vacuum-tube and transistor circuits from the standpoints of response, distortion and stability. Applications include Class A, B and C, grounded-cathode, grounded-grid, cathod-follower and inverse feedback circuits, cascaded amplifiers, and the fundamental theory and characteristics of vacuum tube oscillators and multi-vibrators. Modulated waves, frequency conversion and detection are also considered.
3 class hours; 1 3-hour laboratory period. Credit, 4.

Prerequisite, Electrical Engineering 55. Mr. Langford, Mr. Mohn.

ELECTRICAL ENGINEERING

57. (I) Engineering Analysis

Ordinary differential equations as applied to electrical and mechanical systems; vector algebra and calculus; electro-magnetic field theory through the derivation of Maxwell's field equations and the Poynting and Schelkunoff radiation vectors; reflection and refraction of plane waves; skin effect in round conductors and Bessel's functions.

3 class hours.   Credit, 3.
                                                   Mr. Roys.

Prerequisites: Mathematics 32; Electrical Engineering 42.

58. (II) Electrical Transmission

A continuation of Course 57, consisting of the fundamental theory of waveguides, radiation from antennas, traveling waves in transmission systems, steady state a-c performance of long lines, and the solution of uniform recurrent network problems by means of difference calculus.

3 class hours,   Credit, 3.
                                          Mr. Mohn, Mr. Roys.

Prerequisite, Electrical Engineering 57.

61. (I) 62. (II) Principles of Electrical Engineering

For mechanical, industrial and agricultural engineering students. A study of d-c and a-c circuits and machinery and basic electronics.

3 class hours; 1 3-hour laboratory period.   Credit, 4.
                                       Mr. Edwards, Mr. Trocchi.

Prerequisites; Physics 26; Mathematics 32.

63. (I) and (II) Elements of Electrical Engineering

For civil and chemical engineering students. A study of d-c and a-c circuits and machines with application to industrial problems.

2 class hours; 1 3-hour laboratory period.   Credit, 3.
                                              Mr. Laestadius.

Prerequisites: Physics 26; Mathematics 32.

64. (II) Industrial Electricity

An elective for mechanical, industrial and chemical engineering students which deals principally with the applications of electronics to measurement and control in industry.

2 class hours; 1 3-hour laboratory period.   Credit, 3.
                                              Mr. Laestadius.

Prerequisite, Electrical Engineering 62 or 63.

78. (II) Special Projects

A laboratory course, associated with a selected technical elective (as approved by the student's major adviser), in which the student carries out a study or project of particular interest to himself, with a minimum of supervision, and wherein he is expected to learn to do independent work. A written report is required at the conclusion of the project.

1 3-hour laboratory period.   Credit, 1.
                                            The Department.

Prerequisite, a suitable technical elective concurrently.

79. (I) Electrical Communications I

The general theory of four-terminal, and selective circuits and of the use of distributed parameter systems as circuit elements. Among the special expedients employed are matrices, duality, Foster's reactance theorem, and transmission charts. Applications are made to attenuators, filters, equalizer and delay networks, and to long lines.

3 class hours; 1 3-hour laboratory period. Credit, 4.

Prerequisite, Electrical Engineering 58. MR. LANGFORD.

80. (II) Electrical Communications II

Theory and applications of circuits for radio communication in which wideband and R-F amplifiers, oscillators, modulation, de-modulation, frequency conversion, pulse techniques, noise, interference and information theory are studied.

3 class hours; 1 3-hour laboratory period. Credit, 4.

Prerequisite, Electrical Engineering 56. MR. LANGFORD.

81. (I) Advanced Electrical Machinery

A continuation of Course 54 dealing with modern methods of machine analysis. These are developed and applied to the predetermination of the transient and short circuit behavior and stability of synchronous machines and to variable speed and single phase motors.

3 class hours; 1 3-hour laboratory period. Credit, 4.

Prerequisite, Electrical Engineering 54. MR. KARLSON.

83. (I) Transient Analysis

A study of the transient behavior of electrical, mechanical and thermal systems. The ordinary and partial differential equations associated with the systems are set up and their solutions obtained by the classical, Heaviside operational and Fourier and Laplace transform methods. An introductory survey of functions of a complex variable leads to the evaluation of the inversion integral by means of the method of residues.

3 class hours. Credit, 3.

Prerequisite, Electrical Engineering 58. MR. ROYS.

84. (II) Industrial Electronics

A study of special characteristics of the electron tubes of industry, the theory, design and operation of commercial types of circuits utilizing these tubes, including stroboscope, grid-controlled and polyphase rectifiers, inverters, welding controllers, speed and voltage regulators, high frequency heating circuits, and others.

3 class hours; 1 3-hour laboratory period. Credit, 4.

Prerequisite, Electrical Engineering 55. MR. ROYS.

85. (I) Electrical Measurements

Theory and practice of electric and magnetic measurements; accuracy, precision, and limitations of measurements devices.

2 class hours; 1 3-hour laboratory period. Credit, 3.

Prerequisite, Electrical Engineering 42. MR. LAESTADIUS.

86. (II) Power System Networks

This course is a study of power system networks including power transfer diagrams, voltage studies, system stability criteria, short-circuit calculations, and protective methods.

3 class hours; 1 3-hour laboratory period. Credit, 4.

Mr. Karlson.

Prerequisites, Electrical Engineering 54, 58.

87. (I) Power Applications and Control

A study of the application of electric machines and their controls. Torque relations, typical control systems, theory of relays, combinational and sequential relay systems and counting circuits are among the topics considered.

3 class hours; 1 3-hour laboratory period. Credit, 4.

Mr. Karlson.

Prerequisites, Electrical Engineering 54 and 57.

88. (II) Electric Power Distribution

The general problem of power distribution from bulk substations to the consumer by means of loop and radial systems including such considerations as automatic load transfer, voltage regulation and system protection.

3 class hours. Credit, 3.

Mr. Karlson.

Prerequisite, Electrical Engineering 58.

90. (II) Feedback Control Systems

The analysis and design of basic types of error-sensitive control systems and their components, including servomechanisms. Anlytical and graphical methods for the determination of steady state and transient performance of the several types of controllers are developed. Applications are made to typical systems involving electrical, mechanical and hydraulic components.

3 class hours; 1 3-hour laboratory period. Credit, 4.

Mr. Karlson.

Prerequisite, Electrical Engineering 83.

92. (II) Professional Seminar

Current engineering developments are discussed through student reports. The professional aspects of the electrical engineer's work is stressed. Instruction is given in the preparation of engineering papers for publication and in their presentation before technical audiences.

1 class hour. Credit, 1.

The Department.

94. (II) Microwave Engineering

A review of the fundamental principles of communications and electromagnetic fields and their application to the special problems of the generation, transmission, propagation and reception of microwaves. This also includes characteristics and specifications of standard equipment, and special training in general laboratory and commercial testing techniques.

3 class hours; 1 3-hour laboratory period. Credit, 4.

Mr. Roys.

Prerequisite, Electrical Engineering 79.

96. (II) Principles of Electrical Design

The fundamentals of electric, dielectric, magnetic and heat-flow systems as applied to the design, rating and life of coils, transformers, machinery and other electrical equipment.

2 class hours; 1 3-hour calculation period.   Credit, 3.

MR. ROYS.

Prerequisite, Electrical Engineering 54.

98. (II) Television Engineering

Application of electronics and radio engineering to the special problems of television. Among the topics considered are system theory and analysis, signal sources, video response, noise limitations, synchronization and scanning, color vision and colorimetry, principles of the NTSC system, picture pickup and display tubes, transmission and reception, and monitoring and testing procedures.

3 class hours; 1 3-hour laboratory period.   Credit, 4.

MR. LANGFORD.

Prerequisites, Electrical Engineering 83, and 80 previously or concurrently.

MECHANICAL ENGINEERING

PROFESSOR WEAVER, PROFESSOR BATES, PROFESSOR SWENSON, PROFESSOR KEYSER, ASSOCIATE PROFESSOR DITTFACH, ASSOCIATE PROFESSOR LONGSTAFF, ASSISTANT PROFESSOR EMERSON, ASSISTANT PROFESSOR SOBALA, ASSISTANT PROFESSOR WEIDMANN, ASSISTANT PROFESSOR DAY, ASSISTANT PROFESSOR COSTA, ASSISTANT PROFESSOR PATTERSON, ASSISTANT PROFESSOR HARRINGTON, MR. HOPKINS.

1. (I) Engineering Drawing

The purpose of this course is to develop skill in the use of drafting equipment and to provide a working knowledge of orthographic projection. Included are such topics as lettering, multi-view drawing, sections, dimensions, working drawings and various pictorial representations. The course also includes some work in freehand sketching and ink tracing.

2 3-hour laboratory periods.   Credit, 2.

MR. WEIDMANN.

2. (II) Descriptive Geometry

This course covers the theory of orthographic projection more fully. It includes the representation of the geometric concepts of lines, planes and solids and the solution of engineering problems involving true sizes, angles and shapes by graphical methods.

1 class hour; 2 3-hour laboratory periods.   Credit, 3.

MR. WEIDMANN.

Prerequisite, Mechanical Engineering 1.

23. (Summer) Shop

The course is designed primarily for engineers other than mechanical. Approximately half the semester is spent in welding; in the other half the student gains experience in the machine shop, where he becomes familiar with the various machine and hand tools used in metal working.

3 40-hour weeks.   Credit, 3.

MR. COSTA.

27. (Summer) Shop

The course covers weldability of metals, manual and automatic welding processes. Experience is gained in the manual welding of various metals.

3 40-hour weeks.   Credit, 3.
                                                              MR. PATTERSON.

28. (Summer) Machine Shop

A knowledge of metal-working equipment is obtained by using the fundatal machine tools such as the lathe, planer, shaper, milling machine and drill press. A reasonable amount of bench work is included. Classroom work is devoted to the theory of machine tool operation, fits, tolerances and measurement.

3 40-hour weeks.   Credit, 3.
                                                              MR. COSTA.

39. (I) and (II) Materials of Construction

Properties of engineering materials; failure by (a) exceeding the elastic limit, (b) creep, (c) fatigue, and (d) corrosion. The crystalline nature of metals. Properties and uses of the structural metals, wood, stone, clay products, cementing materials, concrete, plastics, protective coatings, and water.

2 class hours.   Credit, 2.
                                                              MR. KEYSER.

Prerequisites, Chemistry 2 or 4; Physics 27, taken previously or concurrently.

46. (II) Fundamentals of Metallurgy

Physical metallurgy involving crystal structure, solid solutions, diffusion in the solid state, freezing of metals, hardening of metals, annealing, and equilibrium diagrams. These fundamentals are applied to a study of the iron-iron carbide diagrams, time-temperature-transformation relationships for steel, the heat treatment of steel, and heat-treating equipment. Laboratory work is intended to substantiate some of the principles developed in lecture work and to acquire basic skill in metallographic technique.

2 class hours; 1 3-hour laboratory period.   Credit, 3.
                                                              MR. KEYSER.

Prerequisites, Mechanical Engineering 39 or Chemistry 66.

61. (I) Heat Power

A one-semester terminal course for non-mechanical engineering majors, designed to present to the student the fundamental principles involved in the production of power. It consists of the basic theory underlying the field of thermo-dynamics and its application to power machinery. It includes a study of gases, vapors, thermodynamic processes, cycles and power measurement with considerable discussion, both quantitative and qualitative, of the application of the above to gasoline engines, diesel engines, gas turbines, steam turbines, and compressors.

3 class hours.   Credit, 3.
                                                              THE DEPARTMENT.

Prerequisites, Physics 28; Mathematics 6.

63. (I) Engineering Thermodynamics I

This course is a treatment of the application of the laws of heat to various energy-transforming devices. Topics include ideal and actual cycles of steam, internal combustion engines, and air compressors together with problems pertaining to these machines, energy transformations in fluid flow, variable specific heats and mixtures of gases.

4 class hours.   Credit, 4.

MR. SWENSON, MR. LONGSTAFF.

Prerequisites, Physics 28; Mathematics 30 or 31.

64.   (II)   Engineering Thermodynamics II

A continuation of the work of Course 63. Study will be made of liquids and vapors, thermodynamic cycles, energy transformations and the transfer of heat, together with engineering problems pertaining to these devices.

4 class hours.   Credit, 3.

MR. SWENSON, MR. LONGSTAFF.

Prerequisite, Mechanical Engineering 63.

65.   (I)   Heat Engineering I

This course is a survey of the field of applied energy and is designed for engineering students outside of the mechanical engineering field. The application of the laws of heat to energy transforming devices is studied, but not as extensively as in Courses 63 and 64. A study will be made of gases, vapors, fuels, combustion, heat transfer, measurement of power, and internal combustion engines.

3 class hours.   Credit, 3.

THE DEPARTMENT.

Prerequisites, Physics 28; Mathematics 6.

66.   (II)   Heat Engineering II

A continuation of the work of Course 65. Air compressors, fans, refrigeration, and air conditioning turbines, jet propulsion and power plants will be studied.

3 class hours.   Credit, 3.

THE DEPARTMENT.

Prerequisite, Mechanical Engineering 65.

67.   (I)   Mechanical Instrumentation Laboratory

The calibration and application of instruments used in the testing of mechanical engineering apparatus.

1 3-hour laboratory period.   Credit, 1.

THE DEPARTMENT.

Prerequisite, Mechanical Engineering 63 concurrently.

68.   (II)   Kinematics

Principles of mechanism, including velocity and acceleration diagrams, instant centers, gear teeth and gear trains, cams, and various speed transmissions.

2 class hours; 1 3-hour laboratory period.   Credit, 3.

MR. BATES, MR. SOBALA.

Prerequisites, Mechanical Engineering 1; Civil Eng. 52.

75.   (I)   Steam Power Plants

This course is a study of the steam power plant, including boilers, stokers, fuels, combustion, steam generation, prime movers, and auxiliary equipment, and engineering problems involved in design and operation.

3 class hours.   Credit, 3.

MR. SWENSON.

Prerequisite, Mechanical Engineering 64.

76. (II) Refrigeration and Air Conditioning

The course content includes a study of the fundamental principles of thermodynamics as applied to refrigeration and air control. Application of refrigeration to industrial processes and the control of temperature, humidity and motion of air in buildings will be studied.

3 class hours.   Credit, 3.
                                                         MR. SWENSON.
Prerequisite, Mechanical Engineering 64.

77. (I) Internal Combustion Engines

A study is made of spark-ignition and compression-ignition engines including design, fuels, carburetion, ignition, combustion, lubrication, cooling, and engine performance. The gas turbine and jet propulsion will be included.

3 class hours.   Credit, 3.
                                                         MR. DITTFACH.
Prerequisite, Mechanical Engineering 64.

79. (I) Mechanical Engineering Laboratory I

Tests of fuels and lubricants. Performance tests of steam engines and turbines, gasoline and Diesel engines, fans, hydraulic apparatus, refrigeration systems and other typical engineering equipment. Emphasis on laboratory procedure and orderly presentation of results.

2 3-hour laboratory periods.   Credit, 2.
                                                      THE DEPARTMENT.
Prerequisites, Civil Engineering 76 or 75 concurrently; Mechanical Engineering 64 or 66; Mechanical Engineering 67 for Mechanical Engineering majors.

80. (II) Mechanical Engineering Laboratory II

This course continues the work of the first semester in more advanced phases.

2 3-hour laboratory periods.   Credit, 2.
                                                      THE DEPARTMENT.
Prerequisite, Mechanical Engineering 79.

81. (I) Experimental Mechanical Engineering

For non-mechanical engineering majors. Calibration and application of instruments used in the testing of mechanical engineering apparatus. Performance tests on mechanical engineering equipment such as internal combustion engines, steam power apparatus, refrigeration machines, and fans and blowers.

2 3-hour laboratory periods.   Credit, 2.
                                                      THE DEPARTMENT.
Prerequisites, Mechanical Engineering 66; Civil Engineering 75 concurrently.

83. (I) Machine Design

Principles involved in the design of various machine parts including fastenings, shafts, belts, bearings, gears, and pressure vessels.

2 class hours; 1 3-hour laboratory period.   Credit, 3.
                                                         MR. BATES.
Prerequisites, Civil Engineering 51 or 53; Mechanical Engineering 2, 68.

85. Dynamics of Machinery

Gyroscopic effects, governors, dynamic balancing of rotating machinery. Analysis of unbalanced forces in a machine containing parts moving with rotation, reciprocation, and their combination. Elements of vibration theory, vibration isolation, vibration analysis of equivalent masses and shaft systems. Vibration absorbers.

3 class hours. Credit., 3

MR. SOBALA.

Prerequisites, Civil Engineering 52; Mechanical Eng. 68.

86. (II) Advanced Machine Design

A continuation of Course 83. Additional elementary parts are studied which combine into the design of complete machines in the latter part of the course.

2 class hours; 1 3-hour laboratory period. Credit, 3.

MR. BATES.

Prerequisite, Mechanical Engineering 83.

88. (II) Steady Flow Machinery

The principles of thermodynamics are applied to steam and internal combustion turbines, condensers, and other heat transfer apparatus.

3 class hours. Credit, 3.

MR. SWENSON.

Prerequisites, Mechanical Engineering 64 or 66; Civil Engineering 76.

90. (II) Advanced Metallurgy

Advanced topics in engineering metallurgy, such as the effects of alloying elements in steel, aluminum, magnesium, and copper alloys. The significant properties of, the fabricating methods for, and the applications of ferrous and nonferrous metals. Admission by permission of instructor.

2 class hours; 1 3-hour laboratory period. Credit, 3.

MR. KEYSER.

Prerequisite, Mechanical Engineering 46.

91. (I) Professional Seminar

For senior and graduate students only. Presentation of papers on various important subjects in the field of mechanical engineering with principle emphasis on recent developments.

Credit, 1.

THE DEPARTMENT.

94. (I) or (II) Experimental Mechanical Engineering

Special work in mechanical engineering for a senior thesis. Admission by permission of instructor.

Credit, 1-3.

THE DEPARTMENT.

INDUSTRIAL ENGINEERING

25. (I) Manufacturing Processes

The methods of producing and fabricating the basic engineering materials: metals, cementing materials, ceramics, plastics, rubber, and lumber. Production methods (excluding machining) of metal parts and their assembly in a typical mass production industry is discussed. Laboratory periods involve inspection trips and movies.

1 class hour; 1 3-hour laboratory period. Credit, 2.

MR. KEYSER.

26. (Summer) Tool Engineering

This course includes the determination of the manufacturing operations necessary to produce a finished product. This is followed by consideration of the principles embodied in the design of jigs, fixtures, dies, and gauges necessary to perform each operation. The economics of tooling as influenced by intermittent or continuous type manufacturing and the effect of volume are also included.

3 44-hour weeks.   Credit, 3.

MR. COSTA.

51. (I) Industrial Management

A course designed to acquaint the student with the principles of industrial engineering and their application to the solution of the problem of industrial plant operation.

3 class hours.   Credit, 3.

MR. WEAVER.

54. (II) Engineering Economy

This course includes a study of the bases for comparison of alternatives in engineering projects, break-even and minimum cost points, evaluation of proposals for new activities, economy of operations, the evaluation of public activities, the output and life of typical items of engineering and industrial equipment, manufacturing lot sizes, economic purchase quantities, the selection and replacement of structures and machines.

3 class hours.   Credit, 3.

MR. EMERSON.

Prerequisites, Economics 25; Mathematics 6 or 29.

75. (I) Job Evaluation

A study of the principles used to determine an evaluation of all occupations in order to establish an equitable rating between them, to establish sound wage and salary policies.

2 class hours.   Credit, 2.

MR. WEAVER.

Prerequisite, Industrial Engineering 51.

76. (I) Time Study

A study of the principles involved in the establishment of production standards and their application in the management functions of cost accounting, estimating, production control, incentives, budgetary control.

2 class hours; 1 3-hour laboratory period.   Credit, 3.

MR. EMERSON.

Prerequisites, Industrial Engineering 75.

77. (I) Production Control

A study of the principles used to regulate production activities in keeping with the manufacturing plan.

3 class hours.   Credit, 3.

MR. EMERSON.

Prerequisite, Industrial Engineering 51.

78. (II) Factory Planning and Layout

A study of the principles applying to the determination and development of the physical relationship between plant, equipment and operators working toward the highest degree of economy and effectiveness in operation.

1 class hour; 1 3-hour laboratory period. Credit, 2.

MR. WEAVER.

Prerequisites, Mechanical Engineering 2; Industrial Engineering 51.

80. (II) Plant Budgetary Control

A study of the principles used to pre-determine expenses for the factors of production and the comparison of results with the estimates to determine and deal with the causes of expense variations as applied by the operating organization in the industrial plant.

3 class hours. Credit, 3.

MR. WEAVER.

Prerequisite, Industrial Engineering 51.

82. (II) Work Simplification

A study of the principles involved in the simplification of means of doing work and in the application and use of these principles.

1 class hour; 1 3-hour laboratory period. Credit, 2.

MR. WEAVER.

Prerequisite, Mechanical Engineering 68.

86. (II) Industrial Management

Designed for students other than industrial engineers. A broad course dealing with the many problems encountered in a modern industry. Topics include types of organization, management, plant location, arrangement of equipment, product design, methods of production control, costs, wage payment systems and personnel relations.

3 class hours. Credit, 3.

MR. EMERSON.

88. (II) Motion and Time Study

This course covers the combined fields of motion study and time study for junior and senior students outside the industrial engineering field.

2 class hours; 1 3-hour laboratory period. Credit, 3.

MR. EMERSON.

92. (I) Professional Seminar

For seniors and graduate students.

Credit, 1.

THE DEPARTMENT.

ENGLISH

COMPOSITION

1. (I) 2. (II) English Composition

The purpose of the course is to teach effective exposition for use in college
and professional work. College-level readings will be used to achieve this end
and to acquaint the student (1) with the commoner critical terms and literary
forms and (2) with the skills necessary to the comprehension of adult writing.
Scheduled hours include Speech 3. (I) 4. (II).

2 class hours.   Credit, 2.
                                                      THE DEPARTMENT.

81. (I) (II) Creative Writing

A course in critical and imaginative composition based upon the examples
of standard authors and the experience of the student. It provides an opportunity for work in description, narrative, verse and drama as well as in exposition.

3 class hours.   Credit, 3.
                                                      THE DEPARTMENT.
Prerequisite, a mark of A or B in English 2 (U. of M.) or permission of the
head of the department.

83. (I) (II) Technical Writing

For majors in engineering. A course in factual and inductive exposition
with special emphasis upon process reports and theses.

2 class hours.   Credit, 2.
                                                        MR. MITCHELL.
Prerequisites, English 1, 2.

84. (II) Technical Writing

For students not majoring in engineering. A course in factual and inductive exposition with special emphasis upon library research and the preparation
of reports, and theses.

3 class hours.   Credit, 3.
                                                        MR. MITCHELL.
Prerequisites, English 1, 2.

† On leave of absence.

LITERATURE

25. (I) 26. (II) Humane Letters

A general reading course based upon a chronological selection of master-pieces: classical, continental, and English.

3 class hours. Credit, 3.

THE DEPARTMENT.

50. (II) Chaucer

A study of Chaucer's development and preeminence as a creative artist and an attempt to appreciate his humanism.

3 class hours. Credit, 3.

MR. HELMING.

51. (I) The Renaissance in England

A study of various aspects of the Renaissance as revealed in such writers as Spenser, Bacon, Sir Thomas Browne, Burton, and Hobbes. Special emphasis is given to Spenser's *Faerie Queene*.

3 class hours. Credit, 3.

MR. TROY.

53. (I) Lyrical Poetry of the Renaissance in England (1957-58)

A study of lyrical poets such as Sidney, Campion, Jonson, Herrick, Love-lace, Suckling, Carew, Donne, Herbert, Vaughn, Crashaw, Traherne and Mar-vell. Emphasis is given to the "Metaphysical" tradition. Given in alternate years.

3 class hours. Credit, 3.

MR. GOLDBERG, MR. BARRON.

54. (II) Milton

The development of the mind and art of Milton as a Renaissance writer. Emphasis is placed upon *Paradise Lost, Paradise Regained,* and *Samson Agonistes*.

3 class hours. Credit, 3.

MR. GOLDBERG, MR. HELMING, MR. KOEHLER.

55. (I) Shakespeare

This course is based upon the reading of about twenty-five of Shakespeare's plays, and attempts both to indicate the evolution of the dramatist and to emphasize the various phases of his art.

3 class hours. Credit, 3.

MR. RAND.

57. (I) English Literature of the Restoration

A study of the social problems and literary values of the Restoration period as they appear in prose, verse, and drama. Emphasis will be placed on the satire of Dryden; and on the development of the theatre from the Restoration through Congreve and the Comedy of Manners.

3 class hours. Credit, 3.

MR. KOEHLER.

58. (II) Elizabethan Dramatists

A study of English drama from the death of Elizabeth to the closing of the theaters. Special consideration will be given to the plays of Jonson, Beaumont, Fletcher, Webster, Middleton, Massinger, and Shirley.

3 class hours. Credit, 3.

MR. O'DONNELL.

59. (I) English Literature of the Eighteenth Century

A study of the literature of the Augustan Age, with special emphasis on the writing of Swift and Pope.

3 class hours.   Credit, 3.
                                                                  MR. TROY.

60. (II) English Literature of the Eighteenth Century

A continuation of English 59, but may be elected independently.. A study of the literature of the later Eighteenth Century with special emphasis on the Johnson Circle.

3 class hours.   Credit, 3.
                                                                 MR. TROY.

61. (I) Romantic Poetry (1956-57)

A study of the Lake Poets (primarily Wordsworth and Coleridge) and their precursors. Given in alternate years.

3 class hours.   Credit, 3.
                                                                 MR. RAND.

62. (II) Romantic Poetry (1956-57)

A continuation of English 61 but may be elected independently. A study of Byron, Shelley and Keats. Given in alternate years.

3 class hours.   Credit, 3.
                                                                 MISS HORRIGAN.

63. (I) American Poetry

A study of American poetry from Colonial times to 1900, with special emphasis upon the work of Freneau, Bryant, Emerson, Longfellow, Whittier, Poe, Whitman, and Emily Dickinson.

3 class hours.   Credit, 3.
                                        MR. O'DONNELL, MR. WILLIAMS.

65. (I) English Prose of the Nineteenth Century

A study of the chief Romantic prose writers in relation to literary techniques and main currents of epochal thought and feeling. Among the authors treated are Coleridge, Lamb, Hazlitt, DeQuincey, Landor, Carlyle, and Ruskin.

3 class hours.   Credit, 3.
                                                                 MR. GOLDBERG.

66. (II) English Prose of the Nineteenth Century

A continuation of English 65, but may be elected independently. A study of the chief Victorian prose writers in relation to literary techniques and main currents of epochal thought and feeling. Among the authors treated are Macaulay, Newman, Arnold, Mill, Huxley, Pater, and Stevenson.

3 class hours.   Credit, 3.
                                                                 MR. GOLDBERG.

67. (I) American Prose

A course in the chief American prose writers of the nineteenth and twentieth centuries. Among the authors studied are Emerson, Thoreau, Hawthorne, Melville, Mark Twain, Henry Adams, and Henry James.

3 class hours.   Credit, 3.
                                        MR. KAPLAN, MR. O'DONNELL.

68. (II) Modern Drama

This course traces the development of continental English and American drama from the time of Ibsen to the present day. Its purpose is to impart an intelligent and enthusiastic interest in the drama of the twentieth century.

3 class hours.   Credit, 3.

MR. RAND, MR. WILLIAMS.

69. (I) Victorian Poetry (1957-58)

A study of Tennyson and Browning. Given in alternate years.

3 class hours.   Credit, 3.

MR. RAND.

71. (I) Biography

The history of the biography as a literary type; discussion of leading biographers from Boswell to Maurois, with special emphasis upon the development of the modern biographical method.

3 class hours.   Credit, 3.

MR. HELMING.

72. (II) The Bible as Literature

A study of the King James version of the Bible, with emphasis upon the Hebrew as discernible in translation, the poetic qualities characteristic of Tudor England, and the varied influence of the Bible upon subsequent English poetry.

3 class hours.   Credit, 3.

MR. RAND.

73. (I) The Novel from Defoe through the Victorians

The development of the novel; the reading and discussion of eight or nine great English novels of the eighteenth and nineteenth centuries.

3 class hours.   Credit, 3.

MR. ALLEN, MR. HELMING.

74. (II) Greek Classics in Translation

Readings and discussion of the epics of Homer, representative dramas of Aeschylus, Sophocles, Euripides, and Aristophanes, the "Socratic" dialogues of Plato, and Thucydides' history of the Peloponnesian War. Intended to acquaint students with the famous myths and stories of classical antiquity, and the literary forms and ideas which have contributed most to subsequent literatures.

3 class hours.   Credit, 3.

MR. HELMING, MR. TROY.

76. (II) Modern Poetry

This course attempts to trace the spirit of twentieth century poetry from such authors as Hardy, Whitman, and Emily Dickinson to those of the present day.

3 class hours.   Credit, 3.

MR. RAND, MISS HORRIGAN.

77. (I) and (II) The Modern Novel

An analytical presentation of eleven novels written between 1890 and 1950, in which the expanding form and the extension of critical themes will be stressed.

3 class hours.   Credit, 3.

MR. VARLEY.

79. (I) Literary Criticism (1955-56)

A study of major critical attitudes and principles, in relation to philosophic background and to practice. Emphasis is placed upon important critics and theorists from Plato and Aristotle through those of the eighteenth century. Given in alternate years.

3 class hours.   Credit, 3.
                                                      MR. GOLDBERG.

80. (II) Literary Criticism (1955-56)

A continuation of English 79, but may be elected independently. Emphasis is placed upon important critics and theorists of the nineteenth and twentieth centuries. Given in alternate years.

3 class hours.   Credit, 3.
                                                      MR. GOLDBERG.

ENTOMOLOGY

PROFESSOR ALEXANDER, PROFESSOR SWEETMAN, ASSOCIATE PROFESSOR SHAW, ASSOCIATE PROFESSOR HANSON,† ASSISTANT PROFESSOR SMITH, MR. FIELD,* MR. WEIDHAAS.

26. (II) General and Field Entomology

The lectures are devoted to a brief survey of the entire field of entomology; structure and metamorphosis; the more important methods and materials for control of injurious species; a survey of the more conspicuous and important insects with particular attention to the fauna of New England. A laboratory period will be devoted to the preparation and formation of a collection of insects. Until about April 10th, this work will be done indoors and will consist of lectures and practical work preparatory to the field work after that date. Collections made by the students are studied in later courses.

2 class hours; 1 2-hour laboratory period.   Credit, 3.
8:00-8:50 or 10:00-10:50 M. F.; 1:00-2:50 M. Tu. W. Th. F.
                                          MR. ALEXANDER, MISS SMITH.

51. (I) Pests of Special Crops

For students not specializing in entomology who desire a more complete knowledge of the insects connected with their major lines of work. Work in the laboratory consists of identification, life-history studies and control measures of important insect pests. Work of this nature is available on pests of field crops, market-garden crops, fruits, flowers, shade trees and shrubs, forest trees, household articles, domestic animals, and man.

1 class hour; 2 2-hour laboratory periods.   Credit, 3.
10:00-10:50 M.; 1:00-2:50 Tu.; 2:30-3:50 Th.
                                                      MR. WEIDHAAS.
Prerequisite, Entomology 26.

53. (I) Applied Entomology

Studies on the more important insect pests, their life-histories, damage, identification, and methods of control. Special attention is devoted to the use of entomological literature, methods of preparing scientific papers, and the general principles of insect control.

1 class hour; 2 2-hour laboratory periods.   Credit, 3.
10:00-10:50 W.; 3:00-4:50 M. F.   MR. SHAW.
Prerequisite, Entomology 26.

* On leave of absence for military service.
† On leave of absence.

55. (I) 56. (II) Classification of Insects

Laboratory work on the identification of the major orders of insects. In Course 56, the immature stages of insects, with particular stress on their structures and recognition.

3 2-hour laboratory periods. Credit, 3.
8:00-9:50 Tu. Th. S. Mr. ALEXANDER, MISS SMITH.
Prerequisites, Entomology 26; Entomology 57, previously or concurrently.

57. (I) Insect Morphology

The lectures treat of the external and internal anatomy, particularly of the major orders, stress being placed upon the phylogenetic relationships, as backgrounds for parallel and subsequent work in taxonomy and physiology of insects.

1 class hour; 3 2-hour laboratory periods. Credit, 4.
10:00-10:50 F.; 1:00-2:50 M. Tu. Th. Mr. HANSON.
Prerequisite, Entomology 26.

60. (II) Structural Pest Control

For students specializing in entomology, especially those desiring to enter the structural pest field, and others interested in gaining knowledge of methods of combating insect and rodent pests. The emphasis will be placed on the control of those pests attacking buildings and other structures, foods, fabrics, and other stored products in private homes or other establishments. The life history, feeding habits, methods of reproduction, and dispersal of the various species will be stressed in so far as these influence control measures.

2 class hours. Credit, 2.
11:00-11:50 M. F. Mr. SWEETMAN.
Prerequisite, Zoology 1; Entomology 26 desirable.

72. (II) Forest and Shade Tree Insects

The lecture work deals with the principles and methods of controlling insects which attack shade trees, forests and forest products. The laboratory periods are devoted to a study of the more important species, their identification, biology, and specific control measures.

1 class hour: 2 2-hour laboratory periods. Credit, 3.
9:00-9:50 W.; 1:00-2:50 M. F. Mr. HANSON, Mr. WEIDHAAS.
Prerequisite, Entomology 26; 53, 55, 56, and 57 desirable.

74. (II) Medical and Veterinary Entomology

The relationships of insects and their allies to the health of man and animals. The classification, biology and control of these pests is studied in detail.

1 class hour; 2 2-hour laboratory periods. Credit, 3.
10:00-10:50 W.; 3:00-4:50 Tu. Th. Mr. SHAW.
Prerequisite, Entomology 26.

79. (I) Animal Ecology

Designed for students specializing in entomology, zoology, and related fields. The course deals with the relation of animals to their environment, covering the physical factors as temperature, moisture, light, etc., and biotic factors as neighbors, competitors, predators, etc. Both terrestrial and aquatic communities are studied. The student is shown not only that animals do things, but

ENTOMOLOGY

why they make definite responses to the environmental factors. Actual measurements of the environmental factors and responses of the animals in the field and laboratory are included.

2 class hours; 1 2-hour laboratory period. Credit, 3.
9:00-9:50 M. F.; 3:00-4:50 M. MR. SWEETMAN.
Prerequisite, Entomology 26 or Zoology 1 or equivalent.

80. (II) Insect Control

The scientific basis of insect control is considered from the chemical, biological, ecological, mechanical, and legislative approaches. Special emphasis is placed on the composition, manufacture, preparation, and reaction of insecticides, and the use of resistant hosts, micro-organisms and the larger parasites and predators that might be used in the control of insects.

1 class hour; 2 2-hour laboratory periods. Credit, 3.
9:00-9:50 M.; 3:00-4:50 M. F. MR. SWEETMAN.
Prerequisites, Entomology 53, 55, and 57; 79 and 81 desirable.

81. (I) Physiological Entomology

A detailed consideration is given to the organ systems, showing the functions such as nutrition, respiration, and growth, and the relationship of physiology to behavior. A portion of the laboratory time will be devoted to assigned individual problems dealing wth any phase of insect biology or control and conducted on a research basis.

1 class hour; 2 2-hour laboratory periods. Credit, 3.
9:00-9:50 Th.; 3:00 4:50 W. F. MR. SWEETMAN.
Prerequisite, Entomology 26; 55, 56, and 57 desirable.

87. (I) 88. (II) Special Problems in Entomology

Problem work in many fields, as apiculture, biological control and insectary practice, insecticides, morphology, and classification. Intended primarily to introduce qualified students to research methods in some branch of entomology. Excess graduation credits are necessary for election.

Hours by arrangement. Credit, 1, 2, or 3.
THE DEPARTMENT.
Prerequisites, Entomology 26, 53, 55, 57, and should be preceded or accompanied by any other courses in the restricted field of the problem.

89. (I) Entomological Techniques

Theory and practice in the preservation, preparation, and mounting of insects for study and display. Excess graduation credits are necessary for election.

2 2-hour laboratory periods. Credit, 2.
Hours by arrangement. MISS SMITH.
Prerequisites, Entomology 26 and permission of instructor.

90. (II) Evolution

The phylogeny of plants and animals is outlined at some length in conjunction with consideration of factors and forces influencing and guiding evolution. Especial consideration is given throughout the course to the implications and applications of evolutionary concept to human behavior, welfare and philosophy.

2 class hours. Credit, 2.
10:00-10:50 M. F. MR. HANSON.

182

APICULTURE

66. (II) Introductory Beekeeping

This course is designed to give the student a broad grasp of the general field of apiculture. The lectures cover honeybees and their relatives, biology of the bee, methods of management, diseases, pollination, queen rearing, honey produciton, and history of beekeeping. The laboratory will acquaint the student with the structure of the bee, equipment for keeping bees and its construction, costs of beekeeping; plants of value for bees, and as much as possible the actual management of bees in the apiary.

2 class hours; 1 2-hour laboratory period.   Credit, 3.
11:00-11:50 M. F.; 1:00-2:50 M.   Mr. Shaw.

85. (I) Advanced Beekeeping

This course is designed for the student who wants more detailed knowledge of the management of bees. It will cover such topics as fall management, wintering, the care of the honey crop, grading and packaging of honey, judging honey, bee diseases, beeswax, and some simple biometrical problems relating to bees. If possible, one or more visits to commercial apiaries will be made.

1 class hour; 1 2-hour laboratory period.   Credit, 2.
                                                                         Mr. Shaw.
Prerequisite, Entomology 66.

FLORICULTURE

Professor Thayer, Assistant Professor Ross,
Assistant Professor Jester, Mr. Goddard.

26. (II) Garden Materials

A study of the annuals, biennials, herbaceous perennials, bulbs, bedding plants, and roses that are valuable for use in floricultural or landscape gardening work. Methods of propagation, culture, and uses of the various plants are considered as well as identification of materials.

2 class hours; 1 2-hour laboratory period.   Credit, 3.
11:00-11:50 M. F.; 3:00-4:50 Th.   Mr. Goddard.

51. (II) Greenhouse Management

This course is intended to familiarize students with the methods and principles involved in the management of greenhouses and greenhouse crops; history and development of the floricultural industry, preparation of soils, fertilizers, potting, watering, ventilation, control of insects and diseases, methods of plant propagation, forcing plants, soilless methods of plant culture. At some time during the semester the members of the class will be required to take a one-day trip to visit large commercial establishments at an approximate cost of five dollars.

2 class hours; 1 2-hour laboratory period.   Credit, 3.
9:00-9:50 M. F.; 1:00-2:50 F.   Mr. Thayer, Mr. Goddard.

52. (II) Floral Arrangement

A study of the principles involving the arrangement and use of cut flowers and plants; funeral designs, basket and vase arrangements, corsages, wedding bouquets, table decorations, home, church, and other interior decorations. A study of color and color harmony as applied to such work. This course is limited to ten students, preference being given to students specializing in floriculture and landscape architecture.

1 class hour; 2 2-hour laboratory periods.　　　　　　　　　　Credit, 3.
8:00-8:50 Th.; 1:00-2:50 M. F.　　　　　　　　　MR. JESTER, MR. ROSS.

54. (II) Greenhouse Construction and Heating

The location, types, arrangements, construction, cost, equipment, heating, and ventilation of greenhouse structures; the drawings of plans and study of specifications. Special emphasis laid on heating problems.

2 class hours; 1 2-hour laboratory period.　　　　　　　　Credit, 3.
9:00-9:50 M. F.; 3:00-4:50 M.　　　　　　　MR. THAYER, MR. GODDARD.

58. (II) Amateur Floriculture

This course is intended primarily for major students in the School of Home Economics and for other women students. Three phases of floriculture will be considered: (1) the arrangement and use of cut flowers for decorative purposes in the home and elsewhere, (2) house plants, methods of propagation, (3) garden flowers and their uses on the home grounds.

2 class hours; 1 2-hour laboratory period.　　　　　　　　Credit, 3.
10:00-10:50 Tu. Th.; 3:00-4:50 Tu. or 1:00-2:50 Th.
　　　　　　　　　MR. THAYER, MR. ROSS, MR. GODDARD.

75. (I) 76. (II) Commercial Floriculture

A detailed study of the cultural methods for the important commercial cut-flower crops and potted plants. The marketing of flowers and plants, including the management of wholesale markets and retail stores, a study of systems of record keeping, cost analysis, inventory methods, and other phases of this important part of the floricultural industry. Trips may be taken to nearby commercial establishments.

2 class hours; 1 2-hour laboratory period.　　　　　　　　Credit, 3.
9:00-9:50 Tu., Th.; 1:00-2:50 Tu.　　　　　　　　MR. JESTER.
Prerequisite, Floriculture 51.

79. (I) Conservatory Plants (1956-57)

Alternates with Course 81 for students specializing in floriculture. A study of the foliage and flowering plants used in conservatory work; methods of propagation; identification of materials.

1 class hour; 1 2-hour laboratory period.　　　　　　　　Credit, 2.
12:00-12:50 Th.; 1:00-2:50 M.　　　　　　　MR. THAYER, MR. ROSS.

81. (I) Herbaceous Gardens and Borders

Alternates with Course 79 for students specializing in floriculture; given annually for students specializing in landscape architecture. This course is a continuation of Course 26 with emphasis on the use of herbaceous materials in various types of planting of borders and gardens.

1 class hour; 1 4-hour laboratory period.　　　　　　　　Credit, 3.
10:00-10:50 Tu.; 1:00-4:50 Th.　　　　　　　　MR. THAYER.
Prerequisite, Floriculture 26.

82. (II) Seminar

For seniors specializing in floriculture. Presentation and discussion of research work in floriculture and other related fields and individual problems.

1 class hour; 4 laboratory hours.　　　　　　　　　Credit, 3.
11:00-11:50 W.; laboratory hours by arrangement.　　　THE DEPARTMENT.

FOOD TECHNOLOGY

PROFESSOR FELLERS, ASSOCIATE PROFESSOR LEVINE, ASSISTANT PROFESSOR CULBERT-
SON, ASSISTANT PROFESSOR BAKER, ASSISTANT PROFESSOR LIVINGSTON, ASSISTANT
PROFESSOR FAGERSON, MR. LAMPI, MR. JACKSON, MR. KHATCHIKIAN.

51. (I) Introductory Course

This is a general elementary course, primarily for food technology majors,
covering food economics, production, distribution and processing. The applications of fundamental science to the food industries are pointed out. The laboratory exercises cover both the theory and practice of canning, freezing and
dehydration. The principles of packaging are considered. Fruit and vegetable
products are prepared and graded.

2 class hours; 1 2-hour laboratory period. Credit, 3.
8:00-8:50 Tu., Th.; 1:00-2:50 Th. or Fr. MR. FELLERS.

52. (II) Food Products and Adjuncts

This is a continuation of Course 51. The laboratory work includes pickles
and pickle products, maple products, citrus products, fruit syrups, soups, condiments, and the preservation of meat, fish, poultry, and vegetables. The properties
and uses of sugars, syrups, brines, enzymes, acids, salt, pectin, preservatives and
antioxidants are considered. Experience is given in the use and handling of
instruments and equipment.

2 class hours; 1 2-hour laboratory period. Credit, 3.
8:00-8:50 Tu., Th.; 1:00-2:50 W. or Th. MR. FELLERS.
Prerequisite, Food Technology 51.

61. (I) Industrial Technology

A survey of commercial practices in the manufacture and preservation of
food products. This will involve a study of equipment, factory arrangement,
sanitation, government regulations, and the operation of types of commercial
equipment in quantity production.

1 class hour; 1 4-hour laboratory period. Credit, 3.
10:00-10:50 Th.; 1:00-4:50 M. or Tu. MR. LEVINE.
Prerequisites: Food Technology 52; Bacteriology 31.

62. (II) Industrial Technology

This is a continuation of Course 61. The class exercises will deal largely
with a survey study of the sources of raw material, commercial methods of manufacture, packing and distribution of the more common foods. The important
contributions of research to food technology will be studied. Laboratory work
will include the formation of research projects, interpretation of research data,
the use of preservatives, the simple analysis of foods and the commercial practices as applied to preservation of such materials as are available: fish, meats,
poultry, and spring vegetables. The inspection and grading of canned food will
be studied. Various plant visits including a two-day field trip to food plants
in the Boston area will be taken. The trip will cost the student about fifteen
dollars.

1 class hour; 1 4-hour laboratory period. Credit, 3.
10:00-10:50 Th.; 1:00-4:50 M. or Tu. MR. LEVINE.
Prerequisite, Food Technology 61.

185

FOOD TECHNOLOGY

71. (I) 72. (II) Food Science Literature

For seniors who specialize in food technology.

2 class hours.   Credit, 2.
11:00-11:50 M. W.   THE DEPARTMENT.

75. (I) and (II) Food Preservation

For students not majoring in food technology. A survey is made of the causes of food spoilage and of the methods commonly used in preserving foods. The important food products are discussed with emphasis on raw materials used, processing methods and examination of packaged foods. Methods of detecting and preventing spoilage are studied. The laboratory exercises cover the preservation of the major food groups. The theory and use of the pressure cooker are included.

2 class hours; 1 2-hour laboratory period.   Credit, 3.
12:00-12:50 Tu. Th.; 3:00-4:50 M. or Th.   MR. LAMPI.

82. (II) Confections and Cereal Products

The materials offered in this course are as follows: the home manufacture of fruit preserves, candied and glacéed fruits, pastes, confections, candies, and other specialties. Approximately one-half the semester is devoted to elementary work in candy making. This course will also consider the principles of baking, doughs, various cereal products and dry mixes.

2 2-hour laboratory periods.   Credit, 2.
3:00-4:50 W. F.   MR. LEVINE.

85. (I) 86. (II) Marine Products Technology

A survey of marine products of commerce and industry. Canning, curing, and freezing of seafoods. Chemical and micro-biological aspects of the industry. By-products, industrial problems and scientific literature. Emphasis is placed on the New England fisheries. The lectures may be taken without the laboratory hours.

2 class hours; 1 2-hour laboratory period.   Credit, 3 or 2.
                                                               MR. FELLERS.

91. (I) Analysis of Food Products

·Laboratory studies on the grading of foods, examination of foods for adulteration, testing accessory products for quality, and determining the causes of spoilage or deterioration in processed food products. Physical, chemical, microbiological, and microscopical methods will be employed. Training in the use of the A.O.A.C. Standard Methods. Enrollment limited to 18.

1 class hour; 1 4-hour laboratory period.   Credit, 3.
9:00-9:50 Th.; 1:00-4:50 Th. or F.   MR. LIVINGSTON.
Prerequisites: Food Technology 52; Bacteriology 31; Chemistry 30.

92. (II) Objective Analytical Methods and Instrumentation

· For students specializing in food technology. This is a continuation of Course 91. It includes interpretation of analysis, sanitation and food laws, government grading of processed foods, use of manuals and the technical work of trade associations. Laboratory work includes use of all kinds of laboratory and field equipment and apparatus used in food plants.

1 class hour; 1 4-hour laboratory period.   · Credit, 3.
9:00-9:50 Th.; 1:00-4:50 Tu., W., or Th.   MR. LIVINGSTON.·
Prerequisite, Food Technology 91.

96. (II) Introductory Research Methods

For food technology majors. The application of the fundamental sciences to food technology research.

Hours by arrangement. Credit, 2.

THE DEPARTMENT.

98. (II) Sensory Evaluation Methods

An introduction to sensory measurements in the evaluation and acceptance of foods. Panel tests and their statistical interpretation; taste, odor, color, and texture measurements; application to food quality control and grading. For seniors only.

1 class hour; 1 2-hour laboratory period. Credit, 2.

MR. FAGERSON.

FOOD MANAGEMENT

33. (I) Introductory Food Management

An overall study of food service as represented by restaurants, institutions, hotels, and clubs, including the Armed Services. Principles of catering and industry requirements. Food economics and the role of processed foods. Food standards, grades and regulations. Trade practices. Beverage operations and regulations. Elementary principles of management.

3 class hours. Credit, 3.
9:00-9:50 M. W. F. MR. CULBERTSON.

67. (I) Food Preparation and Service

Catering; quantity production with commercial types of equipment—baking, sauces, pastries; radar cookery. Actual participation at one of the University kitchens and in catering at special events.

1 class hour; 1 4-hour laboratory period. Credit, 3.
11:00-11:50 Tu.; laboratory hours by arrangement. MR. CULBERTSON.

68. (II) Kitchen Administration

A general study of problems arising in operation of a commercial kitchen. Attention is given to layouts and floor plans with emphasis on equipment, design, installation, maintenance, sanitation and depreciation. Food control and economy. Considerable time is devoted to personnel procurement and training problems, job breakdown and specifications. Various types of table service and highlights of dining room supervision are included.

2 class hours; 1 2-hour laboratory period. Credit, 3.
11:00-11:50 M. F.; laboratory hours by arrangement. MR. BAKER.

77. (I) Food Service Practices

Functional study of personnel. Duties of managers, stewards, cooks, etc. Menu making; types of catering service. Advertising and promotion methods. Requirements for special functions. Labor procurement and policies. Job training and evaluation. Cost controls.

2 class hours; 1 2-hour laboratory period. Credit, 3.
9:00-9:50 Tu. Th.; laboratory hours by arrangement. MR. CULBERTSON.

78. (II) Stewarding

This is a study of practices used by hotels and restaurants pertaining to purchasing, receiving, and issuing food, beverages, and other supplies. It includes storeroom procedures, issue systems, and internal check methods, principles of food and beverage cost control, menu planning and pricing.

3 class hours. Credit, 3.
11:00-11:50 M. W. F. MR. BAKER.

FORESTRY AND WILDLIFE MANAGEMENT

PROFESSOR HOLDSWORTH, PROFESSOR TRIPPENSEE, PROFESSOR RHODES, ASSOCIATE PROFESSOR RICH, ASSISTANT PROFESSOR MACCONNELL, MR. COLE,* MR. GANLEY, MR. ABBOTT.

25. (I) Wood Anatomy and Identification

A basic anatomical study of wood elements, their various structural characteristics and functions. Relation of structure and properties to use. Microscopic study of wood elements. Practice in identification.

1 class hour; 2 2-hour laboratory periods. Credit, 3.
MR. RICH.

26. (II) Dendrology

The taxonomic features, silvical characteristics and geographical distribution of the principal forest trees of temperate North America, and the description of the forests in which they occur; identification of the native and naturalized woody plants occurring in the forests of the Northeastern United States, in summer and winter conditions, by means of keys and first-hand examination.

2 class hours; 2 2-hour laboratory and field periods. Credit, 3.
MR. RHODES, MR. GANLEY.

51. (I) Forest Management of Watersheds

For students majoring in bacteriology and public health. Admission on recommendation of student's major adviser. A study of forest site—water factor relationships; the improvement of watershed forests through applied silviculture; relative suitability of tree species for watershed uses; forest protection measures.

3 class hours; special field trips. Credit, 3.
MR. RHODES, MR. HOLDSWORTH.

53. (I) Silvics

Forest ecology as a foundation for silvicultural practice: the physiological basis of forest ecology; environmental factors, their effect upon vegetation, and how they are influenced by it; the development and silvical habits of the individual tree; the development, characteristics and classification of forest communities; plant indicators; methods for the study and analysis of vegetation and its environment.

2 class hours; 1 4-hour laboratory and field period. Credit, 3.
MR. RHODES

54. (II) Forest Soils

The structure, development and maintenance of forest soils; their relationship to applied silviculture and forest productivity; the literature of forest soils with special reference to American experience.

3 class hours. Credit, 3.
MR. RHODES

* On leave of absence for military service.

188

55. (I) and (Summer)   The Elements of Forest Mensuration

Methods of determining the volume and value of the forest growing stock; type mapping as it pertains to timber cruising; the field work includes mapping and timber estimating on forests realistic in size and condition and the submission of inventory reports.

2 class hours; 1 4-hour laboratory and field period.   Credit, 3.
Summer course: 3 44-hour weeks.   Mr. MacConnell, Mr. Ganley.

56. (II)   The Principles of Silviculture

The methods of establishing and developing forest stands through the application of correct silvicultural practice. Intermediate cuttings and reproduction systems. Field work in applied silviculture, including the marking of forest stands for silvicultural treatment, is given on University forest property.

2 class hours; 1 4-hour laboratory period.   Credit, 3.
Mr. Rhodes, Mr. Abbott.

57. (I)   Forest Economics and Policy

This course considers the forest as a resource yielding direct forest values and social benefits. The history of American forestry and the development of a forest policy together with the role of the forest in American economy are considered.

3 class hours.   Credit, 3.
Mr. Holdsworth.

59. (I)   Forest Protection

The principle of protecting forests from all harmful agencies but with special reference to the prevention and control of forest fires, insects, and disease. Other agencies are treated in accordance with their importance.

3 class hours.   Credit, 3.
Mr. Abbott.

62. (II)   The Management and Uses of Farm Forests

A study of the production of wood as a crop from forest land associated with farm enterprise. Silvicultural methods to improve wood quality and increase quantity; the measurement of timber volumes and growth rates; the grading, measurement, and use of forest products. Open to non-majors only.

2 class hours; 1 4-hour laboratory period.   Credit, 3.
Mr. Ganley.

71. (I)   Aerial Photogrammetry

Principles of photogrammetry leading to the application of aerial photography in forest management, wildlife biology, engineering, geology, and other fields dealing with large land surfaces. Photographic interpretation and map making from aerial photographs are laboratory activities.

2 class hours; 1 4-hour laboratory period.   Credit, 3.
Mr. MacConnell, Mr. Ganley.

75. (I)   Manufacture and Distribution of Forest Products

A study of the techniques of manufacturing forest products, including production and cost studies; also the seasoning, grading and special processing prerequisite to marketing.

3 class hours.   Credit, 3.
Mr. Rich.

76. (II) Wood Technology

The structure, composition and properties of wood in relation to its economic utilization; wood-liquid relationships as they affect seasoning, preservation, and technological process for industrial purposes. A survey of the technological advances in the use of wood.

3 class hours.

Credit, 3.

MR. RICH.

78. (Summer) Harvesting of Forest Products

Primarily a field course designed to give students practice in the actual harvesting and preparation of direct forest products from the felling of standing timber through the log-making, skidding, transportation and sawing processes to the stacking of lumber. This part of the course is given on University owned forest land and at the mill of a private cooperator. Short field trips are made to active forest properties where harvesting is proceeding and a longer trip is made to New Hampshire and Maine to visit pulpwood and timber operations and manufacturing plants. Lectures and classwork survey the theory and practice of forest harvesting in the several U. S. forest regions.

3 44-hour weeks.

Credit, 3.

MR. GANLEY, MR. MACCONNELL.

80. (II) Principles of Forest Management

The organization of the forest for sustained yield management with a study of the underlying principles. Forest regulation. The preparation of forest management plans.

3 class hours.

Credit, 3.

MR. MACCONNELL.

81. (I) Regional Silviculture

The practice of silviculture as applied in the several forest regions of the United States with special reference to the treatment of the tree species of commercial importance. Emphasis is given to the factors, both natural and economic, which govern silviculture in these regions.

3 class hours.

Credit, 3.

MR. RHODES.

82. (II) Seeding and Planting in the Practice of Forestry

A study of forest tree seeds and their characteristics, production, harvest, storage, and qualities of germination. The production, distribution, and forest use of planting stock.

1 class hour; 2 2-hour laboratory periods.

Credit, 3.

MR. ABBOTT.

85. (I) Air Seasoning and Kiln Drying

A study of the proper conditioning of wood products by air seasoning and kiln drying, of moisture relation in the wood, and of kiln operation.

3 class hours.

Credit, 3.

MR. RICH.

WILDLIFE MANAGEMENT

27. (I) Conservation of Natural Resources

Natural resources of the United States including soil, water, forests, wildlife, and the important minerals, the historic background of their use and their present status in relation to the social and economic welfare. Includes the discussion of various conservation problems in relation to national prosperity.

3 class hours.

Credit, 3.

10:00-10:50 M. W. F.

MR. TRIPPENSEE.

70. (II) Wildlife Management

Life histories, ecology, and management of common game birds and mammals. Includes a study of natural habitats and methods of management.

1 class hour; 2 2-hour laboratory periods. Credit, 3.

MR. TRIPPENSEE.

71. (I) Wildlife Management (1956-57)

Life histories, ecology, and management of waterfowl. Includes a study of natural habitats and method of management. Given in alternate years.

1 class hour; 2 2-hour laboratory periods. Credit, 3.

11:00-11:50 Tu.; 3:00-4:50 Tu. Th. MR. TRIPPENSEE.

72. (II) Forest-Animal Relationships

For students majoring in Forestry. Effects of animals on the forest; the effects of forest practices on wild animal production; economic aspects of forest-animal relationships.

3 class hours. Credit, 3.

10:00-10:50 M. W. F. MR. TRIPPENSEE.

73. (I) Wildlife Management

Life histories, ecology, and management of predaceous birds and injurious mammals. Particularly designed for those who seek employment with rodent control division of U. S. Fish and Wildlife Service.

1 class hour; 2 2-hour laboratory periods. Credit, 3.

MR. TRIPPENSEE.

74. (II) Techniques in Wildlife Management (1954-55)

Admission by permission of instructor. Quantitative field studies of wild animals of forest and farm. Includes cover mapping, habitat studies, census, food habits, and damage of game animals. For students interested in state and federal employment through civil service. Given in alternate years.

1 class hour; 1 4-hour laboratory period. Credit, 3.

1:00-1:50 W.; 1:00-4:50 M. MR. TRIPPENSEE.

75. (I) Wildlife Management (1955-56)

Life histories, ecology, and management of the furbearers. Includes a study of natural habitats, management and fur farm problems. Given in alternate years.

1 class hour; 2 2-hour laboratory periods. Credit, 3.

11:00-11:50 Tu.; 3:00-4:50 Tu. Th. MR. TRIPPENSEE.

84. (II) Seminar (1955-56)

Study and discussion of problems in relation to agriculture, forestry, and the use and control of wildlife resources. For juniors and seniors majoring in wildlife management. Given in alternate years.

3 class hours. Credit, 3.

MR. TRIPPENSEE.

191

GEOLOGY AND MINEROLOGY

PROFESSOR WILSON, ASSISTANT PROFESSOR NELSON, ASSISTANT PROFESSOR JOHANS-
SON, ASSISTANT PROFESSOR WOODLAND, ASSISTANT PROFESSOR SOCOLOW, MR.
RICE, MR. TYNAN, MR. ERICKSON.

1. (I) Physical Geology
An introduction to the agents and processes that modify the earth's crust.
Field trips by arrangement.
2 class hours; 1 quiz hour; 1 2-hour laboratory period.   Credit, 3.
                                                           THE DEPARTMENT.

28. (II) Historical Geology
A survey of geological time, stressing the development of continents and the
history of plants and animals. Field trips by arrangement.
2 class hours; 1 quiz hour; 1 2-hour laboratory period.   Credit, 3.
                                                           THE DEPARTMENT.

50. (I) Engineering Geology
A general course in engineering geology stressing earth structure, the dynamic processes, and agents of weathering. The laboratory work consists of
mineral and rock-determination and map-reading as related to the phenomena
of physical geology.
2 class hours; 1 3-hour laboratory period.   Credit, 3.
                                                    MR. WOODLAND.

51. (I) 52. (II) Mineralogy
A course designed to meet the needs of students majoring in geology and
allied fields. The first semester's work deals with all of the mineral classes with
the exception of the silicate group which has been reserved for the second
semester.
1 class hour; 2 2-hour laboratory periods.   Credit, 3.
                                                    MR. NELSON.

Prerequisites, Chemistry 1 and 2.

54. (II) Economic Geology
A course dealing with the origin, classification, and uses of metallic and
non-metallic mineral deposits.
2 class hours; 1 2-hour laboratory period.   Credit, 3.
                                                    MR. WOODLAND.

56. (II) Lithology
A descriptive study of the classes of rocks with reference to manner of
origin, modes of occurrence, structural features and the chemical and petrographic distinction within each group.
1 class hour; 2 2-hour laboratory periods.   Credit, 3.
                                                    MR. NELSON.

60. (II) Principles of Physical Geography
A systematic study of the world's physiographic provinces, climate, vegetation, soils, mineral resources, and their effects upon mankind. The geographic
relationships to land forms will be stressed.
3 class hours.   Credit, 3.
                        MR. JOHANSSON.

61. (I) Geomorphology (1956-57)

A review of recent studies concerning rock structures, weathering, streams, underground water, shorelines, wind work, volcanoes, and mountains. Field trips by arrangement.

2 class hours; 1 2-hour laboratory period. Credit, 3.

MR. SOCOLOW.

62. (II) Pleistocene Geology (1956-57)

A study of Pleistocene world geology consisting of geological processes, land forms, existing and extinct glaciers, biota and stratigraphy. Field trips by arrangement.

2 class hours; 1 2-hour laboratory period. Credit, 3.

MR. WILSON.

63. (I) Invertebrate Paleontology

A study of the history, development and identification of invertebrate animal fossils. Field trips by arrangement.

1 class hour; 2 2-hour laboratory periods. Credit, 3.

MR. JOHANSSON.

64. (II) Plant Paleontology

A study of the history, development, and identification of plant fossils. Field trips by arrangement.

1 class hour; 2 2-hour laboratory periods. Credit, 3.

MR. WILSON.

71. (I) 72. (II) Special Problems

For seniors specializing in geology.
6 laboratory hours. Credit, 3.
Hours by arrangement. THE DEPARTMENT.

73. (I) Structural Geology

A study of the origin of rock structures, their occurrence, and recognition. Field and laboratory problems emphasize the structure present in the Connecticut valley.

1 class hour; 2 2-hour laboratory periods. Credit, 3.

MR. WOODLAND.

74. (II) Principles of Stratigraphy

An examination of the principles of stratigraphic correlation and their application to the problems of the major rock units of the United States. Field and laboratory work consists primarily of problems related to the eastern United States.

1 class hour; 2 2-hour laboratory periods. Credit, 3.

MR. WILSON.

GERMAN

PROFESSOR ELLERT, ASSOCIATE PROFESSOR SCHROEDER, MR. STAWIECKI, MR. LEA, MISS SCHIFFER, MISS TAPP, VISITING LECTURER PEPPARD.

1. (I) 2. (II) Elementary German

Grammar, prose composition, and reading. No credits in this course may be applied toward a degree until the close of the second semester, except upon special recommendation from the Provost.

3 class hours. Credit, 3.

THE DEPARTMENT.

193

GERMAN

5. (I) 6. (II) Advanced German Prose

Reading of representative German authors: Grammar review.

3 class hours.   Credit, 3.
8:00-8:50 Tu. Th. ` .   MR. LEA.
Prerequisite, Entrance German.

25. (I) 26. (II) Intermediate German

German prose, poetry and drama. Grammar review.

3 class hours.   Credit, 3.
                                                             THE DEPARTMENT.

Prerequisites, German 1 and 2.

28. (II) Scientific German

Intensive and extensive readings of scientific texts in various fields taken
from standard German works.

3 class hours.   Credit, 3.
                                                             THE DEPARTMENT.

Prerequsites, German 25.

51. (I) Nineteenth Century Prose (1956-57)

A study of the *Novelle* from the death of Goethe to 1890 (early realism to
naturalism) with emphasis on literary and social forces in the work of Tieck,
Stifter, Keller, and others. Given in alternate years.

3 class hours.   Credit, 3.
                                                              MR. SCHROEDER.

Prerequisites, German 25 and 26.

52. (II) Poetry and Drama of the Nineteenth Century (1956-57)

A study of the development of the drama and of lyric poetry from 1830
to 1890 with special emphasis on dramatic works of Grillparzer, Hebbel, and
Hauptmann and the poetry of Mörike, Storm, and C. F. Meyer. Given in
alternate years.

3 class hours.   Credit, 3.
                                                             THE DEPARTMENT.

Prerequisites, German 25 and 26.

53. (I) Twentieth Century Prose (1957-58)

Main literary currents in contemporary German prose from Nietzsche to
Hesse with particular attention to the work of Thomas Mann, Kafka, and
Werfel. Given in alternate years.

3 class hours.   Credit, 3.
                                                              MR. SCHROEDER.

Prerequisites, German 25 and 26.

54. (II) Poetry and Drama of the Twentieth Century (1955-56)

Reading and discussion of significant lyrical works of Hofmannsthal, George,
and Rilke, and representative dramas by Hauptmann and Georg Kaiser. Given
in alternate years.

3 class hours.   Credit. 3.
                                                             THE DEPARTMENT.

Prerequisites, German 25 and 26.

55. (I) Storm and Stress

A study of storm and stress in German literature centering in the young Goethe.

3 class hours.   Credit, 3.

Mr. Ellert.

Prerequisites, German 25 and 26.

56. (II) Romanticism (1956-57)

A study of the poetry and prose writings of the romantic period from Novalis to Heine. Given in alternate years.

3 class hours.   Credit, 3.

Mr. Ellert.

Prerequisites, German 25 and 26.

57. (I) Goethe's *Faust*

3 class hours.   Credit, 3.

The Department.

Prerequisites, German 25 and 26.

58. (II) Middle High German (1956-57)

Readings of Middle High German texts in the original with an introduction to the grammar. Given in alternate years.

3 class hours.   Credit, 3.

The Department.

Prerequisites, German 25 and 26.

59. (I) The Germanic Languages (1957-58)

An introduction to general and Germanic philology for German and English majors; a survey of the relationship between German, English, and the other Indo-European tongues and of the historical development of German and English as the two major Germanic literary languages. Given in alternate years.

3 class hours.   Credit, 3.

The Department.

60. (II) The Classical Period (1955-56)

A study of representative works by Lessing, Goethe, and Schiller. Given in alternate years.

Mr. Schroeder.

Prerequisites, German 25 and 26.

68. (II) German Literature of the Middle Ages (1955-56)

A survey of the literature of the German language from the earliest literary documents to the 15th century, with readings in modern German translation of the Nibelungenlied, Gudrun, Parzival, Tristan, Der arme Heinrich, and the lyrics of Walter von der Vogelweide. Given in alternate years.

3 class hours.   Credit, 3.

Mr. Ellert.

79. (I) 80. (II) German Conversation and Composition

Practice in the oral and written language.

4 class hours.   Credit, 3.

3:00-4:50 Tu. Th.   Mr. Schroeder.

Prerequisites, German 25 and 26, or permission of instructor

GOVERNMENT

PROFESSOR ——————, ASSISTANT PROFESSOR GOODWIN, ASSISTANT PROFESSOR TINDER, MR. ALLEN, MR. MAINZER, MR. BRAUNTHAL, MR. STREAMER.

25. (I) and (II) American Government

A study of the principles, machinery, dynamics and problems of government in the United States.

3 class hours.   Credit, 3.
THE DEPARTMENT.

26. (II) European Government

A survey of the politics and governmental institutions of Great Birtain, France, U. S. S. R., and other European countries.

3 class hours.   Credit, 3.
MR. ALLEN, MR. TINDER, MR. BRAUNTHAL.

53. (I) International Relations

The nation-state system and conceptions of national interest in modern world politics. The forms and distribution of power by which states seek to implement national interests. The making of foreign policy and methods of adjusting international conflict. Attention will be given to current international problems.

3 class hours.   Credit, 3.
MR. ALLEN.

54. (II) State Government (1955-56)

A study of state politics, organization and functions, with emphasis on the role of the state in our Federal system. Given in alternate years.

3 class hours.   Credit, 3.
MR. GOODWIN.

55. (S) The Presidency in American Government

The growth of the executive in United States Government. Varying conceptions of the presidential office. Constitutional and political aspects of the office in legislation, administration and conduct of foreign and military affairs. The president as party leader.

5 periods a week for 6 weeks.   Credit, 3.
MR. BRAUNTHAL.

Prerequisite, Government 25.

61. (I) Public Administration

A study of organization and management in modern government, with emphasis on the bureaucracy's role in public policy formation.

3 class hours.   Credit, 3.
MR. MAINZER.

62. (II) Administrative Law

A study of governmental activities in the regulation of industry, agriculture, and labor, with emphasis on the legal framework within which these activities operate. Not offered 1955-56.

3 class hours.   Credit, 3.
MR. MAINZER.

63. (I) Political Parties and Elections

A study of the American political process, with emphasis on parties, pressure groups, and public opinion.

3 class hours. Credit, 3.
MR. GOODWIN.

64. (II) Municipal Government (1956-57)

A survey of the governmental structure and function of American municipalities. Given in alternate years.

3 class hours. Credit, 3.
MR. GOODWIN.

65. (I) Constitutional Law

An historical study of the United States Constitution as interpreted by decisions of the Supreme Court.

3 class hours. Credit, 3.
MR. STEAMER.

66. (II) American Political Thought

A study of the development of American political thought from colonial times to the present.

3 class hours. Credit, 3.
MR. STEAMER.

68. (II) International Law

A study of the origin, character, and function of international law. Not offered 1956-57.

3 class hours. Credit, 3.
MR. BRAUNTHAL.

70. (II) International Organization

A study of international organization in the twentieth century, with emphasis upon the United Nations and regional organizations. Not offered 1955-56.

3 class hours. Credit, 3.
MR. BRAUNTHAL.

71. (I) Ancient and Medieval Political Thought

A study of the development of political thought and its relation to cultural and institutional growth from the time of the Greeks to the end of the Middle Ages.

3 class hours. Credit, 3.
MR. TINDER.

72. (II) Modern Political Thought

A study of the development of political thought and its relation to cultural and institutional growth from the rise of the modern state to the present.

3 class hours. Credit, 3.
MR. TINDER.

73. (I) Comparative Government

A functional analysis of contemporary governments with special attention to the ideology, structure, and dynamics of political parties.

3 class hours. Credit, 3.
MR. ALLEN.

Prerequisite, Government 26.

76. (II) Public Opinion in Politics

A study of opinion and communication as aspects of the political process with emphasis upon communication through mass media. Examination of the relations between mass attitudes and communication and political institutions and the formation of public policy.

3 class hours. Credit, 3.

MR. MAINZER.

93. (I) 94. (II) Seminar

A study of special problems in the field of government.

3 class hours. Credit, 3.

THE DEPARTMENT.

HISTORY

PROFESSOR CALDWELL, PROFESSOR CARY, ASSOCIATE PROFESSOR DAVIS, ASSISTANT PROFESSOR ZEENDER, ASSISTANT PROFESSOR PFLANZE,† ASSISTANT PROFESSOR POTASH,† MR. GAGNON, MR. KINGDON, MR. DIETEL, MR. HIGHAM, MR. HILL, MR. BROWN, MR. GREENBAUM, MR. LEONARD.

5. (I) 6. (II) Modern European Civilization

The first semester covers the period from the later Middle Ages to 1815; the second semester, the period from 1815 to the present. These courses are required of candidates for the B.A. degree but may be elected independently by other students.

3 class hours. Credit, 3.

THE DEPARTMENT.

31. (I) 32. (II) English History

Emphasis on economic, social, and cultural influences, as well as on constitutional development. Either semester may be elected independently.

3 class hours. Credit, 3.

MR. CALDWELL, MR. DIETEL.

51. (I) Ancient History

A general survey of Mesopotamian, Egyptian, Greek, and Roman history, with primary emphasis on cultural and intellectual achievements.

3 class hours. Credit, 3.

MR. DAVIS.

54. (II) The Far East (1956-57)

A general historical introduction to the civilization and contemporary problems of China and Japan. The first half covers the traditional civilization of China and Japan and the early impact of the west to 1890. The second half deals with revolutionary developments of the twentieth century and the place of the Far East in the world balance of power. Given in alternate years.

3 class hours. Credit, 3.

MR. KINGDON.

56. (II) History of Russia (1955-56)

A general historical introduction to the civilization and contemporary problems of Russia. Growth of the Russian state, society, culture and ideology, and their relations to the non-Russian world. Emphasis on the Soviet period. Given in alternate years.

3 class hours. Credit, 3.

MR. GAGNON.

† On leave of absence.

57. (I) 58. (II) Hispanic-American History

The first semester deals with the colonial period: the age of the "conquistadores", political, economic, and cultural developments, and growth of the independence movement; the second semester with the period of national development from 1810 to the present. Emphasis will be given to the history of Mexico and the more important South American countries. Either semester may be elected independently.

3 class hours.   Credit, 3.

Mr. Potash.

59. (I) 60. (II) History of the United States

A survey of the national development including political, social, economic, and cultural factors in the growth of American democracy. The first semester covers the period to 1865; the second, from 1865 to the present. Either semester may be elected independently.

3 class hours.   Credit, 3.

Mr. Cary, Mr. Davis.

62. (II) Medieval History

Europe from the collapse of Roman civilization to the Renaissance. Fusion of the Graeco-Roman inheritance, Christianity, and Germanic traditions in the building of Western European civilization. The medieval outlooks as expressed in the thought and culture of the High Middle Ages.

3 class hours.   Credit, 3.

Prerequisite, History 32.   Mr. Zeender.

69. (I) Europe, 1870-1918

Internal developments of the principal countries, including political and economic changes, social unrest, and intellectual currents; the development of imperialism; a detailed study of conditions and diplomacy which led to the World War; military history of the War.

3 class hours.   Credit, 3.

Prerequisite, History 6.   Mr. Zeender.

70. (II) Europe Since 1918

Approximately half of the course is devoted to international affairs, including the Peace Settlement, the development of German, Italian, and Japanese aggression, and World War II. The other half of the course is a study of internal developments in the principal European nations.

3 class hours.   Credit, 3.

Mr. Caldwell.

71. (I) Main Currents in English Thought, 1600-1900

A study of leaders of thought and the climate of ideas in selected periods, with emphasis on the realtionship of ideas to outstanding historical events.

3 class hours.   Credit, 3.

Mr. Caldwell.

72. (II) History of American Westward Expansion, 1763-1893

Advance of settlement from the Appalachians to the Pacific and influence of the frontier upon social, economic, and political conditions in the country as a whole.

3 class hours.   Credit, 3.

Prerequisite, History 59.   Mr. Davis.

73. (I) History of the Renaissance

The later Middle Ages; the Church at the height of power; the rise of nationalities; the Italian towns; the New Learning and its relation to art, science, invention, geographical discoveries; spread and effects of the Renaissance.

3 class hours. Credit, 3.

MR. KINGDON.

74. (II) Age of Reformation

A study of the religious changes, and the accompanying political upheavals, and the social, economic, and cultural developments in 16th and 17th century Europe.

3 class hours. Credit, 3.

MR. KINGDON.

81. (I) 82. (II) Diplomatic History of the United States

The development of American foreign relations, 1776 to the present. Either semester may be elected independently.

3 class hours. Credit, 2 or 3.

MR. CARY.

Prerequisites, History 59, 60, or permission of the instructor.

91. (I) Seminar

Instruction in bibliography, evaluation of source materials and preparation of reports.

1 class hour. Credit, 1.

THE DEPARTMENT.

92. (II) Historiography

Critical evaluation of representative historians from ancient to modern times.

1 class hour. Credit, 1.

THE DEPARTMENT.

HOME ECONOMICS

PROFESSOR MITCHELL, ASSOCIATE PROFESSOR BRIGGS, ASSOCIATE PROFESSOR MERRIAM, ASSISTANT PROFESSOR COOK, ASSISTANT PROFESSOR DAVIS, ASSISTANT PROFESSOR McCULLOUGH, ASSISTANT PROFESSOR STRATTNER, ASSISTANT PROFESSOR WILHELM, MRS. THIES, MISS HAWES, MRS. SULLIVAN, MRS. DAY, MRS. ESSELEN.

11. (I) Euthenics

A study of the responsibilities and opportunities of women for the improvement of society through creative homemaking, gainful employment, and effective community participation.

Readings, discussions and independent research are designed to help the student begin intelligent preparation for accepting the multiple roles involved in marriage, parenthood, and community citizenship.

3 class hours. Credit, 3.

MISS STRATTNER.

12. (II) Consumer Clothing Problems

This course consists of three fundamental approaches to clothing problems: consumer education in relation to economics in the field of ready-to-wear; a study of art and psychology applied to the selection of apparel; and basic principles of construction.

2 class hours; 1 2-hour laboratory period.   Credit, 3.
MRS. WILHELM, MISS HAWES.

26. (II) Textiles

This course is designed to give the student an introduction to the characteristic properties and uses of natural and synthetic fibers; the conversion of fiber to finished fabrics; fabric identifications; buying and use of fabrics for clothing and home use.

2 class hours; 1 2-hour laboratory period.   Credit, 3.
MISS HAWES.

30. (II) Food Science and Preparation

A study of the fundamental scientific principles and comparative methods of food preparation. The nutritional and economic aspects of foods are also stressed.

2 class hours; 1 3-hour laboratory period.   Credit, 3.
MISS DAVIS.

31. (I) Applied Art

Art principles are studied with many practical applications for selecting and arranging. Specific problems in decorating cloth, wood, and leather afford opportunity for individual expression.

1 class hour; 2 2-hour laboratory periods.   Credit, 3.
MISS BRIGGS, MRS. SULLIVAN.

35. (I) Clothing Construction

Advanced construction and fitting problems with emphasis on new fabrics. In the latter part of the semester provision is made for individual development in the field of clothing in which the student is most interested. Sections offered are: more advanced construction and fitting problems; visual aids for teaching clothing; creative pattern drafting and merchandising women's ready-to-wear.

1 class hour; 2 2-hour laboratory periods.   Credit, 3
MRS. WILHELM, MISS HAWES.

Prerequisite, Home Economics 2 or equivalent.

41. (I) Nutrition and Food Preparation (For Nurses)

This course combines the fundamentals of nutrition with food preparation and meal planning to meet nutritional requirements. The content and emphasis is appropriate for nurses whose responsibilities will be mostly with their patients. Admission by permission of instructor.

3 class hours; 1 2-hour laboratory period.   Credit, 4.
MRS. COOK.

Prerequisites, Chemistry 1 and 2; Zoology 35.

42. (II) Medical Dietetics (For Nurses)

The principles and practice of dietary restrictions and modifications recommended for certain diseases, always keeping in mind the nutritional needs of the individual. Students learn to use current medical literature for supplementary reference in connection with new developments.

2 class hours.   Credit, 2.
MRS. COOK.

Prerequisite, Home Economics 41 or equivalent.

HOME ECONOMICS

51. (I) Meal Planning

Meal planning, serving and etiquette and emphasis on well-balanced meals as to nutritive value and economy of money, time, and labor in preparation. Further study of food principles and techniques of cookery and a unit in food preservation, freezing and canning is included.

2 class hours; 1 3-hour laboratory period.   Credit, 3.
                                                              Miss Davis.

Prerequisite, Home Economics 30; Chemistry 33 or equivalent.

52. (II) Nutrition and Dietetics

A study of the fundamentals of normal nutrition including energy needs, the metabolism of proteins, carbohydrates, fats, vitamins, and minerals; and the quantitative requirements for these various essential nutrients. Laboratory work provides for further study of the composition of foods and their contribution to the diet and the relationship of the nutritive value to cost. Nutritive loss due to cooking, storage, etc., is given consideration.

3 class hours; 1 2-hour laboratory period.   Credit, 3.
                                                              Mrs. Cook.

Prerequisites, Home Economics 30; Chemistry 33 and Zoology 1 or 35.

54. (II) Nutrition

For students who are not majoring in Home Economics and who do not have prerequisites for Home Economics 52. This course is designed to interpret the technical knowledge of foods and nutrition in terms of its practical application for optimum health.

3 class hours.   Credit, 3.
                                                              Mrs. Cook.

56. (II) Meal Planning

This course is designed to meet the needs of those who wish a general knowledge of the basic food principles. It includes latest methods and techniques of cookery, conservation of nutrients, menu planning and food preparation, buying of food, consumer education and table service, decoration and etiquette. It is recommended for students who want a scientific as well as practical knowledge of food and its preparation for everyday use.

2 class hours; 1 3-hour laboratory period.   Credit, 3.
                                                          The Department.

60. (II) Household Equipment

A study of selection, care, and operation of household equipment and the mechanical principles involved. Actual work with equipment and field trips are included.

1 class hour; 1 3-hour laboratory period.   Credit, 2.
                                                             Miss Merriam.

61. (I) Demonstration Techniques

Emphasis is given to the purposes and techniques of demonstration both in preparation of food and the use of equipment, with application to teaching, extension, and business.

2 2-hour laboratory periods.   Credit 2.
                                                             Miss Davis.

Prerequisites, Home Economics 30, 51.

62. (II) Home Furnishing

A study of the fundamental principles which underlie the successful planning and furnishing of a satisfying home. A study of period homes and furnishings is included. Many applications of these principles are worked out in practical problems.

1 class hour; 2 2-hour laboratory periods.   Credit, 3.
                                                                       MISS BRIGGS.

63. (I) Arts and Crafts

Introduction to design and execution in crafts particularly adapted to work with children in schools, playgrounds, summer camps; and for any age in recreational leadership and occupational therapy. Opportunity will be offered for work in several of the following: wood and leather work, block printing, finger-painting, etching, knotting, etc.

1 class hour; 2 2-hour laboratory periods.   Credit, 3.
                                                                       MISS BRIGGS.

70. (II) Child Development

The growth and development of the child, his basic needs, aspects of behavior-routine, creative and social—as they are related to personality development. Planned observation and participation in nursery school.

3 class hours; 1 1-hour laboratory period.   Credit, 3.
                                                                       MRS. THIES.

71. (I) Retail Food Buying

This course is offered jointly by the departments of olericulture, animal husbandry, and poultry husbandry for all students interested in retail marketing. First period: vegetables and fruits, retail buying, varieties and adaptability to various uses, season of availability, grades, packs and packages. Second period: poultry and eggs—dressed poultry is graded and prepared in various ways for the table and home freezing. Demonstrations are given of handling and market classification of eggs. Third period: meats—demonstration and laboratory practices in identification and classification of meat cuts, in preservation (freezing and curing) and in judging quality.

2 class hours; 1 2-hour laboratory period.   Credit, 3.
          MR. SNYDER, MR. VONDELL, MR. ——————.
          MRS. MCCULLOUGH, coordinator.

75. (I) Economics of the Household

A study of personal and family standards of living in the modern home, the economic relations of the household, and the use of time, energy, and money as a means to influence the home situation.

3 class hours.   Credit, 3.
                                                                       MISS MERRIAM.

77. (I) and (II) Home Management Practice

Successive groups of seniors live in the home management house or apartment and assume responsibilities involved in managing a home. Meals are planned on low, medium, and high income levels.

                                                                         Credit, 3.
                                                           MISS MERRIAM, MRS. DAY.
Prerequisites, Home Economics 51 or 56, 52 or 54, and 75, or by special permission.

78. (II) Advanced Textile Design

Weaving and handling of complicated looms. Other types of textile design such as stenciling, silk screen printing, batik, block print, with individual problems dependent on the student's special interests.

1 class hour; 2 3-hour laboratory periods.   Credit, 3.

Prerequisite, Home Economics 31 or its equivalent.   MISS BRIGGS.

80. (II) Family Life

A study of the modern family; ideals and responsibilities of the home and the individual's share in developing positive family relationships.

3 class hours.   Credit, 3.

    MISS STRATTNER.

81. (I) Methods of Teaching Home Economics

A study of the philosophy of general education; the application of home economics to the entire school program; development of curricula based upon student needs; exploration of instructional methods and techniques. This course gives credit toward meeting state standards for teachers.

3 class hours.   Credit, 3.

    MISS STRATTNER.

85. (I) Theory and Practice of Nursery School Management

This course is planned to give students a background in the history and philosophy of the pre-school program; theory and techniques of nursery school practice; children's activities in music, art, literature, and science; fundamentals of play and use of play materials, and methods of observation and recording. Supervised participation in child development laboratory as well as field trips to observe special groups.

2 class hours; 1 3-hour laboratory period.   Credit, 3.

Prerequisite, Home Economics 70.   MRS. THIES.

86. (S) Workshop in Recent Developments in Textiles

This course is a concentrated study of recent developments in the field of textiles. Instruction will include the characteristics and properties of the thermoplastic, protein, cellulose and mineral fibers (natural and synthetic) blends; fabric finishes and fabric care. Some field trips are an important phase of the work.

2 lecture hours and 2 laboratory hours daily for fifteen days.   Credit, 3.

Prerequisite, Home Economics 26 or its equivalent.   MISS HAWES.

87. (I) Principles and Practices of Tailoring

Emphasis on handling of wool in the making of suits and coats.

1 class hour; 2 2-hour laboratory periods.   Credit, 3.

    MRS. WILHELM, MISS HAWES.

Prerequisite, Home Economics 35 or equivalent.

88. (II) Applied Dress Design

Costume design through draping and pattern making. An intensive study is made of texture, line, color and fit as applied to dress design and the figure.

3 2-hour laboratory periods.   Credit, 3.

Prerequisite, Home Economics 35 or equivalent.   MRS. WILHELM.

89. (I) Diet Therapy

The application of nutrition principles to diet in disease. Recent theories of dietary treatment of gastro-intestinal disorders, obesity, anemia, fevers, diabetes, food allergy, cardiovascular and biliary tract diseases are reviewed critically. Students are required to use and be familiar with current medical literature as it applies to nutritional problems in disease and at the same time be open-minded regarding new developments in this field. Scientific and medical terminology is emphasized.

3 class hours. Credit, 3.

MRS. COOK.

Prerequisites, Home Economics 52; Chemistry 79; Zoology 35.

90. (II) Professional Seminars

A one-credit seminar is offered in each of the five fields of subject matter: Nutrition, Textiles, Clothing, Foods, Institutional Administration, Home Management and Equipment, Family Life and Child Development. One seminar is required of each senior and permission may be granted to take as many as three of the five.

Credit, 1-3.

HOME ECONOMICS STAFF.

91. (I) 92. (II) Quantity Food Preparation and Institutional Administration

For qualified juniors or seniors interested in institutional food service. A study of the principles of organization, personnel management, the administration, food costs, operating expenses, and the special functions of the dietitian. Laboratory work is at one of the university dining halls and field trips are planned. It is expected that students will enroll for the work of both semesters. Students wishing to qualify for administrative institutional work are advised to take Accounting 25 and Home Economics 71.

2 class hours, 1 4-hour laboratory period of field work. Credit, 3.

MRS. McCULLOUGH.

Prerequisites, Home Economics 51 and 52.

93. (I) Experimental Foods

The testing and comparing of different food materials and methods of preparation, including advanced work in the science and techniques of cookery. Special individual problems will be studied. The course is helpful to those interested in commercial food testing and valuable to those wishing to develop a scientific approach to the study of foods.

2 class hours; 1 3-hour laboratory period. Credit, 3.

MISS DAVIS.

Prerequisite, Home Economics 30.

94. (S) Workshop in Foods

An intensive course dealing with the planning and preparation of family meals. Consideration will be given to new products, cost levels, new trends toward international foods, and out-door cookery. Designed for home economics teachers and others with a background knowledge of scientific food preparation. Limited to 16 students.

5 hours daily for three weeks. Credit, 3.

MISS DAVIS.

Prerequisite, Home Economics 30 or equivalent.

95. (I) Child Nutrition

A study is made of nutritional needs from prenatal life through infancy and childhood. Methods of judging nutrition, also causes and effects of malnutrition are discussed. Menus for children and measures to insure the consumption of optimal diets are put in practice with laboratory work in the Nursery School.

3 class hours. Laboratory by arrangement. Credit, 3.
Prerequisite, Home Economics 52 or 54. MRS. COOK.

98. (I) and (II) Problems in Home Economics

An intensive study of some phase of home economics. By permission of the Staff adviser.

 Credit, 3.
 HOME ECONOMICS STAFF.

HYGIENE

Hygiene

All freshmen are required to attend a series of lectures on personal hygiene. For men students these lectures are included in the Military program; for women students they are scheduled as a separate course.

 Credit, 1.
 THE HEALTH SERVICE STAFF.

JOURNALISM

PROFESSOR MUSGRAVE.

83. (I) Community Journalism

A study of the weekly newspaper, the small-city daily, and the scholastic press, combined with training in copyediting. The University student publications and town newspapers are used as laboratories.

2 class hours; 1 laboratory period. Credit, 3.
 MR. MUSGRAVE.

85. (I) Introduction to Mass Communication

Designed to acquaint the student with the scope, principles, and practice of contemporary journalism. Stress is placed upon the role of the press as a social institution and upon the relationships between a general education and effective journalism.

3 class hours. Credit, 3.
 MR. MUSGRAVE.

86. (II) Feature Article Writing

Instruction in writing feature or magazine articles, combined with a study of the field of magazine journalism. The practice work is related to problems of interpretive writing and communication. Each student is expected to publish a feature article in a newspaper, a trade journal or other magazines.

3 class hours. Credit, 3.
 MR. MUSGRAVE.

88. (II) Problems in Journalism

The readings cover selected areas of journalistic studies, such as civil rights and the press, language and communication, comparative foreign journalism, history of journalism, communication research methods, the criticism of mass media. Laboratory work for seniors is arranged on daily newspapers. Admission by permission of instructor.

2 class hours; 1 laboratory period. Credit, 3.
 MR. MUSGRAVE.

LANDSCAPE ARCHITECTURE

PROFESSOR OTTO, PROFESSOR BLUNDELL, ASSISTANT PROFESSOR PROCOPIO, ASSISTANT PROFESSOR HAMILTON, MR. MACIVER, MR. KEEGAN.

LANDSCAPE ARCHITECTURE

25. (I) Freehand Drawing and Elementary Design

The work in this course is to supply the student with technical aspects of freehand drawing and design necessary to proficiency in that field.

3 2-hour laboratory periods.   Credit, 3.
1:00-2:50 M. W. F.   MR. KEEGAN.

26. (II) Landscape Drafting

This course continues the work in Landscape Architecture 25, but draws on the mechanical aspects of the designers problems and includes simple projections—orthographic, perspective, and isometric—and architectural shades and shadows.

3 2-hour laboratory periods.   Credit, 3.
1:00-2:50 M. W. F.   MR. KEEGAN.

51. (I) Elements of Topography and Construction

Contour interpolation, grading and drainage, plans, drive design, profiles and sections, computation of earth work. Application of surveying to landscape construction.

3 2-hour laboratory periods.   Credit, 3.
3:00-4:50 M. W. F.   MR. PROCOPIO.
Prerequisites: Civil Engineering 27; Landscape Architecture 26.

52. (II) Construction Details

A series of problems in architectural garden features as walks, steps, walls, gates, pools, and small structures.

3 2-hour laboratory periods.   Credit, 3.
3:00-4:50 M. W. F.   MR. PROCOPIO.
Prerequisites, Landscape Architecture 51.

53. (I) Introductory Design

Fundamental principles of composition with application to problems in the design of gardens and small home grounds.

3 2-hour laboratory periods.   Credit, 3.
1:00-2:50 M. W. F.   MR. OTTO.
Prerequisites, Landscape Architecture 25 and 26 or permission of the instructor.

54. (II) General Design

A series of problems in the design of private properties and public works. Members of this class will be required to take a two-day field trip to visit typical examples of design; approximate cost, $15.00.

3 2-hour laboratory periods.   Credit, 3.
1:00-2:50 M. W. F.   MR. OTTO.
Prerequisites, Landscape Architecture 51, 53, and concurrently 52.

79. (I) Construction and Maintenance (1957-58)

A study of construction methods and materials as applied to the landscape field. Given in alternate years.

3 class hours.
10:00-10:50 M. W. F.

Credit, 3.
MR. PROCOPIO.

80. (II) History and Literature of Landscape Architecture

A review of the history and literature of landscape architecture and allied fields. Compilation of bibliographies of significant works.

2 class hours.
8:00-8:50 Tu. Th.

Credit, 2.
MR. OTTO.

81. (I) 82. (II) Advanced Design

Class B Exchange Problems plus specialized study of landscape details and a summary of general design. Members of the class may be required to take a two-day field trip to visit typical examples of design; approximate cost, $15.00.

3 2-hour laboratory periods.
3:00-4:50 M. W. F.

Credit, 3.
MR. HAMILTON. .

Prerequisites, Landscape Architecture 53 and 54.

83. (I) Architecture (1956-57)

The history of architectural development, including styles of architecture and construction principles of value to landscape architects when working with architectural problems. Given in alternate years.

3 class hours.
8:00-8:50 M. W. F.

Credit, 3.
MR. ——————.

84. (II) Sketching

Drawing and sketching in various mediums from outdoor and indoor subjects.

2 2-hour laboratory periods.

Credit, 2.
MR. MacIVER.

86. (II) City Planning

A critical examination of those factors which influence and guide the physical growth and arrangement of communities in harmony with their social and economic needs.

3 class hours.
8:00-8:50 M. W. F.

Credit, 3.
MR. KEEGAN.

87. (I) Projects in Planning

An application of the principles of modern civic art through a series of problems on the design of various types of urban land areas.

2 3-hour laboratory periods.

Credit, 3.
MR. KEEGAN.

Prerequisite, Landscape Architecture 86.

88. (II) Projects in Planning

A continuation of Landscape Architecture 87.

2 3-hour laboratory periods.

Credit, 3.
MR. KEEGAN.

HORTICULTURE

2. (II) Basic Horticulture

An introductory course for those interested in acquiring some basic knowledge of horticulturally important plants. It is concerned with the structure, flowering and fruiting habits, propagation, training, pruning, and storage of many of our economic plants as well as an introductory discussion of the influence of soil, nutritional status, environmental factors and growth regulating substances on their development.

2 class hours; 1 2-hour laboratory period. Credit, 3.

MR. SOUTHWICK, MR. JOHNSON.

26. (II) Plant Materials

Detailed study of deciduous and evergreen trees, with special reference to their mature form and character, means of identification, natural associations, and uses of the various types of trees in landscape work.

1 class hour; 2 2-hour laboratory periods. Credit, 3.

MR. BLUNDELL.

51. (I) Plant Materials

Detailed study of shrubs and woody vines, and their identification, with special emphasis being given to their adaptability to the various landscape uses, methods of handling, and care.

1 class hour; 2 2-hour laboratory periods. Credit, 3.

MR. BLUNDELL.

52. (II) Planting Design

A study of the utilization of plant materials in combination as applied to the many conditions and demands of landscape work.

1 class hour; 2 2-hour laboratory periods. Credit, 3.

MR. BLUNDELL.

Prerequisites, Horticulture 26 and 51.

LATIN

Instructor in Languages.

1. (I) 2. (II) Elementary Latin

An intensive course in Latin grammar and reading. For those who have had no previous Latin. No credits in this course may be applied toward a degree until the close of the second semester, except upon special recommendation from the Provost.

3 class hours. Credit, 3.

MR. GREENFIELD.

5. (I) 6. (II) Intermediate Latin

An introduction to classical Latin literature: dialogues and oratory (Cicero), the epic (Virgil), lyric poetry (Catullus and Horace), historical prose (Livy), satire, comedy, and other genres.

3 class hours. Credit, 3.

MR. GREENFIELD.

Prerequisites, Latin 1 and 2, or 2 years of high school Latin.

209

MATHEMATICS

PROFESSOR ANDERSEN, PROFESSOR WAGNER, ASSOCIATE PROFESSOR BOUTELLE, ASSO-
CIATE PROFESSOR ROSE, ASSISTANT PROFESSOR SCHOONMAKER, ASSISTANT PRO-
FESSOR CULLEN, MR. SKILLINGS, MR. ALLEN, MR. MIENTKA, MR. MOSER,† MR.
BUSSEL, MR. WATSON, MR. NAYLOR, MR. WALLACE, MISS WELNA, MRS. EP-
STEIN, MR. RICE.

01. (I) Elementary College Algebra

A course intended for those students who offer only one unit of algebra for
entrance. It contains a review of elementary algebra and a more thorough study
of such topics as quadratic equations, exponents and radicals, and progressions.
No college credit is given for this course, but the successful completion of this
course and Mathematics 14 which follows in the second semester, may satisfy the
freshman mathematics requirement unless the student's major requires further
mathematics.

3 class hours. Credit, 0.

THE DEPARTMENT.

1. (I) Introductory Mathematics I

Basic set-theoretic and axiomatic concepts, number systems and equations.
A study of elementary functions, algebraically and by the methods of analytic
geometry.

3 class hours. Credit, 3.

THE DEPARTMENT.

2. (II) Introductory Mathematics II

A terminal course intended for students whose curriculum calls for just
one year of mathematics. A continuation of Mathematics 1, including topics
from the calculus, statistics, and mathematics of finance.

3 class hours. Credit, 3.

THE DEPARTMENT.

Prerequisites, Mathematics 1.

4. (II) Introductory Mathematics IV

A continuation of Mathematics 1 for those students intending to take further courses in mathematics. Analytic geometry and trigonometry.

3 class hours. Credit, 3.

THE DEPARTMENT.

Prerequisite, Mathematics 1.

5. (I) Introductory Engineering Mathematics

Trigonometry and algebra: a rapid basic review, theory of equations, simple
determinants and the slide rule. Plane analytic geometry: the straight line, conic
sections, selected higher plane curves, polar coordinates and parametric equations.

4 class hours. Credit, 4.

THE DEPARTMENT.

6. (II) Introductory Calculus for Engineering

Differentiation, with applications, techniques of integration.

4 class hours. Credit, 4.

Prerequisite, Mathematics 5. THE DEPARTMENT.

† On leave of absence.

7. (I) Algebra and Trigonometry

For all freshmen, except majors in Engineering, who are required to take a full year of college mathematics. Fractions, quadratic equations, exponents, logarithms, variation, determinants of the second and third orders, and plane trigonometry.

3 class hours. Credit, 3.

THE DEPARTMENT.

8. (II) Algebra

This course is designed for the freshmen who do not plan to proceed to Calculus. Theory of equations, progressions, mensuration, number systems, and the elements of statistics and mathematics of investments.

3 class hours. Credit, 3.

THE DEPARTMENT.

10. (II) Algebra and Analytic Geometry

This course is designed for the freshmen who plan to take Calculus. Theory of equations, binominal theorem, determinants of higher order, and plane analytic geometry.

3 class hours. Credit, 3.

THE DEPARTMENT.

12. (II) Functional Mathematics

For freshmen who are not required to take a full year of college mathematics. Fractions, percentage, linear and quadratic equations with applications, exponents, logarithms, slide rule, proportion, graphs, statistics, progressions, and the elements of mathematics of investments.

3 class hours. Credit, 3.

THE DEPARTMENT.

14. (II) Trigonometry and Analytic Geometry

A study of the essential elements of elementary trigonometry and selected topics in algebra.

3 class hours. Credit, 3.

Prerequisite, Mathematics 01. THE DEPARTMENT.

29. (I) Differential Calculus

The basic ideas and methods of the differential calculus.

3 class hours. Credit, 3

Prerequisite, Mathematics 10. THE DEPARTMENT.

30. (II) Integral Calculus

A continuation of Mathematics 29 into the field of the integral calculus, with special emphasis on application to problems.

3 class hours. Credit, 3.

Prerequisite, Mathematics 29. THE DEPARTMENT.

31. (I) Applied Calculus for Engineers

Area, volume, length of curve, centroid, moment of inertia, liquid pressure, work, partial differentiation.

4 class hours. Credit, 4.

Prerequisite, Mathematics 6. THE DEPARTMENT.

211

32. (II) Applied Calculus for Engineers

Multiple integrals, infinite series, expansion of functions, hyperbolic functions, differential equations.

4 class hours.   Credit, 4.

THE DEPARTMENT.

Prerequisite, Mathematics 31.

51. (I) Modern Synthetic Geometry

An extension of the geometry of the triangle and the circle. The course is intended especially for those planning to be high school teachers.

3 class hours.   Credit, 3.

MR. ROSE.

Prerequisite, Mathematics 30.

53. (I) 54. (II) Higher Algebra

Permutations, combinations, probability; mathematical induction, matrices, determinants, linear equations and dependence; quadratic forms and elimination theory; the complex number system; polynomial equations; elementary theory of groups, rings and fields.

3 class hours.   Credit, 3.

THE DEPARTMENT.

Prerequisites, Mathematics 10.

55. (I) Mathematics of Finance

The mathematical principles of simple and compound interest, annuities, depreciation, valuation of bonds, insurance. The development and applications of aids to computation in problems arising from financial transactions.

3 class hours.   Credit, 3.

MR. BOUTELLE.

Prerequisite, Mathematics 7.

56. (II) Finite Differences and Probability (1956-57)

Given in alternate years.

3 class hours.   Credit, 3.

MR. WAGNER.

Prerequisites, Mathematics 30.

60. (II) Spherical Trigonometry and Solid
Analytic Geometry (1955-56)

The trigonometry of the sphere with application to terrestrial and celestial problems. This is followed by a study of higher plane curves and the analytic representation of points, lines, and surfaces in space. Given in alternate years.

3 class hours.   Credit, 3.

MR. BOUTELLE.

Prerequisite, Mathematics 30.

63. (I) Statistics

The fundamental mathematical principles of statistical analysis. The derivation of the basic formulas used, and the study and discussion of such topics as averages, dispersion, skewness, curve fitting, least squares, linear and curvilinear correlation, probability and its application to statistics.

3 class hours.   Credit, 3.

MR. WAGNER.

Prerequisite, Mathematics 30, previously or concurrently.

64. (II) Statistics

A continuation of Mathematics 63, including a study of the joint distribution of two or more random variables; the chi-squared, t-, and F-distributions and their applications; and techniques which do not involve an assumption about the form of the basic distribution.

3 class hours. Credit, 3.

Prerequisites, Mathematics 63, 91.

Mr. ——————.

66. (II) Introduction to Higher Geometry (1955-56)

A study of various methods employed in the modern treatment of the geometry of points, lines, and conics. Such topics as homogenous point and line coordinates, infinite elements; harmonic division; groups of transformations and their invariants; and the elements of projective and other geometrics, will be considered. Given in alternate years.

3 class hours. Credit, 3.

Prerequisite, Mathematics 10.

Mr. Andersen.

71. (I) Vector Analysis (1957-58)

The algebra and calculus of vectors. Applications to physics and other fields will be considered. Given in alternate years.

3 class hours. Credit, 3.

Prerequisites: Mathematics 30; Physics 26.

Mr. Andersen.

72. (II) History of Mathematics (1956-57)

A study of mathematics as it has developed historically. Topics considered include classical problems and concepts of mathematics and the lives and times of the great mathematicians. This course is recommended especially for prospective high school teachers. Given in alternate years.

3 class hours. Credit, 3.

Prerequisite, Mathematics 30.

Mr. Rose.

74. (II) Theory of Numbers (1955-56)

Euclid's Algorism, Theory of Prime Numbers, Aliquot parts, congruences, further topics in number theory. Given in alternate years.

3 class hours. Credit, 3.

Prerequisite, Mathematics 30.

The Department.

81. (I) Differential Geometry (1957-58)

Theory of the geometry of curves and surfaces in three dimensions. Given in alternate years.

3 class hours. Credit, 3.

Prerequisite, Mathematics 30.

The Department.

83. (I) Computational Methods (1956-57)

Errors and approximations in computation, methods of approximating roots of equations, approximation of functions, empirical curve, fitting, approximate integration, and numerical integration of ordinary differential equations. Given in alternate years.

3 class hours. Credit, 3.

Prerequisite, Mathematics 30.

The Department.

MILITARY SCIENCE AND TACTICS

91. (I) (Intermediate) Calculus
Series, expansion of functions, partial differentation, envelopes, and multiple integrals.

3 ·class hours.

Credit, 3.
THE DEPARTMENT.

Prerequisite, Mathematics 30.

92. (II) Differential Equations
3 class hours.

Credit, 3.
THE DEPARTMENT.

Prerequisite, Mathematics 30.

93. (I) Advanced Calculus
The real number system, sequences, elementary theory of functions of one variable and of several variables, Riemannian integration, line integrals, Green's theorem.

3 class hours.

Credit, 3.
THE DEPARTMENT.

Prerequisite, Mathematics 91.

94. (II) Advanced Calculus
Double and triple integrals, improper integrals, gamma functions, Beta functions, elliptic functions, calculus of variations, Fourier Lines, Laplace Transforms.

3 class hours.

Credit, 3.
THE DEPARTMENT.

Prerequisite, Mathematics 93.

95. (I) 96. (II) Readings
A reading course in advanced theoretical topics, intended to furnish a student further preparation for graduate work in mathematics. Topics may be chosen from the fields of algebra, analysis, geometry or applied mathematics. Admission by permission of the head of the department.

3. class hours.

Credit, 3.
THE DEPARTMENT.

MILITARY SCIENCE AND TACTICS

COLONEL TARR, PMST, LIEUTENANT COLONEL GAUTHIER, ASSISTANT PMST, LIEU-TENANT COLONEL EASTLAKE, ASSISTANT PMST, MAJOR TRAGLE, ASSIST-ANT PMST, MAJOR WILSON, ASSISTANT PMST, CAPTAIN HILL, ASSIST-ANT PMST.

1. (I) 2. (II)
Theoretical and practical instruction in leadership, drill and exercise of command; first aid and hygiene; small arms weapons, maps and aerial photographs; military organization; tactics of the rifle squad; combat formations; and military problems and policy of the United States, National Defense Act and ROTC.

3 scheduled hours.

First semester, Credit, 3.
Second semester, Credit, 2.
ARMY INSTRUCTORS.

25. (I)   26. (II)

Theoretical and practical instruction in leadership, drill and exercise of command; the tactics and techniques of armor to include basic communications, basic automotive maintenance, history and missions of armor, familiarization with tank fighting compartment; scouting and patrolling; and crew-served weapons. Emphasis is placed on the functions, duties, and responsibilities of junior noncommissioned officers in the capacity of squad leaders, assistant squad leaders, and guidon bearers.

3 scheduled hours.   Credit, 2.
                                                   ARMY INSTRUCTORS.

51. (I)   52. (II)

Theoretical and practical instruction in leadership, drill and exercise of command; the tactics and techniques of armor to include communications; tank gunnery; automotive maintenance; organization of armored units; platoon tactics; tank driving; troop leading; and map and aerial photographs. Emphasis is placed on the functions, duties, and responsibilities of senior non-commissioned officers.

5 scheduled hours.   Credit, 3.
                                                   ARMY INSTRUCTORS.

75. (I)   76. (II)

Theoretical and practical instruction in leadership, drill and exercise of command; military administration; military law and boards; military teaching methods; psychological warfare; geographical foundations of national power; the tactics and techniques of armor to include combat intelligence, communications, tank gunnery; automotive maintenance; supply and evacuation; tactics; and tank driving. Emphasis is placed on the functions, duties ,and responsibilities of junior commissioned officers.

5 scheduled hours.   Credit, 3.
                                                   ARMY INSTRUCTORS.

AIR SCIENCE

COLONEL SMITH, PAS, LIEUTENANT COLONEL EWBANK, ASSISTANT PAS, MAJOR WELLS, ASSISTANT PAS, CAPTAIN HAMLIN, ASSISTANT PAS, CAPTAIN McCOLLOR, ASSISTANT PAS, CAPTAIN BENTON, ASSISTANT PAS, LIEUTENANT BRIDGES, ASSISTANT PAS.

1. (I)   2. (II)

Theoretical and practical instruction in leadership, drill, and exercise of command, history and development of aviation, fundamentals of global geography, international tensions and security organizations, and instruments of national military security.

3 scheduled hours.   First semester, Credit, 3.
                                          Second semester, Credit, 2.
                                               AIR FORCE INSTRUCTORS.

25. (I)   26. (II)

Theoretical and practical instruction in leadership, drill and exercise of command, careers in the United States Air Force, and elements of aerial warfare, consisting of a study of targets, weapons, aircraft, the air, ocean, bases, and forces.

3 scheduled hours.   Credit, 2.
                                               AIR FORCE INSTRUCTORS.

MUSIC

51. (I) 52. (II)

· Theoretical and practical instruction in leadership, drill and exercise of command, the air force commander and his staff, problem solving techniques, the communication process and air force correspondence, military law, courts and boards, air force base functions, and applied air science, consisting of a study of aircraft engineering, navigation, and weather.

5 scheduled hours. Credit, 3.

AIR FORCE INSTRUCTORS.

75. (I) 76. (II)

Theoretical and practical instruction in leadership, drill and exercise of command, military aspects of world political geography, military aviation, and the evolution of warfare. Emphasis will be placed on preparation for commissioned service, and career guidance.

5 scheduled hours. Credit, 3.

AIR FORCE INSTRUCTORS.

MUSIC

PROFESSOR ALVIANI, MR. CONTINO.

Applied Music

Private lessons in voice, piano, and other instruments at an approximate cost of $30.00 per semester.

15 1-hour lessons. No credit.

25. (I) 26. (II) Fundamentals of Music

A study of the structure of music to meet the practical needs of the listener, performer, or creator. Sight singing, ear training, and keyboard practice are used to give context to the acquired music theory. All music majors are required to study piano while following this course.

1 class hour; 2 2-hour laboratory periods. Credit, 3.
1:00-3:50 Tu.; 1:00-2:50 Th. THE DEPARTMENT.

27. (I) 28. (II) Vocal or Instrumental Music

This course is designed to improve the playing of instruments and/or the use of the singing voice, and to create further appreciation of music by actual performance. Students electing this course should take both Courses 27 and 28. Admission by permission of the instructor.

1 class hour. Credit, 1.
Hour by arrangement. THE DEPARTMENT.

29. (I) 30. (II) Advanced Instrumental or Vocal Ensemble

A continuation of Music 27 and 28 for the training of performers in combination for voices or instruments. Solo performance and program planning are discussed and practiced. Students taking Course 29 should also take Course 30.

1 class hour. Credit, I.
Hour by arrangement. THE DEPARTMENT.

51. (I) and (II) Discovering Music

This elementary course is non-technical and is designed primarily for students desiring a general background and knowledge of this art. With learn-

216

ing to listen as its motive, the course deals with the elements of music, forms in music, music compositions and composers. Excerpts from works most frequently heard and performed will be used as illustrations.

3 class hours.   **Credit, 3.**

THE DEPARTMENT.

52. (II) Discovering Music

A continuation of Music 51. Students may register for this course without Music 51 if permission is granted by the instructor.

3 class hours.   Credit, 3.

THE DEPARTMENT.

55. (I) Organization and Direction of Choral Groups

The aim of this course is to demonstrate the methods of developing school and community choral groups. Techniques and factors of good vocal performance are studied and practiced. The student may conduct choral groups during the semester. Previous musical experience is desirable. Admission by permission of the instructor.

2 class hours.   Credit, 2.

Hour by arrangement.   THE DEPARTMENT.

56. (II) Organization and Direction of Instrumental Groups

Different types of instrumental music, the problems of balancing instrumentation, the functioning of instruments are introduced by the members of the class. Previous musical experience is desirable. Admission by permission of the instructor.

2 class hours.   Credit, 2.

Hours by arrangement.   THE DEPARTMENT.

61. (I) Masterpieces of Music

Selected masterpieces from musical literature are intensively analyzed, and a relationship is drawn between the compositions and the social-cultural periods in the history of music.

3 class hours.   Credit, 3.

9:00-9:50 Tu. Th. S.   THE DEPARTMENT.

Prerequisite, Music 51 or 52 recommended but not required.

62. (I) and (II) Music in the Elementary Grades

Designed for the classroom teacher having little or no formal training in music, this course deals with the principles of musical development with particular emphasis on classroom presentation. Using the class as a laboratory, rote and reading songs are examined and processes of presentation evaluated.

3 class hours.   Credit, 3.

9:00-9:50 M. W. F.   THE DEPARTMENT.

75. (I) 76. (II) Music Theory

The development of skill in the use of music fundamentals. Elementary and advanced harmony are studied and practiced. Techniques of elementary counterpoint are presented to show their relationship to vocal and instrumental music.

2 class hours; 1 2-hour laboratory period.   Credit, 3.

10:00-10:50 Tu. Th.; 1:00-2:50 W.   THE DEPARTMENT.

77. (I) 78. (II) Form and Analysis

An approach to the study of music through observation of its forms, analysis of its rhythms, melodies, and harmonies as used in the vocal and instrumental compositions of various periods in the historical development of music. The theory of conducting is discussed, studied, evaluated, and its techniques practiced.

1 class hour; 2 2-hour laboratory periods. Credit, 3.
10:00-10:50 F.; 10:00-11:50 M. W. THE DEPARTMENT.

79. (I) Score Reading and Analysis

Through listening and reading assignments the characteristics of voices and instruments are studied and the results are applied to practical arranging for vocal and instrumental groups of various types, sizes, and combinations.

3 class hours. Credit, 3.
THE DEPARTMENT.

80. (II) Score Reading and Composition

A continuation of Music 79. In this course the student is expected to study the methods and materials of original composition. Procedures for processing, printing, publishing, and marketing are examined. Laws and regulations governing performance, publication, personnel, and other related activities are discussed.

3 class hours. Credit, 3.
THE DEPARTMENT.

81. (I) Music and History

A comprehensive study of the periods in music history—Renaissance, Baroque, Classic, Romantic, and Modern—so that the student may feel their quality, understand their enthusiasm, recognize their resources and limitations, and identify their habits of thought and style.

3 class hours. Credit, 3.
THE DEPARTMENT.

82. (II) Music and Research Methods

Recommended to students interested in bibliography, references, source materials, rental libraries, etc., who expect to work in the field of music or related fields. In addition to compilation, the student will investigate a special area of study and report the findings in written form.

3 class hours. Credit, 3.
THE DEPARTMENT.

NURSING

PROFESSOR MAHER, ASSOCIATE PROFESSOR GILMORE,
ASSOCIATE PROFESSOR MACDONALD, MISS DIMAGGIO.

26. (II) Orientation to Nursing

An introductory course in nursing developed in three units and designed to orient the beginning student in nursing to the scope and responsibilities of professional nursing.

Unit I considers professional trends and relationships. The student is acquainted with the meaning of professional nursing, trends in nursing education and with her privileges and responsibilities as a member of the nursing and health team.

Unit II aims to familiarize the student with basic teaching principles and methods which will be applied and extended throughout the curriculum in a variety of student teaching relationships. Instruction and practice in group work are included.

Unit III, an introduction to nursing, provides the student with the opportunity to become aware of the health needs of people, to develop interpersonal and technical skills, and to become familiar with the basic principles of nursing care. Experience with patients and allied health workers in selected community agencies is provided.

3 class hours; 2 2-hour laboratory periods. Credit, 4.

THE NURSING DIVISION.

Prerequisites, Psychology 26, 56.

27. (S) Fundamentals of Nursing

This course introduces the student to the nursing care of the patient in the hospital. Emphasis is placed upon the fundamentals of nursing care for all patients and the relationship of the nurse to agencies and personnel providing individual, family and community health services.

12 class hours; 10 clinical practice hours—for 9 weeks. Credit, 9.
Second year. MISS GILMORE AND ASSISTANTS.

28. (S) Social and Historical Foundations of Nursing

A survey course of nursing history from the pre-Christian era to the present. The influence of society upon nursing in the various historical periods is considered in relation to the development of nursing as a profession.

4 class hours—for 9 weeks. Credit, 2.
Second year. MISS MAHER.

51. (I) Medical and Surgical Nursing I

A course planned to help the student develop the ability to give nursing care to patients with representative health problems in the medical and surgical nursing units. Emphasis is placed on the preventive, therapeutic and rehabilitative aspects of medical and nursing care. Pharmacology, diet, therapy, pathology and special therapies are combined within this course in relation to the health problems considered. Special services and personnel within the hospital and community are utilized to enrich the student's concept of comprehensive care for patients. Experience in the medical and surgical units, outpatient service, operating room and diet kitchen is provided.

12 class hours; 12 clinical practice hours—for 24 weeks. Third year. Credit, 16.

MISS GILMORE AND ASSISTANTS; MEDICAL AND ALLIED PROFESSIONAL STAFFS OF COOPERATIVE HOSPITALS AND AGENCIES.

52A. (II) Nursing of Children I

This course provides the student with an opportunity to observe and participate in the care of well children in a nursery school. The student is assisted to understand more fully the child's behavior, to gain further insight into her own behavior and to consider family and community responsibility for preventing emotional disturbance.

15 class hours—for 2 weeks. Third year. Credit, 2.

MISS DiMAGGIO AND PROFESSIONAL STAFFS OF COOPERATIVE AGENCIES.

Prerequisite, Home Economics 70.

NURSING

52B. (I) Nursing of Children II

This course introduces the student to the health needs of children by means of a developmental approach. Emphasis is placed on the importance of child-parent and child-parent-nurse relationship in the care of the child in health and illness.

By studying the needs of children at various stages of development and identifying the needs of the individual child, the student is helped to appreciate her role in helping the child and family to meet the emotional, physical, social and spiritual needs of the hospitalized child.

In the pediatric in-patient and out-patient departments the student is provided with an opportunity to assist in the medical and nursing care given to children. Experience with other community agencies aids in increasing the student's understanding of the community resources which share the responsibility of providing health services for children.

12 class hours; 12 clinical practice hours—for 12 weeks.   Credit, 5.
Fourth year.   MISS DIMAGGIO AND PROFESSIONAL STAFFS
OF COOPERATING HOSPITALS AND AGENCIES.

54. (II) Psychiatric Nursing

Through the presentation and discussion of the dynamics of human behavior, the content of the course is extended to include the fundamentals of psychopathology related to the basic origin of conflict in patients. The specialized abilities and skills of the nurse in providing care to the mentally ill patients are presented in order that the understanding of the patient's behavior will lead to a constructive nurse-patient relationship thereby enabling the students to participate more fully in the therapeutic plan. The relationship of selected patient's behavior pathology to early manifestations of behavior deviation, early diagnosis, treatment, rehabilitation and prevention will be discussed in case conferences. Community responsibility, resources and planning in regard to this major health problem will be explored. Experience in the care of selected patients in a psychiatric hospital is provided.

12 class hours; clinical practice hours—for 12 weeks. Third year.   Credit, 6.
INSTRUCTORS IN PSYCHIATRIC NURSING; MEDICAL AND
ALLIED PROFESSIONAL STAFFS OF THE COOEPRATING
HOSPITALS AND AGENCIES.

56. (II) Tuberculosis Nursing

The principles and practice of nursing the patient with tuberculosis will be utilized as a basis for extending the student's knowledge of tuberculosis; its significance as a major health problem, the special needs of patients with long-term illnesses and the epidemological aspects of communicable diseases. Clinical experience in the care of selected patients with tuberculosis will be combined with clinics, conferences, and group discussion.

12 class hours; 12 clinical practice hours—for 6 weeks. Fourth year.   Credit, 3.
INSTRUCTOR IN TUBERCULOSIS NURSING;
MEDICAL AND ALLIED PROFESSIONAL
STAFFS OF THE COOPERATING HOSPITALS
AND AGENCIES.

57. (II) Maternity Nursing

The course content is developed around the meaning of pregnancy to the patient and the family with special emphasis on the understanding of the mother's physiological and psychological needs before, during, and after the birth of the infant. The specialized abilities of the nurse are taught in relation to an understanding of the phenomena of pregnancy, the birth process, immediate care of the mother and infant, newborn care, the importance for early constructive mother-child relationship and patient teaching. Clinical experience in the clinic, labor and birth room, newborn and premature nurseries, postpartal units and clinics is provided.

12 class hours; 12 clinical practice hours for 12 weeks. Third year. Credit, 5.

INSTRUCTOR IN MATERNITY NURSING; MEDICAL AND ALLIED PROFESSIONAL STAFFS OF THE COOPERATING HOSPITALS AND AGENCIES.

58. (II) Public Health Nursing

An introductory course in public health nursing developed in two units and designed to acquaint the student with the scope of public health nursing and the organizational structure of the various health services within which the public health nurse may function.

Unit 1 reviews national, state and community health programs in relation to the health needs of individuals and families.

Unit II focuses upon the scope and underlying principles of public health nursing practice. The role of the public health nurse in a family centered health service is emphasized. Field instruction is provided in official and non-official public health services.

6 class hours—for 8 weeks. Fourth year.

MISS MAHER; MEDICAL AND PROFESSIONAL STAFFS OF THE COOPERATING PUBLIC HEALTH NURSING SERVICES.

60. (II) Medical and Surgical Nursing II

This course, a continuation of Medical and Surgical Nursing I, provides the student with an opportunity to give nursing care to patients with special health problems requiring greater knowledge and skill. The student takes a more active part in planning nursing care and in individual and group teaching of patients. Clinical practice is provided in special medical and surgical services.

8 class hours; clinical practice 16 hours for 15 weeks. Fourth year. Credit, 8.

MISS GILMORE AND ASSISTANTS; MEDICAL AND ALLIED PROFESSIONAL STAFFS OF THE COOPERATING HOSPITALS AND AGENCIES.

65. (I) Senior Internship

A sixteen week internship offering advanced instruction and practice in an elected clinical specialty through selected cooperating health agencies.

16 weeks. Fifth year. Credit, 4.

THE NURSING DIVISION AND COOPERATING AGENCIES.

66. (II) Senior Nursing Seminar

This course aims to give the student increased understanding of the opportunities, privileges and responsibilities facing the professional nurse in modern society and of the functions of organized professional nursing groups.

Nursing problems are studied through an individual and group approach and an opportunity is afforded the student to apply the principles of methodology and educational research in the study of a specific problem.

4 class hours. Fifth year. Credit, 4.

THE NURSING DIVISION AND CONSULTANTS.

OLERICULTURE

70. (S) Management of the Hospital Nursing Unit

The principles of scientific management are applied to management of patient care in the hospital nursing unit. Directed experience as a team leader in the hospital nursing unit is provided over an eight-week period.

4 class hours, 20 clinical practice hours—for 8 weeks. Fourth year.   Credit, 2.

Miss Gilmore and Assistants; Medical
and Allied Professional Staffs of the
Cooperating Hospitals and Agencies.

71. Newer Concepts in Maternal and Child Care

For graduate nurses. A concept of family centered care is developed through discussion of newer methods of maternal and new born care; consideration of the relationship of basic philosophies and principles of child care to recent developments in the field of pediatric nursing; and a beginning study of the meaning of illness to the child, his parents and the nurse. Admission by permission of the instructor.

Credit, 2.
The Department.

72. Personnel Programs in Schools of Nursing

For graduate nurses. An appraisal of the principles, practices and problems related to the organization and implementation of effective student personnel services within a school of nursing. Techniques used in the selection and counseling of students are demonstrated. Practice is given in the evaluation of selected student personnel programs.

Admission by permission of the instructor.

Credit, 2
The Department.

OLERICULTURE

Professor Snyder, Assistant Professor Tuttle, Mr. ——————.

25. (I) Basic Olericulture

A detailed study of the relationship of water, temperature, humidity, light and other basic factors of the environment to the culture of vegetables and other closely related horticultural crops.

2 class hours; 1 2-hour laboratory period.   Credit, 3.
10:00-10:50 Tu. Th.; 1:00-2:50 F.   Mr. ——————.

51. (I) Nutrition of Vegetable Crops

A critical study of the nutrient requirements of vegetable plants involving soils and their preparation, manures, fertilizers, lime, green manures and crop residues as they relate to intensive cultural practices.

Mr. Tuttle.

52. (II) Commercial Vegetable Production

This course deals with the commercial production of the more important vegetable crops grown out-of-doors and under glass, including the principles basic to vegetable farm organization and management, plant growing, varieties, soil management, cultivation, weed control, irrigation, and other special cultural practices. Trips to nearby farms will be required.

2 class hours; 1 2-hour laboratory period.   Credit, 3.
8:00-8:50 M. F.; 3:00-4:50 F.   Mr. ——————.

73. (I) Produce Marketing Practices

Consideration will be given to the various techniques and methods of preparing produce for market, including harvesting; post harvest handling—washing, waxing, precooling; the use of various gases and growth regulators; packing house facilities and short time storage requirements. Major attention will be given to commercial grades, packs and packages and the various types of produce inspection services.

3 class hours.   Credit, 3.
10:00-10:50 M. W. F.   MR. SNYDER.

74. (II) Merchandising of Perishables

Discussions will include the various techniques, practices and methods used in merchandising horticultural commodities through both wholesale and retail channels. Major emphasis is placed on pre-packaging, promotion and advertising, brands and their use, federal and state regulations, wholesale outlets and operators, methods of sale, retail outlets and selling, roadside and farm markets and transportation.

3 class hours.   Credit, 3.
10:00-10:50 M. W. F.   MR. SNYDER.

75. (I) Systematic Olericulture (1955-1956)

A detailed study of vegetable crops as to their history, nomenclature, classification, structure and identification. Given in alternate years.

2 class hours; 4 laboratory hours.   Credit, 4.
Hours by arrangement.   MR. SNYDER.

80. (II) Special Problems

An advanced study of specific problems relative to the production and marketing of vegetable crops, including a review of basic research reports and current literature.

1 class hour; 4 laboratory hours.   Credit, 3.
Hours by arrangement.   THE DEPARTMENT.

PHILOSOPHY

PROFESSOR SHUTE, ASSISTANT PROFESSOR ROGERS, MR. CARMICHAEL.

25. (I) and (II) Introduction to Philosophy

A study of the distinctive role of philosophy in its relations to the insights of science, religion, and art. The student is introduced to some of the general questions, ideas, theories, and methods of inquiry which have given direction to Western thought, and encouraged to clarify and examine his own ideas regarding knowledge, reality, and value.

3 class hours.   Credit, 3.
                                 THE DEPARTMENT.

63. (I) and (II) Logic

A study of the principles, problems and methods of critical thinking; emphasis upon principles and methods of formal logic; critical study of inductive reasoning and scientific method with applications to current problems.

3 class hours.   Credit, 3.
                MR. ROGERS, MR. CARMICHAEL.

PHILOSOPHY

64. (I) and (II) Ethics

An examination of the many causes and contexts of personal decision and policy formation; an analysis of classical and contemporary theories which attempt to provide an intellectual framework for the guidance and justification of ways of life; and class exploration of concrete cases which focus attention on the realms of value and the place of theory in reflective choice.

3 class hours.   Credit, 3.

THE DEPARTMENT.

65. (I) History of Philosophy—Ancient and Medieval

A survey of development of western thought with emphasis on the cultural factors which generated and interacted with the successive philosophical interpretations of man's experience.

3 class hours.   Credit, 3.

MR. ROGERS.

66. (II) History of Philosophy—Modern

Attention is centered on the impact of modern science on the development of man's comprehensive understanding of the world, of the powers of limitations of knowledge, and of the basis of his valuations.

3 class hours.   Credit, 3.

MR. ROGERS.

72. (II) Philosophy of Science

A study of the backgrounds, presupositions, methods and general theories of modern physical, biological and social sciences. Readings selected from the works of leading scientists and philosophers will be used as the basis of class discussions which will attempt to explore the great achievements of our time and to assess their importance in the student's construction of a mature philosophic orientation.

3 class hours.   Credit, 3.

MR. ROGERS.

74. (II) Oriental Philosophies

A study of the present conflict in ideologies within and between the leading cultures of Asia, understood in the light of their philosophical history. The bearing of philosophical differences between East and West on the problem of mutual understanding.

3 class hours.   Credit, 3.

MR. SHUTE.

81. (I) Philosophy of Religion

A survey of the contrasting types of religious philosophy in the contemporary western world and Asia, with a critical and constructive study of basic issues, such as the meaning of knowledge in the field of religion, the nature of faith, and the religious interpretation of reality.

3 class hours.   Credit, 3.

MR. SHUTE.

82. (II) Aesthetics

A study of the leading modern theories of the nature of art, the analysis of aesthetic experience, the distinctive function of art in culture and personality, and the principles of criticism.

3 class hours.   Credit, 3.

MR. SHUTE.

83. (I) Readings in Ancient Philosophy

Selections are read from Locke, Hume, Kant, and Whitehead, to display
A study is made of the leading philosophical issues discussed by these writers,
with emphasis on ideas which became basic in the development of western
thought.

3 class hours.   Credit, 3.

MR. SHUTE.

84. (II) Readings in Modern Philosophy

Selections are read from Locke, Hume, Kant, and Whitehead, to display
the leading ways in which modern thinkers have looked upon the nature of
the universe and the possibilities and limitations of knowledge.

3 class hours.   Credit, 3.

MR. SHUTE.

85. (I) Metaphysics

The field of metaphysics defined in distinction from the field of science,
contrasting theories of reality offered by contemporary naturalism and idealism,
especially in the light of recent developments in biological and physical science;
analysis of basic ideas which will enable the student to continue a fruitful
development of his own philosophy.

3 class hours.   Credit, 3.

MR. SHUTE.

86. (II) Theory of Knowledge

. Types of knowledge and correlated methods of knowing; questions of certainty, probability, and limits of knowledge; ways of expression, such as mathematical formulae, language, and art, and their involvement in the knowing
process; the nature of the relation between the knowing subject and the known
object.

3 class hours.   Credit, 3.

MR. CARMICHAEL.

PHYSICAL EDUCATION FOR MEN

PROFESSOR McGUIRK, PROFESSOR KAUFFMAN, ASSOCIATE PROFESSOR BRIGGS, ASSISTANT
PROFESSOR RICCI, ASSISTANT PROFESSOR SALWAK, MR. BOSCO, MR. GARBER,
MR. DAMON, MR. DYER.

ACTIVITY COURSES

3. (I) 4. (II) Physical Activity Course

The object of the course is to help every student, through regularity and
continuity of physical activity, to realize not only his physical and mental
capacities, but learn to use them as an intelligent, cooperative, and efficient
citizen. The students are given motor ability tests, expected to learn to swim
and to meet minimum standards in the basic skills through participation in
team sports and exercise.

3 class hours.   Credit, 1.

THE DEPARTMENT.

33. (I) 34. (II) Physical Education

A continuation of Physical Education 3 and 4.

3 class hours.   Credit, 1.

THE DEPARTMENT.

SKILLS AND TECHNIQUES IN PHYSICAL EDUCATION

The following courses are concerned with the methods and techniques of applied physical education. Classroom presentation, field, court, and floor demonstrations are emphasized. These courses are primarily for students enrolled for a Bachelor of Science degree with a major in physical education. Non-major admission only by permission of the instructor.

5. (I) Skills and Techniques

Development of fundamental skills and methods of teaching and organizing groups for participation in track and field, basketball.

60 clock hours per semester. Credit, 1.

Mr. Curran.

6. (II) Skills and Techniques

Fundamental skills in life-saving and water-safety methods. Successful completion resulting in qualifications as American Red Cross Water Safety Instructor.

60 clock hours per semester. Credit, 1.

Mr. Rogers.

35. (I) Skills and Techniques

Development of fundamental skills, methods of teaching and organizing groups for participation in soccer, speedball, volleyball.

60 clock hours per semester. Credit, 1.

Mr. Briggs, Mr. Ricci.

36. (II) Skills and Techniques

Fundamental skills and instruction in techniques of teaching elementary apparatus, tumbling exercises, pyramids, construction of elementary gymnastic routines.

60 clock hours per semester. Credit, 1.

Mr. Bosco.

63. (I) Skills and Techniques

Fundamental skills and techniques of teaching golf and badminton.

60 clock hours per semester. Credit, 1.

Mr. O'Rourke, Mr. Ricci.

64. (II) Skills and Techniques

Fundamentals of movement and rhythmic response basic to elementary dance techniques. Instruction in skills in archery and participation in various types of competitive events.

60 clock hours per semester. Credit, 1.

Mr. Briggs, Mr. Bosco.

83. (I) Skills and Techniques

Fundamental skills, instruction in techniques of teaching tennis and wrestling.

60 clock hours per semester. Credit, 1.

Mr. Kosakowski, Mr. ————.

84. (II) Skills and Techniques

Instruction and participation in indoor and outdoor games of high and low organization. Emphasis on student teaching within class.

60 clock hours per semester. Credit, 1.

Mr. Davis, Mr. Garber.

MAJOR COURSES

21. (I) Introduction to Physical Education

Origins of physical education, fundamental concepts, current status in education, qualifications and professional opportunities in the field.

3 class hours. Credit, 3.

MR. KAUFMANN.

22. (II) First Aid and Safety

Materials applicable to the immediate care of the injured, causes of accidents and procedures designed to develop habits and attitudes leading to safe behaviour through desirable safety practices. Certified by American Red Cross for First Aid Instructor training.

3 class hours. Credit, 3.

MR. BRIGGS.

23. (I) Principles and Practices in Health Education

Principles of maintaining and improving individual health, pupil needs, fundamentals related to planning instruction on the elementary and secondary school level, resources in health education, evaluation of materials.

3 class hours. Credit, 3.

MR. SALWAK.

41. (I) Human Anatomy

A study of the gross structure and function of the human body.

3 class hours. Credit, 3.

MR. RICCI.

42. (II) Kinesiology

A course aimed to give the anatomical application basic to a thorough understanding of the mechanical problems in motor skills.

3 class hours. Credit, 3.

Prerequisite, Physical Education 41. MR. KAUFFMAN.

43. (I) Officiating

Technique and practice in officiating football and soccer.

1 class hour; 1 2-hour laboratory period. Credit, 1.

MR. ————.

44. (II) Officiating

Technique and practice in officiating basketball and baseball.

1 class hour; 1 2-hour laboratory period. Credit, 1.

MR. ————.

53. (II) Physical Education in Elementary Schools

Aims and objectives of modern materials and methods of teaching group games, rhythmic activities, dance relays, stunts and lead-up games for the elementary school.

2 class hours; 1 2-hour laboratory period. Credit, 3.

MR. ————.

54. (II) Physical Education in Secondary Schools

A course in modern methods of teaching physical education in secondary schools. Includes objectives, content material, and organization procedures at the secondary level.

3 class hours. Credit, 3.

MR. RICCI.

55. (I) Organization and Administration of Physical Education

Problems and procedures in physical education, organization of programs, class schedules, classification of students, equipment, records, finance, intramurals, construction and maintenance of gymnasia, swimming pools, locker rooms, and outdoor play areas.

3 class hours. Credit, 3.

MR. McGUIRK.

56. (II) Adaptive Physical Education

A program of developmental activities, games, sports, and rhythms suited to the interests, capacities and limitations of students with disabilities who may not safely engage in unrestricted participation in the vigorous activities of the general physical education program.

2 class hours; 1 2-hour laboratory period. Credit, 3.

Prerequisite, Physical Education 42. MR. GARBER.

57. (I) Methods and Materials; Coaching Football, Basketball

The analysis of and instruction in individual skills and team play, types of offense and defense, teaching techniques.

2 class hours; 1 2-hour laboratory period. Credit, 3.

MR. O'ROURKE, MR. CURRAN.

58. (II) Methods and Materials; Coaching Swimming, Baseball

Designed to develop individual skills and techniques of teaching and coaching swimming and diving, stroke analysis, conduct of meets, water sports. Fundamentals of individual skills, position and team play, offensive and defensive strategy in baseball.

2 class hours; 1 2-hour laboratory period. Credit, 3.

MR. ROGERS, MR. LORDEN.

60. (II) Organized Camping Administration

This course includes the history and philosophy of organized camping, minimum standards of health and safety, modern trends, and the camping industry.

3 class hours. Credit, 3.

MR. BRIGGS.

70. (II) Resources in Recreation

Including types of recreational areas, recreational resources, recreational needs of the people, geography of recreation, competitors of recreational land use, economic aspects of federal, state, and local recreational systems.

3 class hours. MR. BRIGGS.

71. (I) 72. (II) Special Problems Course

Presentation and discussion of research work in physical education, health, or athletics.

3 class hours. Credit. 3.

THE DEPARTMENT.

73. (I) Philosophy and Principles of Physical Education

Contemporary interpretations and critical analysis. The compilation and organization of material in a functional relationship for the foundation of policies and program construction.

3 class hours. Credit, 3.

MR. KAUFFMAN.

74. (II) Tests and Measurements

This course considers the status of measurements in physical education, an historical sketch, typical of contributions in anthropometrics, strength tests, ability and achievement tests, cardiac functional tests, neuro-muscular control tests, and sports technique tests; and it includes the tools of measurement, indices, and the theory and practice of test administration.

2 class hours; 1 2-hour laboratory period. Credit, 3.

MR. SALWAK.

75. (I) Physiology of Exercise

Application of basic physiological concepts to the program of physical education, emphasis upon the physiological effects and adjustments accruing from participation in physical activity. Major factors in diet, conditioning, fatigue, and physical fitness are considered.

3 class hours. Credit, 3.

Prerequisite, Physical Education 42.

80. (II) Driver Education Instructor Course

This course includes driver education and driver training at the instructor's level, and is designed to orient the student to live safely through skillful and efficient behavior on streets and highways. Leads to certification as instructor in driver education and driver training.

2 class hours. Credit, 2.

MR. BRIGGS.

81. (I) Methods and Materials; Coaching Soccer, Track

Analyses of and instruction in individual skills and team play, types of offense and defense, teaching techniques in soccer. Analyses of form and coaching technique in fundamental skills in track and field events.

2 class hour; 1 2-hour laboratory period. Credit, 3.

MR. BRIGGS, MR. ————.

85. (I) Athletic Injuries—Prevention and Care

The use of proper personal and field equipment, support methods, conditioning exercises, the medical examination, therapeutic aids, and the clinical use of physiotherapy equipment.

2 class hours. Credit, 2.

Prerequisite, Physical Education 42. MR. RICCI.

PHYSICAL EDUCATION FOR WOMEN

PROFESSOR TOTMAN, MISS HUBBARD,† MISS RIGGS, MISS OGILVIE,
MISS REID, MISS ROBERTSON, MISS WALLACE.

7. (I) 8. (II) Physical Education

Students are required to participate in one term of dancing, in one team sport, and to pass a safety test in swimming. Except for these requirements, all unrestricted students may select any activity which is offered. Fall season: field hockey, volleyball, soccer, archery, tennis, swimming. Winter season: basketball, volleyball, badminton, swimming, life saving (by permission), modern dance, square dance, calisthenics, posture training. Spring season: softball, soccer, archery, swimming, modern dance.

3 class hours. Credit, 2.

† On leave of absence. THE DEPARTMENT.

27. (I) 28. (II) Physical Education

The activities offered in Courses 7 and 8 are continued. In addition, advanced modern dance is offered in the fall season and water safety instruction in the winter season. Unrestricted students may select any activity which is offered.

3 class hours. Credit, 2.

THE DEPARTMENT.

63. (I) 64. (II) Teaching Sports for Secondary Schools

Designed to give the fundamentals of teaching and officiating of team sports for women appropriate for the secondary school level. Course content includes development and knowledge of techniques, knowledge of rules, teaching progressions, class procedures, and instruction in officiating related to the following activities: hockey, soccer, speedball, volleyball, basketball, and softball.

1 class hour; 3 laboratory hours. Credit, 2.

MISS RIGGS.

65. (I) Play Activities and Games for Elementary Schools

A study of the place of physical education in the schools with emphasis on procedures, organization and teaching techniques. There will be more opportunity to learn games and other play activities for children from 5 to 14 years.

1 class hour; 3 laboratory hours. Credit, 2.

MISS TOTMAN.

66. (II) Rhythms and Dancing for the Elementary School

The course will include the development of rhythmic sense through basic motor skills; dramatizations; the construction of simple dance forms; folk dances and singing games. There will be practice in planning the rhythm and dance program in the elementary school from nursery school through sixth grade.

1 class hour; 3 laboratory hours. Credit, 2.

MISS HUBBARD.

68. (II) Water Safety Instructor Course

This course includes a review of the techniques of senior life saving and gives training in the Red Cross Water Safety Course. A detailed study is made of the organization and teaching of all levels of swimming and diving in various situations. Especial emphasis is given to safety practices. Successful completion results in certification as American National Red Cross Safety instructors.

2 scheduled periods. Credit, 2.

MISS ―――――.

PHYSICS

PROFESSOR POWERS, PROFESSOR ALDERMAN, ASSOCIATE PROFESSOR ROSS, ASSISTANT PROFESSOR MATHIESON, ASSISTANT PROFESSOR FISHER, MR. CROOKER, MR. MAC-MONEGLE.

25. (I) Mechanics, Sound, and Heat

This course is largely a study of the following and related topics; equilibrium of bodies; forms of energy; motion, fluids; surface tension; molecular phenomena; elasticity; wave-motion; sound; thermometry; expansion; hygrometry; transmission of heat; changes of radiation.

3 class hours; 1 2-hour laboratory period. Credit, 4.

THE DEPARTMENT.

Prerequisite, Mathematics 5, 7, or 14.

26. (II)   Light and Electricity

Includes wave-theory of light; optical instruments; analysis of light; interference; polarization; magnetism; electrostatics; production and properties of electric currents; electrical appliances and machines; oscillatory circuits; vacuum tubes, and related topics.

3 class hours; 1 2-hour laboratory period. Credit, 4.

THE DEPARTMENT.

Prerequisite, Physics 25.

27. (I)   General Physics

The topics covered are mechanics, sound, and heat with special emphasis on the mathematical development of statics, centroids, and Gauss' theorem.

3 class hours; 1 2-hour laboratory period. Credit, 4.

THE DEPARTMENT.

Prerequisites, Mathematics 5, 6, or equivalent; Mathematics 31 previously or concurrently.

28. (II)   General Physics

The topics covered are light and electricity with special emphasis on the mathematical development of Gauss' theorem, dielectrics and A.C. electricity.

3 class hours; 1 2-hour laboratory period. Credit, 4.

THE DEPARTMENT.

Prerequisites, Physics 27.

51. (I) 52. (II)   Magnetism, Electricity, Photo-electricity, Thermionics and Applications

Course 51 deals with direct currents (mesh currents often used); Course 52 with alternating currents (low and high frequency), application of thermionics, and photo-electricity. These courses are planned to give the student a good training in the theory and methods of measurement in the indicated and allied subjects. Modern methods are stressed and instruments of precision are used.

2 class hours; 1 2-hour laboratory period. Credit, 3.
8:00-8:50 Tu. Th.; 10:00-11:50 Tu. or 1:00-2:50 W. or Th. MR. POWERS.
Prerequisites, Physics 26 and Mathematics 29 for Course 51; Physics 51 for Course 52.

54. (II)   Meteorology

The course deals with the application of certain concepts of mechanics and thermodynamics to the consideration of various atmospheric phenomena such as condensation, pressure, radiation, motion, fronts, etc. The treatment is theoretical in nature but the observed phenomena are correlated to the theory with a descriptive approach. The laboratory deals with weather observations, preparation of weather charts, and the techniques of weather forecasting.

2 class hours; 1 2-hour laboratory period. Credit, 3.
2:00-2:50 Tu. Th.; laboratory hours by arrangement. MR. CROOKER.
Prerequisites, Physics 26; Mathematics 30.

PHYSICS

55. (I) 56. (II) Mechanics

Development of the fundamental concepts of dynamics with applications to particles and rigid bodies in translation and rotation. One laboratory period may be substituted for one class hour.

3 class hours.   Credit, 3.
9:00-9:50 Tu. Th.; laboratory by arrangement.   Mr. Ross.
Prerequisites, Physics 26; Mathematics 30.

57. (I) Introduction to Astronomy

The general facts and principles of astronomy, mainly qualitative, starting with basic physical principles. Periods of evening observation will be substituted for lecture hours when feasible. This course may not be taken for major credit in Physics.

3 class hours.   Credit, 3.
8:00-8:50 M. W. F.   Mr. Ross.
Prerequisite, Mathematics 7 or equivalent.

58. (II) Photography

Class work and laboratory practice in the fundamentals of photography. Types of cameras, characteristics of photographic emulsions, exposure and exposure meters, processing of negatives and prints, enlarging, composition, photomicrography. Limited to ten students. This course may not be taken for major credit in Physics.

2 class hours; 1 4-hour laboratory period.   Credit, 3.
3:00-3:50 M. W.; 1:00-5:00 F.   Mr. Powers.
Prerequisites, Physics 25, 26; Chemistry 1, 2; Mathematics 10.

60. (II) Sound and Acoustics

A study of vibrations, vibrating bodies, coupled systems, sound structure, and acoustic properties. The work will include many applications of sound to technical and commercial fields.

2 class hours; 1 2-hour laboratory period.   Credit, 3.
                                                              Mr. Alderman.

Prerequisites, Physics 55 or its equivalent.

61. (I) 62. Heat and Thermodynamics

A study of heat exchanges and energy changes due to heat in systems of matter. The subject material and experimental methods are useful in other branches of science.

2 class hours; 1 2-hour laboratory period.   Credit, 3.
10:00-10:50 Tu., Th.; laboratory by arrangement.
                                                              Mr. Alderman.

Prerequisites, Physics 26; Mathematics 30.

63. (I) 64. (II) Optics

An intermediate course in the theory of light. Work in geometrical and physical optics is done. Precision instruments are used in the laboratory.

2 class hours; 1 2-hour laboratory period.   Credit, 3.
1:00-1:50 Tu., Th.; laboratory hours by arrangement.
                                                              Mr. Alderman.

Prerequisites, Physics 26; Mathematics 29.

232

75. (I) 76. (II) Advanced Experimental Work in Selected Topics

These courses are largely experimental and the subject matter is adapted to the needs of the individual student. The research viewpoint is emphasized. The class hour is used for a course in precision of measurements.

1 class hour; 2 2-hour laboratory periods.   Credit, 3.

Mr. Wang.

Prerequisites, Mathematics 29, 30; two of the following year courses: Physics 51-52, 55-56, 61-62, 53-64.

85. (I) 86. (II) Modern Physics

Typical subjects studied are theories of the atom, radiation, quantum theory; spectra, X-ray analysis, nuclear reactions.

3 class hours.   Credit, 3.

9:00-9:50 M. W. F.   Mr. Wang.

Prerequisites, Physics 52, 64, and 12 other junior-senior physics credits; Mathematics 30.

95. (I) 96. (II) Electronics

2 class hours; 1 2-hour laboratory period.   Credit, 3.

10:00-10:50 M. F.; 10:00-11:50 W.   Mr. Wang.

Prerequisites, Physics 51, 52; Mathematics 29, 30.

POMOLOGY

Professor French, Associate Professor Roberts, Mr. J. F. Anderson

26. (II) Small Fruits

A study of the growing of raspberries, blackberries, strawberries, currants, blueberries, cranberries, and grapes, dealing with such questions as varieties, selecting a site for the plantation, soils, fertilizers, pruning, harvesting, and marketing.

2 class hours; 1 2-hour laboratory period.   Credit, 3.

10:00-10:50 M. F.; 1:00-2:50 W. or F.   Mr. Anderson.

25. (I) Introductory Pomology

This course deals with modern tree fruit production including varieties, orchard sites and soils, planting systems, soil management, fertilizers, bearing habits, pruning, pollination, thinning, pest control and handling the crop. The content of this course should be of value to students majoring in allied fields.

2 class hours; 1 2-hour laboratory period.   Credit, 3.

Mr. Anderson.

56. (II) Orchard Pest Control

This course is especially designed to familiarize the student with: (a) spraying and dusting machinery; (b) methods in the application of materials used in orchards, with the important considerations for spraying each fruit and for combating each orchard pest; (c) preparation for use of the common fungicides and insecticides.

2 class hours; 1 2-hour laboratory period.   Credit, 3.

8:00-8:50 Tu., Th.; 1:00-2:50 Tu.   Mr. Roberts.

POMOLOGY

75. (I) Systematic Pomology (1956-57)

A study of the more important kinds and varieties of fruits grown in the United States, their relationships and nomenclature. Particular emphasis is placed upon the identification, classification and value of varieties including a study of the characters of the plant as well as the fruit. Given in alternate years.

1 class hour; 3 2-hour laboratory periods.   Credit, 4.
8:00-8:50 Tu.; 1:00-2:50 M. W. F.   MR. ANDERSON.

77. (I) Fruit Marketing (1957-58)

This course consists of a critical study of the handling of fruit from tree to consumer, including such phases as the physiology of fruit as related to harvesting procedure, also fruit grades and grading, packing, storing and merchandising. Given in alternate years.

2 class hours; 1 2-hour laboratory period.   Credit, 3.
     MR. ROBERTS.

79. (I) Advanced Pomology (1956-57)

Special attention is given to more important findings of research dealing with the interrelation of stock and scion, temperature influences, water relationships and the mineral nutrition of fruit plants. The geography of world fruit production is also considered. Given in alternate years.

2 class hours; 1 2-hour laboratory period.   Credit, 3.
     THE DEPARTMENT.

Prerequisite, Pomology 25 or equivalent.

81. (I) Advanced Pomology (1957-58)

A critical study of the more important research dealing with pollination, fruit set and thinning, preharvest drop, biennial bearing, and the physiology of fruit during storage. The location and objectives of fruit breeding programs in the United States are also discussed. Given in alternate years.

2 class hours; 1 2-hour laboratory period.   Credit, 3.
     THE DEPARTMENT.

Prerequisite, Pomology 25 or equivalent.

84. (II) Special Problems in Pomology

Each student will investigate an individual problem pertinent to his future objectives.

1 class hour; 4 laboratory hours.   Credit, 3.
     THE DEPARTMENT.

Prerequisites, Pomology 79 and 81.

85. (I) 86. (II) Cranberry Problems

For seniors specializing in cranberry technology. Selected readings and individual work to familiarize students with the literature, research, and problems of the cranberry industry.

Hours by arrangement.   Credit, 2.
     MR. FRENCH.

PLANT BREEDING

52. (II) Plant Breeding Methods

An advanced study of genetic topics peculiar to plants, also the methods and problems of the plant breeder. Laboratory work in genetic analysis and the breeding of plants.

2 class hours; 1 2-hour laboratory period.   Credit, 3.
11:00-11:50 M. F.; 3:00-4:50 W.   MR. FRENCH.
Prerequisite, Zoology 53.

81. (I) 82. (II) Special Problems in Plant Breeding

Qualified seniors may carry on advanced study on special topics or undertake such original investigation as time and available material will permit.
Hours by arrangement.   Credit, 2.

Prerequisite, Plant Breeding 52.   MR. FRENCH.

POULTRY HUSBANDRY

PROFESSOR FOX, PROFESSOR SANCTUARY, ASSOCIATE PROFESSOR VONDELL, ASSOCIATE PROFESSOR SMYTH, ASSOCIATE PROFESSOR BANTA.

25. (I) General Poultry

For students not majoring in poultry husbandry. A general course giving an introduction to the breeds of poultry, the principles and practice of breeding, incubation, and poultry nutrition, brooding and rearing, houses and equipment, management practices, disease control, marketing poultry products, and the business of poultry keeping.

2 class hours; 1 2-hour laboratory period.   Credit, 3.
9:00-9:50 M. F.; 10:00-11:50 or 3:00-4:50 T.   MR. FOX.

52. (II) Incubation and Brooding

This course is based upon the actual operation of incubators and brooders. Each year a research project is planned and data obtained concerning the effects of various incubator adjustments upon malpositions and maldevelopment of embryos and the percentage of hatch. Studies of temperature gradients, chick behavior and development are made in brooding with various types of equipment. Analysis is made of common and unusual field problems.

1 class hour; 2 2-hour laboratory periods.   Credit, 3.
11:00-11:50 W.; 3:00-4:50 M.; other hours by arrangements.

MR. SANCTUARY.

53. (I) Poultry Judging

Physiological and anatomical characters are used in production judging. The American Standard of Perfection is employed in a study of the more popular breeds and varieties, and for exhibition judging. Judging teams competing in the Eastern Intercollegiate Contest are trained in this course.

1 class hour; 2 2-hour laboratory periods.   Credit, 3.
8:00-8:50 Tu.; 1:00-2:50 Th. F.   MR. BANTA.

55. (I) Poultry Housing and Sanitation

In this course are considered the biological factors related to the proper physical environment necessary for growth, health, and reproduction. Various systems of ventilation and methods of insulation are studied and demonstrated by models. Humidity, temperature, and condensation studies are made at the poultry plant with varying adjustments of ventilation devices. A study is made of modern equipment. Sanitation from the standpoint of disease prevention practices is also considered.

1 class hour; 1 2-hour laboratory period.   Credit, 2.
9:00-9:50 Th.; 1:00-2:50 Tu.   MR. SANCTUARY.

56. (II) Poultry Nutrition

A study of the scientific principles of nutrition, classification and identification of feedstuffs, formulation and calculation of rations for specific purposes. A class trip may be arranged.

2 class hours; 1 2-hour laboratory period.   Credit, 3.
9:00-9:50 Tu. Th.; 1:00-2:50 W.   MR. BANTA.

75. (I) Marketing Poultry Products

A study of the preparation and grading methods of eggs and poultry products to meet the requirements of the northeastern markets. The laboratories are designed to cover the fields of modern dressing, processing and packaging of poultry; as well as grading, candling and quality studies of eggs. A one-half day class trip to Springfield markets in December is required. Estimated cost, two dollars.

1 class hour; 1 2-hour laboratory period.   Credit, 2.
10:00-10:50 Tu.; 3:00-4:50 W.   MR. VONDELL.

76. (II) Turkey Production

This course includes the production of ducks and geese but most of the time is given to the turkey industry; its importance, breeds, breeding, incubation, brooding, feeding, finishing, marketing, etc.

1 class hour; 1 2-hour laboratory period.   Credit, 2.
1:00-1:50 M.; 3:00-4:50 W.   MR. SMYTH.

77. (I) Poultry Breeding

The improvement of poultry by selection is developed through a study of the principles of heredity. The inheritance of morphological and physiological characters including plumage color, egg production, meat production, hatchability, egg traits, and disease resistance.

2 class hours; 1 2-hour laboratory period.   Credit, 3.
11:00-11:50 M. W.; 1:00-2:50 W.   MR. ————.

78. (II) Seminar and Farm Management

A combination seminar and lecture course designed to give the student a comprehensive view of all phases of the poultry industry. A field trip covering approximately three days will be arranged. Poultry majors with an average of 80 or more in poultry courses may elect an additional problem credit.

3 class hours; 1 2-hour laboratory period may be elected.   Credits, 3, 4.
9:00-9:50 M. W. F.   MR. FOX.

236

PSYCHOLOGY

PROFESSOR NEET, ASSOCIATE PROFESSOR FELDMAN, ASSOCIATE PROFESSOR GOSS, AS-SISTANT PROFESSOR EPSTEIN, ASSISTANT PROFESSOR FIELD, ASSISTANT PROFESSOR ERLICK, MR. CLIFFORD, MR. RHINE, MR. GREENFIELD, MR. MINTZ, MR. SIM-MONS.

26. (I) and (II)   General Psychology

This is an introductory course dealing with the basic principles and applica-tions of psychology with regard to the understanding and control of behavior. Topics considered include the nature and development of behavior, motivation, learning, problems of adjustment, intelligence, aptitudes, and personality.

3 class hours.   Credit, 3.

THE DEPARTMENT.

28. (II)   General Psychology

A continuation of Psychology 26· Topics considered include perception, thinking, emotions, social behavior, individual differences, and adjustment.

3 class hours.   Credit, 3.
9:00-9:50 or 11:00-11:50 M. W. F.   THE DEPARTMENT.
Prerequisite, Psychology 26.

51. (I)   Experimental Psychology

This course is designed to give an understanding of the problems, methods, and data of experimental psychology. One of the basic functions of the course is to acquaint the student with the scientific method as applied to psychological studies of behavior.

2 class hours; 1 2-hour laboratory period.   Credit, 3.
10:00-10:50 Tu. Th.; 1:00-2:50 Tu. W. or Th.   MR. NEET.
Prerequisite, Psychology 26.

56. (I) and (II)   Educational Psychology

A study of psychological facts and principles fundamental to education, teaching, and personal relationships between teacher and pupil. Topics con-sidered in relation to school situations are: physical and mental growth, intelli-gence, motivation, emotions, learning, transfer of training and mental hygiene of teacher and pupil.

3 class hours.   Credit, 3.
9:00-9:50 Tu. Th. S.   MR. RHINE.
Prerequisite, Psychology 26.

61. (I)   Social Psychology

The social behavior of the individual. Topics considered will include methods of studying social behavior, schools of social psychology, social behavior of animals, foundations of personality development, social (cultural) determin-ants of personality, social attitudes and their measurements, effects of collective situations on individual behavior, custom and conformity.

3 class hours.   Credit, 3.
9:00-9:50 M. W. F.   MR. RHINE.
Prerequisite, Psychology 26.

PSYCHOLOGY

62. (II) Social Psychology (1955-56)

A survey of multi-individual phenomena. Topics to be considered are methods of studying collective action, leadership, morale, propaganda, nature and measurement of public opinion, behavior in crowd situations, social conflict and prejudice. Given in alternate years.

3 class hours.   Credit, 3.
11:00-11:50 M. W. F.   MR. RHINE.
Prerequisite, Psychology 26.

63. (I) Physiological Psychology

A study of the relationships between physiological processes and behavior. Major emphasis will be placed upon the structure and mechanisms of the central nervous system and sense organs, endocrine functions, and drives.

3 class hours.   Credit, 3.
11:00-11:50 M. W. F.   MR. FELDMAN.
Prerequisites, Psychology 26; Zoology 35.

72. (II) Advanced Experimental Psychology

The literature, techniques, and apparatus of experimental psychology are considered, and selected projects are carried out individually by the members of the class.

1 class hour; 2 2-hour laboratory periods.   Credit, 3.
10:00-10:50 Th.; 1:00-2:50 Tu. Th.   MR. NEET.
Prerequisites: Psychology 51; Zoology 35.

75. (I) Statistics in Psychology

The application of statistical procedures to the analysis of psychological data and to problems of measurement in psychology and related fields.

2 class hours; 1 2-hour laboratory period.   Credit, 3.
2:00-2:50 M. F.; 2:00-3:50 W.   MR. GOSS.
Prerequisites: Psychology 26; Statistics 77 or Mathematics 62.

81. (I) 82. (I) and (II) Psychological Tests

Different varieties of psychological tests are studied. The first semester surveys the field of testing and introduces the student to tests of intelligence, aptitude, interest, personality, and adjustment. The second semester is devoted to a more intensive study of individual intelligence tests with the aim of teaching the student to administer, score and interpret those in most common use. Either semester may be elected independently.

2 class hours; 1 2-hour laboratory period.   Credit, 3.
Course 81 (I) and 82 (II) 9:00-9:50 Tu. Th.; 3:00-4:50 W.
Course 82 (I) 3:00-3:50 Tu. Th.; laboratory by arrangement.   MR. EPSTEIN.
Prerequisite, Psychology 26.

83. (I) Abnormal Psychology

A study of the principles relative to the causes, symptoms, and treatment of behavior abnormalities. Special attention is given to the following: dynamics of behavior abnormalties, speech problems, emotional extremes, memory losses and other disorders of association, the neuroses and psychoses, and mental deficiency. Hospital trips and clinics.

3 class hours.   Credit, 3.
10:00-10:50 M. W. F.   MR. NEET.
Prerequisite, Psychology 26.

86. (I) and (II) Industrial Psychology

A study of psychology principles and methods in business and industrial situations. Topics considered include: job analysis, job evaluation, employee selection and training, fatigue, techniques of motivation, measurement of morale and problems of leadership.

3 class hours. Credit, 3.
1:00-1:50 M. W. F. or 9:00-9:50 Tu. Th. S. MR. ERLICK.
Prerequisite, Psychology 26.

88. (II) Psychology of Guidance

A study of the psychological principles, techniques and tests necessary in guidance. Practice is given in organizing and evaluating relevant data in the analysis of illustrative cases.

2 class hours; 1 2-hour laboratory period. Credit, 3.
10:00-10:50 Tu. Th.; 2:00-3:50 M. MR. FIELD.
Prerequisites, Psychology 26 and 81 or consent of the instructor.

90. (II) Contemporary Psychologies

A logical, historical, and systematic analysis of contemporary psychological theories, including structuralism, functionalism, Gestalt and organistic psychologies, psychoanalysis, and behaviorisms from Thorndike and Watson to the contemporary scene.

3 class hours. Credit, 3.
2:00-2:50 M. W. F. MR. GOSS.
Prerequisite, Psychology 26.

92. (II) Clinical Psychology

A study of the techniques and methods involved in the diagnosis and treatment of behavior disorders. Diagnostic clinical testing, counselling, and other psychotherapeutic procedures are given consideration. Hospital trips and clinics.

2 class hours; 1 2-hour laboratory period. Credit, 3.
11:00-11:50 M. W. F. MR. EPSTEIN.
Prerequisite, Psychology 83 or consent of the instructor.

93. (II) Psychology of Adolescence (1956-57)

A consideration of the development, and emotional, social and intellectual adjustment of the individual during the adolescent years. Given in alternate years.

3 class hours. Credit, 3.
9:00-9:50 Tu. Th. S. MR. CLIFFORD.

94. (I) and (II) Child Psychology

This course aims to develop an understanding of the behavior of the child. Psychological aspects of the following topics are considered: original nature, maturation and development of behavior, language, habit formation, emotional behavior, development of intelligence and understanding, social behavior, motivation, personality, and mental hygiene. Nursery school observation and practice.

3 class hours. Credit, 3.
10:00-10:50 M. W. F. MR. CLIFFORD.
Prerequisite, Psychology 26.

95. (I) 96. (II) Problems in Psychology.

For qualified seniors. The student will be allowed to do independent work and study on special problems or in certain fields of psychological interest. By arrangement with the members of the department.

Credit, 1.

THE DEPARTMENT.

RECREATION LEADERSHIP

ASSOCIATE PROFESSOR RANDALL.

51. (I) Principles of Recreation

This course considers recreation as an important social force in community life. Emphasis is given to the study and discussion of functional recreation and park programs: their history and philosophy, their relationship with various agencies and related fields, their resources, current problems, and established principles. A field trip is required.

3 class hours.

Credit, 3.

MR. RANDALL.

52. (II) Group Leadership and Camp Counseling

A study of the organized camp and the counselor's part in it, including characteristics, objectives, organization, program, and operating procedures. Major emphasis is given to group leadership, camper guidance, and the acquisition of camping and program skills. Each student is expected to participate in role-playing, program leadership, committee presentations, and two field trips. One of these trips involves a two-night camping experience and the cooking of five meals out-of-doors. Total cost is less than five dollars.

2 class hours; 1 2-hour laboratory period.

Credit, 3.

MR. RANDALL.

74. (II) The Recreation Program

Major emphasis is placed upon a term project in which each student plans a complete and well-rounded recreation program to meet the needs, interests, and abilities of the community which he studied intensively in Sociology 51. Program planning principles and resources are discussed and applied in selected examples. A field trip is required. Students planning to take this course should consult the instructor before the time of pre-registration.

3 class hours.

Credit, 3.

MR. RANDALL.

Prerequisites: Recreation Leadership 51; Sociology 51.

77. (I) Organization and Administration of Community Recreation

A study of staff organization; personnel recruitment, training and supervision; legal aspects; planning and maintenance of areas, facilities and equipment; finances, business procedure, and public relations. Attention is given to public and private recreation agencies. A field trip is required.

3 class hours.

Credit, 3.

MR. RANDALL.

Prerequisite, Recreation Leadership 74.

79. (I) 80. (II) Recreation Leadership Guidance
and Practice

Field experience, involving administrative procedures, in a program leadership capacity in a public or private agency of the student's choice within commuting distance of the university. Supervision is shared by the department and a member of the professional staff of the agency.

Admission by permission of the department.

1 class hour; field work as required.

Mr. Randall and Cooperating Agency.

· RELIGION

Chaplains Father David J. Power, Rabbi Louis Ruchames, the Reverend Albert L. Seely, and visiting lecturers: the Reverend Thayer A. Greene, the Reverend Ewald Mand, Professor Paul Sanders, the Reverend Philip T. Zabriskie.

15. (I) 16. (II) A History of Jewish Thought and Culture

A survey of Jewish thought and culture from the Bible to contemporary times. Particular emphasis will be placed upon the relevance of such thought to contemporary religious and philosophical problems. Among the thinkers to be discussed will be Jeremiah, Ecclesiastes, Philo, Maimonides, Spinoza, Achad-Ha'am, and Will Herberg.

1 hour.
No Credit.
Mr. Ruchames.

17. (I) 18. (II) Basic Beliefs and Practices of Judaism

A study of the fundamental principles and practices of Judaism. An examination of the philosophy of Judaism is followed by an analysis of its customs and ceremonies.

1 hour.
No Credit.
Mr. Ruchames.

20. (II) Introduction to the Old Testament

An introduction to the history, literature, and religion of the Old Testament. The historical problems of the individual books are studied, their message for their own period examined, and their significance for the Christian faith explored. The aim is to give a clear concept of the beginnings of Hebrew religion and thus to help understand and evaluate the Old Testament as an integral part of the Christian Bible and faith.

1 hour.
No Credit.
Mr. Mand.

31. (I) The Life and Message of Jesus

Based primarily on the Synoptic Gospels, the course will interpret the life and ministry of Jesus in the light of his Old Testament heritage and in terms of his unique significance. Being a Christian will be seen from the Biblical viewpoint as commitment to God as known through Jesus Christ.

1 hour.
No Credit.
Mr. Sanders.

35. (I) The Faith of Our Fathers

This course is an examination of the historical origins and development of the Christian Church and the Church's faith from New Testament times through the Reformation. Attention is given to the growth of the Christian faith and to particular individuals such as Paul, Augustine, Aquinas, Luther, and Calvin.

1 hour.
No Credit.
· Mr. Zabriskie.

241

ROMANCE LANGUAGES

41. (I) 42. (II) Catholic Faith and Practice

A seminar with exposition and discussion of questions concerning Roman Catholic dogmas and practices.

1 hour.   No Credit.
FR. POWER.

60. (II) Christian Faith and Human Relations

A study of the relevance of Christian theology to the problems of human existence. Making use of the insights of modern depth psychology in personal relations, the course will deal with what it means to be a person and what this implies for the various relationships of life, i.e., friendship, courtship, marriage, relation to parents and to children. Attention will be given to the insights of Christian theology upon the sexual relationship.

1 hour.   No Credit.
MR. GREENE.

71. (I) 72. (II) Essentials of Protestant Christianity

A study of the main tenets of Protestant belief and action. The aim is to help the student clarify and strengthen his own convictions through examination of topics such as man's knowledge of God, the person and mission of Jesus Christ, the nature of the Church, life after death, and the relation of Christian ethics to personal living and the social order.

1 hour.   No Credit.
MR. SEELY.

Courses in Elementary and Intermediate Hebrew, and Elementary Yiddish are offered by Rabbi Ruchames. These are open to all students.

ROMANCE LANGUAGES

PROFESSOR GODING, ASSOCIATE PROFESSOR FERRIGNO, ASSOCIATE PROFESSOR CLARKE, ASSISTANT PROFESSOR JOHNSON, ASSISTANT PROFESSOR WEXLER, MISS TILLONA,† MR. GREENFIELD, MISS VEUM, MR. FRAKER, MR. MERMIER,† MR. ROUGE, MR. MACCOMBIE, MRS. MAGRI.

FRENCH

1. (I) 2. (II) Elementary French

For those who have had no previous courses in French. Intensive drill for rapid reading, writing, speaking and understanding. No credits in this course may be applied toward a degree until the close of the second semester, except upon special recommendation from the Provost.

3 class hours; 1 laboratory hour.   Credit, 3.
THE DEPARTMENT.

5. (I) 6. (II) Intermediate French

Readings from representative works of French literature. Composition, grammar review, intensive oral practice.

3 class hours; 1 laboratory hour.   Credit, 3.
THE DEPARTMENT.

Prerequisites: French 1 and 2, or permission of the department.

† On leave of absence.

7. (I) 8. (II) Intermediate French; French Life and Culture

Selected readings from representative French literary works and a thorough review and study of grammar. Composition, intensive oral practice.

3 class hours; 1 laboratory hour. Credit, 3.

THE DEPARTMENT.

Prerequisites: 2 or 3 years of high school French and permission of the department.

25. (I) 26. (II) Introduction to French Literature

A study of the outstanding literary trends with readings from representative masterpieces of the literature from the Middle Ages to the present.

3 class hours; 1 laboratory hour. Credit, 3.

THE DEPARTMENT.

Prerequisites: French 7 and 8, or French 5 and 6 and permission of the department.

27. (I) 28. (II) Oral Practice

Intensive oral practice, vocabulary study, grammar essentials for fluent speech. Recommended for those who desire a reasonably good command of the spoken language.

3 class hours; 1 laboratory hour. Credit, 3.

THE DEPARTMENT.

Prerequisites, French 5 and 6 or equivalent or permission of the instructor.

ADVANCED COURSES

Prerequisites, French 7 and 8, or French 5 and 6 and permission of the instructor. Since most of the advanced courses are conducted in French, the student should have a reasonable oral command of the language before electing these courses. For this purpose the student is advised to take French 27 and 28, or, if women, to spend one year in the Maison Francaise.

51. (I) 52. (II) French Literature of the Eighteenth Century (1956-57)

A detailed study of the chief writers and works of the Age of Enlightenment. Given in alternate years.

3 class hours; 1 laboratory hour. Credit, 3.

MR. HULL.

53. (I) 54. (II) French Literature of the Twentieth Century

3 class hours; 1 laboratory hour. Credit, 3.

MISS CLARKE.

55. (I) (56) (II) French Literature of the Seventeenth Century (1955-56)

A survey of the Classic period, with readings from the most representative works. Given in alternate years.

3 class hours; 1 laboratory hour. Credit, 3.

MR. JOHNSON.

57. (I) 58. (II) French Literature of the Nineteenth Century (1956-57)

A detailed study of the more important authors and movements. Given in alternate years.

3 class hours; 1 laboratory hour.   Credit, 3.
                                                                    MR. GODING.

75. (I) 76. (II) Cours de Style

A study of syntax and idioms at an advanced level. The student is taught how to express himself clearly and logically in living French.

3 class hours; 1 laboratory hour.   Credit, 3.
                                          MR. ——————.

79. (I) French Civilization (1957-58)

A study of those elements which lie back of the cultural contribution of France to world civilization. Subjects studied will include arts, sciences, school systems, the press, the family, social classes, influences of history and geography. The assigned readings will be drawn from contemporary French literature. Given in alternate years.

3 class hours; 1 laboratory hour.   Credit, 3.
                                                                   MR. GODING.

80. (II) Advanced Language Study (1955-56)

Methods of teaching; review of grammar and pronunciation.

3 class hours; 1 laboratory hour.   Credit, 3.
                                                                   MR. GODING.

ITALIAN

1. (I) 2. (II) Elementary Italian

For those who have had no previous courses in Italian. The essentials of Italian grammar, intensive drill in pronunciation, conversation and composition. Extensive reading of modern Italian writings. No credits in this course may be applied toward a degree until the close of the second semester except upon special recommendation from the Provost.

3 class hours; 1 laboratory hour.   Credit, 3.
                                                                   MRS. MAGRI.

5. (I) 6. (II) Intermediate Italian

Systematic review of grammar, readings from modern authors, intensive oral drill, continued composition and conversation.

3 class hours; 1 laboratory hour.   Credit, 3.
                                                                 MR. FERRIGNO.

Prerequisites, Italian 1 and 2 or equivalent.

25. (I) 26. (II) Introduction to Italian Literature (1956-57)

This course traces the development of Italian literature from the 13th through the 20th centuries. The course is conducted in Italian. Given in alternate years.

3 class hours; 1 laboratory hour.   Credit, 3.
                                                                 MR. FERRIGNO.

Prerequisites, Itailian 5 and 6 or permission of the department.

244

27. (I) 28. (II) Oral Italian (1957-58)

This course is intended for those students who wish to perfect their knowledge of the spoken language. Given in alternate years.

3 class hours; 1 laboratory hour.   Credit, 3.

MR. FERRIGNO.

Prerequisites, Italian 5 and 6 or permission of the department.

SPANISH

1. (I) 2. (II) Elementary Spanish

For students who have had no training in Spanish. The essentials of Spanish grammar, intensive oral drill in pronunciation, fundamentals of conversation and composition, and extensive reading of short stories. No credits in this course may be applied toward a degree until the close of the second semester, except upon special recommendation from the Provost.

3 class hours; 1 laboratory hour.   Credit, 3.

THE DEPARTMENT.

5. (I) 6. (II) Intermediate Spanish

Systematic grammar review, intensive oral drill, continued composition and conversation; intensive and extensive readings from selected modern texts.

3 class hours; 1 laboratory hour.   Credit, 3.

THE DEPARTMENT.

Prerequisites, Spanish 1 and 2 or two years of high school Spanish.

25. (I) 26. (II) Introduction to Spanish Literature

This course traces the development of Spanish literature from the 12th through the 20th centuries. Readings from some of the most important works. The course is conducted largely in Spanish.

3 class hours; 1 laboratory hour.   Credit, 3.

MR. FERRIGNO.

Prerequisites, Spanish 5 and 6 or permission of the department.

27. (I) 28. (II) Oral Spanish

Primary emphasis is placed on the oral aspects of the language: pronunciation, vocabulary building, reading, comprehension, preparation of speeches, group discussions, and conversations. Considerable attention is also paid to those elements of grammar required for correct and fluent use of the language. Recommended for major students and for those who desire a good command of the language as spoken currently in Spain and Spanish-America.

3 class hours; 1 laboratory hour.   Credit, 3.

MR. WEXLER.

Prerequisites, Spanish 5 and 6 or permission of the department.

63. (I) 64. (II) Advanced Spanish Composition and Syntax (1957-58)

A study of syntax and idioms, and of those more advanced and difficult elements which constitute stylistics. An abundance of original composition leads the student to express himself clearly, logically, and fluently in living

Spanish. Open to juniors and seniors majoring in Spanish and to other qualified students by permission of the department. Given in alternate years.

3 class hours; 1 laboratory hour. Credit, 3.

MR. FERRIGNO.

Prerequisites, Spanish 27 and 28, and at least one course in Spanish literature.

81. (I)   The Romanticists (1956-57)

The course is based on the principal Spanish and Spanish-American writers of the Romantic movement (1808-50 and 1832-88, respectively). Conducted in Spanish. Given in alternate years.

3 class hours; 1 laboratory hour. Credit, 3.

MR. WEXLER.

Prerequisites, Spanish 25 and 26 or permission of the department.

82. (II)   The Modernists (1956-57)

The course is based on the Spanish-American modernism of the period 1888-1910 and on their Peninsular artistic heirs. Conducted in Spanish. Given in alternate years.

3 class hours; 1 laboratory hour. Credit, 3.

MR. WEXLER.

Prerequisites, Spanish 25 and 26 or permission of the department.

83. (I)   84. (II)   The Golden Age (1957-58)

The course is based primarily on the period of maximum creation, 1556-1600. Considerable attention is also paid to the renaissance precursors (1474-1556) and to the writers of the Baroque era (1066-1700). Conducted in Spanish. Given in alternate years.

3 class hours; 1 laboratory hour. Credit, 3.

MR. WEXLER.

Prerequisites, Spanish 25 and 26 or permission of the department.

85. (I)   86 (II)   Cervantes (1956-57)

Reading of Don Quixote. The course is conducted in Spanish. Given in alternate years.

3 class hours; 1 laboratory hour. Credit, 3.

MR. WEXLER.

Prerequisites, Spanish 25 and 26 or permission of the department.

RUSSIAN

Instructor in Languages.

1. (I)   2. (II)   Elementary Russian

Grammar, exercises in composition and conversation, selected readings. No credits in this course may be applied toward a degree until the close of the second semester, except upon special recommendations from the Provost.

3 class hours; 1 laboratory hour. Credit, 3.

MRS. JOA.

Prerequisites, previous language training.

SOCIOLOGY

PROFESSOR KORSON, ASSOCIATE PROFESSOR KING, ASSISTANT PROFESSOR
DRIVER, MR. MANFREDI, MR. WILKINSON, MR. ——————.

25. (I) and (II) Introduction to Sociology

An outline study of the social order, and of the individual considered as a member of his various groups.

3 class hours. Credit, 3.

THE DEPARTMENT.

26. (II) Principles of Sociology

A survey of the theoretical development of major sociological concepts with emphasis on American sociologists and their contributions. Reading and analysis of monographs utilizing the sociological frame of references for selected areas.

3 class hours. Credit, 3.

MR. WILKINSON.

51. (I) Urban Sociology

A comparative study of modern social conditions, and methods of adjustment, with special reference to city environment. Characteristics of the population, urban ecology, and problems of adjustment in the fields of housing, health, education, and recreation are considered.

3 class hours. Credit, 3.
2:00-2:50 Tu. Th., third hour by arrangement. MR. MANFREDI.
Prerequisite, Sociology 25.

52. (II) Rural Sociology

A study of rural society from the standpoint of its population, institutions, standards of living, and their relation to urban society.

3 class hours. Credit, 3.

MR. MANFREDI.

Prerequisite, Sociology 25.

53. (I) An Introductory Study of Cultural Anthropology

A non-technical sociological study of man in preliterate societies.

3 class hours. Credit. 3.

MR. WILKINSON.

Prerequisite, Sociology 25.

56. (II) Race Relations

The social, economic, and political aspects of racial problems in the United States, with particular reference to the Negro and major ethnic groups. A rabbi, minister, and priest are invited to address the class, and visits are made to the respective churches.

3 class hours. Credit. 3.

MR. KORSON, MR. KING.

Prerequisite, Sociology 25.

57. (I) The Family

The study of the development of the customs of courtship and marriage of the contemporary American family. The basic causes of changes and trends of the family are considered. Such topics as mate selection, marriage laws, marital prediction, husband-wife relations, and the role of the child are considered.

3 class hours.   Credit. 3.

MR. KING, MR. KORSON.

Prerequisite, Sociology 25.

62. (II) Population Problems

An analytical study of population trends and problems of the world; the origin, composition, growth, migration, and urbanization of the American population. A consideration of population pressure as a cause of migratory movements.

3 class hours.   Credit, 3.

MR. WILKINSON.

Prerequisite, Sociology 25.

68. (II) Industrial Sociology

A study of the role, status, and function of the worker in the industrial community. A consideration of changing technology, resulting social change and the adjustments made in the industrial community.

3 class hours.   Credit, 3.

MR. KORSON.

Prerequisite, Sociology 25.

75. (I) Social Problems

A consideration of the incidence, distribution and interrelations among the major types of social tensions in human societies. Various theories of causation are evaluated. In addition to regular classroom work, research projects and field trips are required.

3 class hours.   Credit, 3.

MR. DRIVER.

Prerequisite, Sociology 25.

78. (II) Criminology

A study of the nature of crimes and the factors underlying criminal behavior. Attention is also given to the machinery of justice in criminal behavior; the law, the courts, police enforcement, penal and correctional institutions.

3 class hours.   Credit, 3.

MR. DRIVER.

Prerequisite, Sociology 25.

82. (II) Sociological Theory

An examination of the contributions of European and American writers who have concerned themselves with theories of the origin, growth, and development of human social organization.

3 class hours.   Credit, 3.

MR. MANFREDI.

Prerequisite, Sociology 25.

92. (II) Introduction to Social Welfare

For senior majors and others who qualify. Contemporary problems of social concern: causes of poverty; methods of caring for adult and child dependents

and defectives. A consideration of public and private agency administration and techniques, and an examination of federal, state, and local community programs.
3 class hours. Credit, 3.
Prerequisites, Sociology 25, 75. Mr. Driver.

93. (I) 94. (II) Seminar

Admission by permission of instructor. A study of the methods of research employed by social scientists. Students, under direction of the instructor, analyze and organize such sociological material as they gather through their own research. Projects must be approved in advance by the instructor.
Credit, 3.
Hours by arrangement. Mr. Driver.

SPEECH

Professor Niedeck, Assistant Professor Zaitz,† Mr. Peirce, Miss Abramson, and the Instructors in English. Visiting Lecturers Sickles, Hodapp, Cloutier.

3. (I) 4. (II) Public Speaking

This course is designed to give the student introductory instruction and opportunity in oral self-expression and includes both public speaking and literary interpretation. Scheduled under English 1, 2.
1 class hour. Credit, 1.
The Department.

ORAL INTERPRETATION

51. (I) Voice and Diction and Oral Interpretation

The course is divided into five weeks of training and drill in the correct production of speech, followed by ten weeks of practice in the fundamentals of vocal interpretation of literature. It is possible for a student to take the five weeks of voice and diction and receive one credit.
3 class hours. Credit, 1 or 3.
Miss Abramson.

RADIO AND TELEVISION

61. (I) Fundamentals of Broadcasting

A general introduction to broadcasting: practice in preparing, rehearsing, and producing programs of various types.
2 class hours; 1 2-hour labortory period. Credit, 3.
Mr. Zaitz.

62. (II) Advanced Radio Production

An advanced course in broadcasting to provide practice in preparing and producing radio talks, radio plays and documentary programs.
2 class hours; 1 2-hour laboratory period. Credit, 3.
Mr. Zaitz.

63. (I) Television Programming and Production

An exploration of the television medium for orientation in producing, directing and writing: network, local and educational operations both studio and remote.
2 class hours; 1 2-hour laboratory period. Credit, 3.
Mr. Zaitz.

† On leave of absence.

SPEECH

64. (II) Television Programming and Production

Practical television techniques from effective planning through effective execution by people off camera and on camera.

2 class hours; 1 2-hour laboratory period. Credit, 3.

MR. ZAITZ.

Prerequisite, Speech 63.

65. (I) Writing for Television

A consideration of television writing methods for the successful production of all types of formats.

3 class hours. Credit, 3.

MISS ABRAMSON.

66. (II) Film Production and Staging for Television

Preparation and execution of 16mm films for television: the course will prepare a 10-minute film project from the idea to editing, processing, screening and narration.

2 class hours; 1 2-hour laboratory period. Credit, 3.

MR. NIEDECK.

Prerequisite, Speech 63.

THEATRE

71. (I) Scene Design and Construction

Theories and design in the modern theatre with assignments in developing stage settings from sketches to working drawing; from scenery construction to painting.

2 class hours; 1 2-hour laboratory period. Credit, 3.

MR. PEIRCE.

75. (I) Acting and Make-up

The course is roughly divided into ten weeks of study of emotion and imagination in acting, reading lines, rehearsing, diction, and bodily action; and five weeks of study and application of the principles of stage make-up.

2 class hours; 1 2-hour laboratory period. Credit, 3.

MR. NIEDECK.

76. (II) Stage Direction

Study and practice in the fundamentals of directing a play. Recommended for those taking only one course in Drama.

2 class hours; 1 2-hour laboratory period. Credit, 3.

MR. NIEDECK.

78. (II) Stage Lighting

Introduction to lighting a stage. Analysis of basic types of equipment and their application in artistic productions. Simple wiring and installations.

2 class hours; 1 2-hour laboratory period. Credit, 3.

MR. PEIRCE.

RHETORIC AND PUBLIC ADDRESS

91. (I) (II) Extempore Speech

The theory and practice of public speaking for business and professional purposes.

3 class hours. Credit, 3.

MR. NIEDECK.

92. (II) Discussion

Most of the semester is devoted to formal discussion: its organization and presentation. Students are given the opportunity to lead and to participate in discussions of current problems.

3 class hours. Credit 3.

MISS ABRAMSON.

Prerequisite, Speech 91.

94. (II) Persuasion

Advanced study and practice in appeals to beliefs and action through extemporaneous speech.

3 class hours. Credit, 3.

MR. ZAITZ.

Prerequisite, Speech 91.

VETERINARY SCIENCE

PROFESSOR BULLIS, PROFESSOR SMITH.

75. (I) Comparative Veterinary Anatomy

A study of the structure of vertebrates with emphasis upon the comparative structure of domesticated animals, both mammals and birds.

3 class hours. Credit, 3.
11:00-11:50 M. W. F. MR. SMITH.

76. (II) General Veterinary Pathology

An introduction to the study of disease—causes, transmission, structural changes, and defense mechanisms; and the application of these principles to the prevention, control, and eradication of the common communicable and non-communicable diseases of farm animals.

3 class hours. Credit, 3.
11:00-11:50 M. W. F. MR. SMITH.
Prerequisite, Veterinary Science 75.

78. (II) General Veterinary Pathology

This course is similar to Veterinary Science 76 except that diseases of importance to wildlife, and diseases of animals transmissible to man will be considered.

3 class hours. Credit, 3.

MR. SMITH.

Prerequisites, Bacteriology 31, Zoology 35 or 71.

88. (II) Avian Pathology

This course is similar to Veterinary Science 76 but with application to specific communicable and non-communicable diseases of poultry.

3 class hours. Credit, 3.
8:00-8:50 M. W. F. MR. BULLIS.
Prerequisite, Veterinary Science 75.

ZOOLOGY

PROFESSOR WOODSIDE, ASSOCIATE PROFESSOR SNEDECOR, ASSOCIATE PROFESSOR BART-
LETT,† ASSISTANT PROFESSOR TRAVER, ASSISTANT PROFESSOR ROLLASON, ASSIST-
ANT PROFESSOR ANDREWS, ASSISTANT PROFESSOR NUTTING, ASSISTANT PROFESSOR
RAUCH, ASSISTANT PROFESSOR HONIGBERG, ASSISTANT PROFESSOR SWENSON,
ASSISTANT PROFESSOR ROBERTS, MR. SNYDER, MR. MONER.

1. (I) and (II) Introductory Zoology

This course provides an introduction to the principles of biology, with
special reference to the zoological aspects. The structure and activities of a
representative vertebrate animal, the frog, are considered in detail and the
knowledge thus gained is utilized in a comprehensive survey of the major
groups of the animal kingdom. Brief introductions are given to the principles
of classification, nutrition, structure, and functions of protoplasm, genetics,
heredity, development, and evolution.

2 class hours; 1 3-hour laboratory period. Credit, 3.
11:00-11:50 M. W. or 2:00-2:50 M. W. or 3:00-3:50 Tu. Th.; laboratory hours·
as sectioned. THE DEPARTMENT.

25. (I) Survey of the Animal Kingdom

Lectures emphasize those aspects of the zoological sciences which are least
stressed in the introductory course; the principles of classification; ecology;
economic importance; and the history of zoology in relation to man's progress.
The laboratory work will include several exercises in field work; studies on
representatives of phyla not covered previously; the morphological adaptations
of animals to special modes of existence; and some simple zoological techniques.

2 class hours; 1 2-hour laboratory period. Credit, 3.
10:00-10:50 M. F.; 1:00-2:50 Tu. or W. or Th. MR. NUTTING.
Prerequisite, Zoology 1.

35. (I) and (II) Vertebrate Physiology

An introductory course which will include consideration of circulation,
respiration, digestion, metabolism, excretion, chemical and nervous coordination, muscular activity, and reproduction. The laboratory work will acquaint
the student with some of the equipment and methods used in physiological
studies, with emphasis on the experimental approach to the laboratory exercises.

2 class hours; 1 3-hour laboratory period. Credit, 3.
MR. SNEDECOR, MR. SWENSON, MR. ROBERTS.

50. (II) Histology of the Vertebrates

A study of the types of tissues found in the body of vertebrate animals,
and of the organs in which these tissues occur. Tissues and organs of mammals
are emphasized. A knowledge of comparative anatomy is advised.

2 class hours; 1 3-hour laboratory period. Credit, 3.
8:00-8:50 Tu. Th.; 2:00-4:50 Tu. or 1:00-3:50 W. MR. ROLLASON.
Prerequisite, Zoology 1.

51. (I) and (II) Microtechnique of Animal Tissues

The course comprises (1) a consideration of the principles and methods of
microtechnique as applied to animal tissues, and (2) a series of practical exer-

† On leave of absence.

252

cises in the preparation of animal tissues for microscopic examination. Registration is limited to 12 students per semester. Consult instructor for section assignments.

2 2-hour laboratory periods.

Prerequisite, Zoology 1.

Credit, 2.

MR. HONIGBERG.

53. (I) Principles of Genetics

Lectures and laboratory experiments concerning the laws governing the transmission of hereditary factors in plants and animals, expression and action of genes, population genetics, and the relationship of genetics to other biological sciences.

2 class hours; 1 3-hour laboratory period.

Prerequisite, Zoology 1

Credit, 3.

MR. RAUCH.

54. (II) Natural History—Physical

Designed to orient students to the features of sky, climate and terrain which are of prime importance to the teaching naturalist. Collection, recording, preservation, and the use of natural objects will be stressed. Biological data will also be obtained as the season dictates.

1 class hour; 1 4-hour laboratory period.
11:00-11:50 Tu.; 1:00-5:00 F.
Prerequisites, Botany 1; Zoology 1.

Credit, 3.

MR. NUTTING.

55. (I) Natural History—Biotic

An extension of Zoology 54 with emphasis upon the fauna and flora. This course is primarily concerned with the development, local distribution, responses, and interrelationships of these organisms. Their position with respect to the physical environment will be discussed in some detail.

1 class hour; 1 4-hour laboratory period.
11:00-11:50 Tu.; 1:00-5:00 F.
Prerequisites, Botany 26; Geology 27; Zoology 54.

Credit, 3.

MR. NUTTING.

56. (II) Natural History—Field Studies

A program of extensive field work growing out of preparation in Zoology 54 and 55. Emphasis upon seasonal differences in abundance and stage of development of our fauna and flora.

1 class hour; 1 2-hour laboratory period.
1:00-1:50 W.; 2:00-3:50 W.
Prerequisites, Zoology 55 and permission of insructor.

Credit, 2.

MR. NUTTING.

64. (II) Biology of Protozoa (1956-57)

An introduction to the morphology, systematics, physiology, and ecology of protozoa with a consideration of the contributions to the problems of biology made through the study of these organisms. Given in alternate years.

1 class hour; 1 2-hour and 1 3-hour laboratory period.

Prerequisites, Zoology 1 and permission of the instructor.

Credit, 3.

MR. HONIGBERG.

69. (I) Animal Parasitology

Representative protozoan and helminthic parasites of man and domestic animals are studied, with special reference to their morphology and life cycles.

ZOOLOGY

Emphasis is placed upon parasitism as a mode of life; on hostparasite relationships; on vectors, and other modes of transmission; and on methods of control of certain of the more important human parasites.

1 class hour; 2 2-hour laboratory periods.

Prerequisite, Zoology 1.

Credit, 3.
MISS TRAVER.

70. (II) Invertebrate Zoology (1956-57)

A survey of the phyla of invertebrate animals from evolutionary and phlogenetic aspects. Morphology, modes of nutrition and reproduction, interrelationships with other animals, and distributions in time and space, are considered, as well as classification. For each phylum, representatives of the principal classes are studied. Marine, terrestrial and freshwater forms are included. Given in alternate years.

1 class hour; 2 3-hour laboratory periods.

Prerequisite, Zoology 1.

Credit, 3.
MISS TRAVER.

71. (I) Comparative Vertebrate Anatomy

A thorough study of the anatomy of the vertebrates, with emphasis on the evolution, special modifications, and functional interrelationships of each of the organ systems. A systematic approach in both lecture and laboratory work. Animals studied in the laboratory are: protochordates, lamprey, dogfish, mudpuppy, and cat.

2 class hours; 2 3-hour laboratory periods.

1:00-1:50 Tu. Th.; 1:00-3:50 W. F. or 2:00-4:50 Tu. Th.

Prerequisite, Zoology 1.

Credit, 4.
MR. BARTLETT, MR. SNYDER.

72. (II) Vertebrate Embryology

Lectures and laboratory work dealing with the development of representative animals, special emphasis being placed on the amphibian, bird and mammal.

2 class hours; 2 3-hour laboratory periods.

Prerequisite, Zoology 71.

Credit, 4.
MR. WOODSIDE, MR. RAUCH, MR. BARTLETT.

73. (I) General Cytology (1956-57)

A consideration of the morphological features of cells in relation to their function. Lectures, seminar reports and laboratory work will deal with cytoplasmic structure and inclusions and nuclear phenomena. Given in alternate years.

2 class hours; 1 3-hour laboratory period.

Prerequisites, Zoology 50.

Credit, 3.
MR. ROLLASON.

74. (II) Limnology (1955-56)

The study of inland waters, emphasizing the geological, physical, chemical and biological aspects of this problem. Standard methods for making physical and chemical tests and measurements, and for the collection of biological materials, are used by students in the numerous field trips. Biological material collected in the field is studied in the laboratory. Given in alternate years.

2 class hours; 2 3-hour laboratory periods.

Credit, 4.
MISS TRAVER.

in cooperation with the departments of Botany, Entomology, Geology, Public Health, and Zoology.

Prerequisites, Botany 1; Zoology 1; Chemistry 1, 2; and permission to register. Strongly recommended: Botany 25, 26; Entomology 26; Zoology 25; Geology 27, 28; Chemistry 29, 30.

78. (II) Genetics of Animal Populations (1955-56)

The principles of the genetics of animal populations with emphasis upon its basic techniques and methods, its goals and contributions. The population approach to the study of the origin of species and human genetics will be considered also. Given in alternate years. Enrolment is limited to ten.

1 2-hour lecture-discussion period per week. Credit, 2.

MR. RAUCH.

Prerequisites, Zoology 53 or its equivalent and permission of the instructor.

80. (II) Ornithology

An introduction to the study of avian biology with emphasis on structural and functional adaptations, and particularly the behavioral patterns of birds. Laboratory periods include discussions of assigned readings in current literature in addition to field trips for identification and methods of field study.

1 class hour; 2 2-hour laboratory periods. Credit, 3.

8:00-8:50 Th.; 3:00-4:50 M. F. or 9:00-11:00 Tu.; 3:00-4:50 F.

MR. BARTLETT, MR. NUTTING.

Prerequisite, Zoology 1.

81. (I) Vertebrate Zoology

An introduction to the vertebrates, their classification and ecology, with particular emphasis on the fishes. Field trips for the study of local fauna will be included as a part of the laboratory exercises. Course limited to eighteen students.

1 class hour; 2 2-hour laboratory periods. Credit, 3.

9:00-9:50 W.; 1:00-2:50 Tu. Th. MR. ANDREWS, MR. BARTLETT.

Prerequisite, Zoology 1.

82. (II) Mammalogy (1956-57)

The paleontology, taxonomy, speciation, natural history, range and distribution of the class Mammalia. Primary emphasis will be placed upon the study of local fauna, including at least one week-end collecting trip as part of the laboratory exercises. Course limited to fifteen students. Given in alternate years.

2 class hours; 1 2-hour laboratory period. Credit, 3.

MR. SNYDER.

Prerequisites, Zoology 1 and permission of instructor.

83. (I) General and Cellular Physiology

A course designed to introduce the student to modern trends in physiology. Emphasis is on the chemical and physical activities of the single cell. Topics include: protoplasmic organization, cellular metabolism, permeability, bioelectric phenomena, muscle contraction and radiation biology.

3 class hours; 1 3-hour laboratory period. Credit, 4.

MR. SWENSON.

Prerequisites, 1 year of biology; organic chemistry.

84. (II) Comparative Physiology

A course designed to acquaint students with physiological principles involved in adaptations of animals to their environments. In the laboratory, experimental methods used to study adaptive mechanisms will be emphasized.

3 class hours; 1 3-hour laboratory period. Credit, 4.

MR. ROBERTS.

Prerequisites, Zoology 1, 35 or 83.

ZOOLOGY

85. (I) Classes of Arthropods Other Than Insects

Arthropods are studied from the phylogenetic standpoint, with special reference to their relationship to the origin and evolution of insects.

1 class hour; 2 2-hour laboratory periods. Credit, 3.
12:00-12:50 W.; 1:00-2:00 W. F. MR. HANSON.

86. (II) Fishery Biology

Theory in the practice of regulating freshwater fisheries; the physical and biological conditions of the environment and their influence on fish populations.
2 class hours; 1 2-hour laboratory period.
9:00-9:50 Tu. Th.; laboratory hours by arrangement.

MR. ANDREWS.

Prerequisite, Zoology 81 and permission of instructor.

87. (I) Endocrinology

Emphasis will be directed toward the importance of the endocrines in their control over normal functions (growth, metabolism, reproduction, etc.), in a variety of animals.

2 class hours; 1 3-hour laboratory period. Credit, 3.
MR. SNEDECOR.

Prerequisite, Zoology 1.

91. (I) 92. (II) Special Problems in Zoology

Qualified seniors who have met departmental requirements for specialization in the field of zoology may arrange for work on a special problem in zoology.

Credit, 1-3.
THE DEPARTMENT.

Invertebrate Zoology, Marine Biological Laboratory, Woods Hole, Massachusetts.

Credit, 3.

Invertebrate Embryology, Marine Biological Laboratory, Woods Hole, Massachusetts.

Credit, 3.

OFFICERS OF ADMINISTRATION

Office of the President

JEAN PAUL MATHER, B.S.C., M.B.A. (University of Denver), M.A. (Princeton
University), LL.D. (American International College), D.SC. (Lowell
Technological Institute), *President of the University.* South College

AFFIE MAY COOK, *Secretary to the President.* South College

Office of the Secretary

JAMES WILLIAM BURKE, B.S. (University of Massachusetts),
Secretary of the University. South College

Office of the Provost

SHANNON McCUNE, B.A. (College of Wooster), M.A. (Syracuse
University), PH.D. (Clark University), *Provost.* South College

MARSHALL OLIN LANPHEAR, B.S., M.S. (University of Massachusetts),
Registrar. South College

ROBERT STODDART HOPKINS, JR., B.A., M.ED. (Rutgers University),
Dean of Men. South College

HELEN CURTIS, A.B. (Iowa State Teachers College),
A.M. (Columbia University), *Dean of Women.* South College

DONALD WINSLOW CADIGAN, B.S., M.S. (University of Massachusetts),
Associate Registrar. South College

WILLIAM CHANDLER STARKWEATHER, B.S. (University of Massachusetts),
Assistant Registrar. South College

WILLIAM FRANKLIN FIELD, B.S. (West Chester State Teachers College),
ED.M. (Temple University), PH.D. (University of Maryland), *Director
of Guidance.* South College

MILDRED PIERPONT, A.B. (Mount Holyoke College),
Schedule Supervisor. South College

EMILY MAY LARKIN,
Administrative Assistant to the Dean of Men. South College

Office of the Dean of the Graduate School

GILBERT LLEWELLYN WOODSIDE, B.A. (DePauw University), A.M., PH.D.
(Harvard University), *Dean of the Graduate School.* Fernald Hall

MRS. ELIZABETH W. CADIGAN,
Secretary to the Dean of the Graduate School. East Experiment Station

Office of the Treasurer

KENNETH WILLIAM JOHNSON, B.S. (University of Vermont),
Treasurer of the University. South College

257

ADMINISTRATION

L. LAWRENCE TAYLOR, B.B.A. (Northeastern University),
Assistant Treasurer.   South College

FRANCIS JOSEPH TEAHAN,
Administrative Assistant to the Treasurer.   South College

MRS. GAMER H. PAUL, *Secretary to the Treasurer.*   South College

Business Office

HOBART HAYES LUDDEN, B.B.A. (Boston University),
Business Manager.   South College

EDWARD MARCUS MANOOKIAN, *Personnel Officer.*   South College

GEORGE CHARLES BREHM,
Superintendent of Buildings and Grounds.   Service Building

LIONEL GEORGE DAVID, *Engineer.*   Service Building

WALTER OSCAR JOHNSON, B.S. (University of Massachusetts),
Manager of Boarding Halls.   University Commons

HERBERT ALONZO RANDOLPH, *Supervisor of Housing.*   Draper Hall

AUGUSTINE JOSEPH RYAN, A.B. (Dartmouth College), M.B.A. (Harvard
University), *Manager of the University Store.*   North College

Office of Director of Experiment Station

DALE HAROLD SIELING, B.S., M.S. (Kansas State College), PH.D. (Iowa State
College), *Dean of the College of Agriculture and Director of the
Experiment Station.*   East Experiment Station

MARGARET HELEN O'DONNELL,
Administrative Director.   East Experiment Station

MATTHEW LOUIS BLAISDELL, B.S. (University of Massachusetts), *Associate
Professor, Superintendent of Farms and Head of Station Service.*
    Stockbridge Hall

DONALD MARKHAM KINSMAN, B.S. (University of Massachusetts), M.S. (University of New Hampshire), *Assistant Professor, Assistant to Superintendent of Farms.*   Stockbridge Hall

MRS. DOROTHY MALLORY ROSE,
Secretary to the Director.   East Experiment Station

Office of Director of Extension Service

JAMES WILSON DAYTON, B.S. (University of Massachusetts), *Associate Dean
of the College of Agriculture and Director of Extension Service.*
    Stockbridge Hall

IRENE ELISABETH CHANDLER, *Secretary to the Director.*   Stockbridge Hall

Office of Director of Stockbridge School

FRED PAINTER JEFFREY, B.S. (Pennsylvania State University), M.S. (University of Massachusetts), *Associate Dean of the College of Agriculture
and Director of the Stockbridge School.*   Stockbridge Hall

KATHARINE MARY MARTIN, *Secretary to the Director.*   Stockbridge Hall

Office of Publications

ROBERT JOSEPH MCCARTNEY, B.A. (University of Massachusetts),
University Editor. South College

MRS. PEARL THOMAS KLIMCYK,
Secretary to the University Editor. South College

Health Service

ERNEST JAMES RADCLIFFE, M.B., M.D. (University of Toronto),
Senior Physician. Out Patient Department

MALCOLM JAMES CHISHOLM, M.D., C.M. (Dalhousie University),
Assistant Physician. Out Patient Department

Placement Office

EMORY ELLSWORTH GRAYSON, B.S. (University of Massachusetts),
Director of Placement. South College

ROBERT JOHN MORRISSEY, B.S. (State Teachers College, Buffalo, New York),
M.S. (St. Bonaventure College), *Placement Officer for Men.*
South College

MRS. CAROL BURR CORNISH, A.B. (Grinnell College), M.A. (Syracuse University), *Placement Officer for Women.* South College

GEORGE EDWARD EMERY, B.S. (University of Massachusetts),
Assistant Placement Officer. South College

Library

HUGH MONTGOMERY, B.S. (Harvard University), B.S. in L.S.
(Columbia University), *Librarian.* Goodell Library

BENTON LEROY HATCH, B.A. (Yale University),
Assistant Librarian. Goodell Library

MRS. SOSIE KHATCHIKIAN, *Calatoguer.* Goodell Library

MARTIN HUBBARD, A.B. (Bates College), B.S. in ED. (Massachusetts Teachers
College), M.A. (Harvard University) *Chief of Reference and Circulation Services.* Goodell Library

DOROTHY NESTLE, B.S. (University of Massachusetts),
Administrative Secretary. Goodell Library

WILLIAM MCGRATH, B.A. (University of Massachusetts),
Documents Assistant. Goodell Library

EDWARD A. BILLINGS, *General Assistant.* Goodell Library

MRS. HILDEGARDE CHASE, *Catalog Assistant.* Goodell Library

MRS. ELIZABETH GEHLING, *Serials Assistant.* Goodell Library

MRS. HELEN HUBER, *Acquisitions Assistant.* Goodell Library

MRS. SUE MARCOULIER, *Circulation Assistant.* Goodell Library

MRS. JANE PRATT, *Acquisitions Assistant.* Goodell Library

MRS. JANICE TYLER, *Reference Assistant.* Goodell Library

MRS. PATRICIA WEBLER, B.S. (Wisconsin State College at
Milwaukee), *Circulation Assistant.* Goodell Library

ADMINISTRATION

Audio Visual Center

RAYMOND WYMAN, B.S. (University of Massachusetts), ED.M. (Boston University), *Director, Audio Visual Center.* South College

DONALD CURTIS, B.S. (Pennsylvania State University), M.S. (University of Massachusetts), *Assistant Director, Audio Visual Center.*
South College

Alumni Office

ROBERT LEAVITT, B.S. (University of Massachusetts),
Executive Secretary, Associate Alumni. Memorial Hall

Heads of Residence

MRS. MADELINE LEWIS CARTWRIGHT, A.B. (Boston University,
M.A. (Columbia University). Crabtree House

MRS. JEAN THOMPSON CHURCHILL, A.B. (Mt. Holyoke College).
Arnold House

MRS. LUCIE KNOWLES DAVEY. Thatcher House

MME. MARINA SKARZYNSKA GUTOWSKA, PH.D. (University of Warsaw).
Leach House

MRS. AMY STONE JUDGE, A.B. (Mount Holyoke College). Knowlton House

MRS. ELSIE MCCAUSLAND RICH. Hamlin House

MRS. NADINE BOLLES WHIPPLE. Abigail Adams House

Chaplains

REV. DAVID JOHN POWER, A.B. (Georgetown University), (Seminary of Philosophy of Montreal, Grand Seminary of Theology of Montreal), *Chaplain to Catholic Students.* North College

RABBI LOUIS RUCHAMES (Jewish Institute of Religion), PH.D. (Columbia University), *Chaplain to Jewish Students.* Hillel House

REV. ALBERT LYNUS SEELY, B.A. (Oberlin College), B.D. (Yale University), *Chaplain to Protestant Students.* North College

EMERITI

WILLIAM HENRY ARMSTRONG, B.S. (University of Massachusetts), B.S., M.L.A.C.P. (Harvard University), *Assistant Professor of Mechanical Drawing,* Emeritus.

LORIN EARL BALL, B.S. (University of Massachusetts), *Assistant Professor of Physical Education,* Emeritus.

ARTHUR BISHOP BEAUMONT, B.S. (Kentucky State University), PH.D. (Cornell University), *Professor of Agronomy,* Emeritus.

ALEXANDER EDMOND CANCE, A.B. (Macalester College), M.A., PH.D. (University of Wisconsin), *Professor of Economics,* Emeritus.

ORTON LORING CLARK, B.S. (University of Massachusetts), *Associate Professor of Botany,* Emeritus.

PAUL WHEELER DEMPSEY, B.S. (University of Massachusetts), *Assistant Professor of Horticulture,* Emeritus.

LLEWELLYN LIGHT DERBY, B.S. (Springfield College), M.S. (University of Massachusetts), *Associate Professor of Physical Education,* Emeritus.

WALTER SAMUEL EISENMENGER, B.S., M.S. (Bucknell University), A.M., PH.D. (Columbia University), *Professor of Agronomy,* Emeritus.

CLIFFORD J. FAWCETT, B.S. (Ohio State University), *Extension Professor of Animal Husbandry,* Emeritus.

F. ETHEL FELTON, A.B. (Smith College), *Experiment Station Editor,* Emeritus.

CHARLES FREDERIC FRAKER, A.B. (Colorado College), A.M., PH.D. (Harvard University), *Professor of Romance Languages,* Emeritus.

JULIUS HERMAN FRANDSEN, B.S., M.S. (Iowa State College), *Professor of Dairy Industry,* Emeritus.

HENRY JAMES FRANKLIN, B.S., PH.D. (University of Massachusetts), *Professor of Horticulture,* Emeritus.

EDWIN FRANCIS GASKILL, B.S. (University of Massachusetts), *Assistant Professor of Agronomy,* Emeritus.

GUY VICTOR GLATFELTER, B.S. (Pennsylvania State University), M.S. (Iowa State College), *Placement Officer,* Emeritus.

HAROLD MARTIN GORE, B.S. (University of Massachusetts), *Professor of Physical Education for Men,* Emeritus.

JOHN CAMERON GRAHAM, B.S., AGR. (University of Wisconsin), *Professor of Poultry Husbandry,* Emeritus.

MARGARET POMEROY HAMLIN, A.B. (Smith College), *Placement Officer,* Emeritus.

HENRI DARWIN HASKINS, B.S. (University of Massachusetts), *Professor of Agricultural Chemistry,* Emeritus.

EMERITI

ROBERT DORMAN HAWLEY, B.S. (University of Massachusetts), M.B.A. (Boston University), *Treasurer*, Emeritus.

MRS. HARRIET JULIA HAYNES, B.S. (Columbia University), *Extension Professor of Home Economics*, Emeritus.

CURRY STARR HICKS, B.PD., M.ED. (Michigan State Normal College), *Professor of Physical Education*, Emeritus.

ARTHUR DUNHAM HOLMES, B.S. (Dartmouth College), PH.D. (Johns Hopkins University), *Research Professor of Chemistry*, Emeritus.

SAMUEL CHURCH HUBBARD, *Assistant Professor of Floriculture*, Emeritus.

GAY TETLEY KLEIN, B.S. (University of Missouri), M.S. (Kansas State College), *Extension Professor of Poultry Husbandry*, Emeritus.

JOHN BECKLEY LENTZ, A.B. (Franklin and Marshall College), V.M.D. (University of Pennsylvania), *Professor of Veterinary Science*, Emeritus.

FREDERICK ADAMS McLAUGHLIN, B.S. (University of Massachusetts), *Associate Professor of Botany*, Emeritus.

FRANK COCHRANE MOORE, A.B. (Dartmouth College), *Professor of Mathematics*, Emeritus.

WILLARD ANSON MUNSON, B.S., D.AGR. (University of Massachusetts), *Director of Extension Service*, Emeritus.

JOHN BAXTER NEWLON, *Assistant Professor of Engineering*, Emeritus.

SUMNER RUFUS PARKER, B.S. (University of Massachusetts), *Extension Professor of Agriculture*, Emeritus.

CHARLES ADAMS PETERS, B.S. (University of Massachusetts), PH.D. (Yale University), *Professor of Chemistry*, Emeritus.

VICTOR ARTHUR RICE, B.S. (North Carolina State College), M.AGR. (University of Massachusetts), D.AGR. (North Carolina State College), *Professor of Animal Husbandry*, Emeritus.

JACOB KINGSLEY SHAW, B.S. (University of Vermont), M.S., PH.D. (University of Massachusetts), *Research Professor of Pomology*, Emeritus.

EDNA LUCY SKINNER, B.S., M.A. (Columbia University), M.ED. (Michigan State Normal College), *Dean of the School of Home Economics*, Emeritus.

CHARLES HIRAM THAYER, B.AGR. (University of Massachusetts), *Assistant Professor of Agronomy*, Emeritus.

WILBUR HERMAN THIES, B.S., M.S. (Michigan State University), *Extension Professor of Pomology*, Emeritus.

RALPH ALBERT VAN METER, B.S. (Ohio State University), M.S. (University of Massachusetts), PH.D. (Cornell University), LL.D. (Amherst College, University of Massachusetts), *President*, Emeritus.

ROLAND HALE VERBECK, B.S. (University of Massachusetts), *Director of Short Courses*, Emeritus.

WILLIAM GOULD VINAL, B.S., M.A. (Harvard University), PH.D. (Brown University), *Professor of Nature Education*, Emeritus.

WINTHROP SELDEN WELLES, B.S. (University of Illinois), M.ED. (Harvard University), *Professor of Education*, Emeritus.

BASIL BOISE WOOD, A.B. (Brown University), *Librarian*, Emeritus.

FACULTY OF RESIDENT INSTRUCTION

JEAN PAUL MATHER, B.S.C., M.B.A. (University of Denver), M.A. (Princeton University), LL.D. (American International College), D.SC. (Lowell Technological Institute), *President*. South College

SHANNON McCUNE, B.A. (College of Wooster), M.A. (Syracuse University), PH.D. (Clark University), *Provost*. South College

HERSCHEL GEORGE ABBOTT, B.S. (University of Maine), M.F. (Harvard University), *Instructor in Forestry*. Conservation Building

DORIS ELIZABETH ABRAMSON, B.A. (University of Massachusetts), M.A. (Smith College), *Instructor in Speech*. South College

VERNE ALTON ADAMS, B.S. (University of Massachusetts), *Instructor in Dairy and Animal Science*. Stockbridge Hall

GEORGE WILLIAM ALDERMAN, B.A. (Williams College), *Professor of Physics*. Hasbrouck Laboratory

CHARLES PAUL ALEXANDER, B.S., PH.D. (Cornell University), *Professor of Entomology and Head of Department*. Fernald Hall

ELIOT DINSMORE ALLEN, B.A. (Wesleyan University), A.M. (Harvard University), M.A., PH.D. (Princeton University), *Assistant Professor of English*. Chapel

LUTHER ALFRED ALLEN, A.B. (Williams College), M.A. (State University of Iowa), PH.D. (University of Chicago), *Instructor in Government*. North College

STEPHEN IVES ALLEN, A.B. (Amherst College), A.M. (Harvard University), *Instructor in Mathematics*. Mathematics Building

DORIC ALVIANI, MUS.B., ED.M. (Boston University), *Professor of Music*. Memorial Hall

ALLEN EMIL ANDERSEN, A.B., M.A. (University of Nebraska), PH.D. (Harvard University), *Professor of Mathematics and Head of Department*. Mathematics Building

DONALD LINDSAY ANDERSON, B.S. (University of Massachusetts), M.S. (University of Connecticut), PH.D. (Cornell University), *Assistant Professor of Poultry Husbandry*. Stockbridge Hall

JAMES FRANKLIN ANDERSON, B.S., M.S. (West Virginia University), *Instructor in Pomology*. French Hall

JOHN WILLIAM ANDERSON, B.S., M.B.A. (Indiana University), C.P.A. (Maine), *Assistant Professor of Accounting*. Draper Hall

THOMAS JOSEPH ANDREWS, B.S. (University of Massachusetts), A.M. (Williams College), *Assistant Professor of Zoology*. Fernald Hall

ROBESON BAILEY, A.B. (Harvard University), *Visiting Lecturer in English*. Chapel

2

RESIDENT FACULTY

JOHN HARRIS BAKER, B.S. (Cornell University),
Assistant Professor of Food Technology.   Hatch Laboratory

LOUIS NELSON BAKER, B.S. (University of New Hampshire), M.S. (University
of Kentucky), *Assistant Professor of Dairy and Animal Science.*
     . Stockbridge Hall

WALTER MILLER BANFIELD, B.S. (Rutgers University), PH.D. (University of
Wisconsin), *Assistant Professor of Botany.*   Clark Hall

LUTHER BANTA, B.S. (Cornell University),
Assistant Professor of Poultry Husbandry.   Stockbridge Hall

ROLLIN HAYES BARRETT, B.S. (University of Connecticut), M.S.
(Cornell University), *Professor of Farm Management.*   Draper Hall

LEON OSER BARRON, B.A. (University of Massachusetts), M.A. (University of
Minnesota), *Assistant Professor of English.*   Chapel

[1]LAWRENCE MATTHEWS BARTLETT, B.S., M.S. (University of Massachusetts),
PH.D. (Cornell University), *Associate Professor of Zoology.*

MAURICE EDWARD BATES, B.S.E. (M.E.) (University of Michigan), S.M.
(Massachusetts Institute of Technology), PH.D. (University of Michigan), *Professor of Mechanical Engineering.*   Engineering Building

DONALD FRANCIS BENTON, A.B. (Brown University), *Captain, USAFR,*
Assistant Professor of Air Science.   Drill Hall

MATTHEW LOUIS BLAISDELL, B.S. (University of Massachusetts), *Associate*
Professor, Superintendent of Farms and Head of Station Service.
     Stockbridge Hall

LYLE LINCOLN BLUNDELL, B.S. (Iowa State College),
Professor of Horticulture.   Wilder Hall

JAMES SALVATORE BOSCO, B.S. (Springfield College), M.S. (University of
Illinois), *Instructor in Physical Education.*
     Physical Education Building

HAROLD DANFORTH BOUTELLE, B.S., C.E. (Worcester Polytechnic Institute),
Associate Professor of Mathematics.   Mathematics Building

WILLIAM WELCH BOYER, B.S., C.E., M.S., C.E. (North Carolina State College),
Assistant Professor of Civil Engineering.   Engineering Building

GERARD BRAUNTHAL, B.A. (Queens College), M.A. (University of Michigan),
PH.D. (Columbia University), *Instructor in Government.*
     North College

LESLIE GLENN BRIDGES, B.S. (Boston University), *1st Lieutenant, USAFR,*
Assistant Professor of Air Science.   Drill Hall

LAWRENCE ELLIOTT BRIGGS, B.S., M.S. (University of Massachusetts),
Associate Professor of Physical Education.
     Physical Education Building

MILDRED BRIGGS, A.B. (DePauw University), M.S. (Iowa State College),
Associate Professor of Home Economics.   Edna Skinner Hall

RICHARD HOLBROOK BROWN, B.A., M.A., PH.D. (Yale University),
Instructor in History.   Engineering Building

---

[1]On leave of absence, second semester.

KENNETH LLOYD BULLIS, D.V.M. (Iowa State College), M.S. (University of Massachusetts), *Professor of Veterinary Science and Head of Department.* Paige Laboratory

JAMES WILLIAM BURKE, B.S. (University of Massachusetts), *Secretary of the University.* South College

BERNARD PHILIP BUSSEL, B.S. (University of Massachusetts), M.A. (Columbia University), *Instructor in Mathematics.* Mathematics Building

FRED VIRGIL CAHILL, JR., B.A., M.A. (University of Nebraska), PH.D. (Yale University), *Dean of the College of Arts and Science.* North College

THEODORE CUYLER CALDWELL, B.A. (College of Wooster), A.M. (Harvard University), PH.D. (Yale University), *Professor of History.* Chapel

JAMES WILLIAM CALLAHAN, B.S., M.S. (University of Massachusetts), *Instructor in Agricultural Economics.* Draper Hall

GEORGE WESLEY CANNON, B.A. (Dakota Wesleyan University), M.S., PH.D. (University of Illinois), *Associate Professor of Chemistry.*
Goessmann Laboratory

DOUGLAS CARMICHAEL, A.B. (Bowdoin College), A.M. (Harvard University), PH.D. (Indiana University), *Instructor in Philosophy.* North College

LOUIS ALBERT CARPINO, B.S. (Iowa State College), M.S., PH.D. (University of Illinois), *Instructor in Chemistry.* Goessmann Laboratory

ROBERT B. CARSON, B.S., M.S. (Pennsylvania State University), *Lecturer in Public Health.* Marshall Hall Annex

HAROLD WHITING CARY, A.B. (Williams College), A.M. (Harvard University), PH.D. (Yale University), *Professor of History and Head of Department.*
Chapel

KENNETH DELBERT CASHIN, B.S. in CH.E., M.S. in CH.E. (Worcester Polytechnic Institute), PH.D. (Rensselaer Polytechnic Institute), *Assistant Professor of Chemical Engineering.* Engineering Annex

[1]HARRY JOHN CHRISTOFFERS, B.S., M.S. (University of Washington), *Instructor in Chemistry.*

DAVID RIDGLEY CLARK, B.A. (Wesleyan University), M.A., PH.D. (Yale University), *Instructor in English.* Chapel

KATHERINE ALLEN CLARKE, A.B. (Goucher College), M.A. (Middlebury College), *Docteur de l'Universite de Grenoble, Associate Professor of French.* Liberal Arts Annex

EDWARD CLIFFORD, A.B. (Roosevelt College), M.A. (University of Chicago), *Instructor in Psychology.* Liberal Arts Annex

WILLIAM GEORGE COLBY, B.S.A. (University of Illinois), M.S., PH.D. (Rutgers University), *Professor of Agronomy and Head of Department.*
Stockbridge Hall

[2]ALTON BRIGHAM COLE, B.S. (University of Massachusetts), M.F. (Yale University), *Instructor in Forestry.*

DAN STEAD COLLINS, B.S. (University of Pennsylvania), M.A. (University of North Carolina), *Instructor in English.* Chapel

---
[1]On leave of absence.
[2]On leave of absence for military service.

RESIDENT FACULTY

RICHARD MOWRY COLWELL, B.S., M.S. (University of Rhode Island), PH.D.
(University of Massachusetts), *Associate Professor of Accounting.*
Draper Hall

JOSEPH CONTINO, B. MUS. (Oberlin College), M.A. (Columbia University),
Instructor in Music. Memorial Hall

MRS. GLADYS MAE COOK, B.S. (Battle Creek College), M.S. (University of
Massachusetts), *Assistant Professor of Home Economics.*
Edna Skinner Hall

ARMAND J. COSTA, B.A. (American International College),
Assistant Professor of Mechanical Engineering. Engineering Building

BENJAMIN CHARLES CROOKER, JR., B.S. (University of Massachusetts),
Instructor in Physics. Hasbrouck Laboratory

THOMAS ALOYSIUS CULBERTSON, B.S. (University of Massachusetts),
Assistant Professor of Food Technology. Hatch Laboratory

HELEN FRANCES CULLEN, A.B. (Radcliffe College), M.A., PH.D. (University
of Michigan), *Assistant Professor of Mathematics.*
Mathematics Building

ROBERT THOMAS CURRAN, B.S. in BUS.AD. (College of the Holy Cross),
Associate Professor of Physical Education.
Physical Education Building

REYNOLD BERNARD CZARNECKI, B.S. (Pennsylvania State University), M.S.,
PH.D. (University of Illinois), *Assistant Professor of Bacteriology.*
Marshall Hall Annex

DOROTHY DAVIS, B.S. (Syracuse University), M.A. (Columbia University),
Assistant Professor of Home Economics. Edna Skinner Hall

[1]EDWARD LYON DAVIS, A.B. (Harvard University), M.S. (University of
Massachusetts), *Instructor in Botany.*

WILLIAM ALLEN DAVIS, B.A. (Colgate University), A.M. (Harvard
University), *Associate Professor of History.* Chapel

MRS. VERA MARY HILLS DAY, B.A. (Denver University), M.S. (Iowa State
College), *Instructor in Home. Economics.* Edna Skinner Hall

ROBERT WILLIAM DAY, B.S. in M.E. (University of Massachusetts), M.M.E.
(Rensselaer Polytechnic Institute), *Assistant Professor of Mechanical
Engineering.* Gunness Laboratory

LAWRENCE SUMNER DICKINSON, B.S., M.S. (University of Massachusetts),
Professor of Agrostology. Stockbridge Hall

WILLIAM MOORE DIETEL, A.B. (Princeton University), M.A.
(Yale University), *Instructor in History.* Engineering Building

GELLESTRINA TERESA DIMAGGIO, A.B. (Connecticut College for Women),
M.A. (Columbia University), M.N. (Yale University), *Instructor in
Nursing.* Engineering Building

JOHN HARLAND DITTFACH, B.M.E., M.S. (University of Minnesota),
Associate Professor of Mechanical Engineering. Gunness Laboratory

CATHERINE ANNE DOWER, B.A. (Hamline University), M.A. (Smith College),
Instructor in Education. Liberal Arts Annex

[1]On leave of absence.

266

EDWIN DOUGLAS DRIVER, A.B. (Temple University), M.A. (University of Pennsylvania), *Assistant Professor of Sociology.* North College

MRS. MARRON SHAW DUBOIS, B.A. (St. Lawrence University), *Instructor in English.* Chapel

DONALD EGGLESTON EASTLAKE, JR., B.S. in BUS.AD. (Lehigh University), *Lieutenant Colonel, Armor, U.S.A., Assistant Professor of Military Science and Tactics.* Drill Hall

FREDERICK HORTON EDWARDS, B.A.SC. (University of British Columbia), M.A.SC. (Nova Scotia Technical College), *Assistant Professor of Electrical Engineering.* Gunness Laboratory

FRED CHARLES ELLERT, B.S. (University of Massachusetts), M.A. (Amherst College), *Professor of German and Head of Department.* Liberal Arts Annex

J. MURRAY ELLIOT, B.S. (McGill University), M.S. (University of Vermont), *Assistant Professor of Dairy and Animal Science.* Stockbridge Hall

EDWARD DONALD EMERSON, B.S. in M.E. (Harvard University), M.M.E. (University of Delaware), *Assistant Professor of Mechanical Engineering.* Engineering Building

SEYMOUR EPSTEIN, B.A. (Brooklyn College), M.A., PH.D. (University of Wisconsin) *Assistant Professor of Psychology.* Liberal Arts Annex

DWIGHT EDMUND ERLICK, A.B. (Colby College), M.A., PH.D. (Columbia University), *Assistant Professor of Psychology.* Liberal Arts Annex

JOHN NELSON EVERSON, B.S., M.S. (University of Massachusetts), *Assistant Professor of Agronomy.* Stockbridge Hall

WILLIAM LANCELOT EWBANK, B.S. in ED. (Kansas State Teachers College). *Lieutenant Colonel, USAF, Assistant Professor of Air Science.* Drill Hall

ROBERT SIMION FELDMAN, B.S., M.S.; PH.D. (University of Michigan), *Associate Professor of Psychology.* Liberal Arts Annex

CARL RAYMOND FELLERS, A.B. (Cornell University), M.S., PH.D. (Rutgers University), *Professor of Food Technology and Head of Department.* Chenoweth Laboratory

TUAUN HUA FENG, B.S. in C.E. (National Pei-Yang University), M.S., PH.D. (University of Wisconsin), *Assistant Professor of Civil Engineering.* Engineering Building

EDWARD GLENN FENNELL, B.S., M.S. (Bucknell University), ED.D. (Cornell University), *Assistant Professor of Education.* Liberal Arts Annex

JAMES M. FERRIGNO, A.B., A.M., PH.D. (Boston University), *Associate Professor of Romance Languages.* Liberal Arts Annex

RICHARD WILLIAM FESSENDEN, B.S., M.S. (University of Massachusetts). PH.D. (Columbia University), *Professor of Inorganic Chemistry.* Goessmann Laboratory

[2]GORDON FIELD, B.S., M.S. (University of Massachusetts), *Instructor in Entomology.*

---

[2]On leave of absence for military service.

267

ROY MARSHALL FISHER, A.B. (Clark University),
Assistant Professor of Physics. Hasbrouck Laboratory

RICHARD CAROL FOLEY, B.S., M.S. (University of Massachusetts), PH.D. (Rutgers University), *Professor of Dairy and Animal Science.*
Stockbridge Hall

WILLIAM FOOTRICK, B.S., M.P.E. (Springfield College), *Associate Professor of Physical Education.* Physical Education Building

JULIAN M. FORE, B.SC. (Virginia Polytechnic Institute), M.S. (Purdue University), *Professor of Agricultural Engineering and Head of Department.* Stockbridge Hall

THOMAS WALTON FOX, B.S., M.S. (University of Massachusetts), PH.D. (Purdue University), *Professor of Poultry Husbandry and Head of Department.* Stockbridge Hall

CHARLES FREDERIC FRAKER, JR., A.B. (University of Massachusetts), B.MUS. (Yale University), M.A. (Middlebury College), *Instructor in Romance Languages.* Liberal Arts Annex

RALPH LYLE FRANCE, B.S. (University of Delaware), M.S. (University of Massachusetts), *Professor of Bacteriology and Head of Department.*
Marshall Hall

ARTHUR PERKINS FRENCH, B.S. (Ohio State University), M.S. (University of Massachusetts), PH.D. (University of Minnesota), *Professor of Pomology and Plant Breeding and Head of Department of Pomology.*
French Hall

PAUL ADELARD GAGNON, B.S. (University of Massachusetts), M.A. (Harvard University), *Instructor in History.* Chapel

PHILIP LYLE GAMBLE, B.S., M.A. (Wesleyan University), PH.D. (Cornell University), *Professor of Economics and Head of Department.*
North College

ROBERT VERRILL GANLEY, B.S. (University of Massachusetts), M.F. (Duke University), *Instructor in Forestry.* Conservation Building

RICHARD FRANKLIN GARBER, B.S. (Springfield College), M.ED. (Pennsylvania State University), *Instructor in Physical Education.*
Physical Education Building

MARY ELLEN MONICA GARVEY, B.S. (University of Massachusetts),
Associate Professor of Bacteriology. Marshall Hall Annex

ARCHIE PETER GAUTHIER, B.S. (Louisiana State University), *Lieutenant Colonel Armor, USA., Assistant Professor of Military Science and Tactics.* Drill Hall

RICHARD MCIVER GILLIS, B.B.A. (Tulane University), M.B.A. (University of Pennsylvania), *Assistant Professor of Business Finance.* Draper Hall

MARY ELIZABETH GILMORE, B.S. (Simmons College), M.S. (The Catholic University of America), *Associate Professor of Nursing.* Draper Hall

CHESTER STEPHEN GLADCHUK, B.S.ED. (Boston College),
Assistant Football Coach. Physical Education Building

STOWELL COOLIDGE GODING, A.B. (Dartmouth College), A.M. (Harvard University), PH.D. (University of Wisconsin), *Professor of French and Head of Department of Romance Languages.* Liberal Arts Annex

268

GEORGE BENJAMIN GODDARD, B.S. (University of Massachusetts),
Instructor in Floriculture. French Hall

MAXWELL HENRY GOLDBERG, B.S. (University of Massachusetts), M.A., PH.D.
(Yale University), *Professor of English and Head of Department.*
Chapel

GEORGE GOODWIN, JR., B.A. (Williams College), M.A., PH.D. (Harvard University), *Assistant Professor of Government.* North College

ALBERT EDWARD GOSS, B.A., M.A., PH.D. (State University of Iowa),
Associate Professor of Psychology. Liberal Arts Annex

SUMNER MELVIN GREENFIELD, A.B. (Boston College), A.M. (Boston University and Harvard University), *Instructor in Romance Languages*
Liberal Arts Annex

THOMAS AUGUSTUS GROW, B.S. (University of Connecticut), M.S. (Virginia Polytechnic Institute), *Assistant Professor of Civil Engineering.*
Engineering Building

LAWRENCE CARROLL HACKAMACK, B.A. (Culver-Stockton College), M.S. (Western Illinois State College), *Assistant Professor of Industrial Administration.* Draper Hall

WILLIAM HALLER, JR., A.B. (Amherst College), M.A., PH.D. (Columbia University), *Assistant Professor of Economics.* North College

TOM SHERMAN HAMILTON, JR., B.F.A. in LAND ARCH. (University of Illinois), *Assistant Professor of Landscape Architecture.* Wilder Hall

ROSS ELDON HAMLIN, B.S. (Purdue University),
Captain, USAF, Assistant Professor of Air Science. Drill Hall

DENZEL J. HANKINSON, B.S. (Michigan State University), M.S. (University of Connecticut), PH.D. (Pennsylvania State University), *Professor of Dairy and Animal Science and Head of Department.*
Flint Laboratory

[1]JOHN FRANCIS HANSON, B.S., M.S., PH.D. (University of Massachusetts),
Associate Professor of Insect Morphology.

HAROLD ERNEST HARDY, A.B. (Pomona College), PH.D. (University of Minnesota), *Professor of Marketing.* Draper Hall

RICHARDS HARRY HARRINGTON, B.S. (CH.E.), M.S. (CH.E.), SC.D. (University of Michigan), *Assistant Professor of Mechanical Engineering.*
Engineering Building

RICHARD HAVEN, A.B. (Harvard University), M.A. (Princeton University),
B.LITT. (Oxford University), *Instructor in English.* Chapel

SARAH LOUISE HAWES, B.S. (Northern Michigan College of Education), M.S. (Cornell University), *Instructor in Home Economics.*
Edna Skinner Hall

[1]VERNON PARKER HELMING, B.A. (Carleton College), PH.D. (Yale University),
Professor of English.

KARL NEWCOMB HENDRICKSON, B.S., M.S. (University of Maine), *Associate Professor of Civil Engineering.* Engineering Building

---

[1]On leave of absence, second semester.

ROBIN DAVID STEWART HIGHAM, A.B. (Harvard University), M.A. (Claremont Graduate School), *Instructor in History.* Chapel

ALBERT SEYMOUR HILL, A.B. (Boston University), A.M. (Harvard University), *Instructor in History.* Engineering Building

JAMES GERHARD HILL, Captain, Armor, *Assistant Professor of Military Science and Tactics.* Drill Hall

JOHN LORD HOBART, B.S. (University of Massachusetts), *Instructor in Dairy and Animal Science.* Stockbridge Hall

MRS. FLORIANA TARANTINO HOGAN, B.S., A.M., PH.D. (Boston University), *Instructor in English.* Chapel

ROBERT POWELL HOLDSWORTH, B.S. (Michigan State University), M.F. (Yale University), *Professor of Forestry and Head of Department.* Conservation Building

BRONISLAW MARK HONIGBERG, A.B., M.A., PH.D. (University of California), *Assistant Professor of Zoology.* Engineering Building

WALTER HOPKINS, B.S. in M.E. (University of Michigan), *Instructor in Mechanical Engineering.* Engineering Building

LEONTA GERTRUDE HORRIGAN, B.S. (University of Massachusetts), M.A. (Smith College), *Assistant Professor of English.* Chapel

MARSHALL CHAPMAN HOWARD, A.B. (Princeton University), PH.D. (Cornell University), *Assistant Professor of Economics.* North College

[1]ELISABETH VICKERY HUBBARD, B.S. (University of Wisconsin), M.A. (University of Chicago), *Instructor in Physical Education for Women.*

ALEXANDER HULL, JR., B.A., M.A. (University of Washington), *Instructor in French.* Liberal Arts Annex

ANGELO IANTOSCA, S.B. (Massachusetts Institute of Technology), *Visiting Lecturer in Public Health.* Marshall Hall Annex

FRED PAINTER JEFFREY, B.S. (Pennsylvania State University), M.S. (University of Massachusetts), *Associate Dean of the College of Agriculture and Director of the Stockbridge School.* Stockbridge Hall

RANDOLPH ANTHONY JESTER, B.S. (Virginia Polytechnic Institute), M.S. (Rutgers University), *Assistant Professor of Floriculture.* French Hall

WARREN IRVING JOHANSSON, B.S., M.S., PH.D. (University of Massachusetts), *Assistant Professor of Geology and Mineralogy.* Fernald Hall

ROBERT BROWN JOHNSON, A.B. (Ohio University), M.A., PH.D. (University of Wisconsin), *Assistant Professor of Romance Languages.* Liberal Arts Annex

WILLIAM BRADFORD JOHNSON, B.S. (Pennsylvania State University), M.S. (University of Massachusetts), *Instructor in Olericulture.* French Hall

SIDNEY KAPLAN, B.A. (College of the City of New York), M.A. (Boston University), *Assistant Professor of English.* Chapel

JOHN HOPKINS KARLSON, B.S. in E.E. (University of Wisconsin), M.S. in E.E. (Northwestern University), *Assistant Professor of Electrical Engineering.* Gunness Laboratory

---

[1]On leave of absence.

270

SOLIS LEIGHTER KATES, B.S., M.S. (College of the City of New York), PH.D. (Columbia University), *Professor of Clinical Psychology.*
Liberal Arts Annex

SIDNEY WILLIAM KAUFFMAN, B.S., M.ED. (Springfield College), *Professor of Physical Education and Head of Department of Physical Education for Men.* Physical Education Building

JOHN EUGENE KEEGAN, B. ARCH. (Yale University), *Instructor in Landscape Architecture.* Wilder Hall

CAROLYN HELEN KENDROW, B.S., M.S. (University of Massachusetts), *Instructor in Chemistry.* Goessmann Laboratory

CARL ANTON KEYSER, B.S. (Carnegie Institute of Technology), B.S., M.S. (Worcester Polytechnic Institute), *Professor of Metallurgy.*
Engineering Building

MILO KIMBALL, B.S. (Ohio Northern University), B.B.A., M.B.A. (Boston University), *Dean of the School of Business Administration.*
Draper Hall

CLARENCE WENDELL KING, B.A., M.A., PH.D. (Yale University), *Associate Professor of Sociology.* North College

GORDON STEPHENSON KING, B.S. (Michigan State University), *Assistant Professor of Arboriculture.* Wilder Hall

ROBERT McCUNE KINGDON, B.A. (Oberlin College), M.A., PH.D. (Columbia University), *Instructor in History.* Engineering Building

STANLEY KOEHLER, A.B., A.M. (Princeton University), A.M. (Harvard University), PH.D. (Princeton University), *Assistant Professor of English.*
Chapel

JAY HENRY KORSON, B.S. (Villanova College), M.A., PH.D. (Yale University), *Professor of Sociology and Head of Department.* North College

STEPHEN RAYMOND KOSAKOWSKI, *Instructor in Physical Education.* Physical Education Building

THEODORE THOMAS KOZLOWSKI, B.S. (Syracuse University), M.A., PH.D. (Duke University), *Professor of Botany and Head of Department.*
Clark Hall

JOHN ERIC LAESTADIUS, B.E.E., M.S. (The Polytechnic Institute of Brooklyn), *Assistant Professor of Electrical Engineering.* Engineering Building

ROBERT PHILIPS LANE, A.B. (Columbia University), A.M. (Harvard University), *Assistant Professor of English.* Chapel

JOSEPH WALTON LANGFORD, JR., B.S. (University of New Hampshire), S.M. (Massachusetts Institute of Technology), *Associate Professor of Electrical Engineering.* Engineering Building

MARSHALL OLIN LANPHEAR, B.S., M.S. (University of Massachusetts), *Registrar.* South College

EDWARD PETER LARKIN, B.S., M.S., PH.D. (University of Massachusetts), *Instructor in Public Health.* Marshall Hall Annex

HENRY ARTHUR LEA, B.S. in ED., M.A. (University of Pennsylvania), *Instructor in German.* Liberal Arts Annex

WALTER WILFRED LEE, M.B., M.D. (Toronto University), M.P.H. (Harvard University), *Lecturer in Public Health.* Marshall Hall Annex

ROBERT WARD LENTILHON, B.S. (University of Rhode Island), M.B.A. (Boston University), *Assistant Professor of Accounting.*   Draper Hall

ARTHUR SIDNEY LEVINE, B.S., M.S., PH.D. (University of Massachusetts), *Associate Professor of Food Technology.*   Chenoweth Laboratory

ARNOLD EDWIN LEVITT, B.A. (Reed College), M.A., PH.D. (Oregon State College), *Instructor in Chemistry.*   Goessmann Laboratory

HARRY GOTTFRED LINDQUIST, B.S. (University of Massachusetts), M.S. (University of Maryland), *Assistant Professor of Dairy and Animal Science.*
      Flint Laboratory

ADRIAN HERVE LINDSEY, B.S. (University of Illinois), M.S., PH.D. (Iowa State College), *Professor of Agricultural Economics and Head of Department of Agricultural Economics and Farm Management.* Draper Hall

EDGAR ERNEST LINDSEY, B.S. in CH.E. (Georgia School of Technology), D.ENG. (Yale University), *Professor of Chemical Engineering and Head of Department.*   Engineering Building

LOWELL EDWIN LINGO, B.E., M.E. (Yale University), *Assistant Professor of Electrical Engineering.*   Engineering Building

HENRY NELSON LITTLE, B.S. (Cornell University), M.S., PH.D. (University of Wisconsin), *Associate Professor of Chemistry.* Goessmann Laboratory

GIDEON ELEAZAR LIVINGSTON, B.A. (New York University), M.S., PH.D. (University of Massachusetts), *Assistant Professor of Food Technology.*
      Chenoweth Laboratory

ROBERT BLAIR LIVINGSTON, A.B. (Colorado College), M.A., PH.D. (Duke University), *Professor of Botany.*   Clark Hall

JOHN BAILEY LONGSTAFF, B.S. (United States Naval Academy), M.S. (Pennsylvania State University), *Associate Professor of Mechanical Engineering.*   Gunness Laboratory

EARL EASTMAN LORDEN, B.S., M.ED. (University of New Hampshire), *Professor of Physical Education.*   Physical Education Building

JAMES BUREN LUDTKE, B.A., M.A., PH.D. (State University of Iowa), *Associate Professor of Business Finance.*   Draper Hall

JOHN ALBERT MACCOMBIE, B.A. (Yale University), *Instructor in French.*   Liberal Arts Annex

WILLIAM PRESTON MACCONNELL, B.S. (University of Massachusetts), M.F. (Yale University), *Assistant Professor of Forestry.*
      Conservation Building

MARY ELIZABETH MACDONALD, A.B. (Emmanuel College), M.A. (Columbia University), *Associate Professor of Nursing.*   Engineering Building

IAN TENNANT MORRISON MACIVER, *Instructor in Landscape Architecture.*   Wilder Hall

JAMES EDWARD MACMONEGLE, JR., B.S. (University of Massachusetts), *Instructor in Physics.*   Hasbrouck Laboratory

ALBERT PIERPONT MADEIRA, A.B. (Bowdoin College), M.A. (University of New Hampshire), *Instructor in English.*   Chapel

MARY ANN MAHER, B.S., A.M. (Columbia University), *Professor of Nursing and Head of Division of Nursing.*   Engineering Building

272

Lewis Casper Mainzer, b.a. (New York University), m.a. (University of Chicago), *Instructor in Government.* North College

Manley Mandel, b.a. (Brooklyn College), m.s., ph.d. (Michigan State University), *Assistant Professor of Bacteriology.* Marshall Hall

John Francis Manfredi, b.s. (University of Pennsylvania), m.a., ph.d. (Harvard University), *Instructor in Sociology.* North College

Joseph Sol Marcus, b.s. (Worcester Polytechnic Institute), m.s. (University of Massachusetts), *Assistant Professor of Civil Engineering.* Engineering Building

Miner John Markuson, b.s. in arch. (University of Minnesota), *Associate Professor of Agricultural Engineering.* Stockbridge Hall

George Andrews Marston, b.s., c.e. (Worcester Polytechnic Institute), m.s. (University of Iowa), *Dean of the School of Engineering.* Engineering Building

Alfred Herman Mathieson, Jr., s.b. (State Teachers College, East Stroudsburg, Pennsylvania), m.a. (Columbia University), *Assistant Professor of Physics.* Hasbrouck Laboratory

Guenter H. Mattersdorff, a.b., a.m. (Harvard University), *Instructor in Economics.* North College

Rosslyn Clayton McCollor, b.a. (University of Minnesota), *Captain, USAFR, Assistant Professor of Air Science.* Drill Hall

Mrs. Jane Frances McCullough, b.s., m.s. (Ohio University), *Assistant Professor of Home Economics.* Edna Skinner Hall

Shannon McCune, b.a. (College of Wooster), m.a. (Syracuse University), ph.d. (Clark University), *Provost.* South College

Warren Pierce McGuirk, ph.b. (Boston College), ed.m. (Boston University), *Professor of Physical Education and Head of Division.* Physical Education Building

Earl James McWhorter, b.s. (Rensselaer Polytechnic Institute), ph.d. (Cornell University), *Instructor in Chemistry.* Goessmann Laboratory

[2]Guy Rene Mermier, a.b. (Lycee Champollion), certificat de littera-ture et civilisation americaine, diplome d'etudes superior (University de Grenoble), *Instructor in Romance Languages.* Liberal Arts Annex

Oreana Alma Merriam, b.s. (University of Vermont), m.s. (University of Massachusetts), *Associate Professor of Home Economics.* Edna Skinner Hall

Walter Eugene Mientka, b.s. (University of Massachusetts), m.a. (Columbia University), ph.d. (University of Colorado), *Instructor in Mathematics.* Mathematics Building

Harvey Alfred Miller, b.s. (University of Michigan), m.s. (University of Hawaii), ph.d., (Stanford University), *Instructor in Botany.* Clark Hall

[1]Helen Swift Mitchell, a.b. (Mt. Holyoke College), ph.d. (Yale University), *Dean of the School of Home Economics.* Edna Skinner Hall

[1]On leave of absence.
[2]On leave of absence for military service.

JOHN HOWARD MITCHELL, B.S. (Bowdoin College), A.M. (Harvard
University), *Assistant Professor of English.*   Chapel

JOHN WILLIAM MOHN, M.E. (Stevens Institute of Technology), B.S. (Worcester Polytechnic Institute), M.S. (Stanford University), *Associate Professor of Electrical Engineering.*   Engineering Building

JOHN GEORGE MONER, A.B. (Johns Hopkins University), M.A., PH.D. (Princeton University), *Instructor in Zoology.*   Marshall Hall

BRUCE ROBERT MORRIS, A.B. (Western Reserve University), M.A. (Ohio State University), PH.D. (University of Illinois), *Professor of Economics.*
North College

[1]DONALD EUGENE MOSER, A.B. (Amherst College), A.M. (Brown University),
Instructor in Mathematics.

ARTHUR BENSON MUSGRAVE, B.S., M.S. (Boston University), NIEMAN FELLOW
IN JOURNALISM (Harvard University), *Professor of Journalism.*
Chapel

CLAIR WAYLAND NAYLOR, PH.B., M.A. (Yale University),
Instructor in Mathematics.   Mathematics Building

CLAUDE CASSELL NEET, A.B. (University of California, Los Angeles), M.A.,
PH.D. (Clark University), *Professor of Psychology and Head of Department.*   Liberal Arts Annex

ALBERT BIGELOW NELSON, B.S. (Colby College), M.S. (Middlebury College),
Assistant Professor of Geology and Mineralogy.   Fernald Hall

NORTON HART NICKERSON, B.S. (University of Massachusetts), M.A. (University of Texas), PH.D. (Washington University), *Instructor in Botany.*
Clark Hall

ARTHUR ELLSWORTH NIEDECK, B.S. (Ithaca College), M.A. (Cornell University), *Professor of Speech and Head of Department.*
South College

WILLIAM BROWN NUTTING, B.S., M.S. (University of Massachusetts), PH.D.
(Cornell University), *Assistant Professor of Zoology.*   Fernald Hall

GEORGE JAMES OBERLANDER, B.S. (Tufts University), M.S. (University of
Massachusetts), *Instructor in Chemistry.*   Goessmann Laboratory

ANN HELEN O'DONNELL, B.S. (University of Vermont), M.S. (University of
Massachusetts), *Instructor in Education.*   Liberal Arts Annex

WILLIAM GREGORY O'DONNELL, B.S. (University of Massachusetts), M.A.,
PH.D. (Yale University), *Professor of English.*   Chapel

SALLY ANN OGILVIE, B.S., M.ED. (University of North Carolina),
Instructor in Physical Education for Women.   Drill Hall

HELEN FRANCES O'LEARY, B.S. in ED., ED.M. (Boston University),
Assistant Professor of Education.   Liberal Arts Annex

[1]CHARLES FRANK OLIVER, B.S., M.S. (University of Massachusetts),
Assistant Professor of Education.

CHARLES CHRISTOPHER O'ROURKE, B.S. (Boston College),
Head Coach.   Physical Education Building

---

[1]On leave of absence.

ELMER CLAYTON OSGOOD, C.E., D. ENG. (Rensselaer Polytechnic Institute), *Professor of Civil Engineering.* Engineering Building

RAYMOND HERMAN OTTO, B.S. (University of Massachusetts), M.L.A. (Harvard University), *Professor of Landscape Architecture and Head of Department.* Wilder Hall

[2]ERNEST MILFORD PARROTT, B.S. (Union University), M.S. (University of Massachusetts), PH.D. (University of Missouri), *Instructor in Chemistry.*

ROBERT KINCAID PATTERSON, B.S. (University of Maine), *Assistant Professor of Mechanical Engineering.* Gunness Laboratory

HENRY BROWN PEIRCE, JR., B.A. (University of Massachusetts), M.A. (University of Michigan), *Instructor in Speech.* South College

ROBERT CHARLES PERRIELLO, B.S. (University of Massachusetts), *Associate Professor of Bacteriology.* Marshall Hall

[1]OTTO PAUL PFLANZE, B.A. (Maryville College), M.A., PH.D. (Yale University), *Assistant Professor of History*

EDWARD STANLEY PIRA, B.S. (University of Connecticut), *Instructor in Agricultural Engineering.* Stockbridge Hall

[1]ROBERT AARON POTASH, A.B., A.M., PH.D. (Harvard University), *Assistant Professor of History*

FRANK ELWOOD POTTER, B.S. (University of Maine), M.S. (University of Maryland), *Assistant Professor of Dairy and Animal Science.* Flint Laboratory

ALFRED XAVIER POWERS, B.S. in ED. (Fitchburg State Teachers College), *Instructor in Agricultural Engineering.* Stockbridge Hall

WALLACE FRANK POWERS, A.B., A.M., PH.D. (Clark University), *Professor of Physics and Head of Department.* Hasbrouck Laboratory

PAUL NICHOLAS PROCOPIO, B.S., M.S. (University of Massachusetts), *Assistant Professor of Horticulture.* Wilder Hall

ALBERT WILLIAM PURVIS, A.B. (University of New Brunswick), M.ED., D.ED. (Harvard University), *Professor of Education and Head of Department.* Liberal Arts Annex

EUGENE CHARLES PUTALA, B.S., M.S. (University of Massachusetts), *Assistant Professor of Botany.* Clark Hall

FRANK PRENTICE RAND, A.B. (Williams College), A.M. (Amherst College), L.H.D. (University of Massachusetts), *Professor of English.* Chapel

WILLIAM EDWIN RANDALL, JR., B.S. (University of Massachusetts), M.S., PH.D. (University of Wisconsin), *Associate Professor of Recreation Leadership.* North College

HAROLD RAUCH, B.S. (Queens College), M.S. (University of Illinois), PH.D. (Brown University), *Assistant Professor of Zoology.* Fernald Hall

GEORGIA REID, B.S. (State University of New York at Cortland), *Instructor in Physical Education for Women.* Drill Hall

---

[1]On leave of absence.

[2] On leave of absence for military service.

RAMON J. RHINE, A.B. (University of California, Berkeley), M.S. (University of Oregon), PH.D. (Stanford University), *Instructor in Psychology.* Liberal Arts Annex

ARNOLD DENSMORE RHODES, B.S. (University of New Hampshire), M.F. (Yale University), *Professor of Forestry.* Conservation Building

BENJAMIN RICCI, JR., B.S., M.ED. (Springfield College), *Assistant Professor of Physical Education.* Physical Education Building

THOMAS EDWIN RICE, B.S. (University of Massachusetts), *Instructor in Geology and Mineralogy.* Fernald Hall

JOSEPH HARRY RICH, B.S., M.F. (New York State College of Forestry), *Associate Professor of Forestry.* Conservation Building

GEORGE ROBERT RICHASON, JR., B.S., M.S. (University of Massachusetts), *Assistant Professor of Chemistry.* Goessmann Laboratory

MAIDA LEONARD RIGGS, B.S. (University of Massachusetts), *Instructor in Physical Education for Women.* Drill Hall

WALTER STUNTZ RITCHIE, B.S. (Ohio State College), A.M., PH.D. (University of Missouri), *Goessmann Professor of Chemistry and Head of Department.* Goessmann Laboratory

[1]ROBERT LOUIS RIVERS, A.B. (Clark University), M.S. (University of Illinois), *Assistant Professor of Industrial Administration.*

JOHN EDWIN ROBERTS, B.S., M.S. (University of New Hampshire), PH.D. (Cornell University), *Assistant Professor of Chemistry.*
Goessmann Laboratory

JOHN LEWIS ROBERTS, B.S., M.S. (University of Wisconsin), PH.D. (University of California), *Assistant Professor of Physiology.* Marshall Hall

OLIVER COUSENS ROBERTS, B.S. (University of Massachusetts), M.S. (University of Illinois), *Associate Professor of Pomology.* French Hall

GRACE ROBERTSON, A.B. (Barnard College), M.S. (Smith College), *Instructor in Physical Education for Women.* Drill Hall

NEWTON YOUNG ROBINSON, B.S., M.S. (Columbia University), *Instructor in Business Administration.* Draper Hall

DONALD WILLIAM ROGERS, B.S. (Northwestern University), M.A., PH.D. (Yale University), *Assistant Professor of Philosophy.* North College

JOSEPH RICHARD ROGERS, JR., *Associate Professor of Physical Education.*
Physical Education Building

HERBERT DUNCAN ROLLASON, JR., A.B. (Middlebury College), M.A. (Williams College), A.M., PH.D. (Harvard University), *Assistant Professor of Zoology.* Fernald Hall

ISRAEL HAROLD ROSE, B.A., M.A. (Brooklyn College), PH.D. (Harvard University), *Associate Professor of Mathematics.* Mathematics Building

DONALD ERNEST ROSS, B.S. (University of Massachusetts), *Assistant Professor of Floriculture.* French Hall

WILLIAM HAROLD ROSS, B.A., M.A. (Amherst College), PH.D. (Yale University), *Associate Professor of Physics.* Hasbrouck Laboratory

---

[1]On leave of absence.

WILLIAM MARTIN ROURKE, B.A. (Beloit College), M.S. (Northwestern University), *Assistant Professor of Education.*   Liberal Arts Annex

CARL SHERWOOD ROYS, B.S. (Worcester Polytechnic Institute), M.S. in E.E., PH.D. (Purdue University), *Professor of Electrical Engineering and Head of Department.*   Engineering Building

SEYMOUR RUDIN, B.A., M.S. (College of the City of New York), PH.D. (Cornell University), *Instructor in English.*   Chapel

SARGENT RUSSELL, B.S. (University of Maine), M.S. (Cornell University), *Assistant Professor of Agricultural Economics.*   Draper Hall

STANLEY FRANCIS SALWAK, B.S., M.S. (University of Massachusetts), D.ED. (Pennsylvania State University), *Assistant Professor of Physical Education.*   Physical Education Building

WILLIAM CROCKER SANCTUARY, B.S., M.S. (University of Massachusetts), *Professor of Poultry Husbandry.*   Stockbridge Hall

RICHARD CHASE SAVAGE, B.A. (University of North Carolina), M.A. (Columbia University), *Instructor in English.*   Chapel

HENRY HERBERT SCARBOROUGH, JR., B.S. (University of Texas), *Instructor in Botany.*   Clark Hall

EVA SCHIFFER, B.S. (University of Massachusetts), A.M. (Radcliffe College), *Instructor in German.*   Liberal Arts Annex

SIDNEY SCHOEFFLER, B.S. (New York University), A.M. (University of Pennsylvania), PH.D. (The New School for Social Research), C.P.A. (New Jersey), *Associate Professor of Economics.*   North College

NORMAN JAMES SCHOONMAKER, B.S. (University of Massachusetts), S.M. (University of Chicago), PH.D. (University of Pittsburgh), *Assistant Professor of Mathematics.*   Mathematics Building

ADOLF ERNST SCHROEDER, B.A. (University of Illinois), M.A. (Louisiana State University), PH.D. (Ohio State University), *Associate Professor of German.*   Liberal Arts Annex

ARNOLD GIDEON SHARP, B.S. in M.E. (Tufts University), M.S. in M.E. (Worcester Polytechnic Institute), *Assistant Professor of Civil Engineering.*   Gunness Laboratory

FRANK ROBERT SHAW, B.S. (University of Massachusetts), PH.D. (Cornell University), *Associate Professor of Entomology and Beekeeping.*   Fernald Hall

FRANK RUSSELL SHAW, B.E., C.E. (Tulane University), *Lecturer in Public Health.*   Marshall Hall Annex

LAWRENCE WILLIAM SHERMAN, JR., B.S. (Miami University), M.B.A. (Indiana University), *Assistant Professor of Marketing.*   Draper Hall

CLARENCE SHUTE, A.B. (Asbury College), A.M., PH.D. (Columbia University), *Professor of Philosophy.*   North College

DALE HAROLD SIELING, B.S., M.S. (Kansas State College), PH.D. (Iowa State College), *Dean of the College of Agriculture and Direc..r of the Experiment Station.*   East Experiment Station

FRANK ALBERT SINGER, B.S., M.B.A., D.B.A. (Indiana University), *Assistant Professor of Accounting.*   Draper Hall

277

HENRY HILLS SKILLINGS, A.B. (Amherst College), M.A. (Boston University),
Instructor in Mathematics. Mathematics Building

HAROLD WILLIAM SMART, A.B. (Amherst College), LL.B. (Boston University),
Associate Professor of Business Law. Draper Hall

J. HAROLD SMITH, B.S., M.A. (University of Utah), PH.D. (University
of Wisconsin), *Professor of Chemistry.* Goessmann Laboratory

MARION ESTELLE SMITH, B.S., M.S. (University of Massachusetts), PH.D.
(University of Illinois), *Assistant Professor of Entomology.*
Fernald Hall

RUSSELL EATON SMITH, B.S. (University of Massachusetts), V.M.D. (University of Pennsylvania), *Professor of Veterinary Science.*
Paige Laboratory

[1]WALTER WORCESTER SMITH, B.E.E. (Northeastern University),
Assistant Professor of Electrical Engineering.

[1]JAMES GEORGE SNEDECOR, B.S. (Iowa State College), PH.D. (Indiana
University), *Associate Professor of Physiology.*

ERNEST AUGUSTUS SNOW, B.S., M.S. (Harvard University),
Lecturer in Public Health. Fernald Hall

DANA PAUL SNYDER, B.S., M.S. (University of Illinois), PH.D. (University of
Michigan), *Instructor in Zoology.* Fernald Hall

GRANT BINGEMAN SNYDER, B.S.A. (University of Toronto), M.S. (Michigan
State University), *Professor of Olericulture and Head of Department.*
French Hall

DANIEL SOBALA, S.B. (Massachusetts Institute of Technology), *Assistant
Professor of Mechanical Engineering.* Engineering Building

ARTHUR ABRAHAM SOCOLOW, B.S. (Rutgers University), M.A., PH.D. (Columbia University), *Assistant Professor of Geology and Mineralogy.*
Fernald Hall

ODDVAR SOLSTAD, B.S. (Tufts University), M.S. (University of Massachusetts),
Instructor in Chemical Engineering. Engineering Annex

RICHARD ARTHUR SOUTHWICK, B.S., M.S. (University of Vermont),
Instructor in Agronomy. Stockbridge Hall

EDMUND JOSEPH STAWIECKI, B.S. (University of Massachusetts), M.A. (University of Iowa), *Instructor in German.* Liberal Arts Annex

ROBERT J. STEAMER, B.A. (Bucknell University), M.A. (University of Virginia), PH.D. (Cornell University), *Instructor in Government.*
North College

RICHARD STEPHEN STEIN, B.S. (Brooklyn Polytechnic Institute), M.A., PH.D.
(Princeton University), *Assistant Professor of Chemistry.*
Goessmann Laboratory

MARY JANE STRATTNER, B.S. (College of St. Elizabeth), M.A. (University of
Minnesota), *Assistant Professor of Home Economics.* Edna Skinner Hall

HARVEY LEROY SWEETMAN, B.S. (Colorado State College), M.S. (Iowa State
College), PH.D. (University of Massachusetts), *Professor of Entomology.*
Fernald Hall

---

[1]On leave of absence.

JOHN DAVID SWENSON, B.S. (New York University), M.A. (Columbia University), *Professor of Mechanical Engineering.*   Gunness Laboratory

PAUL ARTHUR SWENSON, B.S. (Hamline University), PH.D. (Stanford University), *Assistant Professor of Physiology.*   Marshall Hall

WILLIAM HENRY TAGUE, B.S. (Iowa State College), *Assistant Professor of Agricultural Engineering.*   Stockbridge Hall

RAYMOND PORTER TARR, JR., *Colonel, Infantry, U.S.A., Professor of Military Science and Tactics and Head of Division.*   Drill Hall

CLARK LEONARD THAYER, B.S. (University of Massachusetts), *Professor of Floriculture and Head of Department.*   French Hall

[1]MRS. EMILY PERRY THIES, B.S. (Michigan State University), M.S. (Cornell University), *Instructor in Home Economics.*

[1]ZINA JOAN TILLONA, B.A. (Hunter College), M.A. (Wellesley College), *Instructor in Romance Languages.*   Liberal Arts Annex

GLENN ERIN TINDER, B.A., M.A. (Pomona College), PH.D. (University of California), *Assistant Professor of Government.*   North College

RAY ETHAN TORREY, B.S. (University of Massachusetts), A.M., PH.D. (Harvard University), *Professor of Botany.*   Clark Hall

RUTH JANE TOTMAN, B.S. (Douglass College), M.ED. (University of Pittsburgh), *Professor and Director of Physical Education for Women.*   Drill Hall

HENRY IRVING TRAGLE, *Major, Armor, U.S.A., Assistant Professor of Military Science and Tactics.*   Drill Hall

JAY R TRAVER, B.A., M.A., PH.D. (Cornell University), *Assistant Professor of Zoology.*   Fernald Hall

REUBEN EDWIN TRIPPENSEE, B.S. (Michigan State University), M.S., PH.D. (University of Michigan), *Professor of Wildlife Management.*   Conservation Building

ROBERT FREDERICK TROCCHI, B.S. in E.E. (University of Massachusetts), *Instructor in Electrical Engineering.*   Engineering Building

FREDERICK SHERMAN TROY, B.S. (University of Massachusetts), M.A. (Amherst College), *Professor of English.*   Chapel

[1]ROBERT GARLAND TUCKER, A.B. (Amherst College), A.M. (Harvard University), *Instructor in English.*   Chapel

ALDEN PARKER TUTTLE, B.S. (University of Massachusetts), M.S. (Pennsylvania State University), *Assistant Professor of Vegetable Gardening.*   French Hall

JOHN EDWARD TYLER, JR., A.B., A.M. (College of the Holy Cross), *Instructor in Chemistry.*   Goessmann Laboratory

STANLEY VANCE, B.A. (St. Charles College), A.M., PH.D. (University of Pennsylvania), *Professor of Industrial Administration.*   Draper Hall

HENRY LELAND VARLEY, A.B., A.M. (Wesleyan University), PH.D. (University of Wisconsin), *Associate Professor of English.*   Chapel

ANA MARGARITA VEUM, PROFESSORA NORMAL CON ESPECIALIDAD EN INGLES, *Instructor in Romance Languages.*   Liberal Arts Annex

[1]On leave of absence.

JOHN HENRY VONDELL,
Associate Professor of Poultry Husbandry.   Stockbridge Hall

ROBERT WANNER WAGNER, A.B. (Ohio University), M.A., PH.D. (University of Michigan), *Professor of Mathematics.*   Mathematics Building

ESTHER MARIE WALLACE, B.S. (Boston University), M.S. (Wellesley College), *Instructor in Physical Education for Women.*   Drill Hall

NEAL THOMAS WATSON, B.A. (Duke University), A.M. (Harvard University), *Instructor in Mathematics.*   Mathematics Building

WILLIAM HENRY WEAVER, B.S. in I.E., M.S. in I.E., I.E. (Pennsylvania State University), *Professor of Mechanical Engineering and Head of Department.*   Engineering Building

JOHN AUGUST WEIDHAAS, JR., B.S., M.S. (University of Massachusetts), *Instructor in Entomology.*   Fernald Hall

GEORGE PHILIP WEIDMANN, B.S. (College of the City of New York), M.A. (Columbia University), *Assistant Professor of Mechanical Engineering.*   Engineering Building

HAROLD GEORGE WELLS, JR., B.S. (University of Connecticut), *Major, USAFR, Assistant Professor of Air Science.*   Drill Hall

CECILIA WELNA, B.S. (St. Joseph's College), M.A. (University of Connecticut), *Instructor in Mathematics.*   Mathematics Building

SIDNEY FREDERICK WEXLER, B.S. (New York University), M.A. (University of Colorado), PH.D. (New York University), *Assistant Professor of Romance Languages.*   Liberal Arts Annex

DONALD BATES WHITE, B.B.A. (The University of Texas), Colonel, USAF, *Professor of Air Science and Head of Division.*   Drill Hall

MERIT PENNIMAN WHITE, A.B., C.E. (Dartmouth College), M.S., PH.D. (California Institute of Technology), *Professor of Civil Engineering and Head of Department.*   Engineering Building

MRS. MARGARET KOERBER WILHELM, B.S., M.S. (University of Massachusetts), *Assistant Professor of Home Economics.*   Edna Skinner Hall

THOMAS OBERSON WILKINSON, A.B. (University of North Carolina), M.A. (Duke University), *Instructor in Sociology.*   North College

ROBERT ERWIN WILL, B.A. (Carleton College), M.A. (Yale University), *Instructor in Economics.*   North College

ARTHUR ROBERT WILLIAMS, A.B. (Clark University), A.M., PH.D. (Cornell University), *Assistant Professor of English.*   Chapel

HENRY RITCHIE WILSON, *Major Armor, U.S.A., Assistant Professor of Military Science and Tactics.*   Drill Hall

LEONARD RICHARD WILSON, PH.B., PH.M., PH.D. (University of Wisconsin), *Professor of Geology and Mineralogy and Head of Department.*   Fernald Hall

KAROL STANLEY WISNIESKI, B.S. (University of Massachusetts), M.P.H. (University of Michigan), *Instructor in Bacteriology.* Marshall Hall Annex

BERTRAM GEORGE WOODLAND, B.SC. (University College of South Wales and Monmouthshire, Cardiff, Wales), *Assistant Professor in Geology and Mineralogy.*   Fernald Hall

GILBERT LLEWELLYN WOODSIDE, B.A. (DePauw University), A.M., PH.D. (Harvard University), *Professor of Biology and Head of Department of Zoology; Dean of Graduate School.* Fernald Hall

HENRY BRONISLAW WORONICZ, B.S. (Boston College), *Instructor in Physical Education.* Physical Education Building

MRS. MARTHA ROCKHOLD WRIGHT, B.S. (Miami University), *Instructor in English.* Chapel

RAYMOND WYMAN, B.S. (University of Massachusetts), ED.M. (Boston University), *Assistant Professor of Education and Director, Audio Visual Center.* South College

[1]ANTHONY WILLIAM ZAITZ, B.S.O. (Curry College), M.A. (Boston University), *Assistant Professor of Speech.*

JOHN MICHAEL ZAK, B.S., M.S. (University of Massachusetts), *Assistant Professor of Agronomy.* Stockbridge Hall

JOHN KARL ZEENDER, B.A., M.A. (The Catholic University of America), PH.D. (Yale University), *Assistant Professor of History.* Chapel

PART TIME FACULTY

DAVID CHARLES BARTLETT, B.S. in C.E. (University of Massachusetts), *Instructor in Civil Engineering.* Engineering Building

RUFUS T. BELLAMY, B.A., M.A. (Yale University), *Instructor in English.* Chapel

EDWARD PHILBROOK CLANCY, B.S. (Beloit College), A.M., PH.D. (Harvard University), *Visiting Lecturer in Physics.* Hasbrouck Laboratory

NORMAN L. CLOUTIER, *Visiting Lecturer in Speech.* South College

DAVID GERE DAMON, B.S. (University of Massachusetts), *Instructor in Physical Education.* Physical Education Building

GEORGE BLANDING DYER, JR., B.S. (Springfield College), *Instructor in Physical Education.* Physical Education Building

MRS. ALICE HOPPER EPSTEIN, B.S. (Douglass College), M.S. (University of Wisconsin), *Instructor in Mathematics.* Mathematics Building

NORMAN KENNETH ERICKSON, B.A. (University of Connecticut), *Instructor in Geology and Mineralogy.* Fernald Hall

MRS. KATHERINE LOUISE ESSELEN, B.S., M.S. (University of Massachusetts), *Instructor in Home Economics.* Edna Skinner Hall

RALPH WINTHROP GOODRICH, B.S. (University of New Hampshire), M.A. (University of Connecticut), *Visiting Lecturer in Education.* Liberal Arts Annex

LOUIS SIMPSON GREENBAUM, B.A., M.A. (University of Wisconsin), PH.D. (Harvard University), *Instructor in History.* Engineering Building

NORMAN GREENFELD, B.A., M.A. (Syracuse University), M.S. (University of Massachusetts), *Instructor in Psychology.* Liberal Arts Annex

MRS. MARY E. W. GOSS, B.A., M.A. (State University of Iowa), *Instructor in Sociology.* North College

LLOYD FRANKLIN HAYN, B.A. (Wesleyan University), M.A. (Boston University), *Professor of Economics.* North College

[1]On leave of absence.

281

WILLIAM CARRITHERS HODAPP, A.B. (Centre College), M.A. (University of Indiana), *Visiting Lecturer in Speech.*   South College

RICHARD FIELD JACKSON, B.S., M.S. (University of Massachusetts), *Instructor in Food Technology.*   Chenoweth Laboratory

MRS. VILMA VERONICA JOA, B.S. (University of Tartu), *Instructor in Russian.*   Liberal Arts Annex

JANE T. JUDGE, B.A. (Mt. Holyoke College), M.A. (Smith College), *Instructor in Chemistry.*   Goessmann Laboratory

ROUBEN KHATCHIKIAN, B.S. (Syracuse University), M.S. (University of Tennessee), *Instructor in Food Technology.*   Chenoweth Laboratory

RAUNO ANDREW LAMPI, B.S., M.S. (University of Massachusetts), *Instructor in Food Technology.*   Chenoweth Laboratory

DAVID PHELPS LEONARD, B.A. (Brown University), M.A., PH.D. (University of Michigan), *Visiting Lecturer in History.*   Chapel

MRS. IOLE FIORILLO MAGRI, DOCTOR IN MODERN LANGUAGES (Catholic University of Milan, Italy), M.A. (Mt. Holyoke College), *Instructor in Romance Languages.*   Liberal Arts Annex

IRA MINTZ, B.A. (Long Island University), M.A. (New York University), *Instructor in Psychology.*   Liberal Arts Annex

CLIFFORD NORTON OLIVER, A.B. (Bates College), M.S. (University of Massachusetts), *Instructor in Mathematics.*   Mathematics Building

MURRAY BISBEE PEPPARD, B.A. (Amherst College), M.A., PH.D. (Yale University), *Visiting Lecturer in German.*   Liberal Arts Annex

MRS. LOUISE E. RICE, A.B. (University of Massachusetts), *Instructor in Mathematics.*   Mathematics Building

JEAN ROBERT ROUGE, LICENCE D'ANGLAIS; DIPLOME D'ETUDES SUPERIEURES D'ANGLAIS (Universite de Paris), *Instructor in Romance Languages.*
                                                                    Liberal Arts Annex

VERA A. SICKELS, B.S., M.A. (Columbia University), *Visiting Lecturer in Speech.*   South College

ALVIN JOSEPH SIMMONS, B.S. (Boston College), M.S. (University of Massachusetts), *Instructor in Psychology.*   Liberal Arts Annex

ROBERT L. STAFFANSON, B.M., M.M. (Montana State University), *Instructor in Music.*   Memorial Hall

MRS. MARJORIE FIELD SULLIVAN, B.S. in ED. (Framingham State Teachers College), *Instructor in Home Economics.*   Edna Skinner Hall

MRS. MARY LOUISE TAPP, B.A. (College of St. Rose), M.A. (Middlebury College), *Instructor in German.*   Liberal Arts Annex

EUGENE JOSEPH TYNAN, B.S. (University of Connecticut), *Instructor in Geology and Mineralogy.*   Fernald Hall

ALBERT WILLIS WALLACE, B.S. (Northeastern University), *Instructor in Mathematics.*   Mathematics Building

MRS. FRANCES L. WARNE, B.S. (Cornell University), M.S. (University of Massachusetts), *Instructor in Home Economics.*   Edna Skinner Hall

MARGARET SCOON WILSON, B.A., M.A. (Cornell University), PH.D. (University of Pennsylvania), *Visiting Lecturer in Sociology.*   North College

TEACHING FELLOWS

AHMAD SAID AROURI, B.A. (American International College),
Teaching Fellow in Economics.   North College

FRANK ROWLAND BRIDGES, JR., B.A. (Norwich University), M.S. (University
of Massachusetts), *Teaching Fellow in Bacteriology and Public Health.*
Marshall Hall

JAMES WARREN CHADWICK, JR., B.S. (University of Massachusetts),
Teaching Fellow in Wildlife Management.   Conservation Building

EDWARD JOSEPH CONNORS, JR., B.S. (Marquette University),
Teaching Fellow in Business Administration.   Draper Hall

EVAN CLAIR CRAFTS, B.S. (University of Maine),
Teaching Fellow in Entomology.   Fernald Hall

PAUL JOSEPH CROWLEY, B.S. (University of Massachusetts),
Teaching Fellow in Chemistry.   Goessmann Laboratory

FRANK PETER DI GAMMARINO, B.A. (University of Massachusetts),
Teaching Fellow in Education.   Liberal Arts Annex

RONALD JOSEPH FITZGERALD, B.S. (University of Massachusetts),
Teaching Fellow in Education.   Liberal Arts Annex

CHESTER ANTHONY GIZA, B.S. (University of Massachusetts),
Teaching Fellow in Chemistry.   Goessmann Laboratory

CHARLES LEWIS GOLDMAN, B.S. (Providence College), M.S. (Tufts University), *Teaching Fellow in Bacteriology and Public Health.*
Marshall Hall

SANFORD GOLIN, B.A. (Brown University),
Teaching Fellow in Psychology.   Liberal Arts Annex

JOHN SYLVESTER HALL, B.S. (University of Massachusetts),
Teaching Fellow in Zoology.   Fernald Hall

EDWARD MAURICE HEFFERNAN, B.S. (University of Massachusetts),
Teaching Fellow in Bacteriology and Public Health   Marshall Hall

ALLEN WENTWORTH HIXON, JR., B.S. (University of Massachusetts),
Teaching Fellow in Landscape Architecture.   Wilder Hall

HERBERT MARCUS KAGAN, B.S. (University of Massachusetts),
Teaching Fellow in Bacteriology and Public Health.   Marshall Hall

JOHN FREDERICK KEITH, B.A. (American International College),
Teaching Fellow in Education..   Liberal Arts Annex

WILLIAM THOMAS KENNEDY, B.A. (Adelphi College),
Teaching Fellow in Chemistry.   Goessmann Laboratory

ROBERT JAMES LAVIGNE, B.A. (American International College),
Teaching Fellow in Entomology.   Fernald Hall

JOHN JOSEPH LEE, B.S. (Queens College),
Teaching Fellow in Zoology.   Fernald Hall

HARRY ALDEN LEFFINGWELL, B.A. (University of Rochester),
Teaching Fellow in Geology and Mineralogy.   Fernald Hall

DONALD GEORGE LE GRAND, B.A. (Boston University),
Teaching Fellow in Chemistry.   Goessmann Laboratory

NORMAN HENRY MACLEOD, B.A. (University of Chicago),
Teaching Fellow in Agronomy.   Stockbridge Hall

TEACHING FELLOWS

ROBERT PHILIP McMAHON, B.B.A. (University of Massachusetts),
Teaching Fellow in School of Business Administration. Draper Hall

NOEL JACOB REEBENACKER, B.S. (University of Massachusetts),
Teaching Fellow in Education. Liberal Arts Annex

GLEN ERNEST ROSS, B.A. (University of Colorado),
Teaching Fellow in English. Chapel

RALPH ROTHSTEIN, B.A. (University of Michigan),
Teaching Fellow in Psychology. Liberal Arts Annex

BERNARD L. RYACK, B.S. (University of Connecticut), M.A. (University of
Pennsylvania), *Teaching Fellow in Psychology.* Liberal Arts Annex

JOSEPH DAVID SHORE, B.S. (Cornell University),
Teaching Fellow in Food Technology. Chenoweth Laboratory

SIDNEY GEORGE SPECTOR, B.A. (Harvard University), M.S. (University of
Massachusetts), *Teaching Fellow in Bacteriology and Public Health.*
Marshall Hall

PAUL TAYLOR, B.A. (Suffolk University),
Teaching Fellow in Chemistry Goessmann Laboratory

EARLE ALEXANDER TOMPKINS, JR., B.S. (University of Massachusetts),
Teaching Fellow in Zoology. Fernald Hall

JANE ANN VAN DYKE, B.A. (Beaver College),
Teaching Fellow in Psychology. Liberal Arts Annex

MADELEINE MARIE ODETTE VUATEAU, B.A. (Jeanne de France, Nice),
Teaching Fellow in Romance Languages. Liberal Arts Annex

ENRIQUE YANEZ (CORTEZ), B.S. (Facultad de Agrono-mia, Universidad
Nacional), *Teaching Fellow in Food Technology.*
Chenoweth Laboratory

CHARLES ZAPSALIS, B.S. (Springfield College),
Teaching Fellow in Food Technology Chenoweth Laboratory

284

EXPERIMENT STATION STAFF

DALE HAROLD SIELING, B.S., M.S. (Kansas State College), PH.D. (Iowa State College), *Dean of the College of Agriculture and Director of the Experiment Station.* East Experiment Station

DONALD LINDSAY ANDERSON, B.S. (University of Massachusetts), M.S. (University of Connecticut), PH.D. (Cornell University), *Assistant Research Professor of Poultry Husbandry.* Stockbridge Hall

EDWARD EVERETT ANDERSON, B.S., M.S., PH.D. (University of Massachusetts), *Associate Professor, Research, Food Technology.* Chenoweth Laboratory

JOHN GEDDIE ARCHIBALD, B.S. (Toronto University), M.S. (University of Massachusetts), *Professor, Research, Dairy and Animal Science.* Goessmann Laboratory

JOHN SEARLS BAILEY, B.S. (Michigan State University), M.S. (Iowa State College), *Associate Professor, Research, Cranberry Station.* East Wareham

ALLEN BROWN BARTON, B.S. (University of Minnesota), M.S. (University of Connecticut), *Associate Professor, Research, Agricultural Engineering.* Stockbridge Hall

WILLIAM BERNARD BECKER, B.S. (New York State College of Forestry), M.S., PH.D. (University of Massachusetts), *Assistant Professor, Research, Entomology.* Fernald Hall

EMMETT BENNETT, B.S. (Ohio State University), M.S. (University of Massachusetts), PH.D. (Pennsylvania State University), *Professor, Research, Chemistry.* Goessmann Laboratory

WALLACE GORDON BLACK, B.S., M.S., PH.D. (University of Wisconsin), *Associate Professor, Research, Dairy and Animal Science.* Stockbridge Hall

MATTHEW LOUIS BLAISDELL, B.S. (University of Massachusetts), *Associate Professor; Superintendent of Farms and Head of Station Service.* Stockbridge Hall

PAUL FREDERICK BOBULA, B.S. (University of Massachusetts), M.S. (Ohio State University), *Instructor, Research, Nursery Culture.* Waltham Field Station

MRS. BERYL STONE BOUCHARD, B.S. (University of Massachusetts), *Instructor, Research, Home Economics.* Edna Skinner Hall

ARTHUR ISRAEL BOURNE, A.B. (Dartmouth College), *Professor, Research, Entomology.* Fernald Hall

ALFRED ALEXANDER BROWN, B.S., M.S. (University of Massachusetts), *Professor, Research, Agricultural Economics.* Draper Hall

285

FRANKLIN JAMES CAMPBELL, B.S. (Pennsylvania State University),
Instructor, Research, Floriculture.   Waltham Field Station

FREDERICK BARKER CHANDLER, B.S. (University of Maine), PH.D. (University
of Maryland), *Professor, Research, Cranberry Station.*   East Wareham

CHESTER ELLSWORTH CROSS, B.S., M.S. (University of Massachusetts), PH.D.
(Harvard University), *Professor, Research, Head of Cranberry Station.*
East Wareham

BRADFORD DEAN CROSSMON, B.S., M.S. (University of Connecticut), M.P.A.
(Harvard University), *Associate Professor, Research, Agricultural
Economics.*   Draper Hall

MARILYN BERTHA DERBY, B.S. (University of Massachusetts), M.S. (Cornell
University), *Instructor, Research, Home Economics.*
Edna Skinner Hall

WILLIAM LEONARD DORAN, B.S., M.S. (University of Massachusetts),
Professor, Research, Botany.   Clark Hall

MACK DRAKE, B.S., M.S., PH.D. (Purdue University),
Professor, Research, Chemistry.   Goessmann Laboratory

WILLIAM BRIGHAM ESSELEN, B.S., M.S., PH.D. (University of Massachusetts),
Professor, Research, Food Technology.   Chenoweth Laboratory

GEORGE PETER FADDOUL, D.V.M. (Middlesex University), M.S. (University of
New Hampshire), *Professor, Research, Poultry Disease.*
Waltham Field Station

IRVING SEYMOUR FAGERSON, S.B. (Massachusetts Institute of Technology),
M.S., PH.D. (University of Massachusetts), *Assistant Professor, Research,
Food Technology.*   Chenoweth Laboratory

GORDON WALLACE FELLOWS, A.B. (University of Connecticut),
Instructor, Research, Poultry Disease.   Waltham Field Station

[1]ROBERT ALAN FITZPATRICK, B.S., M.S. (University of Massachusetts),
Assistant Professor, Research, Agricultural Economics.

LESLIE WAYNE FLEMING, A.B., M.A. (University of Kansas),
Instructor, Research, Veterinary Science.   Paige Laboratory

FREDERICK JOHN FRANCIS, B.A., M.A., PH.D. (University of Toronto),
Assistant Professor, Research, Food Technology.
Chenoweth Laboratory

JAMES EVERARD FULLER, A.B., A.M. (Colorado College), PH.D. (Yale University), *Professor, Research, Bacteriology.*   Marshall Hall

WILLIAM JAMES GARLAND, JR.,
Instructor, Research, Entomology.   Waltham Field Station

EUGENE C. GASIORKEWICZ, B.A., M.S. (Marquette University), PH.D. (University of Wisconsin), *Assistant Professor, Research, Botany.*
Waltham Field Station

JULIUS SYDNEY GREENSTEIN, A.B. (Clark University), M.S., PH.D. (University
of Illinois), *Assistant Professor, Research, Dairy and Animal Science.*
Stockbridge Hall

---

[1]On leave of absence.

286

EMIL FREDERICK GUBA, B.S. (University of Massachusetts), PH.D. (University of Illinois), *Professor, Research, Botany.*   Waltham Field Station

JOHN RALPH HAVIS, B.S. (Texas Technical College), M.S., PH.D. (Cornell University), *Professor, Research, Horticulture; Head of Waltham Field Station.*   Waltham Field Station

FRANK ALFRED HAYS, B.S. (Oklahoma Agricultural College), M.A. (University of Nebraska), PH.D. (Iowa State College), *Professor, Research Poultry Husbandry.*   Stockbridge Hall

PORTIA ADELE IERARDI, B.S., M.A. (Boston University), *Experiment Station Editor.*   Munson Hall

ELMAR JARVESOO, AGR.DIP., MAG.AGR. (Tartu University), DR.AGRI. (Berlin University), *Instructor, Research, Agricultural Economics.*   Draper Hall

LINUS HALE JONES, B.S., M.S. (University of Massachusetts), PH.D. (Rutgers University), *Assistant Professor, Research, Botany.*   Clark Hall

PEARL KANE, B.S., M.S. (Pennsylvania State University), *Instructor, Research, Home Economics.*   Edna Skinner Hall

CLIFFORD VAUGHN KIGHTLINGER, B.S., M.S. (Grove City College), *Professor, Research, Agronomy.*   Stockbridge Hall

DONALD MARKHAM KINSMAN, B.S. (University of Massachusetts), M.S. (University of New Hampshire), *Assistant Professor, Assistant to Superintendent of Farms.*   Stockbridge Hall

KAROL JOSEPH KUCINSKI, B.S., M.S., PH.D. (University of Massachusetts), *Assistant Professor, Research, Agronomy.*   Stockbridge Hall

WILLIAM HENRY LACHMAN, JR., B.S., M.S. (Pennsylvania State University), *Associate Professor, Research, Vegetable Gardening.*   French Hall

WARREN LITSKY, A.B. (Clark University), M.S. (University of Massachusetts), PH.D. (Michigan State University), *Associate Professor, Research, Bacteriology.*   Marshall Hall

MRS. MARY EUGENE LOJKIN, B.S., M.S. (Polytechnic Institute, Petrograd), PH.D. (Columbia University), *Assistant Professor, Research, Home Economics Nutrition.*   Edna Skinner Hall

MALCOLM ARTHUR MCKENZIE, PH.B., A.M., PH.D. (Brown University), *Director, Shade Tree Laboratories.*   Shade Tree Laboratories

JOHN WALTER MASTALERZ, B.S. (University of Massachusetts), M.S. (Purdue University), PH.D. (Cornell University), *Assistant Professor, Research. Floriculture.*   Waltham Field Station

WILLIAM SAMUEL MUELLER, B.S. (University of Illinois), M.S. (Rutgers University), PH.D. (University of Massachusetts), *Associate Professor, Research, Dairy and Animal Science.*   Flint Laboratory

MARGARET HELEN O'DONNELL, *Administrative Director of Experiment Station.*   East Experiment Station

LEONARD RAYMOND PARKINSON, B.S. (University of New Hampshire), M.S., PH.D. (University of Massachusetts), *Assistant Professor, Research, Food Technology.*   Hatch Laboratory

RICHARD E. PRIDE, B.S., M.S. (Pennsylvania State University), *Assistant Professor, Research, Horticulture.*   Waltham Field Station

ELIOT COLLINS ROBERTS, B.S. (University of Rhode Island), M.S., PH.D. (Rutgers University), *Assistant Professor, Research, Agronomy.*
Stockbridge Hall

DAVID ROZMAN, B.A., M.A. (University of Wisconsin), PH.D. (Northwestern University), *Professor, Research, Agricultural Economics.*
Draper Hall

EDWARD HARTLEY SEADALE, B.S. (University of Massachusetts), *Instructor, Research, Veterinary Science.*   Paige Laboratory

RUTH EVELYN SHERBURNE, B.S. (Simmons College), *Instructor, Research, Agricultural Economics.*   Draper Hall

J. ROBERT SMYTH, JR., B.S. (University of Maine), M.S., PH.D. (Purdue University), *Associate Professor, Research, Poultry Husbandry.*
Stockbridge Hall

[1]FRANKLIN WALLBURG SOUTHWICK, B.S. (University of Massachusetts), M.S. (Ohio State University), PH.D. (Cornell University), *Professor, Research, Pomology.*   French Hall

HERBERT GEORGE SPINDLER, B.A. (University of Wisconsin), M.B.A. (Boston University), *Assistant Professor, Research, Agricultural Economics.*
Draper Hall

JOSEPH ERIS STECKEL, B.S.A., PH.D. (Purdue University), *Professor, Research, Agronomy.*   Stockbridge Hall

ROBERT LEWIS TICKNOR, B.S. (Oregon State College), M.S., PH.D. (Michigan State University), *Assistant Professor, Research, Nurseryculture.*
Waltham Field Station

WILLIAM EDWARD TOMLINSON, JR., B.S. (Tufts University), M.S. (University of Massachusetts), *Associate Professor, Research, Cranberry Station.*
East Wareham

JONAS VENGRIS, M.AGR. (Agricultural College, Dotnuva, Lithuania), D.AGR.SC. (University of Bonn), *Assistant Professor, Research, Agronomy.*
Stockbridge Hall

WALTER DRURY WEEKS, B.S., M.S. (University of New Hampshire), PH.D. (University of Massachusetts), *Assistant Professor, Research, Pomology.*
French Hall

MRS. ANNE WILLIAMS WERTZ, A.B. (Connecticut College), PH.D. (University of Massachusetts), *Professor, Research, Home Economics Nutrition.*
Edna Skinner Hall

WARREN DRAPER WHITCOMB, B.S. (University of Massachusetts), *Professor, Research, Entomology.*   Waltham Field Station

HAROLD EVERETT WHITE, B.S., M.S. (Purdue University), *Professor, Research, Floriculture.*   French Hall

ROLAND WHALEY WINTERFIELD, B.S. in AGR., D.V.M. (Iowa State College), *Professor, Research, Veterinary Science.*   Paige Laboratory

HRANT MISSAK YEGIAN, B.S. (Iowa State College), M.S. (University of Massachusetts), *Assistant Professor, Research, Agronomy.*   Stockbridge Hall

---

[1]On leave of absence, second semester.

ROBERT ELLSWORTH YOUNG, B.S.A. (Oklahoma Agricultural College), M.S. (Ohio State University), *Professor, Research, Olericulture.*
Waltham Field Station

JOHN WALTER ZAHRADNIK, B.S. (Pennsylvania State University), M.S. (Iowa State College), *Assistant Professor, Research, Agricultural Engineering.*
Stockbridge Hall

BERT MERTON ZUCKERMAN, B.S. (North Carolina State College), M.S. (New York State College of Forestry), PH.D. (University of Illinois), *Assistant Professor, Research, Cranberry Station.*
East Wareham

PART TIME EXPERIMENT STATION STAFF

WILLIAM MAKEPEACE ATWOOD, B.S. (University of Massachusetts),
Instructor, Research, Agronomy.
Stockbridge Hall

JOHANNES DELPHENDAHL, DIP.LDW. (Hohenheim Agricultural College),
Instructor, Research, Agricultural Economics.
Draper Hall

DEWEY BERT DURRETT, B.S. in AGRIC. (West Virginia University),
Instructor, Research, Agricultural Economics.
Draper Hall

ELIZABETH MARY ELBERT, A.B. (University of California), M.S. (Cornell University), *Instructor, Research, Food Technology.*
Chenoweth Laboratory

MRS. GEORGIA PERKINS FRENCH, B.S. (University of Massachusetts),
Instructor, Research, Home Economics.
Edna Skinner Hall

HANS JOA, B.S. (University of Tartu),
Instructor, Research, Agronomy.
Stockbridge Hall

C. MAXWELL MARTIN, B.S. (Sydney Technological College), M.S. (New South Wales University of Technology), *Instructor, Research, Food Technology.*
Chenoweth Laboratory

PHILIP RICHARDSON PEARSON, JR., B.A. (Dartmouth College),
Instructor, Research, Agronomy.
Stockbridge Hall

JOHN MICHAEL WHITE, B.S. (University of Massachusetts),
Instructor, Research, Agronomy.
Stockbridge Hall

EDWARD ALLAN ZANE, B.B.A. (University of Alaska), M.B.A. (Boston University), *Instructor, Research, Argricultural Economics.*
Draper Hall

REGULATORY SERVICE STAFF

JESSIE LOUISE ANDERSON,
  Assistant Professor, Research, Seeds.   West Experiment Station
HAROLD IRWIN BASCH, B.A. (University of Connecticut), M.S. (University of Massachusetts), *Instructor, Research, Veterinary Science.*
  Paige Laboratory
KENNETH LLOYD BULLIS, D.V.M. (Iowa State College), M.S. (University of Massachusetts), *Professor of Veterinary Science and Head of Department.*   Paige Laboratory
CLIFFORD SPENCER CHATER, B.S.A. (University of Rhode Island), M.S. (Kansas State College), *Assistant Professor, Research, Shade Tree Laboratories.*   Waltham Field Station
MIRIAM KEITH CLARKE, A.B. (Mt. Holyoke College), M.S. (University of Massachusetts), *Assistant Professor, Research, Poultry Disease.*
  Paige Laboratory
[2]LEO VINCENT CROWLEY, B.S. (University of Massachusetts),
  Assistant Professor, Research, Feeds and Fertilizers.
JEANNETTE GARDRINE DAVIS, B.S. (University of Massachusetts),
  Instructor, Research, Feeds and Fertilizers.   West Experiment Station
WENDELL PARKER DITMER, B.S. in ED. (Shippenburgh State Teachers College), M.S. (University of Pittsburgh), *Assistant Professor, Research, Seeds.*   West Experiment Station
[2]ELMO JAMES FRESIA, B.S. (University of Massachusetts),
  Instructor, Research, Feeds and Fertilizers.
BERTRAM GERSTEN, B.S. (University of Rhode Island), *Assistant Professor Research, Feeds and Fertilizers.*   West Experiment Station
HENRY WALTER GILBERTSON, B.S. (University of Idaho), M.S. (University of Maryland), *Instructor, Research, Shade Tree Laboratories.*
  Waltham Field Station
RICHARD HAROLD GRAVES, B.S. (University of Massachusetts),
  Instructor, Research, Feeds and Fertilizers.   West Experiment Station
WILLIAM KENNETH HARRIS, D.V.M. (Ohio State University),
  Professor, Research, Mastitis.   Stockbridge Hall
FRANCIS WILLIAM HOLMES, B.A. (Oberlin College), PH.D. (Cornell University), *Assistant Professor, Research, Shade Tree Laboratories.*
  Shade Tree Laboratories
JOHN WILLIAM KUZMESKI, B.S. (University of Massachusetts), *Professor, Research, Feeds and Fertilizers.*   West Experiment Station
WALDO CHANDLER LINCOLN, JR., B.S. (University of Massachusetts),
  Instructor, Research, Seeds.   West Experiment Station

[2]On leave of absence for military service.

290

OLGA MARION OLESIUK, B.A. (Mt. Holyoke College), M.S. (University of Massachusetts), *Assistant Professor, Research, Poultry Disease.*
Paige Laboratory

IONA MAY REYNOLDS, B.S. (University of Massachusetts), *Instructor, Research, Mastitis.*
Paige Laboratory

MARTIN SEVOIAN, B.S. (University of Massachusetts), V.M.D. (University of Pennsylvania), M.S. (Cornell University), *Professor, Research, Veterinary Science.*
Paige Laboratory

C. TYSON SMITH, B.S., M.S. (Princeton University), *Associate Professor, Research, Feeds and Fertilizers.*
West Experiment Station

CHARLES FREDERICK SMYSER, B.S. (University of Maryland), M.S. (University of Connecticut), *Assistant Professor, Research, Veterinary Science.*
Paige Laboratory

GLENN HOWARD SNOEYENBOS, D.V.M. (Michigan State University), *Professor, Research, Avian Pathology.*
Paige Laboratory

ALBERT FRANCIS SPELMAN, B.S. (University of Massachusetts), *Associate Professor, Research, Feeds and Fertilizers.*
West Experiment Station

HENRY VAN ROEKEL, D.V.M. (Iowa State College), M.S. (Virginia Polytechnic Institute), PH.D. (Yale University), *Professor, Research, Veterinary Science.*
Paige Laboratory

291

RESEARCH FELLOWS

HERBERT DAVID BRODY, B.S. (Massachusetts Institute of Technology), M.S. (University of Massachusetts), *Research Fellow in Food Technology.*
Chenoweth Laboratory

FRANZ BRANDL, DIPLOM-INGENIEUR (Agricultural University Bundesreal-gymnasium Linz), *Research Fellow in Food Technology.*
Chenoweth Laboratory

JAMES HAROLD DAVID, B.S. (University of Massachusetts),
Research Fellow in Entomology. Fernald Hall

MARY B. GRIFFIN, B.S. (Teachers College of Connecticut),
Extension Assistant in Sociology. North College

TERRY B. KINNEY, JR., B.S. (University of Massachusetts),
Research Fellow in Poultry Husbandry. Stockbridge Hall

CHARLES EDWIN REDMAN, B.S. (University of Massachusetts),
Research Fellow in Poultry Husbandry. Stockbridge Hall

DONALD JAMES SUTHERLAND, B.S. (Tufts University),
Research Fellow in Entomology. Fernald Hall

EMPLOYEES OF FEDERAL GOVERNMENT

with Headquarters
at the University of Massachusetts

WESLEY ROBERT JONES, B.S. (University of Connecticut), M.S. (University of Massachusetts), *Assistant District Agent, U. S. Fish and Wildlife Service.* South College

ANNE URSULA ROGERS, *Secretary,*
U. S. Fish and Wildlife Service. South College

WILLIAM GULLIVER SHELDON, B.A. (Yale University), M.S., PH.D. (Cornell University), *Leader of the Massachusetts Cooperative Wildlife Research Unit.* Conservation Building

JESSE ALDERMAN TAFT, B.S., M.S. (University of Massachusetts),
Supervisor of Agricultural Teacher-Training. Liberal Arts Annex
(Member of Staff of State Department of Education.)

292

EXTENSION SERVICE STAFF

James Wilson Dayton, b.s. (University of Massachusetts), *Associate Dean of the College of Agriculture and Director of Extension Service.*
Stockbridge Hall

Donald Pearson Allan, b.a. (University of Massachusetts), *Associate Extension Professor, Secretary of Extension Service.* Stockbridge Hall

James Richard Beattie, b.s., m.s. (University of New Hampshire), *Extension Professor of Horticulture.* East Wareham

Ellsworth William Bell, b.s. (Pennsylvania State University), m.s. (University of Vermont), *Extension Professor of Agricultural Economics.* Draper Hall

Alfred Worden Boicourt, b.s., m.s. (Cornell University), *Extension Professor of Horticulture.* Wilder Hall

John Howard Bragg, b.s., m.s. (University of Maine), *Assistant Extension Professor of Marketing.* Draper Hall

Fayette Hinds Branch, b.s. (Cornell University), *Extension Professor of Agricultural Economics.* Draper Hall

Radie Harold Bunn, b.s. (South Dakota State College), *Assistant Extension Professor of Communications.* Munson Hall

Norman Wesley Butterfield, b.s. (University of Massachusetts), m.s. (Purdue University), *Extension Professor of Floriculture.*
Waltham Field Station

Earle Stanton Carpenter, b.s. (University of Massachusetts), m.s. (Iowa State College), *Extension Professor of Communications.* Munson Hall

Byron Earle Colby, b.s. (University of New Hampshire), *Extension Professor of Animal Husbandry.* Stockbridge Hall

Frederick Eugene Cole, b.s. (University of Massachusetts), *Extension Professor of Fruit and Vegetable Marketing.* Draper Hall

Verda Mae Dale, b.s. (Kansas State College), m.s. (Cornell University), *Associate Extension Professor of Home Economics.* Edna Skinner Hall

Virginia Davis, b.s. (Skidmore College), *Assistant Extension Professor of Home Economics.* Edna Skinner Hall

Ralph Wilfred Donaldson, b.s. (Acadia University), b.s.a. (Toronto University), *Extension Professor of Agronomy.* Stockbridge Hall

Winifred Isabel Eastwood, a.b. (Sterling College), m.a. (Columbia University), *Extension Professor; Head, Extension Division of Home Economics.* Edna Skinner Hall

May Stella Foley, b.s. (Michigan State University), m.a. (Columbia University), *Extension Professor of Home Economics.*
Edna Skinner Hall

STANLEY NEWKIRK GAUNT, B.S. (Rutgers University), PH.D. (North Carolina State College), *Extension Professor of Dairy Husbandry.*
Stockbridge Hall

CONSTANTINE JOSEPH GILGUT, B.S., M.S. (University of Massachusetts), A.M., PH.D. (Harvard University), *Extension Professor of Plant Pathology.*
Clark Hall

WELLESLEY CARL HARRINGTON, M.E. (Cornell University),
Extension Professor of Engineering.   Stockbridge Hall

KIRBY MAXWELL HAYES, B.S., M.S. (University of Massachusetts),
Associate Extension Professor of Food Technology.
Chenoweth Laboratory

BARBARA HIGGINS, B.S. (University of Maine), M.S. (Cornell University),
Associate Extension Professor of Home Economics. Edna Skinner Hall

JOHN WARREN HOUGH, B.S. (University of Vermont), M.S. (Cornell University), *Assistant Extension Professor of Poultry Husbandry.*
Stockbridge Hall

MILDRED LOUISE HOWELL, B.S. (Buffalo State Teachers College),
Associate Extension Professor of Home Economics.   Munson Hall

HORACE MANFRED JONES, B.S. (South Dakota State College), *Extension Professor; Head, Extension Division of Youth Work.* Munson Hall

MRS. N. MAY LARSON, B.S. (University of Wisconsin), M.S. (Iowa State College), *Extension Professor of Home Economics.* Edna Skinner Hall

ALLEN SANFORD LELAND, B.S. (University of Massachusetts), *Extension Professor, County Agricultural Program Leader.*   Stockbridge Hall

HARLEY ALANSON LELAND, B.S. (University of Vermont),
Extension Professor of Agriculture.   Munson Hall

WILLIAM JOHN LORD, B.S., M.S. (University of New Hampshire), PH.D. (Pennsylvania State University), *Assistant Extension Professor of Horticulture.*   French Hall

H. RUTH MCINTIRE, B.S. (Cornell University),
Extension Professor of Recreation.   Edna Skinner Hall

WILLIAM EDWARD MEEHL, D.V.M. (Ohio State University), *Extension Professor of Veterinary Science (Poultry).*   Waltham Field Station

ROY EDGAR MOSER, B.S. (Ohio State University), M.S. (Cornell University), *Extension Professor of Agricultural Economics.*   Draper Hall

GILBERT EDWARD MOTTLA, A.B. (Harvard University),
Head, Extension Division of Communications.   Munson Hall

EARLE HARRISON NODINE, B.S. (University of Connecticut), M.ED. (Springfield College), *Associate Extension Professor of Agriculture.*
Munson Hall

GRUNOW OTTO OLESON, B.S., M.S. (University of Wisconsin),
Extension Professor of Communications.   Munson Hall

ROBERT BROWN PARMENTER, B.S.F. (University of Maine),
Extension Professor of Forestry.   Conservation Building

CLARENCE HOWARD PARSONS, B.S., M.S. (University of Massachusetts),
Extension Professor of Dairy Husbandry.   Stockbridge Hall

ROBERT CLEMENS SIMMONS, B.S. in AGR. JOURNALISM (Iowa State College),
Extension Instructor of Communications.   Munson Hall

Rosa Mary Starkey, b.s. (Nasson College), *Assistant Extension Professor of Home Economics.* Edna Skinner Hall

Douglass Neff Stern, b.s. (Lehigh University), v.m.d. (University of Pennsylvania), *Extension Professor of Veterinary Science.*
Paige Laboratory

Cecil Lyman Thomson, b.s.a. (University of Toronto), m.s. (University of Minnesota), *Extension Professor of Vegetable Crops.* French Hall

Herbert Sidney Vaughan, b.s. (University of Massachusetts), m.p.a. (Harvard University), *Head, Extension Division of Agriculture.*
Munson Hall

Mrs. Shirley Smith Weeks, b.s. (Framingham State Teachers College), m.s. (Cornell University), *Assistant Extension Professor of Consumer Education.* Edna Skinner Hall

George William Westcott, b.s., m.s. (Iowa State College), m.p.a., d.p.a. (Harvard University), *Extension Professor of Agricultural Economics.*
Draper Hall

Ellsworth Haines Wheeler, b.s. (University of Massachusetts), m.s., ph.d. (Cornell University), *Extension Professor of Entomology.*
Fernald Hall

Roger Augustus Wolcott, (Massachusetts College of Art), *Assistant Extention Professor of Communications.* Munson Hall

AGENTS WITH HEADQUARTERS
IN COUNTIES

Barnstable County, Barnstable

MYRTIS EDITH BEECHER, B.S.E. (Framingham State Teachers College),
Home Demonstration Agent.

WALTER G. BRUCE, B.S. (University of Massachusetts), *Club Agent.*

¹CARL ARTHUR FRASER, B.S., M.S. (University of Massachusetts), *Club Agent.*

OSCAR SHIRLEY JOHNSON, B.S. (University of Rhode Island),
Associate Agricultural Agent.

BERT TOMLINSON, *County Agent-Manager.*

Berkshire County, Pittsfield

JACQUELINE O. BOLLE, B.S. (Syracuse University), *Assistant Club Agent.*

DICK LEROY BOYCE, B.S. (Cornell University),
Assistant Agricultural Agent.

ROBERT MERRILL HALL, B.S. (University of Rhode Island), *Club Agent.*

MRS. HELEN L. H. JOHNSON, B.S. (Framingham State Teachers College),
Home Demonstration Agent.

JEANNE ELIZABETH MANGUM, B.S. (University of Massachusetts),
Assistant Home Demonstration Agent.

FRANK ALBERT SKOGSBERG, B.V.A. (University of Massachusetts),
County Agent-Manager.

Bristol County, Segreganset

DAVID B. BARROW, B.S. (Cornell University), *Associate Agricultural Agent.*

PHYLLIS JANE BOWDEN, B.S. (Nasson College), *Assistant Club Agent.*

ELMER A. CHAMBERLAIN, B.S. (University of Massachusetts),
Associate Agricultural Agent.

CAROL C. FABER, A.B. (Regis College),
Assistant Home Demonstration Agent.

JOHN F. FARRELL, B.S. (University of Massachusetts), *Associate Club Agent.*

BARBARA RUTH O'BRIEN, B.S. (University of Massachusetts),
Home Demonstration Agent.

HAROLD OLIVER WOODWARD, B.S. (University of Connecticut),
County Agricultural Agent.

---

1 On leave of absence for military service.

Dukes County, Vineyard Haven

JANET DANITIS, B.S. (University of Massachusetts),
Associate Home Demonstration Agent.

MRS. EDITH F. MORRIS, B.S. (Framingham State Teachers College),
Club Agent.

EZRA I. SHAW, B.S. (University of Massachusetts),
County Agricultural Agent.

Essex County, Hathorne

CHARLES EDWARD BLANCHARD, B.S. (University of Massachusetts),
Club Agent.

CALTON OLIVER CARTWRIGHT, B.V.A., M.S. (University of Massachusetts),
Agricultural Agent.

MARGARET MARY FITZPATRICK, B.S. (Framingham State Teachers College),
Associate Club Agent.

DANIEL PATRICK HURLD, JR., B.S. (University of Massachusetts),
Agricultural Agent.

KATHERINE MAY LAWLER, B.S. (Simmons College), M.S. (University of
Massachusetts), *Home Demonstration Agent.*

JOHN EVERETT MILTIMORE, B.S. (University of New Hampshire),
Associate Agricultural Agent.

VERA ARLAYNE SULLIVAN, A.B. (Regis College),
Assistant Home Demonstration Agent.

Franklin County, Greenfield

MILFORD WALTER ATWOOD, B.S. (University of Massachusetts), *Club Agent.*

MARGUERITA COSTANZA, B.S. (Nasson College),
Associate Home Demonstration Agent.

MRS. ELIZABETH ANNE MANNHEIM, B.S. (University of Massachusetts),
Assistant Club Agent.

MRS. MARJORIE HALL McGILLICUDDY, B.S. (Framingham State Teachers
College), *Home Demonstration Agent.*

DONALD TURNER THAYER, B.V.A. (University of Massachusetts),
Associate Agricultural Agent.

OSCAR LEWIS WYMAN, B.S. (University of Maine), *County Agent-Manager.*

Hampden County, West Springfield

WILLIAM J. BENNETT, B.S. (University of Massachusetts),
Associate Agricultural Agent.

*ROBERT ANTHONY BIEBER, B.S. (University of Massachusetts),
Agricultural Agent.

JANICE M. COGSWELL, B.S. (University of Maine),
Associate Home Demonstration Agent.

* Time divided between Hampden and Hampshire Counties.

COUNTY AGENTS

MRS. ETHEL MERLE CROSS, B.S. (Springfield College), *Associate Club Agent.*

ALBERT HENRY FULLER, *Director of County Extension Service.*

CARL ANTON HEDIN, B.S. (Cornell University), *Associate Agricultural Agent.*

MOLLY MARGARET HIGGINS, B.S. (Framingham State Teachers College), *Home Demonstration Agent.*

ROBERT KENDALL MARSH, B.S. (University of Massachusetts), *Club Agent.*

JAMES NATHANIEL PUTNAM, B.S. (University of Massachusetts), *Agricultural Agent.*

Hampshire County, Northampton

REBECCA JANE DEA, B.S. (Nasson College), *Associate Club Agent.*

FLORENCE IRENE GATES, B.S. (Framingham State Teachers College), *Home Demonstration Agent.*

ROGER McKEE HARRINGTON, B.S. (Pennsylvania State University), *Agricultural Agent.*

WALTER MELNICK, B.S. (University of Massachusetts), *County Agent-Manager.*

WILLIAM WARNER METCALFE, B.S. (University of New Hampshire), *Club Agent.*

ELIZABETH A. THAYER, B.S. (Framingham State Teachers College), *Associate Home Demonstration Agent.*

Middlesex County, Concord

MRS. IRENE HOLMES BROWN, B.S. (Framingham State Teachers College), *Assistant Club Agent.*

JOSEPH TRUE BROWN, B.S. (University of New Hampshire), *Director of County Extension Service.*

ALFRED WHITNEY CARLSON, B.S. (Rutgers University), *Agricultural Agent.*

BLANCHE WOODBURY EAMES, B.S. (Framingham State Teachers College), *Home Demonstration Agent.*

MAX GEORGE FULTZ, B.S. (Purdue University), *Agricultural Agent.*

JESSE JAMES, B.S., M.S. (University of Georgia), *Club Agent.*

FRANCIS GOULD MENTZER, JR., B.S. (University of Massachusetts), *Associate Agricultural Agent.*

MRS. JANICE BOWEN MORRIS, B.S. (Russell Sage College), *Assistant Club Agent.*

MRS. ETHEL WADSWORTH VEENENDAAL, B.S. (Cornell University), *Associate Home Demonstration Agent.*

MAURICE C. ROBERTS, B.S. (Michigan State University), *Associate Club Agent.*

JOHN E. STEDMAN, B.S. (University of Rhode Island), *Associate Agricultural Agent.*

Norfolk County, Walpole

CATHERINE COOK, B.S. (Framingham State Teachers College), M.ED. (Boston University), *Associate Club Agent.*

MRS. SANTINA RILEY CURRAN, B.S. (Framingham State Teachers College), *Home Demonstration Agent.*

FRANK LESLIE DAVIS, B.S. (University of Massachusetts), *Agricultural Agent.*

ALBERT JOHN HEALEY, B.S. (University of Massachusetts), *Club Agent.*

PATRICK GILDO SANTIN, B.V.A. (University of Massachusetts), *Associate Agricultural Agent.*

MRS. JEAN ECKERSON WOODWARD, B.S. (Russell Sage College), *Associate Home Demonstration Agent.*

Plymouth County, Brockton

PHYLLIS BRIGHTMAN, B.S. (Temple University), *Assistant Home Demonstration Agent.*

ROBERT BRUCE EWING, *Acting County Agent-Manager and County Club Agent.*

DOMINIC ALEXANDER MARINI, B.S. (University of Massachusetts), *Associate Agricultural Agent.*

EDGAR WINFRED SPEAR, B.S. (University of Massachusetts), *Associate Agricultural Agent.*

BEATRICE ISABELLE WHITE, B.S. (Framingham State Teachers College), *Home Demonstration Agent.*

Worcester County, Worcester

EVERETT S. BRYANT, B.S. (University of Maine), *Associate Agricultural Agent.*

IRENE MARGARET DAVIS, B.S. (Framingham State Teachers College), *Associate Home Demonstration Agent.*

ERNEST ARTHUR GEORGE, B.S. (University of New Hampshire), *Associate Agricultural Agent.*

MRS. RUTH E. GOODWIN, B.S. (University of Maine), *Associate Home Demonstration Agent.*

WILLIAM R. GOSS, B.S. (University of Massachusetts), *Associate Agricultural Agent.*

LEWIS A. HODGKINSON, B.S. (University of Rhode Island), *Associate Agricultural Agent.*

LEON OTIS MARSHALL, B.S. (University of Maine), *Club Agent.*

ELDINE JUNE NYLANDER, B.S. (University of Massachusetts), *Assistant Club Agent.*

WALTER BRUCE SHAW, *Associate Agricultural Agent.*

MRS. EVANGELINE D. STANDISH, B.S. (University of Rhode Island), *Associate Club Agent.*

MILDRED CAROLINE THOMAS, *Home Demonstration Agent.*

CHARLES WINFIELD TURNER, B.S. (University of Rhode Island), M.S. (North Carolina State College), *Director of County Extension Service.*

INDEX

300

INDEX

UNIVERSITY OF MASSACHUSETTS ENROLLMENT — September, 1955

UNDERGRADUATE COLLEGE

CLASS	1956 MEN	1956 WOMEN	1957 MEN	1957 WOMEN	1958 MEN	1958 WOMEN	1959 MEN	1959 WOMEN	TOTAL MEN	TOTAL WOMEN	TOTAL
Arts and Science	197	168	223	209	203	202	218	301	841	880	1,721
Engineering	110	1	165	1	214	5	293	2	782	10	792
Bus. Administration	116	10	158	4	112	13	85	8	471	35	506
Agriculture	84	7	67	6	67	7	82	4	300	24	324
Home Economics	0	38	0	46	0	47	0	52	0	183	183
Physical Education	12	0	14	0	19	0	20	0	65	0	65
Nursing	0	1	0	3	0	10	0	23	0	37	37
Total	519	225	627	270	615	284	698	390	2,459	1,169	3,628
Total by Classes		744		897		899		1,088			3,628
Specials									10	28	38

GRADUATE SCHOOL

	MEN	WOMEN	TOTAL
Regular	204	39	243
Special	60	34	94
			337

STOCKBRIDGE SCHOOL

	1956	1957	TOTAL
Men	153	178	331
Women	4	3	7
			338

SUMMER SCHOOL

578

SUMMARY

Undergraduate College	3,666
Graduate School	337
Stockbridge School	338
TOTAL ENROLLMENT	4,341

Office of Publications
November, 1955

GIFTS AND BEQUESTS

For the information of those who may wish to make a gift or a bequest to this University, the following suggestion is made as to a suitable form which may be used.

There are a number of worth-while activities of the University which are handicapped by lack of funds and for which small endowments would make possible a greater measure of service to our students and to the Commonwealth. The religious work on the Campus is an example. This is now carried on in a very limited way by current private contributions. Further information concerning this and other activities in similar need will be gladly furnished by the President.

SUGGESTED FORM

"I give and bequeath to the Trustees of the University of Massachusetts, at Amherst, Massachusetts, the sum of ....
.... dollars."

(I) (Unrestricted)

"To be used for the benefit of the University of Massachusetts in such manner as the Trustees thereof may direct."

or (2) (Permanent Fund: income unrestricted)

"to constitute an endowment fund to be known as the ....
.................................:.......... Fund, such fund to be kept invested by the Trustees of the University of Massachusetts and the income used for the benefit of the College in such manner as the Trustees thereof may direct."

or (3) (Specific Purposes)

"to be used for the following purposes,"

(Here specify in detail the purposes.)

VOLUME XLVIII   APRIL, 1956   NUMBER 3

Published five times a year by the University of Massachusetts: January, February, April (two), September. Entered at Post Office, Amherst, Mass., as second class matter.

The report of the President for the year ending January 1, 1956, is part of the 93rd annual report of the University of Massachusetts, and as such is Part I of Public Document 31. (Section 8, Chapter 75, of the General Laws of Massachusetts.)

PUBLICATION OF THIS DOCUMENT APPROVED BY GEORGE J. CRONIN, STATE PURCHASING AGENT

2M-4-56-917477

UNIVERSITY OF MASSACHUSETTS

OFFICE OF THE PRESIDENT

February 14, 1956

The Honorable Joseph W. Bartlett
Chairman, Board of Trustees
The University of Massachusetts

Dear Mr. Bartlett:

I am privileged to present to you, to the Board of Trustees, and to the Governor and Citizens of the Commonwealth a Report of Progress for the University of Massachusetts covering the year January 1, 1955 to January 1, 1956.

Respectfully yours,

Jean Paul Mather
Jean Paul Mather
President

Current Enrollment at the University

UNDERGRADUATE COLLEGE

Class	1956 Men	1956 Women	1957 Men	1957 Women	1958 Men	1958 Women	1959 Men	1959 Women	TOTAL Men	TOTAL Women	TOTAL
Arts and Science	197	168	223	209	203	202	218	301	841	880	1721
Engineering	110	1	165	2	214	5	293	2	782	10	792
Business Administration	116	10	158	4	112	13	85	8	471	35	506
Agriculture	84	7	67	6	67	7	82	4	300	24	324
Home Economics	0	38	0	46	0	47	0	52	0	183	183
Physical Education	12	0	14	0	19	0	20	0	65	0	65
Nursing	0	1	0	3	0	10	0	23	0	37	37
TOTAL	519	225	627	270	615	284	698	390	2459	1169	3628

Total by Classes	744	897	899	1088
Specials			10	28

38

3666

GRADUATE SCHOOL

	Men	Women	TOTAL
Regular	204	39	243
Special	60	34	94

337

STOCKBRIDGE SCHOOL

	1956	1957	TOTAL
Men	153	178	331
Women	4	3	7

338

SUMMER SCHOOL

578

Summary

Undergraduate College	3666
Graduate School	337
Stockbridge School	338
Total Enrollment	4341

OFFICE OF PUBLICATIONS, October, 1955

The
Dedication
of an
IDEA

"It is for us the living . . . to be dedicated here to the unfinished work. . . ."

Abraham Lincoln

America's unprecedented rise to world leadership is based on a continent rich in natural resources, on the mingling of vigorous and varied nationalities, and most of all on a political and educational plan which has encouraged the highest development and use of native ability.

The founders of this country recognized that the newly-adopted political system would work only in a democratic environment of free speech, free press, *and generally available education.* On this principle America established its free school system.

When Abraham Lincoln, in 1862, signed the land-grant act which founded the University of Massachusetts, the Federal and State governments joined forces to establish in every state at least one college to furnish "liberal and practical" education to the "industrial classes." Senator Justin Morrill of Vermont, chief advocate of this bill, saw the need for opening the doors of higher education to talent, regardless of wealth. That he had the welfare of the nation as well as the individual in mind is clearly evident in his statement of June 6, 1862 before the House of Representatives of the United States:

"It will add new securities to the perpetuity of republican institutions. Wronging nobody, it will prove a blessing to the whole people now and for ages to come . . . (it) should have been initiated at least a quarter of a century ago and if it had been our taxable resources would now have been far greater than they are."

3

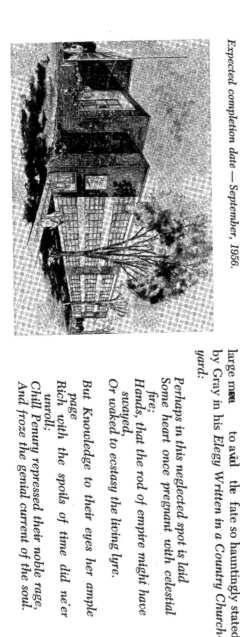

MACHMER HALL
General Classroom Building.
Expected completion date — September, 1956.

Who Should Be Educated

Statistics show that in the present century the average college graduate is paying taxes on $100,000 more income in his lifetime than is the average high school graduate. But far beyond the material income, the great educational system arising from this act, linked with the growth of the elementary and high schools of the nation, has enabled far in large measure to avoid the fate so hauntingly stated by Gray in his *Elegy Written in a Country Churchyard:*

Perhaps in this neglected spot is laid
Some heart once pregnant with celestial
fire;
Hands, that the rod of empire might have
swayed,
Or waked to ecstasy the living lyre.

But Knowledge to their eyes her ample
page
Rich with the spoils of time did ne'er
unroll;
Chill Penury repressed their noble rage,
And froze the genial current of the soul.

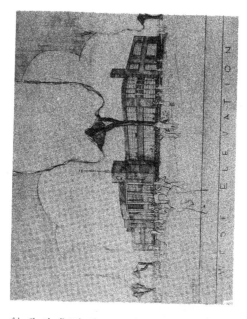

W E S T   E L E V A T I O N

STUDENT UNION

Expected completion — September, 1956.

Today we stand on the threshold of the greatest development of power and the greatest increase in our population ever known. Wrongly used, in a world divided, these forces may bring incalculable misery and loss of civilized values. Rightly used they may bring the greatest blessings ever known to man.

From both a material and a spiritual view, we need higher education for more *able and qualified* young people than ever before. America and the Commonwealth of Massachusetts must lead the way, that people in every land may share in the benefits from a successful meeting of this challenge.

We submit that our progress in culture and productivity will be measured by the availability of higher education for all *able* youth who can benefit by it. Now is the time for a dedicated translation at the University of Massachusetts of America's belief that there shall be no "mute inglorious Miltons", that all our *able* youth — not some — must be given the opportunity to contribute to our common task

according to their inherent ability. We cannot *afford* to say, "Their lot forbade."

The Specifics of Dedication

Since detailed reports from Deans and Directors of the eight Colleges, Schools, and Divisions; the Dean of Men and Dean of Women; the Director of Placement; the Librarian; and the Treasurer have all been filed with proper state authorities, this report will cover the broad policy aspects of the operation, planning, and progress of the University.

Since no new teaching positions were requested in the budget for the period beginning in September 1955 the enrollment was planned for a number smaller than the total of September 1954. This decrease was purposely designed to restore the 13 to 1 student to faculty ratio long established as the

CIRCLED AREAS SHOW 1955 CONSTRUCTION.

fundamental instructional standard for the University and repeatedly recognized by the General Court in approving requests for additional professional staff. Failure to recognize this standard would be a direct dilution of standards for the educational complex of a university offering class, laboratory, and research experiences in more than forty fields of knowledge. Such a complex will always require a greater relative number of professional staff to do an effective job than the public college which does not include highly specialized professional schools, colleges, and graduate studies in its total program.

The enrollment of out-of-state students was prohibited and the admission of transfer students curtailed drastically. This policy, though limited in total educational philosophy and provincial in approach, has been a realistic recognition of the pressure of applications from *highly qualified* resident sons and daughters of Massachusetts taxpayers far in excess of our physical facilities and total staff.

During the legislative session which began in January, 1955 record operating and capital outlay budgets were appropriated for the University. Capital outlay approved placed the total amount appropriated in the two years since July 1954 in excess of total accumulated capital appropriations at cost in the entire history of the University since the founding date of 1863. Particularly significant was a sizable appropriation for laboratory equipment to offset obvious lags in laboratories and classrooms throughout the campus.

As these sizable sums go onto drawing boards and are converted into concrete and stone, it should be recognized that large amounts of these facilities are replacements for obsolete and outmoded temporary structures still in use. This same Report two years ago estimated the instructional facilities to be from five to nine years behind the self-amortizing dormitory facilities for the current student body.

WOMEN'S PHYSICAL EDUCATION BUILDING
Authorized — 1955.

8

However, in addition to replacement, there is inherent in appropriations already passed partial provision for a student body estimated for the fall of 1960 at six thousand students, *provided* future operating budgets cover the staff that is the essential ingredient for such an expansion.

The existence of funds, for example, to erect a Liberal Arts building within the next two years must of necessity be geared to expanding the laboratory and instructional facilities for science as requested in the current budget for 1956. Such planning is basic to the program in force at the University since its inception, which requires two years of enrollment in the generalized and liberalizing arts and sciences in addition to the required studies of any professionalized or specialized school or college within the University.

Master Plan in Preparation

Planning for the present and future has proceeded carefully and systematically throughout the

PROPOSED SCIENCE CENTER
Public Health Wing authorized — 1955.

past year. Through funds wisely provided by the State Division of Building Construction, the architectural firm, Shurcliff and Shurcliff of Boston, completed a preliminary campus planning report in the spring of 1955. This report anticipates a total projected enrollment of 10,000 students by 1965. After careful consideration and review by the campus Planning Council, the Trustees, the faculty and the student body, suggested modifications and improvements have been submitted to Mr. Shurcliff with the hope that a final ten year master plan may evolve. Such planning blueprints the timing and relationship of successive requests to the Legislature, through the Division of Building Construction, for the development of a balanced educational program.

Appointment of Dr. Shannon McCune as Provost and Dr. Fred Cahill as Dean of the College of Arts and Sciences completed the major administrative organization by pulling together the separate Schools of Arts and Sciences, and establishing a top administrative officer over the academic affairs of the University. Both officers have diligently approached the problems of their responsibility. Their dedicated efforts are exemplary of the continuing and everlasting devotion of the entire staff to the meaning and purpose of the University.

Architects have worked during the year toward completion of final plans for bid on the Chemistry addition, the Public Health wing of the Science Center, the Women's Physical Education Building, the Liberal Arts Building, the addition to the Power Plant, and the Vegetable Gardening Building. The Classroom Building and Student Union are well under way at this report. The Union is another self-amortizing building, built with private funds by the Alumni Building Corporation, and amortized by an annual fee of twenty dollars per student voted by the Trustees in a special meeting held in December 1955. At this same meeting the Trustees voted an increase in dormitory rentals of fifteen dollars per student per year, effective in September 1956, to provide more adequate funds for future construction and present maintenance in the face of increasing building and operating costs.

Recognizing that people are the essential ingredient of a great University the Trustees and administration filed identical bi-partisan bills in the House and Senate of the General Court during December 1955, requesting greater flexibility and autonomy in operating personnel policies, under appropriation and state audit. This requested legislation is the most significant single objective of the University looking toward the improved quality as well as quantity of public higher education in the highly competitive years ahead. The University of Massachusetts must be a peer and not a pawn in the great family of state universities now training the leaders and citizens of the nation and the world of tomorrow.

JEAN PAUL MATHER
President

FACADE — MAIN ENGINEERING BUILDING.
New wing dedicated October, 1955.

Personnel Changes

FACULTY

Deaths:

Lawrence V. Loy, EXTENSION PROFESSOR IN CHARGE OF YOUTH PROGRAMS

Harry G. Lindquist, ASSISTANT PROFESSOR OF DAIRY AND ANIMAL SCIENCE

D. Horace Nelson, ASSISTANT PROFESSOR OF DAIRY AND ANIMAL SCIENCE

Retirements:

Charles F. Fraker, HEAD OF DEPARTMENT OF ROMANCE LANGUAGES

Victor A. Rice, HEAD OF DEPARTMENT OF ANIMAL HUSBANDRY

Wilbur H. Thies, EXTENSION SPECIALIST IN POMOLOGY

S. Church Hubbard, ASSISTANT PROFESSOR OF FLORICULTURE

Promotions:

To Dean:

Fred V. Cahill, Jr., ARTS AND SCIENCE

To Head of Department:

Stowell C. Goding, ROMANCE LANGUAGES

Maxwell H. Goldberg, ENGLISH

Arthur E. Niedeck, SPEECH

To Professor:

Carl A. Keyser, METALLURGY

Clarence Shute, PHILOSOPHY

To Associate Professor:

Eliot D. Allen, ENGLISH

Kenneth D. Cashin, CHEMICAL ENGINEERING

Katherine A. Clarke, FRENCH

Sidney Schoeffler, ECONOMICS

To Assistant Professor:

Armand J. Costa, MECHANICAL ENGINEERING

Dwight E. Erlick, PSYCHOLOGY

Tom Sherman Hamilton, Jr., LANDSCAPE ARCHITECTURE

Randolph A. Jester, FLORICULTURE

Robert A. Potash, HISTORY

Bertram C. Woodland, GEOLOGY AND MINERALOGY

Appointments:

Robeson Bailey, VISITING LECTURER IN ENGLISH

Edward P. Clancy, VISITING LECTURER IN PHYSICS

Norman L. Cloutier, VISITING LECTURER IN SPEECH
Ralph W. Goodrich, VISITING LECTURER IN EDUCATION
William C. Hodapp, VISITING LECTURER IN SPEECH
David P. Leonard, VISITING LECTURER IN HISTORY
Murray B. Peppard, VISITING LECTURER IN GERMAN
Robert L. Staffanson, VISITING LECTURER IN MUSIC
Margaret S. Wilson, VISITING LECTURER IN SOCIOLOGY

To Provost:
Shannon McCune

To Head of Department:
Julian M. Fore, AGRICULTURAL ENGINEERING
Gilbert E. Mottla, EXTENSION COMMUNICATIONS
Donald B. White, AIR SCIENCE

To Professor:
Lloyd F. Hayn, ECONOMICS
Solis L. Kates, CLINICAL PSYCHOLOGY
Allen S. Leland, EXTENSION COUNTY AGRICULTURAL PROGRAM LEADER
William E. Meehl, EXTENSION POULTRY PATHOLOGY
Martin Sevoian, VETERINARY SCIENCE RESEARCH

To Assistant Professor:
Donald L. Anderson, POULTRY HUSBANDRY RESEARCH
Donald F. Benton, AIR SCIENCE
John H. Bragg, EXTENSION AGRICULTURAL ECONOMICS
Leslie G. Bridges, AIR SCIENCE
Malcolm J. Chisholm, ASSISTANT PHYSICIAN
Wendell P. Ditmer, SEED CONTROL RESEARCH
Frederick H. Edwards, ELECTRICAL ENGINEERING
Edward G. Fennell, EDUCATION
Richards H. Harrington, MECHANICAL ENGINEERING
James G. Hill, ARMOR
John W. Hough, EXTENSION POULTRY HUSBANDRY
John E. Laestadius, ELECTRICAL ENGINEERING
William J. Lord, EXTENSION POMOLOGY
Frank E. Potter, DAIRY AND ANIMAL SCIENCE
Arthur A. Socolow, GEOLOGY AND MINERALOGY
Mrs. Shirley S. Weeks, EXTENSION HOME ECONOMICS
Bert M. Zuckerman, CRANBERRY STATION RESEARCH

To Instructor:
Verne A. Adams, DAIRY AND ANIMAL SCIENCE
David C. Bartlett, CIVIL ENGINEERING
Harold I. Basch, VETERINARY SCIENCE RESEARCH
Rufus T. Bellamy, ENGLISH
Richard H. Brown, HISTORY
David G. Damon, PHYSICAL EDUCATION FOR MEN

Jeannette G. Davis, FEED AND FERTILIZERS RESEARCH
Mrs. Vera M. H. Day, HOME ECONOMICS
Marilyn B. Derby, HOME ECONOMICS RESEARCH
Catherine A. Dower, EDUCATION
George B. Dyer, PHYSICAL EDUCATION FOR MEN
Elizabeth M. Elbert, FOOD TECHNOLOGY RESEARCH
Norman K. Erickson, GEOLOGY AND MINERALOGY
George B. Goddard, FLORICULTURE
Mrs. Mary E. W. Goss, SOCIOLOGY
Richard H. Graves, FEED AND FERTILIZERS RESEARCH
Louis S. Greenbaum, HISTORY
Norman Greenfeld, PSYCHOLOGY
John L. Hobart, DAIRY AND ANIMAL SCIENCE
Walter Hopkins, MECHANICAL ENGINEERING
John E. Keegan, LANDSCAPE ARCHITECTURE
Rouben Khatchikian, FOOD TECHNOLOGY
John A. MacCombie, FRENCH
James E. MacMonegle, PHYSICS
Mrs. Iole F. Magri, ROMANCE LANGUAGES
C. Maxwell Martin, FOOD TECHNOLOGY RESEARCH
Harvey A. Miller, BOTANY
Ira Mintz, PSYCHOLOGY
John G. Moner, ZOOLOGY
Clifford N. Oliver, MATHEMATICS
Philip R. Pearson, AGRONOMY RESEARCH
Ramon J. Rhine, PSYCHOLOGY
Eva Schiffer, GERMAN

Alvin J. Simmons, PSYCHOLOGY
Dana P. Snyder, ZOOLOGY
Robert J. Steamer, GOVERNMENT
Mrs. Mary L. Tapp, GERMAN
Robert F. Trocchi, ELECTRICAL ENGINEERING
Eugene J. Tynan, GEOLOGY AND MINERALOGY
Mrs. Frances L. Warne, HOME ECONOMICS
Cecilia Welna, MATHEMATICS
John M. White, AGRONOMY RESEARCH

Resignations:
Head of Department:
Herbert N. Stapleton, AGRICULTURAL ENGINEERING
Associate Professor:
Ulrich K. Goldsmith, GERMAN

Assistant Professor:
Theodore L. Batke, CHEMICAL ENGINEERING
Jack F. Davis, PHYSICAL EDUCATION FOR MEN
Bernard Mausner, PSYCHOLOGY
Daniel J. McCarthy, EDUCATION
Gerald J. McLindon, LANDSCAPE ARCHITECTURE
Nathan L. Shipkowitz, VETERINARY SCIENCE RESEARCH
Theodore J. Wang, PHYSICS

Instructor:

Robert J. Allio, MECHANICAL ENGINEERING
Frank D. Bartlett, Jr., ANIMAL HUSBANDRY
Leo P. Beninato, VETERINARY SCIENCE RESEARCH
Robert A. Bennett, VETERINARY SCIENCE
Edward S. Berestka, FEED AND FERTILIZERS RESEARCH
Richard W. Butler, MECHANICAL ENGINEERING
Hall G. Buzzell, MATHEMATICS
James W. Chadwick, Jr., ANIMAL HUSBANDRY
Joan T. Cody, FEED AND FERTILIZERS RESEARCH
Walter E. Conrad, CHEMISTRY
Martin S. Cryan, FOOD TECHNOLOGY
Lyle G. Dearden, ZOOLOGY
Arthur J. Field, SOCIOLOGY
Almon S. Fish, POMOLOGY
John C. Fisher, GEOLOGY AND MINERALOGY
Edith C. Forbes, HOME ECONOMICS
Alice Georgantas, ROMANCE LANGUAGES
Eva R. Grubler, PSYCHOLOGY
Mrs. Katherine W. Irvin, HOME ECONOMICS
Pearl Kane, HOME ECONOMICS RESEARCH
Edwin H. Ketchledge, BOTANY
David W. Knudsen, ELECTRICAL ENGINEERING
Henry Kratz, Jr., GERMAN
Lorraine D. Lavallee, MATHEMATICS
William E. McClellan, GEOLOGY AND MINERALOGY
Donald E. Nevel, CIVIL ENGINEERING

John C. Nicholson, PHYSICS
Donald J. Olsen, HISTORY
Marion B. Rhodes, FEED AND FERTILIZERS RESEARCH
Donald S. Scheufele, CHEMISTRY
Ralph E. Schwartz, MATHEMATICS
Robert C. Simmons, EXTENSION COMMUNICATIONS
Leo F. Solt, HISTORY
Rene S. Taube, ROMANCE LANGUAGES

Leaves of Absence:

Doric Alviani
James F. Anderson
Norman W. Butterfield
Kenneth D. Cashin
Alton B. Cole
Mrs. Gladys M. Cook
Thomas A. Culbertson
Edward L. Davis
William A. Davis
Robert A. Fitzpatrick
Paul A. Gagnon
Mrs. Floriana T. Hogan
E. Vickery Hubbard
Miner J. Markuson
Guy R. Mermier

Helen S. Mitchell
Donald E. Moser
Claude C. Neet
Charles F. Oliver
Otto P. Pflanze
Robert A. Potash
Sargent Russell

Walter W. Smith
James G. Snedecor
Mrs. Emily P. Thies
Zina J. Tillona
Robert G. Tucker
Anthony W. Zaitz
John K. Zeender

ERSITY

ACHUSETTS

SUMMER SESSIONS
1956

Announcement of Courses

Special Summer Session Highlights

EDUCATION WORKSHOP IN THE UNIT METHOD
OF CURRICULA DEVELOPMENT

AMERICAN STUDIES CONCENTRATION

DRIVER EDUCATION INSTRUCTOR COURSE

GRADUATE COURSES IN STATISTICS, FRENCH AND GERMAN

COURSES IN ENGINEERING, FORESTRY, PUBLIC HEALTH AND NURSING

FIELD COURSES IN CONSERVATION OF NATURAL RESOURCES

SPECIAL DAYS DEVOTED TO FOREIGN LANDS AND PEOPLE

ADMINISTRATIVE OFFICERS

J. PAUL MATHER, B.S.C., M.B.A., M.A., LL.D., D.SC................................*President*

SHANNON MCCUNE, B.A., M.A., PH.D....................................*Provost*

GILBERT L. WOODSIDE, B.A., M.A., PH.D.............*Dean of the Graduate School*

MARSHALL O. LANPHEAR, B.S., M.S..................................*Registrar*

DONALD W. CADIGAN, B.S., M.S...........................*Associate Registrar*

ROBERT S. HOPKINS, JR., B.A., M.ED...........................*Dean of Men*

HELEN CURTIS, A.B., A.M...................................*Dean of Women*

JAMES W. BURKE, B.S...*Secretary*

HUGH MONTGOMERY, B.S., B.S. in L.S. ....*Librarian*

KENNETH W. JOHNSON, B.S......................................*Treasurer*

CALENDAR FOR SIX WEEK SESSION

July 2, Monday, 1-5 P.M., Registration, Drill Hall.

July 3, Tuesday, 8 A.M., Classes begin.

July 4, Independence Day, No University exercises.

August 10-11, Friday, Saturday, Final examinations.

August 11, Saturday, 12 noon, end of Summer Session.

* * * *

Registration for other summer courses at Registrar's Office, South College, on the first day of the session.

VOLUME XLVIII   APRIL, 1956   NUMBER 4

Published five times a year by the University of Massachusetts, January, February, April (two), May. Entered at Post Office, Amherst, Mass., as second-class matter.

PUBLICATION OF THIS DOCUMENT APPROVED BY GEORGE J. CRONIN, STATE PURCHASING AGENT

2m-4-56-917368

UNIVERSITY OF MASSACHUSETTS
SUMMER SESSIONS
1956

MAIN SESSION . . . . JULY 2 — AUGUST 11
SPECIAL COURSES . . . . JUNE 3 — SEPTEMBER 14

Programs Offered

The 1956 Summer Sessions at the University provide an opportunity for study in many basic courses and special fields. The program has been planned to serve the needs of teachers and school administrators, as well as undergraduate students and veterans who wish to accelerate their education.

Among the special features is a program of courses and allied activities in American Studies which should be of particular interest to English and History teachers. Four courses in English (English 76, Modern Poetry, English 85 and 86, Major American Writers, and English 87, Problems in American Literary and Linguistics Studies) will be offered; one course in the History of New England to 1860 (History 79); and two courses in American government and political thought (Government 25, American Government; Government 66, American Political Thought). The College English Association, through its national office at the University, is arranging a symposium on American Studies during the session, and several well-known scholars and writers will be in attendance to lead panel discussions and hold conferences with interested students. The University's location in the heart of a region that is rich in cultural association is a very real advantage for the program.

A number of courses taking advantage of the location of the University in the Connecticut Valley will also be offered. These courses will include field work and observation as basic parts of their programs. A course on the Conservation of Natural Resources (Wildlife Management 152) will be taught with the help of a number of distinguished lecturers and leaders in the field of conservation. The basic courses in Botany and Geology will have the surrounding area as their laboratory. Art 33, 34, Freehand Drawing, will emphasize landscape drawing and painting; no prerequisites, other than enthusiasm, are necessary for this course.

A workshop in Education, Education 215, of interest to school administrators and teachers in the fields of elementary and secondary school curriculum will be held June 11-29. Several consultants from the State Department of Education will assist the faculty of the University in conducting the workshop, with emphasis being placed on the planning and construction of units in those fields represented by members of the class. The varied courses in Education will benefit teachers and those who wish to prepare themselves for teaching.

Nursing courses (including instruction and correlated clinical experience) will be given in selected cooperating hospitals and at Vassar College by the nursing faculty of the University and the allied professional staffs of the cooperating agencies.

Special courses in Engineering (chemical, civil, and mechanical), Forestry, and Public Health will also be offered.

In cooperation with the Center for Safety Education of New York University, a two-week Driver Education Instructor course, Physical Education 80,

180, will be offered June 25—July 6. This course prepares teachers seeking certification to teach driver education in secondary schools.

A series of "Days for Asian Understanding" of interest to public school teachers, adults residing in the area, and students and faculty at the University and nearby institutions of higher education are included as part of the main summer session program. The days will be devoted to gaining a better understanding of four Asian countries. Representatives of the embassies of the countries under consideration, foreign students and visitors from the country, and United States government officials and American scholars concerned with the country will spend a day on the campus. The dates selected are Thursdays: July 12, 19, 26, and August 2. A typical day will include a luncheon, afternoon discussion, films, informal visitations and conversation, dinner at the University Commons, and panel discussion in the evening on American foreign policy as related to the country being considered for the day.

Credit for Summer Work

All courses carry degree credit and are equivalent in method, content and credit to courses offered in the University during the regular academic year. Credits obtained in these courses are ordinarily accepted as transfer credits by other colleges and universities. Students desiring to pursue courses for advanced degrees must seek the approval of the Dean of the Graduate School.

Amount of Work Permitted

Students attending the Main Summer Session usually carry two courses, enabling them to earn six or seven semester hours credit. University of Massachusetts undergraduates will receive permission to take more than two courses only if their scholastic average has been 3.0 quality point or better for the last two semesters. A student from another college can enroll for more than two courses only if the appropriate official of his own college submits a statement recommending such a program and certifying that he is an honor student at that institution.

Expenses

Tuition for residents of Massachusetts . . .	$ 5.00 per credit hour
Tuition for non-residents of Massachusetts . .	10.00 per credit hour
Student Health and Activities Fee	2.00
Room rent for six weeks at $4.00 per week . .	24.00
Board for six weeks (Monday through Friday) at $9.50 per week	57.00

Advance Enrollment

To expedite advance enrollment or to obtain approval of admission, students contemplating attendance should notify the Registrar as soon as possible, using the application form on the last page.

Veterans and Residents

Veterans who plan to enroll under the G. I. Bill (P.L. 346, 16, 894, and 550) must present at the time of registration evidence of eligibility (V.A. certificate of eligibility or, if previously enrolled, a clearance through the University

Coordinator). Veterans failing to obtain certification must make payment of tuition and fees.

New students who are not taking courses under G. I. Bills must file certificate of residence with the Treasurer's Office.

Recreation

Under the direction of a faculty-student committee, programs for recreation offering many informal sports such as swimming, softball, baseball, tennis and hiking will be arranged. Special lectures and entertainment, such as a trip to Sturbridge Village and a play at Mountain Park, will also be provided. Dances and one major picnic will be scheduled by the Social Committee.

The surrounding area offers many opportunities for informal picnics and hiking. In addition, square dance festivals are held in nearby towns.

6

COURSE DIRECTORY

The University reserves, for itself and its departments, the right to withdraw or change the announcements made in this catalogue.

Courses numbered 1-99 carry undergraduate credit only. Those numbered 200 or over admit graduate students only. Courses numbered 100-199 are undergraduate courses for which graduate students may receive graduate credit with the completion of additional requirements as determined by the instructor,

ART 33, 34. Freehand Drawing. Either Art 33 or Art 34 may be taken: Art 33 is a non-professional course in elementary drawing and painting in various media in black and white; Art 34 is a non-professional course in which the use of color is stressed in various media and paintings in still-life and landscape subjects are produced. Credit 3
1 - 3:50 MTWTF, Wilder Hall — Mr. MacIver

BOTANY 1. Introductory Botany. The morphology and physiology plants.
1 - 1:50 MTWTF, Clark Hall 105 — Credit 3
2 - 3:50 MTWT, Clark Hall 202 — Mr. Delisle

CHEMISTRY 29. Qualitative Analysis. Systematic semi micro analysis in a study of the principles and laws of the behavior of solutions of electrolytes.
1 - 2:00 MTWTF, Goessmann 26 — Credit 4
2 - 4:50 MTWTF, Goessmann 7 — Mr. Smith
Prerequisites, Chemistry 1 and 2 (or equivalent)

CHEMISTRY 30. Quantitative Analysis. The theory and practice of representative determinations, both gravimetric and volumetric. Credit 4
8 - 9:10 MTWTF, Goessmann 28 — Mr. Roberts
9:20 - 11:50 MTWTF, Goessmann 228
Prerequisite, Chemistry 29

CHEMISTRY 33. Organic Chemistry. A short course intended to satisfy the requirements in this field for all students who do not specialize in Chemistry.
9:20 - 10:30 MTWTF, Goessmann 28 — Credit 4
1 - 4:50 TT, Goessmann 112 — Mr. McWhorter
Prerequisites, Chemistry 1 and 2

ECONOMICS 25. Elements of Economics. Definitions and introductory principles of production, exchange, and the financial organization of society, with a short survey of the economics of distribution and the use of wealth and income. Credit 3
9:20 - 10:30 MTWTF, Engineering Building 16 — Mr. Howard

EDUCATION 51, 151. History of Education. A study of the problems of modern education as seen in historic perspective as part of great social developments. Credit 3
9:20 - 10:30 MTWTF, Gunness Laboratory 10 — Mr. Adams

EDUCATION 61, 161. Elementary School Reading. Methods and materials in a developmental program of reading instruction. Credit 3
9:20 - 10:30 MTWTF, Gunness Laboratory 11 — Miss O'Leary

EDUCATION 62, 162. Elementary School Arithmetic. Methods and materials in teaching arithmetic in elementary grades and correlating it with the total program. Credit 3
10:40 - 11:50 MTWTF, Gunness Laboratory 10 — Mr. Cosgrove

EDUCATION 66, 166.   Preparation and Use of Audio-Visual Aids.   A wide variety of aids studied from the point of view of how they may be used effectively in teaching.   Credit 3
9:20 - 10:30 MTWTF, Engineering Building 28   Mr. Wyman

EDUCATION 181.   Workshop in The Teaching of Modern Foreign Languages in Elementary Schools.   The latest techniques, methods and materials will be presented and demonstrated.   Some roundtable discussions with Education, Romance Language and Psychology departments.   The course is especially designed for present and prospective elementary school teachers and for teachers of a Modern Foreign Language.   Minor credit for students who have a major in a Modern Foreign Language.
10:40 - 11:50 MTWTF, demonstration hours 9:20 - 10:30 MTWTF, Liberal Arts Annex 8   Credit 3
                                                                                                          Mr. Tarrant

EDUCATION 83, 183.   Principles of Secondary Education.   Aims, pupil population, program, guidance, problems and trends of junior and senior high school.   Credit 3
8 - 9:10 MTWTF, Gunness Laboratory 10   Mr. Adams

EDUCATION 209.   Secondary School Administration.   Housing, finance, schedule, library, cafeteria, supervision, and public relations from the standpoint of the junior or senior high school principal.   Credit 3
10:40 - 11:50 MTWTF, Gunness Laboratory 11   Mr. Oliver

EDUCATION 211.   Community Relations for School Personnel.   The development of good public relations, policies and techniques of assisting lay people in interpreting school activities, policies, and objectives.   Credit 3
8 - 9:10 MTWTF, Gunness Laboratory 11   Mr. Oliver

EDUCATION 259.   Teaching Elementary School Science.   Methods and materials and their place in the activity program.   Credit 3
8 - 9:10 MTWTF, Engineering Building 28   Mr. Cosgrove

EDUCATION 265.   Techniques in Remedial Reading.   Methods and materials in diagnosis and remedial instruction.   Credit 3
10:40 - 11:50 MTWTF, Engineering Building 28   Miss O'Leary

EDUCATION 267.   Audio-Visual Laboratory.   Practical experience in setting up and using common audio-visual equipment and materials.   Credit 3
10:40 - 11:50 MTWTF, South College   Mr. Wyman

ENGLISH 2 & SPEECH 4.   English Composition.   Intended to teach straight thinking, sound structure, clear and correct expression.   Credit 3
8 - 9:10 MTWTF, Old Chapel A   Mr. Savage

ENGLISH 25, 26:   Humane Letters.   A general reading course based upon a chronological selection of masterpieces: classical, continental and English.
English 25, 8 - 9:10 MTWTF, Liberal Arts Annex 12A   Credit 3
                                                                                                          Mr. Helming
English 26, 10:40 - 11:50 MTWTF, Old Chapel A   Credit 3
                                                                                                          Mr. Clark

ENGLISH 76, 176.   Modern Poetry.   This course attempts to trace the spirit of twentieth century poetry from such authors as Hardy, Whitman, and Emily Dickinson to those of the present day.   Credit 3
10:40 - 11:50 MTWTF, Old Chapel Seminar   Mr. Dearing

ENGLISH 77, 177. The Modern Novel. An analytical presentation of eleven novels written between 1890 and 1930 in which the expanding form and the extension of critical themes will be stressed. Credit 5
9:20 - 10:30 MTWTF, Old Chapel D   Mr. Lane

ENGLISH 85, 185. Major American Writers. A study of a selected group of the major American writers of the nineteenth and early twentieth century. The authors to be read and discussed will include Emerson, Hawthorne, Longfellow, Lowell, Henry James, Henry Adams, Fitzgerald, and Hemingway. A careful analysis will be made of the varying literary forms given to such dominant themes as nature and the conflict between the individual and society. Credit 3
9:20 - 10:30 MTWTF, Old Chapel B   Mr. O'Donnell

ENGLISH 86, 186. Major American Writers. A study of a selected group of major American writers of the nineteenth and early twentieth century. The authors to be read and discussed include Cooper, Poe, Melville, Thoreau, Whitman, Mark Twain, Stephen Crane, Sinclair Lewis, and Faulkner. A careful analysis will be made of the varying literary forms given to such dominant themes as nature and the conflict between the individual and society. Credit 3
1:20 - 2:30 MTWTF, Old Chapel B   Mr. Kaplan

ENGLISH 87, 187. Problems in American Literary and Linguistics Studies. An exploration of problems connected with the teaching of American language and literature in the context of American culture and in their other cultural inter-relationships; and of problems connected with criticism and research in American literary and linguistic studies. Credit 3
8 - 9:10 MTWTF, Old Chapel B   Mr. Dearing

FRENCH. Graduate Reading Course. For graduate students wishing to prepare for the graduate reading examination. No credit
8 - 9:10 MTWTF, Liberal Arts Annex 12   Mr. Ferrigno

GEOLOGY 1. Physical Geology. An introduction to the agents and processes that modify the earth's crust. Geological phenomena of Connecticut Valley will be stressed. Credit 3
8 - 10:30 MTWTF, Fernald Hall B   Mr. Rice

GERMAN 2. Elementary German. Second semester of elementary German.
10:40 - 11:50 MTWTF, Liberal Arts Annex 1   Credit 3
                                                     Mr. Lea

GERMAN. Graduate Reading Course. For graduate students wishing to prepare for the graduate reading examination. No credit
8 - 9:10 MTWTF, Liberal Arts Annex 1   Mr. Lea

GOVERNMENT 25. American Government. A study of the principles, machinery, dynamics and problems of American national government. Credit 3
9:20 - 10:30 MTWTF, Goessmann 26   Mr. Steamer

GOVERNMENT 26. European Government. A study of the politics and institutions of Great Britain, France, U.S.S.R. and other European countries.
10:40 - 11:50 MTWTF, Goessmann 26   Credit 3
                                                     Mr. Tinder

GOVERNMENT 66. American Political Thought. A study of the development of American political thought from colonial times to the present.
8 - 9:10 MTWTF, Goessmann 26   Credit 3
                                                                      Mr. Steamer

HISTORY 6. Modern European Civilization. A basic survey course covering the period from 1815 to the present.   Credit 3
10:40 - 11:50 MTWTF Old Chapel C   Mr. Zeender

HISTORY 70, 170. Europe Since 1918. Approximately half of the course is devoted to international affairs, the other half to a study of recent internal developments in the principal European countries.   Credit 3
8 - 9:10 MTWTF, Old Chapel C   Mr. Caldwell

HISTORY 79, 179. New England to 1860. A survey of the colonial and early national periods, with emphasis upon the political, social and economic aspects of the life in this region.   Credit 3
9:20 - 10:30 MTWTF, Old Chapel C   Mr. Cary

MATHEMATICS 6. Introductory Calculus for Engineers. May be used as a substitute for Mathematics 29, Differential Calculus. Differentiation, with applications; technique of integration.   Credit 4
Section I, 10:40 - 12:20 MTWTF, Math Building B   Mr. Moser, Mr. Wagner
Section II, 10:40 - 12:20 MTWTF, Math Building G
Prerequisites, Algebra, Trigonometry and Plane Analytic Geometry.

MATHEMATICS 7. Algebra and Trigonometry. Fractions, quadratic equations, exponents, logarithms, variation, determinants of the second and third orders, and plane trigonometry.   Credit 3
9:20 - 10:30 MTWTF, Math Building B   Mr. Moser

PSYCHOLOGY 26. General Psychology. An introductory course dealing with the basic principles and applications of psychology with regard to the understanding and control of behavior.   Credit 3
8 - 9:10 MTWTF, Liberal Arts Annex 27   Mr. Feldman

PSYCHOLOGY 82, 182. Psychological Tests. Different varieties of psychological tests are studied. Practice will be given in administering, scoring, interpreting and evaluating tests.   Credit 3
9:20 - 10:30 MTWTF, Liberal Arts Annex 22   Mr. Epstein
One 3-hour laboratory by arrangement
Prerequisite, Psychology 26

PSYCHOLOGY 94, 194. Child Psychology. The course aims to develop an understanding of the behavior of the child. Psychological aspects of the following are considered: original nature, maturation, play social behavior, personality and mental hygiene.   Credit 3
9:20 - 10:30 MTWTF, Liberal Arts Annex 27   Mr. . . . .
Prerequisite Psychology 26

PSYCHOLOGY 252. Diagnostic Methods I. An intensive study of the methods of administration and of the scoring procedures of a variety of diagnostic methods with emphasis on the Rorschach and Thematic Apperception Test.
10:40 - 11:50 MTWTF, Liberal Arts Annex 22   Credit 3
Prerequisite, Psychology 182   Mr. Epstein

ROMANCE LANGUAGES 215. Seminar in French. A concentrated study of the many highly specialized techniques essential for language proficiency and teaching skills. The seminar offers a complete training leading to the now requisite oral mastery of French, to correct grammatical techniques and analyses, to accurate *explication de texte,* to linguistics and present-day pedagogical procedures. Conducted by specialists in the field of phonetics, linguistics and literature. Procedures will depend upon the most recent funds of information and will be directed toward the most apparent needs of the group.
8 - 9:10 MTWTF, Liberal Arts Annex 8   Credit 2-3
                                                              Mr. Tarrant

SOCIOLOGY 25. Introduction to Sociology. An outline study of the social order and of the individual considered as a member of his various groups.
8 - 9:10 MTWTF, Old Chapel D   Credit 3
                                                      Mr. King

SOCIOLOGY 57, 157 (I) The Family. The study of the development of the customs of courtship and marriage of the contemporary American family. The basic causes of changes and trends of the family are considered. Such topics as mate selection, marriage laws, marital prediction, husband-wife relations, and the role of the child are considered.   Credit 3
10:40 - 11:50 MTWTF, Old Chapel D   Mr. King
Prerequisite, Sociology 25

SPANISH 2. Elementary Spanish. The essentials of Spanish grammar, intensive oral drill and intensive reading of short stories.   Credit 3
10:40 - 11:50 MTWTF, Liberal Arts Annex 12   Mr. Ferrigno
Prerequisite, Spanish 1

SPEECH 91. Extempore Speech. The theory and practice of public speaking for business and professional purposes.   Credit 3
9:20 - 10:30 MTWTF, Old Chapel Auditorium   Mr. Niedeck

STATISTICS 77, 177. Elementary Experimental Statistics. Chi square "t" and analysis of variance tests of significance: frequency distribution, averages, dispersion, regression and simple correlation description; and chart and table presentation are the specific fields covered.   Credit 3
1 - 3 MTWTF, Draper Hall 111   Mr. Russell

WILDLIFE MANAGEMENT 152. Conservation of Natural Resources. A description of, and conservation of basic natural resources including soil, water, forest, wildlife, metallic and non-metallic minerals and the sources of energy including atomic energy. Course includes lectures, demonstrations, and field exercises.   Credit 4
1 - 3 MWF, 1 - 5 TT, Conservation Building   Mr. Trippensee

SPECIAL COURSES

Department of Education

EDUCATION 215. Curriculum Workshop in Elementary and Secondary Schools. For administrators, supervisors, elementary and secondary school teachers; attention given largely to the planning and construction of resource units in those fields represented by the class. Particular attention will be given to the general education fields. The program, comprising class and laboratory hours, is flexible as far as laboratory hours are concerned. Teachers who complete their teaching responsibilities a week after the course begins may still enroll in the workshop by attending the daily group meetings of the class from 4-6 p.m. during the first week. Any laboratory periods not attended during the first week may be made up during the second and third weeks of the workshop. Credit 3

3 weeks. June 11-29

1st week: class hours 4 - 6 p.m.; laboratory 9 - 11 a.m. or 2 - 4 p.m.

2nd and 3d weeks: class hours 10 - 12 a.m.; laboratory 8 - 10 a.m. or 2 - 4 p.m.

Liberal Arts Annex 32 and 30   The Department and consultants
from State Department of Education

School of Engineering

CHEMICAL ENGINEERING 75. Instrumentation. A detailed study of the underlying principles and practices of indicating, recording and controlling instruments used on industrial process equipment. Credit 3

Three 40-hour weeks: Aug. 6-24   Mr. Lindsey and Mr. Goodchild

Engineering Annex

Prerequisites, Physics 27, 28; Chemical Engineering 55, Calculations

CHEMICAL ENGINEERING 88. Chemical Engineering Laboratory. A quantitative study of pilot plant size equipment illustrating some unit operations.

Three 40-hour weeks: Aug. 27-Sept. 14   Credit 3

Engineering Annex   Mr. Cashin and Mr. Goodchild

Prerequisite, Chemical Engineering 56, Unit Operations II

CIVIL ENGINEERING 27. Plane Surveying. The basic principles of mensuration; use of tape, transit, and level; a brief consideration of route surveying for forestry majors. Credit 3

Three 40-hour weeks: July 16-Aug. 3; Aug. 6-24; Aug. 27-Sept. 14

Engineering Building   Mr. Boyer, Mr. Grow

Prerequisite, Mathematics 5, Introductory Engineering Mathematics, or Mathematics 7, Algebra and Trigonometry

CIVIL ENGINEERING 28. Property and Topographic Surveying. A transit and tape property survey requiring reference to Registry of Deeds records; also a topographical survey. Credit 3

Three 40-hour weeks: June 4-22; June 25-July 13

Engineering Building   Mr. Boyer, Mr. Grow

Prerequisite, Civil Engineering 25, Surveying or Civil Engineering 27, Plane Surveying.

12.

CIVIL ENGINEERING 30. Route Surveying Practice. A preliminary survey for a short highway location and the preparation of maps and profile. Credit 3
Three 40-hour weeks: June 4-22; June 25-July 13   Mr. Grow, Mr. Boyer
Engineering Building
Prerequisite, Civil Engineering 25 or 27

MECHANICAL ENGINEERING 23. Shop. Welding and machine shop, use of various machine and hand tools used in metal working.   Credit 3
Three 40-hour weeks: Aug. 6-24; Aug. 27-Sept. 14   Mr. Patterson, Mr. Costa
Engineering Shop

MECHANICAL ENGINEERING 27. Shop. Welding, manual and automatic. For mechanical engineering majors.   Credit 3
Three 40-hour weeks: June 4-22; June 25-July 13   Mr. Patterson, Mr. Pira
Engineering Shop

MECHANICAL ENGINEERING 28. Machine Shop. The fundamental machine tools; lathe, planer, shaper, milling machine and drill press.   Credit 3
Three 40-hour weeks: June 4-22; June 25-July 13   Mr. Hopkins, Mr. Costa
Engineering Shop

Department of Forestry and Wildlife Management

FORESTRY 55, 155. The Elements of Forest Mensuration. Methods of determining the volume and value of the forest growing stock; type mapping; methods of predicting growth of trees and stands.   Credit 3
Three 44-hour weeks: June 4-23   Mr. MacConnell, Mr. Ganley
Conservation Building

FORESTRY 78. Harvesting of Forest Products. Practice in the harvesting and preparation of direct forest products. Field trips to active forest properties and to visit pulpwood operations and manufacturing plants.   Credit 3
Three 44-hour weeks: June 25-July 14   Mr. MacConnell, Mr. Ganley
Conservation Building

Department of Physical Education for Men

PHYSICAL EDUCATION 80, 180. Driver Education and Driver Training. Objectives, scope, content, and problems of driver training; teaching materials; psycho-physical tests; motor vehicle construction, operation, and maintenance; advanced driving practices; administrative standards; practice teaching and behind-the-wheel instruction. Offered in cooperation with the Center for Safety Education, New York University, and the Massachusetts Registry of Motor Vehicles.   Credit 2
8 - 12 MTWTF June 25-July 6   Mr. Stack and Staff
Curry Hicks Gymnasium

Department of Bacteriology and Public Health

PUBLIC HEALTH 92. Supervised Field Training. For Public Health majors only. 13 weeks: June 4-July 6, Marshall Hall Annex then in the field.
Credit 3-6
New England Field Training Staff

School of Nursing

(Continuing courses, with registration restricted to full-time students enrolled in the Basic Collegiate Program of the University of Massachusetts School of Nursing)

NURSING 27. Fundamentals of Nursing. This course introduces the student to the nursing care of the patient in the hospital. Emphasis is placed upon the fundamentals of nursing care for all patients and the relationship of the nurse to agencies and personnel providing individual, family and community health services.

June 11-August 3 at Springfield Hospital   Credit 9
Prerequisite, Nursing 26   Miss Gilmore

NURSING 28. Social and Historical Foundations of Nursing. A survey course of nursing history from the pre-Christian era to the present. The influence of society upon nursing in the various historical periods is considered in relation to the development of nursing as a profession.   Credit 2
June 11-August 3 at Springfield Hospital   Miss Maher
Prerequisite, Nursing 26

NURSING 52A. Nursing of Children I. This course is designed to give the student an increased understanding of the continuing influence of the family on the growing child and the influence of the developing child on his parents and siblings. Through observation and participation in the care of children (two to twelve years of age), case studies and group discussion, the student gains an appreciation of variations in normal growth and development and parent-child relationships.

July 1 to 31 at Vassar Summer Institute   Credit 4
Prerequisites, Home Economics 70, Nursing 26, 27(S), 51

                              Miss DiMaggio and the professional
                              staff of the Vassar Summer Institute

NURSING 57. Maternity Nursing. Unit I of the course in Maternity Nursing is developed around the meaning of pregnancy to the patient and the family with special emphasis on the mother's physiological and psychological needs, before, during and after the birth of the child. Some specialized skills in maternity nursing are taught in relation to an understanding and appreciation of the phenomena of pregnancy and the birth process, the immediate care of mother and infant, newborn care, the importance for early constructive mother-child relationships, and the need for patient teaching.

August 2-31 at Wesson Maternity Hospital, Springfield   Credit 3
Prerequisites, Nursing 26, 27(S), 51   Miss DiMaggio and Miss Wilson

UNIVERSITY OF MASSACHUSETTS SUMMER SCHOOL APPLICATION

Prospective students (except those enrolled at the University during the spring semester) should send this application to the Registrar, University of Massachusetts, as soon as possible. In this way admission to courses with limited enrollment can be assured. Regularly enrolled students at the University will secure a special application form at the Registrar's Office.

Mr.
Name Mrs. ....

Miss   Last   First   Middle

Home address..

Street and number

....

City   State

Indicate educational institutions above secondary school level that you have attended ....

....

What degrees and where earned...

If you are now enrolled at another college, have the following statement completed by your Registrar (a transcript of record is not required):

This is to certify that .... is in good standing

Student's name

at .... and has our approval to take the courses

Name of college

listed on this application.

Signed ....

Will you be studying under the G. I. Bill? ....

Will you require a dormitory room? ....

Will you commute from home? ....

Tentative Program

A normal program consists of two courses. An additional course can be approved only in case the student's academic record is high. (See page 2 under heading, Amount of Work Permitted.)

List the courses for which you wish to be registered.

Courses: Name and number   Descriptive title

OTHER BULLETINS:

UNDERGRADUATE COURSES
GRADUATE COURSES
STOCKBRIDGE SCHOOL

Bulletin

THE UNIVERSITY
OF MASSACHUSETTS

Graduate School Number

1957 - 1958

1958 - 1959

The Graduate School Catalogue for the sessions of 1957-1958, 1958-1959 is part of the Ninety-First Annual Report of the University of Massachusetts and in conjunction with the general catalogue of The University it constitutes Part II of Public Document 31 (Sec. 8, Chapter 75, of the General Laws of Massachusetts).

———◆———

AMHERST, MASSACHUSETTS

Volume XLVIII	November, 1956	Number 5

———◆———

Published five times a year by the University of Massachusetts: February, March, April, September, November. Entered at Post Office, Amherst, Mass., as second-class matter.

PUBLICATION OF THIS DOCUMENT APPROVED BY GEORGE J. CRONIN, STATE PURCHASING AGENT
6m-9-56-918493

ACADEMIC CALENDAR
1956 - 1957

January 2, Wednesday	Last day on which thesis outlin may be handed in by Maste degree candidates who plan finish their work by the 1! Commencement.
January 12, Saturday, 12:00 M.. . . .	Classes stop.
January 14, Monday through January 22, Tuesday	Final examinations.
January 28, Monday	Registration of graduate studer
January 30, Wednesday, 8:00 A.M. . . .	Classes resume.
February 8 or 9, Friday, Saturday . . .	Ph.D. language examinations.
February 22, Friday	Washington's Birthday; a ho day.
March 20, Wednesday	Last day on which graduate st dents may drop courses witho failure.
March 20, Wednesday, 5:00 P.M. to March 25, Monday, 8:00 A.M.. . . .	Spring recess.
April 18, Thursday, 5:00 P.M. to April 23, Tuesday, 8:00 A.M.	Easter recess.
April 26 or 27, Friday, Saturday	Ph.D. language examinations.
May 18, Saturday, 12:00 M.	Classes stop.
May 20, Monday, through May 29 Wednesday	Final examinations.
May 28, Tuesday	Last day for bound theses to I handed in.
May 30, Thursday	Memorial Day; a holiday.
May 31, Friday, through June 2, Sunday . .	Commencement.

ACADEMIC CALENDAR
1957 - 1958

September 9, Monday	Registration of graduate students.
September 11, Wednesday, 8:00 A.M. . .	Classes begin.
October 3, Thursday	Last day on which Ph.D. candidates who plan to complete their work by the June, 1958 Commencement may take the preliminary comprehensive examination.
October 4 or 5, Friday, Saturday	Ph.D. language examinations.
October 12, Saturday	Columbus Day; a holiday.
November 1, Friday	Last day on which graduate students may drop courses without failure.
November 11, Monday	Veteran's Day; a holiday.
November 26, Tuesday, 5:00 P.M. to Monday, December 2, 8:00 A.M. . . .	Thanksgiving recess.
December 6 or 7, Friday, Saturday . .	Ph.D. language examinations.
December 18, Wednesday, 5:00 P.M. to January 2, Thursday, 8:00 A.M. . . .	Christmas recess.
January 2, Thursday	Last day on which thesis outlines may be handed in by Master's degree candidates who plan to finish their work by the 1958 Commencement.
January 11, Saturday, 12:00 M.	Classes stop.
January 13, Monday, through January 21, Tuesday	Final examinations.
January 27, Monday	Registration of graduate students.
January 29, Wednesday, 8:00 A.M.	Classes resume.
February 7 or 8, Friday, Saturday . . .	Ph.D. language examinations.
February 22, Saturday	Washington's Birthday; a holiday.
March 20, Thursday	Last day on which graduate students may drop courses without failure.
March 29, Saturday, 12:00 M. to April 8, Tuesday, 8:00 A.M.	Spring recess.
April 19, Saturday	Patriots Day; a holiday.
April 25 or 26, Friday, Saturday	Ph.D. language examinations.
May 20, Tuesday, 5:00 P.M.	Classes stop.
May 22, Thursday, through May 29, Thursday .	Final examinations.
May 28, Wednesday	Last day for bound theses to be handed in.
May 30, Friday	Memorial Day; a holiday.
May 30, Friday through June 1, Sunday . .	Commencement.

3

ACADEMIC CALENDAR
1958-1959

September 8, Monday . . . . . . Registration of graduate students.

September 10, Wednesday, 8:00 A.M. . . Classes begin.

October 2, Thursday . . . . . . Last day on which Ph.D. candidates who plan to complete their work by the June, 1959 Commencement may take the preliminary comprehensive examination.

October 3 or 4, Friday, Saturday . . . Ph.D. language examinations.

October 13, Monday . . . . . . Columbus Day; a holiday.

November 3, Monday . . . . . . Last day on which graduate students may drop courses without failure.

November 11, Tuesday . . . . . Veteran's Day; a holiday.

November 25, Tuesday, 5:00 P.M. to
December 1, Monday, 8:00 A.M. . . . Thanksgiving recess.

December 5 or 6, Friday, Saturday . . . Ph.D. language examinations.

December 20, Saturday, 12:00 M. to
January 5, Monday, 8:00 A.M. . . . Christmas recess.

January 5, Monday . . . . . . Last day on which thesis outlines may be handed in by Master's degree candidates who plan to finish their work by the 1959 Commencement.

January 10, Saturday, 12:00 M. . . . . Classes stop.

January 12, Monday, through January 20,
Tuesday . . . . Final examinations.

January 26, Monday . . . . . . Registration of graduate students.

January 28, Wednesday, 8:00 A.M. . . . Classes resume.

February 6 or 7, Friday, Saturday . . . Ph.D. language examinations.

February 23, Monday . . . . . . Washington's Birthday; a holiday.

March 20, Friday . . . . Last day on which graduate students may drop courses without failure.

March 21, Saturday, 12:00 M. to
March 31, Tuesday, 8:00 A.M. . . . Spring recess.

April 20, Monday . . . . Patriot's Day; a holiday.

April 24 or 25, Friday, Saturday . . . . Ph.D. language examinations.

May 22, Friday, 5:00 P.M. . . . . . Classes stop.

May 25, Monday, through June 3,
Wednesday . . . . Final examinations.

May 30, Saturday . . . . . . Memorial Day; a holiday.

June 3, Wednesday . . . . . . Last day for bound theses to be handed in.

June 5, Friday, through June 7, Sunday . . Commencement.

THE TRUSTEES OF THE UNIVERSITY

Organization of 1957

6

GENERAL INFORMATION

HISTORY

Graduate courses leading to the degree of doctor of science were offered in botany under President Clark and in chemistry under Professor Goessmann as early as 1876. No candidate, however, completed the requirements for that degree. It was not until 1892, under President Henry H. Goodell, that courses leading to the degree of master of science were offered. This degree was first conferred in June, 1896, on two candidates. Graduate courses leading to the degree of doctor of philosophy were first offered in 1897, with chemistry, botany and entomology as major and minor subjects. The first degree was conferred on one candidate in June, 1902.

In the early years the graduate work was conducted under the direct administration of the President in conjunction with the undergraduate program. The demand for advanced work increased, however, and in June, 1908, the trustees made the Graduate School a separate unit in the University.

LOCATION AND LANDS

The University of Massachusetts is located in Amherst, a town of about ten thousand people, overlooking one of the most picturesque sections of the Connecticut Valley. Amherst is eighty-eight miles from Boston, fifty miles from Worcester, twenty-five miles from Springfield, eighteen miles from Greenfield, and eight miles from Northampton. The campus consists of a tract of approximately seven hundred acres, lying about a mile north of the village center. The University is well provided with modern buildings and equipment, description of which may be found in the general catalog.

PURPOSE AND SCOPE OF THE GRADUATE SCHOOL

The purpose of the Graduate School is to provide qualified students with proper guidance in the methods of advanced study and research. Courses are available leading to the degree of doctor of philosophy, master of arts, master of arts in teaching, master of business administration, master of landscape architecture, master of science, master of science in agricultural engineering, master of science in chemical engineering, master of science in civil engineering, master of science in electrical engineering, and master of science in mechanical engineering.

DOCTOR OF PHILOSOPHY

A Guidance Committee of three will be appointed, or if necessary, reappointed, for each student working towards the doctor's degree as soon as possible after his first registration in the Graduate School, and not later than one month prior to his second registration. This committee will be appointed by the Scholarship Committee of the Graduate Council from members of the graduate faculty, recommended by the Department Head of the student's major department, and will consist of two members of the major department and one other person. The responsibilities of this committee shall be to:

a. Plan the entire Graduate School program of the student.

b. Arrange for the preliminary written comprehensive examination of the student.

c. Plan for the satisfying of the language requirement by the student.

d. Supervise the thesis project and arrange for the final examination. The guidance committee will serve as the thesis committee for the Ph.D. candidate.

e. Report the fulfillment of all requirements to the Head of the major department. The vote of the committee to be unanimous on this.

7

The degree is conferred upon graduate students who have met the following requirements:—

1. The preparation of a dissertation satisfactory to the Guidance Committee and the major department.

2. The earning of at least ninety graduate credits, at least sixty of which must be in the major field, at least fifteen in a minor field or fields related to, but not part of, the major field and not more than thirty in recognition of the dissertation.

3. The passing of a preliminary written comprehensive examination in the major and minor fields, supplemented by an oral examination at the option of the major department, both examinations to be conducted by the major department, to be passed not later than eight months before the completion of the candidate's work.

The department in which the student has enrolled for courses in the minor field has a choice of submitting questions for the comprehensive examination or the certifying of the student as having satisfied all the requirements of each course, except that the examination is required for all courses where the grade in the course was C.

If the student fails a part of the comprehensive examination he may be permitted to make up the deficiency under the direction of his guidance committee. In case of failure of the entire comprehensive examination, a candidate may be permitted a second and final opportunity, but not within twelve months.

4. Satisfying the following language requirement:—two languages, foreign to the candidate and not in the same linguistic group, as recommended by the major department. Proficiency tests should be passed as early as possible and must be passed prior to the preliminary examination. See page 14.

5. The passing of a final examination, at least partly oral, conducted by the Guidance Committee primarily upon, but not limited to, the contents of the candidate's dissertation. The Examining Committee shall consist of the Guidance Committee, the Dean of the Graduate School, and such members of the major department as the Head shall appoint.

6. Satisfying the residence requirement. At least 30 course credits must have been earned at this University. No credit is valid after 9 years.

7. The payment of all fees and expenses.

All the above requirements must be completed by the applicable date listed below

May 28
September 10
February 1

if the degree is to be received at the Commencement following the particular date.

MASTER OF ARTS, MASTER OF SCIENCE, MASTER OF SCIENCE IN AGRICULTURAL
ENGINEERING, MASTER OF SCIENCE IN CHEMICAL ENGINEERING, MASTER
OF SCIENCE IN CIVIL ENGINEERING, MASTER OF SCIENCE IN
ELECTRICAL ENGINEERING, AND MASTER OF SCIENCE
IN MECHANICAL ENGINEERING

The basic requirements for the above degrees are:—

1. Thirty graduate credits, of which not more than six may be transferred from other institutions. Twenty-one of the thirty credits must be in the major field. Courses offered for minor credit only cannot be taken for major credit toward an advanced degree by students majoring in the department or non-departmentalized school concerned. If a thesis is offered, six credits must be earned in courses open to graduate students only; if a thesis is not offered, twelve credits must be earned in courses open to graduate students only. Not more than ten credits may be earned by means of a thesis. No credit is valid after 6 years.

8

2. The thesis is optional with the school or department, but if there is one it shall be under the supervision of a committee appointed by the Scholarship Committee of the Graduate School Council. The thesis must be approved by this committee and by the major department. The candidate must pass a general oral examination to be conducted by the thesis committee. If there is no thesis, the candidate shall take a general examination, written or oral, or both under the supervision of the head of his major department. If a student offers a thesis, problem courses shall be limited to three credits; if a thesis is not offered, the limit shall be six credits.

3. All foreign language requirements are optional with the school or departments.

4. All fees and expenses must be paid before the degree will be conferred.

All of the above requirements must be completed by the applicable date listed below

May 28
September 10
February 1

if the degree is to be received at the Commencement following the particular date.

MASTER OF LANDSCAPE ARCHITECTURE

The degree is conferred upon graduate students who have met the following requirements:—

1. Work covering at least two years, of which a minimum of one and one-half years must be devoted to study in residence, and a minimum of one-half year spent in practice, specific requirements concerning the nature of such practice to be laid down by the department.

2. Submission of a written report on the work done in practice, or an oral examination conducted by the department staff.

3. The earning of not less than forty-five credits of which thirty shall conform essentially to the "fifth year program" (see page 90) the remainder to be selected from the "200 series" on page 88, with minor deviations at the discretion of the department.

4. Preparation of a satisfactory thesis.

5. The passing of final examinations, written and oral.

6. Payment of all fees and expenses.

All of the above requirements must be completed by the applicable date listed below.

May 28
September 10
February 1

if the degree is to be received at the Commencement following the particular date.

MASTER OF BUSINESS ADMINISTRATION

1. The Master of Business Administration degree will be granted to those who satisfactorily complete sixty semester hours of approved course work as follows:

25-6. INTRODUCTION TO ACCOUNTING.	* 6	semester hours.
25-6. ELEMENTS OF ECONOMICS.	* 6	semester hours.
179. ELEMENTS OF STATISTICS.	3	semester hours.
153. MARKETING PRINCIPLES.	3	semester hours.
155. FINANCIAL INSTITUTIONS.	3	semester hours.
163. MANAGEMENT IN INDUSTRY.	3	semester hours.

* Undergraduate credit only.

165.	CORPORATION FINANCE.	3 semester hours.
170.	BUSINESS LAW.	3 semester hours.

The above basic courses may be taken as part of a graduate program or may have been anticipated in undergraduate course work.

201.	THE BUSINESS ENTERPRISE.	3 semester hours.
211.	ACCOUNTING IN MANAGEMENT.	3 semester hours.
222.	MARKETING MANAGEMENT.	3 semester hours.
231.	FINANCIAL MANAGEMENT.	3 semester hours.
242.	PRODUCTION MANAGEMENT.	3 semester hours.
252.	ADMINISTRATIVE PRACTICES.	3 semester hours.
271.	SEMINAR IN BUSINESS ADMINISTRATION.	3 semester hours.
272.	SEMINAR IN BUSINESS ADMINISTRATION.	3 semester hours.
	ELECTIVES: two from those available for graduate credit and approved by the adviser.	6 semester hours.

2. A candidate for the Master of Business Administration *with Honors* must submit an acceptable thesis prepared under the direction of a Supervisor appointed by the Scholarship Committee of the Graduate School Council. The thesis may be substituted for one or both of the elective courses as evaluated by the Committee and the Supervisor. If a thesis be adjudged not distinctive, it will be accepted only in lieu of required course work as evaluated by the Committee and the Supervisor.

3. Each candidate for the M.B.A. degree is required to pass an oral examination.

4. All fees and expenses must be paid before the degree will be conferred.

All of the above requirements must be completed by the applicable date listed below

May 28
September 10
February 1

if the degree is to be received at the Commencement following the particular date.

MASTER OF ARTS IN TEACHING

This is a cooperative program between the College of Arts and Sciences and the School of Education intended primarily for graduates of approved Liberal Arts Institutions who have had little or no course work in professional education. The student will register in the School of Education for either the secondary or elementary teaching program.

The special provisions are:—

1. Secondary school program. Eighteen hours in the fundamental education courses usually required for certification; at least twelve hours in general education courses of which six hours will be in the two hundred category (courses open to graduate students only).

2. Elementary school program. Twenty-four hours in the fundamental education courses usually required for certification; at least twelve hours in general education courses of which six hours will be in the two hundred category.

Provisions applying to both groups:—

1. Ordinarily the program will be undertaken in one year of residence or one year plus a summer session, and for this degree no credit will be valid after two years.

2. All fees and expenses must be paid before the degree will be conferred.

All of the above requirements must be completed by the applicable date listed below

May 28
September 10
February 1

if the degree is to be received at the Commencement following the particular date.

ADMISSION

Requirements for admission:—

1. A Bachelor's Degree or the equivalent from any college or university of recognized standing.

2. An official transcript of all previous college work.

3. A letter of recommendation from the head of the department of the applicant's undergraduate major.

4. A letter of recommendation from someone (not connected with the applicant's undergraduate major) who is qualified to judge the student's ability in academic work.

5. The applicant must have been in the upper half of his graduating class. If the transcript does not indicate the rank of the applicant, it is the duty of the Committee on Admissions to evaluate the transcript.

6. Acceptance by the department and by the Admissions Committee of the Graduate School Council.

Admission to the Graduate School does not imply admission to candidacy for an advanced degree. Such candidacy is subject to specific requirements as laid down by the several departments, and the student must secure the approval of the head of the department in which he desires to major before he can become a candidate for a degree in that subject.

Graduates of Normal Schools are permitted to take courses in the 200 series in the School of Education, but not as candidates for a University of Massachusetts Degree.

With the approval of the Head of the Department concerned and the Dean of the Graduate School, special students are permitted to take graduate courses, but not to exceed a total of 15 credits. Special students may not register for thesis credits. If special students do graduate work of high quality they may apply for admission to regular standing in the Graduate School.

GENERAL STATEMENT

Graduate credit will be allowed for grades of A, B, and C. Not more than six credits of C will be allowed for a Master's degree. Not more than twelve credits of C will be allowed for the Doctor of Philosophy degree. Thesis work must receive a grade of A or B to be accepted by the Graduate School. No graduate credit will be given for courses numbered below 100.

After registration is completed, courses may be added or dropped or changed from credit to audit only upon the approval of the student's adviser and the Dean of the Graduate School. The consent of the instructor also is necessary for the addition of courses. If the student is not passing a course at the time it is dropped, a failure will be recorded. No student, under any conditions, may drop a course after these dates: First semester, November 1; second semester, March 20; Summer School, two weeks from the beginning of the summer session, without a failure unless granted permission by the Scholarship Committee of the Graduate School Council.

Students in the Graduate School may be dismissed for failure to abide by the rules of the University.

The University reserves the right to make changes in the requirements for degrees without notice.

COURSES OFFERED

Courses available as major subjects for the degree of doctor of philosophy:—

Agronomy
Bacteriology
Botany
Chemistry
Economics

Entomology
Food Sciences
Food Technology
Psychology
Zoology

Courses available as major subjects for the master's degree:—

Agricultural Economics
Agricultural Engineering
Agronomy
Bacteriology
Botany
Business Administration
Chemical Engineering
Chemistry
Civil Engineering
Dairy and Animal Science
Economics
Education
Electrical Engineering
English
Entomology
Floriculture
Food Technology

Geology and Mineralogy
History
Home Economics
Landscape Architecture
Mathematics
Mechanical Engineering
Olericulture
Philosophy
Pomology
Poultry Science
Public Health
Psychology
Romance Languages
Sociology
Wildlife Management
Zoology

Courses available as minor subjects:—

Agricultural Economics and
  Farm Management
Agricultural Engineering
Agronomy
Bacteriology
Botany
Business Administration
Chemical Engineering
Chemistry
Civil Engineering
Dairy and Animal Science
Economics
Education
Electrical Engineering
English
Entomology
Floriculture
Food Technology
Forestry
Geology and Mineralogy

German
Government
History
Home Economics
Landscape Architecture
Mathematics
Mechanical Engineering
Olericulture
Philosophy
Physical Education for Men
Physics
Pomology
Poultry Science
Psychology
Public Health
Romance Languages
Sociology
Veterinary Science
Wildlife Management
Zoology

THESES

A thesis must be on a topic in the field of the candidate's major subject, and must indicate that its writer possesses the ability and imagination necessary to do independent constructive thinking. The following rules should be adhered to in the preparation and presentation of a thesis:—

The objective of a thesis should be an attempt to make a real contribution to knowledge and practice. When completed it should be of a quality worthy of publication as a contribution from the department concerned.

The thesis, in its completed form, will be judged largely upon the ability of the author to review literature and reach definite deductions; to formulate a problem, plan a method of attack, and work out a solution; and to summarize his material and draw conclusions. Scholastic attainment in writing and presenting the results of the study will also be an important factor in the evaluation. No thesis markedly poor in its English will be accepted.

A. Master's Theses:

Four copies of each Master's thesis outline are to be transmitted to the Dean of the Graduate School by the head of the department in which the student is majoring. The letter of transmittal should contain the name of the professor within the department who is responsible for the direction of the student's research. This professor will be appointed the Chairman of the student's Thesis Committee. Other possible members of the Thesis Committee might be suggested in the letter of transmittal, but the Scholarship Committee of the Graduate School Council has the responsibility of assigning all faculty members to Thesis Committees. If recommended by the Head of the major department, two of the three members of the Thesis Committee may be members of the major department.

It is the responsibility of the chairman of the Thesis Committee to arrange a conference with other members of the Thesis Committee and the student for the purpose of discussing the research problem before approving the thesis outline. This should be done as soon as possible after the appointment of the Thesis Committee.

The fourth copy of the student's thesis outline is then to be signed by each member of the Thesis Committee to indicate approval of the outline and to indicate the fact that a conference with the student has been held. The fourth copy of the thesis outline is then to be returned to the Dean of the Graduate School.

The outline for the thesis for the Master's Degree must be presented not later than January first of the year in which the student expects to get the degree, or five months before he expects to complete the work for the degree.

B. Master's and Ph.D. Theses:

The Thesis Committee will have direct charge of all matters pertaining to the thesis, and it is recommended that the student use the advice available from this source in the progress of his research. The thesis must have the unanimous approval of this committee and of the major department before arrangements are made for the final examination for the degree.

Three complete, bound copies of the thesis, including drawings and any other accessories, are required by the Graduate School in order that the files in the Graduate office, the library, and the department in which the thesis was prepared may be supplied. The original copy will be deposited in the Library by the Graduate School. The student is responsible for the binding of the thesis.

If the thesis is printed, whether in periodical or book form, the fact that it is a thesis submitted for an advanced degree at the University of Massachusetts shall be explicitly stated in the title itself or as a footnote on the front page.

Because of the time required to give adequate consideration to the research conducted by the student, it is highly desirable that theses be submitted to the committee, in the case of doctor's theses, not later than March 15, and in the case of master's theses, not later than May 15 of the academic year in which the degrees are to be conferred. The theses in their final bound form shall be deposited with the Dean of the Graduate School by May 28. (September 10 for students planning to receive their degrees in the fall; February 1 for students planning to receive their degrees in the winter.)

If typewritten, whether designed for publication or to remain in the typewritten form, the size of the sheet, the arrangement of the title page, the general structure of the thesis, the character of the paper, and the binding must conform to definite standards.

A. *Size of sheet.* Size of sheet must measure 8½ x 11 inches.

B. *Form of title page.* The title page should be distributed as artistically as possible and must be arranged in this order:

    a. Subject.
    b. Name of author.
    c. "Thesis submitted in partial fulfillment of the requirements for the degree of—."
    d. "University of Massachusetts, Amherst."
    e. Date.

C. Following the title page, the arrangement may take such form, variable of course with the subject matter, as is illustrated below:—

    a. An analytical outline of the thesis.
    b. An introductory statement in which the purposes of the author are set forth.
    c. The body of the thesis composed of literature critically reviewed and deductions made, formulation of method of attack or procedure, and results secured. (All literature reviews and any work done by others should be so separated that no question can be raised as to which portion of the thesis represents the original investigation. It should be clearly kept in mind that *compilation* is not considered original investigation.)
    d. Summary and conclusions.
    e. Bibliography. (This should have the approval of the chairman of the thesis committee before final arrangement.)
    f. Acknowledgments.
    g. Statements of approval signed by members of the thesis committee.

D. *Paper.* See sample in the University store.

E. *Binding.* See sample of binding in the Graduate School Office.

All theses are the property of the University.

GRADUATE READING EXAMINATION IN FOREIGN LANGUAGES

1. A Graduate Reading Examination will be given by the German and Romance Language Departments upon written request from the chairman of the Department in which the student in question is doing his graduate work. The request should be sent to the chairman of the language department concerned, via the Dean of the Graduate School, at least ten days before the examination is to be administered.

2. The examination will be given four times during the academic year: The candidate may choose one of two consecutive days in the month concerned. The dates are:

1956	September 28 or 29
	November 30 or December 1
1957	February 8 or 9
	April 26 or 27
	October 4 or 5
	December 6 or 7
1958	February 7 or 8
	April 25 or 26
	October 3 or 4
	December 5 or 6
1959	February 6 or 7
	April 24 or 25
	October 2 or 3
	December 4 or 5

3. Prior to the administration of the reading examination the student may, if he and the representative of the language department agree, have a brief, informal interview so that is can be determined whether he has reached the point at which he is likely to deal competently with Ph.D. reading material in the foreign language.

4. The examination will be a written test of the student's ability to translate accurately from the foreign language into English.

5. The examination will consist of passages taken from books and/or journals pertaining to the major field in which the graduate student is working.

6. One of the passages may be taken from a text prepared by the student, if this text has previously been approved by the language department. The student will not be allowed to use a dictionary for this passage.

7. The student will be permitted to use a dictionary for all sight passages. For this purpose a general dictionary will be made available by the language department. If the student possesses a specialized dictionary and wishes to use it he may do so.

8. The examination will be written in the standard University blue book and it will be kept on file in the office of the Foreign Language Department for at least one year from the date of the examination.

9. The Foreign Language Department keeps a reference file of titles, provided by all department chairmen, of books and periodicals suitable for examination purposes. This file will be available to the graduate student upon request.

10. The examination will be graded PASS or FAIL. It is understood that PASS is of at least grade B caliber.

11. A committee of three members of the language department concerned will grade the examination.

12. The Graduate Office, the chairman of the department requesting the examination, and the graduate student concerned will be notified within ten days of the examination whether the student has passed or failed the examination.

13. In case of failure, a study period of at least four months will be required before a re-examination may be given, unless otherwise agreed upon. In the case of repeated failure, the candidate will not be admitted to the examination for the fourth time unless the language department concerned is satisfied that he has made adequate progress.

15

ESTIMATE OF EXPENSES

A charge of $50 per semester, payable in advance, which covers tuition, laboratory and student health fees, is imposed on students who are residents of Massachusetts. For residents of other states or foreign countries, this charge is $110 per semester. In cases where students carry less than a full schedule of courses, a special tuition rate is provided. Residents of the State pay $5 per credit; nonresidents pay $10. For purposes of definition, all students claiming residence in the State shall at time of admission provide the treasurer's office with an official statement from their town or city clerk as evidence.

Candidates for a Master's degree who have paid a full year's tuition in the Graduate School are not required to pay an additional amount if they later register for a Master's degree.

Candidates for the Doctor of Philosophy degree who have paid two full years' tuition in the Graduate School are not required to pay an additional amount if they later register for the Doctor's thesis.

Board should not be in excess of $14 per week. Rooms for graduate students are not available in the dormitories, but can be rented in private homes at from $25 to $30 per month. The cost of books and incidentals should not exceed $150 per year.

LOTTA CRABTREE FELLOWSHIPS

A limited number of fellowships paying $2000 each are available to students in the broad field of agriculture. Students applying for these fellowships must be interested in earning the Doctor of Philosophy degree for the purpose of serving agricultural pursuits. Application should be made to the Dean of the Graduate School.

TEACHING FELLOWSHIPS

The University offers a number of teaching fellowships for the purpose of assisting with the instructional program of various departments. The stipend is $1400 per year, and appointments absolve students from tuition and are especially suited to those who desire to gain teaching experience and to make themselves at least partly self-supporting while continuing their education. It should be recognized, however, that, in cases where students render this part-time service in return for the financial assistance extended, the residence time requirement for the degree in question is necessarily longer. Teaching fellows may carry up to 13 credits per semester, but the total in any one academic year may not exceed 24 credits. Application for appointment to these fellowships should be made to the Dean of the Graduate School or to the head of the department in which the candidate's major interest lies.

RESEARCH FELLOWSHIPS

A number of research fellowships are available to qualified graduate students. These are made possible because funds are provided by a). various industries, b). the Experiment Station, or c). research grants awarded to members of the Graduate School Faculty either from sources outside the University or from a fund provided by the University and administered by the Research Council. Stipends vary with the type of work and the amount of time involved. Interested students should make application to the head of the department in which they plan to work.

THE CRAMPTON RESEARCH FUND

Interest from the Guy Chester Crampton Research Fund is used to help defray the costs of publication of worthy research papers completed by students or occasionally by staff members. Information concerning the fields of work

laborn-
Mass.
is $100
course,
er credit; non-
-g residence in
with an official

-uition in the
t if they later

two full years'
-nal amount if

-duate students

-ot exceed $150

ble to students

the purpose of
-. The stipend
------n and are
e and to make
education. It
-----r this part-
----idence time
----hing fellows
-----ne academic
fellow-
-----head of the

Inter

-----

for which grants may be made, and instructions for application, may be
from department heads, the chairman of the Crampton Fund Committ
graduate school office.

GRADUATE COURSES DURING THE SUMMER

The University offers opportunities to pursue graduate courses d
summer in connection with the Summer School. Details regardin
offered, facilities for study, etc., may be found in the Summer School
a copy of which is available upon request to the Provost of the Univ

DESCRIPTION OF COURSES ·

Agricultural Economics

ADRIAN H. LINDSEY, major adviser.

COURSES OPEN TO GRADUATE STUDENTS ONLY
(For either major or minor credit)

200. RESEARCH.—Investigations of problems in Agricultural Economics an
Farm Management. Credit,
Mr. LINDSE

202. AGRICULTURAL PRICE THEORY.—The application of economic principl
and measurements to the analysis of agricultural prices. Credit,
Mr. WESTCOT

203. ADVANCED FOOD MARKETING.—Interrelationships of markets and price
marketing margins, efficiency techniques, demand and supply analyses.
Mr. FITZPATRIC
Prerequisite, Agricultural Economics 155 or permission of instructor.

205. RESEARCH METHODS IN PRODUCTION ECONOMICS.—A consideration
procedures and techniques applied in economic analysis of the farm firm inclu
ing budgeting (comparative statics), linear programming and other quantitativ
processes. Credit,
Mr. CROSSMO
Prerequisite, Agricultural Economics 175 or permission of instructor.

300. THESIS, Master's Degree. Credit, 4-1

COURSES OPEN TO BOTH GRADUATE AND
UNDERGRADUATE STUDENTS
(For either major or minor credit)

155. MARKETING.—An analysis of the problems, types of marketing agencie
principal marketing functions, marketing costs and margins, price quotatio
and exchange operations, governmental regulations and the consideration
improvement proposals. Credit,
Mr. LINDSE

156. FUNDAMENTALS OF COOPERATION.—A study of the development of c
operative organizations and the economic analysis of cooperative principl
and operation. Credit,
Mr. LINDSE

157. AGRICULTURAL CREDIT AND LAND APPRAISAL.—The principles and met
ods of land valuation and credit extension. There is also a study of the operatio
of institutions granting credit to agriculture. Credit,
Mr. LINDSE

171. AGRICULTURAL ECONOMIC THEORY.—A comparative and critical stud
of the significant contributions of the leading economists from Adam Smith t
the present. Credit,
Mr. LINDSE

18

175. FARM ORGANIZATION AND MANAGEMENT.—A study of the special problems facing particular farm businesses and the application of economic principles in their solution. Problems include choice of enterprises, selection of particular productive combinations and farm adjustments to changing prices and technology.
Credit, 3.
MR. CROSSMON.

176. ADVANCED FARM MANAGEMENT.—Selected case farms representative of certain types of farming conditions in Massachusetts will be carefully analyzed. Plans for alternative farm adjustments will be projected using the budgetary method.
Credit, 3.
MR. CROSSMON.

Statistics 177. ELEMENTARY EXPERIMENTAL STATISTICS.—"Chi" squire, "t" and analysis of variance tests of significance; frequency distribution, average, dispersion, regression and simple correlation description; and chart and table presentation are the specific fields covered.
Students electing Statistics 177 may not take Statistics 179.
Credit, 3.
MR. RUSSELL.

178. PRINCIPLES OF LAND ECONOMICS.—A study of the utilization of agricultural land and the economic problems of development, settlement, conservation and policy.
Credit, 3.
MR. LINDSEY

Statistics 179. ELEMENTARY ECONOMICS STATISTICS.—"Surveys, tables, charts, frequency distributions, averages, dispersion, standard error and its use, quality control, index numbers, time series, and simple correlation are the specific fields covered."
Credit, 3.
Students electing Statistics 179 may not take Statistics 177.   MR. RUSSELL.

Statistics 180. ADVANCED STATISTICAL METHOD.—Multiple correlation and analysis of variance.
Credit, 3.
MR. LINDSEY and MR. RUSSELL.

182. ADVANCED FARM OPERATION.—A study of farm operations with special emphasis on time and motion experiments.
Credit, 3.
THE DEPARTMENT.

189. SEMINAR.—Public and price policy for agriculture.
Credit, 2-3.
MR. LINDSEY.

190. SEMINAR.—Agricultural Institutions.
Credit, 2-3.
MR. RUSSELL

COURSES IN OTHER DEPARTMENTS FOR WHICH MAJOR CREDIT WILL BE GIVEN

BUSINESS ADMINISTRATION 201. The Business Enterprise.
Credit, 3.
MR. SMART.

BUSINESS ADMINISTRATION 211. Accounting in Management.
Credit, 3.
MR. COLWELL.

AGRICULTURAL ECONOMICS

BUSINESS ADMINISTRATION 222. Marketing Management.   Credit, ᵉ
     MR. HARDY

BUSINESS ADMINISTRATION 231. Financial Management.   Credit, ᵉ
     MR. LUDTKI

BUSINESS ADMINISTRATION 242. Production Management.   Credit, ᵉ
     MR. HACKAMACE

BUSINESS ADMINISTRATION 252. Administrative Practices.   Credit, ᵉ
     THE STAFF

BUSINESS ADMINISTRATION 271. Seminar in Business
Administration I.   Credit, ᵉ
     THE STAFF

BUSINESS ADMINISTRATION 272. Seminar in Business
Administration II.   Credit, ᵉ
     THE STAFF

ECONOMICS 200. Special Studies in Economics.   Credit, 2-5 each semester
     THE STAFF

ECONOMICS 210. History of Economic Thought.   Credit, ᵉ
     MR. VATTER

ECONOMICS 213. Central Banking.   Credit, ᵉ
     MR. GAMBLE

ECONOMICS 227. Mathematical Economics and Economic
Model-Building.   Credit, 3
     MR. SCHOEFFLER

ECONOMICS 260. Monopoly and Public Utility Problems.   Credit, 3
     MR. HOWARD

ECONOMICS 272. Advanced Economic Theory.   Credit, 3
     THE STAFF

ECONOMICS 276. Taxation.   Credit, 3
     MR. GAMBLE

ECONOMICS 293, 295, 297. Courses in Aggregative Economics.
(These courses rotate but not in a consistent cycle.)

ECONOMICS 293. Economic Planning.   Credit, 3
     MR. MORRIS

ECONOMICS 294. Institutional Economics   Credit, 3
     MR. HOWARD

ECONOMICS 295. Full Employment.   Credit, 3
     MR. GAMBLE

ECONOMICS 297. Economic Fluctuations.   Credit, 3
     MR. SCHOEFFLER

ECONOMICS 154.   Money and Monetary Policy.   Credit, 3.
                                                              MR. GAMBLE.

ECONOMICS 155.   Economics of Consumption.   Credit, 3.
                                                              MR. MORRIS.

ECONOMICS 156.   Business Cycles.   Credit, 3.
                                                              MR. HOWARD.

ECONOMICS 170.   Monopolies.   Credit, 3.
                                                              MR. HOWARD.

ECONOMICS 174.   Current Economic Problems.   Credit, 3.
                                                              MR. HOWARD.

ECONOMICS 178.   Public Finance.   Credit, 3.
                                                              MR. GAMBLE.

ECONOMICS 184.   Comparative Economic Systems.   Credit, 3.
                                                              MR. SCHOEFFLER.

Agricultural Engineering

JOHN W. ZAHRADNIK, major adviser.

COURSES OPEN TO GRADUATE STUDENTS ONLY
(For either major or minor credit.)

240. ADVANCED FARM STRUCTURES.—The application of structural theory in the development of high strength structures. The use of building materials and fastening for attaining diaphragms and prestressed components in the development of the structure.
The use of structural factors in the control of environment. Credit, ?
Prerequisite, Agricultural Engineering 173. Mr. BARTON

241. CONTROL OF HEAT AND VAPOR FLOW IN AGRICULTURAL BUILDINGS AND PROCESSES.—Application of mass flow theory to heat and vapor transfer. Thermal and vapor interchange between environment and livestock controlling production rates of metabolic and respiratory heat. The application of instrument and controls. Credit, ?
Prerequisite, Agricultural Engineering 173. Mr. BARTON

250. UNIT OPERATIONS IN AGRICULTURE.—Machine rates and production standards in the production and handling of crops. The uses of climatic data, water control, and production schedules in crop operations. Plant layout and equipment for processing and storage. Energy requirements of alternate methods of processing. Credit, ?
Prerequisite, Permission of Instructor. MR. ZAHRADNIK

260. AGRICULTURAL PROCESSING.—Heat, refrigeration, and vacuum in dehydrating, storing, and concentrating agricultural products. Critical temperatures, latent heats, fermentation, respiration, and equilibrium moisture content as they affect the processes and the end products. The effects of modified atmosphere, adsorbents, and dessicants. The application of instruments and controls.
Prerequisite, Agricultural Engineering 173. Credit, ?
MR. ZAHRADNIK

276. ADVANCED AGRICULTURAL MACHINERY DESIGN.—Stress analysis, periodic vibration, and shock leadings, as related to design of agricultural machinery. The mathematical definition of tillage tool surfaces. Dynamics of suspension devices, automatic release equipment, and hydraulic systems. Credit, ?
Prerequisite, Agricultural Engineering 176. MR. ZAHRADNIK

292. SEMINAR.—Review of current literature on research. Credit, 1
THE STAFF

300. THESIS, MASTER'S DEGREE. Credit, 4-8

COURSES OPEN TO BOTH GRADUATE AND UNDERGRADUATE STUDENTS
(For either major or minor credit.)

171. FARM POWER.—The study of internal combustion engines used in farm tractors and power units. Credit, ?
Prerequisites, Civil Engineering 52 and Mechanical Engineering 65, 68.
MR. TAGUE

173. FARM STRUCTURES.—A study of the strength and durability of building materials, construction systems and the mechanical principles underlying

22

their use in farm-construction. In the drafting room studies will be made of some major farm building and complete working drawings finished in all essential details. Credit, 4.

Prerequisites, Civil Engineering 34, 51, and 61.

176. AGRICULTURAL MACHINERY.—The study of design and operational problems of agricultural field machinery. Credit, 3.

Prerequisites, Civil Engineering 52, Mechanical Engineering 68, 83.

MR. TAGUE.

178. DRAINAGE, RECLAMATION AND CONSERVATION.—The course covers the engineering phase of drainage and reclamation. The various systems are studied, complete layouts established in the field, and problems of flow and run-off given.

Prerequisites, Civil Engineering 27, 75, or 76; Agronomy 2. Credit, 3.

MR. MARKUSON.

185. RURAL ELECTRIFICATION.—A course devoted to the utilization of electricity in agriculture. Credit, 3.

Prerequisite, Electrical Engineering 61, 62. THE STAFF.

COURSES FOR MINOR CREDIT ONLY

(No graduate credit for students majoring in Agricultural Engineering)

151. HOUSE PLANNING.—Plan designs of the small house, will be made. The arrangement of interior equipment, especially in the kitchen, and lighting, heating, water supply, and sewage disposal will be studied, together with a brief history of the house materials, construction methods, equipment, and architectural styles. Consideration will be given to the economics of house building, including financing and to maintenance and overhead expense. Credit, 3.

MR. MARKUSON.

155. FARM SHOP.—For students in agriculture and horticulture. Laboratory exercises cover instruction and practice in the use of carpenter's tools in construction and in bench work, arc and gas welding, pipe fitting, soldering, use of machinist's tools in machinery repair, and the mixing and placing of concrete. Classroom instruction covers materials of construction and the utilization of local and special materials for these purposes. Credit, 3.

MR. PIRA and MR. POWERS.

174. FARM BUILDINGS.—For students without the prerequisites for Agricultural Engineering 173. Credit, 3.

MR. MARKUSON.

180. FOOD PROCESS ENGINEERING.—A study of food processing machinery and instrumentation. Credit, 3.

MR. ZAHRADNIK.

182. REFRIGERATION.—Fundamentals in planning and operating a refrigerated storage with particular reference to size, details of construction, cooling load, and refrigerating machinery and accessories. For non-engineering majors.

Prerequisite, Agricultural Engineering 180. Credit, 2.

MR. ZAHRADNIK.

23

Agronomy

WILLIAM G. COLBY, major adviser.

COURSES OPEN TO GRADUATE STUDENTS ONLY
(For either major or minor credit)

200. SPECIAL PROBLEMS. Credit, 3 or 6
THE STAFF

211. FIELD CROP PRODUCTION.—A survey course which includes the regiona
distribution, the cultural requirements, production, and the utilization of th
principal field crops grown in the U. S. Given in alternate years, beginnin
1955-56. Credit, 3
Mr. COLBY

216. FORAGE CROPS.—A survey course which includes the regional distribution
the cultural requirements and the utilization of the principal forage crops grow
in the U. S. Given in alternate years, beginning 1956-57. Credit, 3
Mr. COLBY

226. CROP IMPROVEMENT.—This is a course in applied genetics involving
study of various plant breeding procedures used in the improvement of importan
agricultural crops. Credit, 3
Prerequisite, Zoology 153, Plant Breeding 152. Mr. YEGIAN

263. CHEMISTRY OF THE SOIL.—The chemistry of soil formation, soil acidity
nutrient element availability, ionic exchange and fixation, biological soils reaction
soil-plant-microorganism relationships, and of organic matter of the soil will b
discussed. The laboratory work will consist of physical, analytical and biochemica
investigations of soils and important soil constituents. Credit,
Mr. STECKEI

264. EXPERIMENTAL METHODS IN AGRONOMY.—The purpose of this cours
is to set forth some of the concepts regarding the application of statistics t
the analysis and interpretation of data obtained in agricultural research. Suc
points as choice of field, design of experiments, effect of competition, interpreta
tion of results, and other special factors that need to be considered in well-planne
experiments are discussed. Credit,
Mr. YEGIAN

290. SEMINAR. Credit, 1 each semeste
THE STAFF

300. THESIS, Master's degree. Credit, 10

400. THESIS, Ph. D. degree. Credit, 30

COURSES OPEN TO BOTH GRADUATE AND UNDERGRADUATE STUDENTS
(For either major or minor credit)

151. FIELD CROPS.—A study of the field crops of the U. S. which will includ
their uses and improvement, with their soil and climatic requirements. Emphas
will be given to the best farm practices of the northeastern states as to rotatio

24

liming, seeding methods, tillage, disease and insect control, and methods of harvesting and storage. As an individual problem, each student must make a detailed plan of crop production for the actual conditions of some New England farm. Credit, 3.

MR. COLBY.

152. FORAGE CROPS.—Analysis of the basic principles involved in the establishment, fertilization, and management of forage grasses and legumes. Three class hours. Credit, 3. Prerequisite, Agronomy 2 or equivalent. MR. COLBY.

153. AGROSTOLOGY.—All factors that influence the successful growing of fine turf grasses are studied and correlated to enable the student to have a practical working knowledge of the construction and maintenance of lawns, sports fields, highways, airport and cemetery turf. Credit, 3. 1957-58 and each alternate year. MR. ROBERTS.

156. AGROSTOLOGY.—This course considers fine turf management as a business and profession. Emphasis is placed on diagnosis and treatment of turf failures; the selection of equipment and supplies and client approach. Field trips and practical exercises arranged. Credit, 3. 1957-58 and each alternate year. MR. ROBERTS.

157. SOIL FORMATION.—Physical, chemical, biological, climatic and geological factors involved in soil formation. The relationship of these factors to the kinds of soils formed in the United States. Credit, 3.

MR. EVERSON.

158. SOIL UTILIZATION.—The relationship of climate and native vegetation to the broader aspects of soil formation; man's use of land resources; soil use and abuse; soil erosion control and its significance to permanent agriculture.

Credit, 3.

MR. EVERSON.

178. FERTILIZERS AND SOIL FERTILITY.—The primary purpose of this course is to relate soils and fertilizers to plant growth. Studies are made of fertilizer practices in the United States and Europe. In the early part of the course consideration is given to the history of fertilizer development, with special emphasis upon early discoveries and causes of failure in early research. Later in the course, studies are made of factors which relate fertilizers and soils to plant growth. Fertilizer formulation technology and practice are considered in detail in the laboratory phase of this course. Credit, 3. Prerequisites, Agronomy 2 or equivalent. MR. EVERSON.

179. SOIL PHYSICS.—For seniors in Agronomy. The factors in soil which control tilth and energy relationships and the laws of physics which govern these factors are discussed. This includes heat, light, color, particle size and charge, water and gas movement, energy relationships and other physical factors effecting changes in the soil. The laboratory is used to familiarize the students with various methods used in measuring these important physical factors. Credit, 3. MR. STECKEL.

184 A. SOIL CHEMISTRY.—For plant science and soil science students. Fundamental inorganic, organic, and biochemical reactions of soils. Plant nutrition and microbiological plant interrelationships. Credit, 3. Prerequisites, Chemistry 29, Botany 168, Agronomy 157. MR. STECKEL.

25

184 B. Soil Chemistry Laboratory.—Primarily for seniors in Agronomy. Methods and techniques used in soil chemistry research and in plant science investigations will be studied. The student will be made familiar with methods of determining exchangeable bases, base exchange capacity, soil phosphate fractionation, and many other determinations peculiar to soil investigations. To be taken concurrently with Agronomy 184 A. Credit, 2.
Prerequisites, Chemistry 29, 30, Botany 168, Agronomy 157. Mr. Steckel.

COURSES IN OTHER DEPARTMENTS FOR WHICH MAJOR CREDIT WILL BE GIVEN

Bacteriology 151, 152, Advanced Bacteriology. Credit, 3.
Miss Garvey.

Botany 202, 203. Advanced Plant Physiology. Credit, 2-4 each semester.
Mr. Kozlowski and Mr. Gentile.

Botany 205, 206. Advanced Plant Pathology. Credit, 2-4 each semester.
Mr. Banfield.

Botany 159, 160. The Angiosperms. Credit, 3-5 each semester.
Mr. Davis.

Botany 166. General Mycology. Credit, 3.
Mr. Banfield.

Botany 167, 168. Introductory Plant Physiology. Credit, 3 each semester.
Mr. Kozlowski.

Botany 175. Methods in Plant Pathology. Credit, 3.
Mr. Banfield.

Botany 181. Plant Ecology. Credit, 3.
Mr. Livingston.

Botany 182. Plant Geography. Credit, 2.
Mr. Livingston.

Botany 189. Plant Cytogenetics. Credit, 3.
Mr. Nickerson.

Chemistry 208. Chemical Spectroscopy. Credit, 3.
Mr. Smith.

Chemistry 237. Biocolloids. Credit, 3.
Mr. Bennett.

Chemistry 151, 152. Organic Chemistry. Credit, 4 each semester.
Mr. Ritchie and Mr. McWhortor.

Chemistry 165, 166. Physical Chemistry. Credit, 4 each semester.
Mr. Smith.

Chemistry 179. Biochemistry. Credit, 4.
Mr. Little

Civil Engineering 280. APPLIED SOIL MECHANICS. Credit, 3.
Mr. HENDRICKSON.

Geology 201. OPTICAL MINERALOGY. Credit, 3.
Mr. NELSON.

Geology 151, 152. MINERALOGY. Credit, 3.
Mr. NELSON.

Geology 156. LITHOLOGY. Credit, 3.
MR. NELSON.

Geology 161. GEOMORPHOLOGY. Credit, 3.
MR. SMITH.

Home Economics 203. ADVANCED NUTRITION—METABOLISM OF THE MAJOR FOODSTUFFS. Credit, 3.
Miss MITCHELL.

Home Economics 204. ADVANCED NUTRITION—VITAMINS AND MINERALS.
Credit, 3.
Miss MITCHELL.

Plant Breeading 152. PLANT BREEDING METHODS. Credit, 3.
Mr. FRENCH.

Plant Breeding 181. PLANT CYTOLOGICAL TECHNIQUES. Credit, 2.
Mr. FRENCH.

Plant Breeding 182. SPECIAL PROBLEM IN PLANT BREEDING. Credit, 2.
Mr. FRENCH.

Poultry Science 203. ADVANCED GENETICS. Credit, 3.
Mr. HAYS.

Poultry Science 204. ADVANCED GENETICS. Credit, 3.
Mr. HAYS.

Bacteriology

RALPH L. FRANCE, major adviser.

Registration by permission of the Department. Prerequisite courses required of graduate students in bacteriology are general chemistry, quantitative and qualitative analysis, organic chemistry, and specified courses in undergraduate bacteriology. Students who have not taken these courses as undergraduates will be required to fulfill these requirements here without graduate credit.

COURSES OPEN TO GRADUATE STUDENTS ONLY
(For either major or minor credit)

200. SPECIAL PROBLEMS.—This course is designed especially to provide research experience for students who do not write a thesis. The problem will be carried out in the same manner as a thesis, except that it will be less extensive. A written report of the completed study will be required. Credit, 3-6.
THE STAFF.

201. HISTORY OF BACTERIOLOGY.—Studies in the development of bacteriology from the late seventeenth century to the present time, especially planned to show the developments of bacteriology in relation to agriculture, public health, the arts, industry and medicine. Credit, 2.
Mr. LITSKY and Mr. FULLER.

202. ADVANCED BACTERIAL PHYSIOLOGY.—Lectures, literature reviews, and laboratory exercises in bacterial nutrition, metabolism and growth. This course will include advanced material not covered in Bacteriology 198. Credit, 3-5.
Prerequisites, Bacteriology 151 and Chemistry 179 or 193. MR. MANDEL.

203. BACTERIAL CYTOLOGY.—Lectures, literature reviews, and laboratory demonstrations, designed to give the student a comprehensive survey of the structure of bacterial cells and the functions of their components. The relationship of bacteria in the field of biology is considered. Credit 3-5.
Prerequisite, College Biology and Bacteriology 31 or equivalent. MR. FULLER.

204. RESEARCH PROJECT.—This course is designed to permit students to do investigational work on bacteriological problems not related to thesis. Limited to 3 credits per semester. For Ph.D. candidates only. Credit, 1-6.
THE STAFF.

205. ADVANCED IMMUNOLOGY.—Consideration will be given to advanced theories and laboratory procedures basic to bacteriology, immunology, and serology. Credit, 3-6.
Prerequisite, Bacteriology 185. Miss GARVEY.

206. MICROBIOLOGICAL FERMENTATIONS.—This course consists of a study of the basic theories as well as the methods and processes by which various chemicals and biological materials are produced on an industrial level through the action of microorganisms. The laboratory experiments are outlined to consider the microorganisms involved, procedures used, and the chemistry of the fermentation reactions. Credit, 3.
Prerequisites, Biological Chemistry and Bacteriology 151 and 152 or equivalents.
MR. CZARNECKI.

207. VIROLOGY.—A comprehensive study of viruses, including laboratory work covering methods for cultivation and identification. Limited to department majors, except by permission of the instructor. Credit, 3.

Mr. LITSKY.

208. SEMINAR.—Lectures and reports on current literature and special topics. (One credit each semester.) Credit, 1-6.

Mr. LITSKY and Mr. FULLER.

213. ANTIBIOTICS.—The historical background and theory of action of antibiotics are correlated with practical laboratory procedures used in the study of their isolation, methods of assay and effects on morphology and survival of bacteria. Credit, 3.
Prerequisite, Bacteriology 51, 52, or equivalent. Mr. CZARNECKI.

214. MICROBIAL GENETICS.—This course will provide a basic understanding of the genetics of bacteria and viruses. Credit, 3.
Prerequisites, Bacteriology 203 and Zoology 153. MR. MANDEL.

215. ANTISEPTICS AND DISINFECTANTS.—This course is designed to give the student a critical evaluation of antiseptics and disinfectants, and the procedures used in testing them. Practical aspects of these compounds are considered as to their general use. Studies of the various classes of antiseptics and disinfectants correlate chemical structure to antibacterial activity, mode of action, speed of action, and specificity. Credit, 3.
Prerequisites, Bacteriology 51, 52 and Chemistry 151, or equivalents.

Mr. LITSKY.

300. THESIS, MASTER'S DEGREE. Credit, 10.

400. THESIS, PH.D. DEGREE. Credit, 30.

COURSES OPEN TO BOTH GRADUATE AND UNDERGRADUATE STUDENTS
(For either major or minor credit)

156. (I) and (II). METHODS FOR BACTERIOLOGICAL PREPARATIONS.—This course is intended for students majoring in bacteriology and public health. The material given in the course includes methods of preparation and sterilization of culture media and equipment; the preparation of stains and reagents; and the use, care, and repair of laboratory instruments. Credit, 2.

THE STAFF.

181. GENERAL APPLIED BACTERIOLOGY.—This course is designed to give the student a working knowledge of routine and special tests used in present day applied bacteriology. Subjects receiving consideration are: methods for determining the sanitary quality of milk and milk products, water and shellfish; eating and drinking utensils; and air. Credit, 3.
Prerequisite, Bacteriology 31, 31A, or permission of instructor. Mr. FRANCE.

182. QUANTITATIVE AND QUALITATIVE BACTERIOLOGY.—Consideration will be given to (1) bacteriological principles which apply to the preservation, fermentation, and spoilage of foods, (2) the sanitary examination of foods, (3) the causes of food poisoning and (4) microbiological assays. Credit, 3.
Prerequisite, Bacteriology 51, or permission of instructor. Miss GARVEY.

29

185. IMMUNOLOGY.—Admission by permission of the instructor. This course includes consideration of host reactions which favor the prevention and cure of disease; qualitative and quantitative estimations of toxins and antitoxins; the use of biological products such as antigens and immune sera in differentia bacteriology and in disease diagnosis; and a consideration of isohemagglutinins as determinants of blood groups. Credit, 3
Prerequisite, Bacteriology 51 or equivalent. Miss GARVEY

190. SANITARY BACTERIOLOGY.—A detailed study of public health laboratory methods. Practical application of methods will be made through field studies By permission of instructor. Credit, 3.
Mr. FRANCE

192. CLINICAL MICROBIOLOGY.—This course is designated for students majoring in medical technology. The purpose of the course is to familiarize the student with routine clinical laboratory procedures. Credit, 3.
By permission of instructor. Mr. FRANCE

195. STUDIES OF SPECIAL MICROBIAL GROUPS.—A study of the biology of certain groups of microorganisms not given consideration, or at the most only briefly mentioned, in other courses offered in the department. The course will cover the autotrophic bacteria, photosynthetic bacteria, actinomycetes, myxobacteria, chlamydobacteria, and spirochaetes. Credit, 3.
One class hour, two 2-hour laboratory periods. Mr. MANDEL.
Prerequisite, Bacteriology 51.

198. BACTERIAL PHYSIOLOGY.—Lectures and laboratory exercises demonstrating the growth and activities of microorganisms as influenced by the environment and genotype and the effect of the microorganisms on the environment. Topics considered include the kinetics, metabolic pathways and effects of radiation.
Prerequisite, Bacteriology 31, Chemistry 179 or equivalent and permission of instructor.
One 4-hour laboratory period; two lecture hours. Credit, 3.
MR. MANDEL.

COURSES IN OTHER DEPARTMENTS FOR WHICH MAJOR CREDIT MAY BE GIVEN

Agricultural Economics 177. STATISTICS. ELEMENTARY EXPERIMENTAL STATISTICS. Credit, 3.
MR. RUSSELL.

Agricultural Economics 179. STATISTICS. ELEMENTARY ECONOMICS STATISTICS. Credit, 3.
Mr. RUSSELL.

Botany 166. GENERAL MYCOLOGY. Credit, 3.
Mr. BANFIELD.

Chemistry 234. ADVANCED BIOCHEMICAL LECTURES. Credit, 3.
Mr. LITTLE.

Chemistry 235. BIOCHEMISTRY LABORATORY METHODS.
Credit, 3-5 each semester.
Mr. LITTLE.

Chemistry 236. ADVANCED BIOCHEMICAL ANALYSIS. Credit, 3-5.
Mr. LITTLE.

Chemistry 237. BIOCOLLOIDS.   Credit, 3.
Mr. BENNETT.

Chemistry 251. SEMINAR.   Credit, 1 each semester.
Mr. RITCHIE.

Entomology 174. MEDICAL ENTOMOLOGY.   Credit, 3.
Mr. SHAW.

Food Technology 210, 211. THERMAL PROCESSING OF FOODS.
Credit, 2, 1st semester.
Credit, 3, 2nd semester.
Mr. ESSELEN.

Food Technology 271, 272. SEMINAR.   Credit, 1-2 each semester.
THE STAFF.

Home Economics 203. ADVANCED NUTRITION—METABOLISM OF MAJOR FOOD-STUFFS.   Credit, 3.
Miss MITCHELL.

Home Economics 204. ADVANCED NUTRITION—VITAMINS AND MINERALS.
Credit, 3.
Miss MITCHELL.

Home Economics 205. LABORATORY METHODS AND TECHNIQUES IN NUTRITION
Credit, 3.
Mrs. WERTZ.

Home Economics 212. NUTRITION SEMINAR.   Credit, 1.
Miss MITCHELL.

Public Health 164. MICROSCOPY OF WATER.   Credit, 3
Mr. SNOW

Zoology 169. ANIMAL PARASITOLOGY.   Credit, 3.
Miss TRAVER.

Zoology 184. CELLULAR PHYSIOLOGY.   Credit, 4.
Mr. SWENSON.

Zoology 248. PHYSIOLOGICAL GENETICS.   Credit, 3.
Mr. RAUCH.

COURSES FOR MINOR CREDIT ONLY

(No graduate credit for students majoring in Bacteriology)

151, 152. ADVANCED BACTERIOLOGY.—Studies on bacterial metabolism and the influence of environmental factors on growth and viability. The differentiation and identification of bacterial species by morphological, cultural, physiological, and serological studies. The combined courses not only give the students a comprehensive picture of the various forms of existing bacteria, but develop a special technique for the isolation, cultivation, and identification of both pathogenic and non-pathogenic species.   Credit, 3 each semester.
By permission of instructor.   Miss GARVEY.

31

Botany

THEODORE T. KOZLOWSKI, major adviser

A thesis will be required of certain candidates for the M.S. in Botany.

COURSES OPEN TO GRADUATE STUDENTS ONLY
(For either major or minor credit)

200. SPECIAL PROBLEMS.—Selected research problems in botany not related to the candidate's thesis.   Credits, 1-5 per semester.

A. Plant Cytology and Genetics.   MR. NICKERSON.

B. Plant Ecology.   MR. LIVINGSTON.

C. Plant Mycology.   Mr. BANFIELD, Mr. GUBA and Mr. GASIORKIEWICZ.

D. Plant Morphology.   MR. DAVIS.

E. Plant Pathology.
    Mr. BANFIELD, Mr. DORAN, Mr. GUBA, Mr. GASIORKIEWICZ.

F. Plant Physiology.   MR. KOZLOWSKI, MR. GENTILE and MR. JONES.

G. Plant Taxonomy.   MR. DAVIS and MR. LIVINGSTON.

202, 203. ADVANCED PLANT PHYSIOLOGY.—Advanced study on metabolism, water relations and mineral nutrition of plants. The course includes lectures, critical analyses of literature, reports and individual conferences.
Prerequisites, one semester of Plant Physiology, one semester of Organic Chemistry.   Credit, 2-4 each semester.
MR. KOZLOWSKI and MR. GENTILE.

204. FOREST PATHOLOGY.—A course dealing with the more common and important fungus diseases and with wood decay caused by saprophytic fungi which affect forest trees.   Credit, 4.
Prerequisite, Botany 151 or equivalent.   MR. BANFIELD.

205, 206.—ADVANCED PLANT PATHOLOGY.—A study of biological problems that underlie the diseased state. Consideration is given to the general parasitological and epidermiological aspects of plant disease from the standpoint of critical examination of the variation in and interaction between host plants, parasites and environment.   Credit, 2-4 each semester.
Prerequisite, Botany 151 and 166 or equivalent.   MR. BANFIELD.

207. ADVANCED PLANT ECOLOGY.—Lectures, conferences, critical reading and reports on advanced considerations of synecology and autecology.   Credit, 3.
MR. LIVINGSTON.

300. THESIS, MASTER'S DEGREE.—Research on an approved problem.
Credit, 10.

400. THESIS, PH.D. DEGREE.—Research on an approved problem.
Credit, 30.

COURSES OPEN TO BOTH GRADUATE AND UNDERGRADUATE
STUDENTS
(For either major or minor credit)

151, 152. PLANT PATHOLOGY.—A basic course in plant pathology dealing with the nature, causes and control of plant diseases. Attention is given to disease symptoms, infection, parasitism, disease transmission, environmental effects and general principles of plant disease control. Credit, 3.

Mr. BANFIELD.

158. MICROTECHNIQUE.—The preparation of microscopic mounts including the use of biological stains with the infiltration, celloidin and paraffin methods, and the use of slide and rotary microtomes. The rewards of careful work are improvement in manipulative technique, better orientation in the field of plant structures, an enhanced aesthetic appreciation and a valuable collection of microscopic mounts. Credit, 2.

MR. PUTALA.

159, 160. THE ANGIOSPERMS. A study of the angiosperm orders from the standpoint of reproductive morphology, ecology, evolution, economics and history. Illustrative types are drawn from the State herbarium, while forms for laboratory dissection are supplied from greenhouses or from preserved materials. A course for horticulturalists as well as botanists. Credit, 3-5 each semester. 1956-57 and each alternate year. MR. DAVIS.

161, 162. COMPARATIVE ANATOMY OF GREEN PLANTS.—The anatomy, evolution, and taxonomy of chlorophyllus plants, including extinct as well as living forms. Lectures interpret anatomical data in accord with such principles as algal tendencies and parallelisms, isomorphic and heteromorphic alternation, the landward migration, telome concept, rise and development of atracheates and tracheates, stelar evolution and wood anatomy, angiosperms as the ultimate evolutionary types. 1957-58 and each alternate year.

Prerequisite, one semester of cryptogamic botany. Credit, 3 each semester.

MR. DAVIS.

163, 164. COMPARATIVE MORPHOLOGY OF FUNGI.—Comparative morphology, life history and habitat of representative species of important orders and families. Laboratory work includes collection, identification, and study of common local forms. Credit, 3 each semester.

Mr. BANFIELD.

166. GENERAL MYCOLOGY.—A general course designed to acquaint the student with various classes of fungi, life history and morphology of representative species, their distribution in nature, their significance in plant and animal disease, and their utilization in industrial fermentations. Credit, 3.

Mr. BANFIELD.

167, 168. INTRODUCTORY PLANT PHYSIOLOGY.—A study of the processes occurring in plants and their relation to the complex of activities constituting plant growth. Credit, 3 each semester.

Mr. KOZLOWSKI.

169. FOREST AND SHADE TREE PATHOLOGY.—The nature, cause and control of the principal types of disease in trees including decay of forest products, standing and structural timber; insects and environment in relation to fungi disease and development; morphology and identification of fungi that induce disease or decay in trees. Credit, 3.

MR. BANFIELD.

175. METHODS IN PLANT PATHOLOGY.—A study of general techniques and specialized methods used in the investigation of plant diseases. 1956-57 and each alternate year. Credit, 3.
Prerequisite, one semester of plant pathology. Mr. BANFIELD.

181. PLANT ECOLOGY.—The relationships of plants to environment including a study of environmental factors (autecology) and of plant communities (synecology). Credit, 3.
Mr. LIVINGSTON.

182. PLANT GEOGRAPHY.—Lectures and assigned readings of descriptive and historical plant geography as well as basic principles governing the natural distribution of plants. Credit, 2.
Mr. LIVINGSTON.

189. PLANT CYTOGENETICS.—The interpretation of hereditary phenomena, in individuals and in populations, in terms of cell structures. A correlation of plant cytology and genetics which includes embryology, hybridization, polyploidy, apomixis, evolutionary trends and distribution patterns. Credit, 3.
Mr. NICKERSON.

190. INSECT TRANSMISSION OF PLANT DISEASES.—A lecture course on intricate interrelationships of insects and microorganisms, with particular emphasis on the basic role played by insects in inception, distribution and perpetuation of plant diseases. Credit, 3.
Mr. BANFIELD.

Business Administration

MILO KIMBALL, adviser.

The program of graduate courses in Business Administration is designed to prepare for positions of responsibility in business, in organizations that serve business, in government, or in business education.

COURSES OPEN TO GRADUATE STUDENTS ONLY

201. THE BUSINESS ENTERPRISE.—The legal-economic-political environment in which business enterprise operates; the risks of enterprise and profits; market demand analysis; cost-price combinations and production policies; the effects of business fluctuations on the individual enterprise; the enterprise system and public policy as expressed in legislation. Credit, 3.
Mr. SMART.

211. ACCOUNTING IN MANAGEMENT.—The theory of accounts applied to management problems; the established methods of accounting in operating situations; the use of quantitative data as bases for policy decisions. Credit, 3.
Mr. COLWELL.

222. MARKETING MANAGEMENT.—A study of the function of marketing from the point of view of the business executive. The broad aspects of product planning and choice of channels of distribution as well as distribution problems are analyzed. The interrelations between research planning, execution and control of marketing activity is carefully considered. Credit, 3.
Mr. HARDY.

231. FINANCIAL MANAGEMENT.—Attention is first centered on financing current operations: financial analysis and planning; credit management; and the sources and management of working capital. Then, long-term financial policies are stressed: the uses of corporate securities; the capital structure; surplus and dividend policies; financing new enterprises; the recapitalization and reorganization of going concerns.   Credit, 3.

Mr. LUDTKE.

242. PRODUCTION MANAGEMENT.—This course deals with the situations which confront executives in charge of manufacturing operations and the direction of people at work. It is designed to develop skill in analyzing production processes in order to determine specific adaptations of production and personnel techniques to the requirements of differing processes.   Credit, 3.

MR. HACKAMACK.

252. ADMINISTRATIVE PRACTICES.—Assuming a knowledge of business processes, this course considers the problems of human relations in business and industry. Consideration is also given to that phase of administration concerned with policy formation.   Credit, 3.

THE STAFF.

271. SEMINAR IN BUSINESS ADMINISTRATION I.—A critical and intensive study of selected problems in Accounting, Finance, Industrial Administration, or Marketing and the application of research methods to these problems.

Credit, 3.
THE STAFF.

272. SEMINAR IN BUSINESS ADMINISTRATION II.—A continuation of the Seminar in Business Administration in the field of the student's special interest.

Credit, 3.
THE STAFF.

300. THESIS, MASTER'S DEGREE.   Credit, 3 or 6

BASIC COURSES REQUIRED OF GRADUATE STUDENTS IN BUSINESS

Accounting

25-6. INTRODUCTION TO ACCOUNTING.—This course aims to give the students a working knowledge of the principles underlying the gathering, recording, and interpretation of accounting data.   Undergraduate credit, 6.

Business Law

170. BUSINESS LAW.—This course consists of a study of the drawing, reading, and interpretation of contracts, and includes agency, sales, and commercial paper.

Credit, 3.

Finance

155. FINANCIAL INSTITUTIONS.—A general course which surveys the development and operations of our financial institutions and provides an integrated study of the entire American financial structure.   Credit, 3.

165. CORPORATION FINANCE.—This course in business finance is concerned with forms of ownership organization, the nature and uses of corporate securities, provision and maintenance of capital, financial expansion and corporate reorganization.   Credit, 3.

Industrial Administration

163. MANAGEMENT IN INDUSTRY.—A study of the principles connected with the organization and management of industrial enterprises.   Credit, 3.

Marketing

153. MARKETING PRINCIPLES.—A study of the forces and conditions which determine prices and the organization and methods concerned with transporting, storing and distributing industrial and consumer goods.   Credit, 3.

ELECTIVE COURSES OPEN TO GRADUATE STUDENTS

Accounting

161. INTERMEDIATE ACCOUNTING.—An application of accounting principles to problems of income determination and the classification and valuation of assets.
Credit, 3.

162. ADVANCED ACCOUNTING.—A continuation of Accounting 161, concerned with the valuation of assets and liabilities, accounting for net worth, statements of application of funds and the analysis of financial statements.   Credit, 3.

164. COST ACCOUNTING.—The use of accounting techniques to determine business costs, including process costs, standard costs, distributive costs and cost problems imposed by government regulation.   Credit, 3.

173. TAX ACCOUNTING.—This course examines the principles of income taxation as applied to individuals and the application of income tax laws in corporate accounting.
Three class hours.   Credit, 3.

176. AUDITING.—A course in the interpretation of accounting records dealing with audit theory and procedure. C.P.A. and American Institute of Accountants examination problems are studied.   Credit, 3.

Finance

176. INSURANCE.—A general course concerning risks encountered by individuals and business enterprises and the methods and institutions evolved to insure against loss. Property, casualty, life and other forms of insurance are studied from the point of view of both the insurance carrier and the insured. Credit, 3.

182. INVESTMENTS.—The principles and techniques that are useful for the analysis and selection of investment media; investment policies of individuals and institutions.   Credit, 3.

Industrial Administration

164. PERSONNEL MANAGEMENT.—A study of the principles of the management of labor relations. Attention is focused on procuring, developing, maintaining and using personnel.   Credit, 3.

166. TRANSPORTATION AND TRAFFIC.—The development of highway, waterway, railway, and air transportation; the operation and control of transportation agencies; the use of freight tariffs, classifications and routing guides; the function of industrial traffic departments.   Credit, 3.

Marketing

154. SALESMANSHIP AND SALES MANAGEMENT.—The principles and practices of personal selling; the management of sales personnel; and the control of sales operations.   Credit, 3.

171. RETAIL MERCHANDISING.—A study of the operation and productive functions of the business of retailing.   Credit, 3.

173. ADVERTISING.—A study of the techniques and media of advertising, its services to business and the organization and economic functions of the advertising industry.   Credit, 3.

176. PURCHASING.—A study of the purchasing problems of industrial enterprises and of their market contacts with their sources of supply.   Credit, 3.

Chemical Engineering

ERNEST LINDSEY, major adviser.

The graduate course in chemical engineering is designed to emphasize advanced study in engineering fundamentals rather than specific technological applications.

To be admitted to full graduate study in this field either of the following requirements should be met:

1. Applicant must have a Bachelor's Degree in Chemical Engineering from a recognized school or,

2. Applicant must show satisfactory academic training or demonstrate proficiency in these subjects as a minimum:

Mathematics: Through Calculus.

Chemistry: Organic, Analytical, Physical.

Engineering Mechanics: Statics, Strength of Materials.

Chemical Engineering: Stoichiometry, Unit Operations, Thermodynamics (including thermodynamics of chemical change).

Electrical Engineering: Elements of circuits and machines.

REQUIRED COURSES

1. Ch. E. 300, Thesis, maximum 10 credits.

2. At least four of the following five courses:

Ch. E. 201, 202, Thermodynamics.

ME. 221, Heat Transfer.

Ch. E. 231, 232, Mass Transfer.

3. Additional courses selected from the following to complete the required 30 credits:

Ch. E. 182, 195; E.E. 201, 202; Math 156, 183, 192, 193, 194; Statistics 177; Chemistry 177, 181, 186, 203, 205, 206, 214, 237; CE. 275; Bacteriology 181, M.E. 183, 190; Physics 185, 186.

COURSES OPEN TO GRADUATE STUDENTS ONLY

(For either major or minor credit)

201. CHEMICAL ENGINEERING THERMODYNAMICS I.—A review of the fundamental laws of thermodynamics followed by a study of some of their applications to chemical engineering: P-V-T relations of fluids, thermodynamic functions, fluid flow, compression and expansion of gases, liquefacation and separation of gases. Prerequisite, Chemical Engineering 181 or equivalent.   Credit, 3.

MR. LINDSEY AND MR. DUUS.

37

202. CHEMICAL ENGINEERING THERMODYNAMICS II.—A continuation of course 201. The study of phase equilibria and chemical reaction equilibria and their applications in chemical processing are taken up. Credit, 3.
Prerequisites, Chemistry 166, Chemical Engineering 181.
MR. LINDSEY AND MR. DUUS.

231. MASS TRANSFER I.—About two-thirds the course is spent on theories of diffusion leading to unified treatment of mass-transfer unit operations: molecular and eddy diffusion mass-, heat-, and momentum transfer analogies, leaching, two-film theory, and related topics. The last third deals with applications of these principles to humidification and gas absorption, with design problems.
Prerequisite, Mechanical Engineering 221. Credit, 3.
MR. CASHIN.

232. MASS TRANSFER II.—A continuation of course 231 in which application of principles to design factors in distillation, liquid-liquid extraction, adsorption, ion exchange, and drying are studied. If time permits gaseous and thermal diffusion will be taken up. Credit, 3.
Prerequisite, Chemical Engineering 231. MR. CASHIN.

300. RESEARCH THESIS.—A theoretical or experimental study of some chemical engineering problem. Credit will be determined by the work done, and by agreement with the Department and the Graduate Thesis Committee.
THE STAFF.

COURSES OPEN TO BOTH UNDERGRADUATE AND GRADUATE STUDENTS
(For either major or minor credit)

182. INDUSTRIAL EQUILIBRIA AND KINETICS.—A study of phase and chemical equilibria and rates of reaction in chemical processes from the industrial point of view. Credit, 3.
Prerequisites, Chemistry 166, Chemical Engineering 181. MR. DUUS.

195. PROCESS EQUIPMENT DESIGN.—The design of process equipment for the chemical industries: riveted pressure vessels, welded pressure vessels, piping, attachments and closures, etc. Credit, 2.
Prerequisites, Chemical Engineering 155, Civil Engineering 153. MR. LINDSEY.

198. ADVANCED UNIT OPERATIONS.—Radiation heat transfer, and multicomponent distillation.
Two class hours. Credit, 2.
Prerequisite, Chemical Engineering 156. MR. CASHIN.

COURSES FOR MINOR CREDIT ONLY

155. UNIT OPERATIONS I.—A study of the fundamental principles underlying the unit operations of fluid flow, heat transfer, and evaporation. A portion of the course is devoted to a study of the thermodynamic properties of matter.
Three class hours; two 3-hour computation periods. Credit, 5.
Prerequisites, Mathematics 30 or 31, Chemistry 30. MR. CASHIN.

156. UNIT OPERATIONS II.—A continuation of course 155 concerning distillation gas absorption, liquid extraction, crystallization, filtration, mixing, crushing, and grinding.

Three class hours; two 3-hour computation periods. Credit, 5.

Prerequisite, Chemical Engineering 155. MR. CASHIN.

158. ORGANIC CHEMICAL TECHNOLOGY.—A study of some unit processes involved in the manufacture of organic chemicals; e.g. nitration, amination, halogenation, oxidation. Credit, 3.

MR. LINDSEY.

177. ELEMENTS OF UNIT OPERATIONS.—For other than chemical engineering majors. An introduction to some of the unit operations of process industries. The emphasis is on principles and types of equipment, rather than on the quantitative aspects and design. Credit, 3.

Prerequisites, Chemistry 30, Physics 25 and 26. Mr. LINDSEY.

181. HEAT-ENERGY RELATIONS.—A study of the energy relations in chemical processes. Includes: types of energy, energy balances, second law, thermodynamic functions, P-V-T-relations of fluids, compression and expansion processes. Credit, 3.

Three class hours. MR. DUUS.

Prerequisites, Chemistry 166, Chemical Engineering 156.

Chemistry

WALTER S. RITCHIE, major adviser.

The Department of Chemistry provides facilities for students intending to complete the requirements for the Master's degree and the Doctor's degree. Students accepted for graduate study are expected to have met the usual requirements for the Bachelor's degree. Those who have not fulfilled these requirements may be admitted on limited status until the deficiencies have been removed.

First year graduate students will take "placement" examinations during the first week of residence. These examinations are for the purpose of evaluating the background of the student, and to assist in the selection of a course of study. Students are admitted to candidacy for a degree only after the satisfactory passing of written comprehensive examinations, at which time thesis problems are assigned in the following fields of chemistry: physical, organic, inorganic, analytical and biochemical.

COURSES OPEN TO GRADUATE STUDENTS ONLY

(For either major or minor credit)

201. INORGANIC PREPARATIONS.—LABORATORY.—The preparation of chemical products from raw materials. The manufacture and testing of pure chemicals. The laboratory work is essentially synthetic in nature and is designed to aid in acquiring a more adequate knowledge of inorganic chemistry than is to be obtained by chemical analysis alone. Credit, 3-5.

Mr. SMITH.

202. INORGANIC CHEMISTRY OF THE LESS FAMILIAR ELEMENTS.—Lectures and collateral reading on the descriptive chemistry of some of the less familiar

elements such as boron, gallium, indium, thallium, the lanthanides, fluorine, titanium, vanadium, tantalum, tungsten, and uranium. Correlations between structure or spatial configurations and chemical properties will be stressed to the extent permitted by modern data. Credit, 3.
1957-58 and each alternate year. MR. ROBERTS.

203. PHYSICAL CHEMICAL MEASUREMENTS.—LABORATORY.—A selection of experiments in Physical Chemistry to meet the needs and background of the individual student. Experiments will be selected from standard texts and from the literature. Credit, 3-5.
Prerequisites, Chemistry 165 and 166 or equivalent. MR. SMITH.

205. CHEMICAL THERMODYNAMICS.—The first and second laws of thermodynamics will be reviewed. The concept of the Boltzmann distribution and the partition function will be introduced, and the calculation of thermodynamic function from these quantities will be discussed. The calculation of equilibrium constants from both thermochemical and spectroscopic data will be considered, as will the application to electrochemistry and ionic equilibria. Credit, 3.
1956-1957 and each alternate year. MR. STEIN.
Prerequisites, Chemistry 165 and 166.

206. GASES, KINETICS, AND CATALYSIS.—Some of the basic concepts of the kinetic theory of gases and the absorption of gases by solids will be discussed. The kinetics of homogeneous gas reactions and chain reactions will be considered as well as the theory of absolute reaction rates. Homogeneous and heterogeneous catalysis, photochemical, radiation induced reactions, and reactions in solution will be discussed. Credit, 3.
1956-1957 and each alternate year. MR. STEIN.
Prerequisite, Chemistry 205 or its equivalent.

208. CHEMICAL SPECTROSCOPY.—This course is designed to give students practice in the use of spectroscopic equipment in solving chemical problems. The lecture work of the course will include discussions of (1) the design and use of instruments, (2) the elementary theory of spectra, and (3) the application of spectroscopy of chemical problems. The laboratory work will include practice in the use of the spectrometer and the spectrograph for the analysis of flame, arc, and spark spectra, and the use of the spectrophotometer for absorption measurements. Photographic procedures will be discussed and used in connection with the operation of the spectrograph. Credit, 3.
1957-58 and each alternate year. MR. SMITH.
Prerequisites, Chemistry 165 and 166, or equivalent.

211, 212. QUANTUM CHEMISTRY.—The application of the quantum theory to chemical problems will be discussed. This will include a discussion of the exact theory for describing the structure of simple atoms, the application of approximate methods for complex atoms and molecules, the chemical bond, resonance, and the interaction of radiation and matter. Credit, 3-6.
1957-1958 and each alternate year. MR. STEIN.
Prerequisites, Chemistry 186, or equivalent.
Differential Equations is desirable.

214. PHYSICAL CHEMISTRY OF HIGH POLYMERS.—Various aspects of the physical chemistry of natural and synthetic polymers will be discussed. Topics to be considered will include: structure of solid polymers, determination of molecular weights, sizes and shapes, mechanical properties of solid polymers, colligative properties of polymer solutions, polyelectrolytes, and physical chemistry of proteins. Credit, 3.
1957-58 and each alternate year. MR. STEIN.
Prerequisite, Chemistry 205 or equivalent.

221. ADVANCED ANALYTICAL CHEMISTRY.—Laboratory consisting of special work to meet the needs of the individual student. It may consist of ultimate analysis, electro-analysis, the analysis of definite classes of materials such as fertilizers, ores, insecticides, alloy or materials containing the rarer elements, and the use of organic reagents.   Credit, 3-5 each semester.
Prerequisite, 183 or equivalent.   Mr. ROBERTS.

223. INTRODUCTION TO MICRO-CHEMISTRY.—Laboratory. Designed to illustrate the applications of micro technique to synthesis, analysis, and characterization. The microscopic work may include the optics of the microscope, micrometry, the microscopic study of fibers, crystals, and physiochemical phenomena and an introduction to microscopical qualitative analysis. The quantitative work may include the determination of carbon, hydrogen, nitrogen, and halogen in organic materials and selected inorganic determinations.
                                                      Credit, 3-5 each semester.
Prerequisite, Chemistry 183, or equivalent.   Mr. ROBERTS.

227. HETEROCYCLIC CHEMISTRY.—The chemistry of the common organic heterocyclic compounds containing nitrogen, oxygen, and sulfur. Includes considerations of mechanisms of the reactions discussed.
Three class hours.   Credit, 3.
Prerequisite, Chemistry 181 or equivalent.   Mr. CANNON.

229, 230. THEORETICAL ORGANIC CHEMISTRY.—Lectures on special topics such as stereochemistry, bond formation, resonance, ionic reactions, free radical reactions, transition state theory, reaction mechanisms, molecular rearrangements, etc.   Credit, 3 each semester.
1956-57 and each alternate year.   MR. CANNON.
Prerequisite, Chemistry 181 or its equivalent.
Chemistry 181 may be taken simultaneously with Chemistry 229.

231. ADVANCED ORGANIC CHEMISTRY.—Laboratory. More difficult synthesis of organic compounds will be assigned to the individual student. These compounds will frequently be those desired as starting materials for research. Their preparation will require the use of the original literature.   Credits, 3-5.
Prerequisite, a year course in Organic Chemistry. Mr. CANNON and Mr. RITCHIE.

232. ORGANIC CHEMISTRY.—An intensive survey of certain reactions of organic chemistry with emphasis on their scope and limitations, recent developments, and mechanisms.   Credit, 3.
1957-58 and each alternate year.   MR. CANNON.
Prerequisite, Chemistry 181.

234. ADVANCED BIOCHEMICAL LECTURES.—Lectures on recent developments in the chemistry of proteins, lipids, carbohydrates, enzymes, and other materials of biological significance.   Credits, 3.
                                                                     Mr. LITTLE.

235. BIOCHEMISTRY LABORATORY METHODS.—Advanced laboratory work on preparation, examination, and analytical techniques for protein, carbohydrate, lipids, enzymes, etc. Methods of colloid chemistry will be included. Individual problems and work will be assigned as far as possible to meet individual requirements.   Credit, 3-5 each semester.
                                                                     Mr. LITTLE.

41

236. ADVANCED BIOCHEMICAL ANALYSIS.—Advanced laboratory course in analytical methods applicable to naturally occurring materials including foods, feeds, etc. Research methods and techniques will be introduced as well as routine methods.   Credit, 3-5.

Mr. LITTLE.

237. BIOCOLLOIDS.—A consideration of the fundamental principles of colloidal behavior and some applications to industry, agriculture, and biology.   Credit, 3. Prerequisite, Chemistry 152, or equivalent.   Mr. BENNETT.

239. CHEMISTRY OF NATURAL PRODUCTS.—The lectures and collateral readings will deal with the chemistry of some classes of natural compounds which are of biochemical and economic interest. Proteins, the sugars, starch, cellulose, polyuronides, lignin, glucosides, alkaloids, enzymes, purines, pyrimidines, and pigments will be considered.   Credit, 2.

MR. LITTLE and MR. McWHORTER.

251. SEMINAR.—Conferences, reports, or lectures.   Credit, 1 each semester.
Maximum credit, 2.
Mr. RITCHIE.

278. ELECTROCHEMISTRY.—A course for students who have had a first course in physical chemistry, or its equivalent. The course will include a study of the fundamentals of oxidation-reduction, galvanic cells, electrolytic cells, conductance transference, and polarography. The concept of activity, and the use of activity co-efficients will be included.   Credit, 2.
1957-58 and each alternate year.

295. RESEARCH PROBLEM.—The student will prepare a proposal for a research problem not directly related to his thesis topic if the latter has been selected. The problem will involve primarily library research. A Committee of three department members will approve the student's topic not later than four weeks from the start of the semester and conduct an oral examination before the end of the semester in which the topic was approved. A written report must be submitted and approved by the committee one week before the examination. Required of all candidates for the Ph.D. in Chemistry and must be completed before the candidate's preliminary examination for the degree.   Credit, 5.

THE DEPARTMENT.

300. THESIS, MASTER'S DEGREE.—The preparation of an acceptable thesis in agricultural, analytical, inorganic, organic, biochemical, or physical chemistry, under the direction of the professor in charge of the work.   Credit, 10.

400. THESIS, PH.D. DEGREE.—The preparation of an acceptable thesis in agricultural, analytical, inorganic, organic, biochemical or physical chemistry, under the direction of the professor in charge of the work.   Credit, 30.

COURSES OPEN TO BOTH GRADUATE AND UNDERGRADUATE STUDENTS
(For either major or minor credit)

177. ADVANCED PHYSICAL CHEMISTRY.—A detailed study of a number of topics such as kinetics, catalysis, chemical thermodynamics and electrochemistry. Three class hours.   Credit, 3.
Prerequisites, Chemistry 165 and 166.   Mr. STEIN.

181. ORGANIC CHEMISTRY.—A rapid and intensive survey of the important reactions of organic chemistry with emphasis on their scope and limitations, recent developments, mechanisms, and theory. Credit, 3.
Three class hours. Mr. CANNON.

182. QUALITATIVE ORGANIC CHEMISTRY.—The characterization of organic compounds by means of physical properties, class reactions, and the preparation of suitable derivatives. Credit, 4.
Two class hours; two 3-hour laboratory periods. Mr. CANNON.

183. ADVANCED QUANTITATIVE ANALYSIS.—The laboratory work will include representative determinations in electrolytic and electrometric methods, and an introduction to colorimetry and other optical methods of analysis. Credit, 3.
Two class hours; one 3-hour laboratory period. Mr. ROBERTS.
Prerequisite, Chemistry 130.

186. THEORETICAL INORGANIC CHEMISTRY.—A survey of inorganic chemistry which is largely theoretical and includes such topics as atomic structure, radiochemistry, periodic classification and relationships, valence concepts, acid-base theory, and the chemistry of coordination compounds. To the extent that time permits these topics will be discussed and illustrated with descriptive chemistry of the familiar elements. Credit, 3.
Three class hours. Mr. SMITH.
Prerequisites, Chemistry 165 and 166.

188. HISTORY OF CHEMISTRY.—An historical and biographical study of chemistry and chemists. Credit, 3.
Three class hours. Mr. RITCHIE.

192. INTRODUCTION RESEARCH.—Admission only by permission of the department.
Ten laboratory periods. Credit, 5.
Hours by arrangement. THE STAFF.

193, 194. GENERAL BIOCHEMISTRY.—These courses offer a broad introduction to the general field of biochemistry for students majoring in chemistry or in the biological sciences and provide a background for more advanced or specialized study in this field. A competent preparation in organic chemistry is required. (Chemistry 51 and 52 or their equivalent.) Credit, 4 each semester.
Three class hours; one 3-hour laboratory period. Mr. LITTLE.

COURSES FOR MINOR CREDIT ONLY
(No graduate credit for students majoring in Chemistry)

151, 152. ORGANIC CHEMISTRY.—A course in the theory of organic chemistry intended to serve the needs of students who will specialize in chemistry, as well as those who may specialize in other fields. Credit, 4.
Three class hours; one 3-hour laboratory period.
MR. RITCHIE and MR. McWHORTER.

163. CHEMISTRY OF WATER, SEWAGE, AND SEWAGE SLUDGE.—The preparation of reagents and standard methods for the analysis of water, sewage, and sewage sludge. Credit, 3.
Two 3-hour laboratory periods. Mr. ⸺.
Prerequisite, Chemistry 30.

165, 166. PHYSICAL CHEMISTRY.—A study of the fundamental theories and laws of physical chemistry.   Credit, 4.
Three class hours; one 3-hour laboratory period.

                                                                    MR. SMITH.

179. BIOCHEMISTRY.—An introduction to general biochemistry and physiological chemistry, with particular emphasis on the extension of fundamental organic chemistry to materials and processes of biological significance; proteins, lipids, carbohydrates, enzymes.   Credit, 4.
Three class hours; one 3-hour laboratory period.   Mr. LITTLE.
Prerequisite, Organic Chemistry.

Civil Engineering

MERIT P. WHITE, major adviser.

COURSES OPEN TO GRADUATE STUDENTS ONLY

(For either major or minor credit)

200. SPECIAL PROBLEMS.   Credit, 3-6.
                                                             THE STAFF.

252. STRUCTURAL DYNAMICS.—This course covers the behavior of simple and complex oscillating systems. It deals particularly with the behavior of structures subjected to periodic forces, to non-periodic forces and to shock loads. Behavior beyond the elastic range is included.   Credit, 3.
Prerequisites, Civil Engineering 51 and 52.   MR. WHITE.

261. MATERIALS TESTING TECHNIQUES.—This course is concerned with the machines and auxiliary equipment used in experimental stress analysis for purposes of research.   Credit, 3.
Prerequisite, Civil Engineering 51.   MR. SHARP.

270. ADVANCED STRUCTURAL THEORY II.—Advanced problems in structural analysis are presented in this course. Topics considered are the analysis of complex rigid frames; influence lines for indeterminate structures; the placing of loads and the determination of stresses in continuous building frames; prestressed concrete.   Credit, 3.
Prerequisites, Civil Engineering 172.   MR. OSGOOD.

271. ARCH ANALYSIS.—Methods of analyzing two-hinged and hingeless arches. A design project is included.   Credit, 3.
Prerequisites, Civil Engineering 70 and 71.   MR. OSGOOD.

275. ADVANCED FLUID MECHANICS.—Theory of hydraulic similitude, dimensional analysis, methods of obtaining dynamic similarity in hydraulic models in actual practice, analysis of typical hydraulic models.   Credit, 3.
Prerequisites, Civil Engineering 75 or 76.   MR. MARCUS.

277. ADVANCED SANITARY ENGINEERING.—This course treats hydraulic and chemical problems encountered in the design and operation of water and sewage works. It also deals with stream sanitation and the latest trends of practice and research in the sanitary engineering field.   Credit, 3.
Prerequisites, Civil Engineering 77, 78.   MR. FENG.

279. THEORETICAL SOIL MECHANICS.—A thorough investigation of the phenomena in soil masses subjected to such forces as seepage, frost, and imposed loads. Credit, 3.

Mr. HENDRICKSON.

280. APPLIED SOIL MECHANICS.—The solution of case problems applying the principles of soil mechanics to the design of embankments, retaining walls, footings, raft foundations, and pile structures. Credit, 3.
Prerequisite, Civil Engineering 279. MR. HENDRICKSON.

300. RESEARCH AND THESIS, MASTER'S DEGREE. Credit, 6.

COURSES OPEN TO BOTH GRADUATE AND UNDERGRADUATE STUDENTS
(For either major or minor credit)

172. ADVANCED STRUCTURAL THEORY I.—Methods of analyzing statically indeterminate structures. Credit, 3.
Prerequisite, Civil Engineering 70. MR. OSGOOD.

179. PRINCIPLES OF SANITARY ENGINEERING.—This course is designed for students in the Department of Public Health. It covers phases of Civil Engineering 77 and 78 with consideration of the non-engineering background of the student. Credit, 3.

MR. FENG.

182. SOIL TESTING.—Sampling, testing, and presentation of reports on the engineering properties of soils. Permeability, consolidation, and shear are the tests covered. Triaxial compression is the principal technique used.
One class hour; two 3-hour laboratory periods. Credit, 3.
Prerequisite, Civil Engineering 80 or equivalent. MR. HENDRICKSON.

188. ADVANCED STRESS ANALYSIS.—Determination of stresses and strains in elements of machines and structures. Credit, 3.
Prerequisite, Civil Engineering 51. MR. WHITE.

196. HYDRAULIC ENGINEERING.—The analysis and design of hydraulic structures such as storage reservoirs, spillways, dams, levees, shore protection and channel works are considered. Credit, 3.
Two class hours; one 3-hour laboratory period. Mr. MARSTON.
Prerequisites, Civil Engineering 73, 76.

198. ADVANCED HIGHWAY ENGINEERING.—Analysis of the engineering aspects of traffic problems such as traffic signal design, street capacities, parking and channelization.
Two class hours; one 3-hour laboratory period. Credit, 3.
Prerequisite, Civil Engineering 55. MR. BOYER.

DAIRY AND ANIMAL SCIENCE

Animal Husbandry

D. J. HANKINSON, major adviser.

Animal Husbandry is a major program of study within the Department of Dairy and Animal Science.

COURSES OPEN TO GRADUATE STUDENTS ONLY

(For either major or minor credit)

Major credit for Animal Husbandry students assumes prerequisites in the animal husbandry field as covered in undergraduate courses in this University. All hours by arrangement.

200. PROBLEMS IN LIVESTOCK PRODUCTION.—This course will deal with some specific problem in feeding, breeding, production or management as relates to the production of some specific livestock product such as milk, wool, or meat. Assistance will be given in outlining the problem and setting up the experimental procedure with the student responsible for collecting and analyzing the data.

Credit, 3-6.
THE STAFF.

205. ADVANCED ANIMAL NUTRITION.—The chemistry of feedstuffs and the chemistry and physiology of digestion, absorption and utilization of energy, proteins, minerals and vitamins in milk, meat, wool, or work production. Recent and current research will be evaluated. Credit, 3.

MR. ARCHIBALD and MR. ELLIOT.
Prerequisites, Animal Husbandry 151 or its equivalent.

211. ADVANCED ANIMAL GENETICS.—This course will stress the statistical approach to Animal Breeding, including the development of selection indexes for various farm mammals, sire indexes and breeding plans based on systems of breeding and selection. Credit, 3.
Prerequisites, Animal Husbandry 176 or equivalent, and Agricultural Economics 177 and 180 or equivalent. MR. GAUNT and MR. BLACK.

216. FERTILITY AND FECUNDITY.—An advanced course in reproductive physiology dealing with the role of heredity, nutrition, pathology and environment in the determination of fertility and fecundity in mammalian forms. Emphasis, in classroom and laboratory, will be placed on current research directed toward control of reproductive function through experimental means. Credit, 3.
Prerequisites, Animal Husbandry 175 or equivalent, and Zoology 187.

MR. BLACK.

220. MILK SECRETION.—A study of milk secretion including the gross and microscopic anatomy of the mammary gland. The development of the gland from birth through parturition and lactation will be studied. The physiology of milk secretion will be reviewed both in relation to the endocrine glands which control it and to more practical aspects of successful dairy cattle. Credit, 3.

MR. FOLEY.

226. THE HISTOLOGY OF DOMESTIC ANIMALS.—An intensive study of the tissues and organs of domestic animals. Special emphasis is placed on those tissues and organ systems which have particular economic or physiological signifi-

DAIRY AND ANIMAL SCIENCE

cance in the fields of livestock production, meats, nutrition, milk secretion and animal breeding. The microscopic structure of the skin and its modifications, fat, muscle, bone, endocrine glands, digestive system and genital systems of farm animals is stressed and related to function.

Prerequisites, Zoology 150, Veterinary Science 175 or equivalent.   Credit, 3.

MR. GREENSTEIN.

229, 230. SEMINAR.—Reports on current literature.   Credit, 1 each semester

THE STAFF.

300. THESIS, MASTER'S DEGREE.   Credit, 5-10.

COURSES IN OTHER DEPARTMENTS FOR WHICH MAJOR CREDIT MAY BE GIVEN

Bacteriology 185. IMMUNOLOGY.   Credit, 3.

MISS GARVEY.

Chemistry 234. ADVANCED BIOCHEMICAL LECTURES.   Credit, 3.

MR. LITTLE.

Chemistry 235. ADVANCED BIOCHEMICAL METHODS.   Credit, 3-5.

MR. LITTLE.

Chemistry 236. ADVANCED BIOCHEMICAL ANALYSIS.   Credit, 3-5.

MR. LITTLE.

Chemistry 237. BIOCOLLOIDS.   Credit, 3.

MR. BENNETT.

Zoology 245. ADVANCED VERTEBRATE PHYSIOLOGY.   Credit, 3.

MR. SNEDECOR.

Zoology 248. PHYSIOLOGICAL GENETICS.   Credit, 3.

MR. RAUCH.

Zoology 172. VERTEBRATE EMBRYOLOGY.   Credit, 4.

MR. WOODSIDE, MR. RAUCH and MR. BARTLETT.

Zoology 178. GENETICS OF ANIMAL POPULATIONS.   Credit, 2.

MR. RAUCH.

Zoology 183. GENERAL AND CELLULAR PHYSIOLOGY.   Credit, 4.

MR. SWENSON.

Zoology 187. ENDOCRINOLOGY.   Credit, 3.

MR. SNEDECOR.

COURSES FOR MINOR CREDIT ONLY

(No graduate credit for students majoring in Dairy and Animal Science)

151. FUNDAMENTALS OF ANIMAL NUTRITION.—This course deals with the nutrients and their metabolism, and the nutritive requirements for maintenance, growth, reproduction, lactation and other body functions. Emphasis will be on ruminants and swine.   Credit, 3.

Three class hours.   MR. ELLIOT.

Prerequisites, Chemistry 33.

152. FEEDS AND FEEDING.—The nature and value of the more important feed-stuffs. Application of principles in balancing rations for the various classes of livestock. Credit, 2.
Prerequisite, Animal Husbandry 151.
Two 2-hour laboratory periods. MR. ELLIOT.

154. MEAT PROCESSING.—For students not majoring in Animal Husbandry by permission of the instructor. A few periods will be devoted to a discussion of the meat packing industry and to the preserving and care of meat products. The remainder will be spent on the classification of meat animals with practice slaughtering and the making of wholesale and retail cuts with stress on identification of retail cuts. A one-day trip through the packing plants of Boston is a requirement of this course and will cost about five dollars. Credit, 2.
One 4-hour laboratory period. MR. ADAMS.

156. BEEF AND SHEEP PRODUCTION.—This course considers the historical and economic development, present status and probable future trends of beef and sheep production in the United States and especially in New England. Considera-tion will be given to types of production, systems and methods of feeding, man-agement and marketing. In the laboratory, practice will be obtained in fitting and showing as well as certain practical techniques such as dehorning, ear-tagging, castrating, foot-trimming, shearing, etc., and the treatment and prevention of external and internal parasites as well as common ailments. Credit, 3.
Two class hours; one 2-hour laboratory period. MR. BAKER.

165. REPRODUCTION IN FARM ANIMALS.—This course deals with the compara-tive aspects of anatomy, embryology, endocrinology and physiology of the re-productive system of farm mammals, concepts of fertility and sterility, and prac-tice in semen collection, artificial insemination and pregnancy diagnosis. A field trip to Shrewsbury to observe operations of the M.S.B.A. bull stud is a require-ment of the course and should not exceed two dollars in cost. Credit, 3.
MR. BLACK.

166. APPLIED ANIMAL GENETICS.—This course is designed to acquaint the student with the workings of heredity and variation in farm mammals and the role of selection procedures and breeding systems in genetic improvement of livestock. Credit, 3.
Three class hours. MR. GAUNT.
Prerequisites, Zoology 153.

174. ADVANCED MEATS.—This course deals with the advanced techniques in preparing, preserving and utilizing the various meat products from cattle, sheep and swine. Credit, 2.
Prerequisites, Animal Husbandry 33 or 154 and permission of instructor.
Two 2-hour laboratory periods. MR. HOBART.

177., 178. DAIRY CATTLE PRODUCTION.—This is an intensive course covering all phases of dairy cattle and milk production. It affords an opportunity to seek the solution to the economic, nutritional, genetic and managerial problems con-cerned in successful dairying. Field trips to leading dairy establishments are components of these courses, the cost estimated to be ten dollars in the fall semester and twenty dollars in the spring semester. Credit, 3 each semester.
Two class hours; one 2-hour laboratory period. MR. FOLEY.

179. HORSE AND SWINE PRODUCTION.—Light horses are emphasized in the horse production portion of the course. The feeding, breeding, training and some equitation are covered. Each student is required to care for a mare for one week. The material devoted to swine husbandry attempts to correlate all management practices and to analyze the various methods of production with emphasis on New England conditions. Field trip costs will not exceed five dollars.
Two class hours; one 2-hour laboratory period. Credit, 3.
MR. BAKER.

Dairy Technology

Dairy Technology is a major program of study within the Department of Dairy and Animal Science.

COURSES OPEN TO GRADUATE STUDENTS ONLY
(For either major or minor credit)

Major credit for Dairy Technology students assumes prerequisites in the dairy technology field as covered in undergraduate courses in this University.

200. PROBLEMS IN DAIRY TECHNOLOGY.—A course for individual study in which the student gives attention to specific current problems involved in the processing of dairy products. Credit, 3.
THE STAFF.

202. ADVANCED DAIRY CHEMISTRY.—A study of the physical, colloidal, and chemical properties of dairy products; the role of milk fat, salts, proteins, carbohydrates, and enzyme systems, and their relation to dairy research. Credit, 3.
Prerequisite, 175 or equivalent.
Two 1-hour lectures; one 3-hour laboratory period. MR. POTTER.

209., 210. SEMINAR.—Reports on current literature. Credit, 1 each semester.
THE STAFF.

300. THESIS, MASTER'S DEGREE. Credit, 10.
THE STAFF.

COURSES OPEN TO BOTH GRADUATE AND UNDERGRADUATE STUDENTS
(For either major or minor credit)

175. DAIRY CHEMISTRY.—Physical and chemical principles which explain the behavior of milk and milk products in the various technological operations. Constituents of milk in relation to other organic compounds; physiochemical aspects of certain dairy phenomena such as foaming, coagulation, etc. The laboratory work will include many of the tests used commercially as well as in dairy research, emphasizing the principles and application of both qualitative and quantitative analysis as well as the technique of operating scientific apparatus.
Enrollment by permission of instructor. Credit, 3.
MR. POTTER.

COURSES IN OTHER DEPARTMENTS FOR WHICH MAJOR CREDIT WILL BE GIVEN

No more than two courses may be selected from the following list of courses:

Bacteriology 202. BACTERIAL PHYSIOLOGY.   Credit, 3-5.
MR. MANDEL.

Bacteriology 203. BACTERIAL CYTOLOGY. .   Credit, 3-5
MR. FULLER.

Chemistry 165, 166. PHYSICAL CHEMISTRY.   Credit, 4 each semester.
MR. SMITH.

Chemistry 193, 194. GENERAL BIOCHEMISTRY.   Credit, 4 each semester.
MR. LITTLE. .

Chemistry 237. BIOCOLLOIDS.   Credit, 3.
MR. BENNETT.

Food Technology 209. THERMAL PROCESSING OF FOODS.   Credit, 2.
MR. ESSELEN.

Food Technology 210. THERMAL PROCESSING OF FOODS.   Credit, 3.
MR. ESSELEN.

Food Technology 221. EDIBLE FATS AND OILS.   Credit, 2.
MR. ANDERSON.

Food Technology 241. FOOD ACCEPTANCE.—Theory and Methodology.
Credit, 3.
MR. FAGERSON.

Home Economics 203. ADVANCED NUTRITION.—Metabolism of major foodstuffs.   Credit, 3.
MISS MITCHELL.

Home Economics 204. ADVANCED NUTRITION.—Vitamins and minerals.
Credit, 3.
MISS MITCHELL.

COURSES FOR MINOR CREDIT ONLY

(No graduate credit for students majoring in Dairy & Animal Science)

152. MARKET MILK.—A study of the various phases of the market milk industry; sanitary production, transportation, pasteurization, and handling in the city plant; marketing, delivery systems, milk and its relation to public health, inspection, milk laws, food value and advertising. Cultured milk and other milk drinks are also included. Some milk plants are visited.   Credit, 4.
MR. EVANS

177. BUTTER AND CHEESE MAKING.—Half of the semester is devoted to butter making; the remainder to cheese making, condensed and powdered milk. The various phases of the butter industry studied are: separators and cream separation; pasteurization, neutralization, and ripening of cream; preparation of starter cultures; churning; marketing and scoring of butter; creamery management. The work in cheese making includes cheddar, cream, Neufchatel, cottage, pro-

cessed cheeses, etc. The manufacture of condensed milk, powdered milk, and commercial casein are also covered. Credit, 4.
Prerequisites, Dairy 25 or permission of instructor.

MR. EVANS and MR. POTTER.

178: ICE CREAM MAKING.—The principles and practices of ice cream making. The effects of such factors as composition, quality, pasteurization, homogenization, aging, and freezing on the finished product are considered. Sherbets, ices, fancy and individual forms, and all flavors of ice cream are studied. Some time is devoted to refrigeration machinery, delivery equipment, and merchandising methods as they are related to the industry. Credit, 4.
Prerequisite, Dairy 25 or permission of instructor. MR. POTTER.

Economics

PHILIP L. GAMBLE, major adviser.

COURSES OPEN TO GRADUATE STUDENTS ONLY

(For either major or minor credit)

200. SPECIAL STUDIES IN ECONOMICS.—The student undertakes a special project under the guidance of a member of the department.
Credit, 2-5 each semester.
THE STAFF.

210. HISTORY OF ECONOMIC THOUGHT.—A general study of economic thought from its ancient beginnings; the contributions of the various schools; recent changes in economic thought. Given as required. Credit, 3.
MR. VATTER.

213. CENTRAL BANKING.—A study of the organization and policies of the major central banks with special reference to the Federal Reserve System. Given as required. Credit, 3.
Mr. GAMBLE.

227. MATHEMATICAL ECONOMICS AND ECONOMIC MODEL-BUILDING.—A study of the various modern applications of mathematics to economic analysis. Special attention is paid to the analysis of interactions among several variables. Both static and dynamic processes will be examined. Given as required.
Admission by consent of instructor. Credit, 3.
Mr. SCHOEFFLER.
Prerequisites, Economics 173 and Mathematics 29 or the equivalent.

260. MONOPOLY AND PUBLIC UTILITY PROBLEMS.—A study of the problem of social control of monopolies and industries affected with a public interest. Given as required. Credit, 3.
Prerequisite, Economics 170. MR. HOWARD.

272. ADVANCED ECONOMIC THEORY.—A study of the various theories of value and distribution. Credit, 3.
Prerequisite, Economics 173. THE STAFF.

276. TAXATION.—A study of the assessment and administration of taxes with particular attention to its economic and social effects of individual taxes and tax systems. Credit, 3.
Prerequisite, Economics 25, 78 or 178. Mr. GAMBLE.

293, 295, 297. COURSES IN AGGREGATIVE ECONOMICS.—(These courses rotate but not in a consistent cycle.)

293. ECONOMIC PLANNING.—Various economic plans in effect or proposed throughout the world. Appraisal of the technique of economic planning. Credit, 3.
Mr. MORRIS.

294. INSTITUTIONAL ECONOMICS.—Study of the major institutions affecting economic problems. Given as required. Credit, 3.
Mr. HOWARD.

295. FULL EMPLOYMENT.—Methods of attaining and maintaining full employment in economy. Credit, 3.
Mr. GAMBLE.

297. ECONOMIC FLUCTUATIONS.—Causes, and methods of control of economic fluctuations. Credit, 3.
Mr. HOWARD.

300. THESIS, MASTER'S DEGREE. Credit, 10.

400. THESIS, PH. D. DEGREE. Credit, 30.

COURSES OPEN TO BOTH GRADUATE AND UNDERGRADUATE STUDENTS
(For either major or minor credit)

Added work required of graduates: (a) extra readings on same or additional assignments, (b) term paper, (c) special problem or project.

154. MONEY AND MONETARY POLICY.—A study of the relationship between money, national and personal income and monetary policy. It includes examination of the relationships between individuals, banks, money markets and central banks. Credit, 3.
Prerequisite, Economics 53 or Finance 53. Mr. GAMBLE.

155. ECONOMICS OF CONSUMPTION.—A study of patterns of consumption, standards of living and the sources and expenditure of individual and family incomes. Credit, 3.
(a and b or c) Mr. MORRIS.

156. BUSINESS CYCLES.—A study of business fluctuations and an analysis of current business cycle theories. Credit, 3.
Mr. HOWARD.

170. MONOPOLIES.—A study of the growth, development and social control of monopolies. Credit, 3
(a, b) Mr. HOWARD.

174. CURRENT ECONOMIC PROBLEMS.—An intensive study of current economic problems. Students will be encouraged to pursue lines of individual interest. Credit, 3
(a, b) Mr. LEVINSON.

177. INTERNATIONAL TRADE.—A study of the policies, principles, and practices of international trade. Credit, 3
(a, b) MR. KINSEY.

178. PUBLIC FINANCE.—A study of the principles underlying public expenditures, public borrowing and taxation. Credit, 3.
(a, b) Mr. GAMBLE

180. LABOR LEGISLATION.—A study of federal and state legislation affecting labor. Credit, 3.
(a, b) MR. WILL.

183. SOCIAL CONTROL OF BUSINESS.—Methods of social control of economic activity including both formal and informal controls. Credit, 3.
(a, b) Mr. HOWARD.

184. COMPARATIVE ECONOMIC SYSTEMS.—An examination of the various forms of economic organization that have been tried and proposed with an analysis of the economic institutions of representative current economics.
(a, b) Credit, 3.
Mr. SCHOEFFLER.

191, 192. SEMINAR. Credit, 1-3.
THE STAFF.

COURSES IN OTHER DEPARTMENTS FOR WHICH MAJOR CREDIT WILL BE GIVEN

Agricultural Economics 200. RESEARCH. Credit, 3.
Mr. LINDSEY.

Agricultural Economics 156. FUNDAMENTALS OF COOPERATION. Credit, 3.
Mr. LINDSEY.

Agricultural Economics 171. AGRICULTURAL ECONOMIC THEORY. Credit, 3.
Mr. LINDSEY.

Agricultural Economics 178. PRINCIPLES OF LAND ECONOMICS. Credit, 3.
Mr. LINDSEY.

Agricultural Economics 180. ADVANCED STATISTICAL METHOD. Credit, 3.
Mr. LINDSEY and Mr. RUSSELL.

Agricultural Economics 189, 190. SEMINAR. Credit, 2-3.
Mr. LINDSEY and Mr. RUSSELL.

Finance 165. CORPORATION FINANCE. Credit, 3.
THE STAFF.

COURSES FOR MINOR CREDIT ONLY
(No graduate credit for students majoring in Economics)

153. MONEY, BANKING AND CREDIT.—A critical survey of the development and operation of the monetary and banking systems of the United States.
Credit, 3.
Mr. GAMBLE.

173. MODERN ECONOMIC THEORY.—A study of current theories about value, distribution and prices. Credit, 3.
Mr. SCHOEFFLER.

179. LABOR PROBLEMS.—An analysis of the background and character of the modern labor problems with special references to the United States. Credit, 3.
(a and b or c) Mr. MORRIS.

Education

ALBERT W. PURVIS, major adviser.

Before being admitted to candidacy for the Master of Science[1] degree with a major in Education, the student must have, in addition to minimum Graduate School requirements:

1. Fifteen hours of such fundamental courses as Education 51, 52, 53, 61, 62, 66, 72, 83, 85, etc., listed in the undergraduate catalog.

2. Experience in teaching. Students entering without teaching experience must arrange for practice teaching as soon as possible.

3. If the major is in secondary education, a major (24 hours) and a minor (12 hours) in the subject-matter fields to be taught.

4. If the major is in elementary school teaching, a minor (18 hours) in some field of general education.

COURSES OPEN TO GRADUATE STUDENTS ONLY
(For either major or minor credit)

200. PROBLEM.—Work necessary to achieve an answer to a particular question in the educational field. Question to be of student's choosing, if possible. It may or may not involve original research and may have only local significance. A bound copy of the typed report must be provided for the Department by the student. Credit, 4.
Prerequisite, Education 291. THE STAFF.

208. THE TEACHER AND SCHOOL ADMINISTRATION.—Problems in admission, promotion, personnel, discipline, extra-curricular activities, supervision, tenure, salary schedules, etc. Credit, 2-3.
Mr. PURVIS.

209. ADMINISTERING SECONDARY SCHOOLS.—Housing, finance, schedule, the library, guidance, cafeteria, public relations. etc. Credit, 2-3.
Mr. OLIVER.

210. ADMINISTERING EXTRA-CURRICULAR ACTIVITIES.—Scheduling, financing, sponsorship, regulation of pupil participation. 1956-57 and each alternate year. Credit, 2-3.
Mr, OLIVER.

211. COMMUNITY RELATIONS FOR SCHOOL PERSONNEL.—Emphasis is placed on the development of good public relations policies and the techniques of assisting lay people in interpreting school activities, policies, and objectives. 1957-58 and each alternate year. Credit, 2-3.
Mr. OLIVER.

[1]For a description of the Master of Arts in Teaching see page 10.

213. ADMINISTERING ELEMENTARY SCHOOLS.—The principal's responsibilities, organization of the school office, scheduling, use of school facilities, curriculum organization, staff relationships, and the place of the school in the community.
Credit, 2-3.
THE STAFF.

214. SUPERVISING ELEMENTARY SCHOOLS.—Principles and problems of supervision in the elementary school; methods and types of supervision as they are related to the modern elementary curriculum, the content fields, the activity program and the area of unitary teaching. Credit, 2-3.
THE STAFF.

215. SEMINAR OR WORKSHOP IN EDUCATION.—Group study of current problems in curriculum, instruction, and administration for school personnel in service.
Credit, 2-6.
THE STAFF.

220. SCHOOL LAWS OF MASSACHUSETTS.—A review of the legal relations of the school personnel covering the usual experiences in school and community, presented in a series of selected cases having the support of court decisions.
Credit, 3.
MR. PURVIS.

254. EVALUATION IN ELEMENTARY SCHOOLS.—Standardized and teacher made tests, rating scales, report cards, growth charts, readiness measures, and diagnosis of educational deficiency in elementary pupils. (To be taken instead of Education 153 by those training for elementary teaching.) Credit, 2-3.
1957-58 and each alternate year. MR. ROURKE.

259. ELEMENTARY SCHOOL SCIENCE.—Methods and materials of instruction.
Credit, 2-3.
MRS. TRUMBULL

265. TECHNIQUES IN REMEDIAL READING.—Methods and materials in diagnosis and remedial instruction. Credit, 2-3.
Prerequisite, Education 161. MISS O'LEARY.

267. AUDIO-VISUAL LABORATORY.—Individual and practical experience in setting up and using common audio-visual equipment and materials. Minor repairs and maintenance will be included. This course should be preceded by Education 166 or a similar course. Credit, 2-3.
MR. WYMAN and MR. CURTIS.

289. COOPERATIVE CURRICULUM PLANNING.—Approved methods of curriculum planning, group work, consensus studies, used by cities and towns in curriculum development. Credit, 2-3.
Prerequisite, Education 188 or 160. 1956-57 and each alternate year.
MR. ROURKE.

291. EDUCATIONAL RESEARCH.—The principles and methods of research with special emphasis upon the technique used in Education. Statistics are studied chiefly from the standpoint of reporting and understanding the results of research. Required in first semester of students who anticipate completion of a thesis or problem in the current year. Credit, 2-3.
MR. PURVIS.

COURSES OPEN TO BOTH GRADUATE AND UNDERGRADUATE STUDENTS

(For either major or minor credit)

151. HISTORY OF EDUCATION. Credit, 2-3.
MR. PURVIS and MR. ADAMS.

152. PRINCIPLES AND METHODS OF TEACHING. Credit, 3.
MR. PURVIS and MR. FENNELL.

153. EDUCATIONAL TESTS AND MEASUREMENTS. Credit, 2-3.
MR. ROURKE.

160. ELEMENTARY SCHOOL CURRICULUM. Credit, 2-3.
MRS. TRUMBULL.

161. ELEMENTARY READING AND LANGUAGE ARTS. Credit, 2-3.
MISS O'LEARY.

162. ELEMENTARY ARITHMETIC. Credit, 2-3.
MRS. TRUMBULL.

164. PRINCIPLES OF ELEMENTARY EDUCATION. Credit, 2-3.
MISS O'LEARY.

166. PREPARATION AND USE OF AUDIO-VISUAL AIDS. Credit, 2-3.
MR. WYMAN and MR. CURTIS.

172. VOCATIONAL EDUCATION IN AGRICULTURE.—By arrangement. Credit, 3.
MR. OLIVER and MR. TAFT.

173. APPRENTICE TEACHING IN AGRICULTURE.—By arrangement. Credit, 6.
MR. OLIVER and MR. TAFT.

175. TECHNIQUE OF TEACHING VOCATIONAL AGRICULTURE.—By arrangement. Credit, 3.
MR. OLIVER and MR. TAFT.

181. WORKSHOP IN THE TEACHING OF MODERN FOREIGN LANGUAGES IN ELEMENTARY SCHOOLS.—The latest techniques, methods and materials will be presented and demonstrated. Some round-table discussions with Education, Romance Language and Psychology Departments. The course is especially designed for present and prospective elementary school teachers and for teachers in a Modern Foreign Language. Minor credit for students who have a major in a Modern Foreign Language. Summer School Only. Credit, 3.
THE STAFF.

183. PRINCIPLES OF SECONDARY EDUCATION. Credit, 2-3.
MR. FENNELL.

188. SECONDARY SCHOOL CURRICULUM. Credit, 2-3.
MR. ROURKE.

COURSES FOR MINOR CREDIT ONLY

(No graduate credit for students majoring in Education)

185. OBSERVATION AND PRACTICE TEACHING.—By arrangement. Credit, 3.
THE STAFF.

Electrical Engineering

CARL S. ROYS, major adviser.

At least 12 credits, including Electrical Engineering 201 and Electrical Engineering 202 and exclusive of thesis, must be obtained in courses open to graduate students only.

COURSES OPEN TO GRADUATE STUDENTS ONLY
(For either major or minor credit)

201. ENGINEERING ANALYSIS I.—Analytical procedures beyond undergraduate levels as applied to the solutions of problems in the various fields of engineering.
Credit, 3.
Prerequisite, Degree of B.S. in Engineering.　　　　MR. ROYS and STAFF.

202. ENGINEERING ANALYSIS II.—A continuation of 201.　　Credit, 3.
Prerequisite, Electrical Engineering 201.　　　　MR. ROYS and STAFF.

204. SERVOMECHANISMS II.—A continuation of Electrical Engineering 190 that covers the principles of quantitative dynamic analyses of closed-cycle control systems in terms of differential equations and complex functions. System synthesis on the basis of specified performance characteristics also is a major objective.
Credit, 3.
Prerequisite, Electrical Engineering 190.　　　　THE STAFF.

221. POWER AND MACHINERY LABORATORY.—This is designed to develop testing techniques through class and laboratory studies of the more advanced topics related to electrical machinery and power systems. When taken concurrently with other courses in power and machinery, the laboratory work may be varied to suit individual needs.
Credit, 3.
One class hour; six hours of laboratory.　　　　MR. KARLSON.
Prerequisite, Electrical Engineering 81.

222. POWER SYSTEMS METERING AND RELAYING.—This course covers metering and protective relaying for electric power systems, and includes modern relay methods used on radial lines, loops and networks, with emphasis upon coordinated protection; circuit interruption problems also are studied.　Credit, 3.
Prerequisite, Electrical Engineering 86.　　　　MR. KARLSON.

223. TRAVELING WAVES IN POWER SYSTEMS.—The fundamental theory of traveling waves and its application to lightning and switching surges in power systems, including reflection and refraction at transition points; insulation levels and coordination; high voltage and current and voltage surge testing standards.
Prerequisite, Electrical Engineering 183.　　　　Credit, 3.
MR. ROYS.

224. POWER SYSTEMS OPERATION AND STABILITY.—A continuation of Electrical Engineering 86 with further applications to power systems under unbalanced steady state and transient conditions. This includes the effects of ground wires, ground impedance and mutual coupling impedances; inductive coordination with communication systems; the effects of saturation and pole saliency in synchronous machines upon steady state and transient stability; variability of load impedance; and multimachine problems.
Credit, 3.
Prerequisite, Electrical Engineering 86.　　　　MR. KARLSON.

241. COMMUNICATIONS NETWORKS.—A continuation of Electrical Engineering 79 covering the principles and applications of network analysis and synthesis, noise and information theory. . Credit, 3.
Prerequisite, Electrical Engineering 79 or its equivalent. MR. ROYS.

243. ELECTROMAGNETIC ENGINEERING I.—The fundamentals of Electromagnetism, including Ampere's and Faraday's Laws, Gauss' Theorem, retarded potential and Hertz' vector, Maxwell's equations and Poynting's vector. These are applied to the propagation, reflection and refraction of electromagnetic waves, radio-frequency lines, wave guides, cavity resonators, antennas and ionospheric reflections. Credit, 3.
Prerequisites, Electrical Engineering 201, 202. MR. ROYS.

246. ELECTROMECHANICAL SYSTEMS AND TRANSDUCERS.—A review of network theory as associated with lumped mechanical systems, vibrating membranes and plates, electromechanical converters and acoustics. Applications are made to microphones, loudspeakers, horns, crystals and electromechanical filters.
Prerequisite, Electrical Engineering 183. Credit, 3.
MR. ROYS.

300. THESIS, MASTER'S DEGREE. GRADUATE RESEARCH.—Independent research under the supervision of a staff member which will serve as the basis for the thesis required for the master's degree in Electrical Engineering. It is expected that a paper covering the project will be presented before the combined A.I.E.E. and I.R.E. student branch at the University. Credit, 3-6.
Consultation and laboratory hours to be arranged.

COURSES OPEN TO BOTH GRADUATE AND UNDERGRADUATE STUDENTS

(For either major or minor credit)

183. TRANSIENT ANALYSIS.—A study of the transient behavior of electrical, mechanical, and thermal systems. The ordinary and partial differential equations associated with the systems are set up and their solutions obtained by the classical, Heaviside Operational and Fourier and Laplace Transform methods. An introductory survey of Functions of a Complex Variable leads to the evaluation of the Inversion Integral by means of the Method of Residues. Credit, 4.
Three class hours; One 3-hour laboratory period. MR. ROYS.
Prerequisite, Electrical Engineering 58.

184. INDUSTRIAL ELECTRONICS.—Special characteristics of the electron tubes of industry; the theory, design and operation of commercial types of equipment utilizing these tubes, including stroboscopes, grid-controlled and polyphase rectifiers, inverters, welding controllers, speed and voltage regulators, high frequency heating circuits, etc. Credit, 4.
Three class hours; one 3-hour laboratory period. MR. ROYS.
Prerequisite, Electrical Engineering 55.

185. ELECTRICAL MEASUREMENTS.—Theory and practice of electric and magnetic measurements; accuracy, precision, and limitations of measurements and devices. Credit, 3.
Two class hours; one 3-hour laboratory period. MR. LAESTADIUS.
Prerequisite, Electrical Engineering 42.

186. POWER SYSTEM NETWORKS.—A study of power system networks including power transfer diagrams, voltage studies, system stability criteria, short-circuit calculations, and protective methods. Credit, 4.
Three class hours; one 3-hour laboratory period. Mr. KARLSON.
Prerequisite, Electrical Engineering 58.

187. POWER APPLICATIONS AND CONTROL.—A study of the application of electric machines and their controls. Torque relations, typical control systems, theory of relays, combinational and sequential relay systems and counting circuits are among the topics considered. Credit, 4.
Three class hours; one 3-hour laboratory period. MR. KARLSON.
Prerequisites, Electrical Engineering 54 and Electrical Engineering 57.

190. FEEDBACK CONTROL SYSTEMS.—The analysis and design of basic types of error-sensitive control systems and their components, including servomechanisms. Analytical and graphical methods for the determination of steady state and transient performance of the several types of controllers are developed. Applications are made to typical systems involving electrical, mechanical, and hydraulic components. Credit, 4.
Three class hours; one 3-hour laboratory period. MR. KARLSON.
Prerequisite, Electrical Engineering 183.

194. MICROWAVE ENGINEERING.—A review of the fundamental principles of communications and electromagnetic fields and their application to the special problems of the generation, transmission, propagation and reception of microwaves. This also includes characteristics and specifications of standard equipment, and special training in general laboratory and commercial testing techniques. Credit, 4.
Three class hours; one 3-hour laboratory period. MR. ROYS.
Prerequisite, Electrical Engineering 79.

196. PRINCIPLES OF ELECTRICAL DESIGN.—The fundamentals of electric, dielectric, magnetic and heat-flow systems as applied to the design, rating and life of coils, transformers, machinery and other electrical equipment. Credit, 3.
Two class hours; one 3-hour laboratory period. Mr. ROYS.
Prerequisite, Electrical Engineering 54.

198. TELEVISION ENGINEERING.—Application of electronics and radio engineering to the special problems of television. Among the topics considered are system theory and analysis, signal sources, video response, noise limitations, synchronization and scanning, color vision and colorimetry, principles of the NTSC system, picture pickup and display tubes, transmission and reception, and monitoring and testing procedures. Credit, 4.
Three class hours; one 3-hour laboratory period. Mr. LANGFORD.
Prerequisites, Electrical Engineering 183 and must be preceded or accompanied by Electrical Engineering 80.

English

MAXWELL H. GOLDBERG, major adviser.

Language requirement: the ability to translate, with the aid of a dictionary, two languages other than English.

COURSES OPEN TO GRADUATE STUDENTS ONLY

(For either major or minor credit)

201. OLD ENGLISH.—A study of Old English grammar with prose translation. This (or 203) required of all English majors. 1957-58 and each alternate year. Credit, 3.

MR. LANE.

203. MIDDLE ENGLISH.—A study of the language of Chaucer and the mediaeval romances. This (or 201) required of all English majors. 1956-57 and each alternate year. Credit, 3.

MR. HELMING.

251. SHAKESPEARE.—A close study of *Henry IV—Part 1, Twelfth Night, King Lear, and Cymbeline*. Given in various years. Credit, 3.
Prerequisite, English 155. THE DEPARTMENT.

254. CARLYLE.—A study of the life and writings of Thomas Carlyle. Biographic, textual, ideational, and esthetic problems will be explored so as to develop competence in research and criticism. Given in various years. Credit, 3.
Prerequisite, English 165 or its equivalent. MR. GOLDBERG.

261. MELVILLE.—An exploration of the life, thought and art of the most complex and representative figure of the American Renaissance. Although emphasis will be placed upon the pre-Civil War novels, the later poetry will also be examined. Given in various years. Credit, 3.
Prerequisite, English 185 or 186. MR. KAPLAN.

264. JOYCE, YEATS, AND ELIOT.—An intensive study of the experiments, in expressing personal experience, that established the Twentieth Century literary myths. Given in various years. Credit, 3.

MR. VARLEY.

300. THESIS, MASTER'S DEGREE. Credit, 9.

COURSES OPEN TO BOTH GRADUATE AND UNDERGRADUATE STUDENTS

(For either major or minor credit)

In these courses English majors are required to supplement the undergraduate assignments with a substantial special study.

150. CHAUCER.—A study of Chaucer's development and preeminence as a creative artist and an attempt to appreciate his humanism. Credit, 3.
Three class hours. MR. HELMING.

151. THE RENAISSANCE IN ENGLAND.—A study of various aspects of the Renaissance as revealed in such writers as Spenser, Bacon, Sir Thomas Browne, Burton, and Hobbes. Special emphasis is given to Spenser's *Faerie Queene*. Credit, 3.
Three class hours. MR. LANE.

153. LYRICAL POETRY OF THE RENAISSANCE IN ENGLAND.—A study of lyrical poets such as Sidney, Campion, Jonson, Herrick, Lovelace, Suckling, Carew, Donne, Herbert, Vaughan, Crashaw, Traherne and Marvell. Emphasis is given to the "Metaphysical" tradition. 1956-57 and each alternate year. Credit, 3.
Three class hours. MR. GOLDBERG, MISS HORRIGAN and MR. BARRON.

154. MILTON.—The development of the mind and art of Milton as a Renaissance writer. Emphasis is placed upon *Paradise Lost, Paradise Regained,* and *Samson Agonistes.* Credit, 3.
Three class hours. MR. GOLDBERG, MR. HELMING and MR. KOEHLER.

155. SHAKESPEARE.—This course is based upon the reading of about twenty-five of Shakespeare's plays, and attempts both to indicate the evolution of the dramatist and to emphasize the various phases of his art. Credit, 3.
Three class hours. MR. RAND.

157. ENGLISH LITERATURE OF THE RESTORATION.—A study of the social problems and literary values of the Restoration period as they appear in prose, verse, and drama. Emphasis will be placed on the satire of Dryden; and on the development of the theatre from the Restoration through Congreve and the Comedy of Manners. Credit, 3.
Three class hours. MR. KOEHLER.

158. ELIZABETHAN DRAMATISTS.—A study of English drama from the death of Elizabeth to the closing of the theaters. Special consideration will be given to the plays of Jonson, Beaumont, Fletcher, Webster, Middleton, Massinger, and Shirley. Credit, 3.
Three class hours. MR. O'DONNELL.

159. ENGLISH LITERATURE OF THE EIGHTEENTH CENTURY.—A study of the literature of the Augustan Age, with special emphasis on the writing of Swift and Pope. Credit, 3.
Three class hours. MR. BARRON.

160. ENGLISH LITERATURE OF THE EIGHTEENTH CENTURY.—A continuation of English 159, but may be elected independently. A study of the literature of the later Eighteenth Century with special emphasis on the Johnson Circle.
Three class hours. Credit, 3.
MR. BARRON.

161. ROMANTIC POETRY.—A study of the Lake Poets (primarily Wordsworth and Coleridge) and their precursors. 1956-57 and each alternate year.
Three class hours. Credit, 3.
MR. RAND.

162. ROMANTIC POETRY.—A continuation of English 161, but may be elected independently. A study of Byron, Shelley and Keats. 1956-57 and each alternate year. Credit, 3.
Three class hours. MISS HORRIGAN.

163. AMERICAN POETRY.—A study of American poetry from Colonial times to 1900, with special emphasis upon the work of Freneau, Bryant, Emerson, Longfellow, Whittier, Poe, Whitman, and Emily Dickinson. Credit, 3.
Three class hours. MR. O'DONNELL and MR. WILLIAMS.

165. ENGLISH PROSE OF THE NINETEENTH CENTURY.—A study of the chief Romantic prose writers in relation to literary techniques and main currents of epochal thought and feeling. Among the authors treated are Coleridge, Lamb, Hazlitt, DeQuincey, Landor, Carlyle, and Ruskin. Credit, 3.
Three class hours. MR. GOLDBERG.

166. ENGLISH PROSE OF THE NINETEENTH CENTURY.—A continuation of English 165, but may be elected independently. A study of the chief Victorian prose writers in relation to literary techniques and main currents of epochal thought and feeling. Among the authors treated are Macaulay, Newman, Arnold, Mill, Huxley, Pater, and Stevenson. Credit, 3.
Three class hours. MR. GOLDBERG.

168. MODERN DRAMA.—This course traces the development of continental English and American drama from the time of Ibsen to the present day. Its purpose is to impart an intelligent and enthusiastic interest in the drama of the twentieth century. Credit, 3.
Three class hours. MR. RAND and MR. WILLIAMS.

169. VICTORIAN POETRY.—A study of Tennyson and Browning. 1957-58 and each alternate year. Credit, 3.
Three class hours. MR. RAND.

171. BIOGRAPHY.—The history of the biography as a literary type; discussion of leading biographers from Boswell to Maurois, with special emphasis upon the development of the modern biographical method. Credit, 3.
Three class hours. MR. HELMING.

172. THE BIBLE AS LITERATURE.—A study of the King James version of the Bible, with emphasis upon the Hebrew as discernible in translation, the poetic qualities characteristic of Tudor England, and the varied influence of the Bible upon subsequent English poetry. Credit, 3.
Three class hours. MR. RAND.

173. THE NOVEL FROM DEFOE THROUGH THE VICTORIANS.—The development of the novel; the reading and discussion of eight or nine great English novels of the eighteenth and nineteenth centuries. Credit, 3.
Three class hours. MR. HELMING and MR. ALLEN.

174. GREEK CLASSICS IN TRANSLATION.—Readings and discussion of the epics of Homer, representative dramas of Aeschylus, Sophocles, Euripides, and Aristophanes, the "Socratic" dialogues of Plato, and Thucydides' history of the Peloponnesian War. Intended to acquaint students with the famous myths and stories of classical antiquity, and the literary forms and ideas which have contributed most to subsequent literatures. Credit, 3.
Three class hours. MR. HELMING and MR. KAPLAN.

176. MODERN POETRY.—This course attempts to trace the spirit of twentieth century poetry from such authors as Hardy, Whitman, and Emily Dickinson to those of the present day. Credit, 3.
Three class hours. MR. RAND and MISS HORRIGAN.

177. THE MODERN NOVEL.—An analytical presentation of eleven or twelve novels written between 1890 and 1920, in which the expanding form and the extension of critical themes will be stressed. Credit, 3.
Three class hours. MR. VARLEY.

178. THE CONTEMPORARY NOVEL.—A continuation of English 177, covering about twelve novels between 1920 and 1950, with some consideration of social issues reflected in the fiction. Credit, 3.
English majors will not elect both English 177 and 178.
English 178 may be elected independently of English 177. MR. VARLEY.
Three class hours.

179. LITERARY CRITICISM.—A study of major critical attitudes and principles, in relation to philosophic background and to practice. Emphasis is placed upon important critics and theorists from Plato and Aristotle through those of the eighteenth century. 1957-58 and each alternate year. Credit, 3. Three class hours. MR. GOLDBERG.

180. LITERARY CRITICISM.—A continuation of English 179, but may be elected independently. Emphasis is placed upon important critics and theorists of the nineteenth and twentieth centuries. 1957-58 and each alternate year. Credit 3. Three class hours. MR. GOLDBERG.

181. CREATIVE WRITING.—A course in critical and imaginative composition based upon the examples of standard authors and the experience of the student. It provides an opportunity for work in description, narrative, verse and drama as well as in exposition. The chief emphasis is on fiction and poetry. Credit, 3. Three class hours. THE DEPARTMENT. Prerequisites, a grade of A or B in English II (U. of M.) or permission of the head of the department.

182. CREATIVE WRITING.—A continuation of English 181, but may be elected independently. Emphasis on Non-Fiction. Credit, 3. Three class hours. THE DEPARTMENT. Prerequisites, a grade of A or B in English II (U. of M.) or permission of the head of the department.

185. MAJOR AMERICAN WRITERS.—A study of a selected group of the major American writers of the nineteenth and early twentieth century. The authors to be read and discussed will include Emerson, Hawthorne, Longfellow, Lowell, Henry James, Henry Adams, Fitzgerald, and Hemingway. A careful analysis will be made of the varying literary forms given to such dominant themes as nature and the conflict between the individual and society. Credit, 3. MR. O'DONNELL.

186. MAJOR AMERICAN WRITERS.—A study of a selected group of major American writers of the nineteenth and early twentieth century. The authors to be read and discussed include Cooper, Poe, Melville, Thoreau, Whitman, Mark Twain, Stephen Crane, Sinclair Lewis, and Faulkner. A careful analysis will be made of the varying literary forms given to such dominant themes as nature and the conflict between the individual and society. Credit, 3. MR. KAPLAN.

187. PROBLEMS IN AMERICAN LITERARY AND LINGUISTIC STUDIES.—Given in various years. Credit, 1-3. THE DEPARTMENT.

188. PROBLEMS IN ENGLISH LITERARY AND LINGUISTIC STUDIES.—Given in various years. Credit, 1-3. THE DEPARTMENT.

Entomology

CHARLES P. ALEXANDER, major adviser

COURSES OPEN TO GRADUATE STUDENTS ONLY

(For either major or minor credit)

(Most courses in the department are given on a 3-year cycle, subject to change on student demand.)

201, 202. ADVANCED INSECT MORPHOLOGY AND PHYLOGENY.—Laboratory, lecture, and reading assignments in morphology and phylogeny of all orders of insects, living and fossil.   Credit, 3 each semester
Prerequisites, Entomology 26, 155, 156, 157 or equivalent.   MR. HANSON.

203. INSECT EMBRYOLOGY.—The embryological development of a generalized type of insect, after which specific insects are considered. Lectures, assigned readings, laboratory work.   Credit, 2.
Prerequisite, ENTOMOLOGY 157.   Mr. SHAW.

204. INSECT HISTOLOGY.—Types of tissues and organs of insects. Laboratory work, discussion and assigned readings.   Credit, 2.
Prerequisites, Entomology 157; Zoology 51.   MR. SHAW.

207. ADVANCED INSECT PHYSIOLOGY.—Discussion and laboratory work dealing with the functions of the organ systems of insects. Emphasis is placed on methods of analysis and study of physiological processes in insects.   Credit, 3.
Prerequisite, Entomology 181 or equivalent.   Mr. SWEETMAN.

210. INSECT INTERRELATIONSHIPS.—A systematic survey of the various ways in which insects live with, make use of, or are utilized by living organisms, including intra-specific relations; the aim is to present an integrated picture of relationships among insects, and between insects and the living world.
Lectures, readings, papers.   Credit, 2.
Prerequisites, Entomology 26 and 179.   Miss SMITH.

211. INSECT BEHAVIOR.—The honey bee is selected as a type for the study of behavior. Lectures; laboratory work to attempt to interpret the reasons for the actions of this insect. Other species may be included for completeness.
Prerequisites, Entomology 26, 166 or equivalent.   Credit, 3.
                                                            Mr. SHAW.

212. GEOGRAPHICAL DISTRIBUTION OF ANIMALS AND PLANTS.—The entire field of distribution of life is considered, including a discussion of physical geography, climate, and other materials basic to the subject.   Credit, 3.
                        2 credits 1st semester, 1 credit 2nd semester.
Prerequisites, Botany 1; Zoology 1.   Mr. ALEXANDER.

214. ADVANCED ANIMAL ECOLOGY.—Basic principles of terrestrial, limnological, and marine ecology. Special emphasis is placed on the influence of causal factors, both physical and biotic, that regulate the activities of all organisms.
Prerequisite, Entomology 179, or equivalent.   Credit, 3.
                                                         Mr. SWEETMAN.

221. ADVANCED CHEMICAL CONTROL OF INSECTS.—The chemistry of insecticides and their physiological effects on insects, man and other animals. Credit, 3.
                                                         Mr. SWEETMAN.
Prerequisites, Entomology 180 and Pomology 156, or equivalent.

223. ADVANCED BIOLOGICAL CONTROL.—The basic fundamental principles, as well as practical application of biological control of insects. A section is devoted to control of pest weeds with insects. Credit, 3.
Prerequisite, Entomology 180, or equivalent. Mr. SWEETMAN.

224. LEGISLATIVE CONTROL OF INSECTS AND INSECTICIDES.—The legal aspects of prevention, control, and eradication of pests; insecticide laws, and health laws regarding use of insecticides. Emphasis is placed on the importance of basic knowledge of the biology and habits of insects and other pest organisms as related to legal and other methods of control and eradication. Credit, 3.
Mr. SWEETMAN.

230. ADVANCED APICULTURE.—This course is designed to provide necessary background for whatever phase of beekeeping the student desires, equipment permitting. Among such topics available are management, biometry, bee poisoning, pollination. Credit, 2-5.
Prerequisites, Entomology 166' 185, or equivalent. Mr. SHAW.

240· COCCIDOLOGY.—Lecture and laboratory work on scale insects; their relationships, structure, habits, technique of mounting, identification, damage, and control. Credit, 2.
Prerequisite, Entomology 26, or equivalent. Mr. HANSON.

241. CLASSIFICATION OF MINOR ORDERS OF INSECTS.—Laboratory work in taxonomy of the many groups with relatively few species. Credit, 2.
Prerequisites, Entomology 26, 155, 156, 157, or equivalent. Mr. HANSON.

242. ADVANCED ARTHROPOD TAXONOMY.—Classification of various groups of insects and insect allies, indicating the latest methods in taxonomy and the principles of classification. In addition to groups listed below, work may be offered in such groups as Ephemerida, Plecoptera, Diptera, Lepidoptera, and others upon special arrangement in advance. Credit, 1-9.
THE STAFF.

A. Culicidae	Miss SMITH
B. Immature stages of insects	Miss SMITH
C. Ticks	Mr. SHAW
D. Siphonaptera	Mr. SHAW
E. Simuliidae	Mr. SHAW
F. Tabanidae	Mr. SHAW
G. Tipulidae	Mr. ALEXANDER
H. Other Groups of Insects	THE STAFF

245. HISTORICAL ENTOMOLOGY.—Lives and works of outstanding entomologists of the world; history of entomology; and classification of insects.
Credit, 3.
(2 credits 1st semester;
1 credit 2nd semester)
Prerequisites, Entomology 26, 153. Mr. ALEXANDER.

248. PRINCIPLES OF SYSTEMATIC ENTOMOLOGY.—Particular stress is placed on a consideration of the International Code of Zoological Nomenclature, and the Opinions thereon; type categories; the species concept; major insect collections; leading entomological specialists. Credit, 3.
(2 credits 1st semester;
1 credit 2nd semester)
Prerequisites, Entomology 26, 155, 156. Mr. ALEXANDER.

ENTOMOLOGY

250. ADVANCED MEDICAL ENTOMOLOGY.—This course is designed to provide training in whatever phase of medical entomology a student selects (materials and references permitting). Such work might include systematic studies of a family or order of insects involved in medical entomology, the biology of any particular group of insects, control measures. Credit, 2-5.
Prerequisites, Entomology 174 or its equivalent. Mr. SHAW.

270. ADVANCED RESEARCH METHODS.—The principles, methods of analysis, and presentation of results of research. A section is devoted to statistical treatment and analysis of research. Credit, 3.
Mr. SWEETMAN.
Prerequisites, Research portion of Entomology 181, or equivalent.

280. SEMINAR.—Reports on the current literature of entomology; special reports by resident and visiting speakers. Credit, 1 each semester.
One class hour. (Maximum for M.S. Candidates, 2)
(Maximum for Ph.D. Candidates, 4)
MR. WEIDHAAS.

300. THESIS, MASTER'S DEGREE.—Original work on one or more topics in insect morphology, systematic entomology, medical entomology, insect physiology, insectides, biological control or apiculture. The thesis requires from one-half to two-thirds of the total working time of the student in his major field. Credit, 10.

400. THESIS, PH.D. DEGREE.—Original work on one or more topics in insect morphology, systematic entomology, medical entomology, insect physiology, insecticides, biological control or apiculture. The thesis requires from one-half to two-thirds of the total working time of the student in his major field.
Credit, 30.

COURSES OPEN TO BOTH GRADUATE AND UNDERGRADUATE STUDENTS

(For either major or minor credit)

185. ADVANCED BEEKEEPING.—A course designed to present more complete knowledge of the more important problems of beekeeping, including management, processing honey and wax, bee diseases, and improvement of honeybees.
Credit, 3.
Prerequisite, Entomology 166. Mr. SHAW.

187, 188. SPECIAL PROBLEMS IN ENTOMOLOGY.—Problem work in many fields, as apiculture, biological control and insectary practice, insecticides, morphology, and classification. Credit, 1, 2, or 3.
Prerequisites, Entomology 26, 53, 155, 157, and should be preceded or accompanied by other courses in the restricted field of the problem.
THE STAFF.

189. ENTOMOLOGICAL TECHNIQUES.—Techniques in the mounting and preservation of insects for study and display by means of fluids, slides, plastics, pinning, and other methods. Credit, 2.
Prerequisite, Entomology 26. Miss SMITH.

190. EVOLUTION.—A course in orientation. Lectures consider evolution of both organic and inorganic matter with attention to the evolution of human behavior and to the effect of evolutionary concepts on human philosophy. Extra supplementary reading required of graduate students. Credit, 2-3.
Mr. HANSON.

COURSES IN OTHER DEPARTMENTS FOR WHICH MAJOR CREDIT WILL BE GIVEN

Zoology 174. LIMNOLOGY. Credit, 4.
MISS TRAVER in cooperation with Departments of Botany,
Entomology, Geology, Public Health and Zoology.

Zoology 185. CLASSES OF ARTHROPODS OTHER THAN INSECTS. Credit, 3.
Mr. HANSON.

Botany 190. INSECT TRANSMISSION OF PLANT DISEASES. Credit, 3.
Mr. BANFIELD.

COURSES FOR MINOR CREDIT ONLY

(No graduate credit for students majoring in Entomology)

151. PESTS OF SPECIAL CROPS. Credit, 3.
Mr. SHAW.

153. APPLIED ENTOMOLOGY. Credit, 3.
Mr. SHAW.

155, 156. CLASSIFICATION OF INSECTS. Credit, 3.
Mr. ALEXANDER, Miss SMITH.

157. INSECT MORPHOLOGY. Credit, 4.
Mr. HANSON.

160. STRUCTURAL PEST CONTROL. Credit, 2.
MR. SWEETMAN.

166. INTRODUCTORY BEEKEEPING. Credit, 3.
Mr. SHAW.

172. FOREST AND SHADE-TREE INSECTS. Credit, 3.
Mr. HANSON.

174. MEDICAL ENTOMOLOGY. Credit, 3.
Mr. SHAW.

179. ANIMAL ECOLOGY. Credit, 3.
Mr. SWEETMAN.

180. BIOLOGICAL CONTROL OR CHEMICAL CONTROL OF INSECTS
Credit, 2 or 3.
Mr. SWEETMAN.

181. PHYSIOLOGICAL ENTOMOLOGY. Credit, 3.
Mr. SWEETMAN.

Floriculture

CLARK L. THAYER, major adviser.

All students who major in this department are required to present a thesis as a part of the major requirements.

FLORICULTURE

COURSES OPEN TO GRADUATE STUDENTS ONLY
(For either major or minor credit)

Horticulture 211, 212. SEMINAR.—Each student will present reviews of assigned papers on topics in Horticulture. Departments of Floriculture, Olericulture and Pomology cooperating. Required of all graduate students majoring in Floriculture, Olericulture and Pomology. Credit, 1 each semester.

THE DEPARTMENTS

226. GARDEN MATERIALS.—Technical studies of a specific genus of plants or a group of plants used in gardening. Credit, 3.
Prerequisite, Floriculture 26. MR. JESTER.

275. ADVANCED COMMERCIAL FLORICULTURE.—Problems dealing with the methods of production of cutflowers and plants under glass. Opportunity is given for a study of factors concerned with methods of marketing such products.
Prerequisites, Floriculture 175 and 176. Credit, 3.
MR. JESTER.

279. CONSERVATORY PLANTS.—Investigations dealing with plant materials which are used primarily in conservatories or in gardens in warm climates.
Prerequisite, Floriculture 179. Credit, 3.
Mr. THAYER.

290. HISTORY OF FLORICULTURE AND FLORICULTURAL LITERATURE.—Consideration of men who have influenced the development of floriculture. Events that have given impetus to the industry. Survey of floricultural literature. Required of all graduate students in the department. Credit, 3.
Mr. THAYER.

297, 298. SEMINAR.—A review of scientific literature in the field of floriculture or in related fields. Credit, 1 each semester.
Mr. WHITE and THE STAFF

300. THESIS, MASTER'S DEGREE.—For students having a major in Floriculture. Based on an original investigation of a problem selected by agreement between the student and the staff. Credit, 10.

COURSES IN OTHER DEPARTMENTS FOR WHICH MAJOR CREDIT WILL BE GIVEN

Agronomy 263. CHEMISTRY OF THE SOIL. Credit, 5.
Mr. STECKEL.

Agronomy 264. EXPERIMENTAL METHODS IN AGRONOMY. Credit, 3.
Mr. YEGIAN.

Botany 158. MICROTECHNIQUE. Credit, 2.
MR. PUTALA.

Botany 159, 160. THE ANGIOSPERMS. Credit, 3-5 each semester.
MR. DAVIS.

Botany 161, 162. THE COMPARATIVE ANATOMY OF GREEN PLANTS.
Credit, 3 each semester.
MR. DAVIS.

Olericulture 201. LITERATURE.   Credit, 3.
                                                 MR. TUTTLE.

Plant Breeding. 152. PLANT BREEDING METHODS.   Credit, 3.
                                                 Mr. FRENCH.

Plant Breeding 181. PLANT CYTOLOGICAL TECHNIQUES. Credit, 2.
                                                 Mr. FRENCH.

Plant Breeding 182. SPECIAL PROBLEMS IN PLANT BREEDING.   Credit, 2.
                                                 Mr. FRENCH.

COURSES FOR MINOR CREDIT ONLY
(No graduate credit for students majoring in Floriculture)

151. GREENHOUSE MANAGEMENT.   Credit, 3.
                                      Mr. THAYER and Mr. JESTER.

152. FLORAL ARRANGEMENT.   Credit, 3
                                                 Mr. Ross.

175, 176. COMMERCIAL FLORICULTURE.   Credit, 3 each semester.
                                                 MR. JESTER.

179. CONSERVATORY PLANTS 1956-57.   Credit, 2.
                                      Mr. THAYER and Mr. Ross.

181. HERBACEOUS GARDENS AND BORDERS.   Credit, 3
                                                 MR. THAYER.

182. SEMINAR (Problem course).   Credit, 3
                                                 Mr. THAYER.

Food Sciences

This is a cooperative major designed for Ph.D. candidates who wish to prepare for research in various phases of the food sciences. It is designed to give a broader and somewhat less intensive scientific base for research or its application in industry than is possible when a student takes most of his major work in one department only. This plan provides for a candidate to place the major emphasis in one of the five departments cooperating which may or may not offer a Ph.D. degree in the department.

The departments cooperating are Bacteriology, Chemistry, Dairy Industry, Food Technology, and the School of Home Economics (Foods and Nutrition). Courses, if properly selected, will satisfy both major and minor requirements. The proportionate contribution of each department will depend upon the student's special interests within the field but a minimum of six credits must be earned in each of the departments contributing to this major.

Candidates for the Ph.D. degree in the Food Sciences are assigned to an advisory committee composed of the heads of the five departments concerned, with the head of the department in which the thesis research is planned serving as chairman. This advisory committee will direct the student's progress, conduct the preliminary examination, and approve the thesis subject. The guidance committee, appointed by the Scholarship Committee of the Graduate School Council with the staff member who is directing the thesis serving as chairman, will have direct charge of all matters pertaining to the thesis investigation.

FOOD SCIENCES

The 30 major course credits required for the Ph.D. must be distributed among at least 3 of the 5 departments concerned. The minimum requirement of six credits in other departments may be satisfied by either major or minor credits. Courses offered by the 5 departments which are acceptable for major credit toward the degree in Food Sciences have been designated by the advisory committee as follows:

400. THESIS, PH.D.   Credit, 30.

Bacteriology

    202. ADVANCED BACTERIAL PHYSIOLOGY.

    203. BACTERIAL CYTOLOGY.

    205. ADVANCED IMMUNOLOGY.

    206. MICROBIOLIGICAL FERMENTATIONS.

    207. VIROLOGY.

    208. SEMINAR.

    213. ANTIBIOTICS.

    214. MICROBIAL GENETICS.

    215. ANTISEPTICS AND DISINFECTANTS.

    156. METHODS FOR BACTERIOLOGICAL PREPARATION.

    182. QUANTITATIVE AND QUALITATIVE BACTERIOLOGY.

    185. IMMUNOLOGY.

    190. SANITARY BACTERIOLOGY.

    196. STUDIES OF SPECIAL MICROBIAL GROUPS.

    198. BACTERIAL PHYSIOLOGY.

Chemistry

    237. BIOCOLLOIDS.

    239. CHEMISTRY OF NATURAL PRODUCTS.

    165, 166. PHYSICAL CHEMISTRY. (For minor credit only)

    179. BIOCHEMISTRY. (For minor credit only)

    183. ADVANCED QUANTITATIVE ANALYSIS.

    193, 194. GENERAL BIOCHEMISTRY

Dairy Industry

    175. DAIRY CHEMISTRY.

    200. PROBLEMS IN DAIRY TECHNOLOGY.

    202. ADVANCED DAIRY CHEMISTRY.

    209, 210. SEMINAR.

Food Technology

    201, 202. SPECIAL INVESTIGATIONS.

    209, 210. THERMAL PROCESSING OF FOODS.

    216. FOOD PACKAGING.

    221. EDIBLE FATS AND OILS.

241. FOOD ACCEPTANCE—THEORY AND METHODOLOGY.

250. FOOD COLORIMETRY.

271, 272. SEMINAR REVIEW OF CURRENT LITERATURE AND RESEARCH.

285, 286. FISHERIES TECHNOLOGY.

161, 162. INDUSTRIAL PRACTICES.

191, 192. FOOD ANALYSIS.

Foods & Nutrition

203. ADVANCED NUTRITION—METABOLISM OF THE MAJOR FOODSTUFFS.

204. ADVANCED NUTRITION—VITAMINS AND MINERALS.

205. LABORATORY METHODS AND TECHNIQUES IN NUTRITION.

207. PROBLEMS IN NUTRITION.

212. NUTRITION SEMINAR.

189. DIET THERAPY.

Food Technology

CARL R. FELLERS, major adviser.

Graduate students who wish to major in Food Technology may not be admitted to candidacy for an advanced degree until such time as the undergraduate requirements in basic sciences and Food Technology have been met substantially.

COURSES OPEN TO GRADUATE STUDENTS ONLY
(For either major or minor credit)

200. RESEARCH PROBLEM.—This course is mainly for candidates for the Master of Science degree. Original research is expected. Two bound copies (flexible binding permissible) are required by the Department. Credit, 3-6.

THE STAFF.

201, 202. SPECIAL INVESTIGATIONS.—A series of individual problems and assignments covering plant layouts, process development, quality control and economics of production. Laboratory, pilot plant and library exercises.

Credit, 1-3 each semester.
THE STAFF.

209, 210. THERMAL PROCESSING OF FOODS.—Biological and Physical Aspects. A study of the factors affecting heat transfer in canned goods. Heating characteristics of canned foods packed in tin, glass, and other containers. Determination of thermal death points of spoilage micro-organisms. Derivation of processing times and temperatures. Causes of spoilage and container failure. Principles of retort operation and control; instrumentation.
First semester—2 lectures or conferences. Credit, 2.
Second semester—1 lecture, one 4-hour laboratory. Credit, 3.
Prerequisites, Food Technology 162 and Bacteriology 182. MR. ESSELEN.

212. FREEZING AND REFRIGERATION.—Lay-out of cold storage plants. Practical refrigeration systems. Equipment and methods used in quick-freezing fruits, vegetables, meats, and marine products. Packaging and quality control. Home freezers and commercial frozen-food lockers. Laboratory and class work.
Prerequisites, Food Technology 152 and Agricultural Engineering 180 or 182.

Credit, 2-4.
MR. FELLERS.

216. FOOD PACKAGING.—A study of the characteristics of all packaging materials including flexible films and how they meet the package requirements of various food products. Methods of testing for structural quality and performance, moisture and gas transmission, and other properties. Consideration of adhesives, lacquers and closures included. Occasional lectures by qualified representatives of industry. Plant visits in non-scheduled hours.

One 4-hour laboratory period; one or more class or discussion hours. Credit, 3.
Prerequisite, Food Techonolgy 162. MR. LEVINE.

221. EDIBLE FATS AND OILS.—The production, processing and uses of edible fats and oils and their chemical nature in relationship to stability. The problem of oxidation and rancidity is considered with emphasis on cause of deterioration and methods of stabilization. Credit, 2.
One class hour, one 2-hour laboratory period.

232. UNIT PROCESSES.—Unit processes pertaining to the food industries are covered. The work includes instrumentation, temperature measurement, blanching, filtration, comminution, deaeration and extraction, processing, cooling, heat transfer, fluid flow, distillation, dehydration, and evaporation. Credit, 2.
Prerequisites, Food Technology 162 and Agricultural Engineering 180.
MR. FAGERSON.

241. FOOD ACCEPTANCE—THEORY AND METHODOLOGY.—A critical analysis of objective and subjective methods of evaluation of the quality of processed foods. Physical and chemical means of expressing quality of a product. Sensory methods including difference-preference tests, panel tests, threshold tests, etc. Application of statistical methods including control chart techniques. Psychological and physiological factors affecting flavor appraisal.
1 lecture; 1 conference.
Prerequisites, Food Technology 192, 162. Credit, 3
MR. FAGERSON.

·250. FOOD COLORIMETRY.—Composition and properties of food colorants. Methods of measurements and specification of color in raw and processed foods. The nature, cause and control of color changes in the handling, processing and storage of food products. The application of the Munsell, C.I.E. and other color systems to commercial quality control and laboratory inspection under governmental grading standards. Credit, 3.
One lecture, one 4-hour laboratory; second semester. MR. LIVINGSTON.
Prerequisite, Food Technology 191 and 192; Chemistry 165 and 166.

271, 272. SEMINAR.—Review of current literature and research.
Credit, 1-2 each semester.
THE STAFF.

285, 286. FISHERIES TECHNOLOGY.—Marine products of commerce. Processed seafoods. Canning, curing, freezing and refrigeration. Spoilage problems. By-products. Chemical and microbiological aspects. Scientific literature. Industrial problems. Credit, 2-3 each semester.
One class hour plus laboratory work to be arranged. MR. FELLERS.

295. BIOLOGICAL AND TOXICOLOGICAL ASSAY OF FOODS.—Provides laboratory training and practice in making animal and microbiological assays of food constituents important in human and animal nutrition. Added chemicals in foods.
Prerequisites, Chemistry 179 and Food Technology 192. Credit, 2-5.
MR. PARKINSON.

300. THESIS, MASTER'S DEGREE.—Research on some suitable problem in Food Technology. Facilities for nutrition research are provided by well-equipped chemical, physical, and small-animal laboratories and poultry plant. Credit, 10.

400. THESIS, PH.D. DEGREE.—Research on some suitable problem in Food Technology. Facilities for nutrition research are provided by well-equipped chemical, physical, and small-animal laboratories and poultry plant. Credit, 30.

COURSES OPEN TO BOTH GRADUATE AND UNDERGRADUATE STUDENTS
(For either major or minor credit)

161, 162. INDUSTRIAL PRACTICES.—Advanced laboratory and pilot plant work in the production of canned, frozen and dehydrated fruits, vegetables, meat, and fish products. The theory and practice in manufacturing jams, jellies and condiments as well as fermented, salted and smoked foods; cereal products and soups. Credit, 3 each semester.
One class hour, one 4-hour laboratory period. Mr. LEVINE.

182. CONFECTIONS AND CEREAL PRODUCTS.—Candy making, maple products, sugar and fountain syrups, corn products such as starch, syrups, dextrose and their uses. Candied fruits and preserves. Flavoring essences, spices, carbonated beverages. This course also considers the principles of baking, doughs, and various prepared cereals and dry mixes. Credit, 3.
One class hour, one 4-hour laboratory period. Mr. LEVINE.

191, 192. ANALYSIS OF FOOD PRODUCTS.—Factory and laboratory methods. Grades and quality factors; physical, chemical, microbiological and microscopical methods, and interpretation of results. Government and trade standards; Federal and State food regulations; mold and insect counts; plant control procedures will be stressed. Food preservatives and flavorings.
Credit, 3 each semester.
Mr. FELLERS and Mr. NEBESKY.
One 4-hour laboratory period, one lecture.
Prerequisites, Chemistry 30, Food Technology 152 or 175.

COURSES IN OTHER DEPARTMENTS FOR WHICH MAJOR CREDIT WILL BE GIVEN

Chemical Engineering 177. ELEMENTS OF UNIT OPERATIONS. Credit, 3.
MR. LINDSEY.

Agricultural Engineering 260. AGRICULTURAL PROCESSING. Credit, 3.
MR. ZAHRADNIK.

Dairy Industry 152. MARKET MILK. Credit, 4.
MR. EVANS.

Dairy Industry 177. BUTTER AND CHEESE MAKING. Credit, 4.
MR. POTTER.

Dairy Industry 178. ICE CREAM MAKING. Credit, 4
MR. POTTER.

Animal Husbandry 154. MEAT PROCESSING. Credit, 2
Mr. BARTLETT.

FOOD TECHNOLOGY

BACTERIOLOGY 206. INDUSTRIAL BACTERIOLOGY.	Credit, 3. Mr. CZARNECKI.
Chemistry 193-194. GENERAL BIOCHEMISTRY.	Credit, 4 or 8. Mr. LITTLE.
Chemistry 237. BIOCOLLOIDS.	Credit, 3. Mr. BENNETT.
Chemistry 239. CHEMISTRY OF NATURAL PRODUCTS	Credit, 3. MR. LITTLE and MR. CONRAD.

Home Economics 205. LABORATORY METHODS AND TECHNIQUES IN NUTRITION.
Credit, 3.
Mrs. WERTZ.

Olericulture 173. MARKETING AND STORAGE OF VEGETABLE CROPS. Credit, 3.
Mr. SNYDER

Olericulture 174. MARKETING PRACTICES.	Credit, 3. Mr. SNYDER.
Poultry Science 201. ADVANCED POULTRY HUSBANDRY.	Credit, 3. THE STAFF.

COURSES FOR MINOR CREDIT ONLY
(No graduate credit for students majoring in Food Technology)

151. FRUIT AND VEGETABLE PRODUCTS.—This is a general elementary course covering food economics, production, distribution and processing. The applications of fundamental science to the food industries are pointed out. The laboratory exercises cover both the theory and practice of canning, freezing, and dehydration. The principles of packaging are considered. Fruit and vegetable products are prepared and graded. Credit, 3.
One class hour, one 4-hour laboratory period. Mr. FELLERS.

152. FOOD PRODUCTS AND ADJUNCTS.—This is a continuation of 151. The laboratory work includes pickles and pickle products, maple products, citrus products, fruit syrups, soups, condiments and the preservation of meats, poultry and vegetables. The properties and uses of sugars, syrups, salt, enzymes, pectin, chemical preservatives and anti-oxidants, are considered. Practice is given in the use and handling of instruments and equipment. Credit, 3.
Two class hours, one 2-hour laboratory period. Mr. FELLERS.

175, 176. FOOD PRESERVATION.—This is a general course in food preservation and is intended only for those who desire a survey of the field in a condensed form. Not open to Food Technology majors. Credit 3, either semester.
One class hour, two 2-hour laboratory periods. Mr. NEBESKY.

195, 196. INTRODUCTORY RESEARCH METHODS.—The application of the fundamental sciences to food technology research. Library and laboratory research on assigned individual problems. Credit, 2 each semester.
By arrangement. Mr. FELLERS, Mr. LEVINE

74

Forestry

COURSES FOR MINOR CREDIT ONLY.

151. FOREST MANAGEMENT OF WATERSHEDS.—A study of forest site and water factor relationships; the measurability of the forest resources and their management toward realizing the multiple values of watersheds. The protection of forested watersheds. Credit, 3.
Three class hours. Mr. RHODES and Mr. HOLDSWORTH.

153. SILVICS.—Forest ecology as the basis for silvacultural practice.
Two class hours; one 4-hour laboratory period. Credit, 3.
Mr. RHODES.

154. FOREST SOILS.—A study of the soils of forests as they influence forest growth and management and as they are influenced by forest trees and forest management. Credit, 3.
Three class hours. MR. MADER.

155. ELEMENTS OF FOREST MENSURATION.—Methods of inventorying the volumes of the timber capital or growing stock and other resources of the forest.
Credit, 3.
Two class hours; one 4 hour laboratory period.
MR. MacCONNELL and MR. BOND.

156. PRINCIPLES OF APPLIED SILVICULTURE.—Forest establishment and cultural development through silvicultural practice. Credit, 3.
Two class hours; one 4-hour laboratory period. Mr. RHODES and Mr. ABBOTT.

157. ECONOMICS OF FORESTRY.—The resource values of the forest with the history of their economic development. Credit, 3.
Three class hours. Mr. HOLDSWORTH.

159. FOREST PROTECTION.—The principle of protecting forests from all harmful agencies. Credit, 3.
Three class hours. Mr. ABBOTT.

171. AERIAL PHOTOGRAMMETRY.—Interpretation and use of aerial photographs in map making and forest land inventory and management. Credit, 3.
Two class hours, one 4-hour laboratory period.
MR. MacCONNELL and MR. BOND.

176. WOOD TECHNOLOGY.—A comprehensive survey of the structure, composition and properties of wood in relation to wood utilization. Credit, 3.
Three class hours. Mr. RICH.

180. PRINCIPLES OF FOREST MANAGEMENT.—The organization of the forest for sustained yields management; preparation of forest management plans.
Three class hours. Credit, 3.
Prerequisites, Forestry 155 and 156. Mr. MacCONNELL.

185. SEASONING OF WOOD.—Methods of air seasoning and kiln drying lumber.
Three class hours. Credit, 3.
Mr. RICH.

Geology and Mineralogy

H. T. U. SMITH, major adviser.

COURSES OPEN TO GRADUATE STUDENTS ONLY.

(For either major or minor credit)

200. SPECIAL PROBLEMS.—For students desiring to pursue special work not covered by courses listed in the curriculum. Permission to take one or both courses must be secured from the head of the department and the instructor under whom the study will be done. The latter will outline and supervise the work. Credit, 2 to 6.

THE STAFF.

201. OPTICAL MINERALOGY.—An introduction to the theory, procedure and technique involved in the study of minerals by means of the petrographic microscope. The laboratory work will include the preparation of thin sections of minerals and rocks, together with a study of their optical properties by means of polarized light. Credit, 3.

Prerequisite, Geology 151. MR. NELSON.

202. ADVANCED PETROLOGY.—A study of physico-chemical principles related to petrogenesis of igneous, metamorphic and sedimentary rocks. The consideration of general principles and specific problems such as differentiation, ore solutions, granitiation, granite tectonics and diagenesis. Credit, 3.

1957-58 and each alternate year. MR. SOCOLOW.

Prerequisite, Geology 201 or equivalent.

212. SEDIMENTATION.—A course dealing with the sources, depositions, modifying conditions, structures and environmental relationships of sediments and their consolidated equivalents. Credit, 3.

MR. DODGE.

213. GEOPHYSICS.—A study of the physics of the earth and of the gravitational, magnetic, electrical, and seismic methods of geophysical exploration. The laboratory work consists of problems and computations. Credit, 3.

Prerequisite, Geology 173. MR. RICE.

214. MINERAL FUELS.—A course dealing with the geological occurrences of coal, gas and oil. The laboratory work consists of problems related to petroleum geology and the recovery of fluid hydrocarbons. Credit, 3.

Prerequisite, Geology 154. MR. SOCOLOW.

221. ANIMAL MICROPALEONTOLOGY.—Principles of animal micropaleontology with emphasis on the use of animal microfossils in stratigraphic investigations.

Credit, 3.

MR. JOHANSSON.

222. PLANT MICROPALEONTOLOGY.—Principles of plant micropaleontology with emphasis on the use of plant microfossils in stratigraphic investigations.

Credit, 3.

MR. —.

241. SEMINAR.—Review of current literature or discussion of selected topics. Credit, 1 each semester. Maximum credit, 2.

THE STAFF.

300. THESIS, MASTER'S DEGREE.—Research on an approved problem.

Credit, 10.

COURSES OPEN TO BOTH GRADUATE AND UNDERGRADUATE STUDENTS

(For either major or minor credit)

173. STRUCTURAL GEOLOGY.—A study of the origin of rock structures, their occurrence and recognition. Undergraduates must have the permission of the instructor before enrolling. Credit, 3.

MR. SOCOLOW.

174. PRINCIPLES OF STRATIGRAPHY.—A study of the principles of stratigraphic correlation as related to the major rock units of the United States. Undergraduates must have the permission of the instructor before enrolling. Credit, 3.

MR. DODGE.

COURSES FOR MINOR CREDIT ONLY

(No graduate credit for students majoring in Geology and Mineralogy)

150. ENGINEERING GEOLOGY.—A general course in engineering geology stressing earth structure, the dynamic processes, and agents of weathering. The laboratory work consists of mineral and rock-determination and map-reading as related to the phenomena of physical geology. Credit, 3.
Two class hours; one 3-hour laboratory period. MR. SOCOLOW.

151, 152. MINERALOGY.—A course designed to meet the needs of students majoring in geology and allied fields. The first semester's work deals with all of the mineral classes with the exception of the silicate group which has been reserved for the second semester. Credit, 3.
One class hour; two 2-hour laboratory periods. MR. NELSON.

154. ECONOMIC GEOLOGY.—A course dealing with the origin, classification, and uses of metallic and non-metallic mineral deposits. Credit, 3.
Two class hours; one 2-hour laboratory period. MR. SOCOLOW.

156. LITHOLOGY.—A descriptive study of the classes of rocks with reference to manner of origin, modes of occurrence, structural features and the chemical and petrographic distinction within each group. Credit, 3.
One class hour; two 2-hour laboratory periods. MR. NELSON.

161. GEOMORPHOLOGY.—A review of recent studies concerning rock structures, weathering, underground water, streams, alpine and continental glaciers, shorelines, and wind work. Credit, 3.
Two class hours; one 2-hour laboratory period. MR. SMITH.

162. PLEISTOCENE GEOLOGY.—A study of Pleistocene world geology consisting of geological processes, land forms, existing and extinct glaciers, biota and stratigraphy. Field trips by arrangement. Credit, 3.
Two class hours; one 2-hour laboratory period. MR. SMITH.

163. INVERTEBRATE PALEONTOLOGY.—A study of the history, development and identification of invertebrate animal fossils. Field trips by arrangement.

Credit, 3.

Mr. JOHANSSON.

164. PLANT PALEONTOLOGY.—A study of the history, development and identification of plant fossils. Field trips by arrangement. Credit, 3.
One class hour; two 2-hour laboratory periods. MR. —.

German

COURSES FOR MINOR CREDIT ONLY

151. NINETEENTH CENTURY PROSE I.—A study of the "Novelle" from the death of Goethe to 1890 (early realism to naturalism) with emphasis on literary and social forces in the work of Tieck, Stifter, Keller, and others. Credit, 3.
Three class hours. Given in 1956-57.

152. POETRY AND DRAMA OF THE NINETEENTH CENTURY II.—A study of the development of the drama and of lyric poetry from 1830 to 1890 with special emphasis on dramatic works of Grillparzer, Hebbel, and Hauptmann and the poetry of Mörike, Storm, and C. F. Meyer. Credit, 3.
Three class hours. Given in 1956-57. THE STAFF.

153. TWENTIETH CENTURY PROSE I.—Main literary currents in contemporary German prose from Nietzsche to Hesse with particular attention to the work of Thomas Mann, Kafka, and Werfel. Credit, 3.
Three class hours. Given in 1955-56. MR. —.

154. POETRY AND DRAMA OF THE TWENTIETH CENTURY II.—Reading and discussion of significant lyrical works of Hofmannsthal, George, and Rilke and representative dramas by Hauptmann and Georg Kaiser. Credit, 3.
Three class hours. Given in 1955-56. THE STAFF.

155. STORM AND STRESS I.—A study of storm and stress in German literature centering in the young Goethe. Credit, 3.
Three class hours. Given in 1955-56. Mr. ELLERT.

156. ROMANTICISM II.—A study of the poetry and prose writings of the romantic period from Novalis to Heine. Credit, 3.
Three class hours. Given in 1956-57. Mr. ELLERT.

157. GOETHE'S FAUST I. Credit, 3.
Three class hours. MR. ELLERT.

158. MIDDLE HIGH GERMAN II.—Reading of Middle High German texts with an introduction to grammar. Credit, 3.
Three class hours. MR. —.

159. THE GERMANIC LANGUAGES I.—An introduction to General and Germanic philology for German and English majors; a survey of the relationship between German, English, and the other Indo-European tongues and of the historical development of German and English as the two major Germanic literary languages. Credit, 3.
Three class hours. THE STAFF.

160. THE CLASSICAL PERIOD II.—A study of representative works by Lessing, Goethe, and Schiller. Credit, 3.
Three class hours. Given in 1955-56. MR. ELLERT.

168. GERMAN LITERATURE OF THE MIDDLE AGES II.—A survey of the literature of the German language from the earliest literary documents to the 15th century, with readings in modern German translation of the Nibelungenlied, Gudrun, Parzival, Tristan, Der arme Heinrich, and the lyrics of Walter von der Vogelweide. Credit, 3.
Three class hours. Given in 1955-56. MR. ELLERT.

222. ADVANCED SPOKEN GERMAN. Credit, 3.
Prerequisites, German 79 and 80 or their equivalent as determined by a qualifying examination. MR. —.

Government

COURSES FOR MINOR CREDIT ONLY

152. AMERICAN FOREIGN POLICY.—An analysis of the principles of American foreign policy. Constitutional, political and administrative considerations which influence the formulation and execution of American foreign policy will be discussed. Special emphasis will be placed on current issues. Credit, 3.
Three class hours. MR. ALLEN.

153. INTERNATIONAL RELATIONS.—The nation-state system and conceptions of national interest in modern world politics. The forms and distribution of power by which states seek to implement national interests. The making of foreign policy and methods of adjusting international conflict. Attention will be given to current international problems. Credit, 3.
Three class hours. MR. ALLEN.

154. STATE GOVERNMENT.—A study of state politics, organization and functions with emphasis on the role of the state in our federal system. 1957-58 and each alternate year. Credit, 3.
Three class hours. MR. GOODWIN.

156. THE LEGISLATIVE PROCESS.—A study of the role of the legislature in national and state government. Among other topics, the functions of legislatures, legislative procedures and the role played by political parties and pressure groups in the legislative process will be surveyed. Emphasis will be placed on research. 1956-57 and each alternate year. Credit, 3.
Three class hours. MR. GOODWIN.

161. PUBLIC ADMINISTRATION.—A study of organization and management in modern government, with emphasis on the bureaucracy's role in public policy formation. Credit, 3
Three class hours. MR. MAINZER.

162. ADMINISTRATIVE LAW.—A study of governmental activities in the regulation of industry, agriculture, and labor, with emphasis on the legal framework within which these activities operate. 1957-58 and each alternate year.
Three class hours. Credit, 3.
MR. MAINZER.

163. POLITICAL PARTIES AND ELECTIONS.—A study of the American political process, with emphasis on parties, pressure groups, and public opinion.
Three class hours.   Credit, 3.
                                                                         MR. GOODWIN.

164. MUNICIPAL GOVERNMENT.—A survey of the governmental structure and function of American municipalities.   Credit, 3.
Three class hours.   MR. GILLESPIE.

165 CONSTITUTIONAL LAW.—An historical study of the United States Constitution as interpreted by decisions of the Supreme Court.   Credit, 3.
Three class hours.

166. AMERICAN POLITICAL THOUGHT.—A study of the development of American political thought from Colonial times to the present.   Credit, 3.
Three class hours.

168. INTERNATIONAL LAW.—A study of the origin, character, and function of international law. 1957-58 and each alternate year.   Credit, 3.
Three class hours.   MR. BRAUNTHAL.

170. INTERNATIONAL ORGANIZATION.—A study of international organization in the twentieth century, with emphasis upon the United Nations and regional organizations. 1956-57 and each alternate year.   Credit, 3.
Three class hours.   MR. BRAUNTHAL.

171. ANCIENT AND MEDIEVAL POLITICAL THOUGHT.—A study of the development of political thought and its relation to cultural and institutional growth from the time of the Greeks to the end of the Middle Ages.   Credit, 3.
Three class hours.   MR. TINDER.

172. MODERN POLITICAL THOUGHT.—A study of the development of political thought and its relation to cultural and institutional growth from the rise of the modern state to the present.   Credit, 3.
Three class hours.   MR. TINDER.

173. COMPARATIVE GOVERNMENT.—A functional analysis of contemporary governments with special attention to the ideology, structure, and dynamics of political parties.   Credit, 3.
Prerequisite, Government 26.   MR. ALLEN.
Three class hours.

176. PUBLIC OPINION IN POLITICS.—A study of opinion and communication as aspects of the political process with emphasis upon communication through mass media. Examination of the relations between mass attitudes and communication and political institutions and the formation of public policy.   Credit, 3.
Three class hours.   MR. MAINZER.

178. MUNICIPAL ADMINISTRATION.—A study of administrative management in American municipalities based on descriptive literature, case materials and personal observation. Particular attention will be given to Massachusetts cities and towns. 1956-57 and each alternate year.   Credit, 3.
Three class hours.   MR. GILLESPIE.

180. MUNICIPAL CORPORATIONS.—A study of the creation and nature of municipal corporations and the legal problems encountered in the conduct of local government. Special reference will be made to Massachusetts municipalities. 1957-58 and each alternate year. Credit, 3.
Three class hours. MR. GILLESPIE.

193, 194. SEMINAR.—A study of special problems in the field of government.
Three class hours. By permission of the Department. Credit, 3.
THE DEPARTMENT.

History

THEODORE C. CALDWELL, major adviser.

In addition to the general requirements for the Master of Arts degree, candidates in History must fulfill the following departmental requirements:

A reading knowledge of one foreign language is required.

The requirement concerning a thesis may be fulfilled by one of the following options: (a) completion of a thesis, for ten credits, (b) completion of two seminar courses, with grades of at least 80, (c) completion of a five credit thesis and one seminar.

A comprehensive written examination, in fields specified by the Department, is required of all candidates.

COURSES OPEN TO GRADUATE STUDENTS ONLY

(For either major or minor credit)

210. THE PROGRESSIVE MOVEMENT AND THE NEW DEAL IN THE UNITED STATES, 1896-1940.—Conditions and ideas in the revolt against conservatism.
Prerequisites, History 159 and 160. Credit, 3.
MR. CARY.

251. SEMINAR IN AMERICAN DIPLOMATIC HISTORY.—Training in historical research. Credit, 3.
Admission by consent of instructor. MR. CARY.

256. SEMINAR IN THE WESTWARD MOVEMENT OF THE UNITED STATES.—Training in historical research. Credit, 3.
Admission by consent of instructor. MR. DAVIS.

300. THESIS, MASTER'S DEGREE. Credits, 5 or 10.

COURSES OPEN TO BOTH GRADUATE AND UNDERGRADUATE STUDENTS

(For either major or minor credit)

The following courses are open to both graduate and undergraduate students who have fulfilled the prerequisites including History 5 or 6 or their equivalent. Graduate students will be expected to do such additional work as shall be prescribed by the instructor.

151. ANCIENT HISTORY.—A general survey of Mesopotamian, Egyptian, Greek and Roman history, with primary emphasis on cultural and intellectual achievements. Credit, 3.
Three class hours. MR. DAVIS.

154. THE FAR EAST IN MODERN TIMES.—A general historical introduction to the civilization and contemporary problems of China and Japan. The first half covers the traditional civilization of China and Japan and the early impact of the west to 1890. The second half deals with revolutionary developments of the twentieth century and the place of the Far East in the world balance of power. 1956-57 and each alternate year. Credit, 3.
Three class hours. MR. McCUNE and MR. KINGDON.

156. THE HISTORY OF MODERN RUSSIA.—A general historical introduction to the civilization and contemporary problems of Russia. Growth of the Russian state, society, culture and ideology, and their relations to the non-Russian world. Emphasis on the Soviet period. 1957-58 and each alternate year. Credit, 3.
Three class hours. MR. GAGNON.

157, 158. HISPANIC-AMERICAN HISTORY.—The first semester deals with the colonial period: the age of the "conquistadores," political, economic, and cultural developments, and growth of the independence movement; the second semester with the period of national development from 1810 to the present. Emphasis will be given to the history of Mexico and the more important South American countries. Either semester may be elected independently.
Three class hours. Credit, 3 each semester.
MR. POTASH.

162. MEDIEVAL HISTORY.—Europe from the collapse of Roman civilization to the Renaissance. Fusion of the Graeco-Roman inheritance, Christianity, and Germanic traditions in the building of Western European civilization. The medieval outlooks as expressed in the thought and culture of the High Middle Ages. Credit, 3.
Three class hours. MR. ZEENDER.

163, 164. HISTORY OF AMERICAN THOUGHT AND CULTURE.—A study of the basic strands of American thought and their reflection in the development of social life and institutions, literature, and the arts. The first course covers the period to 1865. Either semester may be elected independently.
Three class hours. Credit, 3 each semester.
MR. BROWN.

166. THE HISTORY OF MODERN GERMANY.—The evolution of Germany since 1750 in relationship to Western Europe. An analysis of those economic, social, and political, and intellectual influences which determined the unique direction of German cultural development. Culminates in a study of the Nazi revolution and contemporary Germany. Credit, 3.
Three class hours. MR. PFLANZE.

169. EUROPE, 1870-1918.—Internal developments of the principal countries, including political and economic changes, social unrest, and intellectual currents; the development of imperialism; a detailed study of conditions and diplomacy which led to the World War; military history of the War. Credit, 3.
Three class hours. MR. ZEENDER.
Prerequisite, History 6.

170. EUROPE, SINCE 1918.—Approximately half of the course is devoted to international affairs, including the Peace Settlement, the development of German, Italian, and Japanese aggression, and World War II. The other half of the course is a study of internal developments in the principal European nations. Credit, 3.
Three class hours. MR. CALDWELL.

171. MAIN CURRENTS IN ENGLISH THOUGHT, 1600-1900.—A study of leaders of thought and the climate of ideas in selected periods, with emphasis on the relationship of ideas to outstanding historical events. Credit, 3. Three class hours. MR. CALDWELL.

172. HISTORY OF AMERICAN WESTWARD EXPANSION, 1763-1893.—Advance of settlement from the Appalachians to the Pacific and influence of the frontier upon social, economic, and political conditions in the country as a whole. Three class hours. Credit, 3. Prerequisite, History 159, or permission of instructor. MR. DAVIS.

173. HISTORY OF THE RENAISSANCE.—The later Middle Ages; the Church at the height of power; the rise of nationalities; the Italian towns; the New Learning and its relation to art, science, invention, geographical discoveries; spread and effects of the Renaissance. Credit, 3. Three class hours. MR. KINGDON.

174. AGE OF THE REFORMATION.—A study of the religious changes, and the accompanying political upheavals, social, economic, and cultural developments in 16th and 17th century Europe. Credit, 3. Three class hours. MR. KINGDON.

179. NEW ENGLAND TO 1860.—A study of the colonial and early national periods, with emphasis upon the political, social, and economic aspects of life in this region. Credit, 3.
MR. CARY.

181, 182. DIPLOMATIC HISTORY OF THE UNITED STATES.—The development of American foreign relations, 1776 to the present. Either semester may be elected independently. Credit, 3. Three class hours. MR. CARY. Prerequisites, History 159 and 160 or permission of instructor.

COURSE FOR MINOR CREDIT ONLY

(No graduate credit for students majoring in History)

159, 160. HISTORY OF THE UNITED STATES Credit, 3 each semester.
MR. BROWN, MR. CARY and MR. DAVIS.

Home Economics

HELEN S. MITCHELL, major adviser

Graduate work is primarily in the field of Nutrition Research or Home Economics Education with an emphasis on foods and nutrition. Those applying for graduate work in Nutrition should have an undergraduate major in Foods and Nutrition or its equivalent with strong offerings in Organic, Biochemistry, Physiology, and Bacteriology. Students applying for graduate work in Home Economics Education should have an undergraduate major in Home Economics with some courses in Education and Practice Teaching. The major work in this field is offered jointly by the School of Home Economics and the School of Education with certain courses in Education accepted for major credit as listed herewith. Graduate students interested in Child Development and Family Life may wish to avail themselves of the privilege of affiliation at Merrill-Palmer School in Detroit. Such students must take at least 15 credits in residence at the University.

COURSES OPEN TO GRADUATE STUDENTS ONLY

(For either major or minor credit)

200. SPECIAL PROBLEM.—An intensive study of a special problem in the field of Home Economics. This type of problem is recommended instead of a thesis for certain students. Credit, 3-6.

THE STAFF.

203. ADVANCED NUTRITION—METABOLISM OF THE MAJOR FOODSTUFFS.—A study is made of energy metabolism and the metabolism of carbohydrates, fats, proteins, and related substances, their role in human nutrition, and physiological effects of dietary inadequacies. A critical evaluation of food value tables and other reference material is made. Students are expected to give special reports from current literature supplementing class discussion. Credit, 3.

Prerequisites, Biochemistry and/or Physiology. MISS MITCHELL.

204. ADVANCED NUTRITION—VITAMINS AND MINERALS.—A detailed study is made of vitamins and minerals in metabolism, their specific functions in the body and results of mild and severe deficiencies. Special attention is given to current scientific literature on each subject. Credit, 3.

Prerequisite, Biochemistry and/or Physiology. MISS MITCHELL.

205. LABORATORY METHODS AND TECHNIQUES IN NUTRITION.—Laboratory course designed to acquaint qualified students with the different types of laboratory techniques that are currently used in nutrition research. These methods include fluorometric, colorimetric, spectrophotometric, and microbiological determinations of various nutrients in foods and biological fluids. Credit, 3.

1 class hour, one 4-hour lab. Mrs. WERTZ.

Prerequisites, Quantitative Chemistry, Home Ec. 203, 204, or equivalent.

207. PROBLEMS IN NUTRITION.—Qualified students may be permitted to work on a problem of special interest to them in the fields of vitamin and mineral metabolism, basal metabolism, dietary survey techniques, etc. Credit, 3.

Prerequisite, Home Ec. 203 or 204 or equivalent. MRS. WERTZ

209. PROBLEMS IN FOODS.—An advanced study of foods. Designed mainly to equip a student of the science in experimental foods procedures. Special emphasis on individual research problems. Credit, 3.

MISS DAVIS.

Prerequisites, Home Economics 193, Quantitative Chemistry, or equivalent, and permission of instructor.

210. HOME ECONOMICS SEMINAR.—Readings, reports and discussions on the current literature of the following areas—family relations, family economics, and home management. Credit, 3.

MISS MERRIAM AND MISS STRATTNER.

212. NUTRITION SEMINAR.—Readings, discussions and preparation of bibliographies on nutrition problems of current interest. Credit, 1.

MISS MITCHELL.

300. THESIS, MASTER'S DEGREE.—Individual research in the field of nutrition and the preparation of an acceptable thesis reporting results and analysis of such studies. Credit, 10.

COURSES OPEN TO BOTH GRADUATE AND UNDERGRADUATE
STUDENTS

(For either major or minor credit)

178. ADVANCED TEXTILE DESIGN.—Weaving and handling of complicated looms. Other types of textile design such as stencilling, silk screen printing, batik, block print, with individual problems dependent on special student interests. Credit, 3.
One class hour; two 3-hour laboratory periods. Miss BRIGGS.
Prerequisite, Home Economics 26 or equivalent.

181. METHODS OF TEACHING HOME ECONOMICS.—A study is made of general education philosophy; the application of home economics to the entire school program; development of curricula based upon student needs; exploration of instructional methods and techniques. This course gives credit toward meeting state standards for teachers. During the last month a two-hour laboratory period replaces one lecture. Credit, 3.

MISS STRATTNER.

185. THEORY AND PRACTICE OF NURSERY SCHOOL MANAGEMENT.—This course is planned to give students a background in the history and philosophy of the pre-school program; theory and techniques of nursery school practice; children's activities in music, art, literature and sciences; fundamentals of play and use of play material and methods of observation and recording. Supervised participation in child development laboratory as well as field trips to observe special groups. Credit, 3.
Prerequisite, Home Economics 70. MRS. THIES.

187. PRINCIPLES AND PRACTICES OF TAILORING.—Emphasis is placed on handling of wool in the making of suits and coats. Credit, 3.
One class hour; one 4-hour laboratory period. Mrs. WILHELM.
Prerequisite, Home Economics 35 or its equivalent.

188. APPLIED DRESS DESIGN.—Costume design through draping and pattern making. An intensive study is made of texture, line, color, and fit as applied to dress design and the figure. Credit, 3.
One class hour; two 2-hour laboratory periods. Mrs. WILHELM.
Prerequisite, Home Economics 35 or its equivalent.

189. DIET THERAPY.—The application of nutrition principles to diet in disease. Recent theories of dietary treatment of gastro-intestinal disorders, obesity, anemia, fevers, diabetes, food allergy, cardiovascular and biliary tract diseases are reviewed critically. Students are required to use and be familiar with current medical literature as it applies to nutrional problems in disease.
Credit, 3.
Prerequisites, Home Economics 52 or 203 and 204; Physiological Chemistry; Physiology. Mrs. COOK.

190. PROFESSIONAL SEMINARS.—A one-credit seminar is offered in each of the five fields of subject matter: Nutrition, Textiles, Foods, Home Management and Equipment, Family Life and Child Development.
First Semester: Sections A. Child Development and Education (Strattner and Thies).
B. Home Management and Home Planning. (Briggs, Merriam).
C. Textiles and Clothing (Wilhelm and Hawes).

Second Semester: Sections D. Nutrition (Cook and Mitchell).
         E. Foods and Institution Management (Davis
              Forbes, McCullough).
                                             Credit, 1-3.
                              HOME ECONOMICS STAFF.

191, 192. QUANTITY FOOD PREPARATION AND INSTITUTIONAL MANAGEMENT.—
A study of the principles of organization, personnel management, the administra-
tion, food costs, operating expenses, and special functions of the dietitian.
Laboratory work is at one of the university dining halls and field trips are
planned. It is expected that students will enroll for the work of both semesters.
Students wishing to qualify for administrative institutional work are advised to
take Accounting 25 and Home Economics 71.   Credit, 3.
Prerequisite, Home Economics 51 and 52 or equivalent.   Miss STECH.
One class hour; one 5-hour laboratory period, first semester.
Two class hours; one 3-hour laboratory period, second semester.

193. EXPERIMENTAL FOODS.—The testing and comparing of different food
materials and methods of preparation, including advanced work in the science
and techniques of cookery. Special individual problems will be studied.
Two class hours; One 3-hour laboratory period.   Credit, 3.
Prerequisites, Home Economics 30 and 51; Chemistry 33 or equivalent, and permission of the instructor.   Miss DAVIS.

195. CHILD NUTRITION.—A study is made of nutritional needs from prenatal
life through infancy and childhood. Methods of judging nutrition, also causes
and effects of malnutrition are discussed. Menus for children and measures to
insure the consumption of optimal diets are put in practice with laboratory work
in the nursery school.   Credit, 3.
Prerequisite, Home Economics 52 or equivalent.   Mrs. COOK.
Three class hours. Laboratory by arrangement.

198. PROBLEMS IN HOME ECONOMICS.—An intensive study of some phase
of home economics.   Credit, 3.
By permission of the Dean of the School.   THE STAFF.

COURSES IN OTHER DEPARTMENTS FOR WHICH MAJOR CREDIT
                          WILL BE GIVEN

Bacteriology 182. FOOD BACTERIOLOGY.   Credit, 3.
                                                           MISS GARVEY.

Bacteriology 202. BACTERIAL PHYSIOLOGY.   Credit, 3-5.
                                                           MR. MANDEL.

Chemistry 234. ADVANCED BIOCHEMICAL LECTURES.
                                          Credit, 3-5 each semester.
                                                           Mr. LITTLE.

Chemistry 235. BIOCHEMISTRY LABORATORY METHODS.   Credit, 3.
                                                           Mr. LITTLE.

Chemistry 237 BIOCOLLOIDS.   Credit 3.
                                                           Mr. BENNETT.

Chemistry 239. CHEMISTRY OF NATURAL PRODUCTS. Credit, 2.
MR. LITTLE and MR. McWHORTER.

Education 153. EDUCATIONAL TESTS AND MEASUREMENTS. Credit, 2-3.
Mr. ROURKE.

Education 267. AUDIO-VISUAL LABORATORY. Credit, 2-3.
MR. WYMAN and MR. CURTIS.

Education 291. EDUCATIONAL RESEARCH. Credit, 2-3.
Mr. PURVIS.

Food Technology 191, 192. ANALYSIS OF FOOD PRODUCTS.
Credit, 3 each semester.
MR. FELLERS AND MR. NEBESKY.

Food Technology 241. FOOD ACCEPTANCE, THEORY, AND METHODOLOGY.
Credit, 3.
Mr. FAGERSON.

Zoology 183. GENERAL AND CELLULAR PHYSIOLOGY. Credit, 4.
MR. SWENSON.

Zoology 187. ENDOCRINOLOGY. Credit, 3.
MR. SNEDECOR.

Zoology 245. ADVANCED VERTEBRATE PHYSIOLOGY. Credit, 3.
MR. SNEDECOR.

COURSES FOR MINOR CREDIT ONLY
(No graduate credit for students majoring in Home Economics)

152. NUTRITION AND DIETETICS.—A study is made of the fundamentals of
normal nutrition including energy needs, the metabolism of proteins, carbohydrates, fats, vitamins, and minerals; and the quantitative requirements for these
various essential nutrients. Laboratory work provides the further study of the
composition of foods and their contribution to the diet and the relationship
of the nutritive value to cost. Nutritive loss due to cooking, storage, etc., is
given consideration.
Three class hours, one 2-hour laboratory period. Credit, 3.
Prerequisites, Home Ec. 30, Chemistry 33 and Physiology. MRS. COOK.

163. ARTS AND CRAFTS.—Introduction to design and execution in crafts
particularly adapted to work with children in schools, playgrounds, summer
camps; and for any age in recreational leadership and occupational therapy.
Opportunity will be offered for work in several of the following: wood and
leather work, block printing, fingerpainting, etching, knotting, etc. Credit, 3.
Prerequisite, Home Economics 31 or equivalent. Miss BRIGGS.

170. CHILD DEVELOPMENT.—The growth and development of the child, his
basic needs, the aspects of behavior—routine, creative and social—as they are
related to personality development. Planned observation and participation in
the Nursery School.
Three class hours; laboratory by arrangement. Credit, 3.
Mrs. THIES.

175.: ECONOMICS OF THE HOUSEHOLD.—A study is made of personal and family standards of living in the modern home, the economic relations of the household, and the use of time, energy, and money as a means to influence the home situation. Credit, 3.
Prerequisite, Economics 25, or equivalent. MISS MERRIAM.

180. FAMILY LIFE.—A study is made of the modern family; ideals and responsibilities of the home and the individual's share in developing positive family relationships. Credit, 3.
MRS. PIATT.

Landscape Architecture

RAYMOND H. OTTO, major adviser.

COURSES OPEN TO GRADUATE STUDENTS ONLY.

(For either major or minor credit)

200. SPECIAL PROBLEMS.—Individual study by the B. L. A. candidate in lieu of a thesis; or exploratory work preliminary to the thesis by the M.L.A. candidate. Credit, 3.
THE STAFF.

290. THEORY.—Special studies in the history and theory of landscape architecture, and planning. Credit, 3.
MR. HAMILTON.

291. DESIGN.—Individual problems in any or all branches of public and private work. Credit, 3.
Mr. OTTO.

292. CONSTRUCTION.—Including road alignment, computations, and advanced landscape construction. Credit, 3.
Mr. PROCOPIO.

293. PRESENTATION.—Studies in drafting, pen and crayon, rendering, water coloring, etc. Credit, 3.
Mr. MACIVER.

294. PRACTICE.—Professional field work under supervision, conducted upon going projects as opportunity offers. Credit, 3
Mr. BLUNDELL.

297. ARCHITECTURE.—Selected problems as related to landscape architecture. Credit, 3.
MR. GARDNER.

300. THESIS, MASTER'S DEGREE. Credit, 10.

COURSES OPEN TO BOTH GRADUATE AND UNDERGRADUATE STUDENTS

(For either major or minor credit)

175. ART APPRECIATION.—An analysis of the principles of critical judgment underlying the fine arts. Credit, 3.
Mr. OTTO.

178. HISTORY OF ART.—A chronological survey of the arts from early times to the present. Credit, 3.

Mr. HAMILTON.

179. CONSTRUCTION AND MAINTENANCE.—A study of methods and materials of construction, and maintenance procedures. Credit, 3.

Mr. PROCOPIO.

180. LITERATURE OF LANDSCAPE ARCHITECTURE.—A review of the significant literature of all phases of the field, and compiling of bibliographies.

Credit, 2.

Mr. OTTO.

181. ADVANCED DESIGN.—Class "B" Exchange Problems plus specialized study through local projects. Credit, 3.

Mr. HAMILTON.

182. ADVANCED DESIGN. Continuation of 181. Credit, 3.

Mr. HAMILTON.

183. ARCHITECTURE.—Theory and principles of architecture including the development of construction methods and materials. Credit, 3.

MR. GARDNER.

184. SKETCHING.—Presentation of varied subjects in water color and other mediums. Credit, 2.

MR. MACIVER.

186. CITY PLANNING.—A critical examination of those factors which influence and guide the physical growth and arrangement of communities in harmony with their social and economic needs. Open to non-majors. Credit, 3.

MR. BACON.

187. PROJECTS IN PLANNING.—An application of the principles of planning through problems on the design of various types of urban land areas. Credit, 3.

MR. BACON.

188. PROJECTS IN PLANNING—CONTINUATION OF 187. Credit 3.

MR. BACON.

COURSES IN OTHER DEPARTMENTS FOR WHICH MAJOR CREDIT WILL BE GIVEN

Agronomy 153. AGROSTOLOGY. Credit, 3.

MR. ROBERTS.

Agronomy 156. AGROSTOLOGY. Credit, 3.

MR. ROBERTS.

Botany 181. PLANT ECOLOGY. Credit, 3.

Mr. LIVINGSTON.

Floriculture 181. HERBACEOUS GARDENS AND BORDERS. Credit, 3.

MR. THAYER.

89

COURSES FOR MINOR CREDIT ONLY
(No graduate credit for students majoring in Landscape Architecture)

151. ELEMENTS OF TOPOGRAPHY AND CONSTRUCTION.—Contour interpolation, grading and drainage plans, drive design, sections and profiles, computation of earthwork. Credit, 3.

Mr. PROCOPIO.

152. CONSTRUCTION DETAILS.—Problems in structural garden features as walks, steps, walls, gates, pools, and architectural elements. Credit, 3.

MR. PROCOPIO.

153. GARDEN DESIGN.—Fundamental principles of composition as applied to the design of gardens and small properties. Credit, 3.

Mr. OTTO

154. GENERAL DESIGN.—A series of problems in the design of private and public areas. Credit, 3

Mr. OTTO

FOR THE DEGREE OF BACHELOR OF LANDSCAPE ARCHITECTURE

To receive this professional bachelor's degree each candidate will be required:

1. To have received the degree of Bachelor of Science or Bachelor ot Arts from a recognized institution.
2. To have completed as a prerequisite 24 semester credits in landscape architecture, substantially equivalent to the technical courses now required in the undergraduate major in landscape architecture at this college.
3. In addition, to have completed in residence at this institution, 30 credits in landscape architecture and closely related subjects prescribed by the department. (See Fifth Year Program below.)
4. To have received the unanimous approval of the faculty of the department and the vote of approval of the faculty of the Graduate School.

FIFTH YEAR PROGRAM

The regular program of studies for the Fifth Year, subject to minor changes dependent upon courses taken previously, is as follows:

First Semester

201. GENERAL DESIGN.—Class A Exchange problems and advanced local projects. Credit, 3.

Mr. OTTO.

203. ECOLOGY AND PHYSIOGRAPHY.—Plant Associations and ground forms and conditions as related to each other. Credit, 3.

Mr. BLUNDELL.

205. ARCHITECTURE.—Studies in principles and problems of architectural design. Credit, 3.

MR. GARDNER.

207. CONTRACTS, SPECIFICATIONS, ESTIMATING COSTS.—Preparation of supporting data for proposed plans. Credit, 3.

Mr. HAMILTON.

209. LANDSCAPE SKETCHING.—Graphic expression of suitable subjects in various media. Credit, 3
Mr. MacIVER

Second Semester

202. GENERAL DESIGN.—Continuation of 201. Credit, 3.
Mr. OTTO.

204. LANDSCAPE OPERATIONS.—Supervision of local landscape projects.
Credit, 3.
THE STAFF.

206. ARCHITECTURE.—Studies in principles and problems of architectural design. Credit, 3.
MR. GARDNER.

210. ARCHITECTURAL SKETCHING.—Graphic expression of suitable subjects in various media. Credit, 3.
Mr. MacIVER.

212. PROFESSIONAL PRACTICE.—Methods and procedures of the professional office. Credit, 1.
Mr. OTTO

Elective: Suitable subject assigned.

Mathematics

ALLEN E. ANDERSEN, major adviser.

Special Departmental Entrance Requirements:

Candidates for admission who plan to major in this department must have completed at least eighteen semester credit hours in undergraduate mathematics beyond the content of Mathematics 29 and 30 (Differential and Integral Calculus), and also an undergraduate course equivalent to Physics 25 and 26 (Introductory).

Special Degree Requirements:

Six semester credit hours (undergraduate or graduate) in each of the fields of geometry, algebra and applied mathematics and 12 semester credit hours in the field of analysis. A minimum of 12 semester credit hours chosen from courses in this department which are numbered from 200 to 299.

COURSES OPEN TO GRADUATE STUDENTS ONLY

(For either major or minor credit)

200. TOPICS COURSE.—This course is designed to give the student training in independent study. Readings and reports will be assigned. Weekly conferences will be held between student and instructor. Topics may be chosen from the fields of algebra, geometry, theory of functions, and applied mathematics.
Prerequisite, permission of instructor. Credit, 1, 2, or 3.
Mr. ANDERSEN, Miss CULLEN, Mr. ROSE, and Mr. WAGNER.

MATHEMATICS

201, 202. INTRODUCTION TO MODERN ALGEBRA.—Axiomatic foundation of algebra; groups, rings, fields and vector spaces; linear transformations and matrices.　　　　　　　　　　　　　　　　　　　　Credit, 3 each semester.
Three class hours.　　　　　　　　　　　　　　　　　　　　　　　Mr. ROSE.
Prerequisite, permission of instructor.

221, 222. THEORY OF FUNCTIONS OF A REAL VARIABLE.—The real number system, limits, continuity and differentiability of functions of one and two real variables, theories of integration, sequences of functions.
Three class hours.　　　　　　　　　　　　　　　　　　　Credit, 3 each semester.
Prerequisite, Mathematics 191.　　　　　　　　　　　　　　　　　MR. WAGNER.

226. THEORY OF FUNCTIONS OF A COMPLEX VARIABLE.—The complex number system, elementary functions and their mappings, line and contour integrals, expansion and representations of analytic functions, introduction to analytic continuation and Riemannian surfaces.　　　　　　　　　　　Credit, 3.
Three class hours.　　　　　　　　　　　　　　　　　　　　　Miss CULLEN.
Prerequisite, Mathematics 221.

241. TOPOLOGY I.—Point Set Topology: Calculus of sets; Topological, Hausdorff and metric spaces; continuous mappings; homeomorphisms; connectivity and compactness.　　　　　　　　　　　　　　　　　　　Credit, 3.
Prerequisite, Mathematics 194.　　　　　　　　　　　　　　　　Miss CULLEN.

242. TOPOLOGY II.—Combinatorial Topology: Continuous complexes; Jordan's Theorem, Homology and Homotopy.　　　　　　　　　　　Credit, 3.
Prerequisite, Mathematics 241.　　　　　　　　　　　　　　　　Miss CULLEN.

COURSES OPEN TO BOTH GRADUATE AND UNDERGRADUATE STUDENTS
(For either major or minor credit)

151. MODERN SYNTHETIC GEOMETRY.—An extension of the geometry of the triangle and the circle. The course is intended especially for those planning to be high school teachers.]　　　　　　　　　　　　　　Credit, 3.
Three class hours.　　　　　　　　　　　　　　　　　　　　　Mr. ROSE.
Prerequisite, Mathematics 30.

153. 154. HIGHER ALGEBRA.—Permutations, Combinations, probability; mathematical induction, matrices, determinants, linear equations and dependence; quadratic forms and elimination theory; the complex number system; polynomial equations; elementary theory of groups, rings and fields. Credit, 3.
Prerequisite, Mathematics 10.　　　　　　　　　　　　　　　　THE STAFF.

156. FINITE DIFFERENCES AND PROBABILITY.—1956-57 and each alternate year.
Three class hours.　　　　　　　　　　　　　　　　　　　　Credit, 3.
Prerequisite, Mathematics 30.　　　　　　　　　　　　　　　　THE STAFF.

163. STATISTICS I.—The fundamental mathematical principles of statistical analysis. The derivation of the basic formulas used, and the study and discussion of such topics as averages, dispersion, skewness, curve fitting, least squares, linear and curvilinear correlation, probability and its application to statistics.
Three class hours.　　　　　　　　　　　　　　　　　　　　Credit, 3.
Prerequisite, Mathematics 30, previously or concurrently.　　　　Mr. WAGNER.

164. STATISTICS II.—A continuation of Mathematics 163, including a study of the joint distribution of two or more random variables; the chi-squared, t-, and f-distributions and their applications; and techniques which do not involve an assumption about the form of the basic distribution.
Three class hours.   Credit, 3.
Prerequisite, Mathematics 163.   Mr. WAGNER.

166. INTRODUCTION TO HIGHER GEOMETRY.—A study of various methods employed in the modern treatment of geometry of points, lines, and conics. Such topics as homogeneous point and line coordinates; infinite elements; harmonic division; groups of transformations and their invariants; and the elements of projective and other geometries will be considered. 1957-58 and each alternate year.   Credit, 3.
Prerequisite, Mathematics 30.   Mr. ANDERSEN.

171. VECTOR ANALYSIS.—The algebra and calculus of vectors. Applications to physics and other fields will be considered. 1957-58 and each alternate year.
Prerequisites, Mathematics 30, Physics 26.   Credit, 3.
                                                                       Mr. ANDERSEN.

172. HISTORY OF MATHEMATICS.—A study of mathematics as it has developed historically. Topics considered include classical problems and concepts of mathematics and the lives and times of the great mathematicians. This course is recommended especially for prospective high school teachers. 1956-57 and each alternate year.
Three class hours.   Credit, 3.
Prerequisite, Mathematics 30.   Mr. ROSE.

174. THEORY OF NUMBERS.—Euclid's Algorism, Theory of Prime Numbers, Aliquot parts, congruences, further topics in Number Theory.
Three class hours. 1957-58 and each alternate year.   Credit, 3.
Prerequisite, Mathematics 30.   THE STAFF.

181. DIFFERENTIAL GEOMETRY.—Theory of the geometry of curves and surfaces in three dimensions.
Three class hours. 1957-58 and each alternate year.   Credit, 3.
Prerequisite, Mathematics 30.   THE STAFF.

183. COMPUTATIONAL METHODS.—Errors and approximations in computation, methods of approximating roots of equations, approximation of functions, empirical curve fitting, approximate integration, and numerical integration of ordinary differential equations.
Three class hours. 1956-57 and each alternate year.   Credit, 3.
Prerequisite, Mathematics 30.   Mr. BOUTELLE.

192. DIFFERENTIAL EQUATIONS.   Credit, 3.
Three class hours.   THE STAFF.
Prerequisite, Mathematics 30.

193. ADVANCED CALCULUS.—The real number system, sequences, elementary theory of functions of one variable and of several variables, Riemannian integration, line integrals, Green's theorem.
Three class hours.   Credit, 3.
Prerequisite, Mathematics 91.   THE STAFF.

194. ADVANCED CALCULUS.—Double and triple integrals, improper integrals, gamma functions, Beta functions, elliptic functions, calculus of variations, Fourier Series, Laplace Transforms.

Three class hours. Credit, 3.

Prerequisite, Mathematics 193. THE STAFF.

COURSES FOR MINOR CREDIT ONLY

(No graduate credit for students majoring in Mathematics)

155. MATHEMATICS OF FINANCE.—The mathematical principles of simple and compound interest, annuities, depreciation, valuation of bonds, insurance. The development and application of aids to computation in problems arising from financial transactions. Credit, 3.

Prerequisite, Mathematics 7. Mr. BOUTELLE.

160. SPHERICAL TRIGONOMETRY AND SOLID ANALYTICAL GEOMETRY.—The trigonometry of the sphere with applications to terrestrial and celestial problems. This is followed by a study of higher plane curves and the analytic representation of points, lines and surfaces in space. 1957-58 and each alternate year.

Credit, 3·

Prerequisite, Mathematics 30. Mr. BOUTELLE.

191. INTERMEDIATE CALCULUS.—Series, expansion of functions, partial differentiation, envelopes and multiple integrals. Credit, 3.

3 class hours. THE STAFF.

Prerequisite, Mathematics 30.

Mechanical Engineering

WILLIAM H. WEAVER, major adviser.

First Semester	Second Semester
EE 201. ENGINEERING ANALYSIS I. (3)	*EE 202. ENGINEERING ANALYSIS II. (3)
ME 201. ADVANCED THERMODYNAMICS. (3)	ME 221. HEAT TRANSFER. (3)
ME 251. ADVANCED TOPICS IN MACHINE DESIGN. (3)	**ME 241. ADVANCED DYNAMICS. (3)
**ME 211. THEORY OF POWER MACHINES. (3)	ME 300. RESEARCH AND THESIS. (3-5)
ME 300. RESEARCH AND THESIS. (3-5)	***One free elective course subject to approval. This can be either a 100 or 200 series course, technical or non-technical.

*Any other mathematics course open to graduate students only, may be substituted for this.

**Other approved courses may replace these courses, as for example 200 courses in Mathematics, Physics, Civil, Electrical, or Chemical Engineering.

***If the thesis is increased to fulfill the degree requirements of 30 credits, this course may be deleted.

COURSES OPEN TO GRADUATE STUDENTS ONLY
(For either major or minor credit)

200. SPECIAL PROBLEMS IN MECHANICAL ENGINEERING.—Special investigational or research-problems in Mechanical Engineering for graduate students. The scope of this work to be varied to meet specific conditions. Credit, 1-6. Prerequisite as required by the problem. The STAFF.

201. ADVANCED THERMODYNAMICS I.—Advanced course in engineering applications of thermodynamics, including a survey of the physical treatment of thermodynamics.
Prerequisite, Mechanical Engineering 64. Credit, 3.
Mr. SWENSON and Mr. DAY.

202. ADVANCED THERMODYNAMICS II.—A continuation of the work in 201. Mechanical engineering problems in thermodynamics. Credit, 3.
Prerequisite, Mechanical Engineering 201. Mr. SWENSON and Mr. DAY.

211. THEORY OF POWER MACHINES.—The thermodynamic and design aspects underlying power machinery such as gas and steam turbines, internal combustion engines, rotary and reciprocating compressors, jet propulsion and rockets.
Credit, 3.
Prerequisite, Mechanical Engineering 201. Mr. DITTFACH.

221. HEAT TRANSFER.—Fundamentals of heat transfer by convection, conduction and radiation, with engineering applications. Credit, 3.
Prerequisite, Mechanical Engineering 64.
Mr. SWENSON, Mr. DITTFACH, and Mr. DAY.

241. ADVANCED DYNAMICS.—Vibration and stability of systems with many degrees of freedom, normal modes and frequencies; approximate methods. Non-linear systems, self excited vibrations. Gyroscopic effects in mechanical systems. Selected topics of applications to problems in engineering.
Credit, 3.
Prerequisite, Mechanical Engineering 185. MR. WHITE and MR. SOBALA.

251. ADVANCED TOPICS IN MACHINE DESIGN.—Application of advanced theories in elasticity and strength of materials to machine design. Many other theories and their application are included. Credit, 3
Prerequisite, Mechanical Engineering 186. Mr. BATES.

300. RESEARCH AND THESIS.—Independent research under the supervision of a staff member which will serve as the basis for the thesis required for the Master's degree. Consultation and laboratory hours to be arranged. Credit, 3-10.

COURSES OPEN TO BOTH GRADUATE AND UNDERGRADUATE STUDENTS
(For either major or minor credit)

146. FUNDAMENTALS OF METALLURGY.—Physical metallurgy involving crystal structure, solid solutions, diffusion in the solid state, freezing of metals, hardening of metals, annealing, and equilibrium diagrams. These fundamentals are then applied to the study of the iron-iron carbide diagram, the S-curve, heat treatment of steel and the properties and uses of the other principal en-

gineering metals. Laboratory work stresses metallographic and radiographic technique.
Two class hours; one 3-hour laboratory period.   Credit, 3.
Prerequisites, Mechanical Engineering 39 or Chemistry 166.
                                        Mr. KEYSER and Mr. HARRINGTON.

175. STEAM POWER PLANTS.—This course is a study of the steam power plants, including boilers, stokers, fuels, combustion, steam generation, prime movers, and auxiliary equipment, problems involved in design and operation.
Three class hours.   Credit, 3.
Prerequisite, Mechanical Engineering 64.   Mr. SWENSON.

176. REFRIGERATION AND AIR CONDITIONING.—The course content includes a study of the fundamental principles of thermodynamics as applied to refrigeration and air control. Application of refrigeration to industrial processes and the control of temperature, humidity and motion of air in buildings will be studied.
Two class hours, one 3-hour laboratory period.   Credit, 3
Prerequisite, Mechanical Engineering 64.   Mr. DAY and Mr. SWENSON.

177. INTERNAL COMBUSTION ENGINES.—A study is made of spark-ignition and compression-ignition engines including design, fuels, carburetion, ignition, combustion, lubrication, cooling, and engine performance. The gas turbine and jet propulsion will be included.   Credit, 3.
Three class hours.   Mr. DITTFACH.
Prerequisite, Mechanical Engineering 64.

182. FLUID DYNAMICS AND MACHINERY.—Steady one-dimensional compressible flow; compressible flow in channels with friction and heat transfer; boundary layer flow, turbulence, and energy losses; general features of dynamic fluid machines; axial flow fans, pumps, and compressors; centrifugal fans, pumps, and compressors; fluid couplings and torque converters; jet compressors and jet pumps; turbines.   Credit, 3.
Prerequisite, Civil Engineering 76.   Mr. SWENSON.

183. MACHINE DESIGN.—Principles involved in the design of various machine parts including fastenings, shafts, belts, bearings, gears, and pressure vessels.
Two class hours; one 3-hour laboratory period.   Credit, 3.
Prerequisite, Civil Engineering 51 or 53; Mechanical Engineering 68.
                                        Mr. BATES and Mr. PATTERSON.

185. DYNAMICS OF MACHINERY.—Gyroscopic effects, governors, dynamic balancing of rotating machinery. Analysis of unbalanced forces in a machine containing parts moving with rotation, reciprocation, and their combination. Elements of vibration theory, vibration isolation, vibration analysis of equivalent masses and shaft systems. Vibration absorbers.
Three class hours.   Credit, 3.
Prerequisites, Civil Engineering 52, Mechanical Engineering 68.   Mr. SOBALA.

186. ADVANCED MACHINE DESIGN.—A continuation of Course 183. Additional elementary parts are studied which combine into the design of complete machines in the latter part of the course.
Two class hours, one 3-hour laboratory period.   Credit, 3.
Prerequisite, Mechanical Engineering 183.   Mr. BATES.

188. STEADY FLOW MACHINERY.—The principles of thermodynamics are applied to steam and internal combustion turbines, condensors, and other heat transfer apparatus.   Credit, 3.
Three class hours.
Prerequisites, Mechanical Engineering 64 or 66, and Civil Engineering 76.
                                                                Mr. SWENSON.

190. ADVANCED METALLURGY.—Mechanical metallurgy covering the behavior of metals in the plastic state; the shaping of metals by mechanical means such as drawing, rolling, spinning, etc.; the primary methods of metal fabrication such as casting, welding, powder metallurgy, electroforming; the metallurgical applications of radiography.   Credit, 3.
Two class hours, one 3-hour laboratory period.
Prerequisite, Mechanical Engineering 146.   Mr. KEYSER and Mr. HARRINGTON.

194. EXPERIMENTAL MECHANICAL ENGINEERING.—Special work in Mechanical Engineering for a senior thesis.   Credit, 3.
Prerequisite, Permission of Instructor.   The STAFF.

Industrial Engineering

COURSES OPEN TO GRADUATE STUDENTS ONLY
(For either major or minor credit)

200. SPECIAL PROBLEMS IN INDUSTRIAL ENGINEERING.—Special investigational or research problems in industrial engineering for graduate students. The scope of this work to be varied to meet specific conditions.   Credit, 1-6.
Prerequisite as required by the problem.   The STAFF.

Courses Open to Both Graduate and Undergraduate Students
(For either major or minor credit)

175. JOB EVALUTION.—A study of the principles used to determine an evaluation of all occupations in order to establish an equitable rating between them, to establish sound wage and salary policies.   Credit, 2.
Two class hours.
Prerequisite, Industrial Engineering 51.   Mr. WEAVER.

176. TIME STUDY.—A study of the principles involved in the establishment of production standards and their application in the management functions of cost accounting, estimating, production control, incentives, budgetary control.
Two class hours, one 3-hour laboratory period.   Credit, 3.
Prerequisites, Industrial Engineering 175, 182 concurrently except for
Business Administration majors.   Mr. WEAVER and Mr. EMERSON.

177. PRODUCTION CONTROL.—A study of the principles used to regulate production activities in keeping with the manufacturing plan.
Three class hours.   Credit, 3.
Prerequisite, Industrial Engineering 51.   Mr. EMERSON.

178. FACTORY PLANNING AND LAY-OUT.—A study of the principles applying to the determination and development of the physical relationship between plant, equipment and operators working toward the highest degree of economy and effectiveness in operation. Credit, 2.
One class hour, one 3-hour laboratory period.
Prerequisites, Mechanical Engineering 2 and Industrial Engineering 51.
Mr. WEAVER and Mr. SOBALA.

180. PLANT BUDGETARY CONTROL.—A study of the principles used to pre-determine expenses for the factors of production and the comparison of results with the estimates to determine and deal with the causes of expense variations as applied by the operating organization in the industrial plant. Credit, 3.
Three class hours.
Prerequisite, Industrial Engineering 51. Mr. WEAVER.

182. WORK SIMPLIFICATION.—A study of the principles involved in the simplification of means of doing work and in the application and use of these principles.
One class hour, one 3-hour laboratory period. Credit, 2.
Prerequisites, Mechanical Engineering 68 and Industrial Engineering 176. concurrently. Mr. WEAVER.

COURSES IN OTHER DEPARTMENTS FOR WHICH MAJOR CREDIT WILL BE GIVEN

Electrical Engineering 201, 202. ADVANCED ENGINEERING ANALYSIS I, II.
Credit, 3 each semester.
Mr. ROYS and STAFF.

Civil Engineering 188. ADVANCED STRESS ANALYSIS. Credit, 3.
Mr. WHITE.

Olericulture

GRANT B. SNYDER, major adviser

COURSES OPEN TO GRADUATE STUDENTS ONLY

(For either major or minor credit)

201. LITERATURE.—A critical study and analysis of selected scientific papers and reports of past and current research involving vegetable crops. Credit, 3.
Lectures and assigned readings. MR. TUTTLE.

Horticulture 211, 212. SEMINAR.—Each student will be required to present papers on assigned readings related to research work in Horticulture. Departments of Floriculture, Olericulture, and Pomology cooperating.
Credit, 1 each semester.
THE STAFF.

276. ADVANCED VEGETABLE PLANT IMPROVEMENT.—An intensive study of hybridization and selection as related to specific vegetable crops. Special attention will be given to heterosis and its implications in vegetable breeding as well as sterility and its place in seed production of F_1 hybrids. Credit, 3.
Prerequisites, Plant Breeding 152, Zoology 153 or equivalent.
Mr. LACHMAN and Mr. YOUNG.

300. THESIS, MASTER'S DEGREE.—Research on some approved topic relating to a specific phase of Olericulture. Credit, 10.

COURSES OPEN TO BOTH GRADUATE AND UNDERGRADUATE STUDENTS
(For either major or minor credit)

152. ADVANCED COMMERCIAL CULTURE.—A critical analysis of the factors involved in the commercial culture of vegetable crops including soils, nutrition and the relationship of temperature, light and humidity to production techniques and practices both out of doors and in the greenhouse. Credit, 3.
Lectures and laboratory. Mr. THOMSEN and Mr. MAYNARD.

173. MARKETING AND STORAGE OF VEGETABLE CROPS.—A detailed evaluation of factors which may be involved in the market and storage handling of vegetables with particular emphasis on their relationship to quality and deterioration.
Credit, 3.
Mr. SNYDER.

174. MARKETING PRACTICES.—The various practices, techniques and methods that are used in selling and distributing horticultural commodities through the various channels from the farm to the ultimate consumer. Credit, 3.
Mr. SNYDER.

175. ADVANCED SYSTEMATIC OLERICULTURE.—A critical study of vegetable plants as to plant characteristics, nomenclature, identification and classification.
1957-1958. Credit, 3.
Mr. SNYDER.

COURSES IN OTHER DEPARTMENTS FOR WHICH MAJOR CREDIT WILL BE GIVEN

Agronomy 263. CHEMISTRY OF THE SOIL. Credit, 5.
Mr. STECKEL.

Agronomy 264. EXPERIMENTAL METHODS IN AGRONOMY. Credit, 3.
Mr. YEGIAN.

Botany 158. MICROTECHNIQUE. Credit, 2.
Mr. PUTALA.

Food Technology 216. FOOD PACKAGING. Credit, 3.
Mr. LEVINE.

Food Technology 241. FOOD ACCEPTANCE—Theory and Methodology.
Credit, 3.
Mr. FAGERSON.

Plant Breeding 152. PLANT BREEDING METHODS. Credit 3.
Mr. FRENCH.

Plant Breeding 181. PLANT CYTOLOGICAL TECHNIQUES. Credit, 2.
Mr. FRENCH.

Plant Breeding 182. SPECIAL PROBLEM IN PLANT BREEDING. Credit, 2.
Mr. FRENCH.

COURSES FOR MINOR CREDIT ONLY
(No graduate credit for students majoring in Olericulture)

151. PRINCIPLES OF OLERICULTURE. Credit, 3.
Mr. TUTTLE.

Philosophy

CLARENCE SHUTE, major adviser.

COURSES OPEN TO GRADUATE STUDENTS ONLY
(For either major or minor credit)

266. PHILOSOPHY OF EDUCATION.—An evaluation of various educational theories and practices viewed in the light of historical perspective and contemporary thought. Credit, 3.
Mr. ROGERS.

271. SOCIAL PHILOSOPHY.—Starting with an analysis of the present world situation, attention will be given to conflicting claims regarding the basis on which social orders are to be criticized. An attempt will be made to formulate a philosophical foundation for democratic society. Credit, 3.
Mr. ROGERS

286. CONTEMPORARY PHILOSOPHY.—Representative thinkers of the twentieth century will be read, including Bergson, Dewey, Whitehead, and others selected in conference with the class. Credit, 3.
Mr. SHUTE.

289, 290. SEMINAR.—Conferences and reports on special studies in philosophy. Credit, 1-3.
THE STAFF.

300. THESIS, MASTER'S DEGREE. Credit, 10

COURSES OPEN TO BOTH GRADUATE AND UNDERGRADUATE STUDENTS
(For either major or minor credit)

(These courses require extra work for 3 credits)

163. LOGIC.—A study of the principles, problems, and methods of critical thinking with applications to current problems. Credit, 2-3.
Mr. ROGERS and Mr. CARMICHAEL.

164. ETHICS.—An examination of the many causes and contexts of personal decision and policy formation; an analysis of classical and contemporary theories which attempt to provide an intellectual framework for the guidance and justification of ways of life; and class exploration of concrete cases which focus attention on the realms of value and the place of theory in reflective choice.
Credit, 2-3.
Mr. ROGERS and Mr. CARMICHAEL.

165. HISTORY OF PHILOSOPHY:—Ancient and Medieval. A survey of the development of western thought with emphasis on the cultural factors which generated and interacted with the successive philosophical interpretations of man's experience. Credit, 2-3.
Mr. ROGERS.

166. HISTORY OF PHILOSOPHY:—Modern. Attention is centered on the impact of modern science on the development of man's comprehensive understanding of the world, of the powers and limitations of knowledge, and of the basis of his valuations. Credit, 2-3.

Mr. ROGERS.

172. PHILOSOPHY OF SCIENCE.—A study of the backgrounds, presuppositions, methods and general theories of modern physical, biological, and social sciences. Readings selected from the works of leading scientists and philosophers will be used as the basis of class discussions which will attempt to explore the great scientific achievements of our time and to assess their importance in the student's construction of a mature philosophic orientation. Credit, 2-3.

Mr. ROGERS.

174. ORIENTAL PHILOSOPHIES II.—A study of the present conflict in ideologies within and between the leading cultures of Asia, understood in the light of their philosophical history. The bearing of philosophical differences between East and West on the problem of mutual understanding. Credit, 2-3.

Mr. SHUTE.

181. PHILOSOPHY OF RELIGION.—A survey of the contrasting types of religious philosophy in the contemporary western world and Asia, with a critical and constructive study of basic issues, such as the meaning of knowledge in the field of religion, the nature of faith, and the religious interpretation of reality. Credit, 2-3.

Mr. SHUTE.

182. AESTHETICS.—A study of the leading modern theories of the nature of art, the analysis of aesthetic experiences, the distinctive function of art in culture and personality, and the principles of criticism. Credit, 2-3.

MR. SHUTE.

183. READINGS IN ANCIENT PHILOSOPHY.—Selections are read from Plato's dialogues and from the works of Aristotle. A study is made of the leading philosophical issues discussed by these writers, with emphasis on ideas which became basic in the development of western thought. Credit, 2-3.

MR. SHUTE.

184. READINGS IN MODERN PHILOSOPHY.—Selections are read from Locke, Hume, Kant, and Whitehead, to display the leading ways in which modern thinkers have looked upon the nature of the universe and the possibilities and limitations of knowledge. Credit, 2-3.

MR. EHRLICH.

185. METAPHYSICS.—The field of metaphysics defined in distinction from the field of science; contrasting theories of reality offered by contemporary naturalism and idealism, especially in the light of recent developments in biological and physical science; analysis of basic ideas which will enable the student to continue a fruitful development of his own philosophy. Credit, 2-3.

MR. SHUTE.

186. THEORY OF KNOWLEDGE.—Types of knowledge and correlated methods of knowing; questions of certainty, probability, and limits of knowledge; ways of expression, such as mathematical formulae, language, and art, and their involvement in the knowing process; the nature of the relation between the knowing subject and the known object.   Credit, 2-3.

MR. EHRLICH.

COURSES IN OTHER DEPARTMENTS FOR WHICH MAJOR CREDIT
WILL BE GIVEN

Government 171. ANCIENT AND MEDIEVAL POLITICAL THOUGHT.   Credit, 3.
MR. TINDER.

Government 172. MODERN POLITICAL THOUGHT.   Credit, 3.
MR. TINDER.

Physical Education for Men

COURSES FOR MINOR CREDIT ONLY

In addition to the standard requirements of the courses, graduate students must work on a special project requiring research with a resultant term paper

154. (II) PHYSICAL EDUCATION IN SECONDARY SCHOOLS.—A course in modern methods of teaching physical education in secondary schools. Includes objectives, content material, and organization procedures at the secondary level.

Credit, 3.
MR. RICCI

155. (I) ORGANIZATION AND ADMINISTRATION OF PHYSICAL EDUCATION.—Problems and procedures in physical education, organization of programs, class schedules, classification of students, equipment, records, finance, intramurals, construction and maintenance of gymnasia, swimming pools, locker rooms, and outdoor play areas.   Credit, 3

MR. KAUFFMAN.

156. (II) ADAPTIVE PHYSICAL EDUCATION.—A program of developmental activities, games, sports, and rhythms suited to the interests, capacities and limitations of students with disabilities who may not safely engage in unrestricted participation in the vigorous activities of the general physical education program. Prerequisite, Physical Education 42.   Credit, 3.

MR. GARBER.

176. (I) PHILOSOPHY AND PRINCIPLES OF PHYSICAL EDUCATION.—Contemporary interpretations and critical analysis. The compilation and organization of material in a functional relationship for the foundation of policies and program construction.   Credit, 3.

MR. KAUFFMAN.

178. (II) PHYSIOLOGY OF EXERCISE.—Application of basic physiological concepts to the program of physical education, emphasis upon the physiological effects and adjustments accruing from participation in physical activity. Major factors in diet, conditioning, fatigue, and physical fitness are considered.
Prerequisite, Physical Education 42. Credit, 3.
MR. BOSCO.

180. (II) DRIVER EDUCATION INSTRUCTOR COURSE.—This course includes driver education and driver training at the instructor's level, and is designed to orient the student to live safely through skillful and efficient behavior on streets and highways. Leads to certification as instructor in driver education and driver training Credit, 2.
MR. BRIGGS.

187. (I) PHYSICAL EDUCATION IN ELEMENTARY SCHOOLS.—Aims and objectives of modern materials and methods of teaching group games, rhythmic activities, dance relays, stunts and lead-up games for the elementary school. Credit, 3.
MR. FOOTRICK.

Physics

COURSES FOR MINOR CREDIT ONLY

151, 152. MAGNETISM, ELECTRICITY, PHOTO-ELECTRICITY, THERMIONICS AND APPLICATIONS.—Course 151 deals largely with direct currents; Course 152 with alternating currents, applications of thermionics, and photo-electricity.
Two class hours, one 2-hour laboratory period. Credit, 3 each semester.
Prerequisites, Physics 26 and Math. 29. Mr. POWERS.

155, 156.—MECHANICS.—Development of the fundamental concepts of classical dynamics with applications to particles and rigid bodies in translation and rotation. Credit, 3 each semester.
Two class hours; one 2-hour laboratory period. Mr. ROSS.
Prerequisites, Physics 26 and Math. 30.

160. SOUND AND ACOUSTICS.—A study of the vibrations, vibrating bodies, coupled systems, sound structure, and acoustic properties. Credit, 3.
Two class hours; one 2-hour laboratory period. Mr. ALDERMAN.
Prerequisite, Physics 155 or equivalent.

161, 162. HEAT AND THERMODYNAMICS.—A study of heat exchanges and energy changes due to heat in systems of matter. Credit, 3 each semester.
Two class hours, one 2-hour laboratory period. Mr. ALDERMAN.

163, 164. OPTICS.—An intermediate course in the theory of light. Geometrical and physical optics. Credit, 3 each semester.
Two class hours, one 2-hour laboratory period. Mr. ALDERMAN.

175, 176. ADVANCED EXPERIMENTAL WORK IN SELECTED TOPICS.—These courses are largely experimental and the subject matter is adapted to the needs of the individual student. Credit, 3 each semester. One class hour, two 2-hour laboratory periods. THE STAFF. Prerequisites, Physics 151, 152 or 155, 156 or 163, 164; and Math. 29 and 30.

185, 186. MODERN PHYSICS.—Typical subjects studied are theories of the atom, radiation, quantum theory; spectra, X-ray analysis, nuclear reactions. 1957-58 and each alternate year. Credit, 3 each semester. Prerequisites, 18 junior-senior physics credits, including Physics 52 and 64; Math. 30. THE STAFF.

195. 196. ELECTRONICS.—Two class hours; one 2-hour laboratory period. Prerequisites, Physics 151, 152; Math. 29 and 30. Credit, 3 each semester. MR. POWERS.

Pomology

ARTHUR P. FRENCH, major adviser

All students majoring in this department are required to offer a thesis as part of their major requirements.

COURSES OPEN TO GRADUATE STUDENTS ONLY
(For either major or minor credit)

201, 202. POMOLOGICAL RESEARCH.—A critical review of past and current research work in the field of pomology. Topics selected according to the interests and needs of the individual student. Credit, 2 each semester. Prerequisite, Pomology 179 and 181. MR. SOUTHWICK and STAFF.

205. ADVANCED SYSTEMATIC POMOLOGY.—An intensive study of leaf and tree characters of nursery and orchard trees with reference to identification and the relationship of varieties. This work to be undertaken in the summer. Credit, 3. Prerequisite, Pomology 175. Mr. FRENCH.

Horticulture 211, 212. SEMINAR.—Each student will present papers on assigned topics in Horticulture. Departments of Pomology, Floriculture and Olericulture cooperating. Required of all graduate students majoring in Floriculture, Olericulture, and Pomology. Credit, 1 each semester. THE DEPARTMENTS.

300. THESIS, MASTER'S DEGREE. Each student majoring in Pomology will be required to carry out an original investigation on an approved problem and present the results thereof in satisfactory form as a thesis. Credit, 10.

COURSES OPEN TO BOTH GRADUATE AND UNDERGRADUATE STUDENTS
(For either major or minor credit)

179, 181. ADVANCED POMOLOGY.—A consideration of the scientific principles governing the growth and behavior of fruit-bearing plants. Prerequisite, Pomology 25 or equivalent. Credit, 3 each course. Mr. FRENCH, Mr. SOUTHWICK and Mr. WEEKS.

184. SPECIAL PROBLEMS IN POMOLOGY.—Each student will investigate an individual problem and make reports thereon at the weekly class hour.
Prerequisite, Pomology 179, 181 or equivalent. Credit, 3.

Mr. WEEKS and STAFF.

Plant Breeding

Plant Breeding 152. PLANT BREEDING METHODS.—An advanced study of genetic topics peculiar to plants together with consideration of the methods and problems of the plant breeder. Credit, 3.
Prerequisite, Zoology 153 or equivalent. MR. FRENCH.

Plant Breeding 181. PLANT CYTOLOGICAL TECHNIQUES.—The methods of cytology useful to the plant geneticist. Credit, 2.

Mr. FRENCH.

Plant Breeding 182· SPECIAL PROBLEMS IN PLANT BREEDING.—Advanced study of special topics in the field of plant genetics and breeding. Credit, 2.
Prerequisite, Plant Breeding 152. Mr. FRENCH.

COURSES IN OTHER DEPARTMENTS FOR WHICH MAJOR CREDIT WILL BE GIVEN

Agronomy 263. CHEMISTRY OF THE SOIL. Credit, 5.

Mr. STECKEL.

Agronomy 264. EXPERIMENTAL METHODS. Credit, 3.

Mr. YEGIAN.

Botany 202, 203. ADVANCED PLANT PHYSIOLOGY. Credit, 2-4 each semester.

Mr. KOZLOWSKI and Mr. GENTILE.

Chemistry 165, 166. PHYSICAL CHEMISTRY. Credit, 4.

Mr. SMITH.

Chemistry 179. BIOCHEMISTRY. Credit, 4.

Mr. LITTLE.

COURSES FOR MINOR CREDIT ONLY
(No graduate credit for students majoring in Pomology.)

156. ORCHARD PEST CONTROL. Credit, 3.

Mr. ROBERTS.

175. SYSTEMATIC POMOLOGY. Credit, 4.

MR. ANDERSON.

177. COMMERCIAL POMOLOGY. Credit, 3.

Mr. ROBERTS.

Poultry Science

THOMAS W. FOX, major adviser.

The Master of Science degree is offered in the field of genetics, physiology and nutrition.

COURSES OPEN TO GRADUATE STUDENTS ONLY
(For either major or minor credit)

200. SPECIAL PROBLEMS.—Research problems in avian genetics and physiology. Problems such as heat tolerance, metabolism of chicks, factors affecting feathering have been carried out in the past and are mentioned here to illustrate the type of problem that might be undertaken. Credit, 3.

Mr. HAYS, Mr. SMYTH and Mr. ANDERSON.

202. POULTRY RESEARCH PROBLEMS.—A critical review of research in genetics, physiology or nutrition. Required is a comprehensive written report covering some particular phase of the science from its beginning to the present. The final report requires that the student evaluate work in the field and suggest new and unexplored areas. Credit, 3.

Mr. HAYS, Mr. SMYTH and Mr. ANDERSON.

Prerequisites are standard under-graduate courses in poultry husbandry.

203. ADVANCED GENETICS.—A lecture course dealing with the experimental study of genetics in plants and animals. The major aspects of the science are discussed and illustrated to give the student a good working knowledge and to stimulate his interest in this field of biology. Credit, 3.

3 class hours. Mr. HAYS.

Prerequisites, at least one year's training in biology and Zoology 153 or its equivalent.

204. ADVANCED GENETICS.—A continuation of Poultry 203. The first third of the semester will be devoted to human genetics and the last two-thirds to the application of the latest statistical methods in the interpretation of biological data. Credit, 3.

3 class hours. Mr. HAYS.

205. AVIAN GENETICS.—A lecture course covering the genetics of the principal domesticated birds. Special attention is given to methods of experimentation and interpretation of genetic data. The physiology of reproduction of avian species will also be considered in detail.

Prerequisites, at least one year's training in biology and Zoology 153 or its equivalent. Credit, 3.

Mr. SMYTH.

206. AVIAN GENETICS AND PHYSIOLOGY.—This course is a continuation of Poultry 205. Special emphasis will be put on the fields of physiological and population genetics as they apply to poultry genetics and breeding.

3 class hours. Credit, 3.

Prerequisite, Poultry 205. Mr. FOX.

207. ADVANCED POULTRY NUTRITION.—Lectures and reports on research methods and designs for poultry nutrition experiments. Also, discussion of current research developments and theories. Credit, 3. Prerequisites, Chemistry 151, 152, and 179, and Poultry 156 or its equivalent.

Mr. ANDERSON.

300. THESIS, MASTER'S DEGREE. Credit, 10.

COURSES OPEN TO BOTH GRADUATE AND UNDERGRADUATE STUDENTS

(For either major or minor credit)

156. POULTRY NUTRITION.—A study of the scientific principles of nutrition, classification, and identification of feedstuffs, formulation and calculation of rations for specific purposes. Credit, 3.

Mr. ANDERSON.

COURSES IN OTHER DEPARTMENTS FOR WHICH MAJOR CREDIT WILL BE GIVEN

Bacteriology 202. ADVANCED BACTERIAL PHYSIOLOGY. Credit, 3-5.
Mr. MANDEL.

Chemistry 182. QUALITATIVE ORGANIC CHEMISTRY. Credit, 4.
Mr. CANNON.

Chemistry 193, 194. GENERAL BIOCHEMISTRY. Credit, 4 each semester.
Mr. LITTLE.

Chemistry 234. ADVANCED BIOCHEMICAL LECTURES. Credit, 3.
Mr. LITTLE.

Chemistry 235. BIOCHEMICAL LABORATORY METHODS. Credit, 3-5.
Mr. LITTLE.

Chemistry 236. ADVANCED BIOCHEMICAL ANALYSIS. Credit, 3-5.
Mr. LITTLE.

Chemistry 237. BIOCOLLOIDS. Credit, 3.
Mr. BENNETT.

Home Economics 205. LABORATORY METHODS AND TECHNIQUES IN NUTRITION. Credit, 3.
Mrs. WERTZ.

Zoology 173. GENERAL CYTOLOGY. Credit, 3.
Mr. ROLLASON.

Zoology 178. GENETICS OF ANIMAL POPULATIONS. Credit, 2.
Mr. RAUCH.

Zoology 183. GENERAL AND CELLULAR PHYSIOLOGY. Credit, 4.
Mr. SWENSON.

Zoology 184. COMPARATIVE PHYSIOLOGY.	Credit, 4.
	Mr. ROBERTS.
Zoology 187. ENDOCRINOLOGY.	Credit, 3.
	Mr. SNEDECOR.
Zoology 245. ADVANCED VERTEBRATE PHYSIOLOGY.	Credit, 3.
	Mr. SNEDECOR.
Zoology 248. PHYSIOLOGICAL GENETICS.	Credit, 3.
	Mr. RAUCH.

COURSE FOR MINOR CREDIT ONLY
(No graduate credit for students majoring in Poultry Science)

201. ADVANCED POULTRY HUSBANDRY.—A critical review of research in any
one of these fields: (a) genetics and physiology, (b) nutrition, (c) marketing,
or (d) incubation and brooding. Three written reports and a comprehensive
final examination are required. This course is designed for teachers of vocational
agriculture. Credit, 3.
THE STAFF.
Prerequisites are standard undergraduate courses in poultry husbandry.

Psychology

CLAUDE C. NEET, major adviser.

The graduate student majoring in Psychology may orient his program toward
either the Doctor of Philosophy degree or the Master's degree. Emphasis may
be in the area of child-clinical, general experimental, counseling, industrial, or
social psychology.

Students taking the doctorate must satisfy the general requirements of the
Graduate School for the degree. They must also include in their programs of
study the following psychology courses: 175, 207, 213, 226, 295, 296, and 400. In
addition they must elect four of the following courses: 163 172, 202, 203, 204, 206,
and 210. The doctorate program provides practicum courses in each of the applied specialization areas. Institutions and agencies available for such field
work include Belchertown State Hospital, Clarke School for the Deaf, Holyoke
Mental Health Clinic, Monson State Hospital, Northampton State Hospital,
Springfield Child Guidance Clinic, University Guidance and Counseling Services,
University Nursery School, Worcester State Hospital, and various industrial
concerns in nearby towns.

All students qualifying for the Master of Science degree in Psychology must,
in addition to meeting the degree requirements of the Graduate School, take
course 175 and either 200 or 300. They must also pass a written examination
which will cover certain general fields of psychology selected by the Department and certain special fields which may be chosen by the candidate. A final
oral examination, given by the problem or thesis committee and the Department,
is required. Credits taken to satisfy the requirements for the Master's degree
can be applied to the total number of credits required for the doctorate.

Students applying for admission for either the Doctor's or Master's degree
program, in addition to meeting the requirements of the Graduate School, should
have taken an Introductory course and 21 additional undergraduate credits in
Psychology, including a course in laboratory experimental Psychology, and a

course in Statistics. In case the student has not taken this number of credits or lacks these courses, he may be allowed to make up the deficiencies in the Undergraduate School of the University. In exceptional cases, students with entrance deficiencies may, at the end of one semester's study, petition the Department to waive remaining undergraduate deficiencies.

COURSES OPEN TO GRADUATE STUDENTS ONLY
(For either major or minor credit)

200. PROBLEM IN PSYCHOLOGY.—A research project which may be taken in lieu of the master's thesis, or by doctoral students as minor research. Credit, 4-6
THE STAFF.

202. NEURAL CORRELATES OF BEHAVIOR.—A detailed study of the neuroanatomy of senory-motor systems. Emphasis is placed upon the major fiber systems and their role in behavior. 1956-57 and each alternate year. Credit, 3.
Prerequisites, 6 credits of Psychology and 6 credits Zoology or the equivalent.
Mr. FELDMAN.

203. LEARNING I.—A consideration of the basic laws of learning, and of relevant research techniques. 1957-58 and each alternate year. Credit, 3.
Mr. Goss.

204. LEARNING II.—A consideration of the implications of the basic laws of learning for explaining complex behavior. 1957-58 and each alternate year.
Prerequisite, Psychology 203. Credit, 3.
Mr. Goss.

206. DISCRIMINAL PROCESSES.—An analysis of sensory and perceptual processes. The relationships among physical, physiological and behavioral variables are stressed. 1957-58 and each alternate year. Credit, 3.
Prerequisites, 6 hours Psychology and 3 hours Zoology or the equivalent.
Mr. FELDMAN.

207. SYSTEMATIC PSYCHOLOGY.—An analysis of the general structure of psychological theory, and an historical and comparative consideration of the backgrounds, viewpoints on scientific methodology, research interests and techniques, and the component variables, hypotheses, and laws of structural, Gestalt, functional, and behavioristic movements. 1956-57 and each alternate year.
Credit, 3.
Mr. Goss.

210. EMOTION AND MOTIVATION.—A study of the nature, determinants, and interrelationships of emotion and motivation, and of the techniques involved in investigating these phenomena. 1956-57 and each alternate year. Credit, 3.
Mr. NEET.

213. TEST CONSTRUCTION I.—Logic and methods of psychological scaling; media of testing; item, test, and battery construction; relevance and reliability requirements of items, test, and criteria. Credit, 3
Prerequisite, Psychology 175, or taken concurrently. Mr. ERLICK.

PSYCHOLOGY

214. TEST CONSTRUCTION II.—The use of correlational and analysis of variance techniques in test construction. The class will statistically analyze a test which they have constructed. 1956-57 and each alternate year.　　Credit, 3.
Prerequisite, Psychology 213.　　Mr. ERLICK.

221. ADVANCED SOCIAL PSYCHOLOGY.—An investigation of the important areas of social psychology through lectures, discussion, and laboratory exercises. The group will complete two projects or investigations. Topics considered are: experimental study of determinants of social interaction, effect of needs and motives on perception, opinion and attitude measurement, determinants of attitudes, and propaganda.　　Credit, 3.
Two class hours; one 2-hour laboratory　　Mr. LEWIT.
Prerequisite, Psychology 161 or 162.

226. THEORIES OF PERSONALITY.—Problems and sources of data relating to the study of personality. An evaluation of the contributions of psychological theories, and an approach to an integrated theory. 1956-57 and each alternate year.　　Credit, 3.
Prerequisite, Psychology 207.　　Mr. LEWIT.

235. ADVANCED ABNORMAL PSYCHOLOGY.—An intensive study of the behavior disorders and their relationships to normal behavior. Major emphasis is on theories of etiology and symptom formation, and on general problems of therapy.
Prerequisite, Psychology 183, or the consent of the instructor.　　Credit, 3.
　　Mr. NEET.

242. PSYCHOLOGY OF THE PRE-SCHOOL CHILD.—A detailed study of the behavior of the child from the early prenatal period to the school age.　Credit, 3.
Prerequisite, Psychology 194, or the consent of the instructor.　　Mr. CLIFFORD.

245. THE PSYCHOLOGY OF EXCEPTIONAL CHILDREN.—A consideration of the etiology, diagnosis, and treatment of exceptional children. Special emphasis will be placed on intellectual, social, physical and sensory deviations.　Credit, 3.
Prerequisite, Psychology 82 or 182, 83 or 235, 94 or 194. Students having only two of these three prerequisites may take the course on consent of the instructor.
　　Mr. CLIFFORD.

252. DIAGNOSTIC METHODS I.—An intensive study of the methods of administration and of the scoring procedures of a variety of diagnostic methods with emphasis on the Rorschach and Thematic Apperception Test.　Credit, 3.
Prerequisite, Psychology 182.　　Mr. EPSTEIN.

253. DIAGNOSTIC METHODS II.—Basic interpretive procedures of diagnostic devices with emphasis on the Rorschach and Thematic Apperception Test.
Prerequisite, Psychology 252.　　Credit, 3.
　　Mr. EPSTEIN.

254. CASE ANALYSES.—An analysis of individual cases utilizing dynamic principles of behavior to explain selected types of maladjustment. Case material will be used throughout and the student will receive practice in applying principles to individual behavior.　　Credit, 3.
Prerequisites, Psych. 226, 235, 252, and 253　　Mr. KATES.

255. PSYCHOTHERAPY I.—Analyses of techniques of individual psychotherapy. The student may elect concurrently a practicum in psychotherapy in which a therapy case, under supervision, will be carried in one of the following facilities: child guidance clinic, student counseling center, state mental hospital.　Credit, 3.
Prerequisites, Psychology 226, 235, 252, 253, and 254.　　Mr. KATES.

256. PSYCHOTHERAPY II.—Analyses of group and specialized techniques of psychotherapy. The student will elect concurrently a practicum in which supervised practice in one or more group psychotherapeutic methods will be given.
Prerequisites, Psychology 226, 235, 252, 253, 254, and 255.   Credit, 3.
                                                                      Mr. KATES.

265. COUNSELING AND INTERVIEWING TECHNIQUES.—A study of current counseling and guidance techniques employed with groups and individuals including the organization of counseling services, and the use of occupational information and referral sources.   Credit, 3.
Prerequisites, Psychology 181 and 182.   Mr. FIELD.

271. ADVANCED INDUSTRIAL PSYCHOLOGY I.—Human relations in industry. Applications of general and social psychological findings to industry and business, with a concentration on the interdependence of morale, leadership and motivation.   Credit, 3.
Prerequisite, Psychology 186, or the consent of the instructor.   Mr. ERLICK.

283, 284. PRACTICUM—Practice in the application of psychological techniques to the following areas of psychology: child, clinical, guidance and counseling, industrial, and social. Either semester may be elected independently.
                                                          Total credit, 3-12.
                                          THE STAFF, with the Staffs of
                                          cooperating institutions and agencies.

295, 296. RESEARCH METHODOLOGY.—A study and evaluation of research methods and of problems in the major fields of psychology. Two semesters are required of students studying toward the doctorate.   Credit, 2 each semester.
                                                                      THE STAFF.

300. THESIS, MASTER'S DEGREE.—Research, and the preparation of an acceptable thesis.   Credit, 8-10.

400. THESIS, PH.D. DEGREE.—Research, and the preparation of an acceptable thesis.   Credit, 30.

COURSES OPEN TO BOTH GRADUATE AND UNDERGRADUATE STUDENTS
(For either major or minor credit)

156. EDUCATIONAL PSYCHOLOGY.—A study of psychological facts and principles fundamental to education, teaching, and personal relationships between teacher and pupil. Topics considered in relation to school situations are: Physical and mental growth, intelligence, motivation, emotions, learning, transfer of training, and mental hygiene of teacher and pupil.   Credit, 3.
Prerequisite, Psychology 26.   Mr. MINTZ.

161. SOCIAL PSYCHOLOGY.—The social behavior of the individual. Topics considered will include methods of studying social behavior, "schools" of social psychology, social behavior of animals, foundations of personality development, social (cultural) determinants of personality, social attitudes and their measurement, effects of collective situations on individual behavior, customs and conformity.   Credit, 3.
Prerequisite, Psychology 26.   Mr. LEWIT.

162. Social Psychology.—A survey of multiindividual phenomena. Topics to be considered are methods of studying collective action, leadership, morale, propaganda, nature and measurement of public opinion, behavior in crowd situation, social conflict and prejudice. . Credit, 3.
Prerequisite, Psychology 161 or the consent of the instructor. Mr. Lewit.

163. Physiological Psychology.—A study of the relationships between the individual's behavior and his physiological processes. Emphasis will be placed on sensory and motor phenomena, drives, emotional behavior, and learning.
Prerequisites, 6 units of Psychology; Zoology 35. Credit, 3.
Mr. Feldman.

172. Advanced Experimental Psychology.—Experimental design, techniques, and apparatus in psychology are considered, and selected projects are carried out individually by the members of the class. 1957-58 and each alternate year. Credit, 3.
Prerequisites, Psychology 51, and Zoology 35. Mr. Neet.

175. Psychological Statistics.—The application of statistical procedures to the analysis of psychological data and to problems of measurement in psychology and related fields. Credit, 3.
Prerequisite, one semester of statistics, or the equivalent. Mr. Goss.

181. Psychological Tests.—A survey of the construction, development, and use of a variety of psychological tests. Emphasis will be placed upon the administration, scoring, interpretation and evaluation of tests of personality, interests, aptitudes, and group tests of intelligence. Credit, 3.
Prerequisite, Psychology 26. Mr. Mintz.

182. Psychological Tests, Individual Intelligence Tests.—Theories as to the nature and measurement of intelligence. Emphasis is on the administration, scoring and interpretation of individual intelligence tests such as the Stanford-Binet, Wechsler-Bellevue, Merrill-Palmer, and others. Credit, 3.
Prerequisite, Psychology 26. Mr. Epstein and Mr. Kates.

183. Abnormal Psychology.—A study of abnormal behavior. Attention is given to the following: dynamics of behavior abnormalities, the neuroses, psychoses, mental deficiency, speech problems, and sensory and motor disorders. Credit, 3.
Prerequisite, Psychology 26. Mr. Neet.

186. Industrial Psychology.—The course aims to give understanding of psychological principles and methods in business and industrial situations. Topics considered include: employee selection and training, motivation and morale, working conditions, fatigue and accident prevention. Credit, 3.
Prerequisite, Psychology 26. Mr. Erlick.

188. Psychology of Guidance.—A study of the psychological principles, techniques and tests necessary in guidance. Practice is given in organizing and evaluating relevant data in the analysis of illustrative cases. Credit, 3.
Prerequisite, Psychology 181. Mr. Field.

. 190. Contemporary Psychologies.—An introductory historical, logical and systematic analysis of contemporary psychological theories. Credit, 3.
Prerequisite, Psychology 26. Mr. Goss.

192. CLINICAL PSYCHOLOGY.—A study of the development, and present status of the techniques and methods used by the psychologist in the diagnosis and treatment of behavior disorders. Consideration is given to the use of diagnostic tests, psycho-therapy, and the general role of the clinical psychologist.
Prerequisite, Psychology 83 or 183.   Credit, 3.
                                                                  Mr. EPSTEIN.

193. ADOLESCENT PSYCHOLOGY.—The application of the basic principles of learning, primary and secondary motivation, frustration and conflict to the facts and problems of adolescent behavior. 1956-57 and each alternate year.
                                                                    Credit, 3.
Prerequisite, Psychology 26.   Mr. CLIFFORD.

194. CHILD PSYCHOLOGY.—The course aims to develop an understanding of the behavior of the child. Psychological aspects of the following are considered: Original nature, maturation, play, social behavior, personality and mental hygiene. Nursery school observation and practice.   Credit, 3.
Prerequisite, Psychology 26.   MR. CLIFFORD.

Public Health

RALPH L. FRANCE, major adviser.

The following courses are offered to students interested in environmental sanitation and who intend to prepare for positions as industrial and public health sanitarians. With the cooperation of the Massachusetts Department of Public Health and the New England Field Training Center conducted by the United States Public Health Service, field training is integrated into the curriculum. Applicants must have satisfied the entrance requirements of the Graduate School and should have completed an undergraduate major in the physical or biological sciences. Experience as a full time employee in environmental sanitation may be accepted in lieu of specific undergraduate requirements.

COURSES OPEN TO GRADUATE STUDENTS ONLY

(For either major or minor credit)

200. SPECIAL PROBLEMS IN PUBLIC HEALTH.—Special investigational or research problems in public health for advanced students. The scope of this work can be varied to meet specific conditions.   Credit, 3-6.
                                                                   THE STAFF.

201. PUBLIC HEALTH LAW.—A discussion of the laws governing health activities of federal, state and local health agencies including methods of preparation and mediation of health legislation and regulations. Rules of evidence and conduct of witnesses will be included.   Credit, 3.
                                                                 Mr. WISNIESKI.

202. METHODS OF PUBLIC HEALTH EDUCATION.—The object of this course is to give the health educator an opportunity to study, use, and evaluate some of the special methods, tools, and skills in health education. Opportunity for practice in the preparation of health education materials is provided.   Credit, 3.
                                                                 Mr. WISNIESKI.

203. The Planning of Environmental Sanitation Programs.—The practical techniques of putting the principles of environmental sanitation into practice in a health department program are studied. The level of application and the field of application will be determined by the students' own needs. Topics considered are the development of standards, rating systems and field forms, the uses and execution of sanitary surveys, the training of sub-professional sanitarians in areas outside the United States, the planning of schools in food handling, the use of milk-shed rating systems, the job analysis of a balanced sanitation program.   Credit, 3

                                                                    Mr. Wisnieski.

206. Advanced Epidemiology.—Lectures, discussions, and laboratory work on the principles, and methods of epidemiological investigation with laboratory work in assembling and analyzing crude data resulting from field investigations of epidemics.   Credit, 3.
Prerequisite, P. H. 188 or equivalent.   Mr. Lee.

207. Seminar.—Lectures and reports on current literature and special topics. (One each semester.)   Credit, 1-2.
                                                                    The Staff.

300. Thesis, Master's Degree.—Independent research leading to the preparation of a thesis that will make an original contribution to the literature in public health. Results should be suitable for publication. The thesis is optional for M.S. candidates who have had sufficient training in public health before entering the graduate school to profit more from thesis research than from additional courses.   Credit, 10.

COURSES OPEN TO BOTH GRADUATE AND UNDERGRADUATE STUDENTS

(For either major or minor credit)

161, 162. General and Community Sanitation.—A study of the problems of general and community sanitation. Subjects discussed will include insect and rodent control, housing and slum clearance, ventilation, lighting, bathing places, sanitation of eating utensils, nuisances, camp sanitation, industrial hygiene, water supplies, sewerage and sewage, refuse and garbage, food and milk sanitation.
                                                                    Credit, 3.
                                    Mr. Perriello or Mr. Wisnieski.

163. Industrial Hygiene and Sanitation.   Credit, 3.
Permission of instructor.   Mr. Perriello.

164. Microscopy of Water.—Counting and control of plankton in potable waters.   Credit, 3.
Prerequisite, Bacteriology 31A.   Mr. Snow.

184. Public Health Administration.   Credit. 3.
                                                                  Mr. Perriello.

186. Field Studies in Sanitation.—Trips will be taken into the field for the observation of public health practices.   Credit, 2.
Prerequisites, Public Health 161, 162.   Mr. Wisnieski.

188. EPIDEMIOLOGY AND COMMUNICABLE DISEASE CONTROL.—Admission by approval of the instructor.   Credit, 3.
Mr. LEE.

192. SUPERVISED FIELD TRAINING.—To be taken during the summer session. All graduates majoring in sanitary technology must complete a prescribed thirteen-week field training program conducted by the New England Field Training Center under the direction of the Training Division of the Communicable Disease Center, U. S. Public Health Service, with the assistance of the staff and State Department of Health personnel. This course is a prerequisite for placement in federal, state, and municipal agencies.   Credit, 6.
THE STAFF.

COURSES IN OTHER DEPARTMENTS FOR WHICH MAJOR CREDIT WILL BE GIVEN.

Bacteriology 181. GENERAL APPLIED BACTERIOLOGY.   Credit, 3.
Mr. FRANCE.

Bacteriology 182. QUANTITATIVE AND QUALITATIVE BACTERIOLOGY. Credit, 3.
Miss GARVEY.

Bacteriology 190. SANITARY BACTERIOLOGY.   Credit, 3.
Mr. FRANCE.

Bacteriology 215. ANTISEPTICS AND DISINFECTANTS.   Credit, 3.
Mr. LITSKY.

Agricultural Economics 179. ELEMENTARY ECONOMICS STATISTICS.
Credit, 3.
Mr. RUSSELL.

Botany 166. GENERAL MYCOLOGY.   Credit, 3.
Mr. BANFIELD.

Home Economics 203. ADVANCED NUTRITION—METABOLISM OF THE MAJOR FOODSTUFFS.   Credit, 3.
Miss MITCHELL.

Home Economics 204. ADVANCED NUTRITION—VITAMINS AND MINERALS.
Credit, 3.
Miss MITCHELL.

Food Technology 175, 176. FOOD PRESERVATION.   Credit, 3 each semester.
Mr. NEBESKY.

Food Technology 191, 192. ANALYSIS OF FOOD PRODUCTS.
Credit, 3 each semester.
Mr. FELLERS and Mr. NEBESKY.

Dairy 152. MARKET MILK.   Credit, 4.
THE STAFF.

Dairy 209, 210. SEMINAR.   Credit, 1 each semester.
Mr. HANKINSON.

Education 267. AUDIO-VISUAL LABORATORY.   Credit, 2-3.
Mr. WYMAN and Mr. CURTIS.

Zoology 169. ANIMAL PARASITOLOGY.   Credit, 3.
Miss TRAVER.

COURSES FOR MINOR CREDIT ONLY

Government 162. ADMINISTRATIVE LAW.

ENTOMOLOGY 160. STRUCTURAL PEST CONTROL.

Entomology 174. MEDICAL ENTOMOLOGY.

Forestry 151. FOREST MANAGEMENT OF WATERSHEDS.

Animal Husbandry 153. ELEMENTS OF MEAT PACKING.

Civil Engineering 179. PRINCIPLES OF SANITARY ENGINEERING.

Agricultural Engineering 180. FOOD PROCESS ENGINEERING.

Education 166. PREPARATION AND USE OF AUDIO-VISUAL AIDS.

Geology 150. ENGINEERING GEOLOGY.

Veterinary Science 178. GENERAL VETERINARY PATHOLOGY.

Romance Languages

STOWELL C. GODING, major adviser.

Requirements for admission to candidacy for the M.A. in Romance Languages:

1. A working knowledge of Latin.
2. Good oral proficiency in the major language and acceptable oral proficiency in a second Romance Language.
3. A reading knowledge of a second Romance Language or of German.

Course requirements for the M.A. in Romance Languages:

1. Romance Languages 200 or 300.
2. Romance Languages 201-202.
3. Romance Languages 215-216, from 2 to 6 credits, depending on the individual needs and ability of the student.
4. Superior oral proficiency in the major language and good oral proficiency in the second Romance Language.

COURSES OPEN TO GRADUATE STUDENTS ONLY
(For either major or minor credit)

200. PROBLEM COURSE.—Directed study in some phase of linguistics or literature.   Credit, 3-6.

201, 202. INTRODUCTION TO ROMANCE PHILOLOGY.—The development of the Romance Languages from Latin: phonology, morphology, and syntax. Given as needed.   Credit, 3 each semester.

203, 204. OLD FRENCH READINGS.—The evolution of French phonology, morphology, and syntax is traced through the study of some of the earliest monuments of French literature. Given as needed.   Credit, 3 each semester.

205, 206. OLD SPANISH READINGS.—The evolution of Spanish phonology, morphology, and syntax is traced through the study of some of the earliest monuments of Spanish literature.   Credit, 3 each semester.

215. SEMINAR IN FRENCH.—A concentrated study of the many highly specialized techniques essential for language proficiency and teaching skill. The seminar offers a comprehensive training leading to the now requisite oral mastery of French, to correct grammatical techniques and analyses, to accurate explication de texte, to linguistics and to present-day pedagogical procedures. Conducted by specialists in the fields of phonetics, linguistics and literature. Procedures will depend upon the most recent funds of information and will be directed toward the most apparent needs of the group.   Credit, 2-3.

216. SEMINAR IN SPANISH.—Comparable to 215 but in the field of Spanish.
Credit, 2-3.

300. THESIS, MASTER'S DEGREE.   Credit, maximum 10.

COURSES OPEN TO BOTH GRADUATE AND UNDERGRADUATE STUDENTS
(For either major or minor credit)

Courses in French

151, 152. FRENCH LITERATURE OF THE EIGHTEENTH CENTURY.—A detailed study of the chief writers of the Age of Enlightenment. 1956-57 and each alternate year.   Credit, 3 each semester.

153, 154. FRENCH LITERATURE OF THE TWENTIETH CENTURY.—Three class hours; one laboratory hour.   Credit, 3 each semester.

155, 156. FRENCH LITERATURE OF THE SEVENTEENTH CENTURY.—A study of the Classic period with readings from the most representative works. 1957-58 and each alternate year.   Credit, 3 each semester.

157, 158. FRENCH LITERATURE OF THE NINETEENTH CENTURY.—A detailed study of the more important authors and movements. 1956-57 and each alternate year.   Credit, 3 each semester.

175, 176. COURS DE STYLE.—A study of syntax and idiom at an advanced level. The student is taught how to express himself clearly and logically in living French. Given as needed.   Credit, 3 each semester.

179. FRENCH CIVILIZATION.—A study of those elements which lie back of the cultural contribution of France to world civilization. Subjects studied will include arts, sciences, school systems, the press, the family, social classes, influences of history and geography. The assigned readings will be drawn from contemporary French literature. 1957-58 and each alternate year.   Credit, 3.

180. ADVANCED LANGUAGE STUDY.—Methods of teaching; review of grammar and pronounciation; outside reading and reports. 1957-58 and each alternate year.   Credit, 3.

Courses in Spanish

163, 164. ADVANCED SPANISH COMPOSITION AND SYNTAX.—A study of syntax and idioms, and those more advanced and difficult elements which constitute stylistics. 1957-58 and each alternate year.   Credit, 3 each semester.

181. THE ROMANTICISTS.—Readings, lectures and discussions based on the principal Spanish and Spanish-American writers of the Romantic movement (1809-50 and 1832-88, respectively). Oral and written reports. The course is conducted in Spanish. 1956-57 and each alternate year.   Credit, 3.

182. THE MODERNISTS.—Readings, lectures and discussions based on the Spanish-American modernistas of the period 1888-1910 and on their peninsular artistic heirs. Oral and written reports. The course is conducted in Spanish. 1956-57 and each alternate year. · Credit, 3.

183, 184. THE GOLDEN AGE.—Readings, reports, lectures, and discussions based primarily on the period of maximum creation, 1556-1600. Considerable attention is also paid to the Renaissance precursors (1474-1556) and to the writers of the Baroque era (1600-1700). The course is conducted in Spanish. 1957-58 and each alternate year. Credit, 3 each semester.

185, 186. CERVANTES.—Reading of Don Quijote; lectures, discussions, collateral readings and reports. The course is conducted in Spanish. 1956-57 and each alternate year. Credit, 3 each semester.

Sociology

J. H. KORSON, major adviser.

Special Departmental Entrance Requirements:

Candidates for admission who· plan to major in Sociology must have completed an undergraduate major, or have taken a minimum of 15 credits in Sociology. A minimum of three credits in Statistics must be offered. A deficiency in Statistics can be made up by taking Agricultural Economics 179. In certain cases students will be advised to take Agricultural Economics 180. A student lacking this minimum undergraduate training will be expected to make up deficiencies in the undergraduate college of the University. Exceptions to this rule will be made only on petition of the student to the department. Students who desire to direct their training toward Correctional Administration will be expected to take certain courses in Government and Psychology.

In addition to the general requirements for the Master of Arts degree, found elsewhere in this Bulletin, candidates in Sociology are required to take the Graduate Record Examination before admission, or as soon after as possible.

Degree requirements: 30 credits, of which a minimum of 12 are to be earned in courses at the 200 level, 6 of which must be in Sociology 281 and 282. Students who elect the program in Correctional Administration are expected·to earn a minimum of 15 credits at the 200 level. A student may be granted the option of writing a Master's thesis (10 credits) or working on a special problem (3-6 credits). All candidates for the Master of Arts degree must take a final oral examination given by the Department covering their problem or thesis.

COURSES OPEN TO GRADUATE STUDENTS ONLY

(Courses for major or minor credit)

200. SPECIAL PROBLEM.—A special project in Sociology which may serve in lieu of thesis. Credit, 3-6.
Prerequisite, Sociology 193, or equivalent. THE DEPARTMENT.

214. (II) CRIMINOLOGY.—A· consideration of criminological theories, past and present. Special emphasis on present research trends as they relate to theoretical formulations. Given as required. Credit, 3.
Prerequisite, Sociology 78, or equivalent. Mr. DRIVER.

217. (I) JUVENILE DELINQUENCY.—A consideration of various theories of causation and treatment of delinquency. Given as required. Credit, 3.
Prerequisite, Sociology 78, or equivalent. Mr. DRIVER.

268. (II) INDUSTRIAL SOCIOLOGY.—A study of the role, status, and function of the worker in the industrial community. A consideration of the impact of technological change on the community. An analysis of selected occupational functions. Credit, 3.
Prerequisite, Economics 79, or equivalent. Mr. KORSON.

281. (I) HISTORY OF SOCIOLOGICAL THEORY.—A survey of the literature from classical times to the Utilitarians. Credit, 3.
Prerequisite, Sociology 82, or equivalent. Mr. MANFREDI.

282. (II) CONTEMPORARY SOCIOLOGICAL THEORY.—A survey of the literature from Auguste Comte to the present. Credit, 3.
Prerequisite, Sociology 82, or equivalent. Mr. MANFREDI.

291. (I) SOCIAL CHANGE.—Emphasis is placed upon planned innovations and reforms in political, religious and economic areas and upon the possibilities and problems of social planning. Consideration is also given to social changes resulting indirectly from invention and group contact. Credit, 3.
Admission by consent of the instructor. Mr. KING.

298. INTERNSHIP.—Supervised training and practice in the administration of a state correctional institution or organization. Students chosen for this training will serve with one of the following: Women's Reformatory (Framingham), Men's Reformatory (Concord), The Bureau of Classification (Department of Correction), Youth Service Board (Department of Education), The United Prison Association (Boston). A minimum of three months (40-hour weeks) is required and will normally take place the summer following completion of the major part of the student's course work. Credit, 3.
Prerequisites, Sociology 192, 214, 217. THE DEPARTMENT.

300. THESIS, MASTER'S DEGREE. Credit, 10.

(Courses for major or minor credit)

151. URBAN SOCIOLOGY. Credit, 3.
Mr. MANFREDI.

152. RURAL SOCIOLOGY. Credit, 3.
Mr. YPSILANTIS.

153. SOCIAL ANTHROPOLOGY Credit, 3.
Mr. WILKINSON.

156. RACE RELATIONS. Credit, 3.
Mr. KING, Mr. KORSON.

157. THE FAMILY. Credit, 3.
Mr. KING, Mr. KORSON.

162. POPULATION PROBLEMS. Credit, 3.
Mr. WILKINSON.

175. SOCIAL PROBLEMS. Credit, 3.
Mr. DRIVER.

192. SOCIAL WELFARE. Credit, 3.
Mr. YPSILANTIS.

193. SEMINAR RESEARCH METHODS.   Credit, 3.
                                                                  Mr. DRIVER.

194. SEMINAR RESEARCH METHODS.   Credit,3.
                                                                  Mr. DRIVER.

Veterinary Science

COURSES FOR MINOR CREDIT ONLY

175. COMPARATIVE VETERINARY ANATOMY.   Credit, 3.
                                                                  Mr. SMITH.

176. GENERAL VETERINARY PATHOLOGY.   Credit, 3.
                                                                  Mr. SMITH.

178. GENERAL VETERINARY PATHOLOGY.   Credit, 3.
                                                                  Mr. SMITH.

188. AVIAN PATHOLOGY.   Credit, 3.
                                                                  Mr. BULLIS.

Wildlife Management

REUBEN E. TRIPPENSEE, major adviser.

Graduate work in Wildlife Management is closely tied in with the Cooperative Wildlife Research Station which is now a part of the Department of Forestry and Wildlife Management. Financial support for the Unit is received from the U. S. Fish and Wildlife Service, the Wildlife Management Institute and the State Fish and Game Department. Dr. William G. Sheldon, director of the Research Unit spends approximately half of his time assisting the research activities of the students who work under fellowships received through the Unit. The director of research is automatically on the graduate committee of each student who receives funds through the Unit.

Students graduating in Wildlife Management at the University of Massachusetts are strongly urged to pursue graduate work at another University. Opportunities for fellowships in this field are usually available at other Cooperative Units.

COURSES OPEN TO GRADUATE STUDENTS ONLY
(For either major or minor credit)

200. SPECIAL PROBLEMS IN WILDLIFE MANAGEMENT.   Credit, 3 per semester
                                                       maximum credit, 6.
                                                              THE STAFF.

201. NORTH AMERICAN ANIMALS.—A review of the taxonomy, life histories and ecological inter-relationships of certain North American vertebrates.
                                                                  Credit, 3.
                                                                  Mr. TRIPPENSEE.

202. WILDLIFE ADMINISTRATION.—A study of the organization and operation of state and federal agencies and certain associations concerned with wildlife management. Credit, 3.
Prerequisite, Wildlife Management 27 or equivalent. Mr. TRIPPENSEE.

203. WILD ANIMAL ABUNDANCE.—A study of the factors which influence wild animal abundance. Credit, 3.
Mr. TRIPPENSEE.

204. LAND USE AND WILDLIFE.—A study of wildlife populations on different ecological sites with special emphasis on the indirect influence of land use practices and natural vegetative succession. Credit, 3.
Prerequisites, Agronomy 2, Botany 181, Forestry 55 and 56 or equivalents.
Mr. SHELDON and Mr. TRIPPENSEE.

205. MANAGEMENT OF WET LANDS AND WATER IN RELATION TO WILDLIFE. Credit, 3.
Mr. SHELDON and Mr. TRIPPENSEE.

300. THESIS, MASTER'S DEGREE. Credit, 10.

COURSES OPEN TO BOTH GRADUATE AND UNDERGRADUATE STUDENTS
(For either major or minor credit)

170. GAME BIRDS AND MAMMALS.—Life histories, ecology methods of management. Credit. 3.
Mr. TRIPPENSEE.

171. WATERFOWL MANAGEMENT.—Life histories and factors which affect abundance of waterfowl. Credit, 3.
Mr. TRIPPENSEE

173. PREDACEOUS BIRDS AND INJURIOUS RODENTS.—Life histories, ecology and control. Credit, 3.
Mr. TRIPPENSEE.

174. TECHNIQUES IN WILDLIFE MANAGEMENT.—Includes analysis of cover, census methods, food habit studies, and determination of flock and herd age and sex composition of game animals. Credit, 3.
Mr. TRIPPENSEE.

175. MANAGEMENT OF FURBEARERS.—Life histories and management of furbearers and nomenclature of the fur trade. Credit, 3.
Mr. TRIPPENSEE.

COURSES IN OTHER DEPARTMENTS FOR WHICH MAJOR CREDIT WILL BE GIVEN

Agricultural Economics 179. ELEMENTARY ECONOMICS STATISTICS. Credit, 3.
Mr. RUSSELL.

Botany 167, 168. INTRODUCTORY PLANT PHYSIOLOGY. Credit, 3 each semester.
Mr. KOZLOWSKI.

WILDLIFE MANAGEMENT

Botany 181. PLANT ECOLOGY. Credit, 3.
Mr. LIVINGSTON.

Entomology 179. ANIMAL ECOLOGY. Credit, 3.
Mr. SWEETMAN

Entomology 190. EVOLUTION. Credit, 2.
Mr. HANSON.

Entomology 212. GEOGRAPHICAL DISTRIBUTION OF ANIMALS AND PLANTS.
Credit, 3.
Mr. ALEXANDER.

Education 166. PREPARATION AND USE OF AUDIO-VISUAL AIDS. Credit, 2-3.
Mr. WYMAN and Mr. CURTIS.

Forestry 171. AERIAL PHOTOGRAMMETRY. Credit, 3.
Mr. MACCONNELL and Mr. BOND.

Forestry 180. PRINCIPLES OF FOREST MANAGEMENT. Credit, 3.
Mr. MACCONNELL.

Poultry Science. 203, 204. ADVANCED GENETICS. Credit, 3 each semester.
Mr. HAYS.

Zoology 171. COMPARATIVE VERTEBRATE ANATOMY. Credit, 3.
Mr. BARTLETT and Mr. SNYDER.

Zoology 174. LIMNOLOGY.—A study of inland waters. Credit, 4.
Miss TRAVER in cooperation
with the Departments of
Botany, Entomology, Ge-
ology, Public Health and
Zoology.

Zoology 182. MAMMALOGY. Credit, 3.
Mr. SNYDER.

Zoology 183. GENERAL CELLULAR PHYSIOLOGY. Credit, 4.
Mr. SWENSON.

Zoology 184. COMPARATIVE PHYSIOLOGY. Credit, 4.
Mr. ROBERTS.

Zoology 186. FISHERY BIOLOGY. Credit, 3.
Mr. ANDREWS

Zoology 187. ENDOCRINOLOGY. Credit, 3.
Mr. SNEDECOR.

Zoology 200. SPECIAL PROBLEMS. Credit, 3 or 6.
THE STAFF.

Zoology

GILBERT L. WOODSIDE, major adviser.

Graduate students may earn the M.A. degree in Zoology by either of the following plans.

Plan A. Completing thirty graduate credits of which six must be in the 200 category (open to graduate students only). The thirty credits must also include a ten-credit thesis, and the student must pass an oral examination (see page 8).

Plan B. Completing thirty graduate credits, of which fifteen must be in the 200 category (open to graduate students only). No thesis is required but the student must pass a written examination (see page 8).

The requirements for the Ph.D. in Zoology are outlined on page 9.

COURSES OPEN TO GRADUATE STUDENTS ONLY
(For either major or minor credit)

200. SPECIAL PROBLEMS. Credit, 3 or 6.
THE STAFF.

202. ADVANCED INVERTEBRATE ZOOLOGY.—Invertebrate fauna of local ponds, streams and bogs. Morphology, classification, habits and life cycles of such groups as freshwater sponges, flatworms, bryozoans, annelids and crustaceans, with a survey of the important literature on each group. Several field trips. Term paper required.
Discussion period and two 3-hour laboratory periods. Credit, 3.
Prerequisite, Zoology 25, 170 or 174. Miss TRAVER.

204. HELMINTHOLOGY.—The course has two aims: first to acquaint the student with the morphology, classification and life histories of the principal groups of parasitic helminths, only a few of which can be studied in Zoology 169; and second to provide opportunity for the practical application of such knowledge. Included, in addition to the study of the helminth groups, are: methods of preparation of helminths for study; instruction and practice in the use of such reference sources as Biological Abstracts; an individual problem involving the collection, preparation and identification of helminth parasites from some species of animal; and the preparation of a term report embodying these findings. Credit, 3.
One class hour; two 3-hour laboratory periods. Miss TRAVER.
Prerequisites, Zoology 169 or equivalent.

220. EXPERIMENTAL EMBRYOLOGY.—Lectures, seminar reports and laboratory work dealing with the chief factors in the physiology of development: the germ cells, fertilization, establishment of the primary axis, embryonic induction, and differentiation. 1957-58 and each alternate year. Credit, 3.
Prerequisite, Zoology 172 or equivalent.

Mr. WOODSIDE.

245. ADVANCED VERTEBRATE PHYSIOLOGY.—An opportunity for the student to gain experience in small animal surgery and in making standard experimental preparations. Suitable techniques for recording results will be employed, and the proper interpretation of the acquired data will be stressed. Credit, 3.
1957-58 and each alternate year.
One class hour; one 4-hour laboratory period. Mr. SNEDECOR.
Prerequisites, Zoology 35 and 171, or equivalent.

ZOOLOGY

248. PHYSIOLOGICAL GENETICS.—The nature of the gene and its action in the developmental and physiological processes of the organism. Credit, 3. 1957-58 and each alternate year.
Prerequisite, Zoology 153, or equivalent, and permission of instructor.

Mr. RAUCH.

255. DEPARTMENTAL SEMINAR.   Credit, 1 each semester.
Maximum credit, 4.
THE STAFF.

260. PHYSIOLOGY SEMINAR.   Credit, 1 each semester.
Maximum credit, 3.
Mr. SWENSON.

300. THESIS, MASTER'S DEGREE.   Credit, 10.

400. THESIS, PH.D. DEGREE.   Credit, 30.

COURSES OPEN TO BOTH GRADUATE AND UNDERGRADUATE
STUDENTS
(For either major or minor credit)

164. BIOLOGY OF PROTOZOA.—An introduction to the morphology, systematics, physiology, and ecology of Protozoa with a consideration of the contributions to the problems of biology made through the study of these organisms. 1956-57 and each alternate year. Credit, 3.
One lecture hour; one 2-hour and one 3-hour laboratory period. Mr. HONIGBERG.
Prerequisite, Zoology 1 and permission of instructor.

169. ANIMAL PARASITOLOGY.—Representative protozan and helminthic parasites of man and domestic animals are studied, with special reference to their morphology and life cycles. Emphasis is placed upon parasitism as a mode of life, on host-parasite relationship, on vectors, and other modes of transmission, and on methods of control of certain of the more important human parasites. Graduate students taking this course prepare a term paper on some phase of parasitism. Credit, 3.
One class hour; two 2-hour laboratory periods. Miss TRAVER.
Prerequisite, Zoology 1.

170. INVERTEBRATE ZOOLOGY.—A survey of the phyla of invertebrate animals from evolutionary and phylogenetic aspects. Morphology, modes of nutrition and reproduction, interrelationships with other animals, and distribution in time and space are considered as well as classification. For each phylum, representatives of the principal classes are studied. Marine, terrestrial and freshwater forms are included. 1956-57 and each alternate year. Credit, 3.
One class hour; two 3-hour laboratory periods. Miss TRAVER.
Prerequisite, Zoology 1.

173. GENERAL CYTOLOGY.—A consideration of the morphological features of cells in relation to their function. Lectures, seminai reports and individual laboratory work. 1956-57 and each alternate year. Credit, 3.
Prerequisite, Zoology 150. Mr. ROLLASON.

124

174. LIMNOLOGY.—The study of inland waters, emphasizing the geological, physical, chemical and biological aspects of this problem. Standard methods for making physical and chemical tests and measurements, and for the collection of biological materials, are used by students in the numerous field trips. Biological material collected in the field is studied in the laboratory. 1957-58 and each alternate year. Credit, 4.

Two class hours; two 3-hour laboratory periods. Miss TRAVER in cooperation
Prerequisites, Botany 1, Zoology 1, Chemistry 1 with the departments of
and 2 and permission to register. Strongly Botany, Entomology, Ge-
recommended: Botany 25, 26, Entomology 26, ology, Public Health and
Zoology 25, Geology 27, 28, Chemistry 29, 30. Zoology.

178. GENETICS OF ANIMAL POPULATIONS.—The principles of the genetics of animal populations with emphasis upon its basic techniques and methods, its goals and contributions. The population approach to the study of the origin of species and human genetics will also be considered. 1957-58 and each alternate year. Credit, 2.

Enrollment limited to 10. Mr. RAUCH.

One 2-hour lecture-discussion period per week.

Prerequisite, Zoology 153 or equivalent and permission of instructor.

182. MAMMALOGY.—The evolution, distribution, classification and natural history of mammals. In the laboratory special emphasis will be given to study of local fauna. Two or three field trips required. Enrollment limited to 15. 1957-58 and each alternate year. Credit, 3.

Two class hours; one 2-hour laboratory period Mr. SNYDER.

Prerequisite, Zoology 1 and permission of instructor.

183. GENERAL AND CELLULAR PHYSIOLOGY.—A course designed to introduce the student to modern trends in physiology. Emphasis is on the chemical and physical activities of the single cell. Topics include: protoplasmic organization, cellular metabolism, permeability, bioelectric phenomena, muscle contraction and radiation biology. Credit, 4.

Three class hours; one 3-hour laboratory period. Mr. SWENSON.

Prerequisites, one year biology; organic chemistry.

184. COMPARATIVE PHYSIOLOGY.—A course designed to acquaint students with physiological principles involved in adaptations of animals to their environments. In the laboratory, experimental methods used to study adaptive mechanisms will be emphasized. Credit, 4.

Three class hours; one 3-hour laboratory period. Mr. ROBERTS.

Prerequisites, Zoology 1, 35 (or 183).

186. FISHERY BIOLOGY.—Theory in the practice of regulating fresh-water fisheries; the physical and biological conditions of the environment and their influence on fish populations. Credit, 3.

Prerequisite, Zoology 181, or permission of instructor. Mr. ANDREWS.

187. ENDOCRINOLOGY.—The importance of the endocrines in their control over normal functions (growth, metabolism, reproduction, etc.) in a variety of animals. Credit, 3.

Two class hours; one 3-hour laboratory period. Mr. SNEDECOR.

ZOOLOGY

COURSES IN OTHER DEPARTMENTS FOR WHICH MAJOR CREDIT WILL BE GIVEN

Chemistry 193-194. Biochemistry.   Credit, 4 each semester.
Mr. Little.

Entomology 212. Geographical Distribution of Plants and Animals.
Credit, 2, 1st semester; 3, 2nd semester.
Mr. Alexander.

COURSES FOR MINOR CREDIT ONLY

150. Histology of Vertebrates.   Credit, 3.
Mr. Rollason.

153. Genetics.   Credit, 3.
Mr. Rauch.

171. Comparative Vertebrate Anatomy.   Credit, 4.
Mr. Bartlett and Mr. Snyder.

172. Vertebrate Embryology.   Credit, 4.
Mr. Woodside, Mr. Rauch and Mr. Bartlett.

180. Ornithology.   Credit, 3.
Mr. Bartlett and Mr. Nutting.

181. Vertebrate Zoology.   Credit, 3.
Mr. Andrews and Mr. Bartlett.

185. The Classes of Arthropods Other Than Insects.   Credit, 3.
Mr. Hanson

INDEX

INDEX